CCDA Official
Exam Certification Guide
Third Edition

Anthony Bruno, CCIE No. 2738

Steve Jordan, CCIE No. 11293

Cisco Press

800 East 96th Street

Indianapolis, IN 46240 USA

CCDA Official Exam Certification Guide, Third Edition

Anthony Bruno, CCIE No. 2738
Steve Jordan, CCIE No. 11293

Copyright © 2007 Cisco Systems, Inc.

Published by:
Cisco Press
800 East 96th Street
Indianapolis, IN 46240 USA

Printed in the United States of America 1 2 3 4 5 6 7 8 9 0

First Printing June 2007

Library of Congress Cataloging-in-Publication Data

Bruno, A. Anthony.

CCDA official exam certification guide / Anthony Bruno, Steve Jordan. —3rd ed.

p. cm.

ISBN-13: 978-1-58720-177-6 (hardcover w/dvd) 1. Electronic data processing personnel—Certification. 2. Computer networks—Examinations—Study guides. I. Jordan, Steve. II. Title.

QA76.3.B7847 2007

004.6076--dc22

2007015940

ISBN-10: 1-58720-177-1

ISBN-13: 978-1-58720-177-6

Warning and Disclaimer

This book is designed to provide information about the CCDA exam. Every effort has been made to make this book as complete and accurate as possible, but no warranty or fitness is implied.

The information is provided on an "as is" basis. The authors, Cisco Press, and Cisco Systems, Inc. shall have neither liability nor responsibility to any person or entity with respect to any loss or damages arising from the information contained in this book or from the use of the discs or programs that may accompany it.

The opinions expressed in this book belong to the authors and are not necessarily those of Cisco Systems, Inc.

Feedback Information

At Cisco Press, our goal is to create in-depth technical books of the highest quality and value. Each book is crafted with care and precision, undergoing rigorous development that involves the unique expertise of members of the professional technical community.

Reader feedback is a natural continuation of this process. If you have any comments on how we could improve the quality of this book, or otherwise alter it to better suit your needs, you can contact us through e-mail at feedback@ciscopress.com. Please be sure to include the book title and ISBN in your message.

We greatly appreciate your assistance.

Corporate and Government Sales

Cisco Press offers excellent discounts on this book when ordered in quantity for bulk purchases or special sales. For more information, please contact: **U.S. Corporate and Government Sales** 1-800-382-3419 corpsales@pearsontechgroup.com

For sales outside of the U.S. please contact: **International Sales** 1-317-581-3793 international@pearsontechgroup.com

Trademark Acknowledgments

All terms mentioned in this book that are known to be trademarks or service marks have been appropriately capitalized. Cisco Press or Cisco Systems, Inc. cannot attest to the accuracy of this information. Use of a term in this book should not be regarded as affecting the validity of any trademark or service mark.

Publisher: Paul Boger

Executive Editor: Brett Bartow

Managing Editor: Patrick Kanouse

Development Editor: Andrew Cupp

Senior Project Editor: Tonya Simpson

Copy Editor: Gayle Johnson

Publishing Coordinator: Vanessa Evans

Designer: Louisa Adair

Composition: Mark Shirar

Indexer: Tim Wright

Associate Publisher: David Dusthimer

Cisco Representative: Anthony Wolfenden

Cisco Press Program Manager: Jeff Brady

Technical Editors: Mark Gallo, Steve Jordan, and Anthony Sequeira

Americas Headquarters
Cisco Systems, Inc.
170 West Tasman Drive
San Jose, CA 95134-1706
USA
www.cisco.com
Tel: 408 526-4000
800 553-NETS (6387)
Fax: 408 527-0883

Asia Pacific Headquarters
Cisco Systems, Inc.
168 Robinson Road
#28-01 Capital Tower
Singapore 068912
www.cisco.com
Tel: +65 6317 7777
Fax: +65 6317 7799

Europe Headquarters
Cisco Systems International BV
Haarlerbergpark
Haarlerbergweg 13-19
1101 CH Amsterdam
The Netherlands
www-europe.cisco.com
Tel: +31 0 800 020 0791
Fax: +31 0 20 357 1100

Cisco has more than 200 offices worldwide. Addresses, phone numbers, and fax numbers are listed on the Cisco Website at www.cisco.com/go/offices.

About the Authors

Anthony Bruno, CCIE No. 2738, is a senior principal consultant with British Telecom with more than 17 years of experience in the internetworking field. Previously, he worked for International Network Services. His other network certifications include CISSP, CCDP, CCVP, and CWNA. He has consulted for many enterprise and service-provider customers in the design, implementation, and optimization of large-scale data and IP telephony networks. He completed his MSEE at the University of Missouri–Rolla in 1994 and his BSEE at the University of Puerto Rico–Mayaguez in 1990. He is also a part-time instructor for the University of Phoenix–Online, teaching networking courses.

Steve Jordan, CCIE No. 11293, is a senior consultant with British Telecom with more than 11 years of experience in internetworking. Previously, he worked for International Network Services. His other network certifications include CCDP, CCSP, and CCVP. He specializes in security, internetworking, and voice technologies. He has extensive experience with large-scale data center environments and has designed and implemented various network solutions in the manufacturing, telecommunication, and transportation industries. Steve was also a technical reviewer for this book.

About the Technical Reviewers

Mark Gallo is a systems engineering manager at Cisco within the Channels organization. He has led several engineering groups responsible for positioning and delivering Cisco end-to-end systems, as well as designing and implementing enterprise LANs and international IP networks. He has a BS in electrical engineering from the University of Pittsburgh and holds CCNP and CCDP certifications. He resides in northern Virginia with his wife, Betsy, and son, Paul.

Anthony Sequeira, CCIE No. 15626, completed the CCIE in Routing and Switching in January 2006. He is currently pursuing the CCIE in Security. For the past ten years he has written and lectured to massive audiences about the latest in networking technologies. He currently is a senior technical instructor and certified Cisco instructor for Thomson NETg. He lives with his wife and daughter in Florida. When he is not reading about the latest Cisco innovations, he is training for the World Series of Poker or exploring the Florida skies in a Cessna.

Dedications

This book is dedicated to my wife, Yvonne Bruno, Ph.D., and to our daughters, Joanne and Dianne. Thanks for all of your support during the development of this book.

—Anthony Bruno

This book is dedicated to my wife of 13 years, Dorin, and to our sons, Blake, Lance, and Miles, for their support during the writing of this book. For Blake, Lance, and Miles, we can now go fishing and golfing much more! I would also like to dedicate this book to my loving family in Tampa, Florida and Jackson, Mississippi.

—Steve Jordan

Acknowledgments

This book would not have been possible without the efforts of many dedicated people. Thanks to Andrew Cupp, development editor, for his guidance and special attention to detail. Thanks to Tonya Simpson, senior project editor, for her accuracy. Thanks to Brett Bartow, executive editor, for his vision. Thanks to all other Cisco Press team members who worked behind the scenes to make this a better book.

A special thanks my coauthor, Steve Jordan, for stepping in and contributing four chapters in addition to performing the technical review of my chapters. And a special thanks to the other technical reviewers, Mark Gallo and Anthony Sequeira. Their technical advice and careful attention to detail made this book accurate. Also, thanks to DL—you are the best!

—Anthony Bruno

This book would not be possible without all the great people who have assisted me. I would first like to thank Anthony Bruno for inviting me to assist him in this endeavor. Thanks to Brett Bartow, executive editor, for his guidance and support during the project. Thanks to Andrew Cupp, development editor, for supporting my schedule delays and keeping me on track.

Special thanks to the technical reviewers, Mark Gallo and Anthony Sequeira, who helped with the accuracy of this book.

Finally, thanks to all the managers and marketing people at Cisco Press who make all these books possible.

—Steve Jordan

This Book Is Safari Enabled

The Safari® Enabled icon on the cover of your favorite technology book means the book is available through Safari Bookshelf. When you buy this book, you get free access to the online edition for 45 days.

Safari Bookshelf is an electronic reference library that lets you easily search thousands of technical books, find code samples, download chapters, and access technical information whenever and wherever you need it.

To gain 45-day Safari Enabled access to this book:

- Go to http://www.ciscopress.com/safarienabled
- Complete the brief registration form
- Enter the coupon code DNEN-JAPD-QVWI-HCDJ-GFLT

If you have difficulty registering on Safari Bookshelf or accessing the online edition, please e-mail customer-service@safaribooksonline.com.

Contents at a Glance

Contents

Command Syntax Conventions

The conventions used to present command syntax in this book are the same conventions used in the IOS Command Reference. The Command Reference describes these conventions as follows:

- **Bold** indicates commands and keywords that are entered literally as shown. In actual configuration examples and output (not general command syntax), bold indicates commands that are manually input by the user (such as a **show** command).

- *Italic* indicates arguments for which you supply actual values.

- Vertical bars (|) separate alternative, mutually exclusive elements.

- Square brackets ([ ]) indicate an optional element.

- Braces ({ }) indicate a required choice.

- Braces within brackets ([{ }]) indicate a required choice within an optional element.

Foreword

CCDA Official Exam Certification Guide, Third Edition, is an excellent self-study resource for the 640-863 DESGN exam. Passing the exam validates your knowledge of network design for Cisco converged networks based on SONA (the Cisco Service-Oriented Network Architecture). Passing the exam is required for the Cisco Certified Design Associate (CCDA) certification.

Gaining certification in Cisco technology is key to the continuing educational development of today's networking professional. Through certification programs, Cisco validates the skills and expertise required to effectively manage the modern enterprise network.

Cisco Press exam certification guides and preparation materials offer exceptional—and flexible—access to the knowledge and information required to stay current in your field of expertise, or to gain new skills. Whether used as a supplement to more traditional training or as a primary source of learning, these materials offer users the information and knowledge validation required to gain new understanding and proficiencies.

Developed in conjunction with the Cisco certifications and training team, Cisco Press books are the only self-study books authorized by Cisco. They offer students a series of exam practice tools and resource materials to help ensure that learners fully grasp the concepts and information presented.

Additional authorized Cisco instructor-led courses, e-learning, labs, and simulations are available exclusively from Cisco Learning Solutions Partners worldwide. To learn more, visit www.cisco.com/go/training.

I hope that you find these materials to be an enriching and useful part of your exam preparation.

Erik Ullanderson
Manager, Global Certifications
Learning@Cisco
March 2007

Introduction

So you have worked on Cisco devices for a while, designing networks for your customers, and now you want to get certified? There are several good reasons to do so. The Cisco certification program allows network analysts and engineers to demonstrate their competence in different areas and levels of networking. The prestige and respect that come with a Cisco certification will definitely help you in your career. Your clients, peers, and superiors will recognize you as an expert in networking.

Cisco Certified Design Associate (CCDA) is the entry-level certification that represents knowledge of the design of Cisco internetwork infrastructure.

The routing and switching path has various levels of certification. CCDA is the entry-level certification in the network design track. The next step, Cisco Certified Design Professional (CCDP), requires you to demonstrate advanced knowledge of network design. The Cisco Certified Internetwork Expert (CCIE) requires an expert level of knowledge about internetworking.

The test to obtain CCDA certification is called Designing for Cisco Internetwork Solutions (DESGN) Exam #640-863. It is a computer-based test that has 65 questions and a 90-minute time limit. Because all exam information is managed by Cisco Systems and is therefore subject to change, candidates should continually monitor the Cisco Systems site for course and exam updates at http://www.cisco.com/web/learning/le3/learning_career_certifications_and_learning_paths_home.html.

You can take the exam at Prometric or VUE testing centers. You can register with Prometric at http://prometric.com. You can register with VUE at http://www.vue.com/cisco/. The CCDA certification is valid for three years. To recertify, you can pass a current CCDA test, pass a CCIE exam, or pass any 642 or Cisco Specialist exam.

The CCDA exam measures your ability to design networks that meet certain requirements for performance, security, capacity, and scalability. The exam focuses on small- to medium-sized networks. The candidate should have at least one year of experience in the design of small- to medium-sized networks using Cisco products. A CCDA candidate should understand internetworking technologies, including the Enterprise Composite Network Model, routing, switching, WAN technologies, LAN protocols, security, IP telephony, and network management.

Cisco suggests taking the DESGN course before you take the CCDA exam. For more information on the various levels of certification, career tracks, and Cisco exams, go to the Cisco Certifications page at http://www.cisco.com/web/learning/le3/learning_career_certifications_and_learning_paths_home.html.

Strategies for Exam Preparation

The strategy you use for the CCDA test might be slightly different from strategies used by other readers, mainly based on the skills, knowledge, and experience you already have obtained. For instance, if you have attended the DESGN course, you might take a different approach than someone who learned switching via on-the-job training.

Regardless of the strategy you use or your background, this book is designed to help you get to the point where you can pass the exam with the least amount of time required. For instance, there is no need for you to practice or read about IP addressing and subnetting if you fully understand them already. However, many people like to make sure that they truly know a topic and thus read material they already know. This book's features will make you confident that you know some of the material already and also will help you figure out what topics you need to study more.

The following are some additional suggestions for using this book and preparing for the exam:

- Familiarize yourself with the exam topics in Table I-1, and thoroughly read the chapters on topics you are unfamiliar with. Use the assessment tools provided in this book to identify areas where you need additional study. The assessment tools include the "Do I Know This Already?" quizzes, the "Q&A" questions, and the sample exam questions on the CD-ROM.

- Take all quizzes in this book, and review the answers and their explanations. It is not enough to know the correct answer; you also need to understand why it is correct and why the other possible answers are incorrect. Retake the chapter quizzes until you pass with 100 percent.

- Take the CD-ROM test included with this book, and review the answers. Use your results to identify areas where you need additional preparation.

- Review other documents, RFCs, and the Cisco website for additional information. If this book references an outside source, it's a good idea to spend some time looking at it.

- Review the chapter questions and CD-ROM questions the day before your test. Review each chapter's "Foundation Summary" when you are making your final preparations.

- On the test date, arrive at least 20 minutes before your test time. This gives you time to register and glance through your notes before the test without feeling rushed or anxious.

- If you are unsure of the correct answer to a question, attempt to eliminate the incorrect answers.

- You might need to spend more time on some questions than others. Remember, you have a little over 1 minute to answer each question.

How This Book Is Organized

This book is divided into the following parts:

> Part I: General Network Design (Chapters 1 and 2)
> Part II: LAN and WAN Design (Chapters 3 through 6)
> Part III: The Internet Protocol and Routing Protocols (Chapters 7 through 12)
> Part IV: Security, Convergence, and Network Management (Chapters 13 through 16)
> Part V: Comprehensive Scenarios (Chapter 17)
> Part VI: Appendixes (Appendixes A and B)

The "CCDA Exam Topics" section describes the design topics that are covered on the CCDA exam. Before you begin studying for any exam, it is important that you know which topics might be covered. With the CCDA exam, knowing what is on the exam is seemingly straightforward, because Cisco publishes a list of CCDA exam topics. The topics, however, are open to interpretation.

Chapters 1 through 16 cover the Cisco CCDA exam design topics and provide detailed information on each topic. Each chapter begins with a quiz so that you can quickly determine your current level of readiness. Each chapter ends with a review summary and Q&A quiz. Chapter 17, "Comprehensive Scenarios," provides scenario-based questions for further comprehensive study. Some of the questions on the CCDA test might be based on a scenario design.

Finally, in the back of the book you will find an invaluable CD-ROM. The companion CD-ROM contains a powerful testing engine that allows you to focus on individual topic areas or take complete, timed exams. The assessment engine also tracks your performance and provides feedback on a topic-by-topic basis, presenting question-by-question remediation to the text. The practice exam has a database of more than 200 questions, so you can test yourself more than once. Questions can also be delivered in standard exam format or flash card format, and you can choose to randomly generate tests or focus on specific topic areas.

The following summarizes the chapters and appendixes in this book:

- **Chapter 1, "Network Design Methodology,"** discusses obtaining organization requirements, IIR, SONA, PPDIOO methodology, and the process of completing a network design.

- **Chapter 2, "Network Structure Models,"** discusses network hierarchical models and the Enterprise Converged Network Model.

- **Chapter 3, "Enterprise LAN Design,"** covers design models and technologies used in the campus local-area networks.

- **Chapter 4, "Wireless LAN Design,"** covers the technologies and design options for wireless LANs.

- **Chapter 5, "WAN Technologies,"** examines the use of wide-area network technologies for the enterprise edge.

- **Chapter 6, "WAN Design,"** covers WAN designs for the enterprise WAN and enterprise branch.

- **Chapter 7, "Internet Protocol Version 4,"** covers the header, addressing, and protocols used by IPv4.

- **Chapter 8, "Internet Protocol Version 6,"** covers the header, addressing, and protocols used by IPv6.

- **Chapter 9, "Routing Protocol Selection Criteria,"** covers routing protocol characteristics and metrics.

- **Chapter 10, "RIP and EIGRP Characteristics and Design,"** covers the distance vector routing protocols RIPv1, RIPv2, RIPng, EIGRP, and EIGRP for IPv6.

- **Chapter 11, "OSPF and IS-IS,"** covers the link-state routing protocols OSPFv2, OSPFv3, and IS-IS.

- **Chapter 12, "Border Gateway Protocol, Route Manipulation, and IP Multicast,"** covers Border Gateway Protocol, route summarization and redistribution, and multicast protocols.

- **Chapter 13, "Security Management,"** covers network security in terms of security management and policy.

- **Chapter 14, "Security Technologies and Design,"** covers Cisco's security technologies and security solutions for the enterprise edge.

- **Chapter 15, "Traditional Voice Architectures and IP Telephony Design,"** covers traditional TDM-based concepts and solutions, VoIP protocols, and Cisco's Unified IP telephony solutions.

- **Chapter 16, "Network Management Protocols,"** covers network management design, the FCAPS model, SNMP, RMON, and other network management protocols.

- **Chapter 17, "Comprehensive Scenarios,"** provides network case studies for further comprehensive study.

- **Appendix A, "Answers to Chapter 'Do I Know This Already?' Quizzes and Q&A Sections,"** provides the answers to the various chapter quizzes.

- **Appendix B, "The OSI Reference Model, TCP/IP Architecture, and Numeric Conversion,"** reviews the Open Systems Interconnection (OSI) reference model to give you a better understanding of internetworking. It reviews the TCP/IP architecture and also reviews the techniques to convert between decimal, binary, and hexadecimal numbers. Although there might not be a specific question on the exam about converting a binary number to decimal, you need to know how to do so to do problems on the test.

Features of This Book

This book features the following:

- **"Do I Know This Already?" Quizzes**—Each chapter begins with a quiz that helps you determine how much time you need to spend studying that chapter. If you follow the directions at the beginning of the chapter, the "Do I Know This Already?" quiz directs you to study all or particular parts of the chapter.

- **Foundation Topics**—These are the core sections of each chapter. They explain the protocols, concepts, and configuration of the topics in that chapter. If you need to learn about the topics in a chapter, read the "Foundation Topics" section.

- **Foundation Summaries**—Near the end of each chapter, a summary collects the most important information from the chapter. The "Foundation Summary" section is designed to help you review the key concepts in the chapter if you scored well on the "Do I Know This Already?" quiz. This section is an excellent tool for last-minute review.

- **Q&A**—Each chapter ends with a "Q&A" section that forces you to recall the facts and processes described in that chapter. The questions are generally similar than the actual exam. These questions are a great way to improve your recollection of the facts.

- **CD-ROM test questions**—Using the test engine on the CD-ROM, you can take simulated exams. You can also choose to be presented with several questions on a topic that you need more work on. This testing tool provides you with practice to make you more comfortable when you take the CCDA exam.

CCDA Exam Topics

Cisco lists the topics of the CCDA exam on its website at http://www.cisco.com/web/learning/le3/current_exams/640-863.html. The list provides key information about what the test covers. Table I-1 lists the CCDA exam topics and the corresponding parts in this book that cover those topics. Each part begins with a list of the topics covered. Use these references as a road map to find the exact materials you need to study to master the CCDA exam topics. Note, however, that all exam information is managed by Cisco Systems and is subject to change. Therefore, you should continually monitor the Cisco Systems site at www.cisco.com for course and exam updates.

Table I-1 *CCDA Topics and the Parts Where They Are Covered*

Topic	Part
Describe the Methodology Used to Design a Network	
Describe the Cisco Service-Oriented Network Architecture	I
Identify Network Requirements to Support the Organization	I
Characterize an Existing Network	I
Describe the Top Down Approach to Network Design	I
Describe Network Management Protocols and Features	IV
Describe Network Structure and Modularity	
Describe the Network Hierarchy	I
Describe the Modular Approach in Network Design	I
Describe the Cisco Enterprise Architecture	I
Design Basic Enterprise Campus Networks	
Describe Campus Design Considerations	II
Design the Enterprise Campus Network	II
Design the Enterprise Data Center	II
Design Enterprise Edge and Remote Network Modules	
Describe the Enterprise Edge, Branch, and Teleworker Design Characteristics	II
Describe the Functional Components of the Central Site Enterprise Edge	II
Describe WAN Connectivity Between Two Campuses	II
Design the Branch Office WAN Solutions	II
Describe Access Network Solutions for a Teleworker	II
Design the WAN to Support Selected Redundancy Methodology	II
Identify Design Considerations for a Remote Data Center	II
Design IP Addressing and Routing Protocols	
Describe IPv4 & IPv6 Addressing	III
Identify Routing Protocol Considerations in an Enterprise Network	III
Design a Routing Protocol Deployment	III
Design Security Services	
Describe the Security Lifecycle	IV
Identify Cisco Technologies to Mitigate Security Vulnerabilities	IV
Select Appropriate Cisco Security Solutions and Deployment Placement	IV

Table I-1 *CCDA Topics and the Parts Where They Are Covered (Continued)*

Topic	Part
Identify Voice Networking Considerations	
Describe Traditional Voice Architectures and Features	IV
Describe Cisco IP Telephony	IV
Identify the Design Considerations for Voice Services	IV
Identify Wireless Networking Considerations	
Describe Cisco Unified Wireless Network Architectures and Features	II
Design Wireless Network Using Controllers	II
Design Wireless Network Using Roaming	II

In addition, the comprehensive scenarios in Part V test your knowledge of an overall combination of the CCDA exam topics.

If your knowledge of a particular chapter's subject matter is strong, you might want to proceed directly to that chapter's Q&A to assess your true level of preparedness. If you have difficulty with those questions, be sure to read that chapter's "Foundation Topics." Also, be sure to test yourself by using the CD-ROM's test engine.

This part covers the following CCDA exam topics (to view the CCDA exam overview, visit http://www.cisco.com/web/learning/le3/current_exams/ 640-863.html):

- Describe the Cisco Service-Oriented Network Architecture
- Identify Network Requirements to Support the Organization
- Characterize an Existing Network
- Describe the Top Down Approach to Network Design
- Describe the Network Hierarchy
- Describe the Modular Approach in Network Design
- Describe the Cisco Enterprise Architecture

Part I: General Network Design

This chapter covers the following subjects:

- Intelligent Information Network and Service-Oriented Network Architecture

- Prepare, Plan, Design, Implement, Operate, and Optimize Phases

- Identifying Customer Requirements

- Characterizing the Existing Network

- Designing the Network Topology and Solutions

CHAPTER 1

Network Design Methodology

Networks can become complex and difficult to manage. Network architectures and design methodologies help you manage the complexities of networks. This chapter provides an overview of Cisco's Service-Oriented Network Architecture (SONA) as part of Cisco's vision of the Intelligent Information Network (IIN). This chapter also describes the six network life cycle phases and steps in design methodology.

"Do I Know This Already?" Quiz

The purpose of the "Do I Know This Already?" quiz is to help you decide if you need to read the entire chapter. If you already intend to read the entire chapter, you do not necessarily need to answer these questions now.

The ten-question quiz, derived from the major sections in the "Foundation Topics" portion of the chapter, helps you determine how to spend your limited study time.

Table 1-1 outlines the major topics discussed in this chapter and the "Do I Know This Already?" quiz questions that correspond to those topics.

Table 1-1 *"Do I Know This Already?" Foundation Topics Section-to-Question Mapping*

Foundation Topics Section	Questions Covered in This Section
Intelligent Information Network and Service-Oriented Network Architecture	1, 2, 3, 4
Prepare, Plan, Design, Implement, Operate, and Optimize Phases	5, 6
Identifying Customer Requirements	9, 10
Characterizing the Existing Network	7
Designing the Network Topology and Solutions	8

> **CAUTION** The goal of self-assessment is to gauge your mastery of the topics in this chapter. If you do not know the answer to a question or you are only partially sure, you should mark this question wrong for the purposes of the self-assessment. Giving yourself credit for an answer you correctly guess skews your self-assessment results and might give you a false sense of security.

1. What are the three phases of IIN?

   a. Application, Interactive Services, Network Infrastructure

   b. Transport, Service, Application Integration

   c. Policy, System, Service Integration

   d. SONA, Enterprise Architecture, SONA framework

2. What are the three layers of SONA?

   a. Application, Interactive Services, Network Infrastructure

   b. Transport, Service, Application Integration

   c. Policy, System, Service Integration

   d. SONA, Enterprise Architecture, SONA framework

3. Virtualization occurs in which layer of the SONA framework?

   a. Application layer

   b. Virtual layer

   c. Interactive Service layer

   d. Infrastructure Service layer

4. Which of the following is a collaboration application?

   a. Supply chain

   b. IPCC

   c. Product Life Cycle

   d. Human Capital Management

5. Which of the following is the correct order of the six phases of PPDIOO?

   a. Prepare, Plan, Design, Implement, Operate, Optimize

   b. Plan, Prepare, Design, Implement, Operate, Optimize

   c. Prepare, Plan, Design, Implement, Optimize, Operate

   d. Plan, Prepare, Design, Implement, Optimize, Operate

6. The PPDIOO design methodology includes which steps? (Select all that apply.)

   a. Identify customer requirements

   b. Design the network topology

   c. Characterize the network

   d. Optimize the network

7. What are the three primary sources of information in a network audit?

   a. CIO, network manager, network engineer

   b. Network manager, management software, CDP

   c. Network discovery, CDP, SNMP

   d. Existing documentation, management software, new management tools

8. Which design solution states that a design must start from the application layer and finish in the physical layer?

   a. SONA

   b. PPDIOO

   c. IIN

   d. Top-down

9. Budget and personnel limitations are examples of what?

   a. Organization requirements

   b. Organization constraints

   c. Technical goals

   d. Technical constraints

10. Improving network response time and reliability are examples of what?

   a. Organization requirements

   b. Organization constraints

   c. Technical goals

   d. Technical constraints

The answers to the "Do I Know This Already?" quiz appear in Appendix A, "Answers to Chapter Quizzes and Q&A Sections." The suggested choices for your next step are as follows:

- **8 or less overall score**—Read the entire chapter. This includes the "Foundation Topics," "Foundation Summary," and "Q&A" sections.

- **9 or 10 overall score**—If you want more review on these topics, skip to the "Foundation Summary" section and then go to the Q&A section. Otherwise, move to the next chapter.

Foundation Topics

With the complexities of networks, it is necessary to use architectures and methodologies in network design to support business goals. Cisco's Intelligent Information Network (IIN) framework and Service-Oriented Network Architecture (SONA) make it possible to better align IT resources with business priorities. The Cisco Prepare, Plan, Design, Implement, Operate, and Optimize (PPDIOO) network life cycle defines a continuous cycle of phases in a network's life. Each phase includes key steps in successful network planning, design, implementation, and operation. The top-down design approach to network design adapts the network infrastructure to the network applications' needs.

Intelligent Information Network and Service-Oriented Network Architecture

Cisco has developed a strategy to address the increasing demands placed on today's networks. Beyond just basic connectivity, the network plays a crucial role because it touches many components of the infrastructure: end users, servers, middleware, and applications. As demands for networks grow, the network can become complex and difficult to scale and manage. Many applications are not visible to network managers on a limited scale, hampering capacity planning and service performance. Furthermore, the network must be able to respond quickly to denial-of-service (DoS) attacks, viruses, and other security-related events that hamper productivity. Drivers for new network architectures are summarized with

- Application growth

- IT evolution from basic connectivity to intelligent systems

- Increased business expectations from networks

The Cisco IIN framework and SONA make it possible to better align IT resources with business priorities.

IIN Framework

The IIN framework is a vision and architecture that adds intelligence to a network. It is implemented in a phased approach for integrating the network with applications, middleware, servers, and services. The idea is to have a single integrated system to extend intelligence across multiple layers to more closely link the network with the rest of the IT infrastructure. Adding intelligence to the network lets the network actively participate in the delivery of services and applications. IIN defines the evolving role of the network in facilitating the integration of the network with services and applications to better align IT resources with business priorities. It lets organizations quickly adapt to the IT environment and respond to changing business requirements. An IIN's capabilities are as follows:

- **An integrated system**—The network is integrated with applications, middleware, and services.

- **Active participation**—Allows the network to manage, monitor, and optimize application and services delivery.

- **Policy enforcement**—The network enforces policies linking business processes to network rules.

IIN has an evolutionary approach that consists of three phases—Integrated Transport, Integrated Service, and Integrated Application. The goal is for the enterprise to migrate to an intelligent information network.

Integrated Transport involves the convergence of voice, data, and video into a single transport network. The use of Cisco's Unified communications platforms allows the deployment of new applications that enhance communications. Unified messaging is one example of an application where a user can check messages from the IP phone or via email in text or as a voice recording.

Integrated Service merges common elements such as storage and data center server capacity. Virtualization technologies allow the integration of servers, storage, and network elements. With the virtualization of systems with redundant resources, the network can provide services in the event of a local network failure, which enhances business continuity.

The Integrated Application phase allows the network to become application-aware. The network can optimize application performance by integrating application message handling, application optimization, and application security. Cisco calls this technology Application-Oriented Networking (AON).

SONA

SONA is an architectural framework that guides the evolution of enterprise networks to IIN to support new IT strategies. With SONA, distributed applications and services are centrally managed over a common, unified platform. An integrated system allows access to networked applications and services from all locations with greater speed and service quality. Figure 1-1 shows the SONA framework and the offerings included at each layer. SONA networks are based on a three-layer design that incorporates the applications, services, and network. Offerings are contained within each layer:

- **Network Infrastructure layer** contains the Cisco Enterprise Architecture (campus, LAN, WAN, data center, branch) and facilitates the transport of services across the network. It also includes servers, storage, and clients.

■ **Interactive Service layer** optimizes the communication between applications and services using intelligent network functions such as security, identity, voice, virtualization, and quality of service.

■ **Application layer** contains the business and collaboration applications used by end users, such as enterprise resource planning, procurement, customer relationship, unified messaging, and conferencing.

Each layer in this framework is covered in the sections that follow.

Figure 1-1   *SONA Framework*

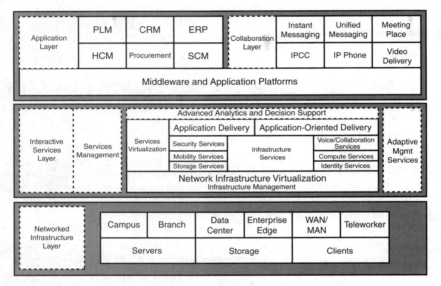

Network Infrastructure Layer

The Network Infrastructure layer contains the Enterprise Network Architecture, which includes the Enterprise Campus, Enterprise Branch, data center, Enterprise Edge, WAN and LAN, and teleworkers. The Cisco Enterprise Architecture is covered in Chapter 2, "Network Structure Models." Servers, storage networks, and end-user clients reside at this layer.

This layer contains switching and routing elements to enhance performance and capabilities, including reliability and security. The network infrastructure is built with redundancy to provide increased reliability. Security configurations are applied to the infrastructure to enforce security policies.

Interactive Service Layer

This layer supports essential applications and the Network Infrastructure layer. Standardized network foundation and virtualization are used to allow security and voice services to scale better. A standardized network architecture can be duplicated and further copied to scale a network. Services provided at this layer fall into two categories: Infrastructure Services and Application Networking Services.

Infrastructure Services

The six infrastructure services are essential in the operation and optimization of network services and applications:

- **Identity services** include authentication, authorization, and accounting (AAA); Network Admission Control (NAC); and Network-Based Application Recognition (NBAR).

- **Mobility services** allow network access regardless of the location. An example is VPN.

- **Storage services** improve storage of critical data. Critical data must be backed up and stored offsite to allow for business continuity and disaster recovery.

- **Compute services** improve computing resources enterprise-wide. High-end servers can be used for virtual machines to scale the amount of servers on the network.

- **Security services** deliver security for all network devices, servers, and users. These services include intrusion detection and prevention devices.

- **Voice and collaboration services** allow user collaboration through all network resources. Cisco's MeetingPlace is an example of a collaboration application.

Application Networking Services

This tier uses middleware applications and Cisco AON to optimize the delivery of applications. Application services deliver application information, optimize application delivery, manipulate application messages, and provide application security and application-level events. Virtualization technologies in this layer are used to maximize resource usage and provide greater flexibility. Servers with multiple virtual machines maximize the use of hardware resources.

Application Layer

The Application layer includes business applications and collaboration applications. Business applications include

- Product Lifecycle Management (PLM)

- Customer Relationship Management (CRM) applications

- Enterprise Resource Planning (ERP) applications

- Human Capital Management (HCM)

- Procurement applications

- Supply Chain Management (SCM)

Collaboration applications include

- Instant messaging (IM)

- Unified messaging (UM)

- IP Contact Center (IPCC)

- Meeting Place

- Video Delivery

Benefits of SONA

The benefits of SONA are as follows:

- **Functionality**—SONA supports the enterprise's operational requirements. The network's services meet the requirements of the business.

- **Scalability**—SONA separates functions into layers, allowing for the growth and expansion of organizational tasks. Modularity and hierarchy allows for network resources to be added to allow growth.

- **Availability**—SONA provides the services from any location in the enterprise and at any time. The network is built with redundancy and resiliency to prevent network downtime.

- **Performance**—SONA provides fast response times and throughput, with quality of service per application. The network is configured to maximize the throughput of critical applications.

- **Manageability**—SONA provides configuration management, performance monitoring, and fault detection. Network management tools are used to detect and correct network faults before applications are affected. Trending tools are used to determine when to add more infrastructure or services to support the increasing demands of applications.

- **Efficiency**—SONA provides the network services with reasonable operational costs and sensible capital investment. Maximum use of existing resources reduces cost and additional equipment is added only when the application demands increase.

Prepare, Plan, Design, Implement, Operate, and Optimize Phases

Cisco has formalized a network's life cycle into six phases: Prepare, Plan, Design, Implement, Operate, and Optimize. These phases are collectively known as PPDIOO. The PPDIOO life cycle provides four main benefits:

- It lowers the total cost of ownership by validating technology requirements and planning for infrastructure changes and resource requirements.

- It increases network availability by producing a sound network design and validating the network operation.

- It improves business agility by establishing business requirements and technology strategies.

- It speeds access to applications and services by improving availability, reliability, security, scalability, and performance.

Figure 1-2 shows the PPDIOO network life cycle.

Figure 1-2   *Cisco PPDIOO Network Life Cycle*

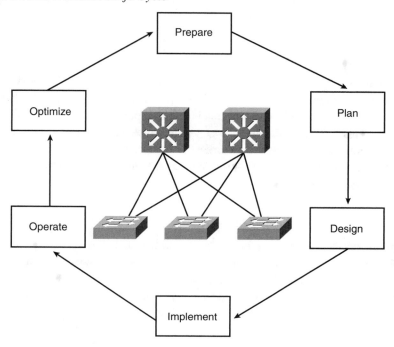

The following sections discuss these phases in detail.

Prepare Phase

The Prepare phase establishes organization and business requirements, develops a network strategy, and proposes a high-level architecture to support the strategy. Technologies that support the architecture are identified. This phase creates a business case to establish a financial justification for a network strategy.

Plan Phase

The Plan phase identifies the network requirements by characterizing and assessing the network, performing a gap analysis against best-practice architectures, and looking at the operational environment. A project plan is developed to manage the tasks, responsible parties, milestones, and resources to do the design and implementation. This project plan is followed during all phases of the cycle.

Design Phase

The network design is developed based on the technical and business requirements obtained from the previous phases. The network design provides high availability, reliability, security, scalability, and performance. The design includes network diagrams and an equipment list. The project plan is updated with more granular information for implementation. After the Design phase is approved, the Implement phase begins.

Implement Phase

New equipment is installed and configured in the Implement phase. New devices replace or augment the existing infrastructure. The project plan is followed during this phase. Planned network changes should be communicated in change control meetings, with necessary approvals to proceed. Each step in the implementation should includes a description, detailed implementation guidelines, estimated time to implement, rollback steps in case of a failure, and any additional reference information. As changes are implemented they are also tested before moving to the Operate phase.

Operate Phase

The Operate phase maintains the network's day-to-day operational health. Operations include managing and monitoring network components, routing maintenance, managing upgrades, managing performance, and identifying and correcting network faults. This phase is the design's final test. During operation, network management stations should monitor the network's general health and generate traps when certain thresholds are reached.

Optimize Phase

The Optimize phase involves proactive network management by identifying and resolving issues before they affect the network. The Optimize phase may create a modified network design if too many network problems arise, to improve performance issues, or to resolve application issues. The requirement for a modified network design leads to the network life cycle beginning.

Design Methodology Under PPDIOO

The following sections focus on a design methodology for the first three phases of the PPDIOO methodology. This design methodology has three steps:

Step 1   Identify network requirements.

Step 2   Characterize the existing network.

Step 3   Design the network topology and solutions.

In step 1, decision makers identify requirements, and a conceptual architecture is proposed. This step occurs in the PPDIOO Prepare phase.

In step 2, the network is assessed, and a gap analysis is performed to determine the infrastructure necessary to meet the requirements. The network is assessed on function, performance, and quality. This step occurs in the PPDIOO Plan phase.

In step 3, the network topology is designed to meet the requirements and close the network gaps identified in the previous steps. A detailed design document is prepared during this phase. Design solutions include network infrastructure, Voice over IP (VoIP), content networking, and intelligent network services. This set occurs in the PPDIOO Design phase.

Identifying Customer Requirements

To obtain customer requirements, you need to not only talk to network engineers, but also talk to business unit personnel and company managers. Networks are designed to support applications; you want to determine the network services that you need to support. The steps to identify customer requirements are as follows:

Step 1   Identify network applications and services.

Step 2   Define the organizational goals.

Step 3   Define the possible organizational constraints.

Step 4   Define the technical goals.

Step 5   Define the possible technical constraints.

You need to identify current and planned applications and determine the importance of each application. Is e-mail as important as customer support? Is IP telephony being deployed? High-availability and high-bandwidth applications need to be identified for the design to accommodate their network requirements.

For organizational goals, you should identify if the company's goal is to improve customer support, add new customer services, increase competitiveness, or reduce costs. It may be a combination of these goals, with some of them being more important than others.

Organizational constraints include budget, personnel, policy, and schedule. The company might limit you to a certain budget or timeframe. The organization may require the project to be completed in an unreasonable timeframe. It may have limited personnel to support the assessment and design efforts, or it might have policy limitations to use certain protocols.

Technical goals support the organization's objectives and the supported applications. Technical goals include the following:

- Improve the network's response time throughput

- Decrease network failures and downtime

- Simplify network management

- Improve network security

- Improve reliability of mission-critical applications

- Modernize outdated technologies (technology refresh)

- Improve the network's scalability

Network design may be constrained by parameters that limit the solution. Legacy applications may still exist that must be supported going forward, and these applications may require a legacy protocol that may limit a design. Technical constraints include

- Existing wiring does not support new technology

- Bandwidth may not support new applications

- Network must support exiting legacy equipment

- Legacy applications must be supported

Characterizing the Existing Network

Characterizing the network is step 2 of the design methodology. In this section you learn to identify a network's major features, tools to analyze existing network traffic, and tools for auditing and monitoring network traffic.

Steps in Gathering Information

When arriving at a site that has an existing network, you need to obtain all the existing documentation. Sometimes no documented information exists. You should be prepared to use tools to obtain information and/or get access to log into the network devices to obtain information. Here are the steps for gathering information:

Step 1   Identify all existing information and documentation.

Step 2   Perform a network audit.

Step 3   Use traffic analysis to augment information on applications and protocols used.

When gathering exiting documentation, you look for site information such as site names, site addresses, site contacts, site hours of operation, and building and room access. Network infrastructure information includes locations and types of servers and network devices, data center and closet locations, LAN wiring, WAN technologies and circuit speeds, and power used. Logical network information includes IP addressing, routing protocols, network management, and security access lists used. You need to find out if voice or video is being used on the network.

Network Audit Tools

When performing a network audit, you have three primary sources of information:

- Existing documentation

- Existing network management software

- New network management tools

After gathering the existing documentation, you must obtain access to the existing management software. The client may already have CiscoWorks tools from which you can obtain hardware models and components and software versions. You can also obtain the existing router and switch configurations.

The network audit should provide the following information:

- Network device list

- Hardware models

- Software versions

- Configurations

- Auditing tool output information

- Interface speeds

- Link, CPU, and memory utilization

- WAN technology types and carrier information

When performing manual auditing on network devices, you can use the following commands to obtain information:

- **show tech-support**

- **show processes cpu**

- **show version**

- **show processes memory**

- **show running-config**

Example 1-1 shows the output of a **show version** command. This command shows the operating system version, the router type, the amount of flash and RAM memory, the router uptime, and interface types.

Example 1-1 **show version** *Command*

```
R2>show version
Cisco IOS Software, 7200 Software (C7200-K91P-M), Version 12.2(25)S9, RELEASE SO
FTWARE (fc1)
Technical Support: http://www.cisco.com/techsupport
Copyright  1986-2006 by Cisco Systems, Inc.
Compiled Tue 28-Mar-06 23:12 by alnguyen


ROM: ROMMON Emulation Microcode
BOOTLDR: 7200 Software (C7200-K91P-M), Version 12.2(25)S9, RELEASE SOFTWARE (fc1
)


 R2 uptime is 5 minutes
System returned to ROM by unknown reload cause - suspect boot_data[BOOT_COUNT] 0
x0, BOOT_COUNT 0, BOOTDATA 19
System image file is "tftp://255.255.255.255/unknown"


This product contains cryptographic features and is subject to United
```

Example 1-1   show version *Command (Continued)*

```
States and local country laws governing import, export, transfer and
use. Delivery of Cisco cryptographic products does not imply
third-party authority to import, export, distribute or use encryption.
Importers, exporters, distributors and users are responsible for
compliance with U.S. and local country laws. By using this product you
agree to comply with applicable laws and regulations. If you are unable
to comply with U.S. and local laws, return this product immediately.

A summary of U.S. laws governing Cisco cryptographic products may be found at:
http://www.cisco.com/wwl/export/crypto/tool/stqrg.html

If you require further assistance please contact us by sending email to
export@cisco.com.

Cisco 7206VXR (NPE400) processor (revision A) with 147456K/16384K bytes of memor
y.
Processor board ID 4294967295
R7000 CPU at 150Mhz, Implementation 39, Rev 2.1, 256KB L2 Cache
6 slot VXR midplane, Version 2.1

Last reset from power-on

PCI bus mb0_mb1 (Slots 0, 1, 3 and 5) has a capacity of 600 bandwidth points.
Current configuration on bus mb0_mb1 has a total of 200 bandwidth points.
This configuration is within the PCI bus capacity and is supported.

PCI bus mb2 (Slots 2, 4, 6) has a capacity of 600 bandwidth points.
Current configuration on bus mb2 has a total of 0 bandwidth points
This configuration is within the PCI bus capacity and is supported.

Please refer to the following document "Cisco 7200 Series Port
Adaptor Hardware Configuration Guidelines" on CCO <www.cisco.com>,
for c7200 bandwidth points oversubscription/usage guidelines.


1 FastEthernet interface
8 Serial interfaces
125K bytes of NVRAM.

65536K bytes of ATA PCMCIA card at slot 0 (Sector size 512 bytes).
8192K bytes of Flash internal SIMM (Sector size 256K).
Configuration register is 0x2102
```

Here are some of the network management tools you can use to obtain network audit information:

- **CiscoWorks** is Cisco's configuration and auditing tool from which you can obtain device inventory and configuration information.

- **WhatsUP Gold/WhatsUP Professional** is IPSwitch's network monitoring tool. It can monitor router bandwidth and do trend analysis. The tool can also monitor servers performing network discovery.

- **Castle Rock SNMPc** monitors network devices, servers, and WAN links. Web reports can be generated.

- **Cacti** is resource monitoring software and a graphing tool.

- **Netcordia NetMRI** is a network analysis product that discovers the network, performs analysis, and makes configuration recommendations.

- **NetQoS NetVoyant** does device performance monitoring and reports on network infrastructure, devices, and services.

- **Other tools** include network protocol analyzers (sniffers) such as Network General Sniffer and WildPackets EtherPeek.

Network Analysis Tools

To obtain application-level information, the IP packet needs to be further inspected. Cisco devices or dedicated hardware or software analyzers capture packets or use SNMP to gather specific information. Network analysis tools include the following:

- **Network-Based Application Recognition (NBAR)** is a Cisco IOS tool used to identify well-known applications and protocols.

- **NetFlow** is IOS software that collects and measures data as it passes through router and switch interfaces.

- **CNS NetFlow Collector Engine** is Cisco hardware that gathers every flow in a network segment.

- **Third-party tools** include Sniffer, Ethernet, and SolarWinds Orion.

Network Checklist

The following is a network checklist that can be used to determine a network's health status:

- No shared Ethernet segments are saturated (no more than 40 percent sustained network utilization). New segments should use switched and not shared technology.

- No WAN links are saturated (no more than 70 percent sustained network utilization).

- The response time is generally less than 100ms (one-tenth of a second). More commonly less than 2ms in a LAN.

- No segments have more than 20 percent broadcasts or multicast traffic. Broadcasts are sent to all hosts in a network and should be limited. Multicast traffic is sent to a group of hosts but should also be controlled and limited to only those hosts registered to receive it.

- No segments have more than one cyclic redundancy check (CRC) error per million bytes of data.

- On the Ethernet segments, less than 0.1 percent of the packets result in collisions.

- A CPU utilization at or over 75 percent for a 5-minute interval likely suggests network problems. Normal CPU utilization should be much lower during normal periods.

- The number of output queue drops has not exceeded 100 in an hour on any Cisco router.

- The number of input queue drops has not exceeded 50 in an hour on any Cisco router.

- The number of buffer misses has not exceeded 25 in an hour on any Cisco router.

- The number of ignored packets has not exceeded 10 in an hour on any interface on a Cisco router.

Designing the Network Topology and Solutions

This section describes the top-down approach for network design, reviews pilot and prototype test networks, and describes the components of the design document. As part of the Design phase of the PPDIOO methodology, a top-down approach is used that begins with the organization's requirements before looking at technologies. Network designs are tested using a pilot or prototype network before moving into the Implement phase.

Top-Down Approach

Top-down design simply means starting your design from the top layer of the OSI model and working your way down. Top-down design adapts the network and physical infrastructure to the network application's needs. With a top-down approach, network devices and technologies are not selected until the applications' requirements are analyzed.

Figure 1-3 shows a top-down structure design process. The design process begins with the applications and moves down to the network. Notice that SONA's Network Infrastructure and Infrastructure Services are incorporated into the design process. Logical subdivisions are then incorporated with specifics.

Figure 1-3   *Top-Down Design Process*

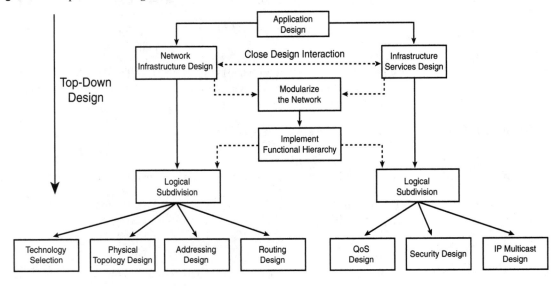

Table 1-2 compares the top-down approach to the bottom-up approach to network design.

Table 1-2   *Top-Down Design Compared to Bottom-Up Design*

Design Approach	Benefits	Disadvantages
Top-down	Incorporates the organization's requirements. Provides the big picture. The design meets current and future requirements.	More time-consuming.
Bottom-up	The design is based on previous experience and allows for a quick solution.	May result in inappropriate design. Organizational requirements are not included.

Pilot and Prototype Tests

As soon as the design is complete and before the full implementation, it is a best practice to test the new solution. This testing can be done in one of two ways: prototype or pilot.

A prototype network is a subset of the full design, tested in an isolated environment. The prototype does not connect to the existing network. The benefit of using a prototype is that it allows testing of the network design before it is deployed before affecting a production network.

A pilot site is an actual "live" location that serves as a test site before the solution is deployed to all locations in an enterprise. A pilot allows real-world problems to be discovered before deploying a network design solution to the rest of the internetwork.

With both a prototype and a pilot, successful testing leads to proving the design and moving forward with implementation. A failure leads to correcting the design and repeating the tests to correct any deficiencies.

Design Document

The design document describes the business requirements; old network architecture; network requirements; and design, plan, and configuration information for the new network. The network architects and analysts use it to document the new network changes, and it serves as documentation for the enterprise. The design document should include the following sections:

- **Introduction** describes the project's purpose and the reasons for the network design.

- **Design Requirements** lists the organization's requirements, constraints, and goals.

- **Existing Network Infrastructure** includes logical (Layer 3) topology diagrams; physical topology diagrams; audit results; routing protocols; a summary of applications; a list of network routers, switches, and other devices; configurations; and a description of issues.

- **Design** contains the specific design information, such as logical and physical topology, IP addressing, routing protocols, and security configurations.

- **Proof of Concept** results from live pilot or prototype testing.

- **Implementation Plan** includes the detailed steps for the network staff to implement the new installation and changes.

- **Appendixes** contains additional information and configurations.

References and Recommended Reading

"The Intelligent Information Network: Introduction," http://www.cisco.com/en/US/netsol/ns648/networking_solutions_intelligent_information_network_home.html

"Service-Oriented Network Architecture: Introduction," http://www.cisco.com/en/US/netsol/ns629/networking_solutions_market_segment_solutions_home.html

"Service-Oriented Network Architecture: What Is It?" http://www.cisco.com/en/US/netsol/ns629/networking_solutions_products_generic_content0900aecd8058763e.html

"What Is IIN?: Introduction," http://www.cisco.com/en/US/netsol/ns650/networking_solutions_market_segment_solution.html

Foundation Summary

The "Foundation Summary" section of each chapter lists the most important facts from the chapter. Although this section does not list every fact from the chapter that will be on the CCDA exam, a well-prepared CCDA candidate should at a minimum know all the details in each "Foundation Summary" before taking the exam.

Table 1-3 describes the IIN phases.

Table 1-3 *IIN Phases*

IIN Phase	Description
Integrated Transport	Convergence of voice, data, and video into a single transport network.
Integrated Service	Merges common elements such as storage, servers, and network elements. Virtualization of systems.
Integrated Application	Allows the network to become application-aware.

Table 1-4 describes the SONA layers.

Table 1-4 *SONA Layers*

SONA Layer	Description
Network Infrastructure layer	Contains the Cisco Enterprise Architecture, servers, storage, and clients.
Interactive Service layer	Optimization of the communication between applications and services using intelligent network functions such as security, identity, voice, virtualization, and quality of service.
Application layer	Contains business and collaboration applications.

Table 1-5 summarizes the SONA infrastructure services.

Table 1-5 *SONA Infrastructure Services*

Infrastructure Service	Description
Identity Services	Includes AAA, NAC, and NBAR
Mobility Services	Access regardless of location

Table 1-5 *SONA Infrastructure Services (Continued)*

Infrastructure Service	Description
Storage Services	Storage of critical data.
Compute Services	Improves compute resources.
Security Services	Security for all resources.
Voice and Collaboration Services	Allows collaboration of users.

Table 1-6 summarizes the phases of the PPDIOO network life cycle.

Table 1-6 *PPDIOO Network Life Cycle Phases*

PPDIOO Phase	Description
Prepare	Establishes organization and business requirements, develops a network strategy, and proposes a high-level architecture.
Plan	Identifies the network requirements by characterizing and assessing the network, performing a gap analysis.
Design	Provides high availability, reliability, security, scalability, and performance.
Implement	Installation and configuration of new equipment.
Operate	Day-to-day network operations.
Optimize	Proactive network management. Modifications to the design.

Table 1-7 summarizes areas in characterizing the network.

Table 1-7 *Characterizing the Network*

	Description
Steps in gathering information	Step 1: Obtain existing information and documentation Step 2: Network audit Step 3: Traffic analysis
Primary sources of network audit information	Existing documentation Existing network management software New network management tools

Table 1-8 compares the top-down design approach to the bottom-up design approach.

Table 1-8 *Top-Down Design Compared to Bottom-Up Design*

Design Approach	Benefits	Disadvantages
Top-down	Incorporates the organization's requirements. Provides the big picture. The design meets current and future requirements.	More time-consuming.
Bottom-up	The design is based on previous experience and allows for a quick solution.	May result in inappropriate design. Organizational requirements are not included.

Table 1-9 summarizes the sections of the design document.

Table 1-9 *Sections of the Design Document*

Section	Description
Introduction	Purpose and goals of the network design.
Design Requirements	Organization requirements and constraints.
Existing Network Infrastructure	Contains diagrams, hardware and software versions, and existing configurations.
Design	New logical topology, design, and IP addressing.
Proof of Concept	Results from pilot or prototype.
Implementation Plan	Detailed steps for implementation.
Appendixes	Supporting information.

Q&A

As mentioned in the introduction, you have two choices for review questions: here in the book or the exam questions on the CD-ROM. The answers to these questions appear in Appendix A.

For more practice with exam format questions, use the exam engine on the CD-ROM.

1. List the three layers of SONA.

2. List the three phases of IIN.

3. List the six infrastructure services.

4. List the drivers for IIN.

5. What name is given to the network's ability to optimize application performance by integrating application message handling and security?

6. List the PPDIOO phases in order.

7. Match each SONA layer with its description.

    i. Network Infrastructure

    ii. Interactive Service

    iii. Application

    a. Virtualization

    b. Contains servers, storage, and switches

    c. Customer relationship and unified messaging

8. SONA guides the evolution of what?

    a. Enterprise networks to integrated network services

    b. Organizations to application service providers

    c. Enterprise networks to intelligent information networks

    d. Enterprise networks to integrated information networks

    e. Cisco Enterprise Architecture to SONA

9. Match each PPDIOO phase with its description.

i. Implement

ii. Optimize

iii. Design

iv. Prepare

v. Operate

vi. Plan

a. Establish requirements

b. Gap analysis

c. Provides high-availability design

d. Installation and configuration

c. Day to day

e. Proactive management

10. Match each infrastructure service with its description.

i. Identity

ii. Mobility

iii. Storage

iv. Compute

v. Security

vi. Voice/collaboration

a. Access from a remote location

b. Improved computational resources

c. Unified messaging

d. AAA, NAC

e. Storage of critical data

f. Secure communications

11. A company location is used to test a new VoIP solution. What is this type of test called?

  a. Prototype

  b. Pilot

  c. Implementation

  d. New

12. An isolated network is created to test a new design. What is this type of test called?

   a. Prototype

   b. Pilot

   c. Implementation

   d. New

13. NBAR, NetFlow, and EtherPeek are examples of what?

   a. Network audit tools

   b. Network analysis tools

   c. SNMP tools

   d. Trending tools

14. Monitoring commands, CiscoWorks, and WhatsUP are examples of what?

   a. Network audit tools

   b. Network analysis tools

   c. SNMP tools

   d. Trending tools

15. Which of the following are technical constraints? (Select all that apply.)

   a. Existing wiring

   b. Existing network circuit bandwidth

   c. Improving the LAN's scalability

   d. Adding redundancy

16. Which of the following are technical goals? (Select all that apply.)

   a. Existing wiring

   b. Existing network circuit bandwidth

   c. Improving the LAN's scalability

   d. Adding redundancy

17. Which of the following are organizational goals? (Select all that apply.)

   a. Improving customer support

   b. Budget has been established

   c. Increasing competitiveness

   d. Completion in three months

   e. Reducing operational costs

   f. Network personnel are busy

18. Which of the following are organizational constraints? (Select all that apply.)

   a. Improving customer support

   b. Budget has been established

   c. Increasing competitiveness

   d. Completion in three months

   e. Reducing operational costs

   f. Network personnel are busy

19. What components are included in the design document? (Select four.)

   a. IP addressing scheme

   b. Implementation plan

   c. List of Layer 2 devices

   d. Design requirements

   e. Selected routing protocols

   f. List of Layer 1 devices

20. Match each design document section with its description.

   i. Introduction

   ii. Design Requirements

   iii. Existing Network Infrastructure

   iv. Design

   v. Proof of Concept

   vi. Implementation Plan

   vii. Appendix

   a. Detailed steps

   b. Current diagram and configuration

   c. Organizational requirements

   d. Goals

   e. Pilot

   f. New logical topology

   g. Supporting information

21. The network health analysis is based on what information?

    a. The number of users accessing the Internet

    b. The statements made by the CIO

    c. Statistics from the existing network

    d. The IP addressing scheme

22. When performing a network audit, you encounter a shared network hub. Collisions exist at 10 percent. What do you recommend?

    a. Replace the 10-Mbps hub with a Fast Ethernet hub.

    b. Replace the hub with a Fast Ethernet switch.

    c. Increase the hub amplification to reduce the number of collisions.

    d. There is no problem with 10 percent collisions in a shared hub.

23. While performing a network audit, you encounter a Frame Relay WAN segment running at a sustained rate of 75 percent from 9 a.m. to 5 p.m. What do you recommend?

    a. Nothing. The daily 24-hour average rate is still 45 percent.

    b. Change from Frame Relay to MPLS.

    c. Increase the provisioned WAN bandwidth.

    d. Deny VoIP calls from 9 a.m. to 5 a.m.

24. What information is included in the network audit report? (Select all that apply.)

    a. Network device list

    b. IOS versions

    c. Router models

    d. Interface speeds

    e. WAN utilization

25. What are the phases of IIN? (Select all that apply.)

    a. Intelligent Transport

    b. Intelligent Application

    c. Integrated Transport

    d. Intelligent Service

    e. Integrated Service

    f. Integrated Application

This chapter covers the following subjects:

- Hierarchical Network Models

- Cisco Enterprise Architecture Model

- Network Availability

CHAPTER 2

Network Structure Models

This chapter reviews the hierarchical network model and introduces Cisco's Enterprise Architecture model. This architecture model separates network design into more manageable modules. This chapter also addresses the use of device, media, and route redundancy to improve network availability.

"Do I Know This Already?" Quiz

The purpose of the "Do I Know This Already?" quiz is to help you decide whether you need to read the entire chapter. If you already intend to read the entire chapter, you do not necessarily need to answer these questions now.

The eight-question quiz, derived from the major sections in the "Foundation Topics" portion of the chapter, helps you determine how to spend your limited study time. Table 2-1 outlines the major topics discussed in this chapter and the "Do I Know This Already?" quiz questions that correspond to those topics.

Table 2-1 *"Do I Know This Already?" Foundation Topics Section-to-Question Mapping*

Foundation Topics Section	Questions Covered in This Section
Hierarchical Network Models	1, 3
Cisco Enterprise Architecture Model	2, 5, 6, 7
Network Availability	4, 8

CAUTION The goal of self-assessment is to gauge your mastery of the topics in this chapter. If you do not know the answer to a question or you are only partially sure, you should mark this question wrong for the purposes of the self-assessment. Giving yourself credit for an answer you correctly guess skews your self-assessment results and might give you a false sense of security.

1. In the hierarchical network model, which layer is responsible for fast transport?

    a. Network

    b. Core

    c. Distribution

    d. Access

2. Which Enterprise Architecture model component interfaces with the service provider (SP)?

    a. Campus infrastructure

    b. Access layer

    c. Enterprise Edge

    d. Edge distribution

3. In the hierarchical network model, at which layer do security filtering, address aggregation, and media translation occur?

    a. Network

    b. Core

    c. Distribution

    d. Access

4. Which of the following is/are method(s) of workstation-to-router redundancy in the access layer?

    a. AppleTalk Address Resolution Protocol (AARP)

    b. Hot Standby Router Protocol (HSRP)

    c. Routing Information Protocol (RIP)

    d. Answers B and C

    e. Answers A, B, and C

5. The network-management module has tie-ins to which component(s)?

    a. Campus infrastructure

    b. Server farm

    c. Enterprise Edge

    d. SP Edge

    e. Answers A and B

    f. Answers A, B, and C

    g. Answers A, B, C, and D

6. Which of the following is an SP Edge module in the Cisco Enterprise Architecture model?

    a. Public Switched Telephone Network (PSTN) service

    b. Edge distribution

    c. Server farm

    d. Core layer

7. In which module would you place Cisco CallManager?

    a. Campus core

    b. E-commerce

    c. Server farm

    d. Edge distribution farm

8. High availability, port security, and rate limiting are functions of which hierarchical layer?

    a. Network

    b. Core

    c. Distribution

    d. Access

The answers to the "Do I Know This Already?" quiz appear in Appendix A, "Answers to Chapter 'Do I Know This Already?' Quizzes and Q&A Sections." The suggested choices for your next step are as follows:

- **6 or less overall score**—Read the entire chapter. It includes the "Foundation Topics," "Foundation Summary," and "Q&A" sections.

- **7 or 8 overall score**—If you want more review on these topics, skip to the "Foundation Summary" section and then go to the "Q&A" section. Otherwise, move to the next chapter.

Foundation Topics

With the complexities of network design, the CCDA needs to understand network models used to simplify the design process. The hierarchical network model was one of the first Cisco models that divided the network into core, distribution, and access layers.

The Cisco Enterprise Architecture is a model that provides a functional modular approach to network design. In addition to a hierarchy, modules are used to organize server farms, network management, campus networks, WANs, and the Internet.

Hierarchical Network Models

Hierarchical models enable you to design internetworks that use specialization of function combined with a hierarchical organization. Such a design simplifies the tasks required to build a network that meets current requirements and can grow to meet future requirements. Hierarchical models use layers to simplify the tasks for internetworking. Each layer can focus on specific functions, allowing you to choose the right systems and features for each layer. Hierarchical models apply to both LAN and WAN design.

Benefits of the Hierarchical Model

The benefits of using hierarchical models for your network design include the following:

- Cost savings

- Ease of understanding

- Modular network growth

- Improved fault isolation

After adopting hierarchical design models, many organizations report cost savings because they are no longer trying to do everything in one routing or switching platform. The model's modular nature enables appropriate use of bandwidth within each layer of the hierarchy, reducing the provisioning of bandwidth in advance of actual need.

Keeping each design element simple and functionally focused facilitates ease of understanding, which helps control training and staff costs. You can distribute network monitoring and management reporting systems to the different layers of modular network architectures, which also helps control management costs.

Hierarchical design facilitates changes. In a network design, modularity lets you create design elements that you can replicate as the network grows. As each element in the network design requires change, the cost and complexity of making the upgrade are contained to a small subset of the overall network. In large, flat network architectures, changes tend to impact a large number of systems. Limited mesh topologies within a layer or component, such as the campus core or backbone connecting central sites, retain value even in the hierarchical design models.

Structuring the network into small, easy-to-understand elements improves fault isolation. Network managers can easily understand the transition points in the network, which helps identify failure points.

Today's fast-converging protocols were designed for hierarchical topologies. To control the impact of routing-protocol processing and bandwidth consumption, you must use modular hierarchical topologies with protocols designed with these controls in mind, such as Open Shortest Path First (OSPF).

Hierarchical network design facilitates route summarization. EIGRP and all other routing protocols benefit greatly from route summarization. Route summarization reduces routing-protocol overhead on links in the network and reduces routing-protocol processing within the routers.

Hierarchical Network Design

As shown in Figure 2-1, a traditional hierarchical LAN design has three layers:

- The core layer provides fast transport between distribution switches within the enterprise campus.

- The distribution layer provides policy-based connectivity.

- The access layer provides workgroup and user access to the network.

Figure 2-1 *Hierarchical Network Design Has Three Layers: Core, Distribution, and Access*

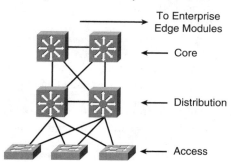

Each layer provides necessary functionality to the enterprise campus network. You do not need to implement the layers as distinct physical entities. You can implement each layer in one or more devices or as cooperating interface components sharing a common chassis. Smaller networks can "collapse" multiple layers to a single device with only an implied hierarchy. Maintaining an explicit awareness of hierarchy is useful as the network grows.

Core Layer

The core layer is the network's high-speed switching backbone that is crucial to corporate communications. The core layer should have the following characteristics:

- Fast transport

- High reliability

- Redundancy

- Fault tolerance

- Low latency and good manageability

- Avoidance of slow packet manipulation caused by filters or other processes

- Limited and consistent diameter

- Quality of service (QoS)

When a network uses routers, the number of router hops from edge to edge is called the *diameter*. As noted, it is considered good practice to design for a consistent diameter within a hierarchical network. The trip from any end station to another end station across the backbone should have the same number of hops. The distance from any end station to a server on the backbone should also be consistent.

Limiting the internetwork's diameter provides predictable performance and ease of troubleshooting. You can add distribution layer routers and client LANs to the hierarchical model without increasing the core layer's diameter. Use of a block implementation isolates existing end stations from most effects of network growth.

Distribution Layer

The network's distribution layer is the isolation point between the network's access and core layers. The distribution layer can have many roles, including implementing the following functions:

- Policy (for example, ensuring that traffic sent from a particular network is forwarded out one interface while all other traffic is forwarded out another interface)

- Redundancy and load balancing

- QoS

- Security filtering

- Address or area aggregation or summarization

- Departmental or workgroup access

- Broadcast or multicast domain definition

- Routing between virtual LANs (VLAN)

- Media translations (for example, between Ethernet and Token Ring)

- Redistribution between routing domains (for example, between two different routing protocols)

- Demarcation between static and dynamic routing protocols

You can use several Cisco IOS Software features to implement policy at the distribution layer:

- Filtering by source or destination address

- Filtering on input or output ports

- Hiding internal network numbers by route filtering

- Static routing

- QoS mechanisms (for example, ensuring that all devices along a path can accommodate the requested parameters)

The distribution layer provides aggregation of routes providing route summarization to the core. In the campus LANs, the distribution layer provides routing between VLANs that also apply security and QoS policies.

Access Layer

The access layer provides user access to local segments on the network. The access layer is characterized by switched and shared-bandwidth LAN segments in a campus environment. Microsegmentation using LAN switches provides high bandwidth to workgroups by reducing collision domains on Ethernet segments. Some functions of the access layer include the following:

- High availability

- Port security

- Broadcast suppression

- QoS

- Rate limiting

- Address Resolution Protocol (ARP) inspection

- Virtual access control lists (VACL)

- Spanning tree

- Trust classification

- Power over Ethernet (PoE) and auxiliary VLANs for VoIP

- Auxiliary VLANs

You implement high-availability models at the access layer. The later section "Network Availability" covers availability models. The LAN switch in the access layer can control access to the port and limit the rate at which traffic is sent to and from the port. You can implement access by identifying the MAC address using ARP, trusting the host, and using access lists.

Other chapters of this book cover the other functions in the list.

For small office/home office (SOHO) environments, the entire hierarchy collapses to interfaces on a single device. Remote access to the central corporate network is through traditional WAN technologies such as ISDN, Frame Relay, and leased lines. You can implement features such as dial-on-demand routing (DDR) and static routing to control costs. Remote access can include virtual private network (VPN) technology.

Hierarchical Model Examples

You can implement the hierarchical model by using either routers or switches. Figure 2-2 is an example of a switched hierarchical design in the enterprise campus. In this design, the core provides high-speed transport between the distribution layers. The building-distribution layer provides redundancy and allows policies to be applied to the building-access layer. Layer 3 links between the core and distribution switches are recommended to allow the routing protocol to take care of load balancing and fast route redundancy in the event of a link failure. The server-distribution layer provides redundancy and allows access to the servers to be filtered. For example, Cisco Unified CallManager servers are placed in the server farm, and the server distribution is used to control access to the IP Telephony servers.

Figure 2-3 shows examples of a routed hierarchical design. In this design, the enterprise network connects to the WAN core. WAN distribution routers provide site redundancy to the remote sites. The selected routing protocol (EIGRP or OSPF) provides Layer 3 load balancing from the remote sites to the core.

Figure 2-2 *Switched Hierarchical Design*

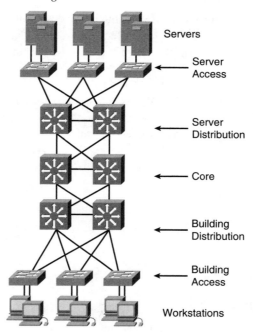

Figure 2-3 *Routed Hierarchical Design*

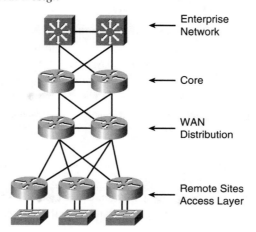

Cisco Enterprise Architecture Model

The Cisco Enterprise Architecture model facilitates the design of larger, more scalable networks. It represents the focused views of the Cisco Service-Oriented Network Architecture (SONA), which concentrates on each area of the network. SONA is covered in Chapter 1, "Network Design Methodology."

As networks become more sophisticated, it is necessary to use a more modular approach to design than just WAN and LAN core, distribution, and access layers. The architecture divides the network into functional network modules. The six modules of the Cisco Enterprise Architecture are

- Enterprise Campus module

- Enterprise Edge module

- Enterprise WAN module

- Enterprise Data Center module

- Enterprise Branch module

- Enterprise Teleworker module

The Cisco Enterprise Architecture maintains the concept of distribution and access components connecting users, WAN services, and server farms through a high-speed campus backbone. The modular approach in design should be a guide to the network architect. In smaller networks, the layers can collapse into a single layer, even a single device, but the functions remain.

Figure 2-4 shows the Cisco Enterprise Architecture model. The Enterprise Campus module contains a campus infrastructure that consists of core, building distribution, and building access layers, with a server farm/data center and edge distribution. Edge distribution provides distribution functions from the campus infrastructure to the Enterprise Edge. The Enterprise Edge module consists of the Internet, e-commerce, VPN, and WAN functions that connect the enterprise to the service provider's facilities. The SP Edge provides Internet, PSTN, and WAN services.

The network-management servers reside in the campus infrastructure but have tie-ins to all the components in the enterprise network for monitoring and management.

The Enterprise Edge connects to the edge-distribution module of the enterprise campus. In small and medium sites, the edge distribution can collapse into the campus-backbone component. It provides connectivity to outbound services that are further described in later sections.

Figure 2-4   *Cisco Enterprise Architecture Model*

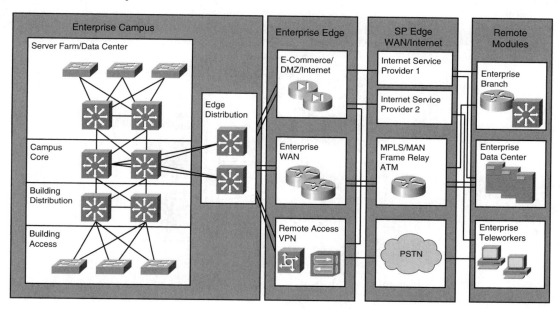

Enterprise Campus Module

The Enterprise Campus consists of the following submodules:

- Campus core

- Building distribution

- Building access

- Edge distribution

- Server farm/data center

Figure 2-5 shows the Enterprise Campus model. The campus infrastructure consists of the campus core, building-distribution, and building-access layers. The campus core provides a high-speed switched backbone between buildings, to the server farm and to the enterprise distribution. This segment consists of redundant and fast convergence connectivity. The building-distribution layer aggregates all the closet access switches and performs access control, QoS, route redundancy, and load balancing. The building-access switches provide VLAN access, PoE for IP phones and wireless access points, broadcast suppression, and spanning tree.

Figure 2-5 *Enterprise Campus Model*

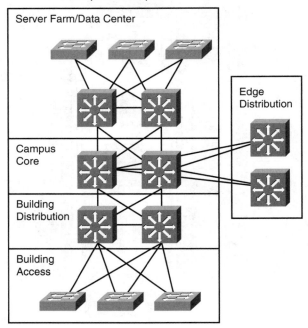

The server farm or data center provides high-speed access and high availability (redundancy) to the servers. Enterprise servers such as file and print servers, application servers, e-mail servers, and Domain Name System (DNS) servers, are placed in the server farm. Cisco Unified CallManager servers are placed in the server farm for IP telephony networks. Network management servers are located in the server farm, but these servers link to each module in the campus to provide network monitoring, logging, trending, and configuration management.

An enterprise campus infrastructure can apply to small, medium, and large locations. In most instances, large campus locations have a three-tier design with a wiring-closet component (building-access layer), a building-distribution layer, and a campus core layer. Small campus locations likely have a two-tier design with a wiring-closet component (Ethernet access layer) and a backbone core (collapsed core and distribution layers). It is also possible to configure distribution functions in a multilayer building-access device to maintain the focus of the campus backbone on fast transport. Medium-sized campus network designs sometimes use a three-tier implementation or a two-tier implementation, depending on the number of ports, service requirements, manageability, performance, and availability required.

Enterprise Edge Module

As shown in Figure 2-6, the Enterprise Edge consists of the following submodules:

- E-commerce networks and servers

- Internet connectivity and DMZ

- VPN and remote access

- Enterprise WAN

Figure 2-6 *Enterprise Edge Module*

E-Commerce

The e-commerce submodule provides highly available networks for business services. It uses the high-availability designs of the server farm module with the Internet connectivity of the Internet module. Design techniques are the same as those described for these modules. Devices located in the e-commerce submodule include

- Web and application servers

- Database servers

- Firewalls

- Network and server intrusion detection systems (IDS)

Internet Edge

The Internet submodule provides services such as public servers, e-mail, and DNS. Connectivity to one or several Internet service providers (ISP) is also provided. Components of this submodule include

- Firewalls

- Internet routers

- FTP and HTTP servers

- SMTP mail servers

- DNS servers

Several models connect the enterprise to the Internet. The simplest form is to have a single circuit between the enterprise and the SP, as shown in Figure 2-7. The drawback is that you have no redundancy or failover if the circuit fails.

Figure 2-7 *Simple Internet Connection*

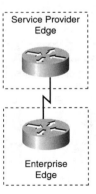

You can use multihoming solutions to provide redundancy or failover for Internet service. Figure 2-8 shows four Internet multihoming options:

- **Option 1**—Single router, dual links to one ISP

- **Option 2**—Single router, dual links to two ISPs

- **Option 3**—Dual routers, dual links to one ISP

- **Option 4**—Dual routers, dual links to two ISPs

Figure 2-8 *Internet Multihoming Options*

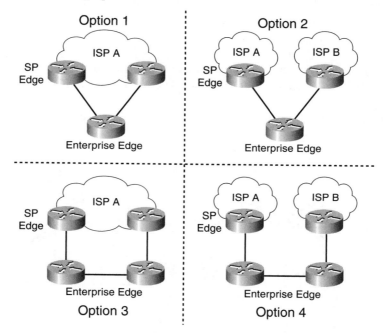

Option 1 provides link redundancy but does not provide ISP and local router redundancy. Option 2 provides link and ISP redundancy but does not provide redundancy for a local router failure. Option 3 provides link and local router redundancy but does not provide for an ISP failure. Option 4 provides for full redundancy of the local router, links, and ISPs.

VPN/Remote Access

The VPN/remote access submodule provides remote-access termination services, including authentication for remote users and sites. Components of this submodule include

- Firewalls

- VPN concentrators

- Dial-in access concentrators

- Adaptive Security Appliances (ASA)

- Network intrusion detection system (IDS) appliances

If you use a remote-access terminal server, this module connects to the PSTN. Today's networks often prefer VPNs over remote-access terminal servers and dedicated WAN links. VPNs reduce communication expenses by leveraging the infrastructure of SPs. For critical applications, the cost savings might be offset by a reduction in enterprise control and the loss of deterministic service. Remote offices, mobile users, and home offices access the Internet using the local SP with secured IP Security (IPsec) tunnels to the VPN/remote access submodule via the Internet submodule.

Figure 2-9 shows a VPN design. Branch offices obtain local Internet access from an ISP. Teleworkers also obtain local Internet access. VPN software creates secured VPN tunnels to the VPN server that is located in the VPN submodule of the Enterprise Edge.

Figure 2-9   *VPN Architecture*

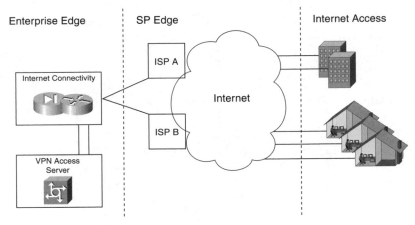

Enterprise WAN

The Enterprise Edge includes access to WANs. WAN technologies include the following:

- MPLS

- Metro Ethernet

- Leased lines

- Synchronous Optical Network (SONET) and Synchronous Digital Hierarchy (SDH)

- PPP

- Frame Relay

- ATM

- Cable

- Digital subscriber line (DSL)

- Wireless

Chapters 5 and 6 cover these WAN technologies. Routers in the Enterprise WAN provide WAN access, QoS, routing, redundancy, and access control to the WAN. For MPLS networks, the WAN routers prioritize IP packets based on configured DSCP values to use one of several MPLS QoS levels. Figure 2-10 shows the WAN module connecting to the Frame Relay SP Edge. The Enterprise Edge routers in the WAN module connect to the SP's Frame Relay switches.

Figure 2-10   *WAN Module*

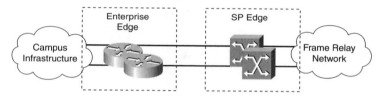

Service Provider (SP) Edge Module

The SP Edge module, shown in Figure 2-11, consists of SP edge services such as the following:

- Internet services

- PSTN services

- WAN services

Enterprises use SPs to acquire network services. ISPs offer enterprises access to the Internet. ISPs can route the enterprise's networks to their network and to upstream and peer Internet providers. Some ISPs can provide Internet services with DSL access. Connectivity with multiple ISPs was described in the "Internet Edge" section.

For voice services, PSTN providers offer access to the global public voice network. For the enterprise network, the PSTN lets dialup users access the enterprise via analog or cellular wireless technologies. It is also used for WAN backup using ISDN services.

WAN SPs offer MPLS, Frame Relay, ATM, and other WAN services for Enterprise site-to-site connectivity with permanent connections. These and other WAN technologies are described in Chapter 5, "WAN Technologies."

Figure 2-11   *WAN/Internet SP Edge Module*

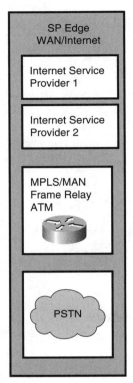

Remote Modules

The remote modules of the Cisco Enterprise Architecture model are the Enterprise Branch, Enterprise Data Center, and Enterprise Teleworker modules.

Enterprise Branch Module

The Enterprise Branch normally consists of remote offices or sales offices. These branch offices rely on the WAN to use the services and applications provided in the main campus. Infrastructure at the remote site usually consists of a WAN router and a small LAN switch, as shown in Figure 2-12. Instead of MPLS or Frame Relay, it is common to use site-to-site VPN technologies to connect to the main campus.

Figure 2-12 *Enterprise Branch Module*

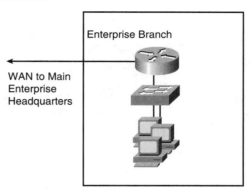

Enterprise Data Center Module

The Enterprise Data Center uses the network to enhance the server, storage, and application servers. The offsite data center provides disaster recovery and business continuance services for the enterprise. Highly available WAN services are used to connect the enterprise campus to the remote Enterprise Data Center. The data center components include

■ **Network devices**—Routers and high-speed switches

■ **High-speed LAN technologies**—Gigabit and 10 Gigabit Ethernet, InfiniBand, optical switching

■ **Interactive services**—Computer infrastructure services, storage services, security, application optimization

■ **DC management**—Fault and trend management and Cisco VFrame for server and service management

Enterprise Teleworker Module

The Enterprise Teleworker module consists of a small office or a mobile user who needs to access services of the enterprise campus. As shown in Figure 2-13, mobile users connect from their homes, hotels, or other locations using dialup or Internet access lines. VPN clients are used to allow mobile users to securely access enterprise applications. The Cisco Teleworker solution provides a solution for teleworkers that is centrally managed using small integrated service routers (ISR) in the VPN solution. IP phone capabilities are also provided in the Cisco Teleworker solution, providing corporate voice services for mobile users.

Figure 2-13   *Enterprise Teleworker Solution*

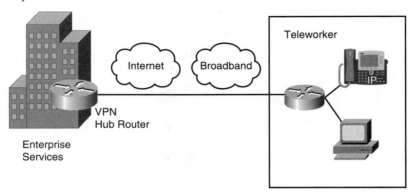

Network Availability

This section covers designs for high-availability network services in the access layer.

When designing a network topology for a customer who has critical systems, services, or network paths, you should determine the likelihood that these components will fail and design redundancy where necessary. Consider incorporating one of the following types of redundancy into your design:

■   Workstation-to-router redundancy in the building-access layer

■   Server redundancy in the server farm module

■   Route redundancy within and between network components

■   Media redundancy in the access layer

The following sections discuss each type of redundancy.

Workstation-to-Router Redundancy

When a workstation has traffic to send to a station that is not local, the workstation has many possible ways to discover the address of a router on its network segment, including the following:

■   ARP

■   Explicit configuration

■   ICMP Router Discovery Protocol (RDP)

■   RIP

- HSRP

- Global Load Balancing Protocol (GLBP)

The following sections cover each of these methods.

ARP

Some IP workstations send an ARP frame to find a remote station. A router running proxy ARP can respond with its data link layer address. Cisco routers run proxy ARP by default.

Explicit Configuration

Most IP workstations must be configured with the IP address of a default router, which is sometimes called the default gateway.

In an IP environment, the most common method for a workstation to find a server is via explicit configuration (a default router). If the workstation's default router becomes unavailable, you must reconfigure the workstation with the address of a different router. Some IP stacks enable you to configure multiple default routers, but many other IP implementations support only one default router.

RDP

RFC 1256 specifies an extension to Internet Control Message Protocol (ICMP) that allows an IP workstation and router to run RDP to let the workstation learn a router's address.

RIP

An IP workstation can run RIP to learn about routers. You should use RIP in passive mode rather than active mode. (Active mode means that the station sends RIP frames every 30 seconds.) Usually in these implementations, the workstation is a UNIX system running the **routed** or **gated** UNIX process.

HSRP

The Cisco HSRP provides a way for IP workstations that support only one default router to keep communicating on the internetwork even if their default router becomes unavailable. HSRP works by creating a phantom router that has its own IP and MAC addresses. The workstations use this phantom router as their default router.

HSRP routers on a LAN communicate among themselves to designate two routers as *active* and *standby*. The active router sends periodic hello messages. The other HSRP routers listen for the hello messages. If the active router fails and the other HSRP routers stop receiving hello messages, the standby router takes over and becomes the active router. Because the new active router assumes both the phantom's IP and MAC addresses, end nodes see no change. They continue to send packets to the phantom router's MAC address, and the new active router delivers those packets.

HSRP also works for proxy ARP. When an active HSRP router receives an ARP request for a node that is not on the local LAN, the router replies with the phantom router's MAC address instead of its own. If the router that originally sent the ARP reply later loses its connection, the new active router can still deliver the traffic.

Figure 2-14 shows a sample implementation of HSRP.

Figure 2-14 *HSRP: The Phantom Router Represents the Real Routers*

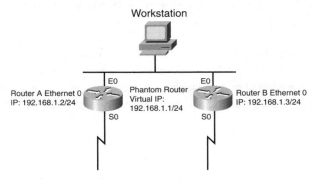

In Figure 2-14, the following sequence occurs:

1. The workstation is configured to use the phantom router (192.168.1.1) as its default router.

2. Upon booting, the routers elect Router A as the HSRP active router. The active router does the work for the HSRP phantom. Router B is the HSRP standby router.

3. When the workstation sends an ARP frame to find its default router, Router A responds with the phantom router's MAC address.

4. If Router A goes offline, Router B takes over as the active router, continuing the delivery of the workstation's packets. The change is transparent to the workstation.

GLBP

GLBP protects data traffic from a failed router or circuit, such as Hot Standby Router Protocol (HSRP), while allowing packet load sharing between a group of redundant routers. The difference in GLBP from HSRP is that it provides for load balancing between the redundant routers. It load balances by using a single virtual IP address and multiple virtual MAC addresses. Each host is configured with the same virtual IP address, and all routers in the virtual router group participate in forwarding packets. GLBP members communicate between each other through hello messages sent every three seconds to the multicast address 224.0.0.102, User Datagram Protocol (UDP) port 3222.

Server Redundancy

Some environments need fully redundant (mirrored) file and application servers. For example, in a brokerage firm where traders must access data to buy and sell stocks, two or more redundant servers can replicate the data. Also, you can deploy CallManager servers in clusters for redundancy. The servers should be on different networks and use redundant power supplies.

Route Redundancy

Designing redundant routes has two purposes: balancing loads and increasing availability.

Load Balancing

Most IP routing protocols can balance loads across parallel links that have equal cost. Use the **maximum-paths** command to change the number of links that the router will balance over for IP; the default is four, and the maximum is six. To support load balancing, keep the bandwidth consistent within a layer of the hierarchical model so that all paths have the same cost. (Cisco Interior Gateway Routing Protocol [IGRP] and Enhanced IGRP [EIGRP] are exceptions because they can load-balance traffic across multiple routes that have different metrics by using a feature called *variance*.)

A hop-based routing protocol does load balancing over unequal-bandwidth paths as long as the hop count is equal. After the slower link becomes saturated, packet loss at the saturated link prevents full utilization of the higher-capacity links; this scenario is called pinhole congestion. You can avoid pinhole congestion by designing and provisioning equal-bandwidth links within one layer of the hierarchy or by using a routing protocol that takes bandwidth into account.

IP load balancing in a Cisco router depends on which switching mode the router uses. Process switching load-balances on a packet-by-packet basis. Fast, autonomous, silicon, optimum, distributed, and NetFlow switching load-balance on a destination-by-destination basis because the processor caches information used to encapsulate the packets based on the destination for these types of switching modes.

Increasing Availability

In addition to facilitating load balancing, redundant routes increase network availability.

You should keep bandwidth consistent within a given design component to facilitate load balancing. Another reason to keep bandwidth consistent within a layer of a hierarchy is that routing protocols converge much faster on multiple equal-cost paths to a destination network.

By using redundant, meshed network designs, you can minimize the effect of link failures. Depending on the convergence time of the routing protocols, a single link failure cannot have a catastrophic effect.

You can design redundant network links to provide a full mesh or a well-connected partial mesh. In a full-mesh network, every router has a link to every other router, as shown in Figure 2-15. A full-mesh network provides complete redundancy and also provides good performance because there is just a single-hop delay between any two sites. The number of links in a full mesh is $n(n–1)/2$, where n is the number of routers. Each router is connected to every other router. A well-connected partial-mesh network provides every router with links to at least two other routing devices in the network.

Figure 2-15   *Full-Mesh Network: Every Router Has a Link to Every Other Router in the Network*

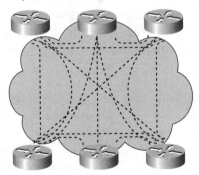

A full-mesh network can be expensive to implement in WANs due to the required number of links. In addition, groups of routers that broadcast routing updates or service advertisements have practical limits to scaling. As the number of routing peers increases, the amount of bandwidth and CPU resources devoted to processing broadcasts increases.

A suggested guideline is to keep broadcast traffic at less than 20 percent of the bandwidth of each link; this amount limits the number of peer routers that can exchange routing tables or service advertisements. When planning redundancy, follow guidelines for simple, hierarchical design. Figure 2-16 illustrates a classic hierarchical and redundant enterprise design that uses a partial-mesh rather than a full-mesh topology. For LAN designs, links between the access and distribution layer can be Fast Ethernet, with links to the core at Gigabit Ethernet speeds.

Figure 2-16   *Partial-Mesh Design with Redundancy*

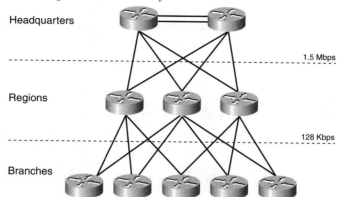

Media Redundancy

In mission-critical applications, it is often necessary to provide redundant media.

In switched networks, switches can have redundant links to each other. This redundancy is good because it minimizes downtime, but it can result in broadcasts continuously circling the network, which is called a *broadcast storm*. Because Cisco switches implement the IEEE 802.1d spanning-tree algorithm, you can avoid this looping in Spanning Tree Protocol (STP). The spanning-tree algorithm guarantees that only one path is active between two network stations. The algorithm permits redundant paths that are automatically activated when the active path experiences problems.

Because WAN links are often critical pieces of the internetwork, WAN environments often deploy redundant media. As shown in Figure 2-17, you can provision backup links so that they become active when a primary link goes down or becomes congested.

Figure 2-17   *Backup Links Can Provide Redundancy*

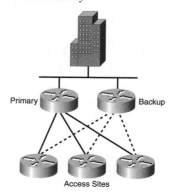

Often, backup links use a different technology. For example, a leased line can be in parallel with a backup dialup line or ISDN circuit. By using *floating static routes*, you can specify that the backup route have a higher administrative distance (used by Cisco routers to select routing information) so that it is not normally used unless the primary route goes down. This design is less available than the partial mesh presented previously. Typically, on-demand backup links reduce WAN charges.

> **NOTE**   When provisioning backup links, learn as much as possible about the physical circuit routing. Different carriers sometimes use the same facilities, meaning that your backup path might be susceptible to the same failures as your primary path. You should do some investigative work to ensure that your backup really is acting as a backup.

You can combine backup links with load balancing and *channel aggregation*. Channel aggregation means that a router can bring up multiple channels (for example, ISDN B channels) as bandwidth requirements increase.

Cisco supports Multilink Point-to-Point Protocol (MPPP), which is an Internet Engineering Task Force (IETF) standard for ISDN B channel (or asynchronous serial interface) aggregation. MPPP does not specify how a router should accomplish the decision-making process to bring up extra channels. Instead, it seeks to ensure that packets arrive in sequence at the receiving router. Then, the data is encapsulated within PPP and the datagram is given a sequence number. At the receiving router, PPP uses this sequence number to re-create the original data stream. Multiple channels appear as one logical link to upper-layer protocols.

References and Recommended Reading

Cisco Enterprise Teleworker Solution, http://www.cisco.com/en/US/netsol/ns340/ns394/ns430/networking_solutions_packages_list.html

Cisco Systems, Inc., "Enterprise Architectures," http://www.cisco.com/en/US/netsol/ns517/networking_solutions_market_segment_solutions_home.html

Cisco Systems, Inc., "Service-Oriented Network Architecture," http://www.cisco.com/en/US/netsol/ns629/networking_solutions_market_segment_solutions_home.html

RFC 3758, Virtual Router Redundancy Protocol (VRRP). Ed Hinden, April 2004

Foundation Summary

The "Foundation Summary" section of each chapter lists the most important facts from the chapter. Although this section does not list every fact from the chapter that will be on your CCDA exam, a well-prepared CCDA candidate should at a minimum know all the details in each "Foundation Summary" before taking the exam.

The CCDA exam requires that you understand the three layers of a hierarchical network design:

- The core layer and campus-backbone component provide fast transport within sites.

- The distribution layer and building-distribution component provide policy-based connectivity.

- The access layer and building-access component provide workgroup and user access to the network.

The Cisco Enterprise Architecture divides the network into six major modules:

- **Enterprise Campus (campus infrastructure, edge distribution, server farm, network management)**—The Enterprise Campus module includes the building-access and building-distribution components and the shared campus backbone component or campus core. Edge distribution provides connectivity to the Enterprise Edge. High availability is implemented in the server farm, and network management monitors the Enterprise Campus and Enterprise Edge.

- **Enterprise Edge (e-commerce, Internet, VPN/remote access, WAN)**—The e-commerce submodule provides high availability for business servers and connects to the Internet submodule.

- **Enterprise WAN**—This module provides Frame Relay or other WAN technology. The VPN submodule provides secure site-to-site remote access over the Internet.

- **Enterprise Branch**—The Enterprise Branch normally consists of remote offices, small offices, or sales offices. These branch offices rely on the WAN to use the services and applications provided in the main campus.

- **Enterprise Data Center**—The Enterprise Data Center consists of using the network to enhance the server, storage, and application servers. The offsite data center provides disaster recovery and business continuance services for the enterprise.

- **Enterprise Teleworker**—The Enterprise Teleworker supports a small office, mobile users, or home users providing access to corporate systems via VPN tunnels.

Figure 2-18 shows an Enterprise composite network model, as described here.

Figure 2-18 *Cisco Enterprise Architecture*

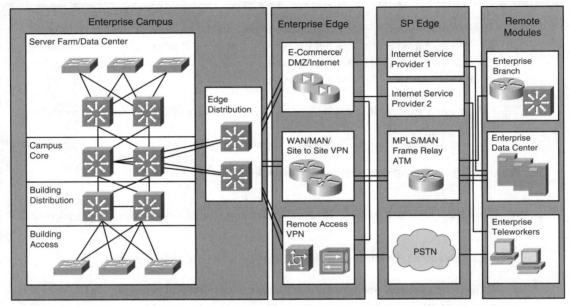

Network availability comes from design capacity, technologies, and device features that implement the following:

- Workstation-to-router redundancy in the building-access module

- Server redundancy in the server-farm module

- Route redundancy within and between network components

- Media redundancy in the access and distribution modules

Q&A

As mentioned in the introduction, you have two choices for review questions: here in the book or the exam questions on the CD-ROM. The answers to these questions appear in Appendix A.

For more practice with exam format questions, use the exam engine on the CD-ROM.

1. True or false: The core layer of the hierarchical model does security filtering and media translation.

2. True or false: The access layer provides high availability and port security.

3. You add CallManager to the network as part of a Voice over IP (VoIP) solution. In which submodule of the Enterprise Architecture should you place CallManager?

4. True or false: HSRP provides router redundancy.

5. Which Enterprise Edge submodule connects to an ISP?

6. List the six modules of the Cisco Enterprise Architecture for network design.

7. True or false: In the Cisco Enterprise Architecture, the network management submodule does not manage the SP Edge.

8. True or false: You can implement a full-mesh network to increase redundancy and reduce a WAN's costs.

9. How many links are required for a full mesh of six sites?

10. List and describe four options for multihoming to the SP between the Enterprise Edge and the SP Edge. Which option provides the most redundancy?

11. To what Enterprise Edge submodule does the SP Edge Internet submodule connect?

12. What are four benefits of hierarchical network design?

13. In an IP telephony network, in which submodule or layer are the IP phones and CallManagers located?

14. Match the redundant model with its description:

i. Workstation-router redundancy

ii. Server redundancy

iii. Route redundancy

iv. Media redundancy

a. Cheap when implemented in the LAN and critical for the WAN

b. Provides load balancing

c. Host has multiple gateways

d. Data is replicated

15. True or false: Small to medium campus networks must always implement three layers of hierarchical design.

16. How many full-mesh links do you need for a network with ten routers?

17. Which layer provides routing between VLANs and security filtering?

   a. Access layer

   b. Distribution layer

   c. Enterprise edge

   d. WAN submodule

18. List the four submodules of the Enterprise Edge.

19. List the three submodules of the SP Edge.

20. List the components of the Internet Edge.

21. Which submodule contains firewalls, VPN concentrators, and ASAs?

   a. WAN

   b. VPN/Remote Access

   c. Internet

   d. Server Farm

22. Which of the following describe the access layer? (Select two.)

    a. High-speed data transport

    b. Applies network policies

    c. Performs network aggregation

    d. Concentrates user access

    e. Provides PoE

    f. Avoids data manipulation

23. Which of the following describe the distribution layer? (Select two.)

    a. High-speed data transport

    b. Applies network policies

    c. Performs network aggregation

    d. Concentrates user access

    e. Provides PoE

    f. Avoids data manipulation

24. Which of the following describe the core layer? (Select two.)

    a. High-speed data transport

    b. Applies network policies

    c. Performs network aggregation

    d. Concentrates user access

    e. Provides PoE

    f. Avoids data manipulation

25. Assuming that there is no Enterprise distribution, which campus submodule connects to the Enterprise Edge module?

    a. SP Edge

    b. WAN submodule

    c. Building Distribution

    d. Campus Core

    e. Enterprise Branch

    f. Enterprise Data Center

26. Which remote module connects to the enterprise via the Internet or WAN submodules and contains a small LAN switch for users?

    a. SP Edge

    b. WAN submodule

    c. Building Distribution

    d. Campus Core

    e. Enterprise Branch

    f. Enterprise Data Center

27. Which three types of servers are placed in the e-commerce submodule?

    a. Web

    b. Application

    c. Database

    d. Intranet

    e. Internet

    f. Public share

Use Figure 2-19 to answer the following questions.

Figure 2-19 *Scenario*

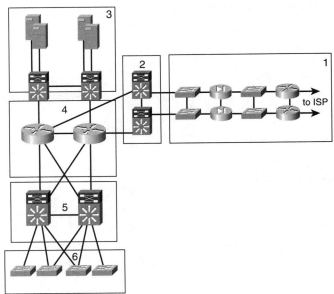

28.   Which is the campus core layer?

29.   Which is the Enterprise Edge?

30.   Which is the campus access layer?

31.   Which is the Enterprise Edge distribution?

32.   Which is the campus distribution layer?

33.   Which is the campus data center?

This part covers the following CCDA exam topics (to view the CCDA exam overview, visit http://www.cisco.com/web/learning/le3/current_exams/ 640-863.html):

- Describe Campus Design Considerations
- Design the Enterprise Campus Network
- Design the Enterprise Data Center
- Describe the Enterprise Edge, Branch, and Teleworker Design Characteristics
- Describe the Functional Components of The Central Site Enterprise Edge
- Describe WAN Connectivity Between Two Campuses
- Design the Branch Office WAN Solutions
- Describe Access Network solutions for a Teleworker
- Design the WAN to Support Selected Redundancy Methodology
- Identify Design Considerations for a Remote Data Center
- Describe Cisco Unified Wireless Network Architectures and Features
- Design Wireless Network Using Controllers
- Design Wireless Network Using Roaming

Part II: LAN and WAN Design

This chapter covers the following subjects:

- LAN Media

- LAN Hardware

- LAN Design Types and Models

C H A P T E R **3**

Enterprise LAN Design

This chapter covers the design of campus local-area networks (LAN). It reviews LAN media, components, and design models. The section "LAN Media" reviews the design characteristics of different Ethernet media technologies.

This chapter covers how you apply Layer 2 switches, Layer 3 switches, and routers in the design of LANs. It reviews several design models for large building, campus, and remote LANs.

"Do I Know This Already?" Quiz

The purpose of the "Do I Know This Already?" quiz is to help you decide whether you need to read the entire chapter. If you intend to read the entire chapter, you do not necessarily need to answer these questions now.

The eight-question quiz, derived from the major sections in the "Foundation Topics" portion of the chapter, helps you determine how to spend your limited study time.

Table 3-1 outlines the major topics discussed in this chapter and the "Do I Know This Already?" quiz questions that correspond to those topics.

Table 3-1 *"Do I Know This Already?" Foundation Topics Section-to-Question Mapping*

Foundation Topics Section	Questions Covered in This Section
LAN Media	2
LAN Hardware	1, 3, 8
LAN Design Types and Models	4, 5, 6, 7

CAUTION   The goal of self-assessment is to gauge your mastery of the topics in this chapter. If you do not know the answer to a question or you are only partially sure, you should mark this question wrong for the purposes of the self-assessment. Giving yourself credit for an answer you correctly guess skews your self-assessment results and might give you a false sense of security.

1. What device filters broadcasts?

   a. Layer 2 switch

   b. Hub

   c. Layer 3 switch

   d. Router

   e. Answers A and C

   f. Answers C and D

   g. Answers A, C, and D

2. What is the maximum segment distance for Fast Ethernet over unshielded twisted-pair (UTP)?

   a. 100 feet

   b. 500 feet

   c. 100 meters

   d. 285 feet

3. What device limits the collision domain?

   a. Layer 2 switch

   b. Hub

   c. Layer 3 switch

   d. Router

   e. Answers A and C

   f. Answers C and D

   g. Answers A, C, and D

4. The summarization of routes is a best practice at which layer?

   a. Access layer

   b. Distribution layer

   c. Core layer

   d. WAN layer

5. What type of LAN switches are preferred in the campus backbone of an enterprise network?

   a. Layer 2 switches

   b. Layer 3 switches

   c. Layer 3 hubs

   d. Hubs

6. What Cisco-proprietary protocol can you use in LAN switches to control multicast traffic at the data link layer within a LAN switch?

  a. IGMP

  b. Cisco Group Management Protocol (CGMP)

  c. MAC filters

  d. Cisco Discovery Protocol (CDP)

7. Marking is also known as what?

  a. Classifying

  b. Pinging

  c. Coloring

  d. Tracing

8. Why is switching preferred on shared segments?

  a. Shared segments provide a collision domain for each host.

  b. Switched segments provide a collision domain for each host.

  c. Shared segments provide a broadcast domain for each host.

  d. Switched segments provide a broadcast domain for each host.

The answers to the "Do I Know This Already?" quiz appear in Appendix A, "Answers to Chapter 'Do I Know This Already?' Quizzes and Q&A Sections." The suggested choices for your next step are as follows:

- **6 or less overall score**—Read the entire chapter. It includes the "Foundation Topics," "Foundation Summary," and "Q&A" sections.

- **7 or 8 overall score**—If you want more review on these topics, skip to the "Foundation Summary" section and then go to the "Q&A" section. Otherwise, move to the next chapter.

Foundation Topics

This chapter covers the design of LANs. It reviews LAN media, components, and design models. Figure 3-1 shows the Enterprise Campus section of the Enterprise Composite Network model. Enterprise LANs have a campus backbone and one or more instances of building-distribution and building-access layers, with server farms and an Enterprise Edge to the WAN or Internet.

Figure 3-1 *Enterprise Campus*

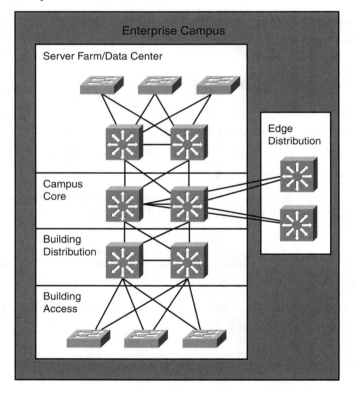

LAN Media

This section identifies some of the constraints you should consider when provisioning various LAN media types. It covers the physical specifications of Ethernet, Fast Ethernet, and Gigabit Ethernet. It also covers the specifications for Token Ring, because you may find this technology on existing networks.

You must also understand the design constraints of wireless LANs in the campus network. Specifications for wireless LANs are covered in Chapter 4, "Wireless LAN Design."

Ethernet Design Rules

Ethernet is the underlying basis for the technologies most widely used in LANs. In the 1980s and early 1990s, most networks used 10-Mbps Ethernet, defined initially by Digital, Intel, and Xerox (DIX Ethernet Version II) and later by the IEEE 802.3 working group. The IEEE 802.3-2002 standard contains physical specifications for Ethernet technologies through 10 Gbps.

Table 3-2 describes the physical Ethernet specifications up to 100 Mbps. It provides scalability information that you can use when provisioning IEEE 802.3 networks. Of these specifications, 10BASE5 and 10BASE2 are no longer used but are included for completeness.

Table 3-2 *Scalability Constraints for IEEE 802.3*

Specification	10BASE5	10BASE2	10BASE-T	100BASE-T
Physical Topology	Bus	Bus	Star	Star
Maximum Segment Length (in Meters)	500	185	100 from hub to station	100 from hub to station
Maximum Number of Attachments Per Segment	100	30	2 (hub and station or hub-hub)	2 (hub and station or hub-hub)
Maximum Collision Domain	2500 meters (m) of five segments and four repeaters; only three segments can be populated	2500 m of five segments and four repeaters; only three segments can be populated	2500 m of five segments and four repeaters; only three segments can be populated	See the details in the section "100-Mbps Fast Ethernet Design Rules" later in this chapter

The most significant design rule for Ethernet is that the round-trip propagation delay in one collision domain must not exceed 512-bit times. This is a requirement for collision detection to work correctly. This rule means that the maximum round-trip delay for a 10-Mbps Ethernet network is 51.2 microseconds. The maximum round-trip delay for a 100-Mbps Ethernet network is only 5.12 microseconds because the bit time on a 100-Mbps Ethernet network is 0.01 microseconds, as opposed to 0.1 microseconds on a 10-Mbps Ethernet network.

10-Mbps Fiber Ethernet Design Rules

Table 3-3 provides some guidelines for fiber-based 10-Mbps Ethernet media for network designs. These specifications are not part of the CCDA test but are included for reference. The 10BASE-FP standard uses a passive-star topology. The 10BASE-FB standard is for a backbone or repeater-based system. The 10BASE-FL standard provides specifications on fiber links.

Table 3-3 *Scalability Constraints for 10-Mbps Fiber Ethernet*

Specification	10BASE-FP	10BASE-FB	10BASE-FL
Topology	Passive star	Backbone or repeater-fiber system	Link
Maximum Segment Length	1000 m	2000 m	2000 m
Allows Cascaded Repeaters?	No	Yes	No
Maximum Collision Domain	2500 m	2500 m	2500 m

100-Mbps Fast Ethernet Design Rules

IEEE introduced the IEEE 802.3u-1995 standard to provide Ethernet speeds of 100 Mbps over UTP and fiber cabling. The 100BASE-T standard is similar to 10-Mbps Ethernet in that it uses carrier sense multiple access collision detect (CSMA/CD); runs on Category (CAT) 3, 4, and 5 UTP cable; and preserves the frame formats. Connectivity still uses hubs, repeaters, and bridges.

100-Mbps Ethernet, or Fast Ethernet, topologies present some distinct constraints on the network design because of their speed. The combined latency due to cable lengths and repeaters must conform to the specifications for the network to work properly. This section discusses these issues and provides sample calculations.

The overriding design rule for 100-Mbps Ethernet networks is that the round-trip collision delay must not exceed 512-bit times. However, the bit time on a 100-Mbps Ethernet network is 0.01 microseconds, as opposed to 0.1 microseconds on a 10-Mbps Ethernet network. Therefore, the maximum round-trip delay for a 100-Mbps Ethernet network is 5.12 microseconds, as opposed to the more lenient 51.2 microseconds in a 10-Mbps Ethernet network.

The following are specifications for Fast Ethernet, each of which is described in the following sections:

- 100BASE-TX

- 100BASE-T4

- 100BASE-FX

100BASE-TX Fast Ethernet

The 100BASE-TX specification uses CAT 5 UTP wiring. Like 10BASE-T, Fast Ethernet uses only two pairs of the four-pair UTP wiring. If CAT 5 cabling is already in place, upgrading to Fast Ethernet requires only a hub or switch and network interface card (NIC) upgrades. Because of the low cost, most of today's installations use switches. The specifications are as follows:

- Transmission over CAT 5 UTP wire.

- RJ-45 connector (the same as in 10BASE-T).

- Punchdown blocks in the wiring closet must be CAT 5 certified.

- 4B5B coding.

100BASE-T4 Fast Ethernet

The 100BASE-T4 specification was developed to support UTP wiring at the CAT 3 level. This specification takes advantage of higher-speed Ethernet without recabling to CAT 5 UTP. This implementation is not widely deployed. The specifications are as follows:

- Transmission over CAT 3, 4, or 5 UTP wiring.

- Three pairs are used for transmission, and the fourth pair is used for collision detection.

- No separate transmit and receive pairs are present, so full-duplex operation is not possible.

- 8B6T coding.

100BASE-FX Fast Ethernet

The 100BASE-FX specification for fiber is as follows:

- It operates over two strands of multimode or single-mode fiber cabling.

- It can transmit over greater distances than copper media.

- It uses media interface connector (MIC), Stab and Twist (ST), or Stab and Click (SC) fiber connectors defined for FDDI and 10BASE-FX networks.

- 4B5B coding.

100BASE-T Repeaters

To make 100-Mbps Ethernet work, distance limitations are much more severe than those required for 10-Mbps Ethernet. Repeater networks have no five-hub rule; Fast Ethernet is limited to two repeaters. The general rule is that 100-Mbps Ethernet has a maximum diameter of 205 meters (m) with UTP cabling, whereas 10-Mbps Ethernet has a maximum diameter of 500 m with 10BASE-T and 2500 m with 10BASE5. Most networks today use switches instead of repeaters, which limits the length of 10BASE-T and 100BASE-TX to 100 m between the switch and host.

The distance limitation imposed depends on the type of repeater.

The IEEE 100BASE-T specification defines two types of repeaters: Class I and Class II. Class I repeaters have a latency (delay) of 0.7 microseconds or less. Only one repeater hop is allowed. Class II repeaters have a latency of 0.46 microseconds or less. One or two repeater hops are allowed.

Table 3-4 shows the maximum size of collision domains, depending on the type of repeater.

Table 3-4 *Maximum Size of Collision Domains for 100BASE-T*

Repeater Type	Copper	Mixed Copper and Multimode Fiber	Multimode Fiber
DTE-DTE (or Switch-Switch)	100 m	Not applicable	412 m (2000 if full duplex)
One Class I Repeater	200 m	260 m	272 m
One Class II Repeater	200 m	308 m	320 m
Two Class II Repeaters	205 m	216 m	228 m

Again, for switched networks, the maximum distance between the switch and the host is 100 m.

Gigabit Ethernet Design Rules

Gigabit Ethernet was first specified by two standards: IEEE 802.3z-1998 and 802.3ab-1999. The IEEE 802.3z standard specifies the operation of Gigabit Ethernet over fiber and coaxial cable and introduces the Gigabit Media-Independent Interface (GMII). These standards are superseded by the latest revision of all the 802.3 standards included in IEEE 802.3-2002.

The IEEE 802.3ab standard specified the operation of Gigabit Ethernet over CAT 5 UTP. Gigabit Ethernet still retains the frame formats and frame sizes, and it still uses CSMA/CD. As with Ethernet and Fast Ethernet, full-duplex operation is possible. Differences appear in the encoding; Gigabit Ethernet uses 8B10B coding with simple nonreturn to zero (NRZ). Because of the 20 percent overhead, pulses run at 1250 MHz to achieve a 1000 Mbps throughput.

Table 3-5 gives an overview of Gigabit Ethernet scalability constraints.

Table 3-5 *Gigabit Ethernet Scalability Constraints*

Type	Speed	Maximum Segment Length	Encoding	Media
1000BASE-T	1000 Mbps	100 m	Five-level	CAT 5 UTP
1000BASE-LX (long wavelength)	1000 Mbps	550 m	8B10B	Single-mode/ multimode fiber
1000BASE-SX (short wavelength)	1000 Mbps	62.5 micrometers: 220 m 50 micrometers: 500 m	8B10B	Multimode fiber
1000BASE-CX	1000 Mbps	25 m	8B10B	Shielded balanced copper

The following are the physical specifications for Gigabit Ethernet, each of which is described in the following sections:

- 1000BASE-LX

- 1000BASE-SX

- 1000BASE-CX

- 1000BASE-T

1000BASE-LX Long-Wavelength Gigabit Ethernet

IEEE 1000BASE-LX uses long-wavelength optics over a pair of fiber strands. The specifications are as follows:

- Uses long wave (1300 nanometers [nm])

- Use on multimode or single-mode fiber

- Maximum lengths for multimode fiber are

    — 62.5-micrometer fiber: 440 m

    — 50-micrometer fiber: 550 m

- Maximum length for single-mode fiber (9 micrometers) is 5 km

- Uses 8B10B encoding with simple NRZ

1000BASE-SX Short-Wavelength Gigabit Ethernet

IEEE 1000BASE-SX uses short-wavelength optics over a pair of multimode fiber stands. The specifications are as follows:

- Uses short wave (850 nm)

- Use on multimode fiber

- Maximum lengths:

  — 62.5-micrometer fiber: 260 m

  — 50-micrometer fiber: 550 m

- Uses 8B10B encoding with simple NRZ

1000BASE-CX Gigabit Ethernet over Coaxial Cable

IEEE 1000BASE-CX standard is for short copper runs between servers. The specification is as follows:

- Used on short-run copper

- Runs over a pair of 150-ohm balanced coaxial cables (twinax)

- Maximum length is 25 m

- Mainly for server connections

- Uses 8B10B encoding with simple NRZ

1000BASE-T Gigabit Ethernet over UTP

The IEEE standard for 1000-Mbps Ethernet over CAT 5 UTP was IEEE 802.3ab; it was approved in June 1999. It is now included in IEEE 802.3-2002. This standard uses the four pairs in the cable. (100BASE-TX and 10BASE-T Ethernet use only two pairs.) The specifications are as follows:

- CAT 5, four-pair UTP

- Maximum length is 100 m

- Encoding defined is a five-level coding scheme

- 1 byte is sent over the four pairs at 1250 MHz

10 Gigabit Ethernet (10GE) Design Rules

The IEEE 802.3ae supplement to the 802.3 standard, published in August 2002, specifies the standard for 10 Gigabit Ethernet. It is defined only for full-duplex operation over optical media. Hubs or repeaters cannot be used because they operate in half-duplex mode. It allows the use of Ethernet frames over distances typically encountered in metropolitan-area networks (MAN) and WANs. Other uses include data centers, corporate backbones, and server farms.

10GE Media Types

10GE has seven physical media specifications based on different fiber types and encoding. Multimode fiber (MMF) and single-mode fiber (SMF) are used. Table 3-6 describes the different 10GE media types.

Table 3-6   *10GE Media Types*

10GE Media Type	Wavelength/Fiber (Short or Long)	Distance	Other Description
10GBASE-SR	Short wavelength MMF	To 300 m	Uses 66B encoding
10GBASE-SW	Short wavelength MMF	To 300 m	Uses the WAN interface sublayer (WIS)
10GBASE-LR	Long wavelength SMF	To 10 km	Uses 66B encoding for dark fiber use
10GBASE-LW	Long wavelength SMF	To 10 km	Uses WIS
10GBASE-ER	Extra-long wavelength SMF	To 40 km	Uses 66B encoding for dark fiber use
10GBASE-EW	Extra-long wavelength SNMP	To 40 km	Uses WIS
10GBASE-LX4	Uses division multiplexing for both MMF and SMF	To 10 km	Uses 8B/10B encoding

Short-wavelength multimode fiber is 850 nm. Long-wavelength is 1310 nm, and extra-long-wavelength is 1550 nm. The WIS is used to interoperate with Synchronous Optical Network (SONET) STS-192c transmission format.

Fast EtherChannel

The Cisco EtherChannel implementations provide a method to increase the bandwidth between two systems by bundling Fast Ethernet or Gigabit Ethernet links. When bundling Fast Ethernet links, use Fast EtherChannel. EtherChannel port bundles allow you to group multiple ports into a single logical transmission path between the switch and a router, host, or another switch. EtherChannels provide increased bandwidth, load sharing, and redundancy. If a link fails in the bundle, the other links take on the traffic load. You can configure EtherChannel bundles as trunk links.

Depending on your hardware, you can form an EtherChannel with up to eight compatibly configured ports on the switch. The participating ports must have the same speed and duplex mode and belong to the same VLAN.

Token Ring Design Rules

Token Ring is not a CCDA test subject but this section is included for reference because you might find Token Ring on existing networks. IBM developed Token Ring in the 1970s. In the 1980s, Token Ring and Ethernet competed as the preferred medium for LANs. The IEEE developed the IEEE 802.5 specification based on the IBM Token Ring specifications. The 802.5 working group is now inactive. The most recent specification is IEEE 802.5-1998. You can find more information at http://www.8025.org.

Table 3-7 lists some media characteristics for designing Token Ring segments.

Table 3-7 *Scalability Constraints for Token Ring*

Specification	IBM Token Ring	IEEE 802.5
Physical Topology	Star	Not specified
Maximum Segment Length	Depends on the type of cable, number of media attachment units (MAU), and so on	Depends on the type of cable, number of MAUs, and so on
Maximum Number of Attachments Per Segment	260 for STP, 72 for UTP	250
Maximum Network Diameter	Depends on the type of cable, number of MAUs, and so on	Depends on the type of cable, number of MAUs, and so on

LAN Hardware

This section covers the hardware devices and how to apply them to LAN design. You place devices in the LAN depending on their roles and capabilities. LAN devices are categorized based on how they operate in the OSI model. This section covers the following devices:

■ Repeaters

■ Hubs

■ Bridges

- Switches

- Routers

- Layer 3 switches

Repeaters

Repeaters are the basic unit in networks that connect separate segments. Repeaters take incoming frames, regenerate the preamble, amplify the signals, and send the frame out all other interfaces. Repeaters operate at the physical layer of the OSI model. Because repeaters are unaware of packets or frame formats, they do not control broadcasts or collision domains. Repeaters are said to be protocol-transparent because they are unaware of upper-layer protocols such as IP, Internetwork Packet Exchange (IPX), and so on.

One basic rule of using Ethernet repeaters is the 5-4-3 Rule, shown in Figure 3-2. The maximum path between two stations on the network should not be more than five segments, with four repeaters between those segments, and no more than three populated segments. Repeaters introduce a small amount of latency, or delay, when propagating the frames. A transmitting device must be able to detect a collision with another device within the specified time after the delay introduced by the cable segments and repeaters is factored in. The 512-bit time specification also governs segment lengths.

Figure 3-2   *Repeater 5-4-3 Rule*

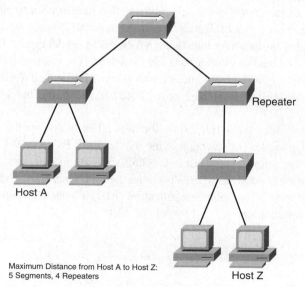

Hubs

With the increasing density of LANs in the late 1980s and early 1990s, *hubs* were introduced to concentrate Thinnet and 10BASE-T networks in the wiring closet. Traditional hubs operate on the physical layer of the OSI model and perform the same functions as basic repeaters. The difference is that hubs have more ports than basic repeaters.

Bridges

Bridges connect separate segments of a network. They differ from repeaters in that bridges are intelligent devices that operate in the data link layer of the OSI model. Bridges control the collision domains on the network. Bridges also learn the MAC layer addresses of each node on each segment and on which interface they are located. For any incoming frame, bridges forward the frame only if the destination MAC address is on another port or if the bridge is unaware of its location. The latter is called *flooding*. Bridges filter any incoming frames with destination MAC addresses that are on the same segment from where the frame arrives; they do not forward these frames.

Bridges are store-and-forward devices. They store the entire frame and verify the cyclic redundancy check (CRC) before forwarding. If the bridges detect a CRC error, they discard the frame. Bridges are protocol-transparent; they are unaware of the upper-layer protocols such as IP, IPX, and AppleTalk. Bridges are designed to flood all unknown and broadcast traffic.

Bridges implement Spanning Tree Protocol (STP) to build a loop-free network topology. Bridges communicate with each other, exchanging information such as priority and bridge interface MAC addresses. They select a root bridge and then implement STP. Some interfaces are in a blocking state, whereas other bridges have interfaces in forwarding mode. Figure 3-3 shows a network with bridges. STP has no load sharing or dual paths, as there is in routing. STP provides recovery of bridge failure by changing blocked interfaces to a forwarding state if a primary link fails. Although DEC and IBM versions are available, the IEEE 802.1d standard is the STP most commonly used.

STP elects a *root bridge* as the tree's root. It places all ports that are not needed to reach the root bridge in blocking mode. The selection of the root bridge is based on the lowest numerical bridge priority. The bridge priority ranges from 0 to 65,535. If all bridges have the same bridge priority, the bridge with the lowest MAC address becomes the root. The concatenation of the bridge priority and the MAC address is the bridge identification (BID). Physical changes to the network force spanning-tree recalculation.

Figure 3-3   *Spanning Tree Protocol*

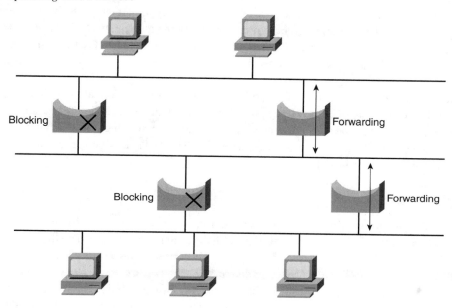

Switches

Switches use specialized integrated circuits to reduce the latency common to regular bridges. Switches are the evolution of bridges. Some switches can run in cut-through mode, where the switch does not wait for the entire frame to enter its buffer; instead, it begins to forward the frame as soon as it finishes reading the destination MAC address. Cut-through operation increases the probability that frames with errors are propagated on the network, because it forwards the frame before the entire frame is buffered and checked for errors. Because of these problems, most switches today perform store-and-forward operation as bridges do. As shown in Figure 3-4, switches are exactly the same as bridges with respect to collision-domain and broadcast-domain characteristics. Each port on a switch is a separate collision domain. By default, all ports in a switch are in the same broadcast domain. Assignment to different VLANs changes that behavior.

Figure 3-4   *Switches Control Collision Domains*

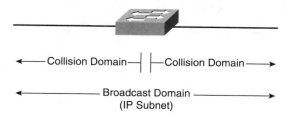

Switches have characteristics similar to bridges; however, they have more ports and run faster. Switches keep a table of MAC addresses per port, and they implement STP. Switches are data link layer devices. They are transparent to protocols operating at the network layer and above. Each port on a switch is a separate collision domain but is part of the same broadcast domain. Switches do not control broadcasts on the network.

The use of LAN switches instead of bridges or hubs is nearly universal. Switches are preferred over shared technology because they provide full bandwidth in each direction when configured in duplex mode. All the devices on a hub share the bandwidth in a single collision domain. Switches can also use VLANs to provide more segmentation. The "LAN Design Types and Models" section in this chapter discusses VLANs.

Routers

Routers make forwarding decisions based on network layer addresses. When an Ethernet frame enters the router, the layer 2 header is removed, the router forwards based on the layer 3 IP address and adds a new layer 2 address at the egress interface. In addition to controlling collision domains, routers bound data link layer broadcast domains. Each interface of a router is a separate broadcast domain. Routers do not forward data link layer broadcasts. IP defines network layer broadcast domains with a subnet and mask. Routers are aware of the network protocol, which means they can forward packets of routed protocols, such as IP and IPX. Figure 3-5 shows a router; each interface is a broadcast and a collision domain.

Figure 3-5 *Routers Control Broadcast and Collision Domains*

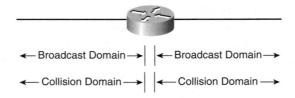

Routers exchange information about destination networks using one of several routing protocols. Routers use routing protocols to build a list of destination networks and to identify the best routes to reach those destinations. The following are examples of routing protocols:

■ Enhanced Interior Gateway Routing Protocol (EIGRP)

■ Open Shortest Path First (OSPF)

■ Border Gateway Protocol (BGP)

■ Routing Information Protocol (RIP)

■ Intermediate System-to-Intermediate System (IS-IS)

Chapter 9, "Routing Protocol Selection Criteria," discusses routing protocols in further detail. Routers translate data link protocols. They are the preferred method of forwarding packets between networks of differing media, such as Ethernet to Token Ring or Ethernet to serial. They also provide methods to filter traffic based on the network layer address, route redundancy, load balancing, hierarchical addressing, and multicast routing.

Layer 3 Switches

LAN switches that can run routing protocols are *Layer 3 switches*. These switches can run routing protocols and communicate with neighboring routers. Layer 3 switches have LAN technology interfaces that perform network layer packet forwarding. The use of switching technologies at the network layer greatly accelerates packet forwarding between connected LANs, including VLANs. You can use the router capacity you save to implement other features, such as security filtering and intrusion detection.

Layer 3 switches perform the functions of both data link layer switches and network layer routers. Each port is a collision domain. You can group ports into network layer broadcast domains (subnets). As with routers, a routing protocol provides network information to other network layer devices (subnets), and a routing protocol provides network information to other Layer 3 switches and routers.

LAN Design Types and Models

LANs can be classified as large-building LANs, campus LANs, or small and remote LANs. The large-building LAN typically contains a major data center with high-speed access and floor communications closets; the large-building LAN is usually the headquarters in larger companies. Campus LANs provide connectivity between buildings on a campus. Redundancy is usually a requirement in large-building and campus LAN deployments. Small and remote LANs provide connectivity to remote offices with a relatively small number of nodes.

Campus design factors include the following categories:

- Network application characteristics

- Infrastructure device characteristics

- Environmental characteristics

Applications are defined by the business, and the network must be able to support them. Applications may require high bandwidth or be time-sensitive. The infrastructure devices influence the design. Decisions on switched or routed architectures and port limitations influence the design. The actual physical distances affect the design. The selection of copper or fiber media may be influenced by the environmental or distance requirements. The following sections show some sample LAN types. Table 3-8 summarizes the different application types.

Table 3-8 *Application Types*

Application Type	Description
Peer-to-peer	Includes instant messaging, file sharing, IP phone calls, and videoconferencing.
Client-local servers	Servers are located in the same segment as the clients or close by.
Client/server farms	Mail, server, file, and database servers. Access is reliable and controlled.
Client-Enterprise Edge servers	External servers such as SMTP, web, public servers, and e-commerce.

Best Practices for Hierarchical Layers

Each layer of the hierarchical architecture contains special considerations. The following sections describe best practices for each of the three layers of the hierarchical architecture: access, distribution, and core.

Access Layer Best Practices

When designing the building access layer, you must take into consideration the number of users or ports required to size up the LAN switch. Connectivity speed for each host should be considered. Hosts might be connected using various technologies such as Fast Ethernet, Gigabit Ethernet, or port channels. The planned VLANs enter into the design.

Performance in the access layer is also important. Redundancy and QoS features should be considered.

The following are recommended best practices for the building access layer:

■ Limit VLANs to a single closet when possible to provide the most deterministic and highly available topology.

■ Use RPVST+ if STP is required. It provides the best convergence.

■ Set VLAN Dynamic Trunking Protocol (DTP) to desirable/desirable with negotiation on.

■ Manually prune unused VLANs to avoid broadcast propagation.

■ Use VTP transparent mode, because there is little need for a common VLAN database in hierarchical networks.

■ Disable trunking on host ports, because it is not necessary. Doing so provides more security and speeds up PortFast.

■ Consider implementing routing in the access layer to provide fast convergence and Layer 3 load balancing.

■ Use the **switchport host** commands on server and end-user ports to enable PortFast and disable channeling on these ports.

Distribution Layer Best Practices

As shown in Figure 3-6, the distribution layer aggregates all closet switches and connects to the core layer. Design considerations for the distribution layer include providing wire-speed performance on all ports, link redundancy, and infrastructure services.

Figure 3-6 *Distribution Layer*

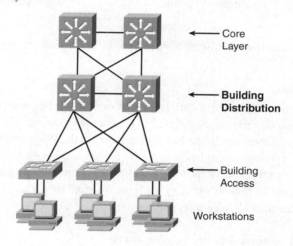

The distribution layer should not be limited on performance. Links to the core must be able to support the bandwidth used by the aggregate access layer switches. Redundant links from the access switches to the distribution layer and from the distribution layer to the core layer allow for high availability in the event of a link failure. Infrastructure services include QoS configuration, security, and policy enforcement. Access lists are configured in the distribution layer.

The following are recommended best practices at the distribution layer:

■ Use first-hop redundancy protocols. Hot Standby Router Protocol (HSRP) or Gateway Load Balancing Protocol (GLBP) should be used if you implement Layer 2 links between the Layer 2 access switches and the distribution layer.

- Use Layer 3 links between the distribution and core switches to allow for fast convergence and load balancing.

- Build Layer 3 triangles, not squares as shown in Figure 3-7.

Figure 3-7 *Layer 3 Triangles*

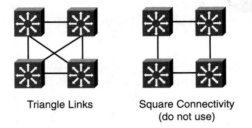

Triangle Links   Square Connectivity
(do not use)

- Use the distribution switches to connect Layer 2 VLANs that span multiple access layer switches.

- Summarize routes from the distribution to the core of the network to reduce routing overhead.

Core Layer Best Practices

Depending on the network's size, a core layer may or may not be needed. For larger networks, building distribution switches are aggregated to the core. This provides high-speed connectivity to the server farm/data center and to the Enterprise Edge (to the WAN and the Internet).

Figure 3-8 shows the criticality of the core switches. The core must provide high-speed switching with redundant paths for high availability to all the distribution points. The core must support gigabit speeds and data and voice integration.

The following are best practices for the campus core:

- Reduce the switch peering by using redundant triangle connections between switches.

- Use routing that provides a topology with no Layer 2 loops which are seen in Layer 2 links using spanning tree protocol.

- Use Layer 3 switches on the core that provide intelligent services that Layer 2 switches do not support.

Figure 3-8 *Core Switches*

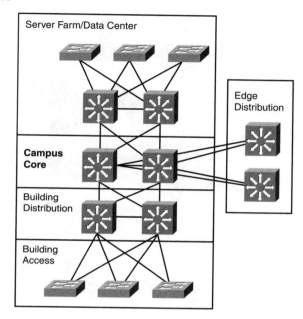

Large-Building LANs

Large-building LANs are segmented by floors or departments. The building-access component serves one or more departments or floors. The building-distribution component serves one or more building-access components. Campus and building backbone devices connect the data center, building-distribution components, and the Enterprise Edge-distribution component. The access layer typically uses Layer 2 switches to contain costs, with more expensive Layer 3 switches in the distribution layer to provide policy enforcement. Current best practice is to also deploy Layer 3 switches in the campus and building backbone. Figure 3-9 shows a typical large-building design.

Each floor can have more than 200 users. Following a hierarchical model of building access, building distribution, and core, Fast Ethernet nodes can connect to the Layer 2 switches in the communications closet. Fast Ethernet or Gigabit Ethernet uplink ports from closet switches connect back to one or two (for redundancy) distribution switches. Distribution switches can provide connectivity to server farms that provide business applications, DHCP, DNS, intranet, and other services.

Figure 3-9   *Large-Building LAN Design*

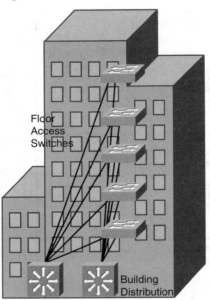

Enterprise Campus LANs

A campus LAN connects two or more buildings within a local geographic area using a high-bandwidth LAN media backbone. Usually the enterprise owns the medium (copper or fiber). High-speed switching devices minimize latency. In today's networks, Gigabit Ethernet campus backbones are the standard for new installations. In Figure 3-10, Layer 3 switches with Gigabit Ethernet media connect campus buildings.

Ensure that you implement a hierarchical composite design on the campus LAN and that you assign network layer addressing to control broadcasts on the networks. Each building should have addressing assigned in such a way as to maximize address summarization. Apply contiguous subnets to buildings at the bit boundary to apply summarization and ease the design. Campus networks can support high-bandwidth applications such as videoconferencing. Remember to use Layer 3 switches with high-switching capabilities in the campus-backbone design. In smaller installations, it might be desirable to collapse the building-distribution component into the campus backbone. An increasingly viable alternative is to provide building access and distribution on a single device selected from among the smaller Layer 3 switches now available.

Figure 3-10 *Campus LAN*

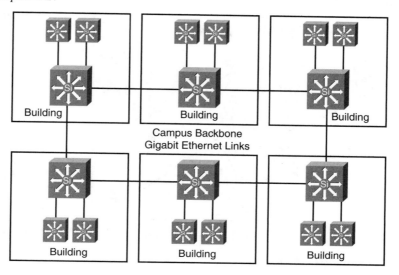

Edge Distribution

For large campus LANs, the Edge Distribution module provides additional security between the campus LAN and the Enterprise Edge (WAN, Internet, and VPNs). The edge distribution protects the campus from the following threats:

- **IP spoofing**—The edge distribution switches protect the core from spoofing of IP addresses.

- **Unauthorized access**—Controls access to the network core.

- **Network reconnaissance**—Filtering of network discovery packets to prevent discovery from external networks.

- **Packet sniffers**—The edge distribution separates the edge's broadcast domains from the campus, preventing possible network packet captures.

Medium Site LANs

Medium-sized LANs contain 200 to 1000 devices. Usually the distribution and core layers are collapsed in the medium-sized network. Access switches are still connected to both distribution/core switches to provide redundancy. Figure 3-11 shows the medium campus LAN.

Figure 3-11 *Medium Campus LAN*

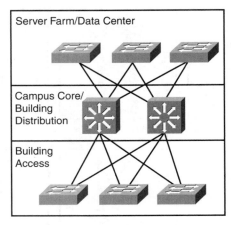

Small and Remote Site LANs

Small and remote sites usually connect to the corporate network via a small router. The LAN service is provided by a small LAN switch. The router filters broadcast to the WAN circuit and forward packets that require services from the corporate network. You can place a server at the small or remote site to provide DHCP and other local applications such as a backup domain controller and DNS; if not, you must configure the router to forward DHCP broadcasts and other types of services. As the site grows, you will need the structure provided by the Enterprise Composite Network model. Figure 3-12 shows a typical architecture of a remote LAN.

Figure 3-12 *Remote Office LAN*

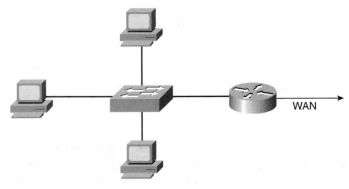

Server-Farm Module

The server-farm or data-center module provides high-speed access to servers for the campus networks. You can attach servers to switches via Gigabit Ethernet or 10 Gigabit Ethernet. Some campus deployments might need EtherChannel technology to meet traffic requirements. Figure

3-13 shows an example of a server-farm module for a small network. Servers are connected via Fast Ethernet or Fast EtherChannel.

Figure 3-13   *Server Farm*

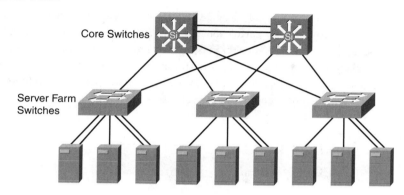

The server-farm switches connect via redundant uplink ports to the core switches. The largest deployments might find it useful to hierarchically construct service to the data center using access and distribution network devices.

Server distribution switches are used in larger networks. Access control lists and QoS features are implemented on the server distribution switches to protect the servers and services and to enforce network policies.

Server Connectivity Options

Servers can be connected in three primary options:

- Single NIC

- Dual NIC EtherChannel

- Content switching

Single NIC connected servers contain Fast or Gigabit Ethernet full-duplex speeds with no redundancy. Servers requiring redundancy can be connected with dual NICs using switch EtherChannel.

Advanced redundancy solutions use content switches that front end multiple servers. This provides redundancy and load balancing per user request.

Enterprise Data Center Infrastructure

Data centers (DC) contain different types of server technologies, including standalone servers, blade servers, mainframes, clustered servers, and virtual servers.

Figure 3-14 shows the Enterprise DC. The DC access layer must provide the port density to support the servers, provide high-performance/low-latency Layer 2 switching, and support dual and single connected servers. The preferred design is to contain Layer 2 to the access layer and Layer 3 on the distribution. Some solutions push Layer 3 links to the access layer. Blade chassis with integrated switches have become a popular solution. Each blade switch houses 16 Intel platforms, each logically connected within the chassis to two access switches.

Figure 3-14 *Enterprise Data Center*

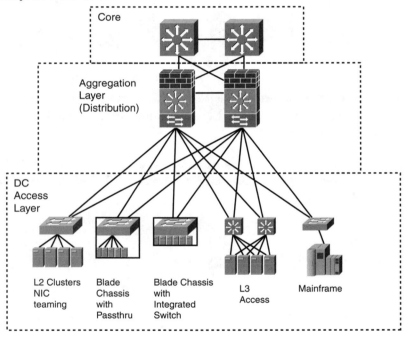

The DC aggregation layer (distribution layer) aggregates traffic to the core. Deployed on the aggregation layer are

- **Load balancers** to provide load balancing to multiple servers

- **SSL offloading devices** to terminate SSL sessions

- **Firewalls** to control and filter access

- **Intrusion detection devices** to detect network attacks

Campus LAN Quality of Service Considerations

For the access layer of the campus LAN, you can classify and mark frames or packets to apply quality of service (QoS) policies in the distribution or at the Enterprise Edge. Classification is a fundamental building block of QoS and involves recognizing and distinguishing between different traffic streams. For example, you distinguish between HTTP/HTTPS, FTP, and VoIP traffic. Without classification, all traffic would be treated the same.

Marking sets certain bits in a packet or frame that has been classified. Marking is also called coloring or tagging. Layer 2 has two methods to mark frames for CoS:

- Inter-Switch Link (ISL)

- IEEE 802.1p/802.1Q

The IEEE 802.1D-1998 standard describes IEEE 802.1p traffic class expediting.

Both methods provide 3 bits for marking frames. The Cisco ISL is a proprietary trunk-encapsulation method for carrying VLANs over Fast Ethernet or Gigabit Ethernet interfaces.

ISL appends tags to each frame to identify the VLAN it belongs to. As shown in Figure 3-15, the tag is a 30-byte header and CRC trailer that are added around the Fast Ethernet frame. This includes a 26-byte header and 4-byte CRC. The header includes a 15-bit VLAN ID that identifies each VLAN. The user field in the header also includes 3 bits for the CoS.

Figure 3-15 *ISL Frame*

The IEEE 802.1Q standard trunks VLANs over Fast Ethernet and Gigabit Ethernet interfaces, and you can use it in a multivendor environment. IEEE 802.1q uses one instance of STP for each VLAN allowed in the trunk. Like ISL, IEEE 802.1Q uses a tag on each frame with a VLAN identifier. Figure 3-16 shows the IEEE 802.1Q frame. Unlike ISL, 802.1Q uses an internal tag. IEEE 802.1Q also supports the IEEE 802.1p priority standard, which is included in the 802.1D-1998 specification. A 3-bit priority field is included in the 802.1Q frame for CoS.

Figure 3-16 *IEEE 802.1Q Frame*

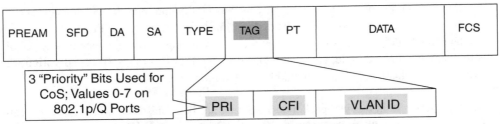

The preferred location to mark traffic is as close as possible to the source. Figure 3-17 shows a segment of a network with IP phones. Most workstations send packets with CoS or IP precedence bits (ToS) set to 0. If the workstation supports IEEE 802.1Q/p, it can mark packets. The IP phone can reclassify traffic from the workstation to 0. VoIP traffic from the phone is sent with a Layer 2 CoS set to 5 or Layer 3 ToS set to 5. The phone also reclassifies data from the PC to a CoS/ToS of 0. With Differentiated Services Code Point (DSCP), VoIP traffic is set to Expedited Forwarding (EF), binary value 101110 (hexadecimal 2E).

Figure 3-17 *Marking of Frames or Packets*

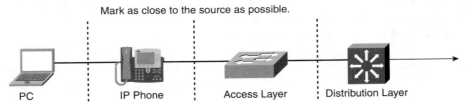

As shown in Figure 3-17, switches' capabilities vary in the access layer. If the switches in this layer are capable, configure them to accept the markings or remap them. The advanced switches in the distribution layer can mark traffic, accept the CoS/ToS markings, or remap the CoS/ToS values to different markings.

Multicast Traffic Considerations

Internet Group Management Protocol (IGMP) is the protocol between end workstations and the local Layer 3 switch. IGMP is the protocol used in multicast implementations between the end hosts and the local router. RFC 2236 describes IGMP version 2 (IGMPv2). RFC 1112 describes the first version of IGMP. IP hosts use IGMP to report their multicast group memberships to routers. IGMP messages use IP protocol number 2. IGMP messages are limited to the local interface and are not routed.

RFC 3376 describes IGMP Version 3 (IGMPv3) IGMPv3 provides the extensions required to support source-specific multicast (SSM). It is designed to be backward-compatible with both prior versions of IGMP. All versions of IGMP are covered in Chapter 12, "Border Gateway Protocol, Route Manipulation, and IP Multicast."

When campus LANs use multicast media, end hosts that do not participate in multicast groups might get flooded with unwanted traffic. Two solutions are

- CGMP

- IGMP snooping

CGMP

Cisco Group Management Protocol (CGMP) is a Cisco-proprietary protocol implemented to control multicast traffic at Layer 2. Because a Layer 2 switch is unaware of Layer 3 IGMP messages, it cannot keep multicast packets from being sent to all ports.

As shown in Figure 3-18, with CGMP, the LAN switch can speak with the IGMP router to find out the MAC addresses of the hosts that want to receive the multicast packets. You must also enable the router to speak CGMP with the LAN switches. With CGMP, switches distribute multicast sessions to the switch ports that have group members.

When a CGMP-enabled router receives an IGMP report, it processes the report and then sends a CGMP message to the switch. The switch can then forward the multicast messages to the port with the host receiving multicast traffic. CGMP Fast-Leave processing allows the switch to detect IGMP Version 2 leave messages sent by hosts on any of the supervisor engine module ports. When the IGMPv2 leave message is sent, the switch can then disable multicast for the port.

IGMP Snooping

IGMP snooping is another way for switches to control multicast traffic at Layer 2. It can be used instead of CGMP. With IGMP snooping, switches listen to IGMP messages between the hosts and routers. If a host sends an IGMP query message to the router, the switch adds the host to the multicast group and permits that port to receive multicast traffic. The port is removed from multicast traffic if an IGMP leave message is sent from the host to the router. The disadvantage of IGMP snooping is that it must listen to every IGMP control message, which can impact the switch's CPU utilization.

Figure 3-18 *CGMP*

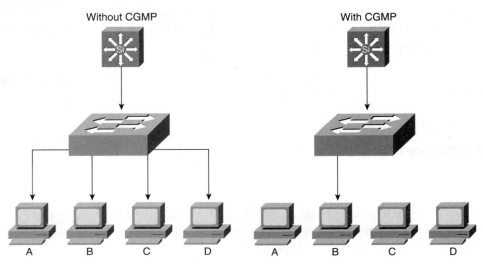

References and Recommended Readings

10Gigabit Alliance, http://www.10gea.org

"Cisco Data Center Network Architecture and Solutions Overview," http://www.cisco.com/application/pdf/en/us/guest/netsol/ns377/c643/cdccont_0900aecd802c9a4f.pdf?pcontent=dc_us&pagename=Data%20Center%20Solutions%20Overview

"CSMA/CD Access Method, IEEE 802.3-2005." New York, NY: Institute of Electrical and Electronics Engineers, 2005

IEEE P802.3ae 10Gb/s Ethernet Task Force, http://grouper.ieee.org/groups/802/3/ae/index.html

"Token-Ring Access Method, IEEE 802.5-1998." Piscataway, New Jersey: Institute of Electrical and Electronics Engineers, 1998

Foundation Summary

The "Foundation Summary" section of each chapter lists the most important facts from the chapter. Although this section does not list every fact from the chapter that will be on the CCDA exam, a well-prepared CCDA candidate should at a minimum know all the details in each "Foundation Summary" before taking the exam.

The CCDA exam requires you to be familiar with the following topics that were addressed in this chapter:

- **LAN media**—Ethernet, Token Ring, and Gigabit LAN media

- **LAN hardware**—Components used in LAN networks

- **LAN design types and models**—Building and campus LAN types and LAN design models

Tables 3-9 through 3-15 provide an overview of the following items that will also assist you in preparing for the CCDA exam:

- Application types

- Overview and comparison of LAN devices

- Summary of LAN types and their characteristics

- Description of the components of the enterprise campus model

- Summary of the modules on the campus infrastructure

Table 3-9 *Application Types*

Application Type	Description
Peer-to-peer	Includes instant messaging, file sharing, IP phone calls, and videoconferencing.
Client-local servers	Servers are located in the same segment as the clients or close by.
Client/server farms	Mail, server, file, and database servers. Access is reliable and controlled.
Client-Enterprise Edge servers	External servers such as SMTP, web, public servers, and e-commerce.

Table 3-10 *Comparison of Transmission Media*

Media	Bandwidth	Distance	Price
Twisted pair	Up to 1 Gbps	100 m	Inexpensive
Multimode fiber	Up to 1 Gbps	2 km (FE) 550 m (GE)	Moderate
Single-mode fiber	10 Gbps	90 km (FE) 40 km (GE)	Moderate to expensive
Wireless	54 Mbps (27 Mbps effective)	500 m at 1 Mbps	Moderate

Table 3-11 *LAN Device Comparison*

Device	OSI Layer	Is Domain Protocol-Transparent or Protocol-Aware?	Boundary	What It Understands
Repeater	Layer 1: physical	Transparent	Amplify signal	Bits
Hub	Layer 1: physical	Transparent	Amplify signal	Bits
Bridge	Layer 2: data link	Transparent	Collision domain	Frames
Switch	Layer 2: data link	Transparent	Collision domain	Frames
Router	Layer 3: network	Aware	Broadcast domain	Packets
Layer 3 switch	Layer 3: network	Aware	Broadcast domain	Packets

Table 3-12 *Campus Layer Design Best Practices*

Campus Layer	Best Practices
Access layer	Limit VLANs to a single closet when possible to provide the most deterministic and highly available topology. Use RPVST+ if STP is required. It provides the best convergence. Set VLAN Dynamic Trunking Protocol (DTP) to desirable/desirable with negotiation on. Manually prune unused VLANs to avoid broadcast propagation. Use VTP transparent mode, because there is little need for a common VLAN database in hierarchical networks. Disable trunking on host ports, because it is not necessary. Doing so provides more security and speeds up PortFast. Consider implementing routing in the access layer to provide fast convergence and Layer 3 load balancing.
Distribution layer	Use first-hop redundancy protocols. Hot Standby Router Protocol (HSRP) or Gateway Load Balancing Protocol (GLBP) should be used if you implement Layer 2 links between the access and distribution. Use Layer 3 links between the distribution and core switches to allow for fast convergence and load balancing. Build Layer 3 triangles, not squares. Use the distribution switches to connect Layer 2 VLANs that span multiple access layer switches. Summarize routes from the distribution to the core of the network to reduce routing overhead.
Core layer	Reduce the switch peering by using redundant triangle connections between switches. Use routing that provides a topology with no spanning-tree loops. Use Layer 3 switches on the core that provide intelligent services that Layer 2 switches do not support.

Table 3-13 *LAN Types*

LAN Type	Characteristics
Large-building network	Large number of users, data center, floor closet switches, multiple LANs within the building, high-speed backbone switching between distribution devices
Campus network	High-speed backbone switching between multiple buildings in a geographic area
Small or remote LAN	Small number of users, small switches

Table 3-14 *Enterprise Campus Model Components*

Component	Description
Campus infrastructure	Core, building distribution, and building access
Server farm	Connects to the campus backbone; has enterprise servers
Edge distribution	Connects the campus backbone to the Enterprise Edge

Table 3-15 *Campus Infrastructure Modules*

Component	Description
Core or campus backbone	High-end Layer 3 switches
Building distribution	Layer 3 or Layer 2 switches providing redundant distribution to the access layer
Building access	Layer 2 access switches

Q&A

As mentioned in the Introduction, you have two choices for review questions: here in the book or the exam questions on the CD-ROM. The answers to these questions appear in Appendix A.

For more practice with exam format questions, use the exam engine on the CD-ROM.

1. True or false: Layer 2 switches control network broadcasts.

2. What technology can you use to limit multicasts at Layer 2?

3. True or false: Packet marking is also called coloring.

4. True or false: Usually the distribution and core layers are collapsed in medium-sized networks.

5. What are two methods to mark frames to provide CoS?

6. Which of the following is an example of a peer-to-peer application?

   a. IP phone call

   b. Client accessing file server

   c. Web access

   d. Using a local server on the same segment

7. What primary design factors affect the design of a campus network? (Select three.)

   a. Environmental characteristics

   b. Number of file servers

   c. Infrastructure devices

   d. Fiber and UTP characteristics

   e. Network applications

   f. Windows, Linux, and mainframe operating systems

8. You need to connect a building access switch to the distribution switch. The cable distance is 135 m. What type of cable do you recommend?

   a. UTP

   b. Coaxial cable

   c. Multimode fiber

   d. Single-mode fiber

9. Which layer of the campus network corresponds to the data center aggregation layer?

    a. Core layer

    b. Distribution layer

    c. Access layer

    d. Server farm

10. Which of the following is an access layer best practice?

    a. Reduce switch peering and routing

    b. Use HSRP and summarize routes

    c. Disable trunking and use RPVST+

    d. Offload SSL sessions and use load balancers

11. Which of the following is a distribution layer best practice?

    a. Reduce switch peering and routing

    b. Use HSRP and summarize routes

    c. Disable trunking and use RPVST+

    d. Offload SSL sessions and use load balancers

12. Which of the following is a core layer best practice?

    a. Reduce switch peering and routing

    b. Use HSRP and summarize routes

    c. Disable trunking and use RPVST+

    d. Offload SSL sessions and use load balancers

13. Which of the following is a DC aggregation layer best practice?

    a. Reduce switch peering and routing

    b. Use HSRP and summarize routes

    c. Disable trunking and use RPVST+

    d. Offload SSL sessions and use load balancers

14. Which of the following are threats to the edge distribution?

    a. IP spoofing

    b. Network discovery

    c. Packet-capture devices

    d. All of the above

15. An enterprise network has grown to multiple buildings supporting multiple departments. Clients access servers that are in local and other buildings. The company security assessment has identified policies that need to be applied. What would you recommend?

    a. Move all departments to a single building to prevent unauthorized access.

    b. Move all servers to one of the LAN client segments.

    c. Move all servers to a server farm segment that is separate from client LANs.

    d. Move all servers to the building distribution switches.

16. Link redundancy and infrastructure services are design considerations for which layer(s)?

    a. Core layer

    b. Distribution layer

    c. Access layer

    d. All of the above

17. Which of the following are server connectivity methods in the server farm?

    a. Single NIC

    b. EtherChannel

    c. Content switch

    d. All of the above

18. What is the recommended method to connect the distribution switches to the core?

    a. Redundant triangle links

    b. Redundant cross-connect links

    c. Redundant Layer 3 squares

    d. Redundant Layer 2 links

19. A campus network of four buildings is experiencing performance problems. Each building contains 400 to 600 devices, all in one IP subnet. The buildings are connected in a hub-and-spoke configuration back to building 1 using Gigabit Ethernet with multimode fiber. All servers are located in building 1. What would you recommend to improve performance?

    a. Connect all buildings in a ring topology

    b. Implement multiple VLANs in each building

    c. Move servers to the buildings

    d. Use single-mode fiber to make the Gigabit Ethernet links faster

20. What of the following is true about data link layer broadcasts?

   a. Not controlled by routers

   b. Not forwarded by routers

   c. Not forwarded by switches

   d. Not controlled by VLANs

21. Match each LAN medium with its original physical specification:

   i. Fast Ethernet

   ii. Gigabit Ethernet

   iii. WLAN

   iv. Token Ring

   v. 10Gigabit Ethernet

   a. IEEE 802.3ab

   b. IEEE 802.11b

   c. IEEE 802.3u

   d. IEEE 802.3ae

   e. IEEE 802.5

22. True or false: Layer 3 switches bound Layer 2 collision and broadcast domains.

23. Match each Enterprise Campus component with its description:

   i. Campus infrastructure

   ii. Server farm

   iii. Edge distribution

   a. Consists of backbone, building-distribution, and building-access modules

   b. Connects the campus backbone to the Enterprise Edge

   c. Provides redundancy access to the servers

24. Match each LAN device type with its description:

   i. Hub

   ii. Bridge

   iii. Switch

   iv. Layer 3 switch

   v. Router

a. Legacy device that connects two data link layer segments

b. Network layer device that forwards packets to serial interfaces connected to the WAN

c. High-speed device that forwards frames between two or more data link layer segments

d. High-speed device that bounds data link layer broadcast domains

e. Device that amplifies the signal between connected segments

25.   Match each application type with its description:

i. Peer-to-peer

ii. Client-local server

iii. Client/server farm

iv. Client-Enterprise Edge

a. Server on the same segment

b. IM

c. Web access

d. Client accesses database server

26.   Match each transmission medium with its upper-limit distance:

i. UTP

ii. Wireless

iii. Single-mode fiber

iv. Multimode fiber

a. 2 km

b. 100 m

c. 90 km

d. 500 m

27.   True or false: IP phones and LAN switches can reassign a frame's CoS bits.

28.   Name two ways to reduce multicast traffic in the access layer.

29.   What are two VLAN methods you can use to carry marking CoS on frames?

30.   True or false: You can configure CGMP in mixed Cisco switch and non-Cisco router environments.

Use Figure 3-19 to answer the following questions.

Figure 3-19   *Enterprise Campus Diagram*

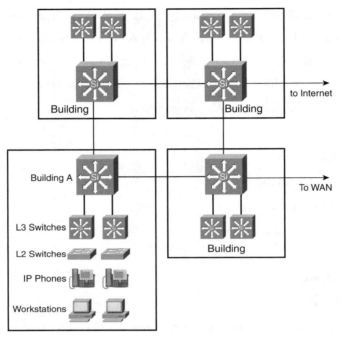

31. What medium would you recommend for the campus LAN backbone?

32. The workstations send frames with the CoS set to 5. What should the IP phones do so that the network gives preference to VoIP traffic over data traffic?

33. If the Layer 2 switches in Building A cannot look at CoS and ToS fields, where should these fields be inspected for acceptance or reclassification: in the building Layer 3 switches or in the backbone Layer 3 switches?

34. Does the network have redundant access to the WAN?

35. Does the network have redundant access to the Internet?

36. Does Figure 3-19 use recommended devices for networks designed using the Enterprise Architecture model?

This chapter covers the following subjects:

- Wireless LAN Technologies

- Cisco Unified Wireless Network

- Wireless LAN Design

CHAPTER 4

Wireless LAN Design

Wireless LANs allow users to connect to network resources and services without using cables. With wireless LANs, users connect to the network in common areas, away from their desk, and in areas that do not easily accommodate the installation of wired cabling, such as outdoors and in designated historical sites. This chapter describes wireless LAN technologies, design, and Cisco solutions.

"Do I Know This Already?" Quiz

The purpose of the "Do I Know This Already?" quiz is to help you decide if you need to read the entire chapter. If you intend to read the entire chapter, you do not necessarily need to answer these questions now.

The eight-question quiz, derived from the major sections in the "Foundation Topics" portion of the chapter, helps you determine how to spend your limited study time.

Table 4-1 outlines the major topics discussed in this chapter and the "Do I Know This Already?" quiz questions that correspond to those topics.

Table 4-1 *"Do I Know This Already?" Foundation Topics Section-to-Question Mapping*

Foundation Topics Section	Questions Covered in This Section
Wireless LAN Technologies	1, 2
Cisco Unified Wireless Network	3, 4, 5
Wireless LAN Design	6, 7, 8

CAUTION   The goal of self-assessment is to gauge your mastery of the topics in this chapter. If you do not know the answer to a question or you are only partially sure, you should mark this question wrong for purposes of the self-assessment. Giving yourself credit for an answer you correctly guess skews your self-assessment results and might give you with false sense of security.

1. What technology provides 54 Mbps of bandwidth using UNII frequencies?

   a. IEEE 802.11b

   b. IEEE 802.11g

   c. IEEE 802.11a

   d. Bluetooth

2. What frequency allotment provides 11 channels for unlicensed use for wireless LANs in North America?

   a. UNII

   b. ISM

   c. Bluetooth

   d. FM

3. What standard is used for control messaging between access points and controllers?

   a. IEEE 802.11

   b. CSMA/CA

   c. IEEE 802.1X

   d. LWAPP

4. Which WLAN controller interface is used for out-of-band management?

   a. Management interface

   b. Service-port interface

   c. AP manager interface

   d. Virtual interface

5. How many access points are supported by a Cisco Catalyst 3750 with an integrated controller?

   a. 6

   b. 50

   c. 100

   d. 300

6. Which WLAN controller redundancy scheme uses a backup WLC configured as the tertiary WLC in the APs?

   a. N+1

   b. N+N

   c. N+N+1

   d. N+N+B

7. What is the recommended maximum number of data devices associated to a WLAN?

    a. 8

    b. 20

    c. 50

    d. 100

8. Which device of Cisco's Wireless Mesh Networking communicates with the rooftop AP?

    a. WLC

    b. WCS

    c. RAP

    d. MAP

The answers to the "Do I Know This Already?" quiz appear in Appendix A, "Answers to Chapter Quizzes and Q&A Sections." The suggested choices for your next step are as follows:

■   **6 or less overall score**—Read the entire chapter. This includes the "Foundation Topics," "Foundation Summary," and "Q&A" sections.

■   **7 or 8 overall score**—If you want more review on these topics, skip to the "Foundation Summary" section and then go to the "Q&A" section. Otherwise, move to the next chapter.

Foundation Topics

Cisco has developed a strategy to address the increasing wireless demands placed on today's networks. The Cisco Unified Wireless Network (UWN) architecture combines elements of wireless and wired networks to deliver scalable, manageable, and secure WLANs. Lightweight Access Point Protocol (LWAPP) allows the placement of lightweight access points that are remotely configured and easily deployable. Cisco provides solutions for client roaming, radio frequency management, and controller designs that make wireless networks scalable. This chapter covers the Cisco UWN architecture as well as general WLAN technologies and design.

Wireless LAN Technologies

This section reviews the Institute of Electronics and Electrical Engineers (IEEE) 802.11 wireless LAN standards, wireless LAN frequencies, access methods, security, and authentication.

Wireless LAN Standards

Wireless LAN (WLAN) applications include inside-building access, LAN extension, outside building-to-building communications, public access, and small office/home office (SOHO) communications. The first standard for wireless LANs is IEEE 802.11, approved by the IEEE in 1997. The current specification is IEEE 802.11-1999, with many amendments thereafter.

IEEE 802.11 implemented wireless LANs at speeds of 1 Mbps and 2 Mbps using Direct Sequence Spread Spectrum (DSSS) and Frequency Hopping Spread Spectrum (FHSS) at the physical layer of the Open System Interconnection (OSI) model. DSSS divides data into separate sections; each section travels over different frequencies at the same time. FHSS uses a frequency-hopping sequence to send data in bursts. With FHSS, some data transmits at Frequency 1, and then the system hops to Frequency 2 to send more data, and so on, returning to transmit more data at Frequency 1.

In 1999, the 802.11b amendment was introduced, providing an 11-Mbps data rate. It provides speeds of 11, 5.5, 2, and 1 Mbps and uses 11 channels of the Industrial, Scientific, and Medical (ISM) frequencies. The interoperability certification for IEEE 802.11b WLANs is wireless fidelity (Wi-Fi). The Wireless Ethernet Compatibility Alliance (WECA) governs the Wi-Fi certification. IEEE 802.11b uses DSSS and is backward-compatible with 802.11 systems that use DSSS.

The IEEE approved a second standard in 1999. IEEE 802.11a provides a maximum 54-Mbps data rate but is incompatible with 802.11b. It provides speeds of 54, 48, 36, 24, 18, 12, 9, and 6 Mbps. IEEE 802.11a uses 13 channels of the Unlicensed National Information Infrastructure (UNII) frequencies and is incompatible with 802.11b and 802.11g. IEEE 802.11a is also known as Wi-Fi5.

In 2003, the IEEE 802.11g standard was approved, providing a 54-Mbps data rate using the ISM frequencies. The advantage of 802.11g over 802.11a is that it is backward-compatible with 802.11b.

The IEEE 802.11n standard is expected to be ratified in 2007; this will provide a maximum data rate of 540 Mbps.

ISM and UNII Frequencies

ISM frequencies are set aside by ITU-R radio regulations 5.138 and 5.150. In the U.S., the Federal Communications Commission (15.247) specifies the ISM bands for unlicensed use. Several bands are specified in the following ranges:

- 900 to 928 MHz

- 2.4 to 2.5 GHz

- 5.75 to 5.875 GHz

Of these, channels located in the 2.4-GHz range are used for 802.11b and 802.11g. As shown in Figure 4-1, 11 overlapping channels are available for use. Each channel is 22 MHz wide. It is common to use channels 1, 6, and 11 in the same areas, because these three channels do not overlap.

Figure 4-1 *ISM 2.4 Channels*

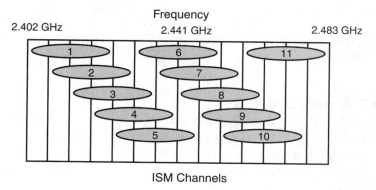

The UNII radio bands were specified for use with 802.11a wireless. UNII operates over three ranges:

- UNII 1—5.15 to 5.25 GHz and 5.25 to 5.35 GHz.

- UNII 2—5.47 to 5.725 GHz. This range is used by High Performance Radio LAN (HiperLAN) in Europe.

- UNII 3—5.725 to 5.875 GHz. This range overlaps with ISM.

UNII provides 12 nonoverlapping channels for 802.11a.

Summary of Wireless LAN Standards

Table 4-2 summarizes WLAN standards, frequencies, and data rates.

Table 4-2   *WLAN Standards Summary*

IEEE Protocol	Standard Release Date	Frequency	Typical Data Rate	Maximum Data Rate
Legacy	1997	ISM	1 Mbps	2 Mbps
802.11a	1999	UNII	25 Mbps	54 Mbps
802.11b	1999	ISM	6.5 Mbps	11 Mbps
802.11g	2003	ISM	25 Mbps	54 Mbps
802.11n	2007 (draft)	ISM or UNII	200 Mbps	540 Mbps

Service Set Identifier (SSID)

WLANs use an SSID to identify the WLAN's "network name." The SSID can be 2 to 32 characters long. All devices in the WLAN must have the same configured SSID to communicate. It is similar to a VLAN identifier in a wired network. The difficulty in large networks is configuring the SSID, frequency, and power settings for hundreds of remotely located access points. Cisco addresses this problem with the Cisco Wireless Control System (WCS). WCS is covered in more detail in the "Cisco UWN Architecture" section.

WLAN Layer 2 Access Method

The IEEE 802.11 Media Access Control (MAC) layer implements carrier sense multiple access collision avoidance (CSMA/CA) as an access method. With CSMA/CA, each WLAN station listens to see whether a station is transmitting. If no activity is occurring, the station transmits. If activity is occurring, the station uses a random countdown timer. When the timer expires, the station transmits.

WLAN Security

WLANs provide an effective solution for hard-to-reach locations and enable mobility to a level that was previously unattainable. However, WLANs without any encryption present a security risk, because publicly available software can obtain the SSIDs. The productivity improvements with WLANs are just beginning, however. The Wired Equivalent Privacy (WEP) security protocol, used in the IEEE 802.11b standard, is considered faulty and vulnerable to numerous attacks. The 802.11b protocol is the most commonly deployed wireless protocol, and although it has the ability to use 64-bit or 128-bit encryption, readily available software can crack the encryption scheme.

In June 2004, the IEEE 802.11i standard was ratified to provide additional security in WLAN networks. IEEE 802.11i is also known as Wi-Fi Protected Access 2 (WPA2). The 802.11i architecture contains the following components:

- 802.1X for authentication (entailing the use of Extensible Authentication Protocol [EAP] and an authentication server)

- Robust Security Network (RSN) for keeping track of associations

- Advanced Encryption Standard (AES) for confidentiality, integrity, and origin authentication

Unauthorized Access

A problem that confronts WLANs comes from the fact that wireless signals are not easily controlled or contained. WEP works at the data link layer, sharing the same key for all nodes that communicate. The 802.11 standard was deployed because it allowed bandwidth speed up to 11 Mbps and it is based on DSSS technology. DSSS also enables APs to identify WLAN cards via their MAC addresses. Because traditional physical boundaries do not apply to wireless networks, attackers can gain access using wireless from outside the physical security perimeter. Attackers achieve unauthorized access if the wireless network does not have a mechanism to compare a MAC address on a wireless card to a database that contains a directory with access rights. An individual can roam within an area, and each AP that comes into contact with that card must also rely on a directory. Statically allowing access via a MAC address is also insecure, because MAC addresses can be spoofed.

Some APs can implement MAC address and protocol filtering to enhance security or limit the protocols used over the WLAN. With hundreds of WLAN clients, MAC address filtering is not a scalable solution. Again, attackers can hack MAC address filtering. A user can listen for transmissions, gather a list of MAC addresses, and then use one of those MAC addresses to connect to the AP.

WLAN Security Design Approach

The WLAN security design approach makes two assumptions, which this chapter describes. The assumptions are that all WLAN devices are connected to a unique IP subnet and that most services available to the wired network are also available to the wireless nodes. Using these two assumptions, the WLAN security designs offer two basic security approaches:

- Use of Lightweight Extensible Authentication Protocol (LEAP) to secure authentication

- Use of virtual private networks (VPN) with IP Security (IPsec) to secure traffic from the WLAN to the wired network

Considering WLAN as an alternative access methodology, remember that the services these WLAN users access are often the same as those accessed by the wired users. WLAN opens a new world of access for the hacker, and you should consider the risks before deployment.

To enhance security, you can implement WLANs with IPsec VPN software, use the IEEE 802.1X-2001 port-based access control protocol, and use dynamic WEP keys.

IEEE 802.1X-2001 Port-Based Authentication

IEEE 802.1X-2001 is a port-based authentication standard for LANs. It authenticates a user before allowing access to the network. You can use it on Ethernet, Fast Ethernet, and WLAN networks.

With IEEE 802.1X-2001, client workstations run client software to request access to services. Clients use EAP to communicate with the LAN switch. The LAN switch verifies client information with the authentication server and relays the response to the client. LAN switches use a Remote Authentication Dial-In User Service (RADIUS) client to communicate with the server. The RADIUS authentication server validates the client's identity and authorizes the client. The server uses RADIUS with EAP extensions to make the authorization.

Dynamic WEP Keys and LEAP

Cisco also offers dynamic per-user, per-session WEP keys to provide additional security over statically configured WEP keys, which are not unique per user. For centralized user-based authentication, Cisco developed LEAP. LEAP uses mutual authentication between the client and the network server and uses IEEE 802.1X for 802.11 authentication messaging. LEAP uses a RADIUS server to manage user information.

LEAP is a combination of 802.1X and EAP. It combines the capability to authenticate to various servers such as RADIUS with forcing the WLAN user to log in to an access point that compares the login information to RADIUS. This solution is more scalable than MAC address filtering.

Because the WLAN access depends on receiving an address, using Dynamic Host Configuration Protocol (DHCP), and the authentication of the user using RADIUS, the WLAN needs constant access to these back-end servers. In addition, LEAP does not support one-time passwords (OTP), so you must use good password-security practices. The password issue and maintenance practice are a basic component of corporate security policy.

Controlling WLAN Access to Servers

In the same way you place Domain Name System (DNS) servers accessible via the Internet on a demilitarized zone (DMZ) segment, you should apply a similar strategy to the RADIUS and DHCP servers accessible to the WLAN. These servers should be secondary servers that are on a different segment (separate VLAN) from their primary counterparts. Access to this VLAN is filtered. Such placement ensures that any attacks launched on these servers are contained within that segment.

You should control network access to the servers. Consider the WLAN an unsecured segment and apply appropriate segmentation and access lists. Such a step ensures that WLAN access is controlled and directed to only those areas that need it. For example, you might not want to permit WLAN access to management servers and HR servers.

You must also protect these servers against network attack. The criticality of these servers makes them an ideal target for denial-of-service (DoS) attacks. Consider using host-based intrusion detection systems (IDS) to detect network attacks against these devices.

Cisco Unified Wireless Network

This section covers the Cisco UWN architecture, LWAPP, WLAN controller components, roaming, and mobility groups. Cisco UWN components provide scalable wireless LAN solutions using WLAN controllers to manage lightweight access points. The CCDA must understand how these components work with each other, how they scale, and how roaming and mobility groups work.

Cisco UWN Architecture

With the explosion of wireless solutions in and out of the enterprise, designers must create solutions that provide mobility and business services while maintaining network security. The Cisco Unified Wireless Network (UWN) architecture combines elements of wireless and wired networks to deliver scalable, manageable, and secure WLANs. As shown in Figure 4-2, the Cisco UWN architecture is composed of five network elements:

- **Client devices**—These include laptops, workstations, IP phones, PDAs, and manufacturing devices to access the WLAN.

- **Access points**—These devices provide access to the wireless network. APs are placed in strategic locations to minimize interference.

- **Network unification**—The WLAN system should be able to support wireless applications by providing security policies, QoS, intrusion prevention, and radio frequency (RF) management. Cisco WLAN controllers provide this functionality and integration into all major switching and routing platforms.

- **Network management**—The Cisco Wireless Control System (WCS) provides a central management tool that lets you design, control, and monitor wireless networks.

■ **Mobility services**—These include guest access, location services, voice services, and threat detection and mitigation.

Figure 4-2 *Cisco UWN Architecture*

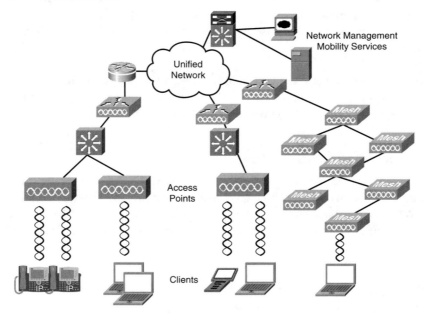

Cisco UWN provides the following benefits:

■ Reduced Total Cost of Ownership (TCO)

■ Enhanced visibility control

■ Dynamic RF management

■ WLAN security

■ Unified wired and wireless network

■ Enterprise mobility

■ Enhanced productivity and collaboration

LWAPP

Lightweight Access Point Protocol (LWAPP) is a draft Internet Engineering Task Force (IETF) standard for control messaging for setup, authentication, and operations between access points (AP) and wireless LAN controllers (WLC).

With Cisco's UWN Split-MAC operation, the control and data messages are split. Lightweight Access Points (LWAP) communicate with the WLCs using control messages over the wired network. LWAPP data messages are encapsulated and forwarded to and from wireless clients. The WLC manages multiple APs, providing configuration information and firmware updates as needed.

LWAP MAC functions are

- **802.11**—Beacons, probe response

- **802.11 Control**—Packet acknowledgment and transmission

- **802.11e**—Frame queuing and packet prioritization

- **802.11i**—MAC layer data encryption/decryption

Controller MAC functions are

- **802.11 MAC Management**—Association requests and actions

- **802.11e Resource Reservation**—To reserve resources for specific applications

- **802.11i**—Authentication and key management

In the LWAPP RFC draft, LWAPP control messages can be transported at Layer 2 tunnels or Layer 3 tunnels. Layer 2 LWAPP tunnels were the first method developed in which the APs did not require an IP address. The disadvantage of Layer 2 LWAPP was that the WLC needed to be on every subnet on which the AP resides. Layer 2 LWAPP is a deprecated solution for Cisco. Layer 3 LWAPP is the preferred solution.

NOTE   Layer 2 LWAPP tunnels use Ethertype code 0xBBBB.

As shown in Figure 4-3, Layer 3 LWAPP tunnels are used between the LWAP and the WLC. Messages from the WLC use UDP port 12223 for control and UDP port 12222 for data messages. In this solution, access points require an IP address, but the WLC does not need to reside on the same segment.

Figure 4-3 *Layer 3 LWAPP*

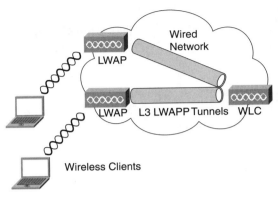

LWAPP Access Point Modes

LWAPP access points operate in one of six different modes:

- **Local mode**—This is the default mode of operation. In this mode, every 180 seconds the AP spends 60 milliseconds on channels it does not operate on. During this 60 ms, the AP performs noise floor measurements, measures interference, and scans for IDS events.

- **Remote Edge AP (REAP) mode**—This mode enables an LWAP to reside across a WAN link and still be able to communicate with the WLC and provide the functionality of a regular LWAP. Currently, REAP mode is supported only on the 1030 LWAPs.

- **Monitor mode**—Monitor mode is a feature designed to allow specified LWAPP-enabled APs to exclude themselves from handling data traffic between clients and the infrastructure. They instead act as dedicated sensors for location-based services (LBS), rogue access point detection, and intrusion detection (IDS). When APs are in Monitor mode, they cannot serve clients and continuously cycle through all configured channels, listening to each channel for approximately 60 ms.

- **Rogue detector mode**—LWAPs that operate in Rogue Detector mode monitor the rogue APs. They do not transmit or contain rogue APs. The idea is that the rogue detector (RD) should be able to see all the VLANs in the network, because rogue APs can be connected to any of the VLANs in the network (thus, we connect it to a trunk port). The switch sends all the rogue AP/client MAC address lists to the RD. The RD then forwards those to the WLC to compare with the MAC addresses of clients that the WLC APs have heard over the air. If the MAC addresses match, the WLC knows that the rogue AP to which those clients are connected is on the wired network.

■ **Sniffer mode**—An LWAPP that operates in Sniffer mode functions as a sniffer and captures and forwards all the packets on a particular channel to a remote machine that runs AiroPeek. These packets contain information on the time stamp, signal strength, packet size, and so on. The Sniffer feature can be enabled only if you run AiroPeek, a third-party network analyzer software that supports decoding of data packets.

■ **Bridge mode**—The Bridge mode feature on the Cisco 1030 (typically indoor usage) and 1500 access points (typically outdoor mesh usage) provides cost-effective, high-bandwidth wireless bridging connectivity. Applications supported are point-to-point bridging, point-to-multipoint bridging, point-to-point wireless access with integrated wireless backhaul, and point-to-multipoint wireless access with integrated wireless backhaul.

LWAPP Discovery

When LWAPs are placed on the network, they first perform DHCP discovery to obtain an IP address. Then Layer 3 LWAPP discovery is attempted. If there is no WLC response, the access point reboots and repeats this process. The Layer 3 LWAPP discovery algorithm is as follows:

1. The AP sends a Layer 3 LWAPP Discovery Request.

2. All WLCs that receive the Discovery Request reply with a unicast LWAPP Discovery Response Message.

3. The AP compiles a list of WLCs.

4. The AP selects a WLC based on certain criteria.

5. The AP validates the selected WLC and sends an LWAPP Join Response. An encryption key is selected, and future messages are encrypted.

Layer 3 Discovery Requests are sent as listed:

■ Local subnet broadcast

■ Unicast LWAPP Discovery Requests to WLC IP addresses advertised by other APs

■ To previously stored WLC IP addresses

■ To IP addresses learned by DHCP option 43

■ To IP addresses learned by DNS resolution of CISCO-LWAPP-CONTROLLER.locadomain

The selected WLC is based on the following:

■ Previously configured primary, secondary, and/or tertiary WLCs

■ The WLC configured as the Master controller

■ The WLC with the most capacity for AP associations

WLAN Authentication

Wireless clients first associate to an access point. Then wireless clients need to authenticate with an authentication server before the access point allows access to services. As shown in Figure 4-4, the authentication server resides in the wired infrastructure. An EAP/RADIUS tunnel occurs between the WLC and the authentication server. Cisco's Secure Access Control Server (ACS) using EAP is an example of an authentication server.

Figure 4-4 *WLAN Authentication*

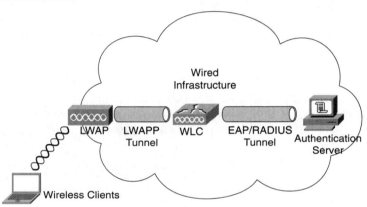

Authentication Options

Wireless clients communicate with the authentication server using EAP. Each EAP type has advantages and disadvantages. Trade-offs exist between the security provided, EAP type manageability, the operating systems supported, the client devices supported, the client software and authentication messaging overhead, certificate requirements, user ease of use, and WLAN infrastructure device support. The following summarizes the authentication options:

- **EAP-Transport Layer Security (EAP-TLS)** is an IETF open standard that is well-supported among wireless vendors but rarely deployed. It uses PKI to secure communications to the RADIUS authentication server using TLS and digital certificates.

- **Protected Extensible Authentication Protocol (PEAP)** is a joint proposal by Cisco Systems, Microsoft, and RSA Security as an open standard. PEAP/MSCHAPv2 is the most common version, and it is widely available in products and widely deployed. It is similar in design to EAP-TTLS, requiring only a server-side PKI certificate to create a secure TLS tunnel to protect user authentication. PEAP-GTC allows more generic authentication to a number of databases such as Novell Directory Services (NDS).

- **EAP-Tunneled TLS (EAP-TTLS)** was codeveloped by Funk Software and Certicom. It is widely supported across platforms and offers very good security, using PKI certificates only on the authentication server.

- **Cisco Lightweight Extensible Authentication Protocol (LEAP)** is an early proprietary EAP method supported in the Cisco Certified Extensions (CCX) program. It is vulnerable to dictionary attacks.

- **EAP-Flexible Authentication via Secure Tunneling (EAP-FAST)** is a proposal by Cisco Systems to fix the weaknesses of LEAP. EAP-FAST uses a Protected Access Credential (PAC), and use of server certificates is optional. EAP-FAST has three phases. Phase 0 is an optional phase in which the PAC can be provisioned manually or dynamically. In Phase 1, the client and the AAA server use the PAC to establish the TLS tunnel. In Phase 2, the client sends user information across the tunnel.

WLAN Controller Components

The CCDA candidate must understand the three major components of WLCs:

- Wireless LANs

- Interfaces

- Ports

Wireless LANs are identified by unique SSID network names. The LAN is a logical entity. Each WLAN is assigned to an interface in the WLC. Each WLAN is configured with radio policies, QoS, and other WLAN parameters.

A WLC interface is a logical connection that maps to a VLAN on the wired network. Each interface is configured with a unique IP address, default gateways, physical ports, VLAN tag, and DHCP server.

The port is a physical connection to the neighboring switch or router. By default, each port is an IEEE 802.1Q trunk port. There may be multiple ports on a WLC into a single port-channel interface. These ports can be aggregated using Link Aggregation (LAG). Some WLCs have a service port that is used for out-of-band management. Figure 4-5 shows the WLC components.

Figure 4-5 *WLAN Controller Components*

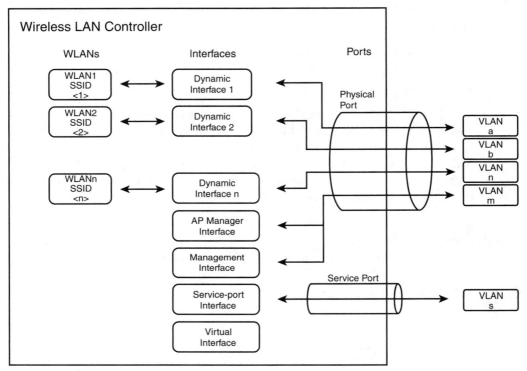

WLC Interface Types

A WLC has five interface types:

- **Management interface** is used for in-band management, connectivity to AAA, and Layer 2 discovery and association.

- **Service-port interface** is used for out-of-band management. It is an optional interface that is statically configured.

- **AP manager interface** is used for Layer 3 discovery and association. It has the source IP address of the AP that is statically configured.

- **Dynamic interface** is analogous to VLANs and is designated for WLAN client data.

- **Virtual interface** is used for Layer 3 security authentication, DHCP relay support, and mobility management.

AP Controller Equipment Scaling

Cisco provides different solutions to support the differing numbers of access points present in enterprise customers. Standalone devices, modules for integrated services routers (ISR), and modules for 6500 switches support numerous APs. Table 4-3 lists the platforms and the number of APs supported.

Table 4-3 *WLAN Controller Platforms*

Platform	Number of Supported Access Points
Cisco 2000 series WLC	6
Cisco WLC for ISRs	6
Catalyst 3750 Integrated WLC	50
Cisco 4400 series WLC	100
Cisco 6500 series WLC Module	300

Roaming and Mobility Groups

The primary reason to have wireless networks is the ability to access network resources from common areas and in areas difficult to run cables. End clients might want to move from one location to another. Mobility allows users to access the network from several locations. Roaming occurs when the wireless client changes association from one access point to another. The challenge is to scale the wireless network to allow client roaming. Roaming can be intracontroller or intercontroller.

Intracontroller Roaming

Intracontroller roaming, shown in Figure 4-6, occurs when a client moves association from one AP to another AP that is joined to the same WLC. The WLC updates the client database with the new associated AP and does not change the client's IP address. If required, clients are reauthenticated, and a new security association is established. The client database remains on the same WLC.

Figure 4-6 *Intracontroller Roaming*

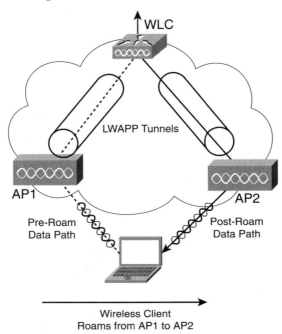

Layer 2 Intercontroller Roaming

Intercontroller roaming occurs when a client moves association from one AP to another AP that is joined to a different WLC. The Layer 2 roam occurs when the client traffic is bridged to the same IP subnet. Figure 4-7 shows Layer 2 intercontroller roaming. Traffic remains of the same IP subnet, and no IP address changes to the client occur. The client database is moved from WLC1 to WLC2. The client is reauthenticated, and a new security session is established.

Layer 3 Intercontroller Roaming

With Layer 3 intercontroller roaming, shown in Figure 4-8, a client moves association from one AP to another AP that is joined to a different WLC. Then the traffic is bridged onto a different IP subnet. When the client associates to AP2, WLC2 then exchanges mobility messages with WLC1. The original client database is not moved to WLC. Instead, WLC1 marks the client with an "Anchor" entry in its database. The database entry is copied to WLC2's database and is marked as a "Foreign" entry. The wireless client maintains its original IP address and is reauthenticated. A new security session is then established.

Figure 4-7 *Layer 2 Intercontroller Roaming*

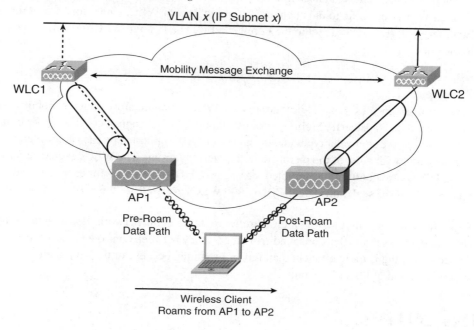

Figure 4-8 *Layer 3 Intercontroller Roaming*

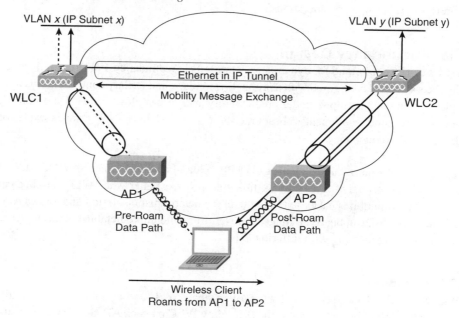

Client traffic then routes in an asymmetric manner. Traffic from the client is forwarded by the Foreign WLC, but traffic to the client arrives at the Anchor WLC, which forwards it through an Ethernet-in-IP (EtherIP) tunnel to the Foreign WLC. The Foreign WLC forwards the data traffic to the client.

Mobility Groups

When you assign WLCs to mobility groups, the WLCs dynamically exchange mobility messages and tunnel data via EtherIP. Mobility groups support up to 24 controllers. The upper limit of APs is bounded by the controller types and the number of APs supported by each controller. Each WLC is configured with a list of the members in the mobility group. The WLCs exchange messages using UDP port 16666 for unencrypted messages or UDP port 16667 for encrypted messages. As an example of the scalability, if 24 Cisco 2000 WLCs are used, 24 * 6 = 144 APs are supported.

Cisco recommends minimizing intercontroller roaming in the network. It is also recommended that there be less than 10 ms of round-trip time latency between controllers. Cisco also states that Layer 2 roaming is more efficient than Layer 3 roaming because of the asymmetric communication of Layer 3 roaming.

Wireless LAN Design

This section covers controller redundancy design, radio frequency groups, site survey, and wireless LAN design considerations.

Controller Redundancy Design

WLCs can be configured for dynamic or deterministic redundancy. For deterministic redundancy, the access point is configured with a primary, secondary, and tertiary controller. This requires more upfront planning but allows better predictability and faster failover times. Deterministic redundancy is the recommended best practice. N+1, N+N, and N+N+1 are examples of deterministic redundancy.

Dynamic controller redundancy uses LWAPP to load-balance APs across WLCs. LWAPP populates APs with a backup WLC. This solution works better when WLCs are in a centralized cluster. This solution is easier to deploy than the deterministic solution and allows APs to load-balance. The disadvantages are longer failover times and unpredictable operation. An example is adjacent APs registering with differing WLCs.

N+1 WLC Redundancy

With N+1 redundancy, shown in Figure 4-9, a single WLC acts as the backup of multiple WLCs. The backup WLC is configured as the secondary WLC on each AP. One design constraint is that the backup WLC may become oversubscribed if there are too many failures of the primary controllers. The secondary WLC is the backup controller for all APs.

Figure 4-9 *N+1 Controller Redundancy*

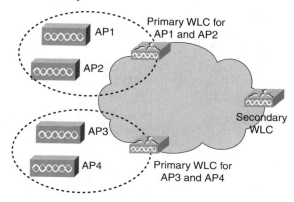

N+N WLC Redundancy

With N+N redundancy, shown in Figure 4-10, an equal number of controllers back up each other. For example, a pair of WLCs on one floor serves as a backup to a second pair on another floor. The top WLC is primary for AP1 and AP2 and secondary for AP3 and AP4. The bottom WLC is primary for AP3 and AP4 and secondary for AP1 and AP2.

Figure 4-10 *N+N Controller Redundancy*

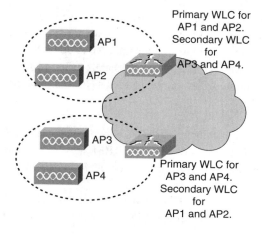

N+N+1 WLC Redundancy

With N+N+1 redundancy, shown in Figure 4-11, an equal number of controllers back up each other (as with N+N), plus a backup WLC is configured as the tertiary WLC for the access points. N+N+1 redundancy functions the same as N+N redundancy plus a tertiary controller that backs up the secondary controllers.

Figure 4-11 *N+N+1 Controller Redundancy*

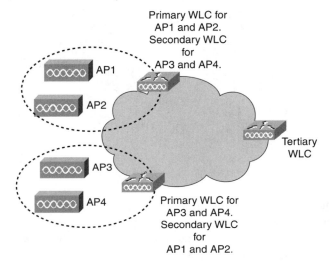

Radio Management and Radio Groups

The limit of available channels in the ISM frequencies used by the IEEE 802.11b/g standard presents challenges to the network designer. There are three nonoverlapping channels (channels 1, 6, and 11). The recommended best practice per AP is up to 20 data devices, or no more than seven concurrent voice over WLAN (VoWLAN) calls using g.711 or eight concurrent VoWLAN calls using g.729. Additional APs should be added as user population grows to maintain this ratio of data and voice per AP.

Cisco Radio Resource Management (RRM) is a method to manage AP radio frequency channel and power configuration. Cisco WLCs use the RRM algorithm to automatically configure, optimize, and self-heal. Cisco RRM functions are as follows:

■ **Radio resource monitoring**—Cisco LWAPs monitor all channels. Collected packets are sent to the WLC, which can detect rouge APs, clients, and interfering APs.

■ **Dynamic channel assignment**—WLCs automatically assign channels to avoid interference.

- **Interference detection and avoidance**—As Cisco LWAPs monitor all channels, interference is detected by a predefined threshold (10 percent by default). Interference can be generated by rouge APs, Bluetooth devices, or neighboring WLANs.

- **Dynamic transmit power control**—The WLCs automatically adjust power levels.

- **Coverage hole detection and correction**—WLCs may adjust the power output of APs if clients report that a low Received Signal Strength Indication (RSSI) level is detected.

- **Client and network load balancing**—Clients can be influenced to associate with certain APs to maintain network balance.

Radio Frequency (RF) Groups

An RF group is a cluster of WLC devices that coordinate their RRM calculations. When the WLCs are placed in an RF group, the RRM calculation can scale from a single WLC to multiple floors, buildings, or even the campus. With an RF group, APs send neighbor messages to other APs. If the neighbor message is above –80 dBm, the controllers form an RF group. The WLCs elect an RF group leader to analyze the RF data. The RF group leader exchanges messages with the RF group members using UDP port 12114 for 802.11b/g and UDP port 12115 for 802.11a.

RF Site Survey

Similar to performing an assessment for a wired network design, RF site surveys are done to determine design parameters for wireless LANs and customer requirements. RF site surveys help determine the coverage areas and check for RF interference. This helps determine the appropriate placement of wireless APs.

The RF site survey has the following steps:

Step 1   **Define customer requirements**, such as service levels and support for VoIP.

Step 2   **Identify coverage areas and user density**, including peak use times and conference room locations.

Step 3   **Determine preliminary AP locations**, which need power, wired network access, mounting locations, and antennas.

Step 4   **Perform the actual survey** by using an AP to survey the location and received RF strength based on the targeted AP placement. Consider the effects of electrical machinery. Microwave ovens and elevators may distort the ration signal from the APs.

Step 5   **Document the findings** by recording the target AP locations, data rates, and signal readings.

Using EoIP Tunnels for Guest Services

Basic solutions use separate VLANs for guest and corporate users to segregate guest traffic from corporate traffic. The guest SSID is broadcast, but the corporate SSID is not. All other security parameters are configured. Another solution is to use Ethernet over IP (EoIP) to tunnel the guest traffic from the LWAPP to an anchor WLC.

As shown in Figure 4-12, EoIP is used to logically segment and transport guest traffic from the edge AP to the anchor WLC. There is no need to define guest VLANs in the internal network, and corporate traffic is still locally bridged. The Ethernet frames from the guest clients are maintained across the LWAPP and EoIP tunnels.

Figure 4-12 *EoIP Tunnels*

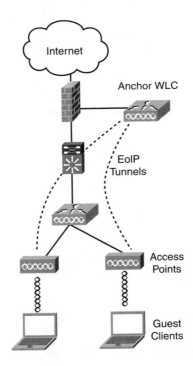

Wireless Mesh for Outdoor Wireless

Traditionally, outdoor wireless solutions have been limited to point-to-point and point-to-multipoint bridging between buildings. With these solutions, each AP is wired to the network. The Cisco Wireless Mesh networking solution, shown in Figure 4-13, eliminates the need to wire each AP and allows users to roam from one area to another without having to reconnect.

Figure 4-13 *Wireless Mesh Components*

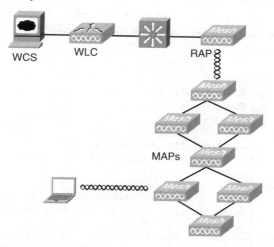

The wireless mesh components are as follows:

- **Wireless Control System (WCS)** is the wireless mesh SNMP management system that allows network-wide configuration and management.

- **Wireless LAN Controller (WLC)** links the mesh APs to the wired network and performs all the tasks previously described for a WLC.

- **Rooftop AP (RAP)** connects the mesh to the wired network and serves as the root (or gateway). It also communicates with the MAPs.

- **Mesh Access Points (MAP)** are remote APs. They communicate with the RAP to connect to the wired network.

Mesh Design Recommendations

The following are Cisco recommendations (and considerations) for mesh design:

- There is a 2- to 3-ms typical latency per hop.

- For outdoor deployment, four or fewer hops are recommended for best performance. A maximum of eight hops is supported.

- For indoor deployment, one hop is supported.

- 20 MAP nodes per RAP are recommended for best performance. Up to 32 MAPs are supported.

Campus Design Considerations

When designing for the Cisco Unified Wireless Network, you need to be able to determine how many LWAPs to place and how they will be managed with the WLCs. Table 4-4 summarizes campus design considerations.

Table 4-4   *WLAN Design Considerations*

Design Item	Description
Number of APs	The design should have enough APs to provide full RF coverage for wireless clients for all the expected locations in the enterprise. Cisco recommends 20 data devices per AP and 7 g.711 concurrent or 8 g.729 concurrent VoWLAN calls.
Placement of APs	APs are placed in a centralized location of the expected area for which they are to provide access. APs are placed in conference rooms to accommodate peak requirements.
Power for APs	Traditional wall power can be used, but the preferred solution is to use power over Ethernet (PoE) to power APs and provide wired access.
Number of WLCs	The number of WLCs depends on the selected redundancy model based on the client's requirements. The number of controllers is also dependent on the number of required APs and the number of APs supported by the differing WLC models.
Placement of WLCs	WLCs are placed on secured wiring closets or in the data center. Deterministic redundancy is recommended, and intercontroller roaming should be minimized. WLCs can be placed in a central location or distributed in the campus distribution layer.

Table 4-5 summarizes AP features for Cisco APs.

Table 4-5   *Supported Features and Specifications for Cisco APs*

Feature	10x0 Series	1121 Series	1130 Series	1230 Series	1240 Series	1300 Series	1500 Series
Autonomous/LWAPP	LWAPP	Both	Both	Both	Both	Both	LWAPP
External antenna	Yes	No	No	Yes	Yes	Yes	Yes
Outdoor install	No	No	No	No	No	Yes	Yes
REAP/Hybrid REAP (H-REAP)	REAP	No	H-REAP	No	H-REAP	No	Yes
Dual radio	Yes	No (only 11b/g)	Yes	Yes	Yes	No (only 11b/g)	Yes

Table 4-5 *Supported Features and Specifications for Cisco APs (Continued)*

Feature	10x0 Series	1121 Series	1130 Series	1230 Series	1240 Series	1300 Series	1500 Series
Power (watts)	13	6	15	14	15	—	—
Memory (Mb)	16	16	32	16	32	16	16
WLANs supported	16	8	8	8	8	8	16

Branch Design Considerations

For branch networks you need to consider the number and placement of APs, which depends on the location and expected number of wireless clients at the branch office. It may not be cost-justifiable to place a WLC at each branch office of an enterprise. One requirement is that the round-trip time (RTT) between the AP and the WLC should not exceed 100 ms. For centralized controllers, it is recommended that you use REAP or Hybrid REAP (H-REAP).

Local MAC

LWAPP supports local media access control (local MAC), which can be used in branch deployments. Unlike with split-MAC, the AP provides MAC management support for association requests and actions. Local MAC terminates client traffic at the wired port of the access point versus at the WLC. This allows direct local access to branch resources without requiring the data to travel to the WLC at the main office. Local MAC also allows the wireless client to function even if a WAN link failure occurs.

REAP

REAP is designed to support remote offices by extending LWAPP control timers. It is the preferred solution for LWAPs to connect to the WLC over the WAN. With REAP control, traffic is still encapsulated over a LWAPP tunnel and is sent to the WLC. Management control and RF management are done over the WAN. Client data is locally bridged. With REAP, local clients still have local connectivity if the WAN fails.

WLCs support the same number of REAP devices as APs. REAP devices support only Layer 2 security policies, do not support NAT, and require a routable IP address.

Hybrid REAP

H-REAP is an enhancement to REAP that provides additional capabilities such as NAT, more security options, and the ability to control up to three APs remotely.

H-REAP operates in two security modes:

- **Standalone mode**—H-REAP does the client authentication itself when the WLC cannot be reached.

- **Connected mode**—The device uses the WLC for client authentication.

H-REAP is more delay-sensitive than REAP. The RTT must not exceed 100 ms between the AP and the WLC.

Branch Office Controller Options

For branch offices, Cisco recommends one of four options:

- **Cisco 2006**—Supports six APs.

- **Cisco 4402-12 and 4402-25**—These devices support 12 and 25 APs, respectively.

- **WLC Module in Integrated Services Router (ISR)**—Supports six APs.

- **3750 with WLAN controller**—Depending on the model, this can support 25 or 50 APs.

References and Recommended Readings

Cisco Outdoor Wireless Network Solution, http://www.cisco.com/en/US/netsol/ns621/ networking_solutions_package.html

Cisco Unified Wireless Network, http://www.cisco.com/en/US/netsol/ns340/ns394/ns348/ns337/ networking_solutions_package.html

Cisco Wireless Control System, http://www.cisco.com/en/US/products/ps6305/index.html

"Enterprise Mobility 3.0 Design Guide," http://www.cisco.com/univercd/cc/td/doc/solution/ emblty30.pdf

IEEE Std 802.11g-2003. Amendment to IEEE Std 802.11, 1999 Edition.

Lightweight Access Point FAQ, http://www.cisco.com/en/US/products/ps6306/ products_qanda_item09186a00806a4da3.shtml

"Light Weight Access Point Protocol (LWAPP), (draft-ohara-capwap-lwapp-02)," http:// tools.ietf.org/html/draft-ohara-capwap-lwapp-02

"Wireless LAN MAC and Physical Layer (PHY) Specifications," IEEE 802.11-1999. Piscataway, New Jersey: Institute of Electrical and Electronics Engineers, 1999.

Foundation Summary

The "Foundation Summary" section of each chapter lists the most important facts from the chapter. Although this section does not list every fact from the chapter that will be on the CCDA exam, a well-prepared CCDA candidate should at a minimum know all the details in each "Foundation Summary" before taking the exam.

Table 4-6 summarizes WLAN standards.

Table 4-6 *WLAN Standards*

IEEE Protocol	Standard Release Date	Frequency	Typical Data Rate	Maximum Data Rate
Legacy	1997	ISM	1 Mbps	2 Mbps
802.11a	1999	UNII	25 Mbps	54 Mbps
802.11b	1999	ISM	6.5 Mbps	11 Mbps
802.11g	2003	ISM	25 Mbps	54 Mbps
802.11n	2007 (draft)	ISM or UNII	200 Mbps	540 Mbps

Table 4-7 summarizes the elements of the Cisco UWN architecture.

Table 4-7 *Cisco UWN Architecture*

Cisco UWN Element	Description
Client devices	These include laptops, workstations, IP phones, PDAs, and manufacturing devices to access the WLAN.
Access points	Provide access to the network.
Network unification	The WLAN system should be able to support wireless applications by providing security policies, QoS, intrusion prevention, RF management, and wireless controllers.
Network management	Cisco Wireless Control System (WCS) provides a central management tool that lets you design, control, and monitor wireless networks.
Mobility services	Include guest access, location services, voice services, and threat detection and mitigation.

Table 4-8 summarizes the LWAPP AP operation modes.

Table 4-8 *LWAPP Access Point Modes*

LWAPP Mode	Description
Local mode	The default mode of operation.
REAP mode	For remote LWAP management across WAN links.
Monitor mode	The APs exclude themselves from handling data traffic and dedicate themselves to location-based services (LBS).
Rogue Detector mode	Monitors for rouge APs.
Sniffer mode	Captures and forwards all packets of a remote sniffer.
Bridge mode	For point-to-point and point-to-multipoint solutions.

Table 4-9 summarizes the wireless controller components.

Table 4-9 *WLC Components*

WLC Component	Description
Wireless LAN	Identified by a unique SSID and assigned to an interface.
Interface	A logical connection that maps to a VLAN in the wired network.
Port	A physical connection to the wired LAN.

Table 4-10 summarizes WLC interface types.

Table 4-10 *WLC Interface Types*

WLC Interface Type	Description
Management interface	For in-band management.
Service-port interface	For out-of-band management.
AP manager interface	For Layer 3 discovery and association.
Dynamic interface	Dedicated to WLAN client data; analogous to VLANs.
Virtual interface	For Layer 3 authentication and mobility management.

Table 4-11 shows how many APs each WLC model supports.

Table 4-11   *WLAN Controller Platform Scalability*

Platform	Number of Supported Access Points
Cisco 2000 series WLC	6
Cisco WLC for ISRs	6
Catalyst 3750 Integrated WLC	50
Cisco 4400 series WLC	100
Cisco 6500 series WLC Module	300

Table 4-12 describes the three types of controller roaming.

Table 4-12   *Controller Roaming Types*

WLC Roaming Type	Description
Intracontroller roaming	The client moves the association from one AP to another AP that is joined to the same WLC. The client entry in the database is updated. No client IP changes occur.
Layer 2 intercontroller roaming	The client moves the association from one AP to another AP that is joined to a different WLC. The Layer 2 roam occurs when the client traffic is bridged to the same IP subnet. The client entry in the database is moved to the new WLC. No IP changes occur.
Layer 3 intercontroller roaming	The client moves the association from one AP to another AP that is joined to a different WLC, and the traffic is bridged onto a different IP subnet. The client entry in the database is copied to the new WLC and is marked as foreign.

Table 4-13 summarizes some of the UDP ports used by WLAN protocols.

Table 4-13   *UDP Ports Used by WLAN Protocols*

WLAN Protocol	UDP Port
LWAPP Control	UDP 12223
LWAPP Data	UDP 12222
WLC Exchange Messages (unencrypted)	UDP 16666
WLC Exchange Messages (encrypted)	UDP 16667
RF Group IEEE 802.11b/g	UDP 12114
RF Group IEEE 802.11a	UDP 12115

Deterministic controller design is the recommended practice in WLAN controller redundancy design. Table 4-14 summarizes WLC redundancy options.

Table 4-14 *WLC Redundancy*

WLC Redundancy	Description
N+1	A single WLC acts as the backup for multiple WLCs. The backup WLC is configured as the secondary on APs.
N+N	An equal number of controllers back up each other.
N+N+1	An equal number of controllers back up each other. The backup WLC is configured as the tertiary on APs.

The Cisco Wireless Mesh networking solution eliminates the need to wire each AP and allows users to roam from one area to another without having to reconnect. Table 4-15 describes the Wireless Mesh Components.

Table 4-15 *Wireless Mesh Components*

Wireless Mesh Component	Description
Wireless Control System (WCS)	The wireless mesh SNMP management system allows network-wide configuration and management.
Wireless LAN Controller (WLC)	Links the mesh APs to the wired network.
Rooftop AP (RAP)	Connects the mesh to the wired network and serves as the root.
Mesh Access Point (MAP)	Remote APs, typically located on top of a pole. Connects to the RAP.

The following points summarize wireless LAN design:

- An RF site survey is used to determine a wireless network's RF characteristics and access point placement.

- Guest services are easily supported using EoIP tunnels in the Cisco Unified Wireless Network.

- Outdoor wireless networks are supported using outdoor access points and Cisco Wireless Mesh Networking access points.

- Campus wireless network design provides RF coverage for wireless clients in the campus using LWAPs. The LWAPs are managed by WLCs.

- Branch wireless network design provides RF coverage for wireless clients in the branch. Central management of REAP or H-REAP access points can be supported.

- The recommended AP limit is roughly seven (g.711) to eight (g.729) voice calls over VoWLAN or up to 20 data devices, because all devices share bandwidth.

Q&A

As mentioned in the Introduction, you have two choices for review questions: here in the book or the exam questions on the CD-ROM. The answers to these questions appear in Appendix A.

For more practice with exam format questions, use the exam engine on the CD-ROM.

1. What is the maximum data rate of IEEE 802.11g?

2. What is the typical data rate of IEEE 802.11n?

3. What are some difficulties with having to manage hundreds of standalone access points?

4. What standard does IEEE 802.11i use for confidentiality, integrity, and authentication?

5. List at least four benefits of Cisco UWN.

6. True or false: With Split-MAC, the control and data frames are load-balanced between the LWAP and the WLC.

7. True or false: With Split-MAC, the WLC, not the LWAP, is responsible for authentication and key management.

8. What LWAPP transport mode is the preferred and most scalable?

    a. Intra

    b. Layer 2

    c. Layer 3

    d. EoIP

9. What is the preferred intercontroller roaming option?

    a. Intra

    b. Layer 2

    c. Layer 3

    d. EoIP

10. What device places user traffic on the appropriate VLAN?

    a. Lightweight AP

    b. WLAN controller

    c. MAP

    d. RAP

11. How many access points are supported in a mobility group using Cisco 4400 series WLCs?

    a. 144

    b. 1200

    c. 2400

    d. 7200

12. What is the recommended number of data devices an AP can support for best performance?

    a. About 6

    b. 7 to 8

    c. 10 to 15

    d. About 20

13. What is the recommended number of VoWLAN devices an AP can support for best performance?

    a. 2 to 3

    b. 7 to 8

    c. 10 to 15

    d. About 20

14. What method is used to manage radio frequency channels and power configuration?

    a. WLC

    b. WCS

    c. RRM

    d. MAP

15. What is the typical latency per wireless mesh hop in milliseconds?

    a. 2 to 3

    b. 7 to 8

    c. 10 to 15

    d. About 20

16. What is the recommended maximum RTT between an AP and the WLC?

    a. 20 ms

    b. 50 ms

    c. 100 ms

    d. 200 ms

17. What is the recommended controller redundancy technique?

   a. N+1+N

   b. Static

   c. Dynamic

   d. Deterministic

18. What is the recommended best practice for guest services?

   a. Use separate VLANs

   b. Use separate routers and access lists

   c. Obtain a DSL connection and bridge to the local LAN

   d. Use EoIP to isolate traffic to the DMZ

19. What is the recommended best practice for branch WLANs?

   a. Use H-REAP with centralized controllers

   b. Use local-MAP

   c. Use wireless mesh design

   d. Use EoIP

20. What are two recommended best practices for WLC design?

   a. Maximize intercontroller roaming

   b. Minimize intercontroller roaming

   c. Use distributed controller placement

   d. Use centralized controller placement

21. How many APs does the Cisco 6500 WLC module support?

   a. 6

   b. 50

   c. 100

   d. 300

22. Match each LWAPP access point mode with its description:

   i. Local

   ii. REAP

   iii. Monitor

   iv. Rogue detector

v. Sniffer

vi. Bridge

a. For location-based services

b. Captures packets

c. For point-to-point connections

d. Default mode

e. Management across the WAN

f. Monitors rouge APs

23. Match each WLC interface type with its description:

i. Management

ii. Service-port

iii. AP manager

iv. Dynamic

v. Virtual

a. Authentication and mobility

b. Analogous to user VLANs

c. Discovery and association

d. Out-of-band management

e. In-band management

24. Match each roaming technique with its client database entry change:

i. Intracluster roaming

ii. Layer 2 intercluster roaming

iii. Layer 3 intercluster roaming

a. The client entry is moved to a new WLC

b. The client entry is updated on the same WLC

c. The client entry is copied to a new WLC

25. Match each UDP port with its protocol:

i. LWAPP data

ii. RF group 802.11b/g

iii. WLC encrypted exchange

iv. LWAPP control

v. WLC unencrypted exchange

a. UDP 12114

b. UDP 12222

c. UDP 12223

d. UDP 16666

e. UDP 16667

26. Match each wireless mesh component with its description:

i. WCS

ii. WLC

iii. RAP

iv. MAP

a. Root of the mesh network

b. Remote APs

c. Networkwide configuration and management

d. Links APs to the wired network

27. How many MAP nodes are recommended per rooftop AP?

a. 6

b. 20

c. 500

d. 100

28. Which of the following shows the correct order of the steps in an RF site survey?

   a. Define requirements, document findings, perform the survey, determine preliminary AP locations, identify coverage areas.

   b. Define requirements, perform the survey, determine preliminary AP locations, identify coverage areas, document findings.

   c. Identify coverage areas, define requirements, determine preliminary AP locations, perform the survey, document findings.

   d. Define requirements, identify coverage areas, determine preliminary AP locations, perform the survey, document findings.

29. What technique performs dynamic channel assignment, power control, and interference detection and avoidance?

   a. LWAPP

   b. RRM

   c. Mobility

   d. LEAP

30. What are the three nonoverlapping channels of IEEE 802.11b/g?

   a. Channels A, D, and G

   b. Channels 1, 6, and 11

   c. Channels 3, 8, and 11

   d. Channels A, E, and G

31. Which of the following statements is true?

   a. IEEE 802.11g is backward-compatible with 802.11b; 802.11a is not compatible with 802.11b.

   b. IEEE 802.11a is backward-compatible with 802.11b; 802.11g is not compatible with 802.11b.

   c. IEEE 802.11b is backward-compatible with 802.11a; 802.11g is not compatible with 802.11b.

   d. IEEE 802.11n is backward-compatible with 802.11a and 802.11g.

32. What is necessary when you use LEAP for authentication?

   a. WLC

   b. WCS

   c. RADIUS server

   d. LWAP

This chapter covers the following subjects:

- WAN Technology Overview

- WAN Design Methodology

- Optimizing Bandwidth Using QoS

CHAPTER 5

WAN Technologies

This chapter reviews wide-area network technologies. Expect plenty of questions about the use of WAN technologies. The CCDA must understand WAN technologies and what makes them different from each other. This chapter also covers WAN design methodologies and how some QoS techniques can make better use of the available bandwidth.

"Do I Know This Already?" Quiz

The purpose of the "Do I Know This Already?" quiz is to help you decide whether you need to read the entire chapter. If you intend to read the entire chapter, you do not necessarily need to answer these questions now.

The ten-question quiz, derived from the major sections in the "Foundation Topics" portion of the chapter, helps you determine how to spend your limited study time.

Table 5-1 outlines the major topics discussed in this chapter and the "Do I Know This Already?" quiz questions that correspond to those topics.

Table 5-1 *"Do I Know This Already?" Foundation Topics Section-to-Question Mapping*

Foundation Topics Section	Questions Covered in This Section
WAN Technology Overview	1, 2, 3, 5, 6, 7, 8
WAN Design Methodology	4, 9
Optimizing Bandwidth Using QoS	10

CAUTION The goal of self-assessment is to gauge your mastery of the topics in this chapter. If you do not know the answer to a question or you are only partially sure, you should mark this question wrong for the purposes of the self-assessment. Giving yourself credit for an answer you correctly guess skews your self-assessment results and might give you a false sense of security.

1. What are two modules or blocks used in the Enterprise Edge?

    a. Internet and Campus Core

    b. Core and Building Access

    c. Internet Connectivity and WAN

    d. WAN and Building Distribution

2. What signaling protocol does Frame Relay use between the switch and the router?

    a. DLCI

    b. LMI

    c. TDM

    d. SONET/SDH

3. How much bandwidth does a T1 circuit provide?

    a. 155 Mbps

    b. 64 kbps

    c. 1.544 kbps

    d. 1.544 Mbps

4. What methodology is used when designing the Enterprise Edge?

    a. Cisco-powered network

    b. ISL

    c. PPDIOO

    d. IEEE

5. SONET/SDH technology is what kind of technology?

    a. Packet-based

    b. Cell-based

    c. Circuit-based

    d. Segment-based

6. Which DSL technology uses higher download speeds than upload speeds and is popular in residential deployments?

    a. IDSL

    b. ADSL

    c. SDSL

    d. TDSL

7.   What Frame Relay DE bit value is of lower importance and can be discarded first?

    a. 2

    b. 1

    c. 0

    d. 2.1

8.   When designing a network for four separate sites, what technology allows a full mesh by using only one link per site instead of point-to-point TDM circuits?

    a. Dark fiber

    b. Cable

    c. ISDN

    d. Frame Relay

9.   The _____ size specifies the maximum number of frames that are transmitted without receiving an acknowledgment.

    a. Segment

    b. Access

    c. TCP

    d. Window

10.   Which of the following adds strict PQ to modular class-based QoS?

    a. LLQ

    b. FIFO

    c. CBWFQ

    d. WFQ

The answers to the "Do I Know This Already?" quiz appear in Appendix A, "Answers to Chapter 'Do I Know This Already?' Quizzes and Q&A Sections." The suggested choices for your next step are as follows:

- **8 or less overall score**—Read the entire chapter. It includes the "Foundation Topics," "Foundation Summary," and "Q&A" sections.

- **9 or 10 overall score**—If you want more review on these topics, skip to the "Foundation Summary" section and then go to the "Q&A" section. Otherwise, move to the next chapter.

Foundation Topics

This chapter covers WAN topics that you need to master for the CCDA exam. It covers the different WAN modules used in the Enterprise Edge. WAN technologies and factors that are used in technology selection are covered. It covers the specifics of several WAN technologies that are available today. The chapter goes on to outline methodologies used for designing WANs. Finally, this chapter covers ways to use quality of service (QoS) to prioritize network traffic and improve the use of available bandwidth.

WAN Technology Overview

WAN technologies provide network connectivity for the Enterprise Edge and remote branch edge locations as well as the Internet. Many WAN choices are available, and new ones are continually emerging. When you're selecting WAN transport technologies, it is important to consider factors such as cost, speed, reliability, hardware, and media. In addition, enterprise branch offices can take advantage of cable and DSL technologies for remote connectivity back to the headquarters or main office.

WAN Defined

Wide-area networks (WANs) are communication networks that can span great distances to provide connectivity. They generally are offered by service providers or carriers. WANs typically carry data traffic, but many now support voice and video as well. Service providers charge fees for providing WAN services or communications to their customers. Sometimes the term "service" is referred to as the WAN communications provided by the carrier.

Figure 5-1 depicts the Enterprise Edge with campus backbone, Internet, and MPLS clouds.

When designing a WAN, you should become familiar with the design's requirements, which are typically derived from these two important goals:

- **Application availability**—Networked applications rely on the network between the client and server to provide its functions to users.

- **Cost and usage**—To select the correct reliable WAN service, you must consider the budget and usage requirements of the WAN service.

Figure 5-1   *Enterprise WAN*

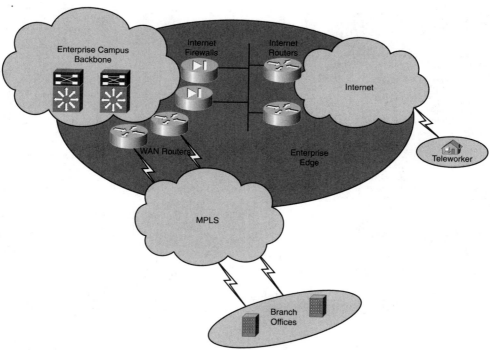

WAN Connection Modules

The Enterprise Edge can have multiple WAN interconnections. Common connectivity modules include but are not limited to the Internet, the demilitarized zone (DMZ), and the WAN. Internet service providers (ISPs) offer many connectivity options for the Internet and DMZ modules of the Enterprise Edge. Internal WAN connectivity between an organization's headquarters and remote sites generally is across a service provider or carrier network. PSTN connectivity still exists for teleworkers and more recently because of the increasing use of VoIP offnet services.

WAN technologies such as Frame Relay exist for point-to-point (P2P) and multipoint WAN services. Service providers also offer full IP WAN solutions such as MPLS where the Enterprise Edge router interacts with service providers at Layer 3. Public WAN connections over the Internet are also available through the use of cable and/or DSL technologies. Typically, these services do not provide any guarantee of network availability, as do Frame Relay and MPLS network solutions.

Figure 5-2 illustrates the use of modules, or blocks, in the Enterprise Edge.

Figure 5-2   *WAN Interconnections*

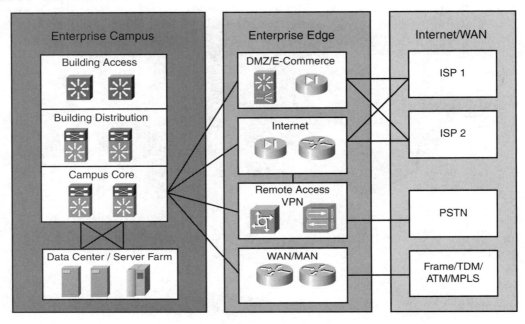

WAN Comparison

Table 5-2 examines some WAN technologies and highlights some common factors that are used to make WAN technology selections. This information also reflects the different characteristics of each WAN technology. However, keep in mind that your service provider offerings limit the WAN technology choices available to you during your selection.

Table 5-2   *WAN Comparison*

WAN Technology	Bandwidth	Reliability	Latency	Cost
Dialup	Low	Low	High	Low
ISDN	Low	Medium	Medium	Low
Frame Relay	Low/Medium	Medium	Low	Medium
TDM	Medium	High	Low	Medium
SONET/SDH	High	High	Low	High
MPLS	High	High	Low	High
Dark fiber	High	High	Low	High

Table 5-2 *WAN Comparison (Continued)*

WAN Technology	Bandwidth	Reliability	Latency	Cost
DWDM	High	High	Low	High
DSL	Low/Medium	Low	Medium	Low
Cable	Low/Medium	Low	Medium	Low
Wireless	Low/Medium	Low	Medium	Medium

The following sections offer more details about each WAN technology covered in Table 5-2.

Dialup

Dialup technology provides connectivity over the PSTN using analog modems. Although the bandwidth is relatively low, the availability of analog is very widespread. Dialup connectivity is ideal for low-bandwidth conversations of 56 kbps or less. Despite the high availability of dialup technology over analog lines, it is generally not a viable option anymore. However, a common use of dialup is when a remote worker or teleworker uses it as a backup network solution if his or her DSL or cable connection goes down.

ISDN

Integrated Services Digital Network (ISDN) is an all-digital phone line connection that was standardized in the early 1980s. ISDN allows both voice and data to be transmitted over the digital phone line instead of the analog signals used in dialup connections. ISDN provides greater bandwidth and lower latency compared to dialup analog technology. ISDN comes in two service types—Basic Rate Interface (BRI) and Primary Rate Interface (PRI).

ISDN is comprised of digital devices and reference points. ISDN devices consist of terminals, terminal adapters, network-termination, line-termination, and exchange-termination equipment. Native ISDN devices are referred to as terminal equipment 1 (TE1), and nonnative ISDN is referred to as terminal equipment 2 (TE2). However, TE2-type devices can be connected to an ISDN system with the help of a terminal adapter (TA).

Working toward the service provider after the TE1 and TE2 devices, the next connection devices are network termination 2 (NT2) and network termination 1 (NT1). These connection devices connect the five-wire to the two-wire local loop. In North America, the NT1 is a CPE device or customer premises equipment. This means that the customer, not the carrier, provides the device. However, in most other parts of the world, the carrier provides the NT1.

> **NOTE** Some Cisco IOS interface cards have the NT1 built in designated by a U, whereas others require an external NT1 device.

ISDN has a series of reference points that define logical interfaces between ISDN devices such as TAs and NT1s:

- **R**—Reference point between non-ISDN equipment and a TA

- **S**—Reference point between terminals and NT2 devices

- **T**—Reference point between NT2 and NT1 devices

- **U**—Reference point between NT1 and the line termination equipment in the carrier's network

Figure 5-3 illustrates how ISDN devices and reference points relate to each other.

Figure 5-3 *ISDN Devices and Reference Points*

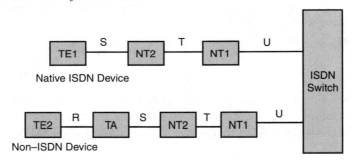

ISDN BRI Service

ISDN BRI consists of two B channels and one D channel (2B+D). Both of the BRI B channels operate at 64 kbps and carry user data. The D channel handles the signaling and control information and operates at 16 kbps. Another 48 kbps is used for framing control and other overhead, for a total bit rate of 192 kbps.

ISDN PRI Service

ISDN PRI service offers 23 B channels and one D channel (23B+D) in both North America and Japan. Each channel (including the D channel) operates at 64 kbps, for a total bit rate of 1.544 Mbps, including overhead. In other parts of the world, such as Europe and Australia, the ISDN PRI service provides 30 B channels and one 64-kbps D channel.

Frame Relay

Frame Relay is a connection-oriented Layer 2 WAN protocol. It is similar to X.25 but has faster performance due to the lack of error checking and retransmitting features. The data link layer establishes connections in Frame Relay using a DTE device such as a router and a DCE device such as a frame switch.

In the early 1980s, networks were growing using more and more point-to-point leased-line connections. Full-mesh connections were used to ensure redundancy between sites. However, full-mesh network configurations presented a larger cost because of the number of leased lines needed. A full mesh requires that each site have a connection to the other sites participating in the full mesh. For example, if you have five WAN sites, each site needs four leased lines to the other sites to complete the full mesh. However, because Frame Relay uses a cloud of switches, each site can use only one connection to the Frame Relay cloud and then can be configured to emulate a full mesh. This reduces the leased-line cost and requires only one leased line per site. This allows the network to achieve full-mesh-like behavior needed for network redundancy.

Frame Relay circuits between sites can be either permanent virtual circuits (PVC) or switched virtual circuits (SVC). PVCs are used more predominantly due to the connections' permanent nature. SVCs, on the other hand, are temporary connections created for each data transfer session.

A point-to-point PVC between two routers or endpoints uses a data-link connection identifier (DLCI) to identify the local end of the PVC. The DLCI is a locally significant numeric value that can be reused through the Frame Relay WAN if necessary.

Local Management Interface

Frame Relay uses a signaling protocol between the Frame Relay router and the Frame Relay switch called the Local Management Interface (LMI). The LMI protocol sends periodic keepalive messages and notifications of additions or removals of PVCs. Three types of LMI protocols are available. The service provider usually informs you on which one to use. LMI also offers a number of features or extensions, including global addressing, virtual circuit status messages, and multicasting. By default, Cisco routers will try all three LMI types until a match is found.

Discard Eligibility

The Discard Eligibility (DE) bit is used in Frame Relay to identify whether a frame has lower importance than other frames. The DE bit is part of the Frame Relay header and can have a value of 1 or 0. Routers or DTE devices can set the value of the DE bit to 1 to indicate that the frame has lower importance than frames marked with a 0. During periods of congestion, the Frame Relay network discards frames marked with the DE bit of 1 before those marked with 0. This reduces the chance of critical data being dropped, because you can identify what traffic gets marked with a DE bit value of 1.

Time-Division Multiplexing

Time-Division Multiplexing (TDM) is a type of digital multiplexing in which multiple channels such as data, voice, and video are combined over one communication medium by interleaving pulses representing bits from different channels. Basic DS0 channel bandwidth is defined at 64 kbps. In North America, a DS1 or T1 circuit provides 1.544 Mbps of bandwidth consisting of 24 time slots of 64 kbps each and an 8-kbps channel for control information. In addition, a DS3 or T3 circuit provides 44.736 Mbps of bandwidth. Other parts of the world, such as Europe, follow E1 standards, which allow for 30 channels at 2.048 Mbps of bandwidth. Service providers can guarantee or reserve the bandwidth used on TDM networks. The customers' TDM transmissions are charged for their exclusive access to these circuits. On the other hand, packet-switched networks typically are shared, thereby allowing the service providers more flexibility in managing their networks and the services they offer.

SONET/SDH

The architecture of Synchronous Optical Network/Synchronous Digital Hierarchy (SONET/SDH) is circuit-based and delivers high-speed services over an optical network. The term SONET is defined by the American National Standards Institute (ANSI) specification, and SDH is defined by the International Telecommunication Union (ITU). SONET/SDH guarantees bandwidth and has line rates of 155 Mbps to more than 10 Gbps. Common circuit sizes are OC-3, or 155 Mbps, and OC-12, or 622 Mbps.

SONET/SDH uses a ring topology by connecting sites and providing automatic recovery capabilities and has self-healing mechanisms. SONET/SDH rings support ATM or packet over SONET (POS) IP encapsulations. The Optical Carrier (OC) rates are the digital bandwidth hierarchies that are part of the SONET/SDH standards. The optical carrier speeds supported are as follows:

- OC-1 = 51.85 Mbps

- OC-3 = 155.52 Mbps

- OC-12 = 622.08 Mbps

- OC-24 = 1.244 Gbps

- OC-48 = 2.488 Gbps

- OC-192 = 9.952 Gbps

- OC-255 = 13.21 Gbps

Figure 5-4 shows an OC-48 SONET ring with connections to three sites that share the ring.

Figure 5-4 *SONET/SDH*

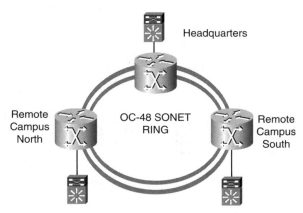

Multiprotocol Label Switching

MPLS is technology for the delivery of IP services using labels (numbers) to forward packets. In normal routed environments, packets are forwarded by the router performing a Layer 3 destination address lookup and rewriting the Layer 2 addresses. MPLS functions by encapsulating packets with headers that include the label information. As soon as packets are marked with a label, specific paths through the network can be designed to correspond to that distinct label. MPLS labels can be based on parameters such as source addresses, Layer 2 circuit ID, or QoS value. The labels can be used to implement traffic engineering by overriding the routing tables. MPLS packets can run over most Layer 2 technologies, such as ATM, Frame Relay, POS, and Ethernet. The goal of MPLS is to maximize switching using labels and minimize Layer 3 routing.

In most MPLS implementations, the equipment is called the customer edge (CE) and provider edge (PE) routers. Typically the customer-owned internal WAN router peers with the CE router. The CE router then connects to the PE router, which is the ingress to the MPLS service provider network. The PE router is in the service provider network.

Figure 5-5 shows an MPLS WAN and how the CE routers connect to the provider.

Figure 5-5 *MPLS*

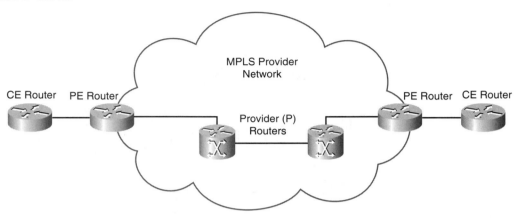

Other WAN Technologies

This section briefly discusses other WAN technologies that are becoming very popular in the network access space as well as some other service provider architectures.

Digital Subscriber Line

Digital Subscriber Line (DSL) is a technology that provides high-speed Internet data services over ordinary copper telephone lines. It achieves this by using frequencies that are not used in normal voice telephone calls.

The term *x*DSL describes the various competing forms of DSL available today. Some of the DSL technologies available include asymmetric (ADSL), symmetric (SDSL), high bit rate (HDSL), very high bit rate (VDSL), rate-adaptive (RADSL) and IDSL (based on ISDN).

Table 5-3 summarizes the types of DSL specifications.

Table 5-3 *DSL Specifications*

Service	Maximum Distance to Central Office	Maximum Upload Speed	Maximum Download Speed	Notes
Full-rate ADSL	18,000 ft (5500 m)	1500 kbps	9 Mbps	Asymmetrical.
ADSL G.lite	18,000 ft (5500 m)	384 kbps	1.5 Mbps	No splitter is required.
RADSL	18,000 ft (5500 m)	384 kbps	8 Mbps	Rate adapts based on distance and quality.

Table 5-3 *DSL Specifications (Continued)*

Service	Maximum Distance to Central Office	Maximum Upload Speed	Maximum Download Speed	Notes
IDSL	35,000 ft (10,070 m)	144 kbps	144 kbps	DSL over ISDN (BRI).
SDSL	22,000 ft (6700 m)	2.3 Mbps	2.3 Mbps	Targets T1 replacement. Symmetrical DSL service.
HDSL	18,000 ft (5500 m)	1.54 Mbps	1.54 Mbps	Four-wire, similar to T1 service.
HDSL-2	24,000 ft (7333 m)	2 Mbps	2 Mbps	Two-wire version of HDSL or four-wire at 2 times the rate.
VDSL	3000 ft (916 m)	16 Mbps	52 Mbps	Few installations.

ADSL is the most popular DSL technology and is widely available. The key to ADSL is that the downstream bandwidth is asymmetric or higher than the upstream bandwidth. Some limitations include that ADSL can be used only in close proximity to the local DSLAM, typically less than 2 km. The local DSLAM, or digital subscriber line access multiplexer, allows telephone lines to make DSL connections to the Internet. Download speeds usually range from 768 kbps to 9 Mbps, and upload speeds range from 64 kbps to 1.5 Mbps. Generally, the equipment used is a DSL modem or (CPE) router that connects back to the ISP's DSLAM.

Although DSL is primarily used in the residential community, this technology can also be used as a WAN technology for an organization. However, keep in mind that because this is a public network connection over the Internet, it is recommended that this technology be used in conjunction with a firewall/VPN solution back into your corporate enterprise network. The high speeds and relatively low cost make this a very popular Internet access WAN technology.

Cable

Broadband cable is a technology used to transport data using a coaxial cable medium over cable distribution systems. The equipment used on the remote-access side is the cable modem, which connects to the Cable Modem Termination System (CMTS) on the ISP side. The Universal Broadband Router (uBR) provides the CMTS services and is deployed at the cable company headend. The uBR forwards traffic upstream through the provider's WAN core or the local PSTN, depending on the services being provided.

The Data Over Cable Service Interface Specifications (DOCSIS) protocol defines the cable procedures that the equipment needs to support. DOCSIS 2.0 was released in 2002 and remains the current version that most cable modems use today. DOCSIS 3.0 specifications released in 2006 include support for IPv6 and channel bonding.

Figure 5-6 illustrates how a cable modem connects to the CMTS.

Figure 5-6 *Data Over Cable*

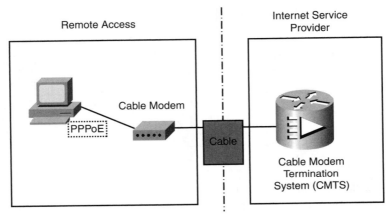

Wireless

Wireless as a technology uses electromagnetic waves to carry the signal between endpoints. Everyday examples of wireless technology include cell phones, wireless LANs, cordless computer equipment, and satellite television.

Here are some examples of wireless implementations:

■ **Mobile wireless**—Consists of cellular applications and mobile phones. Most wireless technologies such as the second and third generations are migrating to more digital services to take advantage of the higher speeds. Mobile wireless technologies include GSM, GPRS, and UMTS:

— **GSM**—Global system for mobile communications. A digital mobile radio standard that uses Time-Division Multiplex Access (TDMA) technology in three bands— 900, 1800, and 1900 MHz. The data transfer rate is 9600 bps and includes the ability to roam internationally.

— **GPRS**—General Packet Radio Service. Extends the capability of GSM speeds from 64 kbps to 128 kbps.

— **UMTS**—Universal Mobile Telecommunications Service. Also known as 3G broadband. Provides packet-based transmission of digitized voice, video, and data at rates up to 2.0 Mbps. UMTS also provides a set of services available to mobile users, location-independent throughout the world.

- **Wireless LAN**—WLANs have increased too in both residential and business environments to meet the demands of LAN connections over the air. Commonly called IEEE 802.11a/b/g or Wi-Fi wireless networks. Currently, 802.11n is in development and provides typical data rates of 200 Mb/s. The growing range of applications includes guest access, voice over wireless, and support services such as advanced security and location of wireless endpoints. A key advantage of WLANs is the ability to save time and money by avoiding costly physical layer wiring installations.

- **Bridge wireless**—Wireless bridges connect two separate wireless networks, typically located in two separate buildings. This technology enables high data rates for use with line-of-sight applications. When interconnecting hard-to-wire sites, temporary networks, or warehouses, a series of wireless bridges can be connected to provide connectivity.

Figure 5-7 shows bridge wireless and wireless LANs.

Figure 5-7 *Wireless Implementations*

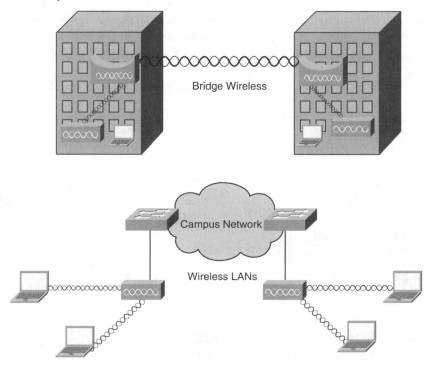

NOTE   Additional information on wireless LANs is provided in Chapter 4, "Wireless LAN Design."

Dark Fiber

Dark fiber is fiber-optic cable that has been installed in the ground or where right-of-way issues are evident. To maintain signal integrity and jitter control over long distances, signal regenerators are used in some implementations. The framing for dark fiber is determined by the enterprise, not the provider. The edge devices can use the fiber just like within the enterprise, which allows for greater control of the services provided by the link. Dark fiber is owned by service providers in most cases and can be purchased similarly to leased-line circuits for use in both the MAN and WAN. The reliability of these types of links also needs to be designed by the enterprise and is not provided by the service provider. This contrasts with SONET/SDH, which has redundancy built into the architecture.

Dense Wave Division Multiplexing

Dense Wave Division Multiplexing (DWDM) increases fiber optic's bandwidth capabilities by using different wavelengths of light called channels over the same fiber strand. It maximizes the use of the installed base of fiber used by service providers and is a critical component of optical networks. DWDM allows for service providers to increase the services offered to customers by adding new bandwidth to existing channels on the same fiber. DWDM lets a variety of devices access the network, including IP routers, ATM switches, and SONET terminals.

Figure 5-8 illustrates the use of DWDM using Cisco ONS devices and a SONET/SDH ring.

Figure 5-8   *DWDM*

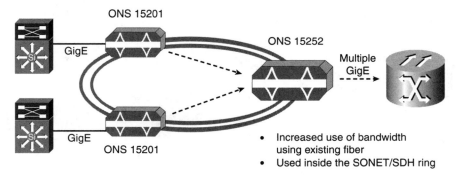

Ordering WAN Technology and Contracts

When you order WAN transport technology, early planning is key. It usually takes at least 60 days for the carrier to provision circuits. Generally, the higher a circuit's capacity, the more lead time is required to provision. When ordering bandwidth overseas, a lead time of 120 days is fairly common.

WAN transport in most cases includes an access circuit charge and, at times, distance-based charges. However, some carriers have eliminated TDM distance-based charges because T1s are readily available from most carriers. In rare cases, construction is necessary to provide fiber access, which requires more cost and time delays. You should compare pricing and available WAN technology options from competing carriers.

When ordering Frame Relay and ATM, a combination of access circuit charges, per-PVC charges, and per-bandwidth Committed Information Rate (CIR) charges are customary. CIR is the rate that the provider guarantees it will provide. Some carriers set the CIR to half the circuit's speed, thereby allowing customers to burst 2 times above the CIR. Frame Relay speeds can be provisioned up to T3 speeds, but typically they are less than 10 Mbps.

MPLS VPNs have been very competitive with ATM and Frame Relay rates. Service providers are offering MPLS VPNs with higher bandwidth at lower rates to persuade their customers away from traditional ATM and Frame Relay services. However, other service providers see more value in MPLS VPNs and price them higher than ATM and Frame Relay because of the added benefits of traffic engineering.

When you're selecting a standard carrier package, it takes about a month to contract a WAN circuit. If you want to negotiate a detailed service level agreement (SLA), expect to take another five months or more, including discussions with the service provider's legal department. The bigger the customer, the more influence it has over the SLAs and the contract negotiations.

Contract periods for most WAN services are one to five years. Contracts are usually not written for longer durations because of the new emerging technologies and better offerings from providers. An exception is dark fiber, which is usually contracted for a 20-year term. In this case you also want to have the right of nonreversion written in the SLA. This means that no matter what happens to the service provider, the fiber is yours for the 20-year period.

Tariffed commercial WAN services are available at published rates but are subject to restrictions. However, carriers are moving toward unpublished rates to be more competitive and to offer more options.

WAN Design Methodology

The methodology used when designing the Enterprise Edge is called prepare, plan, design, implement, operate, and optimize (PPDIOO). Some keys to PPDIOO are the processes of analyzing network requirements, characterizing the existing network, and designing the topology:

- **Analyzing the network requirements** includes reviewing the types of applications, the traffic volume, and the traffic patterns in the network.

- **Characterizing the existing network** reviews the technologies used and the locations of hosts, servers, network equipment, and other end nodes.

- **Designing the topology** is based on the availability of technology, the projected traffic usage, network performance, constraints, reliability, and implementation planning.

New network designs should be flexible and adaptable to future technologies and should not limit the customer's options going forward. Voice over IP (VoIP) is an example of a technology that network designs should be able to support if the customer decides to move to a converged network. The customer should not have to undergo major hardware and software upgrades to implement these types of technologies. Another important consideration is the design's cost-effectiveness throughout the design and implementation stages. For example, the support and management of the network should be an important factor.

Response Time

Response time measures the time between the client user request and the response from the server host. The end user will accept a certain level of delay in response time and still be satisfied. However, there is a limit to how long the user will wait. This amount of time can be measured and serves as a basis for future application response times. Users perceive the network communication in terms of how quickly the server returns the requested information and/or how fast the screen updates. Some applications, such as a request for an HTML web page, require short response times. On the other hand, a large FTP transfer may take a while, but this is generally acceptable.

Throughput

In network communications, throughput is the measure of data transferred from one host to another in a given amount of time. Bandwidth-intensive applications have more of an impact on a network's throughput than interactive traffic such as a Telnet session. Most high-throughput applications usually involve some type of file-transfer activity.

Reliability

Reliability is the measure of a given application's availability to its users. Some organizations require rock-solid application reliability; this has a higher price than most other applications. For example, financial and security exchange commissions require nearly 100 percent uptime for their applications. These types of networks are built with a high amount of physical and logical redundancy. It is important to ascertain the level of reliability needed for a network that is being designed. Reliability goes further than availability by measuring not only whether the service is there but whether it is performing as it should.

Bandwidth Considerations

Table 5-4 compares a number of different WAN technologies, along with the speeds and media types associated with them.

Table 5-4 *Physical Bandwidth Comparison*

Bandwidth	Less Than 2 Mbps	2 Mbps to 45 Mbps	45 Mbps to 100 Mbps	100 Mbps to 10 Gbps
Copper	Serial, ISDN, Frame Relay, TDM, DSL	Frame Relay, Ethernet, DSL, cable, T3	Fast Ethernet	Gigabit Ethernet
Fiber	—	Ethernet	FastEthernet, ATM	Gigabit Ethernet, 10Gigabit Ethernet, ATM, SONET/SDH, POS, dark fiber
Wireless	802.11b	802.11b, wireless WAN (varies)	802.11a/g	802.11n

The WAN designer must engineer the network with enough bandwidth to support the needs of the users and applications that will use the network. How much bandwidth a network needs depends on the services and applications that will require network bandwidth. For example, more bandwidth is needed for VoIP traffic than interactive SSH traffic. A large number of graphics or CAD drawings require an extensive amount of bandwidth compared to simple text-based information being transferred on the network, such as HTML files.

When designing bandwidth for the WAN, remember that implementation and recurring costs are always important factors. QoS techniques become increasingly important when delay-sensitive traffic such as VoIP is using the limited bandwidth available on the WAN.

LAN bandwidth, on the other hand, is inexpensive and plentiful. To provide connectivity on the LAN, you typically need to be concerned only with hardware and implementation costs.

Window Size

The window size defines the upper limit of frames that can be transmitted without getting a return acknowledgment. Transport protocols such as TCP rely on acknowledgments to provide connection-oriented reliable transport of data segments. For example, if the TCP window size is set to 8192, the source stops sending data after 8192 bytes if no acknowledgment has been received from the destination host. In some cases the window size might need to be modified because of unacceptable delay for larger WAN links. If the window size is not adjusted to coincide with the delay factor, retransmissions can occur, which affects throughput significantly. It is recommended that you adjust the window size to achieve better connectivity conditions.

Data Compression

Compression reduces the packet to a smaller size that can be transmitted and then decompressed on the other side of the WAN link. More CPU or hardware time is required to compress and decompress the data, but in return this saves bandwidth and reduces delay on the WAN link.

Compression is available in both software and hardware. Hardware data compression aids the main CPU by offloading the compression and decompression tasks by using the hardware CPU instead. The hardware compression modules can be installed in an available slot on a modular router.

Optimizing Bandwidth Using QoS

QoS is an effective tool for managing a WAN's available bandwidth. Keep in mind that QoS does not add bandwidth; it only helps you make better use of it. For chronic congestion problems, QoS is not the answer; you need to add more bandwidth. However, by prioritizing traffic, you can make sure that your most critical traffic gets the best treatment and available bandwidth in times of congestion. One popular QoS technique is to classify your traffic based on a protocol type or ACL and then give treatment to the class. You can define many classes to match or identify your most important traffic classes. The remaining unmatched traffic then uses a default class in which the traffic can be treated as best effort.

Queuing, Traffic Shaping, and Policing

Cisco has developed many different QoS mechanisms such as queuing, policing, and traffic shaping to enable network operators to manage and prioritize the traffic flowing on the network. Applications that are delay-sensitive require special treatment to avoid dissatisfaction by the user community, such as Voice over X technologies. Two types of output queues are available on routers—the hardware queue and the software queue. The hardware queue uses the strategy of first in, first out (FIFO). The software queue schedules packets first and then places them in the hardware queue. Keep in mind that the software queue is used only during periods of congestion. The software queue uses QoS techniques such as Priority Queuing, Custom Queuing, Weighted Fair Queuing, Class-Based Weighted Fair Queuing, Low-Latency Queuing, and traffic shaping and policing.

Priority Queuing

Priority Queuing (PQ) is a queuing method that establishes four interface output queues that serve different priority levels—high, medium, default, and low. Unfortunately, PQ can starve other queues if too much data is in one queue.

Custom Queuing

Custom Queuing (CQ) uses up to 16 individual output queues. Byte size limits are assigned to each queue so that when the limit is reached, it proceeds to the next queue. The network operator can customize these byte size limits. CQ is more fair than PQ because it allows some level of service to all traffic. This queuing method is considering legacy due to the improvements in the queuing methods.

Weighted Fair Queuing

Weighted Fair Queuing (WFQ) ensures that traffic is separated into individual flows or sessions without requiring that you define access control lists (ACL). WFQ uses two categories to group sessions—high bandwidth and low bandwidth. Low-bandwidth traffic has priority over high-bandwidth traffic. High-bandwidth traffic shares the service according to assigned weight values. WFQ is the default QoS mechanism on interfaces below 2.0 Mbps.

Class-Based Weighted Fair Queuing

Class-Based Weighted Fair Queuing (CBWFQ) extends WFQ capabilities by providing support for modular user-defined traffic classes. CBWFQ lets you define traffic classes that correspond to match criteria, including ACLs, protocols, and input interfaces. Traffic that matches the class criteria belongs to that specific class. Each class has a defined queue that corresponds to an output interface.

After traffic has been matched and belongs to a specific class, you can modify its characteristics, such as assigning bandwidth, maximum queue limit, and weight. During periods of congestion, the bandwidth assigned to the class is the guaranteed bandwidth that is delivered to the class.

One of CBWFQ's key advantages is its modular nature, which makes it extremely flexible for most situations. Many classes can be defined to separate your network traffic as needed. CBWFQ is becoming the "standard QoS mechanism" for networks that are not using VoIP.

Low-Latency Queuing

Low-Latency Queuing (LLQ) adds a strict priority queue to CBWFQ. The strict priority queue allows delay-sensitive traffic such as voice to be sent first, before other queues are serviced. That gives voice preferential treatment over the other traffic types.

Without LLQ, CBWFQ would not have a priority queue for real-time traffic. The additional classification of other traffic classes is done using the same CBWFQ techniques. LLQ is the standard QoS method of choice for Voice over IP networks.

Traffic Shaping and Policing

Traffic shaping and policing are mechanisms that take an action based on the traffic's characteristics, such as DSCP or IP precedence bits set in the IP header.

Traffic shaping slows down the rate at which packets are sent out an interface by matching certain criteria. Traffic shaping uses a token bucket technique to release the packets into the output queue at a preconfigured rate. Traffic shaping helps eliminate potential bottlenecks by throttling back the traffic rate at the source.

Policing tags or drops traffic depending on the match criteria. Generally, policing is used to set the limit of incoming traffic coming into an interface.

When contrasting traffic shaping with policing, remember that traffic shaping buffers packets while policing can be configured to drop packets.

References and Recommended Readings

"Cisco IOS Quality of Service Solutions Configuration Guide Release 12.2," http://www.cisco.com/univercd/cc/td/doc/product/software/ios122/122cgcr/fqos_c/index.htm

"Frame Relay," http://www.cisco.com/univercd/cc/td/doc/cisintwk/ito_doc/frame.htm

"Integrated Services Digital Network," http://www.cisco.com/univercd/cc/td/doc/cisintwk/ito_doc/isdn.htm

Module 4, "Designing Remote Connectivity," Designing for Cisco Internetwork Solution Course (DESGN) v2.0

"TDM: Time Division Multiplex and Multiplexer," http://www.networkdictionary.com/telecom/tdm.php

Foundation Summary

The "Foundation Summary" section of each chapter lists the most important facts from the chapter. Although this section does not list every fact from the chapter that will be on the CCDA exam, a well-prepared CCDA candidate should at a minimum know all the details in each "Foundation Summary" before taking the exam.

This chapter has examined the use of WANs in the Enterprise Edge. It also looked at many of the technologies used in the Enterprise Edge and how they relate to each other. It reviewed the methodology used when designing the Enterprise Edge—PPDIOO. Finally, this chapter discussed several factors that affect bandwidth and ways to optimize bandwidth using QoS techniques.

Table 5-5 examines some WAN technologies and highlights some common factors that are used to make WAN technology selections.

Table 5-5   *WAN Comparison*

WAN Technology	Bandwidth	Reliability	Latency	Cost
Dialup	Low	Low	High	Low
ISDN	Low	Medium	Medium	Low
Frame Relay	Low/Medium	Medium	Low	Medium
TDM	Medium	High	Low	Medium
SONET/SDH	High	High	Low	High
MPLS	High	High	Low	High
Dark fiber	High	High	Low	High
DWDM	High	High	Low	High
DSL	Low/Medium	Low	Medium	Low
Cable	Low/Medium	Low	Medium	Low
Wireless	Low/Medium	Low	Medium	Medium

Table 5-6 summarizes the types of DSL specifications.

Table 5-6 *DSL Specifications*

Service	Maximum Distance to Central Office	Maximum Upload Speed	Maximum Download Speed	Notes
Full-rate ADSL	18,000 ft (5500 m)	1500 kbps	9 Mbps	Asymmetrical.
ADSL G.lite	18,000 ft (5500 m)	384 kbps	1.5 Mbps	No splitter is required.
RADSL	18,000 ft (5500 m)	384 kbps	8 Mbps	Rate adapts based on distance and quality.
IDSL	35,000 ft (10,070 m)	144 kbps	144 kbps	DSL over ISDN (BRI).
SDSL	22,000 ft (6700 m)	2.3 Mbps	2.3 Mbps	Targets T1 replacement. Symmetrical DSL service.
HDSL	18,000 ft (5500 m)	1.54 Mbps	1.54 Mbps	Four-wire, similar to T1 service.
HDSL-2	24,000 ft (7333 m)	2 Mbps	2 Mbps	Two-wire version of HDSL or four-wire at 2 times the rate.
VDSL	3000 ft (916 m)	16 Mbps	52 Mbps	Few installations.

Table 5-7 compares a number of different WAN technologies, along with the speeds and media types associated with them.

Table 5-7 *Physical Bandwidth Comparison*

Bandwidth	Less Than 2 Mbps	2 Mbps to 45 Mbps	45 Mbps to 100 Mbps	100 Mbps to 10 Gbps
Copper	Serial, ISDN, Frame Relay, TDM, DSL	Frame Relay, Ethernet, DSL, cable, T3	Fast Ethernet	Gigabit Ethernet
Fiber	—	Ethernet	FastEthernet, ATM	Gigabit Ethernet, 10Gigabit Ethernet, ATM, SONET/SDH, POS, dark fiber
Wireless	802.11b	802.11b, wireless WAN (varies)	802.11a/g	802.11n

Q&A

As mentioned in the introduction, you have two choices for review questions: here in the book or the exam questions on the CD-ROM. The answers to these questions appear in Appendix A.

For more practice with exam format questions, use the exam engine on the CD-ROM.

1. When using PPDIOO design methodology, what should a network designer do after identifying the customer requirements?

   a. Design the network topology

   b. Design a test network

   c. Plan the implementation

   d. Characterize the existing network

2. Which module within the Enterprise campus connects to the Enterprise Edge module?

   a. Server module

   b. Campus Core

   c. Building Distribution

   d. Remote access/VPN module

3. What WAN technology is most cost effective and suitable for the telecommuter?

   a. MPLS

   b. Dark fiber

   c. ISDN

   d. DSL

4. What two modules are found in the Enterprise Edge?

   a. Campus Core

   b. Building Access

   c. Internet

   d. MAN/WAN

5. Which of the following statements best describes window size for good throughput?

    a. A large window size reduces the number of acknowledgments.

    b. A small window size reduces the number of acknowledgments.

    c. A small window size provides better performance.

    d. None of the above

6. What is the default queuing mechanism for router interfaces below 2.0 Mbps?

    a. Traffic shaping

    b. WFQ

    c. CBWFQ

    d. LLQ

7. Which of the following best describes the PPDIOO design methodology? (Select three.)

    a. Analyze the network requirements

    b. Characterize the existing network

    c. Implement the network management

    d. Design the network topology

8. Which of the following modules belongs in the Enterprise Edge?

    a. Building Distribution

    b. Campus Core

    c. Network Management

    d. DMZ/E-commerce

9. Which network modules connect to ISPs in the Enterprise Edge? (Select two.)

    a. Building Distribution

    b. Campus Core

    c. Internet

    d. DMZ/E-commerce

10. Which Enterprise Edge network module(s) connect(s) using the PSTN connectivity?

    a. Remote Access/VPN

    b. Campus Core

    c. Building Access

    d. DMZ/E-commerce

11. Which Enterprise Edge network module(s) connect(s) using Frame Relay and ATM?

 a. Remote Access/VPN

 b. WAN/MAN

 c. Building Distribution

 d. Server Farm

12. During which part of the PPDIOO design methodology does implementation planning occur?

 a. Analyze the network requirements

 b. Design the topology

 c. Characterize the existing network

 d. None of the above

13. What functional area provides connectivity between the central site and remote sites?

 a. DMZ/E-commerce

 b. Campus Core

 c. Building Distribution

 d. MAN/WAN

14. What WAN technology allows the enterprise to control framing?

 a. Cable

 b. Wireless

 c. DWDM

 d. Dark fiber

15. Which QoS method uses a strict PQ in addition to modular traffic classes?

 a. CBWFQ

 b. Policing

 c. WFQ

 d. LLQ

16. A T1 TDM circuit uses how many timeslots?

17. True or false: ISDN uses LMI for its signaling protocol.

18. True or false: DSL technology is analog technology over coaxial cable.

19. True or false: SONET/SDH supports automated recovery and self-healing mechanisms.

20. True or false: The DE bit set to 0 on a frame indicates to the Frame Relay network that this frame can be dropped.

21. Which wireless implementation is designed to connect two wireless networks in different buildings?

    a. Mobile wireless

    b. GPRS

    c. Bridge wireless

    d. UMTS

22. What improves the utilization of optical fiber strands?

23. On the ISP side of a cable provider, cable modems connect to what system?

24. If Frame Relay, ATM, and SONET technologies are used, what Enterprise Edge network module would they connect to?

    a. WAN/MAN

    b. VPN/Remote Access

    c. Internet

    d. DMZ/E-commerce

25. True or false: Network design requirements are driven by two primary goals: application availability and cost of investment/usage.

26. True or false: Analog dialup technology is a good backup solution for DSL and cable modem access.

27. True or false: Frame Relay SVCs are used more predominantly than PVCs.

28. True or false: ADSL uses the downstream bandwidth, which is higher than the upstream bandwidth, or asymmetrical.

29. What protocol describes data-over-cable procedures that the equipment must support?

This chapter covers the following subjects:

- Traditional WAN Technologies

- Remote-Access Network Design

- VPN Network Design

- WAN Backup Design

- Layer 3 Tunneling

- Enterprise WAN Architecture

- Enterprise Edge Components

- Enterprise Branch Architecture

- Enterprise Teleworker (Branch of One) Design

CHAPTER 6

WAN Design

This chapter reviews wide-area network (WAN) designs for the Enterprise WAN and Enterprise Branch. Expect plenty of questions on both architectures. The CCDA must understand WAN architectures and what makes them different from each other. This chapter also covers hardware and software selections used in WAN design.

"Do I Know This Already?" Quiz

The purpose of the "Do I Know This Already?" quiz is to help you decide whether you need to read the entire chapter. If you intend to read the entire chapter, you do not necessarily need to answer these questions now.

The ten-question quiz, derived from the major sections in the "Foundation Topics" portion of the chapter, helps you determine how to spend your limited study time.

Table 6-1 outlines the major topics discussed in this chapter and the "Do I Know This Already?" quiz questions that correspond to those topics.

Table 6-1 *"Do I Know This Already?" Foundation Topics Section-to-Question Mapping*

Foundation Topics Section	Questions Covered in This Section
Traditional WAN Technologies	1
Remote-Access Network Design	2
VPN Network Design	3
WAN Backup Design	4
Layer 3 Tunneling	—
Enterprise WAN Architecture	5, 6
Enterprise Edge Components	7
Enterprise Branch Architecture	8
Enterprise Teleworker (Branch of One) Design	9, 10

> **CAUTION** The goal of self-assessment is to gauge your mastery of the topics in this chapter. If you do not know the answer to a question or you are only partially sure, you should mark this question wrong for the purposes of the self-assessment. Giving yourself credit for an answer you correctly guess skews your self-assessment results and might give you a false sense of security.

1. Which of the following are examples of packet- and cell-switched technologies used in the Enterprise Edge?

   a. Frame Relay and ATM

   b. ISDN and T1

   c. Cable and DSL

   d. Analog voice and T1

2. Typical remote-access network requirements include which of the following? (Select all that apply.)

   a. Best-effort interactive and low-volume traffic patterns

   b. Voice and VPN support

   c. Connections to the Enterprise Edge using Layer 2 WAN technologies

   d. Connecting the server farm to the campus core

3. Which VPN infrastructure is used for business partner connectivity and uses the Internet or a private infrastructure?

   a. Access VPN

   b. Intranet VPN

   c. Extranet VPN

   d. Self-deployed MPLS VPN

4. What backup option allows for both a backup link and load-sharing capabilities using the available bandwidth?

   a. Dial backup

   b. Secondary WAN link

   c. Shadow PVC

   d. Dial-on-demand routing

5. Which common factor is used for WAN architecture selection that involves eliminating single points of failure to increase uptime and growth?

   a. Network segmentation

   b. Ease of management

   c. Redundancy

   d. Support for growth

6. What WAN/MAN architecture is provided by the service provider and has excellent growth support and high availability?

   a. Private WAN

   b. ISP service

   c. SP MPLS/IP VPN

   d. Private MPLS

7. Which Cisco IOS software family has been designed for the Enterprise Core and the SP edge?

   a. IOS T Releases 12.3, 12.4, 12.3T, and 12.4T

   b. IOS S Releases 12.2SB and 12.2SR

   c. IOS XR

   d. IOS SX

8. When designing Enterprise Branch Architecture using the SONA framework, which of the following are common network components? (Select all that apply.)

   a. Routers supporting WAN edge connectivity

   b. Switches providing the Ethernet LAN infrastructure

   c. Network management servers

   d. IP phones

9. Which design supports 50 to 100 users and provides Layer 3 redundancy features?

   a. Single-tier

   b. Dual-tier

   c. Multi-tier

   d. Branch of One

10. Which branch profile supports 100 to 1000 users, dual routers, dual ASAs, and multilayer switches, including the aggregation of the access layer switch connections?

    a. Single-tier

    b. Dual-tier

    c. Multi-tier

    d. Branch of One

The answers to the "Do I Know This Already?" quiz appear in Appendix A, "Answers to Chapter 'Do I Know This Already?' Quizzes and Q&A Sections." The suggested choices for your next step are as follows:

- **8 or less overall score**—Read the entire chapter. It includes the "Foundation Topics," "Foundation Summary," and "Q&A" sections.

- **9 or 10 overall score**—If you want more review on these topics, skip to the "Foundation Summary" section and then go to the "Q&A" section. Otherwise, move to the next chapter.

Foundation Topics

This chapter covers WAN design topics that you need to master for the CCDA exam. It begins by discussing physical WAN technology and WAN topologies used in the Enterprise Edge. Next is a review of typical remote-access requirements used to design remote-access networks. The chapter goes on to cover the specifics of VPN design and connectivity options available for VPNs.

This chapter also describes the backup strategies used when designing WANs. Then it covers the considerations used in developing WAN architectures. This chapter discusses the hardware and software options used when selecting components for your network design. A section then covers the framework used in designing branch offices. This chapter ends with a review of several options for designing different sizes of branch offices.

Traditional WAN Technologies

When selecting a particular WAN technology, you should be familiar with the three major categories that represent traditional WANs:

- **Circuit-switched**—Data connections that can be brought up when needed and terminated when finished. Examples include ordinary PSTN phone service, analog modems, and ISDN. Carriers reserve that call path through the network for the duration of the call.

- **Leased lines**—A dedicated connection provided by the service provider. These types of connections are point-to-point and generally more expensive. TDM-based leased lines usually use synchronous data transmission.

- **Packet- and cell-switched**—Connections that use virtual circuits (PVC/SVC) established by the service provider. Packet-switched technologies include Frame Relay and cell-switched technologies such as ATM. The virtual circuits are part of the shared ATM/Frame Relay service provider backbone network. This gives the service provider greater flexibility with its service offerings.

WAN Topologies

When designing a WAN, you should become familiar with the basic design approaches for packet-switched networks. These approaches include hub-and-spoke, partial-mesh, and full-mesh topologies, as shown in Figure 6-1.

Figure 6-1   *WAN Topologies*

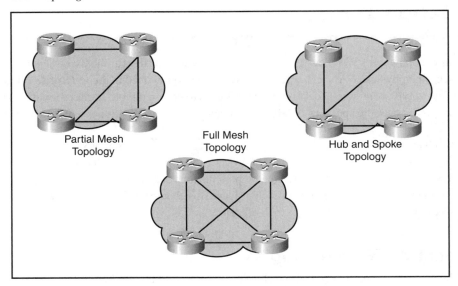

Hub-and-Spoke Topology

A star or hub-and-spoke topology provides a hub router with connections to the spoke routers through the WAN cloud. Network communication between the sites flows through the hub router. Significant WAN cost savings and simplified management are benefits of the hub-and-spoke topology. Hub and spoke topologies also tend to be the most popular WAN topologies.

A major disadvantage of this approach is that the hub router represents a single point of failure. The hub-and-spoke topology limits overall performance when accessing resources at the central hub router from the spoke routers, which affects scalability.

Full-Mesh Topology

With full-mesh topologies, each site has a connection to all other sites in the WAN cloud (any-to-any). As the number of sites grows, so does the number of spoke connections needed. Consequently, the full-mesh topology is not viable in very large networks. However, a key advantage of this topology is that it has plenty of redundancy in the event of network failures. But redundancy implemented with this approach does have a high price associated with it.

Here are some issues inherent with full-mesh topologies:

■   Many virtual circuits (VCs) are required to maintain the full mesh

■   Issues occur with duplication of packets for each site

- Complex configurations are needed

- High cost

Partial-Mesh Topology

A partial-mesh topology has fewer VC connections than a full-mesh topology. Therefore, not all sites in the cloud are required to be connected to each other. However, some sites on the WAN cloud have full-mesh characteristics. Partial-mesh topologies can give you more options and flexibly as far as where you may want to place the high-redundancy VCs given your specific requirements.

Remote-Access Network Design

When designing remote-access networks, the goal is to provide a unified solution that allows for seamless connectivity as if the users are on site. Connection requirements drive the technology selection process. It is important to analyze the application and network requirements in addition to reviewing the available service provider options.

The following summarizes typical remote-access requirements:

- Best-effort interactive and low-volume traffic patterns

- Connections to the Enterprise Edge using Layer 2 WAN technologies (consider capital and recurring costs)

- Voice and VPN support

Remote-access network connections are enabled over permanent always-on connections or dial-on-demand connections:

- Dialup analog, ISDN (dial-on-demand)

- DSL, cable, wireless hotspot (permanent)

VPN Network Design

Virtual private networks typically are deployed over some kind of shared infrastructure. VPNs are similar to tunnels in that they carry traffic over an existing IP infrastructure. VPN infrastructures include the Internet, ATM/Frame Relay WANs, and point-to-point connected IP infrastructures. A disadvantage of using VPNs over public networks is that the connectivity is best-effort in nature and troubleshooting is also very difficult because you don't have visibility into the service provider's infrastructure.

Figure 6-2 shows VPN connectivity options.

Figure 6-2   *VPN Examples*

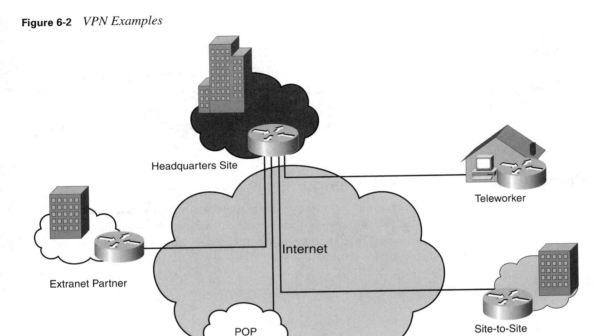

The three VPN groups are divided by application:

■ **Access VPN**—These types of VPN connections give users connectivity over shared networks such as the Internet to their corporate intranets. Users connect remotely using dialup, ISDN, Cable/DSL, or via wireless hotspots. Remote network connectivity into the corporate network over the Internet is typically outsourced to an ISP, and the VPN clients are supported by the internal help desk. Two architectural options are used to initiate the VPN connections: client-initiated or network access server (NAS)-initiated VPN connections. Client-initiated VPN connections let users establish IPsec encrypted sessions over the Internet to the corporate VPN terminating device. NAS-initiated VPN connections are where users first connect to the NAS and then the NAS sets up a VPN tunnel to the corporate network.

- **Intranet VPN**—Intranet VPNs or site-to-site VPNs connect remote offices to the headend offices. Generally, the remote sites use their Internet connection to establish the VPN connection back to the corporate headend office. But they could use a VPN tunnel over an IP backbone provided by the service provider. The main benefits of intranet VPNs are reduced WAN infrastructure, lower WAN charges, and reduction in the cost of ownership.

- **Extranet VPN**—VPN infrastructure for business partner connectivity also uses the Internet or a private infrastructure for network access. Keep in mind that it is important to have secure extranet network policies to restrict the business partners' access.

Overlay VPNs

Overlay VPNs are built using traditional WAN technologies such as Frame Relay and ATM. The service provider provides the virtual circuits to enable connectivity between the locations. The underlying network emulates Layer 3 point-to-point links between sites. Secure VPN tunnels are then built over the IP infrastructure using Generic Routing Encapsulation (GRE) and IPsec protocols. Because the network is secure, the provider has no visibility into the Layer 3 traffic and provides only the transport services. However, this incurs a higher cost because of the bandwidth and virtual circuits needed at each site.

Virtual Private Dialup Networks

Virtual Private Dialup Networks (VPDN) provide remote network access using tunnels over traditional dialup, ISDN, DSL cable, and wireless network access connections. This method involves the ISP terminating network connections and then forwarding the traffic onto the company's corporate network. Virtual tunnels are used between the company sites and the ISP using Layer 2 Forwarding (L2F) or Layer 2 Tunneling Protocol (L2TP) tunnels. Network configuration and security remain under the company's control, not the ISP's.

Peer-to-Peer VPNs

With peer-to-peer VPNs, the service provider plays an active role in enterprise routing. This approach uses modern MPLS VPN technology. Organizations can then use any IP address space, thus avoiding issues with overlapping IP address space. MPLS VPN networks learn routing information from normal IP routing sources; however, they use an additional label to specify the VPN tunnel and the corresponding VPN destination network.

VPN Benefits

The major benefits of using VPNs are flexibility, cost, and scalability. VPNs are easy to set up and deploy in most cases. VPNs enable network access to remote users, remote sites, and extranet business partners. VPNs lower the cost of ownership by reducing the WAN and dialup recurring monthly charges. The geographic coverage of VPNs is nearly everywhere Internet access is available, which makes VPNs highly scalable. In addition, VPNs simplify WAN operations because they can be deployed in a consistent manner.

WAN Backup Design

Redundancy is critical in WAN design for the remote site because of the unreliable nature of WAN links. Most Enterprise Edge solutions require high availability between the primary and remote site. Because WAN links have lower reliability and lack bandwidth, they are good candidates for most WAN backup designs.

Branch offices should have some type of backup strategy in the event of a primary link failure. Backup links can be either dialup or permanent connections.

WAN backup options are as follows:

- **Dial backup**—ISDN provides backup dialup services in the event of a primary failure of a WAN circuit. The backup link is initiated if a failure occurs with the primary link. The ISDN backup link provides network continuity until the primary link is restored, and then the backup link is terminated such as with floating static route techniques.

- **Secondary WAN link**—The addition of a secondary WAN link makes the network more fault-tolerant. This solution offers two key advantages:

  — Backup link—Provides for network connectivity if the primary link fails. Dynamic or static routing techniques can be used to provide routing consistency during backup events. Application availability can also be increased because of the additional backup link.

  — Additional bandwidth—Load sharing allows both links to be used at the same time, increasing the available bandwidth. Load balancing can be achieved over the parallel links using automatic routing protocol techniques.

- **Shadow PVC**—Service providers can offer shadow PVCs, which provide additional PVCs for use if needed. The customer is not charged for the PVC if it does not exceed limits set by the provider while the primary PVC is available. If the limit is exceeded, the service provider charges the customer accordingly.

Load-Balancing Guidelines

Load balancing can be implemented per packet or per destination using fast switching. If WAN links are less than 56 kbps, per-packet load balancing is preferred. Fast switching is enabled on WAN links that are faster than 56 kbps, and per-destination load balancing is preferred.

A major disadvantage of using duplicate WAN links is cost. Duplicate WAN links require additional WAN circuits for each location, and more network interfaces are required to terminate the connections. However, the loss of productivity if a site loses network connectivity and becomes isolated can be greater than the cost of the duplicate WAN link.

WAN Backup over the Internet

Another alternative for WAN backup is to use the Internet as the connectivity transport between sites. However, keep in mind that this type of connection does not support bandwidth guarantees. The enterprise also needs to work closely with the ISP to set up the tunnels and advertise the company's networks internally so that remote offices have reachable IP destinations.

Security is of great importance when you rely on the Internet for network connectivity, so a secure tunnel using IPsec needs to be deployed to protect the data during transport.

Figure 6-3 illustrates connectivity between the headend or central site and a remote site using traditional ATM/FR connections for the primary WAN link. The IPsec tunnel is a backup tunnel that provides redundancy for the site if the primary WAN link fails.

Figure 6-3   *WAN Backup over the Internet*

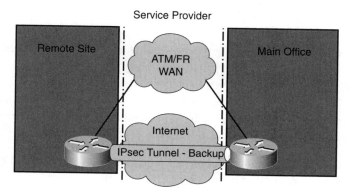

IPsec tunnels are configured between the source and destination routers using tunnel interfaces. Packets that are destined for the tunnel have the standard formatted IP header. IP packets that are forwarded across the tunnel need an additional GRE/IPsec header placed on them as well. As soon as the packets have the required headers, they are placed on the tunnel with a destination address of the tunnel endpoint. After the packets cross the tunnel and arrive on the far end, the GRE/IPsec headers are removed. The packets are then forwarded normally using the original IP packet headers.

Layer 3 Tunneling

Two methods exist for tunneling private networks over a public IP network:

■ **Generic Routing Encapsulation (GRE)**—Developed by Cisco to encapsulate a variety of protocols inside IP tunnels. This approach is simple for basic IP VPNs but lacks in security and scalability. In fact, GRE tunnels do not use any encryption to secure the packets during transport.

■ **IP Security (IPsec)**—IPsec provides secure transmission of data over unsecured networks such as the Internet. IPsec operates in either tunnel mode or transport mode. Packet payloads can be encrypted, and IPsec receivers can authenticate packets' origin. Internet Key Exchange (IKE) and Public-Key Infrastructure (PKI) can also be used with IPsec. IKE is the protocol used to set up a security association (SA) with IPsec. PKI is an arrangement that provides for third-party verification of identities.

Enterprise WAN Architecture

When selecting an enterprise WAN architecture, you should identify and understand the connectivity and business requirements. It is important to review sample network designs that could meet the identified requirements. Here are some common factors that influence decisions for WAN architecture selection:

■ **High availability**—Most businesses need a high level of availability, especially for their critical applications. The goal of high availability is to remove the single points of failure in the design, either by software, hardware, or power. Redundancy is critical in providing high levels of availability. Some technologies have built-in techniques that enable them to be highly available. For technologies that do not, other techniques can be employed, such as using additional WAN circuits and/or backup power supplies.

■ **Support for growth**—Often enterprises want to provide for growth in their WAN architectures, considering the amount of effort and time required to connect additional sites. High-growth WAN technologies can reduce the amount of effort and cost involved in network expansions. WAN technologies that do not provide growth require significantly more effort, time, and cost to add new branches or remote offices.

■ **Ongoing expenses**—Private line and traditional ATM/Frame Relay tend to have higher recurring expenses than Internet-based IP VPNs. Public networks such as the Internet can be used for WAN services to reduce cost, but there are some trade-offs with reliability and security compared to private or ATM/Frame Relay-type transports. Moreover, public networks make it more difficult to provide advanced technologies such as real-time voice and video.

- **Ease of management**—The expertise of the technical staff who are required to maintain and support MAN and WAN technologies varies. Most enterprises have the internal IT knowledge to handle most traditional MAN and WAN upgrades without the need for much training. However, some of the advanced technologies usually reserved for service providers may require additional training for the IT staff if the support is brought in-house. Depending on the technology and the design, you have opportunities to reduce the complexity through network management.

- **Cost to implement**—In most cases, the implementation cost is a major concern. During the design process it is important to evaluate the initial and recurring costs along with the design's benefits. Sometimes an organization can migrate from legacy connectivity to new technology with minimal investment in terms of equipment, time, and resources. In other cases, a network migration can require a low initial cost in terms of equipment and resources but can provide recurring operational savings and greater flexibility over the long term.

- **Network segmentation support**—Segmentation provides for Layer 2/3 logical separation between networks instead of physically separate networks. Advantages include reduced costs associated with equipment, maintenance, and carrier charges. In addition, separate security polices can be implemented per department or by functional area of the network to restrict access as needed.

- **Support for Voice and Video**—There is an increased demand for the support of voice over MAN and WAN technologies. Some WAN providers offer Cisco QoS-Certified IP VPNs, which can provide the appropriate levels of QoS needed for voice and video deployments. In cases where Internet or public network connections are used, QoS cannot always be assured. When voice and video are required for small offices, teleworkers, or remote agents, 768 kbps upstream bandwidth or greater is recommended.

Cisco Enterprise MAN/WAN

The Cisco Enterprise MAN/WAN architecture uses several technologies that work together in a cohesive relationship.

Here is the list of Cisco Enterprise MAN/WAN architectures:

- Private WAN (optional encryption)

- Private WAN with self-deployed MPLS

- ISP service (Internet with site-to-site and remote-access VPN)

- Service provider-managed IP/MPLS VPN

These architectures provide integrated QoS, security, reliability, and ease of management that is required to support enterprise business applications and services. As you can see, alternative technologies to the traditional private WAN can allow for network growth and reduced monthly carrier charges.

Enterprise WAN/MAN Architecture Comparison

Enterprise WAN/MAN architectures have common characteristics that allow the network designer to compare the advantages and disadvantages of each approach. Table 6-2 compares the characteristics of Private WAN, ISP Service, SP MPLS/IP VPN, and Private MPLS architectures.

Table 6-2   *WAN/MAN Architecture Comparison*

Characteristic	Private WAN	ISP Service	SP MPLS/ IP VPN	Private MPLS
High availability	Excellent	Good	Excellent	Excellent
Growth support	Moderate	Good	Excellent	Excellent
Security	IPsec (optional)	IPsec (mandatory)	IPsec (optional)	IPsec (optional)
Ongoing expenses	High	Low	Moderate to high	Moderate to high
Ease of management	High	Medium	Medium	High
Voice/video support	Excellent	Moderate	Excellent	Excellent
Effort to migrate from private WAN	Low	Moderate	Moderate	High

The Cisco Enterprise MAN/WAN architecture includes Private WAN, ISP Service, SP MPLS/IP VPN, and Private MPLS:

■ **Private WAN** generally consists of Frame Relay, ATM, private lines, and other traditional WAN connections. If security is needed, private WAN connections can be used in conjunction with encryption protocols such as Digital Encryption Standard (DES), Triple DES (3DES), and Advanced Encryption Standard (AES). This technology is best suited for an enterprise with moderate growth outlook where some remote or branch offices will need to be connected in the future. Businesses that require secure and reliable connectivity to comply with IT privacy standards can benefit from IPsec encrypted connectivity over the private WAN. Disadvantages of private WANs are that they have high recurring costs from the carriers and they are not the preferred technology for teleworkers and remote call center agents. Some enterprises may use encryption on the network, connecting larger sites and omitting encryption on the smaller remote offices with IP VPNs.

- **ISP Service (Internet with site-to-site and remote-access VPN)** uses strong encryption standards such as DES, 3DES, and AES, which make this WAN option more secure than the private WAN. ISP service also provides compliance with many new information security regulations imposed on some industries, such as healthcare and finance. This technology is best suited for basic connectivity over the Internet. However, if you need to support voice and video, consider IPsec VPN solutions that have the desired QoS support needed to meet your network requirements. The cost of this technology is relatively low. It is useful for connecting large numbers of teleworkers, remote contact agents, and remote offices.

- **SP MPLS/IP VPN** is similar to private WAN technology, but with added scalability and flexibility. MPLS-enabled IP VPNs enable mesh-like behavior or any-to-any branch-type connectivity. SP MPLS networks can support enterprise QoS requirements for voice and video, especially those with high growth potential. SP MPLS features secure and reliable technology with generally lower carrier fees. This makes it a good option for connecting branch offices, teleworkers, and remote call center agents.

- **Private WAN with self-deployed MPLS** usually is reserved for very large enterprises that are willing to make substantial investments in equipment and training to build out the MPLS network. The IT staff needs to be well trained and comfortable with supporting complex networks.

Figure 6-4 illustrates SP MPLS, Private WAN with encryption, and IPsec VPNs WAN architectures.

Figure 6-4 *WAN Architectures*

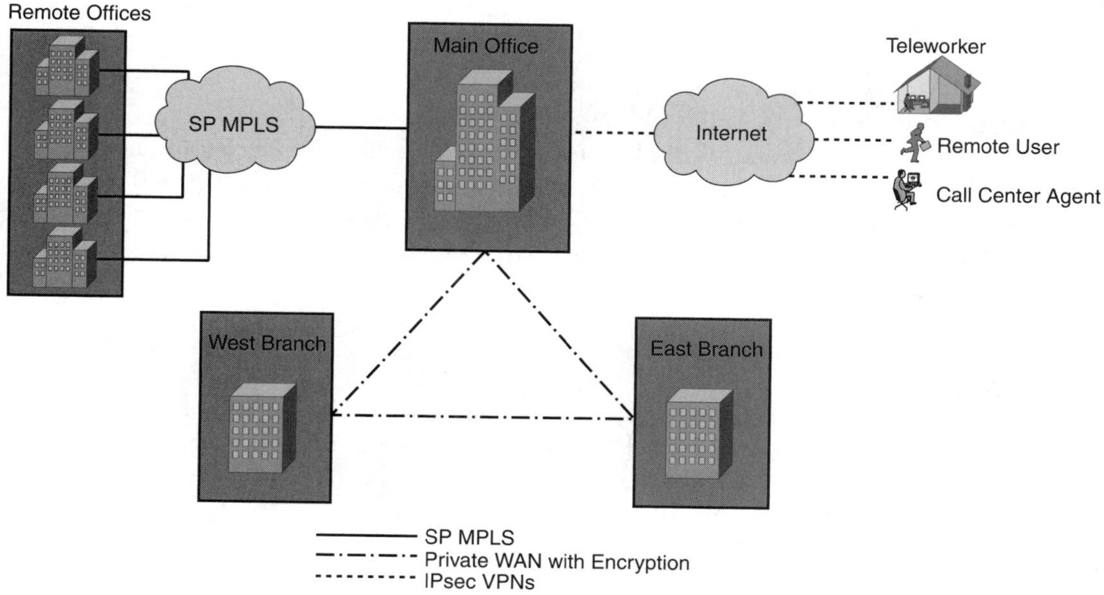

Enterprise Edge Components

When selecting Enterprise Edge hardware and software, you must keep in mind several considerations. Here are some factors to examine during the selection process:

- Hardware selection involves the data link functions and features offered by the device. Considerations include the following:

  — Port density

  — Types of ports supported

  — Modularity (add-on hardware)

  — Backplane and packet throughput

  — Redundancy (CPU and/or power)

  — Expandability for future use

- Software selection focuses on the network performance and the feature sets included in the software. Here are some factors to consider:

  — Forwarding decisions

  — Technology feature support

  — Bandwidth optimization

  — Security vulnerabilities

  — Software issues

Hardware Selection

When evaluating hardware, use the Cisco documentation online to research hardware and determine the equipment's capabilities. Remember to consider the port densities and types of ports the device offers. In addition, other factors to investigate include modularity, packet throughput, redundancy capabilities, and the device's expandability. Finally, keep in mind what power options the hardware supports.

Software Selection

The architecture of Cisco IOS software is designed to meet the requirements of different markets (enterprise, SP, and commercial) and divisions of the network, such as the access, core, distribution, and edge. The Cisco IOS software family consists of IOS T (access), IOS S (Enterprise core, SP edge), and IOS XR (SP Core).

Cisco IOS T supports advanced technology business solutions aimed at access, wireless, data center, security, and Unified Communications (UC). Cisco IOS S focuses on high-end enterprise cores, service provider edge networks, VPNs (MPLS, Layer 2/Layer 3), video, and multicast. Cisco IOS XR is suited for large-scale networks within the service provider core that offer high availability and in-service software upgrades.

The IOS Software families share a common base of technologies. Most of the T family features are also available in the IOS S and IOS XR families.

Figure 6-5 illustrates each of the Cisco IOS software families and where they reside in relationship to each other within the different markets.

Figure 6-5 *Cisco IOS Software Families*

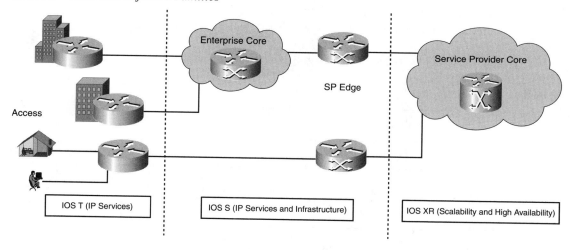

Cisco IOS Packaging

Cisco IOS packaging involves consolidating and organizing the IOS software using consistent and standardized naming across all router platforms. The four base service categories are as follows:

- **IP Base**—Entry-level IOS supporting IP data

- **IP Voice**—Supports converged voice and data

- **Advanced Security**—Security features and VPN

- **Enterprise Base**—Enterprise Layer 3 protocols and IBM support

In addition, three additional premium packages offer new IOS software features that focus on more complex networking environments:

- **SP Services**—Adds features such as MPLS, ATM, SSH, and NetFlow to the lower IP Voice package

- **Advanced IP Services**—Adds support for IPv6 and the features of both the Advanced Security and SP services packages

- **Enterprise Services**—Adds full IBM support and the features of both the Enterprise Base and SP services packages

The features of the lower-tier packages are inherited in the higher-tier packages flowing upward.

At the top is the premium package, Advanced Enterprise Services. It combines all features and supports all routing protocols with voice, security, and VPN technologies.

Figure 6-6 shows the Cisco IOS packaging and how IOS features are inherited.

Figure 6-6   *Cisco IOS Packaging*

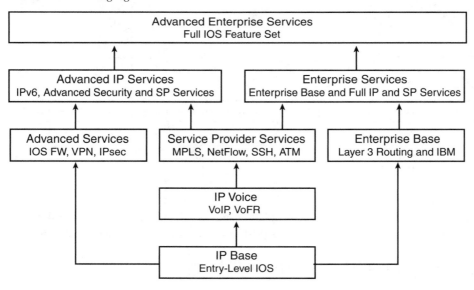

Inheritance of IOS features from one IOS to the next higher level IOS is an important aspect of Cisco IOS packaging. Therefore, as soon as a feature is introduced to an IOS package, it is maintained during upgrades to higher-level IOS packages.

Table 6-3 illustrates the major features and inheritance available with IOS packages.

Table 6-3 *IOS Package Comparison*

Feature Set	IP Data	VoIP, VoFR	ATM, MPLS	AppleTalk, IPX, IBM	Firewall, IDS, VPN
IP Base	×				
IP Voice	×	×			
Advanced Security	×				×
SP Services	×	×	×		
Enterprise Base	×			×	
Advanced IP Services	×	×	×		×
Enterprise Services	×	×	×	×	
Advanced Enterprise Services	×	×	×	×	×

Comparing Hardware and Software

Table 6-4 compares the Cisco router and switch hardware platforms and their associated software families, releases, and functional descriptions.

Table 6-4 *Cisco Router/Switch Platform and Software Comparison*

Router/Switch Hardware	Software	Description
800, 1800, 2800, 3800, 7200	Cisco IOS T Releases 12.3, 12.4, 12.3T, and 12.4T	Access routing platforms supporting fast and scalable delivery of data for enterprise applications.
7x00, 10000	Cisco IOS S Release 12.2SB	Delivers midrange routing services for the Enterprise and SP edge networks.
7600	Cisco IOS S Release 12.2SR	Delivers high-end LAN switching for Enterprise access, distribution, core, and data center. Also supports Metro Ethernet for the SP edge.
12000, CRS-1	Cisco IOS XR	High availability, providing large scalability and flexibility for the SP core and edge.
2970, 3560, 3750	Cisco IOS S Release 12.2SE	Provides low-end to midrange LAN switching for Enterprise access and distribution deployments.

continues

Table 6-4   *Cisco Router/Switch Platform and Software Comparison (Continued)*

Router/Switch Hardware	Software	Description
4500, 4900	Cisco IOS S Release 12.2SG	Provides midrange LAN switching for Enterprise access and distribution in the campus. Also supports Metro Ethernet.
6500	Cisco IOS S Release 12.2SX	Delivers high-end LAN switching for Enterprise access, distribution, core, and data center. Also supports Metro Ethernet for the SP edge.

Enterprise Branch Architecture

Enterprise Branch architectures encompass a wide range of services that customers want to deploy at the edge of the enterprise. These architectures allow for a variety of connection options, and distance typically is not an issue. The services in this architecture give customers new opportunities to increase security, converge their voice and data traffic, improve productivity, and reduce costs.

Cisco Enterprise Branch Architecture is based on Cisco's Service-Oriented Network Architecture (SONA), which includes plug-in modules that provide remote connectivity to network endpoints. The Enterprise Architecture is a flexible and secure framework for extending headend application functionality to the remote site. Common network components that use the SONA framework for the branch include

- Routers supporting the WAN edge connectivity

- Switches providing the Ethernet LAN infrastructure

- Security appliances securing the branch devices

- Wireless APs allowing for roaming mobility

- Call processing providing Unified Communications and video support

- IP phones and PCs for the end-user devices

Branch Design

It is important to characterize the existing network and gather requirements to develop a suitable design for the branch.

Here are some questions you should ask:

- How many locations and existing devices are there (network devices, servers, users)?

- What amount of scalability and growth is expected?

- What level of high availability and/or redundancy is required?

- Is specific server or network protocol support needed?

- Will the network management and/or support be centralized or distributed?

- Are there any network segmentation restrictions, such as DMZ or internal networks versus external networks?

- Will wireless services be needed, and to what extent?

- What is the estimated budget for the branch design?

Enterprise Branch Profiles

The SONA framework has three profiles for the Enterprise Branch. They are based on the number of users located at the branch. The profiles are not intended to be the only architectures for branch offices but rather a common set of services that each branch should include. These profiles serve as a basis on which integrated services and application networking are built. The three profiles for the SONA framework enterprise branch are as follows:

- **Single-tier design**—Up to 50 users (small)

- **Dual-tier design**—Between 50 and 100 users (medium)

- **Multi-tier design**—Between 100 and 1000 users (large)

Figure 6-7 shows the three Enterprise branch profiles and the integrated services layers and application networking services that are provided by the branch infrastructure.

Figure 6-7 *Branch Profiles*

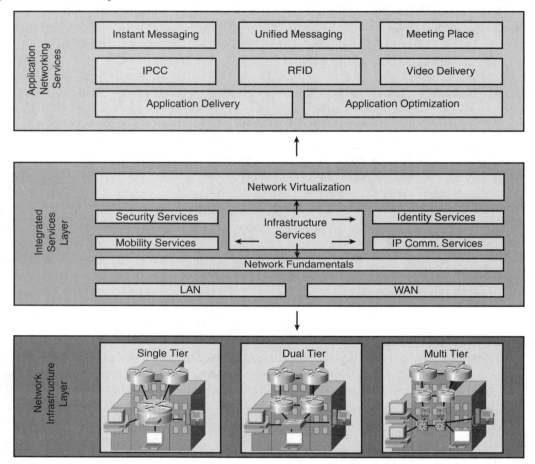

The framework's foundation is the branch profile network infrastructure layer, which includes all the common LAN and WAN components. The integrated services layer is built on top of the infrastructure layer and is composed of security, mobility, UC, and identity services. The application networking services are built above the integrated services layer, which organizes the applications services, such as IM, UCC, unified messaging, video delivery, and application delivery services.

Requirements such as high availability, scalability, and redundancy influence the branch profile selected for a branch office.

To integrate both the WAN edge and LAN infrastructure, an integrated services router (ISR) can be used to provide voice, security, and data services. The integrated services router supports triple-speed interfaces (10/100/1000), high-speed WAN interface cards (HWIC), network modules, and embedded security capabilities.

Single-Tier Design

The single-tier design is recommended for branch offices that do not require hardware redundancy and that have a small user base of up to 50 users. This profile consists of an access router providing WAN services and connections for the LAN services. The access router can connect the Layer 2 switch ports in one of three ways:

■ Using an ISR that has an optional EtherSwitch module that provides 16 to 48 Ethernet ports for client connections.

■ Trunking to an access switch that aggregates the Ethernet connections and can include support for PoE for IP phones and wireless APs.

■ Logical EtherChannel interface between the ISR and the access switches using the EtherSwitch module. The access switches can also provide PoE as needed.

The Layer 3 WAN services are based on the WAN and Internet deployment model. A T1 is used for the primary link, and an ADSL secondary link is used for backup. Other network fundamentals are supported, such as EIGRP, floating static routes, and QoS for bandwidth protection.

The ISR can support the default gateway function and other Layer 3 services such as DHCP, NAT, and IOS Firewall.

The Layer 2 services can be provided by the ISR or access switches such as the 35x0 or 3750 series switches. It is recommended that you use Rapid PVST+ for all Layer 2 branch offices where loops are present. Rapid PVST+ ensures a loop-free topology when multiple Layer 2 connections are used for redundancy purposes.

Figure 6-8 illustrates the single-tier branch design connecting back to the corporate office.

Figure 6-8 *Single-Tier Profile (Small Branch)*

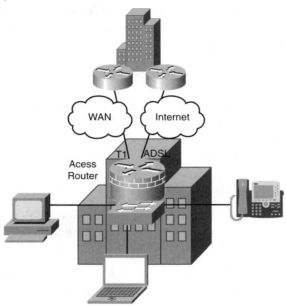

Dual-Tier Design

The dual-tier design is recommended for branch offices of 50 to 100 users, with an additional access router in the WAN edge allowing for redundancy services. Typically two 2821 or 2851 routers are used to support the WAN, and separate access switches are used to provide LAN connectivity.

The infrastructure components are dual-access routers, external Layer 2/Layer 3 switches, laptops, desktops, printers, and IP phones. Dual Frame Relay links are used to connect to the corporate offices via both of the access routers.

Layer 3 services such as EIGRP are deployed. Because there are two routers, HSRP or GLBP can be used to provide redundancy gateway services. QoS can also be used to provide guaranteed bandwidth for VoIP, and policing can be used to restrict certain traffic classes from overwhelming the available bandwidth.

The dual-tier design supports using a higher-density external switch or using the EtherSwitch module with the ISR to create trunks to the external access switches. The Cisco Catalyst 3750 series switches have StackWise technology, allowing multiple switches to be connected and managed as one. This also increases the port density available for end-user connections. With Cisco StackWise technology, customers can connect up to nine 3750 series switches using a variety of fiber and copper ports, allowing greater flexibility with the connection options.

Figure 6-9 illustrates the dual-tier branch design using dual routers back to the corporate office.

Figure 6-9 *Dual-Tier Profile (Medium Branch)*

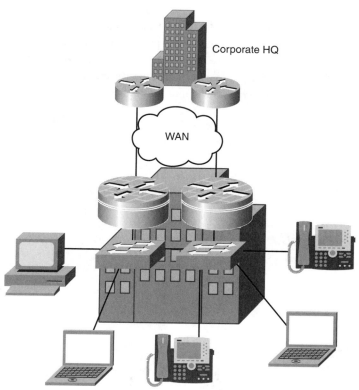

Multi-Tier Design

The multi-tier design is the largest of the branch profiles, supporting between 100 and 1000 users. This design profile is similar to the dual-tier design in that it also provides dual-access routers in the WAN edge. In addition, dual ASAs are used for firewall filtering, and dual distribution switches provide the multilayer switching component. The WAN services use an MPLS deployment model with dual WAN links into the WAN cloud.

Because there are dual routers, the typical redundancy services can also be provided such as EIGRP load balancing and HSRP/GLBP. The ASAs dual configuration allows for ASA failover. QoS services such as shaping and policing can be applied to all the routers and switches as required.

To meet the requirements of the larger user base, a distribution layer of multilayer switches is added to aggregate the connected access switches. A multilayer switch provides the additional

LAN switching capabilities to meet the port density requirements and allowing flexibility to support additional network devices.

A couple of hardware options for this design are the Cisco Catalyst 3750 with StackWise technology or using a modular approach with a Cisco Catalyst 4500. The Cisco 3750 series of switches provide great port densities but do not provide the redundant power without the additional Cisco RPS (external power supply). However, the Cisco 4500 switch platform not only allows for flexibility by adding port densities and interface types but also provides redundant power internally for the entire chassis when using dual power supplies.

If Cisco Catalyst 3560 and 3750 switches are used, additional Layer 2 security features such as dynamic ARP inspection, DHCP snooping, and IP source guard can be used to provide additional security enhancements.

Figure 6-10 illustrates the multi-tier branch design using dual routers, ASAs, and distribution switches.

Figure 6-10 *Multi-Tier Profile (Large Branch)*

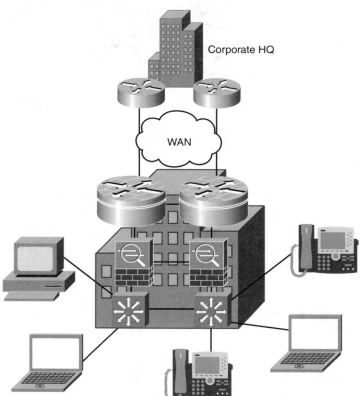

Enterprise Teleworker (Branch of One) Design

At the remote edges of the network is another branch office called the Branch of One, also known as Enterprise Teleworkers. Organizations are continually trying to reduce costs and improve their employees' productivity. By working from home, employees can manage their work schedules more effectively and increase their productivity. This also results in greater job satisfaction and flexibility in the employees' work schedule. The work-from-home teleworker is an extension of the enterprise and serves as the basis for the Enterprise Teleworker solution.

Enterprise Teleworkers or the Branch of One needs to be differentiated from the occasional remote worker. The full-time enterprise teleworker has more extensive application access and requirements than the occasional remote worker. Occasionally remote users connect to the corporate network at a hotspot, but generally they do not have the same application demands of an Enterprise teleworker. Typically the Branch of One user connects to his or her local ISP over a cable or DSL connection and uses an analog phone line as a backup.

References and Recommended Readings

"Enterprise Branch Architecture Design Overview," http://www.cisco.com/univercd/cc/td/doc/solution/enbrover.pdf

Module 4, "Designing Remote Connectivity," Designing for Cisco Internetwork Solution Course (DESGN) v2.0

"WAN and MAN Solutions Overview," http://www.cisco.com/en/US/netsol/ns483/networking_solutions_audience_business_benefit0900aecd8033ea26.html

"What is Cisco SONA?," http://www.cisco.com/application/pdf/en/us/guest/netsol/ns477/c643/cdccont_0900aecd8039b324.pdf

Foundation Summary

The "Foundation Summary" section of each chapter lists the most important facts from the chapter. Although this section does not list every fact from the chapter that will be on the CCDA exam, a well-prepared CCDA candidate should at a minimum know all the details in each "Foundation Summary" before taking the exam.

The CCDA exam requires that you be familiar with the following topics covered in this chapter:

- **Circuit-switched**—Data connections that can be brought up when needed and terminated when finished.

- **Leased lines**—A dedicated connection provided by the service provider.

- **Packet and cell-switched**—Connections that use virtual circuits (PVC/SVC) established by the service provider.

- **Hub-and-spoke (or star) topology**—Provides a hub router with connections to the spoke routers through the WAN cloud.

- **Partial-mesh topology**—Has fewer virtual circuit connections than a full-mesh topology.

- **Full-mesh topology**—Requires that each site be connected to every other site in the cloud.

- **Access VPN**—These types of VPN connections give users connectivity over shared networks such as the Internet to the corporate intranet.

- **Intranet (site-to-site) VPN**—Connect remote offices back to the headend office.

- **Extranet VPN**—VPN infrastructure for business partner connectivity that also uses the Internet or a private infrastructure for access.

- **Dial backup**—ISDN provides backup dialup services in the event of a failure of a primary WAN circuit.

- **Secondary WAN link**—The addition of a secondary WAN link makes the network more fault-tolerant.

- **Shadow PVC**—Service providers can offer shadow PVCs that provide an additional PVC for use if needed.

- **Single-tier design**—Up to 50 users (small)

- **Dual-tier design**—Between 50 and 100 users (medium)

- **Multi-tier design**—Between 100 and 1000 users (large)

- **Branch of One**—Enterprise teleworker

Table 6-5 compares the characteristics of private WAN, ISP service, SP MPLS/IP VPN, and private MPLS architectures.

Table 6-5   *WAN/MAN Architecture Comparison*

Characteristic	Private WAN	ISP Service	SP MPLS/IP VPN	Private MPLS
High availability	Excellent	Good	Excellent	Excellent
Growth support	Moderate	Good	Excellent	Excellent
Security	IPsec (optional)	IPsec (mandatory)	IPsec (optional)	IPsec (optional)
Ongoing expenses	High	Low	Moderate to high	Moderate to high
Ease of management	High	Medium	Medium	High
Voice/video support	Excellent	Moderate	Excellent	Excellent
Effort to migrate from private WAN	Low	Moderate	Moderate	High

Table 6-6 illustrates the major features and inheritance available with IOS packages.

Table 6-6   *IOS Package Comparison*

Feature Set	IP Data	VoIP, VoFR	ATM, MPLS	AppleTalk, IPX, IBM	Firewall, IDS, VPN
IP Base	×				
IP Voice	×	×			
Advanced Security	×				×
SP Services	×	×	×		
Enterprise Base	×			×	
Advanced IP Services	×	×	×		×
Enterprise Services	×	×	×	×	
Advanced Enterprise Services	×	×	×	×	×

Table 6-7 compares the Cisco router and switch hardware platforms and their associated software families, releases, and functional descriptions.

Table 6-7 *Cisco Router/Switch Platform and Software Comparison*

Router/Switch Hardware	Software	Description
800, 1800, 2800, 3800, 7200	Cisco IOS T Releases 12.3, 12.4, 12.3T, and 12.4T	Access routing platforms supporting fast and scalable delivery of data for Enterprise applications.
7x00, 10000	Cisco IOS S Release 12.2SB	Delivers midrange routing services for the Enterprise and SP edge networks.
7600	Cisco IOS S Release 12.2SR	Delivers high-end LAN switching for Enterprise access, distribution, core, and data center. Also supports Metro Ethernet for the SP edge.
12000 CRS-1	Cisco IOS XR	High availability, providing large scalability and flexibility for the SP core and edge.
2970, 3560, 3750	Cisco IOS S Release 12.2SE	Provides low-end to midrange LAN switching for Enterprise access and distribution deployments.
4500, 4900	Cisco IOS S Release 12.2SG	Provides midrange LAN switching for Enterprise access and distribution in the campus. Also supports Metro Ethernet.
6500	Cisco IOS S Release 12.2SX	Delivers high-end LAN switching for Enterprise access, distribution, core, and data center. Also supports Metro Ethernet for the SP edge.

Q&A

As mentioned in the Introduction, you have two choices for review questions: here in the book or the exam questions on the CD-ROM. The answers to these questions appear in Appendix A.

For more practice with exam format questions, use the exam engine on the CD-ROM.

1. What type of WAN technology provides a dedicated connection from the service provider?

   a. Circuit-switched data connection

   b. Leased lines

   c. Packet-switched

   d. Cell-switched

2. What type of topology suffers from a single point of failure?

   a. Hub-and-spoke topology

   b. Full-mesh topology

   c. Partial-mesh topology

   d. None of the above

3. What kind of topology requires that each site be connected to every other site in the cloud?

   a. Hub-and-spoke

   b. Full-mesh

   c. Partial-mesh

   d. All of the above

4. Which WAN technology uses connections that can be brought up when needed, such as ISDN?

   a. Circuit-switched

   b. Leased lines

   c. Packet-switched

   d. Cell-switched

5. Which VPN application gives users connectivity over shared networks?

    a. Intranet VPN

    b. Extranet VPN

    c. Access VPN

    d. None of the above

6. True or false: Overlay VPNs are built using traditional WAN technologies such as Frame Relay and ATM.

7. The service provider plays an active role in enterprise routing with what kind of VPNs?

    a. VPDNs

    b. Peer-to-peer

    c. L2TP

    d. L2F

8. Which backup option provides an additional circuit for use if needed?

    a. Secondary WAN link

    b. Shadow PVC

    c. Dial backup

    d. Load sharing

9. Which WAN backup option uses load sharing in addition to providing backup services?

    a. Dial backup

    b. Shadow PVC

    c. Secondary WAN link

    d. ISDN with DDR

10. True or false: Fast switching is enabled on WAN links that are faster than 56 kbps.

11. True or false: IPsec protects data during transport for WAN backup over the Internet.

12. What two methods are used to enable private networks over public networks?

    a. IPsec

    b. PKI

    c. GRE

    d. PSTN

13. What is not a factor for WAN architecture selection?

    a. Ease of management

    b. Ongoing expenses

    c. Spanning Tree inconsistencies

    d. High availability

14. Which Layer 3 tunneling technique enables basic IP VPNs without encryption?

    a. GRE

    b. IPsec

    c. PKI

    d. IKE

15. True or false: IPsec is optional with a Private WAN architecture.

16. What MAN/WAN architecture uses the Internet with site-to-site VPNs?

    a. Private WAN

    b. ISP Service

    c. SP MPLS/IP VPN

    d. Private WAN with a self-deployed MPLS

17. True or false: Hardware selection involves modularity of add-on hardware but not port densities.

18. True or false: Redundancy but not modularity are key considerations when you're selecting Enterprise Edge hardware.

19. True or false: The Cisco IOS software family IOS T is designed for the SP core.

20. True or false: The Cisco IOS software family IOS T is suited for large networks within the service provider core.

21. What WAN/MAN architecture is usually reserved for very large enterprises that are willing to make substantial investments in equipment and training?

    a. Private WAN

    b. Private WAN with self-deployed MPLS

    c. ISP Service

    d. SP MPLS/IP VPN

22. What entry-level IOS supports IP data?

23. True or false: The premium IOS package is Advanced Enterprise Services.

24. What IOS package supports converged voice and data?

    a. IP Base

    b. Advanced Security

    c. Enterprise Base

    d. IP Voice

25. True or false: The 2970, 3560, and 3750 switches provide low-end to midrange LAN switching for enterprise access and distribution deployments.

26. True or false: Cisco SONA includes plug-in modules for EIGRP and static routing.

27. True or false: Common network components that make up the SONA framework for the branch include IP phones and PCs.

28. Match each Branch profile design with its description:

    a. Single-tier

    b. Dual-tier

    c. Multi-tier

    d. Teleworker

    i. Single-access router

    ii. Cable modem router

    iii. Pair of access routers

    iv. Dual distribution switches

This part covers the following CCDA exam topics (to view the CCDA exam overview, visit http://www.cisco.com/web/learning/le3/current_exams/ 640-863.html):

- Describe IPv4 and IPv6 Addressing
- Identify Routing Protocol Considerations in an Enterprise Network
- Design a Routing Protocol Deployment

Part III: The Internet Protocol and Routing Protocols

This chapter covers the following subjects:

- IPv4 header

- IPv4 addressing

- IP address subnets

- Address assignment and name resolution

CHAPTER 7

Internet Protocol Version 4

This chapter reviews Internet Protocol Version 4 (IPv4) address structures and IPv4 address types. IPv4 is the version of the protocol that the Internet has used since the initial allocation of IPv4 addresses in 1981. The size of the enterprise indicated the address class that was allocated. This chapter covers the IPv4 header to give you an understanding of IPv4 characteristics. The mid-1990s saw the implementation of classless interdomain routing (CIDR), network address translation (NAT), and private address space to prevent the apparent exhaustion of IPv4 address space. Companies implement variable-length subnet masks (VLSM) in their networks to provide intelligent address assignment and summarization. The CCDA needs to understand all these concepts to design IPv4 addressing for a network.

"Do I Know This Already?" Quiz

The purpose of the "Do I Know This Already?" quiz is to help you decide whether you need to read the entire chapter. If you intend to read the entire chapter, you do not necessarily need to answer these questions now.

The ten-question quiz, derived from the major sections in the "Foundation Topics" portion of the chapter, helps you determine how to spend your limited study time.

Table 7-1 outlines the major topics discussed in this chapter and the "Do I Know This Already?" quiz questions that correspond to those topics.

Table 7-1   *"Do I Know This Already?" Foundation Topics Section-to-Question Mapping*

Foundation Topics Section	Questions Covered in This Section
IPv4 Header	4, 10
IPv4 Addressing	1, 5, 9
IPv4 Address Subnets	2, 3, 7
Address Assignment and Name Resolution	6, 8

> **CAUTION** The goal of self-assessment is to gauge your mastery of the topics in this chapter. If you do not know the answer to a question or you are only partially sure, you should mark this question wrong for the purposes of the self-assessment. Giving yourself credit for an answer you correctly guess skews your self-assessment results and might provide you with a false sense of security.

1. Which of the following addresses is an IPv4 private address?

   a. 198.176.1.1

   b. 172.3116.1.1

   c. 191.168.1.1

   d. 224.130.1.1

2. How many IP addresses are available for hosts in the subnet 198.10.100.64/27?

   a. 14

   b. 30

   c. 62

   d. 126

3. What subnet mask should you use in loopback addresses?

   a. 255.255.255.252

   b. 255.255.255.254

   c. 255.255.255.0

   d. 255.255.255.255

4. In what IPv4 field are the precedence bits located?

   a. IP destination address

   b. IP protocol field

   c. Type-of-service field

   d. IP options field

5. What type of address is 225.10.1.1?

   a. Unicast

   b. Multicast

   c. Broadcast

   d. Anycast

6.   What protocol maps IPv4 addresses to MAC addresses?

   a. Domain Name System (DNS)

   b. Address Resolution Protocol (ARP)

   c. Neighbor discovery (ND)

   d. Static

7.   What is a recommended subnet mask to use in point-to-point WAN links?

   a. 255.255.255.0

   b. 255.255.255.255

   c. 255.255.255.224

   d. 255.255.255.252

8.   What is DHCP?

   a. Dynamic Host Control Protocol

   b. Dedicated Host Configuration Protocol

   c. Dynamic Host Configuration Protocol

   d. Predecessor to BOOTP

9.   What is the purpose of NAT?

   a. To translate source addresses to destination addresses

   b. To translate between private and public addresses

   c. To translate destination addresses to source addresses

   d. To translate class of service (CoS) to quality of service (QoS)

10.   The DS field of DSCP is capable of how many codepoints?

   a. 8

   b. 32

   c. 64

   d. 128

The answers to the "Do I Know This Already?" quiz appear in Appendix A, "Answers to Chapter 'Do I Know This Already?' Quizzes and Q&A Sections." The suggested choices for your next step are as follows:

■   **8 or less overall score**—Read the entire chapter. It includes the "Foundation Topics," "Foundation Summary," and "Q&A" sections.

■   **9 or 10 overall score**—If you want more review on these topics, skip to the "Foundation Summary" section, and then go to the "Q&A" section. Otherwise, move to the next chapter.

Foundation Topics

This chapter reviews IPv4 headers, address classes, and assignment methods.

IP is the network-layer protocol in TCP/IP. It contains logical addressing and information for routing packets throughout the internetwork. IP is described in RFC 791, which was prepared for the Defense Advanced Research Projects Agency (DARPA) in September 1981.

IP provides for the transmission of blocks of data, called datagrams or packets, from a source to a destination. The sources and destinations are identified by 32-bit IP addresses. The source and destination devices are workstations, servers, printers, and routers. The CCDA candidate must understand IPv4 logical address classes and assignment. The IPv4 protocol also provides for the fragmentation and reassembly of large packets for transport over networks with small maximum transmission units (MTU). The CCDA candidate must have a good understanding of this packet fragmentation and reassembly.

Appendix B, "The OSI Reference Model, TCP/IP Architecture, and Numeric Conversion," provides an overview of the TCP/IP architecture and how it compares with the OSI model. It also reviews binary numbers and numeric conversion (to decimal), which is a skill needed to understand IP addresses and subnetting.

IPv4 Header

The best way to understand IPv4 is to know the IPv4 header and all its fields. Segments from TCP or the User Datagram Protocol (UDP) are passed on to IP for processing. The IP header is appended to the TCP or UDP segment. The TCP or UDP segment then becomes the IP data. The IPv4 header is 20 bytes in length when it uses no optional fields. The IP header includes the addresses of the sending host and destination host. It also includes the upper-layer protocol, a field for prioritization, and a field for fragmentation. Figure 7-1 shows the IP header format.

Figure 7-1 *IP Header*

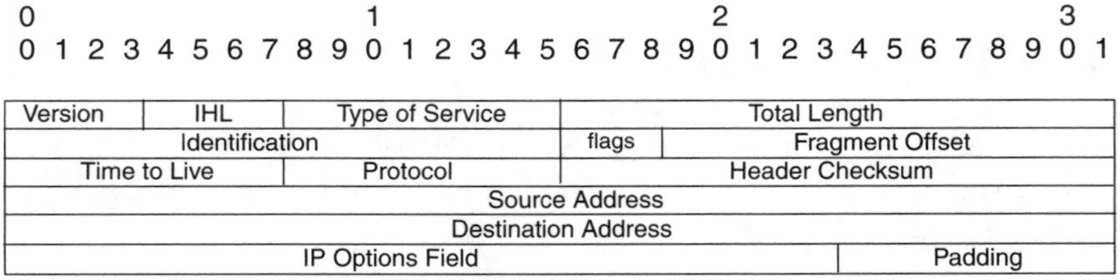

0										1										2										3	
0	1	2	3	4	5	6	7	8	9	0	1	2	3	4	5	6	7	8	9	0	1	2	3	4	5	6	7	8	9	0	1

Version	IHL	Type of Service		Total Length	
Identification			flags	Fragment Offset	
Time to Live		Protocol		Header Checksum	
Source Address					
Destination Address					
IP Options Field				Padding	

The following is a description of each field in the IP header:

- **Version**—This field is 4 bits in length. It indicates the IP header's format, based on the version number. Version 4 is the current version; therefore, this field is set to 0100 (4 in binary) for IPv4 packets. This field is set to 0110 (6 in binary) in IPv6 networks.

- **IHL**—Internet header length. This field is 4 bits in length. It indicates the length of the header in 32-bit words (4 bytes) so that the beginning of the data can be found in the IP header. The minimum value for a valid header (five 32-bit words) is 5 (0101).

- **ToS**—Type of Service. This field is 8 bits in length. Quality of Service (QoS) parameters such as IP precedence or DSCP are found in this field. These are explained further in this chapter.

- **Total length**—This field is 16 bits in length. It represents the length of the datagram or packet in bytes, including the header and data. The maximum length of an IP packet can be $2^{16} - 1 =$ 65,535 bytes. Routers use this field to determine whether fragmentation is necessary by comparing the total length with the outgoing MTU.

- **Identification**—This field is 16 bits in length. It identifies fragments for reassembly.

- **Flags**—This field is 3 bits in length. It indicates whether the packet can be fragmented and whether more fragments follow. Bit 0 is reserved and set to 0. Bit 1 indicates May Fragment (0) or Do Not Fragment (1). Bit 2 indicates Last Fragment (0) or More Fragments to follow (1).

- **Fragment offset**—This field is 13 bits in length. It indicates (in bytes) where in the packet this fragment belongs. The first fragment has an offset of 0.

- **Time to live**—This field is 8 bits in length. It indicates the maximum time the packet is to remain on the network. Each router decrements this field by 1 for loop avoidance. If this field is 0, the packet must be discarded. This scheme permits routers to discard undeliverable packets.

- **Protocol**—This field is 8 bits in length. It indicates the upper-layer protocol. The Internet Assigned Numbers Authority (IANA) is responsible for assigning IP protocol values. Table 7-2 shows some key protocol numbers. A full list can be found at http://www.iana.org/ assignments/protocol-numbers.

Table 7-2 *IP Protocol Numbers*

Protocol Number	Protocol
1	Internet Control Message Protocol (ICMP)
2	Internet Group Management Protocol (IGMP)
6	Transmission Control Protocol (TCP)
17	User Datagram Protocol (UDP)
88	Enhanced IGRP (EIGRP)
89	Open Shortest Path First (OSPF)
103	Protocol-Independent Multicast (PIM)

- **Header checksum**—This field is 16 bits in length. The checksum does not include the data portion of the packet in the calculation. The checksum is recomputed and verified at each point the IP header is processed.

- **Source address**—This field is 32 bits in length. It is the sender's IP address.

- **Destination address**—This field is 32 bits in length. It is the receiver's IP address.

- **IP options**—This field is variable in length. The options provide for control functions that are useful in some situations but unnecessary for the most common communications. Specific options are security, loose source routing, strict source routing, record route, and timestamp.

- **Padding**—This field is variable in length. It ensures that the IP header ends on a 32-bit boundary.

Table 7-3 summarizes the fields of the IP header.

Table 7-3   *IPv4 Header Fields*

Field	Length	Description
Version	4 bits	Indicates the IP header's format, based on the version number. Set to 0100 for IPv4.
IHL	4 bits	Length of the header in 32-bit words.
ToS	8 bits	QoS parameters.
Total length	16 bits	Length of the packet in bytes, including header and data.
Identification	16 bits	Identifies a fragment.
Flags	3 bits	Indicates whether a packet is fragmented and whether more fragments follow.
Fragment offset	13 bits	Location of the fragment in the total packet.
Time to live	8 bits	Decremented by 1 by each router. When this is 0, the router discards the packet.
Protocol	8 bits	Indicates the upper-layer protocol.
Header checksum	16 bits	Checksum of the IP header; does not include the data portion.
Source address	32 bits	IP address of the sending host.
Destination address	32 bits	IP address of the destination host.
IP options	Variable	Options for security, loose source routing, record route, and timestamp.
Padding	Variable	Added to ensure that the header ends in a 32-bit boundary.

ToS

The ToS field of the IP header is used to specify QoS parameters. Routers and layer 3 switches look at the ToS field to apply policies, such as priority, to IP packets based on the settings. The ToS field has undergone several definitions since RFC 791.

Figure 7-2 shows the several formats of the ToS service field based on the evolution of RFCs 791 (1981), 1349 (1992), 2474 (1998), and 3168 (2001). The following paragraphs describe this evolution.

Figure 7-2 *Evolution of the IPv4 ToS Field*

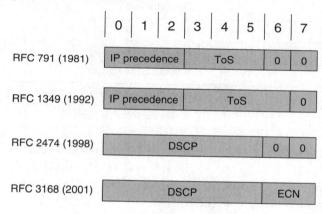

The first 3 (leftmost) bits are the IP precedence bits. These bits define values that are used by QoS methods. The precedence bits especially help in marking packets to give them differentiated treatment with different priorities. For example, Voice over IP (VoIP) packets can get preferential treatment over regular data packets. RFC 791 describes the precedence bits as shown in Table 7-4.

Table 7-4 *IP Precedence Bit Values*

Decimal	Binary	Description
0	000	Routine
1	001	Priority
2	010	Immediate
3	011	Flash
4	100	Flash override
5	101	Critical
6	110	Internetwork control
7	111	Network control

All default traffic is set with 000 in the precedence bits. Voice traffic is usually set to 101 (critical) to give it priority over normal traffic. Applications such as FTP are assigned a normal priority because it tolerates network latency and packet loss. Packet retransmissions are typically acceptable for normal traffic.

RFC 1349 redefined Bits 3 and 6 (expanding for ToS bits) to reflect a desired type of service optimization. Table 7-5 shows the ToS field values that indicate service parameters to use for IP packets.

Table 7-5 *ToS Field Values*

ToS Bits 3 to 6	Description
0000	Normal service
1000	Minimize delay
0100	Maximize throughput
0010	Maximize reliability
0001	Minimize monetary cost

In 1998, RFC 2474 redefined the ToS octet as the Differentiated Services (DS) field and further specified bits 0 through 5 as the Differentiated Services Codepoint (DSCP) to support differentiated services. RFC 3168 (2001) provides updates to RFC 2474 with the specification on an Explicit Congestion Notification (ECN) field.

The DS field takes the format shown in Figure 7-2. The DS field provides more granular levels of packet classification by using 6 bits for packet marking. DS has $2^6 = 64$ levels of classification, which is significantly higher than the eight levels of the IP precedence bits. These 64 levels are called codepoints, and they have been defined to be backward-compatible with IP precedence values. The network designer uses DSCP to give priority to IP packets using Cisco routers. Routers should be configured to map these codepoints to per-hop behaviors (PHB) with queuing or other bandwidth-management techniques. Table 7-6 compares DSCP and IP precedence values used to assign priority and apply policies to IP packets.

Table 7-6 *DSCP and IP Precedence Values*

IP Precedence			DSCP		
Service Type	Decimal	Binary	Class	Decimal	Binary
Routine	0	000	Best effort	0	000 to 000
Priority	1	001	Assured Forwarding (AF) Class 1	8	001 to 000
Immediate	2	010	AF Class 2	16	010 to 000

Table 7-6 *DSCP and IP Precedence Values (Continued)*

IP Precedence			DSCP		
Service Type	Decimal	Binary	Class	Decimal	Binary
Flash	3	011	AF Class 3	24	011 to 000
Flash override	4	100	AF Class 4	32	100 to 000
Critical	5	101	Express Forwarding (EF)	40	101 to 000
Internetwork control	6	110	Control	48	110 to 000
Network control	7	111	Control	56	111 to 000

RFC 2597 defines recommended values for AF codepoints with low, medium, and high packet drop precedence. Table 7-7 shows the recommended AF codepoint values.

Table 7-7 *DSCP AF Packet Drop Precedence Values*

Precedence	AF Class 1	AF Class 2	AF Class 3	AF Class 4
Low drop precedence	001010	010010	011010	100010
Medium drop precedence	001100	010100	011100	100100
High drop precedence	001110	010110	011110	100110

IPv4 Fragmentation

One of the key characteristics of IPv4 is fragmentation and reassembly. Although the maximum length of an IP packet is 65,535 bytes, most of the common lower-layer protocols do not support such large MTUs. For example, the MTU for Ethernet is approximately 1518 bytes. When the IP layer receives a packet to send, it first queries the outgoing interface to get its MTU. If the packet's size is greater than the interface's MTU, the layer fragments the packet.

When a packet is fragmented, it is not reassembled until it reaches the destination IP layer. The destination IP layer performs the reassembly. Any router in the path can fragment a packet, and any router in the path can fragment a fragmented packet again. Each fragmented packet receives its own IP header and is routed independently from other packets. Routers and layer 3 switches in the path do not reassemble the fragments. The destination host performs the reassembly and places the fragments in the correct order by looking at the identification and fragment offset fields.

If one or more fragments are lost, the entire packet must be retransmitted. Retransmission is the responsibility of the higher-layer protocol (such as TCP). Also, you can set the Flags field in the

IP header to "Do Not Fragment" the packet. If the field indicates Do Not Fragment, the packet is discarded if the outgoing MTU is smaller than the packet.

IPv4 Addressing

This section covers the IPv4 address classes, private addressing, and NAT. The IPv4 address space was initially divided into five classes. Each IP address class is identified by the initial bits of the address. Classes A, B, and C are unicast IP addresses, meaning that the destination is a single host. IP Class D addresses are multicast addresses, which are sent to multiple hosts. IP Class E addresses are reserved. Private addresses are selected address ranges that are reserved for use by companies in their private networks. These private addresses are not routed in the Internet. NAT translates between private and public addresses.

An IP addresses is a unique logical number to a network device or interface. An IP address is 32 bits in length. To make the number easier to read, the dotted-decimal format is used. The bits are combined into four 8-bit groups, each converted into decimal numbers—for example, 10.1.1.1. If you are not familiar with binary numbers, Appendix B contains a review of binary and hexadecimal number manipulation.

The following example shows an IP address in binary and decimal formats:

Binary IP address: 01101110 00110010 11110010 00001010
Convert each byte into decimal.

For the first octet:
01101110
0+64+32+0+8+4+2+0 = 110
01101110 = 110

For the second octet:
00110010
0+0+32+16+0+0+2+0 = 50
00110010 = 50

For the third octet:
11110010
128+64+32+16+0+0+2+0 = 242
11110010 = 242

For the fourth octet:
00001010
0+0+0+0+8+0+2+0 = 10
00001010 = 10

The IP address is 110.50.242.10.

IPv4 Address Classes

IPv4 addresses have five classes—A, B, C, D, and E. In classful addressing, the most significant bits of the first byte determine the address class of the IP address. Table 7-8 shows the high-order bits of each IP address class.

Table 7-8   *High-Order Bits of IPv4 Address Classes*

Address Class	High-Order Bits*
A	0xxxxxxx
B	10xxxxxx
C	110xxxxx
D	1110xxxx
E	1111xxxx

*x can be either 1 or 0, regardless of the address class.

Again, the IPv4 Class A, B, and C addresses are unicast addresses. Unicast addresses represent a single destination. Class D is for multicast addresses. Packets sent to a multicast address are sent to a group of hosts. Class E addresses are reserved for experimental use. IANA allocates the IPv4 address space. IANA delegates regional assignments to Regional Internet Registries (RIR). The five RIRs are

- ARIN (American Registry for Internet Numbers)

- RIPE NCC (Reseaux IP Europeens Network Control Center)

- APNIC (Asia Pacific Network Information Center)

- LACNIC (Latin America and Caribbean Network Information Center)

- AfriNIC (African Network Information Centre)

Updates to the IPv4 address space can be found at http://www.iana.org/assignments/ipv4-address-space.

The following sections discuss each of these classes in detail.

Class A Addresses

Class A addresses range from 0 (00000000) to 127 (01111111) in the first byte. Network numbers available for assignment to organizations are from 1.0.0.0 to 126.0.0.0. Networks 0 and 127 are reserved. For example, 127.0.0.1 is reserved for localhost or host loopback. A packet sent to a localhost address is sent to the local machine.

By default, for Class A addresses, the first byte is the network number, and the three remaining bytes are the host number. The format is *N.H.H.H*, where *N* is the network part and *H* is the host part. With 24 bits available, there are $2^{24} - 2 = 16,777,214$ IP addresses for host assignment per Class A network. We subtract two for the network number (all 0s) and broadcast address (all 1s). A network with this many hosts will surely not work with so many hosts attempting to broadcast on the network. This section discusses subnetting later as a method of defining smaller networks within a larger network address.

Class B Addresses

Class B addresses range from 128 (10000000) to 191 (10111111) in the first byte. Network numbers assigned to companies or other organizations are from 128.0.0.0 to 191.255.0.0. This section discusses the 16 networks reserved for private use later.

By default, for Class B addresses, the first two bytes are the network number, and the remaining two bytes are the host number. The format is *N.N.H.H*. With 16 bits available, there are $2^{16} - 2 = 65,534$ IP addresses for host assignment per Class B network. As with Class A addresses, having a segment with more than 65,000 hosts broadcasting will surely not work; you resolve this issue with subnetting.

Class C Addresses

Class C addresses range from 192 (11000000) to 223 (11011111) in the first byte. Network numbers assigned to companies are from 192.0.0.0 to 223.255.255.0. The format is *N.N.N.H*. With 8 bits available, there are $2^8 - 2 = 254$ IP addresses for host assignment per Class C network. $H = 0$ is the network number; $H = 255$ is the broadcast address.

Class D Addresses

Class D addresses range from 224 (11100000) to 239 (11101111) in the first byte. Network numbers assigned to multicast groups range from 224.0.0.1 to 239.255.255.255. These addresses do not have a host or network part. Some multicast addresses are already assigned; for example, 224.0.0.10 is used by routers running EIGRP. A full list of assigned multicast addresses can be found at http://www.iana.org/assignments/multicast-addresses.

Class E Addresses

Class E addresses range from 240 (11110000) to 254 (11111110) in the first byte. These addresses are reserved for experimental networks. Network 255 is reserved for the broadcast address, such as 255.255.255.255. Table 7-9 summarizes the IPv4 address classes. Again, each address class can be uniquely identified in binary by the high-order bits.

Table 7-9 *IPv4 Address Classes*

Address Class	High-Order Bits	Network Numbers
A	0xxxxxxx	1.0.0.0 to 126.0.0.0*
B	10xxxxxx	128.0.0.0 to 191.255.0.0
C	110xxxxx	192.0.0.0 to 223.255.255.0
D	1110xxxx	224.0.0.1 to 239.255.255.255
E	1111xxxx	240.0.0.0 to 254.255.255.255

*Networks 0.0.0.0 and 127.0.0.0 are reserved as special-use addresses.

IPv4 Private Addresses

Some network numbers within the IPv4 address space are reserved for private use. These numbers are not routed on the Internet. Many organizations today use private addresses in their internal networks with NAT to access the Internet. (NAT is covered later in this chapter.) Private addresses are explained in RFC 1918, *Address Allocation for Private Internets*, published in 1996. Private addresses were one of the first steps dealing with the concern that the globally unique IPv4 address space would become exhausted. The availability of private addresses combined with NAT reduces the need for organizations to carefully define subnets to minimize the waste of assigned, public, global IP addresses.

The IP network address space reserved for private internets is 10/8, 172.16/12, and 192.168/16. It includes one Class A network, 16 Class B networks, and 256 Class C networks. Table 7-10 summarizes private address space. Large organizations can use network 10.0.0.0/8 to assign address space throughout the enterprise. Midsize organizations can use one of the Class B private networks 172.16.0.0/16 through 172.31.0.0/16 for IP addresses. The smaller Class C addresses, which begin with 192.168, support only up to 254 hosts each.

Table 7-10 *IPv4 Private Address Space*

Class Type	Start Address	End Address
Class A	10.0.0.0	10.255.255.255
Class B	172.16.0.0	172.31.255.255
Class C	192.168.0.0	192.168.255.255

NAT

NAT devices convert internal IP address space into globally unique IP addresses. NAT was originally specified by RFC 1631; the current specification is RFC 3022. Companies use NAT to translate internal private addresses to public addresses.

The translation can be from many private addresses to a single public address or from many private addresses to a range of public addresses. When NAT performs many-to-one, the process is called port address translation (PAT) because different port numbers identify translations.

As shown in Figure 7-3, the source addresses for outgoing IP packets are converted to globally unique IP addresses. The conversion can be configured statically, or it can dynamically use a global pool of addresses.

Figure 7-3 *Network Address Translation*

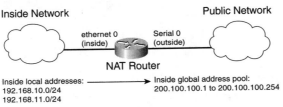

NAT has several forms:

- **Static NAT**—Maps an unregistered IP address to a registered IP address; it is configured manually.

- **Dynamic NAT**—Dynamically maps an unregistered IP address to a registered IP address from a pool (group) of registered addresses. The two subsets of dynamic NAT are overloading and overlapping:

    - **Overloading**—Maps multiple unregistered IP addresses to a single registered IP address by using different ports. This is also known as PAT, single-address NAT, or port-level multiplexed NAT.

    - **Overlapping**—Maps registered internal IP addresses to outside registered IP addresses. It can also map external addresses to internal registered addresses.

When designing for NAT, you should understand the following terminology:

- **Stub domain**—The internal network that might be using private IP addresses.

- **Public network**—Outside the stub domain, it resides in the Internet. Addresses in the public network can be reached from the Internet.

- **Inside local address**—The real IP address of the device that resides in the internal network. This address is used in the stub domain.

- **Inside global address**—The translated IP address of the device that resides in the internal network. This address is used in the public network.

- **Outside global address**—The real IP address of a device that resides in the Internet, outside the stub domain.

- **Outside local address**—The translated IP address of the device that resides in the Internet. This address is used inside the stub domain.

Figure 7-4 illustrates the terms described in the list. The real IP address of the host in the stub network is 192.168.10.100; it is the inside local address. The NAT router translates the inside local address into the inside global address (200.100.10.100). Hosts located in the Internet have their real IP address (outside global address) translated; in the example, 30.100.2.50 is translated into the outside local address of 192.168.100.50.

Figure 7-4 *Terminology Example*

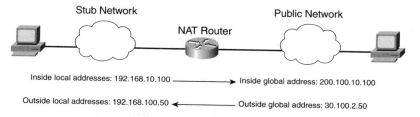

IPv4 Address Subnets

Subnetting plays an important part in IPv4 addressing. The subnet mask helps determine the network, subnetwork, and host part of an IP address. The network architect uses subnetting to manipulate the default mask to create subnetworks for LAN and WAN segments. These subnetworks provide enough addresses for LANs of different sizes. Point-to-point WAN links usually get a subnet mask that allows for only two hosts because only two routers are present in the point-to-point WAN link. You should become familiar with determining subnetwork numbers, broadcast addresses, and host address ranges given an IP address and mask.

Subnet masks are used for Class A, B, and C addresses only. Multicast addresses do not use subnet masks. A subnet mask is a 32-bit number in which bits are set to 1 to establish the network portion of the address, and a 0 is the host part of the address. The mask's bits set to 1 are contiguous on the left portion of the mask; the bits set to 0 are contiguous on the right portion of the mask. Table 7-11 shows the default masks for Class A, B, and C addresses. This section addresses various ways to represent IP subnet masks. Understanding these ways is significant because the representation of a network and its mask can appear differently in Cisco documentation or on the command-line interface.

Table 7-11 *IPv4 Default Network Address Masks*

Class	Binary Mask	Dotted-Decimal Mask
A	11111111 00000000 00000000 00000000	255.0.0.0
B	11111111 11111111 00000000 00000000	255.255.0.0
C	11111111 11111111 11111111 00000000	255.255.255.0

Mask Nomenclature

There are several ways to represent IP subnet masks. The mask can be binary, hexadecimal, dotted-decimal, or a prefix "bit mask." Historically, the most common representation was the dotted-decimal format (255.255.255.0). The prefix bit mask format is now more popular. This format represents the mask by using a slash followed by the number of leading address bits that must be set to 1 for the mask. For example, 255.255.0.0 is represented as /16. Table 7-12 shows most of the mask representations. The /30 mask is common for WAN point-to-point links, and /32 is used for router loopback addresses.

Table 7-12 *Subnet Masks*

Dotted Decimal	Bit Mask	Hexadecimal
255.0.0.0	/8	FF000000
255.192.0.0	/10	FFC00000
255.255.0.0	/16	FFFF0000
255.255.224.0	/19	FFFFE000
255.255.240.0	/20	FFFFF000
255.255.255.0	/24	FFFFFF00
255.255.255.128	/25	FFFFFF80
255.255.255.192	/26	FFFFFFC0
255.255.255.224	/27	FFFFFFE0
255.255.255.240	/28	FFFFFFF0
255.255.255.248	/29	FFFFFFF8
255.255.255.252	/30	FFFFFFFC
255.255.255.255	/32	FFFFFFFF

IP Address Subnet Design Example

This example shows subnetting for a small company. Say the company has 200 hosts and is assigned the Class C network of 195.10.1.0/24. The 200 hosts are in six different LANs.

You can subnet the Class C network using a mask of 255.255.255.224. Looking at the mask in binary (11111111 11111111 11111111 11100000), the first three bytes are the network part, the first 3 bits of the fourth byte determine the subnets, and the five remaining 0 bits are for host addressing.

Table 7-13 shows the subnetworks created with a mask of 255.255.255.224. Using this mask, 2^n subnets are created, where n is the number of bits taken from the host part for the subnet mask. This example uses 3 bits, so $2^3 = 8$ subnets. With Cisco routers, you can use the all-1s subnet (LAN 7) for a subnet. You cannot use the 0s subnet by default, but with Cisco routers, you can use it by configuring the **ip subnet-zero** command. The first column of the table lists the LAN. The second column shows the binary of the fourth byte of the IP address. The third column shows the subnet number, and the fourth and fifth columns show the first host and broadcast address of the subnet.

Table 7-13   *Subnets for Network 195.1.1.0*

LAN	Fourth Byte	Subnet Number	First Host	Broadcast Address
LAN 0	**000**00000	195.10.1.0	195.10.1.1	195.10.1.31
LAN 1	**001**00000	195.10.1.32	195.10.1.33	195.10.1.63
LAN 2	**010**00000	195.10.1.64	195.10.1.65	195.10.1.95
LAN 3	**011**00000	195.10.1.96	195.10.1.97	195.10.1.127
LAN 4	**100**00000	195.10.1.128	195.10.1.129	195.10.1.159
LAN 5	**101**00000	195.10.1.160	195.10.1.161	195.10.1.191
LAN 6	**110**00000	195.10.1.192	195.10.1.193	195.10.1.223
LAN 7	**111**00000	195.10.1.224	195.10.1.225	195.10.1.255

Use the formula $2^n - 2$ to calculate the number of hosts per subnet, where n is the number of bits for the host portion. The preceding example has 5 bits in the fourth byte for host addresses. With $n = 5$, $2^5 - 2 = 30$ hosts. For LAN 1, host addresses range from 195.10.1.33 to 195.10.1.62 (30 addresses). The broadcast address for the subnet is 195.10.1.63. Each LAN repeats this pattern with 30 hosts in each subnet.

The example uses a fixed-length subnet mask. The whole Class C network has the same subnet mask, 255.255.255.224. Routing protocols such as Routing Information Protocol version 1 (RIPv1) and Interior Gateway Routing Protocol (IGRP) can use only fixed-length subnet masks;

they do not support VLSMs, in which masks of different lengths identify subnets within the network. VLSMs are covered later in this chapter.

Determining the Network Portion of an IP Address

Given an address and mask, you can determine the classful network, the subnetwork, and the subnetwork's broadcast number. You do so with a logical AND operation between the IP address and subnet mask. You obtain the broadcast address by taking the subnet number and making the host portion all 1s. Table 7-14 shows the logical AND operation. Notice that the AND operation is similar to multiplying bit 1 and bit 2; if any 0 is present, the result is 0.

Table 7-14 *The AND Logical Operation*

Bit 1	Bit 2	AND
0	0	0
0	1	0
1	0	0
1	1	1

As an example, take the IP address 150.85.1.70 with a subnet mask of 255.255.255.224, as shown in Table 7-15. Notice the 3 bold bits in the subnet mask. These bits extend the default Class C prefix (/24) 3 bits to a mask of /27. As shown in Table 7-15, you perform an AND operation of the IP address with the subnet mask to obtain the subnetwork. You obtain the broadcast number by making all the host bits 1. As shown in bold, the subnet mask reaches 3 bits in the fourth octet. The subnetwork is identified by the five rightmost zeros in the fourth octet, and the broadcast is identified by all ones in the five rightmost bits.

Table 7-15 *Subnetwork of IP Address 150.85.1.70*

	Binary First, Second, and Third Octets	Binary Fourth Octet		Dotted-Decimal IP
IP Address	10010110 01010101 00000001	010	00110	150.85.1.70
Subnet Mask	11111111 11111111 11111111	**111**	00000	255.255.255.224
Subnetwork	10010110 01010101 00000001	010	**00000**	150.85.1.64
	Major network portion	Subnet	Host	
Broadcast Address	10010110 01010101 00000001	010	**11111**	150.85.1.95

VLSMs

VLSMs are used to divide a network into subnets of various sizes to prevent wasting IP addresses. If a Class C network uses 255.255.255.240 as a subnet mask, 16 subnets are available, each with 14 IP addresses. If a point-to-point link needs only two IP addresses, 12 IP addresses are wasted. This problem scales further with Class B and Class A address space. With VLSMs, small LANs can use /28 subnets with 14 hosts, and larger LANs can use /23 or /22 masks with 510 and 1022 hosts, respectively. Point-to-point networks use a /30 mask, which supports two hosts.

VLSM Address-Assignment Example

Take Class B network 130.20.0.0/16 as an example. Using a /20 mask produces 16 subnetworks. Table 7-16 shows the subnetworks. With the /20 subnet mask, the first 4 bits of the third byte determine the subnets.

Table 7-16 *Subnets with the /20 Mask*

Third Byte	Subnetwork
00000000	130.20.0.0/20
00010000	130.20.16.0/20
00100000	130.20.32.0/20
00110000	130.20.48.0/20
01000000	130.20.64.0/20
01010000	130.20.80.0/20
01100000	130.20.96.0/20
01110000	130.20.112.0/20
10000000	130.20.128.0/20
10010000	130.20.144.0/20
10100000	130.20.160.0/20
10110000	130.20.176.0/20
11000000	130.20.192.0/20
11010000	130.20.208.0/20
11100000	130.20.224.0/20
11110000	130.20.240.0/20

With fixed-length subnet masks, the network would support only 16 networks. Any LAN or WAN link would have to use a /20 subnet. This scenario is a waste of address space and therefore is inefficient. With VLSMs, you can further subnet the /20 subnets.

For example, take 130.20.64.0/20 and subdivide it to support LANs with about 500 hosts. A /23 mask has 9 bits for hosts, producing $2^9 - 2 = 510$ IP addresses for hosts. Table 7-17 shows the subnetworks for LANs within a specified subnet.

Table 7-17 *Subnetworks for 130.20.64.0/20*

Third Byte	Subnetwork
01000000	130.20.64.0/23
01000010	130.20.66.0/23
01000100	130.20.68.0/23
01000110	130.20.70.0/23
01001000	130.20.72.0/23
01001010	130.20.74.0/23
01001100	130.20.76.0/23
01001110	130.20.78.0/23

With VLSMs, you can further subdivide these subnetworks of subnetworks. Take subnetwork 130.20.76.0/23 and use it for two LANs that have fewer than 250 hosts. It produces subnetworks 130.20.76.0/24 and 130.20.77.0/24. Also, subdivide 130.20.78.0/23 for serial links. Because each point-to-point serial link needs only two IP addresses, use a /30 mask. Table 7-18 shows the subnetworks produced.

Table 7-18 *Serial-Link Subnetworks*

Third Byte	Fourth Byte	Subnetwork
01001110	00000000	130.20.78.0/30
01001110	00000100	130.20.78.4/30
01001110	00001000	130.20.78.8/30
01001110	00001100	130.20.78.12/30
. . .	. . .	. . .
01001111	11110100	130.20.79.244/30
01001111	11111000	130.20.79.248/30
01001111	11111100	130.20.79.252/30

Each /30 subnetwork includes the subnetwork number, two IP addresses, and a broadcast address. Table 7-19 shows the bits for 130.20.78.8/30.

Table 7-19   *Addresses Within Subnetwork 110.20.78.8/30*

Binary Address	IP Address	Function
10000010 00010100 01001110 00001000	130.20.78.8	Subnetwork
10000010 00010100 01001110 00001001	130.20.78.9	IP address 1
10000010 00010100 01001110 00001010	130.20.78.10	IP address 2
10000010 00010100 01001110 00001011	130.20.78.11	Broadcast address

Loopback Addresses

You can also reserve a subnet for router loopback addresses. Loopback addresses provide an always-up interface to use for router-management connectivity. The loopback address can also serve as the router ID for some routing protocols. The loopback address is a single IP address with a 32-bit mask. In the previous example, network 130.20.75.0/24 could provide 255 loopback addresses for network devices starting with 130.20.75.1/32 and ending with 130.20.75.255/32.

IP Telephony Networks

You should reserve separate subnets for LANs using IP phones. IP phones are normally placed in an auxiliary VLAN that is in a logical segment separate from that of the user workstations. Separating voice and data on different subnets or VLANs also aids in providing QoS for voice traffic in regards to classifying, queuing, and buffering. This design rule also facilitates troubleshooting.

Table 7-20 shows an example of allocating IP addresses for a small network. Notice that separate VLANs are used for the VoIP devices.

Table 7-20   *IP Address Allocation for VoIP Networks*

Building Floor/Function	VLAN Number	IP Subnet
First-floor data	VLAN 11	172.16.1.0/24
Second-floor data	VLAN 12	172.16.2.0/24
Third-floor data	VLAN 13	172.16.3.0/24
First-floor VoIP	VLAN 14	172.16.4.0/24
Second-floor VoIP	VLAN 15	172.16.5.0/24
Third-floor VoIP	VLAN 16	172.16.6.0/24

CIDR and Summarization

CIDR permits the address aggregation of classful networks. It does so by using the common bits to join networks. The network addresses need to be contiguous and have a common bit boundary.

With CIDR, ISPs assign groups of Class C networks to enterprise customers. This arrangement eliminates the problem of assigning too large of a network (Class B) or assigning multiple Class C networks to a customer and having to maintain an entry for each Class C network in the routing tables. It reduces the size of the Internet routing tables and allows for more stable routing topology because the routers do not have the recomputed routing table when more specific routes cycle up and down.

You can summarize four contiguous Class C networks at the /22 bit level. For example, networks 200.1.100.0, 200.1.101.0, 200.1.102.0, and 200.1.103.0 share common bits, as shown in Table 7-21. The resulting network is 200.1.100.0/22, which you can use for a 1000-node network.

Table 7-21 *Common Bits Within Class C Networks*

Binary Address	IP Address
11001000 00000001 01100100 00000000	200.1.100.0
11001000 00000001 01100101 00000000	200.1.101.0
11001000 00000001 01100110 00000000	200.1.102.0
11001000 00000001 01100111 00000000	200.1.103.0

It is important for an Internet network designer to assign IP networks in a manner that permits summarization. It is preferred that a neighboring router receive one summarized route, rather than 8, 16, 32, or more routes, depending on the level of summarization. This setup reduces the size of the routing tables in the network.

For route summarization to work, the multiple IP addresses must share the same leftmost bits, and routers must base their routing decisions on the IP address and prefix length.

Figure 7-5 shows an example of route summarization. All the edge routers send network information to their upstream routers. Router E summarizes its two LAN networks by sending 192.168.16.0/23 to Router A. Router F summarizes its two LAN networks by sending 192.168.18.0/23. Router B summarizes the networks it receives from Routers C and D. Routers B, E, and F send their routes to Router A. Router A sends a single route (192.168.16.0/21) to its upstream router, instead of sending eight routes. This process reduces the number of networks that upstream routers need to include in routing updates.

Figure 7-5 *Route Summarization*

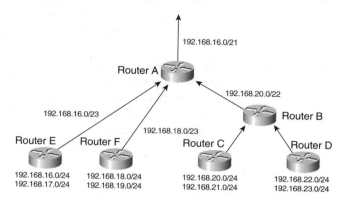

Notice in Table 7-22 that all the Class C networks share a bit boundary with 21 common bits. The networks are different on the 22nd bit and thus cannot be summarized beyond the 21st bit. All these networks are summarized with 192.168.16.0/21.

Table 7-22 *Summarization of Networks*

Binary Address	IP Network
11000000 10101000 00010000 00000000	192.168.16.0
11000000 10101000 00010001 00000000	192.168.17.0
11000000 10101000 00010010 00000000	192.168.18.0
11000000 10101000 00010011 00000000	192.168.19.0
11000000 10101000 00010100 00000000	192.168.20.0
11000000 10101000 00010101 00000000	192.168.21.0
11000000 10101000 00010110 00000000	192.168.22.0
11000000 10101000 00010111 00000000	192.168.23.0

Address Assignment and Name Resolution

IP addresses, subnet masks, default gateways, and DNS servers can be assigned statically or dynamically. You should statically assign most shared network systems, such as routers and servers, but dynamically assign most client systems. This section covers the protocols you use to dynamically assign IP address parameters to a host, which are the Bootstrap Protocol (BOOTP) and the Dynamic Host Configuration Protocol (DHCP). This section also covers DNS and ARP, which are two significant protocols in IP networks. DNS maps domain names to IP addresses, and ARP resolves IP addresses to MAC addresses. These protocols are important in TCP/IP networks because they simplify the methods of address assignment and resolution.

Static and Dynamic IP Address Assignment

Assign the IP addresses of routers, switches, printers, and servers statically. You need to manage and monitor these systems, so you must access them via a stable IP address.

You should dynamically assign end-client workstations to reduce the configuration tasks required to connect these systems to the network. When you assign client workstation characteristics dynamically, the system automatically learns which network segment it is assigned to and how to reach its default gateway as the network is discovered. One of the first methods used to dynamically assign IP addresses was BOOTP. The current method to assign IP addresses is DHCP.

BOOTP

The basic BOOTP was first defined in RFC 951. It has been updated by RFC 1497 and RFC 1542. It is a protocol that allows a booting host to configure itself by dynamically obtaining its IP address, IP gateway, and other information from a remote server. You can use a single server to centrally manage numerous network hosts without having to configure each host independently.

BOOTP is an application-layer protocol that uses UDP/IP for transport. The BOOTP server port is UDP Port 67. The client port is UDP Port 68. Clients send BOOTP requests to the BOOTP server, and the server responds to UDP Port 68 to send messages to the client. The destination IP of the BOOTP requests uses the all-hosts address (255.255.255.255), which the router does not forward. If the BOOTP server is one or more router hops from the subnet, you must configure the local default gateway router to forward the BOOTP requests.

BOOTP requires that you build a MAC-address-to-IP-address table on the server. You must obtain every device's MAC address, which is a time-consuming effort. BOOTP has been replaced by the more sophisticated DHCP.

DHCP

DHCP provides a way to dynamically configure hosts on the network. Based on BOOTP, it is defined in RFC 2131 and adds the capability of reusing network addresses and additional configuration options. DHCP improves on BOOTP by using a "lease" for IP addresses and providing the client with all the IP configuration parameters needed to operate in the network.

DHCP servers allocate network addresses and deliver configuration parameters dynamically to hosts. With DHCP, the computer can obtain its configuration information—IP address, subnet mask, IP default gateway, DNS servers, WINS servers, and so on—when needed. DHCP also includes other optional parameters that you can assign to clients. The configuration information is managed centrally on a DHCP server.

Routers act as relay agents by passing DHCP messages between DHCP clients and servers. Because DHCP is an extension of BOOTP, it uses the message format defined in RFC 951 for BOOTP. It uses the same ports as BOOTP: DHCP servers use UDP Port 67, and DHCP clients use UDP Port 68. Because of these similarities, the configuration to support DHCP in the routers is the same described for BOOTP.

DHCP supports permanent allocation, in which the DHCP server assigns an IP address to the client and the IP address is never reallocated to other clients. With a lease, DHCP can also assign IP addresses for a limited period of time. This dynamic-allocation mechanism can reuse the IP address after the lease expires.

An IP address is assigned as follows:

1. The client sends a **DHCPDISCOVER** message to the local network using a 255.255.255.255 broadcast.

2. BOOTP relay agents (routers) can forward the **DHCPDISCOVER** message to the DHCP server in another subnet.

3. The server sends a **DHCPOFFER** message to respond to the client, offering IP address, lease expiration, and other DHCP option information.

    Other DHCP messages include

    DHCPREQUEST—The client can request additional options or an extension on its lease of an IP address.

    DHCPRELEASE—The client relinquishes the IP address and cancels the remaining lease.

4. If the server is out of addresses or it determines that the client request is invalid, it sends a **DHCPNAK** message to the client.

DNS

DNS servers return destination IP addresses given a domain name. DNS is a distributed database. Separate, independent organizations administer their assigned domain name spaces and can break their domains into a number of subdomains. For example, given www.cisco.com, DNS returns the IP address 198.133.219.25. DNS was first specified by RFCs 882 and 883. The current specifications are specified in RFCs 1034 and 1035.

DNS was implemented to overcome the limitations of managing a single text-host table. Imagine creating and maintaining text files with the names and IP addresses of all the hosts in the Internet! DNS scales hostname-to-IP-address translation by distributing responsibility for the domain name space. DNS follows a reversed tree structure for domain name space, as shown in Figure 7-6. IANA (http://www.iana.org) manages the tree's root.

Figure 7-6 *DNS Tree*

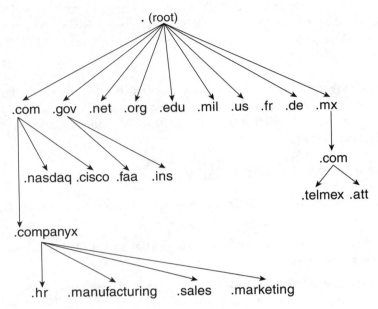

DNS uses TCP and UDP Port 53. UDP is the recommended transport protocol for DNS queries. TCP is the recommended protocol for zone transfers between DNS servers. A zone transfer occurs when you place a secondary server in the domain and transfer the DNS information from the primary DNS server to the secondary server. A DNS query searches for the IP address of an FQDN, such as www.cnn.com.

ARP

When a router needs to send an IP packet over an Ethernet network, it needs to find out what 48-bit MAC physical address to send the frame to. Given the destination IP, ARP obtains the destination MAC. The destination MAC can be a local host or the gateway router's MAC address if the destination IP is across the routed network. ARP is described in RFC 826. The local host maintains an ARP table with a list relating IP address to MAC address.

ARP operates by having the sender broadcast an ARP request. Figure 7-7 shows an example of an ARP request and reply. Suppose a router with the IP address 10.1.1.1 has a packet to send to 10.1.1.10 but does not have the destination MAC address in its ARP table. It broadcasts an ARP request to all hosts in a subnet. The ARP request contains the sender's IP and MAC address as well as the target IP address. All nodes in the broadcast domain receive the ARP request and process it. The device with the target IP address sends an ARP reply to the sender with its MAC address information; the ARP reply is a unicast message sent to 10.1.1.1. The sender now has the target MAC address in its ARP cache and sends the frame.

Figure 7-7 *ARP Request and Reply*

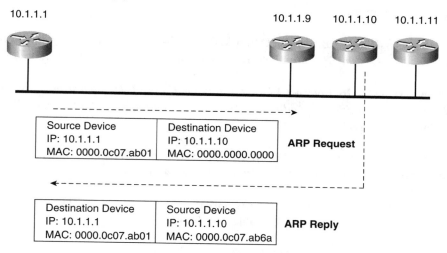

References and Recommended Readings

Almquist, P. RFC 1349, *Type of Service in the Internet Protocol Suite*. Available from http://www.ietf.org/rfc.

Croft, B. and J. Gilmore. RFC 951, *Bootstrap Protocol (BOOTP)*. Available from http://www.ietf.org/rfc.

Davie, B., A. Charny, J.C.R. Bennet, K. Benson, J.Y. Le Boudec, W. Courtney, S. Davari, V. Firoiu, and D. Stiliadis. RFC 3246, *An Expedited Forwarding PHB (Per-Hop Behavior)*. Available from http://www.ietf.org/rfc.

Droms, R. RFC 2131, *Dynamic Host Configuration Protocol*. Available from http://www.ietf.org/rfc.

Egevang, K. and P. Francis. RFC 1631, *The IP Network Address Translator (NAT)*. Available from http://www.ietf.org/rfc.

Heinanen, J., F. Baker, W. Weiss, and J. Wroclawski. RFC 2597, *Assured Forwarding PHB Group*. Available from http://www.ietf.org/rfc.

Information Sciences Institute. RFC 791, *Internet Protocol*. Available from http://www.ietf.org/rfc.

Mockapetris, P. RFC 1034, *Domain Names - Concepts and Facilities*. Available from http://www.ietf.org/rfc.

Mockapetris, P. RFC 1035, *Domain Names - Implementation and Specification*. Available from http://www.ietf.org/rfc.

Nichols, K., S. Blake, F. Baker, and D. Black. RFC 2474, *Definition of the Differentiated Services Field (DS Field) in the IPv4 and IPv6 Headers*. Available from http://www.ietf.org/rfc.

Plummer, D. RFC 826, *Ethernet Address Resolution Protocol: Or Converting Network Protocol Addresses to 48.bit Ethernet Address for Transmission on Ethernet Hardware*. Available from http://www.ietf.org/rfc.

Ramakrishnan, K., S. Floyd, and D. Black. RFC 3168, *The Addition of Explicit Congestion Notification (ECN) to IP*. Available from http://www.ietf.org/rfc.

Rekhter, Y., B. Moskowitz, D. Karrenberg, G.J. de Groot, and E. Lear. RFC 1918, *Address Allocation for Private Internets*. Available from http://www.ietf.org/rfc.

Srisuresh, P. and K. Egevang. RFC 3022, *Traditional IP Network Address Translator (Traditional NAT)*. Available from http://www.ietf.org/rfc.

Foundation Summary

The "Foundation Summary" section of each chapter lists the most important facts from the chapter. Although this section does not list every fact from the chapter that will be on the CCDA exam, a well-prepared CCDA candidate should at a minimum know all the details in each "Foundation Summary" before taking the exam.

This chapter covered the following topics that you will need to master for the CCDA exam:

- **IPv4 header**—Know each field of the IPv4 header.

- **IPv4 addressing**—Know IPv4 address classes, private addressing, and NAT.

- **IPv4 address subnets**—Know VLSMs with a design example.

- **Address assignment and resolution**—Know dynamic IP assignment and address-resolution protocols such as BOOTP, DHCP, DNS, and ARP.

Table 7-23 outlines the IPv4 address classes.

Table 7-23 *IPv4 Address Classes*

Address Class	High-Order Bits	Network Numbers
A	0*xxxxxxx*	1.0.0.0 to 126.0.0.0
B	10*xxxxxx*	128.0.0.0 to 191.255.0.0
C	110*xxxxx*	192.0.0.0 to 223.255.255.0
D	1110*xxxx*	224.0.0.0 to 239.255.255.255
E	1111*xxxx*	240.0.0.0 to 254.255.255.255

Table 7-24 summarizes the IPv4 private address space.

Table 7-24 *IPv4 Private Address Space*

Class Type	Start Address	End Address
Class A	10.0.0.0	10.255.255.255
Class B	172.16.0.0	172.31.255.255
Class C	192.168.0.0	192.168.255.255

Table 7-25 shows subnet mask representations.

Table 7-25 *Subnet Mask Representations*

Dotted Decimal	Prefix	Hexadecimal
255.0.0.0	/8	FF000000
255.128.0.0	/9	FFA00000
255.192.0.0	/10	FFC00000
255.224.0.0	/11	FFE00000
255.240.0.0	/12	FFF00000
255.248.0.0	/13	FFFA0000
255.252.0.0	/14	FFFC0000
255.254.0.0	/15	FFFE0000
255.255.0.0	/16	FFFF0000
255.255.128.0	/17	FFFFA000
255.255.192.0	/18	FFFFC000
255.255.224.0	/19	FFFFE000
255.255.240.0	/20	FFFFF000
255.255.248.0	/21	FFFFFA00
255.255.252.0	/22	FFFFFC00
255.255.254.0	/23	FFFFFE00
255.255.255.0	/24	FFFFFF00
255.255.128.0	/25	FFFFFFA0
255.255.192.0	/26	FFFFFFC0
255.255.255.224	/27	FFFFFFE0
255.255.255.240	/28	FFFFFFF0
255.255.255.248	/29	FFFFFFF8
255.255.255.252	/30	FFFFFFFC
255.255.255.254	/31	FFFFFFFE
255.255.255.255	/32	FFFFFFFF

The following list reviews the various IPv4 address types:

- **Unicast**—The IP address of an interface on a single host. It can be a source or destination address.

- **Multicast**—An IP address that reaches a group of hosts. It is only a destination address.

- **Broadcast**—An IP logical address that reaches all hosts in an IP subnet. It is only a destination address.

Table 7-26 summarizes the fields of the IP header.

Table 7-26 *IPv4 Header Fields*

Field	Length	Description
Version	4 bits	Indicates the IP header's format, based on the version number. Set to 0100 for IPv4.
IHL	4 bits	Length of the header in 32-bit words.
ToS	8 bits	QoS parameters.
Total length	16 bits	Length of the packet in bytes, including header and data.
Identification	16 bits	Identifies a fragment.
Flags	3 bits	Indicates whether a packet is fragmented and whether more fragments follow.
Fragment offset	13 bits	Location of the fragment in the total packet.
Time to live	8 bits	Decremented by 1 by each router. When this is 0, the router discards the packet.
Protocol	8 bits	Indicates the upper-layer protocol.
Header checksum	16 bits	Checksum of the IP header; does not include the data portion.
Source address	32 bits	IP address of the sending host.
Destination address	32 bits	IP address of the destination host.
IP options	Variable	Options for security, loose source routing, record route, and timestamp.
Padding	Variable	Added to ensure that the header ends in a 32-bit boundary.

Table 7-27 compares DSCP and IP precedence values used to assign priority and apply policies to IP packets.

Table 7-27 *DSCP and IP Precedence Values*

IP Precedence			DSCP		
Service Type	Decimal	Binary	Class	Decimal	Binary
Routine	0	000	Best effort	0	000 to 000
Priority	1	001	Assured Forwarding (AF) Class 1	8	001 to 000
Immediate	2	010	AF Class 2	16	010 to 000
Flash	3	011	AF Class 3	24	011 to 000
Flash override	4	100	AF Class 4	32	100 to 000
Critical	5	101	Express Forwarding (EF)	40	101 to 000
Internetwork control	6	110	Control	48	110 to 000
Network control	7	111	Control	56	111 to 000

Q&A

As mentioned in the Introduction, you have two choices for review questions: here in the book or the exam questions on the CD-ROM. The answers to these questions appear in Appendix A.

For more practice with exam format questions, use the exam engine on the CD-ROM.

1. List the RFC 1918 private address space.

2. What is the difference between VLSM and CIDR?

3. Fill in the blank: _____ maps FQDN to IP addresses.

4. True or false: You can use DHCP to specify the TFTP host's IP address to a client PC.

5. True or false: 255.255.255.248 and /28 are two representations of the same IP mask.

6. True or false: Upper-layer protocols are identified in the IP header's protocol field. TCP is protocol 6, and UDP is protocol 17.

7. Fill in the blank: Without any options, the IP header is _____ bytes in length.

8. The IP header's ToS field is redefined as the DS field. How many bits does DSCP use for packet classification, and how many levels of classification are possible?

9. True or false: NAT uses different IP addresses for translations. PAT uses different port numbers to identify translations.

10. True or false: The IP header's header checksum field performs the checksum of the IP header and data.

11. Calculate the subnet, the address range within the subnet, and the subnet broadcast of the address 172.56.5.245/22.

12. When packets are fragmented at the network layer, where are the fragments reassembled?

13. Which protocol can you use to configure a default gateway?

    a. ARP

    b. DHCP

    c. DNS

    d. RARP

14. How many host addresses are available with a Class B network with the default mask?

   a. 63,998

   b. 64,000

   c. 65,534

   d. 65,536

15. Which of the following is a dotted-decimal representation of a /26 prefix mask?

   a. 255.255.255.128

   b. 255.255.255.192

   c. 255.255.255.224

   d. 255.255.255.252

16. Which network and mask summarize both the 192.170.20.16/30 and 192.170.20.20/30 networks?

   a. 192.170.20.0/24

   b. 192.170.20.20/28

   c. 192.170.20.16/29

   d. 192.170.20.0/30

17. Which AF class is backward-compatible with IP precedence bits' flash traffic?

   a. AF2

   b. AF3

   c. AF4

   d. EF

18. Which of the following is true about fragmentation?

   a. Routers between source and destination hosts can fragment IPv4 packets.

   b. Only the first router in the network can fragment IPv4 packets.

   c. IPv4 packets cannot be fragmented.

   d. IPv4 packets are fragmented and reassembled at each link through the network.

19. A packet sent to a multicast address reaches what destination(s)?

   a. The nearest destination in a set of hosts.

   b. All destinations in a set of hosts.

   c. Broadcasts to all hosts.

   d. Reserved global destinations.

20.   What are three types of IPv4 addresses?

Answer the following questions based on the given scenario and figure.

Company VWX has the network shown in Figure 7-8. The main site has three LANs with 100, 29, and 60 hosts. The remote site has two LANs, each with 100 hosts. The network uses private addresses. The Internet service provider assigned the company the network 210.200.200.8/26.

Figure 7-8 *Scenario Diagram*

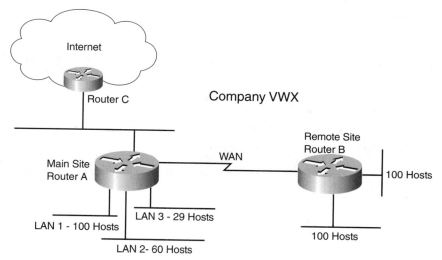

21.   The remote site uses the network prefix 192.168.10.0/24. What subnets and masks can you use for the LANs at the remote site and conserve address space?

   a.   192.168.10.64/26 and 192.168.10.192/26

   b.   192.168.10.0/25 and 192.168.10.128/25

   c.   192.168.10.32/28 and 192.168.10.64/28

   d.   192.168.10.0/30 and 192.168.10.128/30

22.   The main site uses the network prefix 192.168.15.0/24. What subnets and masks can you use to provide sufficient addresses for LANs at the main site and conserve address space?

   a.   192.168.15.0/25 for LAN 1, 192.168.15.128/26 for LAN 2, and 172.15.192.0/27 for LAN 3

   b.   192.168.15.0/27 for LAN 1, 192.168.15.128/26 for LAN 2, and 172.15.192.0/25 for LAN 3

     c. 192.168.15.0/100 for LAN 1, 192.168.15.128/60 for LAN 2, and 172.15.192.0/29 for LAN 3

     d. 192.168.15.0/26 for LAN 1, 192.168.15.128/26 for LAN 2, and 172.15.192.0/29 for LAN 3

23. Which network and mask would you use for the WAN link to save the most address space?

     a. 192.168.11.240/27

     b. 192.168.11.240/28

     c. 192.168.11.240/29

     d. 192.168.11.240/30

24. What networks does Router C announce to the Internet service provider's Internet router?

     a. 210.200.200.8/26

     b. 192.168.10.0/24 and 192.168.11.0/24

     c. 192.168.10.0/25 summary address

     d. 201.200.200.8/29 and 192.168.10.0/25

25. What technology does Router C use to convert private addresses to public addresses?

     a. DNS

     b. NAT

     c. ARP

     d. VLSM

26. What mechanism supports the ability to divide a given subnet into smaller subnets based on need?

     a. DNS

     b. NAT

     c. ARP

     d. VLSM

This chapter covers the following subjects:

- Introduction to IPv6

- IPv6 header

- IPv6 address representation

- IPv6 address types and address allocations

- IPv6 mechanisms

- IPv6 routing protocols

- IPv4 to IPv6 transition strategies and deployments

- IPv6 comparison with IPv4

Internet Protocol Version 6

This chapter reviews Internet Protocol Version 6 (IPv6) address structures, address assignments, representations, and mechanisms used to deploy IPv6. Expect plenty of questions about IPv6 on the exam. The CCDA must understand how an IPv6 address is represented and the different types of IPv6 addresses. This chapter also covers the benefits of IPv6 over IPv4 and compares the protocols.

As IPv6 matures, different deployment models will be used to implement the new protocol with existing IPv4 networks. This chapter covers these models at a high level. This chapter does not discuss the configuration of IPv6 because it is not a requirement for CCDA certification.

"Do I Know This Already?" Quiz

The purpose of the "Do I Know This Already?" quiz is to help you decide whether you need to read the entire chapter. If you intend to read the entire chapter, you do not necessarily need to answer these questions now.

The ten-question quiz, derived from the major sections in the "Foundation Topics" portion of the chapter, helps you determine how to spend your limited study time.

Table 8-1 outlines the major topics discussed in this chapter and the "Do I Know This Already?" quiz questions that correspond to those topics.

Table 8-1   *"Do I Know This Already?" Foundation Topics Section-to-Question Mapping*

Foundation Topics Section	Questions Covered in This Section
IPv6 Header	1, 2
IPv6 Address Representation	5, 8, 9
IPv6 Address Types and Address Allocations	3, 4, 7
IPv6 Mechanisms	10
IPv4 to IPv6 Transition Strategies and Deployments	6

> **CAUTION** The goal of self-assessment is to gauge your mastery of the topics in this chapter. If you do not know the answer to a question or you are only partially sure, you should mark this question wrong for the purposes of the self-assessment. Giving yourself credit for an answer you correctly guess skews your self-assessment results and might provide you with a false sense of security.

1. IPv6 uses how many more bits for addresses than IPv4?

   a. 32

   b. 64

   c. 96

   d. 128

2. What is the length of the IPv6 header?

   a. 20 bytes

   b. 30 bytes

   c. 40 bytes

   d. Same size as the IPv4 header

3. What address type is the IPv6 address FE80::300:34BC:123F:1010?

   a. Aggregatable global

   b. Site-local

   c. Link-local

   d. Multicast

4. What are three types of IPv6 addresses?

   a. Unicast, multicast, broadcast

   b. Unicast, anycast, broadcast

   c. Unicast, multicast, endcast

   d. Unicast, anycast, multicast

5. What is a compact representation of the address 3f00:0000:0000:a7fb:0000:0000:b100:0023?

   a. 3f::a7fb::b100:0023

   b. 3f00::a7fb:0000:0000:b100:23

   c. 3f::a7fb::b1:23

   d. 3f00:0000:0000:a7fb::b1:23

6. What is NAT-PT?

   a. Network address translation-port translation. Translates RFC 1918 addresses to public IPv4 addresses.

   b. Network addressable transparent-port translation. Translates network addresses to ports.

   c. Network address translation-protocol translation. Translates between IPv4 and IPv6 addresses.

   d. Next address translation–port translation

7. What IPv6 address type replaces the IPv4 broadcast address?

   a. Unicast

   b. Multicast

   c. Broadcast

   d. Anycast

8. What is the IPv6 equivalent to 127.0.0.1?

   a. 0:0:0:0:0:0:0:0

   b. 0:0:0:0:0:0:0:1

   c. 127:0:0:0:0:0:0:1

   d. FF::1

9. Which of the following is an "IPv4-compatible" IPv6 address?

   a. ::180.10.1.1

   b. f000:0:0:0:0:0:180.10.1.1

   c. 180.10.1.1::

   d. 2010::180.10.1.1

10. Which protocol maps names to IPv6 addresses?

   a. Address Resolution Protocol (ARP)

   b. Network discovery (ND)

   c. Domain Name System (DNS)

   d. DNSv2

The answers to the "Do I Know This Already?" quiz appear in Appendix A, "Answers to Chapter 'Do I Know This Already?' Quizzes and Q&A Sections." The suggested choices for your next step are as follows:

- **8 or less overall score**—Read the entire chapter. It includes the "Foundation Topics," "Foundation Summary," and "Q&A" sections.

- **9 or 10 overall score**—If you want more review on these topics, skip to the "Foundation Summary" section and then go to the "Q&A" section. Otherwise, move to the next chapter.

Foundation Topics

The following sections cover topics that you need to master for the CCDA exam. The section "IPv6 Header" covers each field of the IPv6 header, which helps you understand the protocol. The section "IPv6 Address Representation" covers the hexadecimal representation of IPv6 addresses and the compressed representation. The section "IPv6 Address Types" covers unicast, multicast, and anycast IPv6 addresses and the current allocations of IPv6 addresses.

The section "IPv6 Mechanisms" covers Internet Control Message Protocol Version 6 (ICMPv6), ND, address assignment and resolution, and IPv6 routing protocols. The section "IPv4 to IPv6 Transition Strategies and Deployments" covers dual-stack backbones, IPv6 over IPv4 tunnels, dual-stack hosts, and network address translation-protocol translation (NAT-PT).

Introduction to IPv6

You should become familiar at a high level with IPv6 specifications, addressing, and design. The driving motivation for the adoption of a new version of IP is the limitation imposed by the 32-bit address field in IPv4. In the 1990s, there was concern that the IP address space would be depleted soon. Although classless interdomain routing (CIDR) and NAT have slowed down the deployment of IPv6, its standards and deployments are becoming mature. IPv6 is playing a significant role in the deployment of IP services for wireless phones. Some countries such as Japan directed IPv6 compatibility back in 2005. Several IPv6 test beds include the 6bone and the 6ren. The 6bone was an IPv6 test bed that focused on testing standards, implementations, and transition and operational procedures. The 6bone has served its purpose and ceased to operate in 2006. The 6ren is an IPv6 network that serves research and educational institutions. Furthermore, the U.S. Federal government has mandated all agencies to support IPv6 by mid 2008.

The IPv6 specification provides 128 bits for addressing, a significant increase from 32 bits. The overall specification of IPv6 is in RFC 2460. Other RFCs describing IPv6 specifications are 3513, 3587, 3879, 2373, 2374, 2461, 1886, and 1981.

IPv6 includes the following enhancements over IPv4:

- **Expanded address space**—IPv6 uses 128-bit addresses instead of the 32-bit addresses in IPv4.

- **Globally unique IP addresses**—The additional address spaces allow each node to have a unique address and eliminate the need for NAT.

- **Fixed header length**—The IPv6 header length is fixed, allowing vendors to improve switching efficiency.

- **Improved option mechanism**—IPv6 options are placed in separate optional headers that are located between the IPv6 header and the transport layer header. The option headers are not required.

- **Address autoconfiguration**—This capability provides for dynamic assignment of IPv6 addresses. IPv6 hosts can automatically configure themselves, with or without a Dynamic Host Configuration Protocol (DHCP) server.

- **Support for labeling traffic flows**—Instead of the type-of-service field in IPv4, IPv6 enables the labeling of packets belonging to a particular traffic class for which the sender requests special handling. This support aids specialized traffic, such as real-time video.

- **Security capabilities**—IPv6 includes features that support authentication and privacy.

- **Maximum transmission unit (MTU) path discovery**—IPv6 eliminates the need to fragment packets by implementing MTU path discovery before sending packets to a destination.

- **Site multihoming**—IPv6 allows multihoming of hosts and networks to have multiple IPv6 prefixes, which facilitates connection to multiple ISPs.

IPv6 Header

This section covers each field of the IPv6 header. The IPv6 header is simpler than the IPv4 header. Some IPv4 fields have been eliminated or changed to optional fields. The fragment offset fields and flags in IPv4 have been eliminated from the header. IPv6 adds a flow label field for quality-of-service (QoS) mechanisms to use.

The use of 128 bits for source and destination addresses provides a significant improvement over IPv4. With 128 bits, there are $3.4 * 10^{38}$ or 34 billion billion billion billion IPv6 addresses, compared to only 4.3 billion IPv4 addresses.

IPv6 improves over IPv4 by using a fixed-length header. The IPv6 header appears in Figure 8-1.

Figure 8-1 *IPv6 Header Format*

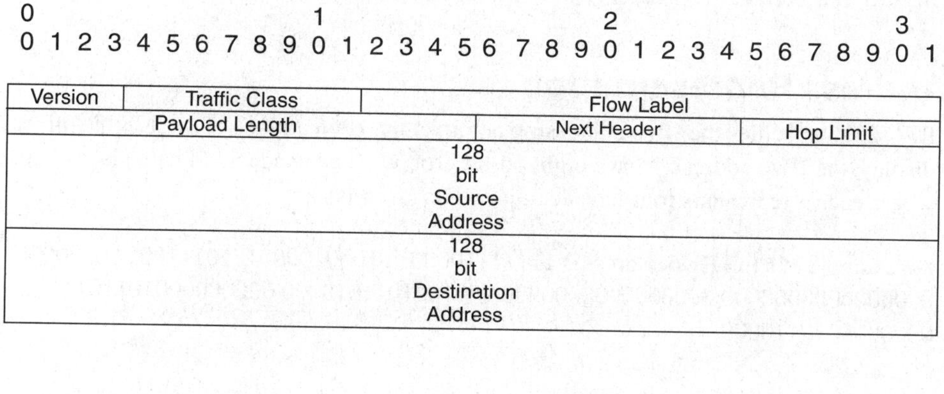

```
0                   1                   2                   3
0 1 2 3 4 5 6 7 8 9 0 1 2 3 4 5 6 7 8 9 0 1 2 3 4 5 6 7 8 9 0 1
```

Version	Traffic Class	Flow Label		
Payload Length			Next Header	Hop Limit
128 bit Source Address				
128 bit Destination Address				

The following is a description of each field in the IP header:

- **Version**—This field is 4 bits long. It indicates the format, based on the version number, of the IP header. These bits are set to 0110 for IPv6 packets.

- **Traffic class**—This field is 8 bits in length. It describes the class or priority of the IPv6 packet and provides functionality similar to the IPv4 type-of-service field.

- **Flow label**—This field is 20 bits in length. It indicates a specific sequence of packets between a source and destination that requires special handling, such as real-time data (voice and video).

- **Payload length**—This field is 16 bits in length. It indicates the payload's size in bytes. Its length includes any extension headers.

- **Next header**—This field is 8 bits in length. It indicates the type of header that follows this IPv6 header. In other words, it identifies the upper-layer protocol. It uses values defined by the Internet Assigned Numbers Authority (IANA).

- **Hop limit**—This field is 8 bits in length. It is decremented by 1 by each router that forwards the packets. If this field is 0, the packet is discarded.

- **Source address**—This field is 128 bits in length. It indicates the sender's IPv6 address.

- **Destination address**—This field is 128 bits in length. It indicates the destination host's IPv6 address.

Notice that although the IPv6 address is four times the length of an IPv4 address, the IPv6 header is only twice the length (40 bytes). Optional network layer information is not included in the IPv6 header; instead, it is included in separate extended headers.

Two important extended headers are the Authentication Header (AH) and the Encapsulating Security Payload (ESP) header. These headers are covered later in the chapter.

IPv6 Address Representation

RFC 2373 specifies the IPv6 addressing architecture. IPv6 addresses are 128 bits in length. For display, the IPv6 addresses have eight 16-bit groups. The hexadecimal value is $x:x:x:x:x:x:x:x$, where each x represents four hexadecimal digits (16 bits).

An example of a full IPv6 address is 1111111000011010 0100001010111001 0000000000011011 0000000000000000 0000000000000000 0001001011010000 0000000001011011 0000011010110000.

The hexadecimal representation of the preceding IPv6 binary number is

FE1A:42B9:001B:0000:0000:12D0:005B:06B0

Groups with a value of 0 can be represented with a single 0. For example, you can also represent the preceding number as

FE1A:42B9:001B:0:0:12D0:005B:06B0

You can represent multiple groups of 16-bit 0s with ::, which might appear only once in the number. Also, you do not need to represent leading 0s in a 16-bit piece. The preceding IPv6 address can be further shortened to

FE1A:42B9:1B::12D0:5B:6B0

> **TIP**   Remember that the fully expanded address has eight blocks and that the double colon represents only 0s. You can use the double colon only once.

You expand a compressed address following the same rules used earlier. For example, the IPv6 address 2001:4C::50:0:0:741 expands as follows:

2001:004C::0050:0000:0000:0741

Because there should be eight blocks of addresses and you have six, you can expand the double colon to two blocks as follows:

2001:004C:0000:0000:0050:0000:0000:0741

IPv4-Compatible IPv6 Addresses

In a mixed IPv6/IPv4 environment, the IPv4 portion of the address requires the last two 16-bit blocks, or 32 bits of the address, which is represented in IPv4 dotted-decimal notation. The remaining portion of the IPv6 address is all 0s. Six hexadecimal 16-bit blocks are concatenated with the dotted-decimal format. The first 96 bits are 0, and the last 32 bits are used for the IPv4 address. This form is $x:x:x:x:x:x:d.d.d.d$, where each x represents the hexadecimal digits and $d.d.d.d$ is the dotted-decimal representation.

An example of a mixed full address is 0000:0000:0000:0000:0000:0000:100.1.1.1; this example can be shortened to 0:0:0:0:0:0:100.1.1.1 or ::100.1.1.1.

IPv6 Prefix Representation

IPv6 prefixes are represented similar to IPv4, with the following format:

IPv6-address/prefix

The *IPv6-address* portion is a valid IPv6 address. The *prefix* portion is the number of contiguous bits that represent the prefix. You use the double colon only once in the representation. An example of an IPv6 prefix is 200C:001b:1100:0:0:0:0:0/40 or 200C:1b:1100::/40.

For another example, look at the representations of the 60-bit prefix 2001000000000ab0:

2001:0000:0000:0ab0:0000:0000:0000:0000/60
2001:0000:0000:0ab0:0:0:0:0/60
2001:0000:0000:ab0::/60
2001:0:0:ab0::/60

The rules for address representation are still valid when using a prefix. The following is not a valid representation of the preceding prefix:

2001:0:0:ab0/60

The preceding representation is missing the trailing double colon:

2001::ab0/60

The preceding representation expands to 2001:0:0:0:0:0:0:0ab0, which is not the prefix 2001:0000:0000:0ab0::/60.

When representing an IPv6 host address with its subnet prefix, you combine the two. For example, the IPv6 address 2001:0000:0000:0ab0:001c:1bc0:08ba:1c9a in subnet prefix 2001:0000:0000:0ab0::/60 is represented as the following:

2001:0000:0000:0ab0:001c:1bc0:08ba:1c9a/60

IPv6 Address Types and Address Allocations

This section covers the major types of IPv6 addresses. IPv4 addresses are unicast, multicast, or broadcast. IPv6 maintains each of these address functions, except that the IPv6 address types are defined a little differently. A special "all-nodes" IPv6 multicast address handles the broadcast function. IPv6 also introduces the anycast address type.

Also important to understand are the IPv6 address allocations. Sections of the IPv6 address space are reserved for particular functions, each of which is covered in this section. To provide you with a full understanding of address types, the following sections describe each type.

As mentioned earlier, there are three types of IPv6 addresses:

- Unicast

- Anycast

- Multicast

IPv6 Unicast Address

The IPv6 *unicast* (one-to-one) address is the logical identifier of a single-host interface. It is similar to IPv4 unicast classful (Class A, Class B, and Class C) addresses. Unicast addresses are divided into global and link-local addresses. A third type, site-local, has been deprecated in RFC 3879. These unicast address types are explained in the following sections.

IPv6 Anycast Address

The IPv6 *anycast* (one-to-nearest) address identifies a set of devices. An anycast address is allocated from a set of unicast addresses. These destination devices should share common characteristics and are explicitly configured for anycast.

You can use the anycast address to identify a set of routers or servers within an area. When a packet is sent to the anycast address, it is delivered to the nearest device as determined by the routing protocol. An example of the use of anycast addresses is to assign an anycast address to a set of servers—one in North America, and the other in Europe. Users in North America would be routed to the North American server, and those in Europe to the European server.

IPv6 Multicast Address

The IPv6 *multicast* (one-to-many) address identifies a set of hosts. The packet is delivered to all the hosts identified by that address. This type is similar to IPv4 multicast (Class D) addresses. IPv6 multicast addresses also supersede the broadcast function of IPv4 broadcasts. You use an "all-nodes" multicast address instead.

Some IPv6 multicast addresses are

FF01:0:0:0:0:0:0:1—Indicates all-nodes address for interface-local scope.
FF02:0:0:0:0:0:0:2—All-routers address for link-local.

IPv6 Address Allocations

The leading bits of an IPv6 address can define the IPv6 address type or other reservations. These leading bits are of variable length and are called the format prefix (FP). Table 8-2 shows the allocation of address prefixes. The IPv6 address space was delegated to IANA. You can find current IPv6 allocations at http://www.iana.org/assignments/ipv6-address-space. Many prefixes are still unassigned.

Table 8-2 *IPv6 Prefix Allocation*

Binary Prefix	Hexadecimal/Prefix	Allocation
0000 0000	0000::/8	Unspecified, loopback, IPv4-compatible
0000 0001	0100::/8	Unassigned
0000 001	0200:/7	Unassigned
0000 010	0400::/7	Reserved for Internetwork Packet Exchange (IPX) allocation
0000 1	0800::/5	Unassigned
0001	1000::/4	Unassigned
001	2000::/3	Global unicast address
010	4000::/3	Unassigned
011	6000::/3	Unassigned
100	8000::/3	Reserved for geographic-based unicast addresses
101	A000::/3	Unassigned
110	C000::/3	Unassigned
1110	E000::/3	Unassigned
1111 0	F000::/5	Unassigned
1111 10	F800::/6	Unassigned
1111 110	FC00::/7	Unassigned
1111 1110 0	FE00::/9	Unassigned
1111 1110 10	FE80:/10	Link-local unicast addresses
1111 1110 11	FEC0::/10	Unassigned; was site-local unicast addresses (deprecated)
1111 1111	FF00::/8	Multicast addresses

Unspecified Address

An unspecified address is all 0s: 0:0:0:0:0:0:0:0. It signifies that an IPv6 address is not specified for the interface. Unspecified addresses are not forwarded by an IPv6 router.

Loopback Address

The IPv6 loopback address is 0:0:0:0:0:0:0:1. This address is similar to the IPv4 loopback address of 127.0.0.1.

IPv4-Compatible IPv6 Address

IPv4-compatible IPv6 addresses begin with 96 binary 0s (six 16-bit groups) followed by the 32-bit IPv4 address, as in 0:0:0:0:0:0:130.100.50.1 or just ::130.100.50.1.

Global Unicast Addresses

IPv6 global addresses connect to the public network. These unicast addresses are globally unique and routable. This address format is initially defined in RFC 2374. RFC 3587 provides updates to the format.

The original specification defined the address format with a three-layer hierarchy: public topology, site topology, and interface identifier. The *public topology* consisted of service providers that provided transit services and exchanges of routing information. It used a Top-Level Aggregator (TLA) identifier and a next-level identifier. A site-level aggregator (SLA) was used for site topology. The *site topology* is local to the company or site and does not provide transit services. The TLA, NLA, and SLA identifiers are deprecated by RFC 3587. RFC 3587 simplifies these identifiers with a global routing prefix and subnet identifier for the network portion of the address.

Figure 8-2 shows the format of the standard IPv6 global unicast address. The global routing prefix is generally 48 bits in length, and the subnet ID is 16 bits. The interface ID is 64 bits in length and uniquely identifies the interface on the link.

Figure 8-2 *IPv6 Global Unicast Address Format*

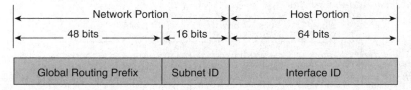

Link-Local Addresses

IPv6 link-local addresses are significant only to nodes on a single link. Routers do not forward packets with a link-local source or destination address beyond the local link. Link-local addresses are identified by leading FE8 hexadecimal numbers. Link-local addresses are configured automatically or manually.

As shown in Figure 8-3, the format of the link-local address is an FP of 1111111010, followed by 54 0s and a 64-bit interface identifier (ID). The interface ID is obtained automatically through communication with other nodes in the link. The interface ID is then concatenated with the link-local address prefix of FE80::/64 to obtain the interface link-local address.

Figure 8-3 *IPv6 Link-Local Address Format*

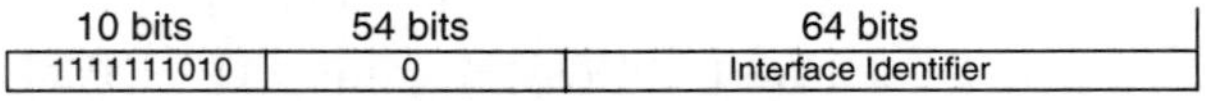

10 bits	54 bits	64 bits
1111111010	0	Interface Identifier

Site-Local Addresses

Site-local addresses were recently removed from IPv6 specifications. They are included here in case you encounter them in other references. IPv6 site-local addresses were meant to be analogous to IPv4 private addresses (RFC 1918). Site-local addresses were meant to be used within an organization and are not globally unique. Site-local addresses are not routable across a public network such as the Internet.

Multicast Addresses

IPv6 multicast addresses perform the same function as IPv4 multicast addresses. Multicast addresses send packets to all hosts in a group. IPv6 multicast addresses are identified by the leading FF hexadecimal numbers (an FP value of 11111111). One additional function of IPv6 multicast is to provide the IPv4 broadcast equivalent with the all-nodes multicast group.

RFC 2373 specifies the format of IPv6 multicast addresses. As shown in Figure 8-4, the fields of the IPv6 multicast address are the FP, a value of 0xFF, followed by a 4-bit flags field, a 4-bit scope field, and 112 bits for the group identifier (ID).

Figure 8-4 *Multicast Address Format*

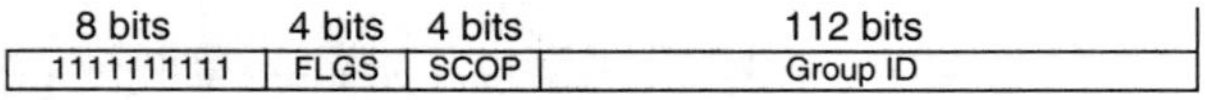

8 bits	4 bits	4 bits	112 bits
1111111111	FLGS	SCOP	Group ID

The FLGS (flags) field consists of three leading 0s followed by a T bit: 000T. If T = 0, the address is a well-known multicast address assigned by the global IANA. If T = 1, the address is not a permanently assigned address.

The SCOP (scope) field limits the scope of the multicast group. Table 8-3 shows the assigned scope values.

Table 8-3 *Multicast Scope Assignments*

SCOP (Binary)	SCOP (Hexadecimal)	Assignment
0000	0	Reserved
0001	1	Node-local scope
0010	2	Link-local scope
0011	3	Unassigned

Table 8-3   *Multicast Scope Assignments (Continued)*

SCOP (Binary)	SCOP (Hexadecimal)	Assignment
0100	4	Admin-local scope
0101	5	Site-local scope
0110	6	Unassigned
0111	7	Unassigned
1000	8	Organization-local scope
1001	9	Unassigned
1010	A	Unassigned
1011	B	Unassigned
1100	C	Unassigned
1101	D	Unassigned
1110	E	Global scope
1111	F	Reserved

The group ID identifies the multicast group within the given scope. The group ID is independent of the scope. A group ID of 0:0:0:0:0:0:1 identifies nodes, whereas a group ID of 0:0:0:0:0:0:2 identifies routers. Some well-known multicast addresses appear in Table 8-4 associated with a variety of scope values.

Table 8-4   *Well-Known Multicast Addresses*

Multicast Address	Multicast Group
FF01::1	All nodes (node-local)
FF02::1	All nodes (link-local)
FF01::2	All routers (node-local)
FF02::2	All routers (link-local)
FF02::5	Open Shortest Path First version 3 (OSPFv3)
FF02::6	OSPFv3 designated routers
FF02::9	Routing Information Protocol (RIPng)
FF02::A	EIGRP routers
FF02::B	Mobile agents
FF02::C	DHCP servers/relay agents
FF02::D	All Protocol Independent Multicast (PIM) routers

IPv6 Mechanisms

The changes to the 128-bit address length and IPv6 header format modified the underlying protocols that support IP. This section covers ICMPv6, IPv6 ND, address resolution, address assignment, and IPv6 routing protocols. These protocols must now support 128-bit addresses. For example, DNS adds a new record locator for resolving fully qualified domain names (FQDN) to IPv6 addresses. IPv6 also replaces ARP with the IPv6 ND protocol. IPv6 ND uses ICMPv6.

ICMPv6

ICMP needed some modifications to support IPv6. RFC 2463 describes the use of ICMPv6 for IPv6 networks. All IPv6 nodes must implement ICMPv6 to perform network layer functions. ICMPv6 performs diagnostics (ping), reports errors, and provides reachability information. Although IPv4 ICMP uses IP protocol 1, IPv6 uses a Next Header number of 58.

Informational messages are

- Echo request

- Echo reply

Some error messages are

- Destination unreachable

- Packet too big

- Time exceeded

- Parameter problem

The destination-unreachable messages also provide further details:

- No route to destination

- Destination administratively prohibited

- Address unreachable

- Port unreachable

Other IPv6 mechanisms use ICMPv6 to determine neighbor availability, path MTU, destination address, or port reachability.

IPv6 Network Discovery (ND) Protocol

IPv6 does not implement the ARP that is used in IPv4. Instead, IPv6 implements the ND protocol described in RFC 2461. Hosts use ND to implement plug-and-play functions that discover all other nodes in the same link, check for duplicate addresses, and find routers in the link. The protocol also searches for alternative routers if the primary fails.

The IPv6 ND protocol performs the following functions:

- **Address autoconfiguration**—The host can determine its full IPv6 address without the use of DHCP.

- **Duplicate address detection**—The host can determine whether the address it will use is already in use on the network.

- **Prefix discovery**—The host finds out the link's IPv6 prefix.

- **Parameter discovery**—The host finds out the link's MTU and hop count.

- **Address resolution**—The host can determine the MAC address of other nodes without the use of ARP.

- **Router discovery**—The host finds local routers without the use of DHCP.

- **Next-hop determination**—The host can determine a destination's next hop.

- **Neighbor unreachability detection**—The host can determine whether a neighbor is no longer reachable.

- **Redirect**—The host can tell another host if a preferred next hop exists to reach a particular destination.

IPv6 ND uses ICMPv6 to implement some of its functions. These ICMPv6 messages are

- **Router Advertisement (RA)**—Sent by routers to advertise their presence and link-specific parameters.

- **Router Solicitation (RS)**—Sent by hosts to request RA from local routers.

- **Neighbor Solicitation (NS)**—Sent by hosts to request link layer addresses of other hosts. Also used for duplicate address detection.

- **Neighbor Advertisement (NA)**—Sent by hosts in response to an NS.

- **Redirect**—Sent to a host to notify it of a better next hop to a destination.

The link address resolution process uses Neighbor Solicitation (NS) messages to obtain a neighbor's link layer address. Nodes respond with a Neighbor Advertisement (NA) message that contains the link layer address.

IPv6 Name Resolution

IPv4 uses A records to provide FQDN name-to-IPv4 address resolution. DNS adds a resource record (RR) to support name-to-IPv6-address resolution. RFC 3596 describes the addition of a new DNS resource record type to support transition to IPv6 name resolution. The new record type is AAAA, commonly known as "quad-A." Given a domain name, the AAAA record returns an IPv6 address to the requesting host.

RFC 2874 specifies another DNS record for IPv6; it defines the A6 resource record. The A6 record provides additional features and is intended as a replacement for the AAAA RR. Current DNS implementations need to be able to support A (for IPv4), A6, and AAAA resource records, with type A having the highest priority and AAAA the lowest.

Path MTU Discovery

IPv6 does not allow packet fragmentation throughout the internetwork. Only sending hosts are allowed to fragment. Routers are not allowed to fragment packets. RFC 2460 specifies that the MTU of every link in an IPv6 must be 1280 bytes or greater. RFC 1981 recommends that nodes should implement IPv6 path MTU discovery to determine whether any paths are greater than 1280 bytes. ICMPv6 packet-too-big error messages determine the path MTU. Nodes along the path send the ICMPv6 packet-too-big message to the sending host if the packet is larger than the outgoing interface MTU.

Figure 8-5 shows a host sending a 2000-byte packet. Because the outgoing interface MTU is 1500 bytes, Router A sends an ICMPv6 packet-too-big error message back to Host A. The sending host then sends a 1500-byte packet. The outgoing interface MTU at Router B is 1300 bytes. Router B sends an ICMPv6 packet-too-big error message to Host A. Host A then sends the packet with 1300 bytes.

Figure 8-5 *ICMPv6 Packet-Too-Big Message*

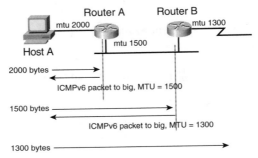

IPv6 Address-Assignment Strategies

An IPv6 host can obtain its address through autoconfiguration or from the DHCP. DHCP is a stateful method of address assignment. IPv6 nodes might or might not use DHCPv6 to acquire IP address information.

Autoconfiguration of Link-Local Address

IPv6 hosts can use a stateless autoconfiguration method, without DHCP, to acquire their own IP address information. Hosts obtain their link-local addresses automatically as an interface is initialized. First, the host performs a duplicate address-detection process. The host joins the all-nodes multicast group to receive neighbor advertisements from other nodes. The neighbor advertisements include the subnet or prefix associated with the link. The host then sends a neighbor-solicitation message with the tentative IP address (interface identifier) as the target. If a host is already using the tentative IP address, that host replies with a neighbor advertisement. If the host receives no neighbor advertisement, the target IP address becomes the link-local address of the originating host.

DHCPv6

DHCPv6 is the updated version of DHCP that provides dynamic IP address assignment for IPv6 hosts. DHCPv6 is described in RFC 3315. It provides the same functions as DHCP, with more control than stateless autoconfiguration, and it supports renumbering without routers. DHCPv6 assignment is stateful, whereas IPv6 link-local autoconfiguration is not.

IPv6 Security

IPv6 has two integrated mechanisms to provide security for communications. It natively supports IP Security (IPSec). IPSec is mandated at the operating-system level for all IPSec hosts. RFC 2401 describes IPSec. Extension headers carry the IPSec AH and ESP header. The AH provides authentication and integrity. The ESP header provides confidentiality by encrypting the payload. For IPv6, the AH defaults to message digest algorithm 5 (MD5), and the ESP encryption defaults to data encryption standard-cipher block chaining (DES-CBC).

A description of the IPSec mechanisms appears in Chapter 13, "Security Solutions." More information also appears in RFC 2402, *IP Authentication Header*, and in RFC 2406, *IP Encapsulating Security Payload (ESP)*.

IPv6 Routing Protocols

New routing protocols have been developed to support IPv6, such as RIPng, Integrated Intermediate System-to-Intermediate System (i/IS-IS), EIGRP for IPv6, and OSPFv3. Border Gateway Protocol (BGP) also includes changes that support IPv6. Enhanced Interior Gateway Routing Protocol (EIGRP) also now supports IPv6.

RIPng for IPv6

RFC 2080 describes changes to RIP to support IPv6 networks, called RIP next generation (RIPng). RIP mechanisms remain the same. RIPng still has a 15-hop limit, counting to infinity, and split horizon with poison reverse. Instead of User Datagram Protocol (UDP) Port 520 for RIPv2, RIPng uses UDP Port 521. RIPng supports IPv6 addresses and prefixes. Cisco IOS Software currently supports RIPng. RIPng uses multicast group FF02::9 for RIP updates to all RIP routers.

EIGRP for IPv6

Cisco has developed EIGRP support for IPv6 networks to route IPv6 prefixes. EIGRP for IPv6 is configured and managed separately from EIGRP for IPv4; no network statements are used. EIGRP for IPv6 retains all the characteristics (network discovery, DUAL, modules) and functions of EIGRP for IPv4. EIGRP uses multicast group FF02::A for EIGRP updates.

OSPFv3 for IPv6

RFC 2740 describes OSPF Version 3 to support IPv6 networks. OSPF algorithms and mechanisms (flooding, designated router [DR] election, areas, shortest path first [SPF] calculations) remain the same. Changes are made for OSPF to support IPv6 addresses, address hierarchy, and IPv6 for transport. Cisco IOS Software currently supports OSPFv3.

OSPFv3 uses multicast group FF02::5 for all OSPF routers and FF02::6 for all designated routers.

IS-IS for IPv6

Specifications for routing IPv6 with integrated IS-IS are currently an Internet draft of the IETF. The draft specifies new type, length, and value (TLV) objects, reachability TLVs, and an interface address TLV to forward IPv6 information in the network. IOS supports IS-IS for IPv6 as currently described in the draft standard.

BGP4 Multiprotocol Extensions for IPv6

RFC 2545 specifies the use of BGP attributes for passing on IPv6 route information. The MP_REACH_NLRI (multiprotocol-reachable) attribute describes reachable destinations. It includes the next-hop address and a list of Network Layer Reachability Information (NLRI) prefixes of reachable networks. The MP_UNREACH_NLRI (multiprotocol-unreachable) attribute conveys unreachable networks. IOS currently supports these BGP4 multiprotocol attributes to communicate reachability information for IPv6 networks.

IPv4 to IPv6 Transition Strategies and Deployments

Several deployment models exist to migrate from an IPv4 network to IPv6. During a transition time, both protocols can coexist in the network. The deployment models are

- IPv6 over dedicated WAN links

- IPv6 over IPv4 tunnels

- IPv6 using dual-stack backbones

- Protocol translation

Each model provides several advantages and disadvantages with which you should become familiar. The following sections describe each model.

IPv6 over Dedicated WAN Links

In this deployment model, all nodes and links use IPv6 hierarchy, addressing, and protocols. It is not a transition model, but a new, separate deployment of IPv6. The WAN in this model uses IPv6. The disadvantage of this model is that additional costs are incurred when separate links are used for IPv6 WAN circuits during the transition to using IPv6 exclusively. As shown in Figure 8-6, a company needs both IPv6 and IPv4 networks in sites A and B during the IPv6 deployment and transition. The networks are connected using separate WANs.

Figure 8-6 *Dedicated IPv6 WAN*

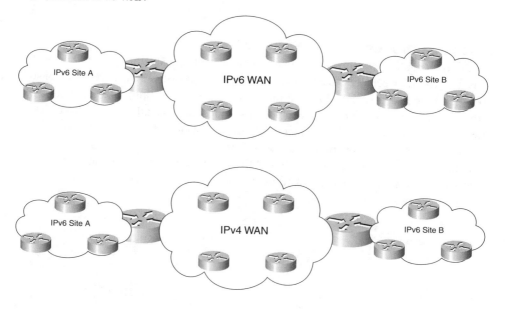

IPv6 over IPv4 Tunnels

In this deployment model, pockets of IPv6-only networks are connected using IPv4 tunnels. With tunneling, IPv6 traffic is encapsulated within IPv4 packets so that they are sent over the IPv4 WAN. The advantage of this method is that you do not need separate circuits to connect the IPv6 networks. A disadvantage of this method is the increased protocol overhead of the encapsulated IPv6 headers. Tunnels are created manually, semiautomatedly, or automatically using 6to4.

RFC 3056 specifies the 6to4 method for transition by assigning an interim unique IPv6 prefix. 2002::/16 is the assigned range for 6to4. Each 6to4 site uses a /48 prefix that is concatenated with 2002.

Figure 8-7 shows a network using IPv4 tunnels. Site A and Site B both have IPv4 and IPv6 networks. The IPv6 networks are connected using an IPv4 tunnel in the WAN.

Figure 8-7   *IPv6 over IPv4 Tunnels*

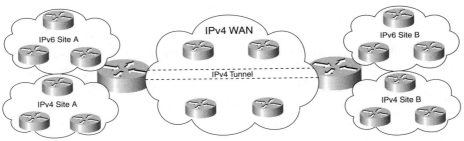

Dual-Stack Backbones

In this model, all routers in the backbone are dual-stack, capable of routing both IPv4 and IPv6 packets. The IPv4 protocol stack is used between IPv4 hosts, and the IPv6 protocol stack is used between IPv6 hosts. This deployment model works for organizations with a mixture of IPv4 and IPv6 applications. Figure 8-8 shows a network with a dual-stack backbone. All the WAN routers run both IPv4 and IPv6 routing protocols. The disadvantages are that the WAN routers require dual addressing, run two routing protocols, and might require additional CPU and memory resources. Another disadvantage is that IPv4-only and IPv6-only hosts cannot communicate with each other directly; dual-stack hosts or network translation is required (covered next) for IPv4 and IPv6 hosts to communicate.

Figure 8-8   *Dual-Stack Backbone*

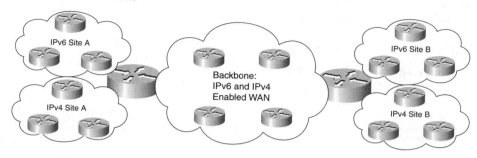

Dual-Stack Hosts

Hosts require dual stacks (IPv4 and IPv6) to communicate with both IPv4 and IPv6 hosts. In this environment, host applications can communicate with both IPv4 and IPv6 stacks. When using dual stacks, a host uses DNS to determine which stack to use to reach a destination. If DNS returns an IPv6 (A6 record) address to the host, the host uses the IPv6 stack. If DNS returns an IPv4 (A record) address to the host, the host uses the IPv4 stack. Using dual stacks is the method recommended for campus and access networks during a transition to IPv6.

Protocol Translation Mechanisms

One of the mechanisms for an IPv6-only host to communicate with an IPv4-only host without using dual stacks is protocol translation. RFC 2766 describes NAT-PT, which provides translation between IPv6 and IPv4 hosts. NAT-PT operates similarly to the NAT mechanisms to translate IPv4 private addresses to public address space. NAT-PT binds addresses in the IPv6 network to addresses in the IPv4 network and vice versa. Figure 8-9 shows a network using NAT-PT.

Figure 8-9   *Network Address Translation-Protocol Translation*

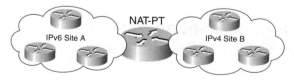

IPv6 Comparison with IPv4

This section provides a summary comparison of IPv6 to IPv4. Become knowledgeable about the characteristics summarized in Table 8-5. The use of 128 bits over 32 bits is an obvious change.

The upper-layer protocol is identified with the next header field in IPv6, which was the protocol type field used in IPv4. ARP is replaced by IPv6 ND.

Table 8-5 *IPv6 and IPv4 Characteristics*

Characteristic	IPv6	IPv4
Address length	128 bits	32 bits
Address representation	Hexadecimal	Dotted-decimal
Header length	Fixed (40 bytes)	Variable
Upper-layer protocols	Next header field	Protocol type field
Link address resolution	ND	ARP
Address configuration	Stateless autoconfiguration or stateful DHCP	Stateful DHCP
DNS (name-to-address resolution)	A6 records	A records
Interior routing protocols	EIGRPv6, OSPFv3, RIPng, IS-IS for IPv6	EIGRP, OSPFv2, RIPv2, IS-IS
Classification and marking	Traffic class and flow label fields, Differentiated Services Code Point (DSCP)	IP precedence bits, type-of-service field, DSCP
Private addresses	Site-local addresses	RFC 1918 private address space
Fragmentation	Sending host only	Sending host and intermediate routers
Loopback address	0:0:0:0:0:0:0:1	127.0.0.1
Address types	Unicast, anycast, multicast	Unicast, multicast, broadcast

References and Recommended Readings

Carpenter, B. and K. Moore. RFC 3056, *Connection of IPv6 Domains via IPv4 Clouds*. Available from http://www.ietf.org/rfc.

Coltun, R., D. Ferguson, and J. Moy. RFC 2740, *OSPF for IPv6*. Available from http://www.ietf.org/rfc.

Conta, A. and S. Deering. RFC 2463, *Internet Control Message Protocol (ICMPv6) for the Internet Protocol Version 6 (IPv6) Specification*. Available from http://www.ietf.org/rfc.

Crawford, M. and C. Huitema. RFC 2874, *DNS Extensions to Support IPv6 Address Aggregation and Renumbering*. Available from http://www.ietf.org/rfc.

Deering, S. and R. Hinden. RFC 2460, *Internet Protocol, Version 6 (IPv6) Specification*. Available from http://www.ietf.org/rfc.

Doyle, J. and J. Carroll. *Routing TCP/IP*, Volume I, Second Edition. Indianapolis: Cisco Press, 2005.

Doyle, J. and J. Carroll. *Routing TCP/IP*, Volume II. Indianapolis: Cisco Press, 2001.

Droms, R., editor, J. Bound, B. Volz, T. Lemon, C. Perkins, and M. Carney. RFC 3315, *Dynamic Host Configuration Protocol for IPv6 (DHCPv6)*. Available from http://www.ietf.org/rfc.

Hinden, R. and S. Deering. RFC 2373, *IP Version 6 Addressing Architecture*. Available from http://www.ietf.org/rfc.

Hinden, R. and S. Deering. RFC 3513, *Internet Protocol Version 6 (IPv6) Addressing Architecture*. Available from http://www.ietf.org/rfc.

Hinden, R., S. Deering, and E. Nordmark. RFC 3587, *IPv6 Global Unicast Address Format*. Available from http://www.ietf.org/rfc.

Hinden R., M. O'Dell, and S. Deering. RFC 2374, *An IPv6 Aggregatable Global Unicast Address Format*. Available from http://www.ietf.org/rfc.

Hopps, C. *Routing IPv6 for IS-IS* (draft). Available from http://www.simpleweb.org/ietf/internetdrafts/complete/draft-ietf-isis-ipv6-03.txt.

Huitema, C. and B. Carpenter. RFC 3879, *Deprecating Site Local Addresses*. Available from http://www.ietf.org/rfc.

"Implementing IPv6 Networks Training." http://www.cisco.com/application/pdf/en/us/guest/tech/tk373/c1482/ccmigration_09186a008019d70b.pdf.

Kent, S. and R. Atkinson. RFC 2401, *Security Architecture for the Internet Protocol*. Available from http://www.ietf.org/rfc.

Kent, S. and R. Atkinson. RFC 2402, *IP Authentication Header*. Available from http://www.ietf.org/rfc.

Kent, S. and R. Atkinson. RFC 2406, *IP Encapsulating Security Payload (ESP)*. Available from http://www.ietf.org/rfc.

Malkin, G. and R. Minnear. RFC 2080, *RIPng for IPv6*. Available from http://www.ietf.org/rfc.

Marques, P. and F. Dupont. RFC 2545, *Use of BGP-4 Multiprotocol Extensions for IPv6 Inter-Domain Routing*. Available from http://www.ietf.org/rfc.

McCann, J., S. Deering, and J. Mogul. RFC 1981, *Path MTU Discovery for IP version 6*. Available from http://www.ietf.org/rfc.

Narten, T., E. Nordmark, and W. Simpson. RFC 2461, *Neighbor Discovery for IP Version 6 (IPv6)*. Available from http://www.ietf.org/rfc.

Thomson, S. and C. Huitema. RFC 1886, *DNS Extensions to Support IP Version 6*. Available from http://www.ietf.org/rfc.

Tsirtsis, G. and P. Srisuresh. RFC 2766, *Network Address Translation – Protocol Translation (NAT-PT)*. Available from http://www.ietf.org/rfc.

Foundation Summary

The "Foundation Summary" section of each chapter lists the most important facts from the chapter. Although this section does not list every fact from the chapter that will be on the CCDA exam, a well-prepared CCDA candidate should at a minimum know all the details in each "Foundation Summary" before taking the exam.

The CCDA exam requires that you be familiar with the three types of IPv6 addresses:

■ **Unicast**—The logical identifier of a single host. Unicast addresses are global unicast or link-local unicast.

■ **Anycast**—Identifies a set of devices. The packet is delivered to the nearest device as determined by the routing protocol.

■ **Multicast**—Identifies a set of hosts. The packet is delivered to all the hosts.

Table 8-6 provides a quick look at the current IPv6 allocations. Be able to identify the allocation based on the leading binary or hexadecimal numbers.

Table 8-6   *IPv6 Prefix Allocations*

Binary Prefix	Hexadecimal/Prefix	Allocation
0000 0000	0000::/8	Unspecified, loopback, IPv4-compatible
0000 0001	0100::/8	Unassigned
0000 001	0200:/7	Unassigned
0000 010	0400::/7	Reserved for Internetwork Packet Exchange (IPX) allocation
0000 1	0800::/5	Unassigned
0001	1000::/4	Unassigned
001	2000::/3	Global unicast address
010	4000::/3	Unassigned
011	6000::/3	Unassigned
100	8000::/3	Reserved for geographic-based unicast addresses
101	A000::/3	Unassigned
110	C000::/3	Unassigned
1110	E000::/3	Unassigned

continues

Table 8-6   *IPv6 Prefix Allocations (Continued)*

Binary Prefix	Hexadecimal/Prefix	Allocation
1111 0	F000::/5	Unassigned
1111 10	F800::/6	Unassigned
1111 110	FC00::/7	Unassigned
1111 1110 0	FE00::/9	Unassigned
1111 1110 10	FE80:/10	Link-local unicast addresses
1111 1110 11	FEC0::/10	Unassigned; was site-local unicast addresses (deprecated)
1111 1111	FF00::/8	Multicast addresses

Table 8-7 is actually a review of Table 8-5. It is presented again in this section because it is essential for the exam. It provides a quick summary of IPv6 characteristics compared to IPv4. Study this table in detail.

Table 8-7   *IPv6 and IPv4 Characteristics*

Characteristic	IPv6	IPv4
Address length	128 bits	32 bits
Address representation	Hexadecimal	Dotted-decimal
Header length	Fixed (40 bytes)	Variable
Upper-layer protocols	Next header field	Protocol type field
Link address resolution	ND	ARP
Address configuration	Stateless autoconfiguration or stateful DHCP	Stateful DHCP
DNS (name-to-address resolution)	A6 records	A records
Interior routing protocols	EIGRP for IPv6, OSPFv3, RIPng, IS-IS for IPv6	EIGRP, OSPFv2, RIPv2, IS-IS
Classification and marking	Traffic class and flow label fields, DSCP	IP precedence bits, type-of-service field, DSCP
Fragmentation	Sending host only	Sending host and intermediate routers
Loopback address	0:0:0:0:0:0:0:1	127.0.0.1
Address types	Unicast, anycast, multicast	Unicast, multicast, broadcast

Table 8-8 describes each field in the 40-byte IP header.

Table 8-8 *IPv6 Header Fields*

IPv6 Header Field	Description
Version	This field is 4 bits in length. It indicates the format, based on the version number, of the IP header. These bits are set to 0110 for IPv6 packets.
Traffic class	This field is 8 bits in length. It describes the IPv6 packet's class or priority and provides similar functionality to the IPv4 type-of-service field.
Flow label	This field is 20 bits in length. It indicates a specific sequence of packets between a source and destination that requires special handling, such as real-time data (voice and video).
Payload length	This field is 16 bits in length. It indicates the payload's size in bytes. Its length includes any extension headers.
Next header	This field is 8 bits in length. It indicates the type of header that follows this IPv6 header.
Hop limit	This field is 8 bits in length. It is decremented by 1 by each router that forwards the packets. If this field is 0, the packet is discarded.
Source address	This field is 128 bits in length. It indicates the sender's IPv6 address.
Destination address	This field is 128 bits in length. It indicates the destination host's IPv6 address.

Q&A

As mentioned in the Introduction, you have two choices for review questions: here in the book or the exam questions on the CD-ROM. The answers to these questions appear in Appendix A.

For more practice with exam format questions, use the exam engine on the CD-ROM.

1. True or false: OSPFv2 supports IPv6.

2. True or false: DNS A6 records are used in IPv6 networks for name-to-IPv6-address resolution.

3. Fill in the blank: IPv6 ND is similar to what _____ does for IPv4 networks.

4. How many bits are there between the colons of IPv6 addresses?

5. The first field of the IPv6 header is 4 bits in length. What binary number is it always set to?

6. True or false: DHCP is required for dynamic allocation of IPv6 addresses.

7. IPv6 multicast addresses begin with what hexadecimal numbers?

8. IPv6 link-local addresses begin with what hexadecimal prefix?

9. True or false: 6to4 allows tunneling of IPv6 through IPv4 networks.

10. List the eight fields of the IPv6 header.

11. Which of the following is not an IPv6 address type?

    a. Unicast

    b. Broadcast

    c. Anycast

    d. Multicast

12. True or false: The IPv6 address 2001:0:0:1234:0:0:0:abcd can be represented as 2001::1234:0:0:0:abcd and 2001:0:0:1234::abcd.

13. What is the subnet prefix of 2001:1:0:ab0:34:ab1:0:1/64?

14. The IPv6 address has 128 bits. How many hexadecimal numbers does an IPv6 address have?

15. What type of IPv6 address is the following?

    FF01:0:0:0:0:0:0:2

16. What is the compact format of the address 2102:0010:0000:0000:0000:fc23:0100:00ab?

    a. 2102:10::fc23:01:ab

    b. 2102:001::fc23:01:ab

    c. 2102:10::fc23:100:ab

    d. 2102:0010::fc23:01:ab

17. When using the dual-stack backbone, which of the following statements is correct?

    a. The backbone routers have IPv4/IPv6 dual stacks, and end hosts do not.

    b. The end hosts have IPv4/IPv6 dual stacks, and backbone routers do not.

    c. Both the backbone routers and end hosts have IPv4/IPv6 dual stacks.

    d. Neither the backbone routers nor end hosts have IPv4/IPv6 dual stacks.

18. How does a dual-stack host know which stack to use to reach a destination?

    a. It performs an ND, which returns the destination host type.

    b. It performs a DNS request that returns the IP address. If the returned address is IPv4, the host uses the IPv4 stack. If the returned address is IPv6, the host uses the IPv6 stack.

    c. The IPv6 stack makes a determination. If the destination is IPv4, the packet is sent to the IPv4 stack.

    d. The IPv4 stack makes a determination. If the destination is IPv6, the packet is sent to the IPv6 stack.

19. Name at least two transition methods or technologies used to migrate from IPv4 to IPv6.

20. Which of the following describe(s) the IPv6 header?

    a. It is 40 bytes in length.

    b. It is of variable length.

    c. The Protocol Number field describes the upper-layer protocol.

    d. The Next Header field describes the upper-layer protocol.

21. Which of the following is true about fragmentation?

    a. Routers between source and destination hosts can fragment IPv4 and IPv6 packets.

    b. Routers between source and destination hosts cannot fragment IPv4 and IPv6 packets.

    c. Routers between source and destination hosts can fragment IPv6 packets only. IPv4 packets cannot be fragmented.

    d. Routers between source and destination hosts can fragment IPv4 packets only. IPv6 packets cannot be fragmented.

22. A packet sent to an anycast address reaches what?

   a. The nearest destination in a set of hosts

   b. All destinations in a set of hosts

   c. Broadcasts to all hosts

   d. Global unicast destinations

23. Which of the following is/are true about IPv6 and IPv4 headers?

   a. The IPv6 header is of fixed length, and the Next Header field describes the upper-layer protocol.

   b. The IPv4 header is of variable length, and the Protocol field describes the upper-layer protocol.

   c. The IPv6 header is of fixed length, and the Protocol field describes the upper-layer protocol.

   d. A and B.

   e. B and C.

Answer the following questions based on the scenario and figure.

A company has an existing WAN that uses IPv4. Sites C and D use IPv4. As shown in Figure 8-10, the company plans to add two new locations (Sites A and B). The new sites will implement IPv6. The company does not want to lease more WAN circuits.

Figure 8-10 *Company Adds Sites A and B*

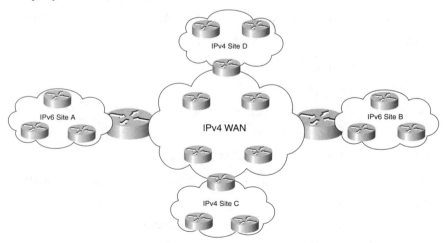

Answer the following questions.

24. What options does the company have to connect Site A to Site B?

25. What mechanism needs to be implemented so that IPv6 hosts can communicate with IPv4 hosts and vice versa?

26. If a dual-stack backbone is implemented, do all WAN routers and all hosts need an IPv6-IPv4 dual stack?

27. If an IPv4 tunnel is implemented between Sites A and B, do all WAN routers require an IPv6-IPv4 dual stack?

This chapter covers the following subjects:

- Routing protocol characteristics

- Routing protocol metrics and loop prevention

- ODR

CHAPTER 9

Routing Protocol Selection Criteria

This chapter covers the metrics used and other characteristics of routing protocols. Routing protocols can be categorized as distance-vector or link-state and as hierarchical or flat. The CCDA must understand how each routing protocol is categorized to select the one that meets the customer's requirements. This chapter covers the routing protocols at a high level. The following chapters dive into more detail on the operations and algorithms used in each routing protocol.

"Do I Know This Already?" Quiz

The purpose of the "Do I Know This Already?" quiz is to help you decide whether you need to read the entire chapter. If you intend to read the entire chapter, you do not necessarily need to answer these questions now.

The eight-question quiz, derived from the major sections in the "Foundation Topics" portion of the chapter, helps you determine how to spend your limited study time.

Table 9-1 outlines the major topics discussed in this chapter and the "Do I Know This Already?" quiz questions that correspond to those topics.

Table 9-1 *"Do I Know This Already?" Foundation Topics Section-to-Question Mapping*

Foundation Topics Section	Questions Covered in This Section
Routing Protocol Characteristics	1, 2, 3, 4, 7, 8
Routing Protocol Metrics and Loop Prevention	6
On-Demand Routing	5

CAUTION   The goal of self-assessment is to gauge your mastery of the topics in this chapter. If you do not know the answer to a question or you are only partially sure, you should mark this question wrong for the purposes of the self-assessment. Giving yourself credit for an answer you correctly guess skews your self-assessment results and might provide you with a false sense of security.

1. Which of the following routing protocols are classful?

    a. Routing Information Protocol Version 1 (RIPv1) and RIPv2

    b. Enhanced Interior Gateway Routing Protocol (EIGRP) and Open Shortest Path First (OSPF)

    c. Intermediate System-to-Intermediate System (IS-IS) and OSPF

    d. RIPv1 only

2. Which type of routing protocol would you use when connecting to an Internet service provider?

    a. Classless routing protocol

    b. Interior gateway protocol

    c. Exterior gateway protocol

    d. Classful routing protocol

3. Which routing protocol is distance-vector and classless?

    a. RIPv2

    b. EIGRP

    c. OSPF

    d. IS-IS

4. Which type of routing protocol sends periodic routing updates?

    a. Static

    b. Distance-vector

    c. Link-state

    d. Hierarchical

5. Which distance-vector routing protocol is used for IPv6 networks?

    a. OSPFv2

    b. RIPng

    c. OSPFv3

    d. BGPv3

6. Which of the following is true regarding routing metrics?

    a. If the metric is bandwidth, the path with the lowest bandwidth is selected.

    b. If the metric is bandwidth, the path with the highest bandwidth is selected.

    c. If the metric is bandwidth, the highest sum of the bandwidth is used to calculate the highest cost.

    d. If the metric is cost, the path with the highest cost is selected.

7. Both OSPF and EIGRP are enabled on a router with default values. Both protocols have a route to a destination network in their databases. Which route is entered into the routing table?

    a. The OSPF route.

    b. The EIGRP route.

    c. Both routes are entered with load balancing.

    d. Neither route is entered; an error has occurred.

8. Which of the following are classless routing protocols?

    a. RIPv1 and RIPv2

    b. EIGRP and RIPv2

    c. IS-IS and OSPF

    d. Answers B and C

The answers to the "Do I Know This Already?" quiz appear in Appendix A, "Answers to Chapter 'Do I Know This Already?' Quizzes and Q&A Sections." The suggested choices for your next step are as follows:

- **6 or less overall score**—Read the entire chapter. It includes the "Foundation Topics," "Foundation Summary," and "Q&A" sections.

- **7 or 8 overall score**—If you want more review on these topics, skip to the "Foundation Summary" section, and then go to the "Q&A" section. Otherwise, move to the next chapter.

Foundation Topics

This chapter covers the high-level characteristics of routing protocols and their metrics. You should become familiar with the different categories of routing protocols and their characteristics for the test. Understand how each metric is used and, based on the metric, which path is preferred. For example, you need to know that a path with the highest bandwidth is preferred over a path with lower bandwidth. This chapter also covers on-demand routing (ODR).

Routing Protocol Characteristics

This section discusses the different types and characteristics of routing protocols.

Characteristics of routing-protocol design are

- **Distance-vector, link-state, or hybrid**—How routes are learned

- **Interior or exterior**—For use in private networks or the public Internet

- **Classless (classless interdomain routing [CIDR] support) or classful**—CIDR enables aggregation of network advertisements (supernetting) between routers

- **Fixed-length or variable-length subnet masks (VLSM)**—Conserve addresses within a network

- **Flat or potentially hierarchical**—Addresses scalability in large internetworks

- **IPv4 or IPv6**—Newer routing protocols are used for IPv6 networks

This section also covers the default administrative distance assigned to routes learned from each routing protocol or from static assignment. Routes are categorized as statically (manually) configured or dynamically learned from a routing protocol. The following sections cover all these characteristics.

Static Versus Dynamic Route Assignment

Static routes are manually configured on a router. They do not react to network outages. The one exception is when the static route specifies the outbound interface: If the interface goes down, the static route is removed from the routing table. Because static routes are unidirectional, they must be configured for each outgoing interface the router will use. The size of today's networks makes it impossible to manually configure and maintain all the routes in all the routers in a timely manner. Human configuration can involve many mistakes, which is why routing protocols exist. They use algorithms to advertise and learn about changes in the network topology.

The main benefit of static routing is that a router generates no routing protocol overhead. Because no routing protocol is enabled, no bandwidth is consumed by route advertisements between network devices. Another benefit of static routing protocols is that they are easier to configure and troubleshoot than dynamic routing protocols. Static routing is recommended for hub-and-spoke topologies with a low-speed remote connection. A default static route is configured at each remote site because the hub is the only route used to reach all other sites. Static routers are also used at network boundaries (Internet or partners) where routing information is not exchanged. These static routes are then redistributed into the internal dynamic routing protocol used.

Figure 9-1 shows a hub-and-spoke WAN where static routes are defined in the remote WAN routers because no routing protocols are configured. This setup eliminates routing protocol traffic on the low-bandwidth WAN circuits.

Figure 9-1 *Static Routes in a Hub-and-Spoke Network*

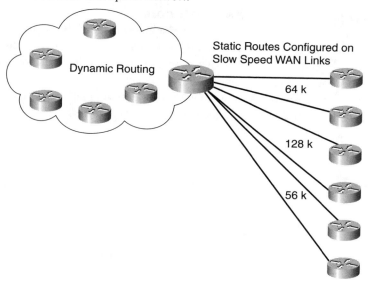

Routing protocols dynamically determine the best route to a destination. When the network topology changes, the routing protocol adjusts the routes without administrative intervention. Routing protocols use a metric to determine the best path toward a destination network. Some use a single measured value such as hop count. Others compute a metric value using one or more parameters. Routing metrics are discussed later in this chapter. The following is a list of dynamic routing protocols:

- RIPv1

- RIPv2

- IGRP

- EIGRP

- OSPF

- IS-IS

- RIPng

- OSPFv3

- EIGRP for IPv6

- Border Gateway Protocol (BGP)

Interior Versus Exterior Routing Protocols

Routing protocols can be categorized as interior gateway protocols (IGP) or exterior gateway protocols (EGP). IGPs are meant for routing within an organization's administrative domain—in other words, the organization's internal network. EGPs are routing protocols used to communicate with exterior domains. Figure 9-2 shows where an internetwork uses IGPs and EGPs with multiple autonomous administrative domains. BGP exchanges routing information between the internal network and an ISP. IGPs appear in the internal private network.

Figure 9-2 *Interior and Exterior Routing Protocols*

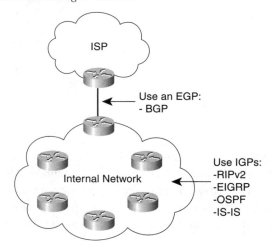

One of the first EGPs was called exactly that—Exterior Gateway Protocol. Today, BGP is the de facto (and the only available) exterior gateway protocol.

Potential IGPs for an IPv4 network are

- RIPv2

- OSPF

- IS-IS

- EIGRP

Potential IGPs for an IPv6 network are

- RIPng

- OSPFv3

- EIGRP for IPv6

RIPv1 is no longer recommended because RIPv2 is the most recent version of RIP. IGRP is an earlier version of EIGRP. IGRP is no longer a CCDA exam topic.

Distance-Vector Routing Protocols

The first IGP routing protocols introduced were distance-vector routing protocols. They used the Bellman-Ford algorithm to build the routing tables. With distance-vector routing protocols, routes are advertised as vectors of distance and direction. The distance metric is usually router hop count. The direction is the next-hop router (IP address) toward which to forward the packet. For RIP, the maximum number of hops is 15, which can be a serious limitation, especially in large nonhierarchical internetworks.

Distance-vector algorithms call for each router to send its entire routing table to only its immediate neighbors. The table is sent periodically (30 seconds for RIP and 90 seconds for IGRP). In the period between advertisements, each router builds a new table to send to its neighbors at the end of the period. Because each router relies on its neighbors for route information, it is commonly said that distance-vector protocols "route by rumor."

Having to wait half a minute for a new routing table with new routes is too long for today's networks. This is why distance-vector routing protocols have slow convergence.

RIPv2 and IGRP can send triggered updates—full routing table updates sent before the update timer has expired. A router can receive a routing table with 500 routes with only one route change, which creates serious overhead on the network—another drawback. Furthermore, RFC 2091 updates RIP with triggered extensions to allow triggered updates with only route changes. Cisco routers support this on fixed point-to-point interfaces.

The following is a list of IP distance-vector routing protocols:

- RIPv1 and RIPv2

- IGRP

- EIGRP (which could be considered a hybrid)

- RIPng

EIGRP

EIGRP is a hybrid routing protocol. It is a distance-vector protocol that implements some link-state routing protocol characteristics. Although EIGRP uses distance-vector metrics, it sends partial updates and maintains neighbor state information just as link-state protocols do. EIGRP does not send periodic updates as other distance-vector routing protocols do. The important thing to consider for the test is that EIGRP could be presented as a hybrid protocol. EIGRP metrics and mechanisms are discussed in Chapter 10, "RIP and EIGRP Characteristics and Design."

Link-State Routing Protocols

Link-state routing protocols address some of the limitations of distance-vector protocols. When running a link-state routing protocol, routers originate information about themselves (IP addresses), their connected links (the number and types of links), and the state of those links (up or down). The information is flooded to all routers in the network as changes in the link state occur. Each router makes a copy of the information received and forwards it without change. Each router independently calculates the best paths to each destination network, using a shortest path tree with itself as the root, and maintains a map of the network.

After the initial exchange of information, link-state updates are not sent unless a change in the topology occurs. Routers do send small Hello messages between neighbors to maintain neighbor relationships. If no updates have been sent, the routing table is refreshed after 30 minutes.

The following is a list of link-state routing protocols (including non-IP routing protocols):

- OSPF

- IS-IS

- OSPFv3

- IPX NetWare Link-Services Protocol (NLSP)

OSPF and IS-IS are covered in Chapter 11, "OSPF and IS-IS."

Distance-Vector Routing Protocols Versus Link-State Protocols

When choosing a routing protocol, consider that distance-vector routing protocols use more network bandwidth than link-state protocols. Distance-vector protocols generate more bandwidth overhead because of the large periodic routing updates. Link-state routing protocols do not generate significant routing update overhead but do use more router CPU and memory resources than distance-vector protocols. Generally, WAN bandwidth is a more expensive resource than router CPU and memory in modern devices.

Table 9-2 compares distance-vector to link-state routing protocols.

Table 9-2 *Distance-Vector Versus Link-State Routing Protocols*

Characteristic	Distance-Vector	Link-State
Scalability	Limited	Good
Convergence	Slow	Fast
Routing overhead	More traffic	Less traffic
Implementation	Easy	More complex
Protocols	RIPv1, RIPv2, IGRP, RIPng	OSPF, IS-IS, OSPFv3

EIGRP is a distance-vector protocol with link-state characteristics (hybrid) that give it high scalability, fast convergence, less routing overhead, and relatively easy configuration.

Hierarchical Versus Flat Routing Protocols

Some routing protocols require a network topology that must have a backbone network defined. This network contains some, or all, of the routers in the internetwork. When the internetwork is defined hierarchically, the backbone consists of only some devices. Backbone routers service and coordinate the routes and traffic to or from routers not in the local internetwork. The supported hierarchy is relatively shallow. Two levels of hierarchy are generally sufficient to provide scalability. Selected routers forward routes into the backbone. OSPF and IS-IS are hierarchical routing protocols.

Flat routing protocols do not allow a hierarchical network organization. They propagate all routing information throughout the network without dividing or summarizing large networks into smaller areas. Carefully designing network addressing to naturally support aggregation within routing-protocol advertisements can provide many of the benefits offered by hierarchical routing protocols. Every router is a peer of every other router in flat routing protocols; no router has a special role in the internetwork. RIPv1, IGRP, and RIPv2 are flat routing protocols. By default, EIGRP is a flat routing protocol, but it can be configured with manual summarization to support hierarchical designs.

Classless Versus Classful Routing Protocols

Routing protocols can be classified based on their support of VLSM and CIDR. Classful routing protocols do not advertise subnet masks in their routing updates; therefore, the configured subnet mask for the IP network must be the same throughout the entire internetwork. Furthermore, the subnets must, for all practical purposes, be contiguous within the larger internetwork. For example, if you use a classful routing protocol for network 130.170.0.0, you must use the chosen mask (such as 255.255.255.0) on all router interfaces using the 130.170.0.0 network. You must configure serial links with only two hosts and LANs with tens or hundreds of devices with the same mask of 255.255.255.0. The big disadvantage of classful routing protocols is that the network designer cannot take advantage of address summarization across networks (CIDR) or allocation of smaller or larger subnets within an IP network (VLSM). For example, with a classful routing protocol that uses a default mask of /25 for the entire network, you cannot assign a /30 subnet to a serial point-to-point circuit. Classful routing protocols are

- RIPv1

- IGRP

Classless routing protocols advertise the subnet mask with each route. You can configure subnetworks of a given IP network number with different subnet masks (VLSM). You can configure large LANs with a smaller subnet mask and configure serial links with a larger subnet mask, thereby conserving IP address space. Classless routing protocols also allow flexible route summarization and supernetting (CIDR). You create supernets by aggregating classful IP networks. For example, 200.100.100.0/23 is a supernet of 200.100.100.0/24 and 200.100.101.0/24. Classless routing protocols are

- RIPv2

- OSPF

- EIGRP

- IS-IS

- RIPng

- OSPFv3

- EIGRP for IPv6

- BGP

IPv4 Versus IPv6 Routing Protocols

With the increasing use of the IPv6 protocol, the CCDA must be prepared to design networks using IPv6 routing protocols. As IPv6 was defined, routing protocols needed to be updated to support the new IP address structure. None of the IPv4 routing protocols support IPv6 networks, and none of the IPv6 routing protocols are backward-compatible with IPv4 networks. But both protocols can coexist on the same network, each with their own routing protocol. Devices with dual stacks recognize which protocol is being used by the IP version field in the IP header.

RIPng is the IPv6-compatible RIP routing protocol. EIGRP for IPv6 is the new version of EIGRP that supports IPv6 networks. OSPFv3 was developed for IPv6, and OSPFv2 remains for IPv4. Internet drafts were written to provide IPv6 routing using IS-IS. Multiprotocol Extensions for BGP provide IPv6 support for BGP. Table 9-3 summarizes IPv4 versus IPv6 routing protocols.

Table 9-3 *IPv4 and IPv6 Routing Protocols*

IPv4 Routing Protocols	IPv6 Routing Protocols
RIPv1, RIPv2	RIPng
EIGRP	EIGRP for IPv6
OSPFv2	OSPFv3
IS-IS	IS-IS for IPv6
BGP	Multiprotocol Extensions for BGP

Administrative Distance

On Cisco routers running more than one routing protocol, it is possible for two different routing protocols to have a route to the same destination. Cisco routers assign each routing protocol an administrative distance. When multiple routes exist for a destination, the router selects the longest match. For example, if to reach a destination of 170.20.10.1 OSPF has a route prefix of 170.20.10.0/24 and EIGRP has a route prefix of 170.20.0.0/16, the OSPF route is preferred because the /24 prefix is longer than the /16 prefix. It is more specific.

In the event that two or more routing protocols offer the same route (with same prefix length) for inclusion in the routing table, the Cisco IOS router selects the route with the lowest administrative distance.

The administrative distance is a rating of the trustworthiness of a routing information source. Table 9-4 shows the default administrative distance for configured (static) or learned routes. In the table, you can see that static routes are trusted over dynamically learned routes. Within IGP routing protocols, EIGRP internal routes are trusted over OSPF, IS-IS, and RIP routes.

Table 9-4 *Default Administrative Distances for IP Routes*

IP Route	Administrative Distance
Connected interface	0
Static route directed to a connected interface	0
Static route directed to an IP address	1
EIGRP summary route	5
External BGP route	20
Internal EIGRP route	90
IGRP route	100
OSPF route	110
IS-IS route	115
RIP route	120
EGP route	140
External EIGRP route	170
Internal BGP route	200
Route of unknown origin	255

The administrative distance establishes the precedence used among routing algorithms. Suppose a router has an EIGRP route to network 172.20.10.0/24 with the best path out Ethernet 0 and an OSPF route for the same network out Ethernet 1. Because EIGRP has an administrative distance of 90 and OSPF has an administrative distance of 110, the router enters the EIGRP route in the routing table and sends packets with destinations of 172.20.10.0/24 out Ethernet 0.

Static routes have a default administrative distance of 1. There is one exception. If the static route points to a connected interface, it inherits the administrative distance of connected interfaces, which is 0. You can configure static routes with a different distance by appending the distance value to the end of the command.

Routing Protocol Metrics and Loop Prevention

Routing protocols use a metric to determine best routes to a destination. Some routing protocols use a combination of metrics to build a composite metric for best path selection. This section describes metrics and also covers routing loop-prevention techniques. You must understand each metric for the CCDA.

Some routing metric parameters are

- Hop count

- Bandwidth

- Cost

- Load

- Delay

- Reliability

- Maximum transmission unit (MTU)

Hop Count

The hop count parameter counts the number of links between routers the packet must traverse to reach a destination. The RIP routing protocol uses hop count as the metric for route selection. If all links were the same bandwidth, this metric would work well. The problem with routing protocols that use only this metric is that the shortest hop count is not always the most appropriate path. For example, between two paths to a destination network—one with two 56-kbps links and another with four T1 links—the router chooses the first path because of the lower number of hops (see Figure 9-3). However, this is not necessarily the best path. You would prefer to transfer a 20-MB file via the T1 links instead of the 56-kbps links.

Figure 9-3 *Hop Count Metric*

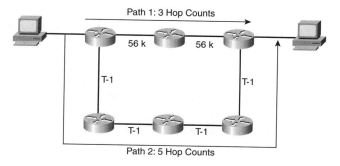

Bandwidth

The bandwidth parameter uses the interface bandwidth to determine a best path to a destination network. When bandwidth is the metric, the router prefers the path with the highest bandwidth to a destination. For example, a Fast Ethernet (100 Mbps) is preferred over a DS-3 (45 Mbps). As shown in Figure 9-3, a router using bandwidth to determine a path would select Path 2 because of the larger bandwidth, 1.5 Mbps over 56 kbps.

If a routing protocol uses only bandwidth as the metric and the path has several different speeds, the protocol can use the lowest speed in the path to determine the bandwidth for the path. EIGRP and IGRP use the minimum path bandwidth, inverted and scaled, as one part of the metric calculation. In Figure 9-4, Path 1 has two segments, with 256 kbps and 512 kbps of bandwidth. Because the smaller speed is 256 kbps, this speed is used as Path 1's bandwidth. The smallest bandwidth in Path 2 is 384 kbps. When the router has to choose between Path 1 and Path 2, it selects Path 2 because 384 kbps is larger than 256 kbps.

Figure 9-4   *Bandwidth Metric Example*

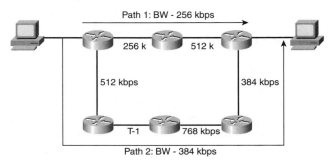

Cost

Cost is the name of the metric used by OSPF and IS-IS. In OSPF on a Cisco router, a link's default cost is derived from the interface's bandwidth.

Cisco's implementation of IS-IS assigns a default cost of 10 to all interfaces.

The formula to calculate cost in OSPF is

$$10^8/\text{BW}$$

where BW is the interface's default or configured bandwidth.

For 10-Mbps Ethernet, cost is calculated as follows:

$$\text{BW} = 10 \text{ Mbps} = 10 * 10^6 = 10{,}000{,}000 = 10^7$$
$$\text{cost (Ethernet)} = 10^8 / 10^7 = 10$$

The sum of all the costs to reach a destination is the metric for that route. The lowest cost is the preferred path.

Figure 9-5 shows an example of how the path costs are calculated. The path cost is the sum of all costs in the path. The cost for Path 1 is $350 + 180 = 530$. The cost for Path 2 is $15 + 50 + 100 + 50 = 215$.

Figure 9-5 *Cost Metric Example*

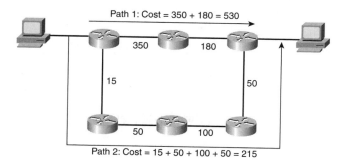

Because the cost of Path 2 is less than that of Path 1, Path 2 is selected as the best route to the destination.

Load

The load parameter refers to the degree to which the interface link is busy. The router keeps track of interface utilization; routing protocols can use this metric when calculating the best route. Load is one of the five parameters included in the definition of the IGRP and EIGRP metric. By default, it is not used to calculate the composite metric. If you have 512-kbps and 256-kbps links to reach a destination, but the 512-kbps circuit is 99 percent busy and the 256-kbps is only 5 percent busy, the 256 kbps link is the preferred path. On Cisco routers, the percentage of load is shown as a fraction over 255. Utilization at 100 percent is shown as 255/255, and utilization at 0 percent is shown as 0/255. Example 9-1 shows the load of a serial interface at 5/255 (1.9 percent).

Example 9-1 *Interface Load*

```
router3>show interface serial 1
Serial1 is up, line protocol is up
  Hardware is PQUICC Serial
  Internet address is 10.100.1.1/24
  MTU 1500 bytes, BW 1544 Kbit, DLY 20000 usec, rely 255/255, load 5/255
```

Delay

The delay parameter refers to how long it takes to move a packet to the destination. Delay depends on many factors, such as link bandwidth, utilization, port queues, and physical distance traveled. Total delay is one of the five parameters included in the definition of the IGRP and EIGRP composite metric. By default, it is used to calculate the composite metric. You can configure an interface's delay with the **delay** *tens-of-microseconds* command, where *tens-of-microseconds* specifies the delay in tens of microseconds for an interface or network segment. As shown in Example 9-2, the interface's delay is 20,000 microseconds.

Example 9-2   *Interface Delay*

```
router3>show interface serial 1
Serial1 is up, line protocol is up
  Hardware is PQUICC Serial
  Internet address is 10.100.1.1/24
  MTU 1500 bytes, BW 1544 Kbit, DLY 20000 usec, rely 255/255, load 1/255
```

Reliability

The reliability parameter is the dependability of a network link. Some WAN links tend to go up and down throughout the day. These links get a small reliability rating. Reliability is measured by factors such as a link's expected received keepalives and the number of packet drops and interface resets. If the ratio is high, the line is reliable. The best rating is 255/255, which is 100 percent reliability. Reliability is one of the five parameters included in the definition of the IGRP and EIGRP metric. By default, it is not used to calculate the composite metric. As shown in Example 9-3, you can verify an interface's reliability using the **show interface** command.

Example 9-3   *Interface Reliability*

```
router4#show interface serial 0
Serial0 is up, line protocol is up
  Hardware is PQUICC Serial
  MTU 1500 bytes, BW 1544 Kbit, DLY 20000 usec, rely 255/255, load 1/255
```

Maximum Transmission Unit (MTU)

The MTU parameter is simply the maximum size of bytes a unit can have on an interface. If the outgoing packet is larger than the MTU, the IP protocol might need to fragment it. If a packet larger than the MTU has the "do not fragment" flag set, the packet is dropped. As shown in Example 9-4, you can verify an interface's MTU using the **show interface** command.

Example 9-4   *Interface MTU*

```
router4#show interface serial 0
Serial0 is up, line protocol is up
  Hardware is PQUICC Serial
  MTU 1500 bytes, BW 1544 Kbit, DLY 20000 usec, rely 255/255, load 1/255
```

Routing Loop-Prevention Schemes

Some routing protocols employ schemes to prevent the creation of routing loops in the network. These schemes are

- Split horizon

- Split horizon with poison reverse

- Counting to infinity

Split Horizon

Split horizon is a technique used by distance-vector routing protocols to prevent routing loops. Routes that are learned from a neighboring router are not sent back to that neighboring router, thus suppressing the route. If the neighbor is already closer to the destination, it already has a better path.

In Figure 9-6, Routers 1, 2, and 3 learn about Networks A, B, C, and D. Router 2 learns about Network A from Router 1 and also has Networks B and C in its routing table. Router 3 advertises Network D to Router 2. Now, Router 2 knows about all networks. Router 2 sends its routing table to Router 3 without the route for Network D because it learned that route from Router 3.

Figure 9-6   *Simple Split-Horizon Example*

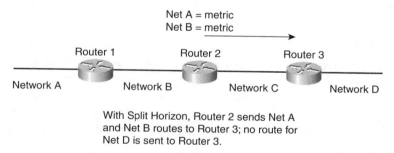

Split Horizon with Poison Reverse

Split horizon with poison reverse is a route update sent out an interface with an infinite metric for routes learned (received) from the same interface. Poison reverse simply indicates that the learned route is unreachable. It is more reliable than split horizon alone. Examine Figure 9-7. Instead of suppressing the route for Network D, Router 2 sends that route in the routing table marked as unreachable. In RIP, the poison-reverse route is marked with a metric of 16 (infinite) to prevent that path from being used.

Figure 9-7 *Split Horizon with Poison Reverse*

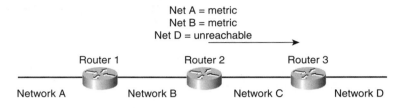

With Poison Reverse, Router 2 sends Net A
and Net B routes to Router 3; also, a
route for Net D with an infinite metric.

Counting to Infinity

Some routing protocols keep track of router hops as the packet travels through the network. In large networks where a routing loop might be present because of a network outage, routers might forward a packet without its reaching its destination.

Counting to infinity is a loop-prevention technique in which the router discards a packet when it reaches a maximum limit. It assumes that the network diameter is smaller than the maximum allowed hops. The router uses the Time-to-Live (TTL) field to count to infinity. The TTL starts at a set number and is decremented at each router hop. When the TTL equals 0, the packet is discarded. For IGRP and EIGRP, the TTL of routing updates is 100 by default.

Triggered Updates

Another loop-prevention and fast-convergence technique used by routing protocols is triggered updates. When a router interface changes state (up or down), the router is required to send an update message, even if it is not time for the periodic update message. Immediate notification about a network outage is key to maintaining valid routing entries within all routers in the network. Some distance-vector protocols, including RIP, specify a small time delay to avoid having triggered updates generate excessive network traffic. The time delay is variable for each router.

Summarization

Another characteristic of routing protocols is the ability to summarize routes. Protocols that support CIDR can perform summarization outside of IP class boundaries. By summarizing, the routing protocol can reduce the size of the routing table, and fewer routing updates on the network occur.

ODR

On-demand routing (ODR) is a mechanism for reducing the overhead with routing. Only Cisco routers can use ODR. With ODR, there is no need to configure dynamic routing protocols or static routes at a hub router. ODR eliminates the need to manage static route configuration at the hub router.

Figure 9-8 shows a hub-and-spoke network where you can configure ODR. The stub router is the spoke router in the hub-and-spoke network. The stub network consists of small LAN segments connected to the stub router and a WAN connection to the hub. Because all outgoing traffic travels via the WAN, no external routing information is necessary.

Figure 9-8 *ODR Hub-and-Spoke Network*

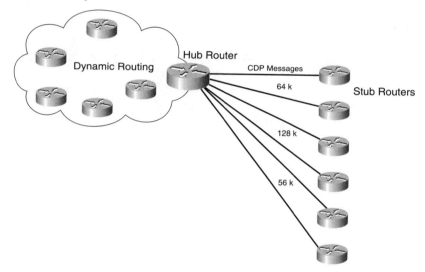

ODR simplifies the configuration of IP with stub networks in which the hub routers dynamically maintain routes to the stub networks. With ODR, the stub router advertises the IP prefixes of its connected networks to the hub router. It does so without requiring the configuration of an IP routing protocol at the stub routers.

ODR uses Cisco Discovery Protocol (CDP) for communication between hub and stub routers. CDP must be enabled for ODR to work. CDP updates every 60 seconds. Because ODR route prefixes are carried in CDP messages, a change is not reported until the CDP message is sent.

The hub router receives the prefix routes from its stub routers. You can configure the hub router to redistribute these prefixes into a dynamic routing protocol to propagate those routes to the rest of the internetwork. Stub routers are configured with a static default route to the hub router.

The benefits of ODR are as follows:

- Less routing overhead than dynamic routing protocols

- No configuration or management of static routes on the hub router

- Reduced circuit utilization

References and Recommended Readings

Bruno, A. *CCIE Routing and Switching Exam Certification Guide*. Indianapolis: Cisco Press, 2002.

Hedrick, C. RFC 1058, *Routing Information Protocol*. Available from http://www.ietf.org/rfc.

Malkin, G. RFC 2453, *RIP Version 2*. Available from http://www.ietf.org/rfc.

Moy, J. RFC 2328, *OSPF Version 2*. Available from http://www.ietf.org/rfc.

Oran, D. RFC 1142, *OSI IS-IS Intra-domain Routing Protocol*. Available from http://www.ietf.org/rfc.

Foundation Summary

The "Foundation Summary" section of each chapter lists the most important facts from the chapter. Although this section does not list every fact from the chapter that will be on the CCDA exam, a well-prepared CCDA candidate should at a minimum know all the details in each "Foundation Summary" before taking the exam.

The CCDA exam requires that you be familiar with the following topics that were covered in this chapter:

- **Routing protocol characteristics**—Characteristics such as static, dynamic, distance-vector, link-state, and interior and exterior protocols

- **Routing protocol metrics**—The metrics used by routing protocols and loop-prevention schemes

- **On-demand routing**—Where to use ODR

Table 9-5 compares distance-vector versus link-state routing protocols.

Table 9-5 *Distance-Vector Versus Link-State Routing Protocols*

Characteristic	Distance-Vector	Link-State
Scalability	Limited	Good
Convergence	Slow	Fast
Routing overhead	More traffic	Less traffic
Implementation	Easy	More complex

Ensure that you know and understand default administrative distances for IP routes. For your convenience, Table 9-6 lists the default administrative distances for IP routes.

Table 9-6 *Default Administrative Distances for IP Routes*

IP Route	Administrative Distance
Connected interface	0
Static route directed to a connected interface	0
Static route directed to the next-hop IP address	1
EIGRP summary route	5
External BGP route	20

continues

Table 9-6 *Default Administrative Distances for IP Routes (Continued)*

IP Route	Administrative Distance
Internal EIGRP route	90
IGRP route	100
OSPF route	110
IS-IS route	115
RIP route	120
EGP route	140
External EIGRP route	170
Internal BGP route	200
Route of unknown origin	255

Table 9-7 summarizes routing protocol characteristics.

Table 9-7 *Routing Protocol Characteristics*

Routing Protocol	Distance-Vector or Link-State	Interior or Exterior	Classful or Classless	Administrative Distance
RIPv1	DV	Interior	Classful	120
RIPv2	DV	Interior	Classless	120
IGRP	DV	Interior	Classful	100
EIGRP	DV (hybrid)	Interior	Classless	90
OSPF	LS	Interior	Classless	110
IS-IS	LS	Interior	Classless	115
BGP	—	Both	Classless	20

The CCDA must know the new routing protocols for IPv6, as listed in Table 9-8.

Table 9-8 *IPv4 and IPv6 Routing Protocols*

IPv4 Routing Protocols	IPv6 Routing Protocols
RIPv1, RIPv2	RIPng
EIGRP	EIGRP for IPv6
OSPFv2	OSPFv3
IS-IS	IS-IS for IPv6
BGP	Multiprotocol Extensions for BGP

Q&A

As mentioned in the Introduction, you have two choices for review questions: here in the book or the exam questions on the CD-ROM. The answers to these questions appear in Appendix A.

For more practice with exam format questions, use the exam engine on the CD-ROM.

1. What two routing protocols do not carry mask information in the route updates?

2. True or false: Link-state routing protocols send periodic routing updates.

3. True or false: RIPv2 was created to support IPv6.

4. True or false: The path with the lowest cost is preferred.

5. True or false: A link with a reliability of 200/255 is preferred over a link with a reliability of 10/255.

6. True or false: A link with a load of 200/255 is preferred over a link with a load of 10/255.

7. On a router, both EIGRP and OSPF have a route to 198.168.10.0/24. Which route is injected into the routing table?

8. On a router, both RIPv2 and IS-IS have a route to 198.168.10.0/24. Which route is injected into the routing table?

9. On a router, EIGRP has a route to the destination with a prefix of /28, and OSPF has a route to the destination with a prefix of /30. Which is used to reach the destination?

10. Which of the following is the best measurement of an interface's reliability and load?

    a. Reliability 255/255, load 1/255

    b. Reliability 255/255, load 255/255

    c. Reliability 1/255, load 1/255

    d. Reliability 1/255, load 255/255

11. Which routing protocols permit an explicit hierarchical topology?

    a. BGP

    b. EIGRP

    c. IS-IS

    d. RIP

    e. OSPF

    f. B and D

    g. C and E

12. What routing protocol parameter is concerned with how long a packet takes to travel from one end to another in the internetwork?

13. For what routing protocol metric is the value of a Fast Ethernet interface calculated as $10^8 / 10^8 = 1$?

14. What is the Cisco default OSPF metric for a Fast Ethernet interface?

15. Match the loop-prevention technique (numerals) with its description (letters):

i. Split horizon

ii. Split horizon with poison reverse

iii. Triggered updates

iv. Counting to infinity

a. Sends an infinite metric from which the route was learned

b. Drops a packet when the hop count limit is reached

c. Suppresses a route announcement from which the route was learned

d. Sends a route update when a route changes

16. True or false: Link-state routing protocols are more CPU- and memory-intensive than distance-vector routing protocols.

17. Which routing protocols would you select if you needed to take advantage of VLSMs? (Select all that apply.)

  a. RIPv1

  b. RIPv2

  c. IGRP

  d. EIGRP

  e. OSPF

  f. IS-IS

18. Which standards-based protocol would you select in a large IPv6 network?

  a. RIPng

  b. OSPFv3

  c. EIGRP for IPv6

  d. RIPv2

19. Which routing protocol is typically deployed by Internet service providers?

  a. EIGRP

  b. OSPFv2

    c. IS-IS

    d. RIPv2

20. Which of the following routing protocols are fast in converging when a change in the network occurs? (Select three.)

    a. RIPv1

    b. RIPv2

    c. EIGRP

    d. OSPF

    e. IS-IS

    f. BGP

21. If you are designing a large corporate network that cannot be designed in a hierarchy, which routing protocol would you recommend?

    a. RIPv1

    b. RIPv2

    c. EIGRP

    d. OSPF

    e. IS-IS

    f. BGP

22. Which routing protocols support VLSMs? (Select all that apply.)

    a. RIPv1

    b. RIPv2

    c. EIGRP

    d. OSPF

    e. IS-IS

    f. All of the above

23. You are connecting your network to an ISP. Which routing protocol would you use to exchange routes?

    a. RIPv1

    b. RIPv2

    c. EIGRP

    d. OSPF

    e. IS-IS

    f. BGP

    g. All of the above

24.   Which routing protocol requires only Cisco routers on the network?

    a. RIPv1

    b. RIPv2

    c. EIGRP

    d. OSPF

    e. IS-IS

    f. BGP

    g. All of the above

25.   Which routing protocol would be supported on an IPv6 network with multiple vendor routers?

    a. RIPv2

    b. EIGRP for IPv6

    c. BGPv6

    d. OSPFv3

    e. RIPv3

    f. All of the above

    g. B and D

26.   What additional protocol is required for ODR to work?

27.   For what network design is ODR preferred?

    a. Mesh topology

    b. Multipoint WAN

    c. Hub-and-spoke topology

    d. All of the above

28.   Which routing protocol represents each column of the following table?

Characteristic	A	B	C	D	E
Supports VLSM	Yes	Yes	Yes	Yes	Yes
Convergence	Fast	Fast	Slow	Fast	Fast
Scalability	High	High	Low	High	High
Supports IPv6	Yes	No	No	No	Yes
Proprietary	Yes	No	No	Yes	No

Answer the following questions based on Figure 9-9.

Figure 9-9 *Scenario Diagram*

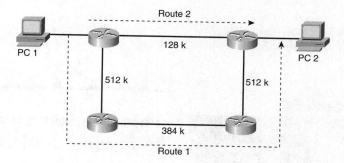

29. A user performs a Telnet from PC 1 to PC 2. If the metric used by the configured routing protocol is the bandwidth parameter, which route will the packets take?

   a. Route 1

   b. Route 2

   c. Neither. The information is insufficient.

   d. One packet will take Route 1, the following packet will take Route 2, and so on.

30. A user performs a Telnet from PC 1 to PC 2. If the metric used by the configured routing protocol is hop count, which route will the packets take?

   a. Route 1

   b. Route 2

   c. Neither. The information is insufficient.

   d. One packet will take Route 1, the following packet will take Route 2, and so on.

31. A user performs a Telnet from PC 1 to PC 2. If the metric used by the configured routing protocol is OSPF cost, which route will the packets take?

   a. Route 1.

   b. Route 2.

   c. Neither. The information is insufficient.

   d. One packet will take Route 1, the following packet will take Route 2, and so on.

This chapter covers the following subjects:

- RIPv1

- RIPv2

- RIPng

- IGRP

- EIGRP for IPv4 Networks

- EIGRP for IPv6 Networks

CHAPTER 10

RIP and EIGRP Characteristics and Design

This chapter reviews distance-vector routing protocols. It covers both versions of the Routing Information Protocol (RIP). Although RIPv1 is no longer a test subject, it is included for reference and because it is still seen on some enterprise networks. This chapter also covers Cisco's Enhanced Interior Gateway Routing Protocol (EIGRP). Cisco's IGRP is also included although it is no longer a test subject. This chapter also covers the routing protocols for IPv6: RIPng and EIGRP for IPv6. The CCDA should understand the capabilities and constraints of each routing protocol.

"Do I Know This Already?" Quiz

The purpose of the "Do I Know This Already?" quiz is to help you decide whether you need to read the entire chapter. If you intend to read the entire chapter, you do not necessarily need to answer these questions now.

The eight-question quiz, derived from the major sections in the "Foundation Topics" portion of the chapter, helps you determine how to spend your limited study time.

Table 10-1 outlines the major topics discussed in this chapter and the "Do I Know This Already?" quiz questions that correspond to those topics.

Table 10-1 *"Do I Know This Already?" Foundation Topics Section-to-Question Mapping*

Foundation Topics Section	Questions Covered in This Section
RIPv2	2, 3, 7
RIPng	5
EIGRP for IPv4 Networks	1, 4, 6, 7, 8
EIGRP for IPv6 Networks	5

CAUTION The goal of self-assessment is to gauge your mastery of the topics in this chapter. If you do not know the answer to a question or you are only partially sure, you should mark this question wrong for the purposes of the self-assessment. Giving yourself credit for an answer you correctly guess skews your self-assessment results and might give you a false sense of security.

1. Which protocol should you select if the network diameter is more than 17 hops?

    a. RIPv1

    b. RIPv2

    c. EIGRP

    d. Answers A and B

    e. Answers B and C

    f. Answers A, B, and C

2. How often does a RIPv2 router broadcast its routing table by default?

    a. Every 30 seconds

    b. Every 60 seconds

    c. Every 90 seconds

    d. RIPv1 does not broadcast periodically.

3. RIPv2 improves on RIPv1 with which of the following capabilities?

    a. Multicast updates, authentication, hop count

    b. Multicast updates, authentication, variable-length subnet mask (VLSM)

    c. Authentication, VLSM, hop count

    d. Multicast updates, hop count

4. Which protocol(s) maintain(s) neighbor adjacencies?

    a. RIPv2 and EIGRP

    b. IGRP and EIGRP

    c. RIPv2

    d. EIGRP

5. Which pair of distance-vector routing protocols supports IPv6 networks?

    a. EIGRP and OSPF

    b. RIPng and EIGRP

    c. RIPv2 and EIGRP

    d. OSPFv2 and EIGRP for IPv6

6. Which parameters are included in the computation of the EIGRP composite metric use by default?

    a. Bandwidth and load

    b. Bandwidth and delay

   c. Bandwidth and reliability

   d. Bandwidth and maximum transmission unit (MTU)

7. Which protocols support VLSMs?

   a. RIPv1 and RIPv2

   b. EIGRP and IGRP

   c. RIPv1 and IGRP

   d. RIPv2 and EIGRP

8. Which routing protocol implements the diffusing update algorithm (DUAL)?

   a. IS-IS

   b. IGRP

   c. EIGRP

   d. OSPF

The answers to the "Do I Know This Already?" quiz appear in Appendix A, "Answers to Chapter 'Do I Know This Already?' Quizzes and Q&A sections." The suggested choices for your next step are as follows:

■ **6 or less overall score**—Read the entire chapter. This includes the "Foundation Topics," "Foundation Summary," and "Q&A" sections.

■ **7 or 8 overall score**—If you want more review on these topics, skip to the "Foundation Summary" section and then go to the "Q&A" section. Otherwise, move to the next chapter.

Foundation Topics

This chapter covers the characteristics of the distance-vector routing protocols that a CCDA can choose from in a network design. *RIPv1* is a routing protocol developed in the late 1980s; it was the only interior gateway protocol (IGP) at that time. *RIPv2* provides enhancements to RIP, such as support for VLSMs.

IGRP is an IGP developed by Cisco in the early 1980s that was not limited to the 15-router-hop constraint in RIP. EIGRP is a hybrid routing protocol that uses distance-vector metrics and link-state routing protocol characteristics. RIPng is the IPv6 implementation of RIP. EIGRP for IPv6 is Cisco's implementation of EIGRP for IPv6 networks.

RIPv1

RFC 1058 from June 1988 defines RIPv1. RIP is a distance-vector routing protocol that uses router hop count as the metric. RIPv1 is a classful routing protocol that does not support VLSMs or classless interdomain routing (CIDR). RIPv1 is no longer a topic on the CCDA test. But reading this section will help you understand the evolution of this routing protocol and help you compare it to the later versions.

There is no method for authenticating route updates with RIPv1. A RIP router sends a copy of its routing table to its neighbors every 30 seconds. RIP uses split horizon with poison reverse; therefore, route updates are sent out an interface with an infinite metric for routes learned (received) from the same interface.

The RIP standard was based on the popular **routed** program used in UNIX systems since the 1980s. The Cisco implementation of RIP adds support for load balancing. RIP load-balances traffic if several paths have the same metric (equal-cost load balancing) to a destination. Also, RIP sends triggered updates when a route's metric changes. Triggered updates can help the network converge faster rather than wait for the periodic update. RIP has an administrative distance of 120. Chapter 9, "Routing Protocol Selection Criteria," covers administrative distance.

RIPv1 summarizes to IP network values at network boundaries. A network boundary occurs at a router that has one or more interfaces that do not participate in the specified IP network. The IP address assigned to the interface determines participation. IP class determines the network value. For example, an IP network that uses 24-bit subnetworks from 180.100.50.0/24 to 180.100.120.0/24 is summarized to 180.100.0.0/16 at a network boundary.

RIPv1 Forwarding Information Base

The RIPv1 protocol keeps the following information about each destination:

- **IP address**—IP address of the destination host or network

- **Gateway**—The first gateway along the path to the destination

- **Interface**—The physical network that must be used to reach the destination

- **Metric**—The number of hops to the destination

- **Timer**—The amount of time since the entry was last updated

The database is updated with the route updates received from neighboring routers. As shown in Example 10-1, the **show ip rip database** command shows a router's RIP private database.

Example 10-1   show ip rip database *Command*

```
router9#  show ip rip database
172.16.0.0/16     auto-summary
172.16.1.0/24     directly connected, Ethernet0
172.16.2.0/24
   [1] via 172.16.4.2, 00:00:06, Serial0
172.16.3.0/24
   [1] via 172.16.1.2, 00:00:02, Ethernet0
172.16.4.0/24     directly connected, Serial0
```

RIPv1 Message Format

The RIPv1 message format is described in RFC 1058 and is shown in Figure 10-1. The RIP messages are encapsulated using User Datagram Protocol (UDP). RIP uses the well-known UDP port 520.

Figure 10-1 *RIPv1 Message Format*

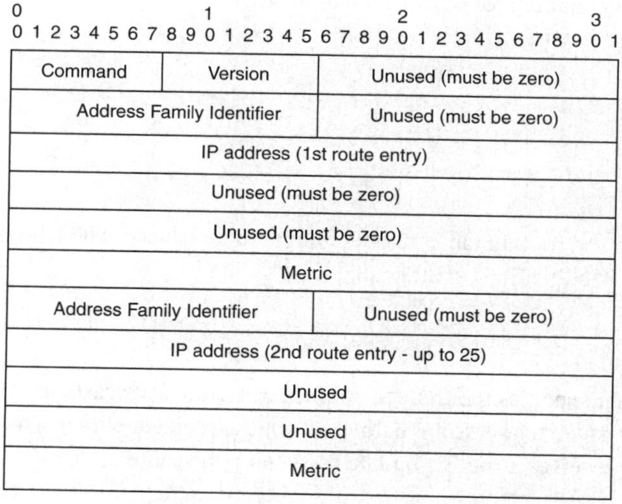

The following describes each field:

- **Command**—Describes the packet's purpose. The RFC describes five commands, two of which are obsolete and one of which is reserved. The two used commands are

  — **Request**—Requests all or part of the responding router's routing table.

  — **Response**—Contains all or part of the sender's routing table. This message might be a response to a request, or it might be an update message generated by the sender.

- **Version**—Set to a value of 1 for RIPv1.

- **Address Family Identifier (AFI)**—Set to a value of 2 for IP.

- **IP address**—The destination route. It might be a network address, subnet, or host route. Special route 0.0.0.0 is used for the default route.

- **Metric**—A field that is 32 bits in length. It contains a value between 1 and 15 inclusive, specifying the current metric for the destination. The metric is set to 16 to indicate that a destination is unreachable.

Because RIP has a maximum hop count, it implements counting to infinity. For RIP, infinity is 16 hops. Notice that the RIP message has no subnet masks accompanying each route. Five 32-bit words are repeated for each route entry: AFI (16 bits); unused, which is 0 (16 bits); IP address; two more 32-bit unused fields; and the 32-bit metric. Five 32-bit words equals 20 bytes for each route entry. Up to 25 routes are allowed in each RIP message. The maximum datagram size is limited to 512 bytes, not including the IP header. Calculating 25 routes by 20 bytes each, plus the RIP header (4 bytes), plus an 8-byte UDP header, you get 512 bytes.

RIPv1 Timers

The Cisco implementation of RIPv1 uses four timers:

- Update
- Invalid
- Flush
- Holddown

RIPv1 sends its full routing table out all configured interfaces. The table is sent periodically as a broadcast (255.255.255.255) to all hosts.

Update Timer

The update timer specifies the frequency of the periodic broadcasts. By default, the update timer is set to 30 seconds. Each route has a timeout value associated with it. The timeout gets reset every time the router receives a routing update containing the route.

Invalid Timer

When the timeout value expires, the route is marked as unreachable because it is marked invalid. The router marks the route invalid by setting the metric to 16. The route is retained in the routing table. By default, the invalid timer is 180 seconds, or six update periods (30 * 6 = 180).

Flush Timer

A route entry marked as invalid is retained in the routing table until the flush timer expires. By default, the flush timer is 240 seconds, which is 60 seconds longer than the invalid timer.

Holddown Timer

Cisco implements an additional timer for RIP, the holddown timer. The holddown timer stabilizes routes by setting an allowed time for which routing information about different paths is suppressed. After the metric for a route entry changes, the router accepts no updates for the route until the holddown timer expires. By default, the holddown timer is 180 seconds.

The output of the **show ip protocol** command, as shown in Example 10-2, shows the timers for RIP, unchanged from the defaults.

Example 10-2 *RIP Timers Verified with* **show ip protocol**

```
router9> show ip protocol
Routing Protocol is "rip"
  Sending updates every 30 seconds, next due in 3 seconds
  Invalid after 180 seconds, hold down 180, flushed after 240
  Outgoing update filter list for all interfaces is
  Incoming update filter list for all interfaces is
  Redistributing: rip
  Default version control: send version 1, receive any version
    Interface           Send  Recv  Triggered RIP  Key-chain
    Ethernet0            1     1 2
    Serial0             1     1 2
  Automatic network summarization is in effect
  Routing for Networks:
    172.16.0.0
  Routing Information Sources:
    Gateway         Distance      Last Update
    172.16.4.2          120       00:00:00
    172.16.1.2          120       00:00:07
  Distance: (default is 120)
```

RIPv1 Design

New networks should not be designed using RIPv1. It does not support VLSMs and CIDR. The IP addressing scheme with RIPv1 requires the same subnet mask for the entire IP network, a flat IP network. As shown in Figure 10-2, when you use RIPv1, all segments must have the same subnet mask.

Figure 10-2 *RIPv1 Design*

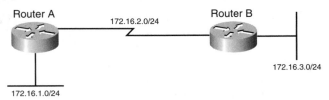

RIPv1 has low scalability. It is limited to 15 hops; therefore, the network diameter cannot exceed this limit. RIPv1 also broadcasts its routing table every 30 seconds. RIP's slow convergence time prevents it from being used as an IGP when time-sensitive data, such as voice and video, is being transmitted across the network. RIPv1 is usually limited to access networks where it can interoperate with servers running **routed** or with non-Cisco routers.

RIPv1 Summary

The characteristics of RIPv1 follow:

■ Distance-vector protocol.

■ Uses UDP port 520.

■ Classful protocol (no support for VLSM or CIDR).

■ Metric is router hop count.

■ Low scalability: maximum hop count is 15; unreachable routes have a metric of 16.

■ Periodic route updates broadcast every 30 seconds.

■ 25 routes per RIPv1 message.

■ Implements split horizon with poison reverse.

■ Implements triggered updates.

■ No support for authentication.

■ Administrative distance for RIP is 120.

■ Used in small, flat networks or at the edge of larger networks.

RIPv2

RIPv2 was first described in RFC 1388 and RFC 1723 (1994); the current RFC is 2453, written in November 1998. Although current environments use advanced routing protocols such as OSPF and EIGRP, some networks still use RIP. The need to use VLSMs and other requirements prompted the definition of RIPv2.

RIPv2 improves on RIPv1 with the ability to use VLSM, with support for route authentication, and with multicasting of route updates. RIPv2 supports CIDR. It still sends updates every 30 seconds and retains the 15-hop limit; it also uses triggered updates. RIPv2 still uses UDP port 520; the RIP process is responsible for checking the version number. It retains the loop-prevention strategies of poison reverse and counting to infinity. On Cisco routers, RIPv2 has the same administrative distance as RIPv1, which is 120. Finally, RIPv2 uses the IP address 224.0.0.9 when multicasting route updates to other RIP routers. As in RIPv1, RIPv2 by default summarizes IP networks at network boundaries. You can disable autosummarization if required.

You can use RIPv2 in small networks where VLSM is required. It also works at the edge of larger networks.

Authentication

Authentication can prevent communication with any RIP routers that are not intended to be part of the network, such as UNIX stations running **routed**. Only RIP updates with the authentication password are accepted. RFC 1723 defines simple plain-text authentication for RIPv2.

MD5 Authentication

In addition to plain-text passwords, the Cisco implementation provides the ability to use Message Digest 5 (MD5) authentication, which is defined in RFC 1321. Its algorithm takes as input a message of arbitrary length and produces as output a 128-bit fingerprint or message digest of the input, making it much more secure than plain-text passwords.

RIPv2 Forwarding Information Base

RIPv2 maintains a routing table database as in Version 1. The difference is that it also keeps the subnet mask information. The following list repeats the table information of RIPv1:

- **IP address**—The IP address of the destination host or network, with subnet mask

- **Gateway**—The first gateway along the path to the destination

- **Interface**—The physical network that must be used to reach the destination

- **Metric**—A number indicating the number of hops to the destination

- **Timer**—The amount of time since the route entry was last updated

RIPv2 Message Format

The RIPv2 message format takes advantage of the unused fields in the RIPv1 message format by adding subnet masks and other information. Figure 10-3 shows the RIPv2 message format.

Figure 10-3 *RIPv2 Message Format*

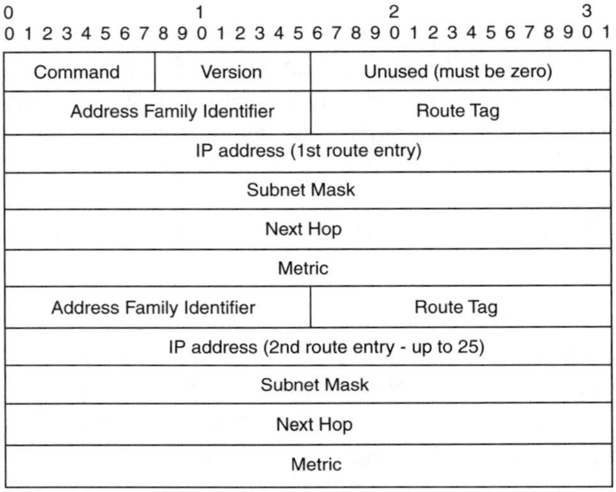

The following describes each field:

- **Command**—Indicates whether the packet is a request or response message. The request message asks that a router send all or a part of its routing table. Response messages contain route entries. The router sends the response periodically or as a reply to a request.

- **Version**—Specifies the RIP version used. It is set to 2 for RIPv2 and to 1 for RIPv1.

- **AFI**—Specifies the address family used. RIP is designed to carry routing information for several different protocols. Each entry has an AFI to indicate the type of address specified. The AFI for IP is 2. The AFI is set to 0xFFF for the first entry to indicate that the remainder of the entry contains authentication information.

- **Route tag**—Provides a method for distinguishing between internal routes (learned by RIP) and external routes (learned from other protocols). You can add this optional attribute during the redistribution of routing protocols.

- **IP address**—Specifies the IP address (network) of the destination.

- **Subnet mask**—Contains the subnet mask for the destination. If this field is 0, no subnet mask has been specified for the entry.

- **Next hop**—Indicates the IP address of the next hop where packets are sent to reach the destination.

- **Metric**—Indicates how many router hops to reach the destination. The metric is between 1 and 15 for a valid route or 16 for an unreachable or infinite route.

Again, as in Version 1, the router permits up to 25 occurrences of the last five 32-bit words (20 bytes) for up to 25 routes per RIP message. If the AFI specifies an authenticated message, the router can specify only 24 routing table entries. The updates are sent to the multicast address of 224.0.0.9.

RIPv2 Timers

RIPv2 timers are the same as in Version 1. They send periodic updates every 30 seconds. The default invalid timer is 180 seconds, the holddown timer is 180 seconds, and the flush timer is 240 seconds. You can write this list as 30/180/180/240, representing the U/I/H/F timers.

RIPv2 Design

Things to remember in designing a network with RIPv2 include that it supports VLSM within networks and CIDR for network summarization across adjacent networks. RIPv2 allows for the summarization of routes in a hierarchical network. RIPv2 is still limited to 16 hops; therefore, the network diameter cannot exceed this limit. RIPv2 multicasts its routing table every 30 seconds to the multicast IP address 224.0.0.9. RIPv2 is usually limited to accessing networks where it can interoperate with servers running **routed** or with non-Cisco routers. RIPv2 also appears at the edge of larger internetworks. RIPv2 further provides for route authentication.

As shown in Figure 10-4, when you use RIPv2, all segments can have different subnet masks.

Figure 10-4 *RIPv2 Design*

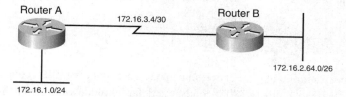

RIPv2 Summary

The characteristics of RIPv2 follow:

- Distance-vector protocol.

- Uses UDP port 520.

■   Classless protocol (support for CIDR).

■   Supports VLSMs.

■   Metric is router hop count.

■   Low scalability: maximum hop count is 15; infinite (unreachable) routes have a metric of 16.

■   Periodic route updates are sent every 30 seconds to multicast address 224.0.0.9.

■   25 routes per RIP message (24 if you use authentication).

■   Supports authentication.

■   Implements split horizon with poison reverse.

■   Implements triggered updates.

■   Subnet mask included in route entry.

■   Administrative distance for RIPv2 is 120.

■   Not scalable. Used in small, flat networks or at the edge of larger networks.

RIPng

RIPng (RIP next generation) is the version of RIP that can be used in IPv6 networks. It is described in RFC 2080. Most of the RIP mechanisms from RIPv2 remain the same. RIPng still has a 15-hop limit, counting to infinity, and split horizon with poison reverse. A hop count of 16 still indicates an unreachable route.

Instead of using UDP port 520 as in RIPv2, RIPng uses UDP port 521. RIPng supports IPv6 addresses and prefixes. RIPng uses multicast group FF02::9 for RIPng updates to all RIPng routers.

RIPng Timers

RIPng timers are similar to RIPv2. Periodic updates are sent every 30 seconds. The default invalid timeout for routes to expire is 180 seconds, the default holddown timer is 180 seconds, and the default garbage-collection timer is 120 seconds.

Authentication

RIPng does not implement authentication methods in its protocol as RIPv2 does. RIPng relies on built-in IPv6 authentication functions.

RIPng Message Format

Figure 10-5 shows the RIPng routing message. Each route table entry (RTE) consists of the IPv6 prefix, route tag, prefix length, and metric.

Figure 10-5 *RIPng Update Message Format*

```
 0           1           2           3
 01234567890123456789012345678901
┌──────────────────┬──────────┬──────────┐
│     Command      │ Version  │ Must     │
│                  │          │ be zero  │
├──────────────────┴──────────┴──────────┤
│ Route entry 1: IPv6 Prefix              │
│ 128 bits                                │
├──────────────────┬──────────┬──────────┤
│    Route tag     │Prefix length│ metric │
├──────────────────┴──────────┴──────────┤
│ Route entry 2: IPv6 prefix              │
│ 128 bits                                │
├──────────────────┬──────────┬──────────┤
│    Route tag     │Prefix length│ metric │
└──────────────────┴──────────┴──────────┘
```

The following describes each field:

- **Command**—Indicates whether the packet is a request or response message. This field is set to 1 for a request and to 2 for a response.

- **Version**—Set to 1, the first version of RIPng.

- **IPv6 prefix**—The destination 128-bit IPv6 prefix.

- **Route tag**—As with RIPv2, this is a method that distinguishes internal routes (learned by RIP) from external routes (learned by external protocols). Tagged during redistribution.

- **Prefix length**—Indicates the significant part of the prefix.

- **Metric**—This 8-bit field contains the router hop metric.

RIPv2 has a Next Hop field for each of its route entries. An RTE with a metric of 0xFF indicates the next-hop address to reduce the number of route entries in RIPng. It groups all RTEs after it to summarize all destinations to that particular next-hop address. Figure 10-6 shows the format of the special RTE indicating the next-hop entry.

Figure 10-6 *RIPng Next-Hop Route Table Entry*

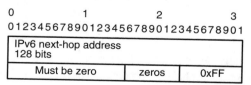

RIPng Design

RIPng has low scalability. As with RIPv2, it is limited to 15 hops; therefore, the network diameter cannot exceed this limit. RIPng also broadcasts its routing table every 30 seconds, which causes network overhead. RIPng can be used only in small networks.

RIPng Summary

The characteristics of RIPng are as follows:

- Distance-vector protocol for IPv6 networks only.

- Uses UDP port 521.

- Metric is router hop count.

- Maximum hop count is 15; infinite (unreachable) routes have a metric of 16.

- Periodic route updates are sent every 30 seconds to multicast address FF02::9.

- Uses IPv6 functions for authentication.

- Implements split horizon with poison reverse.

- Implements triggered updates.

- Prefix length included in route entry.

- Administrative distance for RIPv2 is 120.

- Not scalable. Used in small networks.

IGRP

Cisco Systems developed IGRP to overcome the limitations of RIPv1. IGRP is a distance-vector routing protocol that considers a composite metric that, by default, uses bandwidth and delay as parameters instead of hop count. IGRP is not limited to RIP's 15-hop limit. IGRP has a maximum hop limit of 100 by default and can be configured to support a network diameter of 255.

> **NOTE** IGRP is no longer a CCDA test topic. EIGRP is the enhanced version of IGRP. However, reading this section will provide a good foundation for learning EIGRP in the section that follows.

With IGRP, routers usually select paths with a larger minimum-link bandwidth over paths with a smaller hop count. Links do not have a hop count. They are exactly one hop.

IGRP is a classful protocol and cannot implement VLSM or CIDR. IGRP summarizes at network boundaries. As in RIP, IGRP implements split horizon with poison reverse, triggered updates, and holddown timers for stability and loop prevention. Another benefit of IGRP is that it can load-balance over unequal-cost links. As a routing protocol developed by Cisco, IGRP is available only on Cisco routers.

By default, IGRP load-balances traffic if several paths have equal cost to the destination. IGRP does unequal-cost load balancing if configured with the **variance** command.

IGRP Timers

IGRP sends its routing table to its neighbors every 90 seconds. IGRP's default update period of 90 seconds is a benefit compared to RIP, which can consume excessive bandwidth when sending updates every 30 seconds. IGRP uses an invalid timer to mark a route as invalid after 270 seconds (3 times the update timer). As with RIP, IGRP uses a flush timer to remove a route from the routing table; the default flush timer is set to 630 seconds (7 times the update period and more than 10 minutes).

If a network goes down or the metric for the network increases, the route is placed in holddown. The router accepts no new changes for the route until the holddown timer expires. This setup prevents routing loops in the network. The default holddown timer is 280 seconds (3 times the update timer plus 10 seconds). Table 10-2 summarizes the default settings for IGRP timers.

Table 10-2   *IGRP Timers*

IGRP Timer	Default Time
Update	90 seconds
Invalid	270 seconds
Holddown	280 seconds
Flush	630 seconds

IGRP Metrics

IGRP uses a composite metric based on bandwidth, delay, load, and reliability. Chapter 9 discusses these metrics. By default, IGRP uses bandwidth and delay to calculate the composite metric, as follows:

$$IGRP_{metric} = \{k1 * BW + [(k2 * BW)/(256 - load)] + k3 * delay\} * \{k5/(reliability + k4)\}$$

In this formula, BW is the lowest interface bandwidth in the path, and delay is the sum of all outbound interface delays in the path. The router dynamically measures reliability and load. The values of reliability and load used in the metric computation range from 1 to 255. Cisco IOS routers display 100 percent reliability as 255/255. They also display load as a fraction of 255. They display an interface with no load as 1/255. By default, k1 and k3 are set to 1, and k2, k4, and k5 are set to 0. With the default values, the metric becomes

$$\text{IGRP}_{\text{metric}} = \{1 * \text{BW} + [(0 * \text{BW})/(256 - \text{load})] + 1 * \text{delay}\} * \{0/(\text{reliability} + 0)\}$$
$$\text{IGRP}_{\text{metric}} = \text{BW} + \text{delay}$$

The BW is 10,000,000 divided by the smallest of all the bandwidths (in kbps) from outgoing interfaces to the destination. To find delay, add all the delays (in microseconds) from the outgoing interfaces to the destination, and divide this number by 10. (The delay is in 10s of microseconds.)

Example 10-3 shows the output interfaces of two routers. For a source host to reach network 172.16.2.0, a path takes the serial link and then the Ethernet interface. The bandwidths are 10,000 and 1544; the slowest bandwidth is 1544. The sum of delays is 20000 + 1000 = 21000.

Example 10-3 *show interface*

```
RouterA>  show interface serial 0
Serial0 is up, line protocol is up
  Hardware is HD64570
  Internet address is 172.16.4.1/24
  MTU 1500 bytes, BW 1544 Kbit, DLY 20000 usec,
     reliability 255/255, txload 1/255, rxload 1/255


RouterB>  show interface ethernet 0
Ethernet0 is up, line protocol is up
  Hardware is Lance, address is 0010.7b80.bad5 (bia 0010.7b80.bad5)
  Internet address is 172.16.2.1/24
  MTU 1500 bytes, BW 10000 Kbit, DLY 1000 usec,
     reliability 255/255, txload 1/255, rxload 1/255
```

The IGRP metric is calculated as follows:

$$\text{IGRP}_{\text{metric}} = (10,000,000/1544) + (20000 + 1000)/10$$
$$\text{IGRP}_{\text{metric}} = 6476 + 2100 = 8576$$

You can change the default metrics using the **metric weight** *tos k1 k2 k3 k4 k5* subcommand under **router igrp**. Cisco once intended to implement the tos field as a specialized service in IGRP. However, it was never implemented, so the value of *tos* is always 0. The *k* arguments are the k values used to build the composite metric. For example, if you want to use all metrics, the command is as follows:

```
router igrp n
  metric weight 0 1 1 1 1 1
```

IGRP Design

IGRP should not be used in the design of new networks because it does not support VLSMs. The IP addressing scheme with IGRP requires the same subnet mask for the entire IP network, a flat IP network. IGRP does not support CIDR and network summarization within the major network boundary. IGRP is not limited to a maximum of 15 hops as RIP is; therefore, the network diameter can be larger than that of networks using RIP. IGRP also broadcasts its routing table every 90 seconds, which produces less network overhead than RIP. IGRP is limited to Cisco-only networks.

Drawbacks of IGRP are that it lacks VLSM support and that it broadcasts its entire table every 90 seconds. Its slow convergence makes it too slow for time-sensitive applications. EIGRP is recommended over IGRP.

As shown in Figure 10-7, when you use IGRP, all segments must have the same subnet mask.

Figure 10-7 *IGRP Design*

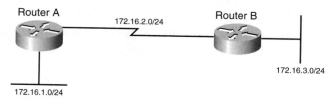

IGRP Summary

The characteristics of IGRP follow:

- Distance-vector protocol.

- Uses IP protocol number 9.

- Classful protocol (no support for CIDR).

- No support for VLSMs.

- Composite metric using bandwidth and delay by default.

- You can include load and reliability in the metric.

- Route updates are sent every 90 seconds.

- 104 routes per IGRP message.

- Hop count is limited to 100 by default and is configurable up to 255.

- No support for authentication.

- Implements split horizon with poison reverse.

- Implements triggered updates.

- By default, equal-cost load balancing. Unequal-cost load balancing with the **variance** command.

- Administrative distance is 100.

- Previously used in large networks; now replaced by EIGRP.

EIGRP for IPv4 Networks

Cisco Systems released EIGRP in the early 1990s as an evolution of IGRP toward a more scalable routing protocol for large internetworks. EIGRP is a classless protocol that permits the use of VLSMs and that supports CIDR for the scalable allocation of IP addresses. EIGRP does not send routing updates periodically, as does IGRP. EIGRP allows for authentication with MD5. EIGRP autosummarizes networks at network borders and can load-balance over unequal-cost paths. Packets using EIGRP use IP 88. Only Cisco routers can use EIGRP.

EIGRP is an advanced distance-vector protocol that implements some characteristics similar to those of link-state protocols. Some Cisco documentation refers to EIGRP as a hybrid protocol. EIGRP advertises its routing table to its neighbors as distance-vector protocols do, but it uses hellos and forms neighbor relationships as link-state protocols do. EIGRP sends partial updates when a metric or the topology changes on the network. It does not send full routing-table updates in periodic fashion as do distance-vector protocols. EIGRP uses DUAL to determine loop-free paths to destinations. This section discusses DUAL.

By default, EIGRP load-balances traffic if several paths have equal cost to the destination. EIGRP performs unequal-cost load balancing if you configure it with the **variance** *n* command. EIGRP includes routes that are equal to or less than *n* times the minimum metric route to a destination. As in RIP and IGRP, EIGRP also summarizes IP networks at network boundaries.

EIGRP internal routes have an administrative distance of 90. EIGRP summary routes have an administrative distance of 5, and EIGRP external routes (from redistribution) have an administrative distance of 170.

EIGRP Components

EIGRP has four components that characterize it:

- Protocol-dependent modules

- Neighbor discovery and recovery

- Reliable Transport Protocol (RTP)

- DUAL

You should know the role of the EIGRP components, which are described in the following sections.

Protocol-Dependent Modules

EIGRP uses different modules that independently support IP, Internetwork Packet Exchange (IPX), and AppleTalk routed protocols. These modules are the logical interface between DUAL and routing protocols such as IPX RIP, AppleTalk Routing Table Maintenance Protocol (RTMP), and IGRP. The EIGRP module sends and receives packets but passes received information to DUAL, which makes routing decisions.

EIGRP automatically redistributes with IGRP if you configure both protocols with the same autonomous system number. When configured to support IPX, EIGRP communicates with the IPX RIP and forwards the route information to DUAL to select the best paths. AppleTalk EIGRP automatically redistributes routes with AppleTalk RTMP to support AppleTalk networks. AppleTalk is not a CCDA objective and is not covered in this book.

Neighbor Discovery and Recovery

EIGRP discovers and maintains information about its neighbors. It multicasts hello packets (224.0.0.10) every 5 seconds on most interfaces. The router builds a table with EIGRP neighbor information. The holdtime to maintain a neighbor is 3 times the hello time: 15 seconds. If the router does not receive a hello in 15 seconds, it removes the neighbor from the table. EIGRP multicasts hellos every 60 seconds on multipoint WAN interfaces (X.25, Frame Relay, ATM) with speeds less than a T-1 (1.544 Mbps), inclusive. The neighbor holdtime is 180 seconds on these types of interfaces. To summarize, hello/holdtime timers are 5/15 seconds for high-speed links and 60/180 seconds for low-speed links.

Example 10-4 shows an EIGRP neighbor database. The table lists the neighbor's IP address, the interface to reach it, the neighbor holdtime timer, and the uptime.

Example 10-4 *EIGRP Neighbor Database*

```
Router#  show ip eigrp neighbor
IP-EIGRP neighbors for process 100
H   Address                  Interface   Hold Uptime    SRTT   RTO  Q  Seq Type
                                         (sec)          (ms)        Cnt Num
1   172.17.1.1               Se0          11 00:11:27    16    200  0  2
0   172.17.2.1               Et0          12 00:16:11    22    200  0  3
```

RTP

EIGRP uses RTP to manage EIGRP packets. RTP ensures the reliable delivery of route updates and also uses sequence numbers to ensure ordered delivery. It sends update packets using multicast address 224.0.0.10. It acknowledges updates using unicast hello packets with no data.

DUAL

EIGRP implements DUAL to select paths and guarantee freedom from routing loops. J.J. Garcia Luna-Aceves developed DUAL. It is mathematically proven to result in a loop-free topology, providing no need for periodic updates or route-holddown mechanisms that make convergence slower.

DUAL selects a best path and a second-best path to reach a destination. The best path selected by DUAL is the *successor*, and the second-best path (if available) is the *feasible successor*. The feasible distance is the lowest calculated metric of a path to reach the destination. The topology table in Example 10-5 shows the feasible distance. The example also shows two paths (Ethernet 0 and Ethernet 1) to reach 172.16.4.0/30. Because the paths have different metrics, DUAL chooses only one successor.

Example 10-5 *Feasible Distance as Shown in the EIGRP Topology Table*

```
Router8#  show ip eigrp topology
IP-EIGRP Topology Table for AS(100)/ID(172.16.3.1)


Codes: P - Passive, A - Active, U - Update, Q - Query, R - Reply,
       r - reply Status, s - sia Status


P 172.16.4.0/30, 1 successors, FD is 2195456
        via 172.16.1.1 (2195456/2169856), Ethernet0
        via 172.16.5.1 (2376193/2348271), Ethernet1
P 172.16.1.0/24, 1 successors, FD is 281600
        via Connected, Ethernet0
```

The route entries in Example 10-5 are marked with a P for the passive state. A destination is in passive state when the router is not performing any recomputations for the entry. If the successor goes down and the route entry has feasible successors, the router does not need to perform any recomputations and does not go into active state.

DUAL places the route entry for a destination into active state if the successor goes down and there are no feasible successors. EIGRP routers send query packets to neighboring routers to find a feasible successor to the destination. A neighboring router can send a reply packet that indicates it has a feasible successor or a query packet. The query packet indicates that the neighboring router does not have a feasible successor and will participate in the recomputation. A route does not return to passive state until it has received a reply packet from each neighboring router. If the router does not receive all the replies before the "active-time" timer expires, DUAL declares the route as stuck in active (SIA). The default active timer is 3 minutes.

EIGRP Timers

EIGRP sets updates only when necessary and sends them only to neighboring routers. There is no periodic update timer.

EIGRP uses hello packets to learn of neighboring routers. On high-speed networks, the default hello packet interval is 5 seconds. On multipoint networks with link speeds of T1 and slower, hello packets are unicast every 60 seconds.

The holdtime to maintain a neighbor adjacency is 3 times the hello time: 15 seconds. If a router does not receive a hello within the holdtime, it removes the neighbor from the table. Hellos are multicast every 60 seconds on multipoint WAN interfaces (X.25, Frame Relay, ATM) with speeds less than 1.544 Mbps, inclusive. The neighbor holdtime is 180 seconds on these types of interfaces. To summarize, hello/holdtime timers are 5/15 seconds for high-speed links and 60/180 seconds for multipoint WAN links less than 1.544 Mbps, inclusive.

NOTE   EIGRP does not send updates using a broadcast address; instead, it sends them to the multicast address 224.0.0.10 (all EIGRP routers).

EIGRP Metrics

EIGRP uses the same composite metric as IGRP, but the BW term is multiplied by 256 for finer granularity. The composite metric is based on bandwidth, delay, load, and reliability. MTU is not an attribute for calculating the composite metric.

EIGRP calculates the composite metric with the following formula:

$$\text{EIGRP}_{metric} = \{k1 * BW + [(k2 * BW)/(256 - \text{load})] + k3 * \text{delay}\} * \{k5/(\text{reliability} + k4)\}$$

In this formula, BW is the lowest interface bandwidth in the path, and delay is the sum of all outbound interface delays in the path. The router dynamically measures reliability and load. It expresses 100 percent reliability as 255/255. It expresses load as a fraction of 255. An interface with no load is represented as 1/255.

Bandwidth is the inverse minimum bandwidth (in kbps) of the path in bits per second scaled by a factor of $256 * 10^7$. The formula for bandwidth is

$$(256 * 10^7)/BW_{min}$$

The delay is the sum of the outgoing interface delays (in microseconds) to the destination. A delay of all 1s (that is, a delay of hexadecimal FFFFFFFF) indicates that the network is unreachable. The formula for delay is

$$[\text{sum of delays}] * 256$$

Reliability is a value between 1 and 255. Cisco IOS routers display reliability as a fraction of 255. That is, 255/255 is 100 percent reliability, or a perfectly stable link; a value of 229/255 represents a 90 percent reliable link.

Load is a value between 1 and 255. A load of 255/255 indicates a completely saturated link. A load of 127/255 represents a 50 percent saturated link.

By default, $k1 = k3 = 1$ and $k2 = k4 = k5 = 0$. EIGRP's default composite metric, adjusted for scaling factors, is

$$\text{EIGRP}_{metric} = 256 * \{ [10^7/BW_{min}] + [\text{sum\_of\_delays}] \}$$

BW_{min} is in kbps, and sum_of_delays is in 10s of microseconds. The bandwidth and delay for an Ethernet interface are 10 Mbps and 1 ms, respectively.

The calculated EIGRP BW metric is

$$256 * 10^7/BW = 256 * 10^7/10{,}000$$
$$= 256 * 10{,}000$$
$$= 256{,}000$$

The calculated EIGRP delay metric is

256 * sum of delay = 256 * 1 ms
= 256 * 100 * 10 microseconds
= 25,600 (in 10s of microseconds)

Table 10-3 shows some default values for bandwidth and delay.

Table 10-3   *Default EIGRP Values for Bandwidth and Delay*

Media Type	Delay	Bandwidth
Satellite	5120 (2 seconds)	5120 (500 Mbps)
Ethernet	25,600 (1 ms)	256,000 (10 Mbps)
T-1 (1.544 Mbps)	512,000 (20,000 ms)	1,657,856
64 kbps	512,000	40,000,000
56 kbps	512,000	45,714,176

As with IGRP, you use the **metric weights** subcommand to change EIGRP metric computation. You can change the k values in the EIGRP composite metric formula to select which EIGRP metrics to use. The command to change the k values is the **metric weights** *tos k1 k2 k3 k4 k5* subcommand under **router eigrp** *n*. The *tos* value is always 0. You set the other arguments to 1 or 0 to alter the composite metric. For example, if you want the EIGRP composite metric to use all the parameters, the command is as follows:

```
router eigrp n
  metric weights 0 1 1 1 1 1
```

EIGRP Packet Types

EIGRP uses five packet types:

- **Hello**—EIGRP uses hello packets in the discovery of neighbors. They are multicast to 224.0.0.10. By default, EIGRP sends hello packets every 5 seconds (60 seconds on WAN links with 1.544 Mbps speeds or less).

- **Acknowledgment**—An acknowledgment packet acknowledges the receipt of an update packet. It is a hello packet with no data. EIGRP sends acknowledgment packets to the unicast address of the sender of the update packet.

- **Update**—Update packets contain routing information for destinations. EIGRP unicasts update packets to newly discovered neighbors; otherwise, it multicasts update packets to 224.0.0.10 when a link or metric changes. Update packets are acknowledged to ensure reliable transmission.

- **Query**—EIGRP sends query packets to find feasible successors to a destination. Query packets are always multicast unless they are sent as a response; then they are unicast back to the originator.

- **Reply**—EIGRP sends reply packets to respond to query packets. Reply packets provide a feasible successor to the sender of the query. Reply packets are unicast to the sender of the query packet.

EIGRP Design

When designing a network with EIGRP, remember that it supports VLSMs, CIDR, and network summarization. EIGRP allows for the summarization of routes in a hierarchical network. EIGRP is not limited to 16 hops as RIP is; therefore, the network diameter can exceed this limit. In fact, the EIGRP diameter can be 225 hops. The default diameter is 100. EIGRP can be used in the site-to-site WAN and IPsec VPNs. In the enterprise campus, EIGRP can be used in data centers, server distribution, building distribution, and the network core.

EIGRP does not broadcast its routing table periodically, so there is no large network overhead. You can use EIGRP for large networks; it is a potential routing protocol for the core of a large network. EIGRP further provides for route authentication.

As shown in Figure 10-8, when you use EIGRP, all segments can have different subnet masks.

Figure 10-8 *EIGRP Design*

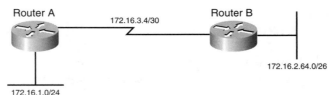

EIGRP Summary

The characteristics of EIGRP follow:

- Hybrid routing protocol (a distance-vector protocol that has link-state protocol characteristics).

- Uses IP protocol number 88.

- Classless protocol (supports VLSMs).

- Default composite metric uses bandwidth and delay.

- You can factor load and reliability into the metric.

- Sends partial route updates only when there are changes.

- Supports MD5 authentication.

- Uses DUAL for loop prevention and fast convergence.

- By default, equal-cost load balancing. Unequal-cost load balancing with the **variance** command.

- Administrative distance is 90 for EIGRP internal routes, 170 for EIGRP external routes, and 5 for EIGRP summary routes.

- High scalability; used in large networks.

- Does not require a hierarchical physical topology.

EIGRP for IPv6 Networks

Cisco has developed EIGRP support for IPv6 networks to route IPv6 prefixes. EIGRP for IPv6 is configured and managed separately from EIGRP for IPv4; no network statements are used. EIGRP for IPv6 retains all the same characteristics (network discovery, DUAL, modules) and functions as EIGRP for IPv4. The major themes with EIGRP for IPv6 are as follows:

- Implements the protocol-independent modules.

- Does EIGRP neighbor discovery and recovery.

- Uses reliable transport.

- Implements the DUAL algorithm for a loop-free topology.

- Uses the same metrics as EIGRP for IPv4 networks.

- Has the same timers as EIGRP for IPv4.

- Uses same concepts of feasible successors and feasible distance as EIGRP for IPv4.

- Uses the same packet types as EIGRP for IPv4.

- Managed and configured separately from EIGRP for IPv4.

- Requires a router ID before it can start running.

- Configured on interfaces. No network statements are used.

The difference is the use of IPv6 prefixes and the use of IPv6 multicast group FF02::A for EIGRP updates. Because EIGRP for IPv6 uses the same characteristics and functions as EIGRP for IPv4 covered in the previous section on EIGRP, they are not repeated here.

EIGRP for IPv6 Design

Use EIGRP for IPv6 in large geographic IPv6 networks. EIGRP's diameter can scale up to 255 hops, but this network diameter is not recommended. EIGRP authentication can be used instead of IPv6 authentication.

EIGRP for IPv6 can be used in the site-to-site WAN and IPsec VPNs. In the enterprise campus, EIGRP can be used in data centers, server distribution, building distribution, and the network core.

EIGRP's DUAL algorithm provides for fast convergence and routing loop prevention. EIGRP does not broadcast its routing table periodically, so there is no large network overhead. The only constraint is that EIGRP for IPv6 is restricted to Cisco routers.

EIGRP for IPv6 Summary

The characteristics of EIGRP for IPv6 are as follows:

- Uses the same characteristics and functions as EIGRP for IPv4.

- Hybrid routing protocol (a distance-vector protocol that has link-state protocol characteristics).

- Uses Next Header protocol 88.

- Routes IPv6 prefixes.

- Default composite metric uses bandwidth and delay.

- You can factor load and reliability into the metric.

- Sends partial route updates only when there are changes.

- Supports EIGRP MD5 authentication.

- Uses DUAL for loop prevention and fast convergence.

- By default, equal-cost load balancing. Unequal-cost load balancing with the **variance** command.

- Administrative distance is 90 for EIGRP internal routes, 170 for EIGRP external routes, and 5 for EIGRP summary routes.

■ Uses IPv6 multicast FF02::A for EIGRP updates.

■ High scalability; used in large networks.

References and Recommended Readings

Bruno, A. *CCIE Routing and Switching Exam Certification Guide*. Indianapolis: Cisco Press, 2002.

Doyle, J. *Routing TCP/IP*, Volume I. Indianapolis: Cisco Press, 1998.

"Enhanced IGRP." http://www.cisco.com/univercd/cc/td/doc/cisintwk/ito_doc/en_igrp.htm.

"Enhanced Interior Gateway Routing Protocol." http://www.cisco.com/en/US/tech/tk365/tk207/technologies_white_paper09186a0080094cb7.shtml.

Hedrick, C. RFC 1058, Routing Information Protocol. Available from http://www.ietf.org/rfc.

"Implementing EIGRP for IPv6." http://www.cisco.com/en/US/partner/products/sw/iosswrel/ps5187/products_configuration_guide_chapter09186a00805fc867.html#wp1049317.

Malkin, G. RFC 1723, *RIP Version 2 - Carrying Additional Information*. Available from http://www.ietf.org/rfc.

Malkin, G. RFC 2453, *RIP Version 2*. Available from http://www.ietf.org/rfc.

Malkin, G. and R. Minnear. RFC 2080, *RIPng for IPv6*. Available from http://www.ietf.org/rfc.

Rivest, R. RFC 1321, *The MD5 Message-Digest Algorithm*. Available from http://www.ietf.org/rfc.

"Routing Information Protocol." http://www.cisco.com/univercd/cc/td/doc/cisintwk/ito_doc/rip.htm.

"Tech Notes: How Does Unequal Cost Path Load Balancing (Variance) Work in IGRP and EIGRP?" http://www.cisco.com/warp/public/103/19.html.

Foundation Summary

The "Foundation Summary" section of each chapter lists the most important facts from the chapter. Although this section does not list every fact from the chapter that will be on your CCDA exam, a well-prepared CCDA candidate should at a minimum know all the details in each "Foundation Summary" before taking the exam.

This chapter has covered the following topics you need to master for the CCDA exam:

- **RIPv2**—The enhancements in Version 2 of RIP to support network designs

- **RIPng**—New RIP for IPv6 networks

- **EIGRP for IPv4**—The enhanced version of IGRP and its uses in network design

- **EIGRP for IPv6**—The modified version of EIGRP that supports IPv6 networks

Table 10-4 compares the routing protocols covered in this chapter.

Table 10-4 *Routing Protocol Comparisons*

Characteristic	RIPv1	RIPv2	RIPng	EIGRP	EIGRP for IPv6
Distance vector	Yes	Yes	Yes	DV/Hybrid	DV/Hybrid
VLSMs	No	Yes	Yes	Yes	Yes
Authentication	No	Yes	No	Yes	Yes
Update timer (sec)	30	30	90	—	—
Invalid timer (sec)	180	180	180	—	—
Flush timer (sec)	240	240	240	—	—
Holddown timer (sec)	180	180	180	—	—
Protocol/port	UDP 520	UDP 520	UDP 521	IP 88	Next Header 88
Admin distance	120	120	120	90	90
IP version	IPv4	IPv4	IPv6	IPv4	IPv6

RIPv1 Summary

The characteristics of RIPv1 follow:

- Distance-vector protocol.

- Uses UDP port 520.

- Classful protocol (no support for VLSMs or CIDR).

- Metric is router hop count.

- Low scalability: maximum hop count is 15; unreachable routes have a metric of 16.

- Periodic route updates broadcast (255.255.255.255) every 30 seconds.

- 25 routes per RIPv1 message.

- Implements split horizon with poison reverse.

- Implements triggered updates.

- No support for authentication.

- Administrative distance for RIP is 120.

- Used in small, flat networks or at the edge of larger networks.

RIPv2 Summary

The characteristics of RIPv2 follow:

- Distance-vector protocol.

- Uses UDP port 520.

- Classless protocol (support for CIDR).

- Supports VLSMs.

- Metric is router hop count.

- Low scalability: maximum hop count is 15; infinite (unreachable) routes have a metric of 16.

- Periodic route updates are sent every 30 seconds to multicast address 224.0.0.9.

- 25 routes per RIP message (24 if authentication is used).

- Supports authentication.

- Implements split horizon with poison reverse.

- Implements triggered updates.

- Subnet mask included in route entry.

- Administrative distance for RIPv2 is 120.

- Not scalable. Used in small, flat networks or at the edge of larger networks.

RIPng Summary

The characteristics of RIPng are as follows:

- Distance-vector protocol for IPv6 networks only.

- Uses UDP port 521.

- Metric is router hop count.

- Maximum hop count is 15; infinite (unreachable) routes have a metric of 16.

- Periodic route updates are sent every 30 seconds to multicast address FF02::9.

- Uses IPv6 functions for authentication.

- Implements split horizon with poison reverse.

- Implements triggered updates.

- Prefix length included in route entry.

- Administrative distance for RIPv2 is 120.

- Not scalable. Used in small networks.

EIGRP for IPv4 Summary

The characteristics of EIGRP follow:

- Hybrid routing protocol (a distance-vector protocol that has link-state protocol characteristics).

- Uses IP protocol number 88.

- Classless protocol (supports VLSMs).

- Default composite metric of bandwidth and delay.

- You can factor load and reliability into the metric.

- Sends route updates to multicast address 224.0.0.10.

- Sends partial route updates only when there are changes.

- Support for MD5 authentication and fast convergence.

- Uses DUAL for fast convergence and loop prevention.

- By default, equal-cost load balancing. Unequal-cost load balancing with the **variance** command.

- Administrative distance is 90 for EIGRP internal routes, 170 for EIGRP external routes, and 5 for EIGRP summary routes.

- High scalability; used in large networks.

- Does not require hierarchical physical topology.

EIGRP for IPv6 Summary

The characteristics of EIGRP for IPv6 are as follows:

- Uses the same characteristics and functions as EIGRP for IPv4.

- Hybrid routing protocol (a distance-vector protocol that has link-state protocol characteristics).

- Uses Next Header protocol number 88.

- Routes IPv6 prefixes.

- Default composite metric uses bandwidth and delay.

- You can factor load and reliability into the metric.

- Sends partial route updates only when there are changes.

- Support for EIGRP MD5 authentication.

- Uses DUAL for loop prevention and fast convergence.

- By default, equal-cost load balancing. Unequal-cost load balancing with the **variance** command.

- Administrative distance is 90 for EIGRP internal routes, 170 for EIGRP external routes, and 5 for EIGRP summary routes.

- Uses IPv6 multicast FF02::A for EIGRP updates.

- High scalability; used in large networks.

Q&A

As mentioned in the Introduction, you have two choices for review questions: here in the book or the exam questions on the CD-ROM. The answers to these questions appear in Appendix A.

For more practice with exam format questions, use the exam engine on the CD-ROM.

1. True or false: RIPv2 broadcasts (255.255.255.255) its routing table every 30 seconds.

2. True or false: By default, EIGRP uses bandwidth, delay, reliability, and load to calculate the composite metric.

3. True or false: EIGRP routers maintain neighbor adjacencies.

4. True or false: EIGRP and RIPv2 support VLSMs and CIDR.

5. True or false: RIPv2 does not have the 15-hop limit of RIPv1.

6. RIP uses which port?

7. RIPng uses which port?

8. EIGRP uses which IP protocol number?

9. Between RIPv1, RIPv2, and EIGRP, which protocol would you recommend for use in a large network?

10. Between RIPv1, RIPv2, and EIGRP, which protocol would you use in a small network that has both Cisco and non-Cisco routers?

11. Which protocol uses the DUAL algorithm for fast convergence?

12. Match the protocol with the characteristic:

    i. EIGRP for IPv6

    ii. RIPv2

    iii. RIPng

    iv. EIGRP

    a. Uses multicast FF02::9

    b. Uses multicast 224.0.0.9

    c. Uses multicast 224.0.0.10

    d. Uses multicast FF02::

13.   Why is EIGRP sometimes considered a hybrid protocol?

14.   A small network is experiencing excessive broadcast traffic and slow response times. The current routing protocol is RIPv1. What design changes would you recommend?

    a. Migrate to RIPv2

    b. Migrate to RIPng

    c. Migrate to EIGRP for IPv4

    d. Migrate to EIGRP for IPv6

15.   Which IPv6 routing protocol does not include authentication within the protocol?

16.   Match the RIP routing table field with its description:

    i. IP address

    ii. Gateway

    iii. Interface

    iv. Metric

    v. Timer

    a. The number of hops to the destination

    b. Next router along the path to the destination

    c. Destination network or host, with subnet mask

    d. Used to access the physical network that must be used to reach the destination

    e. Time since the route entry was last updated

17.   Match the EIGRP component with its description:

    i. RTP

    ii. DUAL

    iii. Protocol-dependent modules

    iv. Neighbor discovery

    a. An interface between DUAL and IPX RIP, IGRP, and AppleTalk

    b. Used to deliver EIGRP messages reliably

    c. Builds an adjacency table

    d. Guarantees a loop-free network

18. With Cisco routers, which protocols use only equal-cost load balancing?

19. With Cisco routers, which protocols allow unequal-cost load balancing?

20. You are designing a global network with more than 500 locations. The network topology is not hierarchical. What routing protocol would you recommend?

   a. RIPv2

   b. EIGRP

   c. OSPF

   d. IS-IS

21. Match each EIGRP parameter with its description:

   i. Feasible distance

   ii. Successor

   iii. Feasible successor

   iv. Active state

   a. The best path selected by DUAL

   b. The successor is down

   c. The lowest calculated metric of a path to reach the destination

   d. The second-best path

22. On an IPv6 network you have RIPng and EIGRP running. Both protocols have a route to destination 10.1.1.0/24. Which route gets injected into the routing table?

   a. The RIPng route

   b. The EIGRP route

   c. Both routes

   d. Neither route. There is a route conflict.

23. A network has a router diameter of 10. Both IPv4 and IPv6 are used. The company does not want to use proprietary routing protocols. Which routing protocol(s) can be used?

    a. RIPv2

    b. RIPng

    c. EIGRP

    d. EIGRP for IPv6

    e. OSPFv2

    f. OSPFv3

    g. Answers A and C

    h. Answers A, B, E, and F

    i. Answers C and D

24. Complete Table 10-5 with the authentication, protocol/port, administrative distance, and IP version of each routing protocol.

Table 10-5 *Protocol Characteristics*

Characteristic	RIPv1	RIPv2	RIPng	EIGRP	EIGRP for IPv6
Authentication					
Protocol/port					
Administrative distance					
IP version					

Use Figure 10-9 to answer the remaining questions.

Figure 10-9 *Path Selection*

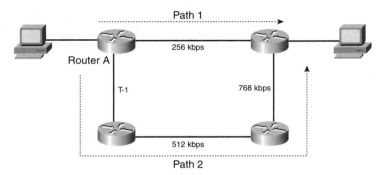

25. By default, if RIPv2 is enabled on all routers, what path is taken?

    a. Path 1

    b. Path 2

    c. Unequal load balancing with Path 1 and Path 2

    d. Equal load balancing with Path 1 and Path 2

26. By default, if RIPng is enabled on all routers, what path is taken?

    a. Path 1

    b. Path 2

    c. Unequal load balancing with Path 1 and Path 2

    d. Equal load balancing with Path 1 and Path 2

27. By default, if EIGRP is enabled on all routers, what path is taken?

    a. Path 1

    b. Path 2

    c. Unequal load balancing with Path 1 and Path 2

    d. Equal load balancing with Path 1 and Path 2

28. EIGRP is configured on the routers. If it is configured with the **variance** command, what path is taken?

    a. Path 1

    b. Path 2

    c. Unequal load balancing with Path 1 and Path 2

    d. Equal load balancing with Path 1 and Path 2

29. By default, if EIGRP for IPv6 is enabled on all routers, and this is an IPv6 network, what path is taken?

    a. Path 1

    b. Path 2

    c. Unequal load balancing with Path 1 and Path 2

    d. Equal load balancing with Path 1 and Path 2

This chapter covers the following subjects:

- OSPFv2

- OSPFv3

- IS-IS

CHAPTER 11

OSPF and IS-IS

This chapter reviews the characteristics and design issues of the Open Shortest Path First Version 2 (OSPFv2) and Intermediate System-to-Intermediate System (IS-IS) protocols. For IPv6 networks, OSPFv3 is also covered. OSPFv2, OSPFv3, and IS-IS are link-state routing protocols. They do not broadcast their route tables as distance-vector routing protocols do. Routers using link-state routing protocols send information about the status of their interfaces to all other routers in the area. Then they perform database computations to determine the shortest paths to each destination.

"Do I Know This Already?" Quiz

The purpose of the "Do I Know This Already?" quiz is to help you decide whether you need to read the entire chapter. If you intend to read the entire chapter, you do not necessarily need to answer these questions now.

The ten-question quiz, derived from the major sections in the "Foundation Topics" portion of the chapter, helps you determine how to spend your limited study time.

Table 11-1 outlines the major topics discussed in this chapter and the "Do I Know This Already?" quiz questions that correspond to those topics..

Table 11-1   *"Do I Know This Already?" Foundation Topics Section-to-Question Mapping*

Foundation Topics Section	Questions Covered in This Section
OSPFv2	1, 2, 4, 6, 7, 8
OSPFv3	10
IS-IS	3, 5, 9

CAUTION   The goal of self-assessment is to gauge your mastery of the topics in this chapter. If you do not know the answer to a question or you are only partially sure, you should mark this question wrong for the purposes of the self-assessment. Giving yourself credit for an answer you correctly guess skews your self-assessment results and might provide you with a false sense of security.

1. Which protocol defines an Area Border Router (ABR)?

   a. Enhanced Interior Gateway Routing Protocol (EIGRP)

   b. OSPF

   c. IS-IS

   d. On-Demand Routing (ODR)

2. Which routing protocols support variable-length subnet masks (VLSM)?

   a. EIGRP

   b. OSPF

   c. IS-IS

   d. A and B

   e. A and C

   f. B and C

   g. A, B, and C

3. Which IGP protocol is a common alternative to EIGRP and OSPF as a routing protocol in service provider networks?

   a. OSPFv2

   b. RIPv2

   c. IGRP

   d. IS-IS

4. What is an ASBR?

   a. Area Border Router

   b. Autonomous System Boundary Router

   c. Auxiliary System Border Router

   d. Area System Border Router

5. What is the default IS-IS metric for a T1 interface?

   a. 5

   b. 10

   c. 64

   d. 200

6. What is the OSPFv2 link-state advertisement (LSA) type for autonomous system (AS) external LSAs?

   a. Type 1

   b. Type 2

    c. Type 3

    d. Type 4

    e. Type 5

7. What address do you use to multicast to the OSPFv2 designated router (DR)?

    a. 224.0.0.1

    b. 224.0.0.5

    c. 224.0.0.6

    d. 224.0.0.10

8. To where are OSPF Type 1 LSAs flooded?

    a. The OSPF area

    b. The OSPF domain

    c. From the area to the OSPF backbone

    d. Through the virtual link

9. In IS-IS networks, the backup designated router (BDR) forms adjacencies to what routers?

    a. Only to the DR.

    b. To all routers.

    c. The BDR becomes adjacent only when the DR is down.

    d. There is no BDR in IS-IS.

10. What OSPFv3 LSA carries address prefixes?

    a. Network LSA

    b. Summary LSA

    c. Inter-Area-Router LSA

    d. Intra-Area-Prefix LSA

The answers to the "Do I Know This Already?" quiz appear in Appendix A, "Answers to Chapter 'Do I Know This Already?' Quizzes and Q&A Sections." The suggested choices for your next step are as follows:

- **8 or less overall score**—Read the entire chapter. It includes the "Foundation Topics," "Foundation Summary," and "Q&A" sections.

- **9 or 10 overall score**—If you want more review on these topics, skip to the "Foundation Summary" section, and then go to the "Q&A" section. Otherwise, move to the next chapter.

Foundation Topics

This chapter covers the link-state routing protocols: OSPFv2, OSPFv3, and IS-IS. These three routing protocols are Interior Gateway Protocols (IGP) used within an autonomous system. OSPF is a popular standards-based protocol used in enterprises. IS-IS is commonly used by large Internet service providers (ISP) in their internal networks.

For the CCDA test, understand the characteristics and design constraints of these routing protocols. You should know the differences between OSPF, IS-IS, and the distance-vector routing protocols covered in Chapter 10, "RIP and EIGRP Characteristics and Design."

OSPFv2

RFC 2328 defines OSPFv2, a link-state routing protocol that uses Dijkstra's shortest path first (SPF) algorithm to calculate paths to destinations. OSPFv2 is used in IPv4 networks. OSPF was created for its use in large networks where RIP failed. OSPF improved the speed of convergence, provided for the use of VLSMs, and improved the path calculation.

In OSPF, each router sends link-state advertisements about itself and its links to all other routers in the area. Note that it does not send routing tables but link-state information about its interfaces. Then, each router individually calculates the best routes to the destination by running the SPF algorithm. Each OSPF router in an area maintains an identical database describing the area's topology. The routing table at each router is individually constructed using the local copy of this database to construct a shortest-path tree.

OSPFv2 is a classless routing protocol that permits the use of VLSMs and classless interdomain routing (CIDR). With Cisco routers, OSPF also supports equal-cost multipath load balancing and neighbor authentication. OSPF uses multicast addresses to communicate between routers. OSPF uses IP protocol 89.

OSPFv2 Concepts and Design

This section covers OSPF theory and design concepts. It discusses OSPF LSAs, area types, and router types. OSPF uses a two-layer hierarchy with a backbone area at the top and all other areas below. Routers send LSAs informing other routers of the status of their interfaces. The use of LSAs and the limitation of OSPF areas are important concepts to understand for the test.

OSPFv2 Metric

The metric that OSPFv2 uses is cost. It is an unsigned 16-bit integer in the range of 1 to 65,535. The default cost for interfaces is calculated based on the bandwidth in the formula $10^8/BW$, where BW is the bandwidth of the interface expressed as a full integer of bps. If the result is smaller than 1, the cost is set to 1. A 10BASE-T (10 Mbps = 10^7 bps) interface has a cost of $10^8/10^7 = 10$. OSPF performs a summation of the costs to reach a destination; the lowest cost is the preferred path. Table 11-2 shows some sample interface metrics.

Table 11-2 *OSPF Interface Costs*

Interface Type	OSPF Cost
10 Gigabit Ethernet	.01 => 1
Gigabit Ethernet	.1 => 1
OC-3 (155 Mbps)	.64516 => 1
Fast Ethernet	$10^8/10^8 = 1$
DS-3 (45 Mbps)	2
Ethernet	$10^8/10^7 = 10$
T1	64
512 kbps	195
256 kbps	390

The default reference bandwidth used to calculate OSPF costs is 10^8 (cost = $10^8/BW$). Notice that for technologies that support speeds greater than 100 Mbps, the default metric gets set to 1 without regard for the network's different capabilities (speed).

Because OSPF was developed prior to high-speed WAN and LAN technologies, the default metric for 100 Mbps was 1. Cisco provides a method to modify the default reference bandwidth. The cost metric can be modified on every interface.

OSPFv2 Adjacencies and Hello Timers

OSPF uses Hello packets for neighbor discovery. The default Hello interval is 10 seconds (30 seconds for nonbroadcast multiaccess [NBMA] networks). Hellos are multicast to 224.0.0.5 (ALLSPFRouters). Hello packets include such information as the router ID, area ID, authentication, and router priority.

After two routers exchange Hello packets and set two-way communication, they establish adjacencies.

Figure 11-1 shows a point-to-point network and an NBMA network.

Figure 11-1 *OSPF Networks*

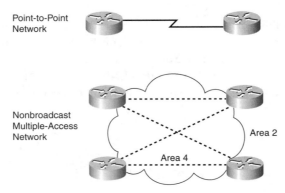

Point-to-Point Network

Nonbroadcast Multiple-Access Network

Area 2

Area 4

For point-to-point networks, valid neighbors always become adjacent and communicate using multicast address 224.0.0.5. For broadcast (Ethernet) and NBMA networks (Frame Relay), all routers become adjacent to the DR and BDR but not to each other. All routers reply to the DR and BDR using the multicast address 224.0.0.6. The later section "OSPF DRs" covers the DR concept.

On OSPF point-to-multipoint nonbroadcast networks, it might be necessary to configure the set of neighbors that are directly reachable over the point-to-multipoint network. Each neighbor is identified by its IP address on the point-to-multipoint network. Non-broadcast point-to-multipoint networks do not elect DRs, so the DR eligibility of configured neighbors is undefined. OSPF communication in point-to-point networks use unicast addresses .

OSPF virtual links unicast OSPF packets. Later in this chapter, the section "Virtual Links" discusses virtual links.

OSPFv2 Areas

As a network grows, the initial flooding and database maintenance of LSAs can burden a router's CPU. OSPF uses areas to reduce these effects. An area is a logical grouping of routers and links that divides the network. Routers share link-state information with only the routers in their areas. This setup reduces the size of the database and the cost of computing the SPF tree at each router.

Each area is assigned a 32-bit integer number. Area 0 (or 0.0.0.0) is reserved for the backbone area. Every OSPF network should have a backbone area. The backbone area is responsible for distributing routing information between areas. It must exist in any internetwork using OSPF over multiple areas as a routing protocol. As you can see in Figure 11-2, communication between Area 1 and Area 2 must flow through Area 0. This communication can be internal to a single router that has interfaces directly connected to Areas 0, 1, and 2.

Figure 11-2 *OSPF Areas*

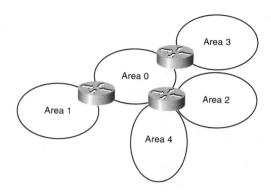

Intra-area traffic is packets passed between routers in a single area.

OSPF Router Types

OSPF classifies participating routers based on their place and function in the area architecture. Figure 11-3 shows OSPF router types.

Figure 11-3 *OSPF Router Types*

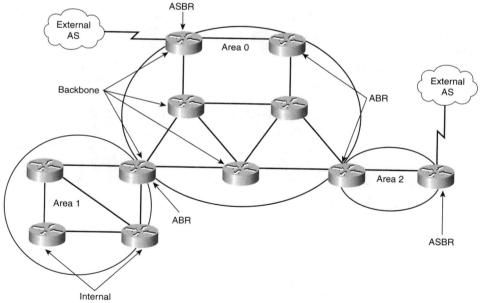

The following list explains each router type in Figure 11-3:

- **Internal router**—Any router whose interfaces all belong to the same OSPF area. These routers keep only one link-state database.

- **ABR**—Routers that are connected to more than one area. These routers maintain a link-state database for each area they belong to. These routers generate summary LSAs.

- **ASBR**—Routers that inject external LSAs into the OSPF database (redistribution). These external routes are learned via either other routing protocols or static routes.

- **Backbone router**—Routers with at least one interface attached to Area 0.

> **TIP** An OSPF router can be an ABR, an ASBR, and a backbone router at the same time. The router is an ABR if it has an interface on Area 0 and another interface in another area. The router is a backbone router if it has one or more interfaces in Area 0. The router is an ASBR if it redistributes external routes into the OSPF network.

OSPF DRs

On multiaccess networks (such as Ethernet), some routers get selected as DRs. The purpose of the DR is to collect all LSAs for the multiaccess network and to forward the LSA to all non-DR routers; this arrangement reduces the amount of LSA traffic generated. A router can be the DR for one multiaccess network and not the DR in another attached multiaccess network.

The DR also floods the network LSAs to the rest of the area. OSPF also selects a BDR; it takes over the function of the DR if the DR fails. Both the DR and BDR become adjacent to all routers in the multiaccess network. All routers that are not DR and BDR are sometimes called DRothers. These routers are only adjacent to the DR and BDR. OSPF routers multicast LSAs only to adjacent routers. DRothers multicast packets to the DR and BDR using the multicast address 224.0.0.6 (ALLDRouters). The DR floods updates using ALLSPFRouters (224.0.0.5).

DR and BDR selection is based on an OSPF DR interface priority. The default value is 1, and the highest priority determines the DR. In a tie, OSPF uses the numerically highest router ID. The router ID is the IP address of the configured loopback interface. The router ID is the highest configured loopback address, or if the loopback is not configured then it's the highest physical address. Routers with a priority of 0 are not considered for DR/BDR selection. The dotted lines in Figure 11-4 show the adjacencies in the network.

Figure 11-4 *DRs*

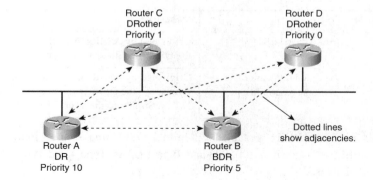

In Figure 11-4, Router A is configured with a priority of 10, and Router B is configured with a priority of 5. Assuming that these routers are turned on simultaneously, Router A becomes the DR for the Ethernet network. Router C has a lower priority, becoming adjacent to Router A and Router B but not to Router D. Router D has a priority of 0 and thus is not a candidate to become a DR or BDR.

If you introduce a new router to the network with a higher priority than that of the current DR and BDR, it does not become the selected DR unless both the DR and BDR fail. If the DR fails, the current BDR becomes the DR.

LSA Types

OSPF routers generate LSAs that are flooded throughout an area or the entire autonomous system. OSPF defines different LSA types for participating routers, DRs, ABRs, and ASBRs. Understanding the LSA types can help you with other OSPF concepts. Table 11-3 describes the major LSA types. There are other LSA types that are not covered in this book.

Table 11-3 *Major LSA Types*

Type Code	Type	Description
1	Router LSA	Produced by every router. Includes all the router's links, interfaces, state of links, and cost. This LSA type is flooded within a single area.
2	Network LSA	Produced by every DR on every broadcast or NBMA network. It lists all the routers in the multiaccess network. This LSA type is contained within an area.
3	Summary LSA for ABRs	Produced by ABRs. It is sent into an area to advertise destinations outside the area.
4	Summary LSA for ASBRs	Originated by ABRs. Sent into an area by the ABR to advertise the ASBRs.

continues

Table 11-3 *Major LSA Types (Continued)*

Type Code	Type	Description
5	AS external LSA	Originated by ASBRs. Advertises destinations external to the OSPF AS, flooded throughout the whole OSPF AS.
7	Not-so-stubby area (NSSA) external LSA	Originated by ASBRs in an NSSA. It is not flooded throughout the OSPF autonomous system, only to the NSSA. Similar to the Type 5 LSA.

Type 1 and Type 2 LSAs are contained within each OSPF area. Routers in different areas pass interarea traffic. ABRs exchange Type 3 and Type 4 LSAs. Type 4 and Type 5 LSAs are flooded throughout all areas.

AS External Path Types

The two types of AS external paths are Type 1 (E1) and Type 2 (E2), and they are associated with Type 5 LSAs. ASBRs advertise external destinations whose cost can be just a redistribution metric (E2) or a redistribution metric plus the costs of each segment (E1) used to reach the ASBR.

By default, external routes are of Type 2, which is the metric (cost) used in the redistribution. Type 1 external routes have a metric that is the sum of the redistribution cost plus the cost of the path to reach the ASBR.

OSPF Stub Area Types

OSPF provides support for stub areas. The concept is to reduce the number of interarea or external LSAs that get flooded into a stub area. RFC 2328 defines OSPF stub areas. RFC 1587 defines support for NSSAs. Cisco routers use totally stubby areas, such as Area 2 as shown in Figure 11-5.

Stub Areas

Consider Area 1 in Figure 11-5. Its only path to the external networks is via the ABR through Area 0. All external routes are flooded to all areas in the OSPF AS. You can configure an area as a stub area to prevent OSPF external LSAs (Type 5) from being flooded into that area. A single default route is injected into the stub area instead. If multiple ABRs exist in a stub area, all inject the default route. Traffic originating within the stub area routes to the closest ABR.

Note that network summary LSAs (Type 3) from other areas are still flooded into the Stub Area 1.

Figure 11-5 *OSPF Stub Networks*

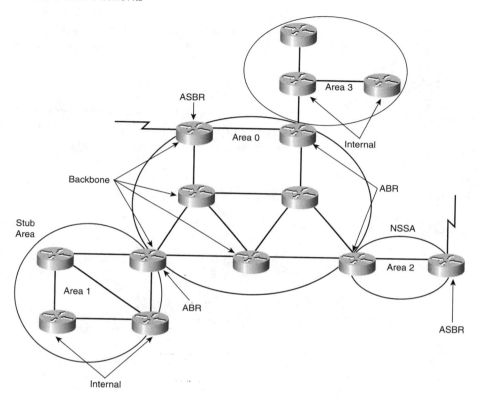

Totally Stubby Areas

Take the Area 1 in Figure 11-5 one step further. The only path for Area 1 to get to Area 0 and other areas is through the ABR. A totally stubby area does not flood network summary LSAs (Type 3). It stifles Type 4 LSAs as well. Like regular stub areas, totally stubby areas do not flood Type 5 LSAs. They send just a single LSA for the default route. If multiple ABRs exist in a totally stubby area, all ABRs inject the default route. Traffic originating within the totally stubby area routes to the closest ABR.

NSSAs

Notice that Area 2 in Figure 11-5 has an ASBR. If this area is configured as an NSSA, it generates the external LSAs (Type 7) into the OSPF system while retaining the characteristics of a stub area to the rest of the AS. There are two options for the ABR. First, the ABR for Area 2 can translate the NSSA external LSAs (Type 7) to AS external LSAs (Type 5) and flood the rest of the internetwork. Second, the ABR is not configured to convert the NSSA external LSAs to Type 5 external LSAs, thus the NSSA external LSAs remain within the NSSA.

Virtual Links

OSPF requires that all areas be connected to a backbone router. Sometimes, WAN link provisioning or failures can prevent an OSPF area from being directly connected to a backbone router. You can use virtual links to temporarily connect (virtually) the area to the backbone.

As shown in Figure 11-6, Area 4 is not directly connected to the backbone. A virtual link is configured between Router A and Router B. The flow of the virtual link is unidirectional and must be configured in each router of the link. Area 2 becomes the transit area through which the virtual link is configured. Traffic between Areas 2 and 4 does not flow directly to Router B. Instead, the traffic must flow to Router A to reach Area 0 and then pass through the virtual link.

Figure 11-6   *OSPF Virtual Link*

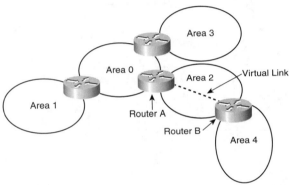

OSPFv2 Router Authentication

OSPFv2 supports the authentication of routes using 64-bit clear text or cryptographic Message Digest 5 (MD5) authentication. Plain-text authentication passwords do not need to be the same for the routers throughout the area, but they must be the same between neighbors.

MD5 authentication provides higher security than plain-text authentication. As with plain-text authentication, passwords don't have to be the same throughout an area, but they do need to be same between neighbors.

OSPFv2 Summary

OSPFv2 is used in large enterprise IPv4 networks. The network topology must be hierarchical. OSPF is used in the enterprise campus building access, distribution, and core layers. OSPF is also used in the enterprise data center, WAN/MAN, and branch offices.

The characteristics of OSPFv2 follow:

- Link-state routing protocol.

- Uses IP protocol 89.

- Classless protocol (supports VLSMs and CIDR).

- Metric is cost (based on interface bandwidth by default).

- Fast convergence. Uses link-state updates and SPF calculation.

- Reduced bandwidth use. Sends partial route updates only when changes occur.

- Routes are labeled as intra-area, interarea, external Type 1, or external Type 2.

- Support for authentication.

- Uses the Dijkstra algorithm to calculate the SPF tree.

- Default administrative distance is 110.

- Uses multicast address 224.0.0.5 (ALLSPFRouters).

- Uses multicast address 224.0.0.6 (ALLDRouters).

- Very good scalability. Recommended for large networks.

OSPFv3

RFC 2740 describes OSPF Version 3 for routing in IPv6 networks. Note that OSPFv3 is for IPv6 networks only and that it is not backward-compatible with OSPFv2 (used in IPv4). OSPF algorithms and mechanisms, such as flooding, router types, designated router election, areas, stub and NSSA, and shortest path first (SPF) calculations, remain the same. Changes are made for OSPF to support IPv6 addresses, address hierarchy, and IPv6 for transport. OSPFv3 uses multicast group FF02::5 for all OSPF routers and FF02::6 for all designated routers.

OSPFv3 Changes from OSPFv2

The following are the major changes for OSPFv3:

- **Version number is 3**—Obviously this is a newer version of OSPF, and it runs over IPv6 only.

- **Support for IPv6 addressing**—New LSAs created to carry IPv6 addresses and prefixes.

- **Per-link processing**—OSPFv2 uses per-subnet processing. With link processing, routers in the same link can belong to multiple subnets.

- **Address semantics removed**—Addresses are removed from the router and network LSAs. These LSAs now provide topology information.

- **No authentication in the OSPFv3 protocol**—OSPFv3 uses the authentication schemes inherited in IPv6.

- **New Link LSA**—For local-link flooding scope.

- **New Intra-Area-Prefix LSA**—Carries all the IPv6 prefix information. Similar to OSPFv2 router and network LSAs.

- **Identifying neighbors by router ID**—Neighbors are *always* identified by the router ID. This does not occur in OSPFv2 point-to-point and broadcast networks.

> **NOTE**   In OSPFv3, the router IDs, area IDs, and LSA link state IDs remain at the size of 32 bits. Larger IPv6 addresses cannot be used.

OSPFv3 Areas and Router Types

OSPFv3 retains the same structure and concepts as OSPFv2. The area topology, interfaces, neighbors, link-state database, and routing table remain the same. RFC 2740 does not define new area types or router types.

The OSPF areas shown in Figure 11-2 and the router types shown in Figure 11-3 remain the same. The router types in relation to the OSPF areas are

- **Internal router**—Any router whose interfaces all belong to the same OSPF area. These routers keep only one link-state database.

- **ABR**—Routers that are connected to more than one area, in which one area is Area 0. These routers maintain a link-state database for each area they belong to. These routers generate summary LSAs.

- **ASBR**—Routers that inject external LSAs into the OSPF database (redistribution). These external routes are learned via either other routing protocols or static routes.

- **Backbone router**—Routers with at least one interface attached to Area 0.

OSPFv3 Link State Advertisements

OSPFv3 retains the LSA types used by OSPFv2 with some modifications and introduces two new LSAs: Link LSA and Intra-Area-Prefix.

All LSAs use a common 20-byte header that indicates the LS type, the advertising router, and the sequence number. Figure 11-7 shows the format of the LSA header.

Figure 11-7 *LSA Header*

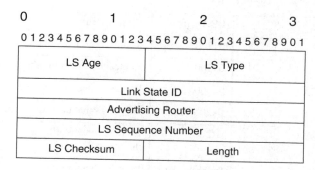

The LS age indicates the time in seconds since the LSA was generated.

The LS type indicates the function performed by this LSA. This field includes a U bit and S2 and S1 bits. When the U bit is set to 0, the LSA is only flooded locally. When the U bit is set to 1, the LSA is stored and flooded. The S1 and S2 bits have the functions indicated in Table 11-4.

Table 11-4 *LSA Header S2 S1 Bits*

S2 S1	Flooding Scope
00	Link-local scope
01	Flood to all routers within the area
10	Flood to all routers within the AS
11	Reserved

The Link State ID is used with the LS type and advertising router to identify the link-state database. The Advertising Router field contains the 32-bit router ID of the router that generated the LSA. The LS Sequence Number is used to detect old or duplicate LSAs. The LS Checksum is for error checking. The Length field indicates the length of the LSA, including the header.

Table 11-5 summarizes the nine LSAs that can be used in OSPF. Most LSAs retain the same function used in OSPFv2 for IPv4. Each OSPFv3 LSA is described in more detail following the table.

Table 11-5 *OSPFv3 LSA Types*

LSA Name	LS Type	Description
Router LSA	0x2001	State of router interfaces
Network LSA	0x2002	Generated by DR routers in broadcast or NBMA networks

continues

Table 11-5 *OSPFv3 LSA Types (Continued)*

LSA Name	LS Type	Description
Inter-Area-Prefix LSA	0x2003	Routes to prefixes in other areas
Inter-Area-Router LSA	0x2004	Routes to routers in other areas
AS-External LSA	0x4005	Routes to networks external to the AS
Group-Membership LSA	0x2006	Networks that contain multicast groups
NSSA Type 7 LSA	0x2007	Routers to networks external to the AS, injected into the NSSA
Link LSA	0x0008	Link-local addresses and list IPv6 prefixes associated with the link
Intra-Area-Prefix LSA	0x2009	IPv6 prefixes associated with a router, a stub network, or an associated transit network segment

Router LSAs describe the cost and state of all the originating router's interfaces. These LSAs are flooded within the area only. Router LSAs are LS type 0x2001. No IPv6 prefixes are contained in this LSA.

Network LSAs are originated by DRs in broadcast or NBMA networks. They describe all routers attached to the link that are adjacent to the DR. These LSAs are flooded within the area only. The LS type is 0x2002. No IPv6 prefixes are contained in this LSA.

Inter-Area-Prefix LSAs describe routes to IPv6 prefixes that belong to other areas. They are similar to OSPFv2 type 3 summary LSAs. The Inter-Area-Prefix LSA is originated by the ABR and has an LS type of 0x2003. It is also used to send the default route in stub areas. These LSAs are flooded within the area only.

Each Inter-Area-Router LSA describes a route to a router in another area. It is similar to OSPF type 4 summary LSAs. It is originated by the ABR and has an LS type of 0x2004. These LSAs are flooded within the area only.

AS-External LSAs describe networks that are external to the autonomous system (AS). These LSAs are originated by ASBRs, have an LS type of 0x4005, and thus are flooded to all routers in the AS.

The group-membership LSA describes the directly attached networks that contain members of a multicast group. This LSA is limited to the area and has an LS type of 0x2006. This LSA is described further in RFC 1584.

Type-7 LSAs describe networks that are external to the AS, but they are flooded to the NSSA area only. NSSAs are covered in RFC 1587. This LSA is generated by the NSSA ASBR and has a type of 0x2007.

Link LSAs describe the router's link-local address and a list of IPv6 prefixes associated with the link. This LSA is flooded to the local link only and has a type of 0x0008.

The Intra-Area-Prefix LSA is a new LSA type that is used to advertise IPv6 prefixes associated with a router, a stub network, or an associated transit network segment. This LSA contains information that used to be part of the router-LSAs and network-LSAs.

OSPFv3 Summary

OSPFv3 is used in large enterprise IPv6 networks. The network topology must be hierarchical. OSPF is used in the enterprise campus building access, distribution, and core layers. OSPF is also used in the enterprise data center, WAN/MAN, and branch offices.

The characteristics of OSPFv3 follow:

- Link-state routing protocol for IPv6.

- Uses IPv6 Next Header 89.

- Metric is cost (based on interface bandwidth by default).

- Sends partial route updates only when changes occur.

- Routes are labeled as intra-area, interarea, external Type 1, or external Type 2.

- Uses IPv6 for authentication.

- Uses the Dijkstra algorithm to calculate the SPF tree.

- Default administrative distance is 110.

- Uses multicast address FF02::5 (ALLSPFRouters).

- Uses multicast address FF02::6 (ALLDRouters).

- Recommended for large IPv6 networks.

IS-IS

IS-IS is an International Organization for Standardization (ISO) dynamic routing specification. IS-IS is described in ISO/IEC 10589, reprinted by the Internet Engineering Task Force (IETF) as RFC 1142. IS-IS is a link-state routing protocol that floods link-state information throughout the network to build a picture of network topology. IS-IS was primarily intended to route OSI Connectionless Network Protocol (CLNP) packets but can also route IP packets. IP packet routing uses Integrated IS-IS, which provides the ability to route protocols such as IP. IS-IS is a common alternative to other powerful routing protocols such as OSPF and EIGRP in large networks. Although it isn't seen much in enterprise networks, IS-IS is commonly used for internal routing in large ISP networks.

IS-IS creates two levels of hierarchy, with Level 1 for intra-area and Level 2 for interarea routing. IS-IS distinguishes between Level 1 and Level 2 intermediate systems (IS). Level 1 ISs communicate with other Level 1 ISs in the same area. Level 2 ISs (routers) are configured for L1/L2 areas, which route between Level 1 areas and form an intra-domain routing backbone. Hierarchical routing simplifies backbone design because Level 1 ISs only need to know how to get to the nearest Level 2 IS.

> **NOTE** In IS-IS, a router is usually the IS, and PCs, workstations, and servers are end systems (ES). End System-to-Intermediate System links are Level 0.

IS-IS Metrics

IS-IS as originally defined uses a composite metric with a maximum path value of 1023. The required default metric is arbitrary and typically is assigned by a network administrator. By convention, it is intended to measure the circuit's capacity to handle traffic, such as its throughput in bits per second. Higher values indicate a lower capacity. Any single link can have a maximum value of 63. IS-IS calculates path values by summing link values. The standard sets the maximum metric values to provide the granularity to support various link types. It also ensures that the shortest-path algorithm used for route computation is reasonably efficient.

In Cisco routers, all interfaces have a default metric of 10. The administrator must configure the interface metric to get a different value. This small metric value range has proven insufficient for large networks. It also provides too little granularity for new features such as traffic engineering and other applications, especially with high-bandwidth links. Cisco IOS Software addresses this issue with the support of a 24-bit metric field, the so-called "wide metric." Wide metrics are also required for route leaking. Using the new metric style, link metrics now have a maximum value of 16,777,215 ($2^{24} - 1$), with a total path metric of 4,261,412,864 ($254 * 2^{24}$ or 2^{32}). Deploying IS-IS in the IP network with wide metrics is recommended for enabling finer granularity and supporting future applications such as traffic engineering.

IS-IS also defines three optional metrics (costs): delay, expense, and error. Cisco routers do not support the three optional metrics. The wide metric noted earlier uses the octets reserved for these metrics.

IS-IS Operation and Design

This subsection discusses IS-IS areas, designated routers, authentication, and the NET. IS-IS defines areas differently from OSPF; area boundaries are links and not routers. IS-IS has no BDRs. Because IS-IS is an OSI protocol, it uses a NET to identify each router.

NET

To configure the IS-IS routing protocol, you must configure a NET on every router. Although configuring NET is not a CCDA test requirement, this information is included for "extra credit."

Although you can configure IS-IS to route IP, the communication between routers uses OSI PDUs. The NET is the OSI address used for each router to communicate with OSI PDUs. A NET address ranges from 8 to 20 bytes. It consists of a domain, area ID, system ID, and selector (SEL), as shown in Figure 11-8.

Figure 11-8 *NET*

Area ID	System ID	SEL
	6 bytes	00

IS-IS routers use the area ID. The system ID must be the same length for all routers in an area. For Cisco routers, it must be 6 bytes in length. Usually, a router MAC address identifies each unique router. The SEL is configured as 00. You configure the NET with the **net** subcommand under the **router isis** command. In the following example, the domain authority and format identifier (AFI) is 49, the area is 0001, the system ID is 00aa.0101.0001, and the SEL is 00:

```
router isis
 net 49.0001.00aa.0101.0001.00
```

IS-IS DRs

As with OSPF, IS-IS selects DRs on multiaccess networks. It does not choose a backup DR as does OSPF. By default, the priority value is 64. You can change the priority value to a value from 0 to 127. If you set the priority to 0, the router is not eligible to become a DR for that network. IS-IS uses the highest system ID to select the DR if there is a tie with the priorities. On point-to-point networks, the priority is 0 because no DR is elected. In IS-IS, all routers in a multiaccess network establish adjacencies with all others in the subnetwork, and IS-IS neighbors become adjacent upon the discovery of one another. Both these characteristics are different from OSPF behavior.

IS-IS Areas

IS-IS uses a two-level hierarchy similar to the OSPF area hierarchy developed later. Routers are configured to route Level 1 (L1), Level 2 (L2), or both Level 1 and Level 2 (L1/L2). Level 1 routers are like OSPF internal routers in a Cisco totally stubby area. An L2 router is similar to an OSPF backbone router. A router that has both Level 1 and Level 2 routes is similar to an OSPF ABR. IS-IS does not define a backbone area, but you can consider the backbone a continuous path of adjacencies among Level 2 ISs.

The L1/L2 routers maintain a separate link-state database for the L1 routes and L2 routes. Also, the L1/L2 routers do not advertise L2 routes to the L1 area. L1 routers do not have information about destinations outside the area and use L1 routes to their L1/L2 router to reach outside destinations.

As shown in Figure 11-9, IS-IS areas are bounded not by the L1/L2 routers but by the links between L1/L2 routers and L2 backbone routers.

Figure 11-9   *IS-IS Areas and Router Types*

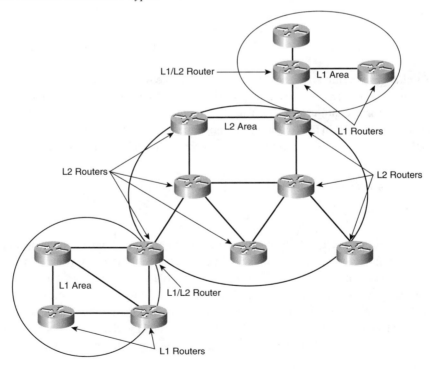

IS-IS Authentication

IS-IS supports three types of clear-text authentication: link authentication, area authentication, and domain authentication. All these types support only clear-text password authentication. Recently, an RFC draft added support for an IS-IS MD5.

Routers in a common subnetwork (Ethernet, private line) use link authentication. The clear-text password must be common only between the routers in the link. Level 1 and Level 2 routes use separate passwords.

With area authentication, all routers in the area must use the same authentication mode and must have the same password.

Only L2 and L1/L2 routers use domain authentication. All L2 and L1/L2 routers must be configured for the same authentication mode and must use the same password.

IS-IS for IPv6

The specification for routing IPv6 with integrated IS-IS is currently an Internet draft (draft-ietf-isis-ipv6-06.txt) of the IETF. The draft specifies new type, length, and value (TLV) objects, reachability TLVs, and an interface address TLV to forward IPv6 information in the network. IOS currently supports IS-IS for IPv6, as described in the draft standard. Because IS-IS for IPv6 is not a focus area for the CCDA, refer to the IETF drafts for further information.

IS-IS Summary

The characteristics of IS-IS follow:

- Link-state protocol.

- Uses OSI CLNP to communicate with routers.

- Classless protocol (supports VLSMs and CIDR).

- Default metric is set to 10 for all interfaces.

- Single metric: single link max = 63, path max = 1023.

- Sends partial route updates only when changes occur.

- Authentication with clear-text passwords and MD5.

- Administrative distance is 115.

- Used in large service provider networks. Not recommended for enterprise networks. Sometimes attractive compared to OSPF and EIGRP.

- Described in ISO/IEC 10589; reprinted by the IETF as RFC 1142.

- IETF draft for routing IPv6 with IS-IS.

References and Recommended Readings

Bruno, A. *CCIE Routing and Switching Exam Certification Guide*. Indianapolis: Cisco Press, 2002.

Coltun, R., D. Ferguson, and J. Moy. RFC 2740, *OSPF for IPv6*. Available from http://www.ietf.org/rfc.

Coltun, R. and V. Fuller. RFC 1587, *The OSPF NSSA Option*. Available from http://www.ietf.org/rfc.

Doyle, J. and J. Carroll. *Routing TCP/IP*, Volume I, Second Edition. Indianapolis: Cisco Press, 2005.

Martey, A. *IS-IS Network Design Solutions*. Indianapolis: Cisco Press, 2002.

Moy, J. RFC 1584, *Multicast Extensions to OSPF*. Available from http://www.ietf.org/rfc.

Moy, J. RFC 2328, *OSPF Version 2*. Available from http://www.ietf.org/rfc.

Oran, D., editor. RFC 1142, *OSI IS-IS Intra-domain Routing Protocol*. Available from http://www.ietf.org/rfc.

Foundation Summary

The "Foundation Summary" section of each chapter lists the most important facts from the chapter. Although this section does not list every fact from the chapter that will be on your CCDA exam, a well-prepared CCDA candidate should at a minimum know all the details in each "Foundation Summary" before taking the exam.

The CCDA exam requires that you be familiar with the following topics covered in this chapter:

- **OSPFv2**—The OSPF link-state routing protocol for IPv4
- **OSPFv3**—OSPF link-state routing protocol for IPv6
- **IS-IS**—The IS-IS link-state routing protocol

Table 11-6 summarizes the OSPF router types. Know how to identify these routers from a description or a diagram. These router types apply to both OSPFv2 and OSPFv3.

Table 11-6 *OSPF Router Types*

OSPF Router Type	Description
Internal router	Router whose interfaces belong to the same OSPF area.
ABR	Router connected to more than one area. It generates summary LSAs.
ASBR	Router that injects external routes into the OSPF protocol.
Backbone router	Routers with at least one interface connected to Area 0.

Table 11-7 summarizes OSPF stub network types. Remember which LSAs are not permitted in each stub type. These stub types apply for both OSPFv2 and OSPFv3.

Table 11-7 *OSPF Stub Network Types*

OSPF Area Stub Type	Description	LSA Types Not Permitted
Stub area	No OSPF external LSAs	Type 5
Totally stubby	No OSPF external and summary LSAs	Type 3, Type 4, and Type 5
NSSA	No OSPF external, Type 7 produced by NSSA	Type 5

Table 11-8 summarizes OSPFv2 LSA types. Understand which routers generate the LSA and what type of information each contains.

Table 11-8 *OSPFv2 Major LSA Types*

Type Code	Type	Description
1	Router LSA	Produced by every router. It includes all the router's links, interfaces, state of links, and cost. This LSA type is flooded within a single area.
2	Network LSA	Produced by every DR on every broadcast or NBMA network. It lists all the routers in the multiaccess network. This LSA type is contained within an area.
3	Summary LSA for ABRs	Produced by ABRs. It is sent into an area to advertise destinations outside the area.
4	Summary LSA for ASBRs	Originated by ABRs. Sent into an area by the ABR to advertise the ASBRs.
5	AS external LSA	Originated by ASBRs. Advertises destinations external to the OSPF AS, flooded throughout the whole OSPF AS.
7	NSSA external LSA	Originated by ASBRs in an NSSA. It is not flooded throughout the OSPF AS, only to the NSSA.

OSPFv2 Summary

Memorize the characteristics of OSPFv2, as listed here:

- Link-state routing protocol.

- Uses IP protocol 89.

- Classless protocol (supports VLSMs and CIDR).

- Metric is cost (based on interface bandwidth by default).

- Fast convergence. Uses link-state updates and SPF calculation.

- Reduced bandwidth use. Sends partial route updates only when changes occur.

- Routes are labeled as intra-area, interarea, external Type 1, or external Type 2.

- Support for authentication.

- Uses the Dijkstra algorithm to calculate the SPF tree.

- Default administrative distance is 110.

- Uses multicast address 224.0.0.5 (ALLSPFRouters).

- Uses multicast address 224.0.0.6 (ALLDRouters).

- Very good scalability. Recommended for large networks.

OSPFv3 Summary

The characteristics of OSPFv3 follow:

- Link-state routing protocol for IPv6.

- Uses IPv6 Next Header 89.

- Metric is cost (based on interface bandwidth by default).

- Sends partial route updates only when changes occur.

- Routes are labeled as intra-area, interarea, external Type 1, or external Type 2.

- Uses IPv6 for authentication.

- Uses the Dijkstra algorithm to calculate the SPF tree.

- Default administrative distance is 110.

- Uses multicast address FF02::5 (ALLSPFRouters).

- Uses multicast address FF02::6 (ALLDRouters).

- Recommended for large IPv6 networks.

Table 11-9 summarizes OSPFv3 LSA types.

Table 11-9 *OSPFv3 LSA Types*

LSA Name	LS Type	Description
Router LSA	0x2001	State of router interface
Network LSA	0x2002	Generated by DR routers in broadcast or NBMA networks
Inter-Area-Prefix LSA	0x2003	Routes to prefixes in other areas
Inter-Area-Router LSA	0x2004	Routes to routers in other areas
AS-External LSA	0x4005	Routes to networks external to the AS
Group-membership LSA	0x2006	Networks that contain multicast groups

continues

Table 11-9 *OSPFv3 LSA Types (Continued)*

LSA Name	LS Type	Description
NSSA Type 7 LSA	0x2007	Routers to networks external to the AS, injected to the NSSA
Link LSA	0x0008	Link-local addresses and list IPv6 prefixes associated with the link
Intra-Area-Prefix LSA	0x2009	IPv6 prefixes associated with a router, a stub network, or an associated transit network segment

IS-IS Summary

Know and understand the characteristics of IS-IS, as summarized in the following list:

- Link-state protocol.

- Uses OSI CLNP to communicate with routers.

- Classless protocol (supports VLSMs and CIDR).

- Default metric is set to 10 for all interfaces.

- Single metric: single link max = 63, path max = 1023

- Sends partial route updates only when changes occur.

- Authentication with clear-text passwords and MD5.

- Administrative distance is 115.

- Used in large networks. Sometimes attractive compared to OSPF and EIGRP.

- Described in ISO/IEC 10589; reprinted by the IETF as RFC 1142.

- Support for IPv6 in draft IETF RFC.

Q&A

As mentioned in the Introduction, you have two choices for review questions: here in the book or the exam questions on the CD-ROM. The answers to these questions appear in Appendix A.

For more practice with exam format questions, use the exam engine on the CD-ROM.

1. True or false: A router needs to have all its interfaces in Area 0 to be considered an OSPF backbone router.

2. True or false: Both OSPF and IS-IS use a designated router in multiaccess networks.

3. Which multicast addresses do OSPFv2 routers use?

4. Which multicast addresses are used by OSPFv3 routers?

5. What are the Cisco administrative distances of OSPF and IS-IS?

6. True or false: By default, IS-IS assigns a cost metric of 10 to a T1 interface and also 10 to an Ethernet interface.

7. Which OSPFv2 router type generates the OSPF Type 3 LSA?

8. Which OSPFv2 router type generates the OSPF Type 2 LSA?

9. What is included in an OSPFv2 router LSA?

10. True or false: An IS-IS L2 router is analogous to an OSPF backbone router.

11. True or false: The router with the lowest priority is selected as the OSPF DR.

12. Match the routing protocol with the description:

    i. EIGRP

    ii. OSPFv2

    iii. RIPv2

    iv. IS-IS

    a. Distance-vector protocol used in the edge of the network

    b. IETF link-state protocol used in the network core

    c. Hybrid protocol used in the network core

    d. OSI link-state protocol

13. What router produces OSPF Type 2 LSAs?

14. True or false: IS-IS uses the IP layer to communicate between routers.

15. What is the default OSPF cost for a Fast Ethernet interface?

16. Which link-state protocols support VLSMs?

17. Which routing protocol do you use in the core of a large enterprise network that supports VLSMs for a network with a mix of Cisco and non-Cisco routers?

18. True or false: An IS-IS L1/L2 router is similar to an OSPF ABR.

19. You use _____ to connect a nondirectly connected OSPF area to the backbone.

20. What is the benefit of designing for stub areas?

21. What constraint does the OSPF network design have for traffic traveling between areas?

22. True or false: The OSPF and IS-IS default costs for Fast Ethernet interfaces are the same.

23. How is OSPFv3 identified as the upper-layer protocol in IPv6?

24. Which routing protocols are recommended for large enterprise networks?

    a. RIPv2

    b. OSPFv2

    c. EIGRP

    d. IS-IS

    e. A and B

    f. B and C

    g. B and D

    h. A, B, C, and D

25. What OSPFv3 has an LS type of 0x0008?

    a. Router LSA

    b. Inter-Area-Router LSA

    c. Link LSA

    d. Intra-Area-Prefix LSA

26. Which routing protocols support VLSMs?

    a. RIPv1

    b. OSPFv2

    c. EIGRP

    d. RIPv2

    e. B and C

    f. B, C, and D

27. Which routing protocols have fast convergence?

    a. RIPv1

    b. OSPFv2

    c. EIGRP

    d. RIPv2

    e. B and C

    f. B, C, and D

28. Which routing protocols have fast convergence?

    a. RIPng

    b. OSPFv3

    c. EIGRP for IPv6

    d. RIPv2

    e. B and C

    f. B, C, and D

29. A retail chain has about 800 stores that connect to the headquarters and a backup location. The company wants to limit the amount of routing traffic used on the WAN links. What routing protocol(s) is/are recommended?

    a. RIPv1

    b. RIPv2

    c. OSPFv2

    d. EIGRP

    e. IS-IS

    f. BGP

    g. B, C, and D

    h. C and D

    i. C, D, and E

30. Which of the following statements is correct?

   a. OSPFv3 provides changes to OSPFv2 for use in IPv4 networks.

   b. OSPFv3 provides changes to OSPFv2 for use in IPv6 networks.

   c. OSPFv3 provides changes to OSPFv2 for use in IPv6 and IPv4 networks.

   d. OSPFng provides changes to OSPFv2 for use in IPv6 networks.

Use Figure 11-10 to answer the next two questions.

Figure 11-10 *Path Selection*

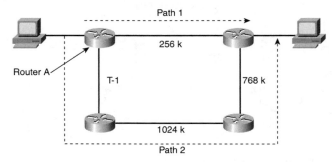

31. If IS-IS is enabled on all routers with the default metrics unchanged, what path is taken?

   a. Path 1

   b. Path 2

   c. Unequal load balance with Path 1 and Path 2

   d. Equal load balance with Path 1 and Path 2

32. If OSPF is enabled on all routers with the default metrics unchanged, what path is taken?

   a. Path 1

   b. Path 2

   c. Unequal load balance with Path 1 and Path 2

   d. Equal load balance with Path 1 and Path 2

Use Figure 11-11 to answer the following question.

Figure 11-11 *OSPF Router Types*

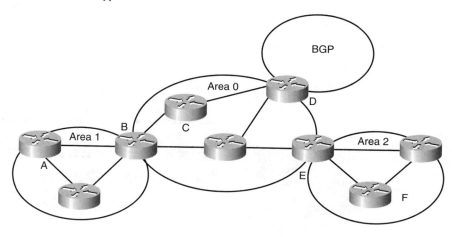

33. Identify the OSPF router types shown in Figure 11-11.

Router A = _____

Router B = _____

Router C = _____

Router D = _____

Router E = _____

Router F = _____

This chapter covers the following subjects:

- BGP

- Route Manipulation

- IP Multicast Review

CHAPTER 12

Border Gateway Protocol, Route Manipulation, and IP Multicast

This chapter covers the Border Gateway Protocol (BGP), which is used to exchange routes between autonomous systems. It is most frequently used between enterprises and service providers. The "Route Manipulation" section covers route summarization and redistribution of route information between routing protocols. The CCDA should know where redistribution occurs when required by the network design. This chapter also reviews policy-based routing (PBR) as a method to change the destination IP address based on policies. Finally, this chapter covers IP multicast protocols.

"Do I Know This Already?" Quiz

The purpose of the "Do I Know This Already?" quiz is to help you decide whether you need to read the entire chapter. If you intend to read the entire chapter, you do not necessarily need to answer these questions now.

The eight-question quiz, derived from the major sections in the "Foundation Topics" portion of the chapter, helps you determine how to spend your limited study time.

Table 12-1 outlines the major topics discussed in this chapter and the "Do I Know This Already?" quiz questions that correspond to those topics.

Table 12-1   *"Do I Know This Already?" Foundation Topics Section-to-Question Mapping*

Foundation Topics Section	Questions Covered in This Section
BGP	1, 2, 7, 8
Route Manipulation	3, 4
IP Multicast Review	5, 6

CAUTION   The goal of self-assessment is to gauge your mastery of the topics in this chapter. If you do not know the answer to a question or you are only partially sure, you should mark this question wrong for the purposes of the self-assessment. Giving yourself credit for an answer you correctly guess skews your self-assessment results and might give you a false sense of security.

1. What protocol do you use to exchange IP routes between autonomous systems?

   a. IGMP

   b. eBGP

   c. IGRP

   d. OSPF

2. What is the current version of BGP?

   a. BGP Version 2

   b. BGP Version 3

   c. BGP Version 4

   d. BGP Version 1

3. Where should routes be summarized?

   a. On the core routers

   b. On the distribution routers

   c. On the access routers

   d. None of the above

4. What is PBR?

   a. Public-Broadcast Routing

   b. Private-Based Routing

   c. Policy-Broadcast Routing

   d. Policy-Based Routing

5. What is IGMP?

   a. Interior Group Management Protocol

   b. Internet Group Management Protocol

   c. Interior Gateway Routing Protocol

   d. Interior Gateway Media Protocol

6. How many bits are mapped from the Layer 3 IPv4 multicast address to a Layer 2 MAC address?

   a. 16 bits

   b. 23 bits

   c. 24 bits

   d. 32 bits

7. What is the administrative distance of eBGP routes?

   a. 20

   b. 100

   c. 110

   d. 200

8. What is CIDR?

   a. Classful Intradomain Routing

   b. Classful Interior Domain Routing

   c. Classless Intradomain Routing

   d. Classless Interdomain Routing

The answers to the "Do I Know This Already?" quiz appear in Appendix A, "Answers to Chapter 'Do I Know This Already?' Quizzes and Q&A Sections." The suggested choices for your next step are as follows:

- **6 or less overall score**—Read the entire chapter. It includes the "Foundation Topics," "Foundation Summary," and "Q&A" sections.

- **7 or 8 overall score**—If you want more review on these topics, skip to the "Foundation Summary" section and then go to the "Q&A" section. Otherwise, move to the next chapter.

Foundation Topics

The "Foundation Topics" section includes discussions of BGP, PBR, route redistribution, and IP multicast protocols. The "BGP" section covers the characteristics and design of BGP. eBGP exchanges routes between autonomous systems. eBGP is commonly used between enterprises and their service providers.

The section "Route Manipulation" covers how you use PBR to change packets' destination addresses based on policies. This section also covers route summarization and redistribution of route information between routing protocols.

The section "IP Multicast Review" covers multicast protocols such as IGMP, Cisco Group Management Protocol (CGMP), and Protocol Independent Multicast (PIM).

BGP

This section covers BGP theory and design concepts. The current version of BGP, Version 4, is defined in RFC 1771 (March 1995). BGP is an interdomain routing protocol. What this means is that you use BGP to exchange routing information between autonomous systems. The primary function of BGP is to provide and exchange network-reachability information between domains or autonomous systems. BGP is a path vector protocol that is suited for setting routing policies between autonomous systems. In the enterprise campus architecture, BGP is used in the Internet connectivity module.

BGP is the de facto standard for routing between service providers on the Internet because of its rich features. You can also use it to exchange routes in large internal networks. The Internet Assigned Numbers Authority (IANA) reserved TCP Port 179 to identify the BGP protocol. BGPv4 was created to provide CIDR, a feature that was not present in the earlier versions of BGP. BGP is a path-vector routing protocol; it is neither a distance-vector nor link-state routing protocol.

> **NOTE**   RFC 1519 describes CIDR, which provides the capability to forward packets based on IP prefixes only, with no concern for IP address class boundaries. CIDR was created as a means to constrain the growth of the routing tables in the Internet core through the summarization of IP addresses across network class boundaries. The early 1990s saw an increase in the growth of Internet routing tables and a reduction in Class B address space. CIDR provides a way for service providers to assign address blocks smaller than a Class B network but larger than a Class C network.

BGP Neighbors

BGP is usually configured between two directly connected routers that belong to different autonomous systems. Each autonomous system is under different technical administration. BGP is frequently used to connect the enterprise to service providers and to interconnect service providers, as shown in Figure 12-1. The routing protocol within the enterprise could be any interior gateway protocol (IGP). Common IGP choices include RIPv2, EIGRP, Open Shortest Path First (OSPF), and Intermediate System-to-Intermediate System (IS-IS). BGPv4 is the only deployed exterior gateway protocol (EGP). AS numbers are a managed resource allocated by the American Registry of Internet Numbers (ARIN). In IP, the AS numbers 64,512 through 65,535 are allocated to IANA and are designated for private use.

Before two BGP routers can exchange routing updates, they must become established neighbors. After BGP routers establish a TCP connection, exchange information, and accept the information, they become established neighbors and start exchanging routing updates. If the neighbors do not reach an established state, they do not exchange BGP updates. The information exchanged before the neighbors are established includes the BGP version number, AS number, BGP router ID, and BGP capabilities.

Figure 12-1 *BGP Neighbors*

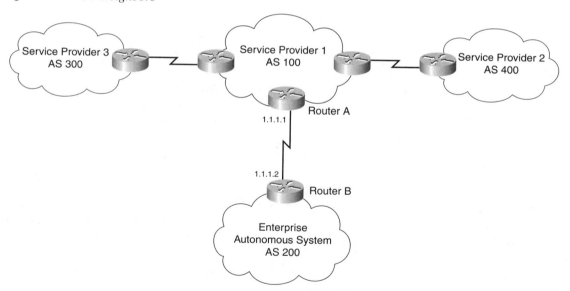

eBGP

eBGP is the term used to describe BGP peering between neighbors in different autonomous systems. As required by RFC 1771, the eBGP peers share a common subnet. In Figure 12-2, all routers speak eBGP with routers in other autonomous systems. Within AS 500, the routers communicate using iBGP, which is covered next.

Figure 12-2 *eBGP Used Between Autonomous Systems*

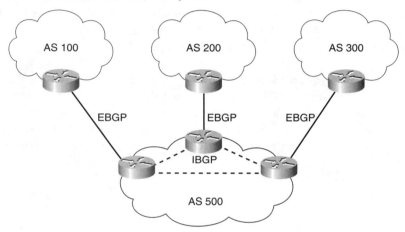

iBGP

iBGP is the term used to describe the peering between BGP neighbors in the same AS. iBGP is used primarily in transit autonomous systems. Transit autonomous systems forward traffic from one external AS to another external AS. If transit autonomous systems did not use iBGP, the eBGP-learned routes would have to be redistributed into an IGP and then redistributed into the BGP process in another eBGP router. Normally the number of eBGP routes is too large for an IGP to handle.

iBGP provides a better way to control the routes within the transit AS. With iBGP, the external route information (attributes) is forwarded. The various IGPs that might be used do not understand or forward BGP attributes, including AS paths, between eBGP routers.

Another use of iBGP is in large corporations where the IGP networks are in smaller independent routing domains along organizational or geographic boundaries. In Figure 12-3, a company has decided to use three independent IGPs: one for the Americas; another for Asia and Australia; and another for Europe, the Middle East, and Africa. Routes are redistributed into an iBGP core.

Figure 12-3 *iBGP in a Large Corporation*

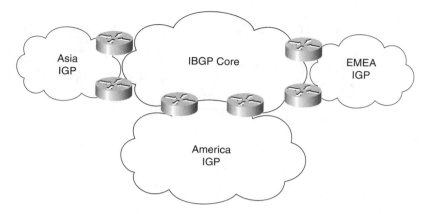

Other Uses of iBGP

The CCDA should know at a high level these other uses for IBGP:

- **Applying policies in the internal AS with the help of BGP path attributes**—BGP path attributes are covered in a later section.

- **QoS Policy Propagation on BGP (QPPB)**—QPPB uses iBGP to spread common QoS parameters from one router to other routers in the network. It classifies packets using IP precedence bits based on BGP community lists, BGP AS paths, and access lists. After packets are classified, QoS features can enforce policies.

- **Multiprotocol BGP peering of Multiprotocol Label Switching (MPLS) Virtual Private Networks (VPN)**—The multiprotocol version of BGP is used to carry MPLS VPN information between all PE routers within a VPN community.

Route Reflectors

iBGP requires that all routers be configured to establish a logical connection with all other iBGP routers. The logical connection is a TCP link between all iBGP-speaking routers. The routers in each TCP link become BGP peers. In large networks, the number of iBGP-meshed peers can become very large. Network administrators can use route reflectors to reduce the number of required mesh links between iBGP peers. Some routers are selected to become the route reflectors to serve several other routers that act as route-reflector clients. Route reflectors allow a router to advertise or reflect routes to clients. The route reflector and its clients form a cluster. All client routers in the cluster peer with the route reflectors within the cluster. The route reflectors also peer with all other route reflectors in the internetwork. A cluster can have more than one route reflector.

In Figure 12-4, without route reflectors, all iBGP routers are configured in an iBGP mesh, as required by the protocol. When Routers A and G become route reflectors, they peer with Routers C and D; Router B becomes a route reflector for Routers E and F. Routers A, B, and G peer among each other.

> **NOTE** The combination of the route reflector and its clients is called a cluster. In Figure 12-4, Routers A, G, C, and D form a cluster. Routers B, E, and F form another cluster.

Figure 12-4 *Route Reflectors*

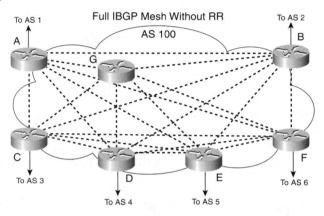

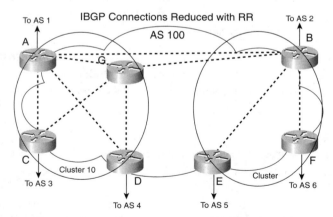

Routers A and G are configured to peer with each other and with Routers B, C, and D. The configuration of Routers C and D is different from the rest; they are configured to peer with Routers A and G only. All route reflectors in the same cluster must have the same cluster ID number.

Router B is the route reflector for the second cluster. Router B peers with Routers A and G and with Routers E and F in its cluster. Routers E and F are route-reflector clients and peer only with

Router B. If Router B goes down, the cluster on the right goes down because no second route reflector is configured.

Confederations

Another method to reduce the iBGP mesh within an AS is BGP confederations. With confederations, the AS is divided into smaller, private autonomous systems, and the whole group is assigned a confederation ID. The private AS numbers or identifiers are not advertised to the Internet but are contained within the iBGP networks. The routers within each private AS are configured with the full iBGP mesh. Each private AS is configured with eBGP to communicate with other semiautonomous systems in the confederation. External autonomous systems see only the AS number of the confederation, and this number is configured with the BGP confederation identifier.

In Figure 12-5, a confederation divides the AS into two.

Figure 12-5 *BGP Confederations*

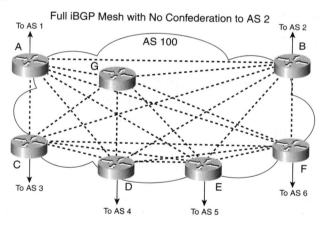

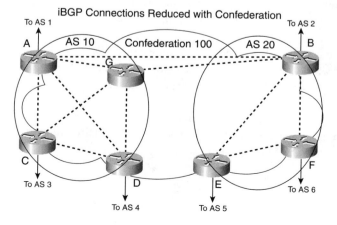

Routers A, B, and G are configured for eBGP between the private autonomous systems. You configure these routers with the **bgp confederation identifier** command. The confederation identifier number is the same for all routers in the network. You use the **bgp confederation peers** command to identify the AS number of other private autonomous systems in the confederation. Because Routers A and G are in AS 10, the peer confederation to Router B is AS 20. Router B is in AS 20, and its peer confederation to Routers A and G is AS 10. Routers C and D are part of AS 10 and peer with each other and with Routers A and G. Routers E and F are part of AS 20 and peer with each other and with Router B.

BGP Administrative Distance

The Cisco IOS Software assigns an administrative distance to eBGP and iBGP routes, as it does with other routing protocols. For the same prefix, the route with the lowest administrative distance is selected for inclusion in the IP forwarding table. Because iBGP-learned routes do not have metrics associated with the route as IGPs (OSPF and EIGRP) do, iBGP-learned routes are less trusted. For BGP, the administrative distances are

- **eBGP routes**—20

- **iBGP routes**—200

BGP Attributes, Weight, and the BGP Decision Process

BGP is a protocol that uses route attributes to select the best path to a destination. This subsection describes BGP attributes, the use of weight to influence path selection, and the BGP decision process.

BGP Path Attributes

BGP uses several attributes for the path-selection process. BGP uses path attributes to communicate routing policies. BGP path attributes include next hop, local preference, AS path, origin, multiexit discriminator (MED), atomic aggregate, and aggregator. Of these, the AS path is one of the most important attributes: It lists the number of AS paths to reach a destination network.

BGP attributes can be categorized as *well-known* or *optional*. Well-known attributes are recognized by all BGP implementations. Optional attributes do not have to be supported by the BGP process; they are used on a test or experimental basis.

Well-known attributes can be further subcategorized as *mandatory* or *discretionary*. Mandatory attributes are always included in BGP update messages. Discretionary attributes might or might not be included in the BGP update message.

Optional attributes can be further subcategorized as *transitive* or *nontransitive*. Routers must advertise the route with transitive attributes to its peers even if it does not support the attribute locally. If the path attribute is nontransitive, the router does not have to advertise the route to its peers.

The following subsections cover each attribute category.

Next-Hop Attribute

The next-hop attribute is the IP address of the next IP hop that will be used to reach the destination. The next-hop attribute is a well-known mandatory attribute. With eBGP, the eBGP peer sets the next hop when it announces the route. Multiaccess networks use the next-hop attribute where there is more than one BGP router.

Local Preference Attribute

The local preference attribute indicates which path to use to exit the AS. It is a well-known discretionary attribute used between iBGP peers and is not passed on to external BGP peers. In Cisco IOS Software, the default local preference is 100. The higher local preference is preferred.

The default local preference is configured on the BGP router with an external path; it then advertises its local preference to internal iBGP peers. Figure 12-6 shows an example of the local preference attribute where Routers B and C are configured with different local preference values. Router A and other iBGP routers then receive routes from both Router B and Router C. Router A prefers using Router C to route Internet packets because it has a higher local preference (400) than Router B (300). The arrows represent the paths taken to go out of the AS.

Figure 12-6 *BGP Local Preference*

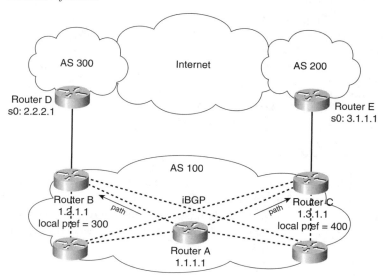

Origin Attribute

Origin is a well-known mandatory attribute that defines the source of the path information. Do not confuse the origin with comparing whether the route is external (eBGP) or internal (iBGP). The origin attribute is received from the source BGP router. There are three types:

- **IGP**—Indicated by an i in the BGP table. Present when the route is learned by way of the **network** statement.

- **EGP**—Indicated by an e in the BGP table. Learned from EGP.

- **Incomplete**—Indicated by a ? in the BGP table. Learned from redistribution of the route.

In terms of choosing a route based on origin, BGP prefers routes that have been verified by an IGP over routes that have been learned from EGP peers, and BGP prefers routes learned from eBGP peers over incomplete paths.

AS Path Attribute

The AS path is a well-known mandatory attribute that contains a list of AS numbers in the path to the destination. Each AS prepends its own AS number to the AS path. The AS path describes all the autonomous systems a packet would have to travel to reach the destination IP network. It is used to ensure that the path is loop-free. When the AS path attribute is used to select a path, the route with the fewest AS hops is preferred. In the case of a tie, other attributes, such as MED, break the tie. Example 12-1 shows the AS path for network 200.50.32.0/19. To reach the destination, a packet must pass autonomous systems 3561, 7004, and 7418. The command **show ip bgp 200.50.32.0** displays the AS path information.

Example 12-1 *AS Path Attribute*

```
Router#show ip bgp 200.50.32.0
BGP routing table entry for 200.50.32.0/19, version 93313535
Paths: (1 available, best #1)
  Not advertised to any peer
  3561 7004 7418
    206.24.241.181 (metric 490201) from 165.117.1.219 (165.117.1.219)
      Origin IGP, metric 4294967294, localpref 100, valid, internal, best
      Community: 2548:182 2548:337 2548:666 3706:153
```

MED Attribute

The MED attribute, also known as a metric, tells external BGP peers the preferred path into the AS when multiple paths into the AS exist. In other words, MED influences which one of many paths a neighboring AS uses to reach destinations within the AS. It is an optional nontransitive attribute carried in eBGP updates. The MED attribute is not used with iBGP peers. The lowest

MED value is preferred, and the default value is 0. Paths received with no MED are assigned a MED of 0. The MED is carried into an AS but does not leave the AS.

Consider the diagram shown in Figure 12-7. With all attributes considered equal, consider that Router C selects Router A as its best path into AS 100 based on Router A's lower router ID (RID). If Router A is configured with a MED of 200, then that will make Router C select Router B as the best path to AS 100. No additional configuration is required on Router B, because the default MED is 0.

Figure 12-7   *MED Attribute*

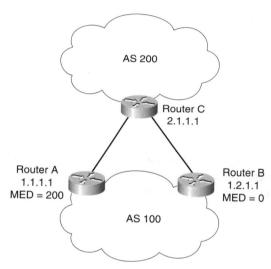

Community Attribute

Although it is not an attribute used in the routing-decision process, the community attribute groups routes and applies policies or decisions (accept, prefer) to those routes. It is a group of destinations that share some common property. The community attribute is an optional transitive attribute of variable length.

Atomic Aggregate and Aggregator Attributes

The atomic aggregate attribute informs BGP peers that the local router used a less specific (aggregated) route to a destination without using a more specific route.

If a BGP router selects a less specific route when a more specific route is available, it must attach the atomic aggregate attribute when propagating the route. The atomic aggregate attribute lets the BGP peers know that the BGP router used an aggregated route. A more specific route must be in the advertising router's BGP table before it propagates an aggregate route.

When the atomic aggregate attribute is used, the BGP speaker has the option to send the aggregator attribute. The aggregator attribute includes the AS number and the IP address of the router that originated the aggregated route. In Cisco routers, the IP address used is the RID of the router that performs the route aggregation. Atomic aggregate is a well-known discretionary attribute, and aggregator is an optional transitive attribute.

Weight

Weight is assigned locally on a router to specify a preferred path if multiple paths exist out of a router for a destination. Weights can be applied to individual routes or to all routes received from a peer. Weight is specific to Cisco routers and is not propagated to other routers. The weight value ranges from 0 to 65,535. Routes with a higher weight are preferred when multiple routes exist to a destination. Routes that are originated by the local router have a default weight of 32,768.

You can use weight instead of local preference to influence the selected path to external BGP peers. The difference is that weight is configured locally and is not exchanged in BGP updates. On the other hand, the local preference attribute is exchanged between iBGP peers and is configured at the gateway router.

When the same destinations are advertised from both Router B and Router C, as shown in Figure 12-8, Router A prefers the routes from Router C over Router B because the routes received from Router C have a larger weight (600) locally assigned.

Figure 12-8 *BGP Weight*

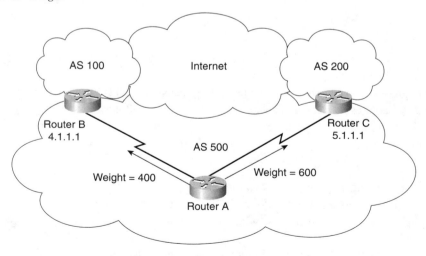

BGP Decision Process

By default, BGP selects only a single path to reach a specific destination (unless you specify maximum paths). The Cisco implementation of BGP uses a simple decision process. When the path is selected, BGP puts the selected path in its routing table and propagates the path to its neighbors.

To select the best path to a destination, Cisco routers running BGP use the following algorithm in the following order:

1. If the specified next hop is inaccessible, drop the path.

2. If the path is internal, synchronization is enabled, and the path is not in the IGP, drop the path.

3. Prefer the path with the largest weight. (This step is Cisco-specific, and weight is localized to the router.)

4. Prefer the path with the largest local preference. iBGP uses this path only to reach the preferred external BGP router.

5. Prefer the path that was locally originated via a **network** or **aggregate** BGP subcommand or through redistribution from an IGP. Local paths sourced by **network** or **redistribute** commands are preferred over local aggregates sourced by the **aggregate-address** command. (This step is Cisco-specific.)

6. If no route was originated, prefer the route that has the shortest AS path. (This step is Cisco-specific.)

7. If all paths have the same AS path length, prefer the path with the lowest origin type. Paths with an origin type of IGP (lower) are preferred over paths originated from an EGP such as BGP, and EGP origin is preferred over a route with an incomplete origin. (This step is Cisco-specific.)

8. If the origin codes are the same, prefer the path with the lowest MED attribute. An eBGP peer uses this attribute to select a best path to the AS. (This step is a tiebreaker, as described in the RFC that defines the BGP.)

9. If the paths have the same MED, prefer the external (eBGP) path over the internal (iBGP) path. (This step is Cisco-specific.)

10. If the paths are still the same, prefer the path through the closest IGP neighbor (best IGP metric). (This step is a tiebreaker, as described in the RFC that defines the BGP.)

11. Prefer the path with the BGP neighbor with the lowest router ID. (The RFC that defines the BGP describes the router ID.)

After BGP decides on a best path, it marks it with a > sign in the **show ip bgp** table and adds it to the IP routing table.

BGP Summary

The characteristics of BGP follow:

- BGP is an exterior gateway protocol (EGP) used in routing in the Internet. It is an interdomain routing protocol.

- BGP is a path vector routing protocol suited for strategic routing policies.

- It uses TCP port 179 to establish connections with neighbors.

- BGPv4 implements CIDR.

- eBGP is used for external neighbors. It is used between different autonomous systems.

- iBGP is used for internal neighbors. It is used within an AS.

- BGP uses several attributes in the routing-decision algorithm.

- It uses confederations and route reflectors to reduce BGP peering overhead.

- The MED (metric) attribute is used between autonomous systems to influence inbound traffic.

- Weight is used to influence the path of outbound traffic from a single router, configured locally.

Route Manipulation

This section covers PBR, route summarization, and route redistribution. You can use PBR to modify the next hop of packets from what is selected by the routing protocol. PBR is useful when the traffic engineering of paths is required. Routes are summarized to reduce the size of routing tables and at network boundaries. Redistribution between routing protocols is required to inject route information from one routing protocol to another. The CCDA must understand the issues with the redistribution of routes.

PBR

You can use PBR to modify the next-hop address of packets or to mark packets to receive differential service. Routing is based on destination addresses; routers look at the routing table to determine the next-hop IP address based on a destination lookup. PBR is commonly used to modify the next-hop IP address based on the source address. You can also use PBR to mark the IP precedence bits in outbound IP packets so that you can apply quality-of-service (QoS) policies. In Figure 12-9, Router A exchanges routing updates with routers in the WAN. The routing protocol might select Serial 0 as the preferred path for all traffic because of the higher bandwidth. The company might have business-critical systems that use the T1 but does not want systems on

Ethernet 1 to affect WAN performance. You can configure PBR on Router A to force traffic from Ethernet 1 out on Serial 1.

Figure 12-9 *Policy-Based Routing*

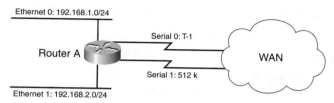

Route Summarization

Large networks can grow very quickly from 500 routes to 1000, to 2000, and so on. Network IP addresses should be allocated to allow for route summarization. Route summarization reduces the amount of route traffic on the network and unnecessary route computation. Route summarization also allows the network to scale as a company grows.

The recommended location for route summarization is to summarize at the distribution layer of the network topology. Figure 12-10 shows a hierarchical network. It has a network core, regional distribution routers, and access routes for sites.

Figure 12-10 *Route Summarization*

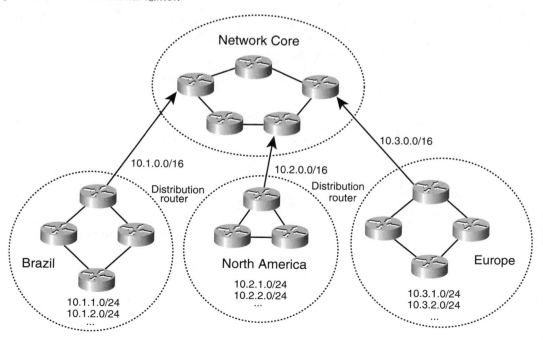

All routes in Brazil are summarized with a single 10.1.0.0/16 route. The North America and European routes are also summarized with 10.2.0.0/16 and 10.3.0.0/16, respectively. Routers in Europe only need to know the summarized route to get to Brazil and North America, and vice versa. Again, design best practices are to summarize at the distribution toward the core. The core only needs to know the summarized route of the regional areas.

Route Redistribution

You configure the redistribution of routing protocols on routers that reside at the Service Provider Edge of the network. These routers exchange routes with other autonomous systems. Redistribution is also done on routers that run more than one routing protocol. Here are some reasons to do redistribution:

■ Migration from an older routing protocol to a new routing protocol.

■ Mixed-vendor environment in which Cisco routers might be using EIGRP and other vendor routers might be using OSPF.

■ Different administrative domain between company departments using different routing protocols.

■ Mergers and acquisitions in which the networks initially need to communicate. In this example two different EIGRP processes might exist.

Figure 12-11 shows an example of the exchange of routes between two autonomous systems. Routes from AS 100 are redistributed into BGP on Router A. Routes from AS 200 are redistributed into BGP on Router B. Then, Routers A and B exchange BGP routes. Router A and Router B also implement filters to redistribute only the desired networks.

Figure 12-11 *Redistribution of BGP Routes*

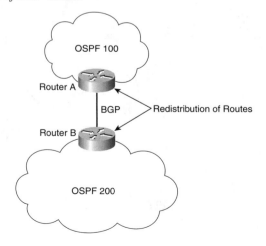

A company might also acquire another company that might be running another routing protocol. Figure 12-12 shows a network that has both OSPF and EIGRP routing protocols. Routers A and B perform redistribution between OSPF and EIGRP. Both routers must filter routes from OSPF before redistributing them into EIGRP and filter routes from EIGRP before redistributing them into OSPF. This setup prevents route feedback.

Figure 12-12 *Redistribution Between IGPs*

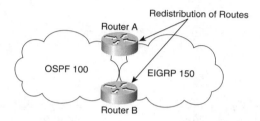

Route feedback occurs when a routing protocol learns routes from another routing protocol and then announces the routes to the other routing protocol. In Figure 12-12, OSPF should not announce the routes it learned from EIGRP, and EIGRP should not announce the routes it learned from OSPF.

You can use access lists, distribution lists, and route maps when redistributing routes. You can use these methods to specify (select) routes for redistribution, to set metrics, or to set other policies for the routes. They are also used to control routes' redistribution direction. Redistribution can be accomplished by two methods:

- Two-way redistribution

- One-way redistribution

In two-way redistribution, routing information is exchanged between both routing protocols. No static routes are used in this exchange. Route filters are used to prevent routing loops. Routing loops can be caused by one route protocol redistributing routes that were learned from a second route protocol back to that second routing protocol.

One-way redistribution only allows redistribution from one routing protocol to another. Normally it is used in conjunction with a default or static route at the edge of a network. Figure 12-13 shows an example of one-way redistribution. The routing information from the WAN routes is redistributed into the campus. But campus routes are not redistributed out to the WAN. The WAN routers use a default gateway to get back to the campus.

Figure 12-13 *One-Way Route Redistribution*

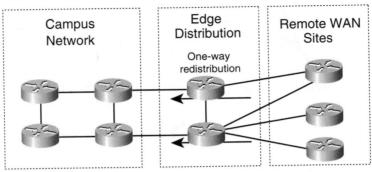

Other locations for one-way redistribution are from building access networks, BGP routes or static routes into the IGP, and from VPN static routes into the IGP.

Default Metric

There is a default metric of 0 when redistributing routes into RIPv2, IS-IS, and EIGRP. You should configure the metric of the redistributed routes to a metric other than 0. You can configure the metric in the **redistribution** command or configure a default metric. You can also use the command in OSPF. IS-IS does not use the **default-metric** command. The **default-metric** command has the following syntax for EIGRP:

```
default-metric bandwidth delay reliability load mtu
```

OSPF Redistribution

This subsection reviews a few things you need to remember when designing a network that will redistribute with OSPF.

When redistributing routes into OSPF, use the **subnets** keyword to permit subnetted routes to be received. If you do not use it, only the major network route is redistributed, without any subnetworks. In other words, OSPF performs automatic summarization to IP classful network values.

By default, redistributed routes are classified as external Type 2 (E2) in OSPF. You can use the **metric-type** keyword to change the external route to an external Type 1 (E1). The network design can take into account the after-redistribution cost (Type 2) or the after-redistribution cost plus the path's cost (Type 1).

In Figure 12-14, Router B is configured to perform mutual redistribution between EIGRP 100 and OSPF process ID 50. In this example, you can use route maps and access lists to prevent routing loops. The route maps permit or deny the networks that are listed in the access lists. The **subnets** keyword redistributes every subnet in EIGRP into OSPF. This book does not cover exact configurations.

Figure 12-14 *OSPF and EIGRP Redistribution*

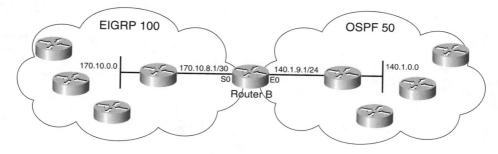

IP Multicast Review

With multicast, packets are sent to a multicast group, which is identified with an IP multicast address. Multicast supports the transmission of IP packets from one source to multiple hosts. Packets with unicast addresses are sent to one device, and broadcast addresses are sent to all hosts; packets with multicast addresses are sent to a group of hosts.

Multicast Addresses

Multicast addressing uses Class D addresses from the IPv4 protocol. Class D addresses range from 224.0.0.0 to 239.255.255.255. IANA manages multicast addresses.

Routing protocols (RIPv2, EIGRP, and OSPF) use multicast addresses to speak to their neighbors. For example, OSPF routers use 224.0.0.6 to speak to the designated router (DR) in a multiaccess network. Class D multicast addresses range from 224.0.0.0 to 239.255.255.255. Multicast addresses in the range of 224.0.0.1 to 224.255.255.255 are reserved for special addresses or network protocol on a multiaccess link. RFC 2365 reserves multicast addresses in the range of 239.192.000.000 to 239.251.255.255 for organization-local scope. Similarly, 239.252.000.000 to 239.252.255.255, 239.254.000.000 to 239.254.255.255, and 239.255.000.000 to 239.255.255.255 are reserved for site-local scope.

Table 12-2 lists some well-known and multicast address blocks.

Table 12-2 *Multicast Addresses*

Multicast Address	Description
224.0.0.0/24	Local network control block
224.0.0.1	All hosts or all systems on this subnet
224.0.0.2	All multicast routers
224.0.0.4	Distance-Vector Multicast Routing Protocol (DVMRP) routers
224.0.0.5	All OSPF routers
224.0.0.6	All OSPF DR routers
224.0.0.9	RIPv2 routers
224.0.0.10	EIGRP routers
224.0.0.13	All PIM routers
224.0.1.0/24	Internetwork control block
224.0.1.39	Rendezvous point (RP) announce
224.0.1.40	RP discovery
224.0.2.0 to 224.0.255.0	Ad hoc block
239.000.000.000 to 239.255.255.255	Administratively scoped
239.192.000.000 to 239.251.255.255	Organization-local scope
239.252.000.000 to 239.254.255.255	Site-local scope

Layer 3 to Layer 2 Mapping

Multicast-aware Ethernet, Token Ring, and Fiber Distributed Data Interface (FDDI) network interface cards use the reserved IEEE 802 address 0100.5e00.0000 for multicast addresses at the MAC layer. This includes Fast Ethernet and Gigabit Ethernet. Notice that for the address, the high-order byte 0x01 has the low-order bit set to 1. This bit is the Individual/Group (I/G) bit. It signifies whether the address is an individual address (0) or a group address (1). Hence, for multicast addresses, this bit is set to 1.

Ethernet interfaces map the lower 23 bits of the IP multicast address to the lower 23 bits of the MAC address 0100.5e00.0000. As an example, the IP multicast address 224.0.0.2 is mapped to the MAC layer as 0100.5e00.0002. Figure 12-15 shows another example looking at the bits of multicast IP 239.192.44.56. The IP address in hexadecimal is EF:C0:2C:38. The lower 23 bits get mapped into the lower 23 bits of the base multicast MAC to produce the multicast MAC address 01:00:5E:40:2C:38.

Figure 12-15 *Mapping of Multicast IP Addressing to MAC Addresses*

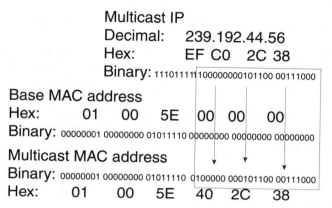

Multicast IP
Decimal: 239.192.44.56
Hex: EF C0   2C 38
Binary: 11101111 100000000101100 00111000

Base MAC address
Hex: 01   00   5E   00   00   00
Binary: 00000001 00000000 01011110 00000000 00000000 00000000

Multicast MAC address
Binary: 00000001 00000000 01011110 01000000 000101100 00111000
Hex: 01   00   5E   40   2C   38

IGMP

IGMP is the protocol used in multicast implementations between the end hosts and the local router. RFC 2236 describes IGMP Version 2 (IGMPv2). RFC 3376 describes IGMP Version 3 (IGMPv3). RFC 1112 describes the first version of IGMP.

IP hosts use IGMP to report their multicast group memberships to routers. IGMP messages use IP protocol number 2. IGMP messages are limited to the local interface and are not routed.

IGMPv1

The first RFC describing IGMP (RFC 1112), written in 1989, describes the host extensions for IP multicasting. IGMPv1 provides simple message types for communication between hosts and routers. These messages are

- **Membership query**—Sent by the router to check whether a host wants to join a multicast group

- **Membership report**—Sent by the host to join a multicast group in the segment

The problem with IGMPv1 is the latency involved for a host to leave a group. With IGMPv1, the router sends membership queries periodically; a host must wait for the membership-query message to leave a group. The query interval is 60 seconds, and it takes three query intervals (3 minutes) for a host to leave the group.

IGMPv2

IGMPv2 improves over IGMPv1 by allowing faster termination or leaving of multicast groups.

IGMPv2 has three message types, plus one for backward compatibility:

- **Membership query**—Sent by the router to check whether a host wants to join a group.

- **Version 2 membership report**—A message sent to the group address with the multicast group members (IP addresses). It is sent to by hosts to join and remain in multicast groups on the segment.

- **Version 2 leave group**—Sent by the hosts to indicate that a host will leave a group; it is sent to destination 224.0.0.2. After the host sends the leave group message, the router responds with a group-specific query.

- **Version 1 membership report**—For backward compatibility with IGMPv1 hosts.

You enable IGMP on an interface when you configure a multicast routing protocol, such as PIM. You can configure the interface for IGMPv1, IGMPv2 or IGMPv3.

IGMPv3

IGMPv3 provides the extensions required to support source-specific multicast (SSM). It is designed to be backward-compatible with both prior versions of IGMP.

IGMPv3 has two message types, plus three for backward compatibility:

- **Membership query**—Sent by the router to check that a host wants to join a group.

- **Version 3 membership report**—A message sent to the group address with the multicast group members (IP addresses). It is sent by hosts to request and remain in multicast groups on the segment.

- **Version 2 membership report**—A message sent to the group address with the multicast group members (IP addresses). It is sent by hosts to request and remain in multicast groups on the segment. This message is used for backward compatibility with IGMPv2 hosts.

- **Version 2 leave group**—Sent by the hosts to indicate that a host will leave a group, to destination 224.0.0.2. The message is sent without having to wait for the IGMPv2 membership report message. This message is used for backward compatibility with IGMPv2 hosts.

- **Version 1 membership report**—This message is used for backward compatibility with IGMPv1 hosts.

You enable IGMP on an interface when you enable a multicast routing protocol, such as PIM. You can configure the interface for IGMPv1, IGMPv2, or IGMPv3.

CGMP

CGMP is a Cisco-proprietary protocol implemented to control multicast traffic at Layer 2. Because a Layer 2 switch is unaware of Layer 3 IGMP messages, it cannot keep multicast packets from being sent to all ports.

As shown in Figure 12-16, with CGMP the LAN switch can speak with the IGMP router to find out the MAC addresses of the hosts that want to receive the multicast packets. With CGMP, switches distribute multicast sessions only to the switch ports that have group members.

Figure 12-16   *CGMP*

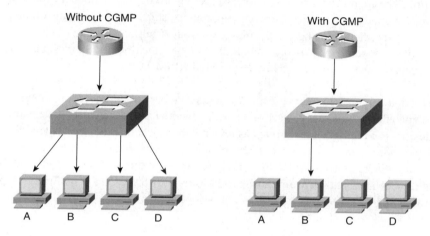

When a router receives an IGMP report, it processes the report and then sends a CGMP message to the switch. The switch can then forward the multicast messages to the port with the host receiving multicast traffic. CGMP fast-leave processing allows the switch to detect IGMP Version 2 leave messages sent by hosts on any of the switch ports. When a host sends the IGMPv2 leave message, the switch can then disable multicasting for the port.

IGMP Snooping

IGMP snooping is another way for switches to control multicast traffic at Layer 2. It listens to IGMP messages between the hosts and routers. If a host sends an IGMP query message to the router, the switch adds the host to the multicast group and permits that port to receive multicast traffic. The port is removed from multicast traffic if the host sends an IGMP leave message to the router. The disadvantage of IGMP snooping is that it has to process every IGMP control message, which can impact the CPU utilization of the switch.

Sparse Versus Dense Multicast Routing Protocols

IP multicast traffic for a particular (source, destination group) multicast pair is transmitted from the source to the receivers using a spanning tree from the source that connects all the hosts in the group. Each destination host registers itself as a member of interesting multicast groups through the use of IGMP. Routers keep track of these groups dynamically and build distribution trees that chart paths from each sender to all receivers. IP multicast routing protocols follow two approaches.

The first approach assumes that the multicast group members are densely distributed throughout the network (many of the subnets contain at least one group member) and that bandwidth is plentiful. The approach with dense multicast routing protocols is to flood the traffic throughout the network and then, at the request of receiving routers, stop the flow of traffic on branches of the network that have no members of the multicast group. Multicast routing protocols that follow this technique of flooding the network include DVMRP, Multicast Open Shortest Path First (MOSPF), and Protocol-Independent Multicast-Dense Mode (PIM-DM).

The second approach to multicast routing assumes that multicast group members are sparsely distributed throughout the network and that bandwidth is not necessarily widely available. Sparse mode does not imply that the group has few members, just that they are widely dispersed. The approach with sparse multicast routing protocols is to not send traffic until it is requested by the receiving routers or hosts. Multicast routing protocols of this type are Core-Based Trees (CBT) and Protocol-Independent Multicast-Sparse Mode (PIM-SM). CBT is not widely deployed and is not discussed in this book.

Multicast Source and Shared Trees

Multicast distribution trees control the path that multicast packets take to the destination hosts. The two types of distribution trees are source and shared. With *source* trees, the tree roots from the source of the multicast group and then expands throughout the network in spanning-tree fashion to the destination hosts. Source trees are also called shortest-path trees (SPT) because they create paths without having to go through a rendezvous point (RP). The drawback is that all routers through the path must use memory resources to maintain a list of all multicast groups. PIM-DM uses a source-based tree.

Shared trees create the distribution tree's root somewhere between the network's source and receivers. The root is called the RP. The tree is created from the RP in spanning-tree fashion with no loops. The advantage of shared trees is that they reduce the memory requirements of routers in the multicast network. The drawback is that initially the multicast packets might not take the best paths to the receivers because they need to pass through the RP. After the data stream begins to flow from sender to RP to receiver, the routers in the path optimize the path automatically to remove any unnecessary hops. The RP function consumes significant memory on the assigned router. PIM-SM uses an RP.

PIM

PIM comes in two flavors: *sparse mode* (PIM-SM) and *dense mode* (PIM-DM). The first uses shared trees and RPs to reach widely dispersed group members with reasonable protocol bandwidth efficiency. The second uses source trees and reverse path forwarding (RPF) to reach relatively close group members with reasonable processor and memory efficiency in the network devices of the distribution trees.

With RPF, received multicast packets are forwarded out all other interfaces, allowing the data stream to reach all segments. If no hosts are members of a multicast group on any of the router's attached or downstream subnets, the router sends a prune message up the distribution tree (the reverse path) to tell the upstream router not to send packets for the multicast group. So, the analogy for PIM-DM is the push method for sending junk mail, and the intermediate router must tell upstream devices to stop sending it.

PIM-SM

PIM-SM is defined in RFC 2362 (experimental). PIM-SM assumes that no hosts want to receive multicast traffic unless specifically requested. In PIM-SM, a router is selected as the RP. The RP gathers the information from senders and makes the information available to receivers. Routers with receivers have to register with the RP. The end-host systems request multicast group membership using IGMP with their local routers. The routers serving the end systems then register as traffic receivers with the RPs for the specified group in the multicast network.

Joining PIM-SM

With PIM-SM, DRs on end segments receive IGMP query messages from hosts wanting to join a multicast group. The router checks whether it is already receiving the group for another interface. If it is receiving the group, the router adds the new interface to the table and sends membership reports periodically on the new interface.

If the multicast group is not in the multicast table, the router adds the interface to the multicast table and sends a join message to the RP with multicast address 224.0.0.13 (all PIM routers) requesting the multicast group.

Pruning PIM-SM

When a PIM-SM does not have any more multicast receiving hosts or receiving routers out any of its interfaces, it sends a prune message to the RP. The prune message includes the group to be pruned or removed.

PIM DR

A designated router is selected in multiaccess segments running PIM. The PIM DR is responsible for sending join, prune, and register messages to the RP. The PIM router with the highest IP address is selected as the DR.

Auto-RP

Another way to configure the RP for the network is to have the RP announce its services to the PIM network. This process is called auto-RP. Candidate RPs send their announcements to RP mapping agents with multicast address 224.0.1.39 (**cisco-rp-announce**). RP mapping agents are also configured. In smaller networks, the RP can be the mapping agent. Configured RP mapping agents listen to the announcements. The RP mapping agent then selects the RP for a group based on the highest IP address of all the candidate RPs. The RP mapping agents then send RP-discovery messages to the rest of the PIM-SM routers in the internetwork with the selected RP-to-group mappings.

PIMv2 Bootstrap Router

Instead of using auto-RP, you can configure a PIMv2 bootstrap router (BSR) to automatically select an RP for the network. The RFC for PIM Version 2, RFC 2362, describes BSR. With BSR, you configure BSR candidates (C-BSR) with priorities from 0 to 255 and a BSR address. C-BSRs exchange bootstrap messages. Bootstrap messages are sent to multicast IP 224.0.0.13 (all PIM routers). If a C-BSR receives a bootstrap message, it compares it with its own. The largest priority C-BSR is selected as the BSR.

After the BSR is selected for the network, it collects a list of candidate RPs. The BSR selects RP-to-group mappings, which is called the RP set, and distributes the selected RPs using bootstrap messages sent to 224.0.0.13 (all PIM routers).

DVMRP

RFC 1075 describes DVMRP. It is the primary multicast routing protocol used in the multicast backbone (MBONE). The MBONE is used in the research community.

DVMRP operates in dense mode using RPF by having routers send a copy of a multicast packet out all paths. Routers that receive the multicast packets then send prune messages back to their upstream neighbor router to stop a data stream if no downstream receivers of the multicast group exist (either receiving routers or hosts on connected segments). DVMRP implements its own unicast routing protocol, similar to RIP, based on hop counts. DVMRP has a 32 hop-count limit. DVMRP does not scale suboptimally. Cisco's support of DVMRP is partial; DVMRP networks are usually implemented on UNIX machines running the **mrouted** process. A DVMRP tunnel is typically used to connect to the MBONE DVMRP network.

IPv6 Multicast Addresses

IPv6 retains the use and function of multicast addresses as a major address class. IPv6 prefix FF00::/8 is allocated for all IPv6 multicast addresses. IPv6 multicast addresses are described in RFC 2373. EIGRP for IPv6, OSPFv3, and RIPng routing protocols use multicast addresses to communicate between router neighbors.

The format of the IPv6 multicast address is described in Chapter 8, "Internet Protocol Version 6." The common multicast addresses are repeated in Table 12-3.

Table 12-3   *Well-Known Multicast Addresses*

Multicast Address	Multicast Group
FF01::1	All nodes (node-local)
FF02::1	All nodes (link-local)
FF01::2	All routers (node-local)
FF02::2	All routers (link-local)
FF02::5	OSPFv3 routers
FF02::6	OSPFv3 designated routers
FF02::9	Routing Information Protocol (RIPng)
FF02::A	EIGRP routers
FF02::B	Mobile agents
FF02::C	DHCP servers/relay agents
FF02::D	All PIM routers

References and Recommended Readings

Border Gateway Protocol. http://www.cisco.com/univercd/cc/td/doc/cisintwk/ito_doc/bgp.htm.

Chandra, R., P. Traina, and T. Li. RFC 1997, *BGP Communities Attribute*. Available from http://www.ietf.org/rfc.

Deering, S. RFC 1112, *Host Extensions for IP Multicasting*. Available from http://www.ietf.org/rfc.

Doyle, J. and J. Carroll. *Routing TCP/IP*, Volume I, Second Edition. Indianapolis: Cisco Press, 2005.

Doyle, J. and J. Carroll. *Routing TCP/IP*, Volume II. Indianapolis: Cisco Press, 2001.

Estrin, D., D. Farinacci, A. Helmy, D. Thaler, S. Deering, M. Handley, V. Jacobson, C. Liu, P. Sharma, and L. Wei. RFC 2362, *Protocol Independent Multicast-Sparse Mode (PIM-SM): Protocol Specification* (experimental). Available from http://www.ietf.org/rfc.

Fenner, W. RFC 2236, *Internet Group Management Protocol, Version 2*. Available from http://www.ietf.org/rfc.

Fuller, V., T. Li, J. Yu, and K. Varadhan. RFC 1519, *Classless Inter-Domain Routing (CIDR): An Address Assignment and Aggregation Strategy*. Available from http://www.ietf.org/rfc.

Halabi, S. *Internet Routing Architectures*. Indianapolis: Cisco Press, 2000.

"Internet Protocol (IP) Multicast Technology Overview" (white paper). Available from http://www.cisco.com/en/US/products/ps5763/products_white_paper0900aecd804d5fe6.shtml.

Meyer, D. RFC 2365, *Administratively Scoped IP Multicast*. Available from http://www.ietf.org/rfc.

Rekhter, Y. and T. Li. RFC 1771, *A Border Gateway Protocol 4 (BGP-4)*. Available from http://www.ietf.org/rfc.

Waitzman, D., C. Partride, and S. Deering. RFC 1075, *Distance Vector Multicast Routing Protocol*. Available from http://www.ietf.org/rfc.

Williamson, B. *Developing IP Multicast Networks*. Indianapolis: Cisco Press, 1999.

Foundation Summary

The "Foundation Summary" section of each chapter lists the most important facts from the chapter. Although this section does not list every fact from the chapter that will be on the CCDA exam, a well-prepared CCDA candidate should at a minimum know all the details in each "Foundation Summary" before taking the exam.

This chapter covered the following topics that you need to master for the CCDA exam:

- **BGP**—The characteristics and design of BGP.

- **Route manipulation**—How you use PBR to change the destination address of packets based on policies. This material also covers route summarization and the redistribution of routes between routing protocols.

- **IP multicast protocols**—Multicast protocols such as IGMP, CGMP, and PIM.

The material summarized next can help you review some of these topical areas.

BGP Summary

The characteristics of BGP follow:

- BGP is an exterior gateway protocol (EGP) used in routing in the Internet. It is an interdomain routing protocol.

- BGP is a path vector routing protocol suited for strategic routing policies.

- BGP uses TCP Port 179 to establish connections with neighbors.

- BGPv4 implements CIDR.

- eBGP is for external neighbors. It's used between separate autonomous systems.

- iBGP is for internal neighbors. It's used within an AS.

- BGP uses several attributes in the routing-decision algorithm.

- BGP uses confederations and route reflectors to reduce BGP peering overhead.

- The MED (metric) attribute is used between autonomous systems to influence inbound traffic.

- Weight is used to influence the path of outbound traffic from a single router, configured locally.

Route Redistribution

Route redistribution can occur

- In mixed vendor environments, where Cisco routers might be using EIGRP and other vendor routers using OSPF.

- In migrations from older routing protocol.

- In different administrative domains.

- From static routes and BGP routes into IGP.

- From VPN static routes into IGP.

- Between campus core and WAN routers.

- From selected building access protocols.

IP Multicast

Table 12-4 summarizes IP multicast protocols.

Table 12-4 *IP Multicast Protocols*

Multicast Protocol	Description
IGMP	Internet Group Management Protocol. Used by IP hosts to report their multicast group memberships to routers.
CGMP	Cisco Group Management Protocol. Used to control multicast traffic at Layer 2.
IGMP snooping	Another method used to control multicast traffic at Layer 2.
PIM	Protocol Independent Multicast. IP multicast routing protocol.
DVMRP	Distance-Vector Multicast Routing Protocol. Primary multicast routing protocol used in the MBONE.

Table 12-5 summarizes IP multicast addresses.

Table 12-5 *IP Multicast Addresses*

Multicast Address	Description
224.0.0.0/24	Local network control block
224.0.0.1	All hosts or all systems on this subnet
224.0.0.2	All routers on this subnet
224.0.0.4	DVMRP routers

Table 12-5 *IP Multicast Addresses (Continued)*

Multicast Address	Description
224.0.0.5	All OSPF routers
224.0.0.6	All OSPF DR routers
224.0.0.9	RIPv2 routers
224.0.0.10	EIGRP routers
224.0.0.13	All PIM routers
224.0.1.0/24	Internetwork control block
224.0.1.39	RP announce
224.0.1.40	RP discovery
224.0.2.0 to 224.0.255.0	Ad hoc block
239.000.000.000 to 239.255.255.255	Administratively scoped
239.192.000.000 to 239.251.255.255	Organization-local scope
239.252.000.000 to 239.254.255.255	Site-local scope

Table 12-6 shows IPv6 multicast addresses.

Table 12-6 *IPv6 Multicast Addresses*

Multicast Address	Multicast Group
FF01::1	All nodes (node-local)
FF02::1	All nodes (link-local)
FF01::2	All routers (node-local)
FF02::2	All routers (link-local)
FF02::5	OSPFv3 routers
FF02::6	OSPFv3 designated routers
FF02::9	Routing Information Protocol (RIPng)
FF02::A	EIGRP routers
FF02::B	Mobile agents
FF02::C	DHCP servers/relay agents
FF02::D	All PIM routers

Q&A

As mentioned in the Introduction, you have two choices for review questions: here in the book or the exam questions on the CD-ROM. The answers to these questions appear in Appendix A.

For more practice with exam format questions, use the exam engine on the CD-ROM.

1. True or false: You use iBGP to exchange routes between different autonomous systems.

2. True or false: BGP Version 4 includes support for CIDR.

3. True or false: eBGP and iBGP redistribute automatically on a router if the BGP peers are configured with the same AS number.

4. Use _____ to modify the next hop of packets based on source IP address.

5. eBGP routes have an administrative distance of ____, and iBGP routes have an administrative distance of ____.

6. True or false: IGMP snooping and CGMP are methods to reduce the multicast traffic at Layer 2.

7. True or false: PIM has a 32 hop-count limit.

8. True or false: PIM-SM routers use the multicast 224.0.0.13 address to request a multicast group to the RP.

9. True or false: AS path is the only attribute BGP uses to determine the best path to the destination.

10. List three IP routing protocols that use multicast addresses to communicate with their neighbors.

11. What IPv6 multicast address does EIGRP use for IPv6?

12. Match the IP multicast address with its description:

    i. 224.0.0.1

    ii. 224.0.0.2

    iii. 224.0.0.5

    iv. 224.0.0.10

    a. All OSPF routers

    b. All routers

    c. EIGRP routers

    d. All hosts

13. Match the BGP attribute with its description:

i. Local preference

ii. MED

iii. AS path

iv. Next hop

a. IP address

b. Indicates the path used to exit the AS

c. Tells external BGP peers the preferred path into the AS

d. List of AS numbers

14. Which Cisco feature can you use instead of local preference to influence the selected path to external BGP routers?

15. What is the purpose of route reflectors?

16. When BGP confederations are used, which number do external peers see?

17. With _____ all routers peer with each other within the private AS, and with _____ client routers peer only with the reflector.

18. Which of the following shows the correct order that BGP uses to select a best path?

   a. Origin, lowest IP, AS path, weight, local preference, MED

   b. Weight, local preference, AS path, origin, MED, lowest IP

   c. Lowest IP, AS path, origin, weight, MED, local preference

   d. Weight, origin, local preference, AS path, MED, lowest IP

19. What feature did BGPv4 implement to provide forwarding of packets based on IP prefixes?

20. What route should be used to summarize the following networks?

10.150.80.0/23, 10.150.82.0/24, 10.150.83.0/24, 10.150.84.0/22

   a. 10.150.80.0/23, 10.150.82.0/23, and 10.150.84.0/22

   b. 10.150.80.0/22 and 10.150.84/22

   c. 10.150.80.0/21

   d. 10.150.80.0/20

21. Match the IPv6 multicast address with its description:

i. FF02::1

ii. FF02::2

iii. FF02::5

iv. FF02::9

v. FF02::A

a. OSPFv3 routers

b. RIPng routers

c. All routers

d. EIGRP routers

e. All nodes

22. Route summarization and redistribution occur in which layer of the hierarchical model?

   a. Building access

   b. Distribution

   c. Core

   d. Server access

23. Which of the following best describes route summarization?

   a. Grouping contiguous addresses to advertise a large Class A network

   b. Grouping noncontiguous addresses to advertise a larger network

   c. Grouping contiguous addresses to advertise a larger network

   d. Grouping Internet addresses

Refer to Figure 12-17 to answer the following questions.

Figure 12-17 *Network Scenario*

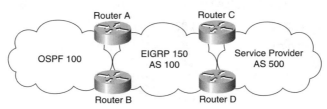

24. Where should you configure BGP?

    a. Routers A and B

    b. Routers C and D

    c. Answers A and B

    d. Routers A and C

25. On which router should you configure redistribution for OSPF and EIGRP?

    a. Router A only

    b. Router B only

    c. Routers A and B

    d. Redistribution occurs automatically.

26. To announce the networks from AS 100 to AS 500, which routing protocols should you redistribute into BGP?

    a. OSPF only

    b. EIGRP only

    c. OSPF and EIGRP

    d. iBGP

27. Where should you use filters?

    a. Routers A and B

    b. Routers C and D

    c. Routers A and C

    d. Answers A and B

This part covers the following CCDA exam topics (to view the CCDA exam overview, visit http://www.cisco.com/web/learning/le3/current_exams/ 640-863.html):

- Describe Network Management Protocols and Features
- Describe the Security Lifecycle
- Identify Cisco Technologies to Mitigate Security Vulnerabilities
- Select Appropriate Cisco Security Solutions and Deployment Placement
- Describe Traditional Voice Architectures and Features
- Describe Cisco IP Telephony
- Identify the Design Considerations for Voice Services

Part IV: Security, Convergence, and Network Management

This chapter covers the following subjects:

- Network Security Overview

- Security Threats

- Security Risks

- Security Policy and Process

- Trust and Identity Management

- Secure Connectivity

- Threat Defense

CHAPTER 13

Security Management

This chapter discusses network security in terms of security management and policy. You will be tested on security threats, risks, policy compliance, and securing network connectivity. You must understand how network security management and policy provide a framework for secure networks. This chapter also covers trust and identity management and threat defense.

"Do I Know This Already?" Quiz

The purpose of the "Do I Know This Already?" quiz is to help you decide whether you need to read the entire chapter. If you intend to read the entire chapter, you do not necessarily need to answer these questions now.

The ten-question quiz, derived from the major sections in the "Foundation Topics" portion of the chapter, helps you determine how to spend your limited study time.

Table 13-1 outlines the major topics discussed in this chapter and the "Do I Know This Already?" quiz questions that correspond to those topics.

Table 13-1 *"Do I Know This Already?" Foundation Topics Section-to-Question Mapping*

Foundation Topics Section	Questions Covered in This Section
Network Security Overview	1
Security Threats	2, 3
Security Risks	4, 5
Security Policy and Process	6, 7
Trust and Identity Management	8
Secure Connectivity	9
Threat Defense	10

> **CAUTION** The goal of self-assessment is to gauge your mastery of the topics in this chapter. If you do not know the answer to a question or you are only partially sure, you should mark this question wrong for the purposes of the self-assessment. Giving yourself credit for an answer you correctly guess skews your self-assessment results and might give you a false sense of security.

1. Which of the following security legislations applies protection to electronic private health information?

   a. SOX

   b. GLBA

   c. HIPAA

   d. EU Data Protection Directive

2. What classification of security threat gathers information about the target host?

   a. Gaining Unauthorized Access

   b. Reconnaissance

   c. Denial of Service

   d. None of the above

3. What type of security threat works to overwhelm network resources such as memory, CPU, and bandwidth?

   a. Denial of Service

   b. Reconnaissance

   c. Gaining Unauthorized Access

   d. NMAP scans

4. What is used to control the rate of bandwidth of incoming traffic?

   a. Unicast RPF

   b. DHCP snooping

   c. Access control lists

   d. Rate limiting

5. What is it called when attackers change sensitive data without proper authorization?

   a. VLAN filtering

   b. ACLs

   c. Integrity violations

   d. Loss of availability

6. What security document focuses on the processes and procedures for managing network events in addition to emergency-type scenarios?

    a. Acceptable-use policy

    b. Incident-handling policy

    c. Network access control policy

    d. Security management policy

7. Which of the following should be included in a security policy? (Choose all that apply.)

    a. Identification of assets

    b. Definition of roles and responsibilities

    c. Description of permitted behaviors

    d. All of the above

8. Authentication of the identity is based on what attributes? (Select all that apply.)

    a. Something the subject knows

    b. Something the subject has

    c. Something the subject is

    d. None of the above

9. What uses two different keys for encryption and relies on Public Key Infrastructure (PKI)?

    a. Asymmetric cryptography

    b. HMAC

    c. IKE

    d. Shared keys

10. Which of the following describe the main areas of focus for the Threat Defense component of Cisco's Self-Defending Network? (Select all that apply.)

    a. Adding full security services for network endpoints

    b. Enhancing the security of the existing network

    c. Enabling integrated security in routers, switches, and appliances

    d. Analyzing the need for transmission integrity

The answers to the "Do I Know This Already?" quiz appear in Appendix A, "Answers to Chapter 'Do I Know This Already?' Quizzes and Q&A Sections." The suggested choices for your next step are as follows:

- **8 or less overall score**—Read the entire chapter. It includes the "Foundation Topics," "Foundation Summary," and "Q&A" sections.

- **9 or 10 overall score**—If you want more review on these topics, skip to the "Foundation Summary" section and then go to the "Q&A" section. Otherwise, move to the next chapter.

Foundation Topics

This chapter covers security management topics that you need to master for the CCDA exam. It begins by explaining the reasons for network security and some ways to prevent attacks. Next, the chapter describes the types of attacks that can compromise network security and classifications of threats. It goes on to cover the risks inherent in network security, along with a series of risk examples. This chapter provides a framework for network security built around a company's security policy.

In addition, this chapter explores how to control and permit network access at any point within the network. Finally, it looks at enabling security in network equipment and traffic isolation techniques.

Network Security Overview

For many years, networks were designed to be fairly open in nature and did not require much security. The greatest area of concern was physical access. Over time, networks grew in size, and complexity increased the need for network security. For today's businesses, security is now a mandatory part of designing IT systems, because the risks are too high if critical data is lost or tampered with. Security teams within organizations must now provide adequate levels of protection for the business to conduct its operations.

Network security is used to defend against network attacks and prevent unauthorized access from intruders. In addition, network security protects data from manipulation and theft. Businesses today also need to comply with company policy and security legislation that is in place to help protect data and keep it private.

Network security needs to be transparent to the end users and should also be designed to prevent attacks by

- Blocking external attackers from accessing the network

- Permitting access to only authorized users

- Preventing attacks from sourcing internally

- Supporting different levels of user access

- Safeguarding data from tampering or misuse

Security Legislation

A number of legislative bodies along with the public have insisted that security controls be in place to protect private information and make certain that it is handled properly. These legislative bodies influence network security by imposing mandates with which organizations are required to comply. These requirements may include protecting customer information with regards to privacy and, in some cases, requiring encryption of the data in question.

The U.S. has a growing body of security legislation that you need to be aware of:

- **U.S. Public Company Accounting Reform and Investor Protection Act of 2002 (Sarbanes-Oxley or SOX)**—Focuses on the accuracy and controls imposed on a company's financial records.

- **Gramm-Leach-Bliley Financial Services Modernization Act of 1999 (GLBA)**—Provides protection against the sale of bank and account information that is regularly bought and sold by financial institutions. GLBA also guards against the practice of obtaining private information through false pretenses.

- **U.S. Health Insurance Portability and Accountability Act (HIPAA)**—Applies to the protection of private health information that is used electronically. The purpose is to enable better access to health information, reduce fraud, and lower the cost of health care in the U.S.

- **EU Data Protection Directive 95/46/EC**—Calls for the protection of people's privacy with respect to the processing of personal data.

Security Threats

It is important to be aware of the different types of attacks that can impact system security. Security threats can be classified into three broad categories:

- **Reconnaissance**—The goal of reconnaissance is to gather as much information as possible about the target host and/or network. Generally this type of information-gathering is done before an attack is carried out.

- **Gaining unauthorized access**—This is the act of attacking or exploiting the target system or host. Operating systems, services, and physical access to the target host have known system vulnerabilities that the attacker can take advantage of and use to increase his or her privileges. Social engineering is another technique for obtaining confidential information from employees by manipulation. As a result of the attacker exploiting the host, confidential information can be read, changed, or deleted from the system.

- **Denial of service (DoS)**—DoS attacks aim to overwhelm resources such as memory, CPU, and bandwidth, thus impacting the target system and denying legitimate users access. Distributed DoS attacks involve multiple sources working together to deliver the attack.

Reconnaissance and Port Scanning

Reconnaissance network tools are used to gather information from the hosts attached to the network. They have many capabilities, including identifying the active hosts and what services the hosts are running. In addition, these tools can find trust relationships, determine OS platforms, and identify user and file permissions.

Some of the techniques that these scanning tools use are TCP connects, TCP SYNs, ACK sweeps, ICMP sweeps, SYN sweeps, and null scans. Here are some of the popular port-scanning tools and their uses:

- **NMAP** (Network Mapper) is designed to scan large networks or even a single host. It is an open-source utility used for network exploration and/or security audits.

- **Superscan** provides high-speed scanning, host detection, Windows host enumeration, and banner grabbing. Superscan is made for Windows clients.

- **NetStumbler** identifies wireless networks using 802.11a/b/g WLAN standards with or without SSID being broadcast. It runs on Windows platforms, including Windows Mobile.

- **Kismet** is an 802.11 wireless sniffer and IDS application that can collect traffic from 802.11a/b/g networks. It collects packets and detects wireless networks—even some that are hidden.

Vulnerability Scanners

Vulnerability scanners determine what potential exposures are present in the network. Passive scanning tools are used to analyze the traffic flowing on the network. Active testing injects sample traffic onto the network. General vulnerability information is published at the following links:

- **CERT CC**—http://www.cert.org

- **MITRE**—http://www.cve.mitre.org

- **Microsoft**—http://www.microsoft.com/technet/security/bulletin/summary.mspx

- **Cisco Security Notices**—http://www.cisco.com/en/US/products/products_security_advisories_listing.html

Here are some tools used for vulnerability scanning:

- **Nessus** is designed to automate the testing and discovery of known vulnerabilities. Nessus is an open-source tool that requires Linux/UNIX or Windows to run.

- **SAINT** (Security Administrator's Integrated Network Tool) is a vulnerability assessment application that runs on UNIX hosts.

- **MBSA** (Microsoft Baseline Security Analyzer) is used to scan systems and identify if patches are missing for Windows products such as operating systems, IIS, SQL, Exchange Server, Internet Explorer, Media Player, and Microsoft Office applications. MBSA also alerts you if it finds any known security vulnerabilities such as weak or missing passwords and other common security issues.

Unauthorized Access

Another threat that you need to be concerned with is attackers gaining access. Hackers use several techniques to gain system access. One approach is when unauthorized people use usernames and passwords to escalate the account's privilege levels. Furthermore, some system user accounts have default administrative username and password pairings that are common knowledge, which makes them very insecure. Trust relationships between systems and applications are another way unauthorized access takes place.

Unauthorized access is also obtained through the use of social engineering—the practice of acquiring confidential information by manipulating legitimate users. Actually, most confidential information such as badges, usernames, and passwords can be uncovered just by walking around an organization. The psychology method is another way of getting confidential information. For example, someone pretending to be from the IT department calls a user and asks for her account information to maintain or correct an account discrepancy.

In addition to these approaches, hackers can obtain account information by using password-cracking utilities or by capturing network traffic.

Security Risks

To protect network resources, processes, and procedures; technology needs to address security risks. Important network characteristics that can be at risk from security threats include data confidentiality, data integrity, and system availability:

- System availability should ensure uninterrupted access to critical network and computing resources to prevent business disruption and loss of productivity.

- Data integrity should ensure that only authorized users can change critical information and guarantee the authenticity of data.

- Data confidentiality should ensure that only legitimate users can view sensitive information to prevent theft, legal liabilities, and damage to the organization.

In addition, the use of redundant hardware and encryption can significantly reduce the risks associated with system availability, data integrity, and data confidentiality.

Targets

Given the wide range of potential threats, just about everything in the network has become vulnerable and is a potential target. Ordinary hosts top the list as the favorite target, especially for worms and viruses. After a host has been compromised, it is frequently used to start new attacks with other nearby systems.

Other high-value targets include devices that support the network. Here is a list of some devices, servers, and security devices that stand out as potential targets:

- **Infrastructure devices**—Routers, switches

- **Security devices**—Firewalls, IDS/IPS

- **Network services**—DHCP and DNS servers

- **Endpoints**—Management stations and IP phones

- **Infrastructure**—Network throughput and capacity

Loss of Availability

Denial-of-service (DoS) attacks try to block or deny access to impact the availability of network services. These types of attacks can interrupt business transactions, cause considerable loss, or damage the company's reputation. DoS attacks are fairly straightforward to carry out, even by an unskilled attacker. Distributed DoS (DDoS) attacks are initiated by multiple source locations within the network to increase the attack's size and impact.

DDoS attacks occur when the attacker takes advantage of vulnerabilities in the network and/or host. Here are some common failure points:

- A network, host, or application fails to process large amounts of data sent to it, which crashes or breaks communication ability.

- A host or application is unable to handle an unexpected condition, such as improperly formatted data and memory or resource depletion.

Nearly all DoS attacks are carried out with spoofing and flooding methods. Here are some ways to combat DoS attacks:

- **DHCP snooping** verifies DHCP transactions and prevents rogue DHCP servers from interfering with production traffic.

- **Dynamic ARP inspection** intercepts ARP packets and verifies that they have valid IP-to-MAC bindings.

- **Unicast RPF** prevents unknown source addresses from using the network as a transport mechanism to carry out attacks.

- **Access control lists (ACLs)** control what traffic is allowed on the network.

- **Rate limiting** controls the rate of bandwidth that incoming traffic is using, such as ARPs and DHCP requests.

Figure 13-1 shows a DoS threat on availability. The attacker is performing a DoS attack on the network and servers using a flood of packets. Keep in mind that this is an external attack; however, an internal attack is also certainly possible.

Figure 13-1 *DoS Threat*

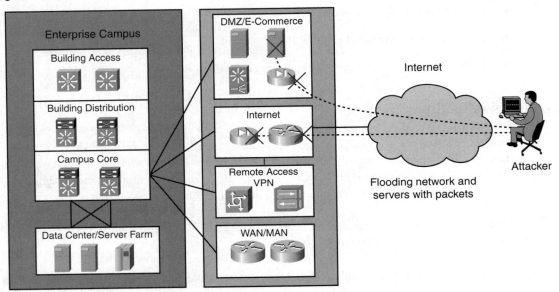

Integrity Violations and Confidentiality Breaches

When attackers change sensitive data without the proper authorization, this is called an integrity violation. For example, an attacker might access financial data and delete critical information. The effect of this change may not be felt for some time or until a significant loss has occurred. Integrity attacks like this are considered by many companies to be one of the most serious threats to their business. Furthermore, identifying these attacks can be very difficult, and the effects can be devastating.

Confidentiality breaches occur when the attacker attempts to read sensitive information. It is difficult to detect these types of attacks, and the loss of data can happen without the owner's knowledge.

It is important to use restrictive access controls to prevent integrity violations and confidentiality attacks. Here are some ways to enforce access control in order to reduce risks:

- Restrict access by separating networks (VLANs) and using packet-filtering firewalls.

- Restrict access with OS-based controls in both Windows and UNIX.

- Limit user access by using user profiles for different departmental roles.

- Use encryption techniques to secure data or digitally sign data.

Figure 13-2 shows an attacker viewing, altering, and stealing competitive information. Pay particular attention to the obstacles the attacker must go through to get to the data.

Figure 13-2　*Confidentiality and Integrity Threats*

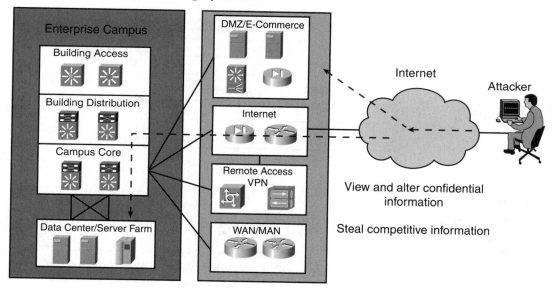

Security Policy and Process

To provide the proper levels of security and increase network availability, a security policy is a crucial element in providing secure network services. In addition, it is important to understand that network security is built around a security policy that is part of a system life cycle.

In terms of network security in the system life cycle, business needs are a key area to consider. Business needs define what the business wants to do with the network.

Risk assessment is another part of the system life cycle. It explains the risks and their costs. Business needs and risk assessment feed information into the security policy.

The security policy describes the organization's processes, procedures, guidelines, and standards. Furthermore, industry and security best practices are leveraged to provide well-known processes and procedures.

Finally, an organization's security operations team needs to have processes and procedures defined. This information helps explain what needs to happen for incident response, security monitoring, system maintenance, and managing compliance.

Figure 13-3 shows the flow of the network security life cycle.

Figure 13-3   *Network Security: System Life Cycle*

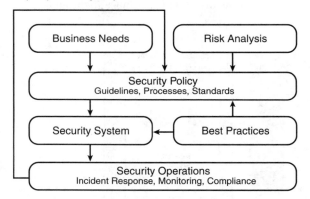

Security Policy Defined

RFC 2196 says, "A security policy is a formal statement of the rules by which people who are given access to an organization's technology and information assets must abide." When developing security policies for an organization, RFC 2196 can serve as a guide for developing security processes and procedures. This RFC lists issues and factors that an organization must consider when setting its policies. Organizations need to make many decisions and come to agreement when creating their security policy.

Basic Approach of a Security Policy

To help create a security policy, here is a generally accepted approach from RFC 2196:

Step 1   Identify what you are trying to protect.

Step 2   Determine what you are trying to protect it from.

Step 3   Determine how likely the threats are.

Step 4   Implement measures that protect your assets in a cost-effective manner.

Step 5   Review the process continuously, and make improvements each time a
weakness is found.

Purpose of Security Policies

One of the main purposes of a security policy is to describe the roles and requirements for securing
technology and information assets. The policy defines the ways in which these requirements will
be met.

There are two main reasons for having a security policy:

- It provides the framework for the security implementation:

  — Identifies assets and how to use them

  — Defines and communicates roles and responsibilities

  — Describes tools and procedures

  — Clarifies incident handling of security events

- It creates a security baseline of the current security posture:

  — Describes permitted and nonpermitted behaviors

  — Defines consequences of asset misuse

  — Provides cost and risk analysis

Here are some questions you may need to ask when developing a security policy:

- What data and assets will be included in the policy?

- What network communication is permitted between hosts?

- How will policies be implemented?

- What happens if the policies are violated?

- How will the latest attacks impact your network and security systems?

Security Policy Components

A security policy is divided into smaller parts that help describe the overall risk management
policy, identification of assets, and where security should be applied. Other components of the
security policy explain how responsibilities related to risk management are handled throughout the
enterprise.

Further documents concentrate on specific areas of risk management:

- **Acceptable-use policy** is a general end-user document that is written in simple language. This document defines the roles and responsibilities within risk management and should have clear explanations to avoid confusion.

- **Network access control policy** defines general access-control principles used and how data is classified, such as confidential, top-secret, or internal.

- **Security management policy** explains how to manage the security infrastructure.

- **Incident-handling policy** defines the processes and procedures for managing incidents and even emergency-type scenarios.

Several other documents supplement these; they vary depending on the organization. The security policy requires the acceptance and support of all employees to make it successful. All the key stakeholders, including members of senior management, should have input into the development of the security policy. In addition, they should continue to participate in the updates to the security policy.

Risk Assessment

Within network security, proper risk management is a technique used to lower risks to within acceptable levels. A well-thought-out plan for network security design implements the components included in the security policy. The security policies that an organization employs use risk assessments and cost-benefit analysis to reduce security risks.

Figure 13-4 shows the three major components of risk assessment. Control refers to how you use the security policy to minimize potential risks. Severity describes the level of the risk to the organization, and probability is the likeliness that an attack against the assets will occur.

Figure 13-4 *Risk Assessment Components*

Risk assessments should explain the following:

- What assets to secure
- The monetary value of the assets
- The actual loss that would result from an attack

- The severity and the probability that an attack against the assets will occur

- How to use security policy to control or minimize the risks

Security costs can be justified by describing the loss of productivity during security incidents.

Generally, network systems are built with just enough security to reduce potential losses to a reasonable level. However, some organizations have higher security requirements, such as complying with SOX or HIPAA regulations, so they need to employ stronger security mechanisms.

A risk index is used to consider the risks of potential threats. The risk index is based on risk assessment components (factors):

- Severity of loss if the asset is compromised

- Probability of the risk actually occurring

- Ability to control and manage the risk

One approach to determining a risk index is to give each risk factor a value from 1 (lowest) to 3 (highest). For example, a high-severity risk would have a substantial impact on the user base and/ or the entire organization. Medium-severity risks would have an effect on a single department or site. Low-severity risks would have limited impact and would be relatively straightforward to mitigate.

The risk index is calculated by multiplying the severity and probability factors and then dividing that by the control factor:

$$\text{risk index} = (\text{severity factor} * \text{probability factor}) / \text{control factor}$$

Table 13-2 shows a sample risk index calculation for a typical large corporation facing a couple of typical risks. If the risk index number calculated is high, there is more risk and thus more impact to the organization. The lower the index number calculated means that there is less risk and less impact to the organization.

Table 13-2 *Risk Index Calculation*

Risk	Severity (S) Range 1 to 3	Probability (P) Range 1 to 3	Control Range 1 to 3	Risk Index (S * P)/ C Range .3 to 9
DoS attack lasting for 1.5 hours on the e-mail server	2	2	1	4
Breach of confidential customer lists	3	1	2	1.5

Continuous Security

As requirements change and new technology is developed, the network security policy should be updated to reflect the changes. Four steps are used to facilitate continuing efforts in maintaining security policies:

Step 1	**Secure**—Identification, authentication, ACLs, stateful packet inspection (SPI), encryption, and VPNs
Step 2	**Monitor**—Intrusion and content-based detection and response
Step 3	**Test**—Assessments, vulnerability scanning, and security auditing
Step 4	**Improve**—Security data analysis, reporting, and intelligent network security

Figure 13-5 shows the four-step process that updates and continues the development of security policies.

Figure 13-5 *Continuous Security*

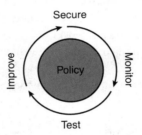

Integrating Security Mechanisms into Network Design

Today's network designs demonstrate an increased use of security mechanisms and have become more tightly integrated with network design. Many security services such as IDS/IPS, firewalls, and IPsec VPN concentrators now reside within the internal network infrastructure. It is recommended that you incorporate network security during the network design planning process. This requires close coordination between the various engineering and operation teams.

Trust and Identity Management

Trust and Identity Management is part of the Cisco Self-Defending Network, which is crucial for the development of a secure network system. It defines who and what can access the network, as well as when, where, and how that access can occur. Access to the business applications and network equipment is based on the user level rights granted to users. Trust and Identity Management also attempts to isolate and keep infected machines off the network by enforcing access control. The three main components of Trust and Identity Management are trust, identity, and access control, as shown in Figure 13-6. The following sections cover these components in detail.

Figure 13-6   *Trust and Identity Management*

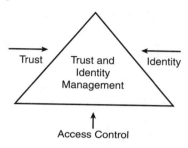

Trust

Trust is the relationship between two or more network entities that are permitted to communicate. Security policy decisions are largely based on this premise of trust. If you are trusted, you are allowed to communicate as needed. However, at times security controls need to apply restraint to trust relationships by limiting access to the designated privilege level. Trust relationships can be explicit or implied by the organization. Some trust relationships can be inherited or passed down from one system to another. However, keep in mind that these trust relationships can also be abused.

Domains of Trust

Domains of Trust are a way to group network systems that share a common policy or function. Network segments have different trust levels, depending on the resources they are securing. When applying security controls within network segments, it is important to consider the trust relationships between the segments. Keep in mind that customers, partners, and employees each have their unique sets of requirements from a security perspective that can be managed independently with Domains of Trust classifications. When Domains of Trust are managed in this way, consistent security controls within each segment can be applied.

Figure 13-7 shows two examples of Trust Domains with varying levels of trust segmented. The lighter shading indicates internal higher security and more secure networks and the darker areas represent less secure areas and lower security.

Figure 13-7 *Domains of Trust*

Example A

Example B

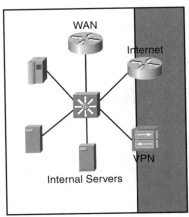

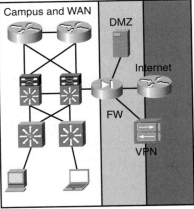

Trust levels such as the internal network can be very open and flexible, whereas the outside needs to be considered unsafe and thus needs strong security to protect the resources. Table 13-3 shows different levels of trust, going from low to high.

Table 13-3 *Domains of Trust: Risks from Low to High*

Domain	Level	Safeguards Required
Production to lab	Low risk	ACLs and network monitoring
Headquarters to branch (IPsec VPN)	Medium risk	Authentication, confidentiality, integrity concerns, ACLs, route filtering
Inside (private) to outside (public)	High risk	Stateful packet inspection, intrusion protection (IPS), security monitoring

Identity

Identity is the "who" of a trust relationship. This can be users, devices, organizations, or all of these. Network entities are validated by credentials. Authentication of the identity is based on the following attributes:

- **Something the subject knows**—Knowledge of a secret, password, PIN, or private key

- **Something the subject has**—Possession of an item such as a token card, smartcard, or hardware key

- **Something the subject is**—Human characteristics such as a fingerprint, retina scan, or voice recognition

Generally, identity credentials are checked by requiring passwords, tokens, or certificates.

Passwords

Passwords are used to give users access and allow them to access network resources. Passwords are an example of the authentication attribute called "something you know." Typically, users do not want to use strong passwords; they want to do what is easiest for them. This presents a problem with security and requires you to enforce a password policy. Passwords should not be common dictionary words and should be time-limited. Passwords should never be shared or posted on a computer monitor.

Tokens

Tokens represent a way to increase security by requiring "two-factor authentication." This type of authentication is based on "something you know" and "something you have." For example, one factor may be a six-digit PIN, and another would be the seven-digit code on the physical token. The code on the tokens changes frequently and is not useful without the PIN. The code plus the PIN is transmitted to the authentication server for authorization. Then the server permits or denies access based on the user's predetermined access level.

Figure 13-8 shows two-factor authentication using a username and password along with a token access code.

Figure 13-8 *Using Tokens*

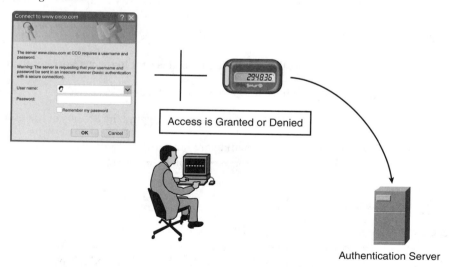

Access is Granted or Denied

Authentication Server

Certificates

Certificates are used to digitally prove your identity or right to access information or services. Certificates, also known as digital certificates, bind an identity to a pair of electronic keys that can be used to encrypt and sign digital information. A digital certificate is signed and issued by a certification authority (CA) with the CA's private key. A digital certificate contains the following:

- Owner's public key

- Owner's name

- Expiration date of the public key

- Name of the certificate authority

- Serial number

- Digital signature of the CA

Certificates can be read or written by an application conforming to the X.509 CCITT international standard.

Access Control

Access control is a security mechanism for controlling admission to networks and resources. These controls enforce the security policy and employ rules about which resources can be accessed. Access control ensures the confidentiality and integrity of the network resources.

The core of network access control consists of the following:

- **Authentication** establishes the user's identity and access to the network resources.

- **Authorization** describes what can be done and what can be accessed.

- **Accounting** provides an audit trail of activities by logging the actions of the user.

Authentication, authorization, and accounting are the network security services supported by AAA that help manage the network access control on your network equipment.

Secure Connectivity

Secure connectivity is a component of the Cisco Self-Defending Network. This component aims to protect the integrity and privacy of organizations' sensitive information. With increased security risks on the rise, it is critical that security be implemented within today's network environments. Internal network segments have traditionally been considered trusted. However, internal threats are now more than ten times more expensive and destructive than external threats. Data that flows across the network needs to be secured so that its privacy and integrity are preserved. These are important concepts to keep in mind when making business decisions about securing connectivity.

The Cisco Secure Connectivity System provides secure transport for data and applications using encryption and authentication techniques. Many security technologies exist for securing data, voice, and video traffic using wired or wireless networks.

Security technologies include

- IP Security (IPsec)

- Secure Shell (SSH)

- Secure Socket Layer (SSL)

- Multiprotocol Label Switching (MPLS) VPNs

- MPLS VPNs with IPsec

Encryption Fundamentals

Cryptography uses encryption to keep data private, thus protecting its confidentiality. The encapsulated data is encrypted with a secret key that secures the data for transport. When the data reaches the other side of the connection, another secret key is used to decrypt the data and reveal the message transmitted. The encryption and decryption can be used only by authorized users. Most encryption algorithms require the user to have knowledge of the secret keys. IPsec is an example of a security protocol framework that uses encryption algorithms to hide the IP packet payload during transmission.

Encryption Keys

An encryption session between two endpoints needs a key to encrypt the traffic and a key to decrypt the traffic at the remote endpoint. There are two ways to send a key to the remote endpoint—shared secrets and Public-Key Infrastructure (PKI):

- Shared secrets

    — Both sides can use the same key or use a transform to create the decryption key.

    — The key is placed on the remote endpoint out of band.

    — This is a simple mechanism, but it has security issues because the key does not change frequently enough.

- PKI

    — It relies on asymmetric cryptography, which uses two different keys for encryption.

    — Public keys are used to encrypt and private keys to decrypt.

    — PKI is used by many e-commerce sites on the Internet.

Figure 13-9 shows what occurs during the encryption process using secret keys.

Figure 13-9 *Encryption Keys*

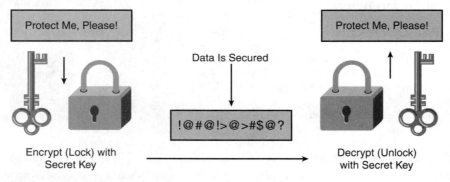

VPN Protocols

The two most common VPN protocols are IPsec and SSL:

- IPsec

    — Uses AH and ESP to secure data

    — Uses Internet Key Exchange (IKE) for dynamic key exchange

    — Endpoints need IPsec software

- SSL

    — Uses TCP port 443 (HTTPS)

    — Provides encrypted VPN connectivity using a web browser

    — All major browsers support SSL VPN

IPsec comes in two forms—IP encapsulating security payload (ESP) and IP authentication header (AH)—which use protocol numbers 50 and 51, respectively. ESP is defined in RFC 2406, and AH is defined in RFC 2402. ESP provides confidentiality, data origin authentication, integrity, and anti-replay service. AH allows for connectionless integrity, origin authentication, and anti-replay protection. These protocols can be used together or independently. Most IPsec clients or routers use IKE to exchange keys and ESP to encrypt the traffic.

SSL VPNs have become increasingly popular because of their clientless nature. A major advantage of SSL VPNs is that you do not need client software—only a web browser that can be accessed wherever an Internet connection exists.

Transmission Confidentiality

To ensure that data is kept private over insecure networks such as the Internet, transmission confidentiality is used. Because the Internet is a public network, ordinary access control mechanisms are unavailable. Therefore, you need to encrypt the data before transporting over any untrusted network such as the Internet.

To provide transmission confidentiality, IPsec VPNs that support encryption can create a secure tunnel between the source and destination. As packets leave one site, they are encrypted; when they reach the remote site, they are decrypted. Eavesdropping in the Internet can occur, but with IPsec encrypted packets, it is much more difficult.

IPsec VPNs commonly use well-known algorithms to perform the confidentiality treatment for packets. The well-known cryptographic algorithms include Triple Data Encryption Standard (3DES), Advanced Encryption Standard (AES), and Rivest Cipher 4 (RC4). These algorithms are thoroughly tested and checked and are considered trusted. However, keep in mind that cryptography can pose some performance problems, depending on the network's state. That is why it is important to carefully analyze the network before deploying VPNs with IPsec.

Data Integrity

Cryptographic protocols protect data from tampering by employing secure fingerprints and digital signatures that can detect changes in data integrity.

Secure fingerprints function by appending a checksum to data that is generated and verified with the secret key. The secret key is known only to those who are authorized. An example of secure fingerprints is Hash-based Message Authentication Code (HMAC), which maintains packet integrity and the authenticity of the data protected.

Digital signatures use a related cryptography method that digitally signs the packet data. A signer creates the signature using a key that is unique and known only to the original signer. Recipients of the message can check the signature by using the signature verification key. The cryptography inherent in digital signatures guarantees accuracy and authenticity because the originator signed it. Financial businesses rely on digital signatures to electronically sign documents and also to prove that the transactions did in fact occur.

Here are some data integrity guidelines to keep in mind:

■ Analyze the need for transmission integrity.

■ Factor in performance, but use the strongest cryptography.

■ Always use well-known cryptographic algorithms.

Threat Defense

As part of the Cisco Self-Defending Network, Threat Defense enhances the security in the network infrastructure by adding increased levels of security protection on network devices, appliances, and endpoints. Both internal and external threats have become much more destructive than in the past. DoS attacks, man-in-the-middle attacks, and Trojan horses have the potential to severely impact business operations. The Cisco Threat Defense system provides a strong defense against these internal and external threats.

Threat Defense has three main areas of focus:

■ **Enhancing the security of the existing network**—Preventing loss of downtime, revenue, and reputation

■ **Adding full security services for network endpoints**—Securing servers and desktops with Cisco Security Agent

■ **Enabling integrated security in routers, switches, and appliances**—Security techniques enabled throughout the network, not just in point products or locations

Physical Security

During your security implementations, it is essential to incorporate physical security to increase the strength of the overall security design. Physical security helps protect and restrict access to network resources and physical network equipment. Sound security policies must defend against potential attacks that can cause loss of uptime or reputation, or even revenue impacts.

Here are some considerations for potential physical threats:

■ Vulnerabilities inherent in systems when attackers access the hardware directly through console access or untrusted software.

■ Access to the network, allowing attackers to capture, alter, or remove data flowing in the network.

■ Attackers may use their own hardware, such as a laptop or router, to inject malicious traffic onto the network.

Here are some physical security guidelines to keep in mind when designing physical security architectures:

- Use physical access controls such as locks or alarms.

- Evaluate potential security breaches.

- Assess the impact of stolen network resources and equipment.

- Use controls such as cryptography to secure traffic flowing on networks outside your control.

Figure 13-10 shows some physical security threat locations that an attacker could potentially exploit.

Figure 13-10 *Physical Security Threats*

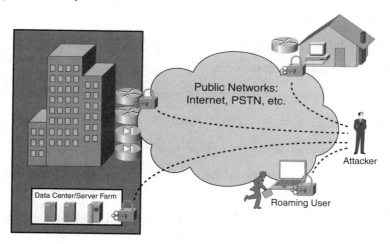

The infrastructure needs to be protected using security features and services to meet the growing needs of business without disruption. Infrastructure protection is the process of taking steps to reduce the risks and threats to the network infrastructure and to maintain the integrity and high availability of network resources.

By using best practices and a security policy, you can secure and harden the infrastructure equipment to prevent potential attacks. To combat network threats, Cisco has enhanced Cisco IOS with security features to support the secure infrastructure and increase the network's availability.

Infrastructure Protection

Here are some solutions for equipment that has built-in integrated security features:

- **Adaptive Security Appliance (ASA)** integrates essential security technologies in one platform (firewall, IPS, IPsec VPN, and SSL VPN).

- **Routers** consolidates IOS firewall, IPS, IPsec VPN, DMVPN, and SSL VPN into the routing platforms to secure the router if attacked.

- **Catalyst switches** combines firewall, IPS, SSL VPN, IPsec VPN, DoS mitigation, and virtual services to build into security zones.

Here are some recommended best practices for infrastructure protection:

- Access network equipment remotely with SSH instead of Telnet.

- Use AAA for access control management.

- Enable SYSLOG collection; review the logs for further analysis.

- Use SNMPv3 for its security and privacy features.

- Disable unused network services such as tcp-small-servers and udp-small-servers.

- Use FTP or SFTP instead of TFTP to manage images.

- Use access classes to restrict access to management and the CLI.

- Enable routing protocol authentication when available (EIGRP, OSPF, IS-IS, BGP, HSRP, VTP).

- Use one-step lockdown in Security Device Manager (SDM) before connecting the router to the Internet.

References and Recommended Readings

IANA protocol numbers, http://www.iana.org/assignments/protocol-numbers

"Managing Risk and Compliance with Cisco Self-Defending Network—U.S.," http://www.cisco.com/en/US/netsol/ns625/networking_solutions_white_paper0900aecd80351e82.shtml

"Managing Security Best Practices with Cisco Self-Defending Network," http://www.cisco.com/en/US/netsol/ns625/networking_solutions_white_paper0900aecd803b5fc9.shtml

Module 6, "Evaluating Security Solutions," Designing for Cisco Internetwork Solution Course (DESGN) v2.0

RFC 2402, *IP Authentication Header*, http://www.ietf.org/rfc/rfc2402.txt

RFC 2406, *IP Encapsulating Security Payload (ESP)*, http://www.ietf.org/rfc/rfc2406.txt

Foundation Summary

The "Foundation Summary" section of each chapter lists the most important facts from the chapter. Although this section does not list every fact from the chapter that will be on the CCDA exam, a well-prepared CCDA candidate should at a minimum know all the details in each "Foundation Summary" before taking the exam.

The CCDA exam requires that you be familiar with the following topics covered in this chapter:

- **U.S. Public Company Accounting Reform and Investor Protection Act of 2002 (Sarbanes-Oxley or SOX)** focuses on the accuracy and the controls imposed on a company's financial records.

- **Gramm-Leach-Bliley Financial Services Modernization Act of 1999 (GLBA)** provides protection against the sale of bank and account information that is regularly bought and sold by financial institutions.

- **U.S. Health Insurance Portability and Accountability Act (HIPAA)** applies to the protection of private health information that is used electronically.

- **EU Data Protection Directive 95/46/EC** calls for the protection of people's privacy with respect to the processing of personal data.

- **Reconnaissance** gathers as much information as possible about the target host and/or network.

- **Gaining unauthorized access** is the act of attacking or exploiting the target host system.

- **Denial of service (DoS)** attacks try to overwhelm resources such as memory, CPU, and bandwidth, thus impacting the attacked system and denying legitimate users access.

- **NMAP** (Network Mapper) scans large networks or one host. It is an open-source utility used for network exploration and/or security audits.

- **Superscan** (made for Windows) provides high-speed scanning, host detection, and Windows host enumeration and banner grabbing.

- **DHCP snooping** verifies DHCP transactions and prevents rogue DHCP servers from interfering with production traffic.

- **Dynamic ARP inspection** intercepts ARP packets and verifies that the packets have valid IP-to-MAC bindings.

- **Unicast RPF** prevents unknown source addresses from using the network as a transport mechanism to carry out attacks.

- **Access control lists (ACLs)** control what traffic is allowed on the network.

- **Rate limiting** controls the rate of bandwidth that incoming traffic is using, such as ARPs and DHCP requests.

- **NetStumbler** identifies wireless networks using 802.11a/b/g WLAN standards.

- **Kismet** is an 802.11 wireless sniffer and IDS that can collect traffic from 802.11a/b/g networks.

- **Acceptable-use policy** is a document that defines the roles and responsibilities within risk management and should have clear explanations to avoid confusion.

- **Network access control policy** is a document that defines general access control principles used and how data is classified, such as confidential, top-secret, or internal.

- **Security management policy** explains how to manage the security infrastructure.

- **Incident-handling policy** defines the processes and procedures for managing incidents and even emergency-type scenarios.

- **Secure**—Identification, authentication, ACLs, stateful packet inspection (SPI), encryption, and VPNs.

- **Monitor**—Intrusion and content-based detection and response.

- **Test**—Assessments, vulnerability scanning, and security auditing.

- **Improve**—Security data analysis, reporting, and intelligent network security.

- **Authentication** establishes the user's identity and access to the network resources.

- **Authorization** describes what can be done and what can be accessed.

- **Accounting** provides an audit trail of activities by logging the actions of the user.

- **Adaptive Security Appliance (ASA)** integrates essential security technologies in one platform (firewall, IPS, IPsec VPN, and SSL VPN).

- **Routers** consolidates IOS firewall, IPS, IPsec VPN, DMVPN, and SSL VPN into the routing platforms to secure the router if it is attacked.

- **Catalyst switches** combines firewall, IPS, SSL VPN, IPsec VPN, DoS mitigation, and virtual services to build into security zones.

Table 13-4 shows a sample risk index calculation for a typical large corporation facing a couple of typical risks. If the risk index number calculated is high, you have more risk and thus more impact to the organization. The lower the index number calculated means that there is less risk and less impact to the organization.

Table 13-4 *Risk Index Calculation*

Risk	Severity (S) Range1 to 3	Probability (P) Range1 to 3	Control Range1 to 3	Risk Index (S * P)/ C Range .3 to 9
DoS attack lasting for 1.5 hours on the e-mail server	2	2	1	4
Breach of confidential customer lists	3	1	2	1.5

Q&A

As mentioned in the Introduction, you have two choices for review questions: here in the book or the exam questions on the CD-ROM. The answers to these questions appear in Appendix A.

For more practice with exam format questions, use the exam engine on the CD-ROM.

1. What technique can be used to protect private information that is transported over the Internet between the headquarters and branch office? (Select the best answer.)

   a. Authentication

   b. Log all data

   c. Encryption

   d. Accounting

2. What would be recommended to protect database servers attached to a switch with a T1 to the Internet? (Select all that apply.)

   a. Firewall

   b. Server Load Balancing (SLB)

   c. Implement host-based security

   d. SPAN

3. What network security issue does 3DES encryption aim to solve?

   a. Data integrity

   b. User authentication

   c. Data authentication

   d. Data confidentiality

4. Users are reporting a DoS attack in the DMZ. All the servers have been patched, and all unnecessary services have been turned off. What else can you do to alleviate some of the attack's effects? (Select all that apply.)

   a. Rate-limit traffic on the firewall's ingress

   b. Use ACLs to let only allowed traffic into the network

   c. Block all TCP traffic from unknown sources

   d. DHCP Snooping for the DMZ segment

5. You are a network engineer for ABC Corp. You need to bring your coworkers up to date on network security threats. What would you discuss with them? (Select all that apply.)

    a. Reconnaissance and gaining unauthorized access

    b. DHCP snooping

    c. Rate limits

    d. DoS

6. True or false: IPsec can ensure data integrity and confidentiality across the Internet.

7. What focuses on the accuracy and controls imposed on a company's financial records?

    a. HIPAA

    b. GLBA

    c. SOX

    d. EU Data Protection Directive

8. What are components of managing the security infrastructure? (Select all that apply.)

    a. Security management policy

    b. Incident-handling policy

    c. Network access control policy

    d. None of the above

9. Which security legislative body calls for the protection of people's privacy?

    a. HIPAA

    b. GLBA

    c. EU Data Protection Directive

    d. SOX

10. True or false: HIPAA protects companies' financial records.

11. True or false: Distributed DoS attacks are when multiple sources work together to deliver an attack.

12. True or false: Social engineering involves manipulating users into giving out confidential information.

13. How can attackers obtain sensitive account information? (Select all that apply.)

    a. Password-cracking utilities

    b. Capturing network traffic

    c. Social engineering

    d. All of the above

14. What best describes how to protect data's integrity?

    a. System availability

    b. Data confidentiality

    c. Ensuring that only legitimate users can view sensitive data

    d. Allowing only authorized users to modify data

15. List some targets that are used for attacks.

16. What provides an audit trail of network activities?

    a. Authentication

    b. Accounting

    c. Authorization

    d. SSHv1

17. What authenticates valid DHCP servers to prevent them from interfering with production?

18. True or False: Unicast RPF is used to prevent unknown source addresses from using the network to route traffic.

19. What can control the rate of traffic that is allowed into the network?

20. What contains the organization's procedures, guidelines, and standards?

21. How can you enforce access control? (Select all that apply.)

    a. Restrict access using VLANs

    b. Restrict access using OS-based controls

    c. Use encryption techniques

    d. All of the above

22. What is a general user document that is written in simple language to describe the roles and responsibilities within risk management?

23. True or false: The network access control policy defines the general access control principles used and how data is classified, such as confidential, top-secret, or internal.

24. What are the four steps used to facilitate continuing efforts in maintaining security policies?

    a. Secure, monitor, maintain, close out

    b. Monitor, test, evaluate, purchase

    c. Improve, test, purchase, evaluate

    d. Secure, monitor, test, improve

25. True or false: As part of the Cisco Self-Defending Network, Trust and Identity Management defines who and what can access the network, as well as when, where, and how that occurs.

26. True or false: A common two-factor authentication technique involves the use of a six-digit PIN from a token in addition to a user password.

27. Match the encryption keys and VPN protocols with their definitions:

i. IPsec

ii. SSL

iii. Shared secret

iv. PKI

a. Both sides use the same key

b. Uses AH and ESP

c. Web browser TCP port 443

d. Asymmetric cryptography

This chapter covers the following subjects:

- Cisco Self-Defending Network

- Trust and Identity Technologies

- Detecting and Mitigating Threats

- Security Management Applications

- Integrating Security into Network Devices

- Securing the Enterprise

CHAPTER 14

Security Technologies and Design

This chapter covers the Cisco Self-Defending Network (SDN) architecture, security technologies, and design options for securing the enterprise. The CCDA candidate can expect many questions related to integrating security technologies and mitigating security exposures. This chapter also focuses on how to integrate security into existing network devices and security platforms throughout your network. Furthermore, the CCDA must understand the different types of security features available and where to deploy them.

"Do I Know This Already?" Quiz

The purpose of the "Do I Know This Already?" quiz is to help you decide whether you need to read the entire chapter. If you intend to read the entire chapter, you do not necessarily need to answer these questions now.

The ten-question quiz, derived from the major sections in the "Foundation Topics" portion of the chapter, helps you determine how to spend your limited study time.

Table 14-1 outlines the major topics discussed in this chapter and the "Do I Know This Already?" quiz questions that correspond to those topics.

Table 14-1 *"Do I Know This Already?" Foundation Topics Section-to-Question Mapping*

Foundation Topics Section	Questions Covered in This Section
Cisco Self-Defending Network	1, 2
Trust and Identity Technologies	3, 4
Detecting and Mitigating Threats	5, 6
Security Management Applications	7
Integrating Security into Network Devices	8
Securing the Enterprise	9, 10

> **CAUTION**   The goal of self-assessment is to gauge your mastery of the topics in this chapter. If you do not know the answer to a question or you are only partially sure, you should mark this question wrong for the purposes of the self-assessment. Giving yourself credit for an answer you correctly guess skews your self-assessment results and might give you a false sense of security.

1. The Cisco Self-Defending Network consists of which of the following components? (Select all that apply.)

   a. Trust and identity management

   b. Secure connectivity

   c. Threat defense

   d. Self healing

2. What network security platform combines a high-performance firewall with an IPS, antivirus, IPsec, and an SSL VPN in a single unified architecture?

   a. Integrated services routers

   b. Cisco Catalyst switches

   c. Adaptive security appliances

   d. NAC

3. Which media-level access control standard developed by IEEE permits and denies access to the network and applies traffic policy based on identity?

   a. AES

   b. 802.1X

   c. NAC

   d. FWSM

4. What mechanism protects networks from threats by enforcing security compliance on all devices attempting to access the network?

   a. NAC

   b. CSA MC

   c. ASDM

   d. SDM

5. Which of the following can be used to perform firewall filtering with the use of ACLs? (Select the best answer.)

   a. ASA

   b. PIX

   c. FWSM

   d. All of the above

6. What Cisco software is loaded on hosts and referred to as HIPS?

   a. Cisco Security Agent

   b. NetFlow

   c. CS-MARS

   d. FWSM

7. Which security management solution integrates the configuration management of firewalls, VPNs, routers, switch modules, and IPS devices?

   a. CSM

   b. SDM

   c. ASDM

   d. ACS

8. When integrating security into the network, which of the following can be used? (Select all that apply.)

   a. PIX

   b. ASA

   c. Cisco IOS IPS

   d. RME

9. Which of the following is used to detect and mitigate threats?

   a. 802.1X

   b. NetFlow

   c. NAC

   d. SSH

10. What Cisco Security Management platform is used to control the TACACS and RADIUS protocols?

   a. SSH

   b. NIPS

   c. ACS

   d. HIPS

The answers to the "Do I Know This Already?" quiz appear in Appendix A, "Answers to Chapter 'Do I Know This Already?' Quizzes and Q&A Sections." The suggested choices for your next step are as follows:

■ **8 or less overall score**—Read the entire chapter. It includes the "Foundation Topics," "Foundation Summary," and "Q&A" sections.

■ **9 or 10 overall score**—If you want more review on these topics, skip to the "Foundation Summary" section and then go to the "Q&A" section. Otherwise, move to the next chapter.

Foundation Topics

This chapter covers security topics that you need to master for the CCDA exam. It begins with a discussion of the Cisco Self-Defending Network and covers the strategy for identifying and responding to security threats. The next section, "Trust and Identity Technologies," discusses the technologies and services used on network security devices such as routers and firewalls. The section, "Detecting and Mitigating Threats," covers the technologies supporting threat defense, such as network- and host-based intrusion prevention systems, ASAs, and Cisco MARS.

The "Security Management Applications" section describes the Cisco Security Management framework of products designed to support the Cisco Self-Defending Network devices. Next, the "Integrating Security into Network Devices" section covers the security features integrated into Cisco network devices, such as routers, firewalls, IPS, endpoint security, and Catalyst Service modules. Finally, the "Securing the Enterprise" section reviews the locations to deploy security devices and solutions in the enterprise campus, data center, and WAN edge.

Cisco Self-Defending Network

The Self-Defending Network is Cisco's strategy for securing an organization's business by identifying, preventing, and adapting to security threats. This level of protection allows organizations to make better use of their network resources, thus improving business processes and increasing revenue.

Operational management and policy control serves as a component of the Self-Defending Network to establish security policies that in turn enforce security access levels. In addition, this serves as the basis for the secure transport of data communications throughout the network.

Security must be fully integrated into all components of the network using advanced technologies and services to protect assets, respond to threats, and ensure confidentiality. The Cisco Self-Defending Network has defined three critical components:

- **Trust and identity management**—Securing critical assets

- **Threat defense**—Responding to the effects of security outbreaks

- **Secure connectivity**—Ensuring privacy and confidentiality of data communications

The underlying foundation of the Cisco Self-Defending Network is the secure network. The Cisco SDN provides transport for all the far-reaching security features and services. These feature and service elements are controlled by the operational management, and the policy control is governed by the organization.

Figure 14-1 shows the Cisco Self-Defending Network framework and how the three critical components tie to management, policy, and the secure network foundation.

Figure 14-1 *Cisco Self-Defending Network*

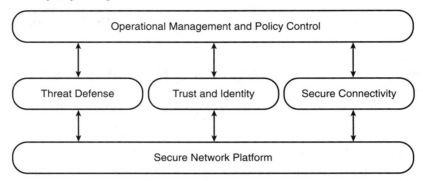

Network Security Platforms

Network security starts with having a secure underlying network. The underlying network provides an ideal place to implement core and advanced security solutions. The center of these secure network solutions includes the Adaptive Security Appliances (ASA), Integrated Services Routers (ISR), and Cisco Catalyst switches that have integrated security embedded in them. These are highly intelligent network security devices with many built-in security features that provide a framework for incorporating security throughout the network. Here is a description of some important security device platforms:

- **Adaptive Security Appliance (ASA)** is a high-performance firewall appliance with intrusion prevention system (IPS), antivirus, IPsec, and SSL VPN technologies integrated into a single unified architecture. ASA also has embedded Network Admission Control (NAC) capabilities.

- **Integrated Services Router (ISR)** combines IOS firewall, VPN, and IPS services across the router portfolio, which enables new security features on existing routers. ISR routers also have NAC enabled.

- **Cisco Catalyst switches** include denial of service (DoS) and man-in-the-middle attack mitigations, integrate the use of service modules for high protection, and provide for secure connectivity.

Self-Defending Network Phases

The Self-Defending Network has three network phases that function together to provide a strong, secure network from the network layer up to the application layer. Here is some more information about each of the network phases:

- **Integrated security**—Security throughout the existing infrastructure in which each network device acts as a point of defense. Hardware devices include routers, switches, wireless, and security appliances supporting firewalling, SSL VPN, IPsec VPN, and encrypted WAN communications.

- **Collaborative security**—Security components that work together with an organization's security policies. Network Admission Control is an example of a control that allows access to endpoints only after they have passed authentication based on security policies.

- **Adaptive threat defense**—Tools used to defend against security threats and varying network conditions. Application awareness defends against Internet-based attacks, and behavioral recognition defends against viruses, spyware, and DoS attacks. Network control provides monitoring functions and manages the security infrastructure, enabling tools for audits and analysis.

Additionally, other security services are contained in this framework, such as Cisco Security Agent, Cisco Trust Agent, NAC, and intrusion prevention. These Self-Defending Network products can be deployed independently or merged to allow for a more complete security solution.

Figure 14-2 illustrates the three Cisco Self-Defending Network phases and where various security technologies, mechanisms, and applications reside.

Figure 14-2 *Self-Defending Network Phases*

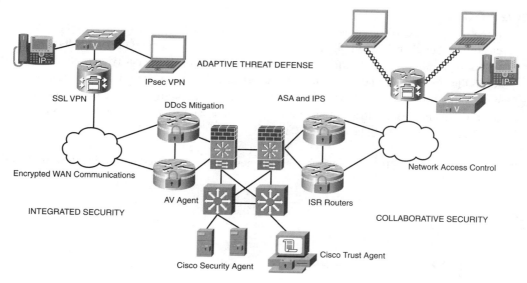

Trust and Identity Technologies

Trust and identity technologies are security controls that enable network traffic security. The following are examples of technologies used to support trust and identity management:

- **Access control lists**—ACLs are used on routers, switches, and firewalls to control access. For example, ACLs are commonly used to restrict traffic on the ingress or egress of an interface by a wide variety of methods, such as using IP addresses and TCP or UDP ports.

- **Firewall**—A security device designed to permit or deny network traffic based on source address, destination address, protocol, and port. The firewall enforces security by using the access and authorization policy to determine what is trusted and untrusted. The firewall also performs stateful packet inspection (SPI), which keeps track of the state of each TCP/UDP connection. SPI permits ingress traffic if the traffic originated from a higher security interface, such as the inside.

- **Network Admission Control (NAC)**—Protects the network from security threats by enforcing security compliance on all devices attempting to access the network.

- **802.1X**—An IEEE media-level access control standard that permits and denies admission to the network and applies traffic policy based on identity.

- **Cisco Identity-Based Network Services (IBNS)**—Based on several Cisco solutions integrated to enable authentication, access control, and user policies to secure network infrastructure and resources.

The following sections cover some of these trust and identity technologies in more detail.

Firewall ACLs

Firewalls are used to control access to and from the Internet and to provide interaction with customers, suppliers, and employees. But because the Internet is insecure, firewalls need to use ACLs to permit and deny traffic flowing through it. Firewalls use security zones to define trust levels that are associated with the firewall's interfaces. For example, the trusted zone is associated with an interface connected to the internal network, and the untrusted zone is associated with an interface connected to outside of the firewall. Common security zones include the inside, outside, and DMZ, but others can be created as needed.

Figure 14-3 shows a PIX firewall with three zones and the permitted policy and flow of the traffic.

Figure 14-3 *Firewall ACLs and Zones*

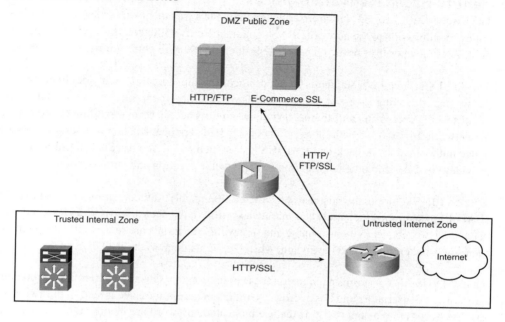

The policy for the firewall shown in Figure 14-3 includes the following:

- Allow HTTP and HTTPS to the Internet

- Allow HTTPS and FTP to the public web and FTP server

- Allow HTTPS to the public e-commerce server

NAC Framework and Appliance

Cisco NAC Framework and Cisco NAC Appliance are two ways to deploy NAC and meet the organization's technology and operational needs. The NAC Framework is an integrated solution led by Cisco that incorporates the network infrastructure and third-party software to impose security policy on the attached endpoints. The NAC Appliance is a self-contained product that integrates with the infrastructure to provide user authentication and enforce security policy for devices seeking entry into the network. NAC Appliances can also repair vulnerabilities before allowing access to the network infrastructure.

NAC can restrict access to noncompliant devices but permits access to trusted wired or wireless endpoints such as desktops, laptops, PDAs, and servers.

Both of these deployment options use the common NAC infrastructure and have considerations for timeframes and customer requirements.

Cisco Identity-Based Network Services

The Cisco Identity-Based Network Services solution is a way to authenticate host access based on policy for admission to the network. IBNS supports identity authentication, dynamic provisioning of VLANs on a per-user basis, guest VLANs, and 802.1X with port security.

The 802.1X protocol is a standards-based protocol for authenticating network clients by permitting or denying access to the network. The 802.1X protocol operates between the end-user client seeking access and an Ethernet switch or wireless access point providing the connection to the network. In 802.1X terminology, clients are called supplicants, and switches and APs are called authenticators. A back-end RADIUS server such as a Cisco Access Control Server (ACS) provides the user account database used to apply authentication and authorization.

With an IBNS solution, the host uses 802.1X and Extensible Authentication Protocol over LANs (EAPoL) to send the credentials and initiate a session to the network. After the host and switch establish LAN connectivity, username and password credentials are requested. The client host then sends the credentials to the switch, which forwards them to the RADIUS ACS.

The RADIUS ACS performs a lookup on the username and password to determine the credentials' validity. If the username and password are correct, an accept message is sent to the switch or AP to allow access to the client host. If the username and password are incorrect, the server sends a message to the switch or AP to block the host port.

Figure 14-4 illustrates the communication flow of two hosts using 802.1X and EAPoL with the switch, AP, and back-end RADIUS server.

Figure 14-4 *802.1X and EAPoL*

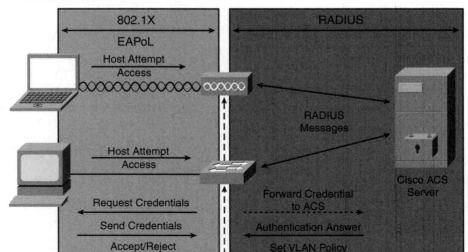

Identity and Access Control Deployments

Validating user authentication should be implemented as close to the source as possible, with an emphasis on strong authentication for access from untrusted networks. Access rules should enforce policy deployed throughout the network with the following guidelines:

- Source-specific rules with *any* type destinations should be applied as close to the source as possible.

- Destination-specific rules with *any* type sources should be applied as close to the destination as possible.

- Mixed rules integrating both source and destination should be used as close to the source as possible.

An integral part of identity and access control deployments is to allow only the necessary access. Highly distributed rules allow for greater granularity and scalability but unfortunately increase the management complexity. On the other hand, centralized rule deployment eases management but lacks flexibility and scalability.

Practicing "defense in depth" by using security mechanisms that back each other up is an important concept to understand. For example, the perimeter Internet routers should employ ACLs to filter packets in addition to the firewall inspecting packets at a deeper level.

Figure 14-5 shows the importance of the authentication databases and how many network components in the Enterprise rely on them for authentication services.

Figure 14-5 *Identity and Access Control*

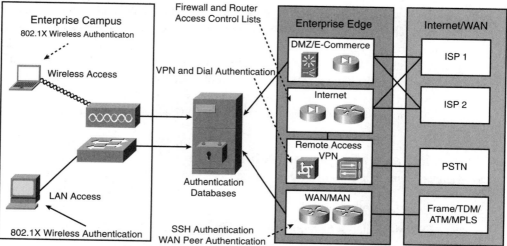

Detecting and Mitigating Threats

The use of threat detection and mitigation techniques enables early detection of and notifications about unwanted malicious traffic. The goals are to detect, notify, and help stop unforeseen and unauthorized traffic. These techniques help increase the network's availability, particularly against unidentified and unexpected attacks. Threat detection and mitigation solutions include the following:

- **Endpoint protection**—Viruses and worms can create havoc by propagating infections from host to host throughout the network. To combat these infestations, endpoint protection such as Cisco's Security Agent is used. It limits the scope of virus outbreaks and is adaptable to new and emerging threats. In addition, antivirus services can aid hosts with detection and removing infections based on known virus pattern markings.

- **Application security and anti-X Defense**—Several new application-layer network products have been released that help address new classes of threats, such as spam, phishing, spyware, packet abuse, and unauthorized point-to-point file sharing. Anti-X defense provides comprehensive antivirus, anti-spyware, file-blocking, anti-spam, URL blocking, and content filtering services. These products supplement traditional firewalls and network-based intrusion detection system (NIDS) solutions with more granular traffic inspection services, thereby quarantining traffic so that it does not propagate throughout the network.

- **Infection containment**—Cisco's ASA, PIX, Firewall Services Module (FWSM), and IOS firewalls protect the network by creating security zones that partition the network into separate segments. The firewall services provide perimeter network security but do not eliminate the need for continuous network monitoring. As part of the Cisco SDN architecture, NAC is also used in the perimeter to perform policy-based admission control, thus reducing potential threats.

- **Inline IPS and anomaly detection**—Cisco has innovated in the area of network intrusion detection systems by being the first to incorporate NIDS into the IOS on routing and switching platforms. In addition, IPS solutions have inline filtering features that can remove unwanted traffic with programmable features that classify traffic patterns. The 4200 IPS sensor appliances, IDSM-2, and the IOS IPS can identify, analyze, and stop unwanted traffic from flowing on the network. Another set of tools used to prevent DDoS attacks and ensure business continuity are the Cisco Traffic Anomaly Detector XT and Guard XT, along with the Cisco Traffic Anomaly Detector Services and Cisco Guard Services module.

Threat Detection and Mitigation Technologies

- Here are some examples of Cisco's Threat Detection and Mitigation technologies:

    — PIX—Firewall appliances

    — FWSM—Catalyst 6500 Firewall Services Module

    — ASA—Adaptive Security Appliance (Robust firewall and/or network-based intrusion prevention system [NIPS])

— IOS firewall—Cisco IOS Software feature set

— IPS sensor appliance—NIPS

— IPS—Intrusion prevention system (IOS feature)

— CSA—Cisco Security Agent (host-based intrusion prevention system [HIPS])

- Network monitoring:

— NetFlow—Stats on packets flowing through router (IOS feature)

— Syslog—Logging data (IOS feature)

— SNMP—Simple Network Management Protocol (IOS feature)

— MARS—Monitoring, Analysis, and Response System

— Cisco Traffic Anomaly Detector Module—Detects high-speed denial-of-service attacks

Threat Detection and Mitigation Solutions

Threat detection and mitigation solutions are deployed throughout the network and can serve as an effective layered defense for secure network communications. For example, let's say your network is being attacked from the Internet, such as a worm or virus outbreak. The Internet WAN routers are your first line of protection and can be used to spot increasing network load or suspicious NetFlow data. After some information has been collected, specific granular ACLs can be used to further identify the attack.

The network IPS provides deep packet inspection to determine the additional details about the attack's signature. HIPS can be deployed using hardware appliances or IOS feature integration; both include signature-based attack detection mechanisms. HIPS also allows for host policy enforcement and verification.

Firewalls can perform stateful packet inspections and block unwanted network traffic locally in the event of an attack. However, it is preferable to engage the ISP and have them block the attack from even entering your network.

To successfully detect threats and mitigate them, it is important to understand where to look for potential threats. The following are good sources of information for detecting and mitigating threats:

- NetFlow

- Syslog

- RMON events

- SNMP thresholds and traps

- CPU and interface statistics

- Cisco Security MARS reporting

Figure 14-6 depicts an attacker sourcing from the Internet and targeting the internal network and how the threat can be detected and mitigated.

Figure 14-6 *Threat Detection and Mitigation*

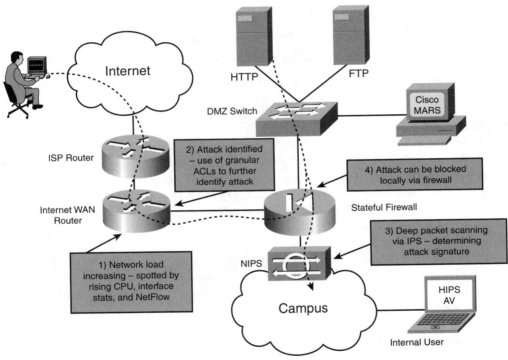

Security Management Applications

Security management applications consolidate network management and monitoring, which allows more secure control of the network. Security management provides several functions:

- Central repository for collecting network information for further analysis of security-related events. In addition, many applications have reporting capabilities to help network managers' present technical information to upper management. Some examples include Authentication, Authorization, and Accounting (AAA) with TACACS and RADIUS servers, Syslog servers, and intrusion detection systems, which enable deep inspection of complex security events.

- Allows for easier deployment of security policies into the security devices via graphical user interface tools. These tools help you maintain the consistency of the security policies across a broad spectrum of network device types.

- Role-based access control for all accounts to separate administrative tasks and user functions.

Security implementations need to be planned properly using the security policies governed by the organization to make good use of the security applications. From time to time, audits are necessary, which requires updates to the security policy and related security management applications. A major risk to security implementations is policy error. Management needs to be cognizant of the security policy and know how to manage incidents properly.

Security Platform Solutions

Cisco has a variety of security management products and technologies that allow scalable administration and enforcement of security policy for the Cisco Self-Defending Network platform. These solutions reduce the operational management and automate many of the common tasks, including configuration, analysis, incident response, and reporting. Some of the security management platforms consist of the following:

- **Cisco Security Manager (CSM)** is an integrated solution for configuration management of firewall, VPN, router, switch module, and IPS devices. CSM has capabilities for security policies to be deployed by device, by group, or globally for all devices.

- **Cisco Secure Access Control Server (ACS)** provides centralized control for administrative access to Cisco devices and security applications. ACS provides for both TACACS and RADIUS security services and supports routers, switches, firewalls, VPN concentrators, content switches, wireless, and VoIP solutions.

- **Cisco Security Monitoring, Analysis, and Response System (Cisco Security MARS)** is an appliance-based solution for network security administrators to monitor, identify, isolate, and respond to security threats. MARS understands the network topology and device configurations from routers, switches, firewalls, and IPS devices. MARS also can model packet flows on the network.

- **Management Center for CSA (CSA MC)** is an SSL web-based tool for managing Cisco Security Agent configurations. CSAs can be grouped to deploy security policies to multiple agents.

- **Cisco Router and Security Device Manager (SDM)** is a web-based tool for routers and supports a wide range of IOS software. SDM improves productivity, simplifies router deployments, and can help troubleshoot network issues. SDM is free software for Cisco router models ranging from the Cisco 830 series to the Cisco 7301.

- **Cisco Adaptive Security Device Manager (ASDM)** is a web-based tool for managing Cisco ASA 5500 series appliances, PIX 500 series appliances (version 7.0 and higher), and Cisco Catalyst 6500 Firewall Services Modules (FWSM version 3.1 and higher). ASDM comes with wizards to automate many common tasks and comprehensive monitoring services.

- **Cisco Intrusion Prevention System Device Manager (IDM)** is a web-based application that configures and manages IPS sensors. IDM runs a web server and is accessible via SSL supporting IPS v5.0 sensors.

Integrating Security into Network Devices

It is crucial to integrate security into all network devices throughout your network. Common device types include

- IOS routers and switches

- PIX firewalls

- Adaptive Security Appliances (ASA)

- VPN concentrators

- Intrusion Prevention Systems (NIPS/HIPS)

- Catalyst 6500 service modules

- Endpoint security

The following sections discuss device security integration in more detail.

IOS Security

Cisco has developed many security features that are integrated into the IOS base software or security-specific feature sets. Here are some of the major areas of security focus that have been included with IOS releases:

- **Cisco IOS Firewall** feature set provides stateful firewall functionality for perimeter routers running IOS. IOS Firewall allows businesses to protect networks from network and application layer attacks, improve uptime, and offer policy enforcement for internal and external connections.

- **Cisco IOS IPS** offers inline deep-packet inspection to successfully diminish a wide range of network attacks. IOS IPS can identify, classify, and block malicious traffic in real time. IOS IPS operates by loading attack signatures on the router and then matching the attacks based on signatures.

- **Cisco IOS IPsec** encrypts data at the IP packet level using a set of standards-based protocols. IPsec provides data authentication, anti-replay, and data confidentially, and is the preferred method of securing VPNs.

- **Cisco IOS Trust and Identity** is a set of services that includes the following:

  — AAA—Framework and mechanisms for controlling device access

  — Secure Shell (SSH)—Used for encrypted router access

  — Secure Socket Layer (SSL)—Secure web application access

  — 802.1X—Standards-based access control protocol to permit or deny network access

  — PKI—Strong authentication for e-commerce applications

ISR Security Hardware Options

The Cisco Integrated Services Routers have additional hardware options that enhance the routers' security capabilities. Here are some of the available hardware options:

- **Built-in VPN Acceleration** is hardware-based encryption that offloads VPN processing from the router's internal CPU to improve VPN throughput.

- **High-Performance AIM** is a VPN encryption advanced integration module used to terminate large numbers of VPN tunnels such as with DMVPN. The module supports 3DES and AES, which increases the router encryption and compression performance.

- **IDS Network Module (NM-CIDS)** provides technologies to prevent a large range of security threats. IDS network modules also include correlation and validation tools to decrease the number of false positives.

- **Secure Voice** is digital signal processor (DSP) slots on the ISR for use with packet voice/fax DSP modules (PVDM). These offer capabilities such as conferencing and transcoding. In addition, Secure Real-time Transport Protocol (SRTP) protects the entire voice payload by encryption, except for the header, which remains in clear text to support QoS.

- **Network Analysis Module** allows capturing of traffic flows from hosts and the decoding of packets for detailed network analysis. It also collects NetFlow data to increase the visibility into application flows.

- **Content Engine Module** is an Integrated Content module for 2800/3800 series routers that supports 40-GB and 80-GB internal hard disks for application and content networking.

> **NOTE**   For a quick reference and complete list of ISR modules, go to http://www.cisco.com/warp/public/765/tools/quickreference/isr.pdf.

Cisco Security Appliances

Cisco Security Appliances provide robust security services and protection, including IPsec VPNs and stateful packet filtering. The following is an overview of Cisco Security Appliances:

- **Adaptive Security Appliance (ASA)**—The ASA is a high-performance multifunction security appliance that offers a comprehensive set of services for securing network environments. The services are customized through product editions tailored for firewall, IPS, anti-X, and VPN. The ASA is a critical component of the Cisco Self-Defending Network that provides proactive threat mitigation, controls application data flows, and delivers flexible VPN and IPS services. In addition, the ASA is very cost-effective and easy to manage, and offers advanced integration modules that enhance the processing capabilities.

- **PIX Security Appliance**—The Cisco PIX series of appliances provides robust firewall services for users and application policy enforcement, attack protection, and security VPN connectivity services. The PIX appliances are easy to deploy and are very cost-effective for most network environments. The appliances range from the desktop PIX 501 (SOHO) up to the modular PIX 535, offering Gigabit network interfaces and failover capabilities.

- **VPN concentrators**—The Cisco VPN 3000 concentrators provide businesses with IPsec and SSL VPN connectivity. VPN concentrators are flexible and offer many deployment scenarios. However, they are commonly used to terminate VPN sessions for remote-access connections. VPN concentrators can also be used to terminate site-to-site tunnels with other VPN concentrators, routers, or even PIX firewalls. The centralized architecture and web-based management ease the administrative burden and consolidate the VPN connectivity for the enterprise. Many organizations are now starting to look at the Cisco ASAs instead of the VPN concentrators due to the increased security options in addition to VPN functionality.

Intrusion Prevention

The Cisco IPS solution integrates passive intrusion detection, inline prevention services, and new technologies to increase accuracy and keep legitimate traffic from being affected. The Cisco IPS 4200 series sensors offer significant protection by detecting and stopping threats from attacking your network. With Cisco IPS, version 5.1 supports inline (IPS) or passive (IDS) capabilities. The IPS appliances support multivector threat identification through detailed inspection of data flows in Layers 2 through 7. Multivector identification secures the network from policy violations, vulnerability exploits, and abnormal reconnaissance activities. The following IPS sensors support bandwidth requirements from 65 Mbps to 1 Gbps:

- **IPS 4215** reviews traffic and provides protection up to 65 Mbps.

- **IPS 4240** reviews traffic and provides protection up to 240 Mbps with support for multiple 10/100/1000 interfaces. IPS 4240-DC supports DC power and is Network Equipment Building Standards (NEBS)-compliant.

- **IPS 4255** delivers 500 Mbps of performance and can be used to protect partially utilized Gigabit connected subnets.

- **IPS 4260** delivers 1 Gbps of performance and can be used on Gigabit subnets with copper or fiber network connections, providing additional flexibility.

Catalyst 6500 Services Modules

The Catalyst 6500 switching platform supports additional security services and functionality through the use of services modules. Several modules enable firewall, IDS, SSL, and network analysis services, in addition to IPsec VPN connectivity and anomaly traffic support.

Catalyst 6500 service modules include the following:

- **Firewall Services Module (FWSM)** is a high-speed firewall module for use in the Cisco Catalyst 6500 and Cisco 7600 series routing platforms. Up to four FWSMs can be installed in a single chassis, providing 5 Gbps of throughput performance per module. For service provider environments, the FWSM supports advanced features such as multiple security contexts for both routed and bridged firewall modes.

- **Intrusion Detection Service Module 2 (IDSM2)** is an IDS module that supports both inline (IPS) and passive (IDS) operation. IDSM2 provides up to 500 Mbps of packet inspection capabilities to efficiently protect your infrastructure.

- **SSL Service Module** is an integrated services module for terminating SSL sessions on Cisco Catalyst 6500 series switch or Cisco 7600 series routing platforms. By offloading the SSL terminations with the SSL module, the web server farms can support more connections, increasing operational efficiency. Up to four SSL modules can be used in a single chassis.

- **IPsec VPN SPA** enables scalable VPN services using the Cisco Catalyst 6500 series switches and Cisco 7600 series routing platforms. The module does not have any interfaces, but instead uses the other module interfaces available on the chassis.

- **Network Analysis Module** provides packet-capture capabilities and visibility into all the layers of the data flows. You can analyze application traffic between hosts and networks. The NAMs support RMON2 and mini-RMON features to provide port-level Layer 2 traffic statistics.

- **Traffic Anomaly Detector Module** uses behavioral analysis and attack recognition technology to identify attack patterns. It monitors traffic destined for application servers and builds detailed profiles based on the normal operating conditions. If the module detects any abnormal behavior in the per-flow data conversations, it considers this behavior a potential attack and responds based on the configured preference. You can have the module send an operator an alert or launch the Cisco Anomaly Guard Module to begin mitigation services.

■ **Anomaly Guard Module** provides the attack response by blocking malicious traffic at Gbps line rates. With multiple layers of defense, it can divert only traffic destined for targeted devices without affecting legitimate traffic.

Endpoint Security

The Cisco Security Agent (CSA) software protects server and desktop endpoints from the latest threats caused by malicious network attacks. CSA can identify and prevent network attacks that are considered unknown or "Day Zero"-type threats. CSAs are packed with many features, including firewall capabilities, intrusion prevention, malicious mobile code protection, operating-system integrity assurance, and audit log consolidation. All these features can be configured and managed through the use of the Management Center for Cisco Security Agents. CSAs can be used with Cisco MARS by sending important endpoints to MARS, thereby improving MARS threat identification and security investigations throughout the network.

The Management Center for Cisco Security Agents provides centralized web-based management for all CSAs deployed in your network. The MC for CSAs comes with more than 20 preconfigured policies that can be used to deploy thousands of agents quickly across the enterprise network. You can create software distribution packages, create or modify security policies, monitor security alerts, and generate reports. It also has features for running the agents in "IDS mode," in which suspicious activity is only alerted to the MC console, not blocked.

Securing the Enterprise

The Cisco Self-Defending Network provides the most comprehensive security systems for securing the enterprise network from the threats of today and tomorrow.

Each location in the enterprise network has unique security requirements because concerns are different and vary by location. However, in most cases customizing network security solutions by functional area offers the best protection for the enterprise network.

The next sections examine some ways to use Cisco security systems in the campus, data center, and enterprise edge.

Implementing Security in the Campus

Security for the campus begins with remembering that you need to implement security throughout your network. Several technologies, protocols, solutions, and devices work together to provide the secure campus. Network security should be implemented in the core, distribution, and access layers and can be grouped into four broad categories:

- **Identity and access control**—802.1X, NAC, ACLs, and firewalls

- **Threat detection and mitigation**—NetFlow, Syslog, SNMP, RMON, CS-MARS, NIPS, and HIPS

- **Infrastructure protection**—AAA, TACACS, RADIUS, SSH, SNMP v3, IGP/EGP MD5, and Layer 2 security features

- **Security management**—CSM, CS-MARS, ACS

Figure 14-7 illustrates the use of Enterprise Campus Security and shows where security technologies, protocols, and mechanisms can be deployed in the enterprise campus.

Figure 14-7 *Enterprise Campus Security*

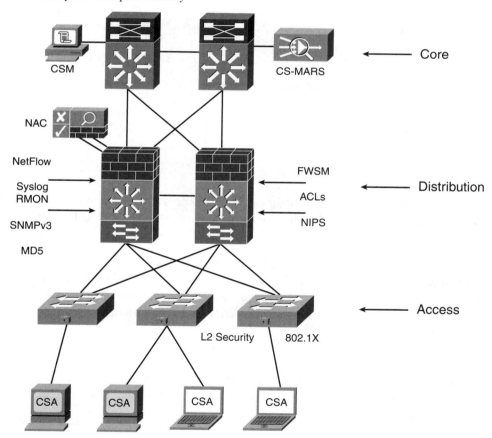

Implementing Security in the Data Center

The Enterprise Data Center hosts critical servers and applications for the main campus and the branch offices. Many of the servers require high availability due to the importance of the information and the high volume of users they serve. Several of the servers may contain sensitive information that is crucial to the business and therefore cannot become compromised. Thus, it needs to be highly secured. Network performance is another area that is critically important, which can limit the choice of protection mechanisms and technologies. Here are some of the risks inherent with Enterprise Data Centers:

- Compromised applications and unauthorized access to critical information

- Exploiting different servers in the business by launching an attack from the compromised servers

To provide adequate security protection, organizations can implement the following:

- **Identity and access control**—802.1X, NAC, ACLs, and firewalls (FWSM/PIX)

- **Threat detection and mitigation**—NetFlow, Syslog, SNMP, RMON, NAM modules, IDS modules, CS-MARS NIPS, and HIPS

- **Infrastructure protection**—AAA, TACACS, RADIUS, SSH, SNMP v3, IGP/EGP MD5, and Layer 2 security features

- **Security management**—CSM, CS-MARS, IDM, and ACS

Figure 14-8 illustrates the use of Enterprise Data Center security and shows where security technologies, protocols, and mechanisms can be deployed in the Enterprise Data Center.

Implementing Security in the Enterprise Edge and WAN

The Enterprise Edge and WAN provide connectivity to other parts of your network over both private and public networks. It is important to consider the available security options when transferring data between locations and over WAN and Internet transports.

Here are some potential risk areas to keep in mind when moving data between locations:

- Attackers obtain access to the network and compromise the confidentiality and integrity of sensitive information with eavesdropping or data manipulation.

- Misconfiguration of the WAN network could cause inappropriate WAN configuration and unwanted connectivity.

Figure 14-8 *Enterprise Data Center Security*

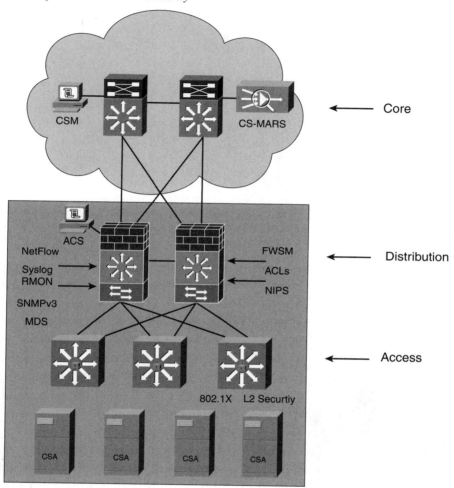

To provide adequate security protection between locations, organizations can implement the following:

- **Identity and access control**—Firewalls, IPsec, SSL VPN, ACLs, and Unicast RPF

- **Threat detection and mitigation**—NetFlow, Syslog, SNMP, RMON, NAM modules, IDS modules, CS-MARS NIPS, and HIPS

- **Infrastructure protection**—AAA, TACACS, RADIUS, SSH, SNMP v3, IGP/EGP MD5, RFC 2827 ingress filtering, and Layer 2 security features

- **Security management**—CSM, CS-MARS, IDM, and ACS

Figure 14-9 illustrates the use of Enterprise Edge and WAN Security, and where security technologies, protocols, and mechanisms can be deployed in the Enterprise Edge and WAN.

Figure 14-9 *Enterprise Edge and WAN Security*

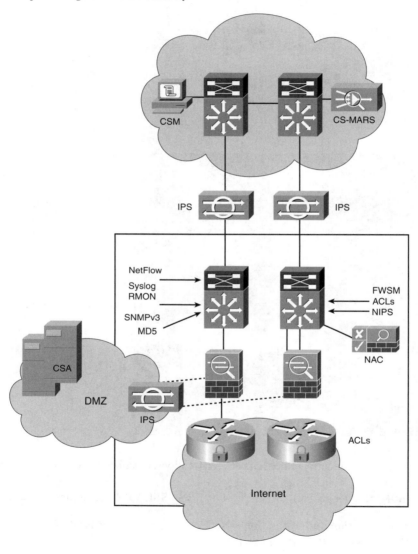

References and Recommended Readings

"The Cisco ASA 5500 as a Superior Firewall Solution," http://www.cisco.com/en/US/netsol/ns340/ns394/ns171/ns413/networking_solutions_white_paper0900aecd8058ec85.shtml

Cisco ISR series at-a-glance, http://www.cisco.com/warp/public/765/tools/quickreference/isr.pdf

"Core Elements of the Cisco Self Defending Network Strategy," http://www.cisco.com/en/US/netsol/ns340/ns394/ns171/ns413/networking_solutions_white_paper0900aecd80247914.shtml

"Deploying Firewalls Throughout Your Organization," http://www.cisco.com/en/US/netsol/ns340/ns394/ns171/ns413/networking_solutions_white_paper0900aecd8057f042.shtml

Module 6 (Evaluating Security Solutions for the Network)—Designing for Cisco Internetwork Solution Course (DESGN) 2.0

"Protecting Against Threats Using the Self-Defending Network," http://www.cisco.com/en/US/netsol/ns340/ns394/ns171/ns413/netbr0900aecd803e3629.html

RFC 2827, *Network Ingress Filtering: Defeating Denial of Service Attacks Which Employ IP Source Address Spoofing*, http://www.faqs.org/rfcs/rfc2827.html

Foundation Summary

The "Foundation Summary" section of each chapter lists the most important facts from the chapter. Although this section does not list every fact from the chapter that will be on your CCDA exam, a well-prepared CCDA candidate should at a minimum know all the details in each "Foundation Summary" before taking the exam.

The CCDA exam requires that you be familiar with the following topics covered in this chapter:

- Critical components of the Self-Defending Network:

    — Trust and identity management—Securing critical assets

    — Threat defense—Responding to the effects of security outbreaks

    — Secure connectivity—Ensuring privacy and confidentiality of data communications

- Cisco Self-Defending Network phases:

    — **Integrated security**—Security throughout the existing infrastructure in which each network device acts as a point of defense

    — **Collaborative security**—Security components that work with an organization's security policies

    — **Adaptive threat defense**—Tools used to defend against security threats and varying network conditions

- Trust and identify technologies:

    — **Access control lists**—ACLs are used on routers, switches, and firewalls to control access

    — **Firewall**—A security device designed to permit or deny network traffic based on source address, destination address, protocol, and port

    — **Network Admission Control (NAC)**—Protects the network from threats by enforcing security compliance on all devices attempting to access the network

    — **802.1X**—An IEEE media-level access control standard that permits and denies access to the network and applies traffic policy based on identity

    — **Cisco Identity-Based Network Services (IBNS)**—Based on several integrated Cisco solutions to enable authentication, access control, and user policies to secure network infrastructure and resources

■ Threat detection and mitigation technologies:

  — PIX—Firewall appliances

  — FWSM—Catalyst 6500 Firewall Services Module

  — ASA—Adaptive Security Appliance (Robust firewall and/or network-based intrusion prevention system [NIPS])

  — IOS firewall—Cisco IOS Software feature set

  — IPS sensor appliance (NIPS)

  — IPS—Intrusion prevention system (IOS feature)

  — CSA—Cisco Security Agent (HIPS)

  — NetFlow—Stats on packets flowing through router (IOS feature)

  — Syslog—Logging data (IOS feature)

  — SNMP—Simple Network Management Protocol (IOS feature)

  — MARS—Monitoring, Analysis, and Response System

  — Cisco Traffic Anomaly Detector Module detects high-speed denial-of-service attacks

■ Security management solutions:

  — **Cisco Security Manager (CSM)** is an integrated solution for configuration management of firewall, VPN, router, switch module, and IPS devices.

  — **Cisco Secure Access Control Server (ACS)** provides centralized control for administrative access to Cisco devices and security applications.

  — **Cisco Security Monitoring, Analysis, and Response System (MARS)** is an appliance-based solution for network security administrators to monitor, identify, isolate, and respond to security threats.

  — **Management Center for CSA (CSA MC)** is an SSL web-based tool for managing Cisco Security Agent configurations.

  — **Cisco Router and Security Device Manager (SDM)** is a web-based tool for routers and supports a wide range of IOS software.

  — **Cisco Adaptive Security Device Manager (ASDM)** is a web-based tool for managing Cisco ASA 5500 series appliances, PIX 500 series appliances (version 7.0 or higher), and Cisco Catalyst 6500 Firewall Services Modules (FWSM version 3.1 or higher).

  — **Cisco Intrusion Prevention System Device Manager (IDM)** is a web-based application that configures and manages IPS sensors.

- Integrating security:

    — Cisco IOS Firewall

    — Cisco IOS IPS

    — Cisco IOS IPsec

    — Cisco IOS trust and identity

    — Cisco IOS Routers and Switches

    — Adaptive Security Appliance (ASA)

    — PIX security appliance

    — VPN concentrator

    — IPS modules

    — Catalyst 6500 series service modules

    — Endpoint Security

- Securing the enterprise:

    — Identity and access control—802.1X, NAC, ACLs, and firewalls

    — Threat detection and mitigation—NetFlow, Syslog, SNMP, RMON, CS-MARS, NIPS, and HIPS

    — Infrastructure protection—AAA, TACACS, RADIUS, SSH, SNMP v3, IGP/EGP MD5, and Layer 2 security features

    — Security management—CSM, CS-MARS, and ACS

Q&A

As mentioned in the Introduction, you have two choices for review questions: here in the book or the exam questions on the CD-ROM. The answers to these questions appear in Appendix A.

For more practice with exam format questions, use the exam engine on the CD-ROM.

1. What security device combines IOS Firewall with VPN and IPS services?

    a. ASA

    b. ISR

    c. Cisco Catalyst switches

    d. IPS

2. What is a standards-based protocol for authenticating network clients?

    a. NAC

    b. PoE

    c. 802.1X

    d. CSM

3. Cisco _____ Framework is an integrated solution led by Cisco that incorporates the network infrastructure and third-party software to impose security policy attached endpoints.

    a. ASA

    b. CSM

    c. ISR

    d. NAC

4. What is an appliance-based solution for network security administrators to monitor, identity, isolate, and respond to security threats? (Select the best answer.)

    a. CS-MARS

    b. CSA MC

    c. ASDM

    d. IDM

5. Cisco IOS Trust and Identity has a set of services that include which of the following? (Select all that apply.)

   a. 802.1X

   b. SSL

   c. AAA

   d. ASDM

6. True or false: SSH provides unencrypted router access.

7. Cisco IOS _____ offers data encryption at the IP packet level using a set of standards-based protocols.

   a. IPS

   b. IPsec

   c. L2TP

   d. L2F

8. True or false: PKI provides strong authentication for e-commerce applications.

9. What provides hardware VPN encryption for terminating a large number of VPN tunnels for ISRs?

   a. FWSM

   b. IDS Network Module

   c. Network Analysis Module

   d. High-Performance AIM

10. True or false: Integrated Content Module for 2800/3800 series routers captures traffic flows from hosts and allows detailed network analysis.

11. True or false: Cisco VPN 3000 concentrators provide robust firewall servers for users and application policy enforcement, attack protection, and security VPN connectivity services.

12. Which of the following services modules do Cisco Catalyst 6500 switches support? (Select all that apply.)

    a. FWSM

    b. IDSM2

    c. VPN3000

    d. ASA

13. What provides attack responses by blocking malicious traffic with Gbps line rates?

    a. Network Analysis Module

    b. Anomaly Guard Module

    c. Content Switch Module

    d. Traffic Anomaly Detector Module

14. Which of the following are identity and access control protocols and mechanisms? (Select all that apply.)

    a. 802.1X

    b. ACLs

    c. NAC

    d. NetFlow

15. True or false: The Cisco Security Agent protects server and desktop endpoints from the latest threats caused by malicious network attacks.

16. What SSL web-based tool is used to manage Cisco Security Agent configurations?

    a. CSM

    b. IDM

    c. ASDM

    d. CSA MC

17. True or false: IDM is a web-based application that configures and manages IPS sensors.

18. True or false: NetFlow is used for threat detection and mitigation.

19. Which of the following is not one of the phases of the Cisco Self-Defending Network?

    a. Integrated Security

    b. Collaborative Security

    c. Network Admission Control

    d. Adaptive Threat Defense

20. True or false: Cisco ASAs, PIX security appliances, FWSM, and IOS firewall are part of Infection Containment.

21. What IOS feature offers inline deep-packet inspection to successfully diminish a wide range of network attacks?

    a. IOS SSH

    b. IOS SSL VPN

    c. IOS IPsec

    d. IOS IPS

22. The 4200 _____ sensor appliances can identify, analyze, and block unwanted traffic from flowing on the network.

23. What provides centralized control for administrative access to Cisco devices and security applications?

    a. CSM

    b. ACS

    c. CS-MARS

    d. CSA MC

24. True or false: ASDM provides management of Cisco ASAs, PIX, and FWSMs.

25. True or false: IPS 4255 delivers 10000 Mbps of performance and can be used to protect partially utilized Gigabit connected subnets.

26. True or false: FWSM is a high-speed firewall module for use in the Cisco Catalyst 6500 and 7600 series routers.

27. Match each protocol, mechanism, or feature with its security grouping:

    i. CSM

    ii. IGP/EGP MD5

    iii. NetFlow

    iv. NAC

    a. Identity and access control

    b. Threat detection and mitigation

    c. Infrastructure protection

    d. Security management

This chapter covers the following subjects:

- Traditional Voice Architectures

- Integrated Multiservice Networks

- IPT Design

CHAPTER 15

Traditional Voice Architectures and IP Telephony Design

The designs of enterprise voice networks are migrating from the traditional use of Private Branch Exchange (PBX) switches to the use of IP telephony architectures such as Cisco Unified CallManager. Enterprise networks now have to be designed with IP telephony in mind. This chapter reviews Public Switched Telephone Network (PSTN) and PBX voice networks, integrated IP telephony, and quality of service (QoS) for IP telephony (IPT) networks.

"Do I Know This Already?" Quiz

The purpose of the "Do I Know This Already?" quiz is to help you decide whether you need to read the entire chapter. If you intend to read the entire chapter, you do not necessarily need to answer these questions now.

The ten-question quiz, derived from the major sections in the "Foundation Topics" portion of the chapter, helps you determine how to spend your limited study time.

Table 15-1 outlines the major topics discussed in this chapter and the "Do I Know This Already?" quiz questions that correspond to those topics.

Table 15-1 *"Do I Know This Already?" Foundation Topics Section-to-Question Mapping*

Foundation Topics Section	Questions Covered in This Section
Traditional Voice Architectures	5, 9
Integrated Multiservice Networks	1, 2, 3, 4, 6, 7
IPT Design	8, 10

CAUTION   The goal of self-assessment is to gauge your mastery of the topics in this chapter. If you do not know the answer to a question or you are only partially sure, you should mark this question wrong for purposes of the self-assessment. Giving yourself credit for an answer you correctly guess skews your self-assessment results and might give you a false sense of security.

1. Which International Telecommunication Union (ITU) standard provides a framework for multimedia protocols for the transport of voice, video, and data over packet-switched networks?

    a. Session Initiation Protocol (SIP)

    b. Voice over IP (VoIP)

    c. H.323

    d. Weighted Fair Queuing (WFQ)

2. What is the default coder-decoder (codec) used with VoIP dial peers?

    a. G.711

    b. G.723

    c. G.728

    d. G.729

3. Real-time Transport Protocol (RTP) operates at what layer of the OSI model?

    a. Application

    b. Session

    c. Transport

    d. Network

4. Which H.323 protocol is responsible for call setup and signaling?

    a. H.245

    b. G.711

    c. H.225

    d. RTCP

5. What unit measures the number of voice calls in one hour?

    a. Kbps

    b. Erlang

    c. DS0

    d. FXS

6. Which feature does not transmit packets when there is silence?

    a. Ear and mouth (E&M)

    b. Voice Activity Detection (VAD)

    c. Dial peers

    d. Digital Silence Suppressor (DSS)

7. What does Compressed Real-time Transport Protocol (CRTP) compress?

   a. RTP headers

   b. RTP, TCP, and IP headers

   c. RTP, User Datagram Protocol (UDP), and IP headers

   d. Real-time Transport Control Protocol (RTCP) headers

8. Which QoS mechanism is recommended for VoIP networks?

   a. Custom queuing

   b. Low-latency queuing (LLQ)

   c. Priority queuing

   d. Switched-based queuing

9. Where is the local loop located?

   a. Between phones and the central office (CO) switch

   b. Between two PBXs

   c. Between the loopback interfaces of two VoIP routers

   d. Between two PSTN switches

10. What is jitter?

   a. The echo caused by mismatched impedance

   b. The loss of packets in the network

   c. The variable delay of received packets

   d. The fixed delay of received packets

The answers to the "Do I Know This Already?" quiz appear in Appendix A, "Answers to Chapter 'Do I Know This Already?' Quizzes and Q&A Sections." The suggested choices for your next step are as follows:

- **8 or less overall score**—Read the entire chapter. It includes the "Foundation Topics," "Foundation Summary," and "Q&A" sections.

- **9 or 10 overall score**—If you want more review on these topics, skip to the "Foundation Summary" section and then go to the "Q&A" section. Otherwise, move to the next chapter.

Foundation Topics

This chapter covers traditional voice architectures, integrated voice design, and QoS in voice networks. The section "Traditional Voice Architectures" covers the architecture of time-division multiplexing (TDM) voice networks. It also discusses PSTN technologies and limitations.

The section "Integrated Multiservice Networks" covers IP telephony design for Cisco Unified Communications. The "IPT Design" section covers QoS mechanisms used in IPT networks and provides IPT design recommendations.

Traditional Voice Architectures

This section reviews technologies and concepts to help you understand traditional voice networks.

The PSTN is the global public voice network that provides voice services. The PSTN is a variety of networks and services that are in place worldwide; it provides a circuit-switched service using Signaling System 7 (SS7) for out-of-band call provisioning through the network. Central office (CO) switches exchange SS7 messages to place and route voice calls throughout the network. The PSTN uses Time-Division Multiplexing (TDM) facilities for calls within the network. From the CO to the customer premises, the call can be analog, ISDN, or TDM digital. Each call consumes 64 Kbps of bandwidth, called digital service zero (DS0).

PBX and PSTN Switches

Traditional switches and PBXs route voice using TDM technology and use 64-kbps circuits. The CCDA must understand some of the differences between these devices. The PBX, as its name states, is used in a private network and uses proprietary protocols. The PBX is located in the enterprise's data center. Each PBX may scale up to 1000 phones. Companies deploy PBX networks to obtain enterprise features and to prevent PSTN long-distance charges.

PBXs are customer-owned voice switches. Enterprise companies install and configure their own PBXs to provide telephony service, four-digit dialing, remote-office extensions, voice mail, and private-line routing within other features. Organizations can reduce toll charges by using private tie-lines between their switches. Calls that are placed between offices through the private voice network are called on-net. If a user needs to place a call outside the private network, the call is routed to the local PSTN. If the call is forwarded to the PSTN, it is called off-net.

Figure 15-1 shows a PBX network for an enterprise. Callers use the PBX network when they place calls from San Diego to Chicago, Atlanta, or Houston. The enterprise reduces toll charges by using its private voice network. A separate private network is in place for data traffic. If a user places a call from San Diego to Los Angeles, it is routed to the PSTN from the San Diego PBX. Then, toll charges are incurred for the call.

Figure 15-1 *PBX Network*

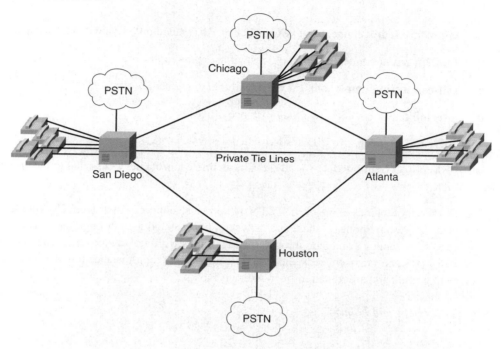

Another issue in the design is the limitation on the number of calls per private line. If the private lines are T1s, they are each limited to carrying 24 concurrent calls at a time. This is because each call takes 64 kbps of bandwidth with the g.711 codec, and 24 calls times 64 kbps/call equals 1.536 Mbps, the bandwidth of a T1.

PSTN switches are not private. They scale up to 100,000 phones and use open standards because they have to communicate with other switches, PBXs, fax machines, and home telephones. PSTN switches normally are located at the CO of the local or interexchange carrier.

Local Loop and Trunks

Depending on the dialed digits, a call routes through the local loop, one or more trunks, and the destination local loop to reach the destination phone. The local loop is the pair of wires that runs from the CO to the home or business office.

Trunks connect two switches. The type of trunk depends on the function of the switches the trunk is connecting. The term *tie-line* is frequently used instead of *trunk* to describe a dedicated line connecting two telephone switches within a single organization. The following is a list of trunk types:

- **Interoffice trunk** connects two CO switches. Also called a PSTN switch trunk.

- **Tandem trunk** connects central offices within a geographic area.

- **Toll-connecting trunk** connects the CO to the long-distance office.

- **Intertoll trunk** connects two long-distance offices.

- **Tie trunk** connects two PBXs. Also called a private trunk.

- **PBX-to-CO trunk or CO-to-PBX business line** connects the CO switch to the enterprise PBX.

Figure 15-2 shows an example of the PSTN. All phones connect to their local CO via the local loop. Calls between Phones 1 and 2 and between Phones 4 and 5 go through interoffice trunks. Calls between Phones 2 and 3 go through tandem trunks within a region. When you place calls between Texas and Massachusetts, they are forwarded to the long-distance toll provider via a toll-connecting trunk and are routed through intertoll trunks.

Figure 15-2 *Local Loops and Trunks*

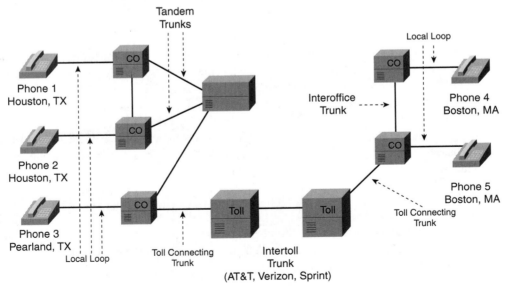

Ports

You can use several ports to connect to voice end stations (phones) and private voice switches:

- **Foreign Exchange Station (FXS)** connects to an end device such as an analog phone or fax machine. It provides line power, dial tone, and ring voltage.

- **Foreign Exchange Office (FXO)** connects to the PSTN. It is an RJ-11 connector that allows an analog connection to be directed to the PSTN's central office or to a station interface on a PBX. The FXO sits on the switch end of the connection. It plugs directly into the line side of the switch, so the switch thinks the FXO interface is a telephone.

- **Ear and Mouth (E&M)** connects private switches. It is an analog trunk used to connect to a voice switch; it supports tie-line facilities or signaling between phone switches. E&M can be connected with two-wire and four-wire. E&M is also called Earth and Magnet.

- **Channelized T1 (or E1)** is commonly used as a digital trunk line to connect to a phone switch where each DS0 supports an active phone call connection. Provides 24 (for T1) or 32 (for E1) channels or DS0 for voice calls. The total bandwidth for a T1 is 1.536 Mbps, and the total bandwidth for an E1 is 2.048 Mbps.

- **ISDN Primary Rate Interface (PRI)** is a digital trunk link used to connect to a phone switch. A separate channel is used for common channel-signaling messages. T1 PRIs provide 23 channels for voice, and E1 PRIs provide 30 channels for voice.

Major Analog and Digital Signaling Types

Signaling is needed to provide the state of telephones, digit dialing, and other information. For a call to be placed, managed, and closed, all of the following signaling categories have to occur:

- **Supervisory** provides call control and phone state (on-hook and off-hook).

- **Addressing** provides dialed digits.

- **Informational** provides information such as dial and busy tones and progress indicators.

These different signaling categories are provided by analog and digital signaling types.

The signaling type depends on the type of connection. The major areas are

- CO to phone (loop and ground start signaling)

- PBX to PBX (E&M)

- T1/E1 Channel Associated Signaling (CAS)

- ISDN PRI Common Channel Signaling (CCS)

- Q Signaling (Q.SIG)

- SS7 interswitch PSTN signaling

Loop-Start Signaling

Loop-start signaling is an analog signaling technique used to indicate on-hook and off-hook conditions in the network. It is commonly used between the telephone set and the CO, PBX, or FXS module. As shown in Figure 15-3, with loop-start the local loop is open when the phone is on-hook. When the phone is taken off-hook, a –48 direct current (DC) voltage loops from the CO through the phone and back. Loop-start signaling is used for residential lines.

Figure 15-3 *Loop-Start Signaling*

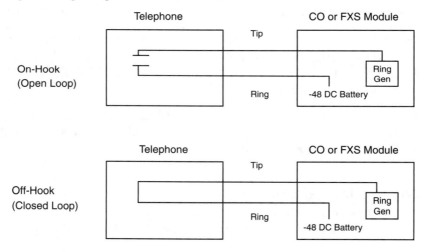

Ground-Start Signaling

Ground-start signaling is an analog signaling technique used to indicate on-hook and off-hook conditions. Ground-start is commonly used in switch-to-switch connections. The difference between ground-start and loop-start is that ground-start requires the closing of the loop at both locations. Ground-start is commonly used by PBXs.

The standard way to transport voice between two telephone sets is to use tip and ring lines. Tip and ring lines are the twisted pair of wires that connect to your phone via an RJ-11 connector. As shown in Figure 15-4, the CO switch grounds the tip line. The PBX detects that the tip line is grounded and closes the loop by removing ground from the ring line.

Figure 15-4   *Ground-Start Signaling*

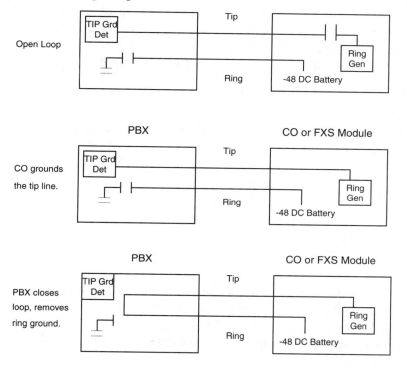

E&M Signaling

E&M is an analog signaling technique often used in PBX-to-PBX tie-lines. E&M is receive and transmit, or more commonly called ear and mouth. Cisco routers support four E&M signal types: Type I, Type II, Type III, and Type V. Types I and II are most popular on the American continents. Type V is used in the United States and Europe.

There are also three forms of E&M dial supervision signaling to seize the E&M trunk:

- **Immediate start**—This is the most basic protocol. In this technique, the originating switch goes off-hook, waits for a finite period of time (for example, 200 ms), and then sends the dial digits without regard for the far end.

- **Wink start**—Wink is the most commonly used protocol. In this technique, the originating switch goes off-hook, waits for a temporary off-hook pulse from the other end (which is interpreted as an indication to proceed), and then sends the dial digits.

- **Delay dial**—In this technique, the originating side goes off-hook, waits for about 200 ms, and then checks whether the far end is on-hook. If the far end is on-hook, it outputs dial digits. If the far end is off-hook, it waits until it goes on-hook and then outputs dial digits.

CAS and CCS Signaling

Digital signaling has two major forms: Channel Associated Signaling (CAS) and Common Channel Signaling (CCS). The major difference is that with CAS the signaling is included in the same channel as the voice call. With CCS the signaling is provided in a separate channel. Table 15-2 shows the common types of CAS and CCS. They are covered in the following sections.

Table 15-2 *Common CAS and CCS Signaling Types*

From	Signaling Type
CAS	T1 or E1 signaling DTMF
CCS	ISDN PRI or BRI QSIG SS7

T1/E1 CAS

Digital T1 CAS uses selected bits within a selected channel to transmit signaling information. CAS is also called robbed-bit signaling or in-band signaling in the T1 implementation. Robbed-bit CAS works with digital voice because losing an occasional voice sample does not affect the voice quality. The disadvantage of robbed-bit CAS is that it cannot be used on channels that might carry voice or data without reducing the data rate to 56 Kbps to ensure that signaling changes do not damage the data stream.

E1 CAS uses a separate channel in the shared medium for CAS, so it does not have this disadvantage. The E1 signaling bits are channel-associated, but they are not in-band.

ISDN PRI/BRI

ISDN T1 PRI provides 23 64-kbps B (bearer) channels for voice, with a separate 64-kbps D (data signaling) channel for signaling. The ISDN E1 PRI provides 30 B channels. The use of messages in a separate channel, rather than preassigned bits, is also called common-channel signaling. Any bit in the signaling channel is common to all the channels sharing the medium rather than dedicated to a particular single channel. ISDN provides the advantage of not changing bits in the channels and thus is useful for data traffic in addition to voice traffic.

The ISDN BRI interface includes two 64-kbps B channels for voice or data and a separate 16-kbps D channel that provides signaling for the interface.

Q.SIG

Q.SIG is the preferred signaling protocol used between PBX switches. It is a standards-based protocol, based on ISDN, that provides services. It is feature-transparent between PBXs. It is interoperable with public and private ISDN networks and provides no restrictions to private dial plans. QSIG is also used between Cisco's Unified CallManager and enterprise PBX in hybrid implementations.

SS7

SS7 is a global ITU standard for telecommunications control that allows voice-network calls to be routed and controlled by call-control centers. SS7 is used between PSTN switches. SS7 implements call setup, routing, and control, ensuring that intermediate and far-end switches are available when a call is placed. With SS7, telephone companies can implement modern consumer-telephone services such as caller ID, toll-free numbers, call forwarding, and so on.

SS7 provides mechanisms for exchanging control, status, and routing messages on public telephone networks. SS7 messages pass over a separate channel than that used for voice communication. You use Common Channel Signaling 7 (CCS7) when speaking about SS7 signaling. CCS7 controls call signaling, routing, and connections between CO, interexchange carrier, and competitive local exchange carrier switches. Figure 15-5 shows the connectivity between SS7 components.

Figure 15-5 *SS7 Signaling Components*

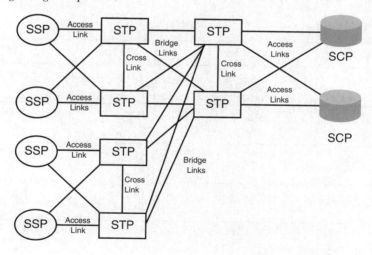

As shown in Figure 15-5, SS7 has the following system components:

- **Signaling Control Point (SCP)**—Databases that provide the necessary information for special call processing and routing, including 800 and 900 call services, credit-card calls, local number portability, cellular roaming services, and advanced call-center applications.

- **Signaling Transfer Point (STP)**—Receives and routes incoming signaling messages toward their destinations. STPs are deployed in mated pairs and share the traffic between them.

- **Signaling Switching Point (SSP)**—Telephone switches equipped with SS7 software and signaling links. Each SSP is connected to both STPs in a mated pair.

Addressing Digit Signaling

There are two methods for submitting analog address digits to place a call:

- Pulse or rotary dialing

- Dual-tone multifrequency (DTMF) dialing

Pulse dialing uses the opening and closing of a switch at the telephone set. A rotary register at the CO detects the opening and closing of the loop. When the number 5 is dialed on a rotary phone, the dial mechanism opens and closes five times, each one-tenth of a second apart.

DTMF uses two tones simultaneously to indicate the dialed number. Table 15-3 shows the phone keypad and the frequencies used. For example, when the number 5 is dialed, the frequencies 770 Hz and 1336 Hz are sent to the CO.

Table 15-3   *DTMF Frequencies*

Frequency	1209 Hz	1336 Hz	1477 Hz
697 Hz	1	ABC 2	DEF 3
770 Hz	GHI 4	JKL 5	MNO 6
852 Hz	PRS 7	TUV 8	WXY 9
941 Hz	*	OPER 0	#

PSTN Numbering Plan

The PSTN uses the ITU E.164 standard for public network addressing. The E.164 standard uses a maximum of 15 digits and makes each phone unique in the PSTN. Examples of E.164 addresses are the residential, business, IP phones, and cell phones that you use every day. Each country is assigned a country code to identify it. The country codes can be one to three digits in length. Table 15-4 shows some examples of country codes.

Table 15-4 *E.164 Country Codes*

Country Code	Country
1	United States, Canada
1-787, 1-939	Puerto Rico
55	Brazil
39	Italy
86	China
20	Egypt
91	India
49	Germany
380	Ukraine
44	United Kingdom
81	Japan
52	Mexico
966	Saudi Arabia

The ITU website that lists country codes is located at http://www.itu.int/itudoc/itu-t/ob-lists/icc/e164_763.html.

Each country divides its network into area codes that identify a geographic region or city. The United States uses the North American Numbering Plan (NANP). NANP has the address format of *NXX-NXX-XXXX*, where *N* is any number from 2 to 9 and *X* is any number from 0 to 9. The first three digits are the area code. The address is further divided into the office code (also known as prefix) and line number. The prefix is three digits, and the line number is four digits. The line number identifies the phone.

An example of a PSTN address in the United States is 1-713-781-0300. The 1 identifies the United States; the 713 identifies an area code in the Houston, Texas, geographical region. The 781 identifies a CO in west Houston. The 0300 identifies the phone.

Another example of a PSTN address is 52-55-8452-1110. The country code 52 identifies the country of Mexico. The area code 55 identifies the geographic area of Mexico City. The office code 8452 and line number 1110 follows.

Other PSTN Services

The PSTN provides a suite of services in addition to call setup and routing:

- Centrex

- Voice mail

- Database services

- Interactive voice response (IVR)

- Automatic call distribution (ACD)

Centrex Services

Companies can use the local phone company to handle all their internal and external calls from the CO. In this voice model, the CO acts as the company's voice switch, with PBX features such as four-digit extension dialing, voice mail, and call holds and transfers. The Centrex service gives the company the appearance of having its own PBX network.

Voice Mail

PSTN service providers can enable voice messaging for customers that request the service. Voice mail provides automated call answering and message recording. Users can then retrieve the message and forward it to other extensions.

Database Services

The PSTN must keep call detail records (CDR) in the database systems. CDR information includes all types of call information, such as called party, caller, time, duration, locations, and user service plans. This information is used for billing and reporting.

IVR

IVR systems connect incoming calls to an audio playback system. IVR queues the calls, provides prerecorded announcements, prompts the caller for key options, provides the caller with information, and transfers the call to another switch extension or agent. IVR is used in customer call centers run by companies in all industries to gather and provide information to the customers before transferring them to agents.

ACD

ACD routes calls to a group of agents. ACD keeps statistics on each agent, such as the number of calls and their duration. Based on the statistics, the ACD system then can evenly distribute the calls to the agents or to the appropriate agent skill group. ACD is used by airline reservation systems, customer service departments, and other call centers.

Voice Terminology

You must consider voice traffic requirements when designing a network. The CCDA must be familiar with the following voice engineering terms.

Grade of Service

Grade of service (GoS) is the probability that a call will be blocked when attempting to seize a circuit. If it is determined that a network has a P.02 GoS, the probability is that 2 percent of all attempted calls will be blocked.

Erlangs

An Erlang is a telecommunications traffic unit of measurement representing the continuous use of one voice path for one hour. This means the use of a single voice resource for one hour (3600 seconds). It describes the total traffic volume of one hour. Erlangs determine voice-call usage for bandwidth requirements for voice network designs, including VoIP. It helps determine if a system has been provisioned with enough resources.

If a group of users makes 20 calls in an hour and each call lasts 10 minutes, the Erlangs are calculated as follows:

20 calls per hour * 10 minutes per call = 200 minutes per hour

traffic volume = (200 minutes per hour) / (60 minutes per hour)
= 3.33 Erlangs

There are three common Erlang models:

- **Erlang B** assumes that a blocked call is blocked, not delayed. It is the most common model used.

- **Extended Erlang B** adds a "retry" percentage to the Erlang B model. It assumes that there is an additional load when calls are reattempted after a failed call.

- **Erlang C** assumes that blocked calls are actually delayed. This model is used in call centers where calls are queued for service.

Centum Call Second (CCS)

A Centum Call Second (CCS) represents one call occupying a channel for 100 seconds. It is the equivalent of 1/36th of an Erlang. In other words, 360 CCS equals 1 Erlang (3600 seconds).

Busy Hour

The busy hour is the specific hour within a 24-hour period in which the highest traffic load occurs. Most calls are placed and are of longer durations during this hour. It is also called peak hour.

Busy Hour Traffic (BHT)

BHT is the amount of voice traffic that occurs in the busy hour, expressed in Erlangs. It is calculated by multiplying the average call duration by the number of calls in the hour and then dividing that by 3600.

For example, if 300 calls occurred during the busy hour, with an average duration of 150 seconds, the BHT is calculated as follows:

BHT = (150 seconds * 300 calls per hour) / (3600 seconds per hour)
BHT = 12.5 Erlangs

Blocking Probability

The blocking probability is the probability that a call will be blocked. A blocking probability of 0.02 means that 2 percent of the calls will be blocked.

Call Detail Records

Call detail records include statistical and other information related to all calls placed. Information included in CDRs includes call time, call duration, source phone number, dialed phone number, and the amount billed. For VoIP networks, the CDR may also include source and destination IP addresses.

Integrated Multiservice Networks

The introduction of packet-voice technology allows the convergence of data and voice networks. This lets companies save toll charges on voice telephone calls. It also reduces companies' total cost of ownership by not having to build and operate separate networks for voice, video, and data.

In multiservice networks, digitized (coded) voice is packaged into packets, cells, or frames; sent as data throughout the networks; and converted back to analog voice. The underlying protocols used for these converged services are

- Voice over Frame Relay (VoFR)

- Voice over Asynchronous Transfer Mode (VoATM)

- Voice over Internet Protocol (VoIP)

Initially, VoFR and VoATM were used but lost ground to VoIP solutions. VoIP is also referred to as IP telephony (IPT) when it is integrated with IP-based signaling and call control. IPT is how almost all new deployments are being implemented.

VoFR

VoFR permits enterprise customers with existing Frame Relay networks to implement packetized voice. Access devices or cards access the Frame Relay network. PBX vendors provide VoFR cards for their switches to support call routing over the Frame Relay network. Figure 15-6 shows three PBXs connected with trunks using VoFR. The PSTN is used for backup if the Frame Relay circuit goes down. The disadvantage of VoFR is that it provides only convergence in the WAN; it still requires local dedicated telephony equipment and networks. It cannot provide convergence to LANs without a network protocol that can span the data link technologies, such as IP.

Figure 15-6 *VoFR Trunks Between PBXs*

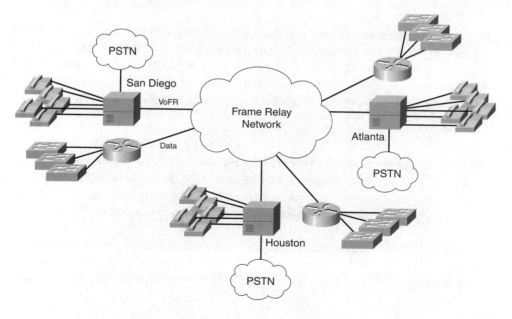

One standard for VoFR is Frame Relay Forum (FRF) 11.1. It establishes specifications for call setup, coding types, and packet formats for VoFR service. It provides the basis for interoperability between vendors.

A number of mechanisms can minimize delay and variable delay (jitter) on a Frame Relay network. The presence of long data frames on a low-speed Frame Relay link can cause unacceptable delays for time-sensitive voice frames. To reduce this problem, some vendors implement smaller frame sizes to help reduce delay and delay variation. FRF.12 is an industry-standard approach to doing this, so products from different vendors can interoperate and consumers will know what type of voice quality to expect. To ensure voice quality, you should set the committed information rate (CIR) of each permanent virtual circuit (PVC) to ensure that voice frames are not discarded.

VoATM

VoATM permits enterprise customers to use their existing ATM networks for voice traffic. ATM inherently provides guaranteed QoS for voice traffic that IP protocols alone cannot provide. ATM can provide the service levels and functionality required to support voice traffic for the WAN. For enterprise networks that have ATM, VoATM provides a mechanism to connect enterprise PBXs via ATM and other VoATM applications.

With ATM, constant bit rate (CBR) or variable bit rate–real time (VBR-rt) classes of service (CoS) provide levels of bandwidth and delay guarantees for voice. Chapter 5, "WAN Technologies," covers ATM.

PBX vendors provide VoATM cards for their switches to support call routing over the Frame Relay network. Figure 15-7 shows three PBXs that are connected via trunks using VoATM. The PSTN is used for backup if the ATM circuit goes down. As with VoFR, the disadvantage of VoATM is that it provides only convergence in the WAN. It cannot provide convergence within the LAN without a network protocol that can span the data link technologies, such as IP.

VoIP

VoIP provides transport of voice over the IP protocol family. IP makes voice globally available regardless of the data link protocol in use (Ethernet, ATM, Frame Relay). With VoIP, enterprises do not have to build separate voice and data networks. Integrating voice and data into a single converged network reduces the costs of owning and managing separate networks.

Figure 15-8 shows a company that has separate voice and data networks. Phones connect to local PBXs, and the PBXs are connected using TDM trunks. Off-net calls are routed to the PSTN. The data network uses LAN switches connected to WAN routers. The WAN for data uses Frame Relay.

Separate operations and management systems are required for these networks. Each system has its corresponding monthly WAN charges and personnel, resulting in additional costs.

Figure 15-7   *VoATM Trunks Between PBXs*

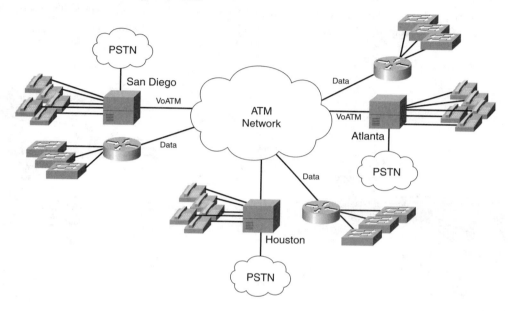

Figure 15-8   *Separate Voice and Data Networks*

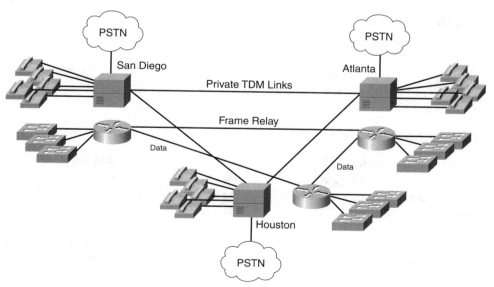

With IP telephony, you can reduce the number of systems, circuits, and support personnel. Figure 15-9 shows a multiservice IP telephony network that employs Ethernet-based phones with server-based call processing with gateway routers. Survivable Remote Site Telephony (SRST) is used for failover or backup to the PSTN if WAN failure occurs. On-net calls travel through the Frame Relay network, and off-net calls are forwarded to the PSTN. The PSTN link is also used if voice overflow or congestion occurs on the WAN network. Calls are then routed to the PSTN.

Figure 15-9 *Converged VoIP Network*

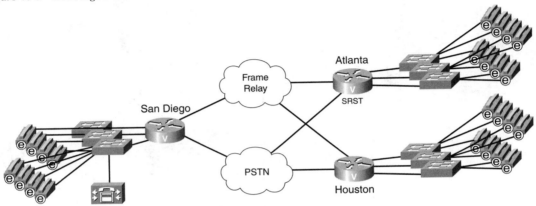

IPT Components

Cisco's IPT architecture divides voice system architectures into four major functional areas, as shown in Figure 15-10:

- Client endpoints
- Call processing
- Service applications
- Voice Enabled Infrastructure

Client endpoints include the IP phones, analog and digital gateways, and digital signal processor (DSP) farms. Included here is Cisco's IP Communicator, which is the software-based IP phone that runs on a PC or laptop. Gateways are used to access PBXs, analog phones, other IP telephony deployments, or the PSTN.

The Cisco Unified CallManager (CM) fulfills the role of call processing. The CM servers are the "brains" of the voice dial plan and are used to establish IPT calls between IP phones.

Figure 15-10   *Cisco IPT Functional Areas*

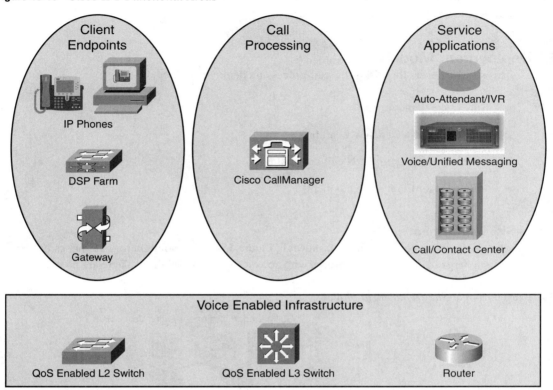

Service applications include IVR, Auto Attendant, and Unity Unified Messaging System for voice mail. Cisco IP Contact Center (IPCC) is used for enterprise call center applications. In addition, a standards-based Telephony Application Programming Interface (TAPI) allows third-party companies to develop applications for the Cisco Unified CallManager.

The voice-enabled infrastructure includes QoS-enabled devices such as LAN switches and routers. These devices are configured to be IPT-aware and provide service guarantees to the VoIP traffic. For example, LAN switches are configured with voice VLANs and Power over Ethernet (PoE) to service the IP phones. Also, WAN routers are configured with queuing techniques to prioritize VoIP streams over other traffic types.

Design Goals of IP Telephony

The overall goal of IP telephony is to replace traditional TDM-based telephony by deploying IPT components on existing IP networks. IPT should be highly available and as reliable as existing voice networks. IPT should provide greater flexibility and productivity while providing lower cost of ownership by using a converged network. IPT also allows third-party software providers to develop new applications for IP phones.

IPT Deployment Models

This section covers the Cisco IPT call-processing deployment models:

- Single-site deployment

- Multisite centralized WAN call processing

- Multisite distributed WAN call processing

- CallManager Express deployment

Single-Site Deployment

The single-site deployment model, shown in Figure 15-11, is a solution for enterprises located in a single large building or campus area with no voice on the WAN links. There are no remote sites.

Figure 15-11 *Single-Site Deployment Model*

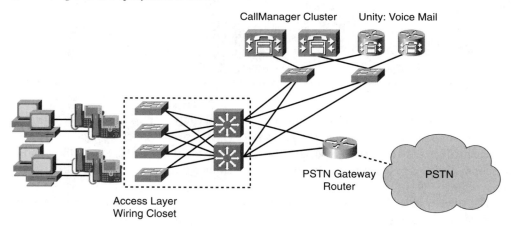

A single CM cluster is deployed for redundancy in the server farm, and Unity is used for voice mail, with or without unified messaging. IP phones are deployed on PoE LAN switches. The Cisco Unified CM supports up to 30,000 IP devices in a cluster. Gateway routers are procured with PRI cards to connect to the enterprise PBX (during migration) or the PSTN.

Multisite Centralized WAN Call-Processing Model

The centralized WAN call-processing model is a solution for medium enterprises with one large location and many remote sites. Figure 15-12 shows the centralized call-processing model. A CM cluster with multiple servers is deployed for redundancy at the large site. Call processing and voice mail servers are located in only the main site. Remote-site IP phones register to the CM cluster located in the main site. PoE switches are used to power all IP phones. Remote sites use voice-enabled gateway routers with SRST for redundancy.

Figure 15-12 *Multisite Centralized WAN CM Deployment Model*

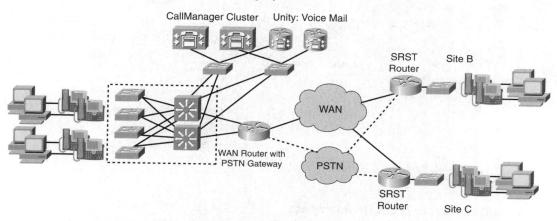

On the WAN, QoS features are configured to prioritize the VoIP packets over other packet types. In the event of WAN failure, SRST configured routers forward calls through the PSTN. The PSTN circuit can be used for local inbound and outbound calls at the remote site. In this model, call admission control (CAC) is configured to impose a limit on the number of on-net calls permitted between sites.

Multisite Distributed WAN Call-Processing Model

The multisite distributed WAN call-processing model is a solution for large enterprises with several large locations. Figure 15-13 shows the distributed WAN model. Up to 30,000 users are supported per CM cluster. Several CM clusters are deployed at the large sites for redundancy, and Unity servers are used for messaging. Intercluster trucks are created to establish communication between clusters. IP phones are deployed on PoE LAN switches.

This model also supports remote sites to be distributed off the large sites. CAC between the CM and Cisco IOS gateway with gatekeeper (GK) is supported. Also, this model supports multiple WAN codecs. Compression of VoIP is done between sites.

Figure 15-13 *Multisite Distributed WAN CM Deployment Model*

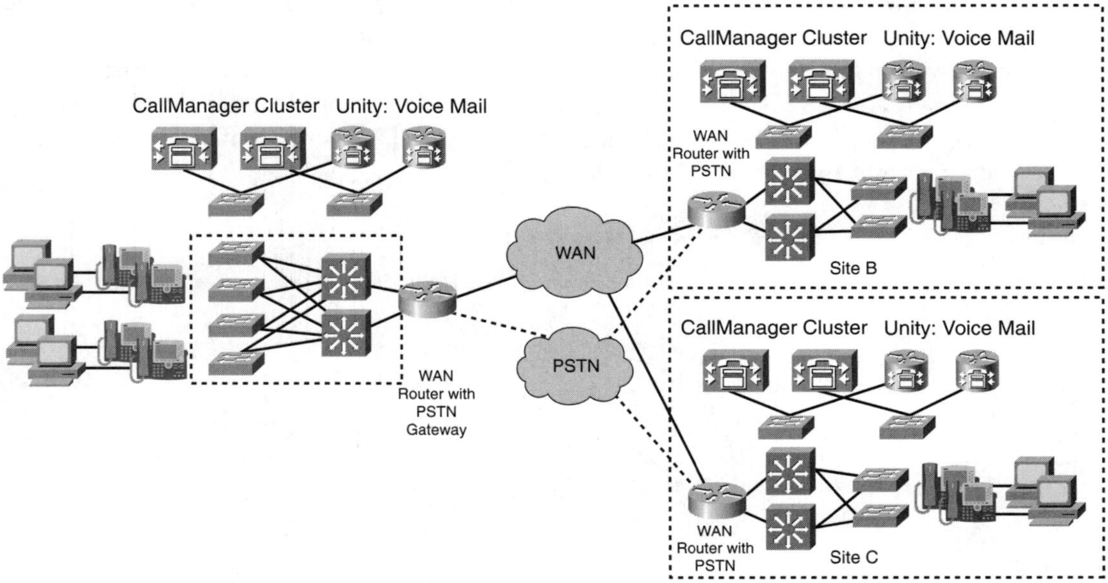

Unified CallManager Express Deployments

Cisco provides Express versions of its CallManager, Unity, and IPCC solutions that are installed in a router. CallManager Express (CME) provides the call processing capabilities of CM on a router. Unity Express and IPCC Express also provide the same services on the router. CME deployments support up to 240 Cisco IP phones. It is a lower-cost solution for small branch offices.

Codecs

Because speech is an analog signal, it must be converted into digital signals for transmission over digital systems. The first basic modulation and coding technique was Pulse Code Modulation (PCM). The international standard for PCM is G.711. With PCM, analog speech is sampled 8000 times a second. Each speech sample is mapped onto 8 bits. Thus, PCM produces (8000 samples per second) * (8 bits per sample) = 64,000 bits per second = 64-kbps coded bit rate. Other coding schemes have been developed to further compress the data representation of speech. Most voice compression codes, such as G.729, begin with a G.711-coded voice stream.

Analog-to-Digital Signal Conversion

The steps involved in converting from analog-to-digital signaling are filtering, sampling, and digitizing. First, signals over 4000 Hz are filtered out of the analog signal. Second, the signal is sampled at 8000 times per second using Pulse Amplitude Modulation (PAM). Third, the amplitude samples are converted to a binary code.

The digitizing process is divided further into two subprocesses:

- **Companding**—This term comes from "compressing and expanding." The analog samples are compressed into logarithmic segments.

- **Quantization and coding**—This process converts the analog value into a distinct value that is assigned a digital value.

Codec Standards

Codecs transform analog signals into a digital bit stream and digital signals back into analog signals. Figure 15-14 shows that an analog signal is digitized with a coder for digital transport. The decoder converts the digital signal into analog form.

Figure 15-14 *Codec*

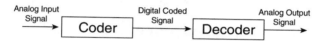

Each codec provides a certain quality of speech. A measure used to describe the quality of speech is the Mean Opinion Score (MOS). With MOS, a large group of listeners judges the quality of speech from 5 (best) to 1 (bad). The scores are then averaged to provide the MOS for each sample. For example, G.711 has a MOS of 4.1, and G.729 has a MOS of 3.92. The default codec setting for VoIP dial peers in Cisco IOS Software is G.729 (g729r8). Other codec standards are shown in Table 15-5. An explanation of the compression techniques is beyond the scope of the CCDA test.

Table 15-5 *Codec Standards*

Codec	Bit Rate	MOS	Description
G.711u	64 kbps	4.1	PCM. Mu-law version used in North America and Japan. Samples speech 8000 times per second, represented in 8 bits.
G.711a	64 kbps	4.1	PCM. A-law used in Europe and international routes.
G.723.1	6.3 kbps	3.9	Multipulse Excitation–Maximum Likelihood Quantization (MPE-MLQ).
G.723.1	5.3 kbps	3.65	Algebraic Code–Excited Linear Prediction (ACELP).
G.726	16/24/32/40 kbps	3.85	Adaptive Differential Pulse-Code Modulation (AD-PCM).
G.728	16 kbps	3.61	Low-Delay CELP (LDCELP).
G.729	8 kbps	3.92	Conjugate Structure ACELP (CS-ACELP).

VoIP Control and Transport Protocols

You use a number of protocols to set up IP telephony clients and calls and to transport voice packets. Some of the most significant protocols are

- **Dynamic Host Configuration Protocol (DHCP)**—To establish IP configuration parameters

- **Domain Name System (DNS)**—To obtain IP addresses of the Trivial File Transfer Protocol (TFTP) server

- **TFTP**—To obtain configurations

- **Skinny Station Control Protocol (SSCP)**—For call establishment

- **Real-time Transport Protocol (RTP)**—For voice stream (VoIP) station-to-station traffic in an ongoing call

- **Real-time Transport Control Protocol (RTCP)**—For call control

- **Media Gateway Control Protocol (MGCP)**—For call establishment with gateways

- **H.323**—For call establishment with gateways from the ITU

- **Session Initiation Protocol (SIP)**—For call establishment with gateways, defined by the Internet Engineering Task Force (IETF)

DHCP, DNS, and TFTP

IP phones use DHCP to obtain their IP addressing information: IP address, subnet mask, and default gateway. DHCP also provides the IP address of the DNS servers and the name or IP address of the TFTP server. You use TFTP to download the IP phone operating system and configuration. Both DHCP and TFTP run over UDP.

SSCP

SSCP is a Cisco-proprietary client/server signaling protocol for call setup and control. SSCP runs over TCP. SSCP is called a "skinny" protocol because it uses less overhead than the call-setup protocols used by H.323. IP phones use SSCP to register with CallManager and to establish calls. SSCP is used for VoIP call signaling and for features such as Message Waiting Indicators. This protocol is not used in the voice media streams between IP phones.

RTP and RTCP

In VoIP, RTP transports audio streams. RTP is a transport layer protocol that carries digitized voice in its payload. RTP is defined in RFC 1889. RTP runs over UDP, which has lower delay than TCP. Because of the time sensitivity of voice traffic and the delay incurred in retransmissions, UDP is used instead of TCP. Real-time traffic is carried over UDP ports ranging from 16,384 to 16,624.

The only requirement is that the RTP data be transported on an even port and that the RTCP data be carried on the next odd port. RTCP is also defined in RFC 1889. RTCP is a session layer protocol that monitors the delivery of data and provides control and identification functions. Figure 15-15 shows a VoIP packet with the IP, UDP, and RTP headers. Notice that the sum of the header lengths is 20 + 8 + 12 = 40 bytes.

Figure 15-15 *IP, UDP, and RTP Headers of a VoIP Packet*

WAN links use RTP header compression to reduce the size of voice packets. This is also called Compressed RTP (CRTP). As shown in Figure 15-16, CRTP reduces the IP/UDP/RTP header from 40 bytes to 2 or 4 bytes—a significant decrease in overhead. CRTP happens on a hop-by-hop basis, with compression and decompression occurring on every link. It must be configured on both ends of the link.

Figure 15-16 *CRTP*

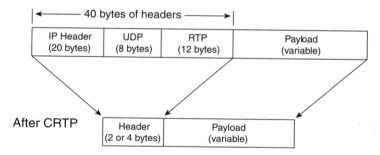

MGCP

MGCP is a client/server signaling protocol used to control gateways in VoIP networks. MGCP is defined in RFC 3435. MGCP's primary function is to control and supervise connection attempts between different media gateways. MGCP gateways handle translation between audio signals and the IP network.

MGCP defines call agents and endpoints. Call agents control the gateways. An endpoint is any gateway interface, such as a PRI trunk or analog interface.

H.323

H.323 is a standard published by the ITU that works as a framework document for multimedia protocols including voice, video, and data conferencing for use over packet-switched networks.

H.323 describes terminals and other entities (such as gatekeepers) to provide multimedia applications. Cisco IOS gateways use H.323 to communicate with Cisco CallManager.

H.323 includes the following elements:

- **Terminals**—Telephones, video phones, and voice mail systems—devices that provide real-time two-way voice.

- **Multipoint Control Units (MCU)**—Responsible for managing multipoint conferences.

- **Gateways**—Composed of a media gateway controller for call signaling and a media gateway to handle media. Provide translation services between H.323 endpoints and non-H.323 devices.

- **Gatekeeper**—Provides call control and signaling services to H.323 endpoints. This function is normally done by an IOS router.

H.323 terminals must support the following standards:

- H.245

- Q.931

- H.225

- RTP/RTCP

H.245 specifies messages for opening and closing channels for media streams and other commands, requests, and indications. It is a conferencing control protocol.

Q.931 is a standard for call signaling used by H.323 within the context of H.225.

H.225 specifies messages for call control, including signaling between endpoints, registration and admissions, and packetization and synchronization of media streams. It performs registration, admission, and status (RAS) signaling for H.323 sessions.

RTP is the transport layer protocol used to transport VoIP packets. RTCP is a session layer protocol.

H.323 includes a series of protocols for multimedia, as shown in Table 15-6.

Table 15-6 *H.323 Protocols*

	Video	Audio	Data	Transport
H.323 protocol	H.261	G.711	T.122	RTP
	H.263	G.722	T.124	H.225
		G.723.1	T.125	H.235
		G.728	T.126	H.245
		G.729	T.127	H.450.1
				H.450.2
				H.450.3
				X.224.0

Gatekeeper Use for Scalability

As a network grows, multiple gateways are placed to communicate with multiple endpoints. Each gateway in a zone needs to be configured with a complete dialing plan. The number of logical connections is calculated with the following formula:

$$L = (N * (N - 1)) / 2$$

where N is the number of gateways in the network.

For example, a network with 7 gateways would have 21 logical connections. With a gatekeeper, simple dial plans are configured on each gateway, and complete dialing is configured on the gatekeeper. This makes network operations and maintenance easier.

SIP

SIP is a protocol defined by the IETF and specified in RFC 2543. It is an alternative multimedia framework to H.323, developed specifically for IP telephony. It is meant to be a replacement to H.323. Cisco now supports SIP on its phones and gateways.

SIP is an application layer control (signaling) protocol for creating, modifying, and terminating Internet multimedia conferences, Internet telephone calls, and multimedia distribution. Communication between members of a session can be via a multicast, a unicast mesh, or a combination.

SIP is designed as part of the overall IETF multimedia data and control architecture that incorporates protocols such as the following:

- Resource Reservation Protocol (RSVP) (RFC 2205) for reserving network resources

- RTP (RFC 1889) for transporting real-time data and providing QoS feedback

- Real-Time Streaming Protocol (RTSP) (RFC 2326) for controlling delivery of streaming media

- Session Announcement Protocol (SAP) (RFC 2974) for advertising multimedia sessions via multicast

- Session Description Protocol (SDP) (RFC 2327) for describing multimedia sessions

SIP supports user mobility by using proxy and redirect servers to redirect requests to the user's current location. Users can register their current locations, and SIP location services provide the location of user agents.

SIP uses a modular architecture that includes the following components:

- **SIP user agent**—Endpoints that create and terminate sessions, SIP phones, SIP PC clients, or gateways

- **SIP proxy server**—Routes messages between SIP user agents

- **SIP redirect server**—Call-control device used to provide routing information to user agents

- **SIP registrar server**—Stores the location of all user agents in the domain or subdomain

- **SIP location services**—Provide logical location of user agents; used by the proxy, redirect, and registrar servers

- **Back-to-back user agent**—Call-control device that allows centralized control of network call flows

IPT Design

This section covers network design issues and solutions that a designer needs to be aware of when designing a network for IPT. Topics such as bandwidth requirements, delay, and QoS schemes should be considered.

Bandwidth

VoIP calls need to meet bandwidth and delay parameters. The amount of bandwidth required depends on the codec used, the Layer 2 protocols, and whether VAD is enabled. For the purpose of call control, you can use the following bandwidth requirements for VoIP design:

■ G.729 calls use 26 kbps

■ G.711 calls use 80 kbps

When you're designing for VoIP networks, the total bandwidth for voice, data, and video should not exceed 75 percent sustained of the provisioned link capacity during peak times. Use the following formula to provision interface speeds:

link capacity = [required bandwidth for voice] + [required bandwidth for video] + [required bandwidth for data]

The remaining bandwidth is used by routing, multicast, and management protocols.

NOTE   G.729 is the recommended codec for calls over the WAN because of its lower bandwidth requirements and higher Mean Opinion Score.

VAD

As we listen and pause between sentences, typical voice conversations can contain up to 60 percent silence in each direction. In circuit-switched telephone networks, all voice calls use fixed-bandwidth 64-kbps links regardless of how much of the conversation is speech and how much is silence. In multiservice networks, all conversation and silence is packetized. Using Voice Activity Detection (VAD), you can suppress packets of silence. Silence suppression at the source IP telephone or VoIP gateway increases the number of calls or data volumes that can be carried over the links, more effectively utilizing network bandwidth. Bandwidth savings are at least 35 percent in conservative estimates. VAD is enabled by default for all VoIP calls.

Table 15-7 shows how much bandwidth is required based on different parameters. Notice that for G.729, bandwidth is reduced from 26.4 kbps to 17.2 kbps with VAD and to 7.3 kbps with VAD and CRTP enabled.

Table 15-7 *VoIP Bandwidth Requirements with CRTP and VAD*

Technique Codec Bit Rate (kbps)	Payload Size (Bytes)	Bandwidth Multilink PPP (MLP) or FRF.12 (kbps)	Bandwidth with CRTP MLP or FRF.12 (kbps)	Bandwidth with VAD MLP or FRF.12 (kbps)	Bandwidth with CRTP and VAD MLP or FRF.12 (kbps)
G.711 (64)	240	76	66	50	43
G.711 (64)	160 (default)	83	68	54	44
G.726 (32)	120	44	34	29	22
G.726 (32)	80 (default)	50	35	33	23
G.726 (24)	80	38	27	25	17
G.726 (24)	60 (default)	42	27	27	18
G.728 (16)	80	25	18	17	12
G.728 (16)	40 (default)	35	19	23	13
G.729 (8)	40	17.2	9.6	11.2	6.3
G.729 (8)	20 (default)	26.4	11.2	17.2	7.3
G.723.1 (6.3)	48	12.3	7.4	8.0	4.8
G.723.1 (6.3)	24 (default)	18.4	8.4	12.0	5.5
G.723.1 (5.3)	40	11.4	6.4	7.4	4.1
G.723.1 (5.3)	20 (default)	17.5	7.4	11.4	4.8

Cisco has developed a tool, available on its website, that can be used to obtain accurate estimates for IPT design. It also adds an additional 5 percent for signaling overhead. The tool is the Voice Codec Bandwidth Calculator and it is available at http://tools.cisco.com/Support/VBC/do/CodecCalc1.do.

Delay Components

The ITU's G.114 recommendation specifies that the one-way delay between endpoints should not exceed 150 ms to be acceptable commercial voice quality. In private networks, somewhat longer delays might be acceptable for economic reasons. Delay components are one of two major types: fixed delay and variable delay.

Fixed delay includes

■ Propagation delay

■ Processing delay

- Serialization delay

- Dejitter delay

Propagation delay is how long it takes a packet to travel between two points. It is based on the distance between the two endpoints. You cannot overcome this delay component. The speed of light is the theoretical limit. A reasonable planning figure is approximately 10 ms per 1000 miles, or 6 ms per 1000 km. This figure allows for media degradation and devices internal to the transport network. Propagation delay is noticeable on satellite links.

Processing delay includes coding, compression, decoding, and decompression delays. G.729 has a delay of 15 ms, and G.711 PCM has a delay of 0.75 ms. The delay created by packetization is also a processing delay. Packetization delay occurs in the process of waiting for a number of digital voice samples before sending out a packet.

Serialization delay is how long it takes to place bits on the circuit. Faster circuits have less serialization delay. Serialization delay is calculated with the following formula:

serialization delay = frame size in bits / link bandwidth in bps

A 1500-byte packet takes (1500 * 8) / 64,000 = 187 ms of serialization delay on a 64 Kbps circuit. If the circuit is increased to 512 kbps, the serialization delay changes to (1500 * 8) / 512,000 = 23.4 ms. Data-link fragmentation using Link Fragmentation and Interleaving (LFI) or FRF.12 mechanisms reduces the serialization delay by reducing the size of the larger data packets. This arrangement reduces the delay experienced by voice packets as data packet fragments are serialized and voice packets are interleaved between the fragments. A reasonable design goal is to keep the serialization delay experienced by the largest packets or fragments on the order of 10 ms at any interface.

Packets can take different, redundant paths to reach the destination. Packets might not arrive at a constant rate because they take different paths, and they might experience congestion in the network. This variable delay is called jitter. The receiving end uses dejitter buffers to smooth out the variable delay of received VoIP packets. Dejitter buffers change the variable delay to fixed delay.

The variable-delay component includes queuing delay. As packets cross a network, they pass through several devices. At every output port of these devices, it is possible that other voice and data traffic is sharing the link. Queuing delay is the delay experienced as a result of other traffic sharing the link. It is the sum of the serialization delays of all the packets scheduled ahead of delayed packets. LFI is used as a solution for queuing delay issues. LFI is covered in the next section.

As the traffic load on a network increases, both the probability of delay and the length of the probable delay increase. The actual queuing delay depends on the number of queues, queue lengths, and queue algorithms. Queuing effects in VoIP networks are covered in the next section.

QoS Mechanisms for VoIP Networks

Cisco provides different QoS tools that you should use on edge and backbone routers to support VoIP networks. This section covers several QoS mechanisms and their impact on VoIP networks:

- CRTP

- LFI

- Priority Queue-WFQ (PQ-WFQ)

- LLQ

- Auto QoS

CRTP

CRTP was covered in an earlier section. It compresses the IP/UDP/RTP headers from 40 bytes to 2 or 4 bytes. It is configured on a link-to-link basis. Cisco recommends using CRTP for links lower than 768 kbps. Do not configure CRTP if the router CPU is above 75 percent utilization.

LFI

LFI is a QoS mechanism used to reduce the serialization delay. In a multiservice network, small VoIP packets have to compete with large data traffic packets for outbound interfaces. If the large data packet arrives at the interface first, the VoIP packet has to wait until the large data packet is serialized. When the large packet is fragmented into smaller packets, the VoIP packets can be interleaved between the data packets. Figure 15-17 shows how LFI works. With no LFI, all VoIP packets and other small packets must wait for the FTP data to be transmitted. With LFI, the FTP data packet is fragmented. The queuing mechanism then can interleave the VoIP packets with the other packets and send them out the interface.

FRF.12 is a fragmentation and interleaving mechanism specific to Frame Relay networks. It is configured on Frame Relay PVCs to fragment large data packets into smaller packets and interleave them with VoIP packets. This process reduces the serialization delay caused by larger packets.

Figure 15-17 *LFI*

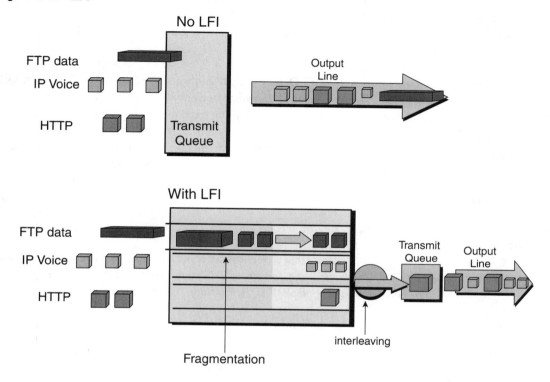

PQ-WFQ

PQ-WFQ is also called IP RTP priority. PQ-WFQ adds a single priority queue to WFQ. The priority queue is used for VoIP packets. All other traffic is queued based on the WFQ algorithm. One variation of PQ-WFQ is Frame Relay RTP priority, which allows strict priority for RTP traffic on Frame Relay PVCs.

With IP RTP priority, the router places VoIP RTP packets in a strict priority queue that is always serviced first. All other (data) traffic is serviced by WFQ. If there is no need for differentiated CoS for data traffic, use IP RTP priority instead of LLQ. If you require differentiated CoS for data traffic, use LLQ.

LLQ

LLQ is also known as Priority Queuing–Class-Based Weighted Fair Queuing (PQ-CBWFQ). LLQ provides a single priority queue, as does PQ-WFQ, but it's preferred for VoIP networks because it can also configure guaranteed bandwidth for different classes of traffic. For example, all voice call traffic would be assigned to the priority queue, VoIP signaling and video would be assigned to a traffic class, FTP traffic would be assigned to a low-priority traffic class, and all other traffic would be assigned to a regular class. With LLQ for Frame Relay, queues are set up on a per-PVC basis. Each PVC has a PQ to support voice traffic. This congestion-management method is considered the most optimal for voice.

If multiple classes are configured for LLQ, they share a single queue but are allocated bandwidth and policed individually. It is recommended that you place only voice in the priority queue, because voice traffic typically is well-behaved, requiring fixed maximum amounts of bandwidth per call. The voice traffic is identified by IP precedence bits set to a value of 5 or a DSCP of Expedited Forwarding (EF) with values of 101xxx. Introducing video or other variable-rate real-time or nonreal-time traffic types could cause unacceptable jitter for the voice traffic. Video traffic normally is set to AF41 (100010). And signaling normally is set to an IP precedence of 3 or a DSCP of 011xxx.

Auto QoS

Auto QoS is a recent Cisco IOS feature that uses a simpler command-line interface (CLI) to enable QoS for VoIP in WAN and LAN environments. Auto QoS significantly reduces the amount of configuration lines necessary to support VoIP in the network.

For the WAN, Auto QoS provides the following capabilities:

- Automatically classifies RTP and VoIP control packets

- Builds VoIP Modular QoS in the Cisco IOS Software

- Provides LLQ for VoIP bearer traffic

- Provides minimum-bandwidth guarantees by using CBWFQ for VoIP control traffic

- Enables WAN traffic shaping where required

- Enables LFI and RTP where required

For the LAN, Auto QoS provides the following capabilities:

- Enforces a trust boundary at the Cisco IP Phone

- Enforces a trust boundary on the Catalyst switch access and uplink and downlink ports

- Enables strict priority queuing and weighted round robin for voice and data traffic

- Modifies queue admission criteria by performing CoS-to-queue mapping

- Modifies queue sizes, as well as queue weights where required

- Modifies CoS-to-DSCP and IP Precedence-to-DSCP mappings

AutoQoS is beneficial for small-to-medium-sized businesses that need to deploy IPT quickly but lack the experience and staffing to plan and deploy IP QoS services.

Auto QoS also benefits large customer enterprises that need to deploy Cisco IPT on a large scale while reducing the costs, complexity, and timeframe for deployment and ensuring that the appropriate QoS for voice applications is being set consistently.

IPT Design Recommendations

The following are some best-practice recommendations when implementing IPT:

- Use separate VLANs/IP subnets for IP phones.

- Use private IP addresses for IP phones.

- Place CallManager and Unity servers on filtered VLAN/IP subnets in the server access in the data center.

- Use IP precedence or DSCP for classification and marking.

- Use LLQ on WAN links.

- Use LFI on slower-speed WAN links.

- Use CAC to avoid oversubscription of priority queues.

IEEE 802.1Q should be configured on the PoE LAN switch ports to allow a voice VLAN for the IP phone and a data VLAN for the PC connected to the IP phone. These VLANs should be on separate IP subnets, and the IP phone should be an RFC 1918 private address subnet. Furthermore, the CallManager servers should be placed on a separate IP subnet in the data center. This lets you restrict access to the IPT environment.

IPT voice packets should be marked with a DSCP of EF (IP precedence 5), and signaling packets should be marked with AF31 (IP precedence 3). This allows QoS schemes to give precedence to the marked packets. LLQ takes the EF marked packets and places them in the strict priority queue, guaranteeing bandwidth for voice. LFI should be configured on WAN links of a size less than 768 kbps to allow smaller IPT packets to get through larger packets. LFI and LLQ also reduce jitter in IPT conversations.

CAC should be used to keep excess voice traffic from the network by rerouting it via alternative network paths or to the PSTN. CAC protects voice traffic from being affected by other voice traffic.

References and Recommended Readings

Andreasen, F., B. Foster, *Media Gateway Control Protocol (MGCP) Version 1.0*, RFC 3435, available from http://www.ietf.org/rfc

Arango, M., A. Dugan, I. Elliott, C. Huitema, S. Pickett, *Media Gateway Control Protocol (MGCP) Version 1.0*, RFC 2705, available from http://www.ietf.org/rfc

Audio-Video Transport Working Group and H. Schulzrinne, *RTP Profile for Audio and Video Conferences with Minimal Control*, RFC 1890, available from http://www.ietf.org/rfc

Audio-Video Transport Working Group, H. Schulzrinne, S. Casner, R. Frederick, and V. Jacobson, *RTP: A Transport Protocol for Real-Time Applications*, RFC 1889, available from http://www.ietf.org/rfc

Handley, M., H. Schulzrinne, E. Schooler, and J. Rosenberg, *SIP: Session Initiation Protocol*, RFC 2543, available from http://www.ietf.org/rfc

Keagy, S. *Integrating Voice and Data Networks*. Indianapolis: Cisco Press, 2000.

Kotha, S. "Deploying H.323 Applications in Cisco Networks" (white paper); available from http://www.cisco.com/warp/public/cc/pd/iosw/ioft/mmcm/tech/h323_wp.htm

Lovell, D. *Cisco IP Telephony*. Indianapolis: Cisco Press, 2002.

McQuerry, S., K. McGrew, S. Foy, *Cisco Voice over Frame Relay, ATM, and IP*. Indianapolis: Cisco Press, 2001.

Reference Guide, Packet Voice Networking. http://www.cisco.com/warp/public/cc/pd/rt/mc3810/prodlit/pvnet_in.htm

Tech Notes: Voice Network Signaling and Control. http://www.cisco.com/warp/public/788/signalling/net_signal_control.html

Voice over IP: Per Call Bandwidth Consumption. http://www.cisco.com/warp/public/788/pkt-voice-general/bwidth_consume.htm

Foundation Summary

The "Foundation Summary" section of each chapter lists the most important facts from the chapter. Although this section does not list every fact from the chapter that will be on the CCDA exam, a well-prepared CCDA candidate should at a minimum know all the details in each "Foundation Summary" before taking the exam.

This chapter covered the following topics that you need to master for the CCDA exam:

- **Traditional voice architectures**—The architecture of TDM voice networks. You must understand PSTN technologies and limitations.

- **Integrated multiservice networks**—IP telephony architectures and components.

- **IPT design**—Design issues, QoS mechanisms, and IPT best practices.

Table 15-8 summarizes technologies and concepts used in voice network design.

Table 15-8 *Voice Technologies*

Technology	Description
BHT	Busy-hour traffic. Expressed in Erlangs.
CCS	Centum Call Second. One call on a channel for 100 seconds.
CDR	Call Detail Record.
FXS	Foreign Exchange Station.
FXO	Foreign Exchange Office.
E&M	Ear and mouth—analog trunk.
Erlang	Measure of total voice traffic volume in one hour. 1 Erlang = 360 CCS.
VAD	Voice Activity Detection.
RTP	Real-time Transport Protocol. Carries coded voice. Runs over UDP.
RTCP	RTP Control Protocol.
Codec	Coder-decoder. Transforms analog signals into digital bit streams.
H.323	ITU framework for multimedia protocols. Used to control Cisco IOS gateways.
MGCP	Media Gateway Control Protocol. Used to control IOS gateways.

continues

Table 15-8 *Voice Technologies (Continued)*

Technology	Description
SIP	Session Initiation Protocol. IETF framework for multimedia protocols.
SS7	Allows voice and network calls to be routed and controlled by central call controllers. Permits modern consumer telephone services. Protocol used in the PSTN.
PSTN	Public Switched Telephone Network.
DTMF	Dual-Tone Multifrequency dialing.
PBX	Private Branch Exchange.
GoS	Grade of service. The probability that a call will be blocked when attempting to seize a circuit.
Centrex	With Centrex services, the CO acts as the company's voice switch, giving the appearance that the company has its own PBX.
IVR	Interactive Voice Response systems provide recorded announcements, prompt callers for key options, and provide information.
ACD	Automatic Call Distribution systems route calls to a group of agents.

Table 15-9 summarizes the different types of codecs used for voice coding.

Table 15-9 *Codec Standards*

Codec	Bit Rate	MOS	Description
G.711u	64 kbps	4.1	PCM. Mu-law version used in North America and Japan. Samples speech 8000 times per second, represented in 8 bits.
G.711a	64 kbps	4.1	PCM. A-law used in Europe and international routes.
G.723.1	6.3 kbps	3.9	Multipulse Excitation–Maximum Likelihood Quantization (MPE-MLQ).
G.723.1	5.3 kbps	3.65	Algebraic Code–Excited Linear Prediction (ACELP).
G.726	16/24/32/ 40 kbps	3.85	Adaptive Differential Pulse-Code Modulation (AD-PCM).
G.728	16 kbps	3.61	Low-Delay CELP (LDCELP).
G.729	8 kbps	3.92	Conjugate Structure ACELP (CS-ACELP).

Table 15-10 summarizes the IPT functional areas.

Table 15-10 *IPT Functional Areas*

IPT Functional Area	Description
Service applications	Unity, IVR, TAPI interface
Call processing	Cisco CM
Client Endpoints	IP phones, digital and analog gateways
Voice Enabled Infrastructure	Layer 2 and Layer 3 switches and routers

Table 15-11 summarizes protocols used in VoIP networks.

Table 15-11 *Significant Protocols in VoIP Networks*

Protocol	Description
DHCP	Dynamic Host Control Protocol. Provides IP address, mask, gateway, DNS address, and TFTP address.
DNS	Domain Name System. Provides the IP address of the TFTP server.
TFTP	Trivial File Transfer Protocol. Provides the IP phone configuration and operating system.
SSCP	Skinny Station Control Protocol. Establishes calls between IP phones and CM.
RTP	Real-time Transport Protocol. Carries codec voice streams.
RTCP	Real-time Transport Control Protocol. Controls RTP streams.
H.323	ITU framework standard. Used to control Cisco IOS gateways.
SIP	Session Initiation Protocol. An IETF replacement for H.323.

Table 15-12 summarizes the different schemes used for QoS.

Table 15-12 *QoS Scheme Summary*

QoS Scheme	Description
CRTP	RTP header compression. Reduces header overhead from 40 bytes to 2 to 4 bytes.
LFI	Link Fragmentation and Interleaving. Fragments large data packets and interleaves VoIP packets between them.
PQ-WFQ	Also known as IP RTP priority. Uses a single strict queue for RTP traffic. All other traffic in WFQ.

continues

Table 15-12 *QoS Scheme Summary (Continued)*

QoS Scheme	Description
LLC	Also known as PQ-CBWFQ. Uses a single strict queue for RTP traffic. Differentiated CoS available for all other traffic.
CAC	Call Admission Control. Reroutes voice calls to the PSTN.

Q&A

As mentioned in the Introduction, you have two choices for review questions: here in the book or the exam questions on the CD-ROM. The answers to these questions appear in Appendix A.

For more practice with exam format questions, use the exam engine on the CD-ROM.

1. True or false: LLQ is recommended for VoIP networks.

2. True or false: H.323 is an IETF standard, and SIP is an ITU standard for multimedia protocols.

3. True or false: An Erlang is a unit that describes the number of calls in an hour.

4. What do you implement to stop packets from being transmitted when there is silence in a voice conversation?

5. The variable delay of received VoIP packets is corrected with what kind of buffers?

6. True or false: Common Channel Signaling uses a separate channel for signaling.

7. True or false: FXO ports are used for phones, and FXS ports connect to the PSTN.

8. True or false: SS7 provides mechanisms for exchanging control and routing messages in the PSTN.

9. An organization uses what kind of system to gather and provide information for the customer before transferring her to an agent?

10. An organization uses what kind of system to route calls to agents based on the agent skill group or call statistics?

11. In addition to codec selection, both _____ and _____ can be used to reduce the bandwidth of VoIP calls.

12. Label each of the following delays as fixed or variable:

    a. Processing

    b. Dejitter buffer

    c. Serialization

    d. Queuing

    e. Propagation

13. How can you reduce serialization delay?

14. Which two queuing techniques use a strict priority queue for RTP traffic?

15. True or false: The maximum one-way delay in the G.114 recommendation for acceptable voice is 200 ms.

16. True or false: FRF.12 is an LFI standard used in networks with VoFR and VoIP over Frame Relay.

17. An assessment of a network determines that the average round-trip time between two sites is 250 ms. Can an IPT solution be implemented between the sites?

18. Match each protocol with its description:

i. DHCP

ii. SSCP

iii. RTP

iv. H.323

v. TFTP

a. Transports coded voice streams

b. Controls Cisco IOS gateways

c. Provides call signaling between Cisco IP phones and CM

d. Provides IP address

e. Provides phone configuration

19. Match each CM deployment model with its description:

i. Single-site deployment

ii. Distributed WAN

iii. Centralized WAN

a. Single CM cluster with SRST at remote sites

b. Single CM cluster implemented in a large building

c. Multiple CM clusters

20. Match each component with its Cisco IPT functional area:

    i. ICM

    ii. Layer 3 switch

    iii. Digital gateway

    iv. Unity

    a. Service applications

    b. Call processing

    c. Client Endpoint

    d. Infrastructure

21. Which standard establishes specifications for call setup and packet formats for VoFR?

22. Which protocol is preferred for inter-PBX trunks?

    a. SS7

    b. RTP

    c. Q.SIG

    d. DTMF

23. CRTP compresses the IP/UDP/RTP header to what size?

    a. 2 or 4 bytes

    b. 2 or 5 bytes

    c. 40 bytes

    d. It compresses the RTP header only

24. The steps of converting an analog signal to digital format occur in which order?

    a. Sampling, filtering, digitizing

    b. Filtering, sampling, digitizing

    c. Digitizing, filtering, sampling

    d. Sampling, digitizing, filtering

25. Digitizing is divided into which two processes?

    a. Filtering and sampling

    b. Expanding and filtering

    c. Companding, and quantizing and coding

    d. Sampling, and quantizing and coding

26. Which of the following are goals of IP telephony?

    a. Use the existing IP infrastructure

    b. Provide lower cost of ownership

    c. Provide greater flexibility in voice communications

    d. All of the above

27. An analysis of a 384-kbps WAN link shows IPT calls being delayed when large file transfers take place. The circuit is running at 45 percent utilization. What QoS scheme(s) should be implemented to alleviate this?

    a. CQ and cRTP

    b. LFI and cRTP

    c. LLQ

    d. All of the above

28. Which codec is recommended for use in WAN links?

    a. G.711

    b. G.723

    c. G.726

    d. G.729

29. Which technology reduces the amount of bandwidth used? (Choose all that apply.)

    a. QoS

    b. LFI

    c. cRTP

    d. VAD

30. Which of the following statements is true?

    a. CAC prevents voice calls from affecting other voice calls.

    b. CAC prevents voice calls from affecting data bandwidth.

    c. CAC prevents data from affecting voice calls.

    d. CAC prevents data from affecting other data traffic.

31. What IPT component contains the dial plan and is used to register IP phones?

    a. Gateway

    b. Unity server

    c. Gatekeeper

    d. Cisco Unified CallManager

Use both the scenario described in the following paragraph and Figure 15-18 to answer the following questions.

The client has an existing Frame Relay network, as shown in Figure 15-18. The network has a large site and 50 small remote sites. The client wants a design for a VoIP network. The client wants to provide differentiated CoS for the voice, Systems Network Architecture (SNA), FTP, and other traffic.

Figure 15-18   *Client's Current Frame Relay Network*

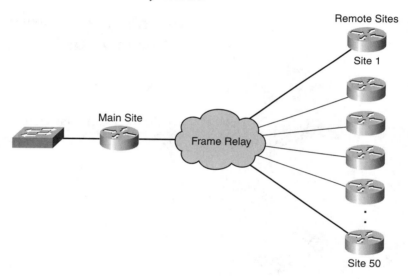

32.   Based on the current network diagram, which Cisco IPT deployment model should you recommend?

33.   What feature should you recommend to provide call processing in the event of a WAN failure?

34.   Which queuing technique should you recommend?

35.   For Site 1, the current data traffic is 512 kbps, and video traffic is 0. What is the minimum bandwidth required to support four concurrent VoIP G.729 calls plus the data traffic to the site?

36.   Should you implement a CallManager cluster?

37.   What feature can you use to reduce bandwidth over the WAN links?

38.   Which LFI technique should you use to reduce the serialization delay?

This chapter covers the following subjects:

■ SNMP

■ Other Network Management Technologies

CHAPTER 16

Network Management Protocols

This chapter introduces the following network management protocols and components: Simple Network Management Protocol (SNMP), Management Information Base (MIB), Remote Monitoring (RMON) protocol, Cisco Discovery Protocol (CDP), and the use of NetFlow and system logging (syslog).

"Do I Know This Already?" Quiz

The purpose of the "Do I Know This Already?" quiz is to help you decide whether you need to read the entire chapter. If you intend to read the entire chapter, you do not necessarily need to answer these questions now.

The ten-question quiz, derived from the major sections in the "Foundation Topics" portion of the chapter, helps you determine how to spend your limited study time.

Table 16-1 outlines the major topics discussed in this chapter and the "Do I Know This Already?" quiz questions that correspond to those topics.

Table 16-1 *"Do I Know This Already?" Foundation Topics Section-to-Question Mapping*

Foundation Topics Section	Questions Covered in This Section
SNMP	1, 2, 3, 4, 6, 8
Other Network Management Technologies	5, 7, 9, 10

CAUTION   The goal of self-assessment is to gauge your mastery of the topics in this chapter. If you do not know the answer to a question or you are only partially sure, you should mark this question wrong for the purposes of the self-assessment. Giving yourself credit for an answer you correctly guess skews your self-assessment results and might give you a false sense of security.

1. Which version of SNMP introduces security extensions for authentication and encryption?

   a. SNMPv1

   b. SNMPv2

   c. SNMPv3

   d. SNMPv4

2. SNMP runs over which protocol?

   a. TCP

   b. UDP

   c. IP

   d. MIB

3. Which SNMP component contains an agent?

   a. Managed device

   b. Agent

   c. NMS manager

   d. MIB

4. Which SNMP component is a collection of information that is stored on the local agent?

   a. Managed device

   b. Agent

   c. NMS manager

   d. MIB

5. CDP is an acronym for which Cisco function?

   a. Collection Device Protocol

   b. Cisco Device Protocol

   c. Campus Discovery Protocol

   d. Cisco Discovery Protocol

6. Which SNMP operation obtains full table information from an agent?

   a. Get

   b. GetNext

   c. GetBulk

   d. Inform

7. RMON1 provides information at what levels of the OSI model?

   a. Data link and physical

   b. Network, data link, physical

   c. Transport and network

   d. Application to network

8. Which of the following is not an SNMP operation?

   a. Get

   b. Community

   c. Set

   d. Trap

9. Which solution gathers information that can be used for accounting and billing applications?

   a. RMON

   b. NetFlow

   c. CDP

   d. Syslog

10. What is CDP?

   a. Client/server protocol

   b. Hello-based protocol

   c. Network management agent

   d. Request-response protocol

The answers to the "Do I Know This Already?" quiz appear in Appendix A, "Answers to Chapter 'Do I Know This Already?' Quizzes and Q&A Sections." The suggested choices for your next step are as follows:

- **8 or less overall score**—Read the entire chapter. It includes the "Foundation Topics," "Foundation Summary," and "Q&A" sections.

- **9 or 10 overall score**—If you want more review on these topics, skip to the "Foundation Summary" section, and then go to the "Q&A" section. Otherwise, move to the next chapter.

Foundation Topics

After a new network is designed, installed, and configured, it must be managed by the operations team. Network management tools are used to gather operating statistics and to manage devices. Statistics are gathered on WAN bandwidth utilization, router CPU and memory utilization, and interface counters. Configuration changes are also made through network management tools such as CiscoWorks. The ISO defines five types of network management processes that are commonly known as FCAPS. These processes are as follows:

- **Fault management**—Refers to detecting and correcting network fault problems

- **Configuration management**—Refers to baselining, modifying, and tracking configuration changes

- **Accounting management**—Refers to keeping track of circuits for billing of services

- **Performance management**—Measures the network's effectiveness at delivering packets

- **Security management**—Tracks the authentication and authorization information

The protocols and tools described is this chapter perform some of these functions. SNMP is the underlying protocol used for network management. Agents are configured in managed devices (routers) that allow the network management system to manage the device. RMON is used for advanced monitoring of routers and switches. CDP is a Cisco proprietary protocol that allows the discovery of Cisco devices. NetFlow is a network monitoring solution that allows for greater scalability than RMON. Syslog allows system messages and error events to be gathered for review.

SNMP

SNMP is an IP application layer protocol that has become the standard for the exchange of management information between network devices. SNMP was initially described in RFC 1157. It is a simple solution that requires little code to implement, which allows vendors to build SNMP agents on their products.

SNMP runs over User Datagram Protocol (UDP) and thus does not inherently provide for sequencing and acknowledgment of packets, but it still reduces the amount of overhead used for management information.

SNMP Components

SNMP has three network-managed components:

- The managed device

- The agent that resides on the managed device

- The network management system (NMS)

Figure 16-1 shows the relationship of these components.

Figure 16-1 *SNMP Components*

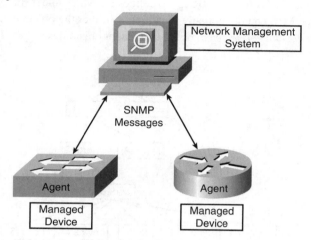

A managed device is a router or LAN switch or any other device that contains an SNMP agent. These devices collect and store management information and make this information available to the NMS. SNMP community strings (passwords) are configured on routers and switches to allow for SNMP management.

The agent is the network management software that resides in the managed device. The agent gathers the information and puts it in SNMP format. It responds to the manager's request for information and also generates traps.

The NMS has applications that are used to monitor and configure managed devices. It is also known as the manager. The NMS provides the bulk of the processing resources used for network management.

MIB

A Management Information Base (MIB) is a collection of information that is stored on the local agent of the managed device. MIBs are organized hierarchically and are accessed by the NMS. MIBs are organized in a treelike structure, with each branch containing similar objects. Each object has a unique object identifier (number) that uniquely identifies the managed object of the MIB hierarchy.

The top-level MIB object IDs belong to different standards organizations, and lower-level object IDs are allocated to associated organizations. Vendors define private branches that include managed objects for their products. Figure 16-2 shows a portion of the MIB tree structure. RFC 1213 describes the MIBs for TCP/IP. Cisco defines the MIBs under the Cisco head object. For example, a Cisco MIB can be uniquely identified by either the object name, *iso.org.dod.private.enterprise.cisco*, or the equivalent object descriptor, *1.3.6.1.4.1.9*.

Figure 16-2 *MIB Tree Structure*

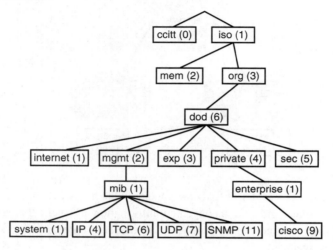

Each individual manageable feature in the MIB is called a MIB variable. The MIB module is a document that describes each manageable feature that is contained in an agent. The MIB module is written in Abstract Syntax Notation 1 (ASN.1). Three ASN.1 data types are required: name, syntax, and encoding. The name serves as the object identifier. The syntax defines the object's data type (integer or string). The encoding data describes how information associated with a managed object is formatted as a series of data items for transmission on the network. More specific information about Cisco MIBs can be found at http://www.cisco.com/public/sw-center/netmgmt/cmtk/mibs.shtml.

SNMP Message Types

SNMPv1 was initially defined by RFC 1157. Since then, SNMP has evolved with a second and third version, each adding new message types. The CCDA should understand each message type and the version associated with each.

SNMPv1

SNMPv1 is defined by RFC 1157. It is a simple request-and-response protocol. The NMS manager issues a request, and managed devices return responses. The date types are limited to

32-bit values. SNMPv1 uses four protocol operations, with five message types to carry out the communication:

- Get Request

- GetNext Request

- Get Response

- Set Request

- Trap

Figure 16-3 shows the SNMPv1 message types.

Figure 16-3   *SNMPv1 Message Types*

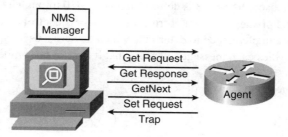

The NMS manager uses the Get operation to retrieve the value-specific MIB variable from an agent. The GetNext operation is used to retrieve the next object instance in a table or list within an agent. The Get Response contains the value of the requested variable.

The NMS manager uses the Set operation to set values of the object instance within an agent. For example, the Set operation can be used to set an IP address on an interface or to bring an interface up or down. Agents use the Trap operation to inform the NMS manager of a significant alarm event. For example, a trap is generated when a WAN circuit goes down.

SNMPv2

SNMPv2 is an evolution of the initial SNMPv1 and is defined in RFCs 1901 and 1902. SNMPv2 offers improvements to SNMPv1, including additional protocol operations. The Get, GetNext, and Set operations used in SNMPv1 are exactly the same as those used in SNMPv1. The SNMP Trap operation serves the same function as in SNMPv1, but it uses a different message format.

SNMPv2 defines two new protocol operations:

- GetBulk

- Inform

The NMS manager uses the GetBulk operation to retrieve large blocks of data, such as multiple rows in a table. This is more efficient than repeating GetNext commands. If the agent responding to the GetBulk operation cannot provide values for all the variables in a list, it provides partial results. The Inform operation allows one NMS manager to send trap information to other NMS managers and to receive information. Another improvement is that data type values can be 64 bits.

SNMPv3

SNMPv3 was developed to correct several deficiencies in the earlier versions of SNMP, security being a primary reason. SNMPv3 is defined in RFCs 3410 through 3415. SNMPv3 provides authentication and privacy by using usernames and access control by using key management. Security levels are implemented to determine which devices a user can read, write, or create. SNMPv3 also verifies each message to ensure that it has not been modified during transmission.

SNMPv3 introduces three levels of security:

- noAuthNoPriv

- authNoPriv

- authPriv

The noAuthNoPriv level provides no authentication and no privacy (encryption). At the authNoPriv level, authentication is provided but not encryption. The authPriv level provides authentication and encryption.

Authentication for SNMPv3 is based on HMAC-MD5 or HMAC-SHA algorithms. The Cipher Block Chaining-Data Encryption Standard (CBC-DES) standard is used for encryption.

Other Network Management Technologies

This section covers RMON, NetFlow, CDP, and syslog technologies used to gather network information.

RMON

RMON is a standard monitoring specification that enables network monitoring devices and console systems to exchange network monitoring data. RMON provides more information than

SNMP, but more sophisticated data collection devices (network probes) are needed. RMON looks at MAC-layer data and provides aggregate information on the statistics and LAN traffic.

Enterprise networks deploy network probes on several network segments; these probes report back to the RMON console. RMON allows network statistics to be collected even if a failure occurs between the probe and the RMON console. RMON1 is defined by RFCs 1757 and 2819, and additions for RMON2 are defined by RFC 2021.

The RMON MIB is located at *iso.org.dod.internet.mgt.mib.rmon* or by the equivalent object descriptor, *1.3.6.1.2.1.16*. RMON1 defines nine monitoring groups; each group provides specific sets of data. One more group is defined for Token Ring. Each group is optional, so vendors do not need to support all the groups in the MIB. Table 16-2 shows the RMON1 groups.

Table 16-2   *RMON1 Groups*

ID	Name	Description
1	Statistics	Contains real-time statistics for interfaces: packets sent, bytes, CRC errors, fragments
2	History	Stores periodic statistic samples for later retrieval
3	Alarm	An alarm event is generated if a statistic sample crosses a threshold
4	Host	Host-specific statistics
5	HostTopN	Most active hosts
6	Matrix	Stores statistics for conversations between two hosts
7	Filters	Allows packets to be filtered
8	Packet Capture	Allows packets to be captured for subsequent analysis
9	Events	Generates notification of events
10	Token Ring	Token Ring RMON extensions

RMON2

RMON1 is focused on the data link and physical layers of the OSI model. As shown in Figure 16-4, RMON2 provides an extension for monitoring upper-layer protocols.

Figure 16-4 *RMON1 and RMON2 Compared to the OSI Model*

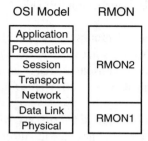

Defined by RFC 2021, RMON2 extends the RMON group with the MIB groups listed in Table 16-3.

Table 16-3 *RMON2 Groups*

ID	Name	Description
11	Protocoldir	Lists the protocols the device supports
12	Protocoldis	Traffic statistics for each protocol
13	Addressmap	Contains network-to-MAC layer address mapping (IP-to-MAC)
14	nlHost	Contains statistics for traffic sent to or from network layer hosts
15	nlMatrix	Contains statistics for conversations between two network layer hosts
16	alHost	Contains Application layer statistics for traffic sent to or from each host
17	alMatrix	Contains Application layer statistics for conversations between pairs of hosts
18	Usrhistory	Contains periodic samples of specified variables
19	Probeconfig	Probe parameter configuration

NetFlow

Cisco's NetFlow allows the tracking of IP flows as they are passed through routers and multilayer switches. NetFlow information is forwarded to a network data analyzer, network planning tools, RMON applications, or accounting and billing applications. NetFlow allows for network planning, traffic engineering, billing, accounting, and application monitoring. NetFlow consists of three major components:

■ Network accounting

■ Flow collector engines

■ Data analyzers

Routers and switches are the network accounting devices that gather the statistics. These devices aggregate data and export the information. Each unidirectional network flow is identified by both source and destination IP addresses and transport layer port numbers. NetFlow can also identify flows based on IP protocol number, type of service, and input interface.

The NetFlow export or transport mechanism sends the NetFlow data to a collection engine or network management collector. Flow collector engines perform data collection and filtering. They aggregate data from several devices and store the information. Different NetFlow data analyzers can be used based on the intended purpose. NetFlow data can be analyzed for performance and planning purposes, security monitoring, RMON monitoring, application monitoring, and billing and accounting.

NetFlow Compared to RMON

NetFlow lets you gather more statistical information than RMON with fewer resources. It provides more data, with date and time stamping. NetFlow has greater scalability and does not require network probes. It can be configured on individual layer 3 interfaces on routers and layer 3 switches. NetFlow provides detailed information on the following:

- Source and destination IP addresses

- Source and destination interface identifiers

- TCP/UDP source and destination port numbers

- Number of bytes and packets per flow

- IP type of service (ToS)

CDP

CDP is a Cisco-proprietary protocol that can be used to discover Cisco network devices. CDP is media- and protocol-independent, so it works over LAN, Frame Relay, ATM, and other media. The requirement is that the media support Subnetwork Access Protocol (SNAP) encapsulation. CDP runs at the data link layer of the OSI model. CDP uses hello messages; packets are exchanged between neighbors, but CDP information is not forwarded.

Being protocol- and media-independent is CDP's biggest advantage over other network management technologies. CDP provides plenty of neighbor information, which is significant for network discovery. It is very useful when SNMP community strings are unknown when performing a network discovery.

When displaying CDP neighbors, you can obtain the following information:

- **Local port**—Local port to connect to the network

- **Device ID**—Name of the neighbor device and MAC address

- **Device IP address**—IP address of the neighbor

- **Hold time**—How long to hold the neighbor information

- **Device capabilities**—Type of device discovered: router, switch, transparent bridge, host, IGMP, repeater

- **Version**—IOS or switch OS version

- **Platform**—Router or switch model number

- **Port ID**—Interface of the neighboring device

Network management devices can obtain CDP information for data gathering. CDP should be disabled on interfaces that face the Internet and other secure networks. CDP works on only Cisco devices.

> **NOTE**   Disable CDP on interfaces for which you do not want devices to be discovered, such as Internet connections.

Syslog

The syslog protocol is currently defined in RFC 3164. Syslog transmits event notification messages over the network. Network devices send the event messages to an event server for aggregation. Network devices include routers, servers, switches, firewalls, and network appliances. Syslog operates over UDP, so messages are not sequenced or acknowledged. The syslog messages are also stored on the device that generates the message and can be viewed locally.

Syslog messages are generated in many broad areas. These areas are called facilities. Cisco IOS has more than 500 facilities. Common facilities include

- IP

- CDP

- OSPF

- TCP

- Interface

- IPsec

- SYS operating system

- Security/authorization

- Spanning Tree Protocol (STP)

Each syslog message has a level. The syslog level determines the event's criticality. Lower syslog levels are more important. Table 16-4 lists the syslog levels.

Table 16-4 *Syslog Message Levels*

Syslog Level	Severity	Level
0	Emergency	System is unusable
1	Alert	Take action immediately
2	Critical	Critical conditions
3	Error	Error messages
4	Warning	Warning conditions
5	Notice	Normal but significant events
6	Informational	Informational messages
7	Debug	Debug level messages

Common syslog messages are interface up and down events. Access lists can also be configured on routers and switches to generate syslog messages when a match occurs. Each syslog message includes a time stamp, level, and facility. Syslog messages have the following format:

mm/dd/yy:hh/mm/ss:FACILITY-LEVEL-mnemonic:description

Syslog messages can create large amounts of network bandwidth. It is important to enable only syslog facilities and levels that are of particular importance.

References and Recommended Reading

"NetFlow Performance Analysis," http://www.cisco.com/en/US/tech/tk812/ technologies_white_paper0900aecd802a0eb9.shtml

MIBs Supported by Product, http://www.cisco.com/public/sw-center/netmgmt/cmtk/mibs.shtml

RFC 1157, *A Simple Network Management Protocol (SNMP)*

RFC 1441, *Introduction to Version 2 of the Internet-standard Network Management Framework*

RFC 1757, *Remote Network Monitoring Management Information Base*

RFC 1901, *Introduction to Community-based SNMPv2*

RFC 1902, *Structure of Management Information for Version 2 of the Simple Network Management Protocol (SNMPv2)*

RFC 2021, *Remote Network Monitoring Management Information Base Version 2 Using SMIv2*

RFC 2576, *Coexistence Between Version 1, Version 2, and Version 3 of the Internet Standard Network Management Framework*

RFC 3164, *The BSD syslog Protocol*

RFC 3410, *Introduction and Applicability Statements for Internet Standard Management Framework*

RFC 3411, *An Architecture for Describing Simple Network Management Protocol (SNMP) Management Frameworks*

RFC 3412, *Message Processing and Dispatching for the Simple Network Management Protocol (SNMP)*

RFC 3414, *User-based Security Model (USM) for Version 3 of the Simple Network Management Protocol (SNMPv3)*

RFC 3416, *Protocol Operations for SNMPv2*

RFC 3418, *Management Information Base for SNMPv2*

Foundation Summary

The "Foundation Summary" section of each chapter lists the most important facts from the chapter. Although this section does not list every fact from the chapter that will be on the CCDA exam, a well-prepared CCDA candidate should at a minimum know all the details in each "Foundation Summary" before taking the exam.

The CCDA exam requires that you be familiar with the following topics covered in this chapter:

- **SNMP**—Underlying protocol for network management

- **MIB**—Stores management information

- **RMON**—Uses network probes for proactive remote monitoring

- **CDP**—Cisco's proprietary protocol for network discovery

- **NetFlow**—More efficient than RMON; collects flow data for performance, billing, planning, and QoS applications

- **Syslog**—Reports state information based on facilities and severity levels

Table 16-5 lists SNMP components.

Table 16-5 *SNMP Components*

SNMP Component	Description
Managed device	Collects and stores management information and contains an agent
Agent	Network management software that gathers information and puts it in SNMP format
NMS	Application used to monitor and configure managed devices

Table 16-6 summarizes SNMP messages.

Table 16-6 *SNMP Messages*

SNMP Message	Description
Get	Retrieves MIB variables from an agent
GetNext	Retrieves the next object instance in a table
Get Response	Response to Get operation commands

continues

Table 16-6 *SNMP Messages (Continued)*

SNMP Message	Description
Set Request	Sets values of the object within an agent
Trap	Sent by the agent to inform the NMS manager of a significant event
GetBulk	SNMPv2 operation to retrieve large blocks of data
Inform	SNMPv2 operation for NMS managers to send trap information to other managers

Table 16-7 summarizes the RMON1 and RMON2 groups.

Table 16-7 *RMON1 and RMON2 Groups*

ID	Name	Group	Description
1	Statistics	RMON1	Contains real-time statistics for interfaces: packets sent, bytes, CRC errors, fragments
2	History	RMON1	Stores periodic statistic samples for later retrieval
3	Alarm	RMON1	An alarm event is generated if a statistic sample crosses a threshold
4	Host	RMON1	Host-specific statistics
5	HostTopN	RMON1	Most active hosts
6	Matrix	RMON1	Stores statistics for conversations between two hosts
7	Filters	RMON1	Allows packets to be filtered
8	Packet capture	RMON1	Allows packets to be captured for subsequent analysis
9	Events	RMON1	Generates notification of events
10	Token Ring	RMON1	Token Ring RMON extensions
11	Protocoldir	RMON2	Lists the protocols the device supports
12	Protocoldis	RMON2	Traffic statistics for each protocol
13	Addressmap	RMON2	Contains network-to-MAC layer address mapping (IP-to-MAC)
14	nlHost	RMON2	Contains statistics for traffic sent to or from network layer hosts
15	nlMatrix	RMON2	Contains statistics for conversations between two network layer hosts

Table 16-7   *RMON1 and RMON2 Groups (Continued)*

ID	Name	Group	Description
16	alHost	RMON2	Contains application layer statistics for traffic sent to or from each host
17	alMatrix	RMON2	Contains application layer statistics for conversations between pairs of hosts
18	Usrhistory	RMON2	Contains periodic samples of specified variables
19	Probeconfig	RMON2	Probe parameter configuration

Table 16-8 summarizes other network management technologies.

Table 16-8   *NetFlow, CDP, and Syslog*

Technology	Description
NetFlow	Collects network flow data for network planning, performance, accounting, and billing applications
CDP	Proprietary protocol for network discovery that provides information on neighboring devices
Syslog	Reports state information based on facility and severity levels

Q&A

As mentioned in the introduction, you have two choices for review questions: here in the book or the exam questions on the CD-ROM. The answers to these questions appear in Appendix A.

For more practice with exam format questions, use the exam engine on the CD-ROM.

1. What does the acronym FCAPS stand for?

2. CDP runs at what layer of the OSI model?

3. Syslog level 5 is what level of severity?

4. True or false: RMON provides more scalability than NetFlow.

5. True false: NetFlow provides detailed information on the number of bytes and packets per conversation.

6. What information can be obtained from a neighbor using CDP?

7. What SNMP message is sent by an agent when an event occurs?

   a. Get

   b. Set

   c. GetResponse

   d. Trap

8. What SNMP message is sent to an agent to obtain an instance of an object?

   a. Get

   b. Set

   c. GetResponse

   d. Trap

9. What SNMP message is used to configure a managed device?

   a. Get

   b. Set

   c. GetResponse

   d. Trap

10. About how many facilities are available for syslog in Cisco routers?

  a. 25

  b. 100

  c. 500

  d. 1000

11. Which SNMPv3 level provides authentication with no encryption?

  a. authPriv

  b. authNoPriv

  c. noAuthNoPriv

  d. noauthPriv

12. What encryption standard does SNMPv3 use?

  a. 3DES

  b. CBC-DES

  c. HMAC-MD5

  d. MD5

13. Which technologies can you use to assess a network and create documentation? (Select two.)

  a. RMON

  b. MIB

  c. CDP

  d. NetFlow

14. Which of the following are true about CDP? (Select three.)

  a. It uses UDP.

  b. It is a data-link protocol.

  c. It provides information on neighboring routers and switches.

  d. It is media- and protocol-independent.

  e. It uses syslog and RMON.

15. RMON2 provides information at what levels of the OSI model?

  a. Data link and physical

  b. Network, data link, and physical

  c. Transport and network only

  d. Application to network

16. Which network management technology operates over TCP?

    a. SNMP

    b. RMON

    c. NetFlow

    d. None of the above

17. Which statement is correct?

    a. SNMPv1 uses GetBulk operations and 32-bit values.

    b. SNMPv2 uses 32-bit values, and SNMPv3 uses 64-bit values.

    c. SNMPv1 uses 32-bit values, and SNMPv2 uses 64-bit values.

    d. SNMPv1 uses GetBulk operations, and SNMPv2 uses Inform operations.

18. Which SNMPv3 level provides authentication and privacy?

    a. authPriv

    b. authNoPriv

    c. noAuthNoPriv

    d. noauthPriv

19. Match the RMON group with its description.

i. Statistics

ii. Matrix

iii. alHost

iv. protocoldir

a. Stores statistics for conversations between two hosts

b. Lists the protocols that the device supports

c. Contains real-time statistics for interfaces: packets sent, bytes, CRC errors, fragments

d. Contains application layer statistics for traffic sent to or from each host

The comprehensive scenarios in this part draw on many different CCDA exam topics to test your overall understanding of the material you will see on the CCDA exam.

Part V: Comprehensive Scenarios

This chapter covers four comprehensive scenarios that draw on several design topics covered in this book:

- Scenario One: Pearland Hospital

- Scenario Two: Big Oil and Gas

- Scenario Three: Beauty Things Store

- Scenario Four: Falcon Communications

The case studies and questions in this chapter draw on your knowledge of CCDA exam topics. Use these exercises to help master the topics as well as to identify areas you still need to review for the exam.

Understand that each scenario presented encompasses several exam topics. Each scenario, however, does not necessarily encompass all the topics. Therefore, you should work through all the scenarios in this chapter to cover all the topics.

Comprehensive Scenarios

Your CCDA exam will probably contain questions that require you to analyze a scenario. This chapter contains four case studies that are similar in style to the ones you might encounter on the CCDA exam. Read through each case study and answer the corresponding questions. You will find the answers to the case study questions at the end of each scenario. Sometimes more than one solution can satisfy the customer's requirements. In these cases, the answers presented represent recommended solutions developed using good design practices. An explanation accompanies the answer where necessary.

Scenario One: Pearland Hospital

Mr. Robertson, the IT director at Pearland Hospital, is responsible for managing the network. Mr. Robertson has requested your help in proposing a network solution that will meet the hospital's requirements. The hospital is growing, and the management has released funds for network improvements.

The medical staff would like to be able to access medical systems using laptops from any of the patient rooms. Doctors and nurses should be able to access patient medical records, x-rays, prescriptions, and recent patient information. Mr. Robertson purchased new servers and placed them in the data center. The wireless LAN (WLAN) has approximately 30 laptops, and about 15 more are due in six months. The servers must have high availability.

Patient rooms are on floors 6 through 10 of the hospital building. Doctors should be able to roam and access the network from any of the floors. A radio-frequency report mentions that a single access point located in each communication closet can reach all the rooms on each floor. The current network has ten segments that reach a single router that also serves the Internet. The router is running Routing Information Protocol Version 1 (RIPv1). The back-end new servers are located in the same segment as those used on floor 1. Mr. Robertson mentions that users have complained of slow access to the servers. He also hands you a table with current IP addresses (see Table 17-1).

Table 17-1 *Current IP Addresses*

Floor	Servers	Clients	IP Network
1	15	40	200.100.1.0/24
2	0	43	200.100.2.0/24
3	0	39	200.100.3.0/24
4	0	42	200.100.4.0/24
5	0	17	200.100.5.0/24
6	0	15	200.100.6.0/24
7	0	14	200.100.7.0/24
8	0	20	200.100.8.0/24
9	0	18	200.100.9.0/24
10	0	15	200.100.10.0/24

Mr. Robertson would like a proposal to upgrade the network with fast switches and to provide faster access to the servers. The proposal should also cover secure WLAN access on floors 6 through 10. Include an IP addressing scheme that reduces the number of Class C networks the hospital uses. Mr. Robertson wants to reduce the number of networks leased from the Internet service provider (ISP).

Scenario One Questions

The following questions refer to Scenario One:

1. What are Pearland Hospital's business requirements?

2. Are there any business-cost constraints?

3. What are the network's technical requirements?

4. What are the network's technical constraints?

5. Prepare a logical diagram of the current network.

6. Does the hospital use IP addresses effectively?

7. What would you recommend to improve the switching speed between floors?

8. Based on the number of servers and clients provided, what IP addressing scheme would you propose?

9. What routing protocols would you recommend?

10. What solution would you recommend for WLAN access and the network upgrade?

11. Draw the proposed network solution.

Scenario One Answers

1. The hospital needs to provide access to patient records, prescriptions, and information from patient rooms.

2. No cost restrictions were discussed.

3. The technical requirements are as follows:

   WLAN access from rooms on floors 6 through 10

   Redundant access to servers in the data center

   Fast switching between LAN segments

4. The technical constraint is as follows:

   Servers must be located in the first floor data-center rooms.

5. Figure 17-1 shows the logical diagram of the current network.

Figure 17-1 *Pearland Hospital Current Network*

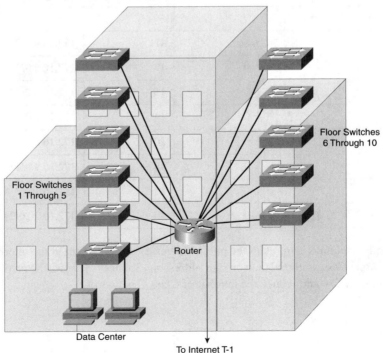

6. The hospital does not use IP addresses effectively. It uses Class C networks on each floor. Each floor wastes more than 200 IP addresses, because each Class C network provides up to 254 IP addresses.

7. Recommend using a high-speed Layer 3 switch for the building LANs. They can use the router for Internet and WAN access.

8. The primary recommendation is to use private addresses for the network. Using private addresses has been a best-practice policy for private internal networks since 1996. With private addresses, the hospital could release eight of the Class C networks to the ISP, retaining two for ISP connectivity.

   With private addresses, the hospital can choose to use 172.16.0.0/16 for private addressing. The addressing scheme shown in Table 17-2 provides sufficient address space for each network.

Table 17-2 *IP Addressing Scheme Using Private Addresses*

Floor	Servers	Clients	IP Network
1	15	0	172.16.0.0/24
1	0	40	172.16.1.0/24
2	0	43	172.16.2.0/24
3	0	39	172.16.3.0/24
4	0	42	172.16.4.0/24
5	0	17	172.16.5.0/24
6	0	15	172.16.6.0/24
7	0	14	172.16.7.0/24
8	0	20	172.16.8.0/24
9	0	18	172.16.9.0/24
10	0	15	172.16.10.0/24
WLAN: 6, 7, 8, 9, 10	0	40	172.16.20.0/24

Another solution is to retain the public addresses and use them in the internal network. This solution is less preferred than private addressing. Table 17-3 shows the recommended address scheme that would reduce the number of Class C networks.

Table 17-3 *IP Addressing Scheme Using Public Address Space*

Floor	Servers	Clients	IP Network
1	0	40	200.100.1.0/26
1	15	—	200.100.1.64/26
2	0	43	200.100.1.128/26
3	0	39	200.100.1.192/26
4	0	42	200.100.2.0/26
5	0	17	200.100.2.64/26
6	0	15	200.100.2.128/26
7	0	14	200.100.2.192/26
8	0	20	200.100.3.0/26
9	0	18	200.100.3.64/26
10	0	15	200.100.3.128/26
WLAN: 6, 7, 8, 9, 10	0	40	200.100.3.192/26

Each subnet has 62 IP addresses for host addressing. Based on the preceding IP addressing scheme, Pearland Hospital does not need networks 200.100.4.0/24 through 200.100.10.0/24.

9. Recommend routing protocols that support variable-length subnet masks (VLSM). The network is small. Recommend RIPv2 or Enhanced Interior Gateway Routing Protocol (EIGRP). Do not recommend Open Shortest Path First (OSPF) because of its configuration complexity.

10. Recommend using two access points on each floor for redundancy. Use a VLAN that spans floors 6 through 10. Change the router to a high-speed Layer 3 switch. Use the router for Internet or WAN access.

11. Figure 17-2 shows the diagram. The router is replaced by the L3 switch to provide high-speed switching between LANs. Each floor has an IP subnet plus a subnet for the WLAN and another for the data center. Each floor has two access points for redundancy. Servers can connect using Fast EtherChannel or Gigabit Ethernet.

Figure 17-2 *Pearland Hospital Proposed Network Solution*

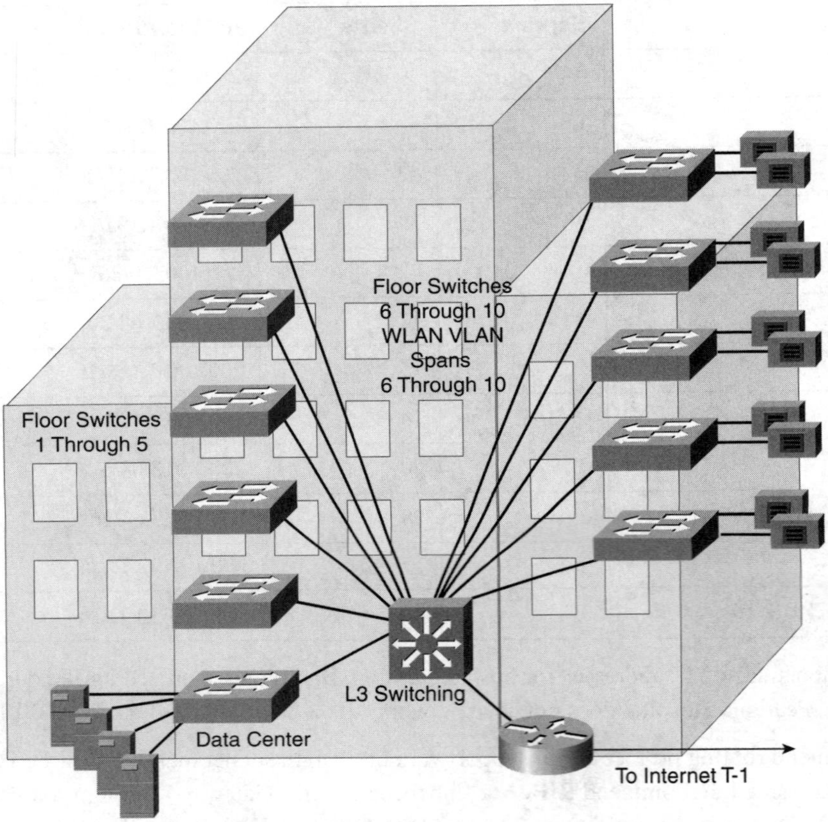

Scenario Two: Big Oil and Gas

Mr. Drew is an IT director at Big Oil and Gas, a medium-sized petrochemical company based in Houston. It also has operations in the Gulf and in South America. Mr. Drew is in charge of the network infrastructure, including routers and switches. His group includes personnel who can install and configure Cisco routers and switches.

The Big Oil and Gas CIO wants to begin migrating from the voice network to an IP telephony solution to reduce circuit and management costs. Existing data WAN circuits have 50 percent utilization or less but spike up to 80 percent when sporadic FTP transfers occur.

Mr. Drew hands you the diagram shown in Figure 17-3. The exiting data network includes 35 sites with approximately 30 people at each site. The network is hub-and-spoke, with approximately 200 people at the headquarters. The WAN links range from 384 kbps circuits to T1 speeds.

Remote-site applications include statistical files and graphical-site diagrams that are transferred using FTP from remote sites to the headquarters.

Figure 17-3 *Big Oil and Gas Current Network*

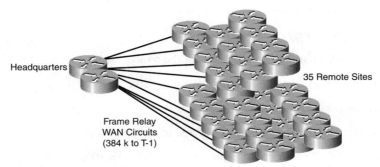

Mr. Drew wants an IP telephony solution that manages the servers at headquarters but still provides redundancy or failover at the remote site. He mentions that he is concerned that the FTP traffic might impact the VoIP traffic. He wants to choose a site to implement a test before implementing IP telephony at all sites.

Scenario Two Questions

The following questions refer to Scenario Two:

1. What are the business requirements for Big Oil and Gas?

2. Are there any business-cost constraints?

3. What are the network's technical requirements?

4. What are the network's technical constraints?

5. Approximately how many IP phones should the network support?

6. What type of IP telephony architecture should you propose?

7. What quality of service (QoS) features would you propose for the WAN?

8. Would you propose a prototype or a pilot?

9. What solution would you suggest for voice redundancy at the remote sites?

10. Diagram the proposed solution.

Scenario Two Answers

1. The company wants to provide voice services in a converged network.

2. The solution should provide reduced costs over the existing separate voice and data networks.

3. The technical requirements are as follows:

   Provide IP telephony over the data network.

   Provide voice redundancy or failover for the remote sites.

   Prevent FTP traffic from impacting the voice traffic.

4. The technical constraint is as follows:

   Call-processing servers need to be located at headquarters.

5. There are 200 IP phones at headquarters, and 35 * 30 = 1050 remote IP phones, for a total of 1250 IP phones.

6. Propose the WAN centralized call-processing architecture with a CallManager (CM) cluster at headquarters.

7. Use low-latency queuing (LLQ) on the WAN links to give the highest priority to voice traffic. Then define traffic classes for regular traffic and FTP traffic. Make bandwidth reservations for the voice traffic and maximum bandwidth restrictions for the FTP traffic. Call Admission Control (CAC) is recommended to limit the number of calls from and to a remote site.

8. To prove that calls can run over the WAN links, implement a pilot site. The pilot would test the design's functionality over the WAN with or without FTP traffic.

9. Recommend the use of Survivable Remote Site Telephony (SRST) to provide voice services in the event of WAN failure, and reroute calls to the Public Switched Telephone Network (PSTN).

10. Figure 17-4 shows the diagram, which shows headquarters and two remote sites for clarity. This architecture is duplicated for all remote sites. Each site uses a voice router that is connected to both the IP WAN and the PSTN. SRST provides voice survivability in the case of WAN failure. A CM cluster is implemented at the headquarters. The CM servers are in the data center in a redundant network.

Figure 17-4 *Headquarters and Two Remote Sites for Clarity*

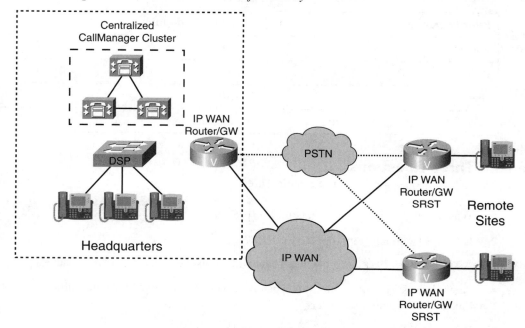

Scenario Three: Beauty Things Store

Beauty Things is a chain of stores that sell beauty supplies. Headquarters is in Houston, Texas, and more than 60 stores are located throughout the U.S. The CIO tells you that they are in the middle of a WAN migration from Frame Relay to MPLS. It will be completed in two months. Most WAN links are less than 384 kbps.

After the WAN migration is complete, the CIO wants to use VoIP for voice calls between stores. He wants to complete the VoIP project within the next six months and within the established budget. Each store will have five concurrent calls back to headquarters.

The WAN provider has four priority queues for traffic: blue, red, green, and yellow. Each is assigned the DSCP codepoints listed in Table 17-4.

Table 17-4 *DSCP Codepoints for Beauty Things*

Priority Queue	DSCP Codepoint
Blue	AF31
Red	EF
Green	AF21
Yellow	Default

Scenario Three Questions

The following questions refer to Scenario Three:

1. What are the business constraints for this project?

2. Is MPLS technology appropriate for VoIP?

3. Assuming a g.729 codec, how much bandwidth must be allocated for VoIP packets per store?

4. Assuming a g.729 codec, how much bandwidth must be reserved for VoIP traffic on the WAN link of the headquarters router?

5. Which MPLS priority queue is assigned for VoIP traffic?

   a. Blue

   b. Red

   c. Green

   d. Yellow

6. Which MPLS priority queue is assigned for FTP traffic?

   a. Blue

   b. Red

   c. Green

   d. Yellow

7. What WAN interface solution must be used to prevent large file transfers from interfering and causing delays of VoIP packets?

   a. Priority queuing

   b. Policy routing

   c. Link fragmentation and interleaving

   d. Serialization delay

8. What is the recommended queuing technique for the WAN interfaces?

    a. PQ

    b. Policy queuing

    c. LLQ

    d. Custom queuing

Scenario Three Answers

1. The WAN project is to be completed in two months. The VoIP project is to be completed in six months and within budget.

2. Yes, MPLS technology is the preferred WAN technology to support VoIP packets. MPLS provides QoS prioritization and guarantees.

3. 130 kbps. This is calculated by taking five concurrent calls times 26 kbps per call.

4. 7.8 Mbps. This is the sum of VoIP traffic per store multiplied by 60 remote stores.

5. B. VoIP traffic is marked with DSCP expedited forwarding, which corresponds to the Red queue.

6. D. FTP traffic does not require prioritization and thus is assigned to the default Yellow queue.

7. C. LFI should be used on WAN links that are less than 768 kbps. It is used to reduce the serialization delay of large packets.

8. C. LLQ is the recommended queuing technique when VoIP packets are present on WAN links.

Scenario Four: Falcon Communications

Falcon Communications has requested an assessment of its current network infrastructure. You are given the diagram shown in Figure 17-5. The current infrastructure contains three 6500 Catalyst switches connected using Layer 2 links. Building access switches, WAN routers, Internet firewalls, the mainframe, and Windows servers all connect to the 6500 switches. Some Fast Ethernet hubs are used on the network.

The IT manager mentions that they experience sporadic network outages several times during the day, and users are complaining that the network is slow. The CIO states that they want to prepare the network, because the company expects to double in size in three years. They also want to prepare the network for IP telephony.

Figure 17-5 *Falcon Communications Current Network*

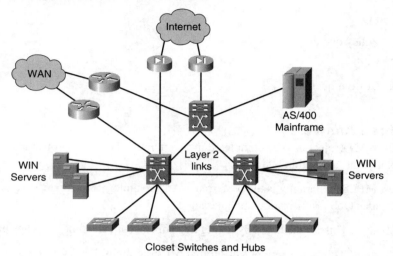

Closet Switches and Hubs

Scenario Four Questions

The following questions refer to Scenario Four:

1. Is this network scalable?
2. What would you recommend for the core switches?
3. What changes are required in the closet switches and hubs?
4. What would you recommend for the WAN routers and Internet firewalls?
5. What would you recommend for the AS/400 and WIN server?
6. What is the role of the distribution layer in the architecture?
7. What are your recommendations for IP addressing?
8. Falcon Communications has a VLAN with a /22 IP subnet that is experiencing network delays. What would you recommend?
9. Diagram your proposed solution.

Scenario Four Answers

1. No. The current Falcon network is not scalable. It is a flat network architecture using Layer 2 links in the core with no hierarchy. It does not have core, distribution, and access layers.
2. Recommend inserting a distribution layer to create a hierarchy between the core and access layers. Use Layer 3 links instead of Layer 2 links to prevent spanning-tree loop broadcast storms.
3. All hubs need to be replaced with switches. All switches should be replaced with PoE switches to provide power to future IP phones and wireless access points. All new switch purchases should be PoE-capable LAN switches.

4. Create an enterprise edge layer that separates the campus LAN and the enterprise edge.

5. Create a server distribution and access layer on which to place all servers and the AS/400 mainframe.

6. The distribution layer has several functions:

   Address summarization

   Security access lists

   Broadcast domain definition

   VLAN routing

   Media translation

7. Recommend allocating /30 subnets for the links between the core and distribution switches. Allocate separate IP subnets for the future IP phones and servers. This lets you apply security policies. Also allocate separate IP subnets for wireless LAN networks.

8. Recommend splitting the IP subnet into four separate /24 IP subnets.

9. The solution shown in Figure 17-6 is a hierarchical network with core, distribution, and access layers. Building access and separate server farms are used. Distribution switches are used to allocate security policies and route summarization. The solution is scalable and will support Falcon Communications' growth plans. PoE switches are deployed to support the future IP telephony deployment.

Figure 17-6 *Falcon Communications Proposed Network Solution*

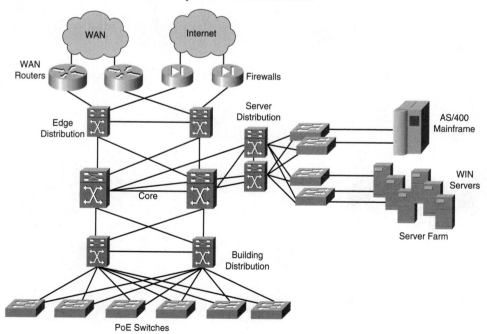

Appendix B provides a review of the OSI model and TCP/IP architecture. Understanding these frameworks will help you comprehend many concepts covered throughout the book. Numeric conversion will help with understanding binary and hexadecimal numbers.

Part VI: Appendixes

Answers to Chapter "Do I Know This Already?" Quizzes and Q&A Sections

Chapter 1

"Do I Know This Already?"

1. B. Integrated Transport, Integrated Service, and Integrated Application are the three phases of IIN.

2. A. Application, Interactive Services, and Network Infrastructure are the layers of SONA.

3. C. Virtualization services occur in the Interactive Service layer of SONA.

4. B. IPCC is a collaboration application. All the others are business applications.

5. A.

6. A, B, C. The PPDIOO methodology has three steps.

7. D. The primary sources of network audits are existing documentation, management software, and new management tools.

8. D. The top-down design approach starts the design from the application layer.

9. B. The examples are organization constraints.

10. C. The examples are technical goals.

Q&A

1. Network Infrastructure layer, Interactive Service layer, and Application layer.

2. Integrated Transport, Integrated Service, and Integrated Application.

3. Identity, Mobility, Storage, Compute, Security, and Voice and Collaboration.

4. Application growth, IT evolution, and increased business expectations from networks.

5. Application-Oriented Network (AON).

6. Prepare, Plan, Design, Implement, Operate, Optimize.

7. i = B, ii = A, iii = C

8. C. SONA evolves enterprise networks to IIN.

9. i = D, ii = F, iii = C, iv = B, v = E, vi = A

10. i = D, ii = A, iii = E, iv = B, v = F, vi = C

11. B. A pilot site is an actual live location for testing.

12. A. A prototype network is a subset of the design in an isolated environment.

13. B.

14. A. Monitoring commands are not SNMP tools.

15. A and B.

16. C and D. The other answers are technical constraints.

17. A, C, E.

18. B, D, F. The other answers are organizational goals.

19. A, B, D, E. Answers C and F are not usually included in the design document.

20. i = D, ii = C, iii = B, iv = F, v = E, vi = A, vii = G

21. C. The network health analysis is based on statistics obtained from the existing network.

22. B. Networks should not contain shared hub segments, and collisions over 1 percent represent an unhealthy segment.

23. C. WAN circuits with sustained utilization of more than 70 percent should have their provisioned bandwidth increased.

24. A, B, C, D, E. All these items are included in a network audit report.

25. C, E, F.

Chapter 2

"Do I Know This Already?"

1. B. The core layer of the hierarchical model is responsible for fast transport.

2. C. The Enterprise Edge consists of e-commerce, Internet connectivity, VPN/remote access, and WAN modules. The Enterprise Edge modules connect to SPs.

3.   C. The distribution layer of the hierarchical model is responsible for security filtering, address and area aggregation, and media translation.

4.   D. HSRP provides default gateway redundancy. Hosts participating in RIP can find alternative gateways.

5.   F. The network-management module monitors all components and functions except the SP Edge.

6.   A. The SP Edge includes Internet, PSTN, and WAN modules.

7.   C. The server farm hosts campus servers including Cisco CallManager servers.

8.   D. The access layer functions are high availability, port security, rate limiting, ARP inspection, virtual access lists, and trust classification.

Q&A

1.   False.

2.   True.

3.   The server farm.

4.   True.

5.   The Internet submodule.

6.   Enterprise Campus, Enterprise Edge, Enterprise WAN, Enterprise Branch, Enterprise Data Center, and Enterprise Teleworker.

7.   True.

8.   False. A full-mesh network increases costs.

9.   Use $n(n-1)/2$, where $n = 6$. $6(6-1)/2 = 30/2 = 15$.

10.   Option 1: Single router, dual links to one ISP

   Option 2: Single router, dual links to two ISPs

   Option 3: Dual routers, dual links to one ISP

   Option 4: Dual routers, dual links to two ISPs

   Option 4 provides the most redundancy, with dual local routers, dual links, and dual ISPs.

11.   The SP Edge Internet submodule connects to the Enterprise Edge Internet submodule.

12.   Cost savings, ease of understanding, easy network growth (scalability), and improved fault isolation.

13. IP phones reside in the building-access layer of the campus infrastructure. The CallManagers are placed in the server farm of the Enterprise Campus.

14. i = C , ii = D, iii = B, iv = A

15. False. Small campus networks can have collapsed core and distribution layers and implement a two-layer design. Medium campus networks can have two-tier or three-tier designs.

16. Use the formula $n(n-1)/2$, where $n = 10$. $10(10-1)/2 = 90/2 = 45$ links.

17. B. The distribution layer provides routing between VLANs and security filtering.

18. E-commerce, Internet, VPN/remote access, and WAN.

19. Internet services, WAN services, and PSTN services.

20. Firewalls, Internet routers, FTP/HTTP servers, SMTP mail servers, and DNS servers.

21. B. The VPN/Remote Access submodule contains firewalls, VPN concentrators, and ASAs.

22. D and E. The access layer concentrates user access and provides PoE to IP phones.

23. B and C. The distribution layer concentrates the network access switches and routers and applies network policies with access lists.

24. A and F. The core layer provides high-speed data transport without manipulating the data.

25. D. The Campus Core connects to the server farm, the Enterprise Edge, and the Building Distribution.

26. E. The infrastructure at the remote site usually consists of a WAN router and a small LAN switch.

27. A, B, C. Web, application, and database servers are placed in the e-commerce submodule.

28. Block 4.

29. Block 1.

30. Block 6.

31. Block 2.

32. Block 5.

33. Block 3.

Chapter 3

"Do I Know This Already?"

1.   F. Routers and Layer 3 switches are Layer 3 devices that control and filter network broadcasts.

2.   C. The maximum distance of 100BASE-T is 100 meters.

3.   G. Every port of a Layer 2 switch, Layer 3 switch, or LAN port on a router is a collision domain.

4.   B. Routes are summarized at the distribution layer.

5.   B. Layer 3 switches are recommended for the backbone of campus networks.

6.   B. CGMP controls multicast traffic at Layer 2.

7.   C. Marking is also known as coloring. Marking sets class-of-service (CoS) bits at Layer 2 or type-of-service (ToS) bits at Layer 3.

8.   B. Each port on a switch is a separate collision or bandwidth domain. All ports on a hub share the same bandwidth domain.

Q&A

1.   False. Layer 2 switches only limit the collision domain.

2.   CGMP.

3.   True.

4.   True.

5.   Inter-Switch Link (ISL) and IEEE 802.1p/802.1Q.

6.   A. IP phone-to-IP phone communication is an example of peer-to-peer communication.

7.   A, C, E. Network applications, infrastructure devices, and environmental characteristics affect network design.

8.   C. Multimode fiber provides the necessary connectivity at the required distance. UTP can reach only 100 m. Single-mode fiber would be more expensive.

9.   B. The DC aggregation layer is similar to the campus distribution layer.

10. C. Disabling trunking on host ports and using RPVST+ are best practices at the access layer.

11. B. The use of HSRP and summarization of routes are best practices in the distribution layer.

12. A. Best practices for the core is the use of triangle connections to reduce switch peering and use routing to prevent network loops.

13. D. Load balancers, SSL offloading, firewalls, and intrusion detection devices are deployed in the DC aggregation layer.

14. D. All are threats to the Enterprise Edge distribution.

15. C. Create a server farm that allows the enforcement of security policies.

16. B. These are design considerations for the distribution layer.

17. D. All are server connectivity options.

18. A. The core and the distribution should be connected using redundant Layer 3 triangular links.

19. B. The building subnets are too large and should be further segmented to reduce the broadcast domain.

20. B. Broadcasts are not forwarded by routers and are controlled by VLANs.

21. i = C, ii = A, iii = B, iv = E, v = D

22. True. Layer 3 switches and routers control both the collision and broadcast domains.

23. i = A, ii = C, iii = B

24. i = E, ii = A, iii = C, iv = D, v = B

25. i = B, ii = A, iii = D, iv = C

26. i = B, ii = D, iii = C, iv = A

27. True. IP phones reclassify incoming frames from the PC. Switches can accept or reclassify incoming frames.

28. CGMP and IP snooping control multicast traffic at Layer 2. The switch and local router exchange CGMP messages. With IGMP snooping, the switch listens to IGMP messages between the host and the router.

29. ISL and IEEE 802.1p/Q are two methods for CoS. ISL was created by Cisco and uses an external tag that contains 3 bits for marking. IEEE 802.1p specifies 3 bits for marking that is carried in the internal tag of IEEE 802.1q. The IEEE 802.1p specification is not included in the IEEE 802.1D-1998 standard.

30. False. You can configure the CGMP only if both the router and switch are Cisco devices.

31. The campus backbone should have high-speed links. Recommend Gigabit Ethernet links.

32. The IP phones should remap the workstation traffic to a value less than the value assigned to voice. Typically, it is recommended that you configure the IP phone to set the CoS to 5 for VoIP traffic.

33. Inspect them at the Layer 3 switches in Building A. Packets should be marked and accepted as close as possible to the source.

34. No. There is no redundancy to the WAN module. A separate link to another building would provide that redundancy.

35. No. There is no redundancy to the Internet module. A separate link from another building would provide that redundancy.

36. Yes. The network uses Layer 2 switches at the building-access layer and Layer 3 switches at the building-distribution and campus-backbone layers.

Chapter 4

"Do I Know This Already?"

1. C. Only 802.11a uses UNII frequencies.

2. B. The Industrial, Scientific, and Medical (ISM) band of frequencies provides 11 channels for wireless LANs.

3. D. Lightweight Access Point Protocol (LWAPP) is a draft Internet Engineering Task Force (IETF) standard for control messaging for setup, authentication, and operations between access points (AP) and wireless LAN controllers (WLC).

4. B. The service-port interface is an optional interface that is statically configured for out-of-band management.

5. B. The Cisco Catalyst 3750 Integrated WLC supports up to 50 APs.

6. C. With N+N+1 redundancy, an equal number of controllers back up each other, as with N+N. Plus, a backup WLC is configured as the tertiary WLC for the access points.

7. B. The recommended best practice is up to 20 WLAN clients.

8. D. Mesh Access Points (MAP) connect to the RAP to connect to the wired network.

Q&A

1. 54 Mbps

2. 200 Mbps

3. Having to configure SSIDs, frequency channels, and power settings for dispersed APs.

4. Advanced Encryption Standard (AES)

5. Reduced TCO
Enhanced visibility control
Dynamic RF management
WLAN security

> Unified wired and wireless network
> Enterprise mobility
> Enhanced productivity and collaboration

6. False. With Split-MAC, control and data traffic frames are split. LWAPs communicate with the WLCs with control messages over the wired network. LWAPP data messages are encapsulated and forwarded to and from wireless clients.

7. True. Controller MAC functions are association requests, resource reservation, and authentication and key management.

8. C. Layer 3 LWAPP tunnels are the preferred solution.

9. B. Layer 2 intercontroller roaming is the preferred intercontroller roaming option.

10. B. The WLC places the user data on the appropriate VLAN and forwards the frame to the wired network.

11. C. Each 4400 series WLC supports 100 APs. 100 APs times 24 controllers in a mobility group equals 2400.

12. D. The recommended number of data devices per AP is 20.

13. B. The recommended number of voice over wireless devices per AP is seven for g.711 and eight for g.729.

14. C. Cisco Radio Resource Management controls AP radio frequency and power settings.

15. A. Typically, there is a 2- to 3-ms latency per hop.

16. C. The RTT between the AP and WLC should not exceed 100 ms.

17. D. Cisco recommends deterministic controller redundancy.

18. D. EoIP is the recommended method for guest services.

19. A. H-REAP with centralized controllers is recommended for branch WLAN design.

20. B and D. Recommended practices are minimizing intercontroller roaming and centralizing controller placement.

21. D. The Cisco 6500 WLC module supports 300 access points.

22. i = D, ii = E, iii = A, iv = F, v = B, vi = C

23. i = E, ii = D, iii = C, iv = B, v = A

24. i = B, ii = A, iii = C

25. i = B, ii = A, iii = E, iv = C, v = D

26. i = C, ii = D, iii = A, iv = B

27. B. For best performance, 20 MAP nodes are recommended per RAP.

28. D. Only answer D has the correct order.

29. B. Radio Resource Management (RRM) functions include radio resource monitoring, dynamic channel assignment, interference detection and avoidance, dynamic transmit power control, coverage hole detection and correction, and client and network load balancing.

30. B. Channels 1, 6, and 11 of the ISM frequencies do not overlap.

31. A. Only answer A is correct.

32. C. LEAP uses mutual authentication between the client and the network server and uses IEEE 802.1X for 802.11 authentication messaging. LEAP uses a RADIUS server to manage user information.

Chapter 5

"Do I Know This Already?"

1. C. DMZ/E-Commerce, Internet, Remote Access VPN, and WAN/MAN are all network modules found in the Enterprise Edge.

2. B. The singling protocol used between the Frame Relay switch and the router is called Local Management Interface (LMI).

3. D. A TDM T1 circuit provides 1.5.44 Mbps of bandwidth.

4. C. The Cisco PPDIOO methodology is used when designing the Enterprise Edge.

5. C. The architecture of Synchronous Optical Network/Synchronous Digital Hierarchy (SONET/SDH) is circuit-based and delivers high-speed services over an optical network.

6. B. With ASDL, the downstream bandwidth is asymmetric, or higher than the upstream bandwidth, and is very popular in residential environments.

7. B. Frame Relay network discards frames marked with the DE bit of 1 before those marked with 0.

8. D. Frame Relay technology supports full mesh configurations when connecting multiple sites together.

9. D. The window size defines the upper limit of frames that can be transmitted without getting a return acknowledgment.

10. A. Low-Latency Queuing (LLQ) adds a strict priority queue to CBWFQ.

Q&A

1. D. After analyzing the customer requirements, the next step is to characterize the existing network.

2. B. The Enterprise Edge modules connect to the enterprise campus via the campus core module.

3. D. The high speeds and relatively low cost of DSL make this a very popular internet access technology for the enterprise telecommuter.

4. C and D. DMZ/E-Commerce, Internet, Remote Access VPN, and WAN/MAN are modules that are found in the Enterprise Edge.

5. A. The window size defines the upper limit of frames that can be transmitted without getting a return acknowledgement. The larger the window size, the smaller number of acknowledgement that need to take place.

6. B. WFQ is the default QoS mechanism on interfaces below 2.0 Mbps.

7. A, B, D. The PPDIOO design methodology includes the process of analyzing network network requirements, characterizing the existing network, and designing the topology.

8. D. DMZ/E-Commerce, Internet, Remote Access VPN, and WAN/MAN are modules that are found in the Enterprise Edge.

9. C and D. DMZ/E-Commerce and Internet are modules that are found in the Enterprise Edge.

10. A. The remote access/vpn module connects to PSTN type connectivity.

11. B. WAN/MAN are modules that use Frame Relay and ATM and are found in the Enterprise Edge.

12. B. After you analyze the network requirements and characterize the existing network, the design of the topology occurs which includes the implementation planning.

13. D. The WAN/MAN functional area or module provides connectivity to the remote sites via Frame Relay, TDM, ATM, or MPLS services.

14. D. The framing for dark fiber is determined by the enterprise not the provider.

15. D. Low Latency Queuing (LLQ) adds a strict priority queue to CBWFQ.

16. 24

17. False. Layer 2 of the ISDN signaling protocol is Link Access Procedure, D channel (LAPD).

18. False. DSL uses digital technology over phone lines.

19. True. SONET/SDH uses a ring topology by connecting sites together and providing automatic recovery capabilities and has self-healing mechanisms.

20.   False. During periods of congestion, the Frame Relay network will discard frames marked with the DE bit of 1 first before those marked with zero.

21.   C. Wireless bridges are used to connect two separate wireless network together typically located in two separate buildings.

22.   DWDM. DWDM maximizes the use of the installed base of fiber used by service providers and is a critical component of optical networks.

23.   CMTS. The equipment used on the remote access side is the cable modem which connects to the Cable Modem Termination System or (CMTS) on the Internet Service provider side.

24.   A. The WAN/MAN module provides connectivity to the remote sites via Frame Relay, TDM, ATM, or SONET network services.

25.   True. Designing WANs use two primary design goals which include application availability and cost and usage.

26.   True. A common use for dial-up is with remote or teleworker using it as a backup network solution in the event that their DSL or cable connection goes down.

27.   False. PVCs are used more predominately due to the permanent nature of the connections.

28.   True. With ASDL, the downstream bandwidth is asymmetric or higher than the upstream bandwidth.

29.   DOCSIS. The Data Over Cable Service Interface Specifications (DOCSIS) protocol defines the cable procedures that the equipment need to support.

Chapter 6

"Do I Know This Already?"

1.   A. Frame Relay and ATM are commonly used to connect to WAN services in the Enterprise Edge.

2.   A, B, C. Typical remote access requirements include best-effort interactive traffic patterns, connections to Enterprise Edge via Layer 2 WAN technologies, and voice and VPN support.

3.   C. Extranet VPN infrastructure uses private and public networks to support business partner connectivity.

4.   B. Secondary WAN links offer both backup and load-sharing capabilities.

5.   C. The goal of high availability is to remove the single points of failure in the design, either by software, hardware, or power. Redundancy is critical in providing high levels of availability.

6. C. SP MPLS MPLS/IP VPN has excellent growth support and high availability services.

7. B. Cisco IOS S Releases 12.2SB and 12.2SR are designed for the Enterprise and SP edge networks.

8. A, B, D. Common components used when designing Enterprise Branch Architecture are routers, switches, and IP phones.

9. B. The dual-tier design is recommended for branch offices of 50 to 100 users, with an additional access router in the WAN edge allowing for redundancy services.

10. C. The multi-tier profile supports between 100 to 1000 users, dual routers, dual firewalls, and multiple distribution switches for aggregation to the access layer switches.

Q&A

1. B. Leased lines are dedicated network connections provided by the service provider.

2. A. A major disadvantage of the hub and spoke topology is that the hub router represents a single point of failure.

3. B. Full-mesh topologies require that each site has a connection to all other sites in the WAN cloud.

4. A. Circuit-switched data connections, such as ISDN service, can be brought up when needed and terminated when finished.

5. C. Access VPN connections give users connectivity over shared networks such as the Internet to their corporate intranets.

6. True. Overlay VPNs are built using traditional WAN technologies such as Frame Relay and ATM.

7. B. With peer-to-peer VPNs, the server provider plays an active role in enterprise routing.

8. B. Service providers can offer shadow PVCs, which provide additional permanent virtual circuit (PVC) for use if needed.

9. C. A secondary WAN links provide advantages that include backup WAN services and load sharing.

10. True. Fast switching is enabled on WAN links that are faster than 56 kbps, and per-destination load balancing is preferred.

11. True. IPsec protocols protect data being transport over the Internet, such as with WAN backup services.

12. A and C. IPsec and GRE are methods that exist for tunneling private networks over a public IP network.

13. C. Factors for WAN architecture selection include ongoing expenses, ease of management, and high availability.

14. A. This approach is simple Layer 3 tunneling for basic IP VPNs without using encryption.

15. True. IPsec encrypted connectivity over the private WAN is optional.

16. B. ISP service uses Internet-based site-to-site VPNs.

17. False. Hardware selection involves modularity of add-on hardware and port densities.

18. False. Redundany and modularity are both considerations when selecting Enterprise Edge hardware.

19. False. The Cisco IOS software family IOS XR is designed for the service provider core.

20. False. The Cisco IOS software family IOS T is designed for access routing platforms for the enterprise.

21. B. A private WAN with self-deployed MPLS is usually reserved for very large enterprises that are willing to make substantial investments in equipment and training to build out the MPLS network.

22. IP Base.

23. True. At the top is the premium package, Advanced Enterprise Services. It combines all features and supports all routing protocols with voice, security, and VPN technologies.

24. D. The IOS package IP Voice supports converged voice and data.

25. True. The Cisco 2970, 3560, and 3750 series switches provide low-end to midrange LAN switching for enterprise access and distribution deployments.

26. False. Cisco Enterprise Branch Architecture is based on Cisco's Service-Oriented Network Architecture (SONA), which includes plug-in modules that provide remote connectivity to network endpoints.

27. True. Common components used when designing Enterprise Branch Architecture are routers, switches, PCs, and IP phones.

28. i = A, ii = C, iii = D, iv = B

Chapter 7

"Do I Know This Already?"

1. C. IPv4 private addresses are contained within 10.0.0.0/8, 172.16.0.0/12, and 192.168.0.0/16.

2. B. There are 5 host bits: $2^5 - 2 = 30$ hosts.

3. D. Loopback addresses should have a /32 mask so that address space is not wasted.

4. C. The precedence bits are located in the type-of-service field of the IPv4 header.

5. B. Multicast addresses range from 224.0.0.1 to 239.255.255.255.

6. B. ARP maps IPv4 addresses to Layer 2 MAC addresses.

7. D. Point-to-point links need only two host addresses; use a /30 mask, which provides $2^2 - 2 = 2$ host addresses.

8. C. DHCP assigns IP addresses dynamically.

9. B. NAT translates between IPv4 private addresses and public addresses.

10. C. The DS field allocates 6 bits in the ToS field, thus making it capable of 64 distinct codepoints.

Q&A

1. 10/8, 172.16/12, and 192.168/16

2. You use VLSM to subdivide a network into subnets of various sizes, whereas CIDR permits the aggregation of classful networks.

3. DNS

4. True. You can use DHCP to specify several host IP configuration parameters, including IP address, mask, default gateway, DNS servers, and TFTP server.

5. False. The bit-number representation of 255.255.255.248 is /29. /28 is the same mask as 255.255.255.240.

6. True.

7. 20 (bytes)

8. DSCP uses 6 bits, which provides 64 levels of classification.

9. True.

10. False. The header checksum field only includes a checksum of the IP header; it does not check the data portion.

11. The subnet is 172.56.4.0/22, the address range is from 172.56.4.1 to 172.56.7.254, and the subnet broadcast is 172.56.7.255.

12. The IP layer in the destination host.

13. B. DHCP configures the IP address, subnet mask, default gateway, and other optional parameters.

14. C. Class B networks have 16 bits for host addresses with the default mask: $2^{16} - 2 = 65,534$.

15. B. A /26 mask has 26 network bits and 6 host bits.

16. C. Network 192.170.20.16 with a prefix of /29 summarizes addresses from 192.170.20.16 to 192.170.20.23.

17. B. AF Class 3 is backward-compatible with IP precedence priority traffic with a binary of 011.

18. A. IPv4 packets can be fragmented by the sending host and routers.

19. B. Multicast addresses are received to a set of hosts subscribed to the multicast group.

20. Unicast, multicast, and broadcast.

21. B. The networks in answer B provide 126 addresses for hosts in each LAN at Site B.

22. A. Network 192.168.15.0/25 provides 126 addresses for LAN 1, network 192.168.15.128/26 provides 62 addresses for LAN 2, and network 192.168.15.192/27 provides 30 addresses for LAN 3.

23. D. You need only two addresses for the WAN link, and the /30 mask provides only two.

24. A. Private addresses are not announced to Internet service providers.

25. B. NAT translates internal private addresses to public addresses.

26. D. VLSM provides the ability to use different masks throughout the network.

Chapter 8

"Do I Know This Already?"

1. C. IPv6 uses 128 bits for addresses, and IPv4 uses 32 bits. The difference is 96.

2. C. The IPv6 header is 40 bytes in length.

3. C. The defining first hexadecimal digits for link-local addresses are FE8.

4. D. IPv6 addresses can be unicast, anycast, or multicast.

5. B. Answers A and C are incorrect because you cannot use the double colons (::) twice. Answers C and D are also incorrect because you cannot reduce b100 to b1.

6. C. NAT-PT translates between IPv4 and IPv6 addresses.

7. B. The IPv6 multicast address type handles broadcasts.

8. B. The IPv6 loopback address is ::1.

9. A. IPv4-compatible IPv6 addresses have the format ::d.d.d.d.

10. C. The DNS maps fully qualified domain names to IPv6 addresses using (AAAA) records.

Q&A

1. False. OSPFv3 supports IPv6. OSPFv2 is used in IPv4 networks.

2. True.

3. ARP

4. 16

5. 0110. The first field of the IPv6 header is the version field. It is set to binary 0110 (6).

6. False.

7. 0xFF (1111 1111 binary)

8. FE8/10

9. True.

10. Version, Traffic Class, Flow Label, Payload Length, Next Header, Hop Limit, IPv6 Source Address, IPv6 Destination Address.

11. B. IPv6 address types are unicast, anycast, and multicast.

12. True. Both compressed representations are valid.

13. 2001:1:0:ab0::/64

14. 32

15. It is a multicast address. All IPv6 multicast addresses begin with hexadecimal FF.

16. C. Answers A, B, and D are incorrect because 0100 does not compact to 01. Answer B is also incorrect because 0010 does not compact to 001.

17. A. The dual-stack backbone routers handle packets between IPv4 hosts and IPv6 hosts.

18. B. DNS indicates which stack to use. DNS A records return IPv4 addresses. DNS AAAA records return IPv6 addresses.

19.   IPv6 over dedicated links
IPv6 over IPv4 tunnels
IPv6 using dual-stack backbones
Protocol-translation mechanisms

20.   A and D.

21.   D. IPv4 packets can be fragmented by the sending host and routers. IPv6 packets are fragmented by the sending host only.

22.   A. Anycast addresses reach the nearest destination in a group of hosts.

23.   D

24.   Implement a dual-stack backbone, or implement IPv4 tunnels between the sites.

25.   NAT-PT is required to provide network address translation and protocol translation between IPv6 and IPv4 hosts.

26.   If a dual-stack backbone is implemented, only the WAN routers require an IPv6-IPv4 dual stack. End hosts do not need a dual stack.

27.   No. All WAN routers still run the IPv4 stack, with two exceptions: the WAN routers at Sites A and B. These routers speak IPv6 within their sites and speak IPv4 to the WAN.

Chapter 9

"Do I Know This Already?"

1.   D. Only RIPv1 is a classful routing protocol. EIGRP, OSPF, IS-IS, and RIPv2 are classless routing protocols.

2.   C. You use an exterior gateway protocol (EGP) to receive Internet routes from a service provider.

3.   A. RIPv2 is a classless distance-vector routing protocol.

4.   B. Distance-vector routing protocols send periodic updates.

5.   B. RIPng is a distance-vector routing protocol that is used in IPv6 networks.

6.   B. If bandwidth is used, the path with the highest bandwidth is selected. If cost is used, the path with the lowest cost is selected.

7.   B. OSPF has an administrative distance of 110. EIGRP has an administrative distance of 90. The route with the lower administrative distance is selected: EIGRP.

8.   D. EIGRP, RIPv2, IS-IS, and OSPF are all classless routing protocols.

Q&A

1. RIPv1 and IGRP. These protocols are classful.

2. False. Distance-vector routing protocols send periodic routing updates.

3. False. RIPng is used with IPv6 networks.

4. True.

5. True. The higher value for reliability is preferred.

6. False. The link with the lower load is preferred.

7. The EIGRP route. EIGRP routes have an administrative distance of 90, and OSPF routes have an administrative distance of 100. The lower administrative distance is preferred.

8. The IS-IS route. IS-IS routes have an administrative distance of 115, and RIP routes have an administrative distance of 120. The lower administrative distance is preferred.

9. The OSPF route, because it has a more specific route.

10. A. The best reliability is 255/255 (100 percent), and the best load is 1/255 (~0 percent).

11. G. IS-IS and OSPF permit an explicit hierarchical topology.

12. Delay measures the amount of time a packet takes to travel from one end to another in the internetwork.

13. OSPF cost. The Cisco default metric is 10^8/BW.

14. The metric is 10^8/BW. If BW = 100 Mbps = 10^8, the metric = $10^8/10^8$ = 1.

15. i = C, ii = A, iii = D, iv = B.

16. True.

17. B, D, E, F.

18. B. OSPFv3 is the only standards-based routing protocol in the list that supports large networks. RIPng has limited scalability.

19. C. IS-IS is deployed by ISPs, not in enterprise networks.

20. C, D, E. Link-state routing protocols plus EIGRP's hybrid characteristics converge faster.

21. C. EIGRP supports large networks and does not require a hierarchical network.

22. B, C, D, E. RIPv1 does not support VLSMs.

23. F. BGP is used to connect to ISPs.

24. C. EIGRP is supported only on Cisco routers.

25. D. OSPFv3 is the only correct answer. RIPv2 is for IPv4 networks. EIGRP is not standards-based. BGPv6 and RIPv3 do not exist.

26. CDP. Cisco Discovery Protocol (CDP) provides for communication between hub and stub routers when using ODR.

27. C.

28. A is EIGRP for IPv6, B is OSPF, C is RIPv2, D is EIGRP, E is OSPFv3.

29. A. The minimum bandwidth via Route 1 is 384 kbps. The minimum bandwidth via Route 2 is 128 kbps. The route with the higher minimum bandwidth is preferred, so the router chooses Route 1.

30. B. Route 2 has fewer router hops than Route 1.

31. A. Route 2 has a higher cost than Route 1. The Route 2 cost is $10^8/128$ kbps = 781.25. The Route 1 cost is $10^8/512$ kbps + $10^8/384$ kbps + $10^8/512$ kbps = 195.31 + 260.41 + 195.31 = 651.03. Route 1 is preferred.

Chapter 10

"Do I Know This Already?"

1. C. RIPv1 and RIPv2 are limited to 15 router hops.

2. A. RIPv2 broadcasts every 30 seconds.

3. B. RIPv2 implements support for VLSMs and an authentication mechanism for route updates and can multicast rather than broadcast updates.

4. D. EIGRP routers maintain adjacencies with their neighboring routers. The adjacencies are kept in a topology table.

5. B. RIPng and EIGRP are the only distance-vector routing protocols that support IPv6.

6. B. By default, EIGRP uses bandwidth and delay in its composite metric.

7. D. RIPv2, EIGRP, OSPF, and IS-IS support VLSMs.

8. C. Only EIGRP implements DUAL. DUAL selects the best path and second-best path to a destination.

Q&A

1. False. RIPv2 multicasts its routing table to 224.0.0.9. It does not send a broadcast to all nodes in the segment.

2. False. By default, EIGRP uses bandwidth and delay to calculate the composite metric.

3.   True. EIGRP routers build a table of adjacent EIGRP neighbors.

4.   True.

5.   False. Both RIPv1 and RIPv2 have a 15-router-hop limit.

6.   RIP uses UDP port 520.

7.   RIPng uses UDP port 521.

8.   EIGRP uses IP protocol 88.

9.   EIGRP is preferred for large networks.

10.   You would use RIPv2 because IGRP and EIGRP are available only on Cisco devices.

11.   EIGRP uses DUAL for fast convergence and loop prevention.

12.   i = D, ii = B, iii = A, iv = C

13.   EIGRP combines characteristics commonly associated with both distance-vector and link-state routing protocols.

14.   C. To reduce the broadcast traffic, use EIGRP for IPv4 as the routing protocol for the network. RIPv2 still generates periodic broadcasts. EIGRP for IPv6 and RIPng are used in IPv6 networks.

15.   RIPng does not include authentication. It uses the authentication schemes of IPv6.

16.   i = C, ii = B, iii = D, iv = A, v = E

17.   i = B, ii = D, iii = A, iv = C

18.   Equal-cost load balancing is a feature of RIPv1 and RIPv2 with Cisco routers.

19.   Unequal-cost load balancing is a feature of IGRP and EIGRP with Cisco routers.

20.   B. EIGRP does not require a hierarchical topology. RIPv2 does not scale for large networks. OSPF and IS-IS require a hierarchical topology. IS-IS is not recommended in enterprise networks.

21.   i = C, ii = A, iii = D, iv = B

22.   B. The EIGRP route has a lower administrative distance.

23.   H. EIGRP is proprietary.

24.

Characteristic	RIPv1	RIPv2	RIPng	EIGRP	EIGRP for IPv6
Authentication	No	Yes	No	Yes	Yes
Protocol/port	UDP 520	UDP 520	UDP 521	IP 88	Next Header 88
Administrative distance	120	120	120	90	90
IP version	IPv4	IPv4	IPv6	IPv4	IPv6

25. A. From Router A, Path 1 is one router hop, and Path 2 is three router hops. RIPv2 selects Path 1 because of the lower metric.

26. A. From Router A, Path 1 is one router hop, and Path 2 is three router hops. RIPng selects Path 1 because of the lower hop count metric.

27. B. From Router A, the lowest bandwidth (BW_{min1}) in Path 1 is 256 kbps; the lowest bandwidth in Path 2 (BW_{min2}) is 512 kbps. With the default delay values, the EIGRP metric calculation would be more sensitive to the bandwidth component of the metric calculation. EIGRP selects the path with the greatest minimum bandwidth.

28. C. By default, EIGRP load-balances using equal-cost paths. EIGRP does unequal load balancing when you use the variance command.

29. B. Regardless of IPv4 or IPv6, EIGRP uses the fastest bandwidth (and lowest delay) for best path calculations. From Router A, the lowest bandwidth (BW_{min1}) in Path 1 is 256 kbps; the lowest bandwidth in Path 2 (BW_{min2}) is 512 kbps. With the default delay values, EIGRP selects the path with the greatest minimum bandwidth: 512 kbps (path 2) is selected over 256 kbps (path 1).

Chapter 11

"Do I Know This Already?"

1. B. OSPF defines ABRs that connect areas to the OSPF backbone.

2. G. EIGRP, OSPF, and IS-IS support VLSMs.

3. D. IS-IS is a common alternative to EIGRP and OSPF for Service Provider networks.

4. B. OSPF defines the ASBR as the router that injects external routes into the OSPF autonomous system.

5. B. The default IS-IS cost metric for any interface type is 10.

6. E. OSPFv2 Type 5 LSAs are AS external LSAs.

7. C. OSPFv2 routers use 224.0.0.6 to communicate with DRs.

8. A. Type 1 LSAs (router LSAs) are forwarded to all routers within an OSPF area.

9. D. IS-IS does not define BDRs.

10. D. Intra-Area-Prefix LSAs carry IPv6 prefixes associated with a router, a stub network, or an associated transit network segment.

Q&A

1. False. A router with one or more interfaces in Area 0 is considered an OSPF backbone router.

2. True.

3. 224.0.0.5 for ALLSPFRouters and 224.0.0.6 for ALLDRouters.

4. FF02::5 for ALLSPFRouters and FF02::6 for ALLDRouters.

5. The administrative distance of OSPF is 110, and the administrative distance of IS-IS is 115.

6. True. By default, IS-IS assigns a cost metric of 10 to all interfaces.

7. OSPF ABRs generate the Type 3 summary LSA for ABRs.

8. OSPF DRs generate Type 2 network LSAs.

9. Included are the router's links, interfaces, state of links, and cost.

10. True.

11. False. The router with the highest priority is selected as the OSPF designated router.

12. i = C, ii = B, iii = A, iv = D

13. OSPF DRs produce OSPF network LSAs for broadcast multi-access networks.

14. False. IS-IS uses Layer 2 OSI PDUs to communicate between routers.

15. Cost is calculated as 10^8/BW, and BW = 100 Mbps = 10^8 bps for Fast Ethernet. Cost = $10^8/10^8 = 1$.

16. OSPF and IS-IS are the only link-state routing protocols, and they both support VLSMs.

17. OSPF. Although RIPv2 and EIGRP support VLSMs, you should use RIPv2 only on the edge. EIGRP is not supported on non-Cisco routers.

18. True. L1/L2 routers maintain separate link-state databases for Level 1 and Level 2 routes. ABRs maintain separate link-state databases for each area they are connected to.

19. Virtual links. You use virtual links to temporarily connect an OSPF area to the backbone.

20. You do not need to flood external LSAs into the stub area, which reduces LSA traffic.

21. All traffic from one area must travel through Area 0 (the backbone) to get to another area.

22. False. For Fast Ethernet, the OSPF cost is 1 and the IS-IS cost is 10.

23. OSPFv3 is identified as IPv6 Next Header 89.

24. F. EIGRP and OSPFv2 are recommended for large enterprise networks.

25. C. Link LSAs are flooded to the local link.

26. F.

27. E. EIGRP and OSPFv2 have fast convergence.

28. E. EIGRP for IPv6 and OSPFv3 have fast convergence for IPv6 networks.

29. H. RIPv1 and RIPv2 generate periodic routing traffic. IS-IS is used in SP networks. BGP is used for external networks.

30. B. OSPFv3 is used in IPv6 networks.

31. A. From Router A, Path 1 has an IS-IS cost of $10 + 10 = 20$. Path 2 has an IS-IS cost of $10 + 10 + 10 + 10 = 40$. Path 1 is selected.

32. B. From Router A, the OSPF cost for Path 1 is $10^8/256$ kbps $= 390$. The OSPF cost for Path 2 is $(10^8/1536$ kbps$) + (10^8/1024$ kbps$) + (10^8/768$ kbps$) = 65 + 97 + 130 = 292$. OSPF selects Path 2 because it has a lower cost.

33. Router A = Internal
    Router B = ABR
    Router C = Backbone
    Router D = ASBR
    Router E = ABR
    Router F = Internal

Chapter 12

"Do I Know This Already?"

1. B. You use External Border Gateway Protocol (eBGP) to exchange routes between autonomous systems.

2. C. The current version of BGP is Version 4. BGPv4 includes support for CIDR.

3. B. It is a best practice to summarize routes on the distribution routers toward the core.

4. D. PBR changes packets' routes based on configured policies.

5. B. You use IGMP between hosts and local routers to register with multicast groups.

6. B. The lower 23 bits of the IP multicast address are mapped to the last 23 bits of the Layer 2 MAC address.

7. A. The administrative distance of eBGP routes is 20. The administrative distance of internal BGP (iBGP) routes is 200.

8. D. CIDR provides the capability to forward packets based on IP prefixes only, with no concern for IP address class boundaries.

Q&A

1. False. You use eBGP to exchange routes between different autonomous systems.

2. True. BGPv4 added support for Classless Interdomain Routing (CIDR), which provides the capability of forwarding packets based on IP prefixes only, with no concern for the address class.

3. True.

4. PBR

5. 20, 200

6. True.

7. False. PIM does not have a hop-count limit. DVMRP has a 32 hop-count limit.

8. True.

9. False. BGP uses several attributes in the BGP decision process.

10. RIPv2, OSPF, and EIGRP.

11. FF02::A

12. i =D, ii = B, iii = A, iv = C

13. i = B, ii = C, iii = D, iv = A

14. Weight. Weight is configured locally and not exchanged in BGP updates. On the other hand, the local preference attribute is exchanged between iBGP peers and is configured at the gateway router.

15. Route reflectors reduce the number of iBGP logical mesh connections.

16. External peers see the confederation ID. The internal private AS numbers are used within the confederation.

17. BGP confederations, route reflectors.

18. B. Only answer B has the correct order of BGP path selection, which is weight, local preference, AS path, origin, MED, and lowest IP.

19. CIDR was first implemented in BGPv4.

20. C.

21. i = E, ii = C, iii = A, iv = B, v = D

22. B.

23. C.

24. B. BGP should be configured between AS 100 and AS 500.

25. C. Both Routers A and B perform the redistribution with route filters to prevent route feedback.

26. B. The OSPF routes are redistributed into EIGRP. Then you can redistribute EIGRP routes into BGP.

27. D. You should use filters on all routers performing redistribution.

Chapter 13

"Do I Know This Already?"

1. C. The U.S. Health Insurance Portability and Accountability Act (HIPAA) applies to the protection of private health information that is used electronically.

2. B. Reconnaissance techniques are used to gather information from hosts attached to the network.

3. A. Denial of service (DoS) attacks aim to overwhelm resources such as memory, CPU, and bandwidth, thus impacting the target system and denying legitimate users access.

4. D. Rate limiting can control the rate of bandwidth that is used for incoming traffic such as ARPs and DHCP requests.

5. C. When an attacker changes sensitive data without the proper authorization, this is called an integrity violation.

6. B. The incident-handling policy defines the processes and procedures for managing incidents and emergency type scenarios.

7. D. Identification of assets, definitions of roles and responsibilities, and a description of permitted behaviors should be included in a security policy.

8. A, B, C. Authentication of an identity is based on something the subject knows, has, or is, such as password, token, and fingerprint, respectively.

9. A. Asymmetric cryptography uses two different keys for encryption and relies on PKI.

10. A, B, C. Threat Defense has three main areas of focus that include enhancing the security of the existing network, adding full security services to network endpoints, and enabling integrated security in routers, switches, and appliances.

Q&A

1. C. Encryption can protect data transported between sites over the Internet.

2. A and C. Firewalls and host-based security have the capabilities to protect database servers, such as in a DMZ segment.

3. D. Encryption is a security technique for protecting the data confidentiality of information.

4. A and B. The use of ACLs and rate limiting can alleviate the effects of a DoS attack being preformed.

5. A and D. DoS, reconnaissance, and gaining unauthorized access are security threats.

6. True. IPsec can ensure data integrity and confidentiality across the Internet.

7. C. SOX focuses on the accuracy and controls imposed on a company's financial records.

8. A, B, C. Managing the security infrastructure has components that include the overall security management policy, incident-handling policy, and network access control policy.

9. C. EU Data Protection Directive calls for the protection of the people's right to privacy with respect to the processing of personal data.

10. False. HIPAA applies to the protection of private health information that is used electronically.

11. True. Distributed DoS attacks are when multiple sources work together to deliver an attack.

12. True. Social engineering involves manipulating users into giving out confidential information.

13. D. Attackers can use password-cracking utilities, capture network traffic, and use social engineering to obtain sensitive information.

14. D. Data integrity allows only authorized users to modify data, ensuring that the data is authentic.

15. Some targets that are used for attacks include routers, switches, firewalls, and servers.

16. B. Accounting provides an audit trail of activities by logging the actions of the user.

17. DHCP snooping authenticates valid DHCP servers, thereby preventing rouge DHCP servers from interfering with real production servers.

18. True. Unicast RPF is used to prevent unknown source addresses from using the network as a transport.

19. Rate limiting can control the rate of traffic that is allowed into the network.

20. The security policy contains the organization's procedures, guidelines, and standards.

21. D. Access control can be enforced by restricting access using VLANs, OS-based controls, and encryption techniques.

22. Acceptable-use policy.

23. True. The network access control policy defines the general access control principles used and how data is classified, such as confidential, top-secret, or internal.

24. D. Secure—Identification, authentication, ACLs, stateful packet inspection (SPI), encryption, and VPNs

    Monitor—Intrusion and content-based detection and response

    Test—Assessments, vulnerability scanning, and security auditing

    Improve—Security data analysis, reporting, and intelligent network security

25. True. The Cisco Self-Defending Network Trust and Identity Management defines who and what can access the network, as well as when, where, and how that access can occur.

26. True. Tokens such as a six-digit PIN and a token code are used in the two-factor authentication technique.

27. i = B, ii = C, iii = A, iv = D

Chapter 14

"Do I Know This Already?"

1. A, B, C. Critical components of the Cisco Self-Defending Network include Trust and Identity Management, Threat Defense, and Secure Connectivity.

2. C. The Cisco ASAs provide high-performance firewall, IPS, anti-X, IPsec, and VPN services.

3. B. 802.1x is an IEEE media-level access control standard that permits and denies admission to the network and applies traffic policy based on identity.

4. A. Network Access Control (NAC) protects the network from security threats by enforcing security compliance on all devices attempting to access the network.

5. D. The Cisco ASA, FWSM, and PIX security appliances all support firewall filtering with ACLs.

6. A. The Cisco Security Agent is software that is installed on hosts to perform host-based intrusion prevention (HIPS).

7. A. CSM is an integrated solution for configuration management of firewall, VPN, router, switch module, and IPS devices.

8. A, B, C. Cisco IOS, PIX, and ASA can all be used to integrate security into the network.

9. B. Netflow provides information for detecting and mitigating threats.

10. C. Cisco ACS is a security management platform for controlling administrative access for Cisco devices and security applications.

Q&A

1. B. Integrated Services Router (ISR) combines IOS firewall, VPN, and IPS services.

2. C. The 802.1X protocol is a standards-based protocol for authenticating network clients by permitting or denying access to the network.

3. D. The NAC Framework is an integrated solution led by Cisco that incorporates the network infrastructure and third-party software to impose security policies on the attached endpoints.

4. A. Cisco Security MARS (CS-MARS) is an appliance-based solution for network security administrators to monitor, identify, isolate, and respond to security threats.

5. A, B, C. Cisco IOS Trust and Identity is a set of services that include AAA, SSH, SSL, 802.1x, and PKI.

6. False. SSH provides encrypted router access.

7. B. Cisco IOS IPsec offers data encryption at the IP packet level using a set of standards-based protocols.

8. True. PKI provides strong authentication services for e-commerce applications.

9. D. High-Performance advanced integration module (AIM) is a hardware module for terminating large numbers of VPN tunnels.

10. False. Integrated Content Modules for 2800/3800 series routers are used for content networking.

11. False. Cisco VPN 3000 concentrators provide businesses with IPsec and SSL VPN connectivity.

12. A, B. Cisco Catalyst 6500 switches support FWSM and IDSM2 services modules.

13. B. The Anomaly Guard Module provides attack responses by blocking malicious traffic at Gbps line rates.

14. A, B, C. Some identity and access control protocols include 802.1X, ACLs, and NAC. NetFlow collects stats on packets flowing through the router.

15. True. The Cisco Security Agent protects server and desktop endpoints from the latest threats caused by malicious network attacks.

16. D. CSA MC is an SSL web-based tool for managing Cisco Security Agent configurations.

17. True. IDM is a web-based application that configures and manages IPS sensors.

18. True. NetFlow is used for threat detection and mitigation.

19. C. The three phases of the Cisco Self-Defending Network include Integrating Security, Adaptive Threat Defense, and Collaborative Security.

20. True. Cisco ASAs, PIX security appliances, FWSM, and IOS firewall are part of Infection Containment.

21. D. IOS intrusion prevention system (IPS) offers inline deep-packet inspection to successfully diminish a wide range of network attacks.

22. IPS. The 4200 IPS sensor appliances can identify, analyze, and block unwanted traffic from flowing on the network.

23. B. Cisco Secure Access Control Server (ACS) provides centralized control for administrative access to Cisco devices and security applications.

24. True. ASDM provides management of Cisco ASAs, PIX, and FWSMs.

25. False. IPS 4255 delivers 1000 Mbps of performance and can be used to protect partially utilized Gigabit connected subnets.

26. True. FWSM is a high-speed firewall module for use in the Cisco Catalyst 6500 and 7600 series routers.

27. i = D, ii = C, iii = B, iv = A

Chapter 15

"Do I Know This Already?"

1. C. H.323 is the ITU standard that provides a framework for the transport of voice, video, and data over packet-switched networks.

2. D. The default codec in Cisco VoIP dial peers is G.729, which has an 8-kbps bit rate.

3. C. RTP operates at the transport layer of the OSI model.

4. C. The H.225 standard defines the procedures for call setup and signaling.

5. B. An Erlang is a unit that describes the number of calls in an hour.

6. B. VAD reduces traffic by not transmitting packets when there is silence in voice conversations.

7. C. CRTP compresses the RTP, UDP, and IP headers.

8. B. LLQ is recommended for VoIP networks.

9. A. The local loop is located between the traditional phone and the CO switch.

10. C. Jitter is the variable delay of packets at the receiving end of a connection, including an IP telephony voice call.

Q&A

1. True. Cisco recommends Low-Latency Queuing for VoIP networks.

2. False. H.323 is an ITU standard, and SIP is an IETF standard for multimedia.

3. True. An Erlang is a telecommunications traffic unit of measurement representing the continuous use of one voice path for one hour.

4. VAD. Voice Activity Detection suppresses packets when there is silence.

5. Dejitter buffers are used at the receiving end to smooth out the variable delay of received packets.

6. True. With CCS, a separate channel (from the bearer channels) is used for signaling.

7. False. You use FXS ports to connect to phones and FXO ports to connect to the PSTN.

8. True. SS7 implements call setup, routing, and control, ensuring that intermediate and far-end switches are available when a call is placed.

9. Interactive Voice Response (IVR) System. IVR systems connect incoming calls to an audio playback system that queues the calls, provides prerecorded announcements, prompts the caller for key options, provides the caller with information, and transfers the call to another switch extension or agent.

10. Automatic Call Distribution (ACD) system. ACD is used by airline reservation systems, customer service departments, and other call centers.

11. CRTP and VAD. Both CRTP and VAD reduce the amount of bandwidth used by VoIP calls. G.729 calls can be reduced from 26.4 kbps to 11.2 with CRTP and to 7.3 with CRTP and VAD.

12. A, B, C, and E are fixed; D is variable. Fixed-delay components include processing, serialization, dejitter, and propagation delays. Variable-delay components include only queuing delays.

13. You reduce the frame size with fragmentation or increase the link bandwidth. The formula is serialization delay = frame size/link bandwidth.

14. PQ-WFQ and LLQ. Both of these queuing techniques use a strict priority queue. LLQ also provides class-based differentiated services.

15. False. The G.114 recommendation specifies 150-ms one-way maximum delay.

16.   True. FRF.12 specifies LFI for Frame Relay networks.

17.   Yes. An RTT of 250 ms means that the average one-way delay is 125 ms, which is less than the recommended maximum of 150 ms.

18.   i = D, ii = C, iii = A, iv = B, v = E

19.   i = B, ii = C, iii = A

20.   i = B, ii = D, iii = C, iv = A

21.   FRF.11

22.   C. Q.SIG is the preferred protocol for inter-PBX trunks.

23.   A. CRTP compresses the IP/UDP/RTP headers from 40 bytes to 2 or 4 bytes.

24.   B. The analog signal is filtered and then sampled, and then samples are digitized.

25.   C. The digitizing process is divided into companding, and quantization and coding.

26.   D. All answers are correct.

27.   B. LFI and cRTP should be implemented to help with the serialization delay on slow-speed WAN circuits. LLQ will not help, because the circuit has no congestion.

28.   D. The G.729 codec is recommended on WAN links because of its lower bandwidth requirements and relatively high MOS.

29.   C and D. cRTP and VAD reduce the amount of IP bandwidth used in IPT calls.

30.   A. CAC prevents new voice calls from affecting existing voice calls.

31.   D. The Cisco Unified CallManager performs the call processing functions of the Cisco IPT solution.

32.   Multisite centralized WAN call processing with a CM cluster at the main site and SRST routers at the remote sites.

33.   SRST enables the remote routers to provide call-handling support for IP phones when they lose connectivity to the CallManagers because of a WAN failure.

34.   LLQ provides a strict queue for RTP (VoIP) traffic and differentiated class of service for all other traffic.

35.   The minimum bandwidth is approximately 640 kbps. Each call is 30 kbps times four, which equals 120 kbps. The exiting 512 kbps of data traffic equals 640 kbps. The circuit should be provisioned at a higher speed to prevent the sustained peak utilization from being higher than 70 percent.

36.   Yes, a CM cluster should be implemented at the main site.

37. CRTP compresses the RTP/UDP/IP headers from 40 bytes to 2 to 4 bytes.

38. FRF.12 is the link and fragmentation technique used in frame relay networks.

Chapter 16

"Do I Know This Already?"

1. C. SNMPv3 introduces authentication and encryption for SNMP.

2. B. SNMP runs over UDP.

3. A. Managed devices contain SNMP agents.

4. D. A MIB is a collection of information that is stored on the local agent of the managed device.

5. D. CDP is Cisco Discovery Protocol.

6. C. The NMS manager uses the GetBulk operation to retrieve large blocks of data, such as multiple rows in a table.

7. A. RMON1 is focused on the data link and physical layers of the OSI model.

8. B. Community is not an SNMP operation.

9. B. NetFlow allows for network planning, traffic engineering, billing, accounting, and application monitoring.

10. B. CDP is a hello-based protocol.

Q&A

1. Fault management, configuration management, accounting management, performance management, and security management.

2. Data link layer.

3. Notice level.

4. False.

5. True.

6. Device ID, IP address, capabilities, OS version, model number, port ID.

7. D. A trap message is sent by the agent when a significant event occurs.

8. A. The NMS manager uses the Get operation to retrieve the value-specific MIB variable from an agent.

9. B. The NMS manager uses the Set operation to set values of the object instance within an agent.

10. C. More than 500 syslog facilities can be configured on Cisco IOS.

11. B. At the authNoPriv level, authentication is provided, but not encryption.

12. B. CBC-DES is the encryption algorithm used by SNMPv3.

13. C and D. Both CDP and NetFlow can be used to discover and document a network.

14. B, C, D.

15. D. RMON2 provides monitoring information from the network to the application layers.

16. D.

17. C.

18. A. The authPriv level provides authentication and encryption.

19. i = C, ii = A, iii = D, iv = B

The OSI Reference Model, TCP/IP Architecture, and Numeric Conversion

The Open Systems Interconnection (OSI) model is a mandatory topic in any internetworking book. The CCDA candidate should understand the OSI model and identify which OSI layers host the different networking protocols. The OSI model provides a framework for understanding internetworking. This appendix provides an overview and general understanding of the OSI reference model.

The Transmission Control Protocol/Internet Protocol (TCP/IP) architecture provides the practical implementation of a layered model. This appendix provides an overview of the TCP/IP layers and how they map to the OSI model.

Also covered in this appendix is the numeric conversion of binary, decimal, and hexadecimal numbers. The ability to covert between binary, decimal, and hexadecimal numbers helps you manipulate IP addresses in binary and dotted-decimal format. Quickly converting these numbers will help you answer test questions.

OSI Model Overview

The International Organization for Standardization (ISO) developed the OSI model in 1984, and revisited it in 1994, to coordinate standards development for interconnected information-processing systems. The model describes seven layers that start with the physical connection and end with the application. As shown in Figure B-1, the seven layers are physical, data link, network, transport, session, presentation, and application.

The OSI model divides the tasks involved in moving data into seven smaller, more manageable layers. Each layer provides services to the layer above, performs at least the functions specified by the model, and expects the defined services from the layer below. The model does not define the precise nature of the interface between layers or the protocol used between peers at the same layer in different instantiations of a protocol stack. The model's design encourages each layer to be implemented independently. For example, you can run an application over IP (Layer 3), Fast Ethernet (Layer 2), Frame Relay (Layer 2), or Gigabit Ethernet (Layer 2). As the packets route through the Internet, the Layer 2 media change independently from the upper-layer protocols. The OSI model helps standardize discussion of the design and construction of networks for developers and hardware manufacturers. It also provides network engineers and analysts with a framework useful in understanding internetworking.

Figure B-1   *Seven-Layer OSI Model*

Layer Number	OSI Layer Name
7	Application
6	Presentation
5	Session
4	Transport
3	Network
2	Data Link
1	Physical

Layered implementations of internetworking technologies do not necessarily map directly to the OSI model. For example, the TCP/IP architecture model describes only four layers, with the upper layer mapping to the three upper layers of the OSI model (application, presentation, and session). The development of IP predates the OSI model. For a more thorough discussion of the TCP/IP model, see Chapter 7, "Internet Protocol Version 4."

The following sections describe and provide sample protocols for each OSI layer.

Physical Layer (OSI Layer 1)

The physical layer describes the transportation of raw bits over physical media. It defines signaling specifications and media types and interfaces. It also describes voltage levels, physical data rates, and maximum transmission distances. In summary, it deals with the electrical, mechanical, functional, and procedural specifications for links between networked systems.

Examples of physical layer specifications are

- EIA/TIA-232 (Electronic Industries Association/ Telecommunications Industry Association)

- EIA/TIA-449

- V.35

- IEEE 802 LAN and metropolitan-area network (MAN) standards

- Physical layer (PHY) groups Synchronous Optical Network/Synchronous Digital Hierarchy (SONET/SDH)

- Maximum cable distances of the Ethernet family, Token Ring, and Fiber Distributed Data Interface (FDDI)

Data Link Layer (OSI Layer 2)

This layer is concerned with the reliable transport of data across a physical link. Data at this layer is formatted into frames. Data link specifications include frame sequencing, flow control, synchronization, error notification, physical network topology, and physical addressing. This layer converts frames into bits when sending information and converts bits into frames when receiving information from the physical media. Bridges and switches operate at the data link layer.

Because of the complexity of this OSI layer, the IEEE subdivides the data link layer into three sublayers for LANs. Figure B-2 shows how Layer 2 is subdivided. The upper layer is the logical link sublayer, which manages communications between devices. The bridging layer, defined by IEEE 802.1, is the middle layer. The lowest layer is the Media Access Control (MAC) sublayer, which manages the protocol access to the physical layer and ultimately the actual media. Systems attached to a common data link layer have a unique address on that data link layer. Be aware that you might find some references describing this layer as having two sublayers: the Logical Link Control (LLC) sublayer and the MAC sublayer.

Figure B-2 *IEEE Data Link Sublayers*

OSI Model	IEEE 802 Specifications
Data Link Layer	802.2 Logical Link
	802.1 Bridging
	Media Access Control

Examples of data link layer technologies are

- Frame Relay

- ATM

- Synchronous Data Link Control (SDLC)

- High-Level Data Link Control (HDLC)

- Point-to-Point Protocol (PPP)

- Ethernet implementations (IEEE 802.3)

- Token Ring (IEEE 802.5)

- Wireless LAN (IEEE 802.11)

Network Layer (OSI Layer 3)

The network layer is concerned with routing information and methods to determine paths to a destination. Information at this layer is called packets. Specifications include routing protocols, logical network addressing, and packet fragmentation. Routers operate at this layer.

Examples of network layer specifications are

- Routed protocols

  — IP

  — Internetwork Packet Exchange (IPX)

  — Connectionless Network Protocol (CLNP)

- Routing protocols

  — Routing Information Protocol (RIP)

  — Open Shortest Path First (OSPF)

  — Enhanced Interior Gateway Routing Protocol (EIGRP)

  — Intermediate System-to-Intermediate System (IS-IS)

Transport Layer (OSI Layer 4)

The transport layer provides reliable, transparent transport of data segments from upper layers. It provides end-to-end error checking and recovery, multiplexing, virtual circuit management, and flow control. Messages are assigned a sequence number at the transmission end. At the receiving end, the packets are reassembled, checked for errors, and acknowledged. Flow control manages the data transmission to ensure that the transmitting device does not send more data than the receiving device can process.

Examples of transport layer specifications are

- Transmission Control Protocol (TCP)

- Real-Time Transport Protocol (RTP)

- Sequenced Packet Exchange (SPX)

- User Datagram Protocol (UDP)

> **NOTE**   Although UDP operates in the transport layer, it does not perform the reliable error-checking functions that other transport layer protocols do.

Session Layer (OSI Layer 5)

The session layer provides a control structure for communication between applications. It establishes, manages, and terminates communication connections called sessions. Communication sessions consist of service requests and responses that occur between applications on different devices.

Examples of specifications that operate at the session layer are

- AppleTalk's Zone Information Protocol (ZIP)

- DECnet's Session Control Protocol (SCP)

- H.245 and H.225

Presentation Layer (OSI Layer 6)

The presentation layer provides application layer entities with services to ensure that information is preserved during transfer. Knowledge of the syntax selected at the application layer allows selection of compatible transfer syntax if a change is required. This layer provides conversion of character-representation formats, as might be required for reliable transfer. Voice coding schemes are specified at this layer. Furthermore, compression and encryption can occur at this layer.

An example of a specification that operates at the presentation layer is Abstract Syntax Notation 1 (ASN.1).

Application Layer (OSI Layer 7)

The application layer gives the user or operating system access to the network services. It interacts with software applications by identifying communication resources, determining network availability, and distributing information services. It also provides synchronization between the peer applications residing on separate systems.

Examples of application layer specifications are

- Telnet

- File Transfer Protocol (FTP)

- Simple Mail Transfer Protocol (SMTP)

- Simple Network Management Protocol (SNMP)

- Network File System (NFS)

- Association Control Service Element (ACSE)

TCP/IP Architecture

The suite of TCP/IP protocols was developed for use by the U.S. government and research universities. The suite is identified by its most widely known protocols: Transmission Control Protocol (TCP) and Internet Protocol (IP). As mentioned, the ISO published the OSI model in 1984. However, the TCP/IP protocols had been developed by the Department of Defense's Advanced Research Projects Agency (DARPA) since 1969. The TCP/IP uses only four layers (as described in RFC 791) versus the seven layers used by OSI. The TCP/IP layers are

- Application

- Host-to-host transport

- Internet

- Network interface

Figure B-3 shows how the TCP/IP layers map to the OSI model.

Figure B-3   *The TCP/IP Architecture and the OSI Model*

OSI Model	TCP/IP Architecture	TCP/IP Protocols
Application	Application	Telnet, SMTP, SNMP, FTP, TFTP, HTTPS, DNS
Presentation		
Session		
Transport	Host-to-Host Transport	TCP, UDP
Network	Internet	IP, ARP, OSPF, ICMP
Data Link	Network Interface	Use of lower layer protocols such as Ethernet and Frame Relay.
Physical		

Network Interface Layer

The TCP/IP network interface (also known as network access) layer maps to the OSI data link and physical layers. TCP/IP uses the lower-layer protocols for transport.

Internet Layer

The Internet layer is where IP resides. IP packets exist at this layer. It directly maps to the network layer of the OSI model. Other TCP/IP protocols at this layer are Internet Control Message Protocol (ICMP), Address Resolution Protocol (ARP), and Reverse ARP (RARP). These protocols are covered in Chapter 7.

Host-to-Host Transport Layer

The host-to-host transport layer of TCP/IP provides two connection services: TCP and UDP. TCP provides reliable transport of IP packets, and UDP provides transport of IP packets without verification of delivery. This layer maps to the OSI transport layer, but the OSI model only defines reliable delivery at this layer.

Application Layer

The TCP/IP application layer maps to the top three layers of the OSI model: application, presentation, and session. This layer interfaces with the end user and provides for authentication, compression, and formatting. The application protocol determines the data's format and how the session is controlled. Examples of TCP/IP application protocols are Telnet, FTP, and Hypertext Transfer Protocol Secure (HTTPS).

The TCP/IP protocols are covered further in Chapter 7.

Example of Layered Communication

Suppose that you use a Telnet application. Telnet maps to the top three layers of the OSI model. In Figure B-4, a user on Host 1 enables the Telnet application to access a remote host (Host 2). The Telnet application provides a user interface (application layer) to network services. As defined in RFC 854, ASCII is the default code format. No session layer is defined for Telnet (not an OSI protocol). Per the RFC, Telnet uses TCP for connectivity (transport layer). The TCP segment is placed in an IP packet (network layer) with a destination IP address of Host 2. The IP packet is placed in an Ethernet frame (data link layer), which is converted into bits and sent onto the wire (physical layer).

When the frame arrives at Router 1, it converts the bits into a frame; removes the frame headers (data link); checks the destination IP address (network); places a serial link header on the packet, making it a serial frame; and forwards the frame to the serial link (data link), which sends it as bits.

Figure B-4 *Telnet Example*

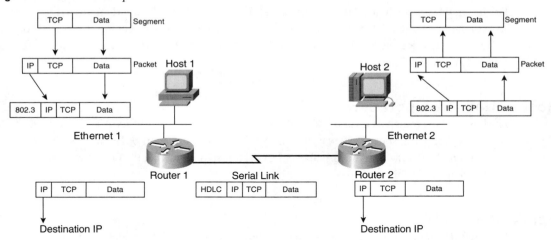

Router 2 receives the bits and converts them into a frame; removes the serial encapsulation headers; checks the destination IP address (network); adds an Ethernet header to the packet, making it a frame; and places the frame on Ethernet 2 (data link). Host 2 receives bits (physical) from the Ethernet cable and converts the bits into a frame (data link). Then, the IP protocol is examined and the packet data is forwarded to TCP, which checks the segment number for errors and then forwards the segment to TCP port 23 (Telnet), which is the application.

Numeric Conversion

This section focuses on the techniques for converting between decimal, binary, and hexadecimal numbers. Although the exam might not have a specific question about converting a binary number to decimal, you need to know how to convert these numbers to do problems on the test. IPv6 addresses are shown in hexadecimal. An IPv4 address could be shown as binary or in traditional dotted-decimal format. MAC addresses and IPv6 addresses are represented in hexadecimal. Some **show** commands have output information in hexadecimal or binary formats.

Hexadecimal Numbers

The hexadecimal numeric system uses 16 digits instead of the 10 digits used by the decimal system. Table B-1 shows the hexadecimal digits and their decimal equivalent values.

Table B-1 *Hexadecimal Digits*

Hexadecimal Digit	Decimal Value
0	0
1	1

Table B-1 *Hexadecimal Digits (Continued)*

Hexadecimal Digit	Decimal Value
2	2
3	3
4	4
5	5
6	6
7	7
8	8
9	9
A	10
B	11
C	12
D	13
E	14
F	15
10	16
11	17
12	18
13	19
14	20

Hexadecimal Representation

It is common to represent a hexadecimal number with "0x" before the number so that it is not confused with a decimal number. The hexadecimal number of decimal 16 is written as 0x10, not 10. Another method is to put a subscript h to the right of the number, such as 10_h. It is also common to use the term "hex" when speaking of hexadecimal. Much of the following text uses "hex."

Converting Decimal to Hexadecimal

First things first: memorize Table B-1. There are two ways to convert larger numbers. The first method is to convert decimal to binary and then convert binary to hex. The second method is to divide the decimal number by 16—the residual is the rightmost hexadecimal digit—and then keep dividing until the number is not divisible anymore. For the first method, use the schemes described in later sections. For the second method, follow the examples described here.

First, divide the decimal number by 16. The remainder of the division is the least-significant (first) hexadecimal digit. Continue to divide the quotients (answer) of the divisions by 16 until the quotient is 0. The remainder value of each later division is converted to a hexadecimal digit and prepended to the previous value. The final remainder is the most-significant digit of the hexadecimal equivalent. For large numbers, you might have to divide many times. This process will be clearer in the following examples.

Conversion Example B-1 *Convert 26 to Its Hex Equivalent*

Divide by 16:

$$
\begin{array}{r}
1\\
16\,\overline{\smash{\big)}\,26}\\
\underline{-16}\\
10 = A_h
\end{array}
$$

Answer: **1A$_h$**

Conversion Example B-2 *Convert 96 to Its Hex Equivalent*

Not divisible by 256; divide by 16:

$$
\begin{array}{r}
6\\
16\,\overline{\smash{\big)}\,96}\\
\underline{-96}\\
0 = 0_h
\end{array}
$$

Answer: **60$_h$**

Conversion Example B-3 *Convert 375 to Its Hex Equivalent*

Divide by 16 first:

$$
\begin{array}{r}
23\\
16\,\overline{\smash{\big)}\,375}\\
\underline{-32}\\
55\\
\underline{-48}\\
7
\end{array}
$$

Now divide 23 by 16:

$$
\begin{array}{r}
1\\
16\,\overline{\smash{\big)}\,23}\\
\underline{-16}\\
7
\end{array}
$$

Now take the residual from the first division (7) and concatentate it with the residual from the second division (7), plus the result of the second division (1), and the answer is 177$_h$.

Conversion Example B-4   *Convert 218 to Its Hex Equivalent*

Divide by 16:

```
              13 = Dh
        ┌─────────
     16 │  218
          -16
        ─────
           58
          -48
        ─────
           10 = Ah
```

Answer: **DAh**

Converting Hexadecimal to Decimal

To convert a hex number to decimal, take the rightmost digit and convert it to decimal (for example, 0xC = 12). Then add this number to the second rightmost digit times 16 and the third rightmost digit times 256. Don't expect to convert numbers larger than 255 on the CCDA exam, because the upper limit of IP addresses in dotted-decimal format is 255 (although Token Ring numbers reach 4096). Some examples follow.

Conversion Example B-5   *Convert 177_h to Decimal*

```
1 x 256 = 256
7 x  16 = 112
7 x   1 =   7
         ─────
          375d
```

Conversion Example B-6   *Convert 60_h to Decimal*

```
6 x 16 =  96
0 x  1 =   0
         ────
          96d
```

Conversion Example B-7   *Convert 100_h to Decimal*

```
1 x 256 = 256
0 x  16 =   0
0 x   1 =   0
         ─────
          256d
```

Conversion Example B-8   *Convert $1DA_h$ to Decimal*

```
 1 x 256 = 256
13 x  16 = 208
10 x   1 =  10
          ─────
           474d
```

Alternative Method for Converting from Hexadecimal to Decimal

Another way is to convert from hex to binary and then from binary to decimal. The following sections discuss converting from binary to decimal.

Binary Numbers

The binary number system uses two digits: 1 and 0. Computer systems use binary numbers. IP addresses and MAC addresses are represented by binary numbers. The number of binary 1s or 0s is the number of *bits*, short for binary digits. For example, 01101010 is a binary number with 8 bits. An IP address has 32 bits, and a MAC address has 48 bits. As shown in Table B-2, IPv4 addresses are usually represented in dotted-decimal format; therefore, it is helpful to know how to convert between binary and decimal numbers. MAC addresses are usually represented in hexadecimal numbers; therefore, it is helpful to know how to convert between binary and hexadecimal.

Table B-2 *Binary Representation of IP and MAC Addresses*

IPv4 Address in Binary	IPv4 Address in Dotted Decimal
00101000 10001010 01010101 10101010	= 40.138.85.170
MAC Address in Binary	**MAC Address in Hexadecimal**
00001100 10100001 10010111 01010001 00000001 10010001	= 0C:A1:97:51:01:91

The CCDA candidate should memorize Table B-3, which shows numbers from 0 to 16 in decimal, binary, and hexadecimal formats.

Table B-3 *Decimal, Binary, and Hexadecimal Numbers*

Decimal Value	Hexadecimal	Binary
0	0	0000
1	1	0001
2	2	0010
3	3	0011
4	4	0100
5	5	0101
6	6	0110
7	7	0111
8	8	1000
9	9	1001

Table B-3 *Decimal, Binary, and Hexadecimal Numbers (Continued)*

Decimal Value	Hexadecimal	Binary
10	A	1010
11	B	1011
12	C	1100
13	D	1101
14	E	1110
15	F	1111
16	10	10000

Converting Binary to Hexadecimal

To convert binary numbers to hex, put the bits in groups of 4, starting with the right-justified bits. Groups of 4 bits are often called *nibbles*. Each nibble can be represented by a single hexadecimal digit. A group of two nibbles is an octet, 8 bits. Examples follow.

Conversion Example B-9   *Convert 0010011101 to Hex*

Group the bits:
00 1001 1101
Answer: **09D$_h$**

Conversion Example B-10   *Convert 0010101001011001000010110001 to Hex*

Group the bits:
0010 1010 0101 1001 0000 1011 0001
Answer: **2A590B1$_h$**

Converting Hexadecimal to Binary

This procedure is also easy. Simply change the hex digits into their 4-bit equivalents. Examples follow.

Conversion Example B-11   *Convert 0DEAD0 to Hex*

Hex: 0   D   E   A   D   0
Binary: 0000 1101 1110 1010 1101 0000
Answer: **000011011110101011010000**

Conversion Example B-12 *Convert AA0101 to Hex*

Hex: A   A   0   1   0   1

Binary: 1010 1010 0000 0001 0000 0001

Answer: **101010100000000100000001**

Converting Binary to Decimal

To convert a binary number to decimal, multiply each instance of 0 or 1 by the power of 2 associated with the position of the bit in the binary number. The first bit, starting from the right, is associated with $2^0 = 1$. The value of the exponent increases by 1 as each bit is processed, working leftward. As shown in Table B-4, each bit in the binary number 10101010 has a decimal equivalent from 0 to 128 based on the value of the bit multiplied by a power of 2 associated with the bit position. This is similar to decimal numbers, in which the numbers are based on powers of 10: 1s, 10s, 100s, and so on. In decimal, the number 111 is $(1*100) + (1*10) + (1*1)$. In binary, the number 11111111 is the sum of $(1*2^7) + (1*2^6) + (1*2^5) + (1*2^4) + (1*2^3) + (1*2^2) + (1*2^1) + (1*2^0) = 128 + 64 + 32 + 16 + 8 + 4 + 2 + 1 = 255$. For 10101010, the result is $128 + 0 + 32 + 0 + 8 + 0 + 2 + 0 = 170$. Examples follow.

Table B-4 *Decimal Values of Bits in a Binary Number*

Power of 2	$2^7 = 128$	$2^6 = 64$	$2^5 = 32$	$2^4 = 16$	$2^3 = 8$	$2^2 = 4$	$2^1 = 2$	$2^0 = 1$
Binary	1	1	1	1	1	1	1	1

NOTE Just memorize 1, 2, 4, 8, 16, 32, 64, and 128. Use it as you read a binary number from right to left. This technique should be helpful in fast conversions.

Conversion Example B-13 *Convert 10110111 to Decimal*

Sum: 128 + 0 + 32 + 16 + 0 + 4 + 2 + 1

Answer = **183**

Conversion Example B-14 *Convert 00011011 to Decimal*

Sum: 16 + 8 + 0 + 2 + 1

Answer = **27**

Conversion Example B-15 *Convert 11111111 to Decimal*

Sum: 128 + 64 + 32 + 16 + 8 + 4 + 2 + 1

Answer = **255**

Converting Decimal to Binary Numbers

This procedure is similar to converting from hex to decimal (by dividing), but now you divide the decimal number by 2. You use each residual to build the binary number by prepending each residual bit to the previous bit, starting on the right. Repeat the procedure until you cannot divide anymore. The only problem is that for large numbers, you might have to divide many times. You can reduce the number of divisions by first converting the decimal value to a hexadecimal value and then converting the intermediate result to the binary representation. After the following example, you will read about an alternate method suitable for use with decimal values between 0 and 255 that can be represented in a single octet.

Conversion Example B-16   *Convert 26 to Binary*

```
         13                           6
    2 |  26                      2 |  13
        -26                          -12
          0                            1
```

The first bit is 0; now divide 13 by 2. [0]   The second bit is 1; now divide 6 by 2. [10]

```
          3                            1
    2 |   6                      2 |   3
         -6                          -2
          0                            1
```

The third bit is 0; now divide 3 by 2. [010]   The fourth bit is 1; the leftmost bit is the division
result at the top, which is one. [11010]

Answer: **11010**

Alternative Method for Converting from Decimal to Binary

The dividing procedure just described works; it just takes a lot of time. Another way is to remember the bit position values within a byte—128, 64, 32, 16, 8, 4, 2, 1—and play with the bits until the sum adds up to the desired number. This method works when you convert integer values between 0 and 255, inclusive. Table B-5 shows these binary numbers and their decimal values.

Table B-5   *Bit Values*

Binary Number	Decimal Value
10000000	128
01000000	64
00100000	32
00010000	16
00001000	8

Table B-5 *Bit Values (Continued)*

Binary Number	Decimal Value
00000100	4
00000010	2
00000001	1

For example, to convert 26, you know that it is a number smaller than 128, 64, and 32, so those 3 bits are 0 (000?????). Now you need to find a combination of 16, 8, 4, 2, and 1 that adds up to 26. This method involves using subtraction to compute the remaining number. Start with the largest number, and make the bit at 16 a 1 (0001????). The difference between 26 and 16 is 10. What combination of 8, 4, 2, and 1 gives 10? 1010. Therefore, the answer is 00011010. You might think this method involves too much guesswork, but it becomes second nature after some practice.

Conversion Example B-17 *Convert 137 to Binary*

> The number is larger than 128; enable that bit. [1???????]
>
> How far is 137 from 128: 9; enable the remaining bits for a value of 9 [1???1001].
>
> The answer is 10001001.

Conversion Example B-18 *Convert 211 to Binary*

> The number is larger than 128; enable that bit. [1???????]
>
> Because 211–128 is greater than 64, enable that bit. [11??????] (Remember that
>
> 11000000 = 192.)
>
> Because 211–192=19, enable bits 16, 2, and 1. [11?1??11]
>
> The answer is 11010011.

In addition to remembering the bit-position values (128, 64, 32, 16, 8, 4, 2, 1), it helps to remember network subnet mask values. Remembering them makes it easier to figure out whether you need to enable a bit. Table B-6 summarizes the binary subnet mask numbers and their decimal values.

Table B-6 *Binary Masks and Their Decimal Values*

Binary Mask	Decimal
10000000	128
11000000	192
11100000	224
11110000	240

Table B-6 *Binary Masks and Their Decimal Values (Continued)*

Binary Mask	Decimal
11111000	248
11111100	252
11111110	254

References and Recommended Readings

ISO/IEC 7498-1: 1994, "Information Processing Systems - OSI Reference Model - The Basic Model."

Postel, J. RFC 791, *Internet Protocol*. Available from http://www.ietf.org/rfc.

Postel, J. RFC 793, *Transmission Control Protocol*. Available from http://www.ietf.org/rfc.

Index

Numerics

A

X-Y-Z

CCNP Prep Center

CCNP Preparation Support from Cisco

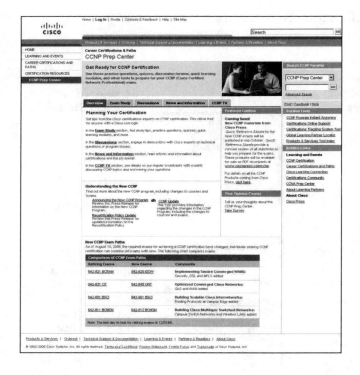

Visit the **Cisco® CCNP® Prep Center** for tools that will help with your CCNP certification studies. Site features include:

- CCNP TV broadcasts, with experts discussing CCNP topics and answering your questions
- Study tips
- Practice questions
- Quizzes
- Discussion forums
- Job market information
- Quick learning modules

The site is free to anyone with a Cisco.com login.

Visit the **CCNP Prep Center** at **http://www.cisco.com/go/prep-ccnp** and get started on your CCNP today!

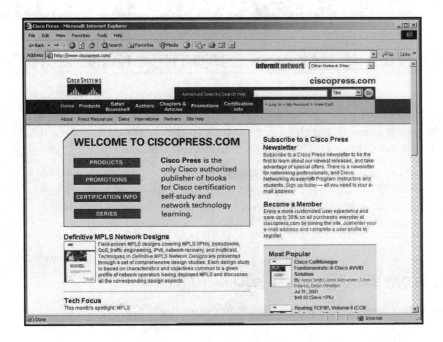

BOOKS ONLINE

ENABLED

THIS BOOK IS SAFARI ENABLED

INCLUDES FREE 45-DAY ACCESS TO THE ONLINE EDITION

The Safari® Enabled icon on the cover of your favorite technology book means the book is available through Safari Bookshelf. When you buy this book, you get free access to the online edition for 45 days.

Safari Bookshelf is an electronic reference library that lets you easily search thousands of technical books, find code samples, download chapters, and access technical information whenever and wherever you need it.

TO GAIN 45-DAY SAFARI ENABLED ACCESS TO THIS BOOK:

● Go to **http://www.ciscopress.com/safarienabled**

● Complete the brief registration form

● Enter the coupon code found in the front of this book before the "Contents at a Glance" page

If you have difficulty registering on Safari Bookshelf or accessing the online edition, please e-mail customer-service@safaribooksonline.com.

DIABETES IN WOMEN

ADOLESCENCE, PREGNANCY, AND MENOPAUSE

THIRD EDITION

DIABETES IN WOMEN

ADOLESCENCE, PREGNANCY, AND MENOPAUSE

THIRD EDITION

E. ALBERT REECE, M.D., PH.D., M.B.A.

Vice Chancellor and Dean
Professor of Obstetrics & Gynecology, Internal Medicine and Biochemistry
University of Arkansas College of Medicine
Little Rock, Arkansas

DONALD R. COUSTAN, M.D.

Chace/Joukowsky Professor and Chair
Department of Obstetrics and Gynecology
Brown Medical School
Obstetrician and Gynecologist in Chief
Women and Infants Hospital of Rhode Island
Providence, Rhode Island

STEVEN G. GABBE, M.D.

Dean, Vanderbilt University School of Medicine
Professor of Obstetrics and Gynecology
Vanderbilt University Medical Center
Nashville, Tennessee

LIPPINCOTT WILLIAMS & WILKINS
A **Wolters Kluwer** Company

Philadelphia · Baltimore · New York · London
Buenos Aires · Hong Kong · Sydney · Tokyo

Acquisitions Editor: Ruth Weinberg
Developmental Editor: Grace Caputo, Erin McMullan
Production Manager: Toni Ann Scaramuzzo
Production Editor: Michael Mallard
Manufacturing Manager: Benjamin Rivera
Cover Designer: Brian Crede
Compositor: Lippincott Williams & Wilkins Desktop Division
Printer: Maple Press

© 2004 by LIPPINCOTT WILLIAMS & WILKINS
530 Walnut Street
Philadelphia, PA 19106 USA
LWW.com

Printed in the USA

Library of Congress Cataloging-in-Publication Data

ISBN: 0-7817-3861-X

Care has been taken to confirm the accuracy of the information presented and to describe generally accepted practices. However, the authors, editors, and publisher are not responsible for errors or omissions or for any consequences from application of the information in this book and make no warranty, expressed or implied, with respect to the currency, completeness, or accuracy of the contents of the publication. Application of this information in a particular situation remains the professional responsibility of the practitioner.

The authors, editors, and publisher have exerted every effort to ensure that drug selection and dosage set forth in this text are in accordance with current recommendations and practice at the time of publication. However, in view of ongoing research, changes in government regulations, and the constant flow of information relating to drug therapy and drug reactions, the reader is urged to check the package insert for each drug for any change in indications and dosage and for added warnings and precautions. This is particularly important when the recommended agent is a new or infrequently employed drug.

Some drugs and medical devices presented in this publication have Food and Drug Administration (FDA) clearance for limited use in restricted research settings. It is the responsibility of the health care provider to ascertain the FDA status of each drug or device planned for use in their clinical practice.

10 9 8 7 6 5 4 3 2 1

CONTENTS

CONTRIBUTORS

Frederick C. Battaglia, M.D. Professor of Pediatrics, Department of Pediatrics, University of Colorado Health Sciences Center, Aurora, Colorado

Peter H. Bennett, M.D., F.R.C.P. Senior Investigator, Phoenix Epidemiology and Clinical Research Branch, NIDDK, NIH, Phoenix, Arizona

Wendy J. Brickman, M.D. Assistant Professor of Pediatrics, Northwestern University Feinberg School of Medicine, Children's Memorial Hospital, Chicago, Illinois

Thomas A. Buchanan, M.D. Departments of Obstetrics and Gynecology and Medicine, Keck School of Medicine, University of Southern California, Los Angeles, California

Marshall W. Carpenter, M.D. Brown University, Women and Infants Hospital of Rhode Island, Providence, Rhode Island

Patrick Catalano, M.D. Professor of Reproductive Biology, Case Western Reserve University; Chairman, Department of Obstetrics and Gynecology, Metro-Health Medical Center, Cleveland, Ohio

Nam H. Cho, M.D., Ph.D., C.C.D. Professor of Preventive Medicine, Ajou University School of Medicine; Director of Clinical Epidemiology, Ajou University Hospital, Suwon, Korea

Larry Cousins, M.D. Division of Perinatology, Mary Birch Hospital for Women, San Diego, California

Donald R. Coustan, M.D. Chace/Joukowsky Professor and Chair, Department of Obstetrics and Gynecology, Brown Medical School; Obstetrician and Gynecologist in Chief, Women and Infants Hospital of Rhode Island, Providence, Rhode Island

Dana Dabelea, M.D., Ph.D. Assistant Professor, Preventive Medicine and Biometrics, University of Colorado Health Sciences Center, Denver, Colorado

Gernot Desoye, Ph.D. Clinic of Obstetrics and Gynecology, Karl-Franzens-University, Vienna, Austria

Esther Eisenberg, M.D., M.P.H. Department of Obstetrics and Gynecology, Vanderbilt University Medical Center, Nashville, Tennessee

Steven C. Elbein, M.D. Department of Endocrinology, John L. McClellan Veterans Hospital, Little Rock, Arkansas

Ulf J. Eriksson, M.D. Professor, Department of Medical Cell Biology, University of Uppsala, Uppsala, Sweden

Steven G. Gabbe, M.D. Dean, School of Medicine, Department of Obstetrics and Gynecology, Vanderbilt University, Nashville, Tennessee

Sandro Gabrielli, M.D. Cattefra Frisiopatologia Prenatale, Clinica Obstetrica e Ginecologia, Universita de Bologna, Bologna, Italy

Henry L. Galan, M.D. Assistant Professor, Department of Obstetrics and Gynecology, Division of Perinatal Medicine, University of Colorado Health Sciences Center, Aurora, Colorado

Philip A. Goldberg, M.D. Department of Internal Medicine, Section of Endocrinology, Yale University School of Medicine, New Haven, Connecticut

Andrea C. Hinton, M.D. Maternal Fetal Medicine Fellow, Department of Obstetrics and Gynecology, University of Cincinnati School of Medicine, Cincinnati, Ohio

Irl B. Hirsch, M.D. Department of Medicine, Division of Metabolism, Endocrinology, and Nutrition, University of Washington School of Medicine; Diabetes Care Center, University of Washington Medical Center, Seattle, Washington

Carol J. Homko, Ph.D., R.N. Temple University Hospital, Philadelphia, Pennsylvania

Lois Jovanovic, M.D. Director and Chief Scientific Officer Sansum Medical Research Institute; Clinical Professor of Medicine, University of Southern California, Los Angeles, California; Adjunct Professor of Biomolecular Science and Engineering, University of California-Santa Barbara, Santa Barbara, California

John L. Kitzmiller, M.D. Los Gatos, California

Siri L. Kjos, M.D. Professor, Department of Obstetrics and Gynecology, Keck School of Medicine, University of Southern California, Los Angeles, California

Mark B. Landon, M.D. Professor and Vice Chairman, Department of Obstetrics and Gynecology, Ohio State University School of Medicine, Columbus, Ohio

Oded Langer, M.D. Babcock Professor and Chairman, Department of Obstetrics and Gynecology, St. Lukes-Roosevelt Hospital Center, University Hospital of Columbia University, New York, New York

Gustavo F. Leguizamón, M.D. Assistant Professor, Department of Obstetrics and Gynecology, CEMIC University, Chief High Risk Pregnancy Unit, CEMIC University Hospital, Buenos Aires, Argentina

Ginny Lewis, M.N., A.R.N.P., C.D.E. Diabetes Care Center, University of Washington Medical Center, Seattle, Washington

Barbara Luke, Sc.D., M.P.H., R.D. Department of Epidemiology and Public Health, University of Miami School of Medicine, Miami, Florida

Jorge H. Mestman, M.D. Professor of Medicine and Obstetrics and Gynecology, Keck School of Medicine, University of Southern California, Los Angeles, California

Boyd E. Metzger, M.D. Tom D. Spies Professor of Medicine, Division of Endocrinology, Northwestern University Feinberg School of Medicine; Attending Physician, Northwestern Memorial Hospital, Chicago, Illinois

Menachem Miodovnik, M.D. Professor and Chair, Department of Obstetrics and Gynecology, Washington Hospital Center, Washington, D.C.

Martin N. Montoro, M.D. Division of Maternal-Fetal Medicine, Women's and Children's Hospital, Los Angeles, California

Leslie Myatt, Ph.D. Department of Obstetrics and Gynecology, University of Cincinnati College of Medicine, Cincinnati, Ohio

William Oh, M.D. Professor of Pediatrics, Brown University, Rhode Island Hospital, Providence, Rhode Island

David J. Pettitt, M.D. Senior Scientist, Clinical Research Department, Sansum Medical Research Institute, Santa Barbara, California

Gianluigi Pilu, M.D. Attending Physician, Department of Obstetrics and Gynecology, University of Bologna School of Medicine, Bologne, Italy

Neda Rasouli, M.D. Instructor, Division of Endocrinology, University of Arkansas for Medical Sciences, Little Rock VA Hospital, Little Rock, Arkansas

E. Albert Reece, M.D., Ph.D. Vice Chancellor and Dean, Professor of Obstetrics & Gynecology, Internal Medicine and Biochemistry, University of Arkansas College of Medicine, Little Rock, Arkansas

Barak M. Rosenn, M.D. Associate Professor of Obstetrics and Gynecology, Columbia University College of Physicians and Surgeons; Director of Obstetrics and Maternal-Fetal Medicine, St. Luke's Roosevelt Hospital Center, New York, New York

Robert S. Sherwin, M.D. Department of Internal Medicine, Section of Endocrinology, Yale University School of Medicine, New Haven, Connecticut

Gerald I. Shulman, M.D. Department of Internal Medicine, Section of Endocrinology, Yale University School of Medicine, New Haven, Connecticut

Baha M. Sibai, M.D. Professor and Chairman, Department of Obstetrics/Gynecology, University of Cincinnati, Cincinnati, Ohio

Kathryn M. Thrailkill, M.D. Associate Professor of Pediatrics, University of Arkansas College of Medicine, Little Rock, Arkansas

PREFACE

The third edition of *Diabetes in Women* provides an updated educational and therapeutic resource for those who care for women with diabetes during adolescence, pregnancy and beyond. While continuing to provide information about diabetes in pregnancy for the healthcare professional, we have widened our scope in this new edition. The risk factors for diabetes are growing in epidemic proportions, and, as a result, it has become more and more common in the United States. We are witnessing an alarming increase of diabetes in the adolescent. Diabetes is now characterized as a major women's health issue and we recognize that diabetes poses particular challenges for women.

As healthcare makes remarkable strides in the control of diabetes, we also recognize that the increase of a woman's life expectancy with the disease presents new challenges. Accordingly, we have expanded this third edition to include the full-spectrum of diabetes in women. The prognosis for women with diabetes continues to improve as does that of their offspring. The revised and current state of knowledge in this edition continues to stress the importance of closely monitored metabolic control in the management of diabetes in pregnancy, but also addresses the entire life cycle of diabetes in adolescence, pregnancy and menopause. The changes recommended by our contributors for the diagnosis of diabetes should prove beneficial to patients, and the value of continued research, innovation and monitoring will constantly change the diabetes landscape.

The enormous increase in both our understanding and knowledge has proved beneficial in fostering new manage-ment strategies for women of all ages with diabetes. Technology, monitoring, quality of care, and up-to-date guidance and information expand the scope of this edition. The data included have served as the bases for the many new medical considerations and guidelines for managing diabetes throughout a woman's life. This third edition recognizes the educational programs, risk assessments and support for quality care and self-management that should assist in increasing the lifespan of women with diabetes.

In aggregate, we have seen overall health improvement for women with diabetes, largely due to better risk assessment, screening, monitoring and management. This edition presents new and updated information on the best treatment options and on dietary management, patient education, genetics, perinatal counseling, diabetes prevention, long-term care of complications, postpartum and menopause. Appropriate care and disease management must be promoted across the span of a woman's life stages. It is our hope that in the ever-changing landscape of information and research, this edition continues to contribute to meet the expanding needs of healthcare professionals.

Gratefully, we acknowledge the contributions of many outstanding experts whose efforts and authoritative reviews and guidance make this publication one which reflects new strategies and practices that will bring new advances in understanding and preventing diabetes.

E. Albert Reece, M.D., Ph.D., M.B.A.
Donald R. Coustan, M.D.
Steven G. Gabbe, M.D.

ACKNOWLEDGMENTS

We would like to express our gratitude to our contributors, who have painstakingly written comprehensive, highly informative, and scholarly chapters. Efforts like these can only be described as labors of love. In addition, all our secretaries and administrative assistants collectively deserve much praise and commendation for the many hours devoted to typing, reviewing, correcting, copying and mailing the many versions of the manuscripts. Finally, we remain indebted to the editors of Lippincott Williams & Wilkins, especially Ms. Lisa McAllister and Ms. Grace Caputo. Overall, their persistent demeanor enabled the timely publication of this book.

We are deeply grateful to all those who collaborated in bringing this project to fruition, from the first edition through the current one.

E. Albert Reece, M.D., Ph.D., M.B.A.
Donald R. Coustan, M.D.
Steven G. Gabbe, M.D.

A Tribute to
Dr. Priscilla White

(March 17, 1900 to December 16, 1989)

Dr. White in 1987.

The past half-century has seen dramatic changes in the management of pregnancy complicated by diabetes, and equally dramatic improvements in outcomes. We of a younger generation of researchers have come late upon the scene, at a time when many of the major advances of the past are taken for granted. For this reason, we feel it appropriate to credit the formative work of early investigators, particularly Dr. Priscilla White, who is acknowledged to be one of the outstanding contributors to the study of diabetes in pregnancy.

In the course of working on the first edition of this book, we were privileged to confer with Dr. White and to hear her personal recollections of 50 years of research and patient care, in which Dr. White captured quite vividly the sadness and gloom, and the dismal reproductive prognosis for diabetic women. As Dr. White remembered:

> Diabetic women were discouraged from becoming pregnant, and termination of pregnancy was often recommended for those who did. Before insulin was available, patients often died during the course of their pregnancy, or their fetuses often died before birth, or as infants Any successful pregnancy was remarkable, so doctors spent almost the entire pregnancy with their patients. We saw them weekly, practically. When they came in labor, I was notified immediately and stayed with them through the entire labor. Delivery was often done prematurely, because if patients were allowed to go to term, the

babies would die. We did see, however, fewer mothers die following the introduction of insulin.

Dr. White spent virtually all her distinguished career in Boston, primarily at the Joslin Clinic caring for pregnant women with diabetes. Her writings have been extensive and have served as mileposts chronically the advances in management and outcome from the early 1920s through the late 1970s. Her system of classification of diabetes among pregnant women was the international standard by which such patients were described.

Her descriptions of the hardships experienced by diabetic individuals prior to the discovery of insulin underscore the tremendous contribution made by Dr. White and her contemporaries. Dr. White will always be respected and remembered with affection by diabetologists, obstetricians, and others who care for diabetic women during their pregnancies. Without the immense strides made by these forerunners, today's advancements might still be out of reach. We presented a copy of the first edition of this book to Dr. White. She graciously accepted our tribute. In 1989, Dr. White died at the age of 89. Fortunately, her contribution lives on!

E. Albert Reece, M.D., Ph.D., M.B.A.
Donald R. Coustan, M.D.
Steven G. Gabbe, M.D.

1

THE HISTORY OF DIABETES MELLITUS

E. ALBERT REECE
STEVEN G. GABBE

The history of diabetes probably dates back to the beginning of humankind, encompassing centuries, generations, and civilizations. A historical review of the events surrounding the evolution of our current knowledge of diabetes mellitus must examine the oldest civilizations, including the Babylonians, Assyrians, Egyptians, Chinese, and Japanese, as well as the contributions of the Greeks, Romans, Europeans, and Americans. This chapter does not attempt to acknowledge all contributors, but rather attempts to develop a cohesive story of the evolution of the field of diabetes mellitus. To place some chronology to events and to put them in the context of the times in which they occurred, it is necessary to describe some societal or political occurrences of those times that had an effect on the development of this field.

EARLY CIVILIZATION AND RECORDS OF DIABETES

Early Egyptian Medicine

Although no consensus exists as to the beginnings of civilization, the period 5000 to 4500 BC is often cited to represent that era. At that time, Babylon was founded by the Sumerians but was later conquered in 3800 BC by the Babylonians and the Assyrians. Babylon was a powerful theocratic empire, with religion dominating politics as well as medicine. Disease was considered to be due to evil spirits or demons that influenced the physical and mental well-being of humans. Beliefs or concepts of this nature led to the beginning of medical astrology. Much of early Babylonian and Assyrian medicine was inscribed on some 800 medical tablets, much of which was translated by Morris Jastrow (1–10).

The Sumerians made inscriptions in clay; the Egyptians used strips of papyrus, reeds fastened together and shaped into rolls, on which they inscribed information. These strips subsequently became permanent records (3). Papyrus Ebers, written about 1500 BC, contains a record of abnormal polyuria, now believed to be related to diabetes (1,3,4) and is probably the first recorded reference to the symptoms of diabetes.

Early Greek Medicine

As previously mentioned, the dominant ideology in early civilization was theocracy, with religion dictating every aspect of human life. It was not until about the time of Hippocrates (466–377 BC) that some separation of medicine from religion occurred. In the Hippocratic writings, no direct reference to diabetes exists, probably because the disease was rare and incurable. The Hippocratic philosophy was to pay little attention to such diseases, although there is some indirect evidence that Hippocrates was familiar with diabetic conditions. In the writing of the Ermerins edition of Hippocrates, a word is used that is translated to mean "to make water much or often." This word was also referred to by Aristotle and may be the condition known to writers of that time as "wasting of the body" (3,5).

Aretaeus of Cappadocia (AD 30–90) was highly respected in his time and was of similar stature in society to Hippocrates. He embraced most but not all of the philosophy of his contemporaries, namely, Hippocrates and Pythagoras. At the time, there was a Pythagorean philosophy, described in the works of Plato (3), that stated:

> He who instead of accepting his destiny endeavors to prolong life by medicine is likely to multiply and magnify his diseases; regimen and not medicine is the true cure when a man has time at his disposal. No attempt should be made to cure a disease system and afford a long and miserable life to the Man himself and to his descendants.

Although Aretaeus did not agree with the above philosophy, he apparently was politically shrewd enough not to disagree with a dominant philosophy in order to maintain the respect of his peers. He was known for his dignity and his love of the art of medicine, his sympathy for sick patients, and his unswerving belief that, whenever possible, medicine should be used to prolong life. In addition, he believed that a physician should also feel obliged to attend to incurable cases even though he may be able to do no more than express sympathy (3,6). One might reflect on such a principle and possibly find it difficult to distinguish from those held by most twentieth century physicians. Although diabetes had always been present, it was Aretaeus who is credited for naming this medical illness. The term *diabetes* means to pass through or to siphon. The following quote by Aretaeus will demonstrate how ill patients with diabetes were and the sense of frustration and hopelessness that such a disease generated, not only to the patient but to the physicians as well (7):

> . . . a wonderful affliction, not very frequently in men, being a melting down of the flesh and limbs into urine. Its cause is of a cold and humid nature as in dropsy, for the patients never stop making water, but the flow is incessant as if from the opening of aqueducts. The nature of the disease is chronic, but the patient is short lived, for the illness is rapid and the death speedy. Moreover, the life is disgusted and painful, thirst unquenchable, with excessive drinking which, however, is disproportionate to the large quantity of urine. If at times they abstain from drinking, the mouth becomes parched and the body dry. The viscera seems scorched up. They are affected with nausea, restlessness and burning thirst and at no distant time they expire.

In another quotation, Aretaeus describes further the symptoms of diabetes, particularly the severe polyuria and the progressive nature of this disease. Except for acquired immunodeficiency syndrome, we can hardly comprehend the sense of hopelessness that such a disease evoked in both patients and physicians (3):

> Diabetes is a wasting of the flesh and limbs into urine from a cause similar to dropsy. The patient never ceasing to make water and the discharge is an incessant sluice let off. The patient does not survive long for the marasmus is rapid and death speedy. The thirst is ungovernable. The copious potations are more than equaled by the diffuse urinary discharge, for more urine flows away, how indeed could the making of water be stopped, or what sense of modesty is paramount to pain? The epithet diabetes has been assigned from the disorder being somewhat like passing of water by a siphon.

We can sense the frustrations in the writings of Aretaeus as he describes the fate of patients with diabetes. Medical therapy was not emphasized for more than one reason. As stated before, the Pythagorean philosophy advocated that medicine should not be used to prolong the sufferings of an incurable disease, and no available cure for diabetes existed.

Early Roman Medicine

Celsus (30 BC to AD 50), a Roman translator of Greek medicine, summarized the medical and surgical progress of both the Hippocratic and the Alexandrian periods. Like Aretaeus, Celsus also described individuals with diabetes as "patients with a discharge of urine greater than the amount of fluid taken in by mouth" (8,9).

Early Arabian Medicine

Arabian medicine was highlighted by an acclaimed physician named Avicenna (AD 980–1027). He was not only a meticulous physician but a prolific writer, authoring more than 100 articles that were compiled to form a canon. Avicenna commented that diabetes may be primary or secondary to another disease. He also observed that diabetic patients have an irregular appetite associated with thirst, mental exhaustion, inability to work, and loss of sexual functions. In essence, Avicenna described many of the features related to diabetes that we are well aware of today. In fact, he observed the carbuncles, furuncles, and a variety of diabetic complications. Avicenna believed that diabetes affected the liver, probably causing enlargement of the organ (1,10).

Early Asian Medicine

The Hindus had three leading medical texts: the Charaka, the Susruta, and the Vagbhata. The Susruta was the book of surgery, and the Charaka the book of medicine. The Hindu medical writings of the sixth century refer to diabetes as honey urine (11):

> A disease of the rich and one that is brought about by gluttony or overindulgence in flour and sugar. This disease is ushered in by the appearance of morbid secretions about the teeth, nose, ears and eyes. The hands and feet are very hot and burning. The surface of the skin is shiny as if oil had been applied to it, this accomplished by the thirst and the sweet taste in the mouth. The different varieties of this disease are distinguished from each other by the symptoms and by the color of the urine. If the disease is produced by phlegm, insects approach the urine. The person is languid. His body becomes flat and there is discharge with mucus from the nose and mouth with dyspeptic symptoms and looseness of the skin. He is always sleeping with cough and difficulty breathing.

The earliest of the Chinese medical texts is based on the works of Huag-ti of 2697 BC. Records were preserved on lacquer on strips of bamboo or palm leaves. These writings represent the counterpart of the Egyptian picture writing. Japanese medicine began much later, with the first medical book dating back to AD 982. The Chinese and Japanese also recognized the symptoms of diabetes but were even less restrained in their description and wrote "the urine of diabetics was very large in amount and it was so sweet that it attracted dogs" (8).

European and American Medicine

Observations of patients having diabetes were also made by Italian, Portuguese, Greek, Dutch, and other Europeans, as well as American physicians. Physicians went beyond merely describing the hopelessness and the osmotic diuretic effect of severe diabetes but began thinking of possible causes and exploring these ideas. Some conducted experiments to simulate the medical illness in order to apply a scientific approach to the understanding of this disease.

Sylvanus (1478–1555) believed that diabetes was a disease of the blood, whereas Cardano (1505–1576) did not accept the dictum that diabetes was a disease of greater fluid output than intake. Therefore, he compiled a table in which he recorded the intake of liquid and urinary output in diabetic patients. Willis Wyatt (1621–1675) of Oxford University claimed diabetes to be a primary disease of the blood. He explained that the sugar present in the urine of patients with diabetes represented excretion of sugar that was initially in the blood. In fact, he made the best qualitative urinalysis studies possible in that time (3).

In 1682, Brunner (12) created an animal model to study diabetes by destroying the pancreas of experimental animals, causing polyuria and polydypsia. Other observations were made that continued to refine the understanding and characterization of diabetes. Dobson (13) in 1776 demonstrated that diabetic urine contained sugar that fermented. In 1888, Cawley (14) diagnosed diabetes for the first time by demonstrating the presence of sugar in the urine. He observed that the disease may result from injury to the pancreas, as had already been observed in experimental animals by Brunner (12).

Throughout this time, diabetes had been recognized and many of its symptoms described. As more observations were made, its clinical and diagnostic features were characterized (15). However, no mention was made of attempts to control the disease. The foundation for systematic treatment of diabetes by restricting the diet should be credited to Rollo (16,17) in 1797. Soon thereafter, Bouchardat (1806–1866) proposed a management of diet and exercise that seems rather contemporary (18). He advocated the use of fresh fats as a substitute for carbohydrate, the avoidance of milk because of its lactose, and the use of alcohol as a fluid. He also invented gluten bread, stressed the use of green vegetables in the diet, and emphasized the importance of "undernutrition." Bouchardat (18) has been credited for professing a modern viewpoint concerning diabetes. Such a therapeutic approach suggests that physicians were then convinced that the disease was caused by the inability of the body to handle carbohydrates properly. Several physicians and investigators subsequently emphasized dietary management of diabetes. Clearly, the Pythagorean era had ended and was replaced by the philosophy of Aretaeus; a potentially incurable disease was now being treated, and diligent efforts were made to prolong life. In any event, as one reads the literature, one understands diabetes as a curable problem, since much effort was dedicated toward this disease. Both clinicians and investigators focused on potential causes and possible cures (3,19). Naunyn (19) devoted most of his life to the study of diabetes. He strongly advised dietary management and suggested the following points (3,19):

1. The alpha and omega care of diabetes is dietetic treatment and not drugs.
2. Diabetic glycosuria increases with time while the weight of the patient decreases.
3. When the diabetic patient is free from sugar, tolerance usually increases; therefore, aim to manage the patient sugar free to prevent glycosuria.
4. Reduction of carbohydrates and proteins is useful for the removal of glycosuria.
5. Sugar-producing foods are carbohydrates and proteins.
6. Determine the exact qualitative and quantitative diet for every diabetic patient who comes under treatment.
7. Patients get along well on 30 to 35 calories/kg body weight.
8. Sugar production from fat does not play such an important role as to influence diabetic glycosuria to a notable extent.
9. For this reason and on account of its high caloric value, fat is the most valuable food for the diabetic.

As we look back at history, we see that the recommendations and observations of Avicenna, Bouchardat, and Naunyn were similar to what we currently recommend for the treatment of diabetes.

EARLY PATHOPHYSIOLOGY

Experimental work as early as 1682 by Brunner (12) demonstrated that the pancreas was the diseased organ in diabetic individuals. In 1869, Langerhans (20) described small islands within the pancreas, now known as islets of Langerhans. He offered no suggestion as to their physiologic significance. Shaffer in 1895 suggested that these islets, when diseased, produced diabetes (3). Six years later in the United States, Opie (21,22) elaborated on the idea that diabetes was due to degeneration of the islets of Langerhans in the pancreas and that these islets had an internal secretion that, when altered in form and function, resulted in diabetes.

Minkowski and von Mering became interested in diabetes research tangentially. They were investigating the role and function of the pancreas in digestion and conducted a pancreatectomy in a dog. The dog was house-trained but nevertheless developed uncontrollable polyuria similar to that seen in diabetic patients. This research subsequently led to the confirmation that removal of the pancreas caused diabetes (7,23–25). Although Langerhans (20) had previously described the islets of Langerhans, neither he nor any other investigator suggested any physiologic significance to these islets until Opie (21,22). The work of Minkowski (25) and the observations by Opie (21,22) began to link islet cell disease and diabetes. In fact, Opie in 1901 (21,22) observed changes in the structure of the islet tissue that could be demonstrated in the pancreas of patients dying of diabetes.

For the next 18 years, many investigators concentrated on the islet cells (25,26). Paulesco, a physiologist in Bucharest, had succeeded in making an extract from the pancreas in 1916, which he called pancreine, that when injected into a diabetic dog gave temporary relief from the symptoms. The German regime stopped his research, and he was not able to resume his scientific work until 1920. It was not until 1921 that he published his paper. Unfortunately, Paulesco never succeeded in obtaining a pure extract suitable for humans (7,27). By the early 1900s, the association of diabetes with pancreatic islet cell disease became an established medical fact. At this point, research was directed at replacement therapy. It became clear that the substance secreted by these islet cells was insufficient in diabetic patients. Zuelzer et al. (1906–1909) prepared an extract from the expressed juice of the pancreas, treated it with alcohol, and dissolved the residue with the salt. This extract was tested in pancreatectomized dogs with hyperglycemia and ketonuria, eight diabetic humans, and four cases of humans with ketosis (3,28). This was clearly the right direction and probably as close as anyone came to the discovery of insulin before Banting and Best. This extract contained a variety of impurities, and after injection, subjects became very ill with chills and fever. The efforts of Zuelzer and colleagues were recognized by MacLeod, in whose laboratory insulin was eventually discovered. MacLeod stated, "Zuelzer in 1908 came very near to isolating what we now call insulin" (7).

DISCOVERY OF INSULIN

A variety of experiments conducted at that time were aimed at further exploring the pathophysiologic bases of diabetes. Banting describes how he became impressed with the work of Barron, particularly with the analogy Barron drew between the degenerative changes induced by experimental ligation of the pancreatic duct or blockage of the duct by gallstones (7,29). As we all know, good science is created in the morning! Such was true with the discovery of insulin. Banting apparently awoke at 2:00 A.M. and was bothered by an idea resulting from his late night reading, so he got up and scribbled on a piece of paper, "Ligate pancreatic duct of dogs, wait 6–8 weeks for degeneration, and remove the residue and extract" (7).

At that time (1920), Banting was a young general practitioner in London and a demonstrator in anatomy. MacLeod was a successful investigator and department chair at the University of Toronto. Banting wrote MacLeod and submitted a proposal for a series of experiments that would cure diabetes. He was rather precise in detailing his needs. He wanted two medical students, a few dogs, laboratory space, and certainly sufficient funding. Such an ambitious proposal by a new investigator submitted to granting agencies of our time would not likely be sup-

ported. In any event, MacLeod allocated two medical student assistants, Charles Best and Clark Noble. Best started first. By the end of the first month, Best had enjoyed the work so much he decided that he would stay for a second month. Shortly after the end of the 8-week period, they were successful in isolating the pancreatic extract that was injected into a pancreatectomized dog. Banting (30) described how he will never forget

> . . . the joy of opening the door of the cage and seeing the dog which had been unable to walk previously, jump on the floor and run around the room in a normal fashion following injection of the extract.

The first patient who received the new extract was Leonard Thompson, a 14-year-old boy (7,30). He was admitted to the Toronto General Hospital with nocturia of 2.5 years' duration and weighed only 29 kg. Because neither Banting nor Best had practice privileges at Toronto General, Dr. Ed Jeffrey, an intern, administered the first dose of insulin on January 11, 1922, which consisted of 7.5 mL of pancreatic extract being injected into each of the patient's buttocks. Leonard was discharged from the hospital on May 15, 1922. He lived a relatively normal life, playing sports and working intermittently. Leonard died at the age of 27 from bronchopneumonia (31).

DIABETES IN PREGNANCY

Before 1856, there are few reports of pregnancy complicating diabetes. Blott wrote that "true diabetes is inconsistent with conception" (7,28). It was not until 1882 that a report by Duncan described 22 pregnancies in the literature, and for the first time, the aforementioned statement of Blott's opinion as well as the dominant philosophy at the time was challenged (32,33). Subsequently, in 1909, Peel collected 66 cases; 27% of the mothers died at the time of labor or within 1 to 2 weeks afterward, and during the following 2 years, 22% more mothers died. One eighth of the pregnancies ended in abortion, and in one third of the pregnancies that went to term, the baby was born dead (7,34). This trend of high maternal and fetal mortality continued until the discovery of insulin. However, physicians were somewhat consoled in that the diabetic pregnancies were rare. In fact, Jellet (7) in a 1905 edition of his manual of midwifery, made the following observation: "First of all, the disease is not a common one, and in the second place, the disability by it is usually so great that as a rule sexual functions including menstruation are arrested." One of the earliest descriptions of gestational diabetes was by Bennewitz of Berlin. He described a 22-year-old woman who developed the classic symptoms of diabetes at 36 weeks' gestation. She suffered an intrapartum fetal death of a 12-lb fetus (35).

As described previously, diabetes was a disease with a dismal prognosis, and reproductive success in these women was not common. Pregnancy worsened the disease and shortened the lives of these patients, many of whom died during or shortly after the pregnancy. In 1920, De Lee (36) wrote that sterility was common among diabetics, probably due to atrophy of the uterus and ovaries, which might also explain the frequent intermittent menses and premature menopause. He continued by saying that abortion and premature labor occurred in 33% of the pregnancies. The children, if pregnancy went to term, often died shortly after birth, with an overall perinatal mortality rate of about 60% to 70%. Diabetes was described as becoming progressively worse with each pregnancy. The nervous system was affected, and about 30% of mothers died, primarily because of diabetic ketoacidosis.

The advent of insulin brought about a dramatic change in the overall outlook for diabetic women and their reproductive potential. There was a dramatic decrease in the maternal mortality from 45% to just over 2% shortly after the introduction of insulin (Fig. 1-1). However, the perinatal mortality did not rapidly change, but rather slowly decreased over time (Fig. 1-2). Problems not altered by the use of insulin included the very large babies and the associated traumatic injury to these fetuses and their mothers during parturition. Other continuing complications were neonatal hypoglycemia, congenital malformations, toxemia of pregnancy, and infections (7,37–41).

In view of the lack of significant improvements in perinatal mortality with the advent of insulin therapy, which contrasted with the reduced maternal mortality observed,

several attempts were made to reduce the fetal death rate. It was observed that there was a significant increase in the stillbirth rate, on the order of 10-fold beyond 36 weeks of gestation. It was said that the fetal mortality rate was about 25% if the birth weight of the baby was approximately 7 pounds (3.2 kg). However, when supervision was poor or totally absent, there was a 70% fetal mortality rate, usually associated with a birth weight of 10 pounds (4.5 kg) or more. Because of these concerns, diabetic patients were routinely delivered at or before 36 weeks by cesarean section or by induction of labor if fetal death had not already occurred, or sooner if maternal complications necessitated early delivery.

Diabetes care soon became centralized, and patients from all over the world were referred to large centers such as King's College in England and the Joslin Clinic in the United States. Various institutional protocols emerged, all aimed at improving fetal outcome. There was a dominant theory originating in Boston that estrogen therapy could improve pregnancy outcome. In 1945, Dr. Priscilla White claimed a 97% fetal survival rate in cases with normal hormone balance and 47% survival in the cases with abnormal hormone balance (42). Subsequent studies, however, showed that estrogens in the doses that were used did not reduce infant mortality in diabetic patients and did not seem to have any beneficial effects on maternal health. In Copenhagen in 1954, Pedersen found that the fetal mortality rate was significantly lower in patients who were being followed over a long period than in those who were first

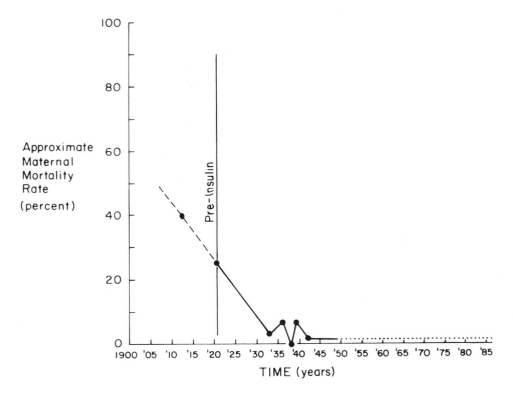

FIGURE 1-1. Maternal mortality before and after the discovery of insulin. A precipitous decline in maternal deaths is depicted shortly after the discovery and use of insulin.

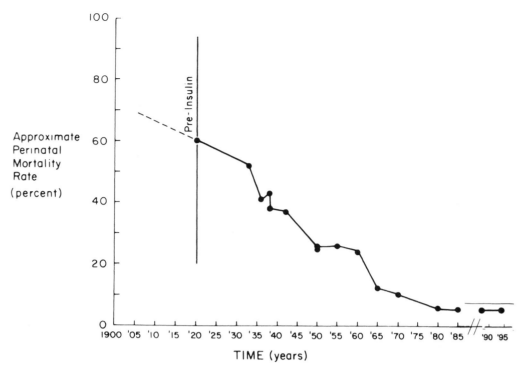

FIGURE 1-2. Perinatal mortality before and after the discovery of insulin. Although a decline in perinatal death was observed, this decline was gradual over time.

seen at or about the time of their delivery (43). Pedersen centralized the care for pregnancies complicated by diabetes at the Rigshospitalet. He identified four prognostically bad signs in pregnancy associated with a significant increase in perinatal mortality: clinical pyelonephritis, ketoacidosis, preeclampsia, and "neglector," a patient who was not compliant irrespective of the cause. As early as the 1950s, there was an emerging philosophy that closer surveillance of patients seemed to result in improved fetal outcome. This led to a management policy of long-term or frequent hospitalizations and early delivery of patients with diabetes.

Other advances included new insulins, particularly the long-acting type and, most recently, human insulin with its low antigenic properties. Other adjunctive tools included estriol measurement, human placental lactogen measurement, assessment of fetal growth with ultrasonography, antepartum fetal heart rate testing, fetal blood sampling techniques during labor, glucose meters, insulin pumps, neonatal intensive care units, and skilled pediatric care. These tools have been used to a lesser or greater extent over the years. Some have been considered to improve perinatal outcome, whereas others, such as estriol and human placental lactogen, have been dropped from clinical use as other newer therapies were found to be of greater value.

In 1977, Karlsson and Kjellmer (44) reported in a retrospective study that there was a linear relationship between glycemic control and perinatal mortality. These findings were corroborated by many other studies and subsequently led to a new trend in diabetes care. Ambient glucose was

stringently maintained as close to nondiabetic levels as possible, with a fairly rapid decline in perinatal mortality rates. These data were reported both in Europe (45) and the United States (46) (Tables 1-1 and 1-2). At the present time, most centers around the country report an average perinatal rate of less than 5%. Patients are living much longer, hence they are experiencing more of the vascular complications of diabetes with its potential effects of pregnancy. In fact, the cause of maternal deaths has shifted from primarily diabetic ketoacidosis to cardiorenal complications (47,48) (Table 1-3).

As many of these complications appeared, an increased incidence in perinatal mortality was found to be associated with patients having complications of diabetes, and recom-

TABLE 1-1. PERINATAL MORTALITY AMONG 1,332 INFANTS OF DIABETIC MOTHERS BORN AT THE RIGSHOSPITAL, 1946–1972

White Classification	Total No. of Infants	Perinatal Mortality(%)
A	181	5.0
B	316	13.9
C	331	18.1
D	425	17.9
F	79	35.4
Total	1,332	16.3

From Pedersen J, Molsted-Pedersen L, Andersen B. Assessors of fetal perinatal mortality in diabetic pregnancy. *Diabetes* 1974;23:302, with permission.

TABLE 1-2. VIABLE FETAL SURVIVAL IN 416 PREGNANCIES WITH MATERNAL VASCULAR DISEASE AT THE JOSLIN CLINIC

	Survival Rate			
	1924–1962		1963–1975	
White Classification	No.	(%)	No.	(%)
R	34	74	48	84
F	126	65	59	72
RF	53	54	30	81
H	0	0	4	100
T	0	0	4	75

From Hare JW, White P. Pregnancy and diabetes complicated by vascular disease. *Diabetes* 1977;26:953, with permission.

mendations were made regarding the avoidance of pregnancy or the termination of pregnancy in patients who had various forms of moderate to severe diabetic vasculopathy (48). It was also believed that diabetes was worsened by the effects of pregnancy. Evolving data to the present time have shown that, except for coronary artery disease, pregnancy is not contraindicated in diabetic patients with vascular complications. Also, the perinatal outcome among these pregnancies does not appear to be significantly different from other insulin-dependent diabetic patients when metabolic control is stringently maintained (49).

There is no doubt that very impressive strides have been made with regard to diabetes in pregnancy, so that at the present time the expectation of the diabetic mother regarding pregnancy performance and fetal outcome can be comparable with that of a nondiabetic patient. There are, however, some unresolved problems, namely, macrosomia and congenital malformations. The incidence of birth defects has not significantly changed over time, and most series report a rate of 6% to 12%. Both clinical and laboratory studies suggest that these malformations are caused by derangement in metabolism during organogenesis (41,50). Recent work has also shown that such malformations can be prevented by the

TABLE 1-3. CAUSE OF DEATH IN 27,966 DIABETIC PATIENTS AT THE JOSLIN CLINIC 1897–1968

Period	Diabetic Ketoacidosis (%)	Cardiorenal Vascular Disease (%)
1897–1914	64.0	18.0
1914–1922	41.5	25.0
1922–1936	8.3	54.4
1937–1949	2.2	69.0
1950–1965	1.0	77.0
1966–1968	1.0	74.0

Modified from Marble A, White P, Bradley RF, et al., eds. *Joslin's diabetes mellitus,* 11th ed. Philadelphia: Lea & Febiger, 1971, with permission.

normalization of metabolism in the preconceptual period (51). Fetal hyperglycemia may contribute to subsequent impaired glucose tolerance associated with defective insulin secretion (52). Although the dramatic increase in type 2 diabetes mellitus observed in the past decade is most likely due to obesity and lack of exercise, such intrauterine exposure may also play a role (53). It is also true, however, that despite encouragement for preconceptional control, patients will become pregnant during unsatisfactory metabolic control. Some studies are now looking at possible therapeutic measures that may either ameliorate or prevent defects caused by hyperglycemia during organogenesis. Recent studies in rodents have demonstrated that fatty acid supplementation can prevent malformations, even in the presence of severe hyperglycemic conditions (41,50).

As we look over the relatively brief history of pregnancy and diabetes, it is apparent that significant strides have been made. It was only in 1776 that Buchan (7,15) wrote:

> In our matrimonial contracts it is amazing so little regard is given to the health and form of the object. Our sportsmen know that the generous courser cannot be bred out of the foundered jade, nor the sagacious spaniel out of the snarling cur. This is settled upon immutable laws. A man who marries a woman of sickly constitution and descended from unhealthy parents, whatever his views may be, cannot be said to act as a prudent part. A diseased woman may prove fertile. Should this be the case, the family must become an infirmary. What prospect of happiness a father of such a family has, we shall leave anyone to judge.

Fortunately, we have surpassed that age when people viewed diabetes as a disease of sorrow and unhappiness with little chance for procreation. Today we can look at such quotes with cynicism.

Although diabetes is probably as old as humankind, some problems still remain without solution. A visionary of our time might see history describing our generation as one in which improved techniques were achieved, leading to better glucose monitoring and control; complex problems relating to pathogenesis of diabetes were unraveled; the various effects of diabetes on organ systems were determined; new methods were introduced for the prevention of diabetes; and the various causes of aberrations of fetal growth and the effects of long-term metabolic control on the development of vasculopathy were explored. We hope the future will also bring about a cure for diabetes, a closed-loop sensor, and insulin pump system or islet cell or stem cell transplantation, or possibly even the microinjection of insulin genes into somatic cells with subsequent autoregulation of insulin production.

REFERENCES

1. Banting FG. The internal secretion of the pancreas. *Am J Physiol* 1922;59:479.

2. Jastrow M. The medicine of the Babylonians and Assyrians. *Proc R Soc Med Lond* 1913–1914;7:109.

3. Barach JH. Historical facts in diabetes. *Ann Med Hist* 1928;10: 387.

4. Ebbell B (translator). *The Papyrus Ebers: the greatest Egyptian medical document.* Copenhagen: Levin & Munksgaard, 1937.

5. Gemmill CL. The Greek concept of diabetes. *Bull NY Acad Med* 1972;48:1033.

6. Aretaeus of Cappadocia. On diabetes. In: Adams F, ed. *The extant works of Aretaeus, the Cappadocian* edited and translated by Adams F. London: Wertheimer for the Sydenham Society, 1856: 338, 485.

7. Peel J. A historical review of diabetes and pregnancy. *J Obstet Gynecol Br Cwlth* 1972;79:385.

8. Ballard JF. A descriptive outline of the history of medicine from its earliest days of 600 BC. *Ann Med Hist* 1924;6:53.

9. Celsus AAC. *De Medicina.* 3 volumes. (English translation by WG Spencer). London: W. Heinemann, 1935–1938.

10. Gruner OC. *Avicenna Ibn Sina. A treatise on the Canon of Medicine incorporating a translation of the first book.* London: Luzac, 1930.

11. Frank LL. Diabetes mellitus in the texts of old Hindu medicine (Charaka, Susruta, Vagbhata). *Am J Gastroenterol* 1957;27:76.

12. Brunner JC. *Experimenta nova circa pancreas.* Amsterdam: H Weststenium, 1683.

13. Dobson M. Experiments and observations on the urine in diabetes. *Med Obs Inq Lond* 1776;5:298.

14. Cawley T. A singular case of diabetes, consisting entirely in the quality of the urine; with an inquiry into the different theories of that disease. *Lond Med J* 1888;9:286.

15. Buchan W. Of the diabetes, and other disorders of the kidneys and bladder. In: *Domestic medicine,* 10th ed. Printed by John Trumbull for Robert Hodge, J.D. M'Dougall and William Green in Boston, 1778:A2.

16. Rollo J. *Cases of the diabetes mellitus,* 2nd ed. London: C Dilly, 1798.

17. Rollo J. *An account of two cases of the diabetes mellitus, with remarks as they arose during the progress of the cure.* London: C Dilly, 1797.

18. Bouchardat A. *Du diabete sucre ou glycourie; son traitement hygienique.* Paris: Germer-Bailliere, 1875.

19. Naunyn B. *Der Diabetes mellitus.* Vienna: A Holder, 1898.

20. Langerhans P. *Beitrage zur mikroskopischen Anatomie der Bauchspeicheldruse* [inaugural dissertation]. Berlin, Buchdruckerei von Gustav Lange, 1869.

21. Opie EL. On the relation of chronic interstitial pancreatitis to the islands of Langerhans and to diabetes mellitus. *J Exp Med* 1900–1901;5:397.

22. Opie EL. The relation of diabetes mellitus to lesions of the pancreas. Hyaline degeneration of the islands of Langerhans. *J Exp Med* 1990–1901;5:527.

23. Mann RJ. Historical vignette: "honey urine" to pancreatic diabetes: 600 BC-1922. *Mayo Clin Proc* 1971;46:56.

24. von Mering J, Minkowski O. Diabetes mellitus nach Pankreasextirpation. *Arch Exp Pathol Pharm Leipzig* 1890;26:371.

25. Minkowski O. Ueber das Vorkommen von Oxybuttersaure im Harn bei Diabetes mellitus. *Arch Exp Pathol Pharm Leipzig* 1884; 18:35.

26. Nelken L. Chairman's remarks. In: Insulin in retrospect. *Isr J Med* 1972;8:467.

27. Paulesco NC. Recherches sur le role du pancreas clans l'assimilation nutritive. *Arch Int Physiol* 1921;17:85.

28. Zuelzer GL. Uber Versuch einer specifischen Ferment-therapie des Diabetes. *Z Exp Pathol Ther Berlin* 1908;5:307.

29. Barron M. The relation of the islets of Langerhans to diabetes, with special reference to cases of pancreatic lithiasis. *Surg Gynecol Obstet* 1920;31:437.

30. Banting FG, Best CH. The internal secretion of the pancreas. *J Lab Clin Med* 1922;7:251.

31. Burrow G, Hazlett B, Phillips MJ. A case of diabetes mellitus. *N Engl J Med* 1982;306:304.

32. Duncan GG. *Diabetes mellitus: principles and treatment.* Philadelphia: WB Saunders, 1951.

33. Duncan JM. On puerperal diabetes. *Trans Obstet Soc Lond* 1882; 24:256.

34. Williams JW. *Obstetrics,* 5th ed. East Norwalk, CT: Appleton & Lange, 1923.

35. Bennewitz HG. Symptomatic diabetes mellitus. [Abstracted from *Osann's 12ter Jahresbericht des Poliklinischen Institutes zu Berlin,* p. 23, Edinburgh Medical and Surgical Journal] 1828;30: 217–218.

36. De Lee JB. *The principles and practice of obstetrics,* 3rd ed. Philadelphia: WB Saunders, 1920.

37. Gabbe SG. A story of two miracles: the impact of the discovery of insulin on pregnancy in women with diabetes mellitus. *Obstet Gynecol* 1992;79:295–299.

38. Joslin EP, Root HF, White P, et al: *The treatment of diabetes mellitus,* 8th ed. Philadelphia: Lea & Febiger, 1948.

39. Papaspyros NS. *The history of diabetes mellitus,* 1st ed. Stuttgart: Thieme, 1952.

40. Papaspyros NS. *The history of diabetes mellitus,* 2nd ed. Stuttgart: Thieme, 1964.

41. Reece EA, Hobbins JC. Diabetic embryopathy: pathogenesis, prenatal diagnosis and prevention. *Obstet Gynecol Surv* 41:325, 1986.

42. White P, Raymond ST, Elliott PJ. Prediction and prevention of late pregnancy accidents in diabetes. *Am J Med Sci* 1939;198:482.

43. Pedersen J. *The pregnant diabetic and her newborn,* 2nd ed. Baltimore: Williams & Wilkins, 1977:201–205.

44. Karlsson K, Kjellmer I. The outcome of diabetic pregnancies in relation to the mother's blood sugar level. *Am J Obstet Gynecol* 1972;112:213.

45. Pedersen J, Molsted-Pedersen L, Andersen B. Assessors of fetal perinatal mortality in diabetic pregnancy. *Diabetes* 1974;23:302.

46. Hare JW, White P. Pregnancy and diabetes complicated by vascular disease. *Diabetes* 1977;26:953.

47. Marble A, White P, Bradley RF, et al., eds. *Joslin's diabetes mellitus,* 11th ed. Philadelphia: Lea & Febiger, 1971.

48. Feudtner C, Gabbe SG. Diabetes and pregnancy: four motifs of modern medical history. *Clin Obstet Gynecol* 2000;43:4–16.

49. Coustan DR, Berkowitz RL, Hobbins JC. Tight metabolic control of overt diabetes in pregnancy. *Am J Med* 1980;68:845.

50. Pinter E, Reece EA, Leranth C, et al. Yolk sac failure in embryopathy due to hyperglycemia: ultrastructural analysis of yok sac differentiation in rat conceptuses under hyperglycemic culture conditions. *Teratology* 1986;33:363.

51. Fuhrmann K, Reiher H, Semmler K, et al. Prevention of congenital malformations in infants of insulin dependent diabetic mothers. *Diabetes Care* 1983;6:219.

52. Sobngwi E, Boudou P, Mauvais-Jarvis F, et al. Effect of a diabetic environment *in utero* on predisposition to type 2 diabetes. *Lancet* 2003;361:1861.

53. Ordovas J, Pittas A, Greenberg AS. Might the diabetic environment in utero lead to type 2 diabetes? *Lancet* 2003;361:1839.

2

THE RISING TIDE OF DIABETES MELLITUS: IMPLICATIONS FOR WOMEN OF ALL AGES

BOYD E. METZGER, NAM H. CHO
WENDY J. BRICKMAN

Diabetes mellitus (DM) is a clinical syndrome characterized by an absolute or relative deficiency of insulin action in responsive organs, thereby exposing all tissues to chronic hyperglycemia. It is estimated that about 17 million persons in the United States have DM (~6.2% of the population) and the prevalence has increased progressively over the past two decades (1,2). Despite the contemporary emphasis on earlier diagnosis and initiation of treatment, approximately one third of individuals are unaware that they have the disease. There is a strong association between age and incidence of type 2 DM, and this contributes to the rapidly growing prevalence of DM in the population at large. Nevertheless, this does not fully account for this epidemic of DM. Indeed, the increase is observed across all ages, and the rapid increase in the frequency of type 2 DM in children is particularly alarming. The contemporary, parallel increase in the prevalence of obesity across all age groups of the U.S. population is striking. Overall, DM shows no gender preference; however, there is a tendency for more type 2 DM to be found in adolescent girls and young adult women, in part related to the fact that systematic screening during pregnancy identifies gestational diabetes mellitus (GDM) in 4% to 8% of the U.S. population (3). GDM is followed by progression to diabetes outside of pregnancy at an accelerated rate.

Similar trends in prevalence of DM have been observed globally, with the most rapid increases in the number of persons identified with DM being reported from areas that have had the most rapid urbanization/westernization of lifestyle. King et al. (4,5) applied prevalence data for DM among adults to United Nations population estimates to ascertain the number of adults with DM globally in 1995 and to project an estimate for the number of persons expected to have DM globally in 2000 and 2025

(Fig. 2-1). As shown, the number is expected to increase from 135 million in 1995 to 300 million by the year 2025.

The economic impact of diabetes is great, estimated at $132 billion in 2002, approximately 10% of the total national expenditures for health care (1). The high cost is driven largely by the direct expenses and loss of productivity associated with the complications of diabetes. Cardiovascular diseases (CVD) make the greatest contribution to the excess morbidity and mortality experienced by people with DM and compared with their peer group, women with DM show the greatest excess CVD risk (6,7).

These trends convey several direct implications for diabetes and pregnancy care. First, the number of pregnancies in women with type 1 DM has increased as management has become more successful, even in the presence of diabetic complications. Furthermore, as indicated below, the incidence of type 1 DM has increased globally in recent years. The number of pregnancies among women with type 2 DM has increased and can be projected to increase more in the future considering the growing incidence of type 2 DM in adolescents. Finally, an apparently rapid increase in the prevalence of GDM poses a serious economic burden on the costs of prenatal and newborn care. However, this is tempered by the continuing controversies about the magnitude and significance of adverse pregnancy outcomes in GDM. Resolution of this important issue awaits the results of ongoing work such as the Hyperglycemia and Adverse Pregnancy Outcome (HAPO) study (8).

In this chapter, we summarize information regarding the nature of these emerging trends and examine their present impact and project their future impact on the lives of women and adolescents that develop type 1 DM, type 2 DM, or GDM.

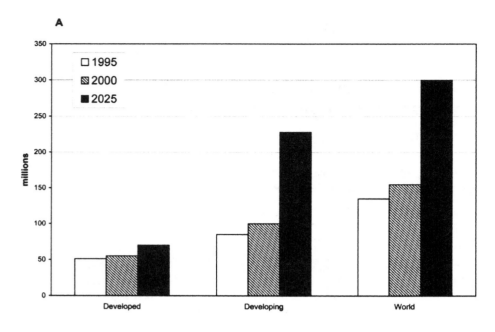

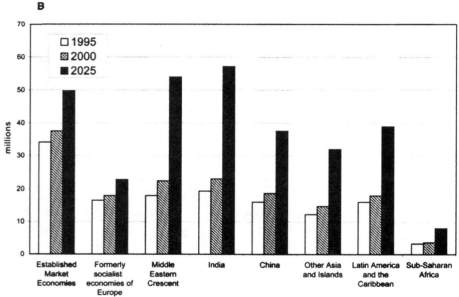

FIGURE 2-1. Number of people with diabetes in the adult population (≥20 years of age) by year and region. **A:** Developed and developing countries and world total. **B:** Major geographic areas. (Adapted from King H, Aubert RE, Herman WH. Global burden of diabetes 1995–2025. Prevalence, numerical estimates, and projections. *Diabetes Care* 1998;21:1414–1431, with permission.)

TYPE 1 DIABETES MELLITUS

Type 1 DM (previously designated insulin-dependent diabetes mellitus, type 1 DM), as it is classically seen in children and adolescents, is abrupt in onset with a clinical course that is characterized by polyuria, polydipsia, polyphagia, weight loss, and fatigue. If the diagnosis is not made at this stage, there is eventual progression to diabetic ketoacidosis (9). Many factors indicate that type 1 DM is an autoimmune disorder that develops in individuals with specific genetic predispositions. There is also much evidence that development of type 1 DM in susceptible per-

sons involves the participation of secondary factors that may be environmental in nature. Thus, the concordance for type 1 DM in identical twins is only 40% to 50% rather than much higher, as would be expected for a condition that is primarily genetic in origin (10). In the following sections, we have summarized some of the evidence that supports the contributions of both genetic and environmental factors in the etiology of type 1 DM. There is strong evidence that the global incidence of type 1 DM has increased in the past several decades (11). The reasons for these phenomena are not entirely clear and we will summarize current hypotheses below.

Global Trends

There have been two workshops on type 1 DM registries: the first in 1983 (12) and another in 1985 (13). As a result, data collection and assessment have become more standardized, and the international patterns and trends in incidence were validated. These efforts have made a significant contribution to understanding the epidemiology of type 1 DM and have facilitated direct comparison of the disease across countries.

In the United States and Western Europe, the current incidence rates for type 1 DM are second only to those of asthma among severe chronic disease of childhood (14). An estimated 13,171 children under 20 years of age develop type 1 diabetes each year (15). An estimated 1.2 million people have type 1 diabetes in the United States today (15). Interestingly, data from the Allegheny County Insulin-Dependent Diabetes Mellitus (IDDM) Registry covering the years 1990 to 1994 suggest a relatively stable age-standardized incidence; however, the incidence of IDDM in 15- to 19-year-old non-whites increased 2.5 times from the time period 1985 to 1989 (16). Whether this is a true increase in autoimmune type 1 diabetes or an increase in another form of diabetes is currently being investigated. However with increased recognition of type 2 diabetes in children, the ability of registries as they have been historically set up to monitor the epidemiology of type 1 diabetes will be challenged. In 1984, Keen and Ekoe (17) stated that, "Insulin-dependent diabetes mellitus is characteristic of Caucasoid people and much less common in, or even absent from, some other ethnic groups." Subsequently, numerous population-based reports indicated that there are marked geographic differences in the incidence of type 1 DM in the world: high risk in Scandinavian countries, moderate risk in Europe and North America, and low risk in Asia (18–24). The highest nationwide incidence rate has been reported in Finland (35.3 per 100,000 person-years) and the lowest in Korea (0.7 per 100,000 person-years) (15,25). This represents a 41-fold difference in incidence rates. There also appears to be an ethnic difference in type 1 DM incidence. In children less than or equal to 14 years of age, incidence (per 100,000/year) in non-Hispanic blacks ranges from 3.3 in San Diego to 11.0 in Philadelphia, whereas the incidence in whites ranges from 13.3 in Philadelphia to 20.6 in Rochester, Minnesota (15,26). In addition to the ethnic differences in incidence of type 1 DM, there is a strong south to north gradient in incidence, with rates increasing with the latitude away from the equator. Furthermore, major differences in incidence rates have also been reported within the same country. Sevenfold difference has been noted within the midwestern region of Poland (27). These earlier trends that indicated variable incidence rates of type 1 DM within Europe have recently been confirmed (28). In an analysis of 37 studies published from 1960 to 1996 from 27 countries, Onkamo et al. (29)

concluded that the incidence of type 1 DM is increasing worldwide, in both low- and high-incidence populations. In a recent comprehensive review, Gale (11) also concluded that the global incidence of type 1 DM has increased substantially over the past several decades.

Despite significant geographic differences in the incidence of type 1 DM, the clinical characteristics and patterns of onset are similar. It has been found consistently that the risk for type 1 DM in boys is slightly in excess of that in girls (18,24). In both sexes, the incidence of type 1 DM in the age groups of 5 to 9 and 10 to 14 years is approximately 2.5 and 3 times higher, respectively, than in the younger age group (0–4 years) (18,24). A seasonal pattern of type 1 DM onset has been observed across continents, with a decrease of incidence in summer months and the highest incidence in winter months (18,24,27,28).

Etiology

These wide variations in incidence have been interpreted as providing evidence of both environmental and genetic factors in the etiology of type 1 DM. Concerted efforts have been mounted among many investigators to identify the putative factors, both environmental and genetic, that are responsible for the clinical development of type 1 DM.

Environmental Associations and "Triggers"

Infection with certain viruses, particularly coxsackie B or mumps, at a critical period of vulnerability has been implicated as an environmental trigger in type 1 DM (30–32). Expression of certain antigens or exposure to related antigens has been postulated to increase vulnerability or protect against type 1 DM (e.g., cow's milk vs. human breast milk) (30–32). Furthermore, the type of early infant diets (33), duration of breast-feeding (33,34), vitamin supplementation, and certain vaccinations (31,35) have been reported to be associated with the development of type 1 DM. As discussed in more detail later (see section on Maternal Influences), the risk for the development of diabetes is higher among offspring of fathers with type 1 DM than among offspring of mothers with type 1 DM.

Genetic Predispositions

The contribution of genetic factors to the etiology of DM has been recognized since ancient times. Initially such impressions were formed primarily from observing familial aggregation of diabetes. The characteristic clinical features, peak incidence of the disease in youth, and association with various autoimmune endocrine diseases helped to identify type 1 DM as a distinct entity before relatively specific markers of the disease were defined. Components of the major histocompatibility complex contribute up to 50% of the genetic risk for type 1 diabetes. Most significant appears to be the class II human leukocyte antigens (HLA) DR and DQ. More specifically, DR3/x, DR4/x or DR3/DR4 and DQβ1*0204 or DQβ1*0302 enhance the individual's risk for type 1 DM that may follow a random environmental event. Both DR2 and DQβ1*0602 are protective against type 1 diabetes (36). Other HLA loci—such as class I (A, B), class II (DP), and now possibly class III polymorphisms (MIC-A)—appear to contribute to the genetic risk for at least a portion of autoimmune diabetes (37–39). How HLA loci contribute to risk is currently under study. Several recent reports examined the association of HLA risk susceptibility with autoimmune response and age at onset of diabetes (40–43).

Currently there is also an attempt to identify other non-HLA genetic loci that contribute to increased susceptibility for type 1 diabetes (37,44). The *IDDM2* locus has been well established to involve a noncoding region of the insulin gene at 11p15 (45). Polymorphisms in this area of variable number of tandem repeats (VNTR) are associated with increased diabetes risk. Multiple other *IDDM* loci have been defined and some candidate genes suggested. The significance of these loci, their polymorphisms, their interactions with each other and the HLA region, and their ability to confer susceptibility to type 1 diabetes need to be studied further.

Although rare, there are several monogenic forms of immune-mediated type 1 diabetes whose genetics have recently been elucidated. This includes mutations in the autoimmune regulator gene (AIRE-1) that maps to chromosome 21 and is responsible for abnormalities seen in autoimmune polyglandular syndrome type 1 (44).

Genetic predisposition to complications of type 1 diabetes is much more elusive than the genetic predisposition to type 1 diabetes. Early data suggest that polymorphisms of several genes may be associated with an increase risk for overt diabetic nephropathy (angiotensin-converting enzyme, apolipoprotein E, and lipoprotein lipase) (46) and coronary artery calcification (hepatic lipase gene) in individuals with type 1 diabetes (47).

Pathophysiology

In the pathogenesis of type 1 DM, the immune response that is postulated to be triggered by an environmental event includes the development of antibodies to a number of cell surface and cytoplasmic antigens including insulin (48), protein tyrosine phosphatase-like molecule islet cell antibody (ICA) 512/IA2 (49,50), and glutamic acid decarboxylase (GAD) (51). Over 90% of individuals presenting with type 1 diabetes have one or more autoantibodies. Until recently, autoimmunity was primarily determined by the detection of circulating ICAs measured with cadaveric pancreatic tissue using immunofluorescence. Recent advances,

however, have led to the development of a high throughput method, allowing for an accurate and economical means of measuring antigens (52).

Identification of antigens has led to new insights into the development of autoimmunity for type 1 diabetes. Several studies have shown that insulin autoantibodies (IAAs) are more common in children diagnosed with diabetes at a younger age than those diagnosed older (40,53). Development of autoimmune antibodies has been detected as early as 3 months of age, and those individuals with high-risk HLA genotypes tend to acquire IAA and GAD autoimmunity prior to ICA seroconversion and IA2 afterward (54). Not all children with autoimmune antibodies develop diabetes, and seroconversion back to negativity is possible, but unlikely (55).

Recent studies have focused on identifying populations at risk for diabetes and improving the prediction of who will develop diabetes, thus allowing better targeting of preventive interventions within a research context. Individuals with multiple diabetes-associated antibodies appear to have a greater chance of developing diabetes (56). Diabetes-free survival curves, according to the number of antibodies found in first-degree relatives of individuals with type 1 diabetes, suggest that the number of diabetes-associated antibodies is associated with greater risk for developing diabetes (57) (Fig. 2-2). The loss of first-phase insulin response, in addition to autoantibodies, also predicts development of diabetes (57,58).

A slowly progressive form of type 1 diabetes, often referred to as latent autoimmune diabetes in adults (LADA), is getting increased recognition in the literature. Adults with LADA have diabetes-associated antibodies, most frequently GAD, and they appear to decompensate to

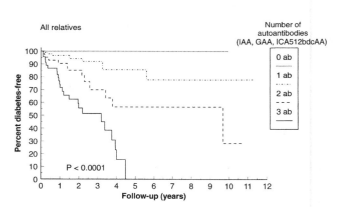

FIGURE 2-2. The diabetes-free survival of first-degree relatives, according to the number of autoantibodies (*ab*) present at baseline, considering insulin autoantibodies, GAD autoantibodies, and islet cell antibody ICA512bdc autoantibodies. Data for all relatives tested. (From Verge CF, Gianani R, Kawasaki E, et al. Prediction of type 1 diabetes in first-degree relatives using a combination of insulin, GAD, and ICA512abc/IA-2 autoantibodies. *Diabetes* 1996;45:926–933, with permission.)

insulin dependence within 2 to 3 years. At least in one population, individuals with LADA have high-risk genotypes similar to those found in adult-onset, rapidly progressing, type 1 diabetes, but are more likely to have single autoantibody positivity (59).

The pathogenesis of type 1 diabetes probably is not isolated to the development of humoral autoimmunity. Some evidence suggests that T cells mediate B-cell destruction as well (60). Triggers of apoptosis and cytokines may also play a role.

TYPE 2 DIABETES MELLITUS

In the United States, type 2 DM accounts for 90% to 95% of all DM (1,2,61,62), and as mentioned previously, undiagnosed diabetes accounts for more than one third of all cases (1,2). Onset and diagnosis of type 2 DM are strongly associated with age; however, the patterns vary substantially among different racial/ethnic groups (e.g., younger onset in Native Americans compared with expectations in non-Hispanic whites) (1,63). On average, more than 80% of cases occur in those over 40 years of age, and a large proportion of affected individuals are asymptomatic (64). Because of the extensive evidence that in recent years the incidence of type 2 DM among younger individuals has increased more rapidly than in the population, this group will be discussed separately.

Global Trends

There are marked differences in the prevalence of type 2 DM between countries, among different ethnic groups in the same geographic region, and within the same ethnic group undergoing internal or external migration. King and associates (4,5) collated data from published reports on the prevalences of type 2 DM and impaired glucose tolerance (IGT) in populations around the world in which a 75-g oral glucose tolerance test was used to evaluate glucose tolerance. These data, estimations from some additional populations, and demographic estimations from the United Nations were used to calculate the global prevalence estimates of diabetes for 1995, 2000, and 2025 mentioned in the introduction to this chapter (4). The key points are illustrated graphically in Fig. 2-1 (4). When adjustments are made to provide a standardized age distribution (5), the lowest prevalences of type 2 DM have been reported in South American Indians of rural Chile, rural Africa, rural areas of the Indian subcontinent, and several populations in the Far East (4,5), whereas the highest prevalences of type 2 DM diabetes have been identified in the North American Pima Indians and Micronesian population of Nauru (65,66). Type 2 DM diabetes is rare or almost unknown in Polynesians when a traditional lifestyle has been maintained. On the other hand, Polynesian populations living in New Zealand have prevalence rates 3 to 10 times those of typical white populations (66,67). A similar striking dichotomy in the prevalence of DM has been found between groups of Pima living in the Southwestern United States and those in rural Northern Mexico (68). An effect of migration on the observed prevalences of type 2 DM is also apparent in other Asian groups with origins in India or Japan (69,70).

Etiology

The etiology of type 2 DM is almost certainly multifactorial in the majority of cases and in some respects is less well understood than the etiology of type 1 diabetes. Contemporary evidence implicates both reduced β-cell function and impaired insulin action as vectors for the myriad factors that can influence glucose homeostasis (71). Impairment of both β-cell function and insulin action play important roles in the development of overt, symptomatic hyperglycemia through a self-perpetuating cycle, designated "glucose toxicity" (72). Both β-cell function and insulin action are strongly influenced by genetic and environmental factors. Polonsky et al. (73) and Gerich's group (74) have summarized the data indicating that disturbances in β-cell function precede the development of DM in susceptible subjects.

Environmental Factors

Epidemiologic studies are playing an increasingly important role in defining the underlying factors that modulate insulin action and β-cell function. A number of epidemiologic studies have identified risk factors (i.e., demographic, genetic, and environmental factors) that are thought to be associated with or play a significant role in the predisposition to type 2 DM (75). For example, increasing age, obesity, family history of DM, racial/ethnic group, exercise level, diet, Western or urban lifestyle, and rural-urban migration are all considered important risk factors for type 2 DM (62–65,75). However, a comprehensive review of the evidence that links risk for DM to these factors is beyond the scope of this report. Furthermore, although considerable progress has been made in identifying epidemiologic risk factors for type 2 DM, interplay between environmental and genetic factors may be of primary importance in the majority of cases. Progress in defining the genetic role in the pathogenesis of type 2 DM will be reviewed below.

Genetic Factors

There is much evidence that the risk for developing type 2 DM is strongly influenced by genetic traits. Maternal factors have been implicated in the predisposition to type 2 DM, but the specific mode of transmission remains unclear. Studies in twins have provided some of the strongest evidence for a genetic basis for type 2 DM. In monozygotic twins, concordance for type 2 DM has ranged from 55% to 100% (10,76–78), rates that are even higher than those observed for type 1 diabetes. In family studies among Mexican Americans, the prevalence of diabetes decreased from 28.2% in first-degree relatives of the proband to 13.3% in second-degree relatives and 11.1% in third-degree relatives (79). In other studies, persons with both a sibling and a parent with type 2 DM were found to have higher fasting plasma glucose (FPG) and insulin concentrations than controls (80). Furthermore, it has been reported that the risk for developing type 2 DM is greater if a sibling is the proband rather than a parent (81,82).

There is considerable evidence that genetic factors play an important part in establishing the degree of insulin resistance in individuals. In one particularly illustrative report (83), Martin and colleagues performed intravenous glucose tests in nondiabetic offspring of two parents with type 2 DM. Insulin-independent glucose uptake and insulin sensitivity index (SI) were estimated with Bergman's minimal model software (MINMOD). Values for SG and SI showed no correlation, and there was no clustering of SG within families. By contrast, values for SI within families were significantly related, and the mean SI values between families were more widely distributed than the values within a given family. However, the families with the most severe insulin resistance, on average, displayed the greatest degree of intrafamily variation in SI values, an observation suggesting heterogeneity of a trait with a strong genetic basis. These points are illustrated clearly in Fig. 2-3 (83). As mentioned earlier, there is also evidence for genetic contributions to familial patterns of β-cell secretory function (73,74).

Despite the finding of higher concordance for DM in twins, and the evidence that has been gathered from other family studies for inheritance of type 2 DM, progress toward identifying specific genetic traits for type 2 DM has been difficult (84). This is undoubtedly related to the fact that type 2 DM is almost certainly polygenic in etiology and the tools for delineating the genetic contributions to complex, multifactorial disorders (e.g., genome-wide scans using microsatellite markers, single nucleotide polymorphisms [SNPs], and complex new analytic techniques such as transmission disequilibrium tests) are still relatively early in their development. Efforts to identify specific genetic defects in type 2 DM are hindered by the lack of specific and accurate markers for type 2 DM other than the development of arbitrarily defined levels of hyperglycemia that represent the outcome, rather than the cause. This is confounded by the fact that the time at which hyperglycemia first develops, and its severity, may be strongly influenced by factors such as obesity that may be partially environmental in origin. Separation of families or other clusters of subjects into groups on the basis of strict clinical, phenotypic, or physiologic/metabolic characteristics such as insulin sensitivity or insulin secretion is a prerequisite to linking the diabetic syndrome to specific genetic traits.

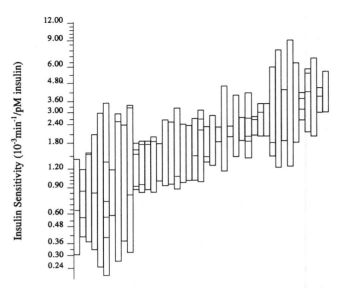

FIGURE 2-3. Insulin sensitivity (S_I, $\log_{10}$) in families with two diabetic parents. The 43 families were ranked from lowest to highest according to the midrange of the log of S_I within each family. The midrange is indicated by a small square in the center of the bar. Horizontal lines across the bar, including those at the upper and lower limits, mark the log of S_I for an individual in that family. (Adapted from Martin BC, Warram JH, Rosner B, et al. Familial clustering of insulin sensitivity. *Diabetes* 1992;41:850–854, with permission.)

Mitochondria-Related Diabetes

Mitochondria play a central, critical role in the metabolic generation of energy, and defects in mitochondrial function impair the generation of adenosine triphosphate (ATP). Pancreatic β-cells have high metabolic activity, and their function is very sensitive to defects in generation of ATP. It is therefore not surprising that DM is commonly observed in the complex mitochondrial disorders that have been described, particularly those due to mutations in mitochondrial DNA (85). Mitochondria have their own genome and are transmitted to the fertilized ovum from the cytoplasm of the oocyte. Thus, mitochondrial DNA is strictly of maternal origin. Diabetes resulting from mutations in mitochondrial DNA is often first detected as GDM. These disorders are discussed in more detail in the section on Maternal Influences.

Maturity-Onset Diabetes of Youth

There is an uncommon variant of DM with features that do not conform to those typical of type 1 or type 2 DM. Because it can usually be diagnosed and often requires treatment prior to 20 to 25 years of age but is not "insulin dependent," it was initially designated as maturity onset diabetes of youth (MODY). The entities of MODY follow an autosomal-dominant mode of inheritance and have alteration of β-cell function as their primary defect (86).

Overweight individuals and minority groups are not over-represented as they are in type 2 diabetes. There are at least six subtypes of MODY (87). MODY 2 involves mutations in the glucokinase gene, which is expressed in liver and pancreatic β-cells and plays a key role in the regulation of glucose metabolism in these tissues (88). Other genes associated with MODY encode transcription factors that are expressed in pancreatic islets: MODY 1, hepatic nuclear factor (HNF)-4α; MODY 3, HNF-1α; MODY 4, insulin promoter factor 1; MODY 5, HNF-1β; and MODY 6, neurogenic differentiation factor 1. The genes are also expressed in other tissues (e.g., liver, kidneys, muscle), and altered liver or renal function may be found in some of the individuals with MODY (87,89). Studies of the function and regulation of these transcription factors are providing basic insights into the regulation of glucose transport and insulin biosynthesis and secretion as well as cellular processes in other tissues.

In the United Kingdom, mutations in HNF-1α appear to be the dominating defect in families with clinical features of MODY (90). This may vary according to the selected population. In addition, it appears a variant of the HNF-1α gene may be associated with earlier-onset type 2 diabetes in the Canadian Oji-Cree population (91). Whether other variants in MODY-associated genes also predispose individuals to type 2 diabetes remains to be clarified.

The results of studies such as those summarized briefly above demonstrate that progress is being made in discerning the biology of islets and toward defining the genetic factors that may be responsible for type 2 DM. However, many investigators are convinced that most type 2 DM is polygenic in origin (84) and that it will continue to be difficult to define a specific cause in many cases. Furthermore, although it is certain that specific genetic factors may predispose to type 2 DM, it is equally clear that environmental factors such as level of physical activity or obesity profoundly influence the appearance and course of clinical diabetes. Much work is still needed to gain a better insight into how genetic and environmental factors interact in type 2 DM.

In Adolescents

The prevalence of type 2 DM is increasing in not only young adults, but also in the pediatric population. In 1994, 16% of new cases in an urban setting were identified as having type 2 diabetes as compared to 2% to 3% prior to 1992 (79,92). Several other recent studies have similarly identified the proportion of new cases of DM referred to a pediatric endocrinology center that are apparently type 2 diabetes in origin. Percentages range from 8% to 45% depending on geographic area and ethnic makeup of the sample (93). As in the adult population, minority groups, such as Hispanic, African American, Asian American, and Native American, appear to be more susceptible to type 2

diabetes. The increase in type 2 diabetes is not unique to North America. High-risk populations and those with increasing obesity in Europe and Asia are also starting to note an increase in cases of type 2 diabetes (94,95).

The prevalence of type 2 diabetes in children has been studied most comprehensively in the Pima Indians, with ascertainment of 53% to 96% of the eligible population. Diabetes has been a devastating disease for the Pima Indian population, with 50% of adults over 35 years of age afflicted (96). The prevalence of type 2 diabetes is higher in Pima Indian girls than boys and has increased significantly in both groups over the past several decades. In 1987 to 1996, the prevalence of type 2 diabetes in 10- to 14-year-old boys and girls was 1.4% and 2.88%, respectively, and for 15- to 19-year-old boys and girls 3.78% and 5.31%, respectively (97).

Unfortunately, no data are available at this time demonstrating the prevalence of type 2 diabetes in children and adolescents in other general populations in North America. The Third National Health and Nutrition Examination Survey covering the years 1988 to 1994 provided useful, though not definitive, information. In the survey, 13 cases of diabetes were found among 2,867 children 12 to 19 years of age (98). Four adolescents were thought to have type 2 diabetes, two cases of which were previously undiagnosed. These findings suggest that the prevalence of type 2 diabetes in the general public is low, and the sample size was not large enough to make stable prevalence estimates in the pediatric population. Furthermore, evaluation of glucose metabolism was based solely on results of a fasting sample in 1,083 subjects and a random sample or 6-hour fasting sample in the remainder. Prevalence rates were most likely underestimated given that the diagnosis of diabetes was not based on data from an oral glucose tolerance test, but rather from either an 8-hour fasting, 6-hour fasting, or random blood sample. Recent studies have also focused on the prevalence of abnormal glucose tolerance in high-risk subjects, rather than the general adolescent population. In an important paper that was published in 2002, Sinha et al. reported results of oral glucose tolerance tests performed on individuals referred to an obesity clinic (99). All children had a body mass index (BMI) >95th percentile for age and gender. They found that 25% of children 4 to 10 years of age and 21% of children 11 to 18 years of age had IGT. Another 4% of adolescents were found to have previously undiagnosed diabetes. Two of the children 4 to 10 years of age with IGT went on to develop diabetes within a 2- to 5-year follow-up time frame.

As in adults, adolescents with polycystic ovary syndrome have a high risk for having IGT independent of BMI (100,101). Perhaps the association of IGT with hyperandrogenism contributes to why more young females than males have been found to have type 2 diabetes.

A significant question remaining to be answered is why there has been an apparent increase in type 2 diabetes among youth? Given that type 2 diabetes, by definition, involves both insulin resistance and a relative insulin deficiency, factors affecting either insulin resistance or insulin secretion could contribute to the increase tendency toward type 2 diabetes.

The dramatic increase in obesity that has been noted in the pediatric population of the United States has been temporally related to the increase in type 2 diabetes and is most commonly implicated in causing the increase in type 2 diabetes. The progressive increase in overweight (defined as BMI >95th percentile for age, gender norms) over the past few decades is shown well in data compiled by the Centers for Disease Control and Prevention from a number of large population based studies. There is also a significant gender and race/ethnic variation, with non-Hispanic black females and Mexican-American males the most overweight (102) (Fig. 2-4).

In fact, several changes in lifestyle have been identified over the past decade that may be contributing to more obesity and the associated higher risk for type 2 diabetes. Increased portion sizes, both at home and in restaurants, have each been implicated in contributing to obesity (103,104). Sugar-sweetened drinks as well as animal protein and fat intake have also been implicated in contributing to obesity and influencing one's risk for type 2 diabetes (95,105). On the other hand, in adults, nut consumption has been shown to reduce one's risk for developing type 2 diabetes, even after correcting for other risk factors, including BMI (106). Less active lifestyles also may be contributing to the increase in obesity we are observing. Increased sedentary activity, identified by television viewing, has been found to be associated with obesity in children and with type 2 diabetes in adults (107,108). This may be a direct effect of less caloric expenditure or from patterns of nutrition often associated with watching television. In addition, physical activity in healthy children has been found to be positively correlated with insulin sensitivity, which further supports sedentary activity as a risk factor for type 2 diabetes in youth (109).

Descriptions of children with type 2 diabetes report a high prevalence of type 2 diabetes among first- and second-degree relatives to be 74% to 100% (93), strongly suggesting an important role for genetic or familial factors. Earlier in this chapter (see also Fig. 2-3) we discussed evidence that genetic factors contribute to both patterns of insulin sensitivity and β-cell function in adults (73,74,110). Of concern are recent findings that abnormalities in insulin secretion may already be evident during adolescence. African-American adolescents, although hyperinsulinemic compared with whites, appear to have inadequate insulin secretion in the face of physiologic insulin resistance seen in puberty (111,112).

Because of the apparently rapid increase in diagnosed cases over the past 10 to 20 years, genetic factors alone are not thought to account for the increase in type 2 diabetes in

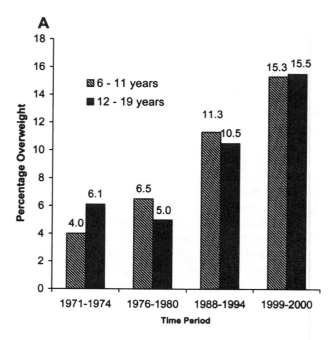

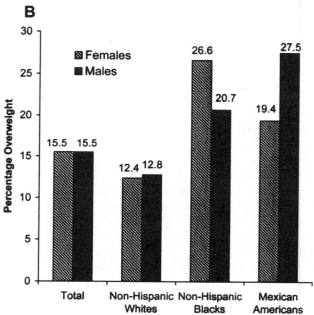

FIGURE 2-4. A: Prevalence of overweight among children and adolescents (body mass index ≥95th percentile for age and gender) over several decades. **B:** Prevalence of overweight in 1999–2000 according to ethnicity and gender. (Adapted from Ogden CL, Flegal DM, Carroll MD, et al. Prevalence and trends in overweight among US children and adolescents, 1999–2000. *JAMA* 2002;288:1728–1732, with permission.)

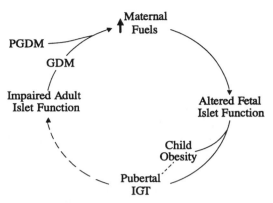

FIGURE 2-5. Diabetes begets diabetes: the alterations of maternal fuel metabolism lead to altered fetal islet function (hyperinsulinism). This intrauterine event predisposes to childhood obesity and adolescent impaired glucose tolerance (*IGT*). Our hypothesis is that it will also lead to impaired adult islet function and IGT or gestational diabetes mellitus (*GDM*).

youth. Potential influences of the increasing frequency and severity of obesity, lessening of physical activity, and diet patterns were discussed in the preceding section. In addition, the impact of the intrauterine environment on an individual's insulin secretion and insulin resistant state is receiving increasing attention. As discussed in more detail in the section on Maternal Influences, exposure to the intrauterine environment of DM appears to predispose the offspring to both obesity and altered glucose homeostasis. Silverman et al. have implicated fetal hyperinsulinism as a risk factor for both childhood obesity and IGT in adolescence (113).

Among the Pima Indians, obesity, *in utero* exposure to diabetes, low birth weight, and high birth weight are each risk factors for the development of diabetes in childhood. Dabelea et al. (97) estimated that over the 30 years of the longitudinal Pima study, the increases in obesity and *in utero* diabetes exposure accounted for the majority of the increase in prevalence of type 2 diabetes.

Increasing obesity, lifestyle habits, and *in utero* environment may each play a role in altering carbohydrate metabolism, leading to changes in insulin resistance or compensatory β-cell function and in some cases the development of type 2 diabetes. Although the actual prevalence of type 2 diabetes in children and adolescents is not known, as noted above, the apparent increase in type 2 diabetes is concerning. More of these children will be entering childbearing age already having type 2 diabetes and will experience not only high-risk pregnancies, but potentially will also face early adulthood marred by complications of type 2 diabetes. Furthermore, the pool of adolescents with altered carbohydrate metabolism that are at risk for GDM is much larger. Consequently, increasing numbers of young women will enter pregnancy with metabolic abnormalities that may increase their risk for developing gestational diabetes. Addi-

tional epidemiologic studies will be needed in the future to follow these changes. More important will be interventions that minimize abnormalities of carbohydrate metabolism and subsequent risk for type 2 diabetes.

DIABETES MELLITUS IN PREGNANCY

Diabetes mellitus complicating pregnancy is heterogeneous with respect to etiology, duration, severity, and the presence of confounding characteristics such as obesity. Precise classification of the cause of DM may not be essential for adequate clinical management during pregnancy. However, it is important for optimal genetic counseling of the family concerning risk of DM in their offspring as well as for advising the mother about her expectations after pregnancy.

Differences in definitions and terminology as well as variances in ascertainment of cases have confounded efforts to compare the prevalence and incidence of various types of DM and glucose intolerance during pregnancy in different areas and among various racial/ethnic groups (3). Women who are known to have DM prior to pregnancy [pregestational diabetes mellitus (PGDM)] are often assumed to have type 1 diabetes, especially if they are receiving treatment with insulin. This may be a valid assumption in populations where the relative prevalence of type 1 diabetes is highest, such as in certain northern Europeans areas like Sweden (19) or Finland (21); however, in populations where type 2 DM is common, more than half of women with PGDM may have type 2 rather than type 1 DM (114–116). GDM is defined as "glucose intolerance with onset or first recognition during pregnancy" (3). Its prevalence generally parallels the incidence of type 2 DM in a given population. Accordingly, GDM is often viewed as a precursor of type 2 DM. Women found to have abnormal glucose tolerance early in pregnancy, especially those with elevated FPG concentrations, are likely to manifest DM when they are initially tested postpartum (117). These subjects may well have type 2 DM antedating pregnancy that has gone undetected, especially if they are not in a healthcare system in which screening for glucose intolerance is universally practiced. Furthermore, a certain proportion of women with GDM can be demonstrated to have immunologic or clinical features suggestive of early type 1 diabetes.

Pregestational Diabetes Mellitus

In the United States, the incidence of PGDM complicating pregnancy has been estimated to be 20 to 50 per 1,000 (118,119). These were based on review of statewide reports of vital statistics, with amplification and verification by chart review in some instances. However, as indicated above, these estimates include varying proportions of subjects that have type 1 or type 2 DM. Furthermore, in such studies, there is substantial evidence for underreporting, especially of those not receiving treatment with insulin. Reports from areas with a high prevalence of type 2 DM provide a strong indication that pregnancy in women with type 2 DM are at high risk for typical diabetes-related adverse perinatal outcomes when the diabetes is poorly controlled (120). The lack of accurate estimates of the frequency and type of DM complicating pregnancy limits the development of reliable data concerning the frequency of various complications (e.g., fetal morbidities such major congenital malformations). Similarly, it is difficult to measure their economic impact or to estimate the amount of health-care resources that might be required to prevent such complications.

Gestational Diabetes Mellitus

Gestational diabetes mellitus, defined as "carbohydrate intolerance with onset or first recognition during pregnancy," has been estimated to occur in approximately 3% to 8% of all pregnancies in the United Sates (3). Marked variation has been reported in the prevalence of GDM worldwide. This was summarized in detail in reports at the 4th International Workshop Conference on GDM (3). From detailed reviews, it appears that several factors contribute to this variation, including differences in definition, diagnostic criteria, methods for screening and ascertainment, as

well as the differences in incidence and prevalence of type 1 and type 2 DM discussed above. The effects of different diagnostic criteria on apparent prevalence of GDM effects are profound and this was recently reviewed in detail (121). Prevalences of GDM reported by racial/ethnic group in studies that used well-defined screening and diagnostic test methods (122–130) are summarized in Table 2-1. It remains difficult to make direct comparisons among all reports, and no attempt has been made to standardize the data with respect to age, as was done in the report of King et al. (4,5). The marked variation in prevalence of GDM among different racial/ethnic groups is evident. Some indication of a migrant effect on prevalence of GDM is apparent in women of Chinese, Korean, or Indian subcontinent origin (123,129,131), as is the case with respect to type 2 DM and IGT in the population at large (4,5,65–70).

There is a general consensus that the prevalence of GDM has increased over the past one to two decades (3) in concert with the increase in prevalence of obesity at younger ages and the increase in type 2 DM among all age groups (2,62,66,92–95). Earlier reports from Melbourne support this contention (123); however, additional reports from observations in other populations are lacking.

Surveys such as NHANES II and III and others (2,61, 64,75,132) illustrate that there is a substantial amount of undiagnosed type 2 DM as well as IGT among persons over

TABLE 2-1. PREVALENCE OF GESTATIONAL DIABETES MELLITUS BY RACIAL/ETHNIC GROUP

Investigator, Year	Subjects (Race/Ethnic)	Screening Method (Glucose Load/Cutoff)	OGTT/Diagnostic Criteria	GDM Prevalence (%)
Green et al. (**122**), 1990	White	50 g/>150 mg/dL[a]	NDDG	1.6
	African American			1.7
	Hispanic			4.2
	Chinese			7.3
Beischer et al. (**123**), 1991	Vietnam-born	NA	50 g/1 h >9 mM[a]	7.3
	Chinese		2 h >7 mmol/L	13.9
	Indian subcontinent			15.0
	Australia and New Zealand			4.3
	Africa and Mauritius			9.4
Dooley et al. (**125**), 1991	White	50 g/≥130 mg/dL[a]	NDDG	2.7
	African American			3.3
	Hispanic			4.4
	Other			10.5
Ranchod et al. (**124**), 1991	Indian	75 g/1 h/≥141 mg/dL	EASD	3.8
			WHO	1.6
Roseman et al. (**126**), 1991	African American	100 g/2 h/≥115 mg/dL[a]	NDDG	2.4
Berkowitz et al. (**127**), 1992	White	50 g/≥135 mg/dL[a]	NDDG	2.3
	African American			3.7
	Hispanic			4.1
Jang et al. (**129**), 1993	Korean	50 g/≥130 mg[a]	NDDG	2.1
Murphy et al. (**128**), 1993	Yup'ik Eskimo	50 g/1 h/≥140 mg/dL[a]	NDDG	5.8
Deerochanawong et al. (**130**), 1996	Thai	75 g/2 h/≥140 mg/dL[a]	WHO IGT	15.7
		100 g/3 h/OGTT[a]	NDDG	1.4

[a]Test administered universally.
EASD, European Association for Study of Diabetes; GDM, gestational diabetes mellitus; IGT, impaired glucose tolerance; NA, not applicable; NDDG, National Diabetes Data Group; OGTT, Oral glucose tolerance test; WHO, World Health Organization.

20 years of age in the United States. On the basis of these findings, it has been suggested that the detection of GDM merely represents the discovery of women in the reproductive age range who have preexisting glucose intolerance (133). Indeed, there appears to be a correlation between the prevalence of GDM and that of type 2 DM in various populations (Table 2-1). When women have been systematically tested serially for glucose intolerance during pregnancy, a significant proportion of GDM has been confirmed in the first trimester (134–136). However, repeated testing throughout pregnancy detects additional cases of GDM up to as late as 36 weeks' gestation (134, 136). Furthermore, a large body of evidence indicates that the insulin resistance of late pregnancy is profound (137–139) and plays an important role in the pathogenesis of GDM. Finally, performing a glucose tolerance test after pregnancy demonstrates normal glucose tolerance in the great majority of women who had GDM. This preponderance of normal glucose tolerance postpartum would not be expected if testing during pregnancy merely led to the identification of preexisting glucose intolerance in the female population. However, GDM is followed by relatively rapid progression to type 2 DM. Within 5 years, up to 50% in several reports (140,141), or even more in at least one study (142), meet the criteria for a diagnosis of DM.

Phenotypic Heterogeneity

Obesity and advanced maternal age are associated with increased risk for GDM (122,123,125,126), as is the case for type 2 DM. Accordingly, GDM is commonly regarded simply as a forerunner of type 2 DM. All cases of GDM do share the fact that they are first recognized during pregnancy, a state of marked "physiologic" insulin resistance. However, this broad definition casts a common title to a very heterogeneous population of subjects (117,125,143). Detailed studies of large numbers of GDM subjects have disclosed considerable phenotypic and genotypic heterogeneity. The severity of carbohydrate intolerance at the time of diagnosis represents one form of phenotypic heterogeneity, and it has served as the basis for the use of FPG to subclassify GDM (117,143,144). Elevated FPG at diagnosis is associated with a higher risk for diabetes postpartum and at an earlier date (117,140). There is also appreciable heterogeneity in age and weight among women with GDM, although it is well known that women with GDM tend to be older, heavier, and shorter than unselected populations of pregnant women (143, 145). Likewise, GDM is heterogeneous with respect to insulin secretion. The majority, but not all subjects with GDM, have impaired first- and second-phase insulin responses to oral (117,143,146) or intravenous challenge (147,148) when compared with age- and obesity-matched normal pregnant women. Although heterogeneity of insulin secretion is substantial, insulin resistance in late

gestation is found in normal pregnant women and in those with GDM (137,147–149). Several studies have reported somewhat greater degrees of insulin resistance among those with GDM when controlled for age and weight (147–149); however, there is much overlap.

Genotypic Heterogeneity

Systematic screening for GDM detects women at risk for progression to overt DM at a relatively early age. Furthermore, as noted above, phenotypic features are heterogeneous and somewhat different than among subjects with typical type 2 DM. It is therefore of interest to examine the various genetic factors that are associated with GDM. One early study reported increased DNA polymorphism in regions flanking the insulin receptor gene to be associated with GDM risk in blacks and non-Hispanic whites (150). Rare cases of DM associated with mutations of mitochondrial DNA, or mitochondria-related DM (85,151,152), may be initially discovered as GDM. MODY (86–91), another uncommon and atypical form of type 2 DM, can also present as GDM.

Admixture of individuals at risk for progression to type 1 DM is potentially another source of genotypic heterogeneity. It is of clinical and prognostic importance to identify such subjects. An increased occurrence of HLA antigens DR3 and DR4 in women with GDM compared with reference populations has been reported in several studies (143,152–154). The prevalence of ICAs in women with GDM has varied with the methods used and the populations tested (143,153–156). In aggregate, the reports suggest a higher prevalence of ICAs among those with more elevated FPG. This contention is supported by data from Copenhagen, one of the areas where the incidence and prevalence of type 1 DM are highest. A higher than expected number of women with documented type 1 DM were found to have experienced their initial clinical presentation during pregnancy (157). In addition, those with GDM who progressed to overt clinical diabetes requiring treatment with insulin tended to do so within the first year after the diagnosis of GDM (158).

These findings of immunologic, genetic, and clinical heterogeneity provide supporting evidence that a small proportion of the gravida with "onset or first recognition of carbohydrate intolerance during pregnancy" may be exhibiting slowly evolving type 1 DM. Prospective identification of the "at-risk" subjects by screening for diabetes autoantibodies, including GAD, may be justified in populations with the highest incidence of type 1 DM.

MATERNAL INFLUENCES

Data from a variety of sources corroborate that maternal or intrauterine factors may influence the risk for developing both type 1 and type 2 DM. There is little, if any, evidence that any form of DM is inherited as an X-linked disorder. However, maternal transmission of diabetes that is linked to mutations in mitochondrial DNA has been described (85,150,151). The first descriptions of a disorder in which DM occurs in combination with a sensorineural hearing loss were made concurrently in Dutch and English families. A mutation has been identified in the mitochondrial gene for transfer RNA [Leu (UUR) at position 3,243] in persons with this syndrome [maternally inherited diabetes and deafness (MIDD)], but it is absent in controls (150). Similar findings have also been reported in Japanese subjects with type 2 DM (151) and subsequently in many regions and ethnic groups (85). Multiple less common variants of MIDD have been described. An estimate of the overall prevalence of mitochondria-related DM suggests that it may account for approximately 1% of type 2 DM in many populations. However, in certain subgroups such as GDM or among diabetic patients with a family history of DM, it may be higher (85).

Type 1 Diabetes Mellitus

The possibility that type 1 DM may develop in their offspring is a major concern of couples when one or both has type 1 DM. Careful review of the patterns of occurrence of type 1 DM in families has established that offspring of fathers with type 1 DM are at significantly higher risk for the development of type 1 DM than is the case when the mother is the parent with the disease (159,160). Bleich et al. (159) reported a 20-year life-table diabetes risk in offspring of diabetic fathers versus mothers of 8.9% ± 1.1% and 3.4% ± 0.6%, respectively.

The risk for developing type 1 diabetes in siblings of a type 1 DM child is increased, but the specific risk is difficult to define. A number of epidemiologic studies have reported that a maternal history of diabetes is associated with an increased risk for type 2 DM (160–163) but a lower risk for type 1 diabetes (159,160) in her children. The mechanism of this "protective" maternal effect is not known. It has been suggested that it may be mediated by alterations in the immunologic system of the fetus that are induced during intrauterine development as a result of the mother's type 1 DM. The Pittsburgh group has reported age-specific incidence rates for siblings compared with the general childhood population based on their large Allegheny County registry data for the years 1965 to 1976 (164). Age-specific relative risk varied from 7- to 18-fold increased risk for siblings. The lifetime cumulative incidence of type 1 DM in siblings of a child with type 1 DM in Europid populations is quoted at 5% to 8%, in contrast to a figure of approximately 0.1% to 0.5% in the general population (165,166). A study from London reported that a sibling of a child with type 1 DM is approximately 15 to 20 times more likely to develop type 1 DM before 20 years

of age (6%) than children from a general population in the same area (167).

Type 2 Diabetes Mellitus and Gestational Diabetes Mellitus

The influence of intrauterine metabolic factors on long-term development of the offspring has been of great interest to many investigators, including our group. Freinkel formulated the hypothesis of "fuel-mediated teratogenesis" (168). It states that maternal fuels may influence development of the fetus by modifying phenotypic gene expression in terminally differentiated, poorly replicating cells. The long-range effects depend on the cells undergoing differentiation, proliferation, or functional maturation at the time of the disturbances in maternal fuel economy. It was postulated that pancreatic β-cells and adipose tissue would be among the tissues vulnerable to functional alterations during later life. The Diabetes in Pregnancy Center (DPC) was established at Northwestern University to test this hypothesis. Reports from this study and others (some are mentioned briefly below) have established linkage between the intrauterine environment and the development of obesity in childhood and IGT in adolescence.

In the relatively homogeneous Pima Indian population, maternal diabetes (exclusively type 2) is associated with an increased risk for both obesity and the development of type 2 DM in young adults (96,97,169,170). At the Northwestern University DPC, maternal histories of diabetes were also observed more frequently than expected among women with GDM (171). Similar results were reported from a population in Berlin (163). Finally, the development of diabetes in the offspring of diabetic rats is influenced by perturbed maternal carbohydrate metabolism, as well as by genetic factors (172,173).

In the Pima population, the risk for developing type 2 DM is greater if the mother had diabetes during pregnancy, rather than developing it after pregnancy (174). This implies that there is a contribution from the abnormal metabolic milieu in addition to the genetic risk. In the Northwestern University DPC cohort, predisposition to obesity and IGT were linked to prenatal metabolic factors, but not the genetic form of the mother's diabetes (they appeared with equal frequency in offspring of mothers with type 1 DM, type 2 DM, or GDM). The risks for obesity in childhood and IGT in adolescence have been independently linked to the presence of fetal hyperinsulinism that had been documented by a high concentration of amniotic fluid insulin in late pregnancy (175,176). Evidence that exposure to excess insulin action *in utero* can exert long-term effects has been obtained with animal models (177,178).

Together these data from humans and animal models implicate exposure to excess insulin action *in utero* in the predisposition to obesity, IGT, and putatively to type 2

DM. We visualize that the chain of events depicted in Fig. 2-5 accounts for our observations. Many of the offspring of diabetic mothers in the Northwestern University DPC study are reaching childbearing age. A substantial number of the Pima offspring of mothers whose glucose tolerance was evaluated during pregnancy have been pregnant. Their risk for having GDM is closely related to the level of glycemia that was found in their mother's pregnancy (174). A substantial proportion of the increasing prevalence of diabetes in Pimas may be attributable to intrauterine exposure to the metabolic environment of diabetes (97). This indeed closes the cycle that is postulated in Fig. 2-5 (i.e., that maternal diabetes does beget more diabetes in her offspring). However, this process is potentially preventable by more effectively normalizing metabolism throughout gestation in PGDM and early diagnosis and correction of metabolic disturbances of GDM. To date, this potential has not been confirmed.

Size at Birth

Since initial focus on the subject by Hales and colleagues (179), it has been firmly established in the past decade that there is an association between small size at birth, adjusted for gestational age (as a result of conditions as diverse as placental insufficiency or chronic maternal malnutrition), and risks for obesity, cardiovascular disease, dyslipidemia, and type 2 DM in later adult life (180). Indeed, among the Pima population, where maternal diabetes is highly prevalent and large size at birth serves as a surrogate for intrauterine exposure to hyperglycemia and is associated with later risks of obesity and diabetes, small size at birth is also associated with an increased risk for diabetes in later life (181).

Although the association between size at birth and disease risk later in life is firmly established, there is much controversy about factors that are responsible for the association. According to one viewpoint, impaired fetal nutrition alone is sufficient to initiate adaptations that ultimately predispose to chronic adult disease (179,180). Others stress the possibility that genetic factors that are determinants of fetal size may increase the potential for survival in the face of adverse nutrition and also account for the association with chronic disease later in life (181–183). Additional prospective, well-characterized studies in other populations are needed.

KEY POINTS

- The prevalences of type 1 DM, type 2 DM, and GDM are all increasing on a global scale, and a dramatic overall increase in the burden of DM is projected in future years.
- Reasons for the increasing prevalence of type 1 diabetes are not clear.

- Environmental and lifestyle factors are implicated in the increase in the prevalence of type 2 DM among all age groups.
- Population-based figures on the frequencies that type 1 and type 2 DM complicate pregnancy are very limited; however, with the increasing prevalences of type 2 DM in adolescents and of GDM, the number of pregnancies and neonates at risk of sequelae from diabetes will continue to grow over the foreseeable future.
- The high risk for developing diabetes outside of pregnancy after women have had GDM makes the postpartum period following GDM a critical time to focus efforts on health maintenance and diabetes prevention.
- Exposure to the maternal metabolic environment of diabetes or to other *in utero* environmental and nutritional factors increases the risk for obesity, diabetes, and cardiovascular disease later in life. More research is needed to identify the factors that are responsible and to develop interventions to prevent these important contributors to the increasing burden of diabetes. Only then will we be able to break the cycle of diabetes leading to increased obesity and diabetes in offspring.

REFERENCES

1. American Diabetes Association. Economic costs of diabetes in the US in 2002. *Diabetes Care* 2003;26:917–932.
2. Harris MI, Flegal KM, Cowie CC, et al. Prevalence of diabetes, impaired fasting glucose, and impaired glucose tolerance in the U.S. adults. The Third National Health and Nutrition Examination Survey, 1984–1994. *Diabetes Care* 1998;21:518–524.
3. Metzger, BE, Coustan DR, for the Organizing Committee. Summary and Recommendations of the Fourth International Workshop-Conference on Gestational Diabetes Mellitus. *Diabetes Care* 1998;21(suppl 2):B161–B167.
4. King H, Rewers M. Global estimates for prevalence of diabetes mellitus and impaired glucose tolerance in adults. *Diabetes Care* 1993;16:157–177.
5. King H, Aubert RE, Herman WH. Global burden of diabetes 1995–2025. Prevalence, numerical estimates, and projections. *Diabetes Care* 1998;21:1414–1431.
6. Abbott RD, Donahue RP, Kannel WB, et al. The impact of diabetes on survival following myocardial infarction in men vs. women. The Framingham Study. *JAMA* 1988;260:3456–3460.
7. Pan WH, Cedres LB, Liu K, et al. Relationship of clinical diabetes and asymptomatic hyperglycemia to risk of coronary heart disease mortality in men and women. *Am J Epidemiol* 1986;123:504–516.
8. HAPO Study Cooperative Research Group. The Hyperglycemia and Adverse Pregnancy Outcome (HAPO) Study. *Int J Gynecol Obstet* 2002;78:69–77.
9. Drash AL. *Clinical care of the diabetic child.* Chicago: Year Book Medical, 1987.
10. Pyke DA. Diabetes. The genetic connections. *Diabetologia* 1979;17:333–343.
11. Gale EAM. The rise of childhood type 1 diabetes in the 20th century. *Diabetes* 2002;51:3353–3361.
12. LaPorte RE, Tajima N, Akerblom HK, et al. Geographic differences in the risk of insulin-dependent diabetes mellitus: the importance of registries. *Diabetes Care* 1985;8(suppl 1):101–107.

13. Patrick SL, Moy CS, LaPorte RE. The world of insulin-dependent diabetes mellitus: what international epidemiologic studies reveal about the etiology and natural history of IDDM. *Diabetes Metab Rev* 1989;5:571–578.

14. Cruickshanks KJ, LaPorte RE, Dorman JE, et al. The epidemiology of insulin-dependent diabetes mellitus: etiology and diagnosis. In: Ahmed PI, Ahmed N, eds. *Coping with juvenile diabetes*. Springfield, IL: Charles C Thomas, 1985:332.

15. LaPorte RE, Matsushima M, Chang YF. Prevalence and incidence of insulin-dependent diabetes. In: Harris MI, et al., eds. *Diabetes in America,* 2nd ed. National Diabetes Data Group, National Institutes of Health (NIH), National Institute of Diabetes, Digestive and Kidney Diseases. NIH Publication No. 95-1468. Washington, DC: US Government Printing Office, 1995:37–46.

16. Libman IM, LaPorte RE, Becker D, et al. Was there an epidemic of diabetes in nonwhite adolescents in Allegheny County Pennsylvania? *Diabetes Care* 1998;21:1278–1281.

17. Keen H, Ekoe JM. The geography of diabetes mellitus. *Br Med Bull* 1984;40:359–365.

18. LaPorte RE, Cruickshanks KJ: Incidence and risk factors for insulin-dependent diabetes. In: Harris MI, Hamman RF, eds. *Diabetes in America.* National Institutes of Health Publication No. 85-1468. Washington, DC: US Government Printing Office, 1985:1–12.

19. Sterky G, Holmgren G, Gustavson KH, et al. The incidence of diabetes mellitus in Swedish children 1970–1975. *Acta Paediatr Scand* 1978;67:139–143.

20. Joner G, Sovik O. Incidence, age at onset and seasonal variation of diabetes mellitus in Norwegian children 1973–77. *Acta Pediatr Scand* 1981;70:329—335.

21. Åkerblom HK, Reunanen A, Kåär ML. The incidence of insulin-dependent diabetes mellitus in 0–4 year-old children in Finland in 1970–80. *Nord Council Arct Med Res Rep* 1980;26:60.

22. Lestradet H, Besse J. Prevalence et incidence du diabete juvenile insulin-dependent en France. *Diabetes Metab* 1977;3:229–234.

23. Gleason RE, Kahn CB, Funk IB, et al. Seasonal incidence of insulin-dependent diabetes in Massachusetts, 1964–1973. *Int J Epidemiol* 1982;11:39–45.

24. LaPorte RE, Fishbein HA, Drash AL, et al. The Pittsburgh insulin-dependent diabetes mellitus (IDDM) registry: the incidence of insulin-dependent diabetes in Allegheny County, Pennsylvania (1965–1976). *Diabetes* 1981;30:279–284.

25. Ko KW, Yang SW, Cho NH. Incidence rate of IDDM in Seoul (1985 to 1988). *Diabetes Care* 1994;17:1473–1475.

26. Lipman TH, Chang YF, Murphy KM. The epidemiology of type 1 diabetes in children in Philadelphia 1990–1994. *Diabetes Care* 2002;25:1969–1675.

27. Rewers M, LaPorte R, Walczak M, et al. Apparent epidemic of insulin-dependent diabetes mellitus in midwestern Poland. *Diabetes* 1987;36:106–113.

28. Green A, Patterson CC. Trends in the incidence of childhood-onset diabetes in Europe 1989–1998. *Diabetologia* 2001;44 (suppl 3):B3–B8.

29. Onkamo P, Vaananen S, Karvonen M, et al. Worldwide increase in incidence of type 1 diabetes—the analysis of the data on published incidence trends. *Diabetologia* 1999;42:1395–1403.

30. Yoon J, Austin M, Onodera T, et al. Virus induced diabetes mellitus isolation of a virus from the pancreas of a child with diabetic ketoacidosis. *N Engl J Med* 1979:300:1173–1179.

31. Helmke K, Otten A, Willems WR, et al. Islet cell antibodies and the development of diabetes mellitus in relation to mumps infection and mumps vaccination. *Diabetologia* 1986;29:30–33.

32. Wagenknecht LE, Roseman JM, Herman WH. Increase incidence of insulin-dependent diabetes mellitus following an epidemic of coxsackie virus B5. *Am J Epidemiol* 1991:133: 1024–1031.

33. Virtanen SM, Rasanen L, Ylonen K, et al. Early introduction of dairy products associated with increased risk of IDDM in Finnish children, the Childhood in Diabetes in Finland Study Group. *Diabetes* 1993;42:1786–1790.

34. Gerstein HC. Cow's milk exposure and type 1 diabetes mellitus: a critical overview of the clinical literature. *Diabetes Care* 1994; 17:13–19.

35. Hyotoy H, Hiltunen M, Reunanen A, et al. Decline of mumps antibodies in type 1 (insulin-dependent) diabetic children and a plateau in the rising incidence of type 1 diabetes after introduction of the mumps-measles-rubella vaccine in Finland, Childhood Diabetes in Finland Study Group. *Diabetologia* 1993;36:1303–1308.

36. Erlich HA, Griffith RL, Bugawan TL, et al. Implication of specific DQB1 alleles in genetic susceptibility and resistance identification of IDDM siblings with novel HLA-DQB1 allele and unusual DR2 and DR1 haplotypes. *Diabetes* 1991;40:478–481.

37. Rich SS, Concannon P. Challenges and strategies for investigating the genetic complexity of common human diseases. *Diabetes* 2002;51(suppl 3):288–294.

38. Gambelunghe G, Ghaderi M, Cosentino A, et al. Association of MHC class I chain-related A (MIC-A) gene polymorphism with type 1 diabetes. *Diabetologia* 2000;43:507–514.

39. Park Y, Lee H, Sanjeevi CB, et al. MICA polymorphism is associated with type 1 diabetes in the Korean population. *Diabetes Care* 2001;24:33–38.

40. Sabbah E, Savola K, Ebeling T, et al. Genetic, autoimmune, and clinical characteristics of childhood- and adult-onset type 1 diabetes. *Diabetes Care* 2000;23:1326–1332.

41. Kimpimake T, Kulmal P, Savola K, et al. Natural History of β-cell autoimmunity in young children with increased genetic susceptibility to type 1 diabetes recruited from the general population. *J Clin Endocrinol Metab* 2002;87:4572–4579.

42. Hathout EH, Hartwick N, Fagoaga OR, et al. Clinical, autoimmune, and HLA characteristics of children diagnosed with type 1 diabetes before 5 years of age. *Pediatrics* 2003;111:860–863.

43. Kukko M, Kimpimäke T, Kulmala A, et al. Signs of beta-cell autoimmunity and HLA-defined diabetes susceptibility in the Finnish Population: the sib cohort from the Type 1 Diabetes Prediction and Prevention Study. *Diabetologia* 2003;46:65–70.

44. Redondo MJ, Eisenbarth GS. Genetic control of autoimmunity in type 1 diabetes and associated disorders. *Diabetologia* 2002; 45:605–622.

45. Bennett ST, Lucassen AM, Gough SC, et al. Susceptibility to human type 1 diabetes at IDDM2 is determined by tandem repeat variation at the insulin gene minisatellite locus. *Nat Genet* 1995;9:284–292.

46. Orchard TJ, Chang YF, Ferrell RE, et al. Nephropathy in type 1 diabetes: a manifestation of insulin resistance and multiple genetic susceptibilities? Further evidence from the Pittsburgh Epidemiology of Diabetes Complication Study. *Kidney Int* 2002;62:963–970.

47. Hokanson JE, Cheng S, Snell-Bergeon JK, et al. A common promoter polymorphism in the hepatic lipase gene (LIPC-480C>T) is associated with an increase in coronary calcification in type 1 diabetes. *Diabetes* 2002;51:1208–1213.

48. Deschamps I, Boitard C, Hors J, et al. Life table analysis of the risk of type I (insulin-dependent) diabetes mellitus in siblings according to islet cell antibodies and HLA markers. *Diabetologia* 1992:35:951–957.

49. Rabin DU, Pleasic SM, Shapiro JA, et al. Islet cell antigen 512 is a diabetes-specific islet autoantigen related to protein tyrosine phosphatases. *J Immunol* 1994;152:3183–3188.

50. Lan M, Lu J, Goto Y, et al. Molecular cloning and identification of a receptor-type protein tyrosine phosphatase, IA-2, from human insulinoma. *DNA Cell Biol* 1994;13:505–514.

51. Clare-Salzler MJ, Tobin AJ, Kaufman DL. Glutamate decarboxylase: an autoantigen in IDDM. *Diabetes Care* 1992;15:132–135.

52. Woo W, LaGasse JM, Zhou Z, et al. A novel high-throughput method for accurate, rapid, and economical measurement of multiple type 1 diabetes autoantibodies. *J Immunol Methods* 2000;244:91–103.

53. Eisenbarth GS. Type I diabetes mellitus. A chronic autoimmune disease. *N Engl J Med* 1986;314:1360–1368.

54. Kupila A, Keskinen P, Simell T, et al. Genetic risk determines the emergence of diabetes-associated autoantibodies in young children. *Diabetes* 2002;51:646–651.

55. Kulmala P, Rahko J, Savola K, et al. Stability of autoantibodies and their relation to genetic and metabolic markers of type 1 diabetes in initially unaffected schoolchildren. *Diabetologia* 2000;43:457–464.

56. LaGasse JM, Brantley MS, Leech NJ, et al. Successful prospective prediction of type 1 diabetes in schoolchildren through multiple defined autoantibodies. *Diabetes Care* 2002;25:505–511.

57. Verge CF, Gianani R, Kawasaki E, et al. Prediction of type 1 diabetes in first-degree relatives using a combination of insulin, GAD, and ICA512abc/IA-2 autoantibodies. *Diabetes* 1996;45:926–933.

58. Chase HP, Cuthbertson DD, Dolan L, et al. First-phase insulin release during the intravenous glucose tolerance test as a risk factor for type 1 diabetes. *J Pediatr* 2001;138:244–249.

59. Hosszúfalusi N, Vatay A, Rajczy K, et al. Similar genetic features and different islet cell autoantibody pattern of latent autoimmune diabetes in adults (LADA) compared with adult-onset type 1 diabetes with rapid progression. *Diabetes Care* 2003;26:452–457.

60. Devendra D, Eisenbarth GS. Immunologic endocrine disorders. *J Allergy Clin Immunol* 2003;111(suppl):624–636.

61. Harris MI. Diabetes in America: diabetes data compiled 1984. National Institutes of Health Publication No. 85-1468;VI-1-31. Washington, DC: US Department of Health and Human Services, US Government Printing Office, 1986.

62. Bennett PH. Epidemiology of diabetes mellitus. In: Rifkin H, Porte D, eds. *Diabetes mellitus theory and practice,* 4th ed. New York: Elsevier, 1990:357–377.

63. Bennett PH, Knowler WC, Rushforth NB, et al. Diabetes and obesity. In: Waldhäusl WK, ed. *Proceedings of the 10th Congress of the International Diabetes Federation.* Amsterdam: Excerpta Medica, 1979:507–511.

64. Harris MI. Undiagnosed NIDDM: clinical and public health issues. *Diabetes Care* 1993;16:642–652.

65. Bennett PH, Rushforth NB, Miller M, et al. Epidemiological studies of diabetes in the Pima Indians. *Rec Prog Horm Res* 1976;32:333–376.

66. Zimmet P, Guinea A, Guthrie W, et al. The high prevalence of diabetes mellitus on a Central Pacific island. *Diabetologia* 1977;13:111–115.

67. Prior IAM, Davidson F. The epidemiology of diabetes in Polynesians and Europeans in New Zealand and the Pacific. *N Z Med J* 1966:65:375–383.

68. Ravussin E, Valencia ME, Esparza J, et al. Effects of a traditional lifestyle on obesity in Pima Indians. *Diabetes Care* 1994;17:1067–1074.

69. Marine N, Edelstein O, Jackson WPU, et al. Diabetes hyperglycaemia and glycosuria among Indians, Malays and Africans (Bantu) in Cape Town, South Africa. *Diabetes* 1969:18:840–857.

70. Kawate R, Nishimoto Y, Yamakido M. Migrant studies among the Japanese in Hiroshima and Hawaii. In: Waldhäusl WK, ed. *Diabetes 1979.* Amsterdam: Excerpta Medica, 1980:526.

71. DeFronzo RA, Bonadonna RC, Ferrannini E. Pathogenesis of NIDDM. A balanced overview. *Diabetes Care* 1992;15:318–368.

72. Leahy JL, Bonner-Weir S, Weir GC. Minimal chronic hyperglycemia is a critical determinant of impaired insulin secretion after incomplete pancreatectomy. *J Clin Invest* 1988;81:1407–1414.

73. Polonsky KS, Sturis J, Bell GI. Seminars in medicine of the Beth Israel Hospital, Boston: non-insulin-dependent diabetes mellitus—a genetically programmed failure of the beta cell to compensate for insulin resistance. *N Engl J Med* 1996;334:777–783.

74. Pimenta W, Korytkowski M, Mitrakou A, et al. Pancreatic beta-cell dysfunction as the primary genetic lesion in NIDDM: evidence from studies in normal glucose-tolerant individuals with a first-degree NIDDM relative. *JAMA* 1995;273:1855–1861.

75. Zimmet PZ. Kelly West Lecture 1991. Challenges in diabetes epidemiology—from West to the rest. *Diabetes Care* 1992;15:232–252.

76. Barnett AH, Eff C, Leslie RDG, et al. Diabetes in identical twins: a study of 200 pairs. *Diabetologia* 1981;20:87–93.

77. Gottlieb MS, Root HF. Diabetes mellitus in twins. *Diabetes* 1968;17:693–704.

78. Newman B, Selby JV, King MC, et al. Concordance for type 2 (non-insulin-dependent) diabetes mellitus in male twins. *Diabetologia* 1987;30:763–768.

79. Mitchell BD, Kammerer CM, Reinhart LJ, et al. NIDDM in Mexican-American families. Heterogeneity by age of onset. *Diabetes Care* 1994;17:567–573.

80. Henriksen JE, Alford E, Handberg A, et al. Increased glucose effectiveness in normoglycemic but insulin-resistant relatives of patients with non-insulin-dependent diabetes mellitus. A novel compensatory mechanism. *J Clin Invest* 1994;94:1196–1204.

81. Leslie RDG, Volkmann HP, Poncher M, et al. Metabolic abnormalities in children of non-insulin-dependent diabetics. *BMJ* 1986;293:840–842.

82. Beaty TH, Neel JV, Fajans SS. Identifying risk factors for diabetes in first degree relatives of non-insulin dependent patients. *Am J Epidemiol* 1982;115:380–397.

83. Martin BC, Warram JH, Rosner B, et al. Familial clustering of insulin sensitivity. *Diabetes* 1992;41:850–854.

84. Lowe WL Jr, ed. *Genetics of diabetes mellitus.* Boston: Kluwer Academic, 2001.

85. Hofmann S, Bauer MF, Gerbitz K-D. Genetics of mitochondria-related forms of syndromic diabetes mellitus. In: Lowe WL Jr, ed. *Genetics of diabetes mellitus.* Boston: Kluwer Academic, 2001:91–108.

86. Fajans SS. Scope and heterogeneous nature of MODY. *Diabetes Care* 1990;13:49–64.

87. Fajans SS, Bell GI, Polonsky KS. Molecular mechanisms and clinical pathophysiology of maturity-onset diabetes of the young. *N Engl J Med* 2001;345:971–980.

88. Matschinsky FM, Glaser B, Magnuson MA. Pancreatic β-cell glucokinase: closing the gap between theoretical concepts and experimental realities. *Diabetes* 1998;47:307–315.

89. Froguel P, Velho G. Lowe WL Jr, ed. *Genetics of diabetes mellitus.* Boston: Kluwer Academic, 2001:79–89.

90. Hattersley AT. Diagnosis of maturity-onset diabetes of the young in the pediatric diabetes clinic. *J Pediatr Endocrinol Metab* 2000;13:1411–1417.

91. Hegele RA, Cao H, Harris SB, et al. The hepatic nuclear factor-1alpha G319S variant is associated with early-onset type 2 diabetes in Canadian Oji-Cree. *J Clin Endocrinol Metab* 1999;84:1077–1082.

92. Pinhas-Hamiel O, Dolan LM, Daniels SR, et al. Increased incidence of non-insulin-dependent diabetes mellitus among adolescents. *J Pediatr* 1996;128:608–615.

93. Fagot-Campagna A, Pettitt DJ, Engelgau MM, et al. Type 2 diabetes among North American children and adolescents: an epi-

demiologic review and a public health perspective. *J Pediatr* 2000;136:664–672.

94. Kiess W, Böttner A, Raile K, et al. Type 2 diabetes mellitus in children and adolescents: a review from a European perspective. *Horm Res* 2003;59(suppl 1):77–84.

95. Kitagawa T, Owada M, Urakami T, et al. Increased incidence of non-insulin dependent diabetes mellitus among Japanese schoolchildren correlates with an increased intake of animal protein and fat. *Clin Pediatr* 1998;37:111–116.

96. Knowler WC, Pettitt DJ, Savage PJ, et al. Diabetes incidence in Pima Indians: contributions of obesity and parental diabetes. *Am J Epidemiol* 1981;113:144–156.

97. Dabelea D, Hanson RL, Bennett PH, et al. Increasing prevalence of type II diabetes in American Indian children. *Diabetologia* 1998;41:904–910.

98. Fagot-Campagna A, Saaddine JB, Flegal KM, et al. Diabetes, impaired fasting glucose, and elevated HbA$_{1c}$ in U.S. adolescents: the Third National Health and Nutrition Examination Survey. *Diabetes Care* 2001;24:834–837.

99. Sinha R, Fisch G, Teague B, et al. Prevalence of impaired glucose tolerance among children and adolescents with marked obesity. *N Engl J Med* 2002;346:802–810.

100. Legro RS, Kunselman AR, Dodson WC, et al. Prevalence and predictors of risk for type 2 diabetes mellitus and impaired glucose tolerance in polycystic ovary syndrome: a prospective, controlled study in 254 affected women. *J Clin Endocrinol Metab* 1999;84:194–199.

101. Palmert MR, Gordon CM, Kartashov AI, et al. Screening for abnormal glucose tolerance in adolescents with polycystic ovary syndrome. *J Clin Endocrinol Metab* 2002;87:1017–1023.

102. Ogden CL, Flegal DM, Carroll MD, et al. Prevalence and trends in overweight among US children and adolescents, 1999–2000. *JAMA* 2002;288:1728–1732.

103. Nielson SJ, Popkin BM. Patterns and trends in food portion sizes, 1977–1998. *JAMA* 2003;289:450–453.

104. Young LR, Nestle M. Expanding portion sizes in the US marketplace: implications for nutrition counseling. *J Am Diet Assoc* 2003;103:231–234.

105. Ludwig DS, Peterson KE, Gortmaker SL. Relation between consumption of sugar-sweetened drinks and childhood obesity: a prospective, observational analysis. *Lancet* 2001;357:505–508.

106. Jiang R, Manson JE, Stampfer MJ, et al. Nut and peanut butter consumption and risk of type 2 diabetes in women. *JAMA* 2002;288:2554–2560.

107. Gortmaker SL, Must A, Sobol AM, et al. Television viewing as a cause of increasing obesity among children in the United States, 1986–1990. *Arch Pediatr Adolesc Med* 1996;150:356–362.

108. Hu FB, Li TY, Colditz GA, et al. Television watching and other sedentary behaviors in relation to risk of obesity and type 2 diabetes in women. *JAMA* 2003;289:1785–1791.

109. Schmitz KH, Jacobs Jr DR, Hong C-P, et al. Association of physical activity with insulin sensitivity in children. *Int J Obes* 2002;26:1310–1316.

110. Elbein SC, Wegner K, Kahn SE. Reduced β-cell compensation to the insulin resistance associated with obesity in members of Caucasian familial type 2 diabetic kindreds. *Diabetes Care* 2000;23:221–227.

111. Arslanian SA. Metabolic differences between Caucasian and African-American children and the relationship to type 2 diabetes mellitus. *J Pediatr Endocrinol Metab* 2002;15(suppl 1):509–517.

112. Goran MI, Bergman RN, Cruz ML, et al. Insulin resistance and associated compensatory responses in African-American and Hispanic children. *Diabetes Care* 2002;25:2184–2190.

113. Silverman BL, Rizzo TA, Cho NH, et al. Long-term effects of the intrauterine environment. *Diabetes Care* 1998;21(suppl 2):B142–B149.

114. Johnstone FD, Nasrat AA, Prescott RJ. The effect of established gestational diabetes on pregnancy outcome. *Br J Obstet Gynaecol* 1990;997:1009–1015.

115. Kadiki OA, Reddy MR, Sahli MA, et al. Outcome of pregnant diabetic patients in Benghazi (Libya) from 1984 to 1991. *Diabetes Res Clin Pract* 1993;21:39–42.

116. Contreras-Soto J, Forsbach G, Vazquez-Rosales J. Noninsulin dependent diabetes mellitus and pregnancy in Mexico. *Int J Gynaecol Obstet* 1991;34:205–210.

117. Metzger BE, Bybee DE, Freinkel N, et al. Gestational diabetes mellitus: correlations between the phenotypic and genotypic characteristics of the mother and abnormal glucose tolerance during the first year postpartum. *Diabetes* 1985;34(suppl 2):111–115.

118. Connell FA, Vadheim, Emanuel I. Diabetes in pregnancy: a population based study of incidence, referral for care and perinatal mortality. *Am J Obstet Gynecol* 1985;51:598–603.

119. Wheeler FC, Gollmar CW, Deeb LC. Diabetes and pregnancy in South Carolina: prevalence, perinatal mortality and neonatal morbidity in 1978. *Diabetes Care* 1982;5:561–565.

120. Cundy T, Gamble G, Townend K, et al. Perinatal mortality in type 2 diabetes mellitus. *Diabet Med* 2000;17:33–39.

121. Metzger BE, Kim YL. Detection and diagnostic strategies for gestational diabetes mellitus. In: Hod M, de Leiva A, Jovanovic L et al., eds. *Textbook of diabetes and pregnancy.* London: Martin Dunitz, Taylor and Francis Group 2003:168.

122. Green JR, Pawson IG, Schumacher LB, et al. Glucose tolerance in pregnancy: ethnic variation and influence of body habitus. *Am J Obstet Gynecol* 1990;163:86–92.

123. Beischer NA, Oats JN, Henry OA, et al. Incidence and severity of gestational diabetes mellitus according to country of birth in women living in Australia. *Diabetes* 1991;40(suppl 2):35–38.

124. Ranchod HA, Vaughan JE, Jarvis P. Incidence of gestational diabetes at Northdale Hospital, Pietermaritzburg. *S Afr Med J* 1991;80:14–16.

125. Dooley SL, Metzger BE, Cho N, et al. The influence of demographic and phenotypic heterogeneity on the prevalence of gestational diabetes mellitus. *Int J Gynecol Obstet* 1991;35:13–18.

126. Roseman JM, Go RCP, Perkins LL, et al. Gestational diabetes mellitus among African-American women. *Diabetes Metab Rev* 1991;7:93–104.

127. Berkowitz GS, Lapinski RH, Wein R, et al. Race/ethnicity and other risk factors for gestational diabetes. *Am J Epidemiol* 1992;135:965–973.

128. Murphy NJ, Bulkow LR, Schraer CD, et al. Prevalence of diabetes mellitus in pregnancy among Yup'ik Eskimos, 1987–1988. *Diabetes Care* 1993;16:315–317.

129. Jang HC, Cho NH, Jung KB, et al. Screening for gestational diabetes. *Int J Gynecol Obstet* 1995;51:115–122.

130. Deerochanawong C, Putiyanum C, Wongsuryrat M, et al. Comparison of National Diabetes Data Group and World Health Organization criteria for detecting gestational diabetes. *Diabetologia* 1996;39:1070–1073.

131. Cho N, Rim C, Jang S, et al. The prevalence of gestational diabetes mellitus: comparison of native Korean, immigrant Korean, and Chicago populations. *Am J Epidemiol* 1994;12:56.

132. Harris MI, Hadden WC, Knowler WC, et al. Prevalence of diabetes and impaired glucose tolerance and plasma glucose levels in U.S. population aged 20–74 yr. *Diabetes* 1987;36:523–534.

133. Harris M. Gestational diabetes may represent discovery of pre-existing glucose intolerance. *Diabetes Care* 1988;11:402–411.

134. Super DM, Edelberg SC, Philipson EH, et al. Diagnosis of gestational diabetes in early pregnancy. *Diabetes Care* 1991;14:288–294.

135. Lavin JP Jr. Screening of high-risk and general populations for

gestational diabetes: clinical application and lost analysis. *Diabetes* 1985;34(suppl 2):24–27.

136. Jovanovic L, Peterson CM. Screening for gestational diabetes: optimum timing and criteria for retesting. *Diabetes* 1985;34 (suppl 2):21–23.

137. Buchanan TA, Metzger BE, Freinkel N, et al. Insulin sensitivity and β-cell responsiveness to glucose during late pregnancy in lean and moderately obese women with normal glucose tolerance or mild gestational diabetes. *Am J Obstet Gynecol* 1990; 162:1008–1014.

138. Catalano PM, Tyzbir ED, Roman NM, et al. Longitudinal changes in insulin release and insulin resistance in nonobese pregnant women. *Am J Obstet Gynecol* 1991;165:1667–1672.

139. Buchanan TA, Catalano PM. The pathogenesis of GDM: implications for diabetes after pregnancy. *Diabetes Rev* 1995;3: 584–601.

140. Metzger BE, Cho NH, Roston SM, et al. Pre-pregnancy weight and antepartum insulin secretion predict glucose tolerance five years after gestational diabetes mellitus. *Diabetes Care* 1993;16: 1598–1605.

141. O'Sullivan JB. Long term follow up of gestational diabetes. In: Camerini-Davalos RA, Cole HS, eds. *Early diabetes in early life.* New York: Academic, 1975:503–510.

142. Kjos SL, Peters RK, Xiang A, et al. Predicting future diabetes in Latino women with gestational diabetes: utility of early postpartum glucose tolerance testing. *Diabetes* 1995;44:586–591.

143. Freinkel N, Metzger BE, Phelps RI, et al. Gestational diabetes mellitus: heterogeneity of maternal age, weight, insulin secretion, HLA antigens, and islet cell antibodies and the impact of maternal metabolism on pancreatic B-cell and somatic development in the offspring. *Diabetes* 1985;34(suppl 2):1–7.

144. Freinkel N. Summary and recommendations of the Second International Workshop-Conference on Gestational Diabetes Mellitus. *Diabetes* 1985;34(suppl 2):123–126.

145. Jang HJ, Min HK, Lee HK, et al. Short stature in Korean women: a contribution to the multifactorial predisposition to gestational diabetes mellitus. *Diabetologia* 1998;41:778–783.

146. Hollingsworth DR, Ney D, Stubblefield N, et al. Metabolic and therapeutic assessment of gestational diabetes by two-hour and twenty-four-hour isocaloric meal tolerance tests. *Diabetes* 1985; 34(suppl 2):81–87.

147. Ryan EA, O'Sullivan MJ, Skyler JS. Insulin action during pregnancy: studies with the euglycemic clamp technique. *Diabetes* 1985;34:380–389.

148. Buchanan TA, Xiang A, Kjos SL, et al. Gestational diabetes: antepartum characteristics that predict postpartum glucose intolerance and type 2 diabetes in Latino women. *Diabetes* 1998;47:1302–1310.

149. Catalano PM, Tyzbir ED, Wolfe R, et al. Carbohydrate metabolism during pregnancy in control subjects and women with gestational diabetes. *Am J Physiol* 1993;264:E60–E67.

150. Ober C, Xiang K-S, Thisted R, et al. Increased risk for gestational diabetes mellitus associated with insulin receptor and insulin-like growth factor II restriction fragment length polymorphisms. *Genet Epidemiol* 1989;6:559–569.

151. van den Ouweland JM, Lemkes HH, Ruitenbeek W, et al. Mutation in mitochondrial tRNA(Leu)(UUR) gene in a large pedigree with maternally transmitted type II diabetes mellitus and deafness. *Nat Gene* 1992;1:368–371.

152. Kadowaki T, Kadowaki H, Mori Y, et al. A subtype of diabetes mellitus associated with a mutation of mitochondria) DNA. *N Engl J Med* 1994;330:962–968.

153. Mawhinney H, Hadden DR, Middleton D, et al. HLA antigens in asymptomatic diabetes. A 10-year follow-up study of potential diabetes in pregnancy and gestational diabetes. *Ulster Med J* 1979;48:166–172.

154. Budowle B, Huddleston JF, Go RCP, et al. Association of HLA-linked factor B with gestational diabetes mellitus in black women. *Am J Obstet Gynecol* 1988;159:805–806.

155. Catalano PM, Tyzbir ED, Sims EAH. Incidence and significance of islet cell antibodies in women with previous gestational diabetes. *Diabetes Care* 1990;13:478–482.

156. Beischer NA, Wein P, Sheedy MT, et al. Prevalence of antibodies to glutamic acid decarboxylase in women who have had gestational diabetes. *Am J Obstet Gynecol* 1995;173:1563–1569.

157. Buschard K, Buch I, Molsted-Pedersen L, et al. Increased incidence of true type I diabetes acquired during pregnancy. *BMJ* 1987;294:275–279.

158. Damm P, Kühl C, Bertelsen A, et al. Predictive factors for the development of diabetes in women with previous gestational diabetes mellitus. *Am J Obstet Gynecol* 1992;167:607–616.

159. Bleich D, Polak M, Eisenbarth GS. Decreased risk of type I diabetes in offspring of mothers who acquire diabetes during adrenarchy. *Diabetes* 1993;42:1433–1439.

160. Pociot F, Norgaard K, Hobolth N, et al. A nationwide population-based study of the familial aggregation of type 1 (insulin-dependent) diabetes mellitus in Denmark. Danish Study Group of Diabetes in Childhood. *Diabetologia* 1993;36: 870–875.

161. Francois R, Picaud JJ, Ruitton-Ugliengo A, et al. The newborn of diabetic mothers. Observations on 154 cases, 1958–1972. *Biol Neonate* 1974;24:1–31.

162. Amendt P, Michaelis D, Hildmann W. Clinical and metabolic studies in children of diabetic-mothers. *Endokrinologie* 1976;67: 351–361.

163. Dörner G, Mohnike A. Further evidence for a predominantly maternal transmission of maturity-onset type diabetes. *Endokrinologie* 1976;68:121–124.

164. Wagener DK, Kuller LH, Orchard TJ, et al. The Pittsburgh diabetes mellitus study. II. Secondary attack rates in families with insulin-dependent diabetes mellitus. *Am J Epidemiol* 1982; 115:868–878.

165. Tillil H, Kobberling J. Age-corrected empirical genetic risk estimates for first degree relatives of IDDM patients. *Diabetes* 1987;36:93–99.

166. Gamble DR. An epidemiological study of childhood diabetes affecting two or more siblings. *Diabetologia* 1980;19: 341–344.

167. Bingley PJ, Gale EAM. Incidence of insulin-dependent diabetes in England: a study in the Oxford region 1985–6. *BMJ* 1989; 298:558–560.

168. Freinkel N. The Banting Lecture 1980: Of pregnancy and progeny. *Diabetes* 1980;29:1023–1035.

169. Pettitt DJ, Baird HR, Aleck KA, et al. Excessive obesity in offspring of Pima Indian women with diabetes during pregnancy. *N Engl J Med* 1983;308:242–245.

170. Pettitt DJ, Aleck KA, Baird HA, et al. Congenital susceptibility to NIDDM. Role of intrauterine environment. *Diabetes* 1988; 37:622–628.

171. Martin AO, Simpson JL, Ober C, et al. Frequency of diabetes mellitus in mothers of probands with gestational diabetes: possible maternal influence on the predisposition to gestational diabetes. *Am J Obstet Gynecol* 1985;151:471–475.

172. Aerts L, Holemans K, Van Assche FA. Maternal diabetes during pregnancy: consequences for the offspring. *Diabetes Metab Rev* 1990;6:147–167.

173. Gauguier D, Nelson I, Bernard C, et al. Higher maternal than paternal inheritance of diabetes in GK rats. *Diabetes* 1994;43: 220–224.

174. Pettitt DJ, Bennett PH, Saad MF, et al. Abnormal glucose tolerance during pregnancy in Pima Indian women: long-term effects on the offspring. *Diabetes* 1991;40(suppl 2):126–130.

175. Metzger BE, Silverman B, Freinkel N, et al. Amniotic fluid insulin concentration as a predictor of obesity. *Arch Dis Child* 1990;65:1050–1052.
176. Silverman BL, Cho NH, Metzger BE. Impaired glucose tolerance in adolescent offspring of diabetic mothers: Relationship to fetal hyperinsulinism. *Diabetes Care* 1995;18:611–618.
177. Susa JB, Boylan JM, Sehgal P, et al. Persistence of impaired secretion in infant rhesus monkeys that had been hyperinsulinemic *in utero*. *J Clin Endocrinol Metab* 1992;75:265–269.
178. Plagemann A, Harder T, Rake A, et al. Hypothalamic insulin and neuropeptide Y in the offspring of gestational diabetic mother rats. *NeuroReport* 1998;9:4069–4073.
179. Hales CN, Barker DJP, Clark PMS, et al. Fetal and infant growth and impaired glucose tolerance at age 64 years. *BMJ* 1991;303:1019–1022.
180. Barker DJP, Gluckman PD, Godfrey KM, et al. Review article: Fetal nutrition and cardiovascular disease in adult life. *Lancet* 1993;341:938–941.
181. McCance DR, Pettitt DJ, Hanson RL, et al. Birth weight and non-insulin-dependent diabetes: thrifty genotype, thrifty phenotype or surviving small baby genotype? *BMJ* 1994;308:942–945.
182. Hattersley AT, Tooke JE. The fetal insulin hypothesis: an alternative explanation of the association of low birth weight with diabetes and vascular disease. *Lancet* 1999;353:1789–1792.
183. Ong KK, Phillips DI, Fall C, et al. The insulin gene VNTR, type 2 diabetes and birth weight. *Nat Genet* 1999;21:262–263.

3

MANAGEMENT OF DIABETES MELLITUS

NEDA RASOULI
STEVEN C. ELBEIN

Diabetes mellitus (DM) is a spectrum of disorders ranging from absolute lack of insulin secretion (type 1 DM) to insulin resistance with various stages of β-cell dysfunction (type 2 DM). Currently, diabetes is classified as type 1 diabetes, type 2 diabetes, other specific types of diabetes, and gestational diabetes (1). This classification scheme was originally developed by the National Diabetes Data Group in 1979 (2) and was revised by an International Expert Committee sponsored by the American Diabetes Association in 1997 (1). This updated classification retained the intermediate stage termed impaired glucose tolerance (IGT) and added an intermediate stage based only on an elevated fasting glucose (110–126 mg/dL), called impaired fasting glucose (IFG). The upper limits for normal glucose were recently revised to 100 mg/dl (49).

Type 1 DM patients require insulin replacement for life due to β-cell destruction and absolute insulin deficiency. Insulin deficiency impairs glucose utilization by insulin requiring tissues, and activates lipolysis in adipose tissue and ketone production in the liver. In the absence of insulin, individuals with type 1 DM may rapidly develop the life-threatening condition of diabetic ketoacidosis (DKA). Type 2 DM, which is the most prevalent form of diabetes, results from a combination of insulin resistance in conjunction with β-cell dysfunction and gradually declining insulin secretion. Type 2 DM often does not require insulin therapy early in the course of disease, when lifestyle changes and oral hypoglycemic agents control hyperglycemia. However, the natural course of type 2 DM is to progressive cell failure and deteriorating glycemic control. Thus, many people with type 2 diabetes will eventually require insulin therapy (3).

Several specific types of diabetes have been defined. Autosomal-dominant, early-onset diabetes may result from defects in genes that alter β-cell function (also known as maturity onset diabetes of youth, or MODY). Defects in mitochondrial DNA may result in maternally inherited diabetes due to β-cell dysfunction as well as

hearing loss. Diseases of the exocrine pancreas and drug-induced diabetes may also mimic idiopathic type 2 DM. Whereas these types of diabetes may not require insulin for survival, insulin is often the optimal treatment for glycemic control.

MANAGEMENT OF METABOLIC ABNORMALITIES IN DIABETES

Diabetes is a metabolic disorder characterized by hyperglycemia and by microvascular and cardiovascular complications that substantially increase the morbidity and mortality associated with the disease. Management of diabetes and prevention of both microvascular and macrovascular complications requires a holistic approach that includes goals beyond normalization of blood glucose, including aggressive lipid management and aggressive control of blood pressure. Aggressive management of blood pressure, lipids, and glycemia reduces cardiovascular events in type 2 DM (4). A current consensus for these goals is summarized in Table 3-1. Each of these elements is discussed below.

TABLE 3-1. GOALS FOR MANAGEMENT OF DIABETES

Glycemic control	
A$_{1c}$	<7%[a]
Preprandial plasma glucose	90–130 mg/dL
Peak postprandial plasma glucose	<180 mg/dL
Blood pressure	<130/80 mm Hg
Lipids	
Low-density lipoprotein	<100 mg/dL
Triglycerides	<150 mg/dL
High-density lipoprotein	>40 mg/dL

[a]A$_{1c}$ <6.5% is recommended by American Association of Clinical Endocrinologists.

GLYCEMIC CONTROL

Glycemic control is fundamental to the management of diabetes. Prospective randomized clinical trials have shown that good glycemic control decreases rates of all microvascular complication (5–7) in both type 1 and type 2 DM. In the Diabetes Control and Complications Trial (DCCT) of type 1 DM, an improvement in glycated hemoglobin measures (HbA$_{1c}$) of only 2% (7% in the intensive treatment group and 9% in the conventional therapy group) resulted in an approximately 50% reduction in rates of progression of retinopathy, albuminuria, and clinical neuropathy at 6.5 years of follow-up (5). Any reduction in glycemia appeared to reduce microvascular complication rates without any apparent threshold for this benefit. Subsequently, similar results were demonstrated in type 2 DM with the United Kingdom Prospective Diabetes Study (UKPDS), despite a difference of only 0.9% in the HbA$_{1c}$ values. Lowering the HbA$_{1c}$ from 7.9% with conventional treatment to 7.0% in the intensive treatment group was accompanied by an approximately 25% reduction in all microvascular end points (6).

In contrast to microvascular complications, demonstration of reduced cardiovascular events by glycemic control alone has been difficult. Although some analyses support a role of glycemic control in reduction of cardiovascular events (8), this reduction did not reach statistical significance in either the DCCT or the UKPDS studies. Reduction of cardiovascular events, which are the leading cause of morbidity and mortality in type 2 DM, requires management of blood pressure and lipid disorders (9).

Monitoring Glycemic Control

The monitoring of glycemic status, both short-term daily variations in glycemia and the long-term glycemic control that has correlated well with microvascular complications, is an essential tool in diabetes management to balance glycemic control with avoidance of hypoglycemia. Short-term assessment requires daily monitoring of capillary blood glucose by the patient (self-monitoring of blood glucose, or SMBG). Alternative methods for continuous glucose monitoring of interstitial fluid glucose has recently become available and will develop further in the near future, but cannot replace SMBG. Glycated protein tests offer the best estimate of long-term control. Good diabetes management generally includes both SMBG and glycated protein levels for type 1 DM or in the intensively controlled type 2 DM subject, whereas an individual with stable glycemic control and type 2 DM treated only with oral agents might achieve safe control with little or no SMBG.

Self-Monitoring of Blood Glucose

SMBG allows patients to evaluate their individual response to therapy, to assess whether glycemic targets are being

achieved, and to respond to glycemic levels with adjustments in premeal insulin or management of hypoglycemic episodes. The frequency and timing of SMBG must be tailored to the regimen and the patient's ability and motivation. Patients with type 2 DM on stable regimens of oral agents may get by with monitoring only during illnesses or times of possible hypoglycemia. Many patients can monitor once daily but rotate the times so that in the course of a week each premeal or bedtime glucose is monitored at least once. Similarly, twice daily monitoring is more useful if different times are monitored each day. For patients attempting to achieve excellent glycemic control and those on multiple daily injections (MDIs), monitoring before and after each meal, at bedtime, and at least weekly at 3:00 A.M. is essential to safe glycemic control.

Monitoring without maintaining an accurate, interpretable log of blood glucoses that allows both the patient and provider to recognize patterns of low or high glucose levels is rarely useful. Many modern meters will download glucoses into software programs that allow a flexible format, but recording glucoses with accompanying information that permits a diary of what events might have led to an unexpected low or high glucose is also important. Providers should periodically check a patient's glucose monitor against a known, calibrated standard to ensure that the readings correspond to laboratory glucose levels.

The large numbers of options that now exist for SMBG are covered in detail elsewhere in this book. Key elements in choosing a meter include ease of use, size, quality of the display, and size of the blood sample. The latter can be critical for some patients, and most recent technologies have reduced sample size to the point that sampling can be performed on body parts other than fingertips, such as arms. These locations are much less sensitive, thus reducing the pain associated with lancing fingertips.

Continuous Glucose Monitoring

Continuous glucose monitoring has recently become possible. This technology cannot yet replace SMBG, and SMBG is required to calibrate these devices. Nonetheless, SMBG gives only a small slice of glycemic control in any given day and provides no information on control during most of the nighttime hours when hypoglycemia is most common. Hence, this new technology represents a valuable adjunct to detect unsuspected hypoglycemia and hyperglycemia. In the future these methods may become widely used and may eventually replace SMBG for day-to-day monitoring in many patients.

Two devices to continuously monitor glucose levels have been approved by the U.S. Food and Drug Administration, both based on the measurement of glucose in the interstitial fluid. The Continuous Glucose Monitoring System (CGMS) (Medtronic MiniMed, Minneapolis, MN) uses a temporary sensor implanted in the subcutaneous tissue, which is connected by a small wire to a pager-sized glucose monitor. Glucose levels are recorded and stored every 5 minutes. At present, no glucose information is given to the patient; thus day-to-day monitoring and adjustment is not possible. Monitoring is typically performed for 72 hours and subsequently downloaded from the device's memory. A different technology is implemented in the GlucoWatch Automatic Glucose Biographer (Cygnus, Inc., Redwood City, CA), which is similar in appearance to a wristwatch. The GlucoWatch measures glucose in interstitial fluid extracted through the skin with an electric current. The device automatically measures glucose every 20 minutes for a 12-hour period, and displays the most recent glucose level. Like the CGMS system, calibration by SMBG is required, and monitoring is for relatively short periods of time, but results are available to the patient. An audible alarm may be set to sound if any reading is above or below preset levels. The frequent and automatic nature of the GlucoWatch readings allows better detection of hypoglycemia than can be achieved by most patients using SMBG in current medical practice (10).

Glycated Protein Testing

Measurement of glycated proteins provides information on the average glycemia over weeks and months by a single measurement. The most commonly used measure is glycated hemoglobin, which is often reported as the hemoglobin A_{1c} or simply HbA_{1c}. HbA_{1c} testing should be performed routinely in all patients with diabetes, at initial assessment, and then approximately every 3 months thereafter to assess glycemic control. Because the HbA_{1c} test reflects a mean glycemia over the preceding 2 to 3 months, recurrent episodes of both hyper- and hypoglycemia may result in an HbA_{1c} at goal, when in fact control is poor. To overcome such misleading conclusions, the HbA_{1c} should be viewed as complementary to SMBG and other short-term measures rather than as a replacement for daily self-monitoring. An alternative to the glycated hemoglobin is fructosamine, a glycated protein measure that reflects glycemic control over the previous 1 to 2 weeks. This measure may be of value when measures of shorter term control are advantageous, such as in preconception control or during pregnancy. The fructosamine may also be useful in situations in which the HbA_{1c} may be inaccurate, such as in hemoglobinopathies or hemolytic anemias.

BLOOD PRESSURE CONTROL

Hypertension (blood pressure ≥140/90 mm Hg) is a common comorbidity of diabetes, affecting 20% to 60% of people with diabetes, depending on age, obesity, and ethnicity. Hypertension is also a major risk factor for cardiovascular disease and microvascular complications such as

retinopathy and nephropathy. In type 1 DM, hypertension often reflects underlying nephropathy. In type 2 DM, hypertension is often present at diagnosis as one element of the metabolic syndrome. Several studies have demonstrated significant improvement in both microvascular and macrovascular complications with tight blood pressure control (11,12). To reduce complications, an American Diabetes Association consensus panel has recommended that blood pressure in diabetic subjects be maintained below 130/80 mm Hg.

Limited data are available from trials comparing different classes of drugs in patients with diabetes and hypertension (13). Several studies have shown benefits of angiotensin-converting enzyme (ACE) inhibitors or angiotensin receptor blockers (ARBs) in preserving kidney function in individuals with microalbuminuria or proteinuria. Early therapy with ACE inhibitors has been shown to decrease the risk for progression of nephropathy in patients with both type 1 and type 2 DM (14), and to also decrease cardiovascular events in type 2 DM with or without hypertension (15). Angiotensin II receptor blockers (ARBs) have been shown similarly to reduce the rate of progression of nephropathy in patients with type 2 diabetes (16–18). Thus, these agents are widely viewed as the standard of care. Nonetheless, several recent studies have raised doubts about these recommendations. The UKPDS Hypertension in Diabetes study showed no significant differences in outcome between individuals assigned to treatment based on an ACE inhibitor compared with those individuals assigned to primary treatment with a β-blocker (19). More recently, the Antihypertensive and Lipid-Lowering Treatment to Prevent Heart Attack Trial (ALLHAT) revealed that a thiazide diuretic (chlorthalidone) was superior to both an ACE inhibitor and a calcium channel blocker in preventing cardiovascular disease (20).

Most diabetic patients, particularly those with type 2 DM, require more than one antihypertensive drug to reach the target goal. Based on currently available data, we recommend initial therapy with an ACE inhibitor or ARB, with the addition of a thiazide diuretic as second-line treatment unless ACE inhibitors are contraindicated. Further analyses of the results of the ALLHAT study results are needed to reconcile the beneficial cardiovascular effects of thiazides with the previous superior performance of ACE inhibitors in renal protection.

LIPID MANAGEMENT

Patients with type 2 DM have an increased prevalence of lipid abnormalities that contributes to higher rates of cardiovascular disease. Patients with type 2 DM most commonly have increased triglyceride levels and decreased high-density lipoprotein (HDL) cholesterol levels. Lipid management aimed at lowering low-density lipoprotein

(LDL) cholesterol, raising HDL cholesterol, and lowering triglycerides has been shown to reduce macrovascular disease and mortality in patients with type 2 DM, particularly those who have had prior cardiovascular events. Although limited data are available from clinical trials, especially in diabetic patients without clinical cardiovascular disease, aggressive therapy of diabetic dyslipidemia is recommended because of the high mortality rate associated with cardiovascular events. Target lipid levels are shown in Table 3-1. Although nutrition assessment and intervention, increased physical activity, and weight loss may allow some patients to reach these lipid levels, many patients require pharmacotherapy despite reaching glycemic goals.

Treatment with 3-hydroxy-3-methylglutaryl coenzyme A (HMG CoA) reductase inhibitors (statins) yielded a significant reduction in coronary and cerebrovascular events in diabetic patients in secondary prevention studies (21,22), and a similar trend of reduced cardiac events was observed in a small subgroup of diabetic patients in a primary prevention trial (23). Notably, the number of women who had an acute major coronary event in this study was small, and there was insufficient power to detect a difference among treatment groups for women (24). Reductions in cardiovascular end points were also achieved by using the fibric acid derivative gemfibrozil in two trials (25,26). The choice between these agents is unclear, but generally primary elevations in triglycerides, as are often seen in type 2 DM, are best treated with a fibric acid derivative (gemfibrozil or fenofibrate), whereas elevations in LDL or non-HDL cholesterol are best treated with a statin. Combinations of these agents are often required to control lipid levels in patients with type 2 DM.

MEDICAL NUTRITION THERAPY

Dietary consultation is an essential part of diabetes management and education (27). Diabetes control is rarely achieved for either type 1 or type 2 DM without good meal timing and food choices. Dietary consultation includes a nutritional assessment to evaluate the patient's food intake, lifestyle, and readiness to make changes. For most patients with type 2 DM, nutritional counseling will include caloric restriction and weight loss. In contrast, diets for type 1 DM are often weight maintaining and usually do not involve caloric restrictions, particularly for young, active patients. Achieving the nutrition-related goals requires a team effort that includes a motivated patient and a registered dietitian, preferably one who is also a certified diabetes educator. Dietary assessment and counseling should be part of the regular follow-up for most diabetic patients. In addition to diet, regular physical activity is recommended for all patients with type 2 DM, both to improve metabolic control by improving insulin action and to reduce the risk for cardiovascular disease (28).

PHARMACOTHERAPY OF DIABETES

Insulin Therapy and Management of Type 1 Diabetes

The injection of insulin is essential for the management of patients with type 1 DM. The treatment goal is to mimic the normal physiology as closely as feasible and to reduce glycemic levels to as close to normal as possible without inducing hypoglycemia. Normally, the pancreas secretes insulin throughout the day in response to blood glucose. In the postmeal state, additional insulin is secreted in response to meal protein and carbohydrate to maintain the blood glucose very close to optimal levels (<140 mg/dL) despite changes in nutrient intake. To mimic this pattern, pharmacotherapy must also use a basal/bolus approach. This approach provides sufficient insulin throughout the day to cover basal (fasting) needs, including nocturnal requirements, supplemented by appropriate amounts of insulin to mimic the normal prandial response. Options to achieve this goal have expanded, with new insulin preparations, including new insulin analogues for conventional multiinjection regimens (intensive conventional therapy or MDIs), and improved pump technology for continuous subcutaneous insulin infusion (CSII). The choice among the options reviewed briefly below must be tailored to the patient's needs, abilities, and lifestyle. A full discussion of the management is beyond the scope of this chapter. Intensive multiinjection or continuous subcutaneous infusion is best handled by experienced, multidisciplinary diabetes care teams.

Available Insulin Preparations

Currently available insulin preparations are isolated from pork pancreas or are synthesized using recombinant DNA technology. Recently, both very short-acting and long-acting (basal) insulin analogues, which modify the primary amino acid sequence of the insulin molecule, have been approved for use. A summary of the available insulin preparations and their pharmacologic properties are shown in Table 3-2. Because of lower rates of insulin antibody for-

TABLE 3-2. TYPES OF AVAILABLE INSULIN

Insulin	Class	Origin	Peak Action
Regular	Short acting	Human, pork	2–4 h
Lispro; Aspart	Rapid acting	Analogue (rDNA)	1–2 h
NPH, Lente	Intermediate acting	Human, pork	6–12 h
Ultralente	Long acting	Human, mixed beef/pork	14–24 h
Glargine	Long acting	Analogue (rDNA)	24 h

NPH, neutral protamine Hagedorn; rDNA, recombinant DNA.

mation and wider availability, initiation of insulin therapy or changes in insulin therapy should use human insulin preparations or insulin analogues. All insulin preparations are safe to use in pregnancy or for preconception diabetes control, although most newer rapid-acting analogue insulins have not been extensively studied. Rapid-acting insulin analogues typically peak at 60 to 90 minutes, short-acting insulins (human and pork regular) show peak activity at 2 to 4 hours, intermediate-acting preparations [neutral protamine Hagedorn (NPH), lente] peak at 6 to 12 hours, and long-acting insulins (ultralente, glargine) last at least 24 hours and peak at 14 to 24 hours. Long-acting insulin therapy is generally "peakless" once steady-state therapy is attained. In addition to these single preparations, insulin therapy for type 2 DM most often includes simple, two-shot regimens comprising mixed insulins. Commercially available mixed insulin preparations include 70% NPH/30% regular, 50% NPH/50% regular, and 75% protamine lispro/25% lispro, among others.

Subcutaneous Insulin Therapy

Insulin therapy is the cornerstone of management of type 1 DM, and is often required to supplement oral therapy or manage type 2 DM. To mimic endogenous insulin secretion, a long-acting insulin is used to provide a steady-state supply of basal insulin and short-acting insulin is injected before each meal to control postprandial hyperglycemia. Alternatively, a mixture of short- and intermediate-duration insulins may be administered twice a day, or a short-acting insulin may be administered continuously by a pump to provide both basal and bolus therapy. Recently developed shorter acting insulin analogues, such as lispro and aspart, offer some advantages over earlier formulations in these regimens. They have a more rapid onset and shorter duration of action compared with regular insulin, which allows the insulin to be given closer to the meal time. Their short duration of action may also more closely mimic endogenous insulin secretion, but in return often results in inadequate insulin between meals to maintain glycemic control and to suppress ketone production. Hence, popular regimens that provide NPH only at bedtime often fail in type 1 DM when rapid-acting analogue insulin preparations are used before meals. Until recently, the only options to permit use of insulin lispro or insulin aspart for bolus therapy were to combine short-acting analogues with twice-daily intermediate insulin (NPH) or twice daily ultralente insulin. The recent release of the long-acting, relatively peakless insulin glargine permits once-daily basal therapy and overcomes these problems.

A detailed description of regimens available for conventional insulin therapy is beyond the scope of this chapter, but will be reviewed briefly. For late-onset type 1 DM or type 2 DM, where some endogenous insulin secretion is often still present, twice-daily intermediate (NPH) insulin may achieve excellent control without premeal bolus ther-

apy. Typically, NPH is best administered in the morning before breakfast to cover daytime basal requirements, some breakfast requirements, and lunchtime. A second injection is given at bedtime (9–11 P.M.) to cover nocturnal basal requirements, which decrease to a nadir at 3 A.M. and then increase until 7 A.M. ("dawn phenomenon"). If this regimen proves inadequate, a short-acting insulin (regular, lispro, or aspart) may be given before supper. Similarly, a rapid-acting insulin may be added prior to breakfast if prelunch glucose levels are consistently elevated. If insulin is given as a premixed preparation (intermediate and short-acting insulin mix), injections must be given before breakfast and before supper. These regimens have the disadvantage that the suppertime intermediate insulin typically induces hypoglycemia at 3:00 A.M., thus limiting morning glycemic control. In pregnancy, accelerated starvation increases the likelihood of early morning hypoglycemia. It is therefore advisable to administer NPH insulin at bedtime. Regimens with premixed insulin may work for type 2 DM, but rarely meet the recommended glycemic goals in type 1 DM. Nonetheless, they may be the best option for those who lack the ability to mix insulin or to take multiple injections, including individuals with impaired vision or manual dexterity. When these "split/mix" regimens fail to achieve the goal of an HbA$_{1c}$ at or below 7.0%, as they often do in completely insulin-dependent type 1 DM, therapy with MDIs often achieves near-normal glycemic control in both type 1 DM and type 2 DM. These regimens combine either an intermediate or a long-acting insulin (e.g., NPH or glargine) given once daily to provide basal insulin with a short-acting insulin before each meal to provide prandial insulin. Adjustment and monitoring of such regimens requires an experienced health-care team.

Typical regimens begin with daily insulin amounts of 0.5 to 0.8 U/kg. Most patients with type 1 DM will require close to 0.5 to 0.6 U/kg, divided such that 30% to 40% is basal and the remainder is split according to the size of the meals. Rapid-acting insulin is best avoided at bedtime, because it often induces nocturnal hypoglycemia. Self-monitoring of blood glucose is essential to achieving good glycemic control, and generally must follow the intensity of the regimen. Thus, two-shot regimens often require only daily or twice-daily monitoring, whereas MDI therapies generally require monitoring before and after each meal, often with variation in the insulin dose to address variations in blood glucose or carbohydrate intake. Additionally, 3:00 A.M. and fasting glucose levels must be balanced to achieve the ideal basal insulin dose. Thus, occasional (weekly in our practice) 3 A.M. glucose checks are essential to adjust and monitor this regimen.

Continuous Subcutaneous Insulin Infusion

CSII is an alternative to MDIs as an effective means of achieving near-normal glycemic control. In CSII, the pump delivers a small amount of insulin on a continuous basis. Because the basal amount may be adjusted throughout the day, according to the patient's typical activity and insulin requirements, changes in insulin requirements due to activity or nocturnal changes are easily accommodated. Bolus therapy must be programmed into the pump before each meal by the patient. Typically, the bolus amount is determined by the amount of carbohydrate in the meal to be consumed, and the patient must "count" the carbohydrate and take an amount of insulin set by the amount of carbohydrate in the meal. This amount of insulin is then adjusted for the blood glucose level prior to the meal. Although CSII has the advantage of flexibility and the ability to deal with changing basal insulin requirement, the superiority of CSII over MDIs in reducing the microvascular complications of diabetes was not demonstrated in the DCCT.

Typically, CSII is used for type 1 DM, although some patients with type 2 DM who require intensive therapy for glycemic control may benefit from the flexibility of CSII. This method of control may be particularly beneficial in preconception planning and during pregnancy. In a metaanalysis of 12 clinical trials (29) comparing glycemic control during CSII to conventional intensive therapy, the HbA$_{1c}$ was reduced by 0.5% (0.2%–0.7%) with CSII compared with MDIs despite a 14% average reduction in daily insulin dose. The ideal candidate for CSII must be strongly motivated to improve glucose control, be willing to monitor and record glucose levels at least 4 to 6 times daily, and have an experienced and available healthcare provider. The key to success is close interaction with a diabetes management team that includes a physician who is comfortable with CSII management, a certified diabetes educator who has been properly trained in CSII management, and a dietitian. As with all methods of intensive therapy, the risk for hypoglycemia increases with tight control. With CSII, further problems may result from the lack of a subcutaneous insulin depot. Thus, any failure of CSII, such as poor absorption, leakage of insulin from the infusion site, or pump malfunction, will result in rapid increases in glycemia and possibly rapid onset of diabetic ketoacidosis. The health-care costs of CSII therapy are considerably higher than those of MDIs, and may be a consideration for many patients.

Management of Type 2 Diabetes

Oral Antihyperglycemic Agents

In principle, oral agents should be initiated only after attempts to achieve glycemic goals with lifestyle modification, including diet, exercise, and weight reduction, have failed. Unfortunately, the patient who can meet glycemic goals with lifestyle modification is unusual, and sustained weight reduction is rarely achieved. Furthermore, current options for oral hypoglycemic agents are compatible with weight loss. Consequently, most clinicians and endocri-

nologists now initiate treatment at diagnosis for all but the mildest cases of type 2 DM, with the hope that medication can be discontinued subsequently. Currently available medications fall into three broad classes: insulin secretagogues, insulin sensitizers, and α-glucosidase inhibitors. Within each of these classes are several options, thus leading to a panoply of options for initial monotherapy and subsequent combination therapy. Additionally, many of these agents may be combined successfully with insulin to achieve glycemic goals. A complete catalog of these options is beyond the scope of this chapter, and few studies have compared the efficacy of various treatment regimens. As monotherapy, the sulfonylurea insulin secretagogues and insulin sensitizers (biguanides, thiazolidinediones) are equally effective in lowering fasting glucose and HbA$_{1c}$.

Currently available insulin secretagogues include the sulfonylurea agents (glyburide, glipizide, glimepiride) and the more recently marketed meglitinides (nateglinide, repaglinide). Both classes of drugs act through the β-cell potassium channel to depolarize the β-cell and stimulate insulin secretion in a non-glucose-dependent manner. The primary difference between these agents is in the onset and duration of action, although differential binding to the cardiac (SUR2) receptors among drugs in this class has been a recent source of concern that might eventually alter treatment recommendations. The meglitinides are nonsulfonylurea drugs that have a more rapid onset and shorter duration of action. Consequently, these agents must be given before each meal, but the short duration of action theoretically results in less postprandial hypoglycemia. Although first-generation sulfonylurea agents (chlorpropamide, tolbutamide, tolazamide) remain available, these agents have problematic durations of action, side effects, and drug interaction profiles that we believe limit their utility in the current market. Insulin secretagogues are only effective in the presence of adequate β-cell insulin secretory reserve, and thus are best used early in the course of type 2 DM or for mild to moderate hyperglycemia. Major complications are hypoglycemia and weight gain, which may be less problematic with newer generation sulfonylurea agents and meglitinides. The second generation sulfonylurea agents are particularly cost effective and have an excellent safety profile.

Insulin-sensitizing agents include the biguanides (metformin) and the thiazolidinediones (pioglitazone, rosiglitazone). Biguanides improve insulin sensitivity primarily by decreasing hepatic glucose output, whereas thiazolidinediones have their primary effect in improving peripheral insulin sensitivity. Both agents have the advantage that they do not cause hypoglycemia, because they do not induce insulin secretion. Metformin is an ideal agent for obese and insulin-resistant patients. Although equal in effect to sulfonylurea agents, metformin causes neither hypoglycemia nor weight gain. However, gastrointestinal symptoms including diarrhea and dyspepsia, can be limiting, and lactic acidosis is a rare but potentially fatal complication (30). To reduce the risk for lactic acidosis, metformin should not be prescribed to patients with decreased renal function, abnormal liver function, patients at risk for volume contraction, such as severe congestive heart failure, or patients who engage in binge alcohol intake.

Thiazolidinediones, the newest class of agents to be added to the diabetes armamentarium, act through the peroxisome proliferator–activated receptor-γ. These agents are powerful insulin sensitizers in some patients, but may fail to be effective in up to 30% of patients for unclear reasons. Furthermore, these agents do not reach full effectiveness for up to 6 weeks. Furthermore, unlike metformin, thiazolidinedione agents may cause profound weight gain, although this gain is almost exclusively in subcutaneous tissue and paradoxically does not appear to impact insulin sensitivity. These agents may be used in patients with renal insufficiency, but they can exacerbate congestive heart failure and they often cause edema. Whereas metformin did not preserve β-cell function in the United Kingdom Prospective Diabetes Study, preliminary data suggest that thiazolidinedione agents might preserve β-cell mass, but more studies are needed.

Alpha-glycosidase inhibitors (miglitol, acarbose) inhibit the absorption of carbohydrates in the small intestine, thus lowering postprandial glycemia. Gastrointestinal side effects are common, and these agents are less effective than those discussed above in lowering HbA$_{1c}$. However, they do not cause hypoglycemia or weight gain, and are safe in renal failure and congestive heart failure. They generally must be reserved for mild type 2 DM, or as combination therapy with insulin sensitizers.

Principles of Type 2 Diabetes Mellitus Therapy

Current practice dictates that pharmacologic therapy begins with a single agent, usually either a secretagogue or an insulin sensitizer. Sulfonylureas and metformin are equally effective (31). In most patients monotherapy eventually fails to maintain control. Modern practice often combines oral agents in synergistic classes to regain control before adding insulin. Commonly used combinations include an insulin secretagogue and metformin or a thiazolidinedione, but combinations of metformin and a thiazolidinedione have also been effective in some patients. Because type 2 DM results in progressive β-cell failure (32), many patients with type 2 DM will eventually require insulin therapy, either alone or in addition to oral agents. Most regimens combine nighttime insulin with daytime sulfonylurea agents, biguanides, or a thiazolidinedione. Thus, most practitioners stage therapy from initial monotherapy to combination oral therapy, combinations of oral agents and insulin, and finally multiple insulin injections.

Diabetes Screening and Prevention

Type 2 diabetes is one of the most costly chronic diseases. The prevalence of type 2 DM is increasing to epidemic proportions in the United States. The microvascular and macrovascular complications resulting from the disease are a significant cause of morbidity and mortality. The early stages of the disease are often asymptomatic, and many patients already have microvascular complications at the time of diagnosis (33). Epidemiologic studies suggest that one of every two diabetic individuals is undiagnosed. These patients are at increased risk for stroke, coronary heart disease, peripheral vascular disease, and microvascular complications. Because the early detection and prompt treatment of type 2 DM is expected to decrease the complications of diabetes, screening of high-risk populations is appropriate. Nonetheless, we currently lack data from prospective studies on the benefits and the cost effectiveness of screening. The American Diabetes Association has recommended that screening be considered at 3-year intervals beginning at age 45 years, particularly in those with a body mass index over 25 kg/m^2 (34). Testing should be considered at a younger age or more frequently in individuals with one or more of the other risk factors shown in Table 3-3. Recent recommendations for screening nonpregnant individuals in clinical practice are based on a fasting plasma glucose of 126 mg/dL or greater. Alternatively, a 2-hour postchallenge glucose of 200 mg/dL or greater during a 75-g oral glucose tolerance test is also strongly suggestive of type 2 DM. Both tests should be confirmed on another day. Individuals with a fasting plasma glucose value of 100 to 126 mg/dL are considered to have IFG, whereas those individuals with a 2-hour glucose value of 140 to 200 mg/dL during a 75-g glucose tolerance test are defined as having IGT. Both groups, along with individuals with a history of gestational diabetes, are at high risk to progress to type 2 DM and should be monitored subsequently.

Several recent trials have shown that lifestyle modification will decrease the rate of progression to type 2 DM in high-

TABLE 3-3. SCREENING CRITERIA FOR TYPE 2 DIABETES

Age ≥45 years
Overweight (BM ≥25 kg/m²)
Family history of type 2 diabetes
Habitual physical inactivity
Ethnicity (e.g. African Americans, Hispanic Americans, Native Americans, Asian Americans, and Pacific Islanders)
Previously identified IFG or IGT
History of gestational diabetes or delivery of a baby weighing >9 lbs
Hypertension (≥140/90 mm Hg)
HDI ≤35 mg/dL and/or triglyceride ≥250 mg/dL
Polycystic ovary syndrome
History of vascular disease

BMI, body mass index; HDL, high-density lipoprotein; IFG, impaired fasting glucose; IGT, impaired glucose tolerance.

risk individuals by over 50% (35), even with modest reductions in body weight of 10% or less (36,37). Nonetheless, achievement of sustained weight loss and increased physical activity is rarely achieved in practice, even when the goals are modest. This situation is not aided by the lack of health-care resources for lifestyle modification. Pharmacologic therapy without reliance on an exercise or dietary change has also lowered the risk for future type 2 DM in several studies, albeit not to the same extent. Metformin reduced the risk for diabetes by 31% in the Diabetes Prevention Program (37). Other studies have suggested reductions in progression to type 2 DM of 30% to 50% with the α-glucosidase inhibitor acarbose (38), the antiobesity agent orlistat (39), and the thiazolidinedione troglitazone (40), which is no longer available. Additional studies with the thiazolidinedione rosiglitazone, an ACE inhibitor (ramipril), and an insulin secretagogue (nateglinide) are ongoing. A recommendation on when to begin pharmacologic therapy in addition to or instead of lifestyle modification, and what therapy to choose, must await completion of ongoing trials.

SPECIAL CONSIDERATIONS FOR WOMEN

Diabetes management is rarely gender specific, but a few issues are largely unique to treatment of women. Insulin sensitivity is well known to vary with menstruation, generally improving in the follicular phase and decreasing in the proliferative phase. For some women, particularly those with type 1 DM on intensive regimens (MDI, CSII), insulin doses must be adjusted to account for these changes. Women with polycystic ovary syndrome (PCOS) represent a unique challenge. Over 50% of patients with PCOS are insulin resistant (41), and combined with prevalent defects in insulin secretion, these women are at high risk for development of type 2 DM (42). Agents that improve insulin sensitivity, particularly metformin and thiazolidinediones, improve both ovulation and diabetic control and might potentially prevent or delay the onset of diabetes in these patients (43,44). Women with a history of gestational diabetes mellitus represent another high-risk group. The incidence of diabetes in this population ranges from 6% to 60% (45), and again results from combined insulin resistance and β-cell dysfunction (46). Currently treatment is focused on lifestyle modification, but a recent study suggested that thiazolidinediones might reduce future diabetes by up to 50% (40). As discussed earlier, such therapy is not yet standard of care in high-risk populations, but based on findings in the Diabetes Prevention Program, metformin therapy should be considered when lifestyle modification is not successful.

FUTURE DEVELOPMENTS IN CLINICAL MANAGEMENT

A number of new developments promise to change the methods of treating at least some individuals with diabetes. Pul-

monary delivery of short-acting insulin using an inhaler is the most immediately promising of these developments, and may soon offer an alternative to MDIs. Two formulations of inhalable insulins are currently under investigation, and early studies suggest that these preparations will have more rapid onset of action in addition to the convenience of eliminating multiple injections. The development of an artificial pancreas by relaying the information from a glucose sensor to an insulin delivery system has been a long-standing hope, but required a reliable continuous glucose-monitoring device. Such devices are now available, but still require frequent calibration. Because these devices measure interstitial fluid glucose, they track 10 to 15 minutes behind the blood glucose, which would delay any insulin response to blood glucose. Nonetheless, the availability of closed-loop systems that sense interstitial glucose and deliver insulin is within the realm of possibility in the near future.

Islet cell transplantation began in the early 1970s, but transplants rarely resulted in sustained insulin independence. Recently, new immunosuppressive protocols, methods for islet preparation, and larger numbers of transplanted islets have promised much greater success (47,48) and have renewed interest in islet transplantation as a therapeutic option. Islets are implanted into the portal vein, where they embolize to the liver and develop a blood supply. Trials are now ongoing using these new methods. Nonetheless, this technology will remain limited by the availability of human islet tissue and the necessity of long-term immunosuppressive therapy.

KEY POINTS

- Management of diabetes and prevention of both microvascular and macrovascular complications requires a holistic approach that includes goals beyond normalization of blood glucose, including aggressive lipid management and aggressive control of blood pressure (Table 3-1).
- Insulin therapy is essential in type 1 DM patients and the goal is to reduce glycemic levels to as close to normal as possible without inducing hypoglycemia. The basal/prandial approach in insulin therapy (MDI or CSII) is the best way to achieve glycemic control.
- Although monotherapy with an oral agent is effective at early stages of type 2 DM, the gradual decline in β-cell function over time usually necessitates combination oral therapy and finally insulin treatment to maintain glycemic control.
- Risk factors for type 2 DM include obesity, inactivity, family history of diabetes, certain ethnicity, history of gestational diabetes and PCOS. Because early type 2 DM is usually asymptomatic, regular screening by fasting glucose is recommended for all high-risk individuals.
- Lifestyle modification is fundamental to the prevention and treatment of type 2 DM; based on recent trials,

pharmacologic therapy of "prediabetes" is less effective but might be considered when lifestyle modification cannot be achieved.

REFERENCES

1. Report of the Expert Committee on the Diagnosis and Classification of Diabetes Mellitus. *Diabetes Care* 1997;20(7):1183–1197.
2. Classification and diagnosis of diabetes mellitus and other categories of glucose intolerance. National Diabetes Data Group. *Diabetes* 1979;28(12):1039–1057.
3. Turner RC, Cull CA, Frighi V, et al. Glycemic control with diet, sulfonylurea, metformin, or insulin in patients with type 2 diabetes mellitus: progressive requirement for multiple therapies (UKPDS 49). UK Prospective Diabetes Study (UKPDS) Group. *JAMA* 1999;281(21):2005–2012.
4. Gde P, Vedel P, Larsen N, et al. Multifactorial intervention and cardiovascular disease in patients with type 2 diabetes. *N Engl J Med* 2003;348(5):383–393.
5. The effect of intensive treatment of diabetes on the development and progression of long-term complications in insulin-dependent diabetes mellitus. The Diabetes Control and Complications Trial Research Group. *N Engl J Med* 1993;329(14):977–986.
6. UK Prospective Diabetes Study (UKPDS) Group. Intensive blood-glucose control with sulphonylureas or insulin compared with conventional treatment and risk of complications in patients with type 2 diabetes (UKPDS 33). *Lancet* 1998;352(9131):837–853.
7. UK Prospective Diabetes Study (UKPDS) Group. Effect of intensive blood-glucose control with metformin on complications in overweight patients with type 2 diabetes (UKPDS 34). *Lancet* 1998;352(9131):854–865.
8. Lawson ML, Gerstein HC, Tsui E, et al. Effect of intensive therapy on early macrovascular disease in young individuals with type 1 diabetes. A systematic review and meta-analysis. *Diabetes Care* 1999;22(suppl 2):B35–B39.
9. Stratton IM, Adler AI, Neil HA, et al. Association of glycaemia with macrovascular and microvascular complications of type 2 diabetes (UKPDS 35): prospective observational study. *BMJ* 2000;321(7258):405–412.
10. Potts RO, Tamada JA, Tierney MJ. Glucose monitoring by reverse iontophoresis. *Diabetes Metab Res Rev* 2002;18(suppl):49–53.
11. Hansson L, Zanchetti A, Carruthers SG, et al. Effects of intensive blood-pressure lowering and low-dose aspirin in patients with hypertension: principal results of the Hypertension Optimal Treatment (HOT) randomised trial. HOT Study Group. *Lancet* 1998;351(9118):1755–1762.
12. UK Prospective Diabetes Study Group. Tight blood pressure control and risk of macrovascular and microvascular complications in type 2 diabetes: UKPDS 38. *BMJ* 1998;317(7160):703–713.
13. Arauz-Pacheco C, Parrott MA, Raskin P. The treatment of hypertension in adult patients with diabetes. *Diabetes Care* 2002;25(1):134–147.
14. Lewis EJ, Hunsicker LG, Bain RP, et al. The effect of angiotensin-converting-enzyme inhibition on diabetic nephropathy. The Collaborative Study Group. *N Engl J Med* 1993;329(20):1456–1462.
15. Heart Outcomes Prevention Evaluation Study Investigators. Effects of ramipril on cardiovascular and microvascular outcomes in people with diabetes mellitus: results of the HOPE study and MICRO-HOPE substudy. *Lancet* 2000;355(9200):253–259.
16. Parving HH, Lehnert H, Brochner-Mortensen J, et al. The effect of irbesartan on the development of diabetic nephropathy in patients with type 2 diabetes. *N Engl J Med* 2001;345(12):870–878.
17. Brenner BM, Cooper ME, de Zeeuw D, et al. Effects of losartan on renal and cardiovascular outcomes in patients with type 2 diabetes and nephropathy. *N Engl J Med* 2001;345(12):861–869.
18. Lewis EJ, Hunsicker LG, Clarke WR, et al. Renoprotective effect of the angiotensin-receptor antagonist irbesartan in patients with nephropathy due to type 2 diabetes. *N Engl J Med* 2001;345(12):851-860.
19. UK Prospective Diabetes Study Group. Efficacy of atenolol and captopril in reducing risk of macrovascular and microvascular complications in type 2 diabetes: UKPDS 39. *BMJ* 1998;317(7160):713–720.
20. The ALLHAT Officers and Coordinators for the ALLHAT Collaborative Research Group. The Antihypertensive and Lipid-Lowering Treatment to Prevent Heart Attack Trial. Major outcomes in high-risk hypertensive patients randomized to angiotensin-converting enzyme inhibitor or calcium channel blocker vs diuretic: the Antihypertensive and Lipid-Lowering Treatment to Prevent Heart Attack Trial (ALLHAT). *JAMA* 2002;288(23):2981–2997.
21. Rala K, Pedersen TR, Kjekshus J, et al. Cholesterol lowering with simvastatin improves prognosis of diabetic patients with coronary heart disease. A subgroup analysis of the Scandinavian Simvastatin Survival Study (4S). *Diabetes Care* 1997;20(4):614–620.
22. Sacks FM, Pfeffer MA, Moye LA, et al. The effect of pravastatin on coronary events after myocardial infarction in patients with average cholesterol levels. Cholesterol and Recurrent Events Trial investigators. *N Engl J Med* 1996;335(14):1001–1009.
23. Downs JR, Clearfield M, Weis S, et al. Primary prevention of acute coronary events with lovastatin in men and women with average cholesterol levels: results of AFCAPS/TexCAPS. Air Force/Texas Coronary Atherosclerosis Prevention Study. *JAMA* 1998;279(20):1615–1622.
24. Clearfield M, Downs JR, Weis S, et al. Air Force/Texas Coronary Atherosclerosis Prevention Study (AFCAPS/TexCAPS): efficacy and tolerability of long-term treatment with lovastatin in women. *J Womens Health Gender-Based Med* 2001;10(10):971–981.
25. Frick MH, Elo O, Haapa K, et al. Helsinki Heart Study: primary-prevention trial with gemfibrozil in middle-aged men with dyslipidemia. Safety of treatment, changes in risk factors, and incidence of coronary heart disease. *N Engl J Med* 1987;317(20):1237–1245.
26. Rubins HB, Robins SJ, Collins D, et al. Gemfibrozil for the secondary prevention of coronary heart disease in men with low levels of high-density lipoprotein cholesterol. Veterans Affairs High-Density Lipoprotein Cholesterol Intervention Trial Study Group. *N Engl J Med* 1999;341(6):410–418.
27. Franz MJ, Bantle JP, Beebe CA, et al. Evidence-based nutrition principles and recommendations for the treatment and prevention of diabetes and related complications. *Diabetes Care* 2002;25(1):148–198.
28. Exercise and NIDDM. *Diabetes Care* 1990;13(7):785–789.
29. Pickup J, Keen H. Continuous subcutaneous insulin infusion at 25 years: evidence base for the expanding use of insulin pump therapy in type 1 diabetes. *Diabetes Care* 2002;25(3):593–598.
30. Brown JB, Pedula K, Barzilay J, et al. Lactic acidosis rates in type 2 diabetes. *Diabetes Care* 1998;21(10):1659–1663.
31. Johansen K. Efficacy of metformin in the treatment of NIDDM. Meta-analysis. *Diabetes Care* 1999;22(1):33–37.
32. UK Prospective Diabetes Study Group. UK Prospective Diabetes Study 16. Overview of 6 years' therapy of type II diabetes: a progressive disease. *Diabetes* 1995;44(11):1249–1258.
33. Harris MI. Undiagnosed NIDDM: clinical and public health issues. *Diabetes Care* 1993;16(4):642–652.
34. American Diabetes Association. Screening for Type 2 Diabetes. *Diabetes Care* 2003;26(suppl):21–24.
35. Pan XR, Li GW, Hu YH, et al. Effects of diet and exercise in preventing NIDDM in people with impaired glucose tolerance. The

Da Qing IGT and Diabetes Study. *Diabetes Care* 1997;20(4): 537–544.

36. Tuomilehto J, Lindstrom J, Eriksson JG, et al. Prevention of type 2 diabetes mellitus by changes in lifestyle among subjects with impaired glucose tolerance. *N Engl J Med* 2001;344(18): 1343–1350.

37. Knowler WC, Barrett-Connor E, Fowler SE, et al. Reduction in the incidence of type 2 diabetes with lifestyle intervention or metformin. *N Engl J Med* 2002;346(6):393–403.

38. Chiasson JL, Josse RG, Gomis R, et al. Acarbose for prevention of type 2 diabetes mellitus: the STOP-NIDDM randomised trial. *Lancet* 2002;359(9323):2072–2077.

39. Scheen AJ. Prevention of type 2 diabetes in obese patients: first results with orlistat in the XENDOS study. *Rev Med Liege* 2002; 57(9):617–621.

40. Buchanan TA, Xiang AH, Peters RK, et al. Preservation of pancreatic beta-cell function and prevention of type 2 diabetes by pharmacological treatment of insulin resistance in high-risk hispanic women. *Diabetes* 2002;51(9):2796–2803.

41. Dunaif A, Segal KR, Futterweit W, et al. Profound peripheral insulin resistance, independent of obesity, in polycystic ovary syndrome. *Diabetes* 1989;38(9):1165–1174.

42. Chang RJ, Nakamura RM, Judd HL, et al. Insulin resistance in nonobese patients with polycystic ovarian disease. *J Clin Endocrinol Metab* 1983;57(2):356–359.

43. Knowler WC, Barrett-Connor E, Fowler SE, et al. Reduction in the incidence of type 2 diabetes with lifestyle intervention or metformin. *N Engl J Med* 2002;346(6):393–403.

44. Ehrmann DA, Schneider DJ, Sobel BE, et al. Troglitazone improves defects in insulin action, insulin secretion, ovarian steroidogenesis, and fibrinolysis in women with polycystic ovary syndrome. *J Clin Endocrinol Metab* 1997;82(7):2108–2116.

45. Hadden DR. Geographic, ethnic, and racial variations in the incidence of gestational diabetes mellitus. *Diabetes* 1985;34 (suppl):8–12.

46. Buchanan TA. Pancreatic B-cell defects in gestational diabetes: implications for the pathogenesis and prevention of type 2 diabetes. *J Clin Endocrinol Metab* 2001;86(3):989–993.

47. Shapiro AM, Lakey JR, Ryan EA, et al. Islet transplantation in seven patients with type 1 diabetes mellitus using a glucocorticoid-free immunosuppressive regimen. *N Engl J Med* 2000;343(4):230–238.

48. Ryan EA, Lakey JR, Paty BW, et al. Successful islet transplantation: continued insulin reserve provides long-term glycemic control. *Diabetes* 2002;51(7):2148–2157.

49. Follow-up Report on the Diagnosis of Diabetes Mellitus. *Diabetes Care* 2003;26(11):3160–67.

DIABETES CARE FOR ADOLESCENTS

KATHRYN M. THRAILKILL

Adolescence is a developmental period characterized by numerous changes, including periods of physiologic, hormonal, nutritional, cognitive, psychological, social, and legal transition, all of which can impact on diabetes care. Adolescence is also a critical age for implementation of many health screening regimens important in long-term diabetes management. The intent of this chapter is to discuss these unique aspects of diabetes management, as they relate to the adolescent patient. While type 2 diabetes mellitus (DM) accounts for greater than 90% of all cases among the population at large, and type 2 DM is discussed widely throughout this text, among children and adolescents, more than 80% of patients with DM carry a diagnosis of type 1 DM. Therefore, except where otherwise specified, this chapter will focus on the evaluation and management of type 1 DM in the adolescent patient.

The Third National Health and Nutrition Examination Survey (NHANES III) revealed a prevalence of diabetes (all types) in individuals 12 to 19 years of age of 4.1 per 1,000 (1). Over 13,000 new cases of type 1 DM will be diagnosed each year in the United States in children under 20 years of age (2). Compared with the incidence of other chronic childhood diseases, including childhood cancer (~1 in 7,000) and cystic fibrosis (~1 in 3,900), only asthma is more prevalent as a chronic childhood disorder, existing in 10% of the childhood population.

The following pages will review the unique features of pubertal physiology, as well as its potentially adverse consequences for diabetes management during adolescence. Aspects of disease morbidity for the adolescent will be discussed, particularly as they relate to the distinctive presentation of acute and chronic diabetes-related complications during the adolescent years. In addition, modifications of diabetes therapy necessary during puberty will be reviewed, with specific reference to intensifying diabetes management at this age, as well as the unique nutritional requirements of adolescent patients. Specific behavior and maturational aspects of adolescent development that are known to impact on diabetes control and morbidity will be reviewed. The balance between adolescent autonomy versus adherence to medical recommendations will be examined and the

impact of eating disorders (EDs) on diabetes management will be discussed. Finally, we will examine the developing epidemic of type 2 DM among adolescents, and review the diagnostic dilemma of differentiating between type 1 and type 2 DM in this age group, with specific reference to the epidemiology, pathophysiology, presentation, and medical management of type 2 DM.

ADOLESCENT PHYSIOLOGY

Growth and Associated Alterations in Growth Hormone and Growth Factor Secretion in Diabetes Mellitus

Type 1 diabetes mellitus is a disease of insulin deficiency, resulting from the autoimmune-mediated destruction of pancreatic β-cells. However, several lines of evidence suggest that regional deficiency of insulin in the portal circulation, a condition that persists in all conventionally treated patients with type 1 DM, produces a secondary disruption of the growth hormone (GH)–insulin-like growth factor (IGF)–IGF binding protein (IGFBP) axis (for detailed review, see reference 3). In fact, type 1 DM is characterized by a state of GH resistance, characterized by GH hypersecretion, reduced circulating levels of IGF-1 (4–6), IGFBP-3 (7,8) and growth hormone binding protein (GHBP) (9–11), yet elevated levels of IGFBP-1 (12). Together, these changes create a deficiency of "free IGF-1" and reduced IGF-1 bioavailability in the patient with type 1 DM. The magnitude of these GH-IGF-IGFBP axis abnormalities correlates inversely with the degree of endogenous β-cell secretion (13,14).

The role of portal insulinopenia in contributing to somatotropin axis abnormalities is confirmed by studies examining the effects of differing modes of diabetes treatment on their ability to correct the GH-IGF-IGFBP axis. When comparing studies of intensified peripheral insulin administration (15,16), with studies using intraperitoneal insulin delivery (8), and finally, with infusion of insulin directly into the portal system (17), one can appreciate incremental corrections in serum concentrations of GH,

IGF, and IGFBPs across these treatment modalities. Only direct intraportal insulin delivery, however, results in normalization of the GH-IGF-IGFBP axis. Consistent with this, patients with type 1 DM who remain C-peptide positive have higher circulating IGF-1 levels than those who do not (18). Moreover, when patients with type 1 DM are treated with a combination of recombinant human IGF-1 (rhIGF-1) in addition to standard insulin therapy, serum IGF-1 concentrations increase, GH levels decrease, and derangements in IGFBP secretion are partially rectified (19–21).

Adolescence is associated with marked increases in growth velocity, resulting from a two- to threefold increase in daily growth hormone secretion during the pubertal years. Unfortunately, the unique hormonal milieu of puberty, while important for growth, is nonetheless deleterious for optimal glycemic control. Preexisting diabetes-related abnormalities in the somatotropin axis are exaggerated during adolescence (13). GH hypersecretion is accentuated during mid to late puberty in the diabetic adolescent. While the liver remains resistant to GH action, muscle and other nonresistant tissues succumb to the insulin antagonistic actions of such high GH levels. Exaggerated nocturnal secretion of GH, in particular, accentuates fasting hyperglycemia characteristic of the dawn phenomenon, and contributes to nocturnal ketogenesis. Chronic GH excess contributes to higher average hemoglobin A_{1c} (HbA_{1c}) values, and the tendency toward relatively more rapid decompensation into diabetic ketoacidosis (DKA). Finally, GH-IGF axis abnormalities not only exacerbate hyperglycemia in the diabetic adolescent, but also may independently contribute to the pathogenesis of emerging diabetes-specific complications, including diabetic neuropathy, nephropathy, and retinopathy. (See section on Emergence of Microvascular Complications.)

Clearly, deterioration in glycemic control during the adolescent years is not solely the consequence of "noncompliance" or adolescent-related behavioral changes, but is, in part, the result of worsening disruption of the GH-IGF-IGFBP system. The impact of pubertal physiology on metabolic control was exemplified in the Diabetes Control and Complications Trial (DCCT) (22), wherein even highly motivated adolescent subjects randomized to the intensive treatment study arm could only achieve HbA_{1c} values that were, on average, approximately 1% higher than their adult counterparts. In comparison, in several studies, adolescents treated with a combination of rhIGF-1 and intensified insulin therapy have been shown to experience significant reductions in HbA_{1c}, without concurrent hypoglycemia or weight gain (19,23).

Beyond its impact on glucose control, one can question whether dysregulation of the somatotropin axis negatively impacts on adolescent growth and development. Historical literature of growth among children with type 1 DM, reflecting decades in which glucose control was much less

stringent than current practice, suggested that the diagnosis of type 1 DM was associated with short stature (24–26), failure to thrive, delayed puberty (26,27), or, in extreme cases, Mauriac syndrome of short stature, hepatomegaly, and delayed adolescence (28,29). More recent investigations, however, demonstrate that these associations are no longer expected. Beyond approximately 3 years of age, studies of growth in type 1 DM reveal that at the time of diagnosis, the heights of children and adolescents actually exceed their nondiabetic peers by a small increment (30–34). This difference can be attributed to a similar difference in parental stature, suggesting that the genetic potential for taller stature may infer an increased risk for DM (30). The onset of puberty and the timing of pubertal progression are normal (35,36) or, at most, minimally delayed (37) in teenagers with type 1 DM. However, the peak height velocity (PHV) during the pubertal growth spurt is reduced in adolescents with diabetes, more so in girls than in boys (33–36). Consequently, adolescents experience some reduction in height standard deviation score during puberty (35). Because prepubertal diabetic adolescents are relatively tall, however, final adult height in this population remains within normal percentiles (36). Therefore, significant growth failure in adolescents with type 1 DM should prompt further evaluation to eliminate concurrent hypothyroidism or celiac disease in these individuals.

Several explanations have been offered for the relatively slower pubertal growth noted among adolescent girls. As discussed later (see section on the Hormonal Milieu of Puberty), mild hyperandrogenism emerges in adolescent girls, contributing to bone age advancement (35) and earlier growth cessation in this group. Alternatively, because PHV is negatively correlated in some studies with HbA_{1c} (35), the relatively greater deterioration in glycemic control noted in adolescent girls, compared with adolescent boys, could contribute to a worse growth outcome. It is now well established that the insulin resistance characteristic of puberty in both diabetic and nondiabetic adolescents (38) is, on average, more pronounced in girls (39,40).

Sex Steroids and Puberty in Type 1 Diabetes Mellitus

Adolescence is also highlighted by sexual maturation and increased circulating concentrations of sex steroids. With good glycemic control, the onset of puberty and the progression of sexual maturation are near normal or only minimally delayed in adolescents with type 1 DM. The average age of reported menarche is near 13.5 years (37,41), compared with 12.8 to 13 years for white nondiabetic girls (37,42).

Among adult women with type 1 DM, a higher prevalence of hyperandrogenic disorders has been noted, including polycystic ovary syndrome (PCOS) and hirsutism (43). The antecedent to these changes may already be apparent in the adolescent girl, in the form of mild ovarian hyperandrogenism. Menstrual irregularity is notably more common among postmenarchal girls with type 1 DM, compared with nondiabetic adolescent girls (41,44,45). Increased levels of total and free testosterone (46), decreased levels of sex hormone–binding globulin (SHBG) (44,47), and increased ratios of testosterone to SHBG (47) have all been demonstrated in insulin-treated pubertal girls with type 1 diabetes, compared with nondiabetic adolescent girls. Functional ovarian hyperandrogenism can also be demonstrated by gonadotropin-releasing hormone stimulation testing in up to 50% of oligomenorrheic adolescents with type 1 DM (48), and PCOS can often be confirmed in adolescents girls with type 1 DM and menstrual irregularities (44).

Because subcutaneous insulin delivery results in supraphysiologic peripheral insulin exposure, such derangements may be a consequence of insulin-mediated stimulation of ovarian androgen synthesis. Moreover, improvement in glycemic control in patients with type 1 DM can be associated with further increases in the levels of free testosterone (49). Circulating concentrations of free androgen are also affected by dysregulation of SHBG concentrations in the patient with type 1 DM. Hepatic SHBG secretion is inhibited by hepatic insulin exposure (50), and SHBG concentrations reflect hepatic insulinization (51). Reports of SHBG concentrations in diabetic adolescents vary widely, describing normal (46,52), increased (51), and decreased (47) SHBG levels, likely reflecting differences in study design, gender, and metabolic control of each study population. Nevertheless, acute hyperinsulinemia has been shown to produce a decrease in SHBG concentration (53), SHBG levels are inversely correlated with daily insulin dose (47), and diabetic women with amenorrhea have significantly lower serum levels of SHBG than either regularly cycling diabetic or nondiabetic women (54). Together, these findings suggest that therapeutic modalities creating hyperinsulinemia in the adolescent girl with type 1 DM may promote hyperandrogenic disorders in ways that are mechanistically similar to the development of PCOS in the individual with hyperinsulinemia, insulin resistance, and type 2 DM.

ADOLESCENT MORBIDITY

Diabetic Ketoacidosis

Diabetic ketoacidosis is an acute and life-threatening complication of type 1 DM precipitated by insufficiency of insulin administration relative to concurrent metabolic needs. DKA is the most common cause of death in diabetic children, and accounts for approximately 50% of deaths in diabetic individuals under 24 years of age (55).

Unfortunately, the incidence of DKA increases notably during the adolescent years. A threefold increase in the incidence of DKA in female patients with type 1 DM 13 years of age and older, compared with girls less than 7 years of age, has been observed (56). Similarly, in a study of 61 youths 9 to 16 years of age at the Joslin Diabetes Center, investigators reported that 28% of patients in this age group experienced a single episode of DKA, whereas 15% of patients had recurrent episodes of DKA (57). This is in contrast to estimates among adult patients of 5 to 13 episodes of DKA per 1,000 patients per year (58).

General risk factors for DKA in the adolescent include female gender, a longer duration of DM, higher HbA$_{1c}$, underinsurance, and the presence of concurrent psychiatric disorders (56,59). Additional factors contributing to an increase in DKA during adolescence, in particular, include emerging noncompliance with diabetes treatment recommendations, "junk food" binging, concurrent bulimia, glucosuric purging (see section on Impact of Eating Disorders on Diabetes Management), the physiological insulin resistance of puberty, and the potential for errors in insulin pump management in the relatively inexperienced insulin pump user. Among adolescents with recurrent DKA, certain individual and family psychosocial predictors have also been identified, including (a) a higher incidence of behavior problems; (b) lower self-esteem; (c) a lower level of social competence; (d) higher levels of reported family conflict; and (e) lower reports of family cohesion, expressiveness, family organization, and family warmth (57,60). In addition, specific psychiatric disorders have been associated with DKA in adolescents, including anxiety disorders, phobias, depression, and attention/disruptive behavior disorders (60). Finally, recurrent DKA is more frequent among adolescent girls than among boys (57,61) .

Events precipitating DKA in the adolescent patient frequently include the deliberate or inadvertent omission of insulin in conjunction with emotional stressors (55). The new diagnosis of disease, concurrent infection in a patient with poor glycemic control, or trauma are also precipitating events in many adolescents.

Using this information, it should be possible to identify individuals, frequently girls, who are at increased risk for recurrent DKA, and to provide preventive psychological and psychosocial interventions aimed at alleviating known risk factors. Individuals with a history of poor glycemic control and known psychological or psychiatric disturbances should be targeted for intervention.

With general trends toward intensification of pediatric diabetes management and improvements in clinical care over the past 15 to 20 years, the overall incidence of DKA among adolescents with previously diagnosed DM may be decreasing (59). However, a recent report of 15-year trends in DKA among pediatric patients in Australia suggests that hospitalizations for DKA attributable to newly diagnosed diabetes are increasing (59). Moreover, the frequency of serious complications of DKA, including cerebral edema, remains constant (59), and DKA remains a significant cause of diabetes-related mortality among young patients (62).

Consequently, the potential for DKA remains a serious health risk of adolescent patients.

Emergence of Microvascular Complications

Diabetic Nephropathy

Among patients with type 1 DM, diabetic nephropathy develops in approximately 40% of patients with a 20-year history of disease. Moreover, diabetic nephropathy is the most common cause of end-stage renal disease (ESRD) in the United States, contributing to 30% to 40% of all newly diagnosed cases of ESRD (63). In the United States, costs associated with ESRD for patients with diabetes are estimated at $51,000 per patient-year. Yearly costs of care for diabetic patients with renal failure have been estimated at $3–4 billion (64). Together, these statistics highlight the significant medical and financial impact of diabetic nephropathy in this country.

The development of diabetic nephropathy has been described as a five-stage process, progressing from a condition of glomerular hyperfiltration and nephromegaly (stage 1), to glomerular basement membrane (GBM) thickening and mesangial expansion (stage 2), to microalbuminuria and eventual decline in glomerular filtration rate (GFR) (stage 3), to frank proteinuria with severe hypertension and sequelae of moderate to severe renal insufficiency (stage 4), to eventual ESRD (stage 5) (64). It has been hypothesized that the early changes in GBM thickness and content ultimately affect filtration properties of the GBM, leading first to increased urinary albumin excretion (UAE) and eventually to frank proteinuria.

About 20% to 40% of patients with newly diagnosed type 1 DM already demonstrate evidence of increased renal size on imaging studies, and increased GFR (65). Moreover, 5% to 10% of all children and adolescents with type 1 DM exhibit persistent microalbuminuria (66–71). Microalbuminuria in the preteen has been considered rare. However, Jones et al. conducted a longitudinal study of 233 children with type 1 DM, measuring albumin:creatinine ratios (ACRs) on early morning urine samples (72). They found that among children 4 to 11 years of age followed for 8 years (final age 12–18 years), approximately 15% developed persistently elevated ACRs, while another 12% demonstrated intermittently elevated ACRs. Of those children with persistently elevated ACRs, one third presented before puberty, and two thirds within the first 4 years of diagnosis; 10 children showed a progressive increase in ACR, and 7 had at least one episode of spot-urine macroalbuminuria. Although less stringent, and considerably less predictive, studies using screening ACR suggest that incipient diabetic nephropathy may be quite prevalent in the peripubertal patient. In fact, normoalbuminuric subjects, including prepubertal children and adolescents, exhibit GBM thickening

and mesangial expansion (73,74), confirming that renal structural abnormalities precede clinically detectable increases in UAE. The International Diabetic Nephropathy Study, a large, longitudinal study of the natural history of nephropathy, is currently underway and will track the development of diabetic renal lesions in patients with type 1 DM, as demonstrated by the results of two renal biopsies performed 5 years apart (75). Baseline information from this study has shown that renal lesions (increased GBM width, increased fractional volume of mesangium and mesangial matrix) are clearly present in young normoalbuminuric patients, and are evident as early as 2 to 8 years after disease onset (76).

Among those individuals who develop renal dysfunction, several risk factors for the development of renal disease have been identified, including duration of diabetes, age at diagnosis, race, systemic or glomerular hypertension, poor glycemic control, genetic predisposition to kidney disease, and dietary composition (69,70,77,78). Racial differences in the development of ESRD have been clearly observed, with Native Americans, Hispanics, and African Americans demonstrating significantly higher rates of developing ESRD compared with their white counterparts (77,79). A genetic basis for the development of nephropathy is also evident in data demonstrating that the cumulative risk for diabetic nephropathy among siblings of probands with nephropathy is approximately 70%, whereas the risk among siblings of individuals without nephropathy is only about 25% (80). Polymorphisms in genes of the renin-angiotensin system family have been implicated in this increased risk (78,81). Finally, although patients with both type 1 and type 2 DM demonstrate evidence of nephropathy, for unknown reasons, fewer patients with type 2 DM go on to develop frank ESRD.

Among adolescents, numerous physiologic changes characteristic of puberty may accentuate these other well-established risk factors. Glycemic control frequently deteriorates during puberty, promoting the effect of chronic hyperglycemia on emerging renal pathology. Burgeoning sex steroid secretion affects a variety of physiologic pathways that may contribute to diabetic nephropathy, including the renin-angiotensin system, the protein kinase C pathway, and the nitric oxide system (78). Early renal hypertrophy and changes in renal architecture may also be exacerbated by the unique pubertal physiology of the somatotropin axis. As noted earlier, type 1 diabetes is characterized by a state of hepatic GH resistance, resulting in high circulating concentrations of GH, but diminished circulating concentrations of IGF-1. During the adolescent growth spurt, dysregulation of GH secretion is exaggerated. The kidney, however, retains its sensitivity to GH. Unlike the liver, messenger RNA levels for renal GHBP (a putative index of GH receptor number) are not decreased in diabetic animals (82,83), and mesangial cells from diabetic nonobese diabetic (NOD) mice constitutively oversecrete IGF-1 (84). In fact, the kidney is a target tissue of local IGF action. Specifically, IGF-1 promotes renal cell mitogenesis, nephron hypertrophy and tubular phosphate transport (85). A variety of animal model and human studies of diabetes confirm that conditions which either indirectly (via GH) or directly increase IGF-1 [i.e., acromegaly or systemic administration of IGF-1 (85)] promote increases in renal blood flow, glomerular filtration rate, and kidney volume (86), whereas conditions of GH deficiency [GH-deficient diabetic rats (87)] impede these changes. Similarly, diabetic mice treated with GH receptor antagonists (82,88) or somatostatin analogues (89), as well as knockout mice with GH receptor or GHBP gene disruption (88), are all protected from diabetes-induced renal/glomerular hypertrophy and increases in GFR and UAE. These findings support the speculation that diabetes-induced changes in systemic GH exposure and intrarenal IGF-1 availability, leading to enhanced IGF action within kidney parenchyma, may contribute to the development of diabetic kidney disease. If such is the case, enhanced synthesis of systemic GH and renal IGF-1 during the adolescent growth spurt could contribute to the emergence of diabetic nephropathy at this age. Consistent with this concept, earlier studies have demonstrated that among microalbuminuric diabetic children and adolescents, UAE values are positively correlated with GH secretion rates (66), whereas more recent studies confirm a strong correlation between urinary IGF-1 and GH excretion and microalbuminuria (86).

The onset and progression of diabetic nephropathy can be impeded using current strategies aimed at curtailing proteinuria. Such interventions have the greatest impact if begun early in the evolution of the disease (77). Therefore, it is imperative that early screening and treatment implementation be a high priority in the care of adolescents. Microalbuminuria is defined as an albumin excretion rate of 20 to 199 μg/min, as measured in at least two of three consecutive, nonketotic urine specimens, typically obtained over a 3- to 6-month period. Longitudinal studies in type 1 DM suggest that in patients who demonstrate microalbuminuria and receive no specific therapy, approximately 80% will experience consistent increases in proteinuria, exhibiting overt renal disease or macroalbuminuria (≥300 mg/24 h or ≥200 μg/min) within a 10- to 15-year time frame (77). Overt nephropathy then predictably leads to diminishing glomerular filtration rates, and in type 1 DM, without intervention, 50% to 75% of these individuals will go on to develop ESRD. In contrast, UAE rates of less than 30 μg/min can be converted to normal in approximately one third of patients with institution of strict metabolic control and correction of hypertension with angiotensin-converting enzyme (ACE) inhibitors. Current clinical recommendations include an annual test for the presence of microalbuminuria in type 1 diabetic patients who have had diabetes over 5 years and in all type 2 diabetic patients starting at the time of diagnosis (77) (Table 4-1). Consequently, all diabetic adolescents, excluding only those most recently diagnosed with type 1 DM, will require vigilant screening for and prompt treatment of diabetes-related renal abnormalities (see Chapter 29).

Diabetic Retinopathy

Diabetic retinopathy (DR) is the leading cause of blindness in the United States; in nearly 8% of individuals who are legally blind, diabetes is the cause. Some degree of diabetic retinal changes develop in 30% to 60% of adults within 10 to 15 years of diagnosis of type 1 DM (90–92) and in nearly all patients with a 20-year history of disease (91). Fortunately, in the majority of these individuals, only background retinopathy, a non-vision-threatening condition, will be detected. However, more aggressive, sight-threatening degrees of retinopathy cause no visual impairment or ophthalmologic symptoms in their earliest stages. Consequently, early detection of DR is possible only through scheduled preventive screening examinations.

The American Diabetes Association recommends (92) that patients greater than or equal to 10 years of age with

TABLE 4-1. SCREENING FOR DIABETIC MICROVASCULAR DISEASE IN ADOLESCENTS

Condition	Screening Test	Frequency	Age to Begin
Hypertension	Blood pressure assessment	All routine visits	At diagnosis
Increased UAE	Spot urine (μg/mg creatinine) or 24-h collection (μg/min or mg/24 h)	Yearly	After 5 years of disease duration (77)
Retinopathy	Dilated ophthalmologic examination[a]	Yearly	After 3–5 years of disease duration (92)
Distal polyneuropathy	Clinical examination of the foot[b]	Yearly	(Not specified)
Pupillary AN	Pupillary size, shape and reflexes (194)	Yearly	After 5 years of disease duration (194)
Cardiac AN	R-R variation with respiration (ECG), HR/BP response to standing, or 24-h Holter recording	Yearly	Onset of puberty (122) or after 5 years of disease duration (194)

[a]Baseline opthalmologic evaluation is typically recommended soon after diagnosis, following stabilization of glucose control, to exclude refractive errors, cataract formation or other eye disorders.
[b]Including visual inspection, vibration perception, light touch perception, and ankle tendon reflexes.
AN, acanthosis nigricans; BP, blood pressure; ECG, electrocardiography; HR, heart rate; R-R, R-R interval on ECG; UAE, urinary albumin excretion.

type 1 DM should begin a schedule of yearly dilated, comprehensive eye examinations within 3 to 5 years of disease onset (Table 4-1). Screening prior to age 10 has not been encouraged because, historically, prepubertal diabetes was considered less predisposing to risk. More recent research, however, suggests that prepubertal disease duration should not be overlooked. Studies using highly sensitive fluorescein angiography suggest that minimal retinal changes may be present in 10% of children and adolescents with diabetes within the first year of diagnosis, and may exist in some youths at the time of diagnosis (93). In a large study of Australian patients 6 to 20 years of age, with disease duration of 0.02 to 18.4 years, early retinopathy was detected by fundus photography in 27% of patients (94). Particularly concerning, however, was the recognition that early retinopathy was detected in 9% of patients who were under 11 years of age at the time of examination. Moreover, when comparing patients with a similar duration of diabetes, comparable rates of retinopathy were reported among a subgroup of patients who were currently prepubertal (27% with DR) and a subgroup who were pubertal (29% with DR) (95). The contribution of prepubertal duration of diabetes to DR risk has been similarly noted in large studies of pediatric patients with type 1 DM independently conducted in Israel, Sweden, Germany, and the United States (96–98). The earlier-than-anticipated development of retinal changes has been increasingly recognized. In one study, DR was reported in 43% of young patients with type 1 DM after 4 years of disease (99). Even proliferative diabetic retinopathy (PDR) has been reported as early as 2 years after the diagnosis of autoimmune DM (100). Together, these studies support the concept that subclinical eye disease may be present in many more adolescent patients than previously appreciated. Therefore, some would encourage the initiation of routine screening as early as 2 years after diagnosis. In fact, the International Society for Pediatric and Adolescent Diabetes (ISPAD) subcategorizes their recommendations for retinopathy screening as follows (101).

■ For prepubertal onset of diabetes: 5 years after onset or at age 11 years, or at puberty (whichever is earlier), and annually thereafter.
■ For pubertal onset of diabetes: 2 years after onset, and annually thereafter.

The overall incidence of retinopathy among adults with type 1 DM has been estimated at 50% (102). However, among adolescent populations with long-standing diabetes, retinal abnormalities have been noted with similar frequency (103), confirming that age-independent risk factors are important. Known risk factors for DR include (a) poor glycemic control, as indicated by chronically elevated HbA$_{1c}$ values; (b) increasing duration of disease; (c) markers of insulin resistance, including waist-to-hip ratios and triglyceride levels; (d) a history of smoking; and (e) the presence of microalbuminuria (92). In addition, hypertension

"is an established risk factor for the development of macular edema and is associated with the presence of PDR" (92). Susceptibility to DR has also been associated with certain HLA-DR alleles (104) and specific aldose reductase gene polymorphisms (105).

As is the case for diabetic nephropathy, features of both pubertal physiology and adolescent behavior may promote the emergence of retinal disease in this age group. As noted above, glycemic control clearly deteriorates during adolescence, and this alone may promote the emergence of eye disease. Experimentation with cigarette smoking may also have a detrimental impact on the onset and progression of retinopathy in diabetic adolescents, as has been established for adult smokers (106). A role for the GH-IGF-1 axis in the development and progression of DR has also been inferred, ever since hypophysectomy was first introduced as a treatment for DR (107); the precise role, however, remains highly controversial. A variety of studies suggest that the development of DR may result from associated changes in intraocular IGF bioavailability (108–109). A number of clinical studies, however, appear to challenge this concept. In a large population-based study of diabetics, Wang et al. examined the relationship between serum IGF-1 levels and the incidence and progression of DR over a 6-year period (110). They found no association between serum IGF-1 levels and the incidence or progression of retinopathy among over 1,200 adult-onset and childhood-onset diabetic patients. Similar findings were reported in a smaller study of young patients with type 1 DM and rapidly progressive severe retinopathy (111). Moreover, others have failed to demonstrate differences in vitreous IGF-1 concentrations in diabetics with PDR compared with nondiabetic controls (112). Therefore, despite the fact that the onset of puberty can accelerate the progression of retinal changes, a clear link between this phenomenon and puberty-associated changes in GH secretion has not been established.

Diabetic Neuropathy

Approximately half of all patients with diabetes eventually develop diabetic polyneuropathy. Among young patients with type 1 DM, neurophysiologic (or subclinical) peripheral neuropathy has been reported in 10% to 30% of individuals (71,113–115), with similar frequencies detected in prepubertal and postpubertal patients (71). In fact, it has been suggested that subclinical peripheral neuropathy is the most frequently detected microvascular complication among young patients with relatively short-term duration of diabetes (71), and sensory and autonomic nerve dysfunction have been detected even in children with newly diagnosed diabetes mellitus (116). Deterioration in nerve conduction velocity in distal motor and sensory nerves (113), increased vibration perception threshold (102,113, 117), and increased current perception threshold (118) have all been reported in adolescents, and strongly associated with short-term poor metabolic control (113,114, 118). Such neurophysiologic changes in peripheral nerve function typically exist in the absence of, and predate clinical signs of, neuropathy. However, clinical neuropathy, most commonly abolition of ankle jerk reflexes (113) and limited joint mobility (117), have been reported in up to 10% of pediatric patients.

Diabetic autonomic neuropathy, or impaired function of the autonomic nervous system, is a recognized adult complication of DM, present in 5% to 10% of the adult population with diabetes (79,119,120). Effects on the cardiovascular, genitourinary, gastrointestinal, and ophthalmologic systems and sweat glands can contribute to cardiac arrhythmia, hypertension, myocardial infarction, impotence, gastroparesis, and anhidrosis or hyperhidrosis. Unfortunately, reports on the autonomic function of diabetic adolescents are limited. Increasing evidence suggests, however, that subclinical neuronal abnormalities are present quite early on, with parasympathetic abnormalities preceding sympathetic abnormalities (121). Even among children and adolescents with good glycemic control, or receiving intensive diabetes management, early indicators of autonomic neuropathy are not infrequently present, including (a) reductions in heart rate variability by 24-hour Holter monitoring (122,123); (b) QTc interval prolongation (124); (c) elevated ambulatory blood pressure values (117,125); (d) reduced papillary adaptation to darkness (117,125,126); (d) bladder dysfunction (127); and (e) gallbladder dilatation (128). Cardiac autonomic dysfunction has also been reported in adolescents with newly diagnosed type 1 DM (129).

As noted earlier (see section on Growth and Associated Alterations in Growth Hormone and Growth Factor Secretion), type 1 DM is characterized both by a reduction in total IGF-1 concentrations, as well as a decrease in bioavailable (or free) IGFs (3). However, IGFs are neurotrophic growth factors, with demonstrated effects on sensory, motor, and sympathetic neurons. Specifically, IGFs stimulate motor neuron proliferation and differentiation, enhance motor neuron sprouting, increase myelination and inhibit demyelination, reduce neuron apoptosis during normal development, enhance axonal regeneration after injury, and protect neurons from toxicity induced by chemicals, cytokines, and cancer chemotherapy (130). Therefore, a role for IGF deficiency in the pathogenesis of diabetic neuropathy has been postulated. In fact, several nerve-specific abnormalities in IGF bioavailability have been demonstrated in studies of both animal and human diabetes (131–135). In addition, advancing age, acute weight loss, and short stature among children are all risk factors for the development of diabetic neuropathy, and are all conditions that independently cause a further reduction in circulating levels of IGF-1 (136). Together, these studies suggest that low systemic and neuronal levels of IGF-1 may contribute to the development of diabetic neuropathy, although this link is not established. Known risk factors for the development of diabetic neuropathy among young patients include a history of poor metabolic control (114,118,137–139), duration of diabetes (114,137–139), height (114,137,139) cigarette smoking (137,139), and the advancement of pubertal stage (118,122).

Neurophysiologic evidence of peripheral and autonomic nerve dysfunction can be demonstrated in adolescents demonstrating no or little clinical neurologic abnormality. However, the natural history and long-term consequences of these early changes remain unclear. Studies demonstrating improvement of subclinical abnormalities in newly diagnosed patients entering a "honeymoon" phase (116) suggest that the early effects of severe hyperglycemia may be reversible. Consequently, appropriate recommendations for surveillance of neuropathy in childhood and adolescents are lacking. It would seem prudent, however, that in the face of poor metabolic control, or within 3 to 5 years of disease onset, adolescents should be queried and examined for evidence of pain, paresthesias, dysesthesias, diminished light touch or vibration sense, postural hypotension, or gastroparesis. Additional recommendations for surveillance are outlined in Table 4-1.

MEDICAL MANAGEMENT OF ADOLESCENTS

Intensive Insulin Regimens

The adverse effects of puberty on glycemic control have been well documented, with clear peaks in average HbA$_{1c}$ levels reported during midpuberty among adolescent populations (140,141). Equally noteworthy, however, is the now unequivocal importance of tight glycemic control on minimizing or delaying the development of microangiopathy in these patients (22). Consequently, adolescence has become a critical time for modifying management goals so as to counteract the glycemic deterioration of puberty, and to maintain near normoglycemia. Intensive management strategies, if not already initiated, are particularly important at this age.

Current options for intensification of care include both multiple daily injection (MDI) regimens and continuous subcutaneous insulin infusion (CSII) therapy, commonly known as insulin pump therapy. With proper implementation and surveillance, both forms can lead to improved glycemic control and a reduction in HbA$_{1c}$ levels (142,143). The beneficial consequences of lower HbA$_{1c}$ levels can include a reduction in microvascular and macrovascular abnormalities, improved wound healing, enhanced hypoglycemia awareness, and reduced comorbidity of severe hypoglycemia. Glycemic goals of intensive insulin therapy are outlined in Table 4-2.

An insulin pump is an open-loop system that utilizes input from the pump wearer to modify insulin delivery.

TABLE 4-2. GLYCEMIC GOALS OF INTENSIVE INSULIN THERAPY FOR ADOLESCENTS (TYPE 1 DIABETES MELLITUS)

Timepoint	Normal Range	FSBG Goal
Fasting glucose (mg/dL)	<110[a]	70–130
Premeal FSBG (mg/dL)	—	70–140
2-hour postprandial BG (mg/dL)	<140[a]	<180
Bedtime FSBG (mg/dL)	—	100–150
HbA$_{1c}$ (%)	<6.0	<7.0

[a]Plasma glucose.
FSBG, fasting serum blood glucose.

Insulin delivery is matched to anticipated insulin requirements using two concurrent programs. Basal infusions provide a continuous rate of insulin delivery designed to maintain glycemic control during periods of food absence. Basal insulin delivery functions to restrain hepatic glucose output, keeping glucose output in equilibrium with glucose uptake by tissues. Basal rates can be preprogrammed and set to incorporate numerous rate adjustments throughout the day, accommodating differences in energy expenditure, daily circadian rhythms (i.e., dawn phenomenon), and daily protein intake. In contrast, bolus infusions provide intermittent pulses of insulin, typically given prior to meals, to meet the insulin requirements of consumed carbohydrates. Appropriately balancing bolus insulin delivery with dietary intake requires that the user become familiar with product nutrition labels and be able to accurately estimate carbohydrate content of consumed meals and snacks. Bolus doses are chosen to match the anticipated carbohydrate content of the upcoming meal. In current practice, rapid-acting human insulin analogues (insulin aspart, insulin lispro) are typically used in pumps to provide for rapid absorption and onset of action (10–20 minutes), a well-timed postprandial peak effect (approximately 1 hour), and a limited duration of action (~3 hours), all of which are beneficial for closely matching glucose absorption. In addition, by using insulin with a relatively short duration of action, the wearer can promptly reprogram any component of therapy to adjust for unanticipated or sudden changes in intake, exercise, or daily schedule.

MDI therapy uses multiple-component insulin regimens, given as three to five or more injections per day, to variably approximate the basal and bolus concept. Basal insulin therapy is given either as intermediate-acting insulin [neutral protamine Hagedorn (NPH) or lente], long-acting insulin (ultralente) or a long-acting insulin analogue (glargine), typically in one or two daily doses. Multiple doses of rapid-acting insulin (insulin aspart or insulin lispro) or short-acting insulin (regular insulin) are superimposed on the basal pattern to provide for augmented postprandial insulin effects. Use of rapid-acting insulin analogues as a component of MDI can promote a more

physiologic match between peak insulin concentration and postprandial insulin requirement. However, because basal insulin therapy relies on insulin products with a 12- to 24-hour duration of action, rapid proactive dose adjustments can be problematic. Moreover, a therapy using multiple overlapping mixed injections can create prolonged periods of excessive insulin exposure when not required. Over time, this prolonged hyperinsulinemia can promote weight gain, and may contribute to unanticipated hypoglycemia.

Implementation of either MDI or CSII can result in improved metabolic control. However, in head-to-head comparisons among adolescent patients, use of CSII has been shown to produce greater short-term reductions in HbA$_{1c}$, with 50% less hypoglycemia, less weight gain, and better patient acceptance than MDI (141,142). Moreover, use of CSII by adolescent patients can result in sustained lowering of HbA$_{1c}$ levels over several years (143). Both forms of therapy can accommodate some day-to-day variation in meal timing and portion size. CSII, however, can allow for greater hour-by-hour flexibility. Pharmacokinetic advantages of CSII over MDI include (a) the use of only rapid-acting forms of insulin, allowing for more predictable subcutaneous absorption; (b) the use of only one injection site for 3 days, allowing for less frequent injections, and less site-specific variation in absorption; (c) the elimination of a subcutaneous insulin depot, reducing the likelihood of unnecessary excess insulin action at times when it is not needed, and allowing for less reactive lipohypertrophy; and (d) the use of programmable insulin delivery, allowing for a more physiologic match of insulin delivery to insulin need. Additional lifestyle advantages of CSII include the availability of greater flexibility in day-to-day scheduling, less hypoglycemia apprehension, and the greater portability of therapy. The potential for progressive weight gain (if dietary intake is not controlled) and more rapid deterioration into ketoacidosis, however, may make CSII less appropriate for some.

Nutritional Requirements of the Adolescent with Diabetes

General guidelines for the recommended daily allowances for energy during adolescence are widely referenced relative to chronologic age, gender, or pubertal status. Recommended basal energy intake relative to body weight for adolescents 11 to 18 years of age include 40 to 47 kcal/kg/day for girls and 45 to 55 kcal/kg/day for boys (144). Estimated energy requirements based on stature include 10 to 19 kcal/cm of height for girls and 13 to 23 kcal/cm for boys (144). These recommendations accommodate the increased energy requirements of puberty, and can translate into daily energy needs of 2,400 to 3,400 kcal/day. Such recommendations do not, however, account for the added fuel utilization of exercise, or counteract the energy losses due to glucosuria.

Regular exercise and sustained physical activity should be encouraged for all adolescents in accordance with the physical activity recommendations of the Centers for Disease Control and Prevention (i.e., 30 minutes of moderately intense physical activity daily) (145). The adolescent with diabetes should be advised that his or her illness alone poses no contraindication to exercise or sports participation, although a limited number of specific activities might be avoided due to safety concerns associated with a concurrent severe hypoglycemic event (i.e., scuba diving). In fact, added benefits of exercise for the diabetic individual include cardiovascular risk reduction, improved insulin sensitivity, and weight maintenance. To participate fully, however, supplemental energy intake during periods of exercise will be required, because muscle glycogen stores and initial blood glucose supplies are depleted during the first 45 to 60 minutes of vigorous exercise. Consequently, an additional 30 to 60 g of carbohydrate intake every hour, ideally distributed at 30-minute intervals, will be necessary for prolonged periods of moderate- to high-intensity exercise. In addition, supplemental carbohydrate-containing foods should be consumed within 3 to 4 hours after exercise completion to replenish muscle glycogen stores. Failure to do so can precipitate delayed exercise-induced hypoglycemia.

Adolescence is also a period in which several specific nutrient requirements are accentuated. Daily requirements for these nutrients during adolescence are outlined in Table 4-3. The adolescent growth spurt is a period of particularly high calcium requirement. Greater than 90% of peak adult bone mass is typically achieved by the end of the second decade of life, and 45% of this bone mass is acquired during the adolescent growth spurt. Maximizing peak adult bone mass is one critical protective factor in the prevention of osteoporosis. Because the risk for osteoporosis is increased among individuals with type 1 DM (146,147), optimal bone mineralization during puberty becomes all the more important. During puberty, normal skeletal mineralization is dependent on a calcium acquisition rate of 400 to 500 mg/day. To achieve this, the National Institutes of Health Consensus Development Conference Statement on Optimal Calcium Intake recommended a daily calcium

intake of 1,200 to 1,500 mg for adolescents (148). However, greater than 70% of adolescent girls may fail to achieve this recommendation (149–151), largely due to a decrease in dairy food consumption. Substitution of diet soft drinks for milk by diabetic adolescents striving to improve glycemic control will further impact negatively on bone health by decreasing calcium intake, increasing phosphoric acid consumption, and promoting calcium excretion through caffeine-related diuresis. In addition, daily urinary calcium excretion is increased as a consequence of diabetes alone, particularly among girls (152). Consequently, oral calcium supplementation to meet dietary requirements should be strongly considered for the diabetic adolescent, and some would advocate that recommendations for dietary calcium intake be increased to 1,400 to 1,600 mg/day (151).

Intake of certain vitamins and minerals important for growth, sexual maturation, and reproductive success, particularly vitamins A, C, and D, folic acid, and zinc, are also inadequate during the adolescent growth spurt (153). Moreover, iron requirements increase during adolescence because of concomitant increases in blood volume, hemoglobin concentration, and lean body mass. Following menarche, adolescent girls experience additional menses-related iron losses. Data from NHANES III indicated that 14.2% of adolescent girls and 12.1% of adolescent boys were found to be iron deficient (154), and approximately 2.4% of adolescent girls 12 to 19 years of age exhibit iron-deficiency anemia (155). The recommended daily intake of iron during adolescence is 12 to 15 g/day. In addition, adequate intake of vitamin C is necessary for efficient iron absorption (Table 4-3).

Consumption of dietary fat in excess of daily recommendations (i.e., <30% of daily calories from fat and <10% of total calories from saturated fat) is particularly problematic during adolescence. It has been estimated that more than 84% of children and adolescents consume an excess of total fat, and greater than 91% consume an excess of saturated fats (156). Factors contributing to high-fat diets

TABLE 4-3. NUTRITIONAL RECOMMENDATIONS FOR ADOLESCENTS WITH DIABETES

Nutrient	Recommended Daily Requirement	Typical Daily Intake	Sources
Calcium	1,200–1,500 mg/day	700–900 mg/day	Dairy products Ca-fortified foods
Iron	12 (M)–15 (F) mg/day	—	Lean red meats Iron-fortified foods
Vitamin C	75 (F)–90 (M) mg/day	—	Raw fruits/vegetables
Zinc	12–15 mg/day	For ~75% of adolescent girls, intake is inadequate	Meat, eggs, seafood dairy products
Fiber	20–25 g/day	10–15 g/day	Whole grains Raw fruits/vegetables

M, male; F, female.

include both the participation in federal school breakfast and lunch programs in which a typical meal contains over 38% (153) total fat, and the increased consumption of fast food meals both on a regular basis and in conjunction with adolescent social events and participation in sports. Typical fast food meals from popular commercial chains, even if consumed with an artificially sweetened beverage, contain 40% to 54% of calories from fat and 28% to 35% of total fats from saturated fats. The average adolescent visits a fast food restaurant more than twice a week (157). The increasing prevalence of vending machines also promotes dietary fat intake. Vending machine purchases contribute to 3% of teen eating occasions, adding candy (32% of purchases) and salty snacks (26% of purchases) to the adolescent diet (157). For individuals with controlled type 1 DM, plasma lipid levels are comparable with those among the general population. Therefore, recommendations for the limitation of fat intake do not differ from those for the population at large. Nevertheless, because diabetes is an independent risk factor for the development of cardiovascular disease, attention to the macrovascular and obesity-related consequences of a high-fat diet is important.

Finally, adolescence is a time during which numerous aberrant dietary behaviors emerge (see section on Impact of Eating Disorders on Diabetes Management), including both common practices of skipping meals and experimenting with fad diets, as well as severe nutritional pathology (i.e., anorexia nervosa [AN] and bulimia nervosa), all of which can be particularly problematic for the adolescent with DM.

Impact of Eating Disorders on Diabetes Management

The therapy for type 1 DM requires strict surveillance of dietary intake, regularity in eating habits, and the particular avoidance of dietary sweets. Moreover, intensification of diabetes management, while leading to improved control, can be associated with increased and often unacceptable weight gain, particularly among adolescents (158). Such circumstances are precursors to disordered eating behaviors, even among normal adolescents. Therefore, concern has arisen over a possible predisposition for EDs among patients with type 1 DM.

In fact, both type 1 DM and EDs are relatively common diagnoses, occurring in 0.5% and 1.0% of adolescents, respectively. Therefore, some overlap in disease is expected. Reports in the literature of the prevalence of EDs among preadolescent and adolescent patients with type 1 DM, however, are contradictory. To date, most studies do not demonstrate an increase in the prevalence of "classic" EDs (i.e., AN or bulimia nervosa) (159–165) among diabetic adolescents, although a lesser number of studies dispute this claim (166–168). In one of the largest retrospective studies, Nielsen et al. (159) examined data from the Danish nationwide psychiatric admission case register from 1970 to 1984, and

found only 23 patients with a concurrent diagnosis of DM and AN, among 500 females with type 1 DM and 658 females with AN, concluding that the concurrence of these disorders was rare. Similarly, Wing et al. (160), surveying 202 adolescents with type 1 DM, found no increase in the incidence of bulimia, whereas Birk et al. (161), in a survey of 385 females 13 to 45 years of age, reported rates of AN and BN that were within the range reported in the general population.

In contrast to classic AN or bulimia nervosa, less specific eating psychopathology may be a common occurrence among adolescent girls with type 1 DM. Insulin manipulation (either omission or underdosing) appears to be a relatively common method of weight management used by adolescent and young adult females with type 1 DM. Studies have demonstrated that 5% to 39% of patients with type 1 DM have intentionally underdosed their insulin therapy for the purpose of weight control (163,167,169). Inconsistencies in the literature regarding the prevalence of disturbed eating behaviors might be explained by the fact that eating behaviors detected using various ED survey tools often reflect higher scores on the dietary subscales, items that might intentionally be scored in a positive manner in a compliant patient with DM. Even so, disturbed eating behaviors are not commonly reported by young men, suggesting that some psychological disturbances related to eating behaviors do exist with higher frequency in adolescent and young adult women.

Biggs et al. (170) studied 42 females 16 to 40 years of age with type 1 DM to determine those characteristics distinguishing individuals who withhold insulin as a form of weight control from those who do not. Patients who withheld insulin were (a) more concerned with dieting; (b) demonstrated greater disturbance with body image; (c) were more likely to engage in binge eating; (d) demonstrated feelings of inadequacy, alienation, and negative attitudes toward their illness; (e) lied to physicians more frequently about compliance; and (f) were reluctant to develop close social relationships. Affenito et al. (169) examined the effects of subclinical disorders of eating behavior (i.e., those patients not meeting the *Diagnosis and Statistical Manual of Mental Disorders* criteria, but demonstrating behaviors consistent with partial criteria) on glycemic control, and compared this group with patients who had a clinical ED. Women with clinical EDs were found to have a greater number of diabetes-related hospital admissions and severe hypoglycemic reactions, compared with subclinical and control groups. However, they found that patients with a subclinical ED also demonstrated an increased frequency of noncompliance with blood glucose testing, higher HbA$_{1c}$ levels, and more frequent intentional insulin misuse. In fact, 80% of patients with a subclinical ED reported past misuse of insulin, as a method of purging calories. Such studies would suggest that higher-end estimates of the prevalence of intentional insulin misuse during adolescence might be more correct.

A number of factors inherently contribute to the risk for altered eating attitudes among patients with type 1 DM, including a tendency toward food preoccupation, the need for chronic dietary constraint and disengagement from internal hunger and satiety cues, and the weight gain associated with insulin treatment. Cycles of weight gain and loss may be particularly problematic for these patients. Patients frequently gain or regain considerable weight immediately following the diagnosis of type 1 DM. Recognizing that approximately one third of all newly diagnosed pediatric diabetes occurs during the adolescent years, acute changes in body image and self-perception may become permanently intertwined with the negativity of this chronic diagnosis. Additional weight gain associated with puberty is also problematic. Exaggerated weight gain in girls with type 1 DM, compared with boys, during the adolescent years is well documented (171). As noted earlier, GH hypersecretion of puberty contributes to insulin resistance. A natural therapeutic response to the resultant chronic and fasting hyperglycemia is intensification of control. Results of the DCCT, however, demonstrated that intensive therapy was associated with an average 3.25-kg weight gain over 5 years in adolescent subjects (158). Finally, unlike other adolescents, patients with type 1 DM have the availability of induced glucosuria as a unique, prompt, and effective purging method for weight control.

Several groups have documented deterioration in metabolic control in association with EDs, specifically noting higher average HbA1c values, among diabetic patients with EDs, compared with those without. Mean HbA1c values in the range of 9% to 15% are reported among those patients with EDs (162,163,169,172–174); these results are typically 1% to 3% above the reported average HbA1c for each study's diabetic comparison group without EDs. With respect to intentional underuse of insulin for weight control, several studies also report an increase in average HbA1c values (162,165,169), although a few investigations found no differences in metabolic control associated with the misuse of insulin (173). In a study by Rodin et al. (174), patients with EDs also rated themselves as less compliant with blood glucose self-monitoring, urine testing, daily schedule adherence, and compliance with exercise and dietary prescriptions. Overall, it appears that the concurrence of EDs with type 1 DM is predictive of poor metabolic control and the tendency toward generalized noncompliance with diabetes management recommendations.

In addition to poor metabolic control, short-term medical consequences of EDs include (a) recurrent, severe hypoglycemia, often with reports of intermittent loss of consciousness; (b) frequent DKA secondary to intentional insulin omission; and (c) growth retardation or pubertal delay, primarily among patients displaying features of AN. Concurrence of EDs with DM has also been associated with a higher risk for long-term microvascular complications. Rydall et al. studied 91 women with type 1 DM at baseline and 4 years later, not only to determine the prevalence and persistence of disordered eating behaviors among this group, but also to establish the association of these behaviors with the occurrence of DR and nephropathy (172,175). They found that 85% of those patients defined as having highly disordered eating behaviors at follow-up demonstrated some degree of retinopathy, compared with 43% of the moderately disordered eating, and 24% of the nondisordered eating groups. In fact, disordered eating behaviors had a greater predictive power than duration of diabetes on development of retinopathy. Differences in UAE rates did not meet statistical significance. Nonetheless, 43%, 20%, and 18% of patients with highly, moderately, and nondisordered eating, respectively, were found to have microalbuminuria at follow-up. The concurrence of type 1 DM and AN has been associated with a 15-fold increase in overall mortality compared with diabetes alone (159).

Ascertainment of body weight and shape preoccupation, binge eating behaviors, and insulin omission or underutilization for the purpose of weight control are key aspects of an interval health assessment for the adolescent girl with DM. When such features are noted in conjunction with suboptimal glycemic control, or a history of recurrent DKA or severe hypoglycemia, the likelihood of an ED is high. Suspicion or confirmation of an ED in a diabetic adolescent necessitates psychiatric referral and appropriate psychiatric assessment and intervention. A complete discussion of treatment approaches to EDs among diabetic patients is beyond the scope of this text. Patients with severely disturbed eating behaviors require intense individualized therapy, with attention to family involvement in treatment. Milder cases, particularly when detected early, however, may respond to outpatient intervention in the diabetes clinic, focused on modification of eating attitudes and perceptions of body image and self-esteem.

In summary, although neither AN nor bulimia nervosa are particularly prevalent among patients with type 1 DM, subclinical disturbed eating attitudes and behaviors appear to be common in young women with type 1 DM, and are associated with specific patterns of family dysfunction and individual psychiatric symptoms. Induced glucosuria due to insulin omission or underutilization is the weight control method of choice among such individuals. It is important to recognize the development of these symptoms, because such behaviors are associated with poor glycemic control and, ultimately, with the premature onset of diabetic microvascular complications.

ADOLESCENT DEVELOPMENT

Autonomy versus Management Adherence

Adolescence is a time during which parents begin to relinquish their role in diabetes management and the adolescent both strives to and is expected to assume greater responsibility for diabetes self-care. This change is initiated by both developmental and practical adjustments. Developmentally, adolescence is a stage characterized by increasing autonomy, independence, control, self-awareness and abstract thought. In addition, owing to the nature of educational, social, and leisure activities, adolescents spend less time at home, and less time under direct adult supervision. Consequently, responsibility for implementation of diabetes care is gradually shifted to the adolescent patient. Concurrently, however, adolescence is also characterized by diminished respect for authority, increasing acquiescence to peer group influence, some degree of distorted body image, feelings of immortality, and experimentation with health-compromising behaviors. These latter attributes can present a direct contradiction to health-care recommendations for good diabetes management. Coupled with a puberty-associated decrease in insulin sensitivity, the need to "rebel" against preexisting health and behavioral expectations can lead to notable deterioration in glycemic control during the adolescent years.

Several studies have documented that adolescents, as a group, are less likely to adhere to management recommendations than either younger or older patients (176,177). Up to one fourth of adolescents acknowledge missing insulin injections, and nearly one third admit to falsification of the blood glucose records reported to their health-care practitioner (176), although parents significantly underestimate the frequency with which teenagers engage in these mismanagement behaviors (176).

Therefore, optimal care for the adolescent patient with diabetes requires an approach that simultaneously recognizes and encourages the emerging independence and self-reliance of the adolescent, while expecting some cooperative but less obtrusive oversight of parents. The adolescent patient needs assistance in establishing and periodically reviewing his or her daily priorities, and in encouraging the incorporation of appropriate diabetes management tasks. New education focusing on the potentially deleterious consequences of risk-taking behaviors and the need for periodic preventative health screening should be provided. Involvement in teenage support groups, diabetes camps, and adolescent-oriented educational seminars can be both encouraging and provide needed peer group associations. And, where necessary, specialized psychological evaluation and counseling can be provided to address issues of chronic nonadherence with medical recommendations, or problems of substance abuse or disordered eating behaviors.

EMERGENCE OF TYPE 2 DIABETES MELLITUS

Historically, the diagnosis of diabetes in an individual under 20 years of age was categorized as type 1 DM. However, the emerging epidemic of type 2 DM in adolescence and child-

hood, and the emerging distinction in drug therapies available for these diseases, have highlighted the need for accurate diagnosis of the adolescent patient.

A generalized increase in the incidence of type 2 DM has been observed over the past quarter century, particularly among the more developed and affluent nations of the world. Changes in food abundance, economic well-being, energy expenditure of industrialized compared with agrarian employment, and genetic factors all contribute to this trend. Racial groups at highest risk for type 2 DM in the United States include Native Americans, Hispanic Americans, and African Americans, with adult disease susceptibility rates that are 3-fold, 2-fold, and 0.5-fold higher, respectively, than non-Hispanic whites (178).

Alarmingly, the incidence of type 2 DM is also increasing among children and adolescents; within these minority communities, the prevalence of type 2 DM is fast approaching the prevalence of type 1 DM among adolescents. Recent reports suggest that anywhere from 8% to 45% of children with newly diagnosed diabetes have nonimmune-mediated disease (179), depending on the race and ethnicity of a particular study group. Among North American Indian adolescents 15 to 19 years of age, the prevalence of type 2 DM has been reported at 50.9 per 1,000 for Pima Indians, 4.5 per 1,000 for U.S. American Indians as a whole, and 2.3 per 1,000 for Canadian Indians in Manitoba (180), exceeding the general U.S. prevalence of type 1 DM of 1.7 cases per 1,000 people under the age of 20. Among academic pediatric diabetes centers in Florida, a state with over 30% minority composition, the percentage of diabetic patients diagnosed with type 2 DM increased from 8.7% in 1994 to 23.7% in 1998 (181).

Considering that adolescents as a group are not economically or socially independent of their family unit, unique lifestyle risk factors contributing to the increase in type 2 DM in this age group may be difficult to delineate. The development of obesity at this age, however, is universally accepted as a predisposing condition. It is clear that a generalized trend toward increased caloric intake, increased high-fat, fast food–prevalent diets, and an overall decrease in the level of exercise have contributed to an epidemic of obesity in the United States (182–184), with similar trends reported among Canadian (185), Chinese (186), Finnish (187), Indian (188), and Australian youth. In a study of the economic burden of obesity in American youths 6 to 17 years of age, the annual hospital costs for obesity-associated disease increased from $35 million during 1979 to 1981, to $127 million during 1997 to 1999 (189). This increase in obesity heralds the increase in type 2 DM.

The onset of puberty is also a culprit in the development of type 2 DM in adolescents. The underlying pathophysiology of type 2 DM in children and adolescents is considered to be the same as in adults. Specifically, insulin resistance (genetically determined, and exaggerated by weight gain) leads to hyperinsulinemia (yet normoglycemia), which leads to β-cell secretory inadequacy (producing postprandial hyperglycemia), which ultimately leads to β-cell secretory failure (and fasting hyperglycemia). The increase in GH secretion during midpuberty accentuates insulin resistance (see section on Puberty and Associated Alterations in Growth Hormone and Growth Factor Secretion). As noted in the American Diabetes Association Consensus Statement on type 2 DM in Children and Adolescents (179), "insulin-mediated glucose disposal is on average 30% lower in adolescents between Tanner stages II and IV compared with prepubertal children in Tanner stage I and compared with young adults." Moreover, girls are more insulin resistant than boys at every Tanner stage. Similar puberty-based differences in insulin sensitivity have been reconfirmed among an exclusively African-American adolescent population (190). It is not surprising, therefore, that among children and adolescents, a marked increase in the diagnosis of type 2 DM is noted at the time of puberty, and the peak ages for the diagnosis of type 2 DM among minors is 12 to 16 years.

Distinguishing between type 1 DM and type 2 DM in the newly presenting hyperglycemic adolescent can be challenging. Historical and clinical features used to clarify the diagnosis are outlined in Table 4-4. In general terms, the adolescent with type 1 DM typically presents following a relatively precipitous illness, characterized by polyuria, polydipsia, polyphagia, and weight loss in a previously normal weight individual. Ketonuria or DKA is frequently observed, and serologic evidence of pancreatic autoimmu-

nity and insulin deficiency are expected. In contrast, the adolescent with type 2 DM often presents with milder, more long-standing symptoms of hyperglycemia, noted in a significantly overweight individual who has a strong family history of type 2 DM and who displays acanthosis nigricans or other clinical evidence of hyperinsulinemia. The incidental diagnosis of type 2 DM in an asymptomatic individual is also common. As outlined in Table 4-5, however such dividing lines are frequently blurred, and certain features may overlap between diseases. Consequently, categorization of an individual patient may be based on a constellation of features that weigh more heavily in one direction or the other. And, in some patients, the diagnosis may only be revealed over time, as one follows the natural history of illness in a given individual.

Several general features of type 2 DM in adolescents can be recognized, however. Among a pediatric cohort, the mean age of onset is 13 to 14 years. The incidence of type 2 DM is higher among girls, with varying female:male ratios of 1.3:1 to 4:1 reported (180). Acanthosis nigricans is present in 60% to 90% of patients at the time of diagnosis, and estimates of body mass index range between 30 and 40 (191). Ancillary chief complaints leading to the diagnosis of type 2 DM can include vaginal moniliasis and cutaneous Candida infections. Concurrent diagnoses not infrequently include hypertension, hyperlipidemia, PCOS, microalbuminuria, and sleep apnea (191).

Because the onset of type 2 DM can be insidious, unlike type 1 DM, screening of asymptomatic adolescents is rec-

TABLE 4-4. DISTINGUISHING BETWEEN TYPE 1 AND TYPE 2 DIABETES MELLITUS (DM)

	Type 1 DM	Type 2 DM
Age at onset	Throughout childhood, peak onset at school entry and at puberty; diagnosis rare after 20 years	Puberty and into adulthood
Race/ethnicity	All races, though rare in Asians	Native American, Hispanic American, African American, Asian; less common though possible in whites
Clinical presentation	Acute onset, brief duration of symptoms, weight loss, frequent ketosis or DKA	Mild onset, insidious presentation, long-standing symptoms
Associated history	Family history of autoimmune diseases 5% with first- or second-degree relative with type 1 DM	Genetic predisposition (74%–100% have first- or second-degree relative with type 2 DM)
Associated clinical signs	Typically normal BMI Vitiligo (infrequent)	Obesity Acanthosis nigricans
Laboratory confirmation		
Autoimmune markers	Islet cell, anti-GAD antibody (>80% of patients)	Antibodies infrequent
Ketosis	Present, severe DKA possible	Typically absent or mild
C-peptide	Low or undetectable	Elevated
Insulin	Decreased/normal	Variable-increased/reduced
Secretion/Sensitivity IGF-A1	Below normal at diagnosis	Age-appropriate or elevated
Possible ancillary diagnoses	Autoimmune thyroid disease Celiac disease Other autoimmune diagnoses	Hypertension Hyperlipidemia Polycystic ovary syndrome

BMI, body mass index; DKA, diabetic ketoacidosis; GAD, glutamic acid decarboxylase; IGF, insulin-like growth factor.

TABLE 4-5. HETEROGENEITY OF DISEASE, AS DEMONSTRATED BY OVERLAPPING FEATURES

	Type 1 Diabetes Mellitus	Type 2 Diabetes Mellitus
Weight	~20% of patients may have "concurrent" obesity at presentation.	85% of patients are overweight or obese at diagnosis, but ~35% may have a BMI <28.
Ketonuria	Frequent	⅓ may have ketonuria at diagnosis, and 5–25% may present with DKA (179).
C-peptide	A modest B-cell reserve can persist for several years in some patients.	C-peptide levels may be deceptively low at the time of acute decompensation, due to glucose toxicity.
Pancreatic autoimmunity	Expected	Reported in 10%–30% of white adults with type 2 diabetes mellitus (195)
Mortality	DKA + cerebral edema	HHNK + cerebral edema
Therapy	Will require lifelong insulin therapy	May require insulin initially, and later in life

BMI, body mass index; DKA, diabetic ketoacidosis; HHNK, hyperglycemic hyperosmotic nonketotic coma.

ommended. In 2000, a consensus statement of the American Diabetes Association, prepared in conjunction with the National Institute of Diabetes and Digestive and Kidney Diseases, the Centers for Disease Control and Prevention, and the American Academy of Pediatrics (179) was published, detailing testing recommendations for at-risk individuals. The recommended criteria for testing are given in Table 4-6. For individuals meeting these criteria, screening with a fasting plasma glucose every 2 years should begin at age 10 or at the onset of puberty, whichever comes first.

Because the pathophysiology of type 2 DM in adolescents is similar to that in adults, options for pharmaceutical therapy and treatment recommendations are comparable to adult guidelines (191) (see Chapter 3). Dietary modification and exercise are major components of therapy, and at young ages, substantial weight loss alone may significantly forestall the need for pharmacologic intervention. Lifestyle modifications, however, are often particularly difficult during adolescence and achieve greater success if directed at the family as a whole. Oral hypoglycemic agents, including metformin, sulfonylureas, and thiazolidinediones have all been used in adolescent treatment of type 2 DM, although rigorous clinical

TABLE 4-6. TYPE 2 DIABETES MELLITUS (DM) SCREENING RECOMMENDATIONS

Overweight individuals, defined as:
  BMI >85th percentile for age and sex
  Weight for height >85th percentile
  Weight >120% of ideal weight for height
Plus two other risk factors
  Family History of type 2 DM in First- or second-degree relative
  Increased racial/ethnic risk (Native Americans, Hispanic Americans, African Americans, Asians/South Pacific Islanders)
  At risk for insulin resistance (AN, HTN, dyslipidemia, PCOS)

AN, acanthosis nigricans; BMI, body mass index; HTN, hypertension; PCOS, polycystic ovary syndrome.
Data from the American Diabetes Association Consensus Statement. Type 2 diabetes in children and adolescents. *Diabetes Care* 2000;23:381–389.

investigation of safety and efficacy is limited (181,192). However, treatment of type 2 DM by pediatric endocrinologists remains in its infancy, and inconsistencies are apparent. In a recent review by Silverstein et al., the current clinical practices of pediatric endocrinologists with respect to the treatment of type 2 DM were reviewed. Among members of the Lawson Wilkins Pediatric Endocrine Society in North America, survey responses indicated that 44% of pediatric patients with type 2 DM were treated with oral hypoglycemic agents, whereas 48% were treated with insulin (181). Of the 44% treated with oral hypoglycemic agents, 71% received metformin, 46% received sulfonylureas, 9% thiazolidinediones, and 4% meglitinide. Among three university-based pediatric endocrinology practices in Florida, 50% of patients were treated with oral hypoglycemic therapy, 23% received insulin alone, 9% received a combination of oral hypoglycemic agents and insulin, and 11% were treated with diet and exercise (181). In contrast, among pediatric patients followed by the Division of Endocrinology and Metabolism at the Children's Hospital Los Angeles, 68% of patients were on oral agents alone, 19% were on insulin alone, and 13% were on combination therapy (193). Despite a growing trend toward the use of oral agents in adolescents, safety and efficacy data for many of these agents have not been established in minors. Moreover, many recent studies foreshadow the potential for latent adverse events if treatments with these agents are initiated at a young age.

SUMMARY

In the life of a patient with diabetes, adolescence is a period highlighted by metabolic deterioration, due to concurrent physiologic, behavioral, developmental, and cognitive changes characteristic of this age group. Due to changes in hormonal physiology, and to glycemic control, adolescence is a time of emerging microvascular and macrovascular morbidity. Together, these features make care of the adolescent patient a challenging endeavor, for the patient, for the family, and for the health-care team. The need for improved metabolic control, using intensive management strategies such as CSII or MDI and age-specific nutritional recommendations, becomes critical. In addition, medical care must factor in the unique developmental makeup of the adolescent patient, so as to engender trust, and promote increasing participation in diabetes self-care. The diagnosis of diabetes in this age group can also be problematic. Superimposed on the heightened incidence of type 1 DM during puberty is the recent epidemic of type 2 DM presenting during the adolescent years. Careful attention must be directed to arriving at an accurate diagnosis, recognizing that divergent treatment approaches are necessary to manage these two disorders effectively.

KEY POINTS

■ Adolescence is a developmental period characterized by physiologic, hormonal, nutritional, cognitive, and psychological changes, as well as periods of social and legal transition, all of which can impact on diabetes management and disease morbidity.

■ Inherent dysregulation of the somatotropin axis in type 1 DM is greatly exaggerated during puberty, contributing to a puberty-associated deterioration in glycemic control, relative insulin resistance, exaggerated dawn phenomenon, nocturnal ketogenesis, and more frequent DKA.

■ Features of both pubertal physiology and adolescent behavior contribute to the emergence of microvascular complications during adolescence. Therefore, early clinical screening for evidence of diabetic nephropathy, retinopathy, and neuropathy should be a high priority in the care of the adolescent patient.

■ Diabetes management at this age typically necessitates some intensification of care, perhaps best accomplished using modalities such as CSII therapy.

■ Subclinical disturbed eating attitudes and behaviors appear to be common in young women with type 1 DM; patterns of deliberate insulin omission or underutilization as a means of weight control, along with a history of chronic hyperglycemia or recurrent DKA, may forewarn the clinician of an ED.

■ Greater than 80% of pediatric patients with diabetes exhibit type 1 DM. Nevertheless, there is an alarming recent increase in the incidence of type 2 DM among adolescents. Hyperglycemia detected in the setting of a milder, insidious disease presentation, obesity, and acanthosis nigricans among individuals of high-risk minority populations suggest a diagnosis of type 2 DM.

ACKNOWLEDGMENTS

I am very appreciative of the critical review and editorial comments provided by Drs. John Fowlkes, Paul Frindik, Stephen Kemp, and Clay Bunn.

REFERENCES

1. Fagot-Campagna A, Saaddine JB, Flegal KM, et al. Diabetes, impaired fasting glucose and elevated HbA1c in U.S. Adolescents: The Third National Health and Nutrition Examination Survey. *Diabetes Care* 2001;24:834–837.

2. American Diabetes Association. Diabetes statistics. In: *Diabetes 2001 vital statistics*. Alexandria, VA: American Diabetes Association, 2001:13–27.

3. Thrailkill K. Insulin-like growth factor-I in diabetes mellitus: its physiology, metabolic effects and potential clinical utility. *Diabetes Technol Ther* 2000;2:69–80.

4. Taylor AM, Dunger DB, Grant DB, et al. Somatomedin-C/IGF-1 measured by radioimmunoassay and somatomedin bioactivity in adolescents with insulin-dependent diabetes compared with puberty matched controls. *Diabetes Res* 1988;9:177–181.

5. Amiel SA, Sherwin RS, Hintz, RL, et al. Effects of diabetes and its control on insulin-like growth factors in the young subject with type 1 diabetes. Diabetes 1984;3:1175–1179.

6. Tan K, Baxter RC. Serum insulin-like growth factor I levels in adult diabetic patients: the effect of age. *J Clin Endocrinol Metab* 1986;63:651–655.

7. Batch JA, Baxter RC, Werther G. Abnormal regulation of insulin-like growth factor binding proteins in adolescents with insulin-dependent diabetes. *J Clin Endocrinol Metab* 1991;73: 964–968.

8. Hanaire-Broutin H, Sallerin-Caute B, Poncet MF, et al. Insulin therapy and GH-IGF-I axis disorders in diabetes: impact of glycaemic control and hepatic insulinization. *Diabetes Metab* 1996;22:245–250.

9. Menon RK, Arslanian S, May B, et al. Diminished growth hormone–binding protein in children with insulin-dependent diabetes mellitus. *J Clin Endocrinol Metab* 1992;74:934–938.

10. Holl RW, Siegler B, Scherbaum WA, et al. The serum growth hormone–binding protein is reduced in young patients with insulin-dependent diabetes mellitus. *J Clin Endocrinol Metab* 1993;76:165–167.

11. Mercado M, Molitch ME, Baumann G. Low plasma growth hormone binding protein in IDDM. *Diabetes* 1992;41:605–609.

12. Brismar K, Gutniak M, Povoa G, et al. Insulin regulates the 35 kD IGF binding protein in patients with diabetes mellitus. *J Endocrinol Invest* 1988;11:599–602.

13. Dunger DB, Acerini CL. IGF-I and diabetes in adolescence. *Diabetes Metab* 1998;24:101–107.

14. Hall K, Brismar K, Grissom F, et al. IGFBP-1 production and control mechanisms. *Acta Endocrinol (Copenhagen)* 1991;124: 48–54.

15. Bereket A, Lang CH, Blethen SL, et al. Effect of insulin on the insulin-like growth factor system in children with new-onset insulin-dependent diabetes mellitus. *J Clin Endocrinol Metab* 1995;80:1312–1317.

16. Rieu M, Binoux M. Serum levels of insulin-like growth factor (IGF) and IGF binding protein in insulin-dependent diabetics during an episode of severe metabolic decompensation and the recovery phase. *J Clin Endocrinol Metab* 1985;60:781–785.

17. Shisko PI, Dreval AV, Abugova IA, et al. Insulin-like growth factors and binding proteins in patients with recent-onset type 1 (insulin dependent) diabetes mellitus: influence of diabetes control and intraportal insulin infusion. *Diabetes Res Clin Pract* 1994;25:1–12.

18. Wurtzberger MI, Prevelic GM, Sonksen PH, et al. The effect of recombinant human growth hormone on regulation of growth hormone secretion and blood glucose insulin dependent diabetes. *J Clin Endocrinol Metab* 1993;77:267–272.

19. Cheetham TD, Holly JM, Clayton K, et al. The effects of repeated daily recombinant human insulin-like growth factor I

administration in adolescent with type 1 diabetes. *Diabet Med* 1995;12:885–892.

20. Carroll PV, Umpleby M, Ward GS, et al. rhIGF-I administration reduces insulin requirements, decreases growth hormone secretion, and improves the lipid profile in adults with IDDM. *Diabetes* 1997;46:1453–1458.

21. Thrailkill K, Quattrin T, Baker L, et al. Dual hormonal replacement therapy with insulin and recombinant human insulin-like growth factor (IGF)-I in insulin-dependent diabetes mellitus: Effects on the growth hormone/IGF/IGF-binding protein system. *J Clin Endocrinol Metab* 1997;82:1181–1187.

22. The Diabetes Control and Complications Trial Research Group. The effect of intensive treatment of diabetes on the development and progression of long-term complications in insulin-dependent diabetes mellitus. *N Engl J Med* 1993;329: 977–986.

23. Quattrin T, Thrailkill K, Baker L, et al. Dual hormonal replacement with insulin and recombinant human insulin-like growth factor in IDDM: effects on glycemic control, IGF-I levels and safety profile. *Diabetes Care* 1997;20:374–380.

24. Joslin EP, Root HF, White P. The growth, development and prognosis of diabetic children. *JAMA* 1925;85:420.

25. Wagner R, White P, Bogan IK. Diabetic dwarfism. *Am J Dis Child* 1942;63:667.

26. Ibrahim II, Sakr R, Ghaly IM, et al. Endocrine profiles in pediatric andrology. II. Insulin-dependent diabetic adolescents. *Arch Androl* 1983;11:45–51.

27. Tattersall RB, Pyke DA. Growth in diabetic children; studies in identical twins. *Lancet* 1973;11:1105–1109.

28. Mauriac P. Hepatomegalies de l'enfance avec troubles de la croissance et du metabolisme des glucides. *Paris Med* 1934;2:525.

29. Lee RGL, Bode HH. Stunted growth and hepatomegaly in diabetes mellitus. *J Pediatr* 1977;91:82–84.

30. DiLiberti JH, Carver K, Parton E, et al. Stature at time of diagnosis of type 1 diabetes mellitus. *Pediatrics* 2002;109:479–483.

31. Blom L, Persson LA, Dahlquist G. A high linear growth is associated with an increased risk of childhood diabetes mellitus. *Diabetologia* 1992;35:528–533.

32. Holl RW, Grabert M, Heinze E, et al. Age at onset and long-term metabolic control affect height in type-1 diabetes mellitus. *Eur J Pediatr* 1998;157:972–977.

33. Salardi S, Tonioli S, Tassoni P, et al. Growth and growth factors in diabetes mellitus. *Arch Dis Child* 1987;62:57–62.

34. Edelsten AD, Hughes IA, Oakes S, et al. Height and skeletal maturity in children with newly-diagnosed juvenile onset diabetes. *Arch Dis Child* 1981;56:40–44.

35. Ahmed ML, Connors MK, Drayer NM, et al. Pubertal growth in IDDM is determined by HbA1c levels, sex and bone age. *Diabetes Care* 1998;21:831–835.

36. Salerno M, Argenziano A, Di Maio S, et al. Pubertal growth, sexual maturation and final height in children with IDDM. Effects of age at onset and metabolic control. *Diabetes Care* 1997;20:721–724.

37. Schriock EA, Winter RJ, Traisman HS. Diabetes mellitus and its effects on menarche. *J Adolesc Health Care* 1984;5:101–104.

38. Amiel SA, Sherwin RS, Simonson DC, et al. Impaired insulin action in puberty. A contributing factor to poor glycemic control in adolescents with diabetes. *N Engl J Med* 1986;315: 215–219.

39. Moran A, Jacobs DR Jr, Steinberger J, et al. Association between the insulin resistance of puberty and the insulin-like growth factor-I/growth hormone axis. *J Clin Endocrin Metab* 2002;87:4817–4820.

40. Acerini CL, Williams RM, Dunger DB. Metabolic impact of puberty on the course of type 1 diabetes. *Diabetes Metab* 2001;27(suppl):19–25.

41. Yeshaya A, Orvieto R, Dicker D, et al. Menstrual characteristics of women suffering from insulin-dependent diabetes mellitus. *Int J Fertil Menopausal Stud* 1995;40:269–273.

42. Herman-Giddens ME, Slora EJ, Wasserman RC, et al. Secondary sexual characteristics and menses in young girls seen in office practice: a study from the Pediatric Research Office Settings Network. *Pediatrics* 1997;99:505–512.

43. Escobar-Morreale HF, Roldan B, Barrio R, et al. High prevalence of the polycystic ovary syndrome and hirsutism in women with type 1 diabetes mellitus. *J Clin Endocrinol Metab* 2000;85: 4182–4187.

44. Adcock CJ, Perry LA, Lindsell DR, et al. Menstrual irregularities are more common in adolescents with type 1 diabetes: association with poor glycaemic control and weight gain. *Diabet Med* 1994;11:465–470.

45. Snajderova M, Martinek J, Horejsi J, et al. Premenarchal and postmenarchal girls with insulin-dependent diabetes mellitus: ovarian and other organ-specific autoantibodies, menstrual cycle. *J Pediatr Adolesc Gynecol* 1999;12:209–214.

46. Meyer K, Deutscher J, Anil M, et al. Serum androgen levels in adolescents with type 1 diabetes: relationship to pubertal stage and metabolic control. *J Endocrinol Invest* 2000;23:362–386.

47. Rudberg S, Persson B. Indications of low sex hormone binding globulin (SHBG) in young females with type 1 diabetes, and an independent association to microalbuminuria. *Diabet Med* 1995;12:816–822.

48. Virdis R, Zampolli M, Street ME, et al. Ovarian 17 alpha-hydroxyprogesterone responses to GnRH analog testing in oligomenorrheic insulin-dependent diabetic adolescents. *Eur J Endocrinol* 1997;136:624–629.

49. Christensen L, Hagen C, Henriksen JE, et al. Elevated levels of sex hormones and sex hormone binding globulin in male patients with insulin dependent diabetes mellitus. Effect of improved blood glucose regulation. *Dan Med Bull* 1997;44: 547–550.

50. Pugeat M, Cousin P, Baret C, et al. Sex hormone-binding globulin during puberty in normal and hyperandrogenic girls. *J Pediatr Endocrinol Metab* 2000;13:1277–1279.

51. Yki-Jarvinen H, Makimattila S, Utriainen T, et al. Portal insulin concentrations rather than insulin sensitivity regulate serum sex hormone–binding globulin and insulin-like growth factor binding protein 1 *in vivo*. *J Clin Endocrinol Metab* 1995;80: 3227–3232.

52. Holly JM, Dunger DB, al-Othman SA, et al. Sex hormone binding globulin levels in adolescent subjects with diabetes mellitus. *Diabet Med* 1992;9:371–374.

53. Ebeling P, Stenman UH, Seppala M, et al. Androgens and insulin resistance in type 1 diabetic men. *Clin Endocrinol (Oxf)* 1995;43:601–607.

54. Djursing H, Hagen C, Nyboe Andersen A, et al. Serum sex hormone concentrations in insulin dependent diabetic women with and without amenorrhea. *Clin Endocrinol (Oxf)* 1985;23: 147–154.

55. White NH, Santiago JV. Diabetic ketoacidosis in children. In: DeFronzo RA, ed. *Current management of diabetes mellitus.* St. Louis: CV Mosby, 1998:13–20.

56. Rewers A, Chase HP, Mackenzie T, et al. Predictors of acute complications in children with type 1 diabetes. *JAMA* 2002; 287:2511–2518.

57. Dumont RH, Jacobson AM, Cole C, et al. Psychosocial predictors of acute complications of diabetes in youth. *Diabet Med* 1995;12:612–618.

58. DeFronzo RA. Diabetic ketoacidosis in adults. In: DeFronzo RA, ed. *Current management of diabetes mellitus.* St. Louis: CV Mosby, 1998:20–26.

59. Bui TP, Werther GA, Cameron FJ. Trends in diabetic ketoaci-

dosis in childhood and adolescence: a 15-yr experience. *Pediatr Diabetes* 2002;3:82–88.

60. Liss DS, Waller DA, Kennard BD, et al. Psychiatric illness and family support in children and adolescents with diabetic ketoacidosis: a controlled study. *J Am Acad Child Adolesc Psychiatry* 1998;37:536–544.

61. Wright AD, Hale PJ, Singh BM, et al. Changing sex ratio in diabetic ketoacidosis. *Diabet Med* 1990;7:628–632.

62. Laron-Kenet T, Shamis I, Weitzman S, et al. Mortality of patients with childhood onset (0–17 years) type 1 diabetes in Israel: a population-based study. *Diabetologia* 2001;44:B81–B86.

63. DeFronzo RA. Diabetic nephropathy: diagnostic and therapeutic approach. In: DeFronzo RA, ed. *Current management of diabetes mellitus.* St. Louis: CV Mosby, 1998:134–144.

64. Feld LG. Diabetic nephropathy. In: Barratt TM, Avner ED, Harmon WE, eds. *Pediatric nephrology.* Baltimore: Lippincott Williams & Wilkins, 1999:633–640.

65. Koulouridis E. Diabetic nephropathy in children and adolescents and its consequences in adults. *J Pediatri Endocrinol Metab* 2001;14:1367–1377.

66. Salardi S, Cacciari E, Pascucci MG, et al. Microalbuminuria in diabetic children and adolescents. Relationship with puberty and growth hormone. *Acta Paediatr Scand* 1990;79:437–443.

67. Moore TH, Shield JP. Prevalence of abnormal urinary albumin excretion in adolescents and children with insulin dependent diabetes: the MIDAC study. Microalbuminuria in Diabetic Adolescents and Children (MIDAC) research group. *Arch Dis Child* 2000;83:239–243.

68. Riihimaa PH, Knip M, Hirvela H, et al. Metabolic characteristics and urine albumin excretion rate in relation to pubertal maturation in type 1 diabetes. *Diabetes Metab Res Rev* 2000;16:269–275.

69. Levy-Marchal C, Sahler C, Cahane M, et al., for the GECER Study Group. Risk factors for microalbuminuria in children and adolescents with type 1 diabetes. *J Pediatr Endocrinol Metab* 2000;13:613–620.

70. Holl RW, Grabert M, Thon A, et al. Urinary excretion of albumin in adolescents with type 1 diabetes: persistent versus intermittent microalbuminuria and relationship to duration of diabetes, sex, and metabolic control. *Diabetes Care* 1999;22:1555–1560.

71. Bognetti E, Calori G, Meschi F, et al. Prevalence and correlates of early microvascular complications in young type 1 diabetic patients: role of puberty. *J Pediatr Endocrinol Metab* 1997;10:587–592.

72. Jones CA, Leese GP, Kerr S, et al. Development and progression of microalbuminuria in a clinic sample in patients with insulin dependent diabetes mellitus. *Arch Dis Child* 1998;78:518–523.

73. Ellis EN, Warady BY, Wood EG, et al. Renal structural-functional relationships in early diabetes mellitus. *Pediatr Nephrol* 1997;11:584–591.

74. Berg UB, Torbjörnsdotter TB, Jaremko G, et al. Kidney morphological changes in relation to long-term renal function and metabolic control in adolescents with IDDM. *Diabetologia* 1998;41:1047–1056.

75. Mauer M, Drummond K, for the International Diabetic Nephropathy Study Group. The early natural history of nephropathy in type 1 diabetes. I. Study design and baseline characteristics of the study participants. *Diabetes* 2002;51:1572–1579.

76. Drummond K, Mauer M, for the International Diabetic Nephropathy Study Group. The early natural history of nephropathy in type 1 diabetes. II. Early renal structural changes in type 1 diabetes. *Diabetes* 2002;51:1580–1587.

77. American Diabetes Association Position Statement. Diabetic nephropathy. *Diabetes Care* 2002;25(suppl 1):85–89.

78. Lane PH. Diabetic kidney disease: impact of puberty. *Am J Physiol Renal Physiol* 2002;283:F589–F600.

79. American Diabetes Association. Diabetes complications. In: *Diabetes 2001 vital statistics.* Alexandria, VA: American Diabetes Association, 2001:43–74.

80. Quinn M, Angelico MC, Warram JH, et al. Familial factors determine the development of diabetic nephropathy in patients with IDDM. *Diabetologia* 1996;39:940–945.

81. Rudberg S, Rasmussen LM, Bangstad HJ, et al. Influence of insertion/deletion polymorphism in the ACE-I gene on the progression of diabetic glomerulopathy in type 1 diabetic patients with microalbuminuria. *Diabetes Care* 2000;23:544–548.

82. Landau D, Segev Y, Eshet R, et al. Changes in the growth hormone–IGF-I axis in non-obese diabetic mice. *Int J Exp Diabetes Res* 2000;1:9–18.

83. Segev Y, Landau D, Rasch R, et al. Growth hormone receptor antagonism prevents early renal changes in nonobese diabetic mice. *J Am Soc Nephrol* 1999;10:2374–2381.

84. Elliot SJ, Striker LJ, Hattori M, et al. Mesangial cells from diabetic NOD mice constitutively secrete increased amounts of insulin-like growth factor-I. *Endocrinology* 1993;133:1783–1788.

85. Hirschberg R, Kopple JD. Insulin-like growth factor I and renal function. *Diabetes Rev* 1995;3:177–195.

86. Cummings EA, Sochett EB, Dekker MG, et al. Contribution of growth hormone and IGF-I to early diabetic nephropathy in type 1 diabetes. *Diabetes* 1998;47:1341–1346.

87. Gronbaek H, Vomers P, Bjorn SF, et al. Effect of GH/IGF-I deficiency on long-term renal changes and urinary albumin excretion in diabetic dwarf rats. *Am J Physiol* 1997;272:E918–E924.

88. Flyvbjerg A. Potential use of growth hormone receptor antagonist in the treatment of diabetic kidney disease. *Growth Horm IGF Res* 2001;11(suppl):115–119.

89. Landau D, Segev Y, Afargan M, et al. A novel somatostatin analogue prevents early renal complications in the nonobese diabetic mouse. *Kidney Int* 2001;60:505–512.

90. Harris MI, Klein R, Cowie CC, et al. Is the risk of diabetic retinopathy greater in non-Hispanic blacks and Mexican Americans than in non-Hispanic whites with type 2 diabetes. A US population study. *Diabetes Care* 1998;21:1230–1235.

91. Aiello LP, Gardner TW, King GL, et al. Diabetic retinopathy. *Diabetes Care* 1998;21:143–156.

92. American Diabetes Association Position Statement. Diabetic retinopathy. *Diabetes Care* 2002;25(suppl 1):90–93.

93. Salardi S, Rubbi F, Puglioli R, et al. Diabetic retinopathy in childhood: long-term follow-up by fluorescein angiography beginning in the first months of disease. *J Pediatr Endocrinol Metab* 2001;14:507–515.

94. Donaghue KC, Fairchild JM, Chan A, et al. Diabetes complication screening in 937 children and adolescents. *J Pediatri Endocrinol Metab* 1999;12:185–192.

95. Donaghue KC, Fung AT, Hing S, et al. The effect of prepubertal diabetes duration on diabetes. Microvascular complication in early and late adolescence. *Diabetes Care* 1997;20:77–80.

96. Holl RW, Lang GE, Grabert M, et al. Diabetic retinopathy in pediatric patients with type 1 diabetes: effect of diabetes duration, prepubertal and pubertal onset of diabetes, and metabolic control. *J Pediatr* 1998;132:790–794.

97. Kalter-Leibovici O, Leibovici L, Loya N, et al. The development and progression of diabetic retinopathy in type I diabetic patients: a cohort study. *Diabet Med* 1997;14:858–866.

98. Kernell A, Dedorsson I, Johansson B, et al. Prevalence of diabetic retinopathy in children and adolescents with IDDM. A population-based multicenter study. *Diabetologia* 1997;40:307–310.

99. North RV, Farrell U, Banford D, et al. Visual function in young IDDM patients over 8 years of age. A 4-year longitudinal study. *Diabetes Care* 1997;20:1724–1730.

100. Bouhanick B, Bellanne-Chantelot C, Salle A, et al. Proliferative retinopathy in patients with type 1 diabetes of less than 5 years duration. *Diabetes Metab* 2002;28:141–144.

101. Swift PGF, ed. *ISPAD guidelines 2000.* Zeist, the Netherlands: Medical Forum International, 2000.

102. Chaturvedi N, Sjoelie AK, Porta M, et al. Markers of insulin resistance are strong risk factors for retinopathy incidence in type 1 diabetes. *Diabetes Care* 2001;24:284–289.

103. Olsen BS, Sjoelie A, Hougaard P, et al. A 6-year nationwide cohort study of glycaemic control in young people with type 1 diabetes. Risk markers for the development of retinopathy, nephropathy and neuropathy. Danish Study Group of Diabetes in Childhood. *J Diabetes Complications* 2000;14:295–300.

104. Falck AA, Knip JM, Ilonen JS, et al. Genetic markers in early diabetic retinopathy of adolescents with type I diabetes. *J Diabetes Complications* 1997;11:203–207.

105. Demaine A, Cross D, Millward A. Polymorphisms of the aldose reductase gene and susceptibility to retinopathy in type 1 diabetes mellitus. *Invest Ophthalmol Vis Sci* 2000;41:4064–4068.

106. Danne T, Kordonouri O, Enders I, et al. Monitoring for retinopathy in children and adolescents with type 1 diabetes. *Acta Paediatr Suppl* 1998;425:35–41.

107. Luft R, Olivecrona H, Sjögren B. Hypophysectomy in man. *Nord Med* 1952;47:351.

108. Boulton M, Gregor Z, McLeod D, et al. Intravitreal growth factors in proliferative diabetic retinopathy: correlations with neovascular activity and glycaemic management. *Br J Ophthalmol* 1997;81:228–233.

109. Danis RP, Bingaman DP. Insulin-like growth factor-1 in retinal microangiopathy in the pig eye. *Ophthalmology* 1997;104:1661–1669.

110. Wang Q, Dills DG, Klein R, et al. Does insulin-like growth factor I predict incidence and progression of diabetic retinopathy? *Diabetes* 1995;44:161–164.

111. Agardh CD, Agardh E, Eckert B, et al. Growth hormone levels in the basal state and after thyrotropin-releasing hormone stimulation in young type 1 (insulin-dependent) diabetic patients with severe retinopathy. *Diabetes Res* 1992;19:81–85.

112. Lee HC, Lee KW, Chung CH, et al. IGF-I of serum and vitreous fluid in patients with diabetic proliferative retinopathy. *Diabetes Res Clin Pract* 1994;24:85–88.

113. Riihimaa PH, Suominen K, Tolonen U, et al. Peripheral nerve function is increasingly impaired during puberty in adolescents with type 1 diabetes. *Diabetes Care* 2001;24:1087–1092.

114. el Bahri-Ben MF, Gouider R, Fredj M, et al. Childhood diabetic neuropathy: a clinical and electrophysiological study. *Funct Neurol* 2000;15:35–40.

115. Donaghue KC, Fung AT, Fairchild JM, et al. Prospective assessment of autonomic and peripheral nerve function in adolescents with diabetes. *Diabet Med* 1996;13:65–71.

116. Solders G, Thalme B, Aguirre-Aquino M, et al. Nerve conduction and autonomic nerve function in diabetic children. A 10-years follow-up study. *Acta Paediatr* 1997;86:361–366.

117. Karavanaki K, Baum JD. Prevalence of microvascular and neurologic abnormalities in a population of diabetic children. *J Pediatr Endocrinol Metab* 1999;12:411–422.

118. Barkai L, Kempler P, Vamosi I, et al. Peripheral sensory nerve dysfunction in children and adolescents with type 1 diabetes mellitus. *Diabet Med* 1998;15:228–233.

119. Dyck PJ, Kratz KM, Karnes JL, et al. The prevalence by staged severity of various types of diabetic neuropathy, retinopathy, and nephropathy in a population-based cohort: the Rochester Diabetic Neuropathy Study. *Neurology* 1993;43:817–824.

120. Flynn MD, O'Brien IA, Corrall RJ. The prevalence of autonomic and peripheral neuropathy in insulin-treated diabetic subjects. *Diabet Med* 1995;12:310–313.

121. Karavanaki-Karanassiou K. Autonomic neuropathy in children and adolescents with diabetes mellitus. *J Pediatr Endocrinol Metab* 2001;14:1379–1386.

122. Massin MM, Derkenne B, Tallsund M, et al. Cardiac autonomic dysfunction in diabetic children. *Diabetes Care* 1999;22:1845–1850.

123. Faulkner MS, Hathaway DK, Milstead EJ, et al. Heart rate variability in adolescents and adults with type 1 diabetes. *Nurs Res* 2001;50:95–104.

124. Suys BE, Huybrechts SJ, DeWolf D, et al. QTc interval prolongation and QTc dispersion in children and adolescents with type 1 diabetes. *J Pediatr* 2002;141:59–63.

125. Lafferty AR, Werther GA, Clarke CF. Ambulatory blood pressure, microalbuminuria, and autonomic neuropathy in adolescents with type 1 diabetes. *Diabetes Care* 2000;23:533–538.

126. Karachaliou FH, Karavanaki K, Greenwood R, et al. Consistency of microvascular and autonomic abnormalities in diabetes. *Arch Dis Child* 1996;75:124–128.

127. Barkai L, Szabo L. Urinary bladder dysfunction in diabetic children with and without subclinical cardiovascular autonomic neuropathy. *Eur J Pediatr* 1993;152:190–192.

128. Arslanoglu I, Unal F, Sagin F, et al. Real-time sonography for screening of gallbladder dysfunction in children with type 1 diabetes mellitus. *J Pediatr Endocrinol Metab* 2001;14:61–69.

129. Verrotti A, Chiarelli F, Morgese G. Autonomic dysfunction in newly diagnosed insulin-dependent diabetes mellitus children. *Pediatr Neurol* 1996;14:49–52.

130. Dore S, Kar S, Quirion R. Rediscovering an old friend, IGF-I: potential use in the treatment of neurodegenerative diseases. *Trends Neurosci* 1997;20:326–331.

131. Wuarin L, Guertin DM, Ishii DN. Early reduction in insulin-like growth factor gene expression in diabetic nerve. *Exp Neurol* 1994;130:106–114.

132. Wuarin L, Namdev R, Burns JG, et al. Brain insulin-like growth factor-II mRNA content is reduced in insulin-dependent and non-insulin dependent diabetes mellitus. *J Neurochem* 1996;67:742–751.

133. Busiguina S, Chowen JA, Argente J, et al. Specific alterations of the insulin-like growth factor I system in the cerebellum of diabetic rats. *Endocrinology* 1996;137:4980–4987.

134. Bitar MS, Pilcher CW. Attenuation of IGF-I antinociceptive action and a reduction in spinal cord gene expression of its receptor in experimental diabetes. *Pain* 1998;75:69–74.

135. Migdalis IN, Kalageropoulou K, Kalantzis L, et al. Insulin-like growth factor-I and IGF-I receptors in diabetic patients with neuropathy. *Diabetes Med* 1995;12:823–827.

136. Ishii DN. Implication of insulin-like growth factors in the pathogenesis of diabetic neuropathy. *Brain Res Brain Res Rev* 1995;20:47–67.

137. Forrest KY, Maser RE, Pambianco G, et al. Hypertension as a risk factor for diabetic neuropathy: a prospective study. *Diabetes* 1997;46:665–670.

138. Valensi P, Giroux C, Seeboth-Ghalayini B, et al. Diabetic peripheral neuropathy: effects of age, duration of diabetes, glycemic control and vascular factors. *J Diabetes Complications* 1997;11:27–34.

139. Tesfaye S, Stevens LK, Stephenson JM, et al. Prevalence of diabetic peripheral neuropathy and its relation to glycaemic control and potential risk factors: the EURODIAB IDDM Complications Study. *Diabetologia* 1996;39:1377–1384.

140. Tylleskar K, Tuvemo T, Gustafsson J. Diabetes control deteriorates in girls at cessation of growth: relationship with body mass index. *Diabet Med* 2001;18:811–815.

141. Mann MP, Johnston DI. Total glycated haemoglobin (HbA1) levels in diabetic children. *Arch Dis Child* 1982;57:434–437.

142. Boland EA, Grey M, Oesterle A, et al. Continuous subcutaneous

insulin infusion. A new way to lower risk of severe hypoglycemia, improve metabolic control, and enhance coping in adolescents with type 1 diabetes. *Diabetes Care* 1999;22:1779–1794.

143. Ahern JAH, Boland EA, Doane R, et al. Insulin pump therapy in pediatrics: a therapeutic alternative to safely lower HbA1c levels across all age groups. *Pediatr Diabetes* 2002;3:10–15.

144. Spear BA. Adolescent growth and development. *J Am Diet Assoc* 2002;102(suppl):23–29.

145. Centers for Disease Control and Prevention. Guidelines for school and community programs to promote lifelong physical activity among young people. MMWR 1997;46:1–36.

146. Kemink SA, Hermus AR, Swinkels LM, et al. Osteopenia in insulin-dependent diabetes mellitus; prevalence and aspects of pathophysiology. *J Endocrinol Invest* 2000;23:295–303.

147. Tuominen JT, Impivaara O, Puukka P, et al. Bone mineral density in patients with type 1 and type 2 diabetes. *Diabetes Care* 1999;22:1196–2000.

148. National Institutes of Health. *Consensus Development Conference Statement: optimal calcium intake.* Bethesda, MD: National Institutes of Health, June 6–8, 1994.

149. Albertson AM, Tobelmann RC, Marquart L. Estimated dietary calcium intake and food sources for adolescent females: 1980–92. *J Adolesc Health* 1997;20:20–26.

150. McDowell MA, Briefel RR, Alaimo K, et al. Energy and macronutrient intakes of persons ages 2 months and over in the United States: Third National Health and Nutrition Examination Survey, Phase 1, 1988–1991. *Adv Data* 1994;24:1–24.

151. Key JD, Key LL Jr. Calcium needs of adolescents. *Curr Opin Pediatr* 1994;6:379–382.

152. Brown IR, McBain AM, Chalmers J, et al. Sex difference in the relationship of calcium and magnesium excretion to glycaemic control in type 1 diabetes mellitus. *Clin Chim Acta* 1999;283:119–128.

153. Miller EC, Maropis CG. Nutrition and diet-related problems. *Adolesc Med* 1998;25:193–210.

154. Spear BA. Adolescent growth and development. *J Am Diet Assoc* 2002;102(suppl):23–29.

155. Dallman PR, Looker AC, Carroll M, et al. Influence of age on laboratory criteria for the diagnosis of iron deficiency and iron deficiency anemia in infants and children. In: Hallburg L, ed. *Proceedings of the Symposium on Iron Nutrition in Health and Disease.* London: John Libbey & Co, 2002.

156. Lewis CJ, et al. Healthy People 2000: report on the 1994 nutrition progress review. *Nutr Today* 1994;29:6–14.

157. Story M, Neumark-Sztainer D, French S. Individual and environmental influences on adolescent eating behaviors. *J Am Diet Assoc* 2002;102(suppl):40–51.

158. The DCCT Research Group. Effect of intensive diabetes treatment on the development and progression of long-term complications in adolescent with insulin-dependent diabetes. Diabetes Control and Complications Trial. *J Pediatr* 1994;125:177–188.

159. Nielsen S, Emborg C, Molbak AG. Mortality in concurrent type 1 diabetes and anorexia nervosa. *Diabetes Care* 2002;25:309–312.

160. Wing RR, Nowalk MP, Marcus MD, et al. Subclinical eating disorders and glycemic control in adolescents with type 1 diabetes. *Diabetes Care* 1986;9:162–167.

161. Birk R, Spencer ML. The prevalence of anorexia nervosa, bulimia, and induced glycosuria in IDDM females. *Diabetes Educ* 1989;15:336–341.

162. Peveler RC, Fairburn CG, Boller I, et al. Eating disorders in adolescents with IDDM. *Diabetes Care* 1992;15:1356–1360.

163. Meltzer LJ, Bennett Johnson S, Prine JM, et al. Disordered eating, body mass, and glycemic control in adolescents with type 1 diabetes. *Diabetes Care* 2001;24:678–682.

164. Striegel-Moore RH, Nicholson TJ, Tamborlane WV. Prevalence of eating disorder symptoms in preadolescent and adolescent girls with IDDM. *Diabetes Care* 1992;15:1361–1368.

165. Bryden KS, Neil A, Mayou RA, et al. Eating habits, body weight and insulin misuse. *Diabetes Care* 1999;22:1956–1960.

166. Neumark-Sztainer D, Story M, Toporoff E, et al. Psychological predictors of binge eating and purging behaviors among adolescents with and without diabetes mellitus. *J Adolesc Health* 1996;19:289–296.

167. Stancin T, Link DL, Reuter JM. Binge eating and purging in young women with IDDM. *Diabetes Care* 1989;12:601–603.

168. Engstrom I, Kroon M, Arvidsson CG, et al. Eating disorders in adolescent girls with insulin-dependent diabetes mellitus: a population-based case-control study. *Acta Paediatr* 1999;88:175–180.

169. Affenito SG, Backstrand JR, Welch GW, et al. Subclinical and clinical eating disorders in IDDM negatively affect metabolic control. *Diabetes Care* 1997;20:182–184.

170. Biggs MM, Basco MR, Patterson G, et al. Insulin withholding for weight control in women with diabetes. *Diabetes Care* 1994;17:1186–1189.

171. Domargard A, Sarnblad S, Kroon M, et al. Increased prevalence of overweight in adolescent girls with type 1 diabetes mellitus. *Acta Paediatr* 1999;88:1223–1228.

172. Rydall AC, Rodin GM, Olmsted MP, et al. Disordered eating behavior and microvascular complications in young women with insulin-dependent diabetes mellitus. *N Engl J Med* 1997;336:1849–1854.

173. Jones JM, Lawson ML, Daneman D, et al. Eating disorders in adolescent females with and without type 1 diabetes: cross sectional study. *BMJ* 2000;320:1563–1566.

174. Rodin G, Craven J, Littlefield C, et al. Eating disorders and intentional insulin undertreatment in adolescent females with diabetes. *Psychosomatics* 1991;32:171–176.

175. Daneman D, Olmsted M, Rydall A, et al. Eating disorders in young women with type 1 diabetes. Prevalence, problems and prevention. *Horm Res* 1998;50(suppl 1):79–86.

176. Weissberg-Benchell J, Glasgow AM, Tynan WD, et al. Adolescent diabetes management and mismanagement. *Diabetes Care* 1995;18:77–82.

177. Johnson SB, Silverstein J, Rosenbloom A, et al. Assessing daily management in childhood diabetes. *Health Psychol* 1986;5:545–564.

178. Barrett EJ, Nadler JL. Non-insulin-dependent diabetes mellitus. In: Besser GM, Thorner MO, eds. *Comprehensive clinical endocrinology,* 3rd ed. Edinburgh: Elsevier Science, 2002:303–318.

179. American Diabetes Association Consensus Statement. Type 2 diabetes in children and adolescents. *Diabetes Care* 2000;23:381–389.

180. Fagot-Campagna A, Pettitt DJ, Engelgau MM, et al. Type 2 diabetes among North American children and adolescents: an epidemiologic review and a public health perspective. *J Pediatr* 2000;136:664–672.

181. Silverstein JH, Rosenbloom AL. Treatment of type 2 diabetes mellitus in children and adolescents. *J Pediatri Endocrinol Metab* 2000;13:1403–1409.

182. Crespo CJ, Smit E, Troiano RP, et al. Television watching, energy intake and obesity in US children: results from the third National Health and Nutrition Examination Survey, 1988–1994. *Arch Pediatr Adolesc Med* 2001;155:360–365.

183. Ogden CL, Flegal KM, Carroll MD, et al. Prevalence and trends in overweight among US children and adolescents, 1999–2000. *JAMA* 2002;288:1728–1732.

184. Troiano RP, Flegal KM. Overweight children and adolescents: description, epidemiology, and demographics. *Pediatrics* 1998;101:497–504.

185. Tremblay MS, Katzmarzyk PT, Willms JD. Temporal trends in overweight and obesity in Canada, 1981–1996. *Int J Obes Relat Metab Disord* 2002;26:538–543.

186. Luo J, Ju FB. Time trends in obesity in pre-school children in China from 1989 to 1997. *Int J Obes Relat Metab Disord* 2002;26:553–558.

187. Kautiainen S, Rimpela A, Vikat A, et al. Secular trends in overweight and obesity among Finnish adolescents in 1997–1999. *Int J Obes Relat Metab Disord* 2002;26:544–552.

188. Ramachandran A, Snehalatha C, Vinitha R, et al. Prevalence of overweight in urban Indian adolescent school children. *Diabetes Res Clin Pract* 2002;57:185–190.

189. Wang G, Dietz W. Economic burden of obesity in youths aged 6–17 years: 1979–1999. *Pediatrics* 2002, 109.

190. Saad RJ, Danadian K, Lewy V, et al. Insulin resistance of puberty in African-American children: lack of compensatory increase in insulin secretion. *Pediatric Diabetes* 2002;3:4–9.

191. Love K, Zeitler P. Type 2 diabetes and insulin resistance in adolescents. *Endocrinologist* 2001;11:35–40.

192. Jones KL, Arslanian S, Peterokova VA, et al. Effect of metformin in pediatric patients with type 2 diabetes: a randomized controlled trial. *Diabetes Care* 2002;25:89–94.

193. Kaufman FR. Diabetes in children and adolescents. *Med Clin North Am* 1998;82:721–738.

194. Vinik AI, Suwanwalaikorn A. Autonomic Neuropathy. In: DeFronzo RA, ed. *Current management of diabetes mellitus.* St. Louis: CV Mosby, 1998:165–176.

195. Brooks-Worrell BM, Juneja R, Minokadeh A, et al. Cellular immune responses to human islet proteins in antibody-positive type 2 diabetic patients. *Diabetes* 1999;48:983–988.

5

GENETICS, PERINATAL COUNSELING, AND DIABETES EDUCATION

E. ALBERT REECE
CAROL HOMKO

GENETICS OF DIABETES MELLITUS

Significant advances in the understanding of genetic factors in diabetes mellitus, particularly type 1 diabetes, have been achieved in the past 25 years (1). Diabetes mellitus is not one single disease but a group of disorders that share glucose intolerance in common. These disorders are also genetically heterogeneous. In an attempt to classify the different forms of diabetes, the National Diabetes Data Group (2) introduced a classification in 1979, which Hollingsworth and Resnik (3) subsequently modified (Table 5-1). Generally, diabetes can be categorized into four groups: (a) insulin-dependent diabetes mellitus (type 1); (b) non-insulin-dependent diabetes mellitus (type 2); (c) gestational diabetes mellitus (GDM; type 3); and (d) diabetes associated with other conditions or genetic syndromes (secondary diabetes; type 4).

TABLE 5-1. CLASSIFICATION OF GLUCOSE INTOLERANCE

Nomenclature	Old Names
Type 1: Insulin-dependent diabetes mellitus	Juvenile diabetes Juvenile-onset diabetes Ketosis-prone diabetes
Type 2: Non-insulin-dependent diabetes mellitus, nonobese, obese	Adult-onset diabetes Maturity-onset diabetes Ketosis-resistant diabetes Stable diabetes, maturity-onset diabetes of youth
Type III: Gestational or carbohydrate intolerance, nonobese, obese	Gestational diabetes mellitus
Type IV: Secondary diabetes	Conditions and syndromes associated with impaired glucose tolerance

Modified from Hollingsworth DR, Resnik R, eds. *Medical counseling before pregnancy.* New York: Churchill Livingstone, 1988, with permission.

Since the early 1970s, it has been known that type 1 diabetes is a human leukocyte antigen (HLA)-linked disorder, whereas type 2 is not, supporting the genetic distinctions between these two clinically separate classifications. The magnitude of the differences in genetic factors that lead to either type 1 or type 2 diabetes was demonstrated by twin studies (4,5). When one member of a monozygotic twin pair has type 1, the probability that the second twin will develop the disease is between 20% and 50%, suggesting that genetic factors are required but not sufficient. By contrast, the risk for developing type 2 is almost 100% in monozygotic cotwins of type 2 patients (6,7) (Table 5-2).

Besides twin studies, classic familial pedigree and population studies have also been used to study the genetics of diabetes. Recently, a variety of newer physiologic, serologic, and molecular approaches has also been applied. It is clear from these works that a variety of etiologic and pathophysiologic mechanisms are involved in each of the different forms of type 1 and type 2. The distinction between the different types of diabetes is crucial for genetic counseling, even though this differentiation is not always clinically feasible.

HLA and Disease Susceptibility

The major genetic susceptibility to type 1 diabetes is provided by genes near or within the HLA region (8). The HLA region, otherwise known as the major histocompatibility complex (MHC), is a family of closely linked genes located on the short arm of chromosome 6 (Fig. 5-1). This single genetic region occupies about 1/3,000th of the human genome and controls antigens that are the primary targets of cell-mediated and antibody-mediated reactions to transplanted tissue (9). The MHC plays a critical role in immune functions, regulating immune cooperation between monocytes and lymphocytes. Furthermore, it is believed that MHC molecules play a significant role in susceptibility to certain diverse diseases, possibly via an immunoregulatory role (10,11).

TABLE 5-2. PREDOMINANT CHARACTERISTICS OF TYPE 1 AND TYPE 2 DIABETES

Characteristics	Type 1	Type 2
Revalence	0.1%–0.5%	5%–10%[a]
Weight at onset	Nonobese	Often obese
Age at onset	Usually young, <30 yr	Usually older, >40 yr
Seronal variations	Yes	No
Insulin level	Low or absent	Variable
Ketosis	Most often	Unusual
Major histocompatibility complex gene associations	HLA-DR4, HLA-DR3, HLA-DQ	None
Twin studies	30%–50% concordance	80%–100% concordance
Anti–islet cell antibodies	Positive in 70% of new type 1 diabetics or prediabetics	None

[a]Prevalence in Western countries.
From Hagay Z, Reece EA, Hobins JC. Diabetes mellitus in pregnancy and periconceptional genetic counseling. *Am J Perinatol* 1992;9:88, with permission.

The HLA complex is composed of several closely linked loci (i.e., selected chromosomal regions), the best known of which are the HLA-A, -B, -C, and -D/DR loci. Each of these loci is composed of several different alleles, which code for various antigens that can be distinguished serologically or by mixed lymphocyte culture (9). An important feature of the HLA system is linkage disequilibrium, which occurs when the association of two alleles from different regions is observed at a much higher frequency than predicted by the individual allele frequencies in that population (9,12) (Fig. 5-2).

Three major classes of HLA gene products have been described (11,13,14) (Fig. 5-1). Class I gene products are surface antigens controlled by the 1-HA-A, -B, and -C genes. These surface antigens are found on all nucleated cells and platelets. Each of these class I genes is highly polymorphic, meaning many separate alleles have been identified in humans at each of these loci. At least 23 alleles for HLA-A, 50 for HLA-B, and 8 for HLA-C have been described.

Control of class II gene products occurs within the HLA-D region. These molecules are expressed primarily on the surface of antigen-presenting cells such as B lympho-

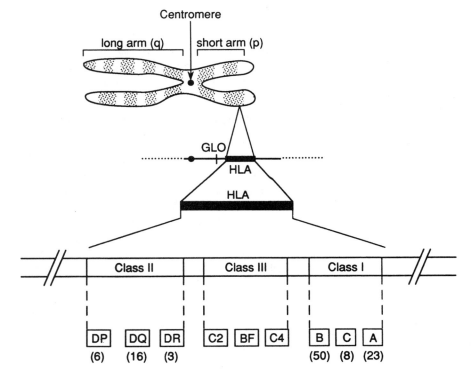

FIGURE 5-1. The HLA gene complex located on the short arm of human chromosome 6. The numbers in parentheses indicate the minimum number of alleles per locus. (From Hagay Z, Reece EA, Hobbins JC: Diabetes mellitus in pregnancy and periconceptional genetic counseling. Am J Perinat 9:88, 1992.)

Text

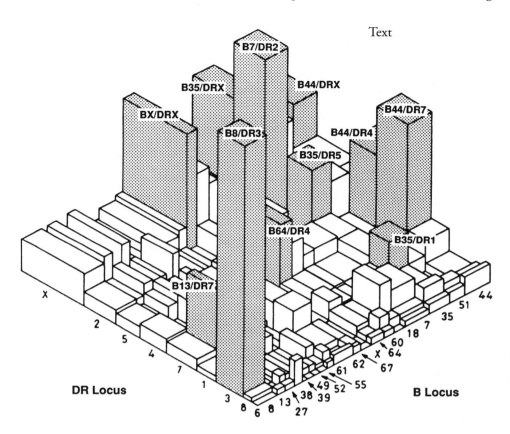

FIGURE 5-2. Schematic presentation of linkage disequilibrium between the alleles of HLA-DR and HLA-B loci. (Modified from Tiwari JL, Terasaki PI. Endocrinology. IN: HLA and disease associations. New York, Springer Verlag, 1985:1.)

cytes, macrophages, and activated T lymphocytes. Biochemical and DNA molecular studies have indicated the presence of at least three distinct loci within the HLA-D region, referred to as DP, DQ, and DR. Each of these regions is further divided into sand-subunits, encoded by the respective A and B genes. For the class II HLA-DR subregion, the allelic products defined by serology were given numbers from DR1 to DRW14. Many alleles from the DP and DQ loci have been cloned and sequenced (15,16). The genomic organization of the currently identified class II loci is presented in Fig. 5-3. The primary biologic significance of both class I and class II gene products probably relates to

their role as receptor elements in antigen recognition and immune response. Class I epitopes contribute to the immune system by presenting foreign (or self) antigens to cytotoxic T lymphocytes, whereas class II gene products present antigens to T-helper cells (Table 5-3).

Between classes I and II are the genes encoding class III molecules, which are not directly involved with the immune reaction. In 1964, Lilly et al. (17) observed that the MHC of mice (the H2 system) controls the genetic susceptibility to viral leukemogenesis. In 1972, an association between certain HLA factors and disease states was observed in humans: HLA-B8 and celiac disease (18) and

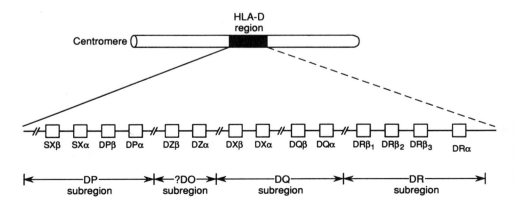

FIGURE 5-3. The HLA-D region with its subregions on the short arm of chromosome 6. (Modified from Hitman GA: Progress with the genetics of insulin-dependent diabetes mellitus. Clin Endocrinol 25:463, 1986.)

TABLE 5-3. THREE DISTINCT TYPES OF MAJOR HISTOCOMPATIBILITY COMPLEX ANTIGENS

	Class I Antigens	Class II Antigens	Class III Antigens
Genetic control	HLA-A, -B, and -C	HLA-DR, -DP, and -DQ	HLA-C2, -C4, and -BF
Tissue distribution	All nucleated cells and platelets	B cells, activated T cells, monocytes/ macrophages; some have marrow-precursor cells	Plasma protein
Function	Important in tissue transplantation and presentation of antigen to cytotoxic T cells	Associated with activation of immune system and present antigen to T-helper cells	Perform several biologic functions related to the mechanism of defense against infection (i.e., enhance phagocytosis)

From Reece EA, Hagay Z, Hobbins I. Insulin-dependent diabetes mellitus and immunogenetics: maternal and fetal considerations. *Obstet Gynecol Surv* 1991;46:257, with permission.

HLA-B13 and B17 and psoriasis (19,20). During the following years, several additional associations between HLA loci and disease were described (Table 5-4). A significant association with disease suggests either a causative role for the gene polymorphism or linkage between the marker allele and a disease susceptibility allele. It is now clear that certain HLAs are associated with disease susceptibility to a greater extent than any other known genetic marker in humans (21).

In Table 5-4, an individual's chances of acquiring a specified disease, if the indicated antigen is inherited, is expressed as the relative risk. For example, those who have inherited the HLA-B27 allele have an 87 times greater chance of developing ankylosing spondylitis than those who have not inherited this gene. It should be stressed that for each disease, only the antigen with the strongest association is recorded in Table 5-4.

The association of HLA and disease may have important implications for diagnosis, prognosis, and possible pharmacologic prophylaxis. In many cases, this association helped to clarify disease heterogeneity; however, the areas that have so far profited most markedly from the discovery of these associations are probably the "genetically inherited" diseases, especially type 1 diabetes (21). In type 1, the disease is not inherited per se; it is the susceptibility to the disease that is inherited, and the development of the disease is dependent on other genetic factors and possibly environmental factors as well (Table 5-5).

Genetic Factors Involved in Type 1 Diabetes Mellitus

HLA Association with Type 1 Diabetes Mellitus

Singal and Blajchman (8) were the first to report an association between type 1 diabetes and class I antigens, specifically B15 in Canadian patients. This was corroborated 1 year later both in Denmark and Britain, where studies showed a significant increase of FRA-B15 and HLA-B8 in type 1, whereas HLA-B7 showed a negative association (22,23). The association of these class I antigens and type 1 is now known to be due to linkage disequilibrium between class I and class II alleles. Thus, significant linkage disequilibrium was found between HLA-B7 and HLA-DR2, B8 and DR3, and B15 and DR4 (Fig. 5-2). Studies of the DR region (class II antigens) have shown stronger association with type 1 than the B locus; although approximately 60% of type 1 patients possess HLA-B8 or -1315, more than 90% possess DR3 or DR4 (24). The higher frequency of certain HLA-DR molecules in type 1 compared with the HLA-B locus indicates that the DR subregion of class II is more closely linked to type 1 than the class I loci (25). The relative risk for developing type 1 is increased to about 15-

TABLE 5-4. ASSOCIATION BETWEEN HUMAN LEUKOCYTE ANTIGEN (HLA) AND SELECTED DISEASES

Disease	HLA	Frequency of Antigen (%)		
		In Patients	In Controls	Relative Risk
Congenital adrenal hyperplasia	B47	9	0.6	15.4
Ankylosing spondylitis	B27	90	9.4	87.4
Type 1 diabetes	DR3 and DR4	91	57.3	7.9
Systemic lupus erythematosus	DR3	70	28.2	5.8
Multiple sclerosis	DR2	59	25.8	4.1
Hasimoto thyroiditis	DR5	19	6.9	3.2

Modified from Svejgaard A, Platz P, Ryder LP. HLA and disease 1982: a survey. *Immunol Rev* 1983;70:10, with permission.

TABLE 5-5. PROPOSED SIX STAGES IN THE PATHOGENESIS OF TYPE 1 DIABETES MELLITUS (DM)

Stage and Occurrence	Comments
Stage I: Genetic susceptibility	Most likely polygenic
	HLA association with type 1 (chromosome 6); 95% of whites with type 1 express HLA-DR3 or -DR4, or both
	Non-HLA association with type 1; immunoglobulin loci (encoded on chromosomes 2, 14); polymorphic region 58 of the insulin gene (chromosome 11); T-cell receptor (chromosome 7, 14)
Stage II: Triggering factors	Environmental factors: toxic chemicals (?), viruses such as coxsackie B, rubella, mumps (?), stress (?)
Stage III: Active autoimmunity	Many immunologic abnormalities may precede overt DM by >9 years; anti–islet cell antibodies may be present in up to 70% of pre-DM patients
Stage IV: Progressive loss of glucose-stimulated insulin secretion	Reduction in β-cell mass, evident from abnormal intravenous glucose tolerance test in ≥50% of first-degree relatives (type 1) with islet-cell antibodies
Stage V: Early onset of overt DM	≥10% of β-cells remain
	Trials of immunotherapy (such as steroids and cyclosporine) have been Attempted
Stage VI: Overt DM with complete P-cell destruction	Several years may elapse between stages V and VI

From Hagay Z, Reece EA, Hobbins JC. Diabetes mellitus in pregnancy and periconceptional genetic counseling. *Am J Perinatol* 1992;9:88, with permission.

fold in individuals who coinherit both DR3 and DR4 alleles, in contrast to the lower risk associated with individuals homozygous for either of these two alleles (25–28). Conversely, the estimated relative risk for developing type 1 was increased only about threefold in HLA-B8 and -B15-positive individuals (8,23). It is possible to calculate the absolute risk for inheriting type 1 diabetes according to various HLA haplotypes (29). For example, individuals with DR2 have a lower absolute risk for type 1 (1:2,500) than the risk in the general population (1:500). Individuals with DR3/DR4 have the highest risk (1:42) for developing type 1 diabetes (29) (Table 5-6). However, this association with the HLA-D region is not exclusively associated with type 1 diabetes, because DR3 and DR4 are also found in approximately 50% of healthy individuals (24). Many investigators concur that DR3 and DR4 (as defined by conventional serology) are not themselves the only susceptibility alleles, and it has been suggested that perhaps susceptibility is due

TABLE 5-6. ABSOLUTE RISKS FOR TYPE 1 DIABETES FOR WHITES OF VARIOUS HUMAN LEUKOCYTE ANTIGEN (HLA) GENOTYPES[a]

HLA Genotype	Absolute Risk
DR3/DR3	1:125
DR3/DRX[b]	1:500
DR4/DR4	1:147
DR4/DRX	1:476
DR3/DR4	1:42
DRX/DRX	1:5565

[a]Based on type 1 prevalence rate of 1 in 500.
[b]X, non-DR3; non-DR4 antigen.
Modified from Maclaren NK, Henson V. The genetics of insulin-dependent diabetes. *Growth Genet Horm* 1986;2:1, with permission.

to certain subsets of DR3 and DR4 molecules or is influenced by more than one locus in the HLA region.

The rapid evolution of recombinant DNA technology and the development of genetic probes for the HLA region have initiated a new approach to the study of the genetics of type 1 (30). Studies using monoclonal antibodies directed against distinct allelic products have indicated that HLA-DQ may actually be more closely linked to the disease susceptibility locus than HLA-DR (31). Sheehy et al. (32) reported that a DR4 haplotype carries a higher risk for type 1 if it encodes a particular DQ subtype, DQW3.2 (now classified as DQB1*0302 33). Furthermore, sequence analysis of the HLA-DQ3 gene product suggested that a single amino acid (aspartic acid) at position 57 is uniquely important for determining susceptibility or resistance to type 1 diabetes (32–35). These groups of investigators have shown that among type 1 patients, the DQ alleles do not have aspartic acid at position 57. They suggest that the DQB allelic polymorphisms, particularly at position 57, determine the susceptibility or the lack thereof for type 1. Moreover, these investigators suggested that an individual carrying one aspartic acid 57–negative and one aspartic acid 57–positive allele (DQBl*0302 and DQBl*0301), a so-called heterozygote state, has a much lower risk for developing type 1. However, individuals homozygous for an aspartic acid 57–negative allele had a high prevalence of type 1. In this study of 39 type 1 patients, 35 were aspartic acid negative homozygous. They concluded that full HLA susceptibility is dependent on the individual having two aspartic acid 57–negative DQ alleles, especially if they are from the DR4 or DR3 haplotypes. Although a similar finding was found in DR4-positive Northern Indian Asians (36), this association was not confirmed transracially (37,38), and DQB1*0302 is therefore unlikely to be a primary disease susceptibility determinant.

Because the structure, function, and expression of the α and β chains of the class II molecule are interdependent, a possible candidate for a gene product that can modify the function of the DQ β chain is the α chain. Transracial studies have implicated DQA1*0301 as the primary allele associated with type 1 diabetes in Japanese (39), black Americans (40), Northern Indians (41), and whites (42,43). In whites, this allele encodes arginine at position 52, and it has been postulated that disease susceptibility correlates with expression of a DQ molecule bearing Arg 52 on the α chain and lacking Asp 57 on the β chain (42). This finding has not been confirmed in other races (37,39).

In summary, the association between specific HLA regions and type 1 susceptibility is now defined more precisely. The susceptibility area is located within the D region and specifically in or close to DR3 and/or DR4 and/or DQ-α or β alleles. However, it is still not known whether the DR and/or DQA or DQB antigens themselves predispose to type 1 or if the susceptibility is due to as-yet-undefined diabetes susceptibility genes located close to and inherited with these antigens.

HLA Susceptibility and β-Cell Destruction in Type 1 Diabetes Mellitus

The development of type 1 diabetes can be divided into six stages conceptually, beginning with genetic susceptibility and ending with complete β-cell destruction. It now seems clear that genetic predisposition (i.e., HLA-linked susceptibility) when combined with other factors (i.e., environmental) leads to clinical diabetes. The aforementioned data indicate that type 1 may be due to immune disease of the pancreatic β-cells. Insulitis is regarded as a process in which insulin-secreting cells are gradually destroyed. Most theories attempting to explain autoimmunity either implicate primary dysfunction within the immune system as the cause or suggest primary islet cell anatomy damage, which may lead to secondary autoimmune destruction. Stage I represents genetic susceptibility inherent in some subjects in whom environmental factors (stage II) such as stress and viral infections occur. These insults trigger the development of β-cell immunity (stage III) in which immunologic abnormalities can precede the development of overt type 1 diabetes. In fact, immunologic abnormalities that can precede type 1 diabetes include anticytoplasmic islet cell antibodies (ICAs), antiinsulin antibodies, and lymphocyte inhibition of insulin secretion (44–46). Initially, individuals with immunologic abnormalities have normal insulin secretion. In stage IV, glucose-stimulated insulin secretion is progressively lost, although overt diabetes does not immediately occur (47). This selective loss of response to glucose may reflect a reduction of β-cell mass. In stage V, overt diabetes is first recognized while some residual insulin secretion remains but eventually results in complete β-cell destruction (stage VI).

The immune response to foreign organisms depends on the responsiveness of the MHC to a given stimulus. The fundamental role of MHC genes is in the identification and distinction of foreign from self. T cells of the immune system can recognize and respond to an antigen only if they are presented in combination with an HLA molecule on the surface of antigen-presenting cells (48–50) (Fig. 5-4). The mechanism by which genes within the MHC of humans influence autoimmune processes is not clear. One recent suggestion by Todd (51) is that there is an impairment in the tolerance of the immune system so that self is recognized as foreign. However, tolerance may be maintained by a third class of T lymphocytes called suppressor T cells. These cells are able to suppress the proliferation of T-helper cells but may require HLA-DQ for their suppression. This suggests that type 1 patients with aspartic 57-negative DQ molecules have abnormal tolerance, perhaps leading to self-destruction of pancreatic β-cells.

Another theory regarding the pathogenesis of type 1 involves aberrant expression of HLA-D region gene products on the surface of cells outside the immune system. For example, the aberrant expression of these gene products on pancreatic β-cells may result in cell destruction. Class II antigens are normally limited to macrophages, B lymphocytes, and activated T lymphocytes. It has been suggested that under pathologic conditions, other cell types may become class II positive, such as in Hashimoto thyroiditis and Graves disease. Bottazzo et al. (52) have demonstrated DR expression on β-cells of the pancreatic islets of a young girl with type 1 diabetes in the very early stages of the dis-

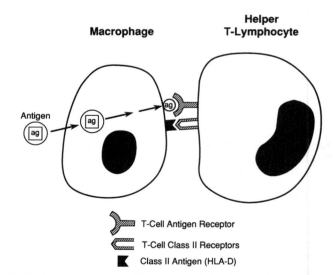

FIGURE 5-4. Schematic illustration of the interaction between the macrophage and the helper T lymphocyte. The latter recognizes and responds to antigens if it sees both the foreign antigen and DR antigen on the surface of macrophages. (From Reece EA, Hagay Z, Hobbins J: Insulin-dependent diabetes mellitus and immunogenetics: maternal and fetal considerations. Obstet Gynecol Surv 46:257, 1991.)

ease. However, endocrine cells in the islets of a control pancreas were invariably DR negative. Thus, expression of class II antigens on the surface of antigen-presenting cells capable of attracting T-helper cells specific for these antigens resulted in the autoimmune destruction of the β-cells.

Non-HLA Associations with Type 1 Diabetes Mellitus

There is ample evidence to support the idea that type 1 diabetes is a genetically programmed autoimmune disease, and its association with HLA has provided new ways to explore certain aspects of the mode of disease inheritance. Nonetheless, although HLA association is strong, it does not explain or account for all the genetic predisposition to type 1. For instance, many individuals with both DR3 and DR4 do not develop type 1, whereas many diabetic individuals possess neither of these antigens (15). Another interesting example is the finding of higher incidences of type 1 among black Americans compared with African blacks with similar HLA antigenic frequencies (53). It has been estimated that loci in the HLA region account for 30% to as much as 70% of the genetic predisposition. This suggests that genetic factors other than HLA contribute to susceptibility to type 1 diabetes (53,54). The search for non-HLA susceptibility genes has focused predominantly on the following three areas:

1. Immunoglobulin heavy chain (Gm) and light chain (Km) regions encoded on chromosomes 14 and 2, respectively
2. The insulin gene (INS), located on the short arm of chromosome 11; particularly the polymorphic 5′ region
3. The T-cell receptor β chain region on chromosome 7 and α chain region on chromosome 14

Field et al. (55) and Rich et al. (56) reported an association between the DR type, particular genes in the immunoglobulin heavy chain (Gm) region, and type 1 diabetes susceptibility. Field et al. proposed that genes encoding Gm allotypes (or genes in linkage disequilibrium with them) may contribute to susceptibility to type 1 diabetes through interaction with HLA (55). This finding was not corroborated subsequently in a fairly large sample of affected families. However, a significant association was observed between 5′ insulin region alleles and type 1 diabetes, although the significance of this relationship is not clear.

Because the autoimmune process leading to type 1 diabetes is specific to the β-cells of the pancreas that produce insulin, abnormalities of insulin secretion or processing are possible etiologic factors. Thus, the insulin (INS) gene remains a candidate for susceptibility to type 1 diabetes. The major polymorphism in the INS gene region is located 58 to the start of the transcription region of the INS gene on the short arm of chromosome 11(11p15.5) (57). In whites, the size of this variable number tandem repeat falls into two main classes: small alleles of approximately 40

repeats (class I alleles) and large alleles of approximately 170 repeats (class II) (33). Many population association studies have shown an increase in the frequency of the class I allele in patients with type 1 diabetes compared with controls (58). However, linkage analyses in multiplex families have failed to confirm this finding (59). Julier et al. (60) were able to detect linkage by considering only parents heterozygous for the common disease-associated alleles. In that study, the parental origin of the INS gene appeared to be important in imparting disease susceptibility, suggesting a role for genomic imprinting.

Other candidate genes for susceptibility to type 1 diabetes include those coding for T-cell receptors, because type 1 diabetes appears to be T cell mediated. T-cell receptors are surface molecules composed of both α and β chains, each with constant and variable regions. These receptors mediate antigen recognition by T lymphocytes.

There are only limited numbers of studies analyzing polymorphisms of both α and β subunit genes of the T-cell receptors (8). Both association and linkage analyses of polymorphisms of the genes coding for the α subunit and susceptibility to type 1 diabetes have been negative (61). An early association study of polymorphisms within the T-cell receptor β chain gene suggested a higher frequency of heterozygosity among diabetic individuals compared with controls (62). Later studies using larger populations and linkage analysis, however, failed to confirm this observation (63). There is no convincing evidence that genes in the T-cell receptor α or β chain regions influence predisposition to type 1 diabetes, either directly or indirectly through interaction with HLA region genes. However, Field (64) showed that diabetic individuals who are positive for the IgG$_2$ allotype G2m(23) have significantly different frequencies of a T-cell receptor β chain restriction fragment length polymorphism than those who are negative for the allotype, suggesting an interaction between T-cell receptor β genes and immunoglobulin heavy chain genes.

In summary, other candidate genes related to susceptibility to type 1 diabetes are characterized by the relative inconsistencies of the findings compared with those for HLA. However, it seems that all three genes—the immunoglobulin, the T-cell receptor, and the insulin gene—play a certain role in the immunopathogenesis of type 1 diabetes. It seems likely that as the approaches and tools for mapping such susceptibility genes become more clearly defined, the identification of further susceptibility determinants will be accomplished in the near future (65).

Genetic Counseling

Type 1 Diabetes Mellitus

Although great progress has been made in the understanding of the genetics of type 1 diabetes mellitus, the exact mode of inheritance of the disease remains controversial. It is possible that manifestations of type 1 diabetes require the interaction of at least five different genes (on chromosomes 2, 6, 7, 11, and 14) along with environmental factors. Hence, it is clear why genetic counseling in type 1 diabetes is not simple.

Because the exact mechanism of inheritance of type 1 diabetes is not known, genetic counseling is based on empirical risk. For example, the estimated overall risk of siblings of the type 1 proband developing the disease ranges from 4.6% to 6.6% (66,67). HLA typing of the entire family permits more precise estimates, because the risk for a sibling is related to the number of haplotypes that the sibling shares with the diabetic proband.

If disease occurs independently of HLA, then the expected frequency of affected sibling pairs sharing one, two, or no haplotypes will be 50%, 25%, and 25%, respectively. However, the expected frequencies assuming linkage of susceptible genes to HLA should be increased for sibling pairs sharing two haplotypes and decreased if only one or no haplotype was shared. In fact, this is precisely what has been found in family studies of type 1 diabetes: observed frequencies among affected sibling pairs are 58.5% being HLA identical, 37.3% sharing one haplotype, and 4.2% for HLA nonidentical. Table 5-7 displays the distribution of the number of HLA haplotypes shared among sibling pairs with type 1 diabetes according to observed frequency versus the expected proportions if disease was independent of HLA.

Thompson et al. (68), in an extensive international multicenter study involving 1,792 white probands with type 1 diabetes, calculated the risk to siblings on the basis of DR type of the proband and haplotype sharing of the sibling and probands (Table 5-8). It is apparent that for an HLA-identical sibling, the risk is 13.1%; but if only one haplotype is shared, the risk is 4.6%. The risk for siblings sharing no haplotype with the proband and therefore not depending on the DR genotype of the proband is 1.8%. This risk is greater than the prevalence of the disease (0.4%) in the general population and may indicate that additional factors

TABLE 5-8. ESTIMATES OF RISKS TO SIBLINGS OF TYPE 1 DIABETES PROBANDS ON THE BASIS OF DR TYPE OF PROBAND AND HAPLOTYPE SHARING

Proband DR Type	Risk of Siblings According to Number of Haplotypes Shared (%)		
	2	1	0
DR3/DR4	19.2	3.7	1.3
DR4/DR4	7.4	3.5	1.0
DR4/X	11.1	6.8	1.6
DR3/DR3	14.1	3.9	2.4
DR3/X	11.2	4.9	2.8
X/X[a]	5.7	3.3	3.8
Overall risk	13.1	4.6	1.8

[a]X, non-DR3; non-DR4 antigen.
From Reece EA, Hagay Z, Hobbins J. Insulin-dependent diabetes mellitus and immunogenetics: maternal and fetal considerations. *Obstet Gynecol Surv* 1991;46:257, with permission.

are involved in the disease predisposition. It is also evident from Table 5-7 that siblings who share two haplotypes with a DR3/DR4 proband have the highest risk (19.2%) for developing type 1 diabetes. This is in agreement with other studies that showed increased risk for type 1 diabetes for DR3/DR4 heterozygotes in comparison with either DR3/DR3 or DR4/DR4 homozygotes (1,25,27).

What is the risk for offspring developing the disease if a parent has type 1 diabetes? In the past, the most common answer was that the cumulative risk for type 1 diabetes by age 20 to 30 years is in the range of 16% (69,70). However, Warram et al. (71) studied the incidence of type 1 diabetes in offspring of patients with the disease. They found that by the age of 20 years, 6.1% of the offspring of the diabetic fathers had diabetes. By contrast, only 1.3% of the offspring of the diabetic mothers had the disease by the age of 20 years. Hence, type 1 diabetes is transmitted less frequently to the offspring of diabetic mothers than to those of diabetic fathers. The mechanism responsible for this preferential transmission is not clear. A possible explanation offered is the lower frequency of recombination between linked loci during gametogenesis in men than in women (72). Another possible mechanism is one that depends on the intimate relationship between the mother and fetus, as evidenced by increased pregnancy loss rate in mothers with type 1 diabetes (71).

TABLE 5-7. DISTRIBUTION OF THE NUMBER OF HUMAN LEUKOCYTE ANTIGEN (HLA) HAPLOTYPES SHARED AMONG TYPE 1 SUBPAIRS ACCORDING TO THE OBSERVED VERSUS EXPECTED PROPORTIONS

Siblings	No. of Haplotypes Shared (%) with Proband		
	0	1	2
Expected percentage of type 1 in siblings if disease is independent of HLA	25	50	25
Observed percentage in type 1 siblings	4.2	37.3	58.5

From Reece EA, Hagay Z, Hobbins J. Insulin-dependent diabetes mellitus and immunogenetics: maternal and fetal considerations. *Obstet Gynecol Surv* 1991;46:257, with permission.

Type 2 Diabetes Mellitus

There are clear genetic and immunologic differences between type 1 and type 2 diabetes mellitus. The latter is not linked with HLA, and no specific genetic markers have been found. Furthermore, type 2 diabetes does not seem to be an autoimmune or endocrine disease. Current available information indicates that type 2 diabetes is due to both impaired insulin secretion and insulin resistance (73). Although the genetic markers for type 2 diabetes are not yet defined, it is evident from family and twin studies that the genetic component of type 2 diabetes is much stronger. As mentioned previously, monozygotic twins have a much higher rate of concordance for type 2 diabetes (almost 100%) than for type 1 diabetes (20%–50%) (6,7). Based on twin studies, one may expect that there is a consistent pattern of inheritance in type 2 diabetes; unfortunately, this is not the case. Environmental factors also play an important role in the etiology of type 2 diabetes, as reflected in the rapid changes in frequency in type 2 diabetes seen in migrant populations and the major effect of obesity on its frequency and clinical course.

It is likely that there is genetic heterogeneity in type 2 diabetes, and the modes of inheritance, for the most part, are poorly defined. However, there is a special subgroup of type 2 diabetes in which the disease develops not in midlife but much earlier, in adolescence or young adulthood (74,75). This subgroup is referred to as maturity-onset diabetes of youth. This disease is transmitted as an autosomal-dominant trait, with as many as 50% of offspring inheriting the disease or manifesting glucose intolerance (75,76). Another example of genetic heterogeneity in type 2 diabetes is found in differences in familial aggregations [i.e., among nonobese diabetic individuals, 15% of first-degree relatives (siblings, parents, or offspring) are also affected compared with 7.3% of first-degree relatives of obese diabetic individuals] (77) (Table 5-9).

The empirical risk for relatives with type 2 diabetes developing the disease is thus much higher than that of rel-

atives with type 1 diabetes. The transmission of the disease to first-degree relatives of type 2 probands is almost 15%, and as many as 30% will have impaired glucose tolerance. When both parents have type 2 diabetes, the chance for developing the disease is much higher and reaches 60% to 75% (78). Given the magnitude of these risks, periodic screening of first-degree relatives with oral glucose tolerance tests is not unreasonable. Those found to have impaired glucose tolerance should be advised to attain ideal body weight. Obesity is certainly a risk factor among this group that should be avoided.

Gestational Diabetes Mellitus

Carbohydrate intolerance of variable severity discovered or presumably arising during pregnancy is defined as GDM. Glycemic control is often achieved by diet or insulin therapy, or both (2,79). GDM patients are usually identified by means of an oral glucose tolerance test. Fifteen percent or more of those patients will require insulin treatment in the pregnancy, either because of fasting or postprandial hyperglycemia (79). These differences demonstrate that the severity of metabolic disturbances can vary between patients with GDM. This raises the question of whether this group of patients consists of a single homogeneous entity. At one time, GDM was believed to be a variant of type 2 diabetes. Available data, however, support the concept that GDM is a heterogeneous disorder representing, at least in part, patients who are destined to develop diabetes in later life, either type 1 or type 2 (79–82). The exact percentage difference of each subgroup is unknown, but it seems that most of the cases represent a preclinical state of type 2 diabetes.

Long-term follow-up of patients who had GDM showed an increased incidence of acquiring diabetes during middle age or later (30%–50%) (83). However, this risk can be modified by weight reduction in later years. The possibility that GDM may represent some patients who are destined to develop type 1 diabetes later in life was raised by the following factors: first, type 1 diabetes may occur in the age group of pregnancy (hence, the disease may arise as a result of the stress of pregnancy); second, it has become clear that autoimmunity plays a key role in type 1 diabetes, and the disease process is believed to be a slow destructive process of β-cells in the pancreas (82,84) (Table 5-4). Immunologic studies have shown that as many as 30% of GDM patients may have circulating ICAs (82,85), and anti-ICAs have been found in high proportions of patients with pre–type 1 diabetes (86–94). Tarn and co-workers (89) reported that up to 54% of first-degree relatives of individuals with type 1 diabetes who were found to be positive for complement-fixing ICAs on three or more occasions developed type 1 diabetes within a maximum of 8 years of follow-up. Furthermore, they showed that GDM patients who were ICA positive had a higher prevalence of HLA-DR3 or DR4 than those who were ICA negative, and more than half of them

TABLE 5-9. EMPIRICAL RISK FOR OFFSPRING OF TYPE 1 AND TYPE 2 DIABETICS DEVELOPING DIABETES

Affected Parents	Empirical Risk Estimates of Offspring
Type 1 Diabetes	
Diabetic mother	1%
Diabetic father	6%
Parents unaffected but previous sibling affected	Overall 5–6%; No. haplotypes shared with proband: 1 haplotype = 5% 2 haplotype = 13% No haplotypes = 2%
Both parents affected	33%
Type 2 Diabetes	
Maturity-onset diabetes of the young	50%
Obese	7%
Nonobese	15%
First-degree relatives	15%–30%
Both parents affected	60%–75%

From Hagay Z, Reece EA, Hobbins JC. Diabetes mellitus in pregnancy and periconceptional genetic counseling. *Am J Perinatol* 1992;9:88, with permission.

developed type 1 diabetes 11 years after the diagnosis of GDM (89). In a study of Pima Indians (91) (a group in whom the incidence of type 2 diabetes is high), there was a higher prevalence of diabetes in the offspring of women who had type 2 diabetes during pregnancy than in the offspring of women who developed diabetes only after the pregnancy (45% vs. 8.6% at age 20–24 years). The investigators suggested that the intrauterine environment is an important determinant of the development of diabetes and its effect is additive to genetic factors.

The previously mentioned data support the concept that GDM is clearly heterogeneous and composed of patients who are prone to develop either type 1 or type 2 diabetes later in life. Further studies are needed to clarify this heterogeneity.

DIABETES EDUCATION AND PERINATAL COUNSELING

Pregnant women with diabetes are faced with the emotional stress of dealing with a serious condition that has many potential implications for both their own as well as their infant's well-being and safety. In addition, they are faced with the increased demands of an intensive self-management regimen. The physiologic and social difficulties associated with these pregnancies require a knowledgeable health-care team that can both understand the complexities of the medical issues and at the same time provide effective support. The ensuing text highlights the educational and counseling needs of the women with diabetes throughout gestation and the postpartum period.

Multidisciplinary Team Approach

Over the past decade, multidisciplinary team management has become increasingly accepted as an effective and efficient alternative for the provision of the multidimensional care and support that is demanded by the diabetic pregnancy. This approach emphasizes diabetes education, nutrition management and psychosocial support to complement the traditional medical approach that focuses on diagnosis and therapy. The multidisciplinary team includes the patient and her significant other as well as a perinatalogist, endocrinologist, obstetrician, dietitian, diabetes nurse educator, neonatologist, and other specialists as needed. These specialists, with their different areas of expertise, work together to provide optimal, individualized care and education around prenatal needs and diabetes management (95).

The Diabetes Control and Complications Trial provided evidence of the significance of the team approach and the vital role of the diabetes educator/specialist (96,97). Diabetes educators possess a thorough knowledge of the current principles of diabetes care and management as well as the principles of teaching and learning. Diabetes educators

can offer valuable and continuous guidance and support to women as they adjust to the rigors of an intensive treatment regimen and changes of pregnancy. However, their most essential role is to organize and coordinate the education process for the woman with diabetes before, during, and after pregnancy.

Patient Empowerment

Active patient participation is essential for the success of a pregnancy complicated by diabetes. Traditional approaches to diabetes education have been compliance based. Such an approach aims to improve patient adherence to the treatment recommendations of health-care professionals. It is based on the assumption that health-care professionals are the diabetes experts and that pregnant women with diabetes should comply with their treatment recommendations to improve glucose control and prevent perinatal complications.

In the early 1990s the Education Committee of the University of Michigan Diabetes Research and Training Center concluded that this traditional compliance-based educational approach was an inappropriate conceptual structure for the practice and evaluation of diabetes patient education. They developed a different approach called "patient empowerment" (98,99). Patient empowerment posits that the purpose of diabetes patient education is to ensure that the choices patients make every day in living with and caring for diabetes are informed choices. This approach assumes that most persons with diabetes are responsible for making important and complex decisions while carrying out the daily treatment of their diabetes. It also assumes that because patients are the ones who experience the consequence of having and treating diabetes, they have both the right and responsibility to be the primary decision makers regarding their own diabetes care.

The knowledge needed to perform self-care falls into two global domains. The first domain is expertise about diabetes. The second domain is psychosocial challenges and skills. The empowerment philosophy is based on the assumption that to be healthy, people need to have the psychosocial skills to bring about changes in their personal behavior, their social situations, and the institutions that influence their lives. These skills play an important role in the development and implementation of a successful diabetes self-care plan that both enhances the patient's health and quality of life. Therefore, diabetes education during pregnancy must address not only blood glucose management but also the psychosocial challenges of a pregnancy complicated by chronic disease (98,99).

Diabetes Education

Patient education is integral to a successful pregnancy complicated by diabetes. The woman must be skilled and knowledgeable to participate fully in the necessary decisions about self-care. The physicians, diabetes educators, and other professionals must form a unified teaching team to assure that the patient has consistent and accurate information. The diabetes health-care team must integrate medical priorities and concerns as well as the woman's abilities, willingness, and readiness into an individualized diabetes education plan.

Providing diabetes self-management education requires attention to patient assessment, individualized instruction, and evaluation of patient response. Teaching and learning are generally divided into three domains: knowledge, psychomotor skills, and affective or attitudinal learning. Before beginning, the educator must assess the woman's attitudes and health beliefs about diabetes and pregnancy. Patients' experience with diabetes or other health problems can shape their attitudes and affect their readiness to learn and apply diabetes self-management skills. The support of families, particularly the father of the baby, can have a significant positive impact on an individual's attitudes and readiness to learn. It is therefore important that the father and other family members be involved in the educational process. Social/cultural and religious beliefs can also influence the patient's interest and willingness to learn and must be considered when developing the educational plan.

Adults are usually self-directed and must feel a need to learn before they are able to participate fully in the educational process (100). Diabetes education is much more rewarding and enjoyable for both the educator and the participant when the participant is an active and committed learner. Practice and rehearsal have been shown to increase the retention of knowledge and skills. Repetition of the performance of a single task builds a person's self-efficacy, which in turn affects task persistence, initiation and endurance, all of which are believed to promote behavior change. Complex behaviors are best broken down into small steps and learned successively. Learning is reinforced by feedback. Making women aware of their incremental progress can encourage continued learning and helps to develop self-efficacy.

In summary, diabetes education is an important component of the care and management for the patient with diabetes. A thorough discussion of complications, risks, and required management should be provided to all diabetic women and their partners so that informed and responsible decisions regarding pregnancy can be made. A sample educational curriculum is presented in Table 5-10. To be most effective, patient education should be thought of as an ongoing process that plays a lifelong role for women with diabetes. All members of the treatment team are teachers, and each contact with the woman is an opportunity to teach or to evaluate the effect of teaching.

Pregnancy can provide the ideal opportunity for education and counseling aimed at motivating the patient to improve long-term diabetes control. Although the establishment of maternal euglycemia has dramatically improved

TABLE 5-10. PATIENT EDUCATION OUTLINE FOR PREGNANT WOMEN WITH DIABETES

I. Prepregnancy counseling
  A. Relationship of diabetes control to congenital malformations
  B. Effect of pregnancy on vascular complications
  C. Appropriate use of contraception
  D. Early identification of pregnancy
II. Patient education: pregnancy
  A. General overview
    1. Effects of diabetes on pregnancy
    2. Effects of pregnancy on diabetes
    3. Relationship of diabetes control to improved perinatal outcome
  B. Review of self-management skills
    1. Nutrition counseling
    2. Exercise
    3. Blood glucose monitoring
  C. Fetal monitoring
    1. Perinatal testing
    2. Fetal movements counts
  D. Preparation for labor and delivery
III. Postpartum teaching
  A. Postpartum glycemic control
  B. Breast-feeding
  C. Birth control
  D. Gestational diabetes
    1. Risk for developing GDM in subsequent pregnancies
    2. Risk for developing overt diabetes
    3. Promotion of healthy lifestyle changes
    4. Annual blood glucose testing

outcomes in pregnancies complicated by diabetes, the benefits of strict metabolic control go far beyond pregnancy. Evidence from the Diabetes Control and Complications Trial suggest that tight glycemic control should be maintained for life (96). This trial conclusively demonstrated that intensive diabetes therapy effectively delays the onset and slows the progression of microvascular complications in patients with type 1 diabetes. For women who have not previously been maintained on intensive therapy regimens, pregnancy may provide the impetus and opportunity to initiate such therapy.

FAMILY PLANNING

Effective contraception, pregnancy planning, and preconception care are all important components of a comprehensive reproductive care program for women with diabetes. Every physician visit offers an excellent opportunity for regular discussions of the need for preconception glucose control and for development of a care plan for future pregnancies.

Prepregnancy Planning

Preconception planning is important to prevent undesired pregnancies and to allow conception to occur only after the achievement of stringent metabolic control. The incidence of congenital anomalies among children of diabetic women is four to ten times higher than among their nondiabetic counterparts. Current evidence suggests that normalization of blood glucose in the preconceptional period and the maintenance of normal glycemic control throughout the critical phase of organogenesis results in a reduced incidence of anomalies. The other advantages of prepregnancy glycemic control include improved cooperation among those involved in the care of these patients, an increased proportion of planned pregnancies, earlier antenatal care, and identification of infertility.

However, despite the data demonstrating the protective effect of strict glycemic control before conception, many women with diabetes still seek medical care only after they learn that they are pregnant. It has been demonstrated that women with diabetes who seek care preconception are more likely to have discussed preconception care with their health-care providers and to have been encouraged to seek this care. It would appear that the emphasis that we as health-care providers place on preconception counseling very likely plays a crucial role in whether or not our female patients seek this care (101). Therefore, health-care providers need to deliver and reinforce this message at every contact with female patients with diabetes of childbearing age. This is especially true for unmarried women of lower socioeconomic status without private physicians, who have been demonstrated to be the least likely to obtain preconception care (101).

Maternal Complications

Women with diabetes are living longer and hence more women with vascular complications are becoming pregnant. The major cause of maternal death has shifted from diabetic ketoacidosis to cardiorenal complications (102). In the past, diabetic women with vasculopathy were counseled to avoid pregnancy or terminate pregnancy if it occurred. New data, however, suggest that with the possible exception of coronary artery disease, women with vasculopathy may be counseled toward more favorable outcomes (103).

The chronic complications of diabetes, however, may in fact be affected by pregnancy. Evidence suggests that pregnancy per se is an independent risk factor that accelerates diabetic retinopathy (104,105). Furthermore, both hyperglycemia and hypertension have been shown to potentiate this acceleration (105,106). This information serves to underscore the importance of women with proliferative retinopathy seeking preconception care and achieving euglycemia before pregnancy. A study published by Reece and colleagues (107) in 20 women with advanced diabetic retinopathy demonstrates that with appropriate contemporary management, satisfactory retinal and perinatal outcomes are possible. None of their patients experienced progressive visual changes that were not amenable to photocoagulation

therapy, and successful perinatal outcomes were reported in 94% of their sample. In addition, there is evidence to suggest that regression of retinal changes is common during the postpartum period (108).

The effect of pregnancy on diabetic nephropathy is less clear but is believed not to accelerate the rate of progression to end-stage renal disease (109–111). However, nephropathy has important implications during pregnancy because of its association with an increased risk for preeclampsia, accelerated hypertension, fetal growth restriction, fetal distress, preterm delivery, and perinatal death. At least in women with mild to moderate renal insufficiency, successful perinatal outcomes are possible with meticulous attention to blood glucose and blood pressure control as well as fetal surveillance (107,110). Diabetic women with vascular disease need sensitive but explicit counseling to make informed decisions regarding their reproductive futures. Because the risk for vascular complications increases with duration of disease, women with pregestational diabetes may not be well advised to delay childbearing until their later years.

Contraceptive Choices

When considering the potential risks of contraception in women with diabetes mellitus, the clinician must also consider the other major alternative, which is a possibly undesired pregnancy. Despite advances in obstetric care and diabetes management, the risks for morbidity and mortality are increased for the woman with diabetes and her offspring. Today, many contraceptive options are available for women with diabetes that do not increase the risk for the vascular complications of diabetes.

The vast majority of the more than 30 formulations of oral contraceptives available on the American market contain various doses of synthetic estrogen and progestin. Most of the preparations are considered to be low dose, containing less than 0.05 mg of ethinyl estradiol or mestranol. The major metabolic side effects of progestins include decreased glucose tolerance as the result of increased peripheral insulin resistance. Also, progestins decrease high-density lipoprotein cholesterol and increase low-density lipoprotein cholesterol. Estrogens, however, increase insulin sensitivity in muscle and adipose cells and favorably alter lipid levels. Therefore, the combinations of estrogen and progesterone in most preparations are thought to balance the metabolic effects of each other (112). Studies in nondiabetic women have demonstrated that low-dose oral contraceptives have little effect on glucose tolerance or serum insulin and glucagon levels (113). Both human (114,115) and animal (116) studies have failed to demonstrate accelerated atherosclerosis with oral contraceptive use or increased risk of myocardial infarction in former oral contraceptive users (117,118).

Low-dose oral contraceptives can be selectively used in women with pregestational diabetes as well as in women with a history of gestational diabetes. Most recent studies of low-dose oral contraceptives in women with diabetes have demonstrated little if any change in glucose tolerance or insulin requirements. Although the data available to evaluate the effect of oral contraceptive use on diabetic complications are limited to retrospective and cross-sectional studies, no association between vasculopathy and prior history or years of oral contraceptive use has been demonstrated.

Diabetic women placed on oral contraceptive therapy should be evaluated after the first cycle of oral contraceptive use and every 3 to 4 months thereafter. Evaluations should include monitoring of weight, blood pressure, lipid levels, postprandial glucose levels, and hemoglobin A_{1c} (112,113). In women with a history of GDM, annual testing for diabetes is recommended regardless of contraceptive method.

Long-acting progestins are currently available on the U.S. market and offer another alternative for the woman with diabetes. Depo Provera (Pharmacia & Upjohn, Peapack, NJ, U.S.A.) is administered as an intramuscular injection every 3 months. Studies in nondiabetic women have demonstrated a statistically significant but not clinically significant deterioration in glucose tolerance.

In the past, intrauterine devices have not been recommended for use in women with diabetes because the potential increased risk for infection was considered unacceptable. However, two subsequent studies evaluating the newer, medicated, copper intrauterine devices did not find an increased risk for pelvic inflammatory disease after the postinsertion period in women with type 1 and type 2 diabetes (119,120). Therefore, women with diabetes who are at very low risk for sexually transmitted disease may consider this additional option. Women should receive antibiotic prophylaxis at the time of insertion and be followed closely to ensure the detection and early treatment of infection (113).

Other options include barrier methods such as the diaphragm, condom, spermicidal jelly or foam, contraceptive sponge, and cervical cap. Because these methods produce no metabolic alterations, they can be used safely in women with diabetes. However, these methods are user dependent and have a much higher failure rate than the previously discussed options. Last, permanent sterilization is a reasonable option for women who have completed their childbearing and desire no more children.

KEY POINTS

■ Our current knowledge thus far has led us to understand that diabetes mellitus is not a single disease. Therefore, its inheritance pattern will be influenced by its heterogeneity as well as its multifactorial origin.

■ Genes within the HLA region contribute to the development of type 1 diabetes. It seems that 60% of the genetic basis of type 1 diabetes is related to the HLA gene locus on chromosome 6 and another 40% is non-HLA associated (i.e., chromosomes 2, 7, 11, and 14).

■ Twin study data demonstrate that type 2 diabetes is transmitted at a higher rate to twins than observed in type 1 diabetes, suggesting a greater genetic contribution in type 2 diabetes. However, the genetic factors involved in this latter group are largely unknown.

■ Genetic counseling for most patients and families should involve a discussion of the empirical risks, followed by recommendations of a lifestyle that will avoid high-risk factors.

■ Multidisciplinary team management has been increasingly accepted as an effective and efficient alternative for the provision of the multidimensional care and support that is demanded by the diabetic pregnancy. This approach emphasizes diabetes education, psychosocial support, and counseling to complement traditional medical management.

■ Active patient participation is essential for the success of a pregnancy complicated by diabetes. Educational approaches that empower women with diabetes to initiate self-directed behavior change will lead to enhanced pregnancy outcomes.

■ A systematic approach to family planning and repeated encouragement by providers of the importance of preconception care must be included as essential components of comprehensive diabetes care.

■ Strict glycemic control in the perinconceptional period and throughout gestation can reduced the risk for congenital malformations, neonatal morbidities, and perinatal mortality.

■ The goal of maintaining normal blood glucose levels throughout pregnancy is the standard of care for pregnancies complicated by diabetes.

■ The achievement of euglycemia requires frequent daily self-blood glucose determinations in both the fasted and postprandial states.

■ Hemoglobin A_{1c} and fructosamine assays are useful indicators of overall glycemic control in the diabetic pregnancy.

REFERENCES

1. Hitman GA. Progress with the genetics of insulin-dependent diabetes mellitus. *Clin Endocrinol* 1986;25:463.
2. National Diabetes Data Group. Classification and diagnosis of diabetes mellitus and other categories of glucose intolerance. *Diabetes* 1979;28:1039.
3. Hollingsworth DR, Resnik R, eds. Medical counseling before pregnancy. New York: Churchill Livingstone, 1988.
4. Gottlieb MS, Root HF. Diabetes mellitus in twins. *Diabetes* 1968;17:693.
5. Tattersall RB, Pyke DA. Diabetes in identical twins. *Lancet* 1972;2:1120.
6. Pyke DA. Diabetes: the genetic connections. *Diabetologia* 1979; 17:333.

7. Barnett AH, Eff C, Leslie RDG, et al. Diabetes in identical twins. *Diabetologia* 1981;20:87.

8. Singal DP, Blajchman MA. Histocompatibility (L-A) antigens, lymphocytotoxic antibodies and tissue antibodies in patients with diabetes mellitus. *Diabetes* 1973;22:429.

9. Sachs D. The majority histocompatibility complex. In: Paul WE, ed. *Fundamental immunology.* New York: Raven, 1984: 303.

10. Zinkernagel RM. Associations between major histocompatibility antigens and susceptibility to disease. *Annu Rev Microbiol* 1979;33:201.

11. Sondel PM. In: Graziano FM, Lemanske RF, eds. *Immunogenetics: the major histocompatibility complex.* Baltimore: Williams & Wilkins, 1989;89.

12. Benacerraf B. Role of MHC gene products in immune regulation. *Science* 1980;212:1229.

13. Gjerset GF, Slichter SJ, Hansen JA. HLA, blood transfusion and the immune system. *Clin Immunol Allergy* 1984;4:503.

14. Scott DW, Dawson JR. *Key facts in immunology.* New York: Churchill Livingstone, 1985.

15. Kaufman JF, Auffray B, Korman AJ, et al. The class II molecules of the human and murine major histocompatibility complex. *Cell* 1984;36:1.

16. Bach FH, Sachs DH. Current concepts: immunology transplantation. *N Engl J Med* 1987;317:489.

17. Lilly T, Boyse EA, Old LJ. Genetic basis of susceptibility to viral leukemogenesis. *Lancet* 1964;2:1207.

18. Falchuk ZM, Rogentine GN, Strober W. Predominance of histocompatibility antigen HLA8 in patients with gluten-sensitive enteropathy. *J Clin Invest* 1972;51:1602.

19. Svejgaard A, Nielsen LS, Svejgaard E, et al. HLA in psoriasis vulgaris and in pustular psoriasis—population and family studies. *Br J Dermatol* 1974;91:145.

20. White SH, Newcomer VC, Mickey MR, et al. Disturbance of HLA antigen frequency in psoriasis. *N Engl J Med* 1972;287:740.

21. Svejgaard A, Platz P, Ryder LP. HLA and disease 1982: a survey. *Immunol Rev* 1983;70:10.

22. Nerup J, Platz P, Anderson OO, et al. HLA-antigens and diabetes mellitus. *Lancet* 1974;2:864.

23. Cudworth AG, Woodrow JC. HLA system and diabetes mellitus. *Diabetes* 1975;24:245.

24. Wolf E, Spencer KM, Cudworth AG. The genetic susceptibility to type I (insulin-dependent) diabetes: analysis of the HLA-DR association. *Diabetologia* 1983;24:224.

25. Sachs JA, Cudworth AG, Jaruquemada D, et al. Type I diabetes and the HLA D locus. *Diabetologia* 1980;418:41.

26. Thompson G. Handbook of experimental immunology. Vol. 10. Oxford, UK: Blackwell Scientific, 1986.

27. Svejgaard A, Platz P, Ryder LP. Insulin-dependent diabetes mellitus. In: Terasaki PI, ed. *Histocompatibility testing.* Los Angeles: UCLA Tissue Typing Laboratory, 1980:638.

28. Thompson G. HLA-DR antigens and susceptibility to insulin-dependent diabetes mellitus. *Am J Hum Genet* 1984;36:1309.

29. Maclaren NK, Henson V. The genetics of insulin-dependent diabetes. *Growth Genet Horm* 1986;2:1.

30. Todd JA. Genetic analysis of susceptibility to type I diabetes. *Springer Semin Immunopathol* 1992;14:33.

31. Kim SJ, Holbeck SL, Nisperos B, et al. Identification of a polymorphic variant associated with HLA-BQW3 and characterized by specific restriction sites within the DQ beta-chain gene. *Proc Natl Acad Sci U S A* 1985;82:8139.

32. Sheehy J, Rowe JR, Nepom BS. Defining the IDDM-susceptible genotype. *Diabetes* 1988;37:91A.

33. Bodner JG, Marsh SGE, Parham P, et al: Nomenclature for factors of the HLA system. *Hum Immunol* 1989;28:326.

34. Todd JA, Bell JI, McDevitt HO. HLA-DQB gene contributes

35. Todd JA, Bell JI, McDevitt HO. A molecular basis for genetic susceptibility to insulin-dependent diabetes mellitus. *Trends Genet* 1988;4:129.

36. Fletcher J, Odugbesan O, Mijovic C, et al. Class II HLA DNA polymorphisms in type I (insulin-dependent) diabetic patients of North Indian origin. *Diabetologia* 1988;31:343.

37. Penny M, Jenkins D, Mijovic CH, et al. Susceptibility to IDDM in a Chinese population: role of HLA class II alleles. *Diabetes* 1992;41(8):914.

38. Jacobs KH, Jenkins D, Mijovic CH, et al. An investigation of Japanese subjects maps susceptibility to type I (insulin-dependent) diabetes mellitus close to the DQA1 gene. *Hum Immunol* 1992;33:53.

39. Todd JA, Fukui Y, Kitagawa T, et al. The A3 allele of the HLA-DQA1 locus is associated with susceptibility to type I diabetes in Japanese. *Proc Natl Acad Sci U S A* 1990;87:1094.

40. Mijovic CH, Jenkins D, Jacobs KH, et al. HLA-DQA1 and DQ3, alleles associated with genetic susceptibility to IDDM in a black population. *Diabetes* 1991;40:748.

41. Jenkins D, Mijovic C, Jacobs KH, et al. Allele-specific gene probing supports the DQ molecule as a determinant of inherited susceptibility to type I (insulin-dependent) diabetes mellitus. *Diabetologia* 1991;34:109.

42. Khalil I, d'Auriol L, Gobet M, et al. A combination of HLA-DQ Asp57-negative and HLA-DQ Arg52 confers susceptibility to insulin-dependent diabetes mellitus. *J Clin Invest* 1990;85:1315.

43. Kockum I, Wassmuth R, Holmberg E, et al. HLA-DQ primarily confers protection and HLA-DR susceptibility in type I (insulin-dependent) diabetes studied in population-based affected families and controls. *Am J Hum Genet* 1993;53:150.

44. MacCuish AC, Barnes EW. Pancreatic islet cell in insulin-dependent disease. *Lancet* 1974;2:1529.

45. Palmer JP, Asplin CM, Clemons P, et al. Insulin antibodies in insulin-dependent diabetics before insulin treatment. *Science* 1983;222:1337.

46. Dobersen MJ, Scharff JE, Ginsberg-Fellner F, et al. Cytotoxic autoantibodies to beta cells in the serum of patients with insulin-dependent diabetes mellitus. *N Engl J Med* 1980;303:1493.

47. Srikanta S, Ganda OP, Rabizadeh A, et al. First-degree relatives of patients with type I diabetes: islet-cell antibodies and abnormal insulin secretion. *N Engl J Med* 1985;313:461.

48. Schwartz RH. T-lymphocyte recognition of antigen in association with gene products of the major histocompatibility complex. *Annu Rev Immunol* 1985;3:237.

49. Sette A, Buus S, Colon S, et al. Structural characteristics of an antigen required for its interaction with 1a and recognition by T cells. *Nature* 1987;328:395.

50. Marrack P, Kappler I. The antigen specific major histocompatibility complex-restricted receptor on T cells. *Adv Immunol* 1986;38:1.

51. Todd JA. Genetic control of autoimmunity in type I diabetes. *Immunol Today* 1990;11:112.

52. Bottazzo GF, Dean BM, McNally JM, et al. *In situ* characterization of autoimmune phenomena and expression of HLA molecules in the pancreas in diabetic insulitis. *N Engl J Med* 1985; 313:353.

53. Risch N. Assessing the role of HLA-linked and unlinked determinants of disease. *Am J Hum Genet* 1987;40:1.

54. Rotter JI, Landau EM. Measuring the genetic contribution of a single locus to multilocus disease. *Clin Genet* 1984;26:529.

55. Field LL, Anderson CE, Neiswanger K, et al. Interaction of HLA and immunoglobulin antigens in type I (insulin-dependent) diabetes. *Diabetologia* 1984;27:504.

56. Rich SS, Weitkamp LR, Guttormsen S, et al. Gm, Km and HLA in insulin-dependent diabetes mellitus: a log-linear analysis of association. *Diabetes* 1986;35:927.

57. Bell GI, Horita S, Karam JH. A highly polymorphic locus near the human insulin gene is associated with insulin-dependent diabetes mellitus. *Diabetes* 1984;33:176.

58. Hitman GA, Tarn AC, Winter RM, et al. Type I (insulin-dependent) diabetes and a highly variable locus close to the insulin gene on chromosome 11. *Diabetologia* 1985;28:218.

59. Tuomilehto-Wolf E, Tuomilehto J, Cepaitis Z, et al. New susceptibility haplotype for type I diabetes. *Lancet* 1989;2:299.

60. Julier C, Hyer RN, Davies J, et al. Insulin-IGF2 region on chromosome 11p encodes a gene implicated in HLA-DR4 dependent diabetes susceptibility. *Nature* 1991;354:155.

61. Concannon P, Wright JA, Wright LG, et al. T cell receptor genes and insulin dependent diabetes mellitus (IDDM): no evidence for linkage from affected sib-pairs. *Am J Hum Genet* 1990;47:45.

62. Millward BA, Leslie RDG, Welsh HI, et al. T-cell receptor beta chain gene polymorphisms are associated with insulin-dependent diabetes in identical twins. *Clin Exp Immunol* 1987;70:152.

63. Field LL, Anderson CE, Neiswanger K, et al. Interaction of HLA and immunoglobulin antigens in type I (insulin-dependent) diabetes. *Diabetologia* 1984;27:504.

64. Field LL. Non-HLA region genes in insulin-dependent diabetes mellitus. *Baillieres Clin Endocrinol Metab* 1991;5:413.

65. Bell JI. Polygenic disease. *Curr Opin Genet Dev* 1993;3:466.

66. Chern MM, Anderson VE, Barbosa J. Empirical risk for insulin-dependent diabetes (IDDM) in sibs: further definition of genetic heterogeneity. *Diabetes* 1982;31:1115.

67. Tillil H, Kobberling J. Age-corrected empirical genetic risk estimates for first-degree relatives of IDDM patients. *Diabetes* 1987;36:93.

68. Thompson G, Robinson WP, Kuhner MK, et al. Genetic heterogeneity, modes of inheritance, and risk estimates for a joint study of Caucasians with insulin-dependent diabetes mellitus. *Hum Genet* 1988;43:799.

69. Wagener DK, Sacks JM, Laporte RE, et al. The Pittsburgh study of insulin-dependent diabetes mellitus: risk for diabetes among relatives of IDDM. *Diabetes* 1982;31:136.

70. Kobberling J, Bruggeboes B. Prevalence of diabetes among children of insulin-dependent diabetic mothers. *Diabetologia* 1980;18:459.

71. Warram JH, Krolewski AS, Gottlieb MS, et al. Differences in risk of insulin-dependent diabetes in offspring of diabetic mothers and diabetic fathers. *N Engl J Med* 1984;311:149.

72. Vadheim CM, Rotter JI, MacLaren NH, et al: Preferential transmission of diabetic alleles within the HLA gene complex. *N Engl J Med* 1986;315:1314.

73. Cahill GF Jr. Heterogeneity in type II diabetes [Editorial]. *West J Med* 1985;142:240.

74. Tattersall RB, Fajans SS. A difference between the inheritance of classical juvenile-onset and maturity-onset diabetes of young people. *Diabetes* 1975;24:44.

75. O'Rahilly S, Spivey RS, Holman RR, et al. Type II diabetes of early onset: a distinct clinical and genetic syndrome? *BMJ* 1987;294:923.

76. Heiervang E, Folling I, Sovik D, et al. Maturity-onset diabetes of the young. Studies in a Norwegian family. *Acta Paediatr Scand* 1989;78:74.

77. Permutt MA, Andreone T, Chirgwin J, et al. The genetics of type I and type II diabetes: analysis by recombinant DNA methodology. *Adv Exp Med Biol* 1985;189:89.

78. Zimmet P, Taft P. The high prevalence of diabetes mellitus in Nauru, a central Pacific island. *Adv Metab Disord* 1978;9:225.

79. Freinkel N, Josimovich J, for the Conference Planning Committee. American Diabetes Association workshop conference on gestational diabetes: summary and recommendations. *Diabetes Care* 1980;3:499.

80. Ober C, Wason CJ, Andrew K, et al. Restriction fragment length polymorphisms of the insulin gene hypervariable in gestational onset diabetes mellitus. *Am J Obstet Gynecol* 1987;157:1364.

81. Freinkel N, Metzger BE, Phelps RL, et al. Gestational diabetes mellitus. Heterogeneity of maternal age, weight, insulin secretion, HLA antigens, and islet cell antibodies and the impact of maternal metabolism on pancreatic B-cell and somatic development in the offspring. *Diabetes* 1985;34:1.

82. Ginsberg-Fellner F, Mark EM, Nechemias C, et al. Islet cell antibodies in gestational diabetics. *Lancet* 1980;2:362.

83. O'Sullivan JB. Subsequent morbidity among gestational diabetic women. In: Sutherland HW, Stowers JM, eds. *Carbohydrate metabolism in pregnancy and the newborn.* Edinburgh: Churchill Livingstone, 1984:174.

84. Freinkel N, Metzger BE. Gestational diabetes: problems in classification and implications for long-range prognosis. In: Vranic M, Hollenberg CH, Steiner G, eds. *Comparison of type I and type II diabetes. Similarities and dissimilarities in etiology, pathogenesis, and complications.* New York: Plenum, 1985:47.

85. Stowers JM, Sutherland HW, Kerridege DR: Long-range implications for the mother: the Aberdeen experience. *Diabetes* 1985;34:106.

86. Powers AC, Eisenbarth GS. Autoimmunity to islet cells in diabetes mellitus. *Annu Rev Med* 1985;36:31.

87. Vardi P, Dib SA, Tuttlemen M, et al. Competitive insulin autoantibody assay. Prospective evaluation of subjects at high risk for development of type I diabetes mellitus. *Diabetes* 1987;36:1286.

88. Ginsberg-Fellner F, Witt ME, Franklin BH, et al. Triad of markers for identifying children at high risk of developing insulin-dependent diabetes mellitus. *JAMA* 1985;254:1469.

89. Tarn AC, Thomas JM, Dean BM, et al. Predicting insulin-dependent diabetes. *Lancet* 1980;1:845.

90. Srikanta S, Ricker AT, McCullock DK, et al. Autoimmunity to insulin, beta cell dysfunction, and development of insulin-dependent diabetes mellitus. *Diabetes* 1986;35:139.

91. Pettit DJ, Aleck KA, Baird HR, et al. Congenital susceptibility to NIDDM. Role of intrauterine environment. *Diabetes* 1988;37:622.

92. Hagay Z, Reece EA, Hobbins JC. Diabetes mellitus in pregnancy and periconceptional genetic counseling. *Am J Perinatol* 1922;9:88.

93. Reece EA, Hagay Z, Hobbins J. Insulin-dependent diabetes mellitus and immunogenetics: maternal and fetal considerations. *Obstet Gynecol Surv* 1991;46:257.

94. Tiwari JL, Terasaki PI. Endocrinology. In: *HLA and disease associations.* New York: Springer-Verlag, 1985:1.

95. Bailey BK, Cardwell MS. A team approach to managing preexisting diabetes complicated by pregnancy. *Diabetes Educ* 1996;22:111.

96. Diabetes Control and Complications Trial Study Group. The effect of intensive treatment of diabetes on the development and progression of long-term complications in insulin dependent diabetes mellitus. *N Engl J Med* 1993;329:977.

97. Diabetes Control and Complications Trial Research Group. The impact of the trial coordinator in the Diabetes Control and Complications Trial (DCCT). *Diabetes Educ* 1993;19:509.

98. Anderson RM. Patient empowerment and the traditional medical model: a case of irreconcilable differences? *Diabetes Care* 1995;18:412.

99. Anderson RM, Funnell MM, Bultler PM, et al. Patient empowerment: results of a randomized controlled trial. *Diabetes Care* 1995;18:943.

100. Walker EA. Characteristics of the adult learner. *Diabetes Educ* 1999;25(suppl 6):16.
101. Janz NK, Herman WH, Becker MP. Diabetes and pregnancy: factors associated with seeking preconception care. *Diabetes Care* 1995;18:157.
102. Marble A, White P, Bradley RF, et al., eds. *Joslin's diabetes mellitus,* 11th ed. Philadelphia: Lea & Febiger, 1971.
103. Reece EA, Homko CJ. Diabetes-related complications of pregnancy. *J Natl Med Assoc* 1993;85:537.
104. Klein BE, Moses SE, Klein R. Effect of pregnancy on progression of diabetic retinopathy. *Diabetes Care* 1990;13:34.
105. Chew EY, Mills JL, Metzger BE, et al. Metabolic control and progression of retinopathy. The diabetes in early pregnancy study. National Institute of Child Health and Human Development Diabetes in Early Pregnancy Study. *Diabetes Care* 1995;18:631.
106. Rosenn B, Midovnik M, Kranias G, et al. Progression of diabetic retinopathy in pregnancy: association with hypertension in pregnancy. *Am J Obstet Gynecol* 1992;166:1214.
107. Reece EA, Lockwood CJ, Tuck S, et al. Retinal and pregnancy outcomes in the presence of diabetic proliferative retinopathy. *J Reprod Med* 1994;39:799.
108. Axer-Siegel R, Hod M, Fink-Cohen S, et al. Diabetic retinopathy during pregnancy. *Ophthalmology* 1996;103:1815.
109. Reece EA, Leguizamon G, Homko C. Pregnancy performance and outcomes associated with diabetic nephropathy. *Am J Perinatol* 1998;15:413.
110. Reece EA, Winn HN, Hayslett JP, et al. Does pregnancy alter the rate of progression of diabetic nephropathy? *Am J Perinatol* 1990;7:193.
111. Reece EA, Leguizamon G, Homko C. Stringent control in diabetic nephropathy associated with optimization of pregnancy outcome. *J Matern Fetal Med* 1998;7:213.
112. Kjos SL. Postpartum care of women with diabetes. *Clin Obstet Gynecol* 2000;43:75.
113. Kjos SL. Contraception in diabetic women. *Obstet Gynecol Clin North Am* 1996;23:243.
114. Peterson KR, Skouby SO, Sidelman J, et al. Effects of contraceptive steroids on cardiovascular risk factors in women with insulin-dependent diabetes mellitus. *Am J Obstet Gynecol* 1994;171;400.
115. Peterson KR, Skouby SO, Sidelman J, et al. Assessment of endothelial function during oral contraception in women with insulin-dependent diabetes mellitus. *Metabolism* 1994;43:1379.
116. Clarkson TB, Shively CA, Morgan TM, et al. Oral contraceptives and coronary artery atherosclerosis of cynomolgus monkeys. *Obstet Gynecol* 1990;75:217.
117. Klein BEK, Moss SE, Klein R. Oral contraceptives in women with diabetes. *Diabetes Care* 1990;13:895.
118. Garg SK, Chase HP, Marshal G, et al. Oral contraceptives and renal and retinal complications in young women with insulin-dependent diabetes mellitus. *JAMA* 1994;271:1099.
119. Kimmerle R, Weiss R, Berger M, et al. Effectiveness, safety, and acceptability of a copper intrauterine device (XCU Safe 300) in type 1 diabetic women. *Diabetes Care* 1993;16:1227.
120. Kjos SL, Ballagh SA, La Cour M, et al. The copper T380A intrauterine device in women with type II diabetes mellitus. *Obstet Gynecol* 1994;84:1006.

PRECONCEPTIONAL CARE OF WOMEN WITH DIABETES

BARAK M. ROSENN
MENACHEM MIODOVNIK

Diabetes mellitus is one of the most common medical disorders of this era, affecting approximately 11 million people in the United States, or 4% of the population. Approximately 90% of these patients have type 2 diabetes and only 10% have type 1 diabetes. In the 18- to 44-year-old group, the prevalence of diabetes is lower, affecting approximately 1.5% of the population, but the representation of type 1 diabetes is disproportionately larger because of the overall tendency of type 1 diabetes to occur at an earlier age. Thus, 1 to 2 of every 100 pregnant women may have preexisting diabetes, and many of these have type 1 diabetes. As more women postpone childbearing to a later stage in their lives, and as techniques of assisted reproduction allow women to conceive well beyond the age of 40, the prevalence of type 2 diabetes among pregnant women is continuously increasing. The current epidemic of obesity and type 2 diabetes among younger Americans exacerbates this phenomenon.

For the woman with diabetes who is planning a pregnancy, two main concerns need to be addressed. First, how will diabetes affect the pregnancy and the health of the infant? Second, how will pregnancy affect the course of the diabetic disease? Additionally, she will want to understand what steps must be taken in order to optimize the outcome of her pregnancy. The purpose of this chapter is to assist the clinician in providing preconceptional care to the woman with diabetes. It will outline how this patient should be evaluated, how to address the patient's concerns regarding the course and outcome of her pregnancy and the effects of pregnancy on diabetes, and how to optimize the preconceptional management of these patients.

GENERAL MATERNAL EVALUATION

Preconceptional or prenatal care should include an evaluation of maternal status with respect to her diabetes and any existing complications. Some patients are highly motivated, visit their physician according to schedule, use their glucose meters on a regular and frequent basis, maintain good glycemic control, adhere to a prescribed diet, and exercise regularly. Unfortunately, most patients do not fall into this category. Many have very poor control of their diabetes, and may be unaware of end organ complications. Furthermore, a significant proportion of the population may actually have undiagnosed glucose intolerance and even overt type 2 diabetes for several years before being diagnosed and treated appropriately. Therefore, evaluation of the patient's status and risk in terms of diabetic complications should include the following components:

1. Evaluation of glycemic control, including hemoglobin A1c concentration and review of daily, self-monitoring of blood glucose concentrations obtained at least five to seven times a day and recorded with a memory glucose meter.
2. Evaluation of blood pressure, including assessment of postural hypotension.
3. Evaluation of renal status: 24-hour urine collection for determination of creatinine clearance and total protein excretion along with serum creatinine and blood urea nitrogen (BUN) concentrations. The possibility of a urinary tract infection should be excluded if proteinuria is present.
4. Evaluation of retinal status, preferably by an ophthalmologist who specializes in retinal disease. Documentation is best accomplished by a written description of findings accompanied by color photographs of the fundi for comparison with later examinations.
5. An EKG should be obtained on all women aged 35 years or older, those with hypertension, nephropathy, or peripheral vascular disease, those who are obese or have hypercholesterolemia, and those who have had diabetes for more than 10 years. Abnormal findings on EKG or suspicious symptomatology should be followed by a stress test.
6. Clinical evaluation of peripheral and autonomic neuropathy, such as sensory loss in the lower extremities, heat intolerance, postural hypotension, and gastroparesis.

7. Clinical evaluation of hypoglycemic symptoms, their frequency, severity, and typical manifestations.
8. Clinical evaluation of peripheral vascular disease.
9. Evaluation of thyroid status (TSH and free T_4) in patients with type 1 diabetes.

Having evaluated the patient's disease status, some prognostication into the expected course of pregnancy and the expected maternal and fetal outcome can be made, and these can be discussed with the patient and her family. It should, however, be appreciated that there are currently many gaps in our knowledge, and much of our clinical practice is guided by subjective experience rather than by objective data. Nevertheless, it is clear that strict glycemic control is the key to optimizing pregnancy outcome, because glycemic control is so closely linked with the risk of potential complications.

CONCEPTION AND EMBRYOPATHY

Does Diabetes Affect a Woman's Ability to Conceive?

A variety of abnormalities in female reproductive function have been described in retrospective studies of women with diabetes. These include delayed menarche and early menopause (1), delayed ovulation, and an increased incidence of menstrual cycle irregularities (2) that may occur with a frequency twice that of control subjects (3). In a retrospective analysis (4), a positive correlation between increased duration of diabetes and later onset of menarche was observed, even when the subject's maternal menarche was taken into account. A survey among women of reproductive age with diabetes (5) found that approximately 20% failed to conceive within 2 years of attempting, a rate that is higher than expected among the nondiabetic population. Failure to conceive was associated with earlier onset of diabetes and with higher daily doses of insulin.

The mechanisms underlying impaired fertility in women with diabetes are not entirely clear. They may be related to abnormal function of the hypothalamic–pituitary axis, such as a decreased luteinizing hormone response to gonadotropin-releasing hormone (6), reductions in basal concentrations of luteinizing hormone and follicle-stimulating hormone (2,7), low thyrotropin concentrations leading to low circulating thyroxine and impaired prolactin synthesis or release (8), or impaired synthesis of corticosterone (9). Diabetes may also modify female reproductive function through the direct effect on insulin-dependent mechanisms of cells in the ovary itself. Indeed, ovarian weights are reduced in rats with alloxan-induced diabetes, possibly because of decreased responsiveness of the ovaries to gonadotropins (10). It has also been observed that granulosa cells isolated from women with diabetes demonstrate impaired insulin-stimulated synthesis of progesterone, even in cases of fair diabetic control (11).

Thus, it appears that the hyperglycemic milieu in diabetes may affect various aspects of reproductive function. Consequently, improvement of glycemic control should, theoretically, increase the rate of conception in these women. Indeed, using life table analysis, we found that our population of women with diabetes had a lower cumulative pregnancy rate at each assessment time point over a 24-month period compared with nondiabetic women. In addition, the rate of conception was higher in women with good glycemic control as assessed by HbA1c concentrations (unpublished data).

Does Diabetes Increase Risk of Early Pregnancy Loss?

Whether women with diabetes have an increased rate of spontaneous abortion (SAB) has been a matter of controversy. A comprehensive review (12) of 58 studies spanning 37 years (1940 to 1988) found an overall rate of 10%, which is probably not different from the rate of SAB in the general population. Most of these studies, however, suffer from methodologic shortcomings that cloud their interpretation. The rate of SAB in prospective, well-designed studies of pregnancies in women with type 1 diabetes has ranged from 15% to 30% (13–16). A recently published large retrospective study from Denmark found that the rate of SAB among women with type 1 diabetes was 17.5% compared to 10% to 12% in the nondiabetic population (17). Several investigators have reported an association between SAB and poor glycemic control in the first trimester, as reflected by higher HbA1c concentrations (13,16,18–20). Further, SAB was related to glycemic control in the period close to conception rather than the period immediately before the abortion itself (21).

The increased risk of SAB in diabetic pregnancies is most likely related to the toxic milieu to which the developing embryo is exposed. This may result in degeneration of the embryo and the appearance of a blighted ovum or in a malformation incompatible with intrauterine life. Other possible mechanisms underlying SAB in the face of poor glycemic control may be abnormal placentation (22) and vascularization (23), and perhaps an increased incidence of chromosomal abnormalities. Whether there is a threshold of hyperglycemia above which the risk of SAB is increased in women with diabetes is a matter of controversy. The Diabetes in Early Pregnancy (DIEP) study (14) demonstrated that increasingly higher first-trimester HbA1c concentrations were associated with increasing rates of SAB with no evidence of a threshold effect. A similar dose-response association between poor glycemic control and fetal wastage was demonstrated by Nielsen et al. (24). A threshold effect has clearly been demonstrated in human pregnancies (19,25–27) and in mice (28), and it is clear that improving glycemic control prior to conception is associated with a lower incidence of SAB (22,29,30).

Does Diabetes Increase Risk of Congenital Malformations?

Congenital malformations (CM) have emerged as the single most important cause of perinatal mortality among infants of mothers with diabetes, accounting for 50% of perinatal deaths, compared with 20% to 30% in infants of nondiabetic mothers (31). Women who have pregestational diabetes (either type 1 or type 2) are at increased risk for having a malformed fetus (32–37). Even women with fasting hyperglycemia first detected during pregnancy, who more likely than not had undiagnosed pregestational diabetes, have an increased incidence of congenital malformations in their offspring (38,39). These observations underscore the notion that a hyperglycemic milieu during embryogenesis is the underlying factor associated with the increased incidence of malformations.

Several studies have established the relationship between CM and poor glycemic control in women with diabetes, demonstrating that higher first-trimester HbA1c concentrations are associated with an increased risk of CM (16,19,40–45). Three studies have also demonstrated a threshold effect of poor glycemic control with respect to the increased risk of CM (19,25,27). The presence of diabetic vasculopathy in the mother has also been associated with an increased risk of CM in some studies (40–42), but not in others (19).

Even though centers specializing in the intensive treatment of pregnant women with diabetes have observed a decline in the incidence of CM since the early 1980s (46,47), the overall incidence of malformations as reported in published surveys remains between 4.2% to 9.4% (16,48–50), several times higher than in the background population. Thus, prevention of major CM in pregnancies in women with diabetes should focus on preconceptional and early postconceptional glycemic control. Clearly, the patient with poor glycemic control and abnormally high blood HbA1c concentrations is at increased risk for having an infant with CM.

In a study by Rosenn et al. (51), minor CM in infants of women with type 1 diabetes were associated with poor glycemic control late in the first trimester and early in the second trimester, corresponding to the late embryonic and early fetal development periods. These observations, however, were not confirmed in a retrospective analysis of diabetic pregnancies (52).

Despite the apparent advantages in achieving good glycemic control before conception, most women with diabetes still conceive before entering a regimen of strict glycemic control. Specialized centers have devoted much effort and resources in an attempt to shift the balance in this paradigm. In addition to the obvious benefits of such an approach in terms of clinical outcome, an analysis of the cost/benefit ratio for preconceptional care demonstrates that intensive medical care before conception results in sig-

nificant cost savings compared with prenatal care only (53,54). These savings are due to fewer hospitalizations during pregnancy and decreased intensity of care and length of stay, both for mothers who received preconceptional care and for their newborn infants.

The desired levels of glycemic control for women with diabetes during the preconceptional period and during pregnancy have not yet been determined. Although there are no specifically defined targets of preconceptional glycemic control derived from prospective, randomized clinical trials, most perinatologists advocate strict glycemic control for these women (see below). Although strict glycemic control is beneficial in terms of pregnancy outcome, these benefits must be weighed against the potential for increased morbidity associated with hypoglycemia in women with type 1 diabetes.

MATERNAL HYPOGLYCEMIA

Does Pregnancy Increase Risk of Maternal Hypoglycemia?

Type 1 diabetes is associated with defective glucose counterregulation and hypoglycemia unawareness (55). Impairment of glucagon secretion from the pancreatic islet alpha cells usually occurs within 5 years of onset of diabetes, although the mechanisms underlying this deficiency are unknown. Many patients, particularly those with long-standing disease of 10 years or more, also manifest a deficient counterregulatory epinephrine response to hypoglycemia: secretion of epinephrine is both delayed (occurs at lower glucose concentrations) and diminished (lower peak epinephrine responses) compared with normal controls (56–58). Defective epinephrine secretion in response to hypoglycemia in these individuals is associated with the syndrome of hypoglycemia unawareness, lack of perceived autonomic responses to hypoglycemia such as palpitations, tremor, and sweating. Consequently, many subjects fail to recognize the impending dangers of falling blood glucose concentrations and do not react to prevent the progression to neuroglycopenia. Once in the altered mental state associated with neuroglycopenia, the ability to recognize this dangerous situation and to take action becomes increasingly difficult, and the patient may deteriorate to a state of seizures, coma, or even death.

In addition to defects in counterregulation that occur as a result of the disease process in diabetes, institution of intensive insulin therapy *per se* may alter the counterregulatory response to hypoglycemia. Indeed, patients with well-controlled diabetes often tolerate subnormal plasma glucose concentrations without any symptoms of hypoglycemia. In such patients, a lower glucose concentration may be required to elicit symptoms and hormonal counterregulatory responses compared to patients who are less strictly controlled (59,60). Thus, a vicious cycle of iatrogenic hypoglycemia is set into motion in patients with type 1 diabetes placed on intensive insulin therapy (61): strict glycemic control predisposes to hypoglycemia, which is most severe in patients with compromised counterregulatory responses and hypoglycemia unawareness. Intensive insulin therapy further compromises counterregulatory responses, and increases the risk of hypoglycemia. The resulting recurrent episodes of hypoglycemia compromise counterregulatory responses even further.

Because pregnant women with type 1 diabetes are commonly treated with intensive insulin therapy, it is not surprising that hypoglycemia is a common complication. In addition to the mechanisms described previously, it has been shown that during pregnancy counterregulatory hormonal responses are diminished even further (62). Indeed, several investigators have reported high rates of moderate and severe hypoglycemia in women with type 1 diabetes treated with intensive insulin therapy during pregnancy. Coustan et al. (63) reported a 72% rate of moderate hypoglycemia and a 46% rate of severe hypoglycemia among 22 pregnant women with type 1 diabetes randomized to insulin pump therapy or intensive conventional insulin. Evers et al. (64) surveyed a cohort of 278 pregnant women with type 1 diabetes and found that the rate of severe hypoglycemia increased from 25% before pregnancy to 41% during the first trimester. In a report by Kitzmiller et al. (65), of 84 women who conceived after attending a preconception clinic, 58% had 1 to 17 hypoglycemic episodes per week during the first 7 weeks of pregnancy. Rayburn et al. (66) reported that 36% of pregnant women with type 1 diabetes had severe symptomatic hypoglycemia during pregnancy, with the peak incidence occurring during sleep between midnight and 8:00 A.M. Similar results were reported by Steel et al. (67). Hellmuth et al. (68) obtained hourly overnight blood glucose concentrations in 43 women during the first trimester, and found that 37% had nocturnal hypoglycemia that was asymptomatic in all but one patient. Kimmerle et al. (69) reported a 41% rate of severe hypoglycemia among their population of 77 women with type 1 diabetes, with most of the episodes occurring during the first half of pregnancy. In a study of 84 pregnant women with type 1 diabetes, Rosenn et al. (70) found that significant hypoglycemia that requires assistance from another person occurred in 71%, with a peak incidence between 10 and 15 weeks. Thirty-four percent of the subjects had at least one episode of severe hypoglycemia resulting in seizures, loss of consciousness, injury, emergency glucagon administration, or intravenous glucose treatment. Of note, Gabbe et al. (71) have reported that a small group of women who used an insulin pump throughout pregnancy had no episodes of severe hypoglycemia, and those who switched to insulin pump therapy during pregnancy had a notable decrease in the incidence of severe hypoglycemia. Thus, insulin pump therapy during pregnancy might help to overcome the oscillations in glucose levels that appear to play a role in the frequency and severity of hypoglycemia.

Can Hypoglycemia Have an Adverse Effect on the Developing Fetus?

Although concerns regarding the hazards of hypoglycemia are primarily related to the pregnant mother with diabetes, the potential effects of maternal hypoglycemia on the developing fetus need to be considered. *In vivo* and *in vitro* studies of rat and mice embryos have demonstrated an association between short- or long-term hypoglycemia and an increased rate of fetal malformations (72–75). However, the impact of maternal hypoglycemia on human fetal development and neonatal outcome has not been extensively studied. An early report on women undergoing psychiatric treatment with insulin shock therapy suggested an association between severe hypoglycemia induced during the first trimester and an adverse pregnancy outcome (76). Since that report, however, not one of the studies involving pregnant women with type 1 diabetes has found any association between maternal hypoglycemia and adverse fetal outcome (63,65–70). In two separate reports, hypoglycemia in the third trimester in women with type 1 diabetes was associated with pathologic changes in fetal baseline heart rate (77) and heart rate variability (78). In clinical studies involving moderate hypoglycemia induced in pregnant women with type 1 diabetes, however, no pathologic changes were observed in fetal behavior or in fetal heart rate (79,80). Rather, Bjorklund et al. (81) demonstrated increased fetal movements and heart rate reactivity, as well as no adverse effects on umbilical artery flow velocity waveforms during moderate hypoglycemia. Lapidot et al. (82) studied fuel utilization in the brains of near-term fetal rabbits under conditions of maternal hypoglycemia. These investigators suggested that in the face of hypoglycemia, the fetal brain is capable of utilizing lactate as a source of energy, rendering the fetus relatively unaffected by maternal hypoglycemia.

ADVANCED DIABETES: MICROVASCULAR AND MACROVASCULAR COMPLICATIONS

Until recently, women with advanced diabetes were frequently advised to avoid pregnancy for fear of aggravating the underlying disease and its complications, as well as resulting in poor perinatal outcome. In reality, many women with advanced diabetes who receive specialized prenatal care, can, in most instances, expect a successful pregnancy without significantly compromising their health or the well-being of their offspring.

DIABETIC NEPHROPATHY

Diabetic nephropathy is a progressive disease that affects 30% to 40% of patients with diabetes and is the most common cause of end-stage renal disease in the United States.

Clinically, diabetic nephropathy progresses through four distinct phases (83). Initially, there is a phase of glomerular hyperfiltration that is manifested by an increased glomerular filtration rate believed to result in renal structural damage. Within a few years, minute amounts of protein appear in the urine, a phase of microalbuminuria, defined variably as 30 to 300 mg of albumin excretion per 24 hours, or 20 to 200 mcg per minute. After a few years, overt nephropathy develops (>300 mg albumin excretion per 24 hours) characterized by excretion of progressively larger amounts of protein. Ultimately, progressive renal insufficiency and end-stage renal disease occur, which manifest as decreasing creatinine clearance, increasing serum creatinine, and uremia. In type 1 diabetes, diabetic nephropathy rarely manifests within the first 10 years of diabetes, but by 30 years, most of the 30% to 40% of those destined to develop nephropathy will already have done so. In patients with type 2 diabetes, microalbuminuria is often present at the time the patient is diagnosed with the disease. In the recent past, progression of nephropathy generally proceeded to end-stage renal disease with creatinine clearance declining at a rate of approximately 10ml/minute every year, so that by the end of 10 years, most patients had reached the stage of renal failure requiring dialysis or renal transplant. Over the past decade, however, it has become clear that the development and progression of nephropathy can be modified by maintaining strict glycemic control (84–87) and by meticulous control of blood pressure (88,89). It is now recommended that blood pressure be maintained below 130/80 mm Hg (90). Furthermore, it has become clear that antihypertensive treatment of patients with nephropathy using angiotensin-converting enzyme inhibitors (ACE inhibitors) or calcium-channel blockers has a beneficiary effect on nephropathy, even in the absence of hypertension (90).

Why Should Pregnancy Affect Nephropathy?

At least four factors that are associated with pregnancy could, hypothetically, increase the risk of nephropathy.

1. During normal pregnancy, there is a 40% to 60% increase in glomerular filtration rate (91). Since it is generally accepted that the primary insult leading to diabetic nephropathy is glomerular hyperfiltration, this could accelerate the development and the progression of nephropathy.
2. Pregnancy-induced hypertension and preeclampsia affect 15% to 20% of all women with diabetes, and an even greater proportion of those with nephropathy (92,93). Because systemic hypertension plays an important role in the progression of nephropathy, hypertensive disorders of pregnancy might be expected to exert a detrimental effect in this context.
3. Because diets with high protein content can result in increased glomerular filtration rates, increased dietary protein intake, such as recommended during pregnancy, may exacerbate glomerular hyperfiltration and accelerate the course of diabetic nephropathy.
4. Because they have adverse effects in pregnancy, ACE inhibitors which may slow the progression of nephropathy, are discontinued in pregnancy.

Conversely, the strict glycemic control that is commonly recommended and instituted during pregnancy may actually have a beneficial effect on nephropathy. Therefore, it is difficult to predict the overall effect of pregnancy on the course of diabetic renal disease. To date, there have been only a few studies involving relatively few pregnant women that have examined the short- and long-term effects of pregnancy on renal function, and most have not included non-pregnant controls.

How Does Pregnancy Affect the Course of Diabetic Nephropathy?

Pregnancy in women with microalbuminuria or overt nephropathy is often associated with a marked increase in proteinuria. This, however, is generally an acute and transient phenomenon. In most cases, even when massive proteinuria develops during pregnancy, it usually subsides after delivery and returns to prepregnancy levels. Of more concern to the patient is an issue that is much more difficult to determine, namely, the ultimate long-term effects of pregnancy on the course of diabetic nephropathy.

To date, ten longitudinal, uncontrolled studies have attempted to address this issue. Because of their design, none of these studies can account for all the possible confounding factors that might affect the outcome, and most studies include a relatively small number of subjects, which explains some of the conflicting conclusions. Seven of these studies (94–99) determined that pregnancy did not alter the expected rate of decline in renal function, while one study (100) concluded that this is true only for women with early mild nephropathy. Two studies have suggested that pregnancy may accelerate the decline in renal function in women with advanced nephropathy, that is, women who have not only proteinuria but also higher serum creatinine concentrations (above 1.4 mg/dL) or decreased creatinine clearance (below 75 ml/minute) (101,102).

Further support for the premise that pregnancy does not alter the course of diabetic nephropathy comes from four cross-sectional studies (103–106) that examined the prevalence of diabetic nephropathy among parous women compared to nulliparous women, and found no differences between the groups. Similarly, two small, prospective, controlled studies (105,107) compared the incidence of diabetic nephropathy among parous women and nulliparous women over a short period of time, and found no differ-

TABLE 6-1. ASSOCIATION OF PREGNANCY WITH THE DEVELOPMENT OF DIABETIC NEPHROPATHY

Authors	No. of Subjects	Follow-Up (mo)	Increased Risk	Type of Study
Carstensen et al., 1982 (106)	22	7–211	No	Cross-sectional
Chaturvedi et al., 1995 (104)	582	NA	No	Cross-sectional
Hemachandra et al., 1995 (105)	80	NA	No	Cross-sectional
Hemachandra et al., 1995 (105)	30	12 (mean)	No	Case control
Miodovnik et al., 1996 (108)	136	36–193	No	Observational
Miodovnik et al., 1998 (107)	23	14–43	No	Prospective

NA, not applicable.

ences between the two. Another large, retrospective study (108) determined that parity has no effect on the development or the progression of diabetic nephropathy.

Taken together, most of the aforementioned studies suggest that pregnancy is not associated with development of nephropathy or with accelerated progression of preexisting nephropathy, but some data suggest that in patients with moderate or advanced renal disease, pregnancy may have a detrimental effect on progression to end-stage renal disease. This fact should be taken into account when counseling this selective group of high-risk patients. These data are summarized in Tables 6-1 and 6-2.

Does Diabetic Nephropathy Affect Pregnancy Outcome?

The presence of diabetic nephropathy significantly affects the outcome of pregnancy, primarily due to the following three factors:

1. Pregnant women with diabetic nephropathy have an increased risk of developing hypertensive complications. Many of these women have preexisting chronic hypertension, and even in those who do not, preeclampsia is a common complication of pregnancy. Although the diagnosis of preeclampsia and superimposed preeclampsia in women who have preexisting proteinuria or hyperten-

sion may be sometimes difficult, it appears that pre-eclampsia develops in up to 50% of women with nephropathy (97,98,100,109–113).
2. In women with nephropathy, there is an increased risk of fetal prematurity due to deteriorating maternal status or fetal jeopardy. Approximately 25% to 30% of these pregnancies are delivered before 34 weeks gestation, and approximately 50% are delivered before 37 weeks (94,96–100,109–113).
3. Fetal distress and fetal growth restriction occur in approximately 20% of pregnancies of women with diabetic nephropathy. Chronic hypertension, decreased creatinine clearance, worsening nephropathy, and superimposed preeclampsia are all associated with this increased risk (94,99).

In general, the worst perinatal outcomes occur in women who have measurable impairment in renal function, with decreased creatinine clearance and increased serum creatinine concentrations. Aggressive control of maternal hypertension is of utmost importance to optimize pregnancy outcome, but the choice of antihypertensive medications is somewhat limited. As noted above, the use of ACE inhibitors during pregnancy is contraindicated due to their potential adverse effects on the fetus. The most widely used medications are methyldopa, nifedipine, and alpha-adrenergic blockers, to maintain a targeted blood pressure in the range of 130/80 mmHg.

TABLE 6-2. ASSOCIATION OF PREGNANCY WITH PROGRESSION OF DIABETIC NEPHROPATHY

Authors	No. of Subjects	Follow-Up (mo)	Accelerated Progression	Progressed to End-Stage Renal Disease
Kitzmiller et al., 1981 (94)	23	9–35	No	3
Dicker et al., 1986 (95)	5	6–12	No	0
Grenfell et al., 1986 (96)	20	6–120	No	2
Reece et al., 1988 (97)	31	1–86	No	6
Reece et al., 1990 (98)	11	10–45	No	0
Kimmerle et al., 1995 (99)	29	4–108	No	8
Gordon et al., 1996 (100)	34	34 (mean)	Yes	3
Purdy et al., 1996 (101)	11[a]	6–138	Yes	7
Mackie et al., 1996 (102)	6[a]	6–96	No	3
Miodovnik et al., 1996 (108)	46	43–182	No	12
Kaaja et al., 1996 (103)	6	84	No	—

[a]Study subjects with moderate renal dysfunction at beginning of follow-up.

During the past 2 decades, survival of infants born to mothers with diabetic nephropathy has been consistently close to 100%. However, the increased rate of prematurity in this population is associated with a higher risk of long-term infant morbidity. Thus, although women with diabetic nephropathy may expect to deliver a viable fetus and take home a reasonably healthy infant, such patients are most likely to have a complicated course of pregnancy, requiring expert care and intensive management.

DIABETIC RETINOPATHY

Diabetic retinopathy is the leading cause of blindness in the United States, and ultimately affects the majority of patients with diabetes. The etiology of diabetic retinopathy is not well understood, but the process involves progression from background retinopathy, with development of capillary microaneurysms, excessive vascular permeability, and the formation of vascular occlusions, to the phase of proliferative retinopathy, with blood vessel proliferation and formation of fibrous tissue, contraction of fibrous tissue and the vitreous, and the onset of hemorrhage leading ultimately to blindness. After 20 years of diabetes, practically 100% of patients who had onset of diabetes before age 30 develop diabetic retinopathy, and approximately 50% of them have proliferative retinopathy. Thus, most pregnant women with early onset type 1 diabetes have some degree of diabetic retinopathy, and some may have already advanced to proliferative disease (114).

The risk of progression from nonproliferative to proliferative diabetic retinopathy (in nonpregnant patients) is directly related to the degree of retinopathy at the time of evaluation: patients who have severe nonproliferative disease have a higher risk of progressing to proliferative retinopathy than patients with mild nonproliferative disease (115). Regular periodic fundal examinations are extremely important in patients with diabetes, because laser photocoagulation is an effective therapy for proliferative retinopathy that can often prevent further progression of the disease. This, in combination with other treatment modalities, such as vitrectomy, has greatly improved the prognosis for patients with diabetic retinopathy.

Why Should Pregnancy Affect Retinopathy?

In the nonpregnant population with diabetes, most studies demonstrate that the presence and severity of retinopathy is related to poor glycemic control (116–118). Moreover, several recent large prospective, randomized clinical trials have demonstrated that intensified glycemic control of diabetes is associated with significantly slower development and progression of retinopathy in patients with type 1 and type 2 diabetes (84,85,119). Since the current consensus is to institute strict glycemic control in pregnant women with diabetes, this is expected to have a beneficial effect on retinopathy. At the same time, other studies have shown that rapid normalization of blood glucose can cause acute progression of retinopathy (120), so that institution of strict glycemic control during pregnancy may actually be associated with deterioration of retinopathy. Nevertheless, recent evidence indicates that, over a longer period of follow-up of up to 4 years, despite rapid initial progression, patients who have been managed with intensive insulin therapy have overall slower progression of retinopathy compared to patients managed less intensively (115).

In addition to institution of strict glycemic control, other changes occurring during pregnancy may affect retinopathy. It has been suggested that circulating and local factors such as growth hormone (121), insulin-like growth factor 1 (122), and other angiogenic factors produced by the placenta in abundance may, theoretically, affect the progression of retinopathy (123). Hypertension has also been consistently linked to the severity of retinopathy. The relation of hypertension to retinopathy may be particularly important during pregnancy because 10% to 20% of women with diabetes develop pregnancy-induced hypertension (92). Indeed, the development of pregnancy-induced hypertension or preeclampsia is associated with an increased risk for progression of retinopathy during pregnancy (124,125). Another theoretical concern related to pregnancy is that the abrupt increases in blood pressure that occur with maternal expulsive efforts during delivery may cause acute retinal hemorrhages in mothers with preproliferative changes. This concern, however, has not been substantiated by the limited available data addressing this issue.

How Does Pregnancy Affect Retinopathy?

Several studies have addressed this question and have reached varying conclusions (124–137). Some of this variance may be attributed to differences in study design and limited follow-up, but taken together, the following conclusions may be drawn:

1. It appears that progression of retinopathy is related to the severity of preexisting disease: women with no background retinopathy or with mild retinopathy are less likely to have progression than those with more advanced retinopathy. Nevertheless, approximately 5% to 10% of patients with no retinal disease or with background retinopathy before pregnancy may develop proliferative retinopathy during pregnancy requiring photocoagulation. It is impossible to determine whether such progression reflects the natural course of their disease and would have occurred even without pregnancy. These findings are summarized in Table 6-3.
2. Several studies have demonstrated that in many patients regression of retinal changes occurs during the postpar-

TABLE 6-3. PROGRESSION OF RETINOPATHY DURING PREGNANCY ACCORDING TO INITIAL RETINAL STATUS

Authors	No. of Pregnancies	No Retinopathy	Background Retinopathy	Proliferative Retinopathy
Horvat et al., 1980 (126)	160	13/118 (11%)	11/35 (31%)	1/7 (14%)
Moloney and Drury, 1982 (127)	53	8/20 (40%)	15/30 (50%)	1/3 (33%)
Dibble et al., 1982 (128)	55	0/23 (0%)	3/19 (16%)	7/13 (54%)
Price et al., 1984 (129)	31	0/14 (0%)	0/10 (0%)	5/7 (71%)
Ohrt, 1984 (130)	100	4/50 (8%)	15/48 (31%)	1/2 (51%)
Jovanovic and Jovanovic 1984 (131)	21	0/0 (0%)	0/11 (0%)	4/10 (40%)
Phelps et al., 1986 (132)	38	3/13 (23%)	13/20 (65%)	5/5 (100%)
Serup, 1986 (133)	45	6/19 (32%)	11/21 (52%)	0/5 (0%)
Rosenn et al., 1992 (124)	154	18/78 (23%)	28/68 (41%)	5/8 (63%)
Chew et al., 1995 (134)	155	4/39 (10%)	31/101 (31%)	—[a]
Axer-Siegel et al., 1996 (135)	65	10/38 (26%)	17/22 (77%)	2/5 (40%)
Lovestam-Adrian et al., 1997 (125)	55	10/39 (26%)	3/14 (21%)	5/12 (42%)[b]
Lapolla et al., 1998 (136)	16	0/9 (0%)	1/7 (14%)	0/0 (0%)
Temple et al., 2001 (137)	179	6/163 (3.7%)	3/10 (30%)	0/6 (0%)
Total	1127	82/623 (13.2%)	151/416 (36.3%)	36/83 (43.4%)

[a]Women with proliferative retinopathy were excluded from the study.
[b]Includes women with severe nonproliferative retinopathy.

tum period. These observations suggest that short-term observations related to pregnancy may not predict the overall long-term effects of pregnancy on diabetic retinopathy.

3. The quality of glycemic control at conception, and the degree of change in glycemic control during pregnancy, reflected in the drop of hemoglobin A_1 concentration, are directly associated with progression of retinopathy. Obviously, these two factors are closely associated, and it is impossible to determine the independent effect of each on the progression of retinopathy. Consequently, it is possible that gradual institution of good glycemic control prior to pregnancy may offer the best opportunity to avoid progression of retinopathy during pregnancy.

4. Progression of retinopathy is more likely to occur in patients with hypertensive disorders. Studies have shown that 50% to 60% of women with chronic hypertension or pregnancy-induced hypertension had progression of retinopathy during pregnancy.

Unlike nephropathy, the presence of retinopathy *per se* does not seem to have an adverse effect on pregnancy outcome. Some women have coexisting retinopathy and nephropathy, but it appears that in these patients, the increased risk of adverse pregnancy outcome is related to the presence of nephropathy and not retinopathy.

HYPERTENSION

Hypertension is a very common comorbidity among the diabetic population, with a prevalence of up to three times higher than that of nondiabetic age-matched groups (138).

The presentation and the natural history of hypertension, however, are different in type 1 and type 2 diabetes. In type 1 diabetes, blood pressure is typically normal at the time of diagnosis and usually remains normal unless albuminuria develops. Hypertension in these patients reflects the development of diabetic nephropathy after several years of disease, and ultimately affects approximately 30% of individuals (139). In type 2 diabetes, hypertension may be present at the time of diagnosis or even before the development of hyperglycemia (140). Although many of these patients have risk factors that are independently associated with hypertension, such as obesity, older age, and African-American ethnicity, the prevalence of hypertension is still 1.5 times higher among the diabetic population even after adjusting for age and weight (140). Epidemiologic evidence indicates that hypertension in individuals with diabetes greatly increases the risks of cardiovascular disease, nephropathy, and retinopathy (141). Aggressive management of hypertension is associated with a significant reduction in cardiovascular disease and mortality (142,143), as well as progression of nephropathy and retinopathy both in patients with type 1 (144,145) and type 2 (142) diabetes. Even though 140/90 mmHg is defined as the threshold of hypertension in the general population, a cutoff point of 130/80 mmHg has been recommended for individuals with diabetes due to the high cardiovascular risk associated with blood pressure above these values (146).

Superimposed preeclampsia in women with chronic hypertension is more common (20%) than preeclampsia in previously normotensive women (7%). In addition, maternal morbidity and mortality are greater in superimposed preeclampsia than in preeclampsia in normotensive women. Furthermore, perinatal morbidity and mortality are significantly higher in infants born to hypertensive mothers, particularly those with proteinuria. There are currently insufficient data to determine whether diabetes confounds the effects of chronic hypertension on the outcome of pregnancy.

In pregnant women with chronic hypertension treated with antihypertensive medications, blood pressure values are usually controlled to no less than 140/90 mmHg in order to maintain adequate placental perfusion, and to decrease the risk of fetal growth restriction. However, in women with diabetes and chronic hypertension, aggressive control of hypertension should be initiated preconceptionally in order to decrease long-term macrovascular and microvascular complications, maintaining blood pressure values below 130/80 mmHg. Whether such aggressive management should be continued during pregnancy is still an unresolved issue that warrants further investigation.

CORONARY ARTERY DISEASE

Women with diabetes have a threefold increased risk of atherosclerosis and fatal myocardial infarction. In women who have preexisting coronary artery disease, the cardiovascular changes associated with pregnancy and delivery can result in inadequate myocardial oxygenation, leading to myocardial infarction and heart failure. Increased cardiac output, decreased systemic vascular resistance with shunting of blood away from the coronary arteries, increased oxygen consumption during physical activity, increased vascular return during uterine contractions, and acute blood loss at delivery may all contribute to an absolute or relative decrease in the ability of the coronary blood flow to meet the demands of the myocardium. Additionally, these women are extremely vulnerable to myocardial damage and pulmonary edema in the immediate postpartum period. After a vaginal delivery, there is an immediate 60% to 80% increase in cardiac output (147) due to release of venocaval obstruction, autotransfusion of utero-placental blood, and rapid mobilization of extravascular fluid, resulting in increased venous return and stroke volume. These fluid shifts are less pronounced after cesarean delivery using controlled analgesia.

Of particular concern in these patients are the consequences of hypoglycemia. As mentioned previously, institution of strict glycemic control in pregnant women with type 1 diabetes is associated with a significant risk of hypoglycemia, primarily during the first half of pregnancy. Activation of the counterregulatory responses to hypoglycemia will cause release of catecholamines, resulting in tachycardia, possible arrhythmia, and increased demands on the myocardium. These changes are particularly hazardous in a patient with underlying coronary artery disease and may result in an acute myocardial infarction.

Diabetic Coronary Artery Disease and Outcome of Pregnancy

The information in the medical literature concerning pregnancy in women with diabetes and coronary heart disease is limited, and is composed primarily of case reports (148–161). To our knowledge, there have been 20 cases reported in the literature between 1953 and 1998, of mothers with diabetes who suffered a myocardial infarction (MI) or ischemic cardiac event before, during, or shortly after pregnancy. Among the 13 women whose event occurred during pregnancy or in the puerperium, 7 mothers and 7 infants died. Among the 7 women whose myocardial event occurred prior to pregnancy, all of the mothers and infants survived. The difference in outcome between women who had a MI prior to pregnancy and those who had a MI during pregnancy or the puerperium, may reflect the cardiovascular demands of pregnancy, but might also be due to selection bias: it is possible that the pregnant women with a prior MI had only minimal or no preexisting cardiac dysfunction prior to pregnancy. It is also noteworthy, that prior to 1980, the overall maternal mortality rate was 70% (7 out of 10 women), while among cases reported after 1980, the mortality rate has dropped to 0% (0 out of 10). This may reflect improved care, heightened awareness of the risks associated with these pregnancies, better counseling for women with diabetic coronary artery disease, or reporting bias of unexpectedly successful outcomes despite preexisting coronary artery disease.

DIABETIC NEUROPATHY

Little, if anything, is known about the effects of diabetic neuropathy on pregnancy and the possible effects of pregnancy on neuropathy. Some studies suggest that a short-term increase in the incidence of polyneuropathy may occur in association with pregnancy, but that in the long term, pregnancy does not lead to an increase in the prevalence of this complication (104,105).

The presence of autonomic neuropathy with gastroparesis is particularly relevant to pregnancy in that, with the hyperemesis of pregnancy, it results in exacerbation of nausea and vomiting. This may result in irregular absorption of nutrients, inadequate nutrition, and aberrant glucose control. Exacerbation of autonomic neuropathy during pregnancy has been reported by some authors (162,163), whereas others have noticed transient improvement in symptoms during pregnancy (164). Overall, it seems that pregnancy does not alter the natural course of diabetic autonomic neuropathy (165), a complication associated with severe morbidity and mortality. From the few reported cases of pregnancy in women with autonomic neuropathy, it may be concluded that, although a successful outcome of the pregnancy is possible, there is a significant risk of maternal morbidity.

DIABETES MELLITUS AND OBSTETRIC COMPLICATIONS

Does Diabetes Increase the Risk of Preeclampsia?

Diabetes mellitus has long been considered a risk factor for the development of preeclampsia. The rate of preeclampsia in women with diabetes is generally accepted as being higher than the 5% to 7% rate in the general population (166). Cousins (92) reviewed the English literature from 1965 to 1985 and reported that the incidence of preeclampsia was highly correlated with advanced White class, with an average rate of 15.7% in classes B to RF. A similar correlation of preeclampsia with White class was found by Jervell et al. (167) and by Diamond et al. (168). Hiilesmaa et al. (169) followed 683 pregnant women with type 1 diabetes and found that preeclampsia developed in 12.8% (excluding those with nephropathy) compared to 2.7% among 854 nondiabetic controls. Poor glycemic control, nulliparity, retinopathy, and duration of diabetes were independent predictors of preeclampsia. In a prospective study involving 491 women with type 1 diabetes, Hanson and Persson (170) found a 21% rate of preeclampsia or pregnancy-induced hypertension (PIH), a fourfold increase compared with the general population in Sweden. The frequency of preeclampsia/PIH increased progressively with advanced White class. Similarly, Reece et al. (40) reported that acute hypertensive complications occurred in 51.6% of pregnant women with diabetic microvascular disease, compared with 32.9% among those without microvascular disease. Specifically, in women with diabetic nephropathy, most authors report a high incidence of preeclampsia/PIH or superimposed preeclampsia, in excess of 30% (94,96,97,99,100,109–113).

An association between preeclampsia and poor glycemic control has been reported by several authors: Sibai et al. (171) found that among a group of 462 pregnant women with preexisting diabetes, the rate of preeclampsia was 20%, and this complication was significantly more common among those with microvascular disease. Hsu et al. (172) found a 32.5% rate of preeclampsia among 123 pregnant women with type 1 diabetes, associated with high HbA1c levels at any time during pregnancy. Reducing HbA1c by improving glycemic control both before and during pregnancy resulted in a significantly lower incidence of preeclampsia. In a later publication (173), the same authors reported that 45% of the women with high HbA1c (>8%) levels had preeclampsia, compared with 24% of women with normal HbA1c levels. Specifically, preeclampsia was strongly associated with high HbA1c levels between 16 and 20 weeks gestation.

Siddiqi et al. (174) found that the rate of PIH in a study population of 175 women with type 1 diabetes was 15.4% and was significantly associated with nulliparity, poor glycemic control in the first and second trimesters, and advanced White class. Similarly, Hanson et al. (175) found a 20.6% rate of PIH/preeclampsia among their population of 491 women with type 1 diabetes, compared with 5% among the background population, and found that PIH/preeclampsia was significantly associated with longer duration of diabetes, higher initial HbA1c in pregnancy, and presence of microvascular disease.

Despite the abundance of data pointing to an increased incidence of preeclampsia among pregnant women with diabetes and to an association with advanced disease and poor glycemic control, some authors have reported conflicting findings. Gabbe et al. (176) found no significant increase in the incidence of PIH among patients with diabetes (13% vs. 10% in the general population in their report) and no increase of PIH in White classes D to R. In a small series reported by Coustan et al. (177), the incidence of PIH was 5.5%. Kitzmiller et al. (178) reported PIH in 5% of their patients with diabetes, not significantly different from the 3.8% rate of PIH in their general nondiabetic population. Martin et al. (179) reported a 20% incidence of PIH in diabetes (twice that in the general population in their report) but found no correlation with glycemic control. These apparently conflicting findings may be due, at least in part, to methodologic discrepancies.

Few studies have examined the association of microalbuminuria and preeclampsia. Combs et al. (180) observed an increased risk of preeclampsia if microalbuminuria exceeded 190 mg protein per 24 hours. Similarly, Ekbom et al (181) noted that microalbuminuria prior to pregnancy is the strongest predictor of preeclampsia in type 1 diabetes.

It is unclear why diabetes affects the risk of preeclampsia. Although the etiology of preeclampsia has yet to be elucidated, it seems to involve compromise of the normal process of adaptation of maternal vasculature in pregnancy. Poor glycemic control in women with diabetes during pregnancy may be associated with restriction of the normally occurring physiologic vascular changes and consequently with the development of preeclampsia. The association between preeclampsia and advanced White class may be related to the pathophysiologic process of microvascular disease. This process may involve autoregulative and adaptive mechanisms of the maternal vasculature in pregnancy, thus predisposing the mother to preeclampsia.

Does Diabetes Increase the Risk of Preterm Delivery?

Preterm labor leading to the delivery of a preterm, low birth weight infant remains one of the foremost obstetric problems worldwide. Preterm delivery occurs in approximately 10% to 11% of all pregnancies in the United States, accounting for more than 75% of all perinatal morbidity and mortality (182). Conflicting data exist regarding the incidence of spontaneous premature labor in pregnancies complicated by diabetes: similar rates (177), as well as increased (170,183) or decreased (184) rates, have been reported. Published studies are confounded by the high rate of iatrogenic prematurity in these pregnancies. Even as late as the 1970s, premature delivery was advocated for infants of mothers with diabetes because of the risk of intrauterine fetal death, especially after the 37th week of gestation (185). Improved techniques for antepartum fetal surveillance, however, as well as meticulous glycemic control, have decreased the risk of intrauterine demise. Consequently, the incidence of iatrogenic prematurity in pregnancies among women with diabetes has also declined.

Greene et al. (186) reported that 26.2% of women with type 1 diabetes delivered before 37 completed weeks of gestation, compared with 9.7% of nondiabetic women. Preeclampsia was the most significant risk factor associated with premature delivery. Compared with the general population, most of the excess risk of prematurity in mothers with diabetes was confined to patients with hypertension or advanced White class. Reece et al. (40) found no association between preterm labor and microvascular disease, but noted that preterm delivery was more common among women in poor metabolic control during the third trimester (31%) than in women with satisfactory control (11%). Similarly, Rosenn et al. (93) observed that 30% of women with type 1 diabetes delivered before 37 weeks gestation, and 9.4% delivered before 34 weeks, compared with 12% and 5.3%, respectively, in the nondiabetic population. In this study, improved glycemic control was associated with a lower risk of premature delivery. Kovilam et al. (187) found that each increment of 1% in the glycohemoglobin concentration during pregnancy conveyed a 37% increase in the risk of preterm delivery. In a large prospective observational study that included 461 women with pregestational diabetes and 2738 controls, Sibai et al (188) documented that women with diabetes had significantly higher rates of both spontaneous (16.1% vs. 10.5%) and indicated (21.9% vs. 3.4%) preterm delivery compared to controls. Weiss et al. (189) measured cord blood levels of insulin in newborn infants of mothers with diabetes, and found that among infants with high cord blood insulin levels the rate of preterm delivery was 71%, compared with 5% among infants with normal levels.

The association of preterm labor with poor glycemic control is an observation that eludes a straightforward rationale. Although the etiology of preterm labor has yet to be determined, it is possible that various pathophysiologic conditions may act independently toward a common mechanism, such as local release of prostaglandins in uterine muscle, resulting in preterm labor. Prostaglandin production is increased in platelets from patients with diabetes (190), but there are no data suggesting increased production of prostaglandins in the uterus or amnion of the diabetic pregnancy. Furthermore, it is impossible to exclude the possibility that patients with poor glycemic control are also those in whom behavioral and other factors may increase the risk of preterm labor.

Does Diabetes Increase the Risk of Polyhydramnios?

Polyhydramnios is considered a frequent complication of diabetic pregnancy. In a review by Cousins (92), the overall incidence of polyhydramnios was 17.6% in patients with White classes B and C and 18.6% in patients with classes D, R, and F. High rates of polyhydramnios were also reported by Lufkin et al. (191) (29% compared with 0.9% in control subjects) and by Kitzmiller et al. (178) (31%). Rosenn et al. (93) found that the rate of polyhydramnios was 26.4% among women with type 1 diabetes, compared with 0.6% in control subjects. Polyhydramnios was associated with poor glycemic control throughout the entire pregnancy, especially during the first two trimesters. Similarly, Reece et al. (40) observed polyhydramnios in 17% of women with poor third trimester metabolic control, compared to 1% among adequately controlled women.

Although the diagnosis of polyhydramnios is subject to observer bias, the use of the amniotic fluid index (192) in sonography improves the objectivity of data on amniotic fluid volume in diabetic and nondiabetic pregnancies. The observed rate of polyhydramnios in control populations may be an underestimation of the true rate because women with uncomplicated pregnancies do not usually undergo sonographic examinations as frequently as pregnant women with diabetes. It is unclear why polyhydramnios is more common in women with diabetes and why it is associated with poor glycemic control. Polyhydramnios in these circumstances may be related to an increased glucose content in the amniotic fluid, creating an osmotic pressure that, with equilibration, results in an increased volume of amniotic fluid. In addition, if maternal hyperglycemia is associated with fetal hyperglycemia, this could be associated with fetal polyuria and, hence, cause polyhydramnios. Whether this is indeed the case remains to be determined. In at least one report, increased amniotic fluid volume was not associated with increased output of fetal urine measured sonographically (193).

Does Diabetes Increase the Risk of Infectious Morbidity?

Patients with diabetes are at high risk for infection (194). Several deficiencies in the immune mechanism involving defective leukocyte and lymphocyte activity may explain a propensity to infection (195–197). These abnormalities appear to be linked to poor glycemic control (198,199). Pregnancy is also generally thought to constitute a state of relative immune deficiency, specifically, impaired cell-mediated immunity (200). Thus, pregnancy in the patient with diabetes is likely to represent an additional risk factor for infection.

There are few studies on the rate of specific infections in diabetic pregnancies. Vejlsgaards (201) reported an increased incidence of urinary tract infection in gravid women with diabetes compared with nondiabetic gravid women. In a study restricted to postpartum infections, Diamond et al. (202) also observed an increased rate of postpartum wound infection, endometritis, or both in pregnant women with diabetes. Cousins (92), in his meta-analysis, found that pyelonephritis was reported in 2.2% of pregnant women with class B and C diabetes and in 4.9% of women with class D, F, and R. Pedersen and Molsted-Pedersen (203) found that pyelonephritis was more common among class F women and stated that this condition is associated with increased perinatal mortality.

Glycemic control was not evaluated in the aforementioned studies, but Rayfield et al. (204) demonstrated a direct correlation between the overall prevalence of infection and the mean plasma glucose concentration. Stamler et al. (205) found that 83% of women with type 1 diabetes had at least one episode of antenatal infection, compared with 26% of nondiabetic women. The rate of postpartum infection was five times higher in women with diabetes, and they were susceptible to more kinds of infections.

MANAGEMENT GUIDELINES FOR PRECONCEPTION CARE

Using a multidisciplinary approach that includes a diabetes nurse educator, nutritionist, and physician, glycemic control should be achieved by the use of an appropriate meal plan, self-monitoring of blood glucose (fasting before and after meals and at bedtime) using a reflectance meter equipped with memory, self-administration and ongoing adjustment of insulin, and a program of regular physical exercise. Patients with type 1 diabetes may require more frequent determination of blood glucose concentrations, including at 2 to 3 A.M., to avoid episodes of hypoglycemia. Improvement of glycemic control should be achieved in a gradual manner, minimizing the risks of hypoglycemia and exacerbation of retinopathy. Women with type 2 diabetes treated with oral hypoglycemic agents pose a specific dilemma: Although these medications have not been found to increase the risk of congenital malformations, there are only data on their safety in early pregnancy. Therefore, most

practitioners convert from oral hypoglycemic agents to insulin therapy in these patients. During this phase of glycemic control, the patient should be using an effective method of birth control to avoid an unplanned pregnancy. Ultimately, the levels of pre- and post-prandial glucose concentrations outlined in Table 6-4 should be achieved.

Insulin therapy should be adjusted to achieve these levels of glycemia control. This usually involves three to four injections of insulin a day, comprised of various combinations of rapid-, short-, and intermediate-acting insulins.

The patient should be followed on a regular and frequent basis, and should have feedback on her glycemic control at least every 1 to 2 weeks. Assessment of overall glycemic control can be achieved by measuring HbA1c and obtaining the weekly or bi-weekly average glucose concentration from the glucose meter. Once the vast majority of glucose measurements are within the desired range and the concentration of HbA1c has decreased to no more than 1% above the upper limit of normal, the patient should be encouraged to conceive. Failure to conceive within 6 months should prompt a referral to a reproductive endocrinologist for evaluation of infertility.

Women who are using ACE inhibitors should be allowed to continue their medications until pregnancy has been confirmed. Every effort should be made to diagnose pregnancy as early as possible so that the use of these medications may be discontinued.

Based on the observations reviewed in the previous sections, several general guidelines can serve as a basis for the management of women with diabetic nephropathy or microalbuminuria (Table 6-5); diabetic retinopathy (Table 6-6); and diabetic coronary artery disease (Table 6-7), which continues to be extremely hazardous despite recently published encouraging results of pregnancy outcome.

KEY POINTS

- Preconceptional evaluation of a woman with diabetes should include evaluation of glycemic control, blood pressure, retinal disease, renal status, thyroid function, ischemic heart disease, peripheral and autonomic neuropathy, peripheral vascular disease, and hypoglycemic symptoms.
- The key to improving outcome of pregnancy in women with diabetes is strict glycemic control. Women with dia-

TABLE 6-4. GOALS FOR SELF-MONITORED GLYCEMIC CONTROL

	Capillary Whole-Blood Glucose	Capillary Plasma Glucose
Fasting	<95 mg/dL (<5.3 mmol/L)	<105 mg/dL (<5.8 mmol/L)
Before meals	70–100 mg/dL (3.9–5.6 mmol/L)	80–110 mg/dL (4.4–6.1 mmol/L)
1 h after meals	<120 mg/dL (<6.7 mmol/L)	<135 mg/dL (<7.5 mmol/L)
2 h after meals	<140 mg/dL (<7.8 mmol/L)	<155 mg/dL (<8.6 mmol/L)

TABLE 6-5. GUIDELINES FOR MANAGEMENT OF WOMEN WITH DIABETIC NEPHROPATHY

■ Initial evaluation of the patient should be performed as outlined in the section on evaluation at the beginning of this chapter. If serum creatinine is 1.5 mg/dL or above, or if creatinine clearance is 75 ml/min or less, the patient and her family should be advised that the risk of maternal and fetal complications is high, and that it is possible pregnancy will accelerate progression of nephropathy towards end/stage renal disease. The physician should make every effort to ensure that the patient fully comprehends the significance of these risks.

■ Patients with hypertension should be managed aggressively to maintain blood pressure values under 130/80 mmHg. Patients with chronic hypertension who are treated with ACE inhibitors should be switched to an alternative medication as soon as the pregnancy test becomes positive. Methyldopa can be used at doses of up to 3 gm/d, and nifedipine or beta-adrenergic blockers can be used when control of blood pressure cannot be achieved with methyldopa.

■ A 24-h collection of urine should be obtained at the first prenatal visit and at least once each trimester for determination of total protein content and creatinine clearance. A urine culture should be obtained simultaneously to rule out the coexistence of a urinary tract infection. Proteinuria may often increase during pregnancy to nephrotic ranges, but will usually subside following delivery, and is not, in itself, an indication for delivery. In the presence of massive proteinuria, serum albumin levels should be monitored. Peripheral edema often becomes a severe problem that requires supportive management.

ACE, angiotensin-converting enzyme.

betes should be urged to seek counseling and achieve good glycemic control prior to conception.

■ Strict preconceptional and periconceptional glycemic control can minimize the excess risks of spontaneous abortion and congenital malformations in diabetic pregnancies.

■ Most women with type 1 diabetes experience an exacerbation of hypoglycemic symptoms during pregnancy, particularly during the first few months.

TABLE 6-6. GUIDELINES FOR MANAGEMENT OF WOMEN WITH DIABETIC RETINOPATHY

■ Whenever possible, women with diabetic retinopathy should be encouraged to obtain preconceptional ophthalmologic evaluation prior to pregnancy. Preconceptional management also allows gradual institution of strict glycemic control prior to pregnancy that may decrease the risk of progression related to abrupt glycemic control.

■ Women with proliferative retinopathy should undergo phototherapy and other treatment prior to pregnancy, and not conceive before the proliferative process has been completely stabilized.

■ During the preconceptional control period and during pregnancy, any complaints related to changes in vision should be addressed immediately by referring the patient to an ophthalmologist.

TABLE 6-7. GUIDELINES FOR MANAGEMENT OF WOMEN WITH DIABETIC CORONARY ARTERY DISEASE

■ Preconceptional evaluation should include a thorough evaluation by a cardiologist to determine the extent of coronary artery disease and myocardial function.

■ Following initial evaluation, either preconceptionally or as early in pregnancy as possible, the patient should be made aware of the serious maternal risks associated with pregnancy. The risk of maternal death should be explicitly discussed with the patient and her family. It is impossible to quantify this risk but it is most likely related to the degree of cardiac dysfunction.

■ The option of termination of pregnancy should be specifically discussed with the patient and her partner.

■ Every effort should be made to attain adequate glycemic control without risking hypoglycemia. Targets of glycemic control should be adjusted in those patients who have a history of frequent hypoglycemia, or who experience hypoglycemic episodes during pregnancy.

■ The patient should be counseled that she will need to deliver at a tertiary care center.

■ A method for permanent sterilization should be discussed with the patient well in advance, so that the procedure might be performed following delivery.

■ Hypoglycemia does not appear to have adverse effects on the developing fetus.

■ Most studies suggest that pregnancy is not associated with development of nephropathy or with accelerated progression of preexisting mild nephropathy.

■ In patients with moderate or advanced renal disease, pregnancy may have a detrimental effect on progression to end-stage renal disease.

■ Impaired renal function, particularly when complicated by hypertension, is associated with an increased risk of prematurity and adverse perinatal outcome.

■ Progression of retinopathy during pregnancy is related to the severity of preexisting disease, is more likely to occur in patients with hypertensive disorders, and is likely to regress during the postpartum period.

■ The quality of glycemic control at conception and the degree of change in glycemic control during pregnancy are directly associated with progression of retinopathy.

■ In women with diabetes and chronic hypertension, aggressive control of hypertension should be initiated preconceptionally in order to decrease long-term macrovascular and microvascular complications.

■ There is a high risk of maternal mortality in pregnant women with ischemic heart disease, particularly during the immediate postpartum period.

■ Maternal diabetes appears to increase the risk of several major obstetric complications, including preeclampsia, premature labor, polyhydramnios, and infectious complications.

■ Poor maternal glycemic control is directly correlated with the increased risk of obstetric complications.

REFERENCES

1. Bergqvist N. The gonadal function in female diabetics. *Acta Endocrinol (Copenhagen)* 1954;19:1.
2. Djursing H, Nyholm HC, Hagen C, et al. Clinical and hormonal characteristics in women with anovulation and insulin-treated diabetes mellitus. *Am J Obstet Gynecol* 1982;143:876.
3. Kjaer K, Hagen C, Sando SH, et al. Infertility and pregnancy outcome in an unselected group of women with insulin-dependent diabetes mellitus. *Am J Obstet Gynecol* 1992;166:1412.
4. Chitkara VK, Biro FM, Franklin A, et al. Duration of diabetes delays onset of menarche. *Adolesc Med* 1991;7:4a.
5. Briese V, Muller H. Diabetes mellitus: an epidemiologic study of fertility, contraception and sterility. *Geburtshilfe Frauenheilkd* 1995;55:270.
6. Kirchick HJ, Keyes PL, Frye BE. An explanation for anovulation in immature alloxan-diabetic rats treated with pregnant mare's serum gonadotropin: reduced pituitary response to gonadotropin releasing hormone. *Endocrinology* 1979;105:1343.
7. Djursing H, Hagen C, Nyholm HC, et al. Gonadotropin responses to gonadotropin-releasing hormone and prolactin responses to thyrotropin-releasing hormone and metoclopramide in women with amenorrhea and insulin-treated diabetes mellitus. *J Clin Endocrinol Metab* 1983;56:1016.
8. Djursing H, Nyholm HC, Hagen C, et al. Depressed prolactin levels in diabetic women with anovulation. *Acta Obstet Gynecol Scand* 1982;61:403.
9. Valdes CT, Elkind-Hirsch KE, Rogers DG. Diabetes-induced alterations of reproductive and adrenal function in the female rat. *Neuroendocrinology* 1990;51:406.
10. Liu TYF, Lin HS, Johnson DC. Serum FSH, LH, and the ovarian response to exogenous gonadotropins in alloxan diabetic immature female rats. *Endocrinology* 1972;91:1172.
11. Diamond MP, Lavy G, Polan ML. Progesterone production from granulosa cells of individual human follicles derived from diabetic and non-diabetic subjects. *Int J Fertil* 1989;34:204.
12. Kalter H. Diabetes and spontaneous abortion: a historical review. *Am J Obstet Gynecol* 1987;156:1243.
13. Miodovnik M, Skillman C, Holroyde JC, et al. Elevated maternal glycohemoglobin in early pregnancy and spontaneous abortion among insulin-dependent diabetic women. *Am J Obstet Gynecol* 1985;153:439.
14. Mills JL, Simpson JL, Driscoll SG, et al. Incidence of spontaneous abortion among normal women and insulin-dependent diabetic women whose pregnancies were identified within 21 days of conception. *N Engl J Med* 1988;319:1617.
15. Miodovnik M, Mimouni F, Tsang RC, et al. Glycemic control and spontaneous abortion in insulin-dependent diabetic women. *Obstet Gynecol* 1986;68:366.
16. Casson IF, Clarke CA, Howard CV, et al. Outcomes of pregnancy in insulin dependent diabetic women: results of a five year population cohort study. *BMJ* 1997;31:275.
17. Lorenzen T, Pociot F, Johannesen J. A population-based survey of frequencies of self-reported spontaneous and induced abortion in Danish women with type 1 diabetes mellitus. Danish IDDM Epidemiology and Genetics Group. *Diabetic Med* 1999;16:472.
18. Mills JL, Knopp RH, Simpson JL, et al. Lack of relation of increased malformation rates in infants of diabetic mothers to glycemic control during organogenesis. *N Engl J Med* 1988;318:671.
19. Greene MF, Hare JW, Cloherty JP, et al. First-trimester hemoglobin A1 and risk for major malformation and spontaneous abortion in diabetic pregnancy. *Teratology* 1989;39:225.
20. Wright AD, Nicholson HO, Pollock A, et al. Spontaneous abortion and diabetes mellitus. *Postgrad Med J* 1983;59:295.
21. Mimouni F, Tsang RC. Pregnancy outcome in insulin-dependent diabetes: temporal relationships with metabolic control during specific pregnancy periods. *Am J Perinatol* 1988;5:334.
22. Rosenn B, Miodovnik M, Combs CA, et al. Preconception management of insulin-dependent diabetes: improvement of pregnancy outcome. *Obstet Gynecol* 1991;77:846.
23. Bendon RW, Mimouni F, Khoury J, et al. Histopathology of spontaneous abortion in diabetic pregnancies. *Am J Perinatol* 1990;7:207.
24. Nielsen GL, Sorensen HT, Nielson PH, et al. Glycosylated hemoglobin as predictor of adverse fetal outcome in type 1 diabetic pregnancies. *Acta Diabetol* 1997;34:217.
25. Rosenn B, Miodovnik M, Combs CA, et al. Glycemic thresholds for spontaneous abortion and congenital malformations in insulin-dependent diabetes mellitus. *Obstet Gynecol* 1994;84:515.
26. Mello G, Parretti E, Mecacci F, et al. Glycemic thresholds in spontaneous abortion during the first trimester in pregnant women with insulin dependent diabetes. *Minerva Ginecol* 1997;49:365.
27. Hanson U, Persson B, Thunell S. Relationship between haemoglobin A$_{1c}$ in early type 1 (insulin-dependent) diabetic pregnancy and the occurrence of spontaneous abortion and fetal malformation in Sweden. *Diabetologia* 1990;33:100.
28. Torchinsky A, Toder V, Carp H, et al. In vivo evidence for the existence of a threshold for hyperglycemia-induced major fetal malformations: relevance to the etiology of diabetic teratogenesis. *Early Pregnancy* 1997;3:27.
29. Dicker D, Feldberg D, Samuel N, et al. Spontaneous abortion in patients with insulin-dependent diabetes mellitus: the effect of preconceptional diabetic control. *Am J Obstet Gynecol* 1988;158:1161.
30. Miodovnik M, Mimouni F, Siddiqi TA, et al. Spontaneous abortions in repeat diabetic pregnancies: a relationship with glycemic control. *Obstet Gynecol* 1990;75:75.
31. Kalter H. Perinatal mortality and congenital malformations in infants born to women with insulin-dependent diabetes mellitus: United States, Canada and Europe, 1940–1988. *MMWR Morb Mortal Wkly Rep* 1990;39:363.
32. Kucera J. Rate and type of congenital anomalies among offspring of diabetic women. *J Reprod Med* 1971;7:61.
33. Becerra JE, Khoury MJ, Cordero JF, et al. Diabetes mellitus during pregnancy and the risks for specific birth defects: a populations-based case-control study. *Pediatrics* 1990;85:1.
34. Cousins L. Congenital anomalies among infants of diabetic mothers: etiology, prevention, prenatal diagnosis. *Am J Obstet Gynecol* 1983;147:333.
35. Schaefer-Graf UM, Buchanan TA, Xiang A, et al. Patterns of congenital anomalies and relationship to initial internal fasting glucose levels in pregnancies complicated by type 2 and gestational diabetes. *Am J Obstet Gynecol* 2000, 182;313.
36. Towner D, Kjos SL, Leung B, et al. Congenital Malformations in Pregnancies Complicated by NIDDM. *Diabetes Care* 1995;18:1446.
37. Rosenn BM, Miodovnik M, Khoury JC, et al. Pregnancy outcome in women with type 2 diabetes mellitus. *Am J Obstet Gynecol* 1996:147:394..
38. Schaefer UM, Songster G, Xiang A., et al. Congenital malformations in offspring of women with hyperglycemia first detected during pregnancy. *Am J Obstet Gynecol* 1997;177:1165.
39. Sheffield JS, Butler-Koster EL, Casey BM, et al. Maternal diabetes mellitus and infant malformations. *Am J Obstet Gynecol* 2002;100:925.

40. Reece EA, Sivan E, Francis G, et al. Pregnancy outcomes among women with and without diabetic microvascular disease (White's classes B to FR) versus non-diabetic controls. *Am J Perinatol* 1998;15:549.

41. Miodovnik M, Mimouni F, Dignan PSJ, et al. Major malformations in infants of IDDM women: vasculopathy and early first-trimester poor glycemic control. *Diabetes Care* 1988;11:713.

42. Miller E, Hare JW, Cloherty JP, et al. Elevated maternal hemoglobin A1c in early pregnancy and major congenital anomalies in infants of diabetic mothers. *N Engl J Med* 1981;304:1331.

43. Ylinen K, Aula P, Stenman UH, et al. Risk of minor and major fetal malformations in diabetics with high haemoglobin A1c in early pregnancy. *BMJ* 1984;289:345.

44. Lucas MJ, Leveno KJ, Williams ML, et al. Early pregnancy glycosylated hemoglobin, severity of diabetes, and fetal malformations. *Am J Obstet Gynecol* 1989;161:426.

45. Suhonen L, Hiilesmaa V, Teramo K. Glycaemic control during early pregnancy and fetal malformations in women with type 1 diabetes mellitus. *Diabetologia* 2000;43:79.

46. Miodovnik M, Rosenn B, Siddiqi T, et al. Increased rate of congenital malformations (CM) and perinatal mortality (PM) in infants of mothers with insulin dependent diabetes (IDDM): myth or reality? *Am J Obstet Gynecol* 1998;178:S52(abst).

47. Damm P, Molsted-Pedersen L. Significant decrease in congenital malformations in newborn infants of an unselected population of diabetic women. *Am J Obstet Gynecol* 1989;161(5):1163–1167.

48. Hawthorne G, Robson S, Ryall EA, et al. Prospective population bases survey of outcome of pregnancy in diabetic women: results of the Northern Diabetic Pregnancy Audit, 1994. *BMJ* 1997;315:279.

49. Nordstrom L, Spetz E, Wallstrom K, et al. Metabolic control and pregnancy outcome among women with insulin-dependent diabetes mellitus: a twelve-year follow-up in the country of Jamtland, Sweden. *Acta Obstet Gynecol Scand* 1998;77:284.

50. The DCCT Research Group. Pregnancy outcomes in the Diabetes Control and Complications Trial. *Am J Obstet Gynecol* 1996;174:1343.

51. Rosenn B, Miodovnik M, Dignan PSJ, et al. Minor congenital malformations in infants of insulin-dependent diabetic women: association with poor glycemic control. *Obstet Gynecol* 1990;76:745.

52. Hod M, Merlob P, Friedman S, et al. Prevalence of minor congenital anomalies in newborns of diabetic mothers. *Eur J Obstet Gynecol Reprod Biol* 1992;44:111.

53. Elixhauser A, Weschler JM, Kitzmiller JL, et al. Cost-benefit analysis of preconception care for women with established diabetes mellitus. *Diabetes Care* 1993;16:1146.

54. Herman WH, Janz NK, Becker MP, et al. Diabetes and pregnancy: preconception care, pregnancy outcomes, resource utilization and costs. *J Reprod Med* 1999;44:33.

55. Cryer PE, Gerich J. Hypoglycemia in insulin-dependent diabetes mellitus: Insulin excess and defective glucose counter-regulation. In: Rifkin H, Porte D, eds. *Ellenberg and Rifkin's Diabetes Mellitus: Theory and Practice*, 4th ed. New York: Elsevier, 1990:526–546.

56. White NH, Skor DA, Cryer PE, et al. Identification of type 1 diabetic patients at increased risk for hypoglycemia during intensive therapy. *N Engl J Med* 1983;308:485–491.

57. Boden G, Reichard GA Jr, Hoeldtke RD, et al. Severe insulin-induced hypoglycemia associated with deficiencies in the release of counterregulatory hormones. *N Engl J Med* 1981;305:1200–1205.

58. Bolli G, DeFeo P, Compagnucci P, et al. Abnormal glucose counterregulation in insulin-dependent diabetes mellitus: interaction of anti-insulin antibodies and impaired glucagon and epinephrine secretion. *Diabetes* 1983;32:134–141.

59. Amiel SA, Tamborlane WV, Simonson DC, et al. Defective glucose counterregulation after strict control of insulin-dependent diabetes mellitus. *N Engl J Med* 1987;316:1376–1383.

60. Amiel SA, Sherwin RS, Simonson DC, et al. Effect of intensive insulin therapy on glycemic thresholds for counterregulatory hormone release. *Diabetes* 1988:37:901–907.

61. Cryer PE. Iatrogenic hypoglycemia as a cause of hypoglycemia-associated autonomic failure in IDDM: a vicious cycle. *Diabetes* 1992;41:255–260.

62. Rosenn B, Miodovnik M, Berk M, et al. Counterregulatory responses to hypoglyceia in pregnant women with insulin-dependent diabetes mellitus. Abstracts of the 40th annual meeting of the Society for Gynecologic Investigation, Toronto, Canada, 1993.

63. Coustan DR, Reece EA, Sherwin RS, et al. A randomized clinical trial of the insulin pump vs. intensive conventional therapy in diabetic pregnancies. *JAMA* 1986;255:631.

64. Evers IM, ter Braak EW, de Valk HW, et al. Risk indicators predictive for severe hypoglycemia during the first trimester of type 1 diabetic pregnancy. *Diabetes Care* 2002;25:554.

65. Kitzmiller JL, Gavin LA, Gin GD, et al. Preconception care of diabetes: glycemic control prevents congenital anomalies. *JAMA* 1991;265:731.

66. Rayburn W, Piehl E, Jacober S, et al. Severe hypoglycemia during pregnancy: its frequency and predisposing factors in diabetic women. *Int J Gynaecol Obstet* 1986;24:263.

67. Steel JM, Johnstone FD, Hepburn DA, et al. Can prepregnancy care of diabetic women reduce the risk of abnormal babies? *BMJ* 1990;301:1070.

68. Hellmuth E, Damm P, Molsted-Pedersen L, et al. Prevalence of nocturnal hypoglycemia in first trimester of pregnancy in patients with insulin treated diabetes mellitus. *Acta Obstet Gynecol Scand* 2000;79:958.

69. Kimmerle R, Heinemann L, Delecki A, et al. Severe hypoglycemia, incidence and predisposing factors in 85 pregnancies of type I diabetic women. *Diabetes Care* 1992;15:1034.

70. Rosenn B, Miodovnik M, Holcberg G, et al. Hypoglycemia: the price of intensive insulin therapy in insulin-dependent diabetes mellitus pregnancies. *Obstet Gynecol* 1995;85:417.

71. Gabbe SG, Holing E, Temple P, et al. Benefits, risks, costs, and patients satisfaction associated with insulin pump therapy for the pregnancy complicated by type 1 diabetes mellitus. *Am J Obstet Gynecol* 2000;182:1283.

72. Smoak IW, Sadler TW. Embryopathic effects of short-term exposure to hypoglycemia in mouse embryos in vitro. *Am J Obstet Gynecol* 1990;163:619.

73. Akazawa M, Akazawa S, Hashimoto M, et al. Effects of brief exposure to insulin-induced hypoglycemic serum during organogenesis in rat embryo culture. *Diabetes* 1989;38:1573.

74. Buchanan TA, Schemmer JK, Freinkel N. Embryotoxic effects of brief maternal insulin-hypoglycemia during organogenesis in the rat. *J Clin Invest* 1986;78:643.

75. Ellington SK. Development of rat embryos cultured in glucose-deficient media. *Diabetes* 1987;36:1372.

76. Impastato DJ, Gabriel AR, Lardaro HH. Electric and insulin shock therapy during pregnancy. *Dis Nervous System* 1964;25:542.

77. Langer O, Cohen WR. Persistent fetal bradycardia during maternal hypoglycemia. *Am J Obstet Gynecol* 1984;149:688.

78. Stangenberg M, Persson B, Stange L, et al. Insulin-induced hypoglycemia in pregnant diabetics. *Acta Obstet Gynecol Scand* 1983;62:249.

79. Diamond MP, Reece EA, Caprio S, et al. Impairment of counterregulatory hormone responses to hypoglycemia in pregnancy women with insulin-dependent diabetes mellitus. *Am J Obstet Gynecol* 1992;166:70.

80. Rosenn B, Miodovnik M, Khoury J, et al. Counterregulatory response to hypoglycemia in pregnant women with insulin-dependent diabetes mellitus. *Obstet Gynecol* 1996;87:568.

81. Bjorklund AO, Adamson UKC, Almstrom NHH, et al. Effects of hypoglycaemia on fetal heart activity and umbilical artery Doppler velocity waveforms in pregnant women with insulin-dependent diabetes mellitus. *Br J Obstet Gynaecol* 1996;103:413.

82. Lapidot A, Haber S. Effect of acute insulin-induced hypoglycemia on fetal versus adult brain fuel utilization, assessed by (13)C MRS isotopomer analysis of [U-(13)C]glucose metabolites. *Dev Neurosci* 2000;22:444.

83. Selby JV, FitzSimmons SC, Newman JM, et al. The natural history and epidemiology of diabetic nephropathy. Implications for prevention and control. *JAMA* 1990;263:1954.

84. Reichard P, Britz A, Carlsson P, et al. Metabolic control and complications over 3 years in patients with insulin dependent diabetes (IDDM): the Stockholm Diabetes Intervention Study (SDIS). *J Intern Med* 1990;228:511.

85. Diabetes Control and Complications Trial Research Group. The effect of intensive treatment of diabetes on the development and progression of long-term complications in insulin-dependent diabetes mellitus. *N Engl J Med* 1993;329:977.

86. McCance DR, Hadden DR, Atkinson AB, et al. The relationship between long-term glycemic control and diabetic nephropathy. *QJM* 1992;82:53.

87. Reichard P, Rosenqvist U. Nephropathy is delayed by intensified insulin treatment in patients with insulin-dependent diabetes mellitus and retinopathy. *J Intern Med* 1989;226:81.

88. Parving H-H. Impact of blood pressure and antihypertensive treatment on incipient and overt nephropathy, retinopathy, and endothelial permeability in diabetes mellitus. *Diabetes Care* 1991;14:260.

89. Jerums G, Allen TJ, Tsalamandris C, et al. The Melbourne Diabetic Nephropathy Study Group: angiotensin converting enzyme inhibition and calcium channel blockade in incipient diabetic nephropathy. *Kidney Int* 1992;41:904.

90. American Diabetes Association. Clinical practice recommendations 2003: diabetic nephropathy. *Diabetes Care* 2003;26[Suppl 1]:94.

91. Davison JM, Dunlop W. Changes in renal hemodynamics and tubular function induced by normal human pregnancy. *Semin Nephrol* 1984;4:198.

92. Cousins L. Pregnancy complications among diabetic women: review 1965–1985. *Obstet Gynecol Surv* 1987;43:10.

93. Rosenn B, Miodovnik M, Combs CA, et al. Poor glycemic control and antepartum obstetric complications in women with insulin-dependent diabetes. *Int J Gynecol Obstet* 1993;43:21.

94. Kitzmiller JL, Brown ER, Phillippe M, et al. Diabetic nephropathy and perinatal outcome. *Am J Obstet Gynecol* 1981;141:741.

95. Dicker D, Feldberg D, Peleg D, et al. Pregnancy complicated by diabetic nephropathy. *J Perinat Med* 1986;14:299.

96. Grenfell A, Brudenell JM, Doddridge MC, et al. Pregnancy in diabetic women who have proteinuria. *QJM* 1986;59:379.

97. Reece EA, Coustan DR, Hayslett JP, et al. Diabetic nephropathy: pregnancy performance and fetomaternal outcome. *Am J Obstet Gynecol* 1988;159:56.

98. Reece EA, Winn HN, Hayslett JP, et al. Does pregnancy alter the rate of progression of diabetic nephropathy? *Am J Perinatol* 1990;7:193.

99. Kimmerle R, Zass RP, Cupisti S, et al. Pregnancies in women with diabetic nephropathy: long-term outcome for mother and child. *Diabetologia* 1995;38:27.

100. Gordon M, Landon MB, Samuels P, et al. Perinatal outcome and long-term follow-up associated with modern management of diabetic nephropathy. *Obstet Gynecol* 1996;87:401.

101. Purdy LP, Hantsch CE, Molitch ME, et al. Effect of pregnancy on renal function in patients with moderate-to-severe diabetic renal insufficiency. *Diabetes Care* 1996;19:1067.

102. Mackie AD, Doddridge MC, Gamsu HR, et al. Outcome of pregnancy in patients with insulin-dependent diabetes mellitus and nephropathy with moderate renal impairment. *Diabetic Med* 1996;13:90.

103. Kaaja R, Sjoberg L. Hellsted T, et al. Long-term effects of pregnancy on diabetic complications. *Diabetic Med* 1996;13:165.

104. Chaturvedi N, Stephenson JM, Fuller JH. The relationship between pregnancy and long-term maternal complications in the EUROBIAB IDDM Complications Study. *Diabetic Med* 1995;12:494.

105. Hemachandra A, Ellis D, Lloyd CE, et al. The influence of pregnancy on IDDM complications. *Diabetes Care* 1995;18:950.

106. Carstensen LL, Frost-Larsen K, Fugleberg S, et al. Does pregnancy influence the prognosis of uncomplicated insulin-dependent diabetes mellitus? *Diabetes Care* 1982;5:1.

107. Miodovnik M, Rosenn BM, Berk M, et al. The effect of pregnancy on microvascular complications of insulin-dependent diabetes (IDDM): a prospective study. *Am J Obstet Gynecol* 1998;178:S53.

108. Miodovnik M, Rosenn BM, Khoury JC, et al. Does pregnancy increase the risk for development and progression of diabetic nephropathy? *Am J Obstet Gynecol* 1996;174:1180.

109. Rosenn BM, Miodovnik M, Khoury JC, et al. Outcome of pregnancy in women with diabetic nephropathy. *Am J Obstet Gynecol* 1997;176:S179.

110. Dunne FP, Chowdhury TA, Hartland A, et al. Pregnancy outcome in women with insulin-dependent diabetes mellitus complicated by nephropathy. *QJM* 1999;92:451.

111. Khoury JC, Miodovnik M, LeMasters G, et al. Pregnancy outcome and progression of diabetic nephropathy. What's next? *J Matern Fetal Neonatal Med* 2002;11:238.

112. Bar J, Ben-Rafael Z, Padoa A, et al. Prediction of pregnancy outcome in subgroups of women with renal disease. *Clin Nephrol* 2002;53:437.

113. Ekbom P, Damm P, Feldt-Rasmussen B, et al. Pregnancy outcome in type I diabetic women with microalbuminuria. *Diabetes Care* 2001;24:1739.

114. American Diabetes Association. Clinical practice recommendations 2003: diabetic retinopathy. *Diabetes Care* 2003;26[Suppl 1]:99.

115. DCCT Research Group. Progression of retinopathy with intensive versus conventional treatment in the diabetes control and complications trial. *Ophthalmology* 1995;102:647.

116. Alvarsson ML, Grill VE. Effect of long term glycemic control on the onset of retinopathy in IDDM subjects: a longitudinal and retrospective study. *Diabetes Res* 1989;10:75.

117. Klein R, Klein BEK, Moss SE, et al. Glycosylated hemoglobin predicts the incidence and progression of diabetic retinopathy. *JAMA* 1988;260:2864.

118. Brinchmann-Hansen O, Dahl-Jorgensen K, Sandvik L, et al. Blood glucose concentrations and progression of diabetic retinopathy: the seven year results of the Oslo Study. *BMJ* 1992;304:19.

119. Kroc Collaborative Study Group. Blood glucose control and the evolution of diabetic retinopathy and albuminuria. *N Engl J Med* 1984;311:365.

120. Dahl-Jorgensen K, Brinchmann-Hansen O, Hanssen KF, et al. Rapid tightening of blood glucose leads to transient deterioration of retinopathy in insulin-dependent diabetes mellitus: the Oslo Study. *BMJ* 1985;290:811.

121. Sevin R. The correlation between human growth hormone (HGH) concentration in blood plasma and the evolution of diabetic retinopathy. *Ophthalmologica* 1972;165:71.

122. Arner P, Sjoberg S, Gjotterberg M, et al. Circulating insulin-like growth factor I in type 1 (insulin-dependent) diabetic patients with retinopathy. *Diabetologia* 1989;32:753.

123. Castellon R, Hamdi HK, Sacerio I, et al. Effects of angiogenic growth factor combinations on retinal endothelial cells. *Exp Eye Res* 2002;74:523.

124. Rosenn B, Miodovnik M, Kranias G, et al. Progression of diabetic retinopathy in pregnancy: association with hypertension in pregnancy. *Am J Obstet Gynecol* 1992;166:1214.

125. Lovestam-Adrian M, Agardh CD, Aberg A, et al. Preeclampsia is a potent risk factor for deterioration of retinopathy during pregnancy in type 1 diabetic patients. *Diabetic Med* 1997;14:1059.

126. Horvat M, Maclean H, Goldberg L, et al. Diabetic retinopathy in pregnancy: a 12-year prospective survey. *Br J Ophthalmol* 1980;64:398.

127. Moloney JBM, Drury MI. The effect of pregnancy on the natural course of diabetic retinopathy. *Am J Ophthalmol* 1982;93:745.

128. Dibble CM, Kochenour NK, Worley RJ, et al. Effect of pregnancy on diabetic retinopathy. *Obstet Gynecol* 1982;59:699.

129. Price JH, Hadden DR, Archer DB, et al. Diabetic retinopathy in pregnancy. *Br J Obstet Gynaecol* 1984;91:11.

130. Ohrt V. The influence of pregnancy on diabetic retinopathy with special regard to the reversible changes shown in 100 pregnancies. *Acta Ophthalmol* 1984;62:603.

131. Jovanovic R, Jovanovic L. Obstetric management when normoglycemia is maintained in diabetic pregnant women with vascular compromise. *Am J Obstet Gynecol* 1984;149:617.

132. Phelps RL, Sakol P, Metzger BE, et al. Changes in diabetic retinopathy during pregnancy. *Arch Ophthalmol* 1986;104:1806.

133. Serup L. Influence of pregnancy on diabetic retinopathy. *Acta Endocrinol (Copenhagen)* 1986;104:1806.

134. Chew EY, Mills JL, Metzger BE, et al. Metabolic control and progression of retinopathy: the Diabetes in Early Pregnancy Study. National Institute of Child Health and Human Development Diabetes in Early Pregnancy Study. *Diabetes Care* 1995;18:631.

135. Axer-Siegel R, Hod M, Fink-Cohen S, et al. Diabetic retinopathy during pregnancy. *Ophthalmology* 1996;103:1815.

136. Lapolla A, Cardone C, Negrin P, et al. Pregnancy does not induce or worsen retinal and peripheral nerve dysfunction in insulin-dependent diabetic women. *J Diabetes Complications* 1998;12:74.

137. Temple RC, Aldridge VA, Sampson MJ, et al. Impact of pregnancy on the progression of diabetic retinopathy in type 1 diabetes. *Diabetic Med* 2001;18:573.

138. Wingard DL, Barrett-Connor E. Heart disease and diabetes. In: *Diabetes in America.* Washington, DC: U.S. Government Printing Office, 1995:429–448 (NIH pub. no. 95–1468).

139. Nishimura R, LaPorte RE, Dorman JS, et al. Mortality trends in type 1 diabetes: the Allegheny County (Pennsylvania) Registry 1965–1999. *Diabetes Care* 2001;24:823.

140. Hypertension in Diabetic Study (HDS): prevalence of hypertension in newly presenting type 2 diabetic patients and the association with risk factors for cardiovascular and diabetic complications. *J Hyperten* 1993;11:309.

141. Knuiman MW, Welborn TA, McCann VJ, et al. Prevalence of diabetic complications in relation to risk factors. *Diabetes* 1986;35:1332.

142. UK Prospective Diabetes Study Group. Tight blood pressure control and risk of macrovascular and microvascular complications in type 2 diabetes: UKPDS 38. *BMJ* 1998;317:703.

143. Hansson L, Zanchetti A, Carruthers SG, et al. Effects of intensive blood-pressure lowering and low-dose aspirin on patients with hypertension: principal results of the Hypertension Optimal Treatment (HOT) randomized trial. *Lancet* 1998;351:1755.

144. Lewis EJ, Hunsicker LG, Bain RP, et al. The effect of angiotensin-converting enzyme inhibition on diabetic nephropathy. *N Engl J Med* 1993;329:1456.

145. Hermans MP, Birchard SM, Colin I, et al. Long-term reduction of microalbuminuria after 3 years of angiotensin-converting enzyme inhibition by perindopril in hypertensive insulin treated diabetic patients. *Am J Med* 1992[Suppl. 4B]:102.

146. Bakris GL, Williams M, Dworkin L, et al. Preserving renal function in adults with hypertension and diabetes: a consensus approach. *Am J Kid Dis* 2000;36:646.

147. Ueland K, Metcalfe J. Circulatory changes in pregnancy. *Clin Obstet Gynecol* 1975;18:41.

148. Siegler AM, Hoffman J, Bloom O. Myocardial infarction complicating pregnancy. *Obstet Gynecol* 1956;7:306.

149. Delaney JJ, Ptacek J. Three decades of experience with diabetic pregnancies. *Am J Obstet Gynecol* 1970;106:550.

150. White P. Life cycle of diabetes in youth: 50th anniversary of the discovery of insulin (1921–1971). *J Am Med Womens Assoc* 1972;27:293.

151. Hibbard LT. Maternal mortality due to cardiac disease. *Clin Obstet Gynecol* 1975;18:27.

152. Hare JW, White P. Pregnancy in diabetes complicated by vascular disease. *Diabetes* 1977;26:953.

153. Silfen SL, Wapner RJ, Gabbe SG. Maternal outcome in class H diabetes mellitus: case reports. *Obstet Gynecol* 1980;55:749.

154. Reece EA, Egan JFX, Coustan DR, et al. Coronary artery disease in diabetic pregnancies. *Am J Obstet Gynecol* 1986;154:150.

155. Gast MJ, Rigg LA. Class H diabetes and pregnancy. *Obstet Gynecol* 1985;66:5S.

156. Sheikh AU, Harper MA. Myocardial infarction during pregnancy: management and outcome of two pregnancies. *Am J Obstet Gynecol* 1993;169:279.

157. Spencer J, Gadalla F, Wagner W, et al. Cesarean section in a diabetic patient with a recent myocardial infarction. *Can J Anaesth* 1994;41:516.

158. Wilson JD, Moore G, Chipps D. Successful pregnancy in patients with diabetes following myocardial infarction. *Aust N Z J Obstet Gynaecol* 1994;34:604.

159. Pombar X, Strassner HT, Fenner PC. Pregnancy in a woman with Class H diabetes and previous coronary artery bypass graft: part 2. A case report and review of the literature. *Obstet Gynecol* 1995;85:825.

160. Gordon MC, Landon MB, Boyle J, et al. Coronary artery disease in insulin-dependent diabetes mellitus of pregnancy (class H): a review of the literature. *Obstet Gynecol Surv* 1996;51:437.

161. Darias R, Herranz L, Garcia-Ingelmo MT, et al. Pregnancy in a patient with type 1 diabetes mellitus and prior ischaemic heart disease. *Eur J Endocrinol* 2001;144:309.

162. Steel JM. Autonomic neuropathy in pregnancy [Letters and comments]. *Diabetes Care* 1989;12:170.

163. Macleod AF, Smith SA, Sonksen PH, et al. The problem of autonomic neuropathy in diabetic pregnancy. *Diabetic Med* 1990;7:80.

164. Scott AR, Tattersall RB, McPherson M. Improvement of postural hypotension and severe diabetic autonomic neuropathy during pregnancy [Letters and comments]. *Diabetes Care* 1988;11:369.

165. Airaksinen KEJ, Salmela PI. Pregnancy is not a risk factor for a deterioration of autonomic nervous function in diabetic women. *Diabetic Med* 1993;10:540.

166. Roberts JM. Pregnancy-related hypertension. In: Creasy RK, Resnik R, eds. *Maternal–Fetal Medicine: Principles and Practice,* 4th ed. Philadelphia: WB Saunders, 1999:836.

167. Jervell J, Moe N, Skjaeraasen J, et al. Diabetes mellitus in pregnancy: management and results at Rikshospitalet, Oslo, 1970–1977. *Diabetologia* 1979;16:151.

168. Diamond MP, Shah DM, Hester RA, et al. Complication of insulin-dependent diabetic pregnancies by preeclampsia and/or chronic hypertension: analysis of outcome. *Am J Perinatol* 1985; 2:263.

169. Hiilesmaa V, Suhonen L, Teramo K. Glycaemic control is associated with preeclampsia but not with pregnancy-induced hypertension in women with type I diabetes mellitus. *Diabetologia* 2000;43:1534.

170. Hanson U, Persson B. Outcome of pregnancies complicated by type 1 insulin-dependent diabetes in Sweden: acute pregnancy complications, neonatal mortality and morbidity. *Am J Perinatol* 1993;10:330.

171. Sibai BM, Caritis S, Hauth J, et al. Risks of preeclampsia and adverse neonatal outcomes among women with progrestational diabetes mellitus. National Institute of Child and Human Development Network of Maternal–Fetal Medicine Units. *Am J Obstet Gynecol* 2000;182:364.

172. Hsu CD, Tan HY, Hong SF, et al. Strategies for reducing the frequency of preeclampsia in pregnancies with insulin-dependent diabetes mellitus. *Am J Perinatol* 1996;13:265.

173. Hsu CD, Hong SF, Nickless NA, et al. Glycosylated hemoglobin in insulin-dependent diabetes mellitus related to preeclampsia. *Am J Perinatol* 1998;15:199.

174. Siddiqi T, Rosenn B, Mimouni F, et al. Hypertension during pregnancy in insulin-dependent diabetic women. *Obstet Gynecol* 1991;77:514.

175. Hanson U, Persson B. Epidemiology of pregnancy-induced hypertension and preeclampsia in type 1 (insulin-dependent) diabetic pregnancies in Sweden. *Acta Obstet Gynecol Scand* 1998;77:620.

176. Gabbe S, Mestman J, Freeman R, et al. Management and outcome of pregnancy and diabetes mellitus, classes B to R. *Am J Obstet Gynecol* 1977;129:723.

177. Coustan D, Berkowitz R, Hobbins J. Tight metabolic control of overt diabetes in pregnancy. *Am J Med* 1980;68:845.

178. Kitzmiller J, Cloherty J, Younger M, et al. Diabetic pregnancy and perinatal morbidity. *Am J Obstet Gynecol* 1978;131:560.

179. Martin FIR, Heath P, Mountain KR. Pregnancy in women with diabetes mellitus: fifteen years' experience: 1970–1985. *Med J Aust* 1987;146:187.

180. Combs CA, Rosenn B, Kitzmiller JL, et al. Early-pregnancy proteinuria in diabetes related to preeclampsia. *Obstet Gynecol* 1993;82:802.

181. Ekbom P, Damm P, Nogaard K, et al. Urinary albumin excretion and 24-hour blood pressure as predictors of pre-eclampsia in type 1 diabetes. *Diabetologia* 2000;43:927.

182. Creasy RK, Iams JD. Preterm labor and delivery. In: Creasy RK, Resnik R, eds. *Maternal–Fetal Medicine: Principles and Practice*, 4th ed. Philadelphia: WB Saunders, 1999:498.

183. von Kries R, Kimmerle R, Schmidt JE, et al. Pregnancy outcomes in mothers with pregestational diabetes: a population-based study in North Rhine (Germany) from 1988 to 1993. *Eur J Pediatr* 1997;156:963.

184. Zalut J, Reed KL, Shenker L. Incidence of premature labor in diabetic patients. *Am J Perinatol* 1985;2:276.

185. Tsang RC, Ballard JL, Braun C. The infant of the diabetic mother: today and tomorrow. *Clin Obstet Gynecol* 1981;24:125.

186. Greene MF, Hare JW, Krache M, et al. Prematurity among insulin-requiring diabetic gravid women. *Am J Obstet Gynecol* 1989;161:106.

187. Kovilam O, Khoury J, Miodovnik M, et al. Spontaneous preterm delivery in the type 1 diabetic pregnancy: the role of glycemic control. *J Matern Fetal Neonatal Med* 2002;11:245.

188. Sibai BM, Caritis SN, Hauth JC, et al. Preterm delivery in women with pregestational diabetes mellitus or chornic hypertension relative to women with uncomplicated pregnancies. The National Institute of Child Health and Human Development Maternal–Fetal Medicine Units Network. *Am J Obstet Gynecol* 2000;183:1520.

189. Weiss PA, Kainer F, Haas J. Cord blood insulin to assess the quality of treatment in diabetic pregnancies. *Early Hum Dev* 1998;51:187.

190. Halushka PV, Luric D, Colwell JA. Increased synthesis of prostaglandin-E–like material by platelets from patients with diabetes mellitus. *N Engl J Med* 1977;297:1306.

191. Lufkin G, Nelson R, Hill L, et al. An analysis of diabetic pregnancies at Mayo Clinic, 1950–79. *Diabetes Care* 1984;7:539.

192. Moore TR, Cayle JE. The amniotic fluid index in normal human pregnancy. *Am J Obstet Gynecol* 1990;162:1168.

193. Van Otterlo L, Wladimiroff J, Wallenburg H. Relationship between fetal urine production and amniotic fluid volume in normal pregnancy and pregnancy complicated by diabetes. *Br J Obstet Gynaecol* 1977;84:205.

194. Krall LP, ed. *Joslin Diabetes Manual*, 12th ed. Philadelphia: Lea & Febiger, 1989.

195. Mowat AG, Baum J. Chemotaxis of polymorphonuclear leukocytes from patients with diabetes mellitus. *N Engl J Med* 1971;284:621.

196. MacCuish AC, Urbaniak SJ, Campbell CJ, et al. Phytohemagglutinin transformation and circulating lymphocyte subpopulations in insulin-dependent diabetic patients. *Diabetes* 1974;23: 708.

197. Bagdade JD, Stewart M, Walters E. Impaired granulocyte adherence: a reversible defect in host defense in patients with poorly controlled diabetes. *Diabetes* 1978;27:677.

198. Bagdade JD, Root RK, Bulger RJ. Impaired leukocyte function in patients with poorly controlled diabetes. *Diabetes* 1974;23:9.

199. Nolan CN, Beaty HN, Bagdade JD. Further characterization of the impaired bactericidal function of granulocytes in patients with poorly controlled diabetes. *Diabetes* 1978;27:889.

200. Falkoff R. Maternal immunologic changes in pregnancy: a critical appraisal. *Clin Rev Allergy* 1987;5:287.

201. Vejlsgaards R. Studies on urinary infections in diabetes. *Acta Medica Scandinavica* 1973;193:33.

202. Diamond MP, Entman SS, Salyer SL, et al. Increased risk of endometritis and wound infection after cesarean section in insulin-dependent diabetic women. *Am J Obstet Gynecol* 1986; 155:297.

203. Pedersen J, Molsted-Pedersen L. Prognosis of the outcome of pregnancy in diabetics. *Acta Endocrinol (Copenhagen)* 1965;50: 70.

204. Rayfield EJ, Ault MJ, Keusch GT, et al. Infection and diabetes: the case for glucose control. *Am J Med* 1982;72:439.

205. Stamler EF, Cruz ML, Mimouni F, et al. High infectious morbidity in insulin-dependent diabetic pregnant women: an understated complication. *Am J Obstet Gynecol* 1990;163:1217.

LONG-TERM CARE OF MEDICAL COMPLICATIONS OF DIABETES

IRL B. HIRSCH
GINNY LEWIS

After the introduction of insulin in the early 1920s, it could be argued that there were few major developments for the treatment of diabetes and its complications for many decades. The use of protamine insulins in the mid-1930s can now be seen as directing insulin management in the wrong direction by administering insulin once or twice daily (as opposed to multiple injections). Of course, it was not until the end of the century that the medical community understood that multiple injections mimicking normal insulin secretion was a better way to provide insulin. Perhaps one of the biggest advances in diabetes therapy after the discovery of insulin was the introduction of antibiotics, as infectious complications of diabetes in those days had a significant associated mortality. It was not until the 1990s, however, that medical technology allowed improved blood glucose control. Therapies were available for both blood pressure and cholesterol reductions, and the pathogenesis of diabetes-related complications were understood so that these problems could be screened and treated. This chapter reviews many of the advances in this field.

PREVENTING DIABETES COMPLICATIONS

Perhaps the greatest controversy in the field of diabetes since the first insulin injection was administered in January 1922 was the impact of glycemic control on diabetes complications. The definitive answer was difficult to determine due to the lack of tools to both maintain and monitor meticulous glycemic control. The introduction of self-monitoring of blood glucose (SMBG) at home, hemoglobin A1c testing, and insulin pump therapy in the early 1980s finally made it possible for large numbers of people with diabetes to achieve near-normal levels of blood glucose (1). Nevertheless, hypoglycemia continued to be the limiting factor for most of these people (2). These advances also had a major impact on people with type 2 diabetes who did not require insulin therapy. Furthermore, the introduction of

metformin in the mid-1990s and the thiazolidinediones later in the decade gave us many more options for achieving improved diabetes control.

Until the report of the Diabetes Control and Complications Trial (DCCT) in 1993, there were no large prospective clinical trials that could conclusively note the precise relationship between hyperglycemia and either microvascular or macrovascular disease. Prior to this time, there were cross-sectional population-based surveys that suggested the increased frequency of diabetic retinopathy with increasing duration of diabetes, particularly with type 1 diabetes (3,4). Another important finding from these early observations was that regardless of diabetes duration, approximately 40% of patients with diabetes will not develop proliferative diabetic retinopathy. Furthermore, initial studies from the Steno Hospital in Denmark (5) and the Joslin Clinic in Boston (6) concluded that approximately 35% to 40% of patients with type 1 diabetes will develop diabetic nephropathy, but the rest seem to be protected despite decades of follow-up. Why some patients appear to be protected from certain diabetes-related complications is a question that has not been adequately answered.

In the 1980s numerous trials reported a relationship between glycemic control and microvascular complications. Most of these studies were in subjects with type 1 diabetes. Several of these reports were retrospective, and the prospective trials generally included small numbers of patients and were inconclusive. In 1993 the DCCT ended much of the controversy, at least for type 1 diabetes (7). This 10-year multicenter trial consisted of 1441 subjects, 99% of whom completed the study. There were a total of 9300 patient-years of observation in the DCCT. This represents 10-fold more study years than all other controlled clinical trials combined. Patients were randomly assigned to a conventional treatment of up to two insulin injections per day, or an intensive treatment regimen consisting of either three or four daily insulin injections or an insulin pump. The group assigned to intensive therapy was asked to perform SMBG before meals and at bedtime.

At the end of the 6.5 years, there was a significant difference in median HbA1c levels between the two groups (7.2% vs. 8.9%, p<0.001) (7). This less than 2% difference in HbA1c had a tremendous impact on diabetes-related complications: the rate of the appearance of diabetic retinopathy was decreased by 76% with intensive therapy, while the rate of retinopathy progression was reduced by 64% and the need for photocoagulation for proliferative disease was lowered by 59%. While the appearance of microalbuminuria was decreased by 39%, the risk reduction for clinical nephropathy (over 300 mg/day of albuminuria) was 54%. The appearance of clinical neuropathy was also lowered by 60%. The DCCT finally ended the debate about the relationship of microvascular complications with glycemic control in type 1 diabetes. It should be noted, however, that the questions about macrovascular events could not be answered by this trial due to the small number of events in this young population.

The relationship between glycemic control and diabetes-related complications in type 2 diabetes is also better understood. Due to the fact that macrovascular complications account for the majority of the mortality in this disease, concern about how our treatments might impact cardiovascular disease has been a concern for decades. A large American study in the 1960s concluded that sulfonylurea tolbutamide was associated with increased cardiovascular events (8). The other concern was that insulin therapy, administered to a population already obese, would lead to further weight gain and increased cardiovascular disease. These concerns were for the most part eliminated with the 1998 report of the United Kingdom Prospective Diabetes Study (UKPDS) (9,10). In this landmark clinical trial that recruited over 5200 patients, an "intensive policy" of diabetes treatment included patients who were randomized initially to monotherapy with either sulfonylurea, metformin, or insulin therapy. The "conventional policy" group was initially randomized to a diet and exercise program. By the end of this 10-year follow-up study, the subjects in the intensive policy group had overall better outcomes. For those patients who had a body weight less than 120% of ideal (and metformin was not used), a HbA1c of 7.0% compared to 7.9% reduced all microvascular endpoints by 25%, photocoagulation for proliferative retinopathy by 29%, and cataract surgery by 24% (9). There was also a 16% reduction in myocardial infarction but this did not reach statistical significance (p=0.052). For the obese cohort for which metformin was one of the treatment arms, the subjects receiving metformin had a HbA1c of 7.4% compared to 8.0% for the conventionally treated group (10). This relatively small difference resulted in a 42% risk decrease in diabetes-related death and a 36% reduction in all-cause mortality. Microvascular endpoints were also significantly lowered with metformin therapy (10). Importantly, these positive results were not seen with sulfonylurea therapy or insulin therapy for this obese group, suggesting

metformin should be the drug of choice for newly diagnosed obese patients with type 2 diabetes.

Taken together, these two large clinical trials suggest that meticulous glycemic control can impact diabetes complications. Hyperglycemia appears to have a quantitatively greater impact on microvascular disease than macrovascular events. On the other hand, the morbidity of retinopathy, nephropathy, and neuropathy are significant, and as we continue to focus on the prevention and treatment of myocardial infarction and stroke, improved survival will result in more cases of microvascular problems if hyperglycemia is not effectively treated.

In the next four sections, each major complication for patients with diabetes is reviewed. Each section discusses the critical issues for screening and treatment that all providers caring for these patients need to consider.

CARDIOVASCULAR DISEASE

Patients with type 2 diabetes are two to four times more likely to die from cardiovascular disease (CVD) than their nondiabetic counterparts. By far, CVD is the leading cause of death in this population as it is responsible for 77,000 annual deaths (11). It has also been reported that an individual with type 2 diabetes without a previous myocardial infarction has the same risk of having a myocardial infarction as a nondiabetic individual who has already had a heart attack. For patients with type 2 diabetes, mortality rates from an acute myocardial infarction are about twice as high (12). While these statistics are staggering, it is also important to note that even when traditional risk factors are controlled for (hypertension, smoking, hypercholesterolemia, and physical inactivity), there is still excess CVD in patients with diabetes (11).

The mechanisms by which diabetes increases CV risk are complex. Nonenzymatic glycation of protein appears to promote atherosclerosis. The resultant insoluble proteins, called advanced glycation end products (AGEs), are increased. AGEs accelerate atherosclerosis in a variety of ways. In addition, glycation of lipoproteins enhances their atherogenic potential. Both the degradation and release of LDL cholesterol are impaired by glycation, while glycated HDL results in increasing HDL clearance.

A clustering of risk factors for CVD is now termed the *metabolic syndrome*, previously known as the *syndrome of insulin resistance* or *syndrome X*. The components of this syndrome are noted in Table 7-1. Various components of this syndrome may be present in an individual at any one time. It is thought that insulin resistance is the key underlying factor in this syndrome. Compensatory hyperinsulinemia develops and is a marker of the insulin-resistant state. Unfortunately, there is much confusion about this, principally because insulin resistance is not easily measured. Thus, in many reports insulin has been measured as a sur-

TABLE 7-1. COMPONENTS OF THE METABOLIC SYNDROME

1. Insulin resistance
2. Hyperinsulinemia
3. Glucose intolerance or type 2 diabetes
4. Hypertension
5. Dyslipidemia: hypertriglyceridemia and low HDL cholesterol
6. Small, dense, LDL particles
7. Increased uric acid
8. Increased plasminogen activator factor
9. Coronary artery disease

rogate for insulin resistance. These studies have often shown a correlation between hyperinsulinemia and CVD outcome. Yet, while hyperinsulinemia is not an independent risk factor for CVD, insulin resistance may be. In many studies, including the UKPDS (9), exogenous hyperinsulinemia has not been shown to be a risk for CVD.

Medications

During the past few years there have been several large clinical trials assessing different pharmacologic strategies to reduce CVD in people with diabetes. Several classes of drugs have been tested, and now the main challenge is translating the results of these studies to the level of the physicians providing the care to these patients. Each class will be described separately and is further summarized in Table 7-2.

Angiotensin Converting Enzyme Inhibitors

Angiotensin converting enzyme (ACE) inhibitors have been used for the treatment of diabetic nephropathy since the mid-1980s, and by the early 1990s clinical trials had clearly shown them to be superior to other agents for retarding the progression of renal disease in this population (13). The impact of ACE inhibitors on CVD was not fully realized until 2000 with the publication of the Heart Outcomes Prevention Evaluation (HOPE) study and the microalbuminuria, cardiovascular, and renal outcomes (MICRO)

HOPE substudy (14). In the HOPE investigation, over 3,500 people with diabetes were randomized to receive the ACE inhibitor ramipril at 10 mg daily or a placebo. After 4.5 years, ramipril lowered the risk of myocardial infarction by 22%, stroke by 33%, cardiovascular death by 37%, total mortality by 24%, and overt nephropathy by 24%. What was even more surprising was that ramipril also reduced the need for photocoagulation for proliferative diabetic retinopathy. Clearly, ramipril has macrovascular and microvascular protection for patients with diabetes. The investigators could not extrapolate that other ACE inhibitors would have the same benefit, but most reports do not differentiate one ACE inhibitor from another. This is an issue since several ACE inhibitors are now generic and thus the savings for using other ACE inhibitors could be substantial.

Another interesting role of ACE inhibitors is that they appear to improve survival rates if used early in the course of acute myocardial infarction (15). Patients without diabetes do not appear to have any benefit from these agents.

Angiotensin Receptor Blockers

Related to the ACE inhibitors are the angiotensin receptor blockers (ARBs). In the Losartan Intervention for Endpoint (LIFE) trial, an analysis of patients with diabetes, hypertension, and left ventricular mortality was recently reported (16). In this trial, the ARB losartan was found to be more effective than the β-blocker atenolol at reducing cardiovascular and total mortality. In 1,195 patients with diabetes, those treated with losartan resulted in a 37% and 39% decrease of cardiovascular and total mortality, respectively. Thus, in patients with diabetes, hypertension, and left ventricular hypertrophy, ARBs appear to be more beneficial than β-blockers.

Statins

The role of statins has also been clarified during the past few years. The data strongly suggest that patients with diabetes and either relatively normal cholesterol levels (17,18)

TABLE 7-2. THE ROLE OF VARIOUS DRUGS FOR TREATMENT OF DIABETES COMPLICATIONS

Drug Class	Diabetic Retinopathy	Diabetic Nephropathy	Acute MI	CHF	CV Mortality Prevention	Diabetes Prevention
ACEI	B	A	A	A	A	B
ARB	NA	A	NA	NA	A[a]	B
Statins	NE	B	B	B	A	NE
Aspirin	NE	NE	A	NE	A	NE
β-blocker	NE[b]	NE[b]	A	A	A	NE

ACEI, angiotensin-converting enzyme inhibitor; ARB, angiotensin receptor blocker; CHF, congestive heart failure; CV, cardiovascular; MI, myocardial infarction; NA, not available; NE, no effect.
Notes: Level of evidence A, positive effect; primary endpoint of a randomized controlled clinical trial. Level of evidence B, positive effect; secondary endpoint or post-hoc analysis.
[a]In diabetic patients with hypertension and left ventricular hypertrophy.
[b]No effect independent of primary blood pressure lowering.

or hypercholesterolemia (19,20) benefit from LDL cholesterol reduction with statins. Although the LDL cholesterol target for patients with diabetes is less than 100 mg/dL, these new data suggest that statins should be the first line of therapy for this and in fact may be of benefit even in the absence of hypercholesterolemia. This topic was clarified with the report of the Heart Protection Study (HPS) in 2002 (21). Patients with known diabetes or heart disease over the age of 40 were placed either on simvastatin or on placebo and were followed for a mean of 5 years. Significant reductions were seen in a number of endpoints, including mortality and rate of major vascular events. All-cause mortality was reduced by 13% in the simvastatin group. Major vascular events were significantly decreased by 24% to 25% across a number of subgroup analyses, including patients with diabetes. Importantly, this improvement of vascular events was not altered by baseline lipid levels, suggesting that people with diabetes over the age of 40 should be considered to receive statins independent of their cholesterol levels.

Aspirin

The role of aspirin in the prevention and treatment of CVD is also better understood. Aspirin has been shown to be effective in people with diabetes for both primary prevention and secondary intervention (22). A meta-analysis of 145 prospective controlled trials of aspirin therapy in men and women with known CVD reported by the Antiplatelet Trialists showed a reduction of vascular events by about 25% for both those with and without diabetes (23). There was a trend for increased risk reduction with aspirin doses of 325 mg/day or less. Similar reductions in CVD risk have been reported for a variety of other large trials. The current recommendations are for men and women with diabetes aged over 30 years to use 81 to 325 mg/day of aspirin as primary prevention if they have any of the other traditional cardiovascular risk factors (24). This would include almost all people with diabetes in this age group. All individuals with diabetes and known CVD should use aspirin therapy as secondary intervention unless there are known contraindications such as aspirin allergy (24).

Screening

One of the more difficult clinical controversies is the role of screening for coronary artery disease (CAD) in asymptomatic individuals with type 2 diabetes. Based on U.S. surveys, evidence of CAD is present in 7.5% to 20% of people with diabetes aged more than 45 years (25). The problem is that there are a number of factors that can interfere with the specificity, sensitivity, and implications of noninvasive diagnostic tests for CAD in this population. Hypertension, cardiomyopathy (even in its mildest form), autonomic neuropathy, renal insufficiency, and endothelial dysfunction

TABLE 7-3. INDICATIONS FOR CARDIAC TESTING IN PATIENTS WITH DIABETES

1. Typical or atypical cardiac symptoms
2. Resting electrocardiograph suggestive of ischemia or infarction
3. Peripheral or carotid occlusive arterial disease
4. Sedentary lifestyle, age ≥35 years, and plans to begin an exercise program
5. Two or more of the risk factors below in addition to diabetes:
   a. Total cholesterol ≥240 mg/dL, LDL cholesterol ≥160 mg/dL, or HDL cholesterol <35 mg/dL
   b. Blood pressure >140/90
   c. Smoking
   d. Family history of premature CAD
   e. Proteinuria or microalbuminuria

CAD, coronary artery disease.
From American Diabetes Association. Consensus development conference on the diagnosis of coronary artery disease in people with diabetes. *Diabetes Care* 1998;21:1551–1559, with permission.

can all alter current cardiac testing, including nuclear medicine evaluations (26). However, given the tremendous benefits of identifying CAD with the potential for life-saving revascularization, in addition to the potential for better adherence to known pharmacologic interventions and risk-modifying behaviors, the American Diabetes Association and American College of Cardiology published a consensus conference in 1999 (27). It should also be pointed out that besides the drug treatments noted above, with a known diagnosis of CAD, the patient can also receive other beneficial therapies, such as β-blockers and nitrates.

There are currently numerous noninvasive tests for CAD available. Each has its advantages and disadvantages, and which test is used will depend on a given patient's situation (27). The current indications for cardiac testing for patients with diabetes are noted in Table 7-3.

Because of the explosion of recent clinical trials, prevention and treatment of CAD for people with diabetes have become clearer. First, Table 7-4 notes the treatment targets that this high-risk population must attempt to achieve (28). Next, independent of blood pressure, LDL cholesterol, and hyperglycemia, there are certain pharmacologic interventions that have also been proven to make dramatic reduc-

TABLE 7-4. TREATMENT TARGETS FOR PEOPLE WITH DIABETES

1. HbA1c <7%
2. Blood pressure   <130/80
3. LDL cholesterol   <100 mg/dL
4. Triglycerides   <150 mg/dL
5. HDL cholesterol   >45 mg/dL
6. Yearly screening for diabetic retinopathy with a dilated retinal exam
7. Yearly assessment for albuminuria
8. Annual comprehensive foot exam

tions in cardiovascular events and mortality (Table 7-2). The immediate goal at this point in time should be to provide this information to physician providers and patients with diabetes.

DIABETIC RETINOPATHY

Diabetic retinopathy is the leading cause of new cases of blindness in patients with diabetes aged 20 to 74 in the United States (29). Diabetes accounts for 12% of new cases of blindness annually, while approximately 8% of people who are legally blind have diabetes (25). While diabetic retinopathy is the most common cause of vision loss, cataracts, glaucoma, and macular edema are also more prevalent in individuals with diabetes. The prevalence of retinopathy is related to duration of diabetes, with the presence of comorbidities such as hypertension, renal disease, hypercholesterolemia and the level of glycemic control also affecting the onset and progression of retinopathy (29–31). In type 1 diabetes, retinopathy rarely appears prior to puberty or in the first 3 to 5 years following diagnosis (29). Over the next 20 years, the incidence of retinopathy increases. Over 80% of patients have some degree of retinopathy after 20 years of diabetes (30). In patients with type 2 diabetes, the formal diagnosis of diabetes may be preceded by long periods of hyperglycemia. These individuals often present with existing microvascular and macrovascular complications. Up to 21% of patients with type 2 diabetes will have retinopathy at the time of diagnosis (29). Puberty and pregnancy can increase the progression of retinopathy (29).

Diabetic retinopathy is a disease of the microvascular system, progressing from mild nonproliferative retinopathy (NPDR) with increased vascular permeability, followed by severe NPDR with capillary closure and microaneurysms, to proliferative diabetic retinopathy (PDR) with increased new vessel formation and scarring (29,31). Untreated PDR results in the greatest risk for vision loss.

The incidence and severity of diabetic retinopathy can be reduced with appropriate screening, prevention, and treatment methods. Early detection is critical to appropriate management. Screening and follow up recommendations from the American Diabetes Association 2003 clinical practice recommendations (29) include the following:

- Patients with type 1 diabetes who are more than 10 years of age should have an initial dilated and comprehensive eye exam within 3 to 5 years of diagnosis.
- Patients with type 2 diabetes should have an initial dilated and comprehensive eye examination at the time of diabetes diagnosis.
- Women with preexisting diabetes who are contemplating pregnancy should have a dilated and comprehensive eye exam prior to conception.

- Women with preexisting diabetes who become pregnant should have a dilated and comprehensive exam in the first trimester of pregnancy. Follow-up exams are at the discretion of the physician based on the results of the initial exam.
- An ophthalmologist or optometrist skilled in diabetic retinopathy should perform subsequent exams for patients with type 1 and type 2 diabetes annually. More frequent exams may be needed if retinopathy is present or progressing (29).

The primary goal of routine screening and treatment is to decrease the risk for severe vision loss. With early identification of diabetic retinopathy, appropriate candidates for photocoagulation therapy can be identified and treatment started earlier in the course of the disease. The Diabetic Retinopathy Study (DRS) (32) was the first multicenter trial to demonstrate a reduced risk of vision loss with early panretinal photocoagulation. The Early Treatment Diabetic Retinopathy Study (ETDRS) (33) further defined the stages of diabetic retinopathy at which panretinal photocoagulation was indicated.

Besides the relationship between glycemic control and retinopathy noted above, there is evidence showing that a rapid reduction in HbA1c can cause worsening of retinopathy. A particularly fast reduction in an extremely high HbA1c level (>10%) provides the greatest risk for this to occur (34). Several mechanisms have been proposed, but this phenomenon is probably related to the impact of hypoxia due to a change in retinal blood flow as glycemic control is improved. Although speculative, this may in fact be one of the etiologies of the worsening of retinopathy during pregnancy. There is also a growing body of evidence that PDR in general and its worsening in particular is related to an increase in vascular endothelial growth factor (VEGF) levels, a peptide that also appears to be regulated by angiotensin. Although it is difficult to give precise recommendations for how quickly it is safe to improve glucose control, patients with preexisting retinopathy should be carefully monitored by an ophthalmologist as the HbA1c decreases.

A relationship between hypertension and development of diabetic retinopathy has been established in a number of studies. Aiello et al. (30) summarized a number of these studies that demonstrate the association between blood pressure and development or progression of retinopathy. Approximately two-thirds of the studies reviewed demonstrated an association between systolic blood pressure, diastolic blood pressure, or both. The UKPDS also found a relationship between hypertension and diabetic retinopathy that was independent of glycemic control (9).

The concern regarding the use of aspirin therapy in patients with diabetic retinopathy was addressed by the Early Treatment Diabetic Retinopathy Study (ETDRS) in 1991 (33). This study showed no change in progression of diabetic retinopathy or increase in vitreous hemorrhage for patients with NPDR and less than high-risk PDR. There is no contraindication for using aspirin therapy in patients with diabetic retinopathy when indicated for other medical conditions (29,31,33).

A relationship has been established between the development of anemia and progression of diabetic retinopathy (30). An increase in neovasculization is stimulated by retinal hypoxia. The ETDRS found low hematocrit to be an independent risk factor for development of high-risk PDR (35). For patients with retinopathy and low hemoglobin levels, there is a five-fold increased risk to progress to severe retinopathy (30). Awareness toward screening and appropriate treatment for anemia needs to be considered in the health care maintenance for women with retinopathy.

DIABETIC NEPHROPATHY

Diabetic nephropathy is a microvascular complication of diabetes whose outcome can be significantly altered with early diagnosis and intervention. The DCCT and the UKPDS have clearly demonstrated the effects of early intervention on decreasing the development and progression of diabetic nephropathy (7,9,10). Approximately 20% to 30% of patients with Type 1 and Type 2 diabetes will develop some form of kidney disease (36). Diabetic nephropathy accounts for about 40% of new cases of end-stage renal disease (ESRD) in the United States (36). Due to the increased prevalence for type 2 diabetes, this population accounts for over half the patients starting on dialysis (36). There is also significant ethnic variability with African Americans,

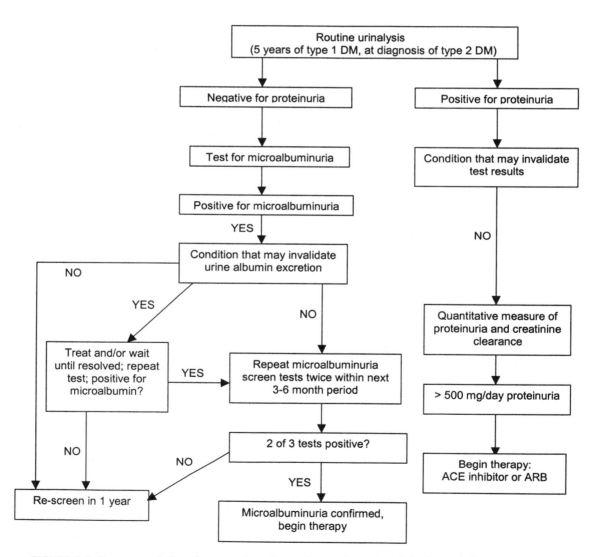

FIGURE 7-1. Recommendations for screening, diagnosing, and treating diabetic renal disease.

Native Americans, and Hispanics having a higher risk for developing ESRD (36).

The first clinical evidence of nephropathy is the appearance of microalbumin in the urine (>30 mg/24 hr). This early stage is referred to as microalbuminuria or incipient nephropathy (36). If left untreated, it will progress to overt nephropathy with urine microalbumin at more than 300 mg/24 hr within 10 to 15 years. Once overt nephropathy occurs, glomerular filtration rates will gradually decrease, with ESRD occurring in approximately 50% of patients with type 1 diabetes in 10 years (36). The rate of decrease in the glomerular filtration rate varies from patient to patient. Microalbuminuria is also a marker for increased risk of cardiovascular disease (36). Therefore, once microalbuminuria has been identified, controlling for cardiovascular risk factors is also important.

Early detection through screening programs allows early intervention and the greatest possibility for preventing diabetic nephropathy. Screening for albuminuria should begin at the time of diagnosis for individuals with type 2 diabetes, starting with an initial routine urinalysis. If the protein is positive on routine urinalysis, then a quantitative test should be done to determine the degree of microalbuminuria. If the initial urinalysis is negative, a more specific test for microalbumin should be performed (36). In type 1 diabetes, complications rarely occur before 5 years duration of diabetes; therefore routine screening can be initiated at that point. Screening for microalbumin can be accomplished by a random albumin/creatinine spot ratio (normal <30 mg/gm creatinine; overt nephropathy >300 mg/gm creatinine); or by a timed collection (normal <20 mcg/min; overt nephropathy >200 mcg/min). The 24-hour timed urine collection for albumin and creatinine clearance (normal ≤30 mg/24 hr; overt nephropathy ≥300 mg/24 hr) (36) is still considered the "gold standard" for clinical care, but is usually too burdensome for routine screening. Interfering factors that may elevate the urine albumin include hematuria, fever, infection, pyuria, exercise within 24 hours of the test, marked hyperglycemia, marked hypertension, and congestive heart failure (36). Due to the variability in test results (coefficients of variation can exceed 25%), abnormal results need to be confirmed before considering the patient to have crossed diagnostic thresholds (36). Urine albumin screening should occur annually. Once microalbuminuria has been identified, recommendations for follow-up are not as clear; however, continued screening to assess the effects of therapy or further progression of the disease is prudent at least annually or more frequently as therapy indicates.

Treating microalbuminuria involves managing blood pressure, blood glucose, and cholesterol. Once again the DCCT and UKPDS provide excellent data supporting intensive glycemic control (7,9,10). Current guidelines from the American Diabetes Association suggest achieving a HbA1C of 7% or less, and maintaining strict blood pressure control with values less than 130/80. Multiple studies

including DCCT, UKPDS, and MICRO-HOPE (37) have assessed the effect of ACE inhibitors and angiotensin ARBs on the progression of diabetic nephropathy. There is now abundant evidence demonstrating the beneficial effects of the ACE inhibitors as part of a program for primary prevention, with the use of ACE inhibitors or ARBs as part of a secondary prevention program to delay progression to overt nephropathy (38). These studies also support the beneficial effects of these drugs as independent from blood pressure control alone (39). Fig. 7-1 summarizes recommendations for screening, diagnosing and treating diabetic renal disease.

DIABETIC NEUROPATHY

Diabetes is the leading cause of neuropathy in the United States (40). The prevalence of diabetic neuropathy is not well understood. Studies have described the prevalence as ranging from 28.5% to over 60% of patients with type 1 and type 2 diabetes (25,40). Much of the lack of prevalence data is due to inconsistent definitions for peripheral neuropathy and inconsistent diagnostic criteria used in the studies. Prevalence increases with duration of diabetes (40). Neuropathy can affect any part of the nervous system. Diabetic neuropathy is usually divided into peripheral and autonomic neuropathy. Peripheral neuropathy is further divided into sensory and motor neuropathy. Autonomic neuropathy can present with cardiac symptoms such as resting tachycardia and orthostatic hypotension or as gastrointestinal neuropathy with esophageal dysmotility, delayed gastric emptying, nausea, vomiting, diarrhea, or constipation. Some patients with autonomic neuropathy also exhibit hyperhydrosis with excessive sweating during meals.

The etiology for diabetic neuropathy is multifactorial (40–42). Hyperglycemia interferes with cell metabolism by stimulating the polyol pathway through increased action of the aldose reductase enzyme, which creates an increase in sorbitol. This decreases available free nerve myoinositol. There is an increase in the glycation of nerve proteins, causing an increase in AGEs. The overall effect is impaired nerve conduction (40–42). Diabetic peripheral neuropathy occurs in a distal to proximal distribution with an initial "stocking–glove" distribution (40). Early recognition of peripheral neuropathy and management of risk factors is widely regarded as important for reducing the number of foot ulcers and amputations (43). The American Diabetes Association has developed screening guidelines for the assessment and risk identification of peripheral neuropathy (43). All people with diabetes are to have an annual foot examination to include the following:

- Measure of protective sense
- Assessment of foot structure and biomechanics
- Assessment of vascular status

■ Assessment of skin integrity (43)

Screening tools for peripheral neuropathy are available and are relatively easy and cost effective to perform in the primary care setting (40,44). A recent study reviewed four simple tests for evaluating protective sense; the 10-gram Semmes–Weinstein monofilament (von Frey hairs; Stoelting Company, Wood Dale, IL), a sterile Neurotip for superficial pain sensation, and a 128-Hz tuning fork using the timed method and the on–off method for testing vibratory sense (44). This investigation found that any one of these measures (with the exception of the timed vibratory method, which yielded less consistent results), provides an adequate assessment of protective sense (44). These methods offer a simple, inexpensive approach for in-office assessment of peripheral neuropathy.

Assessment of autonomic neuropathy is often subjective, based on patient symptoms. Resting tachycardia is a frequent symptom for cardiac autonomic neuropathy. Postural blood pressure can be used to identify orthostatic hypotension. Symptoms of gastroparesis include a sense of postprandial bloating, early satiety, nausea, vomiting, diarrhea, and constipation (45,46). Erratic blood glucose control is often an outcome from delayed gastric emptying (45). Prevention and management of both peripheral and autonomic neuropathy begin with meticulous blood glucose management.

Treatment for peripheral neuropathy is a combination of pain control and symptom control. A number of pharmacologic options have been used to relieve the pain and numbness associated with peripheral neuropathy, including tricyclic antidepressants, selective serotonin re-uptake inhibitors, anticonvulsants, mexitetine, tramadol, levodopa, gamma-linolenic acid, alpha-lipoic acid, dextromethor-

phan, and topical capsaicin (40,47). Nonpharmacology treatments include transcutaneous electrical nerve stimulation and acupuncture (40,47,48). Tricyclic antidepressants, such as amitriptyline, nortriptyline, and desipramine, have been studied extensively and shown to have some effectiveness (47,49–51). Doses have varied widely depending on patient response to treatment. More recently, the anticonvulsant gabapentin has been shown to reduce peripheral neuropathy pain in doses ranging from 900 mg per day to 3,600 mg per day in divided doses (51,52).

Treatment for autonomic neuropathy is based on controlling symptoms and improving gastric emptying (46). For patients with a mild form of gastroparesis, dietary interventions such as small, frequent, low-fat meals may be adequate to relieve symptoms (46). Pharmacologic intervention continues to be the primary treatment using prokinetic agents such as metoclopramide and cisapride (46). Table 7-5 lists the standard prokinetic medications including dosage schedules and potential side effects (46). Of the prokinetic agents listed, metoclopramide is the only medication approved by the U.S. Food and Drug Administration for diabetic gastroparesis (46). Cisapride has been removed from the U.S. market due to concerns about cardiac arrhythmias associated with drug interactions and other medical conditions (46). However, cisapride is still available on a limited basis directly from the manufacturer. Several studies have demonstrated the efficacy of domperidone for treating gastroparesis; however, it has not been approved in the United States (46).

For patients unresponsive to dietary or pharmacologic intervention, surgical approaches such as venting gastrostomy or jejunostomy are an alternative (46). The gastrostomy can be left open to decrease nausea, vomiting, and bloating after meals. The jejunostomy provides a route for

TABLE 7-5. AGENTS FOR TREATMENT OF DIABETIC GASTROPARESIS

Medications	Mode of Action	Dosing	Side Effects
Cisapride[a]	5-HT4 agonist, promotion of acetylcholine release; stimulant of smooth muscle contraction; 5-HT3 antagonist	10–20 mg po bid to qid	Cramping, diarrhea, headaches, arrhythmias
Metoclopramide	Dopamine D2 antagonist; 5-HT4 agonist, promotion of acetylcholine release; 5-HT3 antagonist	5–20 mg po qid; 10 mg IV/IM every 3 h prn; 5–10 mg SC tid or qid	Dystonia, tardive dyskinesia, depression, drowsiness, hyperprolactinemia
Domperidone	Peripheral D2 antagonist	10–40 mg po qid	Hyperprolactinemia, very rare dystonia
Erythromycin	Motilin receptor agonist	50–250 mg po qid; 1–2 mg/kg IV every 8 h	Nausea, vomiting, cramping, tachyphylaxis
Bethanechol	Muscarinic agonist	25 mg po qid; 2.5 mg SC qid	Nausea, vomiting, cramping, diaphoresis, flushing

[a]Has been withdrawn from the market in the United States. Available through manufacturer only.
bid, twice daily; IM, intramuscularly; IV, intravenously; po, mouth; prn, as needed; qid, four times daily; SC, subcutaneously; tid, three times daily.
From Rabine JC, Barnett JL. Management of the patient with gastroparesis. *J Clin Gastroenterol* 2001;32:12, with permission.

adequate nutrition and hydration when needed (46). Gastric pacing is a new surgical approach that has shown promise in decreasing symptoms of gastroparesis; however, no controlled clinical trials are available (46,53).

KEY POINTS

- The UKPDS and DCCT have demonstrated that glycemic control makes a difference in the development of microvascular and macrovascular complications for both type 1 and type 2 diabetes.
- CVD is the leading cause of death in patients with diabetes. Strategies for reducing CVD risk for patients with diabetes involve lifestyle and pharmacology management.
- Blood pressure should be measured at every visit. Patients should be treated to a blood pressure goal of lower than 130/80.
- ACE inhibitors have both macrovascular and microvascular protection for patients with diabetes.
- In patients with diabetes, hypertension, and left ventricular hypertrophy, angiotensin receptor blockers appear to be more beneficial than β-blockers.
- Lowering LDL cholesterol and triglycerides and increasing HDL cholesterol are associated with a decrease in cardiovascular events. Adults should have a lipid panel measured annually or every 2 years in adults with low-risk lipid panels. Current goals include LDL lower than 100 mg/dl; triglycerides lower than 150 mg/dl; and HDL greater than 40 mg/dl.
- The data strongly suggest patients with diabetes and either relatively normal cholesterol levels or hypercholesterolemia benefit from LDL cholesterol reduction with statins.
- Aspirin has been shown to be effective in people with diabetes for both primary prevention and secondary intervention.
- With early identification of diabetic retinopathy, appropriate candidates for photocoagulation therapy can be identified and treatment started earlier in the course of the disease.
- Patients with type 1 diabetes who are more than 10 years of age should have an initial dilated eye examination within 3 to 5 years of diagnosis and annually thereafter. Patients with type 2 diabetes should have an initial dilated eye examination at the time of diabetes diagnosis and annually thereafter. Women with preexisting diabetes who are contemplating pregnancy should have a dilated eye exam prior to conception.
- Annual screening for microalbuminuria should begin at the time of diagnosis for individuals with type 2 diabetes and after 5 years duration of diabetes in patients with type 1 diabetes.
- A visual inspection of the patient's feet should be done at each routine visit. A comprehensive foot exam should be done annually, including a measure of protective sense, assessment of foot structure and biomechanics, assessment of vascular status, and assessment of skin integrity.

REFERENCES

1. Schade DS, Santiago JV, Skyler JS, and Rizza RA. Intensive insulin therapy. Medical Examination Publishing Co., Inc. (an Excerpta Medica company) 1983.
2. Cryer PE. Hypoglycemia is the limiting factor in the management of diabetes. *Diabetes Metab Res Rev* 1999;15:42–46.
3. Palmberg P, Smith M, Waltman S, et al. The natural history of retinopathy in insulin-dependent juvenile-onset diabetes. *Opthlamology* 1981;88:613–618.
4. Klein R, Klein BEK, Moss SE, et al. The Wisconsin epidemiologic study of diabetic retinopathy. II. Prevalence and risk of diabetic retinopathy when age at diagnosis is less than 30 years. *Arch Opthlamol* 1982;102:520–526.
5. Anderson AK, Christiansen JS, Anderson JK, et al. Diabetic nephropathy in type 1 (insulin-dependent) diabetes: an epidemiological study. *Diabetologia* 1983;25:496–501.
6. Kussman MJ, Goldstein HH, Gleason RE. The clinical course of diabetic nephropathy. *JAMA* 1976;236:1861–1863.
7. Diabetes Control and Complications Trial Research Group. The effect of intensive treatment of diabetes on the development and progression of long-term complications in insulin-dependent diabetes mellitus. *N Engl J Med* 1993;329:977–986.
8. Goldner MG, Knatterud GL, Prout TE. Effects of hypoglycemic agents on vascular complications in patients with adult-onset diabetes. 3. Clinical implications of UGDP results. *JAMA* 1971;218:1400–1410.
9. UK Prospective Diabetes Study (UKPDS) Group. Intensive blood-glucose control with sulphonylureas or insulin compared with conventional treatment and risk of complications in patients with type 2 diabetes (UKPDS 33). *Lancet* 1998;352:837–853.
10. UK Prospective Diabetes Study (UKPDS) Group. Effect of intensive blood-glucose control with metformin on complications in overweight patients with type 2 diabetes (UKPDS 34). *Lancet* 1998;352:854–865.
11. Geiss LS, Herman WH, Smith PJ. Mortality in non-insulin-dependent diabetes. In: National Diabetes Data Group, ed. *Diabetes in America*, 2nd ed. Bethesda, MD: National Institutes of Health, National Institute of Diabetes, Digestive, and Kidney Diseases, 1995:233–252.
12. Jacoby RM, Nesto RW. Acute myocardial infarction in the patient with diabetes: pathophysiology, clinical course, and prognosis. *J Am Coll Cardiol* 1992;20:736–744.
13. Lewis EJ, Hunsicker LG, Bain RP, Rohde RD. The effect of angiotensin-converting enzyme inhibition on diabetic nephropathy. The Collaborative Study Group. *N Engl J Med* 1993;329:1456–62.
14. Heart Outcomes Prevention Evaluation (HOPE) Study Investigators. Effects of ramipril on cardiovascular and microvascular outcomes in people with diabetes mellitus: results of the HOPE study and MICRO-HOPE substudy. *Lancet* 2000;355:253–259.
15. Zuanetti G, Latini R, Maggioni AP, et al. Effect of the ACE inhibitor lisinopril on mortality in diabetic patients with acute myocardial infarction: data from the GISSI-3 study. *Circulation* 1997;96:4239–4245.
16. Lindholm LH, Ibsen H, Dahlof B, et al. Cardiovascular morbidity and mortality in patients with diabetes in the Losartan Intervention for Endpoint Reduction in Hypertension Study (LIFE): a randomised trial against atenolol. *Lancet* 2002;359:1004–1010.

17. Goldberg RB, Mellies MJ, Sacks FM, et al. Cardiovascular events and their reduction with pravastatin in diabetic and glucose-intolerant myocardial infarction survivors with average cholesterol levels: subgroup analyses in the cholesterol and recurrent events (CARE) trial. The Care Investigators. *Circulation* 1998; 98:2513–2519.

18. Downs JR, Clearfield M, Weis S, et al. Primary prevention of acute coronary events with lovastatin in men and women with average cholesterol levels: results of AFCAPS/TexCAPS. Air Force/Texas Coronary Atherosclerosis Prevention Study. *JAMA* 1998;279:1615–1622.

19. Pyorala K, Pedersen TR, Kjekshus J, et al. Cholesterol lowering with simvastatin improves prognosis of diabetic patients with coronary heart disease. A subgroup analysis of the Scandinavian Simvastatin Survival Study (4S). *Diabetes Care* 1997;20: 614–620.

20. Prevention of cardiovascular events and death with pravastatin in patients with coronary heart disease and a broad range of initial cholesterol levels. The Long-Term Intervention with Pravastatin in Ischaemic Disease (LIPID) Study Group. *N Engl J Med* 1998;339:1349–1357.

21. HPSCG. MRC/BHF Heart Protection Study of cholesterol lowering with simvastatin in 20,536 high-risk individuals: a randomized placebo-controlled trial. *Lancet* 2002;360:7–22.

22. Colwell JA. Aspirin therapy in diabetes (technical review). *Diabetes Care* 1997;20:1767–1771.

23. Antiplatelet Trialists' Collaboration. Collaborative overview of randomized trials of antiplatelet therapy I: prevention of death, myocardial infarction, and stroke by prolonged antiplatelet therapy in various categories of patients. *BMJ* 1994;308:71–72, 81–106.

24. American Diabetes Association. Aspirin therapy in diabetes (position statement). *Diabetes Care* 2002;25[Suppl 1]:78–79.

25. American Diabetes Association. *Diabetes Vital Statistics, 2001.* Alexandria, VA: American Diabetes Association, 2001.

26. Nesto RW. Screening for asymptomatic coronary artery disease in diabetes. *Diabetes Care* 1999;22:1393–1395.

27. American Diabetes Association. Consensus development conference on the diagnosis of coronary artery disease in people with diabetes. *Diabetes Care* 1998;21:1551–1559.

28. American Diabetes Association. Standards of medical care for patients with diabetes mellitus. *Diabetes Care* 2002;25:33–49.

29. American Diabetes Association. Position statement: diabetic retinopathy. *Diabetes Care* 2003;26:226–229.

30. Aiello LP, Cahill MT, Wong JS. Systemic considerations in the management of diabetic retinopathy. *Am J Ophthalmol* 2001; 132:760–776.

31. Aiello LP, Gardner TW, King GL, et al. Diabetic retinopathy. *Diabetes Care* 1998;21:143–156.

32. Diabetic Retinopathy Study Research Group. Photocoagulation treatment of proliferative diabetic retinopathy. Clinical application of Diabetic Retinopathy Study (DRS) findings, DRS report number 8. *Ophthalmology* 1981;88:583–600.

33. Early Treatment Diabetic Retinopathy Study Research Group. Early photocoagulation for diabetic retinopathy. ETDRS report number 9. *Ophthalmology* 1991;98[Suppl5]:766–785.

34. Chantelau E, Kohner EM. Why some cases of retinopathy worsen with diabetic control improves. *BMJ* 1997;315: 1105–1106.

35. Davis MD, Fisher MR, Gangnon RE, et al. Risk factors for high-risk proliferative diabetic retinopathy and severe visual loss: early treatment diabetic retinopathy study report number 8. *Invest Ophthalmol Vis Sci* 1998;39:233–252.

36. American Diabetes Association. Clinical Practice Recommendations. Diabetic nephropathy. *Diabetes Care* 2002;25[Suppl 1]: 585–589.

37. Fournier A, Presne C, Makdassi R, et al. Renoprotection with antihypertensive agents. *Lancet* 2002;359:1694–1695.

38. Tobe SW, McFarlane PA, Naimark DM. Microalbuminuria in diabetes mellitus. *CMAJ* 2002;167:499–509.

39. Sica DA, Bakris GL. Type 2 diabetes: RENAAL and IDNT—the emergence of new treatment options. *J Clin Hypertension* 2002;4: 52–57.

40. Simmons Z, Feldman EL. Update on diabetic neuropathy. *Curr Opin Neurol* 2002;15:595–603.

41. Pfeifer MA. Painful or insensitive lower extremity. In: Lebovitz HE, ed. *Therapy for Diabetes Mellitus and Related Disorders.* Alexandria, VA: American Diabetes Association, 1994.

42. King RHM. The role of glycation in the pathogenesis of diabetic polyneuropathy. *J Clin Pathol Mol Pathol* 2001;54:400–408.

43. American Diabetes Association. Preventive foot care in people with diabetes. *Diabetes Care* 2002;25[Suppl 1]:69–70.

44. Perkins BA, Olaleye D, Zinman B, et al. Simple screening tests for peripheral neuropathy in the diabetes clinic. *Diabetes Care* 2001;24:250–256.

45. Kong MF, Horowitz M, Jones, KL, et al. Natural history of diabetic gastroparesis. *Diabetes Care* 1999;22:503–507.

46. Rabine JC, Barnett JL. Management of the patient with gastroparesis. *J Clin Gastroenterol* 2001;32:11–18.

47. Jensen PG, Larson JR. Management of painful diabetic neuropathy. *Drugs Aging* 2001;18:737–749.

48. Baheti DK. Neuropathic pain—recent trends in management. *J Indian Med Assoc* 2001;99:692,694–695,697.

49. Max MB, Culnane M, Schafer SC, et al. Amitriptyline relieves diabetic neuropathy pain in patients with normal or depressed mood. *Neurology* 1987;37:589–596.

50. Max MB, Lynch SA, Muir J, et al. Effects of desipramine, amitriptyline, and fluoxetine on pain in diabetic neuropathy. *N Engl J Med* 1992;326:1287–1288.

51. Backonja M, Beydoun A, Edwards KR, et al. Gabapentin for the symptomatic treatment of painful neuropathy in patients with diabetes mellitus: a randomized control trial. *JAMA* 1998;280: 1831–1836.

52. Hemstreet B, Lapointe M. Evidence for the use of gabapentin in the treatment of diabetic peripheral neuropathy. *Clin Ther* 2001;23:520–531.

53. Fain JA, Tonzi MK. Understanding gastroparesis: a case study. *Gastroenterol Nurs* 2002;25:154–160.

MENOPAUSE AND DIABETES

ESTHER EISENBERG

Recent medical advances have led to improvements in the care of women with both type 1 and type 2 diabetes mellitus, enabling them to live well beyond menopause. As women approach the menopausal years, many questions arise about the relationship and interaction of diabetes and menopause. Does having diabetes affect the age of menopause? Do menopausal women have an increased tendency to develop diabetes? What are the effects of menopause in diabetic women? Is hormone replacement therapy safe to treat menopausal symptoms among diabetic women? What are the effects of hormone replacement therapy in diabetic women? These questions are explored in this chapter.

Menopause is defined by the last menstrual period. This is one of the final events in the reproductive progression that starts with the development of secondary sexual characteristics and progresses through puberty, menarche, reproduction, and, ultimately, to ovarian follicular depletion. Perimenopause, the variable time of ovarian hormonal changes preceding the menopause and the first year after menopause, is characterized by irregular menses, hot flashes, and the recrudescence of depressive symptoms if one is prone to these (1,2). Postmenopause is marked by estrogen deficiency that often is associated with vasomotor symptoms and urogenital and vaginal atrophy. Over time, the continued lack of estrogen leads to increased bone resorption, osteopenia, and eventual osteoporosis. Estrogen deficiency has also been associated in observational studies with an increased incidence of cardiovascular disease and Alzheimer's disease, although estrogen replacement has not been shown in controlled trials to improve these outcomes (3). In fact, large randomized controlled studies have shown that women with and without underlying cardiovascular disease who use hormone replacement therapy (HRT) may have a slight increase in untoward cardiovascular events. These include myocardial infarction or death in the first year of use of HRT comprised of continuous conjugated equine estrogen (CEE) combined with medroxyprogesterone acetate (MPA) (4,5). Treatment of diabetic women with HRT has not been studied in large, randomized controlled trials.

EFFECTS OF DIABETES ON MENOPAUSE

Type 1 Diabetes and Onset of Menopause

Menarche occurs in women with type 1 diabetes on average about 1 year later than in normal nondiabetic women. Women with type 1 diabetes also are more likely than their nondiabetic counterparts to report menstrual irregularities during their reproductive years (6). Menstrual regularity is related to glycemic control during adolescence in young women with type 1 diabetes. Postmenarcheal diabetic women who have elevated glycosylated hemoglobin (HbA1c) levels greater than 10% have been observed to have an increased prevalence of menstrual disturbances consisting of amenorrhea and oligomenorrhea (7). Moreover, compared to nondiabetic women, women with type 1 diabetes have an increased risk of menstrual irregularities and are twice as likely as nondiabetic women to experience an early menopause. The mean age of menopause has been studied in only a small number of women with type 1 diabetes. Menopause occurred at a mean age of 41.6 years in 15 women with type 1 diabetes compared to a mean age of 49.9 years in their nondiabetic sisters and a mean age of 48 years in other nondiabetic women (6,8). Diabetic women who had menstrual irregularities before age 30 had more than a twofold risk of early menopause, and those who had a unilateral oophorectomy had almost a 10-fold risk of early menopause compared to other women with type 1 diabetes. The reasons for an earlier age of onset of menopause in women with type 1 diabetes are unknown, although various explanations for more rapid ovarian follicular depletion have been proposed. These include a direct toxic effect of hyperglycemia on the viability of the oocyte and an increased association of other autoimmune disorders such as an increased production of immunoglobulins by the immune system that are directed against sites at the ovary in diabetic women. The role of glycemic control in relation to the age of onset of menopause is not clear.

Although studies of age at menarche and menopause in type 1 diabetic women are sparse, if indeed the age at menarche is later and the age at menopause is earlier than the norm, then the window of reproductive potential is shorter in these women. Moreover, when a diabetic woman's glycemic control is poor, aberrations of menstrual cyclicity, including anovulation, amenorrhea, and abnormal uterine bleeding, occur more frequently, which also limit reproductive potential.

Type 2 Diabetes and Onset of Menopause

The effect of adult onset or type 2 diabetes on the timing of menopause has not been well studied. An association of earlier onset of menopause has been observed in a cross-sectional study of 51 mid-life women with type 2 diabetes. These women had an earlier mean age at menopause of 45.7 years, whereas nondiabetic control women had a mean age of menopause of 48 years. Earlier age at diagnosis of diabetes was associated with earlier age at menopause. The women in this study had similar levels of obesity with a mean body mass index (BMI) of 29.9 and 29.6, respectively (9), suggesting that diabetes is an independent risk factor for earlier age at menopause. When age at menopause was studied in 404 mid-life diabetic women, excluding those who had a history of previous irregular uterine bleeding or irregular menses (most likely excluding those women with poor glycemic control), women with type 2 diabetes who had regular menstrual cycles were found to undergo menopause at a similar age compared to nondiabetic women (10). It is possible that hyperglycemia or hyperinsulinemia is related to ovarian follicular depletion; however, this remains to be established. Women with polycystic ovarian syndrome (PCOS) predominantly exhibit hyperinsulinemia and hyperandrogenism. A puzzling observation in women with a history of PCOS is that they undergo menopause at a later age than women of similar BMI who do not have PCOS (11,12). Possible explanations are that increased numbers of follicles and increased ovulations occur in women with PCOS, or that the process of apoptosis is altered or inhibited in PCOS.

PCOS and Increased Risk of Type 2 Diabetes

Women with PCOS have a 5- to 10-fold or greater risk of developing type 2 diabetes, and nearly one-third of women with PCOS have impaired glucose tolerance or diabetes by age 35 (12,13). When perimenopausal women with a history of PCOS were compared to normal women of comparable BMI, waist circumference, blood pressure, lipid profiles, and similar family history of type 2 diabetes, hypertension or coronary artery disease, a four-fold increased prevalence of diabetes was found in the women with PCOS (11). After menopause, the prevalence of type 2 diabetes in women with a history of PCOS is 15% while age-matched nondiabetic women have a prevalence of diabetes of 2.3% (12). Having a family history of type 2 diabetes in addition to PCOS is associated with a greater risk

of developing type 2 diabetes than either of these risk factors alone (13). Current recommendations include screening of women with PCOS for impaired glucose tolerance. This screening should be repeated when these women become menopausal.

MENOPAUSE AND THE RISK OF DIABETES

Epidemiologic studies have shown that the incidence of type 2 diabetes mellitus is rising. The number of women over age 45 with diabetes mellitus has increased 10-fold in the past century. The development of diabetes in genetically predisposed individuals is strongly influenced by environmental factors, including the increased incidence of obesity and sedentary tendencies of modern society. Increasing age has been associated with higher levels of plasma glucose in menopausal women. Moreover, fasting insulin and postglucose load insulin and glucose levels are seen to increase significantly with increasing BMI and waist/hip ratio (14). Postmenopause is associated with an increase in a woman's weight. This weight increase has often been attributed to the use of menopausal hormone replacement therapy. In fact, randomized controlled studies of postmenopausal women taking hormone replacement compared to those not taking hormones have shown that women who do not take HRT tend to gain more weight than women who use HRT (15).

Obesity

A quantification of body size, BMI utilizes the measure of weight normalized for height, calculated as weight in kilograms divided by the square of the height in meters (kg/m^2). Normal BMI ranges from 18.5 kg/m^2 to 25 kg/m^2. A person is considered overweight when the BMI is between 25 and 30 kg/m^2. Obesity is defined as a BMI above 30 kg/m^2. In the United States, an estimated 22.9 million women were obese in 2001, and this prevalence is increasing at a rapid rate. The prevalence of diagnosed diabetes rose from 4.9% in 1990 to 7.9% in 2001 in the overall U.S. population, an increase of 61%. Thus, in 2001, an estimated 16.7 million adults in the United States were diagnosed with diabetes of whom 9.8 million were women. Adults with BMI over 40 (morbidly obese) had a greater than seven-fold odds ratio of having diabetes. This does not include those individuals with undiagnosed diabetes, which may account for 35% of all persons with the disease (16). Over the last decade, the average BMI increased from 27.6 to 29 kg/m^2 in women between the ages of 40 and 59, which translates to an average weight increase of about 7 to 10 pounds (17).

Obesity and weight gain are associated with an increased risk of diabetes (18). Not only is the total amount of body fat important, but also the regional distribution of fat to the central abdomen is inversely related to insulin sensitivity in women in the early post-menopausal period. Thus, insulin sensitivity is significantly correlated to abdominal adiposity as measured by sagittal diameter on computed tomography scans, but not significantly correlated to total fat or percent body fat (19). Similarly, postmenopausal women with abdominal obesity, as measured by waist circumference (WC) greater than 80 cm, had higher fasting insulin and triglyceride levels, a higher incidence of glucose intolerance, and higher systolic blood pressure compared to similar women with lower WC. These relationships were independent of BMI (20). Reduction in the amount of central abdominal fat is likely to improve insulin sensitivity and reduce the risk of developing diabetes. Moreover, intentional weight loss reduces the risk that an overweight person will develop diabetes (21) and his/her mortality rate (22). Identifying obese individuals who are insulin resistant will distinguish those who are likely to benefit from weight loss. Women who are insulin resistant may have the following laboratory findings: (a) a high plasma triglyceride level (greater than 150 mg/dL) and a low HDL cholesterol concentration (less than 40 mg/dL); (b) hypertension; and (c) impaired glucose tolerance as measured by an elevated glucose response to a 75-g oral glucose load, or a fasting plasma glucose level between 110 and 126 mg/dL (23).

Activity Levels

Sedentary behaviors such as watching television and sitting at work have been associated with an increased risk of diabetes in women. A large cohort study of over 68,000 nurses showed that each 2-hour increment of television viewing was associated with a 14% increase in the risk of diabetes, and each 2-hour increment of sitting at work was associated with a 7% increase in diabetes. Conversely, each 2 hours spent standing or walking at home was associated with a 12% reduction in diabetes and each hour per day of brisk walking was associated with a 34% decrease in diabetes. Curtailing sedentary behaviors and adopting a moderately active lifestyle of fewer than 10 hours per week of television viewing and more than 0.5 hours per day of brisk walking was predicted to reduce the incidence of new cases of diabetes by 43% (24).

Other behaviors are associated with a reduced risk of diabetes in mid-life and postmenopausal women. The consumption of five or more servings of nuts or peanut butter per week is associated with a lower risk of diabetes (25). Drinking two drinks per day of alcohol (30 grams) reduces fasting insulin levels and improves insulin sensitivity (26).

Diabetes may be prevented by dietary change and exercise. Women with a mean age of 50 and BMI of 34 who were at high risk for developing diabetes were able to prevent the development of diabetes by 54% with intensive lifestyle changes, including a healthy low-calorie, low-fat diet designed to reduce body weight by 7% as well as moderate physical activity for at least 150 minutes per week. Alternatively, treatment with the insulin-sensitizing biguanide drug metformin, at a dosage of 850 mg twice daily, reduced the incidence of diabetes in women by 28% compared to no treatment (27).

Menopausal Hormone Replacement Therapy and Lower Risk of Diabetes

Hormone replacement therapy has both positive and negative effects on overall health. These include a reduction in serum levels of high-density and low-density lipoproteins but an increase in triglyceride levels; lowering of fibrinogen but an increase in venous thrombosis. HRT use may lower the risk of future diabetes. A reduction in fasting glucose and insulin levels in women treated with HRT is one beneficial effect of HRT that has been observed in large randomized controlled trials (28,29). In the Post-menopausal Estrogen/Progestin Interventions (PEPI) trial, the HRT combination of CEE and micronized progesterone was found to have the most beneficial effect on fasting glucose levels and response to glucose challenge. A subgroup analysis of the Heart and Estrogen/Progestin Replacement Study (HERS) showed that postmenopausal women with underlying coronary artery disease who were treated with daily combined CEE and MPA had a 35% lower incidence of diabetes over a 4-year period compared to similar women who were treated with placebo. Of the 2,029 postmenopausal women without diabetes at baseline, 6.2% receiving CEE–MPA hormones and 9.5% of those receiving placebo ultimately developed diabetes during the 4-year study period. In a longitudinal investigation of postmenopausal women in the Strong Health Study, among 13 American Indian tribes whose prevalence of type 2 diabetes ranges from 40% to 70%, postmenopausal estrogen use did not significantly increase the risk of diabetes. However, increasing duration of estrogen use in this population was associated with a greater risk of type 2 diabetes (30). Thus, estrogen treatment may differ from HRT with regard to its effects on glucose homeostasis, or varied effects may be observed in different populations of women.

Even though several studies have indicated that HRT may lower the risk of diabetes, it should not be used solely for prevention, as additional risks of HRT must be weighed along with potential benefits. Nonetheless, HRT is not contraindicated in women at high risk for diabetes. In women whose menopausal symptoms interfere with quality of life or activities of daily living, HRT may be prescribed without known deleterious effects on glucose metabolism. In addition, in women with type 2 diabetes, HRT should not be withheld because of concerns about the effects on blood glucose levels, as glycemic control is improved by HRT and estrogen replacement (31) (see below).

HORMONE REPLACEMENT THERAPY IN MENOPAUSAL WOMEN WITH DIABETES

Diabetic women are less than half as likely to be prescribed HRT as other menopausal women (32). Considerably fewer women with diabetes mellitus (17%) were noted to use HRT than women without diabetes (39%) in a telephone survey of postmenopausal women (33). In postmenopausal women with well-controlled type 2 diabetes, HRT may be used to relieve vasomotor symptoms and vaginal atrophic changes of menopause, in view of studies that show no adverse effect on blood glucose levels and suggest improvement in overall glycemic control and insulin sensitivity. Variable effects of HRT on lipid parameters have been observed in diabetic postmenopausal women. Some reports show an improvement in lipid parameters (31,34–36) Others suggest that diabetic women may exhibit a less than optimal effect of HRT on their lipids, including a blunted HDL response and an exaggerated increase in triglyceride response to estrogen therapy (37). Thus, lipids should be monitored after initiation of HRT.

Although an increase in myocardial infarction was observed in postmenopausal women treated with HRT in the Women's Health Initiative study (4), a contrary observation that postmenopausal estrogens do not increase the risk of myocardial infarction in diabetic women (38) was found in a case control study of postmenopausal estrogen use and the risk of myocardial infarction in treated diabetic women. Clearly, additional data are needed from randomized controlled trials of HRT in postmenopausal diabetic women to better define risks in this group.

HRT Effects on Glycemic Control in Postmenopausal Women with Type 2 Diabetes

Most of the information about HRT in postmenopausal diabetic women refers to type 2 diabetes. A large cross-sectional study of postmenopausal diabetic women enrolled in the Kaiser Permanente Medical Care Program of Northern California showed that diabetic women currently using HRT had HbA1c levels that were significantly lower than those in women not using HRT. This lower HbA1c level was observed whether or not the women were using solely estrogen replacement or HRT. Moreover, HRT remained independently associated with a lower HbA1c level after adjusting for age, ethnicity, education, obesity, hypoglycemic therapy, duration or diabetes self-monitoring of blood glucose, and exercise (39). Similarly, a prospective crossover study of HRT in 14 overweight type 2 diabetic women noted a reduction in central adiposity, improved lipid metabolism, and HbA1c levels after 6 months of HRT use when compared to these parameters after 6 months of observation (40). Estrogen replacement therapy, likewise, has been found to decrease glycosylated hemoglobin levels and has beneficial effects on blood lipoprotein levels in postmenopausal women with type 2 diabetes (34,35).

This difference in HbA1c levels not only implies better glycemic control, but also potentially translates into a reduction in complications of diabetes including microvascular complications and myocardial infarction. The mechanism by which estrogen improves glycemic control may be related to improved insulin sensitivity and possible suppression of hepatic glucose production (41).

ADDITIONAL MEDICAL CONSIDERATIONS IN MENOPAUSAL WOMEN WITH TYPE 2 DIABETES

Postmenopausal women with diabetes often have associated obesity, elevated triglyceride levels and hypertension, and additional risk factors for heart disease. In fact, menopausal women with diabetes have a 75% chance of death from cardiovascular disease. These considerations are examined in other sections of this book.

Endometrial Cancer

Specific considerations for postmenopausal diabetic women are an increased risk of postmenopausal bleeding and endometrial cancer (42). The triad of diabetes, obesity, and hypertension are significant markers of risk for endometrial cancer. Endometrial cancer risk, obesity, diabetes, and hypertension were examined in a population-based study of postmenopausal Swedish women aged 50 to 74. Obese women (BMI 30 to <34) had a three-fold increased risk of endometrial cancer, while those with marked obesity (BMI ≥34) had a six-fold increased risk of endometrial cancer compared to lean women (BMI <22.5). Type 2 diabetes was associated with a 1.5-fold increased risk for endometrial cancer and type 1 diabetes with a 13.3-fold increased risk. Hypertension was found to increase the risk of endometrial cancer only among women with obesity (43). The increased risk of endometrial cancer in diabetic women is not explained solely by obesity, since an increased risk for endometrial cancer has been observed after adjustment for BMI (44). In the setting of limited physical activity, the risk for endometrial cancer increases even more (45). Any episode of abnormal uterine bleeding in a postmenopausal diabetic woman requires evaluation with transvaginal sonography of the endometrium and/or endometrial biopsy (46–49).

Osteoporosis and Fracture

Accumulating evidence indicates that postmenopausal women with diabetes are at increased risk for fracture (50,51) compared to nondiabetic women. The risk for hip fracture has been found to be extremely high for women with type 1 diabetes. However, women with type 2 diabetes also have a moderately increased risk for hip fracture. In the type 2 diabetic woman, longer duration of type 2 diabetes, use of insulin or oral hypoglycemic medication and recent onset of diabetes have been associated with a higher incidence of hip fracture, while type 2 diabetic women who were not treated with pharmacologic agents had a risk of hip fracture similar to nondiabetic women, perhaps reflecting that severity of disease is associated with greatest risk (52).

Postmenopausal women with type 1 diabetes have a significantly lower bone mineral density (BMD) at the femoral neck compared to healthy postmenopausal women (53,54). In contrast, postmenopausal women with type 2 diabetes have often been found to have higher BMD measurements compared to other postmenopausal women (54–57). Nevertheless, several reports and prospective studies indicate a marked increased risk of hip fractures and more than a doubling of the risk of foot fractures in type 2 diabetics compared to nondiabetic women (50,58,59). Possible explanations for the higher risk of specific fractures despite a higher bone mineral density in older women with type 2 diabetes include poor vision, peripheral neuropathy (60), and problems with balance and functional impairment, or poor bone quality resulting in increased bone fragility despite normal bone density. A prospective study of fractures in older diabetic individuals showed that fractures were significantly associated with several factors related to diabetes including the presence of diabetic retinopathy, cataracts involving at least 25% of the lens area, use of insulin treatment, and a longer duration of diabetes (61).

Strategies to prevent falls and attention to vision as well as evaluation and treatment of low bone mineral density are important preventive measures in this population.

UNDIAGNOSED DIABETES

In 1998, the prevalence of diabetes in individuals aged 60 to 74 was 23.4%, and almost half were undiagnosed (62). Many menopausal women with type 2 diabetes are unidentified and untreated. Consequently, they are at increased risk for the complications of diabetes that are directly related to hyperglycemia and hyperinsulinemia. Ethnic and racial differences in the prevalence of diabetes are observed in older women as well. Currently, type 2 diabetes remains undiagnosed in approximately one-third of all older people with diabetes. In a recent study of 3,075 well-functioning people aged 70 to 79, the prevalence of diabetes was 15.3% in white women (7.8% diagnosed and 7.4% undiagnosed) and 27.8% in black women (21.6% diagnosed and 6.2% undiagnosed) (63). Factors associated with undiagnosed diabetes included a history of hypertension, higher BMI, and larger waist circumference. These data point to the importance of screening postmenopausal women for diabetes.

The efficacy of screening for diabetes varies by age and an individual's additional risk factors for diabetes. Identifying and treating a woman with diabetes has far-ranging long-term preventive consequences. In people over 45 years old, a new case of diabetes was identified in 2.8% when an additional risk factor of hypertension, family history of diabetes mellitus, or obesity was present. However, without additional risk factors, the yield of a fasting blood sugar for screening was extremely low at 0.2% (64).

Postmenopausal women who have an elevated BMI, hypertension, family history of diabetes, or personal history of PCOS should be screened for diabetes and treated if diabetes is diagnosed. Once an elevated fasting blood glucose level or impaired glucose tolerance is identified, a more compelling case can be made for lifestyle modification and increased physical activity.

KEY POINTS

- Menstrual regularity is directly related to glycemic control during adolescence in insulin-dependent diabetic women.
- Compared with nondiabetic women, women with type 1 diabetes have an increased risk of menstrual irregularities and are twice as likely as nondiabetic women to experience an early menopause.
- Women with PCOS have a 5- to 10-fold or greater risk of developing type 2 diabetes, and nearly one-third of women with PCOS have impaired glucose tolerance or diabetes by age 35.
- The development of diabetes in genetically predisposed individuals is strongly influenced by environmental factors. A large contributing factor is the increased incidence of obesity and sedentary tendencies of modern society.
- Postmenopause is associated with an increase in a woman's weight. Randomized controlled studies of postmenopausal women taking hormone replacement compared to those not taking hormones have shown that women who do not take HRT tend to gain more weight than women who use HRT.
- During the past decade, the average BMI increased from 27.6 to 29 kg/m^2 in women between the ages of 40 and 59, which translates to an average weight increase of about 7 to 10 pounds.
- Sedentary behaviors such as watching television and sitting at work have been associated with an increased risk of diabetes in women. Curtailing sedentary behaviors and adopting a moderately active lifestyle of fewer than 10 hours per week of television viewing and more than 0.5 hour per day of brisk walking was predicted to reduce the incidence of new cases of diabetes by 43%.
- In postmenopausal women with well-controlled type 2 diabetes, HRT may be used to relieve vasomotor symp-

toms and vaginal atrophic changes of menopause, as studies show no adverse effect of HRT on blood glucose levels and possible improvement in overall glycemic control and insulin sensitivity. Even though several large randomized controlled trials have indicated that HRT may lower the risk of diabetes, it should not be used solely for prevention, as additional risks of HRT must be weighed along with potential benefits.

■ Specific considerations for postmenopausal diabetic women are an increased risk of postmenopausal bleeding and endometrial cancer. Any episode of abnormal uterine bleeding in a postmenopausal diabetic woman requires evaluation with transvaginal sonography of the endometrium and/or endometrial biopsy.

■ Accumulating evidence indicates that postmenopausal women with diabetes are at increased risk for fracture compared to nondiabetic women.

REFERENCES

1. Soules MR, Sherman S, Parrott E, et al. Executive summary: Stages of Reproductive Aging Workshop (STRAW), Park City, Utah, July 2001. *Menopause* 2001;8:402–407.
2. Soules MR, Sherman S, Parrott E, et al. Executive summary: Stages of Reproductive Aging Workshop (STRAW). *Fertil Steril* 2001;76:874–878.
3. Nelson HD, Humphrey LL, Nygren P, et al. Postmenopausal hormone replacement therapy: Scientific review. *JAMA* 2002; 288:872–881.
4. Rossouw JE, Anderson GL, Prentice RL, et al. Risks and benefits of estrogen plus progestin in healthy postmenopausal women: principal results from the Women's Health Initiative randomized controlled trial. *JAMA* 2002;288:321–333.
5. Hulley S, Grady D, Bush T, et al. Randomized trial of estrogen plus progestin for secondary prevention of coronary heart disease in postmenopausal women. Heart and Estrogen/Progestin Replacement Study (HERS) Research Group. *JAMA* 1998;280: 605–613.
6. Dorman JS, Steenkiste AR, Foley TP, et al. Menopause in type 1 diabetic women. Is it premature? *Diabetes* 2001;50:1857–1862.
7. Schroeder B, Hertweck SP, Sanfillipo JS, et al. Correlation between glycemic control and menstruation in diabetic adolescents. *J Reprod Med* 2000;45:1–5.
8. Strotmeyer ES, Steenkiste AR, Foley TP, et al. Menstrual cycle differences between women with type 1 diabetes and women without diabetes. *Diabetes Care* 2003;26:1016–1021.
9. Malacara JM, Huerta R, Rivera B, et al. Menopause in normal and uncomplicated NIDDM women: physical and emotional symptoms and hormone profile. *Maturitas* 1997;28:35–45.
10. Lopez-Lopez R, Huerta R, Malacara JM. Age at menopause in women with type 2 diabetes mellitus. *Menopause* 1999;6:174–78
11. Cibula D, Cifkova R, Fanta M, et al. Increased risk of non-insulin dependent diabetes mellitus, arterial hypertension and coronary artery disease in perimenopausal women with a history of the polycystic ovary syndrome. *Hum Reprod* 2000;15:785–789.
12. Dahlgren E, Johansson S, Lindstedt G, et al. Women with polycystic ovary syndrome wedge resected in 1856 to 1965: a long term follow-up focusing on natural history and circulating hormones. *Fertil Steril* 1992;57:505–513.
13. Legro RS, Kunselman AR, Dodson WC, et al. Prevalence and predictors of risk for type 2 diabetes mellitus and impaired glucose tolerance in polycystic ovary syndrome: a prospective, controlled study in 254 affected women. *Endocrinol Metab* 1999;84: 165–169.
14. Barrett-Connor E, Schrott HG, Greendale G, et al. Factors associated with glucose and insulin levels in healthy postmenopausal women. *Diabetes Care* 1996;19:333–340.
15. Esplanand MA, Stefanick ML, Kritz-Silverstein D, et al. Effect of postmenopausal hormone therapy on body weight and waist and hip girths. *J Clin Endocrinol Metab* 1987;82:1549–1556.
16. Mokdad AH, Ford ES, Bowman BA, et al. Prevalence of obesity, diabetes, and obesity-related health risk factors, 2001. *JAMA* 2003;289:76–79.
17. Friedman JM. A war on obesity, not the obese. *Science* 2003;299:855–858.
18. Ford ES, Williamson DF, Liu S. Weight change and diabetes incidence: findings from a national cohort of US adults. *Am J Epidemiol* 1997;146:214–222.
19. Sites CK, Calles-Escandon J, Brochu M, et al. Relation of regional fat distribution to insulin sensitivity in postmenopausal women. *Fertil Steril* 2000;73:61–65.
20. Hwa CM, Fuh JL, Hsiao CF, et al. Waist circumference predicts metabolic cardiovascular risk in postmenopausal Chinese women. *Menopause* 2003;10:73–80.
21. Will JC, Williamson DF, Ford ES, et al. Intentional weight loss and 13-year diabetes incidence in overweight adults. *Am J Public Health* 2002;92:1245–1248.
22. Gregg EW, Gerzoff RB, Thompson TJ, et al. Intentional weight loss and death in overweight and obese U.S. adults 35 years of age and older. *Ann Intern Med* 2003;138:383–389.
23. Reaven GM. Importance of identifying the overweight patient who will benefit most by losing weight. *Ann Intern Med* 2003; 138:420–423.
24. Hu FB, Li TY, Colditz GA, et al. Television watching and other sedentary behaviors in relation to risk of obesity and type 2 diabetes mellitus in women. *JAMA* 2003;289:1785–1791.
25. Jiang R, Manson JE, Stampfer MJ, et al. Nut and peanut butter consumption and risk of Type 2 diabetes in women. *JAMA* 2002; 288:2554–2560.
26. Davies MJ, Baer CJ, Judd JT, et al. Effects of moderate alcohol intake on fasting insulin and glucose concentrations and insulin sensitivity in postmenopausal women. A randomized controlled trial. *JAMA* 2002;287:2559–2562.
27. Knowler WC, Barrett-Connor E, Fowler SE, et al. Reduction in the incidence of Type 2 diabetes with lifestyle intervention or metformin. *N Engl J Med* 2002;346:393–403.
28. Kanaya AM, Herrington D, Vittinghoff E, et al. Glycemic Effects of Postmenopausal Hormone Therapy: The Heart and Estrogen/progestin Replacement Study. *Ann Intern Med* 2003; 138:1–9.
29. Espeland MA, Hogan PE, Fineberg SE, et al. Effect of postmenopausal hormone therapy on glucose and insulin concentrations. PEPI Investigators. Postmenopausal Estrogen/Progestin Interventions. *Diabetes Care* 1998;21:1589–1595.
30. Zhang Y, Howard BV, Cowan L, et al. The effect of estrogen use on levels of glucose and insulin and the risk of type 2 diabetes in American Indian postmenopausal women: the Strong Heart Study. *Diabetes Care* 2002;25:500–504.
31. Palin SL, Kumar S, Sturdee DW, et al. HRT in women with diabetes-review of the effects on glucose and lipid metabolism. *Diabetes Res Clin Pract* 2001;54:67–77.
32. Feher MD, Isaacs AJ. Is hormone replacement therapy prescribed for postmenopausal diabetic women? *Br J Clin Pract* 1996;50: 431–432.
33. Keating NL, Cleary PD, Rossi AS, et al. Use of hormone replacement therapy by postmenopausal women in the United States. *Ann Intern Med* 1999;130:545–553.

34. Andersson B, Mattsson LA, Lennart H, et al. Estrogen replacement therapy decreases hyperandrogenicity and improves glucose homeostasis and plasma lipids in postmenopausal women with noninsulin-dependent diabetes mellitus. *J Clin Endocrinol Metab* 1997;82:638–643.
35. Friday KE, Dong C, Fontenot RU. Conjugated equine estrogen improves glycemic control and blood lipoproteins in postmenopausal women with type 2 diabetes. *J Clin Endocrinol Metab* 2001;86:48–52.
36. Cornu C, Mercier C, Ffrench P, et al. Postmenopause hormone treatment in women with NIDDM or impaired glucose tolerance: the MEDIA randomized clinical trial. *Maturitas* 2000;37:95–104.
37. Robinson JG, Brancat FL, Folsom AR, et al. Can postmenopausal hormone replacement improve plasma lipids in women with diabetes? *Diabetes Care* 1996;19:480–485.
38. Kaplan RC, Heckbert SR, Weiss MS, et al. Postmenopausal estrogens and risk of myocardial infarction in diabetic women. *Diabetes Care* 1998;21:1117–1121.
39. Ferrara, A, Karter AJ, Ackerson LM, et al. Hormone replacement therapy is associated with better glycemic control in women with type 2 diabetes: the Northern California Kaiser Permanente Diabetes Registry. *Diabetes Care* 2001;24:1144–1150.
40. Samaras K, Hayward CS, Sullivan D, et al. Effects of postmenopausal hormone replacement therapy on central abdominal fat, glycemic control, lipid metabolism, and vascular factors in type 2 diabetes: a prospective study. *Diabetes Care* 1999;22:1401–1407.
41. Matute ML, Kalkhoff RK. Sex steroid influence on hepatic gluconeogenesis and glucogen formation. *Endocrinology* 1973;92:762–768.
42. Weber AM, Belinson JL, Piedmonte MR. Risk factors for endometrial hyperplasia and cancer among women with abnormal bleeding. *Obstet Gynecol* 1999;93:594–598.
43. Weiderpass E, Persson I, Adami HO, et al. Body size in different periods of life, diabetes mellitus, hypertension and risk of postmenopausal endometrial cancer (Sweden). *Cancer Causes Control* 2000;11:185–192.
44. Anderson KE, Anderson E, Mink PJ, et al. Diabetes and endometrial cancer in the Iowa women's health study. *Cancer Epidemiol Biomarkers Prev* 2001;10:611–616.
45. Furberg AS, Thune I. Metabolic abnormalities (hypertension, hyperglycemia and overweight), lifestyle (high energy intake and physical inactivity) and endometrial cancer risk in a Norwegian cohort. *Int J Cancer* 2003;104:669–676.
46. Karlsson B, Granberg S, Wikland M, et al. Transvaginal ultrasonography of the endometrium in women with postmenopausal bleeding: a Nordic multicenter study. *Am J Obstet Gynecol* 1995;172:1488–1494.
47. Langer RD, Pierce JJ, O'Hanlan KA, et al. Transvaginal ultrasonography compared with endometrial biopsy for the detection of endometrial disease. *N Engl J Med* 1997;337:1792–1798.
48. Paley PJ. Screening for the major malignancies affecting women: Current guidelines. *Am J Obstet Gynecol* 2001;184:1021–1030.
49. Foley DV, Masukawa T. Endometrial monitoring of high-risk women. *Cancer* 1981;48[Suppl 2]:511–514.
50. Schwartz AV, Sellmeyer DE, Ensrud KE, et al. Older women with diabetes have an increased risk of fracture: a prospective study. *J Clin Endocrinol Metab* 2001;86:32–38.
51. Schwartz AV, Hillier TA, Sellmeyer DE, et al. Older women with diabetes have a higher risk of falls: a prospective study. *Diabetes Care* 2002;25:1749–1754.
52. Nicodemus KK, Folson AR, Iowa Women's Health Study. Type 1 and type 2 diabetes and incident hip fractures in postmenopausal women. *Diabetes Care* 2001;24:1192–1197.
53. Rachon D, Mysliwska J, Suchecka-Rachon K. Serum interleukin-6 and bone mineral density at the femoral neck in postmenopausal women with type 1 diabetes. *Diabetic Med* 2003;20:475–480.
54. Chrisensen JO, Svendsen OL. Bone Mineral in Pre-and Postmenopausal women with insulin-dependent and non-insulin-dependent diabetes mellitus. *Osteoporos Int* 1999;10:307–311.
55. Akin O, Gol K, Erkaya S. Evaluation of bone turnover in postmenopausal patients with type 2 diabetes mellitus using biochemical markers and bone mineral density measurements. *Gynecol Endocrinol* 2003;17:19–29.
56. Hanley DA, Brown JP, Tenenhouse A, et al. Associations among disease conditions, bone mineral density, and prevalent vertebral deformities in men and women 50 years of age and older: cross-sectional results from the Canadian Multicentre Osteoporosis Study. *J Bone Miner Res* 2003;18:784–790.
57. Leidig-bruckner G, Ziegler R. Diabetes mellitus a risk for osteoporosis? *Exp Clin Endocrinol Diabetes* 2001;109[Suppl 2]:493–514.
58. Ottenbacher KJ, Ostir GV, Peek MK, et al. Diabetes mellitus as a risk factor for hip fracture in Mexican American older adults. *J Gerontol A Biol Sci Med Sci* 2002;57:648–653.
59. Forsen L, Meyer HE, Midthjell K, et al. Diabetes mellitus and the incidence of hip fracture: results from the Nord-Trondelag Health Survey. *Diabetologia* 1999;42:920–925.
60. Rix M, Andreassen H, Eskildsen P. Impact of peripheral neuropathy on bone density in patients with type 1 diabetes. *Diabetes Care* 1999;22:827–831.
61. Ivers RQ, Cumming RG, Mitchell P, et al. Diabetes and risk of fracture: the Blue Mountain Eye Study. *Diabetes Care* 2001;24:1198–1203.
62. Ruwaard D, Hoogenveen RT, Verkleij H, et al. Forecasting the number of diabetic patients in The Netherlands in 2005. *Am J Public Health* 1993;83:989–995.
63. Franse LV, Di Bari M, Shorr RI, et al. Type 2 diabetes in older well-functioning people: who is undiagnosed? Data from the health, aging, and body composition study. *Diabetes Care* 2001;24:2065–2070.
64. Lawrence JM, Bennett P, Young A, et al. Screening for diabetes in general practice: cross sectional population study. *BMJ* 2001;323:548–551.

9

CARBOHYDRATE, LIPID, AND AMINO ACID METABOLISM

PHILIP A. GOLDBERG
GERALD I. SHULMAN
ROBERT S. SHERWIN

NORMAL BODY FUEL METABOLISM

Regulation of Body Fuel Metabolism

In humans, normal regulation of fuel metabolism involves a complex orchestra of interactions among exogenous fuels, hormones, and the exchange of substrates between relevant body organs. *Insulin* is the primary "conductor" of this orchestra, controlling the body's storage and metabolism of fuels during various conditions of fuel supply and demand. *Glucagon* and other metabolic hormones play supportive roles. Following a meal, augmented insulin secretion facilitates the uptake and storage of glucose, fatty acids, and amino acids into insulin-sensitive tissues. Conversely, insulin deficiency leads to the mobilization of endogenous fuels and to the reduced storage of ingested nutrients. Insulin exerts both anabolic and anticatabolic effects on its three primary target tissues (Table 9-1). In the liver, it suppresses endogenous glucose production and promotes the synthesis of glycogen and fat. In skeletal muscle and adipose tissue, insulin promotes the storage of glycogen and fat, respectively, while inhibiting glycogenolysis, lipolysis, and protein catabolism.

In the resting state, the human body requires approximately one kcal per minute (1,440 kcal per day) to satisfy basal energy requirements (1). With physical activity and/or prolonged exposure to cold temperatures, these requirements may increase two- or three-fold (2), necessitating rapidly accessible energy stores. In humans, *glycogen* is the primary storage molecule for carbohydrates. However, the human liver is capable of storing less than 500 kcal as glycogen; for this reason, liver glycogen stores are rapidly depleted within hours of beginning a fast. On the other hand, adipose tissue can house 100,000 or more kcal of stored fuel, enough to provide energy for months of survival during a prolonged fast. The following sections describe normal human fuel metabolism during the various conditions of fuel supply and demand.

Postabsorptive State

The hours following an overnight fast and preceding the morning meal are referred to as the *postabsorptive state*. During this time, concentrations of hormones (insulin and glucagon) and substrates (glucose, amino acids, and fatty acids) that responded to prior meal ingestion have returned to baseline, and the basal rate of total body fuel consumption is closely matched by the rate of endogenous fuel production. The postabsorptive state thus serves as a useful reference point for discussing normal and pathologic alterations in fuel metabolism.

Glucose

After an overnight fast, a decline in circulating insulin levels leads to a marked reduction in glucose uptake by peripheral insulin-sensitive tissues (e.g., skeletal muscle and fat), and favors the mobilization of free fatty acids (FFA) as energy-yielding fuels. Glucose consumption continues in non-insulin-sensitive tissues (e.g., the brain, renal medulla, formed blood elements) and in the gut, so that total body glucose utilization persists at a rate of 200 to 250 grams per day (3). In the postabsorptive state, the primary site of glucose consumption is the central nervous system (CNS), which is critically dependent on a continuous supply of glucose for oxidative metabolism. Despite the lack of exogenous fuel and ongoing glucose utilization, circulating blood glucose levels remain stable in the postabsorptive state, since the liver (and to a lesser extent, the kidney) releases glucose at a rate sufficient to match that of consuming tissues.

Glycogenolysis and *gluconeogenesis* are the two major processes involved in endogenous glucose production. In the postabsorptive state, more than 50% of hepatic glucose production is derived from glycogenolysis, with gluconeogenesis contributing most of the remaining half (4). The synthesis of glucose from lactate accounts for at least 50% of the gluconeogenic component; the remaining glucose is

TABLE 9-1. METABOLIC ACTIONS OF INSULIN

	Target Organ		
	Liver	**Adipose Tissue**	**Muscle**
Anticatabolic effects	↓ Glycogenolysis ↓ Gluconeogenesis ↓ Ketogenesis	↓ Lipolysis	↓ Proteolysis
Anabolic effects	↑ Glycogen synthesis ↑ Fat synthesis	↑ Fat synthesis ↑ Glycerol synthesis	↑ Glucose uptake ↑ Glycogen synthesis ↑ Protein synthesis

synthesized mostly from the conversion of glucogenic amino acids (e.g., alanine). The conversion of fat-derived glycerol and recycled pyruvate contribute less than 3% of total hepatic glucose production (5). Figure 9-1 summarizes normal glucose homeostasis in the postabsorptive state.

Regarding hormonal regulation of the postabsorptive state, glucagon serves mainly to maintain the constant release of glucose from the liver, while insulin suppresses hepatic glucose production. Compelling evidence that basal glucagon secretion is important for maintaining hepatic glucose production derives from studies in which somatostatin is infused to suppress glucagon production, while insulin levels are maintained by an exogenous insulin infusion. In this circumstance, a sustained 75% reduction in hepatic glucose production occurs (6). The restraining influence of basal concentrations of insulin on postabsorptive glucose production is evident in the opposite experiment, where plasma insulin levels are suppressed by somatostatin, while circulating glucagon levels are maintained using an exogenous glucagon infusion. Under these

conditions, there is a prompt increase in hepatic glucose production (7). Overall, then, hepatic glucose production appears to be regulated by a "push-pull" system under the influence of the opposing actions of insulin (inhibitory) and glucagon (stimulatory). In the postabsorptive state, hormonal regulation of glucose homeostasis is directed primarily at adjusting endogenous glucose production to match target organ demands.

Amino Acids

Following an overnight fast, skeletal muscle (the primary reservoir of total body protein stores) is in negative nitrogen balance, as evidenced by a net release of amino acids into the circulation (8). This net proteolysis is facilitated by declining insulin levels. Because plasma amino acid levels remain relatively constant, the increased amino acid release must be accompanied by augmented amino acid uptake by nonmuscular tissues; this uptake occurs primarily in the liver, and to a lesser extent in the kidney and gut. In sum-

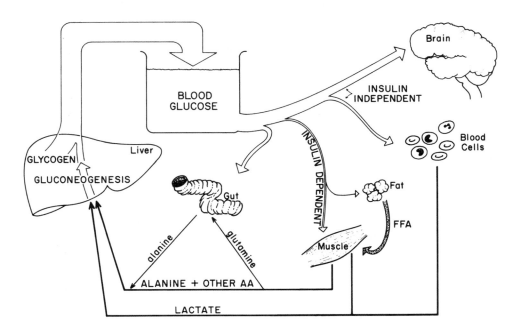

FIGURE 9-1. Glucose homeostasis in the postabsorptive state in normal humans. FFA, free fatty acids; AA, amino acids.

mary, during the postabsorptive state there is a net flux of amino acids from skeletal muscle to the liver. During hepatic metabolism of these amino acids, carbon atoms are utilized for gluconeogenesis, and nitrogenous waste products (urea and ammonia) are generated.

Although virtually all of the possible amino acids are released by skeletal muscle, *alanine* and *glutamine* predominate, accounting for more than 50% of amino acids released (9). Alanine is a primary substrate for hepatic gluconeogenesis. Glutamine serves both as a precursor for renal ammonia synthesis and as an energy-yielding fuel for the gut. Because alanine and glutamine account for less than 15% of amino acid residues in skeletal muscle protein, their release in higher concentrations (>50%) has been explained on the basis of *de novo* synthesis in muscle tissue.

The carbon skeleton of alanine is derived from *pyruvate* (Fig. 9-2); the majority of the pyruvate used for alanine synthesis is supplied by glycolysis (10). The branched chain amino acids (BCAAs; leucine, isoleucine, and valine) appear to serve as the predominant nitrogen sources for alanine production (11) (Fig. 9-2); in contrast to other amino acids, BCAAs are metabolized to a greater extent in muscle than in liver. BCAA oxidation in muscle appears to be sufficient to provide nearly all of the nitrogen required for alanine formation (12), and is a powerful determinant of the availability of alanine for hepatic gluconeogenesis. In marked contrast to alanine, the carbon skeleton (as well as the nitrogen source) of glutamine is most likely derived from the *in situ* catabolism of amino acids in skeletal muscle (13).

The pattern of amino acid uptake by the liver and gut complements that of skeletal muscle release; that is, alanine and glutamine are predominantly generated (14). Alanine is primarily used by the liver, whereas glutamine is taken up

mostly by the gut (15) (Fig. 9-1). However, glutamine does contribute to hepatic glucose (and urea) production, because a portion of the glutamine taken up by the gut is converted to alanine and released directly into the portal vein. The rate at which alanine and other amino acids are converted to glucose is in large part determined by the balance between glucagon (stimulatory) and insulin (inhibitory) concentrations in the portal vein. High insulin-to-glucagon ratios suppress BCAA oxidation, thereby reducing alanine availability for hepatic glucose production (16). The restraining effects of insulin on protein catabolism also limit the release of glucogenic amino acids from skeletal muscle, thereby complementing insulin's restraining effect on hepatic gluconeogenesis.

Fatty Acids

Following an overnight fast, a fall in circulating insulin levels facilitates the release of FFA from adipose tissue (Fig. 9-3). In the fat cell, insulin is an effective inhibitor of *hormone-sensitive lipase*, which catalyzes the hydrolysis of stored triglycerides to liberate glycerol and FFA. This antilipolytic action occurs at insulin concentrations far lower than those required to stimulate glucose transport (17).

The levels of insulin normally present in the postabsorptive state are sufficiently low to permit a flux of FFA from fat stores to extracerebral tissues, such as skeletal muscle, heart, renal cortex, and liver (Fig. 9-3). In these tissues, fatty acids serve as a principal energy-yielding fuel. In the postabsorptive state, the consumption of FFA by skeletal muscle is also an important factor in limiting muscle *glucose* uptake and oxidation. FFA reduce glycolytic flux and slow the entry of glucose-derived pyruvate into the Kreb's cycle (18). The magnitude of the insulin decline in portal blood after an overnight fast is not, however, of sufficient magnitude to significantly stimulate hepatic ketone production from FFA.

Metabolic Adaptation during Short-term Starvation

Because liver glycogen stores are limited to ~70 grams (19)—while total body (basal) glucose consumption occurs at approximately 200 to 250 grams per day—hepatic glycogen stores are rapidly dissipated early during a fast (20). As a result, the initial phase of starvation is characterized by accelerated gluconeogenesis to meet ongoing tissue demands for glucose, primarily from the CNS. During early starvation, the maintenance of glucose homeostasis is mediated by both hepatic and extrahepatic events. There is increased release of alanine and other glycogenic amino acids from skeletal muscle (21) as well as an increased rate of hepatic conversion of alanine to glucose (8). The latter effect is *not* solely a function of

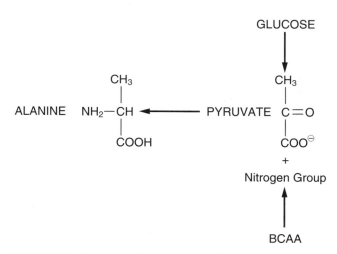

FIGURE 9-2. Alanine synthesis in muscle. The carbon skeleton of alanine is mainly derived from glucose, whereas branched chain amino acids (BCAA) play the dominant role in donating nitrogen atoms.

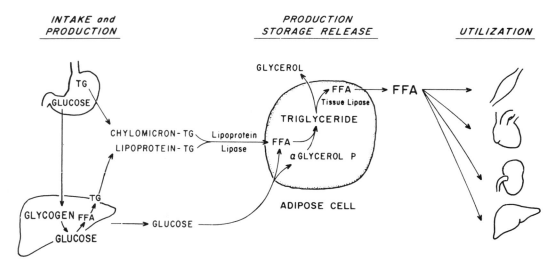

INTAKE *and* PRODUCTION

PRODUCTION STORAGE RELEASE

UTILIZATION

FIGURE 9-3. Fat synthesis, storage, and release in normal humans. Within the liver, insulin stimulates the conversion of glucose to free fatty acids (FFA) and the esterification of FFA to form triglycerides (TG). Both exogenously dietary triglycerides (chylomicron-TG) and endogenously synthesized triglycerides (lipoprotein-TG) contribute to fatty acid delivery to adipose tissue. Insulin accelerates adipocyte uptake of FFA through its stimulatory effect on lipoprotein lipase. Fat storage within adipose tissue is also enhanced by insulin's glycerogenic effects, as well as by its antilipolytic actions (inhibition of tissue lipase). When insulin levels fall, FFA are released from adipose tissue and are used for fuel by muscle, heart, kidney, and liver.

increased substrate availability, since plasma levels of alanine and other glycogenic amino acids actually fall during fasting, despite their increased release from skeletal muscle stores (22). These observations suggest that intrahepatic gluconeogenic mechanisms are stimulated during a short-term fast.

An additional factor contributing to glucose homeostasis during early starvation is an increased rate of lipolysis—and subsequent release of FFA—from adipose tissue. The oxidation of FFA by skeletal muscle conserves glucose for use by the CNS, whereas FFA oxidation by the liver activates key gluconeogenic enzymes and furnishes the energy and reducing power necessary for additional hepatic glucose synthesis (23).

The metabolic adaptations of early starvation (namely, increased gluconeogenesis, glycogenolysis, amino acid mobilization, and lipolysis) are facilitated by a decline in insulin secretion below postabsorptive levels, as well as by a modest increase in portal glucagon (24,25). Suppressed insulin secretion appears to be controlled primarily by a drop in arterial glucose concentrations, while the rise in glucagon is predominantly attributable to slowed glucagon metabolism (25). As shown in Fig. 9-4, hypoinsulinemia contributes in several complementary ways to promote gluconeogenesis; other than directly stimulating gluconeogenic enzymes, it enhances the delivery of glycogenic amino acids from muscle to liver and increases lipolysis and FFA availability. Hypoinsulinemia also reduces peripheral glucose consumption. In contrast, elevated glucagon levels act predominantly at the level of the liver.

Not surprisingly, the progressive rise in circulating *ketones* during starvation is also regulated by insulin and glucagon levels (26). The development of hyperketonemia involves (a) increased delivery of FFA from adipose tissue; (b) increased hepatic oxidation of FFA ("ketogenic capacity"); and (c) decreased ketone uptake by peripheral tissues. Hypoinsulinemia stimulates each of these processes, while

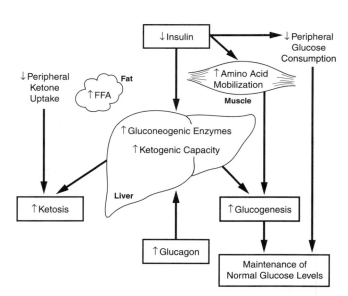

FIGURE 9-4. Interaction of insulin suppression and glucagon stimulation in promoting gluconeogenesis and ketosis during starvation. FFA, free fatty acid.

hyperglucagonemia contributes mainly by enhancing the ketogenic capacity of the liver (26) (Fig. 9-4). Growth hormone may also play a role in ketogenesis by stimulating lipolysis (27).

Exercise

As in starvation, during exercise there is a need to generate endogenous fuels to meet increased tissue demands. Because muscle glycogen stores are rapidly depleted by anerobic glycolysis, energy for working muscle must be supplied via blood-borne substrates. During exercise, fuels are supplied primarily by the liver, which can increase its production of glucose by 300% to 500% (28). Hepatic glucose production is precisely regulated to maintain normal circulating glucose levels despite increased glucose uptake by skeletal muscle. During exercise, FFA are also mobilized from adipose tissue, to minimize the depletion of the liver's limited glycogen stores. (Remember, these glycogen stores are best reserved for use by the CNS.) As exercise continues for prolonged periods, the consumption of FFA assumes an increasingly important role in meeting the energy requirements of working skeletal muscle (29) (Fig. 9-5). This spares the liver from further demands for glucose production, which, after prolonged exercise, occurs to an increasing extent from gluconeogenic precursors such as protein-derived amino acids (29).

During exercise, insulin secretion diminishes, the sympathetic nervous system is activated, and there is an incremental rise is several "counterregulatory" hormones including glucagon, cortisol, growth hormone, and catecholamines (epinephrine, norepinephrine). These hormones peak during high-intensity exercise (30). This hormonal milieu promotes the mobilization of glucose and FFA from the liver and adipose tissue, respectively, providing the necessary fuels for working muscle tissue. Nonhormonal mechanisms are also important during exercise; current evidence suggests that the increased fuel consumption by exercising muscle is mediated largely via local nonhormonal mechanisms, including increased transloca-

tion of glucose transport proteins (i.e., GLUT 4) to cell surfaces (31). The precise mechanisms for this translocation are poorly understood, but are likely mediated via activation of AMP kinase (32).

Glucose Ingestion

Glucose ingestion induces a variety of homeostatic mechanisms that serve to minimize rises in plasma glucose and to maintain normoglycemia. They include (a) suppression of endogenous glucose production by the liver; (b) stimulation of glucose uptake by splanchnic tissues (mostly the liver); and (c) stimulation of peripheral glucose uptake, most notably in skeletal muscle. These homeostatic processes are activated by rising insulin levels and/or by hyperglycemia itself. Specifically, inhibition of hepatic glucose production is exquisitely sensitive to small rises in portal insulin (33,34), but may also occur in response to hyperglycemia *per se* when portal insulin levels are clamped (35). Glucose uptake by splanchnic tissues is stimulated by rising glucose concentrations, and to some extent by hyperinsulinemia (36); basal insulin levels are required for glucose to exert this effect (37). By contrast, peripheral glucose uptake is promoted primarily by hyperinsulinemia and, to a lesser extent, by hyperglycemia itself (36). Note that considerably larger amounts of insulin are required to increase peripheral glucose uptake than to suppress hepatic glucose production (33).

While glucose is the dominant mediator of insulin secretion, there are other important effectors involved. Insulin responses to oral glucose are substantially higher than to an intravenous glucose load, mostly due to the secretion of incretins (e.g., glucagon-like peptide 1, gastrointestinal peptide) (38), and parasympathetic innervation from the gut (39). These incretins and neural signals are thought to "prime" pancreatic β-cells for augmented insulin release during ingested meals.

Following glucose ingestion, the liver and skeletal muscle play the predominant roles in the body's homeostatic

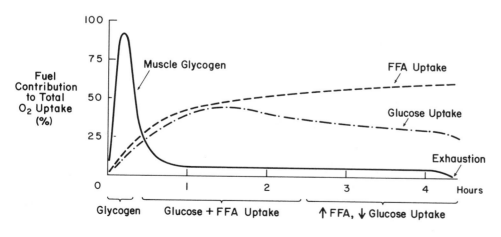

FIGURE 9-5. Time-dependent changes in the contribution of muscle glycogen and blood-borne fuels to the energy requirements of leg muscles during bicycle exercise. FFA, free fatty acid.

response. Approximately two-thirds of an exogenous glucose load is deposited in skeletal muscle, while the remaining third is taken up by splanchnic tissues (e.g., liver and gut) (40). When one considers that the liver also reduces endogenous production of glucose by more than 50%, the net effect is a substantial splanchnic retention of glucose, which is similar in magnitude to the amount of glucose deposited in skeletal muscle tissue. The normal homeostatic response to an exogenous glucose load is summarized in Fig. 9-6.

It is important to recognize that responses to an oral glucose load (e.g., a glucose tolerance test) are *not* representative of blood glucose excursions observed in healthy individuals during ordinary meals. During circumstances of *mixed meal* intake (carbohydrates, fats, and proteins), blood glucose levels generally vary by no more than 30 to 40 mg/dL over 24 hours. This "fine tuning" is primarily determined by the exquisite sensitivity of the liver to minimal changes in insulin secretion. When small amounts of glucose are consumed, peripheral insulin levels rise only modestly (less than twofold). However, because insulin is released directly into the portal vein, portal insulin concentrations rise several times higher. Consequently, hepatic glucose production is suppressed, while peripheral glucose uptake (which requires higher insulin levels for activation) is only modestly increased, if at all (41). Thus, as compared with the liver, skeletal muscle and adipose tissue are involved to a more limited extent in the metabolic adjustment to very small glucose loads. This phenomenon is a direct consequence of the disparity of the dose-response curves of hepatic and peripheral tissues to insulin (33).

Protein Ingestion

Because muscle is in negative nitrogen balance in the fasting state, the repletion of muscle nitrogen depends upon a

net uptake of amino acids after protein ingestion. This transfer of amino acids from the gut into muscle tissue is facilitated by the action of insulin. In the presence of insulin, muscle proteolysis is suppressed (42), producing positive muscle nitrogen balance despite a lack of stimulated total body protein synthesis (43). Interestingly, mixed meals of carbohydrate and protein result in greater insulin production than protein meals alone, further facilitating insulin-mediated protein anabolism.

In healthy subjects, ingestion of a pure protein meal is followed by a large output of amino acids from the splanchnic bed. Valine, leucine, and isoleucine (the BCAAs) account for more than 60% of amino acids entering the systemic circulation, even though they contribute only 20% of the amino acids in the protein meal (44). Simultaneous with the release of amino acids from the splanchnic bed, there is increased uptake of amino acids into skeletal muscle; again, BCAAs account for more than half of the amino acid uptake (44). BCAAs therefore constitute the primary substrates for the immediate repletion of muscle nitrogen following protein intake. Furthermore, because BCAAs comprise only 20% of the amino acid residues in muscle protein (12), it is likely that they are catabolized within muscle as a source of energy. Interestingly, high intracellular levels of BCAAs in muscle induced by protein feeding may have importance beyond the delivery of nitrogen. There is evidence that BCAAs have the unique capacity to directly stimulate net protein accumulation through complementary mechanisms of inhibiting of protein catabolism and stimulating protein synthesis (45,46).

Fat Ingestion

The rise in plasma insulin following the ingestion of a mixed meal accelerates tissue uptake of ingested triglyceride

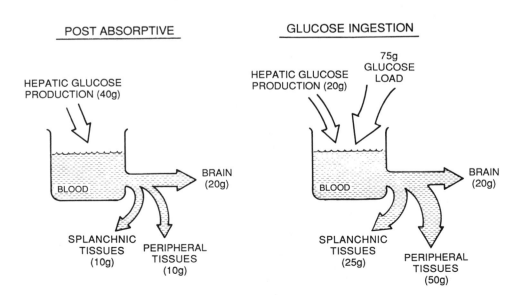

FIGURE 9-6. Cumulative rates of hepatic glucose production and glucose disposal by non–insulin-dependent tissues (e.g., brain), the splanchnic bed, and peripheral insulin-sensitive tissues (e.g., muscle) during a 4-hour period either in the postabsorptive state (fast) or following ingestion of a 75-gram glucose load in normal subjects. After glucose ingestion, hepatic glucose production is reduced by 50%, and glucose uptake is increased in both splanchnic (2.5-fold) and peripheral (five-fold) tissues.

(TG), and serves to promote fat synthesis and storage in both the liver and adipose tissue. Insulin uses several complementary mechanisms of action to achieve these lipogenic effects (Fig. 9-3).

Following ingestion, triglycerides are hydrolyzed to FFA by intestinal lipases. Once absorbed in the small intestine, the FFA are then reesterified into *chylomicron-TG*, which enters the blood via the lymphatics. In capillary endothelium, insulin stimulates *lipoprotein lipase*, which hydrolyzes chylomicron-TG (and endogenous lipoprotein-TG) back into FFA, which in turn are taken up by adipocytes for triglyceride synthesis and eventual storage (47). This effect is complemented by insulin's potent inhibitory effect on *hormone-sensitive lipase* within the adipocyte (preventing TG hydrolysis), as well as by insulin's glycerogenic effects. Insulin stimulates glucose entry into adipocytes via GLUT-4 translocation to the adipocyte surface; a large proportion of the glucose taken up by the adipocyte is used to make α-*glycerophosphate*, which in adipose tissue is necessary for the esterification of fatty acids to form triglycerides (48).

The net effects of the antilipolytic, fat synthetic, and glycerogenic actions of meal-stimulated insulin elevations are to increase total fat synthesis and storage, to reduce circulating FFA, and to inhibit the formation of ketone bodies. Fig. 9-3 summarizes the complex pathways of fat synthesis, storage, and release during normal human metabolism.

Role of Gender in Glucose Homeostasis

Historically, the assessment of fuel metabolism has typically been performed without regard to the hormonal milieu of sex-specific steroids. Recently, however, converging lines of evidence suggest the existence of important gender-related differences in fuel metabolism. In response to exogenous insulin infusions, total whole-body glucose uptake (and glucose uptake per unit of insulin) is greater in males than females, perhaps due in part to their larger total body muscle mass (49–51). Additionally, it is known that the metabolic response to prolonged fasting differs by gender. In men, fasting induces a slow, gradual drop in circulating glucose, and levels rarely fall below 50 mg/dL. In women, there is an accelerated decline in fasting glucose levels, which often fall into the 40- to 50-mg/dL range after 48 to 72 hours (52). Although the explanation for these differences has not been established, it has been suggested that the smaller muscle mass of women may be responsible, and that the generation of glucogenic amino acids from muscle may be less in fasted females than males. In support of this theory, it has been demonstrated that the fast-induced decline in circulating alanine is more pronounced in women than in men (52). Despite converging evidence that women achieve lower glucose levels during prolonged fasting than men, the literature contains conflicting data regarding the effect of gender on counterregulatory hormone responses to

hypoglycemia. Several reports have demonstrated that epinephrine, norepinephrine, and growth hormone responses to hypoglycemia and other stimuli are significantly higher in males (53,54). Other investigators, however, have failed to demonstrate such differences (55); these discrepancies remain unsatisfactorily explained.

Finally, the female menstrual cycle also appears to exert some effects on body fuel metabolism. Assessments of carbohydrate metabolism during hyperglycemia have demonstrated increased glucose uptake during the preovulatory period (56–58). However, no detectable differences in the basal rate of glucose turnover, insulin-stimulated glucose uptake, or insulin-induced suppression of hepatic glucose output have been observed between the two phases of the menstrual cycle (59–61). Counterregulatory hormone responses to hypoglycemia also appear to be similar in the follicular and luteal phase (62).

LACK OF INSULIN ACTION IN DIABETES MELLITUS

Diabetes mellitus is a chronic syndrome in which a complex interaction of hereditary and environmental factors leads to inadequate insulin *action*, due to decreased insulin secretion and/or decreased insulin sensitivity (*insulin resistance*) in target tissues. In patients with type 1 diabetes, a complex interplay of genetic, environmental, and autoimmune factors selectively destroys pancreatic β-cells, producing a profound insulin secretory defect, often with secondary insulin resistance. Patients with type 2 diabetes, in contrast, have less severe insulin deficiency but greater impairment in insulin action. Regardless of causation, the metabolic consequences of diabetes mellitus primarily reflect the degree to which there exists absolute or relative insulin deficiency. Insulin's critical role in the pathophysiology of diabetes derives from its function as the primary regulatory hormone for human fuel metabolism.

Insulin Secretion in Diabetes

In patients with diabetes, defects of insulin secretion range from a complete lack of insulin to a partial secretory deficiency that becomes apparent only during periods of increased insulin demand, such as aging, physical stress, illness, or pregnancy.

In type 1 patients, insulin secretory defects are typically progressive and severe. While most type 1 patients produce some degree of endogenous insulin for several years (despite the need for early insulin supplementation) (63), endogenous insulin secretion is ultimately lost as functioning β-cells are selectively destroyed. Interestingly, the extent to which endogenous insulin secretion is maintained appears to be an important factor in determining the stability of long-term metabolic control in these patients (64).

In patients with type 2 diabetes, defects of insulin secretion are typically less severe. Whereas glucose-stimulated insulin secretion is usually impaired, fasting insulin levels may be normal or even high, reflecting the pancreas's attempt to overcome peripheral insulin resistance. In type 2 patients, the magnitude of the insulin secretory defect correlates with the severity of fasting hyperglycemia. In mild cases (i.e., fasting plasma glucose >126 mg/dL), there is often selective impairment of the first-phase insulin response. In such individuals, the loss of β-cell responsiveness is *specific to glucose*; that is, the β-cells respond normally to other insulin secretogogues such as amino acids and β-adrenergic stimulation (65). Consequently, insulin deficiency is much less pronounced during the ingestion of mixed meals as compared with during pure sugar ingestion (66). In type 2 patients with more severe fasting hyperglycemia (≥200 mg/dL), the β-cells' capacity to respond to increased circulating glucose levels is more severely affected. These observations suggest that a specific abnormality in β-cell glucose recognition occurs in the earliest stages of type 2 diabetes, and that this defect worsens as the disease course progresses.

The classic reports by Yalow and Berson (67) emphasized the presence of hyperinsulinemia in patients with type 2 diabetes. This seeming paradox was later shown to be more apparent than real, when viewed in the context of body weight and ambient blood glucose levels. More than 80% to 85% of patients with type 2 diabetes are obese. It is now known that obesity *per se* is accompanied by hyperinsulinemia, and is associated with insulin resistance on the part of target tissues (68). When a comparison is made between obese type 2 diabetic patients and weight-matched nondiabetic controls, it is clear that insulin levels in obese diabetic patients are lower than those observed in obese subjects with normal glucose tolerance (69). Hyperglycemia itself also plays a role in generating hyperinsulinemia in type 2 patients. In other words, when glucose levels are raised in nondiabetic subjects (to simulate the glucose tolerance curve of diabetic patients), the deficient insulin response observed in diabetic patients becomes more readily apparent.

Insulin Resistance in Diabetes

Insulin's biologic activity relates not only to its circulating concentrations, but also to its functional ability to activate cellular events. On a cellular level, the first step of insulin action involves its binding to a specific *insulin receptor* on the target cell surface. This ligand-receptor interaction triggers a cascade of complex cellular changes, termed *postreceptor events*, which produce the eventual metabolic response. The concentrations of insulin required to activate metabolic processes vary significantly with respect to both target tissues and fuel substrates involved. For example, a doubling of systemic insulin levels achieves near-maximal suppression of lipolysis, but has little effect on glucose uptake by skeletal muscle and other peripheral tissues (70). The insulin concentrations needed to promote protein anabolism or to suppress hepatic glucose production fall between these extremes (33,71). As a result of this marked variability, the metabolic consequences of incomplete insulin deficiency vary substantially among the various body fuels and target tissues involved.

Type 2 diabetes is characterized by insulin resistance or the impaired effectiveness of the insulin molecule to exert metabolic effects (72). Peripheral tissues such as skeletal muscle are preferentially affected; in these tissues, the insulin dose-response curve for augmenting glucose uptake is shifted to the right, and maximal response is also reduced, particularly in the setting of severe hyperglycemia (73). Other insulin-stimulated processes, such as the inhibition of hepatic glucose production, also show reduced sensitivity to insulin in type 2 patients. In contrast to skeletal muscle, however, hepatic insulin resistance is more readily overcome by larger concentrations of circulating insulin (74).

Early studies of insulin resistance focused on defects of the insulin receptor. Although insulin receptor abnormalities are present in some patients with type 2 diabetes (e.g., leprechaunism), it is now recognized that post-receptor defects play the more dominant role in explaining insulin resistance (74). Intracellular free fatty acid metabolites appear to promote insulin resistance through complex mechanisms, including a reduced capacity for GLUT 4 translocation to the cell surface (74). In addition, the coexistence of obesity clearly accentuates the severity of the resistant state. In particular, *visceral* fat deposits have a higher lipolysis rate and are more insulin resistant than peripheral fat stores. In the setting of excess visceral adiposity, elevated FFA levels promote further fat deposition in liver and muscle, generating a vicious cycle of worsening insulin resistance (75).

Interestingly, insulin sensitivity is also impaired in patients with type 1 diabetes (76) and in animals rendered partially insulin deficient by subtotal pancreatectomy. In these circumstances, the insulin resistance is to a large extent responsive to more intensive insulin therapy (77). Thus, even in type 1 diabetes, insulin resistance may hinder therapeutic measures directed at improving glycemic control.

ALTERATIONS IN BODY FUEL METABOLISM IN DIABETES MELLITUS

As discussed above, the metabolic alterations observed with diabetes primarily reflect the degree to which there is absolute or relative insulin deficiency. Viewed in the context of insulin as the primary fuel storage hormone, insulin deficiency results in a diminished ability to effectively store body fuels, largely due to inadequate disposal of ingested meals; hyperglycemia, hyperaminoacidemia, and hypertriglyceridemia result. In its most severe form (diabetic ketoacidosis), insulin absence leads to glucose overproduction and to the marked acceleration of catabolic processes including glycogenolysis, lipolysis, and proteolysis.

Postabsorptive State

Following an overnight fast, most diabetic patients exhibit persistent fasting hyperglycemia. In patients with more severe hyperglycemia, rates of endogenous fuel production exceed rates of consumption, resulting in glycosuria and additional energy wasting. In this way, diabetes can be thought of as a state of "accelerated starvation," a situation not unlike the one observed during normal pregnancy.

Glucose

When absolute or relative insulin deficiency occurs in the postabsorptive state, elevated fasting glucose levels ensue. When these elevations are mild (100 to 125 mg/dL), patients are said to have *impaired fasting glucose (IFG)* levels. Once fasting levels exceed 126 mg/dL, the diagnosis of diabetes mellitus is established (78). In nondiabetic individuals, minimal hyperglycemia is sufficient to fully suppress hepatic glucose production (41). In diabetics, however (or in patients with IFG), hepatic glucose production is inadequately suppressed at each given level of hyperglycemia (79), resulting in a constant state of relative or absolute glucose overproduction (Fig. 9-7). In type 1 patients, a more severe portal insulin deficiency results in more consistently elevated hepatic glucose production. In this circumstance, insulin deficiency may lead to hypersecretion of glucagon and growth hormone, further accentuating glucose overproduction by the liver (80,81).

In diabetic patients, gluconeogenesis accounts for a substantially larger proportion of hepatic glucose production as compared with normal subjects, in whom glycogenolysis accounts for more than half of fasting glucose production

(82). For example, in patients with type 1 diabetes, the absence of insulin's restraining effect allows for increased hepatic uptake of glycogenic substrates and for increased conversion of these substrates into glucose. By contrast, the magnitude and pattern of amino acid release from muscle in type 1 diabetic subjects are similar to those of healthy controls (82), implying that intrahepatic effects are primarily responsible for the augmented gluconeogenesis. It is possible that increased recycling of glycolytic intermediates (e.g., lactate) may occur as well. Finally, observations of increased gluconeogenesis in type 2 diabetes are consistent with the fact that in the liver, greater amounts of insulin are necessary to inhibit gluconeogenesis as compared with glycogenolysis (83).

In the extreme situation of total insulin lack, rapidly increasing blood glucose levels fail to elicit an appropriate insulin response. This insulin absence, together with the excessive release of counterregulatory hormones (glucagon, cortisol, growth hormone, and catecholamines), leads to accelerated gluconeogenesis and a three-fold (or more) increase in hepatic glucose production. Finally, in the setting of both insulin deficiency and severe insulin resistance (produced by the insulin-antagonistic hormones), compensatory increases in peripheral glucose disposal are essentially paralyzed. The clinical correlates of these metabolic events are profound hyperglycemia and glycosuria, as is observed in cases of diabetic ketoacidosis (DKA) or the hyperosmolar hyperglycemic state (HHS). If even minimal insulin levels are present, clinically significant ketogenesis can usually be suppressed; this is the essential pathophysiologic difference between DKA and the HHS.

Amino Acids

In the postabsorptive state, diabetic patients have elevated circulating amino acid levels. Closer examination reveals that this hyperaminoacidemia is due almost entirely to higher levels of the branched chain amino acids (BCAAs) (82) (Fig. 9-8). By contrast, plasma alanine levels may be reduced, particularly when insulin deficiency is severe (84). The specific tissue site accounting for the rise in plasma BCAAs has not been fully clarified. For example, there is no demonstrable increase in the net release of BCAAs from either leg (82) or splanchnic tissues in diabetic subjects (84). Nevertheless, recent studies using radioactive tracers demonstrate that the delivery of BCAAs into the circulation is augmented in poorly controlled type 1 diabetic patients (85). Considering that the BCAAs are essential amino acids, these studies imply that total body protein breakdown is increased in such patients. In the clinical setting, these protein fluxes are not usually detected, perhaps because of compensatory increases in protein synthesis to minimize body protein loss. This compensation is presumably lost when insulin deficiency becomes very severe, as evidenced by the stunted growth of young diabetic patients in the preinsulin era, and by the marked protein wasting of type 1 patients with ketoacidosis.

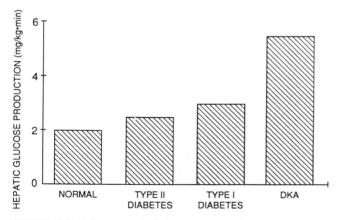

FIGURE 9-7. Influence of diabetes and diabetic ketoacidosis (DKA) on fasting hepatic glucose production.

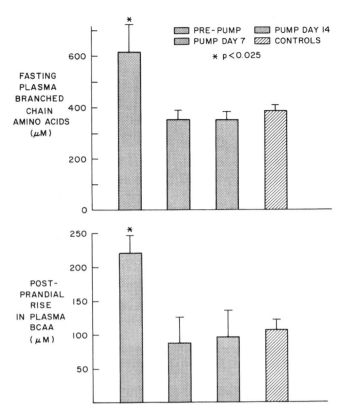

FIGURE 9-8. Fasting and postprandial increments (after mixed meal ingestion) in branched-chain amino acids (BCAA) in type 1 diabetic patients and healthy controls. The diabetic patients were studied at baseline (during poor glycemic control), and following 7 and 14 days of intensive insulin therapy using a portable insulin pump. (Based on data of Tamborlane WV, Sherwin RS, Genel M, et al. Restoration of normal lipid and amino-acid metabolism in diabetic patients treated with a portable insulin-infusion pump. *Lancet* 1979;1:1258, with permission.)

In type 1 diabetic patients, elevated circulating levels of BCAAs also facilitate their accelerated oxidation (16,85). The increased *in situ* catabolism of these amino acids provides muscle tissue with the nitrogen groups necessary for alanine synthesis (11), thereby increasing substrate availability for gluconeogenesis. In this way, the accelerated breakdown of muscle amino acids contributes indirectly to hyperglycemia.

The described abnormalities of BCAA metabolism are frequently absent in patients with type 2 diabetes. This is likely because the metabolism of BCAAs is dependent on lower insulin levels than those required for peripheral glucose metabolism (42).

Free Fatty Acids

Circulating FFA levels are frequently elevated in postabsorptive diabetic patients (86). This phenomenon appears to be a consequence of accelerated mobilization of body fat stores, and can primarily be attributed to diminished

insulin action. In type 2 diabetic subjects, FFA elevations occur in the presence of normal or increased insulin levels (86), suggesting resistance to insulin's inhibitory effect on lipolysis. The increased availability of FFA leads to their oxidation by skeletal muscle, which in turn leads to a diminished rate of glucose oxidation (18). Although FFA cannot be directly converted to glucose, they promote hyperglycemia in diabetic patients by providing the liver with energy-yielding fuel and cofactors to support gluconeogenesis. FFA also interfere with glucose disposal in skeletal muscle (87) by activating cellular processes that interfere with insulin signaling.

In type 2 diabetes, the presence of endogenous insulin secretion allows for sufficient portal insulin levels to suppress ketogenic processes in the liver. In patients with type 1 diabetes, however, mobilized FFA are more readily converted to ketone bodies. The lack of insulin in the portal circulation suppresses fat synthesis in the liver, and thus lowers intrahepatic levels of malonyl co-enzyme A. Together with an increased availability of carnitine, these processes stimulate the activity of hepatic acylcarnitine transferase, which facilitates the transfer of long chain fatty acids into mitochondria, where they are broken down via β-oxidation and converted to ketone bodies (26) (Fig. 9-9). Hypoinsulinemia also favors decreased ketone utilization by peripheral tissues, contributing to hyperketonemia. By virtue of insulin's inhibitory effect on ketone turnover, hypoinsulinemia in the type 1 diabetic patient enhances the magnitude of the ketosis for any given level of ketone production (88). As a result, blood ketones may be elevated in poorly controlled type 1 diabetic patients; however, the magnitude of this elevation is generally not sufficient to significantly alter normal acid-base balance, and usually causes no symptoms.

Finally, patients with diabetes commonly exhibit elevated fasting concentrations of lipoproteins. Most striking is the elevation in *very low-density lipoprotein* (VLDL) triglyceride, which can be seen in many types of diabetic patients. In type 2 patients, for instance, elevated portal insulin levels may promote VLDL triglyceride synthesis. In type 1 patients, in contrast, there is deficient lipoprotein lipase activity, leading to decreased triglyceride clearance from the circulation (89–91).

Glucose Ingestion

In nondiabetic subjects, the ingestion of glucose triggers a variety of homeostatic responses aimed at minimizing the postprandial rise in blood glucose concentrations. These responses include suppression of endogenous glucose production and stimulation of glucose uptake by splanchnic and peripheral tissues. Because these homeostatic changes are largely dependent on insulin, diabetes, even in its mildest forms, is almost invariably accompanied by postprandial hyperglycemia.

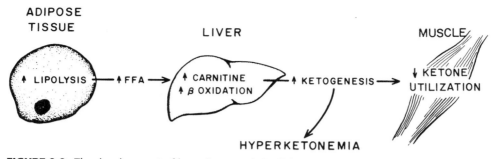

FIGURE 9-9. The development of hyperketonemia in diabetic patients is a consequence of three distinct metabolic events: (a) accelerated delivery of free fatty acids (FFA) from adipose tissue; (b) augmented β-oxidation of FFA to ketones as a result of elevated cartinine levels and reduced concentrations of malonyl co-enzyme A; and (c) reduced ketone utilization in skeletal muscle. Each of these processes is inhibited by the action of insulin.

In patients with *impaired glucose tolerance (IGT)*, relative insulin deficiency is by definition apparent only after carbohydrate ingestion, when augmented peripheral glucose uptake is required to compensate for increased glucose availability. In patients with IGT, postabsorptive (fasting) glucose levels are normal, because basal insulin secretion is adequate to inhibit hepatic glucose production (Table 9-2); remember that this process is sensitive to minor changes in insulin levels. IGT patients generally have impaired early insulin secretory responses to glucose, as well as markedly diminished peripheral insulin sensitivity (73). Postprandial hyperglycemia in these patients mainly derives from reduced glucose uptake by skeletal muscle (and to a lesser extent, by the liver and other peripheral tissues). According to current American Diabetes Association criteria, IGT is diagnosed in nonpregnant patients when glucose levels 2 hours after a 75-gram oral glucose load fall between 140 and 199 mg/dL (in patients with fasting glucose levels below 126 mg/dL). If these 2-hour glucose levels exceed 200 mg/dL, diabetes mellitus has been established (78).

In patients with overt type 2 diabetes, a similar but more pronounced pattern is observed (92). These patients have both increased insulin resistance and a further blunted insulin secretory response; as a result, they can no longer overcome their defects in peripheral insulin action by secreting larger amounts of insulin (73). Type 2 patients do, however, have sufficient *portal* insulin levels to permit hyperglycemia itself to suppress hepatic glucose production, and to some extent promote hepatic glucose uptake (Table 9-2). These conditions do tend to reduce postprandial glucose excursions to some degree, at least when compared to the responses of insulin-deficient type 1 patients.

The type 1 diabetic patient characteristically shows the most marked and prolonged elevations in blood glucose concentrations following carbohydrate ingestion. These patients, because they fail to secrete any endogenous insulin, have considerably lower portal insulin levels than patients with type 2 diabetes, and their loss of this portal-peripheral insulin gradient is not readily reversed by subcutaneous insulin therapy. Consequently, the insulin-deprived liver fails to suppress hepatic glucose production, and fails to promote hepatic glucose uptake in response to rising glucose levels (82). In addition, glucose uptake by peripheral tissues is further impaired by the total lack of an insulin secretory response, and because of the development of worsening insulin resistance following chronic insulin deprivation (76) (Table 9-2). The net result of this multifaceted disturbance is a gross defect in metabolic glucose disposal that can only be partially compensated for by increased renal glycosuria.

The impact of glucose ingestion on FFA metabolism is also worth a brief discussion. In normal subjects, the rise in plasma insulin following glucose ingestion also inhibits lipolysis, which in turn decreases the availability of FFA for oxidation in skeletal muscle. This diminished availability of FFA facilitates glucose uptake and oxidation into skeletal muscle, because FFA oxidation interferes with both glycolysis and the movement of glucose-derived pyruvate into the Kreb's cycle (87). In type 2 diabetic subjects, despite some availability of insulin, there is much less suppression of lipolysis during glucose ingestion due to insulin resistance (86); as a result, there is an accumulation of FFA. Similar metabolic changes are observed in type 1 patients, mostly

TABLE 9-2. HOMEOSTATIC RESPONSE TO GLUCOSE INGESTION IN PATIENTS WITH IMPAIRED GLUCOSE TOLERANCE OR DIABETES MELLITUS

	Impaired Glucose Tolerance	Type 2 Diabetes	Type 1 Diabetes
Suppression of hepatic glucose production	NL	NL or ↓	↓↓
Stimulation of splanchnic glucose uptake	NL	NL	↓↓
Stimulation of peripheral glucose uptake		↓↓	↓↓

NL, normal; ↓, below normal; ↓↓, well below normal.

due to insulin lack, although insulin resistance may contribute in these patients as well. In summary, the failure of diabetic patients to suppress fat oxidation during glucose consumption results in excess circulating FFA, which worsen peripheral insulin resistance and block the uptake and oxidation of glucose entering skeletal muscle.

Protein Ingestion

In addition to defects in protein metabolism reflected in the postabsorptive state (increased use of amino acids for gluconeogenesis, increased release of BCAAs), patients with *type 1* diabetes also have impaired repletion of muscle nitrogen stores after protein ingestion. Following ingestion of a protein meal, the net splanchnic release of individual amino acids in type 1 diabetic subjects is similar to that observed in healthy controls (44). However, postprandial amino acid elevations are exaggerated (44) due completely to excess circulating levels of BCAAs (Fig. 9-8). In normal subjects, there is an ongoing net uptake of BCAAs by muscle tissues to prevent hyperaminoacidemia. In diabetic patients, however, this net uptake is only transiently observed (44), resulting in excess circulating BCAA levels. Type 1 diabetes thus may be viewed as a disorder of protein tolerance as well as glucose tolerance. This view is consistent with the known capacity of insulin to inhibit the net release of BCAAs from

skeletal muscle (93). Because the capacity to release insulin in response to systemic hyperaminoacidemia is usually intact in patients with type 2 diabetes (66) comparable defects in protein disposal generally do not occur in type 2 patients.

In diabetic subjects, protein feeding also contributes to abnormalities in glucose regulation. In normal subjects, protein ingestion induces a modest rise in insulin secretion, which offsets the stimulatory effects of glucagon (and the amino acid load itself) on hepatic glucose production (44). As a result, blood glucose levels remain at basal values. By contrast, in diabetic subjects protein ingestion produces a large (albeit transient) increase in hepatic glucose production, mostly due to elevated glucagon levels without the restraining effects of insulin (44). Consequently, diabetic patients experience substantial hyperglycemia following protein ingestion (Fig. 9-10), which is exaggerated by ongoing hepatic glucose production and peripheral insulin resistance.

Fat Ingestion

The consumption of fatty foods leads to the formation of *chylomicrons*, which provide a means of transferring triglycerides from the gut into adipose tissue. The ultimate disposal of exogenous triglycerides (and endogenous triglycerides) is regulated by the activity of insulin-sensitive *lipoprotein lipase*

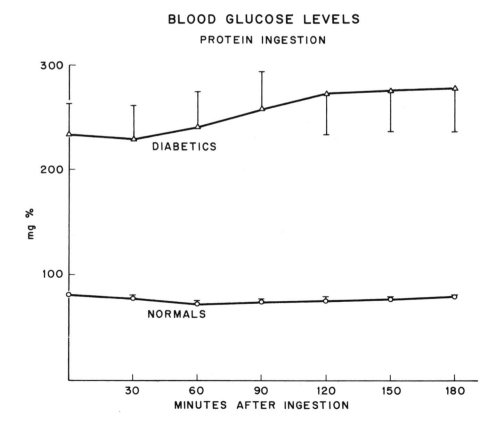

FIGURE 9-10. Hyperglycemic effect of protein feeding in patients with type 1 diabetes.

(Fig. 9-3). In diabetic patients, then, postprandial elevations of plasma triglycerides may be increased and/or prolonged, mostly due to defective triglyceride disposal.

As discussed above, increased circulating FFA after a fatty meal can inhibit glucose uptake and oxidation by skeletal muscle, because FFA oxidation interferes with both glycolysis and the movement of glucose-derived pyruvate into the Kreb's cycle (87). In diabetic patients, then, fat ingestion can contribute to further worsening of glucose dysregulation.

Exercise

After vigorous exercise, diabetic patients may experience a rapid decline in blood glucose levels; this observation has been the traditional basis for recommending exercise to patients with diabetes. This acute glucose-lowering action is more pronounced in insulin-treated patients, and occurs only if insulin therapy is sufficient to prevent marked hyperglycemia and ketosis (94). The importance of insulin availability in mediating these effects is underscored by two important observations in insulin-dependent patients. First, the magnitude of the blood glucose decline is clearly greater if exercise coincides with the peak action of the insulin preparation used. Second, exercise may accelerate insulin absorption from subcutaneous injection sites, predictably producing a more pronounced drop in circulating glucose levels (95).

Studies using radiolabeled glucose have helped to elucidate the mechanism of the glucose-lowering effect of acute exercise in diabetic patients. Normally, exercise leads to a marked increase in glucose uptake by skeletal muscle (28). Blood glucose levels remain stable, because hepatic glucose production increases to compensate for increased rates of peripheral glucose consumption. This process is mediated by a decline in circulating insulin levels and by activation of the sympathetic nervous system, as well as by the release of counterregulatory hormones (30). In diabetic patients receiving exogenous insulin (i.e., in patients without endogenous insulin regulation), circulating insulin levels may remain inappropriately high during exercise. Concurrently, exercise may enhance the absorption of insulin from subcutaneous injection sites. The resulting relative hyperinsulinemia prevents the normal compensatory increase in hepatic glucose production, and may also potentiate glucose uptake by exercising muscle (96). The net effect is a potentially dangerous fall in circulating blood glucose levels (Fig. 9-11).

The clinical utility of the acute glucose-lowering effects of exercise in type 1 diabetes is limited. Unless exercise is regular and of appropriate intensity and duration, there is little long-term "carry-over" that can be expected to improve long-term glycemic control. Furthermore, the magnitude of these effects is not easily titrated; as a result, hypoglycemia is a frequent complication of vigorous exer-

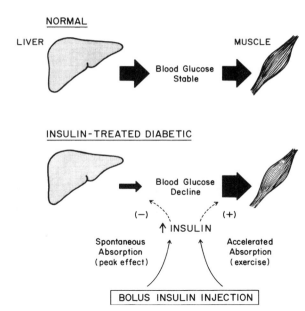

FIGURE 9-11. Mechanism of exercise-induced hypoglycemia in insulin-treated diabetic patients. In insulin-treated diabetic patients, insulin levels fail to drop during exercise. Concurrently, exercise may lead to enhanced absorption of exogenous insulin from subcutaneous injection sites. The resulting relative hyperinsulinemia prevents the normal compensatory increase in hepatic glucose production, and may also potentiate glucose uptake by exercising muscle. The net effect is a fall in circulating blood glucose levels.

cise in type 1 patients. The rapid rise in counterregulatory hormones that ensues, coupled with the increased responsiveness of diabetic patients to these hormones (81) and the tendency to overeat when hypoglycemic symptoms occur, can lead to rebound hyperglycemia. Thus, in clinical practice, acute intermittent exercise may actually cause large fluctuations in blood glucose levels, rather than its desired effect of improving glycemic control.

In poorly regulated ketotic diabetics, exercise tends to accentuate both hyperglycemia and ketonemia, particularly if the exercise is prolonged (97). These observations may be explained by hypoinsulinemia and/or the exaggerated release of counterregulatory hormones in response to exercise (98). These hormonal changes (coupled with the diabetic hyperresponsiveness to counterregulatory hormones) potentiate exercise-induced increases in hepatic glucose production, and can also stimulate lipolysis and ketone production by the liver (Fig. 9-12). Because exercise-induced stimulation of glucose uptake in skeletal muscle occurs *independently* of insulin (as described above), glucose consumption by exercising muscle is relatively unaffected during poor glycemic control, and thus does not contribute significantly to rising blood glucose levels (99).

Baseline differences in rates of gluconeogenesis between nondiabetic and type 1 diabetic subjects are also further exaggerated during exercise. During short-term exercise in nondiabetic subjects, increased hepatic glucose production

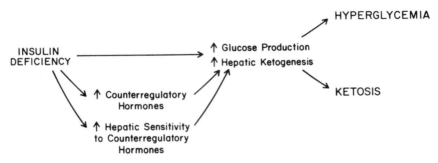

FIGURE 9-12. Mechanism of exercise-induced hyperglycemia and ketosis in poorly controlled type 1 diabetic patients. In poorly regulated type 1 patients, exercise can accentuate insulin deficiency, resulting in the exaggerated release of counter-regulatory hormones in response to exercise. These hormonal changes (coupled with the diabetic hyper-responsiveness to counter-regulatory hormones) may potentiate exercise-induced increases in hepatic glucose production, and can stimulate hepatic lipolysis and ketone production. Hyperglycemia and ketosis result.

is mediated by accelerated glycogenolysis; rates of gluconeogenesis generally remain unchanged (28). By contrast, diabetic patients demonstrate a rapid increase in gluconeogenesis during exercise; in normal subjects, these changes can be induced only by prolonged (2 to 4 hours) periods of exercise (94). In summary, the effect of exercise in insulin-deficient diabetic patients is to exaggerate the excessive rate of gluconeogenesis that characterizes diabetes.

There appears to be a more favorable risk-benefit ratio for exercise in patients with type 2 diabetes, as compared with insulin-dependent patients. In type 2 patients, regular aerobic exercise improves insulin sensitivity, and can have beneficial effects on both long-term glycemic control and cardiovascular outcomes (100). Also, since type 2 patients maintain some degree of endogenous insulin regulation, there is a reduced tendency for dangerous glycemic excursions during exercise. As a result, a program of aerobic exercise is routinely recommended for the majority of patients with type 2 diabetes. For type 1 patients, a regular exercise program is also advocated, predominantly for the prevention of cardiovascular disease.

Effect of Intensive Insulin Therapy on Body Fuel Metabolism

As described above, poorly controlled diabetes mellitus is characterized by a variety of metabolic and hormonal abnormalities that contribute to its long-term complications. Recent clinical advances, including improved methods for quantifying glycemic control and improved insulin delivery, have allowed us to investigate the extent to which these abnormalities and complications can be reversed by physiologic insulin delivery. Many clinical studies have demonstrated that *intensive insulin therapy* (i.e., multiple injections or the use of an insulin pump) can restore blood glucose levels to near-normal values (101–103). Because intensive regimens provide a relatively constant basal level of insulin throughout the night (in amounts sufficient to

restrain hepatic glucose production), postabsorptive glucose concentrations can be effectively normalized. Postprandial glucose elevations can also be dramatically reduced, but postprandial values are more resistant to optimal control.

In nondiabetic subjects, postprandial glycemic excursions are curtailed by the insulin-driven suppression of endogenous hepatic glucose production (41). This regulation is typically lost in "conservatively" treated type 1 patients, in whom the liver is less sensitive to small increments in circulating insulin (104) and is unable to respond to hyperglycemia *per se* (82). Following intensive insulin therapy, hepatic insulin sensitivity improves (35,104); as a result, the endogenous contribution to circulating glucose levels can be more effectively suppressed, blunting postprandial glycemic excursions. Additionally, the administration of rapidly acting insulin before meals allows for adequate portal insulin levels to promote hepatic glucose uptake. As mentioned above, however, these improvements are often not sufficient to restore postprandial glucose to normal levels. With regular insulin preparations, the rise in circulating insulin levels after subcutaneous insulin injection is delayed, and peak levels are lower than those observed in normal subjects (105). Newer rapid-acting insulin analogs have partially addressed these deficiencies. In addition, insulin resistance in peripheral tissues is only partially reversed by intensive insulin therapy (106). Because skeletal muscle is the primary site of exogenous glucose disposal (40), it is not surprising that elevated postprandial glucose levels frequently persist in patients undergoing intensive insulin therapy.

With respect to other insulin-sensitive fuels, intensive insulin therapy also reverses elevations in basal BCAA concentrations (107) (Fig. 9-8), likely as a result of diminished alanine delivery into plasma (85). Intensive treatment also blunts excessive postprandial BCAA levels following the ingestion of a mixed meal (107). With regard to fat metabolites, pathologic elevations of FFA and triglyceride levels can also be reversed by intensive metabolic therapy (105,107).

Finally, intensive insulin therapy appears to have important effects on the release of counterregulatory hormones (see below). Elevations in growth hormone and glucagon levels observed in patients with poorly controlled diabetes are diminished after institution of strict glycemic control (80,108); excessive increments in catecholamine and growth hormone released during mild exercise are also reversed (98) (Fig. 9-13). It follows, therefore, that some of the metabolic benefits of intensive insulin regimens may be derived from the lowering of counterregulatory hormone levels. Moreover, when growth hormone is infused in hourly pulses to diabetic subjects using a portable insulin pump, serum growth hormone is raised to levels similar to those observed in patients with poorly controlled diabetes. Under these conditions, glycemic control markedly deteriorates, with a concurrent increase in circulating levels of ketones and FFA (80). In other words, growth hormone elevations can themselves reproduce the entire spectrum of

poor diabetic control, even in the face of previously optimized insulin therapy.

Glucose Counterregulation

The recent clinical emphasis on intensive insulin therapy has improved long-term outcomes in patients with diabetes, but has also produced an increased incidence of hypoglycemic events, particularly in type 1 patients who lack the ability to regulate endogenous insulin secretion (109). Hypoglycemia is uncomfortable and can precipitate adrenergic responses, leading to adverse cardiovascular events; during severe episodes, it can result in altered consciousness, seizures, coma, or even death. In the clinical setting, hypoglycemia (and patients' fear of hypoglycemia) is the predominant rate-limiting factor to achieving glycemic control in patients with insulin-dependent diabetes.

In normal subjects, hypoglycemia invokes a rapid, multitiered response intended to restore normal circulating glucose levels. In this setting, time is of the essence, since proper functioning of the CNS is tightly dependent on a constant supply of circulating glucose. Spontaneous recovery from hypoglycemia involves both increased endogenous glucose production and reduced peripheral glucose utilization. Three fundamental mechanisms are responsible for this process: (a) dissipation of endogenous insulin; (b) subjective awareness of hypoglycemia, producing hunger to trigger carbohydrate ingestion; and (c) counterregulatory hormone activity. When plasma glucose levels fall into the low-normal range, *glucagon* is released from pancreatic α-cells. In conjunction with falling levels of endogenous insulin, glucagon stimulates glucose production, mainly by activating hepatic glycogenolysis; gluconeogenesis is also facilitated by the low insulin-to-glucagon ratio. *Catecholamines* are also released, producing the "alarm" symptoms of hypoglycemia (hunger, tremor, palpitations, diaphoresis) and further stimulating glucose output through activation of hepatic glycogenolysis, mobilization of substrates for gluconeogenesis, and further suppression of endogenous insulin production. Catecholamines also antagonize the peripheral effects of insulin, thereby contributing to decreased peripheral glucose utilization (110). If hypoglycemia is sustained (i.e., more than 3–4 hours), additional counterregulatory mechanisms become important, including *growth hormone* release and activation of the hypothalamic-pituitary-adrenal axis (i.e., *cortisol* production), both of which serve to further stimulate hepatic glucose output and inhibit peripheral glucose utilization.

In a significant number of (predominantly type 1) diabetic patients, the problem of hypoglycemia is compounded by the syndrome of *hypoglycemia unawareness*. This syndrome is associated with a number of known clinical risk factors, including tight glucose control (e.g., intensive insulin therapy), extended disease duration, and recent episodes of antecedent hypoglycemia (111,112). The precise mecha-

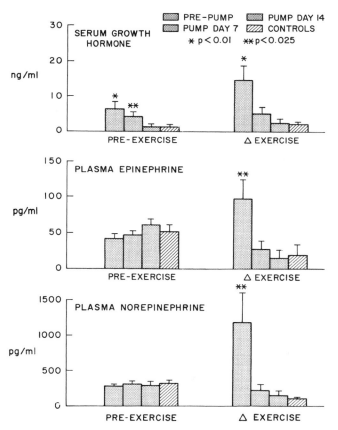

FIGURE 9-13. Resting levels and exercise-induced increments of growth hormone, epinephrine, and norepinephrine in type 1 diabetic and healthy control subjects. The diabetic patients were studied before (during poor glycemic control) and after 7 and 14 days of intensive therapy using a portable insulin pump. (Based on data of Tamborlane WV, Sherwin RS, Koivisto V, et al. Normalization of the growth hormone and catecholamine response to exercise in juvenile-onset diabetics treated with a portable insulin infusion pump. *Diabetes* 1979;28:785, with permission.)

nisms underlying the syndrome of hypoglycemia unawareness are poorly understood; however, the syndrome is clearly associated with defective glucose counterregulation, with antecedent hypoglycemia as a primary causative factor (113,114). Defective glucagon responses develop in the majority of type 1 patients as early as 2 to 5 years after diagnosis; when this occurs, counterregulation becomes critically dependent on an intact sympatho-adrenal axis (i.e., epinephrine) (115). Unfortunately, many diabetic patients develop a blunted sympatho-adrenal response as well (116,117); as a result, they experience reduced awareness of hypoglycemia, placing them at even higher risk for severe hypoglycemia. This phenomenon may be mediated, at least in part, by activation of the hypothalamic-pituitary-adrenal (HPA) axis.

The clinical impact of hypoglycemia unawareness takes on particular importance during pregnancy, where intensive insulin treatment regimens have become standard clinical practice. The detrimental impact of maternal hypoglycemia on a developing fetus is incompletely understood.

KEY POINTS

- In the setting of normal body fuel metabolism, insulin is the primary "conductor" of a complex orchestra of interactions among exogenous fuels, hormones, and the constant exchange of substrates among relevant body organs, the liver, muscle, and adipose in particular.
- In patients with diabetes mellitus, a lack of insulin action leads to accelerated use of stored fuels, and to the improper storage of ingested body fuels, resulting in elevated circulating levels of glucose and free fatty acids. These elevated substrate levels contribute to the long-term clinical complications seen in diabetic patients.
- Diabetes mellitus is characterized by defects in insulin secretion and/or insulin resistance. It consists of two distinct diseases. Type 1 diabetes, which results from autoimmune destruction of the insulin-producing pancreatic β-cells, and type 2 diabetes, which most often begins with insulin resistance and becomes manifest when the β-cells fail to adequately compensate. For individual patients with type 2 diabetes, there is marked heterogeneity with regard to the severity of each defect.
- Intensive therapy of diabetes mellitus results in near normalization of body fuel metabolism, and can reduce the long-term clinical complications of diabetes.
- Hypoglycemia (and the resulting induction of hypoglycemia unawareness) is the rate-limiting step to achieving tight glucose control in diabetic patients.

REFERENCES

1. Ravussin E, Lillioja S, Anderson TE, et al. Determinants of 24-hour energy expenditure in man. Methods and results using a respiratory chamber. *J Clin Invest* 1986;78:1568.
2. Sims EA, Danforth E Jr. Expenditure and storage of energy in man. *J Clin Invest* 1987;79:1019.
3. Sacca L, Vigorito C, Cacala M, et al. Mechanisms of epinephrine-induced glucose intolerance in normal humans: role of the splanchnic bed. *J Clin Invest* 1982;69:284.
4. Rothman DL, Magnusson I, Katz DL, et al. Quantitation of hepatic glycogenolysis and gluconeogenesis in fasting humans with ¹³C NMR. *Science* 1991;254:573.
5. Felig P. The glucose-alanine cycle. *Metabolism* 1973;22:179.
6. Cherrington AD, Liljenquist JE, Shulman GI, et al. Importance of hypoglycemia-induced glucose production during isolated glucagon deficiency. *Am J Physiol* 1979;236:263.
7. Sherwin RS, Tamborlane W, Hendler R, et al. Influence of glucagon replacement on the hyperglycemic and hyperketonemic response to prolonged somatostatin infusion in normal man. *J Clin Endocrinol Metab* 1977;45:1104.
8. Felig P. Amino acid metabolism in man. *Annu Rev Biochem* 1975;44:933.
9. Felig P, Pozefsky T, Marliss E, et al. Alanine: key role in gluconeogenesis. *Science* 1970;167:1003.
10. Chang TW, Goldberg AL. The origin of alanine produced in skeletal muscle. *J Biol Chem* 1967;253:3677.
11. Haymond MW, Miles TM. Branched chain amino acids as a major source of alanine nitrogen in man. *Diabetes* 1982;31:86.
12. Odessey R, Khairallah EA, Goldberg AL. Origin and possible significance of alanine production by skeletal muscle. *J Biol Chem* 1974;249:7623.
13. Chang TW, Goldberg AL. The metabolic fates of amino acids and the formation of glutamine in skeletal muscle. *J Biol Chem* 1978;253:3685.
14. Felig P, Owen OE, Wahren J, et al. Amino acid metabolism during prolonged starvation. *J Clin Invest* 1969;48:584.
15. Elwyn D, Parikh HC, Shoemaker WC. Amino acid movements between gut, liver and periphery in unanesthetized dogs. *Am J Physiol* 1968;215:1260.
16. Buse MG, Herlong HF, Weigand DA. The effects of diabetes, insulin, and the redox potential on leucine metabolism by isolated rat hemidiaphragm. *Endocrinology* 1976;98:1166.
17. Zierler L, Rabinowitz D. Effects of very small concentrations of insulin on forearm metabolism: persistence of its action on potassium and free fatty acids without its effect on glucose. *J Clin Invest* 1964;43:950.
18. Randle P, Garland JPB, Hales CN, et al. The glucose-fatty acid cycle: its role in insulin sensitivity and the metabolic disturbances of diabetes mellitus. *Lancet* 1963;1:785.
19. Hultman E, Nilsson LH. Liver glycogen in man: effect of different diets and muscular exercise. *Adv Exp Med Biol* 1971;11:143.
20. Rothman DL, Magnusson I, Katz LD, et al. Quantitation of hepatic glycogenolysis and gluconeogenesis in fasting humans with 13C NMR. *Science* 1991;254:573.
21. Pozefsky T, Tancredi RG, Moxley RT, et al. Effects of brief starvation on muscle amino acid metabolism in nonobese man. *J Clin Invest* 1976;57:444.
22. Felig P, Marliss E, Owen OE, et al. Role of substrate in the regulation of hepatic gluconeogenesis in fasting man. *Adv Enzyme Regul* 1969;7:41.
23. Cahil GF Jr. Starvation in man. *N Engl J Med* 1970;282:668.
24. Cahill GH Jr, Herrera MG, Morgan AP, et al. Hormone-fuel interrelationships during fasting. *J Clin Invest* 1966;45:1751.
25. Fisher M, Sherwin RS, Hendler R, et al. Kinetics of glucagon in man: effects of starvation. *Proc Natl Acad Sci U S A* 1976;73:1734.
26. McGarry JD, Wright P, Foster D. Hormonal control of ketogenesis: rapid activation of hepatic ketogenic capacity in fed rats by anti-insulin serum and glucagon. *J Clin Invest* 1975;55:1202.

27. Sherwin RS, Shulman GI, Hendler R, et al. Effect of growth hormone on oral glucose tolerance and circulating metabolic fuels in man. *Diabetologia* 1983;24:155.

28. Wahren J, Felig P, Ahlborg G, et al. Glucose metabolism during leg exercise in man. *J Clin Invest* 1978;50:2715.

29. Ahlborg G, Felig P, Hagenfeldt L, et al. Substrate turnover during prolonged exercise in man. *J Clin Invest* 1974;53:1080.

30. Galbo G, Richter J, Hilsted J, et al. Hormonal regulation during prolonged exercise. *Ann N Y Acad Sci* 1977;301:72.

31. Goodyear LJ, Kahn BB. Exercise, glucose transport, and insulin sensitivity. *Ann Rev Med* 1998;49:235.

32. Goodyear LJ. AMP-activated protein kinase: a critical signaling intermediary for exercise-stimulated glucose transport? *Exerc Sport Sci Rev* 2000;28:113.

33. Rizza R, Mandarino L, Gerich J. Dose-response characteristics for effects of insulin on production and utilization of glucose in man. *Am J Physiol* 1981;240:1630.

34. Steele R. Influence of glucose loading and/or injected insulin on hepatic glucose output. *Ann N Y Acad Sci* 1959;82:420.

35. Sacca L, Hendler R, Sherwin RS. Hyperglycemia inhibits glucose production in man independent of changes in glucoregulatory hormones. *J Clin Endocrinol Metab* 1978;47:1160.

36. DeFronzo RA, Ferrannini E, Hendler R, et al. Influence of hyperinsulinemia, hyperglycemia, and the route of glucose administration on splanchnic glucose exchange. *Proc Natl Acad Sci U S A* 1977;75:5173.

37. Saccá L, Cicala M, Trimarco B, et al. Differential effects of insulin on splanchnic and peripheral glucose disposal after an intravenous glucose load in man. *J Clin Invest* 1982;70:117.

38. Tillil H, Shapiro ET, Miller MA, et al. Dose-dependent effects of oral and intravenous glucose on insulin secretion and clearance in normal humans. *Am J Physiol* 1988;254:349.

39. Rasmussen H, Zawalich KC, Ganesan S, et al. Physiology and pathophysiology of insulin secretion. *Diabetes Care* 1990;13:655.

40. Katz LK, Glickman MG, Rapoport S, et al. Splanchnic and peripheral disposal of oral glucose in man. *Diabetes* 1983;32:675.

41. Felig P, Wahren J. Influence of endogenous insulin secretion on splanchnic glucose and amino acid metabolism in man. *J Clin Invest* 1971;50:1702.

42. Fukagawa NK, Minaker KL, Rowe JW, et al. Insulin-mediated reduction of whole body total protein breakdown. Dose response effects on leucine metabolism in postaborptive man. *J Clin Invest* 1985;76:2306.

43. Tessari P, Trevisan R, Inchiostro S, et al. Dose-response curves of effects of insulin on leucine kinetics in humans. *Am J Physiol* 1986;251:334.

44. Wahren J, Felig P, Hagenfeldt J. Effect of protein ingestion on splanchnic and leg metabolism in normal man and in patients with diabetes mellitus. *J Clin Invest* 1976;57:987.

45. Buse MG, Reid SS. Leucine: a possible regulator of protein turnover in muscle. *J Clin Invest* 1975;56:1250.

46. Sherwin RS. Effect of starvation on the turnover and metabolic response to leucine. *J Clin Invest* 1978;61:1471.

47. Sadur CN, Eckel RH. Insulin stimulation of adipose tissue lipoprotein lipase: use of the euglycemic clamp technique. *J Clin Invest* 1982;69:1119.

48. Robinson J, Newsholme EA. Glycerol kinase activities in rat heart and adipose tissue. *Biochem J* 1967;104:2C.

49. Yki-Jarvinen H. Sex and insulin sensitivity. *Metabolism* 1984;33:1011.

50. Hale PJ, Wright JV, Nattrass M. Differences in insulin sensitivity between normal men and women. *Metabolism* 1985;34:1133.

51. Arslanian SA, Heil BV, Becker DJ, et al. Sexual dimorphism in insulin sensitivity in adolescents with insulin-dependent diabetes mellitus. *J Clin Endocrinol Metab* 1991;72:920.

52. Haymond MW, Kan IE, Clarke WL, et al. Differences in circulating gluconeogenic substrates during short-term fasting in men, women, and children. *Metabolism* 1982;31:33.

53. Diamond MP, Jones T, Caprio S, et al. Gender influences counterregulatory hormone responses to hypoglycemia. *Metabolism* 1993;42:1568.

54. Frankenhaeuser M, Dunne E, Lundberg U. Sex differences in sympathetic-adrenal medullary reactions induced by different stressors. *Psychopharmacology* 1976;47:1.

55. Amiel SA, Maran A, MacDonald IA. Sex differences in counterregulatory hormone responses but not glucose kinetics during insulin induced hypoglycemia. *Diabetes* 1991;40[Suppl 1]:2221.

56. Diamond MP, Simonson DC, DeFronzo RA. Menstrual cyclicity has a profound effect on glucose homeostasis. *Fertil Steril* 1989;52:204.

57. Valdes CT, Elkind-Hirsch KE. Intravenous glucose tolerance test insulin sensitivity changes derived during the menstrual cycle. *J Clin Endocrinol Metab* 1991;72:642.

58. Singh BM, Nattrass M. Alterations in insulin action during the menstrual cycle in normal women. *Diabetes Nutr Metab* 1989;2:39.

59. Diamond MP, Jacob RJ, Connolly-Diamond M, et al. Glucose metabolism during the menstrual cycle: assessment by the euglycemic, hyperinsulinemic clamp technique. *J Reprod Med* 1993;38:417.

60. Yki-Jarvinen H. Insulin sensitivity during the menstrual cycle. *J Clin Endocrinol Metab* 1984;59:350.

61. Toth EL, Suthijumroom A, Crockford PM, et al. Insulin action does not change during the menstrual cycle in normal women. *J Clin Endocrinol Metab* 1987;64:74.

62. Diamond MP, Grainger DA, Rossi G, et al. Counter-regulatory response to hypoglycemia in the follicular and luteal phases of the menstrual cycle. *Fertil Steril* 1993;60:988.

63. Block MB, Mako ME, Steiner DF, et al. Circulating C-peptide immunoreactivity: studies in normals and diabetic patients. *Diabetes* 1972;21:1013.

64. Shima K, Tanaka R, Morishita S, et al. Studies on the etiology of "brittle" diabetes: relationship between diabetic instability and insulinogenic reserve. *Diabetes* 1977;26:717.

65. Robertson RP, Porte D Jr. The glucose receptor: a defector mechanism in diabetes mellitus distinct from the beta adrenergic receptor. *J Clin Invest* 1973;52:870.

66. Coulston GLA, Chen Y-DI, Reaven GM. Does day-long absolute hypoinsulinemia characterize the patient with non-insulin-dependent diabetes mellitus? *Metabolism* 1983;32:754.

67. Yalow RS, Berson SA. Immunoassay of endogenous plasma insulin in man. *J Clin Invest* 1960;39:1157.

68. Lockwood DH, Amatruda TM. Cellular alterations responsible for insulin resistance in obesity and type II diabetes mellitus. *Am J Med* 1983;75:23.

69. Kipnis DM. Insulin secretion in normal and diabetic individuals. *Ann Intern Med* 1970;16:103.

70. Zierler L, Rabinowitz D. Effects of very small concentrations of insulin on forearm metabolism: persistence of its action on potassium and free fatty acids without its effect on glucose. *J Clin Invest* 1964;43:950.

71. Fukagawa NK, Minaker KL, Rowe JE, et al. Insulin-mediated reduction of whole body protein breakdown: dose-response effects on leucine metabolism in postabsorptive man. *J Clin Invest* 1985;76:2306.

72. DeFronzo RA, Ferrannini E, Koivisto V. New concepts in the pathogenesis and treatment of non-insulin-dependent diabetes mellitus. *Am J Med* 1983;74:52.

73. Olefsky TM, Ciaraldi TP, Kolterman OG. Mechanism of insulin resistance in non-insulin-dependent (type II) diabetes. *Am J Med* 1985;79:12.

74. Shulman GI. Cellular mechanisms of insulin resistance. *J Clin Invest* 2000;106:171.

75. Petersen KF, Hendler R, Price T, et al. 13C/31P NMR studies on the mechanism of insulin resistance in obesity. *Diabetes* 1998;47:381.

76. DeFronzo RA, Hendler R, Simonson D. Insulin resistance is a prominent feature of insulin-dependent diabetes. *Diabetes* 1982;31:795.

77. Scarlett JA, Gray RS, Griffin J, et al. Insulin treatment reverses the insulin resistance of type II diabetes mellitus. *Diabetes Care* 1982;5:353.

78. Expert Committee on the Diagnosis and Classification of Diabetes Mellitus. Report of the expert committee on the diagnosis and classification of diabetes mellitus. *Diabetes Care* 2002;25[Suppl 1]:5.

79. DeFronzo RA, Simonson D, Ferrannini E. Hepatic and peripheral insulin resistance: a common feature in non-insulin-dependent and insulin-dependent diabetes. *Diabetologia* 1982;23:313.

80. Press M, Tamborlane WV, Sherwin RS. Importance of raised growth hormone levels in mediating the metabolic derangements of diabetes. *N Engl J Med* 1984;310:810.

81. Shamoon H, Hendler R, Sherwin RS. Altered responsiveness to cortisol, epinephrine, and glucagon in insulin-infused juvenile-onset diabetics: a mechanism for diabetic instability. *Diabetes* 1980;29:284.

82. Wahren J, Felig P, Cerase E, et al. Splanchnic and peripheral glucose and amino acid metabolism in diabetes mellitus. *J Clin Invest* 1972;51:1870.

83. Chiasson JL, Liljenquist JE, Finger FE, et al. Differential sensitivity of glycogenolysis and glucogenogenesis to insulin infusion in dogs. *Diabetes* 1976;25:283.

84. Nikou P, Philippidis H, Palaiologos G. Serum alanine concentration in diabetic children under insulin treatment. *Horm Metab Res* 1975;7:207.

85. Gertner J, Press M, Mathews D, et al. Improvements in leucine kinetics with continuous subcutaneous insulin infusion. *Diabetes* 1984;33[Suppl 1]:2.

86. Greenfield M, Kolterman O, Olefsky J, et al. Mechanism of hypertriglyceridemia in diabetic patients with fasting hyperglycemia. *Diabetologia* 1980;18:441.

87. Ferrannini E, Barrett EJ, Bevilacqua S, et al. Effect of fatty acids on glucose production and utilization in man. *J Clin Invest* 1983;72:1737.

88. Sherwin RS, Hendler R, Felig P. Effect of diabetes mellitus and insulin on the turnover and metabolic response to ketones in man. *Diabetes* 1976;26:776.

89. Bagdad JD, Porte D Jr, Bierman EL. Acute insulin withdrawal and the regulation of plasma triglyceride removal in diabetic subjects. *Diabetes* 1968;17:127.

90. Nikkila EA, Huttunen JK, Ehnholm C. Postheparin plasma lipoproteinlipase and hepatic lipase in diabetes mellitus: relationship to plasma triglyceride metabolism. *Diabetes* 1977;26:11.

91. Tobey TA, Greenfield M, Kraemer F, et al. Relationship between insulin resistance, insulin secretion, very low density lipoprotein kinetics, and plasma triglyceride levels in normotriglyceridemic man. *Metabolism* 1981;30:165.

92. DeFronzo RA, Gunnarsson R, Björkman O, et al. Effects of insulin on peripheral and splanchnic glucose metabolism in non-insulin-dependent (type II) diabetes mellitus. *J Clin Invest* 1985;76:149.

93. Pozefsky T, Felig P, Tobin J, et al. Amino acid balance across the tissues of the forearm in postabsorptive man: effects of insulin at two dose levels. *J Clin Invest* 1969;48:2273.

94. Wahren J, Hagenfeldt L, Felig P. Splanchnic and leg exchange of glucose, amino acids, and free fatty acids during exercise in diabetes mellitus. *J Clin Invest* 1975;55:1303.

95. Koivisto VA, Felig P. Effects of leg exercise on insulin absorption in diabetic parents. *N Engl J Med* 1978;298:79.

96. DeFronzo R, Felig P, Ferrannini E, et al. Synergistic interaction between exercise and insulin on peripheral glucose uptake. *J Clin Invest* 1981;69:1468.

97. Berger M, Berchtold P, Coppers HJ, et al. Metabolic and hormonal effects of muscular exercise in juvenile type diabetes. *Diabetologia* 1977;13:355.

98. Tamborlane WV, Sherwin RS, Koivisto V, et al. Normalization of the growth hormone and catecholamine response to exercise in juvenile-onset diabetics treated with a portable insulin infusion pump. *Diabetes* 1979;28:785.

99. Wahren J, Felig P, Hagenfeldt L. Physical exercise and fuel homeostasis in diabetes mellitus. *Diabetologia* 1978;14:213.

100. American Diabetes Association. Diabetes mellitus and exercise: position statement. *Diabetes Care* 2000;23[Suppl 1]50.

101. Pickup JC, Keen H, Parsons JA, et al. Continuous subcutaneous insulin infusion: improved blood glucose and intermediary metabolite control in diabetics. *Lancet* 1979;1:1255.

102. Tamborlane WV, Sherwin RS, Genel M, et al. Reduction to normal of plasma glucose in juvenile diabetes by subcutaneous administration of insulin with a portable infusion pump. *N Engl J Med* 1979;300:573.

103. Champion MC, Shephard GAA, Rodger NW, et al. Continuous subcutaneous infusion of insulin in the management of diabetes mellitus. *Diabetes* 1980;29:206.

104. Amiel SA, Tamborlane WV, Simonson DC, et al. Defective glucose counterregulation after strict glycemic control of insulin-dependent diabetes mellitus. *N Engl J Med* 1987;316:1376.

105. Verdonk C, Tamborlane W, Hendler R, et al. Does insulin treatment of diabetes cause hyperinsulinemia and hypoaminoacidemia? *Clin Res* 1981;29:425.

106. Simonson DC, Tamborlane WV, Sherwin RS, et al. Improved insulin sensitivity in patients with type I diabetes mellitus after CSII. *Diabetes* 1985;34[Suppl 3]:80.

107. Tamborlane WV, Sherwin RS, Genel M, et al. Restoration of normal lipid and amino-acid metabolism in diabetic patients treated with a portable insulin-infusion pump. *Lancet* 1979;1:1258.

108. Raskin P, Pietri A, Unger R. Changes in glucagon levels after four to five weeks of glucoregulation by portable insulin infusion pumps. *Diabetes* 1979;29:1033.

109. Diabetes Control and Complications Trial (DCCT) Research Group. Hypoglycemia in the Diabetes Control and Complications Trial. *Diabetes* 1997;46:271.

110. De Feo P, Perriello G, Torlon E, et al. Contribution of adrenergic mechanisms to glucose counterregulation in normal humans. *Am J Physiol* 1991;261:75.

111. Clarke W, Gonder-Frederick LA, Richards PE, et al. Multifactorial origin of hypoglycemic symptom unawareness in IDDM. *Diabetes* 1991;40:680.

112. Simonson DC, Tamborlane WV, DeFronzo RA, et al. Intensive insulin therapy reduces counterregulatory hormone responses to hypoglycemia in patients with type I diabetes. *Ann Intern Med* 1985;103:184.

113. Davis M, Shamoon H. Counterregulatory adaptation to recurrent hypoglycemia in normal humans. *J Clin Endocrinol Metab* 1991;73:995.

114. Cryer PE. Iatrogenic hypoglycemia as a cause of hypo-

glycemia-associated autonomic failure in IDDM. *Diabetes* 1992;41:255.

115. Bolli G, De Feo P, Compagnucci P, et al. Important role of adrenergic mechanisms in acute glucose counterregulation following insulin-induced hypoglycemia in type I diabetes: evidence for an effect mediated by beta-adrenoreceptors. *Diabetes* 1982;31:641.

116. Kleinbaum J, Shamoon H. Impaired counterregulation of hypoglycemia in insulin-dependent diabetes mellitus. *Diabetes* 1983;32:493.

117. Amiel SA, Sherwin RS, Simonson DC, et al. Effect of intensive insulin therapy on glycemic thresholds for counterregulatory hormone release. *Diabetes* 1988;37:901.

METABOLIC CHANGES DURING NORMAL AND DIABETIC PREGNANCIES

PATRICK M. CATALANO
THOMAS A. BUCHANAN

There are significant alterations in maternal metabolism during pregnancy that provide adequate nutritional stores in early gestation to meet the increased maternal and fetal demands of late gestation and lactation. Although we are apt to think of diabetes mellitus as a disorder exclusively of maternal glucose metabolism, in fact diabetes mellitus affects all aspects of maternal nutrient metabolism. In this chapter, we consider maternal glucose metabolism as it relates to pancreatic β-cell function, insulin clearance, and endogenous (i.e., primarily hepatic) glucose production and peripheral glucose utilization and their regulation by insulin. We also address maternal protein and lipid metabolism, placental transport function, and potential mechanisms related to alterations in maternal metabolism during pregnancy. The long-term impacts of these metabolic abnormalities are discussed elsewhere in this text.

NORMAL METABOLISM

Glucose Metabolism

Early gestation can be viewed as an anabolic condition in the mother because of the increases in maternal fat stores and small increases in insulin sensitivity. Hence, nutrients are stored in early gestation in order to meet the increased fetal anabolic demands of late gestation. In contrast, late pregnancy is characterized by increased insulin resistance. This increase in insulin resistance results in increases in maternal glucose and free fatty acid concentrations allowing for greater substrate availability for fetal growth. Longitudinal studies in women with normal glucose tolerance have shown significant progressive alterations in all aspects of glucose metabolism as early as the end of the first trimester (1).

There is a progressive decrease in fasting glucose with advancing gestation. The mechanism is complex and not well understood. Potential contributing factors include the increase in plasma volume in early gestation, increased feto-placental glucose utilization in late gestation, and restraint

of glucose production relative to circulating glucose concentrations. Kalhan (2) and Cowett (3), using stable isotope methodologies, were the first to describe increased fasting hepatic glucose production in late pregnancy. Additionally, Catalano et al. (4), using a stable isotope of glucose in a prospective longitudinal study design, reported a 30% increase in maternal fasting hepatic glucose production with advancing gestation (Fig. 10-1). The increase remained significant after adjustment for maternal weight gain. The enhanced fasting hepatic glucose production occurred despite a significant elevation in fasting insulin concentration, thereby indicating a decrease in maternal hepatic insulin sensitivity in women with normal glucose tolerance. Additionally, in obese women with normal glucose tolerance, there was a decreased ability of infused insulin to fully suppress hepatic glucose production in late gestation as compared with pregravid and early pregnancy measurements. These findings indicate a further decrease in hepatic insulin sensitivity (5) in obese women. The fact that the liver does not fully compensate for the reduced glucose concentrations suggests some restraint on glucose production compared to the nonpregnant condition. Indeed, the fall in plasma glucose that occurs between 14 and 18 hours of fasting in the third trimester results from a fall in endogenous glucose production in the face of constant glucose clearance (6). Reduced availability of alanine as a substrate for gluconeogenesis, resulting both from impaired hepatic extraction of alanine (7) and from a reduced supply of alanine in the circulation (8,9), has been implicated as a contributing factor to the fasting hypoglycemia of pregnancy. Enhanced β-cell function resulting in elevated fasting insulin concentrations relative to the ambient glucose concentrations most likely contributes to fasting hypoglycemia as well.

Estimates of peripheral insulin sensitivity in pregnancy have included the measurement of insulin response to a fixed oral or intravenous glucose challenge or the ratio of insulin to glucose under a variety of experimental conditions. In recent years, newer methodologies such as computer model-

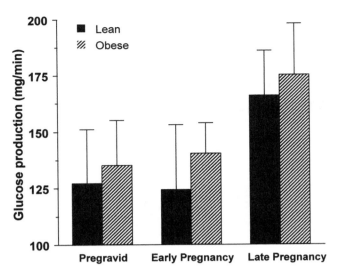

FIGURE 10-1. Basal endogenous (primarily hepatic) glucose production (mean ± SD) in lean and obese women with normal glucose tolerance described in Fig. 10-2. (From Catalano PM, Tyzbir ED, Wolfe RR, et al. Carbohydrate metabolism during pregnancy in control subjects and women with gestational diabetes. *Am J Physiol* 1993;264:60–67; and Catalano PM, Huston L, Amini SB, et al. Longitudinal changes in glucose metabolism during pregnancy in obese women with normal glucose tolerance and gestational diabetes. *Am J Obstet Gynecol* 1999;180:903–916, with permission.)

ing of an intravenous glucose tolerance test (10) and the euglycemic-hyperinsulinemic clamp (11) have improved our ability to quantify peripheral insulin sensitivity. In lean women in early gestation, Catalano et al. (12) reported a 40% decrease in maternal insulin sensitivity, defined as a decrease in the glucose infusion rate during the euglycemic-hyperinsulinemic clamp in order to maintain euglycemia (90mg/dl). However, despite a constant insulin infusion based on subject weight or surface area, maternal insulin concentrations vary among euglycemic clamps done at different times in pregnancy due to changes in the relationship between body size and plasma volume as well as changes in insulin clearance with advancing gestation. Additionally, complete suppression of hepatic glucose production did not occur during insulin infusion in obese women (5). Therefore, in order to compare insulin sensitivity at different times during pregnancy and in nonpregnant women, net glucose utilization rates must be expressed relative to steady-state insulin concentrations. The effects of insulin on glucose utilization and production can be assessed separately if labeled glucose is infused during the clamps. When glucose turnover rates were expressed relative to steady-state insulin levels during the clamp procedures, there was only a 10% decrease in insulin sensitivity from pregravid to early gestation in lean subjects (Fig. 10-2A). In contrast, there was a 15% increase

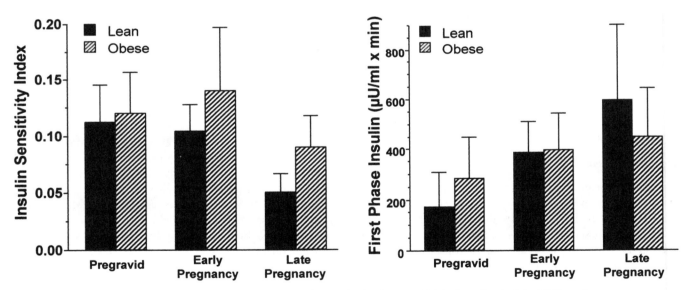

FIGURE 10-2. Insulin secretion and insulin sensitivity (mean ±SD) in lean (body fat <25%) and obese (body fat >25%) in Caucasian women who maintained normal glucose tolerance during pregnancy. Intravenous glucose tolerance tests and euglycemic, hyperinsulinemic clamps were performed before pregnancy ("pregravid"), and during gestational weeks 12 to 14 ("early pregnancy") and 34 to 36 (late pregnancy). **A:** Insulin-mediated glucose uptake during the steady-state period of glucose clamps ([glucose infusion rate + residual endogenous glucose production rate] / state insulin concentration). **B:** First-phase insulin response to intravenous glucose (incremental insulin area during first 5 minutes after glucose injection). (From Catalano PM, Tyzbir ED, Wolfe RR, et al. Carbohydrate metabolism during pregnancy in control subjects and women with gestational diabetes. *Am J Physiol* 1993;264:60–67; and Catalano PM, Huston L, Amini SB, et al. Longitudinal changes in glucose metabolism during pregnancy in obese women with normal glucose tolerance and gestational diabetes. *Am J Obstet Gynecol* 1999;180:903–916, with permission.)

in insulin sensitivity or decreased resistance in obese women in early pregnancy as compared with pregravid estimates (13). Hence, the decrease in insulin requirements in early gestation observed in some women requiring insulin may be a consequence of a relative increase in insulin sensitivity, particularly in obese women with decreased insulin sensitivity prior to conception.

As compared with the metabolic alterations in early pregnancy, there is uniformity of opinion regarding the decrease in peripheral insulin sensitivity in late gestation. Burt (14) was the first to demonstrate that pregnant women experienced less hypoglycemia in response to exogenous insulin in comparison with nonpregnant subjects. Additionally, Spellacy et al. (15) reported an increase in insulin response to a glucose challenge in late gestation. Later research by Fisher et al. (16), using a high-dose glucose infusion test; Buchanan et al. (17), using the Bergman computer modeling of the intravenous glucose tolerance test; and Ryan et al. (18) and Catalano et al. (1), using the euglycemic-hyperinsulinemic clamp all have demonstrated a decrease in insulin sensitivity in late gestation ranging from 33% to 78%. The decrease in insulin sensitivity is profound relative to other conditions, approaching the degree observed in individuals with established type 2 diabetes (Fig. 10-3). It should be noted that the quantitative estimates of insulin sensitivity from glucose clamps conducted at a single insulin concentration could underestimate the degree of insulin resistance because there is a large increase during pregnancy in glucose disposal that does not require insulin (i.e., utilization by the fetus and placenta). Hay et al. (19) reported that in the pregnant ewe model, approximately one-third of maternal glucose utilization was accounted for by uterine, placental, and fetal tissue. Additionally, Marconi et al. (20) reported that based on human fetal blood sampling, fetal glucose concentration was a function of fetal size and gestational age in addition to maternal glucose concentration. These problems do not apply to measurements of insulin sensitivity performed by computer modeling of intravenous glucose tolerance test (IVGTT) data, since that approach assesses insulin-dependent and insulin-independent net glucose disposal separately (10).

The physiologic factors responsible for the insulin resistance of pregnancy are not known with certainty, but the changes appear to be related to the metabolic effects of several hormones and cytokines that are elevated in the maternal circulation during pregnancy. Potential hormones include human placental lactogen (HPL), progesterone, prolactin, and cortisol. Evidence to support an impact of those hormones on insulin action in pregnancy comes from three sources. First, the pattern of insulin resistance during pregnancy tends to parallel the growth of the fetoplacental unit and the levels of hormones secreted by the placenta (21,22). Second, administration of hormones such as HPL (22,23), progesterone (24,25), or glucocorticoids (23) to nonpregnant individuals induces metabolic changes (e.g., hyperinsulinemia without hypoglycemia) that are consistent with a blunting of insulin action. Third, *in vitro* exposure of insulin target cells such as adipocytes to hormones that are elevated during pregnancy has been reported to impair insulin-mediated glucose uptake by those cells (26).

Recently, Kirwan et al. (27) have reported that circulating tumor necrosis factor alpha (TNF-α) concentrations had an inverse correlation with insulin sensitivity as estimated from euglycemic clamp studies. During late pregnancy, there is a significant inverse relationship between TNF-α and insulin sensitivity. Furthermore, among leptin, cortisol, HPL, human chorionic gonadotropin, estradiol, progesterone, and prolactin, TNF-α was the only significant predictor of the change in insulin sensitivity from pregravid through late gestation. In a related series of experiments, placental TNF-α was measured using a dually perfused *in vitro* human placental cotyledon model. In this model, 94% of placental TNF-α was released into the maternal circulation and 6% was released to the fetal side. Hence, it appears that the progressive decrease in insulin sensitivity in pregnancy results from the metabolic action of hormones and cytokines secreted from the feto-placental unit. The potential role of other factors, such as free fatty acids (FFA) may also contribute to the insulin resistance of pregnancy.

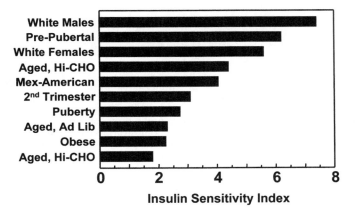

FIGURE 10-3. Range of insulin sensitivity in people with normal glucose tolerance. Whole-body insulin sensitivity index (min^{-1} per μU/ml $\times$ 10^{-4}) was assessed by minimal model analysis of intravenous glucose tolerance tests in ten groups of people with normal glucose tolerance. Note the wide range of insulin sensitivity despite the relatively narrow range of circulating glucose concentrations among the groups. Hi-CHO, data collected after ingestion of high-carbohydrate diet; Ad Lib, data collected on unrestricted diet. (Adapted from Bergman RN. Toward physiological understanding of glucose tolerance: minimal model approach. *Diabetes* 1989;38:1512–1527, with permission.)

The cellular determinants of insulin resistance during pregnancy are not well characterized. In theory, one or more of the steps in the insulin-signaling cascade involved in insulin-stimulated glucose uptake or suppression could be impaired in pregnant individuals. Insulin binding to skeletal muscle, the target tissue that is quantitatively most important for total-body insulin-mediated glucose uptake, has been reported to be similar in nonpregnant and pregnant women (28), suggesting that the peripheral insulin resistance of pregnancy occurs at steps downstream from cell-surface receptor binding of insulin.

Studies in human skeletal muscle and adipose tissue have demonstrated that defects in the insulin signaling cascade may be related to decreased insulin sensitivity in pregnancy (Fig. 10-4). The intracellular actions of insulin are mediated by autophosphorylation of the insulin receptor β (IR-β) subunit on tyrosine followed by activation of the insulin receptor tyrosine kinase (IRTK), which phosphorylates insulin receptor substrates, particularly insulin receptor substrate 1 (IRS-1). Tyrosine phosphorylation of the insulin receptor and of IRS-1 is required for activation of the enzyme phosphatidyl-inositol-3-kinase (PI-3-kinase), a necessary step for several effects of insulin, including translocation of glucose transporter 4 (Glut-4) to the cell surface where glucose transport occurs. Garvey et al. (29) reported that there were no significant differences in GLUT4 concentration in skeletal muscle from pregnant and nonpregnant women. Based on the studies of Friedman et al. (30), there appear to be defects in the downstream insulin-signaling cascade relating to pregnancy. Pregnant women have reduced IRS-1 protein compared with nonpregnant women. The down-regulation of the IRS-1 protein closely

parallels the decreased ability of insulin to induce additional steps in the insulin-signaling cascade that lead to glucose transport. Indeed down-regulation of IRS-1 protein closely parallels the ability of insulin to stimulate 2-deoxy glucose uptake *in vitro*.

As noted previously, TNF-α has been correlated with the changes in insulin sensitivity during pregnancy. Furthermore, TNF-α is associated with decreased insulin sensitivity in a number of conditions, including obesity (31), aging (32), and sepsis (33). *In vitro* studies have shown that TNF-α down-regulates insulin receptor signaling in cultured adipocytes (34) and skeletal muscle cells (35). TNF-α activates a pathway that increases sphingomyelinases and ceramides, which interfere with insulin receptor autophosphorylation. Recently, it has been shown that TNF-α promotes serine phosphorylation of IRS-1, thus impairing its association with the insulin receptor (36). In pregnancy, there is evidence that insulin receptor and IRS-1 tyrosine phosphorylation are impaired, and serine phosphorylation is increased in late-gestation skeletal muscle (37,38). Therefore, the increased TNF-α concentrations in late pregnancy may attenuate the insulin-signaling cascade and result in the observed decrease of insulin sensitivity.

In summary, based on available data, there are significant alterations in insulin sensitivity in normal pregnancy. In early pregnancy, insulin sensitivity may increase, decrease, or remain the same. The alterations in early pregnancy are related to maternal pregravid insulin sensitivity and the mechanisms remain speculative. In late gestation, there are significant decreases in insulin sensitivity. The stimulus for decreased insulin sensitivity in muscle and adipose tissue appears to be placental cytokine production, that is, TNF-

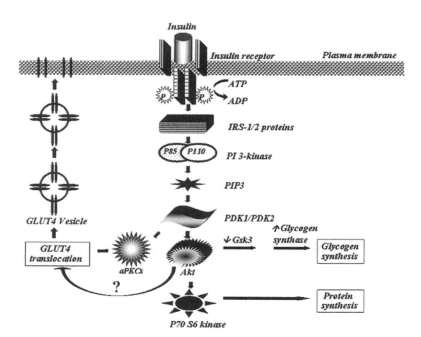

FIGURE 10-4. Schematic model of the insulin signaling pathway in skeletal muscle. ATP, adenosine triphosphate; ADP, adenosine diphosphate; P, phosphorylation; IRS-1/2, insulin receptor substrate 1 and 2; PI 3-kinase, phosphoinositol 3-kinase; p85, PI 3-kinase regulatory subunit; p110, PI 3-kinase catalytic subunit; PIP3, phosphatidylinositol(3,4,5)triphosphate; PDK1/PDK2, phosphoinositide-dependent protein kinase 1 and 2; Akt, serine/threonine kinase; Gsk3, glycogen synthase kinase 3; aPKC, atypical protein kinase C subfamily; GLUT4, glucose transporter.

α and leptin. There is an improvement in insulin sensitivity and concomitant decrease in serum concentration of these cytokines postpartum. Additionally, the processes by which TNF-α affects the IRS-1 function in the insulin-signaling cascade appear to be present during gestation. The mechanisms resulting in decreased hepatic insulin sensitivity are less well characterized, but the increase in maternal FFA concentration certainly may play a role.

There are progressive increases in insulin secretion in response to an intravenous glucose challenge with advancing gestation (Fig. 10-2B). The increases in insulin concentration are more pronounced in lean as compared to obese women, most probably because lean women begin their pregnancies with better insulin sensitivity and have greater decreases in insulin sensitivity as compared to obese women with normal glucose tolerance.

The normal response of β-cells to insulin resistance is to increase insulin secretion, thereby minimizing the impact of insulin resistance on circulating glucose levels (39–41). Increased insulin secretion during pregnancy most likely represents such compensation for progressive insulin resistance rather than vice versa, since insulin resistance occurs in the absence of endogenous insulin secretion (i.e., in type 1 diabetes) (42). However, the observation that insulin secretion may be increased as much as 50% early in the second trimester (Fig. 10-2B) before insulin resistance of pregnancy becomes manifest, suggests that the hormonal milieu of pregnancy may exert a primary effect to increase insulin secretion independent of insulin resistance. The mechanisms that lead to enhanced insulin secretion in pregnancy, whether primary or as compensation for insulin resistance, are not known completely. A likely contributing factor is an increase in β-cell mass that appears, on the basis of animal studies (43–45), to result from a combination of β-cell hypertrophy and hyperplasia. Hyperplasia of pancreatic islets has also been observed in human pregnancy (46). The increased β-cell mass may contribute to the pattern of increased fasting insulin concentrations despite normal or lowered fasting glucose concentrations that have been observed in late pregnancy. Increased β-cell mass may also contribute to an enhanced insulin response to secretogogues during pregnancy. The magnitude of the enhanced β-cell responsiveness (i.e., two- to three-fold above nonpregnant levels) (12,13,17,18) cannot be explained on the basis of a 10% to 15% increase in β-cell mass (47). Thus, the responsiveness of individual β-cells to nutrients must also be increased during pregnancy. Limited information is available regarding the cellular mechanisms responsible for the increased β-cell responsiveness. Two groups (48,49) have reported increased activities of protein kinase A or C in pancreatic tissue from pregnant compared to nonpregnant rats. Another report (50) revealed enhanced cell-to-cell communication in pancreatic islets from pregnant compared to nonpregnant animals. The relation of these phenomena to enhanced insulin secretion *in vivo* is not known.

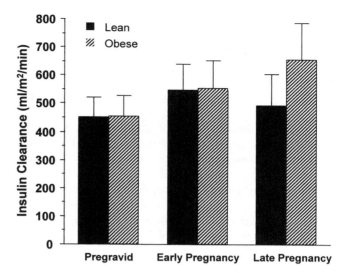

FIGURE 10-5. Whole body insulin clearance rates (mean ±SD) measured during hyperinsulinemic clamps in lean and obese women with normal glucose tolerance described in Fig. 10-2. (From Catalano PM, Huston L, Amini SB, et al. Longitudinal changes in glucose metabolism during pregnancy in obese women with normal glucose tolerance and gestational diabetes. *Am J Obstet Gynecol* 1999;180:903–916; and Catalano PM, Drago NM, Amini SB. Longitudinal changes in pancreatic β cell function and metabolic clearance rate of insulin in pregnant women with normal and abnormal glucose tolerance. *Diabetes Care* 1998;21:403–408, with permission.)

Data regarding insulin clearance in pregnancy are scant. In separate studies, Bellman and Hartman (51), Lind et al. (52), and Burt and Davidson (53) reported no difference in the insulin disappearance rate when insulin was infused intravenously in late gestation in comparison with nongravid subjects. In contrast, Goodner and Freinkel (54), using a radiolabeled insulin, described a 25% increase in insulin turnover in a pregnant as compared with a nonpregnant rat model. Catalano et al. (55) using the euglycemic-clamp model reported a 20% increase in insulin clearance in lean women and a 30% increase in insulin clearance in obese women by late pregnancy (Fig. 10-5). Although the placenta is rich in insulinase, the exact mechanism for the increased insulin clearance reported in some studies remains speculative.

Amino Acid Metabolism

In addition to glucose, which is the primary energy source of feto-placental tissues, accretion of protein is essential for fetal growth. There is increased nitrogen retention in pregnancy in both maternal and fetal compartments. It is estimated that there is approximately a 0.9-kg accretion of maternal protein by 27 weeks (56). It has also been reported that there is a significant decrease in most fasting maternal amino acid concentrations in early pregnancy prior to the accretion of significant maternal or fetal tissue (57). These anticipatory changes in fasting amino acid metabolism occur after a shorter period of fasting in comparison with nonpregnant women. Additionally, maternal amino acid concentrations were significantly decreased in mothers of small for gestational age neonates in comparison with maternal concentrations in appropriately grown neonates (58).

Circulating amino acid concentrations reflect the balance between protein breakdown and synthesis. Those parameters are best measured by using stable isotopes of representative amino acids. Duggleby and Jackson (59) have estimated that the rate of protein synthesis during the first trimester of pregnancy is similar to rates in nonpregnant women. However, there is a 15% increase in synthesis during the second trimester and a further increase in the third trimester by about 25% compared to nonpregnant, nonlactating women. Additionally, there are marked interindividual differences at each time point. These differences appear to have a strong relationship with fetal growth. For example, mothers who had increased protein turnover in mid-pregnancy had babies with increased lean body mass after adjustment for significant co-variables (60).

Amino acids can be used either for protein accrual or oxidized as an energy source. The only reliable means to assess amino acid oxidation is to measure the rate of urea synthesis directly. Estimating urea synthesis using stable isotopes has been performed in a number of studies. Based on the results of Duggleby and Jackson (59), there appears to be a modest shift in oxidation in early pregnancy with an accrual of amino acids for protein synthesis in late gestation. Furthermore, Kalhan et al. (61) reported that there are significant pregnancy-related adaptations in maternal protein metabolism early in gestation prior to any significant increase in fetal protein accretion.

Amino acids are transported across a concentration gradient from mother to fetus via the placenta by means of energy-requiring amino acid transporters. Amino acid transporters are highly stereospecific, but they have low substrate specificity. Additionally, they may vary with location between the microvillus (MVM) and basal membranes (BM) (62), depending on the system type. Lower amino acid concentrations have been reported in growth-restricted neonates in comparison with appropriately grown neonates, and decreased amino acid transporter activity has been implicated as a possible mechanism. However, the potential role, if any, of placental amino acid transporters in macrosomic infants is currently unknown (63).

Lipid Metabolism

While there is ample literature regarding the changes in glucose metabolism during gestation, data regarding the alterations in lipid metabolism are meager by comparison. Knopp et al. (64) have reported that there is a two- to fourfold increase in total triglyceride concentration and a 25% to 50% increase in total cholesterol concentration during gestation. Additionally, there is a 50% increase in LDL cholesterol and a 30% increase in HDL cholesterol by mid-gestation that decreases slightly in the third trimester. Maternal triglyceride and VLDL triglyceride levels in late gestation are positively correlated with maternal estriol and insulin concentrations. Relative to lipid insulin resistance, Sivan et al. (65) examined the effect of insulin on FFA turnover in obese women in late pregnancy and postpartum using stable isotopes of glycerol during a euglycemic clamp. There were no significant differences in basal FFA turnover oxidation or concentration during the second and third trimesters of pregnancy and postpartum. However, lipolysis was significantly less suppressed during insulin infusion during the third trimester as compared with the second trimester and postpartum. Additionally, Catalano et al. (66) reported on the longitudinal changes in suppression of FFA from pregravid through late pregnancy. There was a significant decreased ability of insulin to suppress FFA concentrations in late gestation. These data demonstrate that in addition to glucose insulin resistance in late gestation, there is evidence for "lipid" insulin resistance as well. Furthermore, Xiang et al. (67) observed a significant correlation between basal FFA concentrations and hepatic glucose production. The increase in maternal lipid concentrations, in particular FFA, in late gestation has been hypothesized as a possible mechanism for the decrease in insulin sensitivity of maternal glucose utilization and production (65).

DIABETES MELLITUS

Diabetes mellitus is a chronic metabolic disorder characterized by hyperglycemia resulting from either absolute or relative insulin deficiency. Although hyperglycemia is the common thread of various forms of diabetes mellitus, the pathophysiology of the hyperglycemia remains heterogeneous. Based on our current understanding of the pathogenesis of reduced insulin secretion, diabetes is classified into two major types: type 1, formerly referred to as insulin-dependent diabetes or juvenile-onset diabetes; and type 2, formerly referred to as non-insulin-dependent or adult-onset diabetes. In type 1 diabetes, the insulin deficiency usually results from autoimmune destruction of pancreatic β-cells, leading to severe or complete insulin deficiency. In type 2 diabetes, the insulin deficiency occurs on a background of insulin resistance. Whether the insulin deficiency or the insulin resistance is the predisposing factor continues to be debated, although there is mounting evidence that insulin resistance leads to β-cell dysfunction. Patients who already have abnormal glucose tolerance usually have both insulin resistance and inappropriately low insulin secretion (12,13,67,68). Recent longitudinal studies by Goldfine et al. (69) reveal that people destined to develop type 2 diabetes can have insulin resistance with normal insulin secretion when their glucose levels are normal 10 to 20 years before the onset of diabetes. That observation suggests that insulin resistance is a prerequisite for type 2 diabetes and that the progressive β-cell dysfunction that characterizes the disease is acquired on the background of insulin resistance. Evidence from the Troglitazone in Prevention of Diabetes (TRIPOD) study suggests that the insulin resistance may reveal the defect in insulin secretion in susceptible individuals (70). In that study, treating insulin resistance in Hispanic women with prior gestational diabetes (GDM) lowered secretory demands on their β-cells and stopped the loss of β-cell function for 4.5 years. Both type 1 and type 2 diabetes may be etiologically heterogeneous and further subclassification is likely as the root causes are identified. Indeed, maturity onset diabetes of the young (MODY), an autosomal dominant form of diabetes once considered an early onset form of type 2 diabetes, is now known to result from several specific gene mutations that appear to affect insulin secretion (71), providing a third general category of β-cell defects that are caused by genetic variants with a large negative impact on β-cell function in the absence of insulin resistance.

All forms of diabetes can occur during pregnancy. Previously, the classification by White (72), first proposed in the 1940s, has been used to communicate succinctly the duration of diabetes, its onset in relation to pregnancy, and the presence or absence of chronic diabetic complications. As understanding of the pathogenesis of diabetes and the effects of specific complications on pregnancy outcomes has improved, the White classification has become less useful. It is more appropriate to characterize pregnancies with maternal diabetes according to (a) the time of diagnosis in relationship to the pregnancy (pregestational vs. GDM); (b) etiology of β-cell dysfunction and hyperglycemia (e.g., immune [type 1], nonimmune with insulin resistance [type 2], known genetic causes [MODY and mitochondrial DNA abnormalities]); and (c) presence or absence of chronic diabetic complications such as retinopathy, nephropathy, and atherosclerosis. The remainder of this chapter is devoted to the maternal metabolic abnormalities that characterize diabetes during pregnancy.

METABOLIC CHANGES IN PREGESTATIONAL DIABETES

Pregestational Type 1 Diabetes

The metabolic impact of pregnancy has predictable effects on patients with preexisting diabetes mellitus. Immune destruction of β-cells leaves the body with no means to compensate for the metabolic effects of the feto-placental unit on maternal carbohydrate, fat, and amino acid metabolism. As a result, concentrations of glucose, fatty acids, ketones, triglycerides, and many amino acids may be ele-

vated in the maternal circulation. As discussed elsewhere in this book, those metabolites can alter embryonic and fetal development, leading to many of the perinatal complications of maternal diabetes. Restoration of a normal relationship between circulating insulin levels and maternal insulin requirements can greatly reduce the impact of maternal diabetes on intrauterine development from conception onward. At present, this restoration is achieved by provision of insulin in a physiologic pattern and in sufficient amounts to normalize maternal intermediary metabolism. Glucose is the most readily measured of the metabolites affected by maternal diabetes, and glucose provides a "benchmark" for assessment of metabolic regulation in diabetic pregnancies. However, other metabolites may have an effect on embryonic (73) and fetal (74–76) development, which may explain why careful glycemic control does not invariably eliminate fetal complications in diabetic pregnancies. Additionally, current methods of insulin delivery are not well suited to minute-by-minute normalization of maternal glycemia, leaving even the best glucose regulation inferior to what a normal pancreas can achieve.

Type 1 diabetes accounts for less than 10% of cases of diabetes in the population, but a slightly greater fraction in women of reproductive age due to the relatively young age of onset of type 1 as compared to type 2 diabetes. Type 1 diabetes is usually characterized by abrupt clinical onset at a young age, following a period of immune destruction of β-cells that may have lasted years or decades. The β-cell destruction continues after the clinical onset of diabetes, usually leading to absolute insulinopenia with lifelong requirements for insulin replacement. Although type 1 diabetes is typically a disease of youth, it has been reported to occur at virtually any age. The disease is particularly common in whites, especially those of Northern European ancestry. Most evidence indicates a genetic predisposition related to an individual's HLA type as well as other loci that have not been fully identified. Disease concordance in monozygotic twins is 33% to 50%, suggesting that environmental triggers are required to initiate the disease in genetically predisposed individuals. The triggers have not been identified. Because of their complete dependence on exogenous insulin, pregnant women with type 1 diabetes are at increased risk for the development of diabetic ketoacidosis, a condition that results when lipolysis and ketone production are unchecked by insulin. Ketoacidosis can occur more rapidly and at lower glucose concentrations than is common for nonpregnant individuals. Additionally, because intensive insulin therapy is used in women with type 1 diabetes to decrease the risk of embryonic and fetal complications, these women are at increased risk for hypoglycemia. The risk may be particularly high in the first trimester when food intake may be inconsistent and tissue sensitivity to insulin enhanced. Studies by Diamond et al. (77) and Rosenn et al. (78) have shown that women with type 1 diabetes are at increased risk for hypoglycemia during pregnancy because of diminished counterregulatory epinephrine and glucagon responses to hypoglycemia. The deficiency in counterregulatory response may also be in part due to an independent effect of pregnancy.

The alterations in glucose metabolism in women with type 1 diabetes are not well characterized. Because of maternal insulinopenia, insulin response during gestation can only be estimated relative to pregravid requirements. Estimates of the changes in insulin requirements are complicated by the degree of preconceptional glucose control and frequent presence of insulin antibodies. Weiss and Hofman (79) reported on the change in insulin requirements in women with type 1 diabetes and strict glucose control either prior to conception or at 10 weeks gestation. There was a 12% decrease in insulin requirement from 10 to 17 weeks gestation and a 50% increase in insulin requirement from 17 weeks until delivery as compared with pregravid requirement. After 36 weeks gestation, there was a decrease in insulin requirement (Fig. 10-6). In the Diabetes in Early Pregnancy Study (DIEP), Jovanovic et al. (80) also reported that there was a mid-first trimester decline in insulin requirements in type 1 diabetic pregnant women. A 5% decrease in insulin requirement after 36 weeks gestation was also noted by McManus and Ryan (81). The decrease in insulin requirement was associated with a longer duration of diabetes mellitus but not with adverse perinatal outcome. The mechanisms for the decrease in insulin requirement in early pregnancy in women with type 1 diabetes are not well characterized. This may be the result of the increased pregravid insulin sensitivity as discussed previously. Additionally, the decrease in insulin requirement in early pregnancy in women with type 1 diabetes may be a reflection of amelioration of a component of insulin resistance due to glucose toxicity caused

by previously poor glucose control (82). Lastly, Jovanovic et al. (80) have speculated that the fall in insulin requirements in these women may be mediated through a decline in progesterone, an anti-insulin hormone during the luteal-placental shift at 8 to 10 weeks gestation.

Schmitz et al. (42) have evaluated the longitudinal changes in insulin sensitivity in women with type 1 diabetes in early and late pregnancy as well as postpartum in comparison with nonpregnant women with type 1 diabetes. In the pregnant women with type 1 diabetes, there was a 50% decrease in insulin sensitivity only in late gestation. There was no significant difference in insulin sensitivity in pregnant women with type 1 diabetes in early pregnancy or within 1 week of delivery as compared with nonpregnant women with type 1 diabetes. Therefore, based on the available data, women with type 1 diabetes appear to have a similar decrease in magnitude in insulin sensitivity as compared with women with normal glucose tolerance.

Pregestational Type 2 Diabetes

Women with type 2 diabetes also manifest an increase in insulin resistance during pregnancy. They enter pregnancy substantially more insulin resistant than patients with type 1 diabetes, but end up with only slightly greater insulin resistance by the third trimester. Thus, the net change in insulin resistance and increase in insulin requirement is less in the type 2 patients, but the final level of resistance and insulin requirement may be the same or more than in type 1 patients. Indeed, total daily requirements in women with type 2 diabetes may reach 1.5 to 2.0 U/kg of body weight by the third trimester.

Patients with type 2 diabetes are not at high risk for ketoacidosis. However, the accelerated lipolysis and ketogenesis of pregnancy have an important implication for the dietary treatment of patients with type 2 diabetes during pregnancy. Caloric restriction and weight loss have been shown to improve insulin sensitivity and ameliorate the hyperglycemia of nonpregnant patients with type 2 diabetes (83,84). However, caloric restriction during pregnancy can lead to ketonuria and mild ketonemia in the absence of hyperglycemia ("starvation ketosis"), particularly if the restriction in calories and carbohydrates is large. Although starvation ketosis does not pose any significant risk to mothers, at least three studies have linked ketonuria or mild ketonemia during pregnancy to impaired motor and intellectual development of young children (85–87). Thus, prescription of diets with sufficient calorie or carbohydrate restriction to induce even mild ketosis is discouraged during pregnancy.

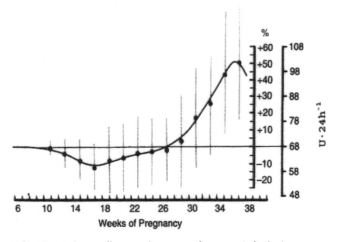

FIGURE 10-6. Insulin requirements (mean ±SD) during pregnancy in 12 patients with type 1 diabetes antedating pregnancy. All 12 had strict metabolic control initiated before the 10th gestational week. The solid line (0%, 68 units per day) represents insulin requirements at the initiation of therapy. (From Weiss PAM, Hofman H. Intensified conventional insulin therapy for the pregnant diabetic patient. *Obstet Gynecol* 1984;64:629–637.)

Gestational Diabetes

GDM is the presence of glucose concentrations that are at the upper end of the population distribution for glucose in pregnant women and first detected during pregnancy. Like any form of hyperglycemia, GDM results from an imbalance between tissue insulin requirements for glucose regulation and the ability of the pancreatic β-cells to meet those requirements. The insulin deficiency, which is relative rather than absolute, can result from any of the disease processes that lead to diabetes in nonpregnant individuals. A small fraction of patients have evidence of autoimmunity directed against pancreatic β-cells—10% and 35% when measured by immunofluorescence techniques to detect antibodies against pancreatic islets (88,89) but only 2% to 13% when measured as antibodies to specific β-cell antigens (90,91). Some of these deficiencies may be population dependent. Other patients have genetic variants that have been identified as causes of diabetes in the general population, including autosomal dominant or maternal/mitochondrial inheritance patterns (92–98). Most cases appear to result from inadequate insulin secretion that arises in women with chronic insulin resistance and, therefore, appears to be related to type 2 diabetes. The remaining discussion focuses on insulin resistance and β-cell defects in those women who account for 80% to 90% of women with GDM.

Insulin Resistance

Ryan et al. (18) were the first to report a 40% decrease in whole-body insulin sensitivity in women with severe GDM in comparison with a pregnant control group in late pregnancy using glucose clamp methodology. Catalano et al. (12,13), using similar techniques enhanced by the use of labeled glucose infusions, described the longitudinal changes in insulin sensitivity in both lean and obese women who develop GDM in comparison with a control group matched for body composition. Women who developed GDM had a lower insulin sensitivity than weight-matched controls (Fig. 10-7). The difference was most evident before and during early pregnancy. By late gestation the acquired insulin resistance of pregnancy was marked in both groups so that the intergroup differences were less pronounced but still statistically significant. Of interest, there was an (15% to 20%) increase in insulin sensitivity prior to conception and through early pregnancy (12–14 weeks), particularly in those women with the lowest insulin sensitivity prior to conception, that is, lean women with GDM and obese women with normal glucose tolerance who developed GDM. The changes in insulin sensitivity from the time prior to conception through early pregnancy were inversely correlated with changes in maternal weight gain and energy expenditure (99). The relationship between these alterations in insulin's effect on glucose metabolism, weight gain, and energy expenditure may help explain the decreases in maternal weight gain and insulin requirements in women with diabetes in early gestation (79,99). Xiang et al. (67) also used glucose clamps with labeled glucose to study a large cohort of Hispanic women with GDM and matched

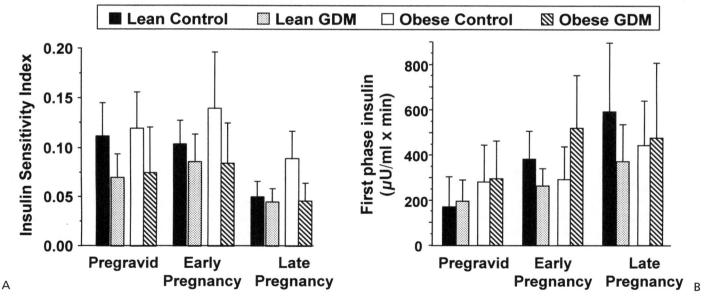

FIGURE 10-7. Insulin secretion and insulin sensitivity in the lean and obese control women presented in Fig. 10-2 and in age, ethnicity and body composition matched women who developed gestational diabetes. **A:** Insulin sensitivity. **B:** First-phase insulin response. See Fig. 10-2 for details regarding the measurements. (From Catalano PM, Tyzbir ED, Wolfe RR, et al. Carbohydrate metabolism during pregnancy in control subjects and women with gestational diabetes. *Am J Physiol* 1993;264:60–67; and Catalano PM, Huston L, Amini SB, et al. Longitudinal changes in glucose metabolism during pregnancy in obese women with normal glucose tolerance and gestational diabetes. *Am J Obstet Gynecol* 1999;180:903–916, with permission.)

controls in the third trimester. Even among the subset of women with GDM who did not have diabetes soon after pregnancy, insulin sensitivity in the third trimester was reduced by a small amount compared with women with normal glucose tolerance.

In the study by Xiang et al. (67), insulin resistance was observed not only for stimulation of glucose utilization, but also for suppression of glucose production. The effect was tightly linked to suppression by insulin of FFA production/release, which was also impaired in women with GDM. Reduced suppression of hepatic glucose production by infused insulin has also been noted in lean as well as obese women with GDM in late gestation. In contrast, glucose production after an overnight fast has been found by some (67), but not others (12,13,16), to be elevated in women with GDM despite higher basal insulin concentrations than those observed in women with normal glucose tolerance. These findings support a role for hepatic insulin resistance in the overnight-fasted state as well.

Studies in human skeletal muscle and adipose tissue have demonstrated that there are defects in the postreceptor insulin-signaling cascade in women with GDM in addition to those described in pregnant women with normal glucose tolerance. Based on the studies of Friedman et al. (30), all pregnant women appeared to have a decrease in insulin receptor substrate-1 (IRS-1) expression. As discussed previously, the down-regulation of the IRS-1 protein closely parallels the decreased ability of insulin to induce additional steps in the insulin-signaling cascade, the movement of the GLUT-4 transfer to the cell surface membrane, thereby facilitating glucose transport into the cell (Fig. 10-4). In addition to the above mechanisms, in women with GDM there is a distinct decrease in the ability of the IR-β—that component of the insulin receptor not on the cell surface—to undergo tyrosine phosphorylation. This additional defect in the insulin-signaling cascade is not found in either pregnant or nonpregnant women with normal glucose tolerance (30), and results in a 25% lower glucose transport activity.

Other potential defects in the insulin-signaling cascade in women with GDM include a decreased ability of insulin to fully stimulate tyrosine phosphorylation of the IR-β. Tyrosine phosphorylation of insulin receptor substrate proteins is balanced by dephosphorylation reactions carried out by cellular and membrane-bound protein phosphatases. Vandate has been shown to inhibit protein-tyrosine phosphatase activity. During *in vitro* studies by Shao et al. (100), vandate failed to normalize glucose transport activity in women with GDM, suggesting that decreased glucose uptake in women with GDM is not the result of impaired tyrosine phosphorylation alone. Additionally, the same investigators have reported that in women with GDM, plasma cell membrane glycoprotein-1 (PC-1), an inhibitor of insulin receptor tyrosine kinase (IRTK) activity, was increased in comparison with pregnant and nonpregnant control subjects. The increase in PC-1 content suggests

excessive phosphorylation of serine/threonine residues in skeletal muscle insulin receptors, thus contributing to decreased IRTK activity, that is, decreased insulin sensitivity (101). Of interest, TNF-α, described earlier as a placental factor that might decrease maternal insulin sensitivity, has been shown to act as a serine/threonine kinase, thereby inhibiting IRS-1 and insulin receptor tyrosine phosphorylation. Thus, these receptor defects may contribute in part to the pathogenesis of GDM and an increased risk of type 2 diabetes later in life.

Beta Cell Defects

As stated previously, β-cell defects in GDM could reflect the spectrum of β-cell abnormalities that lead to diabetes in nonpregnant individuals. Few studies of insulin secretion in GDM have focused on specific subtypes of the disease, so information about causes of poor insulin secretion in specific subtypes is scant. In women with circulating markers of pancreatic autoimmunity, poor insulin secretion is likely the result of ongoing β-cell destruction, although this issue has not been investigated in humans. Likewise, poor insulin secretion in women with genetic markers for autosomal dominant or maternally inherited diabetes likely reflects abnormalities of β-cell function that have been described in association with those diseases outside of pregnancy (102,103), but the issue remains poorly investigated. Virtually all studies of women with GDM reveal β-cell function that is decreased, generally in the range of 30% to 70%, relative to women who maintain normal glucose tolerance during pregnancy. Since most studies have found chronic insulin resistance in women with GDM or a history thereof, it is likely that most β-cell dysfunction in GDM occurs on a background of insulin resistance. Indeed, when insulin sensitivity and secretion have been compared between normal women and those with GDM during and after pregnancy, the failure of β-cell function to compensate for insulin resistance in GDM has been similar to controls (12,18). In Fig. 10-7A, the longitudinal data of Catalano et al. (13,14) reveal that women with GDM follow a pattern of change in insulin sensitivity that parallels controls, a slight increase in early gestation and large fall by late gestation, albeit at lower insulin sensitivity overall. Their β-cell function, assessed as acute insulin response to intravenous glucose (Fig. 10-7B), likewise follows a pattern that is similar to controls, a slight increase early in gestation before insulin sensitivity declines and then a further increase in late gestation when insulin sensitivity falls, but lower insulin secretion overall relative to the decreased insulin sensitivity. The fact that insulin secretion is reduced in women with GDM despite their insulin resistance means that their β-cell defect is even greater than can be appreciated by insulin levels or responses alone. Most importantly, women with GDM do increase their insulin secretion during pregnancy, just as normal women do. The point is further supported by the findings of Homko et al. (104) (Fig. 10-8). Their data, which were obtained using fixed hyperglycemia to match the glucose stimulus to β-cells in all subjects, also reveal that women with GDM increase their insulin secretion during pregnancy in a pattern that is similar to, but at lower levels than, women who maintain normal glucose levels in pregnancy. Calculation of the relative defect in β-cell compensation for insulin resistance between GDM and control women reveals a similar defect—41% during pregnancy and 50% after pregnancy. This consistency in the magnitude of the β-cell defect, combined with the fact that women with GDM do increase their insulin responses during pregnancy (Figs. 10-7 and 10-8), demonstrates that GDM is not simply a fixed limitation in insulin secretory reserve that becomes manifest as hyperglycemia when insulin needs increase during pregnancy. Instead, as proposed by Harris (105), it appears that GDM represents detection during pregnancy of chronic metabolic abnormalities that antedate pregnancy but are detected when pregnancy leads to the first evaluation of glucose tolerance in otherwise healthy young women.

The common association between a β-cell defect detected during pregnancy (i.e., under conditions of acquired insulin resistance) in women who also have chronic insulin resistance may provide clues to the cause of

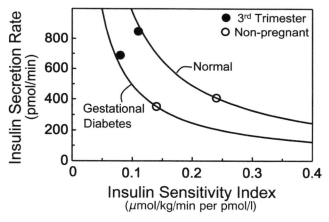

FIGURE 10-8. Insulin sensitivity and insulin secretion in normal women and women with gestational diabetes during the third trimester and after pregnancy. Insulin secretion rates were calculated from plasma C-peptide and insulin concentrations during steady-state hyperglycemia (180 mg/dl) created by variable-rate glucose infusions. Insulin sensitivity was calculated as follows: (glucose disposal rate) / (plasma insulin concentration) during the same glucose infusions. Curved lines represent the product of the means of insulin sensitivity and insulin secretion, a measure of β-cell compensation for insulin resistance (122) in each group when they were not pregnant. (Data from Homko C, Sivan E, Chen X, et al. Insulin secretion during and after pregnancy in patients with gestational diabetes mellitus. *J Clin Endocrinol Metab* 2001;86:568–573, with permission. Adapted from Buchanan TA. Pancreatic B-cell defects in gestational diabetes: implications for the pathogenesis and prevention of type 2 diabetes. *J Clin Endocrinol Metab* 2001;86:989–993, with permission.)

the β-cell defect in GDM. One possibility is that women who have chronic insulin resistance and a separate β-cell problem are the individuals whose glucose levels rise to the level of GDM at a relatively young age. However, recent studies of Hispanic women in the United States of Mexican and Central American ancestry with GDM indicate that their β-cell defect is either caused or worsened by insulin resistance. The epidemiologic observation, made in a cohort of nearly 700 individuals with GDM followed for 5 to 6 years after the index pregnancy (106), was that weight gain and an additional pregnancy independently increased the risk of diabetes (three-fold for a pregnancy and two-fold for 10 pounds of weight gain). That observation led to an intervention study, the TRIPOD study (70), in which nonpregnant women with recent GDM were given a thiazolidinedione drug to ameliorate their insulin resistance. The immediate response of most subjects was to reduce their insulin secretion, although approximately one-third of the women failed to do so because the drug did not affect their insulin resistance. During a median 30 months of follow-up, diabetes rates were reduced 55% compared to placebo-treated patients. The protection from diabetes was very closely linked to the degree of reduction of endogenous insulin requirements when patients were initially placed on the drug, persisted for 8 months after the drug was stopped and insulin resistance returned, and was associated with stabilization of β-cell function for 4.5 years, while placebo-treated patients lost 39% of their β-cell function. These findings demonstrate that reducing secretory demands placed on the β-cell by chronic insulin resistance can arrest falling β-cell function, thereby preventing diabetes. The findings indicate that chronic insulin resistance causes or worsens the β-cell dysfunction that leads to GDM and subsequent type 2 diabetes in Hispanic women. The general implication (Fig. 10-9) is that insulin resistance provides the "stress" needed to initiate or enhance a progressive loss of β-cell function in susceptible individuals. The progressive loss of function leads to a gradual loss of glucose tolerance diagnosed as GDM during pregnancy and, eventually, to type 2 diabetes. This model provides a strong rationale for avoiding insulin resistance to prevent GDM in the first place and type 2 diabetes after GDM, especially given that the risk of diabetes after GDM is on the order of 20% to 50% within 5 years. Whether the biology of the β-cell defect observed in Hispanic women who develop GDM applies to other ethnic groups as well remains to be tested.

Because circulating glucose concentrations are distributed in a unimodal rather than a bimodal fashion in most populations, the distinction between normal and abnormal glucose tolerance in pregnancy is made by drawing a line across a continuum of circulating glucose concentrations. As a result, the diagnosis of GDM is likely to identify a significant number of women with a true genetic risk of subsequent diabetes, as well as some women whose glucose tolerance is simply at the upper end of the normal distribution

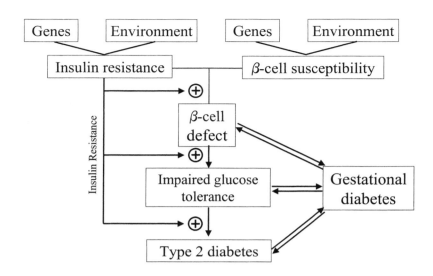

FIGURE 10-9. Schematic diagram of pathogenesis of gestational and type 2 diabetes, based predominantly on observations made on Hispanic American women. Two factors, insulin resistance and susceptibility of β-cells to fail under the high secretory demands of insulin resistance, are required to initiate and sustain a progressive loss of β-cell function. Glucose levels rise as β-cell function declines. Testing of glucose levels and tolerance in pregnancy leads to detection of the β-cell defects. Treatment of insulin resistance can arrest the process. (From Buchanan TA, Xiang AH, Peters RK, et al. Preservation of pancreatic beta-cell function and prevention of type 2 diabetes by pharmacological treatment of insulin resistance in high-risk Hispanic women. *Diabetes* 2002;51:2796–2803, with permission.)

for the population. That concept is supported by two findings. First, Buchanan (107) has reported that approximately 25% of a group of white, black, and Hispanic women with GDM had insulin secretory responses to glucose that were normal for their degree of insulin resistance in late pregnancy. Those women had mild GDM and might be expected to be at low risk of diabetes when they are not pregnant (108–111). Second, as indicated by the long-term follow-up studies of O'Sullivan (112), a significant number of women with GDM may never develop diabetes after pregnancy. Thus, not all women with GDM can be regarded as truly abnormal in their regulation of circulating glucose concentrations.

DIABETIC PREGNANCIES

Amino Acid Metabolism

The data regarding amino acid metabolism in pregnant women with GDM were limited and at times contradictory. Issues relating to maternal body mass index, the need for insulin therapy, stable isotope methodology, and ethnic variations are all potential confounders relating to interpretation of the data. Butte et al. (113) and Metzger et al. (114) have reported higher plasma amino acid concentrations in women with GDM as compared with a control group with normal glucose metabolism. Estimates of proteolysis or protein turnover are often conducted using stable isotopes of amino acids. Zimmer et al. (115) reported no significant difference in fasting leucine and phenylalanine turnover in women with GDM and a control group. However, the investigators noted that basal insulin concentrations were three to five times greater in the women with GDM compared with the controls, indicating that hyperinsulinemia was required to maintain normal amino acid turnover. In contrast, Kalhan et al. (116) reported that both

leucine turnover and oxidation were greater in obese women with GDM compared with less obese control subjects. Butte et al. (113) evaluated basal amino acid turnover in women with GDM and normal glucose tolerance in late pregnancy and again postpartum. Again, there was no difference in basal protein metabolism—that is, proteolysis estimated as nitrogen flux using [15N]-labeled leucine—between GDM and control subjects. Nitrogen flux was lower during pregnancy but not significantly different between groups. There was a positive correlation between maternal fasting serine concentrations and fetal weight. The authors speculated that amino acids such as arginine may be a stimulus for fetal islet cell stimulation with resulting fetal macrosomia. In women with well-controlled type 1 diabetes, Whittaker et al. (117) reported no significant difference in basal or insulin-stimulated protein metabolism.

Lastly, transport of amino acids from mother to fetus is mediated by transporters localized in the MVM exposed to the maternal circulation and BM facing the fetal circulation. Jansson et al. (118) evaluated MVM system-A amino acid transporters in placental tissue for macrosomic and nonmacrosomic women with normal glucose tolerance and women with type 1 diabetes and GDM. System-A amino acid transporters are expressed in almost all human tissues and transport a broad range of neutral amino acids. They reported that MVM system-A amino acid transporters were increased 65% to 80% in placental tissue obtained from women with diabetes, independent of fetal macrosomia. In contrast, the MVM system-A activity was not significantly different in placental tissue from macrosomic and nonmacrosomic infants of women with normal glucose tolerance. There was, however, an increase in MVM leucine transport in macrosomic infants of women with GDM. BM amino acid transport was not affected by diabetes. The authors concluded that the increase in MVM amino acid transport may be required for increased placental metabolic needs. These data are in contrast to Kuruvilla et al. (119), who observed decreased MVM system A activity in placental tissue from women with diabetes and macrosomic neonates. Differences in methodologies may account for the discrepancies.

In summary, based on available data, protein metabolism, as estimated using stable isotope methodology to estimate amino acid turnover, may be equivalent or increased in women with GDM as compared with a normoglycemic group. However, the increased insulin concentrations required to maintain appropriate amino acid turnover may be a manifestation of compensated, amino acid insulin resistance of pregnancy. Although basal amino acid concentrations may correlate with birth weight, the role of amino acid transporter number and function are yet to be clarified.

Lipid Metabolism

There is evidence during pregnancy for a decreased insulin sensitivity in lipid metabolism for women with diabetes as compared with women with normal glucose tolerance. Women with type 2 diabetes, because they are frequently obese and more insulin resistant, often have hypertriglyceridemia and associated reductions in high-density lipoproteins (HDL) (120). These abnormalities are also observed when these women become pregnant. In women with type 2 diabetes and GDM, Knopp et al. (120) reported an associated increase in triglyceride levels and a decrease in HDL concentrations. However, Montelongo et al. (121) reported little change in basal FFA concentrations after a 12-hour fast through all three trimesters.

Relative to postabsorptive lipid metabolism/insulin sensitivity (i.e., the ability of insulin to inhibit lipolysis), Xiang et al. (67) described FFA concentrations that were greater after an overnight fast in the third trimester in Hispanic women with GDM as compared with a matched control group. During hyperisulinemia in the high physiological range, suppression of FFA was similar in the two groups, so steady-state FFA levels remained higher in the women with GDM. This pattern was the same when only GDM subjects who had normal glucose tolerance postpartum were compared to controls. In a small number of subjects evaluated longitudinally from before pregnancy through late gestation, Catalano et al. (66) reported that in control subjects there was a significant decline in insulin suppression of FFA with advancing gestation and the percent suppression of FFA was significantly lower in GDM as compared with control subjects. Additionally, in a cross-sectional analysis, the same authors reported a significant decrease in IRS-1 and a significant increase in IRS-2 and the P85-α subunit of PI-3-kinase in subcutaneous adipose tissue biopsies from women with GDM in comparison with pregnant control subjects. These changes in insulin-signaling protein concentrations may contribute to the decreased ability of insulin to suppress FFA in women with GDM. Decreased peroxisome proliferator–activated receptor gamma (PPAR-

γ) mRNA and protein concentrations were also reported in adipose tissue of these same women with GDM as compared to nonpregnant controls. This, in addition to decreases in lipoprotein lipase mRNA, is consistent with the increased lipid insulin resistance in late pregnancy and may contribute to the decrease in adipose tissue mass, increasing FFA concentrations and fat oxidation observed in late pregnancy, particularly in women with GDM.

KEY POINTS

- In women with normal glucose tolerance there is a progressive, 40% to 50% decrease in both peripheral (skeletal muscle) and endogenous (primarily hepatic) insulin sensitivity with advancing gestation.
- There is a significant two- to three-fold increase in pancreatic β-cell function during pregnancy that is in large part due to compensation for insulin resistance, but that may include a component of pregnancy-enhanced β-cell function directly. There is also a 20% to 30% increase in insulin clearance with advancing gestation.
- Recently, cytokines—specifically, TNF-α and leptin (possibly of placental origin and in addition to the increase in FFA)—have been implicated as predictors of the insulin resistance during gestation.
- The decreased insulin sensitivity of pregnancy appears to be a postreceptor phenomenon. IRS-1 protein concentration is decreased during pregnancy.
- The decreased insulin sensitivity of pregnancy is not limited to carbohydrate metabolism, but also may affect amino acid (increased protein turnover) and lipid metabolism (increased lipolysis).
- In women with type 1 diabetes, there appears to be a decrease in insulin sensitivity in pregnancy that is similar in magnitude to the decrease observed in women with normal glucose tolerance.
- In women with type 2 diabetes, there is decreased insulin sensitivity prior to conception in comparison with a matched control group. Insulin sensitivity decreases further during pregnancy. Insulin requirements during pregnancy may be 50% to 100% greater in women with type 2 and women with type 1 diabetes.
- Most women who develop GDM have decreased insulin sensitivity both before and during gestation as compared to an appropriately weight-matched control group. Women with GDM also have approximately 50% less insulin secretion relative to their insulin resistance when compared to women with normal glucose tolerance. The defect is similar in magnitude during and after pregnancy, suggesting that the metabolic defects of GDM exist outside of pregnancy. Thus, it appears that GDM is predominantly glucose intolerance, that is, first clinically detected during pregnancy, because that is when glucose tolerance is measured in all healthy pregnant women.

- In addition to the decrease in skeletal muscle IRS-1, women with gestational diabetes have additional defects in the insulin-signaling cascade. These include a decrease in the ability of IR-β to undergo tyrosine phosphorylation, resulting in a 25% decrease in glucose transport activity.

- The effects of insulin on amino acid and lipid insulin sensitivity during pregnancy are also reduced in women with GDM in comparison to women with normal glucose metabolism.

- These metabolic alterations during gestation in women with diabetes alter the environment of the developing fetus, thereby increasing the risk not only for poor short-term fetal outcomes such as macrosomia and hypoglycemia, but may have profound long-term implications.

REFERENCES

1. Catalano PM, Tyzbir ED, Roman NM, et al. Longitudinal changes in insulin release and insulin resistance in non-obese pregnant women. *Am J Obstet Gynecol* 1991;165:1667–1672.
2. Kalhan SC, D'Angelo LJ, Savin SM, et al. Glucose production in pregnant women at term gestation: Sources of glucose for human fetus. *J Clin Invest* 1979;63:388–394.
3. Cowett RA, Susa JB, Kahn CB, et al. Glucose kinetics in non-diabetic and diabetic women during the third trimester of pregnancy. *Am J Obstet Gynecol* 1983;146:773–780.
4. Catalano PM, Tyzbir ED, Wolfe RR, et al. Longitudinal changes in basal hepatic glucose production and suppression during insulin infusion in normal pregnant women. *Am J Obstet Gynecol* 1992;167:913–919.
5. Sivan E, Chen X, Homko CJ, et al. Longitudinal study of carbohydrate metabolism in healthy obese women. *Diabetes Care* 1997;20:1470–1475.
6. Bruschetta H, Buchanan TA, Steil GM, et al. Reduced glucose production accounts for the fall in plasma glucose during brief extension of an overnight fast in women with gestational diabetes. *Clin Res* 1994;42:27.
7. Kalhan SC, Gilfillian CA, Tserng KY, et al. Glucose–alanine relationship in normal human pregnancy. *Metabolism* 1988;37:152–158.
8. Felig P, Kim YJ, Lynch V, et al. Amino acid metabolism during starvation in human pregnancy. *J Clin Invest* 1972;51:1195–1202.
9. Metzger BE, Agnoli FS, Hare JW, et al. Carbohydrate metabolism in pregnancy. X. Metabolic disposition of alanine by the perfused liver of the fasting pregnant rat. *Diabetes* 1973;22:601–612.
10. Pacini G, Bergman RN. MINMOD: A computer program to calculate insulin sensitivity and pancreatic responsivity from the frequently sampled intravenous glucose tolerance test. *Comput Methods Programs Biomed* 1986;23:113–122.
11. DeFronzo RA, Tobin JD, Andres R. Glucose clamp technique: A method for quantifying insulin secretion and resistance. *Am J Physiol* 1979;237:214–223.
12. Catalano PM, Tyzbir ED, Wolfe RR, et al. Carbohydrate metabolism during pregnancy in control subjects and women with gestational diabetes. *Am J Physiol* 1993;264:60–67.
13. Catalano PM, Huston L, Amini SB, et al. Longitudinal changes in glucose metabolism during pregnancy in obese women with normal glucose tolerance and gestational diabetes. *Am J Obstet Gynecol* 1999;180:903–916.
14. Burt RL. Peripheral utilization of glucose in pregnancy. III Insulin intolerance. *Obstet Gynecol* 1956;2:558–664.
15. Spellacy WN, Goetz FC, Greenberg BZ, et al. Plasma insulin in normal "early" pregnancy. *Obstet Gynecol* 1965;25:862–865.
16. Fisher PM, Sutherland HW, Bewsher PD. The insulin response to glucose infusion in normal human pregnancy. *Diabetologia* 1980;19:15–20.
17. Buchanan TZ, Metzger BE, Freinkel N, et al. Insulin sensitivity and β-cell responsiveness to glucose during late pregnancy in lean and moderately obese women with normal glucose tolerance or mild gestational diabetes. *Am J Obstet Gynecol* 1990;162:1008–1014.
18. Ryan EA, O'Sullivan MJ, Skyler JS. Insulin action during pregnancy. Studies with the euglycemic clamp technique. *Diabetes* 1985;34:380–389.
19. Hay WW, Sparks JW, Wilkening RB, et al. Partition of maternal glucose production between conceptus and maternal tissues in sheep. *Am J Physiol* 1983;245:347–350.
20. Marconi AM, Paolini C, Buscaglia M, et al. The impact of gestational age and fetal growth on the maternal-fetal glucose concentration difference. *Obstet Gynecol* 1996;87:937–942.
21. Freinkel N. The Banting Lecture 1980. Of pregnancy and progeny. *Diabetes* 1980;29:1023.
22. Samaan N, Yen SCC, Gonzalez D. Metabolic effects of placental lactogen in man. *J Clin Endocrinol Metab* 1968;28:485.
23. Kalkhoff RK, Richardson BL, Beck P. Relative effects of pregnancy human placental lactogen and prednisolone on carbohydrate tolerance in normal and subclinical diabetic subjects. *Diabetes* 1969;18:153.
24. Beck P. Progestin enhancement of the plasma insulin response to glucose in rhesus monkeys. *Diabetes* 1969;18:146.
25. Kalkhoff RK, Jacobson M, Lemper D. Progesterone, pregnancy and the augmented plasma insulin response. *J Clin Endocrinol* 1970;31:24.
26. Ryan EA, Enns L. Role of gestational hormones in the induction of insulin resistance. *J Clin Endocrinol Metab* 1988;67:341.
27. Kirwan JP, Hauguel-de Mouzon S, Lepercq J, et al. TNFα is a predictor of insulin resistance in human pregnancy. *Diabetes* 2002;51:2207–2213.
28. Damm P, Handberg A, Kuhl C, et al. Insulin receptor binding and tyrosine kinase activity in skeletal muscle from normal pregnant women and women with gestational diabetes. *Obstet Gynecol* 1993;82:251.
29. Garvey WT, Maianu L, Hancock JA, et al. Gene expression of GLUT4 in skeletal muscle from insulin-resistant patients with obesity, IGT, GDM, and NIDDM. *Diabetes* 1992;41:465–475.
30. Friedman JE, Ishizuka T, Shao J, et al. Impaired glucose transport and insulin receptor tyrosine phosphorylation in skeletal muscle from obese women with gestational diabetes. *Diabetes* 1999;48:1807–1814.
31. Hotamisligil GS, Peraldi P, Budavari A, et al. IRS-1 mediated inhibition of insulin receptor tyrosine kinase activity in TNF-α and obesity-induced insulin resistance. *Science* 1996;271:665–668.
32. Kirwan JP, Krishnan RK, Weaver JA, et al. Human aging is associated with altered TNF-α production during hyperglycemia and hyperinsulinemia. *Am J Physiol* 2001;281:1137–1143.
33. Ling PR, Bistrian BR, Mendez B, et al. Effects of systemic infusions of endotoxin, tumor necrosis factor, and interleukin-1 on glucose metabolism in the rat: relationship to endogenous glucose production and peripheral tissue glucose uptake. *Metabolism* 1994;43:279–284.
34. Hotamisligil GS, Murray DL, Choy LN, et al. Tumor necrosis

factor alpha inhibits signaling from the insulin receptor. *Proc Natl Acad Sci U S A* 1994;91:4854–4858.

35. del Aguila LF, Claffey KP, Kirwan JP. TNF-a impairs insulin signaling and insulin stimulation of glucose uptake in C2C12 muscle cells. *Am J Physiol* 1999;276:849–855.

36. Rui L, Aguirre V, Kim JK, et al. Insulin/IGF-1 and TNF-α stimulate phosphorylation of IRS-1 at inhibitory ser (307) via distinct pathways. *J Clin Invest* 2001;107:181–189.

37. Friedman JE, Ishizuka T, Shao J, et al. Impaired glucose transport and insulin receptor tyrosine phosphorylation in skeletal muscle from obese women with gestational diabetes. *Diabetes* 1999;49:1807–1814.

38. Shao J, Catalano PM, Yamashita H, et al. Decreased insulin receptor tyrosine kinase activity and plasma cell membrane glycoprotein-1 overexpression in skeletal muscle from obese women with gestational diabetes mellitus (GDM): evidence for increased serine/threonine phosphorylation in pregnancy and GDM. *Diabetes* 2000;490:603–610.

39. Bergman RN, Phillips LS, Cobelli C. Physiologic evaluation of factors controlling glucose disposition in man. Measurement of insulin sensitivity and beta-cell sensitivity from the response to intravenous glucose. *J Clin Invest* 1981;68:1456–1467.

40. Buchanan TA. Carbohydrate metabolism in pregnancy: Normal physiology and implications for diabetes mellitus. *Isr J Med Sci* 1991;27:432–441.

41. Kahn SE, Prigeon RL, McCulloch DK, et al. Quantification of the relationship between insulin sensitivity and B-cell function in human subjects: evidence for a hyperbolic function. *Diabetes* 1993;42:1663–1672.

42. Schmitz O, Klebe J, Moller J, et al. In vivo insulin action in type 1 (insulin-dependent) diabetic pregnant women as assessed by the insulin clamp technique. *J Clin Endocrinol Metab* 1985;61:877–881.

43. Green IC, El Seifi S, Perrin D, et al. Cell replication in the islets of Langerhans of adult rats: effects of pregnancy, ovariectomy and treatment with steroid hormones. *J Endocrinol* 1981;88:219–224.

44. Van Assche FA. Quantitative morphological and histoenzymatic study of the endocrine pancreas in nonpregnant and pregnant rats. *Am J Obstet Gynecol* 1974;118:39–41.

45. Aerts L, Van Assche FA. Ultrastructural changes of the endocrine pancreas in pregnant rats. *Diabetologia* 1975;11:285–289.

46. Van Assche FA, Aerts L, De Prins F. A morphological study of the endocrine pancreas in human pregnancy. *Br J Obstet Gynaecol* 1978;85:818–820.

47. Van Assche FA, Aerts L, De Prins F. A morphological study of the endocrine pancreas in human pregnancy. *Br J Obstet Gynaecol* 1978;85:818–820.

48. Hubinot CJ, Duframe SP, Malaisse WJ. Effect of pregnancy upon the activity of protein kinase A and C in rat pancreatic islets. *Horm Metab Res* 1985;17:104–109.

49. Tanigawa K, Tsuchiyama S, Kato Y. Differential sensitivity of pancreatic β-cells to phorbol ester TPA and Ckinase inhibitor H7 in nonpregnant and pregnant rats. *Endocrinol J* 1990;37:883–891.

50. Sheridan JD, Anaya PA, Parsons JA, et al. Increased dye coupling in pancreatic islets from rats in late term pregnancy. *Diabetes* 1988;37:908–911.

51. Bellman O, Hartman E. Influence of pregnancy on the kinetics of insulin. *Am J Obstet Gynecol* 1975;122:829–833.

52. Lind T, Bell S, Gilmore E. Insulin disappearance rate in pregnant and nonpregnant women and in nonpregnant women given GHRIH. *Eur J Clin Invest* 1977;7:47–51.

53. Burt RL, Davidson IWF. Insulin half-life and utilization in normal pregnancy. *Obstet Gynecol* 1974;43:161–170.

54. Goodner CJ, Freinkel N. Carbohydrate metabolism in pregnancy: the degradation of insulin by extracts of maternal and fetal structures in the pregnant rat. *Endocrinology* 1959;65:957–967.

55. Catalano PM, Drago NM, Amini SB. Longitudinal changes in pancreatic b cell function and metabolic clearance rate of insulin in pregnant women with normal and abnormal glucose tolerance. *Diabetes Care* 1998;21:403–408.

56. Hytten FE. Nutrition. In: Hytten F, Chamberlain G, eds. *Clinical Physiology in Obstetrics.* Oxford: Blackwell Scientific, 1980:163–192.

57. Metzger BD, Unger RH, Freinkel N. Carbohydrate metabolism in pregnancy. XIV. Relationships between circulation glucagon, insulin, glucose and amino acids in response to a "mixed meal" in late pregnancy. *Metabolism* 1977;26:151–156.

58. McClain PE, Metcoff J, Crosby WM, et al. Relationship of maternal amino acid profiles at 25 weeks of gestation to fetal growth. *Am J Clin Nutr* 1978;31:401–407.

59. Duggleby SC, Jackson AA. Protein, amino acid and nitrogen metabolism during pregnancy: how might the mother meet the needs of her fetus? *Curr Opin Clin Nutr Metab Care* 2002;5:503–509.

60. Duggleby SC, Jackson AA. Relationship of maternal protein turnover and lean body mass during pregnancy and birth weight. *Clin Sci (Lond)* 2001;101:65–72.

61. Kalhan SC, Rossi KQ, Gruca LL, et al. Relation between transamination of branched-chair amino acids and urea synthesis: evidence from human pregnancy. *Am J Physiol* 1998;275:423–431.

62. Ogata ES. The small for gestational age neonate. In: Cowett RM, ed. *Principles of Perinatal-Neonatal Metabolism,* 2nd ed. New York: Springer-Verlag, 1998:1097–1104.

63. Liechty EA, Boyle DW. Protein metabolism in the fetal placental unit. In: Cowett RM, ed. *Principles of Perinatal-Neonatal Metabolism,* 2nd ed. New York: Springer-Verlag, 1998:369–387.

64. Knopp RH, Humphrey J, Irvin S. Biphasic metabolic control of hypertriglyceridemia in pregnancy. *Clin Res* 177;25:161.

65. Sivan E, Homko CJ, Chen X, et al. Effect of insulin in fat metabolism during and after normal pregnancy. *Diabetes* 1999;44:384–388.

66. Catalano PM, Nizielski SE, Shao J, et al. Down regulation of IRS-1 and PPARγ in obese women with gestational diabetes: relationship to free fatty acids during pregnancy. *Am J Physiol (Endocrin Metab)* 2002;282:522–533.

67. Xiang AH, Peters RH, Trigo E, et al. Multiple metabolic defects during late pregnancy in women at high risk for type 2 diabetes. *Diabetes* 1999;48:848–854.

68. Ryan EA, Imes S, Liu D, et al. Defects in insulin secretion and action in women with a history of gestational diabetes. *Diabetes* 1995;44:506–512.

69. Goldfine AB, Bouche C, Parker RA, et al. Insulin resistance is a poor predictor of type 2 diabetes in individuals with no family history of disease. *Proc Natl Acad Sci U S A* 2003;100:2724–2729.

70. Buchanan TA, Xiang AH, Peters RK, et al. Preservation of pancreatic beta-cell function and prevention of type 2 diabetes by pharmacological treatment of insulin resistance in high-risk Hispanic women. *Diabetes* 2002;51:2796–2803.

71. Herman WH, Fajans SS, Ortiz FJ, et al. Abnormal insulin secretion, not insulin resistance is the genetic or primary defect of MODY in RW pedigree. *Diabetes* 1994;43:40–46.

72. White P. Pregnancy complicating diabetes. *Am J Med* 1949;7:609–616.

73. Sadler TV, Hunter ES III, Wynn RE, et al. Evidence for multifactorial origin of diabetes-induced embryopathies. *Diabetes* 1989;38:70.

74. Kalkhoff RK. Impact of maternal fuels and nutritional state on fetal growth. *Diabetes* 1991;40[Suppl 2]:61.

75. Metzger BE. Biphasic effects of maternal metabolism on fetal growth. Quintessential expression of fuel-mediated metabolism. *Diabetes* 1991;40[Suppl 2]:99.

76. Knopp RH, Bergelin RO, Wahl PW, et al. Relationship of infant birth size to maternal lipoproteins, apoproteins, fuels, hormones, clinical chemistries, and body weight at 36 weeks gestation. *Diabetes* 1985;34[Suppl 2]:71.

77. Diamond MP, Reece EA, Caprios L, et al. Impairment of counter regulatory hormone responses to hypoglycemia in pregnant women with insulin-dependent diabetes mellitus. *Am J Obstet Gynecol* 1992;166:70–77.

78. Rosenn BM, Miodovnik M, Khoury JC, et al. Counter regulatory hormonal responses to hypoglycemia during pregnancy. *Obstet Gynecol* 1996;87:568–574.

79. Weiss PAM, Hofman H. Intensified conventional insulin therapy for the pregnant diabetic patient. *Obstet Gynecol* 1984;64: 629–637.

80. Jovanovic L, Knopp RH, Brown Z, et al. Declining insulin requirements in the late first trimester of diabetic pregnancy. *Diabetes Care* 2001;24:1130–1136.

81. McManus RM, Ryan EA. Insulin requirements in insulin-dependent and insulin-requiring GDM women during the final month of pregnancy. *Diabetes Care* 1992;15:1323–1327.

82. Rossetti L, Giaccari A, DeFronzo RA. Glucose toxicity. *Diabetes Care* 1990;13:610–630.

83. Henry RR, Schaeffer L, Olefsky JM. Glycemic effects of intensive calorie restriction and refeeding in noninsulin dependent diabetes mellitus. *J Clin Endocrinol Metab* 1985;61:917.

84. Wing RR. Behavioral treatment of obesity. Its application to type II diabetes. *Diabetes Care* 1993;16:193.

85. Churchill JA, Berendez HW, Nemore J. Neuropsychological deficits in children of diabetic mothers. *Am J Obstet Gynecol* 1966;105:257.

86. Stehbens JA, Baker GL, Kitchell M. Outcome at ages 1, 3, and 5 years of children born to diabetic women. *Am J Obstet Gynecol* 1977;127:408.

87. Rizzo T, Metzger BE, Burns WJ, et al. Correlation between antepartum maternal metabolism and intelligence of offspring. *N Engl J Med* 1991;325:911.

88. Steel JM, Irvine WJ, Clark BF. The significance of pancreatic islet cell antibody and abnormal glucose tolerance during pregnancy. *J Clin Lab Immunol* 1980;4:83–86.

89. Ginsberg-Fellner F, Mark EM, Nechemias C, et al. Autoantibodies to islet cells: comparison of methods [Letter]. *Lancet* 1982;2:1218.

90. Mauricio D, de Leiva A. Autoimmune gestational diabetes mellitus: a distinct clinical entity. *Diabetes Metab Res Rev* 2001;17: 422–428.

91. Catalano PM, Tyzbir ED, Sims EAH. Incidence and significance of islet cell antibodies in women with previous gestational diabetes mellitus. *Diabetes Care* 1990;13:478–482.

92. Saker PJ, Hattersley AT, Barrow B, et al. High prevalence of a missense mutation of the glucokinase gene in gestational diabetes due to a founder-effect in a local population. *Diabetalogia* 1996;39:1125–1128.

93. Allan CJ, Argyropoulos G, Bowker M, et al. Gestational diabetes mellitus and gene mutations which affect insulin secretion. *Diabetes Res Clin Pract* 1997;36:135–141.

94. Ellard S, Beards F, Allen LI, et al. A high prevalence of glucokinase mutations in gestational diabetic subjects selected by clinical criteria. *Diabetologia* 2000;43:250–253.

95. Chen Y, Liao WX, Roy AC, et al. Mitochondrial gene mutations in gestational diabetes mellitus. *Diabetes Res Clin Pract* 2000;48:29–35.

96. Aggarwal P, Gill-Randall R, Wheatley T, et al. Identification of mtDNA mutation in a pedigree with gestational daibetes, deafness, Wolff–Parkinson–White syndrome and placenta accreta. *Hum Hered* 2001;51:114–116.

97. Stoffel M, Bell KL, Blackburn CL, et al. Identification of glucokinase mutations in subjects with gestational diabetes mellitus. *Diabetes* 1993;42:937–940.

98. Zaidi FK, Wareham NJ, McCarthy M, et al. Homozygosity for a common polymorphism in the islet-specific promoter of the glucokinase gene is associated with a reduced early insulin response to oral glucose in pregnant women. *Diabetic Med* 1997;14:228–234.

99. Catalano PM, Roman-Drago N, Amini SB, et al. Longitudinal changes in body composition and energy balance in lean women with normal and abnormal glucose tolerance during pregnancy. *Am J Obstet Gynecol* 1998;179:156–165.

100. Shao J, Catalano PM, Yamashita H, et al. Vandate enhances but does not normalize glucose transport and insulin receptor phosphorylation in skeletal muscle from obese women with gestational diabetes. *Am J Obstet Gynecol* 2000;183:1263–1270.

101. Shao J, Catalano PM, Yamashita H, et al. Decreased insulin receptor tyrosine kinase activity and plasma cell membrane glycoprotein-1 over expression in skeletal muscle from obese women with gestational diabetes (GDM): evidence for increased serine/threonine phosphorylation in pregnancy and GDM. *Diabetes* 2000;49:603–610.

102. Byrne MM, Sturis J, Menzel S, et al. Altered insulin secretory responses to glucose in diabetic and nondiabetic subjects with mutations in the diabetes susceptibility gene MODY3 on chromosome 12. *Diabetes* 1996;45:1503–1510.

103. Bell GI, Pilkis SJ, Weber IT, et al. Glucokinase mutations, insulin secretion, and diabetes mellitus. *Ann Rev Physiol* 1996; 58:171–186.

104. Homko C, Sivan E, Chen X, et al. Insulin secretion during and after pregnancy in patients with gestational diabetes mellitus. *J Clin Endocrinol Metab* 2001;86:568–573.

105. Harris MI. Gestational diabetes may represent discovery of preexisting glucose intolerance. *Diabetes Care* 1988;11:402–411.

106. Peters RK, Kjos SL, Xiang A, et al. Long-term diabetogenic effect of a single pregnancy in women with prior gestational diabetes mellitus. *Lancet* 1996;347:227–230.

107. Buchanan TA. Carbohydrate metabolism in pregnancy: normal physiology and implications for diabetes mellitus. *Isr J Med Sci* 1991;27:432.

108. Kjos SL, Buchanan TA, Montoro M, et al. Serum lipids within 36 months of delivery in women with recent gestational diabetes mellitus. *Diabetes* 1991;40[Suppl 2]:142.

109. Kjos SL, Buchanan TA, Peters R, et al. Postpartum glucose tolerance testing identifies women with recent gestational diabetes who are at highest risk for developing diabetes within five years. *Diabetes* 1994;43[Suppl 1]:136.

110. Metzger BE, Bybee DE, Freinkel N, et al. Gestational diabetes mellitus. Correlations between the phenotypic and genotypic characteristics of the mother and abnormal glucose tolerance during the first year postpartum. *Diabetes* 1985;43[Suppl 2]:111.

111. Catalano PM, Vargo KM, Bernstein IM, et al. Incidence and risk factors associated with abnormal postpartum glucose tolerance in women with gestational diabetes. *Am J Obstet Gynecol* 1991;165:914.

112. O'Sullivan JB. The Boston gestational diabetes studies: review and perspectives. In: Sutherland HW, Stowers JM, Pearson DWM, eds. *Carbohydrate Metabolism in Pregnancy and the Newborn.* London: Springer-Verlag, 1989:287–294.

113. Butte NF, Hsu HW, Thotathuchery M, et al. Protein metabolism in insulin-treated gestational diabetes. *Diabetes Care* 1999; 22:806–811.

114. Metzger BE, Phelps RL, Freinkel N, et al. Effects of gestational diabetes on diurnal profiles of plasma glucose, lipids and individual amino acids. *Diabetes Care* 1980;3:402–09.
115. Zimmer DM, Golichowski AM, Karn CA, et al. Glucose and amino acid turnover in untreated gestational diabetes. *Diabetes Care* 1996;19:591–596.
116. Kalhan SC, Denne SC, Patel DM, et al. Leucine kinetics during a brief fast in diabetes in pregnancy. *Metab Clin Exp* 1994; 43:378–384.
117. Whittaker PG, Lee CH, Taylor R. Whole body protein kinetics in women: effect of pregnancy and IDDM during anabolic stimulation. *Am J Endocrinol Metab* 2000;279:978–988.
118. Jansson T, Ekstrand Y, Bjorn C, et al. Alterations in the activity of placental amino acid transporters in pregnancies complicated by diabetes. *Diabetes* 2002;51:2214–2217.
119. Kuruvilla AG, D'Souza SW, Glazier JD, et al. Altered activity of the system A amino acid transporter in microvillus membrane vesicles from placentas of macrosomic babies born to diabetic women. *J Clin Invest* 1994;94:689–695.
120. Knopp RH, Chapman M, Bergelin RO, et al. Relationship of lipoprotein lipids to mild fasting hyperglycemia and diabetes in pregnancy. *Diabetes Care* 1980;3:416–420.
121. Montelongo A, Lasuncion MA, Pallardo LF, et al. Longitudinal study of plasma lipoproteins and hormones during pregnancy in normal and diabetic women. *Diabetes* 1992;41:1651–1659.
122. Bergman RN. Toward physiological understanding of glucose tolerance. Minimal model approach. *Diabetes* 1989;38:1512–1527.
123. Buchanan TA. Pancreatic B-cell defects in gestational diabetes: implications for the pathogenesis and prevention of type 2 diabetes. *J Clin Endocrinol Metab* 2001;86:989–993.

11

THE PLACENTA

GERNOT DESOYE
LESLIE MYATT

The placenta is a fetal tissue separating the maternal and fetal circulation. Because of this position, it is exposed to the regulatory influence of hormones, cytokines, growth factors and substrates present in both circulations. Whereas the effect of maternally derived factors and their changes in diabetes on placental function have received considerable interest in the past decades, the fetal-placental interaction in diabetes has been largely neglected. However, even well-controlled diabetes in pregnancy is associated with some hyperglycemia and hyperinsulinemia in the fetus. Both can act on glucose transporters and insulin receptors (1) on the fetal aspect of the human placenta as molecular targets, and one can anticipate these to elicit some changes in the placenta. The effects of the diabetic environment on placental structure and function strongly depend on the quality of glycemic control achieved during critical periods in placental development, on the modality of treatment, and on the time period of severe departures from excellent metabolic control. In the following chapter, current research findings are reviewed, and, when possible, are synthesized into hypothetical concepts. For detailed and comprehensive information, the reader is referred to some recent pertinent reviews (2–4).

PLACENTAL DEVELOPMENT, MORPHOLOGY, AND COMPOSITION

Placental development may be affected by any metabolic or endocrine insult at early stages of gestation (5). Development can be retarded in the first trimester, paralleling fetal growth delay as reflected by a lower placental weight and protein content (6,7), lower circulating levels of placenta specific hormones such as placental lactogen (8), and by a reduction of trophoblast cell number as a result of hyperglycemia (9). There is a large body of literature describing a number of placental lesions in diabetes mellitus, including plethora, choriangiosis, edema, hypo- and hyperramification of the terminal villi, infarction, fetal-placental sclerosis, fibrotic villi, and villous basement membrane changes (10). Teasdale systematically reviewed these findings in the early

1980s (11–13) and concluded that the placental exchange area (fetal vascular and villous surfaces) was increased in diabetes. Subsequently, the realization that tight glycemic control is necessary throughout gestation to prevent poor perinatal outcomes led to steadily improved glycemic control. Placental structure has now been reexamined in this light. Despite improvement in glycemic control in the past decades, a tendency toward heavier placentas in overt and gestational diabetes has been observed, especially when the fetuses are heavier (1,14–16).

Microscopic morphology is essentially normal in women with well-controlled diabetes, regardless of the type of diabetes (17), but some distinct alterations may be found. The most prominent changes are the 30% to 50% increase in total surface area in the periphery of the villous tree. Villous growth in diabetes is anisomorphic, resulting in a relatively smaller increment in surface for a given volume (18). Villi are better vascularized in diabetes, with greater capillary length, surface area, and mean diameter (19). Vascular growth is exclusively longitudinal without vascular remodeling (20), although this is not a consistent finding (14,21). The endothelial cell growth may be stimulated by overproduction of angiogenic factors such as fibroblast growth factor-2 (22), vascular endothelial growth factors, or placental insulin-like growth factors. Endothelial cell junctions are altered, which may change placental barrier function (23). These structural changes are independent of the severity and duration of the disease. They occur predominantly on the fetal aspect of the placenta. Together with changes in the fetal erythrocytes, they result in a shorter diffusion distance for oxygen (24–26) and may represent part of an adaptive response of the placenta to fetal hypoxia that accompanies many diabetic pregnancies, because of trophoblast basement membrane thickening and excessive fetal aerobic metabolism (Fig. 11-1). Varying reports may reflect differing degrees of glycemic control and differing sampling techniques. Despite implementation of tight control, normoglycemia may not be achieved, and the rate at which physiologic control is reached may still lead to glycemic effects. There may thus remain subtle changes in placental

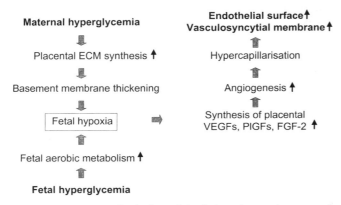

FIGURE 11-1. Hypothetical model of the placental structural adaptive response to hypoxia by increasing the surface area of exchange to ensure adequate oxygen delivery to the fetus at the cost of increased maternal-fetal nutrient flow. *ECM,* extracellular matrix, predominantly collagen type IV.

structure/function in diabetic pregnancies that can have profound effects.

Placentomegaly, if it occurs, is the result of an increase in mesenchymal tissue mass reflected by higher DNA content (27,28). The placentas in diabetes also contain more triglycerides and phospholipids, unchanged cholesterol content (29), and changes in the content of n-3 long-chain polyunsaturated fatty acids with increases in 22:5 n-3, but decreases in 20:5 n-3 and 22:6 n-3 fatty acids (29).

The trophoblast basement membrane is thicker, because of increased amounts of collagen type IV (30). The thicker basement membrane impairs transport of diffusible substances (31,32). Collagen types IV, V, and VI contain more carbohydrates because of nonenzymatic glycosylation resulting from maternal or fetal hyperglycemia (33). The total glycosaminoglycan content of the villous connective tissue is also increased in diabetes due to a higher proportion of hyaluronic acid and heparan sulfate, whereas the proportion of dermatan sulfate is markedly decreased (34).

TRANSPORT AND METABOLISM

Oxygen and Iron

Fetal hypoxia is the result of increased fetal oxygen consumption for glucose oxidation and reduced oxygen supply because of structural and blood flow changes. Whether oxygen-sensitive production of erythropoietin in the placenta (35) is the source of increased fetal levels (36,37) in diabetes is unknown. Augmented erythropoiesis increases fetal iron demand, which can be met by transplacental transfer of transferrin. In diabetes, placental transferrin receptor expression is increased (38) and may result from an increase in factors regulating transferrin receptor expression (39). However, the binding affinity may be reduced, because of more pronounced receptor glycosylation (40).

Glucose

Maternal-fetal glucose transfer in general follows a downhill gradient. Several glucose transporters have been identified in the human term placenta (GLUT-1, GLUT-3, GLUT-4, GLUT-8, GLUT-12) (41–44). GLUT-1 and GLUT-8 are ubiquitously expressed in all cells of the human placenta. GLUT-1 is the predominant transporter on the trophoblast, with a 3:1 asymmetric distribution between the microvillous and basal membrane (45), and accounts for glucose uptake into the trophoblast and subsequent transfer to the fetus. The role of GLUT-8 is unknown. Its expression is down-regulated in diabetes (44), whereas total placental levels of GLUT-1, GLUT-3, and GLUT-4 are unchanged (46,47), although this is controversial for GLUT-1 (48,49). GLUT-3 as well as the insulin-sensitive glucose transporters GLUT-4 and GLUT-12 are predominantly located on the fetal aspect of the placenta (i.e. endothelial cells and stroma), where they may facilitate glucose uptake from the fetal circulation.

Transplacental transport has a high capacity. Saturation is reached at glucose levels above 20 mM (360 mg/dL) (50), allowing for unlimited and rapid transfer. GLUT-1 is regulated by ambient glucose levels. Hyperglycemia reduces GLUT-1 transcript and protein levels (51) and translocates GLUT-1 from the surface to intracellular sites (52), resulting in a loss of functional GLUT-1 on the trophoblast surface. This loss of GLUT-1 at the cell surface alters glucose uptake only at concentrations close to or above 15 mM (270 mg/dL) (52), a concentration that should not be reached in diabetic patients whose glucose levels are well controlled. The GLUT-1 response to hyperglycemia is found at term but not in the first trimester (53). At the beginning of pregnancy, GLUT-1 is regulated by ketone bodies (54) and insulin (53).

Total glucose transfer across total placenta (i.e., corrected for placental weight differences) is unchanged in gestational diabetic women treated with diet (55) or insulin (32), making it unlikely that alterations in maternal-fetal transport contribute to fetal macrosomia in diabetes. Some glucose is also transported back from the fetus into the placenta (56), and the backflux is increased in diabetes (57). GLUT-1, the high-affinity GLUT-3, and the insulin-regulatable transporters GLUT-4 and GLUT-12 may extract glucose from the fetal circulation at the placental endothelium where glucose will be stored as glycogen. Placental glycogen levels in diabetes are increased (1,27,58). The endothelium is richly endowed with the glycogen precursor glycogenin (59). Glycogen stores in diabetes are deposited predominantly around fetoplacental vessels (58,60) and can be the result of fetal hyperinsulinemia (61). Because the placenta is the only fetal tissue capable of storing excessive glucose (62,63), it was proposed that excess fetal glucose is extracted by the placenta and converted to glycogen (Fig. 11-2). Only when the placental glycogen stores are saturated will fetal glucose

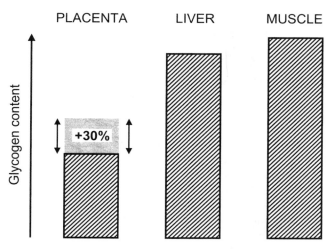

FIGURE 11-2. Among fetal tissues, only the placenta stores more glycogen in diabetes. This capacity to store extra glucose allows the placenta to serve as a buffer for some fetal hyperglycemia as it occurs in diabetes even when maternal glycemia is adequately controlled (62–64).

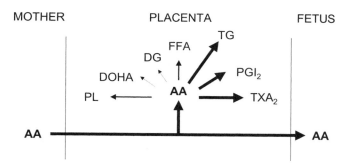

FIGURE 11-3. Placental arachidonic acid (*AA*) uptake, transfer, and metabolism in diabetes is either increased (*thick arrows*), decreased (*thin arrows*), or unchanged (*dotted arrows*) as compared with control placentas. The arrow length for metabolites indicates extent of arachidonic acid uptake into the various lipid and eicosanoid fractions in diabetes. *PL*, phospholipids; *DOHA*, dihydroxy fatty acid; *DG*, diglyceride; *FFA*, free fatty acid; *TG*, triglyceride. (Data from references 31 and 76.)

levels then increase and lead to hyperinsulinemia (64). Because of low glucose-6-phosphatase levels (65), breakdown of placental glycogen in cases of fetal emergency energy demand will result in lactate rather than glucose. However, in diet-treated gestational diabetes, lactate release into the fetal and maternal circulation is reduced (32,55).

In contrast to liver and adipose tissue, glucose metabolism in the diabetic placenta is rather stable in general, despite the changes in the maternal and fetal metabolic and hormonal milieu. Activity of enzymes related to glucose catabolism (i.e., glycolysis) and the reduced form of nicotinamide adenine dinucleotide phosphate (NADPH)-generating pathways is increased (66). The increased NADPH levels may be used for synthesis of fatty acids; reduction of oxidized glutathione by glutathione peroxidase and for monooxygenases that are involved in biosynthesis of cholesterol, progesterone (67), collagens (30); and in detoxification processes.

Lipids

The maternal sources of fetal lipids include triglycerides in lipoproteins, phospholipids, cholesterol esters, and free fatty acids. Diabetes is associated with alterations in the level and composition of maternal lipids. Levels of free fatty acids and triglycerides are elevated. Triglyceride transport across the placenta involves several lipases facilitating entry and release of triglycerides (68). Three lipases have been identified in the placenta (69). A pH 4 lipase activity is higher in diabetes correlating with birth weight (70) and is reduced in fetal growth restriction (71).

Free fatty acids traverse the placenta along a maternal-fetal concentration gradient (72). Maternal plasma concen-

trations of myristate, palmitate, stearate and linoleate correlate with those in the umbilical vein (73). After entry into the placenta, intermediate esterification of free fatty acids to triglycerides may occur, followed by lipolysis and release into the fetal circulation. Fatty acid partitioning and the activity of these pathways depends on ambient glucose levels (74). A proportion of the fatty acids traversing the placenta may be stored within the tissue; docosahexaenoic acid is preferentially accrued (75). Diabetes is associated with higher placental levels of linoleate (29). Arachidonic acid uptake into the placenta from type 1 diabetics is increased and is predominantly incorporated into placental triglycerides (31). Eicosanoid formation from arachidonic acid is three to six times higher in diabetes with a preferential conversion into thromboxane A_2 over prostacyclin (76) (Fig. 11-3). This imbalance in eicosanoid production may contribute to the reduction in umbilical blood flow in some diabetic pregnancies.

Fetal levels of low-density lipoprotein cholesterol and high-density lipoprotein-3 cholesterol are similar in type 1 diabetes and nondiabetic pregnancies, but high-density lipoprotein-2 cholesterol levels are elevated in diabetes (77). The contribution of maternal-fetal cholesterol transfer is unknown, but receptors and binding proteins for lipoproteins have been identified in the placenta and trophoblast, respectively (78–86). Cholesterol partitioning in the placental pool that is fed by maternal and *de novo* synthesized cholesterol and potential diabetes-related changes are unknown, but some components of the diabetic milieu alter placental receptors for very-low-density lipoproteins (82) and lectinlike oxidized low-density lipoproteins (85).

Amino Acids

Maternal amino acids provide by far the major source of nitrogen, and thus are taken up by both the placenta and the fetus. The amino acid transport systems in the human term placenta resemble those described for various other tissues and cells (86). Their activity may be coupled to an inward Na$^+$-gradient. The placenta expresses Mg^{2+}-dependent Na$^+$/K$^+$-ATPase (EC 3.6.1.36), the ubiquitous sodium transport system, with an almost fourfold higher activity in the basal as compared with the microvillous trophoblast membrane (87). As a result of abnormal enzymatic function, total activity of this enzyme is reduced in placentas of type 1 diabetic pregnancies (88). Available data on the transport systems in the human placenta suggest that these are unaltered in diabetes (89–91), although distinct changes in intrinsic activity, but not in total uptake, have been noted (91). Because of the complexity of amino acid transport systems with partly overlapping specificity, any generalization must be made with caution, if at all. In addition, duration and severity of diabetes may also have a strong influence on the transporters. Moreover, different diabetes-associated factors may lead to opposing alterations, and the net result will then be determined by the impact of one of these as exemplified by L-arginine uptake into a trophoblast model. L-arginine uptake is increased by long-term hyperglycemia and decreased by hyperinsulinemia (92).

Nucleosides

Placentomegaly and excessive fetal growth will require increased synthesis of DNA and RNA, which in turn will require an ample supply of nucleosides and ribose as building blocks. Because of increased activity of the placental pentose phosphate pathway in diabetes (66), more ribose may be delivered for placental demand. Sodium-independent nucleoside transporters will facilitate nucleoside passage from the mother to the fetus along a downhill concentration gradient. They have been identified at the microvillous and basal membrane of the syncytiotrophoblast and appear to be unchanged in diabetes (93). In contrast, in the endothelium of the umbilical cord, these transporters are down-regulated (94).

PLACENTAL BLOOD FLOW IN DIABETES

It has long been recognized that adequate placental growth and blood flow are necessary for optimal fetal growth and a successful pregnancy. Because placental blood flow determines the transport of flow-limited substances such as oxygen and glucose, it has received heightened scrutiny recently due to the increased awareness that life *in utero* can have a major impact on the development of adult disease. There are several situations where abnormalities of placental blood flow are associated with adverse fetal outcomes. These disorders include preeclampsia, intrauterine fetal growth restriction, and poorly controlled pregestational diabetes mellitus. Trophoblast invasion may be impaired. The

incidence of abnormal pregnancies related to invasion defects such as spontaneous abortions (95), preeclampsia (96), and intrauterine growth restriction (97) in the second half of gestation is higher in diabetic than in nondiabetic mothers. Hyperglycemia does not appear to be the underlying cause (98), but insulin (99,100), leptin (101), and isoprostanes (102) may be responsible factors. This hypothesis is as yet speculative because there has been no study of trophoblast invasion of the placental bed in diabetic pregnancy. However, some placentas from pregnancies complicated by type 1 diabetes do show fibrinoid necrosis and atherosis in their decidual bed, as observed in preeclampsia (103). There is a relationship between the severity of this pathology and abnormal uterine arcuate artery systolic/diastolic ratios in type 1 diabetic patients (104). This does not appear to grossly affect fetal blood flow in the placenta. Doppler flow indices of both placental and fetal circulations were essentially normal in diabetic pregnancies except for cases complicated by preeclampsia or intrauterine growth restriction (105), suggesting that hyperglycemia per se does not overtly alter placental blood flow. Recently, Fadda et al. (106) again reported that Doppler indices were essentially normal in gestational diabetes except for a small number of cases with perinatal complications. *In vitro* hyperglycemia per se does not affect fetal-placental flow until glucose levels exceed 8.9 mM (160 mg/dL) (107). This does not preclude more subtle effects on placental blood flow, particularly in the fetal-placental circulation, which may then be more susceptible to insult.

AUTACOIDS IN THE PLACENTA IN DIABETES

The human placenta lacks local autonomic vascular control; thus, circulating humoral factors or local autocrine-paracrine agents are essential for placental hemodynamic control (108). There may be differences in sensitivity in various regions of the placental vasculature from the umbilical cord down to the villous tree in response to autacoids. These regions may then be differentially affected by hyperglycemia. Indeed, the relative production of the vasodilator prostacyclin to the vasoconstrictor thromboxane changes throughout the fetal placental circulation, favoring prostacyclin in the cord artery. In diabetic placentas, there is a tendency toward higher thromboxane levels (i.e. favoring vasoconstriction) (109). This does not appear to be related to maternal glycemic control, as suggested by *in vitro* culture studies (110), but may be related to oxidative stress. Kuhn et al. (76) have shown a predominance of thromboxane and hydroxyeicosatetraenoic acid production by perfused placenta from the diabetic pregnancy. The nitric oxide radical (NO) may play an important role in the regulation of fetal-placental blood flow because it has been shown *in vitro* to maintain low basal tone and attenuate the vasoconstrictive effects of thromboxane and endothelin (111). The constitutive endothelial isoform of nitric oxide synthase (eNOS) is expressed in fetal-placental vascular endothelium and in syncytiotrophoblasts (112,113). Significantly greater eNOS mRNA expression was found in women with maternal diabetes delivering at term as compared with normal pregnant women (114). Di Iulio et al. (115), however, observed no differences in the activity of total or calcium-independent NO synthase in homogenates of placentas from gestational diabetes, type 1 diabetes, or controls. However, differences in specific locations may have been obscured by homogenization. Whereas no differences in NO synthase activity were noted between control placentas and those from patients with gestational diabetes in the umbilical cord artery and vein, and the chorionic plate artery and vein, significantly less activity was found in the stem villous vessels of placentas from women with gestational diabetes (116). These findings suggest there may be regional differences in expression in the placenta affected by diabetes.

Increased concentrations of adrenomedullin are observed in amniotic fluid of diabetic women (type 1 or gestational diabetes) (117), indicating that placental adrenomedullin production is upregulated in diabetic pregnancy, perhaps to prevent excessive vasoconstriction.

OXIDATIVE STRESS IN THE PLACENTA IN DIABETES

Oxidative stress is simply described as an imbalance in the production of reactive oxygen species over the ability of antioxidants to clear them. There is increasing recognition now that preeclampsia—which complicates 5% to 7% of all pregnancies and is the leading cause of fetal growth restriction, indicated premature delivery, and maternal death—is a syndrome characterized by profound dysfunction of the vascular endothelium (118), which itself may be due to oxidative stress (119). Like preeclampsia, diabetes is also characterized as a state of endothelial dysfunction, with considerable evidence that reactive oxygen species play an important role. In diabetes, oxygen free radicals are thought to be produced as a result of prolonged periods of exposure to hyperglycemia, which is known to cause nonenzymatic glycation of plasma proteins (120). Diabetes may be associated with increased advanced glycosylation end product formation on the fetal aspect of the placenta (121). These glycated products undergo further spontaneous reaction, leading to the production and release of free radicals including superoxide. Indeed, glycated protein prepared from diabetic serum is able to generate superoxide at physiologic pH. In addition, stimulation of the mitochondrial electron transport chain by hyperglycemia generates superoxide (122). Superoxide, in the absence of appropriate levels of scavengers may lead to an imbalance between prooxidants and antioxidants and produce a state of oxidative stress.

Pregnancies complicated by preeclampsia are associated with elevated blood and tissue levels of lipid peroxidation products (123), reinforcing the role of oxidative stress in the etiology of preeclampsia. Pregnant individuals with diabetes develop preeclampsia at higher rates (124). Increased lipid peroxide levels may be the result of decreased antioxidant activities. In contrast to other embryonic tissues (125,126) in which diabetes-associated generation of oxygen free radicals results in high-amplitude mitochondrial swelling, the human trophoblast appears to be resistant to such changes regardless of gestational age (127,128). Although trophoblast mitochondria can generate oxygen free radicals (129), they are morphologically normal (128).

ANTIOXIDANT CAPACITY

In response to increased prooxidant challenge, antioxidants may be increased as a compensatory response but are subsequently reduced in the chronic state as they are overwhelmed. In the fetoplacental vascular endothelium of diabetic pregnancies, we found increased expression of the manganese superoxide dismutase isoform (130). Reductions in total free radical–trapping antioxidant capacities such as the scavenger activity of superoxide dismutase and catalase, glutathione metabolism, or vitamin E levels, as well as an increase in lipid peroxides, have been seen in patients with preeclampsia (131) or diabetes (132). Administration of antioxidants, vitamin C, and vitamin E reduced placental lipid peroxidation in the perfused human placenta from women with preeclampsia (133). These data suggest that treatment with antioxidants may be useful in preventing or reversing the altered vascular reactivity in diabetes or preeclampsia.

NITRIC OXIDE AND SUPEROXIDE IN THE PLACENTA

The diabetic state may lead to increased production of superoxide or increased nitric oxide formation by increased enzymatic activity of endothelial or inducible isoforms of nitric oxide synthase. Superoxide can arise from glycated plasma proteins and from many other cellular sources, including the mitochondrial electron transport chain. At low concentrations, nitric oxide can function as an antioxidant by inhibiting the mitochondrial electron transport chain (129). However, nitric oxide is inactivated by superoxide anion, which therefore limits its bioactivity. This interaction, however, yields peroxynitrite anion (ONOO) a powerful oxidant of a variety of biomolecules (134). Peroxynitrite is known to cause lipid peroxidation, inhibit the mitochondrial electron transport system, as well as nitrotyrosine residues and oxidize sulfhydryl groups from proteins, hence altering their activity or disrupting signal transduction pathways (135). In the isolated perfused rat heart, administration of peroxynitrite impairs relaxation (136). Peroxynitrite causes vascular dysfunction in rats by selective impairment of adrenoreceptors when given systemically (137). In a series of descriptive studies, we showed increased expression of nitrotyrosine residues, which are formed by the interaction of peroxynitrite with tyrosine moieties in the fetal vasculature and villous stroma of placentas from women with preeclampsia and diabetes (130,138) (Fig. 11-4). Significantly more intense nitrotyrosine immunostaining was apparent in the vascular endothelium of placentas from patients with preeclampsia and in the vascular endothelium of villous stroma of placentas from women with diabetes (130). The immunostaining in stroma may be due to local generation of peroxynitrite due to hyperglycemia-associated oxidative stress in the stroma, or to diffusion of peroxynitrite produced in vascular endothelium at high concentrations in the underlying stroma. Indeed, peroxynitrite may diffuse up to several cell diameters in distance. Interestingly, in a study of 10 women with White class C and D diabetes, under good glycemic control during pregnancy, there were still increased levels of nitrotyrosine in the placental villous vascular endothelium and stroma (130). Therefore, we may have observed subclinical disease process despite the presence of good glycemic control or inability to achieve optimal control in the fetal compartment. Overall, however, these findings suggest the involvement of peroxynitrite in the pathologic processes of placental injury in diabetes and preeclampsia.

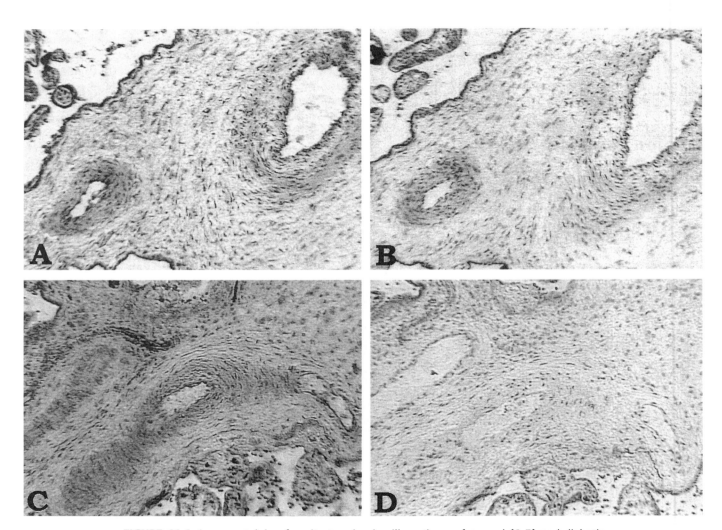

FIGURE 11-4. Immunostaining for nitrotyrosine in villous tissue of normal **(A,B)** and diabetic **(C,D)** pregnancies. Frozen sections were immunostained with monoclonal nitrotyrosine antibody **(A,C)** or no primary antibody **(B,D)** using the Vectastain ABC kit (original magnification ×125). (Reprinted from Lyall F, Gibson JL, Greer IA, et al. Increased nitrotyrosine in the diabetic placenta: evidence for oxidative stress. *Diabetes Care* 1998;21:1753–1758, with permission.)

SIGNIFICANCE OF PEROXYNITRITE ACTION

The functional significance of the presence of altered tyrosine residues on proteins in the fetoplacental vasculature remains to be fully elucidated. In a subsequent study (139), we sought to directly determine whether peroxynitrite caused a functional deficit in the placental vascular bed in placentas of pregnancies complicated by preeclampsia or diabetes by comparing the responses to increasing concentrations of the vasoconstrictors U46619 and angiotensin-II and the vasodilators glyceryl trinitrate and prostacyclin. In addition, we determined the response to these agents in normal placentas before and after treatment with authentic peroxynitrite. Interestingly, we found that the responses to both vasoconstrictors and vasodilators were significantly attenuated in placentas from patients with diabetes and preeclampsia. Similarly, the responses to U46619, glyceryl trinitrate, and prostacyclin, but not angiotensin-II, were significantly attenuated in a normal placenta following peroxynitrite treatment (139). Other groups have made observations that support these conclusions. A significant attenuation of the vasoconstrictor response to U46619 in the fetoplacental circulation of women with preeclampsia was reported (140), although no effect was seen on vasodilator responses to prostacyclin. Similarly, Wilkes et al. (141) found responses to U46619 to be attenuated in the fetoplacental vasculature of pregnancies complicated by diabetes accompanied by reduction of the affinity of thromboxane receptors. Thus, diminished responses to vasoactive agents may be observed in resistance vessels of placentas from women with diabetes and preeclampsia (Fig. 11-5) and may

lead to compromise of the fetus if the placental vasculature cannot adapt sufficiently in times of stress. Immunostaining for nitrotyrosine residues confirmed that nitrotyrosine residues were present in the placentas from pregnancies complicated by preeclampsia and diabetes, but also that peroxynitrite treatment of the placental vasculature led to the formation of nitrotyrosine residues (139). Taken together, these data suggest but do not prove a cause-and-effect relationship whereby peroxynitrite formation in the placental vasculature is capable of attenuating vascular responses. This hypothesis does not preclude other pathophysiologic processes such as progressive glycation and cross-linking of connective tissue proteins of the fetoplacental vasculature, which can produce vascular stiffness, from also contributing to the altered vascular reactivity.

In vitro, the placental vasculature of diabetic pregnancies displays altered vascular activity despite apparently good fetal outcomes *in vivo.* When studying placental vascular responses to hypoxia *in vitro,* Figueroa et al. (142) found that gestational diabetes resulted in enhanced relaxation to hypoxia in placental arteries and veins and enhanced contraction to reoxygenation or hydrogen peroxide. The presence of nitrotyrosine residues may be a marker of subclinical disease or indicate that, despite the vascular dysfunction, there is still adequate reserve supporting fetal survival. However, this dysfunctional vasculature may prevent the placenta from responding adequately to increased demands for oxygen and nutrient transfer when the fetus is severely stressed, perhaps explaining the increased morbidity and mortality and some of the unexpected fetal demises that occur near term in pregnancies complicated by diabetes.

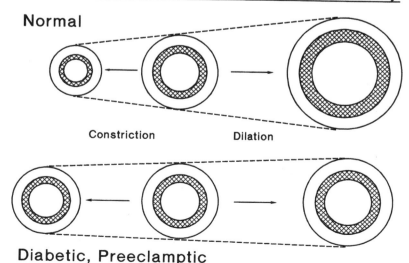

Potential Effect of Vascular Dysfunction on Vessel Reactivity

Normal

Constriction   Dilation

Diabetic, Preeclamptic

FIGURE 11-5. Vascular dysfunction in the placenta from pregnancies complicated by diabetes or preeclampsia due to oxidative stress may cause diminished vascular reactivity to the same stimuli when compared with normotensive pregnancies, thus compromising the ability to respond to demand for changes in blood flow.

TARGETS OF PEROXYNITRITE

The deleterious effects of reactive oxygen species have been studied in many systems. Peroxynitrite can injure the mitochondrial electron transport system, resulting in inhibition of cellular respiration (143), and may also initiate lipid peroxidation. Peroxynitrite can also increase DNA breaks, which can lead to initiation of a futile DNA repair cycle by activation of poly(ADP-ribose) polymerase, resulting in depletion of cellular NAD$_+$ and ATP stores (144). In particular, the modification of tyrosine-containing proteins by nitration of aromatic amino acids may affect signal transduction pathways (135). The decrease in reactivity of the fetoplacental vasculature observed in pregnancies affected by type 1 diabetes mellitus or preeclampsia (139) may be the result of peroxynitrite-mediated alterations of signal transduction pathways, including vascular receptors and changes in the contractile apparatus of the vascular smooth muscle. It has been shown that peroxynitrite may selectively inactivate the prostacyclin receptor (145). It is possible that different vascular receptors show different sensitivities to peroxynitrite. This may explain the apparent lack of effect on responses to angiotensin-II observed following *in vitro* incubation with peroxynitrite. Current approaches to identifying the protein targets of peroxynitrite action in the vasculature have used a candidate molecule approach. Advances in proteomics now allow us to potentially isolate proteins and subsequently identify them.

KEY POINTS

- Placental changes in diabetes depend on quality of glycemic control of the mother and fetus.
- Structural changes are found predominantly in the fetal aspect of the placenta.
- Structural and functional changes may act to increase oxygen delivery to the fetus.
- Increased activity of NADPH-generating pathways is observed.
- Maternal-fetal glucose transport is unchanged.
- Storage of some of the excess fetal glucose occurs within the placenta.
- Alterations in fatty acid uptake, metabolism, and transport are observed.
- Transfer of amino acids and nucleosides appears stable.
- Blood flows are grossly normal except in preeclampsia with or without intrauterine growth restriction.
- Placenta shows oxidative stress and vascular dysfunction.
- Increased production of reactive oxygen and nitrogen species has been documented.
- Peroxynitrite may cause vascular dysfunction.

REFERENCES

1. Desoye G, Hofmann HH, Weiss PA. Insulin binding to trophoblast plasma membranes and placental glycogen content in well-controlled gestational diabetic women treated with diet or insulin, in well-controlled overt diabetic patients and in healthy control subjects. *Diabetologia* 1992;35:45–55.
2. Desoye G, Shafrir E. Placental metabolism and its regulation in health and diabetes. *Mol Aspects Med* 1994;15:505–682.
3. Desoye G, Shafrir E. The human placenta in diabetic pregnancy. *Diabet Rev* 1996;4:70–89.
4. Hauguel-de Mouzon S, Shafrir E. Carbohydrate and fat metabolism and related hormonal regulation in normal and diabetic placenta. *Placenta* 2001;22:619–627.
5. Bjork O, Persson B. Placental changes in relation to the degree of metabolic control in diabetes mellitus. *Placenta* 1982;3:367–378.
6. Brown ZA, Mills JL, Metzger BE, et al. Early sonographic evaluation for fetal growth delay and congenital malformations in pregnancies complicated by insulin-requiring diabetes. *Diabetes Care* 1992;15:613–619.
7. Robinson J, Canavan JP, el Haj AJ, et al. Maternal diabetes in rats. I. Effects on placental growth and protein turnover. *Diabetes* 1988;37:1665–1670.
8. Pedersen JF, Sorensen S, Molsted-Pedersen L. Serum levels of human placental lactogen, pregnancy-associated plasma protein A and endometrial secretory protein PP14 in first trimester of diabetic pregnancy. *Acta Obstet Gynecol Scand* 1998;77:155–158.
9. Desoye G, Weiss U, Schmut O, et al. Distinct effects of hyperglycemia in vitro on trophoblast proliferation and mitochondrial activity of placental trophoblasts at various stages of first trimester human pregnancy. *Diabetes* 2000;49(suppl 1):A.49.
10. Benirschke K, Kaufmann P. *Pathology of the human placenta,* 4th ed. New York: Springer-Verlag, 2000.
11. Teasdale F. Histomorphometry of the placenta of the diabetic women: class A diabetes mellitus. *Placenta* 1981;2:241–251.
12. Teasdale F. Histomorphometry of the human placenta in class B diabetes mellitus. *Placenta* 1983;4:1–12.
13. Teasdale F. Histomorphometry of the human placenta in class C diabetes mellitus. *Placenta* 1985;6:69–81.
14. Clarson C, Tevaarwerk GJ, Harding PG, et al. Placental weight in diabetic pregnancies. *Placenta* 1989;10:275–281.
15. Makhseed M, Musini VM, Ahmed MA, et al. Placental pathology in relation to the White's classification of diabetes mellitus. *Arch Gynecol Obstet* 2002;266:136–140.
16. Taricco E, Radaelli T, Nobile de Santis MS, et al. Fetal and placental weights in relation to maternal characteristics in gestational diabetes. *Placenta* 2003;24:343–347.
17. Mayhew TM, Sisley I. Quantitative studies on the villi, trophoblast and intervillous pores of placentae from women with well-controlled diabetes mellitus. *Placenta* 1998;19:371–377.
18. Mayhew TM. Patterns of villous and intervillous space growth in human placentas from normal and abnormal pregnancies. *Eur J Obstet Gynaecol Reprod Biol* 1996;68:75–82.
19. Mayhew TM, Sorensen FB, Klebe JG, et al. Growth and maturation of villi in placentae from well-controlled diabetic women. *Placenta* 1994;15:57–65.
20. Mayhew TM. Enhanced fetoplacental angiogenesis in pre-gestational diabetes mellitus: the extra growth is exclusively longitudinal and not accompanied by microvascular remodelling. *Diabetologia* 2002;45:1434–1439.
21. Jirkovska M, Kubinova L, Janacek J, et al. Topological properties and spatial organization of villous capillaries in normal and diabetic placentas. *J Vasc Res* 2002;39:268–278.
22. Arany E, Hill DJ. Fibroblast growth factor-2 and fibroblast growth factor receptor-1 mRNA expression and peptide localization in placentae from normal and diabetic pregnancies. *Placenta* 1998;19:133–142.
23. Babawale MO, Lovat S, Mayhew TM, et al. Effects of gesta-

tional diabetes on junctional adhesion molecules in human term placental vasculature. *Diabetologia* 2000;43:1185–1196.

24. Mayhew TM, Sorensen FB, Klebe JG, et al. The effects of mode of delivery and sex of newborn on placental morphology in control and diabetic pregnancies. *J Anat* 1993;183:545–552.

25. Mayhew TM, Sorensen FB, Klebe JG, et al. Oxygen diffusive conductance in placentae from control and diabetic women. *Diabetologia* 1993;36:955–960.

26. Mayhew TM, Jackson MR, Boyd PA. Changes in oxygen diffusive conductances of human placentae during gestation (10–41 weeks) are commensurate with the gain in fetal weight. *Placenta* 1993;14:51–61.

27. Diamant YZ, Metzger BE, Freinkel N, et al. Placental lipid and glycogen content in human and experimental diabetes mellitus. *Am J Obstet Gynecol* 1982;144:5–11.

28. Winick M, Noble A. Cellular growth in human placenta. II. Diabetes mellitus. *J Pediatr* 1967;71:216–219.

29. Lakin V, Haggarty P, Abramovich DR, et al. Dietary intake and tissue concentration of fatty acids in omnivore, vegetarian and diabetic pregnancy. *Prostagland Leukot Essent Fatty Acids* 1998;59:209–220.

30. Laureti E, De Galateo A, Giorgino F. The concentration of hydroxyproline, lipids and hexoses in normal and diabetic placentas in the third month of pregnancy. *Boll Soc Ital Biol Sper* 1982;58:702–707.

31. Kuhn DC, Crawford MA, Stuart MJ, et al. Alterations in transfer and lipid distribution of arachidonic acid in placentas of diabetic pregnancies. *Diabetes* 1990;39:914–918.

32. Osmond DT, King RG, Brennecke SP, et al. Placental glucose transport and utilisation is altered at term in insulin-treated, gestational-diabetic patients. *Diabetologia* 2001;44:1133–1139.

33. Ioka H, Moriyama I, Kyuma M, et al. Nonenzymatic glucosylation of human placental trophoblast basement membrane collagen. Relation to diabetic pathology. *Acta Obstet Gynaecol Jpn* 1987;39:400–404.

34. Wassermann L, Schlesinger H, Abramovich A, et al. Glycosaminoglycan pattern sin diabetic and toxemic term placentas. *Am J Obstet Gynecol* 1980;138:769–773.

35. Conrad KP, Benyo DF, Westerhausen-Larsen A, et al. Expression of erythropoietin by the human placenta. *FASEB J* 1996;10:760–768.

36. Widness JA, Teramo KA, Clemons GK, et al. Direct relationship of antepartum glucose control and fetal erythropoietin in human type 1 (insulin-dependent) diabetic pregnancy. *Diabetologia* 1990;33:378–383.

37. Salvesen DR, Brudenell JM, Snijders RJ, et al. Fetal plasma erythropoietin in pregnancies complicated by maternal diabetes mellitus. *Am J Obstet Gynecol* 1993;168:88–94.

38. Petry CD, Wobken JD, McKay H, et al. Placental transferrin receptor in diabetic pregnancies with increased fetal iron demand. *Am J Physiol* 1994;267:E507–514.

39. Georgieff MK, Berry SA, Wobken JD, et al. Increased placental iron regulatory protein-1 expression in diabetic pregnancies complicated by fetal iron deficiency. *Placenta* 1999;20:87–93.

40. Georgieff MK, Petry CD, Mills MM, et al. Increased N-glycosylation and reduced transferrin-binding capacity of transferrin receptor isolated from placentae of diabetic women. *Placenta* 1997;18:563–568.

41. Hauguel-de Mouzon S, Challier JC, Kacemi A, et al. The GLUT3 glucose transporter isoform is differentially expressed within human placental cell types. *J Clin Endocrinol Metab* 1997;82:2689–2694 .

42. Xing AY, Challier JC, Lepercq J, et al. Unexpected expression of glucose transporter 4 in villous stromal cells of human placenta. *J Clin Endocrinol Metab* 1998;83:4097–4101.

43. Gude NM, Rogers S, Best JD, et al. Reduced glucose uptake and expression of a novel glucose transporter in placentas from gestational diabetic pregnancies. *Placenta* 2001;22:A.56.

44. Charron MJ, Challier JC, Weldon R, et al. GLUT8 glucose transporter, a novel candidate to regulate placental glucose fluxes in diabetic pregnancies. *Diabetes* 2004 (in press).

45. Jansson T, Wennergren M, Illsley NP. Glucose transporter protein expression in human placenta throughout gestation and in intrauterine growth retardation. *J Clin Endocrinol Metab* 1993;77:155415–155462.

46. Jansson T, Ekstrand Y, Wennergren M, et al. Placental glucose transport in gestational diabetes mellitus. *Am J Obstet Gynecol* 2001;184:111–116.

47. Sciullo E, Cardellini G, Baroni MG, et al. Glucose transporter (Glut1, Glut3) mRNA in human placenta of diabetic and nondiabetic pregnancies. *Early Pregnancy* 1997;3:172–182.

48. Gaither K, Quraishi AN, Illsley NP. Diabetes alters the expression and activity of the human placental GLUT1 glucose transporter. *J Clin Endocrinol Metab* 1999;84:695–701.

49. Jansson T, Wennergren M, Powell TL. Placental glucose transport and GLUT 1 expression in insulin-dependent diabetes. *Am J Obstet Gynecol* 1999;180:163–168.

50. Hauguel S, Desmaizieres V, Challier JC. Glucose uptake, utilization, and transfer by the human placenta as functions of maternal glucose concentration. *Pediatr Res* 1986;20:269–273.

51. Hahn T, Barth S, Weiss U, et al. Sustained hyperglycemia *in vitro* down-regulates the GLUT1 glucose transport system of cultured human term placental trophoblast: a mechanism to protect fetal development? *FASEB J* 1998;12:1221–1231.

52. Hahn T, Hahn D, Blaschitz A, et al. Hyperglycaemia-induced subcellular redistribution of GLUT1 glucose transporters in cultured human term placental trophoblast cells. *Diabetologia* 2000;43:173–180.

53. Gordon MC, Zimmerman PD, Landon MB, et al. Insulin and glucose modulate glucose transporter messenger ribonucleic acid expression and glucose uptake in trophoblasts isolated from first-trimester chorionic villi. *Am J Obstet Gynecol* 1995;173:1089–1097.

54. Shubert PJ, Gordon MC, Landon MB, et al. Ketoacids attenuate glucose uptake in human trophoblasts isolated from first-trimester chorionic villi. *Am J Obstet Gynecol* 1996;175:56–62.

55. Osmond DT, Nolan CJ, King RG, et al. Effects of gestational diabetes on human placental glucose uptake, transfer, and utilisation. *Diabetologia* 2000;43:576–582.

56. Schneider H, Reiber W, Sager R, et al. Asymmetrical transport of glucose across the *in vitro* perfused human placenta. *Placenta* 2003;24:27–33.

57. Thomas CR, Eriksson GL, Eriksson UJ. Effects of maternal diabetes on placental transfer of glucose in rats. *Diabetes* 1990;32:276–282.

58. Robb SA, Hytten FE. Placental glycogen. *Placenta* 1976;83:43–53.

59. Hahn D, Blaschitz A, Korgun ET, et al. From maternal glucose to fetal glycogen: expression of key regulators in the human placenta. *Mol Hum Reprod* 2001;7:1173–1178.

60. Jones CJP, Desoye G. Glycogen distribution in the capillaries of the placental villus in normal, overt and gestational diabetic pregnancy. *Placenta* 1993;14:505–517.

61. Goltzsch W, Bittner R, Bohme HJ, et al. Effect of prenatal insulin and glucagon injection on the glycogen content of rat placenta and fetal liver. *Biomed Biochim Acta* 1987;46:619–622.

62. Shelley HJ. Carbohydrate reserves in the newborn infant. *BMJ* 1964;1:273–275.

63. Villee CA. The intermediary metabolism of human fetal tissues. *Cold Spring Harb Symp Quant Biol* 1954;19:186–199.

64. Desoye G, Korgun ET, Ghaffari-Tabrizi N, et al. Is fetal macrosomia in adequately controlled diabetic women the result of a

placenta defect?—a hypothesis. *J Mat Fet Neonat Med* 2002; 11:258–261.

65. Barash V, Riskin A, Shafrir E, et al. Kinetic and immunologic evidence for the absence of glucose-6-phosphatase in early human chorionic villi and term placenta. *Biochim Biophys Acta* 1991;1073:161–167.

66. Diamant YZ, Kissilevitz R, Shafrir E. Changes in the activity of enzymes related to glycolysis, gluconeogenesis and lipogenesis in placentae from diabetic women. *Placenta* 1984;5:55–60.

67. Coughlan MT, Oliva K, Georgiou HM, et al. Glucose-induced release of tumour necrosis factor-alpha from human placental and adipose tissues in gestational diabetes mellitus. *Diabet Med* 2001;18:921–927.

68. Shafrir E, Barash V. Placental function in maternal-fetal transport in diabetes. *Biol Neonate* 1987;51:102–112.

69. Waterman IJ, Emmison N, Dutta-Roy AK. Characterisation of triacylglycerol hydrolase activities in human placenta. *Biochim Biophys Acta* 1997;1394:169–176.

70. Kaminsky S, Sibley P, Maresh M, et al. The effects of diabetes on placental lipase activity in the rat and human. *Pediatr Res* 1992;30:541–543.

71. Kaminsky S, D'Souza SW, Massey RF, et al. Effect of maternal undernutrition and uterine artery ligation on placental lipase activities in the rat. *Biol Neonate* 1991;60:201–206.

72. Hull D, Elphick MC. Evidence for fatty acid transfer across the human placenta. *Ciba Found Symp* 1979;63:75–91.

73. Hendrickse W, Stammers JP, Hull D. The transfer of free fatty acids across the human placenta. *Br J Obstet Gynaecol* 1985;92: 945–952.

74. Ogburn PL Jr, Rejeshwari M, Turner SI, et al. Lipid and glucose metabolism in human placental culture. *Am J Obstet Gynecol* 1988;159:629–635.

75. Larque E, Demmelmair H, Berger B, et al. *In vivo* investigation of the placental transfer of ^{13}C-labelled fatty acids in human. *J Lipid Res* 2003;44:49–55.

76. Kuhn DC, Botti JJ, Cherouny PH, et al. Eicosanoid production and transfer in the placenta of the diabetic pregnancy. *Prostaglandins* 1990;40:205–215.

77. Kilby MD, Neary RH, Mackness MI, et al. Fetal and maternal lipoprotein metabolism in human pregnancy complicated by type I diabetes mellitus. *J Clin Endocrinol Metab* 1998;83:1736–1741.

78. Wadsack C, Hammer A, Levak-Frank S, et al. The selective cholesteryl ester uptake from high-density lipoprotein by human first trimester and term trophoblast. A preferential routing for cholesteryl ester supply during fetal development? *Placenta* 2003;24:131–143.

79. Fischer U, Birkenmeier G, Horn LC. Localization of alpha(2)-macroglobulin receptor/low-density lipoprotein receptor in third-trimester human placentas: a preliminary immunohistochemical study. *Gynecol Obstet Invest* 2001;52:22–25.

80. Lafond J, Charest MC, Alain JF, et al. Presence of CLA-1 and HDL binding sites on syncytiotrophoblast brush border and basal plasma membranes of human placenta. *Placenta* 1999; 20:583–590.

81. Tsatas D, Baker MS, Rice GE. Tissue-specific expression of the relaxed conformation of plasminogen activator inhibitor-2 and low-density lipoprotein receptor-related protein in human term gestational tissues. *J Histochem Cytochem* 1997;45:1593–1602.

82. Wittmaack FM, Gafvels ME, Bronner M, et al. Localization and regulation of the human very low density lipoprotein/apolipoprotein-E receptor: trophoblast expression predicts a role for the receptor in placental lipid transport. *Endocrinology* 1995;136:340–348.

83. Furuhashi M, Seo H, Mizutani S, et al. Expression of low density lipoprotein receptor gene in human placenta during pregnancy. *Mol Endocrinol* 1989;3:1252–1256.

84. Alsat E, Bouali Y, Goldstein S, et al. Low-density lipoprotein binding sites in the microvillous membranes of human placenta at different stages of gestation. *Mol Cell Endocrinol* 1984;38: 197–203.

85. Halvorsen B, Staff AC, Henriksen T, et al. 8-iso-prostaglandin F(2alpha) increases expression of LOX-1 in JAR cells. *Hypertension* 2001;37:1184–1190.

86. Christensen HN. Role of amino acid transport and countertransport in nutrition and metabolism. *Physiol Rev* 1990;70: 43–77.

87. Kelley LK, Smith CH, King BF. Isolation and partial characterization of the basal cell membrane of human placental trophoblast. *Biochim Biophys Acta* 1983;734:91–98.

88. Zolese G, Rabini RA, Fumelli P, et al. Modifications induced by insulin-dependent diabetes mellitus on human placental Na[+]/K[+]-adenosine triphosphatase. *J Lab Clin Med* 1997;130: 374–380.

89. Dicke JM, Henderson GI. Placental amino acid uptake in normal and complicated pregnancies. *Am J Med Sci* 1988;295: 223–227.

90. Kuruvilla AG, D'Souza SW, Glazier JD, et al. Altered activity of the system A amino acid transporter in microvillous membrane vesicles from placentas of macrosomic babies born to diabetic women. *J Clin Invest* 1994;94:689–695.

91. Foster MR, Birdsey TJ, Bruce C, et al. Evaluation of amino acid transport in cytotrophoblast cells isolated from placentas of diabetic women. *Placenta* 2001;22:A.57.

92. Eaton BM, Sooranna SR. *In vitro* modulation of L-arginine transport in trophoblast cells by glucose. *Eur J Clin Invest* 1998; 28:1006–1010.

93. Osses N, Sobrevia L, Cordova C, et al. Transport and metabolism of adenosine in diabetic human placenta. *Reprod Fertil Dev* 1995;7:1499–1503.

94. Sobrevia L, Jarvis SM, Yudilevich DL. Adenosine transport in cultured human umbilical vein endothelial cells is reduced in diabetes. *Am J Physiol* 1994;267:C39–C47.

95. Buchanan AT, Kitzmiller JL. Metabolic interactions of diabetes and pregnancy. *Annu Rev Med* 1994;45:245–260.

96. Garner PR, D'Alton ME, Dudley DK, et al. Preeclampsia in diabetic pregnancies. *Am J Obstet Gynecol* 1990;163:505–508.

97. Moore TA. Fetal growth in diabetic pregnancy. *Clin Obstet Gynecol* 1997;40:771–786.

98. Weiss U, Arikan G, Haas J, et al. Hyperglycemia *in vitro* alters the invasion of trophoblast from human first trimester placenta into extracellular matrix. *Diabetes* 2000;49(suppl 1):A316.

99. Shaw LM. Identification of insulin receptor substrate 1 (IRS-1) and IRS-2 as signaling intermediates in the alpha6beta4 integrin-dependent activation of phosphoinositide 3-OH kinase and promotion of invasion. *Mol Cell Biol* 2001;21:5082–5093.

100. Mandl M, Haas J, Bischof P, et al. IGF-I and insulin effects on model cell lines for first trimester trophoblast are modified by serum. *Histochem Cell Biol* 2002;117:391–399.

101. Castellucci M, De Matteis R, Meisser A, et al. Leptin modulates extracellular matrix molecules and metalloproteinases: possible implications for trophoblast invasion. *Mol Hum Reprod* 2000; 6:951–958.

102. Staff AC, Ranheim T, Henriksen T, et al. 8-Iso-prostaglandin f(2alpha) reduces trophoblast invasion and matrix metalloproteinase activity. *Hypertension* 2000;35:1307–1313.

103. Kitzmiller JL, Watt N, Driscoll SG. Decidual arteriopathy in hypertension and diabetes in pregnancy: immunofluorescent studies. *Am J Obstet Gynecol* 1981;141:773–779.

104. Barth WH Jr, Genest DR, Riley LE, et al. Uterine arcuate artery Doppler and decidual microvascular pathology in pregnancies complicated by type I diabetes mellitus. *Ultrasound Obstet Gynecol* 1996;8:98–103.

105. Salvesen DR, Higueras MT, Mansur CA, et al. Placental and fetal Doppler velocimetry in pregnancies complicated by maternal diabetes mellitus. *Am J Obstet Gynecol* 1993;168:645–652.

106. Fadda GM, D'Antona D, Ambrosini G, et al. Placental and fetal pulsatility indices in gestational diabetes mellitus. *J Reprod Med* 2001;46:365–370.

107. Roth JB, Thorp JA, Palmer SM, et al. Response of placental vasculature to high glucose levels in the isolated human placental cotyledon. *Am J Obstet Gynecol* 1990;163:1828–1830.

108. Myatt L. Control of vascular resistance in the human placenta. *Placenta* 1992;13:329–341.

109. Saldeen P, Olofsson P, Parhar RS, et al. Prostanoid production in the umbilicoplacental arterial tree relative to impaired glucose tolerance. *Early Hum Dev* 1998;50:175–183.

110. Rakoczi I, Tihanyi K, Gero G, et al. Release of prostacyclin (PGI$_2$) from trophoblast in tissue culture: the effect of glucose concentration. *Acta Physiol Hung* 1988;71:545–549.

111. Myatt L, Brewer AS, Langdon G, et al. Attenuation of the vasoconstrictor effects of thromboxane and endothelin by nitric oxide in the human fetal-placental circulation. *Am J Obstet Gynecol* 1992;166:224–230.

112. Myatt L, Brockman DE, Eis ALW, et al. Immunohistochemical localization of NOS in the human placenta. *Placenta* 1993;14:487–495.

113. Eis ALW, Brockman DE, Pollock JS, et al. Immunohistochemical localization of endothelial nitric oxide synthase in human villous and extravillous trophoblast populations and expression during syncytiotrophoblast formation *in vitro*. *Placenta* 1995;16:113–126.

114. Rossmanith WG, Hoffmeister U, Wolfahrt S, et al. Expression and functional analysis of endothelial nitric oxide synthase (eNOS) in human placenta. *Mol Hum Reprod* 1999;5:487–494.

115. Di Iulio JL, Gude NM, King RG, et al. Human placental nitric oxide synthase activity is not altered in diabetes. *Clin Sci (Lond)* 1999;97:123–128.

116. Dollberg S, Brockman DE, Myatt L. Nitric oxide synthase activity in umbilical and placental vascular tissue of gestational diabetic pregnancies. *Gynecol Obstet Invest* 1997;44:177–181.

117. Di Iorio R, Marinoni E, Urban G, et al. Fetomaternal adrenomedullin levels in diabetic pregnancy. *Horm Metab Res* 2001;33:486–490.

118. Roberts J, Redman C. Preeclampsia: more than pregnancy-induced hypertension. *Lancet* 1993;341:1447–1454.

119. Roberts J, Taylor R, Goldfien A. Clinical and biochemical evidence of endothelial cell dysfunction in the pregnancy syndrome preeclampsia. *Am J Hypertens* 1991;4:700–708.

120. Tames F, Mackness M, Arrol S, et al. Non-enzymatic glycation of apolipoprotein B in the sera of diabetic and non-diabetic subjects. *Atherosclerosis* 1992;93:237–244.

121. Avila C, Tanji M, D'Agati V, et al. Localization of advanced glycation end-products (AGEs) and its receptor (RAGE) in placenta of gestational and pre-gestational diabetes. *J Soc Gynecol Invest* 1999;6(suppl):153A.

122. Nishikawa T, Edelstein D, Du XL, et al. Normalizing mitochondrial superoxide production blocks three pathways of hyperglycaemic damage. *Nature* 2000;404:787–790.

123. Kato H, Yoneyama Y, Araki T. Fetal plasma lipid peroxide levels in pregnancies complicated by preeclampsia. *Gynecol Obstet Invest* 1997;43:158–161.

124. Caritis S, Sibai B, Hauth J, et al. Low dose aspirin to prevent preeclampsia in women at high risk. *N Engl J Med* 1998;338:701–705.

125. Yang X, Borg LAH, Siman CM, et al. Maternal antioxidant treatments prevent diabetes-induced alterations of mitochondrial morphology in rat embryos. *Anatom Rec* 1998;251:303–315.

126. Yang X, Borg LAH, Eriksson UJ. Altered mitochondrial morphology of rat embryos in diabetic pregnancy. *Anatom Rec* 1995;241:255–267.

127. Jones CJ, Weiss U, Siman CM, et al. Mitochondria from human trophoblast and embryonic liver cells are resistant to hyperglycaemia-associated high-amplitude swelling. *Diabetologia* 2001;44:389–391.

128. Pustovrh C, Jawerbaum A, Sinner D, et al. Membrane-type matrix metalloproteinase-9 activity in placental tissue from patients with pre-existing and gestational diabetes mellitus. *Reprod Fertil Dev* 2000;12:269–275.

129. Goda N, Suematsu M, Mukai M, et al. Modulation of mitochondrion-mediated oxidative stress by nitric oxide in human placental trophoblastic cells. *Am J Physiol* 1996;217:H1893–H1899.

130. Lyall F, Gibson JL, Greer IA, et al. Increased nitrotyrosine in the diabetic placenta: evidence for oxidative stress. *Diabetes Care* 1998;21:1753–1758.

131. Wang Y, Walsh SW. Antioxidant activities and mRNA expression of superoxide dismutase, catalase, and glutathione peroxidase in normal and preeclamptic placentas. *J Soc Gynecol Invest* 1996;3:179–184.

132. Maxwell SR, Thomason H, Sandler D, et al. Antioxidant status in patients with uncomplicated insulin-dependent and non-insulin-dependent diabetes mellitus. *Eur J Clin Invest* 1997;27:484–490.

133. Poranen AK, Ekblad U, Uotila P, et al. The effect of vitamin C and E on placental lipid peroxidation and antioxidative enzymes in perfused placenta. *Acta Obstet Gynecol Scand* 1998;77:372–376.

134. Beckman JS, Beckman TW, Chen J, et al. Apparent hydroxyl radical production by peroxynitrite: implications for endothelial injury from nitric oxide and superoxide. *Proc Natl Acad Sci U S A* 1990;87:1620–1624.

135. Ischiropoulos H, Zhu L, Chen J, et al. Peroxynitrite-mediated tyrosine nitration catalyzed by superoxide dismutase. *Arch Biochem Biophys* 1992;298:431–437.

136. Villa LM, Salas E, Darley-Usmar VM, et al. Peroxynitrite induces both vasodilatation and impaired vascular relaxation in the isolated perfused rat heart. *Proc Natl Acad Sci U S A* 1994;91:12383–12387.

137. Benkusky NA, Lewis SJ, Kooy NW. Peroxynitrite-mediated attenuation of alpha- and beta-adrenoceptor agonist-induced vascular responses *in vivo*. *Eur J Pharmacol* 1999;364:151–158.

138. Myatt L, Rosenfield RB, Eis AL, et al. Nitrotyrosine residues in placenta. Evidence of peroxynitrite formation and action. *Hypertension* 1996;28:488–493.

139. Kossenjans W, Eis A, Sahay R, et al. Role of peroxynitrite in altered fetal-placental vascular reactivity in diabetes or preeclampsia. *Am J Physiol Heart Circ Physiol* 2000;278:H1311–H1319.

140. Read MA, Leitch IM, Giles WB, et al. U46619-mediated vasoconstriction of the fetal placental vasculature in vitro in normal and hypertensive pregnancies. *J Hypertens* 1999;17:389–396.

141. Wilkes BM, Mento PF, Hollander AM. Reduced thromboxane receptor affinity and vasoconstrictor responses in placentae from diabetic pregnancies. *Placenta* 1994;15:845–855.

142. Figueroa R, Omar HA, Tejani N, et al. Gestational diabetes alters human placental vascular responses to changes in oxygen tension. *Am J Obstet Gynecol* 1993;168:1616–1622.

143. Radi R, Rodriguez M, Castro L, et al. Inhibition of mitochondrial electron transport by peroxynitrite. *Arch Biochem Biophys* 1994;308:89–95.

144. Zhang J, Dawson VL, Dawson TM, et al. Nitric oxide activation of poly(ADP-ribose) synthetase in neurotoxicity. *Science* 1994;263:687–689.

145. Zou MH, Leist M, Ullrich V. Selective nitration of prostacyclin synthase and defective vasorelaxation in atherosclerotic bovine coronary arteries. *Am J Pathol* 1999;154:1359–1365.

THE BIOLOGY OF NORMAL AND ABNORMAL FETAL GROWTH AND DEVELOPMENT

HENRY L. GALAN
FREDERICK C. BATTAGLIA

FETAL AND PLACENTAL GROWTH

There are many reasons to consider fetal and placental growth in a book focused on maternal diabetes. No disease process in obstetrics has brought out more clearly how maternal nutritional and metabolic changes may impact the growth and development of the fetus and placenta. This chapter will consider briefly normal fetal and placental growth and then focus on the fetuses of diabetic mothers, whether it is large for gestational age (LGA) or small for gestational age (SGA).

Normal Growth and Development

In uncomplicated pregnancies, the growth of the fetus and placenta follows a predictable course. The placenta reaches its mature size far more quickly than the fetus. Placental growth characteristics differ by species; in humans, the placenta continues to grow throughout the pregnancy, although it has almost reached its term size by the end of the second trimester. Coincident with this growth in weight, there is the orderly development of the villous tree and its accompanying fetal vasculature. These changes are vital for the placenta to increase its total functional capacity during gestation. Figure 12-1 depicts the increase in surface area and in umbilical blood flow during gestation in normal pregnancy. The increase in surface area does not include the amplification introduced by the development of the microvilli on the maternal surface of the trophoblast (1). Teasdale found that the amplification factor introduced by the microvilli does not increase with gestational age, but actually decreases. Thus, this factor cannot account for the

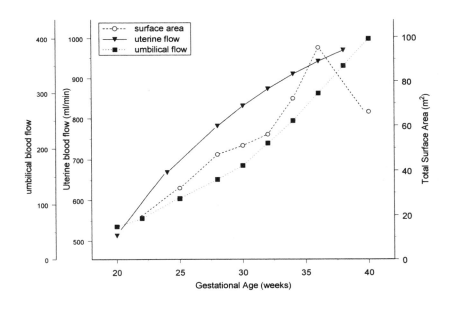

FIGURE 12-1. Total surface area including contribution of microvilli is taken from Teasdale (1). Uterine blood flow from Konje et al. (51). Umbilical blood flow from Barbera et al. (52) Umbilical blood flow and total surface area increase exponentially with gestation but uterine flow increases gradually, reflecting the relatively large metabolic requirements of the placenta in early gestation.

tremendous increase in placental functional capacity during gestation. In addition to the structural alterations in circulatory and surface area already discussed, changes in transporter activity impact the permeability of the placenta to nutrients such as glucose and amino acids.

Normal Fetal Growth

When we consider human fetal growth, it is important to recognize those characteristics of fetal growth that are shared by most mammals. There are also characteristics that are unique to human fetal development. Among the more general features of fetal growth is that most of the increase in fetal weight occurs after placental growth is almost complete. This difference in growth rates makes it clear that the functional capacity per gram of the placenta increases markedly during the latter third of gestation. There are also marked increases in perfusion of the placenta both within the uterine circulation and within the umbilical circulation. Susa and Langer, in a previous edition of this chapter (2), pointed out that 95% of the eventual fetal weight occurs in the last half of gestation and is influenced by a variety of factors, not the least of which is the maternal supply of nutrients and oxygen. It is clear that achieving a normal fetal growth rate requires changes in both perfusion and permeability.

The addition of new tissue involves the accretion of extra- and intracellular water and electrolytes, as well as protein and fat. The accumulation of extra- and intracellular water does not occur at the same rate. In all mammals, during gestation the fraction of total body water that is intracellular increases and that of extracellular fluid decreases. These changes in water and electrolytes are the basis for the changes in fetal metabolic rate during gestation (3,4). As shown in Fig. 12-2, taken from studies in ovine pregnancy (5,6), when fetal oxygen consumption (VO₂) is expressed per kilogram fetal weight, there is a relatively small change in VO₂ during gestation. This observation is consistent with fetal heart rate data, which show a relatively small decrease in fetal heart rate during gestation (6) However, if VO₂ is expressed per gram dry weight, the change is quite large, comparable with the relationship between VO₂ and body size in postnatal life. In essence, early development is characterized by having relatively few cells in a large volume of extracellular fluid (5).

The unique characteristics of human development include the growth of a large brain and the accretion of a large depot of white fat. *In utero,* brain growth is fairly constant among all mammals in grams per day (7). This is reflected in the longer gestation of primates compared with other mammals of similar size (7). In humans, gestation is much longer than in mammals producing a newborn of comparable weight.

The deposition of fat represents over half the caloric accretion from 27 weeks until term and approximately 90%

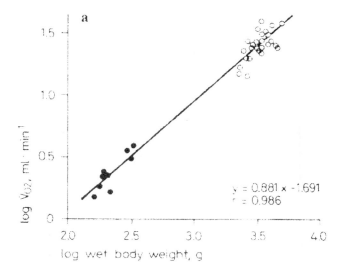

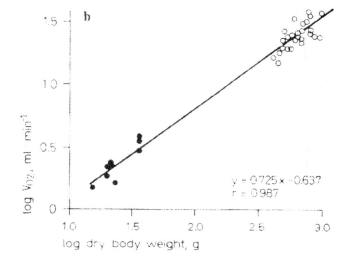

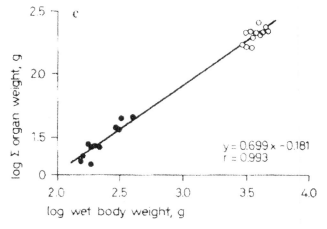

FIGURE 12-2. Relationships between log fetal oxygen consumption (VO₂) and log wet body weight **(A)**, log VO₂ and log dry body weight **(B)**, and log summed wet weights of liver, kidneys, heart, and brain (organ weight) and wet body weight **(C)** in mid (v) and late (V) gestation fetuses. [Data from Bell AW, Battaglia FC, Makowski EL, et al. Relationship between metabolic rate and body size in fetal life. *Biol Neonate* 1985;47(2):120–123.]

of the added calories in the last few weeks of pregnancy (8). This pattern of fat accretion in human pregnancy is particularly important as it applies to diabetes in pregnancy. Figure 12-3, taken from the study of Sparks et al. (8), brings out the striking accumulation of white fat depots in the human fetus in late gestation. This pattern of fat accretion for the human fetus has many clinical implications. For one thing, it means that the recognition of intrauterine growth restriction (IUGR) is far more likely to be made in late gestation, when a decrease in fat stores is clinically obvious. In early gestation (e.g., 20–30 weeks) there is little fat deposition present even in normally grown preterm infants, which makes recognition of IUGR more difficult. Early studies by Ogata et al. using serial ultrasound measurements of fetal abdominal circumference in diabetic pregnancies brought out the fact that a clear-cut deviation from normal growth was not apparent until at least 30 weeks' gestation (9) (Fig. 12-4). For pregnancies complicated by diabetes, whether type 1, type 2, or gestational diabetes, macrosomia is the most frequent problem encountered, and these large infants have significantly increased fat stores compared with other

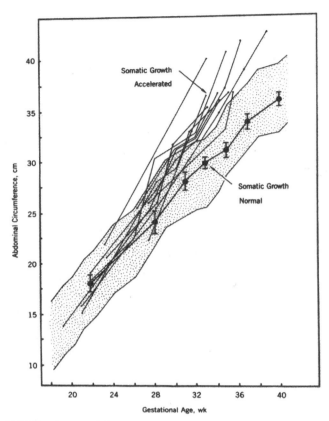

FIGURE 12-4. Serial measurements of the fetal abdominal circumference during pregnancies complicated by diabetes. The 95% confidence band for normal pregnancies is also shown. (Reprinted from Ogata E, Sabbagha R, Metzger B. Serial ultrasonography to assess evolving fetal macrosomia. Studies in 23 pregnant diabetic women. *JAMA* 1980;243:2405, with permission.)

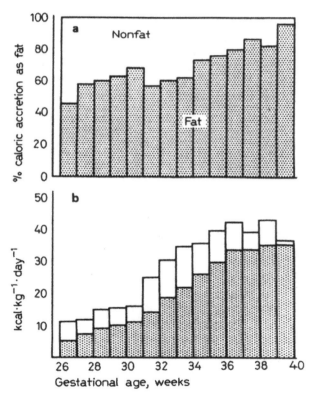

FIGURE 12-3. A, B: A daily rate of caloric increase (kcal/kg/day) for each week of gestation from 27 weeks to term. The daily rate of increases for fat and nonfat dry weight (g/kg/day) were multiplied by 9.5 and 4.5 kcal/g, respectively, to obtain the caloric accretion rates. **B:** These values as percentages of the total caloric accretion. [Data from Sparks JW, Girard JR, Battaglia FC. An estimate of the caloric requirements of the human fetus. *Biol Neonate* 1980;38(3–4):113–119.]

LGA babies (10–12). As such, determination of fetal fat stores could provide information on glycemic control in the diabetic patient. In the past decade, efforts have been made to determine fetal fat stores via ultrasonography.

In 1997, Bernstein et al. reported the use of ultrasonography to assess anthropometric measurements of fetal body composition (11) by comparing fat (subcutaneous tissue) and lean body mass (estimated fetal weight, femur length) measurements across gestation in normal fetuses, and showed significant correlations with both birth weight and estimates of neonatal lean and fat mass. As a natural extension of the Bernstein study, Galan et al. demonstrated that lean and fat measurements obtained by ultrasonography could be used to account for differences in birth weights between two populations at different altitudes (12). In the latter study, rather than using femur length or estimated fetal weight as the index of lean mass, the researchers used the area of muscle and bone on an axial view of the fetal thigh as well as measurements of abdominal subcutaneous thickness. Both sites confirmed differences between the two populations in fetal fat concentration. Thus, ultrasound estimates of subcutaneous tissue and, indirectly, fetal fat stores may provide a measure of glycemic control in pregnancies complicated by diabetic vasculopathy and differentiate the IUGR fetus with reduced fat stores from other SGA fetuses with normal fat stores.

ABNORMAL FETAL GROWTH

Abnormal fetal growth encompasses both ends of the growth spectrum: the problem of IUGR and that of excessive growth or macrosomia. Because excessive growth is a far more common problem in pregnancies complicated by diabetes, it will be discussed first.

Large-for-Gestational-Age Infants

LGA infants are those above the 90th percentile in fetal weight for gestational age. *Macrosomia* is frequently used interchangeably with *LGA*. Ventura et al. reported on the extremes of growth that included a definition of high birth weight or macrosomia as a weight greater than 4,000 g, which accounted for 10% of the 3,880,894 births in 1997 (13). Traumatic birth injury (shoulder dystocia, brachial plexus injury, facial nerve injury, and cephalohematomas) is more common when the pregnancy is complicated by diabetes and further increased in macrosomic infants of diabetic mothers (IDMs) (14,15). In 1991, Langer et al. reported on a 15-year experience with macrosomia (estimated fetal weight >4,000 g) at the University of Texas Health Sciences Center in San Antonio. They found the overall incidence of macrosomia to be 20.6% among patients with diabetes compared with 7.6% among normal women (14). Shoulder dystocia occurred significantly more frequently in IDMs when the birth weights were greater than 4,250 g. In clinical practice, this has become a commonly used fetal weight cut-off for recommending an elective cesarean section in the diabetic patient. Although the term *macrosomia* is useful from a birth injury standpoint, it is limited by a specific birth weight cut-off without regard to gestational age. Thus, it may not reflect the excess of fetal somatic growth earlier in gestation because a baby born at 34 weeks may still be LGA, but not macrosomic by that definition.

LGA infants include those who have grown large as a consequence of pathology (e.g., IDMs or infants with Wiedemann-Beckwith syndrome) and those infants who are growing normally but are large as part of the distribution of normally growing infants. Diabetes in pregnancy, including gestational diabetes, increases the frequency of excessive fetal and placental growth.

One of the most interesting aspects of diabetes in pregnancy is that it was the first problem to provide evidence of changes in the normal pattern of fetal development that lead to problems in neonatal adjustment. The LGA baby of a patient with diabetes, whether type 1, type 2, or gestational diabetes, reflects the excessive fetal growth that is always associated with remodeling of fetal tissues during fetal development. These changes distinguish the LGA IDM from other LGA infants. The remodeling affects most tissues of the body, although principally three tissue beds are affected, and it is these that led to its recognition. These abnormalities are not classic congenital anomalies occurring during embryogenesis, but structural remodeling occurring during the fetal phase of development. The three tissue beds that are structurally altered and that affect adversely neonatal adaptation include (a) pancreatic islets; (b) cardiac tissue, including myocytes, septal tissue, and the pulmonary vascular smooth muscle; and (c) adipose tissue. Pedra et al. reported that approximately 50% of fetal hypertrophic cardiomyopathy, not associated with multiple pregnancy, was attributable to maternal diabetes and represented the largest single etiologic group (16). As mentioned earlier, hyperplasia and hypertrophy of adipocytes also leads to increased fetal fat deposition. Okereke et al. (17) found a significant increase in fat mass and in percentage body fat for infants of mothers with gestational diabetes compared with infants of uncomplicated pregnancies (17). The increase in fat concentration is particularly interesting because it cannot be attributed to macrosomia per se but speaks to altered tissue growth just as the cardiac changes do. These investigators reported higher leptin concentrations in the infants of gestational diabetics, as have other investigators (17).

These complications can be reduced by good management of diabetic control during pregnancy, but they are never completely eliminated. There are no longer any significant differences in neonatal mortality between LGA and appropriate-for-gestational age (AGA) babies in late gestation (18). This finding attests to the fact that good obstetric management can have a profound impact on outcome. However, neonatal hypoglycemia, primary pulmonary hypertension, and cardiomyopathy are all reflections of this altered fetal growth.

Diabetes is a disease that impacts both embryologic as well as fetal development. Embryologically, diabetes mellitus is a known risk factor for the development of cardiac defects *in utero* and is an indication for targeted fetal echocardiography. These defects include ventriculo- and atrioseptal defects, valvular defects, and outflow tract abnormalities, including transposition of the great vessels (19). In addition to the increased risk for cardiac defects, uncontrolled maternal diabetes is known to alter normal fetal development in many tissues, including vascular and cardiac. It may accelerate fetal cardiac growth and result in diastolic cardiac dysfunction, leading to cardiomyopathy depicted clinically as congestive heart failure and ventricular outflow tract obstruction later in gestation (20–22). Echocardiographic features include an increase in myocardial thickness, specifically septal hypertrophy, ventricular stiffness, and abnormal myocardial contractility. While the effects of diabetes on the fetal heart have been well described, it is of interest to note that little is known about the abnormal pulmonary blood flow and potential pulmonary vascular remodeling in newborns of poorly controlled diabetic mothers encountered in the neonatal intensive care setting. That some degree of pulmonary vascular remodeling and hypertension exists in these fetuses is consistent with the documented echocardiographic studies and remains an area open to investigation.

Although the fetus of the well-controlled diabetic mother is at increased risk for accelerated cardiac growth, if the diabetes remains well-controlled, cardiac function will likely remain stable and will not deteriorate. Jaeggi et al. recently compared echocardiographic findings between fetuses of nondiabetic mothers and of women with well-controlled type 1 diabetes. Although fetuses of well-controlled diabetic mothers showed a progressive increase of the interventricular septal thickness at 20 to 35 weeks' gestation, there was no change in functional echocardiographic features, including diastolic function (mitral and tricuspid valve Doppler flow ratios), afterload (umbilical artery pulsatility index), and systolic function (shortening fractions and outputs). In a similar fashion, the fetus of the well-controlled diabetic patient without microvascular disease demonstrates flow velocity waveform Doppler profiles in the umbilical artery that are normal, which indicates that the resistance to blood flow in the placenta is normal (23,24). The importance of tight maternal glycemic control is further emphasized by these findings.

Neonatal hyperviscosity and polycythemia can be related to chronic fetal hypoxia. The hypercoagulability of the IDM is not well understood. When coupled with polycythemia, it can lead to thrombotic complications, including thromboses of the cerebral venous circulation.

Intrauterine Growth Restriction

IUGR represents a subset of SGA. Just as with LGA infants, some SGA infants are normally developed and are simply part of the normal distribution of birth weights at any given gestational age. IUGR refers to those babies whose growth has been significantly impaired for reasons of maternal, placental, or fetal pathology. The diagnosis of IUGR requires two pieces of information. One of these is gestational age. The other is an estimate of fetal weight obtained from ultrasound biometry. Alternately, one can rely on measurement of abdominal circumference alone, determined with ultrasonography, and consider those infants with an abdominal circumference less than 2 SD for gestational age as potentially growth-restricted infants. If further ultrasound studies reveal other aspects of pathology, such as reduced fetal fat concentration, or Doppler studies demonstrate fetal arterial velocimetry changes, the diagnosis of IUGR is confirmed.

IUGR is a relatively infrequent complication of maternal diabetes regardless of whether the diabetes is gestational or pregestational. Approximately 50 years ago, White developed a classification scheme for gestational and pregestational diabetic patients in an effort to improve perinatal mortality (25). This classification emphasized that the risk for fetal injury is proportional to the severity of the maternal disease. Class A diabetes is gestational diabetes; class B and C diabetes, pregestational diabetes that does not have vascular complications; and classes D, E, F, H, R, and T diabetes, patients with pregestational diabetes with varying degrees of vascular disease and end-organ injury. It is generally accepted that patients with vascular disease of any etiology are at risk for IUGR. More specifically, chronic hypertension, a common feature in diabetics with advanced microvascular disease, is a well known risk factor for IUGR (26). Despite this information, it is interesting that some published data show no increased risk for an SGA fetus even in more advanced stages of diabetes, as shown in Table 12-1. However, the White's classification system does not take into account whether there is chronic hypertension and whether the chronic hypertension is well treated or not.

In addition, there are other published studies suggesting that the occurrence of IUGR is increased in diabetic patients with advanced vascular disease. In 2001, McElvy et al. reported on the incidence of IUGR in diabetic patients with progressive or stable retinopathy. Using logistic regression analysis, they found independent associations for progressive retinopathy and chronic hypertension with IUGR (27). In a study by Dicker et al., the incidence of IUGR was significantly more common in patients whose diabetes was complicated by vasculopathy when compared with those without vasculopathy (8 of 22 vs. 0 of 86, respectively; $p < 0.001$) (23). In another study by Ekbom et al., IUGR occurred significantly more often in patients with type 1 diabetes who demonstrated nephropathy compared to those with either microalbuminuria or normal urinary albumin excretion (28). One must keep in mind that with diabetes, babies are frequently macrosomic and only infrequently growth restricted using strict percentile cutoffs, as shown in Table 12-1. However, there may be a substantial number of growth-restricted babies whose fetal size falls

TABLE 12-1. INCIDENCE OF LGA AND SGA BABIES IN PREGNANCIES COMPLICATED BY GESTATIONAL AND PREGESTATIONAL DIABETES USING WHITE'S CLASSIFICATION SCHEME

	Gestational	Class B, C	Class D, F, R	Total
LGA (>90th percentile)	22%	31%	22%	24%
SGA (<10th percentile)	4%	5%	5%	4%

Adapted from Creasy and Resnik, Maternal-Fetal Medicine, chapter 53, page 967, WB Saunders, 1999, which was adapted from California Department of Health Services, Maternal and Child Health Branch: Status Report of the Sweet Success California Diabetes and Pregnancy Program 1986–89, Sacramento, March 31, 1991.

within the normal range, but are in fact growth restricted based on criteria such as umbilical artery Doppler velocimetry or fat deposition. Therefore, these infants are at risk for the morbidities associated with IUGR. Although there are mixed reports in the literature regarding IUGR and advanced diabetes, it is clear that with diabetes, fetal growth disturbances (SGA and LGA) are common, and that fetal growth surveillance, either by clinical acumen or ultrasonography, is warranted.

Doppler Velocimetry and Fetal Assessment

A number of abnormalities have been described in the placenta of the diabetic patient, including accumulation of nonparenchymal and parenchymal villous tissue, spiral vessel lumen narrowing, and obliteration of fetal stem arteries (29,30). Vascular structural abnormalities such as these can impact the resistance of blood flow through the placenta. Indices of blood flow resistance can be easily determined through the use of Doppler velocimetry. Pulsed-wave Doppler velocimetry of the umbilical artery produces a velocity profile waveform that contains a distinct systolic and diastolic component reflecting activity of the fetal cardiac cycle and the resistance to blood flow downstream within the placenta. Trudinger et al. demonstrated that the

umbilical artery systolic to diastolic (S/D) ratio was elevated above the 95th percentile in 85% of cases where the fetus was growth restricted (31). The increase in the S/D ratio was due to a decrease in diastolic velocity, which was in turn due to an increase in blood flow resistance within the placenta. Umbilical artery Doppler velocimetry has been proven to be a useful adjunct to the nonstress test and biophysical profile for antenatal testing in high-risk pregnancies. More specifically, umbilical artery Doppler reduces perinatal mortality in growth-restricted fetuses by one third when used in combination with other tests (32).

While the first reported use of Doppler in the umbilical artery occurred in the 1970s, the first published reports of umbilical artery Doppler studies in the diabetic pregnancy did not occur until the late 1980s. In a recent review, Reece et al. summarized the literature and utility of umbilical artery Doppler in the diabetic patient (33). In 1991, Degani et al. performed umbilical artery Doppler in patients following a fasting blood glucose and a 1-hour glucose challenge test to determine if there was a correlation between Doppler findings and blood glucose. An increase of 30 mg/dL or more in maternal plasma glucose concentration resulted in a significant increase in the umbilical artery pulsatility index. The effect of chronic glucose elevation on umbilical artery Doppler velocimetry is less clear. There are nine published reports that address glycemic con-

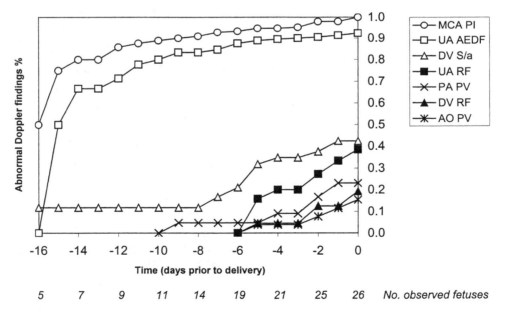

FIGURE 12-5. Cumulative onset time curves of Doppler abnormalities for each fetal vessel examined. Time 0 refers to the date of delivery. ○, MCA PI; □, UA AEDF; △, DV S/a; ■, UA RF; ×, PA PV; ▲, DV RF; ✳, AO PV. (UA, umbilical artery; MCA, middle cerebral artery; DV, ductus venosus; PA, pulmonic outflow tracts; AO, aortic outflow tracts; UA AEDF, absent end-diastolic flow; DV RF, reverse flow; UA RF, reverse end-diastolic flow; DV S/a, abnormal S/a ratio; AO PV, abnormal peak velocity; PA PV, abnormal peak velocity) [Reprinted from Ferrazzi E, Bozzo M, Rigano S, et al. Temporal sequence of abnormal Doppler changes in the peripheral and central circulatory systems of the severely growth-restricted fetus. *Ultrasound Obstet Gynecol* 2002;19(2):140–146, with permission.]

trol, maternal microvascular disease, and umbilical artery Doppler findings (23,24,34–40).

Four of these studies showed a correlation between the umbilical artery S/D ratio and glycemic control, whereas five did not. This difference could be explained in part by relatively good glucose control in the majority of patients. What is evident from these studies is that diabetic women with vasculopathy appear to have increased umbilical artery S/D ratios and that these elevated umbilical artery S/D ratios correlate with adverse outcomes. The adverse outcomes included IUGR, respiratory distress syndrome, stillbirth, nonreassuring fetal heart rate tracings, and metabolic abnormalities.

A study by Bracero et al. addressing Doppler velocimetry and placental morphology in diabetic patients requiring insulin further supports the idea that it is vasculopathy and vascular dysfunction that is responsible for Doppler abnormalities in umbilical artery flow (41). In this group of 25 type 1 diabetic patients, 14 patients had normal Doppler velocimetry and 11 abnormal velocimetry. No differences between the groups for placental weight, number of tertiary stem villi, number of small muscular arteries, or mean arterial width were found. This suggests a functional rather than structural process in the placenta that accounts for the Doppler findings. Compared with the diabetic group with normal Doppler findings, the group with abnormal Doppler findings had poorer glycemic control, were delivered earlier, and also had a significant increase in low birth weight, neonatal hyperbilirubinemia, cesarean delivery for nonreassuring fetal heart rate tracings, and a neonatal intensive care unit stay of more than 2 days.

As suggested by Reece et al. (33), Doppler velocimetry as an adjunct to antenatal testing in the diabetic patient should be interpreted with caution and primarily reserved for those patients who demonstrate microvascular disease where Doppler indices might show evidence of increased vascular resistance within the placenta. It is worth pointing out that measurement of velocity waveforms in the umbilical artery represents only part of an overall fetal Doppler surveillance. In a recent study, Ferrazzi et al. (42) determined velocity waveforms at eight sites in the fetal circulation longitudinally in a group of patients with IUGR. Figure 12-5 shows the individual vessels interrogated and when those vessels become abnormal as a function of time as the fetus progressed to a nonreassuring, nonreactive nonstress test. This study emphasizes that there is an orderly sequence of change within the fetal circulation in these pregnancies as fetal status progressively deteriorates. At present, there is no comparable detailed study of the fetal circulation in diabetic pregnancies, controlled or uncontrolled.

Metabolic Changes in the Fetus

The changes in the fetus of the diabetic woman are driven by the increased delivery of nutrients from the maternal to the fetal compartment across the placenta, which leads to chronic fetal hyperinsulinemia. The Pedersen hypothesis, resting on the critical role of fetal hyperinsulinemia, has become an accepted explanation for much of the change in fetal development. This hypothesis assumes an increased delivery of virtually all nutrients to the fetus, including amino acids and glucose. The presence of fetal hyperinsulinemia in diabetic pregnancies has been well established and has been reviewed by Catalano et al. (43). Despite its general acceptance, increased umbilical uptake of all amino acids and glucose has been difficult to establish in pregnancies complicated by diabetes, because the rate at which nutrients enter the fetal circulation from the placenta is difficult to measure in human pregnancies. However, animal studies suggest that there is likely to be considerable selectivity in terms of which nutrients are taken up in larger amounts. Studies of *in vivo* transplacental transport of amino acids in ovine pregnancy have shown that when maternal concentrations of all amino acids are increased, there is a selective increase in some fetal amino acid concentrations, but not in all of them, reflecting competitive inhibition by amino acids with high affinity for shared transporters (44–46). Similarly, studies of maternal hyperglycemia have shown quite different effects on fetal glucose uptake for acute compared with chronic maternal hyperglycemia (47,48). However, the presence of fetal hyperinsulinemia in pregnancies complicated by diabetes establishes the presence of chronically elevated nutrients that themselves can act as secretogogues, whether glucose or one or more amino acids. Disorders of fetal growth in many tissues can be due to both increased concentrations of nutrients and the endocrine changes that the nutrients induce. For example, increased fetal leptin concentrations and increased uptake of carbon into the fetal circulation combine to produce the increased fat depots of the IDM.

Changes in fetal tissue growth and the metabolic consequences of the IDM can interact to cause considerable morbidity in the neonatal period. For example, polycythemia and hyperviscosity may lead to a significant reduction in cerebral and myocardial plasma flow. If the IDM develops postnatal hypoglycemia, low neonatal plasma glucose concentration and reduced plasma flow lead to a marked reduction in glucose delivery to the brain and heart. In the neonatal period, the heart, as well as the brain, are carbohydrate dependent. If cardiomyopathy is present, this combination of metabolic and growth disturbances can lead to cardiac dysfunction. The older pediatric literature contained examples of polycythemic IDMs dying with an enlarged heart and hypoglycemia. The control of neonatal glucose concentration is quite effective in intensive care nurseries today, and the IDM with polycythemia and cardiomyopathy requires tight regulation of glucose concentration in the first week of life. Hypercoagulability in the fetus of the diabetic mother can produce a variety of thrombotic problems in both the arterial and venous circulations of the neonate. In fact, arterial thrombi can lead to *in utero* complications (49).

A great deal of research focuses on the question of whether abnormal fetal growth carries with it long-term implications for childhood and adult health. We shall not attempt to review all of this in this chapter because most of the focus has been on pregnancies complicated by IUGR. However, the longitudinal studies of Silverman et al. (50) are of note. They reported that the children of both pregestational and gestational diabetic women have a higher incidence of obesity at 14 to 17 years of age (body mass index of 24.6 ± 5.8 vs. 20.9 ± 3.4 in controls) and that 36% have impaired glucose tolerance. Thus, the long-term implications of fetal obesity and macrosomia are becoming established.

KEY POINTS

- Fetal growth is uniquely characterized by the deposition of a large amount of white fat depots in the last trimester.
- IDM pregnancies are associated with increased fetal size and with a high frequency of fetal growth abnormalities, including β-cell hyperplasia and cardiac septal hypertrophy.
- IUGR fetuses represent a subset of SGA fetuses. They can be diagnosed *in utero* by ultrasonography and the clinical severity characterized by Doppler studies of the fetal circulation and fetal heart rate.
- There is an orderly sequence of changes in fetal velocimetry for various fetal vessels in IUGR pregnancies that are indicative of progressive disease, and in the majority of IUGR cases, these changes occur prior to fetal heart rate or biophysical profile changes.
- Umbilical flow measurements and hepatic umbilical venous flow measurements have shown that there are a subset of IUGR pregnancies in which these flows are markedly reduced.

REFERENCES

1. Teasdale F, Jean-Jacques G. Morphometric evaluation of the microvillous surface enlargement factor in the human placenta from mid-gestation to term. *Placenta* 1985;6(5):375–381.
2. Susa J, Langer O. Diabetes and fetal growth. In: Reece E, Coustan D, eds. *Diabetes mellitus in pregnancy.* New York: Churchill Livingstone, 1995:79–92.
3. Behrman R, Seeds A Jr, Battaglia FC, et al. The normal changes in mass and water content in fetal rhesus monkey and placenta throughout gestation. *J Pediatr* 1964;65(1):38–44.
4. Frijs-Hansen B. Changes in body water compartments during growth. *Acta Paediatr* 1957;110(suppl):1–68.
5. Bell AW, Battaglia FC, Makowski EL, et al. Relationship between metabolic rate and body size in fetal life. *Biol Neonate* 1985;47(2):120–123.
6. Meier PR, Manchester D, Battaglia FC, et al. Fetal heart rate in relation to body mass. *Proc Soc Exp Biol Med* 1983;172:107–110.
7. Hofman M. Evolution of brain size in neonatal and adult placental mammals: a theoretical approach. *J Theoret Biol* 1983;105:317–332.
8. Sparks JW, Girard JR, Battaglia FC. An estimate of the caloric requirements of the human fetus. *Biol Neonate* 1980;38(3–4):113–119.
9. Ogata E, Sabbagha R, Metzger B. Serial ultrasonography to assess evolving fetal macrosomia. Studies in 23 pregnant diabetic women. *JAMA* 1980;243:2405–2408.
10. Bernstein I, Catalano P. Influence of fetal fat on the ultrasound estimation of fetal weight in diabetic mothers. *Obstet Gynecol* 1992;79(4):561–563.
11. Bernstein I, Goran J, Amini S, et al. Differential growth of fetal tissues during the second half of pregnancy. *Am J Obstet Gynecol* 1997;176(1):28–32.
12. Galan H, Rigano S, Radaelli T, et al. Reduction of subcutaneous mass, but not lean mass, in normal fetuses in Denver, Colorado. *Am J Obstet Gynecol* 2001;185:834–838.
13. Ventura S, Martin J, Curtin S, et al. Births: final data for 1997. *Natl Vital Stat Rep* 1999;47(18):1–96.
14. Langer O, Berkus M, Huff R, et al. Shoulder dystocia: should the fetus weighing >4000 grams be delivered by cesarean section. *Am J Obstet Gynecol* 1991;165:831–837.
15. Mimouni F, Miodovnik M, Rosenn B, et al. Birth trauma in insulin dependent diabetic pregnancies. *Am J Perinatol* 1992;9(3):205–209.
16. Pedra S, Smallhorn J, Ryan G, et al. Fetal cardiomyopathies: pathogenic mechanisms, hemodynamic findings and clinical outcome. *Circulation* 2002;106(5):585–591.
17. Okereke N, Uvena-Celebrezze J, Hutson-Presley L, et al. The effect of gender and gestational diabetes mellitus on cord leptin concentration. *Am J Obstet Gynecol* 2002;187(3):798–803.
18. Lemons J, Bauer C, Oh W, et al. Very low birth weight outcomes of the National Institute of Child Health and Human Development Neonatal Research Network, January 1995 through December 1996. *Pediatrics* 2001;107(1):e1.
19. Meyer-Wittkopf M, Simpson J, Sharland G. Incidence of congenital heart defects in fetuses of diabetic mothers: a retrospective study of 326 cases. *Ultrasound Obstet Gynecol* 1996;8:8–10.
20. Mehta S, Nuamah I, Kalhan S. Altered diastolic function in asymptomatic infants of mothers with gestational diabetes. *Diabetes* 1991;40:56–60.
21. Rizzo G, Arduini D, Romanini C. Cardiac function in fetuses of type I diabetic mothers. *Am J Obstet Gynecol* 1991;164:837–843.
22. Veille J, Hanson R, Sivakoff M, et al. Fetal cardiac size in normal, intrauterine growth retarded, and diabetic pregnancies. *Am J Perinatol* 1993;10:275–279.
23. Dicker D, Goldman J, Yeshaya A, et al. Umbilical artery velocimetry in insulin-dependent diabetes mellitus pregnancies. *J Perinat Med* 1990;18:391–395.
24. Johnstone F, Steel J, Haddad N, et al. Doppler umbilical artery flow velocity waveforms in diabetic pregnancy. *Br J Obstet Gynaecol* 1992;99:135–140.
25. White P. Classification of obstetric diabetes. *Am J Obstet Gynecol* 1978;130(2):228–230.
26. Easterling T, Benedetti T, Carlson K, et al. The effect of maternal hemodynamics on fetal growth in hypertensive pregnancies. *Am J Obstet Gynecol* 1991;165:902–906.
27. McElvy S, DeMarini S, Miodovnik M, et al. Fetal weight and progression of diabetic retinopathy. *Obstet Gynecol* 2001;97:587–592.
28. Ekbom P, Damm P, Feldt-Rasmussen B, et al. Pregnancy outcome in type 1 diabetic women with microalbuminuria. *Diabetes Care* 2001;24:1739–1744.
29. Fox H. Pathology of the placenta in maternal diabetes mellitus. *Obstet Gynecol* 1969;34:792–797.

30. Teasdale F. Histomorphometry of the human placenta in class B diabetes mellitus. *Placenta* 1983;4:1–12.
31. Trudinger BJ, Giles W, Cook C. Uteroplacental blood flow velocity-time waveforms in normal and complicated pregnancy. *Br J Obstet Gynaecol* 1985;92:39–45.
32. Alfirevic Z, Neilson J. The current status of Doppler sonography in obstetrics. *Curr Opin Obstet Gynecol* 1996;8(2):114–118.
33. Reece E, Homko C, Wiznitzer A. Doppler velocimetry and the assessment of fetal well-being in normal and diabetic pregnancies. *Ultrasound Obstet Gynecol* 1994;4:508–514.
34. Bracero L. Umbilical artery velocimetry in diabetes and pregnancy. *Obstet Gynecol* 1986;68:654–658.
35. Bracero L, Jovanovic L, Rochelson B, et al. Significance of umbilical and uterine artery velocimetry in the well-controlled pregnant diabetic. *J Reprod Med* 1989;34(4):273–276.
36. Bracero L, Schulman H. Doppler studies of the uteroplacental circulation in pregnancies complicated by diabetes. *Ultrasound Obstet Gynecol* 1991;1:391–394.
37. Ishimatsu J, Yoshimura O, Manabe A, et al. Umbilical artery blood flow velocity waveforms in pregnancy complicated by diabetes mellitus. *Arch Gynecol Obstet* 1991;248(3):123–127.
38. Kofinas A, Penry M, Swain M. Uteroplacental Doppler flow velocity waveform analysis correlates poorly with glycemic control in diabetic pregnant women. *Am J Perinatol* 1991;8(4):273–277.
39. Landon M, Gabbe S, Bruner J, et al. Doppler umbilical artery velocimetry in pregnancy complicated by insulin-dependent diabetes mellitus. *Obstet Gynecol* 1989;73(6):961–965.
40. Reece EA, Homko C. Doppler ultrasonography in pregnancies complicated by diabetes mellitus. *Proceedings of the First International Symposium on Diabetes in Pregnancy.* Tel-Aviv, Israel, March 30 to April 3, 1992.
41. Bracero L, Beneck D, Schulman H. Doppler velocimetry, placental morphology and outcome in insulin-dependent diabetes. *Ultrasound Obstet Gynecol* 1993;3:236–239.
42. Ferrazzi E, Bozzo M, Rigano S, et al. Temporal sequence of abnormal Doppler changes in the peripheral and central circulatory systems of the severely growth-restricted fetus. *Ultrasound Obstet Gynecol* 2002;19(2):140–146.
43. Catalano P, Ishizuka T, Friedman J. Glucose metabolism in pregnancy. In: Cowett R, ed. *Principles of perinatal-neonatal metabolism.* New York: Springer-Verlag, 1998:183–206.
44. Jozwik M, Teng C, Wilkening R, et al. Effects of branched-chain amino acids on placental amino acid transfer and insulin and glucagon release in the ovine fetus. *Am J Obstet Gynecol* 2001; 185:487–495.
45. Jozwik M, Teng C, Timmerman M, et al. Uptake and transport by the ovine placenta of neutral nonmetabolizable amino acids with different transport system affinities. *Placenta* 1998;19(7):531–538.
46. Wilkes P, Meschia G, Teng C, et al. The effect of an elevated maternal lysine concentration upon placental lysine transport in pregnant sheep. *Am J Obstet Gynecol* 2003;189(5):1494–1500.
47. Simmons M, Battaglia FC, Meschia G. Placental transfer of glucose. *J Dev Physiol* 1979;1:227–243.
48. Anderson M, He J, Flowers-Ziegler J, et al. Effects of selective hyperglycemia and hyperinsulinemia on glucose transporters in fetal ovine skeletal muscle. *Am J Physiol* 2001;281(4):R1256–R1263.
49. Long D, Lorant D. Multiple arterial thrombi and *in utero* leg gangrene in an infant of a diabetic mother. *J Perinatol* 2002;22(5):424–427.
50. Silverman B, Rizzo T, Cho N, et al. Long-term effects of the intrauterine environment. The Northwestren University Diabetes in Pregnancy Center. *Diabetes Care* 1998;21(suppl 2):B142–B149.
51. Konje JC, Kaufmann P, Bell SC, et al. A longitudinal study of quantitative uterine blood flow with the use of color power angiography in appropriate for gestational age pregnancies. *Am J Obstet Gynecol* 2001;185(3):608–613.
52. Barbera A, Galan HL, Ferrazzi E, et al. Relationship of umbilical vein blood flow to growth parameters in the human fetus. *Am J Obstet Gynecol* 1999;181(1):174–179.

13

CONGENITAL MALFORMATIONS: EPIDEMIOLOGY, PATHOGENESIS, AND EXPERIMENTAL METHODS OF INDUCTION AND PREVENTION

E. ALBERT REECE
ULF J. ERIKSSON

Most neonatal problems have gradually declined during the past century. The clinical significance of birth defects, therefore, has now assumed greater importance because mortality rates attributed to congenital malformations have decreased far less than other causes of death (1). Thus, the relative impact of major congenital malformations has continued to grow (2–5). Congenital anomalies occur in about 3% of all infants born in the United States, accounting for about 21% of infant mortality (2,3). The causes are heterogeneous, and some categorization has been proposed. Kalter and Warkany (2,3) divided malformations into those (a) caused by single major mutant genes, (b) due to interaction between hereditary tendencies and genetic factors, (c) associated with chromosomal aberrations, (d) attributed to discrete environmental factors, and (e) with no identified causes.

Diabetes mellitus is one of the most common maternal illnesses resulting in anomalous offspring (6–39). The frequency of major congenital anomalies among infants of diabetic mothers (IDMs) has been estimated at 6% to 10%, representing a two- to three-fold increase over the frequency in the general population and accounting for 40% of all perinatal deaths among these infants (6,38,40–48).

These congenital malformations have become a serious problem with both social and financial implications. Despite extensive human and animal studies, the precise pathogenesis remains unknown, as several reviews have shown (41,43,49–53).

Unfortunately, the origin of the dysmorphogenesis dates back to a very early developmental period when the pregnancy is hardly diagnosable (54). Current clinical and experimental evidence suggests that the maternal metabolic milieu has a direct influence on the embryo during a critical and vulnerable developmental period in early pregnancy (55,56). Clinical and experimental studies have also impli-

cated alterations in maternal metabolic fuels (i.e., manifested as hyperglycemia, hyperketonemia, or altered branched chain amino acid [BCAA] levels to be involved in the induction of congenital malformations during the critical phase of organogenesis) (57–64).

In particular, in experimental studies, increased ambient concentrations of glucose (65–74), beta-hydroxybutyrate (69,71,74–85), or BCAA (74,84) has been shown to cause embryonic dysmorphogenesis in vitro. Experimental hyperglycemia and hyperketonemia result in a deficiency state of arachidonic acid (AA) (86–89) and certain prostaglandins (90,91). Increased ambient glucose concentration may also cause excessive accumulation of sorbitol (92–96) and decreased concentration of myoinositol (MI) (90,94, 96–102), as well as increased generation of free oxygen radicals (73,74,84,102) in embryonic tissue in conjunction with the induction of embryonic dysmorphogenesis (Table 13-1).

This chapter reviews much of the available information on diabetic embryopathy, provides a brief summary of neural tube development and yolk sac function during

TABLE 13-1. ETIOLOGIC FACTORS ASSOCIATED WITH DIABETIC EMBRYOPATHY

Altered metabolic fuels
Maternal hyperglycemia
Maternal hyperketonemia
Maternal hypoglycemia
   Free oxygen radicals
Somatomedin inhibitors
   Genetic susceptibility
   Other maternal factors

Reece EA, Hobbins JC. Diabetic embryopathy: pathogenesis, prenatal diagnosis and prevention. *Obstet Gynecol Surv* 1986;41:32, with permission (129).

organogenesis, discusses experimental studies of induction and prevention of hyperglycemia-related malformations, and examines possible pathogenic mechanisms of embryopathy, with special regard to the function of the yolk sac and the transport of nutrients and antioxidants from mother to embryo.

EPIDEMIOLOGY OF DIABETES-RELATED BIRTH DEFECTS

Statistical analyses reveal a shift in the percentages of assigned causes of infant deaths and demonstrates that the contribution made by congenital malformations is formidable and has now become a recognized public health problem (1–3). Maternal diabetes mellitus is one of the known causes of congenital malformations, which, at the present time, account for about one-half of the perinatal mortality among offspring of diabetic women (11,22,43,54,103). Before the discovery of insulin, the outcome of diabetic pregnancies was extremely poor. In fact, Duncan in 1882 (104) reported a dismal picture of rapid death for both mother and fetus, with a perinatal mortality rate of 70% and maternal mortality in the range of 30% to 40% (105). After the introduction of insulin, maternal mortality rates declined precipitously, but the perinatal mortality rate declined very slowly, eventually reaching the present rate of 4% to 13% (9,16,17,41,103,106–110). This decline in mortality as well as morbidity is thought to result from a combination of improved protocols for insulin administration, centralization of care, and aggressive perinatal/neonatal management (21,22,103,111,112). Unfortunately, the incidence of congenital malformations among IDMs has not changed and, at the present time, accounts for a relatively greater proportion of morbidity and mortality of IDMs than previously (2,18,35–39,43,105,106,108,110, 113,114).

The first association between congenital malformations and diabetes in pregnancy is credited to LeCorche in 1885 (115). Since that time, there has been controversy regarding the incidence and potential causes of anomalous development. In the preinsulin and early insulin periods, White (116) reported that the diabetes-related malformation rate was 3.4%, a figure she later recognized was understated (117–119). In a personal discussion that one of us (E.A.R.) had with Dr. White a few years before her death, she recalled noting an increased malformation rate in offspring of diabetics, even in the early to mid-1920s. Although the association between maternal diabetes and birth defects was recognized, the magnitude and potential causality were not appreciated until Mølsted-Pedersen et al. (6) demonstrated that the incidence of malformations was three times higher than in the nondiabetic population.

The results of the Perinatal Collaborative Project derived from hospitals throughout the United States were reported

by Chung and Myrianthopoulos in 1975 (42), in which they analyzed 47,000 nondiabetic pregnancies, 372 pregnancies of women with gestational diabetes mellitus (GDM) and 577 pregnancies complicated by overt diabetes, and demonstrated that 17% of the infants of mothers with overt diabetes and 8.4% of those of nondiabetic women had malformations. However, the malformation rate in the offspring of the nondiabetic mother was higher than is usually seen in other series. It is possible that minor malformations were included. In any event, the difference was statistically significant. In 1976, Soler et al. (106) reported having studied 701 diabetic pregnancies between 1950 and 1974, whereas Drury et al. (10) reported 300 diabetic pregnancies studied between 1969 and 1976. They found malformation rates of 8% and 6.4%, respectively, in IDMs, compared with 1% to 2% in the general population (10,106). In Scandinavia, slightly lower malformation rates have been reported in pregnancies complicated by diabetes (19,21,22), whereas in the United States, the incidence of malformations varies considerably, from almost 20% in the Atlanta Birth Defect Case Control study (120) to nearly normal levels in a recent study of prepregnancy control in California (103). In most studies, however, the frequency of malformations observed during the neonatal period among IDMs ranges from 4% to 13% (9,16,17,40,41,49,57,103, 106–110,121,122).

The issue of GDM being associated with congenital anomalies is controversial (14,40,123,124). Prospective studies have suggested the possibility of increased rates of malformations in offspring of women with GDM (10,40). Adashi et al. (124) in an 18-month study surveyed 113 diabetic pregnancies: 81 diet-controlled women with GDM, 6 women with insulin-requiring GDM, and 26 women with pregestational type 1 diabetes. The rate of congenital malformation was 5.3% in the diet-controlled GDM group, compared with no malformations in offspring of women with either GDM or pregestational diabetes receiving insulin (124). Several other studies, however, do not support this increased rate of structural anomalies (18,40,42). Hadden (18) reported comparable rates of anomalies between women with GDM and the general population. Other studies also report the lack of increased risk of fetal abnormalities in infants of mothers with GDM (40,42). It is possible that the results of the former study are somewhat skewed because of the few women with type 1 diabetes.

TYPES OF BIRTH DEFECTS
Structural Abnormalities

There is great diversity in the types of malformations observed among IDMs, and analysis of collected data from many centers reveal no diabetes-specific anomalies (23,25, 26,35,37–41,43,51,54,125–129). These defects appear to be indistinguishable from malformations related to other

TABLE 13-2. CONGENITAL ANOMALIES IN IDMS

Skeletal and central nervous system
  Caudal regression syndrome
  Neural tube defects excluding anencephaly
  Anencephaly with or without herniation of neural elements
  Microcephaly
Cardiac
  Transportation of the great vessels with or without
    ventricular septal defect
  Ventricular septal defects
  Coarctation of the aorta with or without ventricular septal or
    patent ductus arteriosus
  Atrial septal defects
  Cardiomegaly
Renal anomalies
  Hydronephrosis
  Renal agenesis
  Ureteral duplication
Gastrointestinal
  Duodenal atresia
  Anorectal atresia
  Small left colon syndrome
Other
  Single umbilical artery

From Reece EA, Hobbins JC. Diabetic embryopathy: pathogenesis, prenatal diagnosis and prevention. *Obstet Gynecol Surv* 1986;41:325, with permission.

genetic or environmental causes (130). Despite these data, some authors have erroneously suggested that caudal regression syndrome or sacral agenesis was pathognomonic of a diabetes-induced malformation (16,43,54).

Diabetes-related malformations are typically major anomalies, which often involve multiple organs, causing disability or death (40,42,51,75). The most frequent types of malformations found in IDMs involve the central nervous system (CNS) and cardiovascular, gastrointestinal, genitourinary, and skeletal systems (40–42,51) (Table 13-2).

Malformations of the Central Nervous System

Neural axis malformations constitute a significant proportion of abnormalities of IDMs (1,6,40–42,57,131–135). The most common types in this group are anencephaly, acrania, meningocele, meningomyelocele, arrhinencephaly, microcephaly, and holoprosencephaly. Malformations of the CNS can involve any aspect of the neural axis (7,40–43,57,132–137). Some authors report a much higher incidence of anencephaly than meningocele: Kucera (41) noted a 6:1 ratio, whereas Chung and Myrianthopoulos (42) found an 8:1 ratio. Barr et al. (136) and Miller et al. (57) observed holoprosencephaly, a relatively rare defect, to be increased in IDMs. The overall incidence of neural tube defects among offspring of type 1 diabetic women is considerably higher than in nondiabetic individuals (134). Mills (43) reported a threefold difference, whereas Milun-

sky (134) found a 20-fold increase among IDMs. Zacharias et al. (135) reported, in a predominantly black indigent inner-city population, that the incidence of neural tube defects among diabetic offspring was significantly higher than in nondiabetic individuals. These various studies demonstrate that neural tube defects are increased in pregnancies complicated by diabetes irrespective of the socioeconomic status or ethnic background of the populations studied.

Cardiac Anomalies

There is a general agreement that an increased incidence of cardiac anomalies occurs among offspring of women with type 1 diabetes (25,41,43,51,138–144). The types of malformations vary with different studies. The most frequent types of cardiac anomalies seen are ventricular septal defect, transposition of the great vessels, coarctation of the aorta, single ventricle, hypoplastic left ventricle, and pulmonic valve atresia (6,25,41,43,51,127,138–145). Mølsted-Pedersen et al. (6) demonstrated a direct relationship between the overall rate of congenital heart disease in IDMs and an increasing degree of maternal vascular complications. Neave (127), in a prospective study, documented a positive correlation between the severity of malformations and the duration of maternal diabetes mellitus. Rowland et al. (139) reported an incidence of congenital heart disease of approximately 4% in a series of 470 IDMs. This represents a fivefold higher incidence than that seen in the general population (8 per 1,000). Mølsted-Pedersen et al. (6) found an incidence of only 1.7% in a series of 853 IDMs. Diversity in the various types of cardiac malformations has also been reported (6). For example, Rowland et al. (139) noted that 50% of the cardiac anomalies were a transposition of the great vessels, ventricular septal defect, and coarctation of the aorta, whereas Herre and Horky (138) found 73% of congenital heart disease being accounted for by aortic abnormalities (138,139). Kucera (41) and Mills (43) reported an increased frequency of situs inversus, whereas Driscoll (145) and Mølsted-Pedersen et al. (6) showed ventricular septal defect to be the most common single cardiac anomaly.

Despite these diversities in the type and incidence of cardiac anomalies, the overall rate of occurrence is significantly higher than in the general population.

Renal Anomalies

An increased rate of genitourinary anomalies among IDMs was first noted by Kucera (41). The most frequent types of renal anomalies are renal agenesis, multicystic kidney, double ureters, and hydronephrosis (41,43,129,146). These anomalies may exist alone or in combination with other abnormalities such as Potter facies, duodenal atresia, and Meckel's diverticulum (146).

Skeletal Anomalies

The most frequent types of skeletal anomalies are sacral hypoplasia and agenesis, hypoplastic limbs, and pes equinovarus (7,40,41,43,51,145,147). Sacral agenesis is a rare condition, first described by Hohl in 1857 (148). This malformation, although occurring at a higher frequency in the offspring of diabetic women, does occur in infants of nondiabetic mothers as well (147). In this light, as noted above, sacral agenesis cannot be considered pathognomonic for diabetes-induced malformations. Welch and Aterman (147) indicated that confusion exists with regard to the etiology and identity of this well-known syndrome. They concluded that caudal regression syndrome is influenced by at least two factors: a maternal tendency toward diabetes and the effect of a specific human leukocyte antigen (HLA) allele. This conclusion was based on the observation of this syndrome occurring in IDMs and also in a familial pattern in nondiabetic pregnancies as well (147). These skeletal anomalies are often part of a group of defects involving multiple organs (149).

Other Anomalies

Single umbilical artery occurs in about 6.4% of IDMs, representing a five-fold increase over that seen in the general population (129,150). This malformation, however, occurs in offspring of both diabetic and nondiabetic mothers and is associated with structural anomalies including polydactyly, vertebral anomalies, clubfoot, and multiple anomalies of the heart and great vessels (125,150).

Polyhydramnios commonly occurs in pregnant women with diabetes. This condition can be associated with CNS and gastrointestinal abnormalities (6,13,129). The etiology of polyhydramnios is unclear. However, suggested pathogenic mechanisms include increased osmolality, decreased fetal swallowing, high gastrointestinal tract obstructions, and fetal polyuria secondary to fetal hyperglycemia. Experimental work, however, has not provided strong evidence for any of these explanations (129).

Functional Abnormalities

Results of neurologic follow-up studies of IDMs have been controversial (128,151–162). Altered intellectual or psychomotor behavior in later adult life has been screened for intensely, with very diverse results. Several reports have suggested that IDMs may show signs of impaired intellectual or psychomotor development (151–155,160,161). Yssing (153) and Hayword et al. (154) found a high incidence of cerebral handicaps, and Churchill et al. (151) reported that in mothers whose pregnancies were complicated by acetonuria, intellectual impairment was more likely to be observed in the offspring. A prospective study by Stephens et al. (155) also found an increase in intellectual delay at 3

and 5 years of age in IDMs whose mothers had acetonuria. Petersen et al. (160) examined 4-year-old children of diabetic mothers and found affected development (Denver Developmental Screening Tests) in 11 of 34 children who had experienced growth delay during the first 8 to 14 weeks of pregnancy. By contrast, only 4 of the 50 children with no history of early growth delay showed affected development (160).

There are also several negative reports failing to demonstrate any alteration in the psychomotor or intellectual development of the children of diabetic mothers compared with normal mothers (156–159). Naeye (128) demonstrated no difference in IQ between offspring of diabetic and nondiabetic mothers. A follow-up study by Persson and Gentz (158) conducted from 1969 to 1972 in offspring of women with type 1 diabetes and GDM women reported that the neuropsychological development in both groups of infants was within normal limits. Neither group found a correlation between intellectual status and White classification, gestational age, or insulin requirements of the mother during pregnancy (128,158).

A relationship between the IQ of the child and maternal levels of ketone bodies in the two last trimesters has been demonstrated (162,163). Rizzo et al. (163) investigated the effect of maternal metabolism in pregnancies complicated by diabetes on the cognitive and behavioral function of 223 offspring. They found that the children's mental developmental indices and Stanford–Binet scores at 2 years of age correlated inversely with third-trimester plasma β-hydroxybutyrate levels, although they were within normal limits. The above differences among investigations may be accounted for, in part, by the fact that maternal serum ketone concentrations remained below the threshold for ketonuria as reflected in the results of earlier studies. Experimentally, a good model does not exist for assessing fetal behavioral changes in pregnancies complicated by diabetes. In the only published study to date, there were only marginal and transient signs of disturbed behavior in the offspring of manifestly diabetic rats (164).

It has been suggested that functional abnormalities may occur even in the absence of structural anomalies. Widness et al. (165) found a 30% increase in the level of erythropoietin in a fairly large series of IDMs, whereas Perrine et al. (166) reported a consistent delay in the switch from μ-globin to β-globin. These latter findings may be related to suppression of γ-globin gene expression (166). These observations are relatively new and may provide insight into important developmental mechanisms at the molecular level.

From the aforementioned description, several conclusions can be made regarding diabetes-related anomalies: most organ systems are involved structurally or functionally; there are no diabetes-specific malformations; and developmental disturbances occur during organogenesis.

PATHOGENESIS

Clinical and Experimental Observations

Many etiologic factors have been proposed regarding the mechanism of diabetes-related birth defects. This phenomenon is complicated by the fact that diabetes is not a simple disorder of carbohydrate metabolism but, rather, involves the impairment of lipid and protein metabolism as well.

At the present time, the metabolic alterations associated with hyperglycemia and occurring during early embryonic development are considered the major teratogens (40,42,49–51,58—60,121,167–173). Indeed, several clinical reports have suggested that hyperglycemia acts as a primary teratogen (8,34). This is inferred from clinical demonstrations of a positive correlation between maternal glycosylated hemoglobin (HbA1c) levels in early pregnancy and fetal malformation rate (16,17,26,34,55, 57,112,174–180), and the decreased rate of fetal dysmorphogenesis achieved by intensified control of the maternal diabetic state during this time period (179,181–184). Experimental results support this notion of hyperglycemia as a teratogen, since high glucose levels, (63,185) or maternal diabetes *in vivo*, (59,60,63,69,74,81,92,94,95, 99,164,170,173,185–223) as well as exposure to high glucose concentration (65,66,69,73,84,86,87,90,93,96,100, 102,224–233) or diabetic serum (53,62,66,81,91,231, 234–242) *in vitro* cause embryonic maldevelopment.

Multifactorial analysis of maternal parameters in the pregnant diabetic rat has shown a correlation between maternal levels of glucose, ketone bodies (β-hydroxybutyrate), branched chain amino acids and adverse embryo outcome (malformation and resorption rates) (63). Furthermore, *in vitro* studies indicate that diabetic serum is teratogenic to rodent embryos even when the glucose level is normal (53,62,240,241).

It has also been shown that diabetic pregnant women with a minimal elevation in HbA1c levels still have an increased risk for offspring with congenital malformations, and that the risk is not related to the HbA1c concentration (34,61). Furthermore, several studies have indicated that metabolites other than glucose (e.g., lactate, pyruvate, ketone bodies, several amino acids, glycerol, and free fatty acids) may be altered in diabetic individuals, despite normoglycemia (243–252). The conclusion from these studies is that hyperglycemia may be a major teratogen in diabetic pregnancy and that alterations in several maternal and fetal metabolites (i.e., β-hydroxybutyrate and BCAA) are additional teratogens.

It has been suggested that in some cases hypoxemia due to vascular disease may exist, further complicating the already present metabolic alterations (6). The findings of both clinical and experimental studies have led to the current belief that diabetes-related malformations result from a disruption of developmental processes during organogenesis by metabolic perturbations, primarily hyperglycemia

(49,87,111,121,122,171,228–230,253–257). Mills et al. (54), using a developmental morphologic dating system of each organ primarily involved in diabetes-related anomalies, demonstrated that these birth defects occur before the 7th week of pregnancy.

HbA_{1c} is expressed as the percentage of total hemoglobin A and provides an integrated retrospective index of glycemic status over the 4 to 8 weeks preceding its determination (258). The introduction of HbA_{1c} has permitted investigators to confirm the presence of hyperglycemia during very early gestation (55,57). Miller et al. (57) and Leslie et al. (55) reported a significantly higher incidence of major congenital anomalies occurring in the offspring of diabetic women who had elevated first-trimester HbA_{1c} levels. These results illustrate that embryos exposed to metabolic derangements during this period of organogenesis are at increased risk for teratogenic insults. The above finding would imply a possible role of nonenzymatic glycosylation of proteins in the induction of malformations. However, experimental work from Sadler and Horton (259) does not support this hypothesis. They found that hyperglycemia produces no significant increase in nonenzymatic glycosylation of embryonic, visceral yolk sac, or serum proteins during the culture period, suggesting that this mechanism is not responsible for hyperglycemia-induced malformations in culture (259). Unfortunately, our understanding of the role of glycosylated proteins is cloudy because so few studies are confined to the critical period of organogenesis when embryos are most susceptible to insults.

Studies have examined the relationship of hyperglycemia, duration of diabetes, vascular complications, and the White classification with the occurrence of anomalies (6,8,57). Karlsson and Kjellmer (8), in a 10-year study of pregnancies complicated by diabetes, found a higher rate of malformations among patients with hyperglycemia, longstanding diabetes, and diabetic vasculopathy than among those without the above complications. They, along with Mølsted-Pedersen et al. (6), noted an increased incidence of malformations among White classes D through F as compared with White classes A through C. Using glycosylated hemoglobin at the 14th week of pregnancy, Miller et al. (57) observed that the frequency of malformations was correlated not with the White classification but with the degree of glucose control: $HbA_{1c} < 6.9\%$ = 0% anomalies; 7.0% to 8.5% = 5% anomalies; > 10% = 22.4% anomalies. These findings are consistent with Greene et al. (112), who reported a risk of malformations of 3.0% with HbA_1 = 9.3% and 40% with HbA_1 = 14.4%.

Features other than hyperglycemia have been implicated in the teratogenicity of the maternal environment in the pregnancy complicated by diabetes. In clinical studies, near-normalized glucose levels do not completely protect or predict congenital malformations (61). Furthermore, as noted above, recent animal studies have suggested the existence of other maternal teratogens (62), such as elevated β-hydroxybutyrate, triglycerides, and BCAA concentrations (63,73).

It has been suggested that hypoglycemia or hypoglycemic reactions of diabetic women may be causative in the induction of congenital malformations. Human data on this subject are fragmentary (6) because so few controlled studies are available. In a review of the subject, Reece et al. (260) analyzed case reports in the psychiatric literature of anomalous offspring in nondiabetic women receiving insulin shock therapy during pregnancy (7,137). However, later case reports by Impastato et al. (261) found no structural anomalies among the offspring of 19 women who received insulin coma therapy before 10 weeks' gestation.

Findings are also inconclusive when the data specific to diabetes in pregnancy are reviewed. Rowland et al. (139) reported a four-fold increase in heart disease in IDMs when the pregnancy was complicated by hypoglycemia. In contrast to these findings, Mølsted-Pedersen et al. (6) reported that only 8 of 65 diabetic mothers with malformed infants had insulin-related hypoglycemic reactions during the first trimester of pregnancy. Findings by Mølsted-Pedersen et al. (6) are supported by several clinical trials that have demonstrated no increase in the incidence of congenital anomalies despite severe and frequent maternal hypoglycemia (262–264). Furthermore, because frequent hypoglycemic episodes occur in humans rather commonly with tight glucose control and this stringent metabolic control is associated with a decrease in the malformation rate, hypoglycemia is not likely to be a major contributor to the genesis of congenital anomalies in humans.

Hypoglycemia is teratogenic *in vitro*, as evidenced by the malformed embryos resulting from culture in a medium in which the glucose concentration was reduced to less than 2 to 3 mmol/L (36 to 54 mg/dL) (265–268). Data on hypoglycemia and outcome of pregnancy in intact animals are limited. Landauer (269) and Zwilling (270) suggested that insulin (rather than hypoglycemia) would be teratogenic, based on studies in which they injected large doses of insulin into eggs and found skeletal malformations in the chickens. Similar findings in the same animal have been reported by others (271,272). Insulin has also been injected in high doses in pregnant rabbits (273–275) and resulted in congenital malformations. Similar experiments have been performed on mice (276) and rats (274–280) with almost identical results. There also exists a negative experimental *in vivo* study in which no malformations could be demonstrated despite massive insulin doses given to the mother (281). The teratogenic role of insulin in clinical settings is doubtful, as maternal insulin is considered to traverse the placenta very sparingly, and fetal pancreatic β-cells do not elaborate insulin until about 12 weeks of gestation, which is beyond the period of organogenesis (6,282,283).

The question of a genetic contribution to congenital malformations in IDMs has also been raised. Eriksson et al. (198) reported that the frequency of congenital malformations in the offspring of streptozocin-induced diabetic rats

differed among Sprague–Dawley substrains. This difference existed despite similar levels of glycemic control. In the U substrain, a 19% frequency of skeletal malformations and an increased frequency of resorbed fetuses was observed, whereas the H strain showed no skeletal malformations and few resorbed fetuses. More recently, Eriksson et al. (69) studied hybrids from the U and H strains to determine the relative contributions of maternal and fetal genotypes. Offspring of H female rats showed a low frequency of skeletal malformations and resorptions, regardless of embryonic genotype, whereas fetuses of U/U and H/U female rats demonstrated higher malformation and resorption rates. These rates were further increased if the embryos were more than 75% U genotype. Therefore, in the rat model, teratogenicity in the susceptible mother appears to be potentiated by the presence of genetically predisposed embryos (69). In a subsequent study, it was shown that the susceptibility to diabetes-induced congenital malformations in the offspring of U, H, and inbred lines of U rats was associated with a specific isoenzyme of catalase (284), a finding in line with other studies suggesting a role for metabolism of free oxygen radicals in the teratogenicity of diabetic pregnancy.

In contrast to these animal data, human studies have not directly supported a genetic influence in the pathogenesis of diabetic embryopathy. Studies by Chung and Myrianthopoulos (42) from the Perinatal Collaborative Study and by Comess et al. (40) from the Pima Indian study compared the incidences of congenital malformations in offspring of diabetic and nondiabetic fathers. They did not find a statistically significant difference between these two groups, thus suggesting that genes predisposing to diabetes in the father do not result in excess congenital malformations (40,42). These results, along with the diversity in the types of malformations and the absence of repetitive and identical anomalies among siblings, do not support, although they do not entirely exclude, some genetic factor as a major determinant for congenital malformations (40).

Other factors that have been suggested to play a possible role in diabetes-induced teratogenesis include low levels of zinc and other trace metals (285–288), altered metabolism of glycosaminoglycans (217), and increased concentration of somatomedin inhibitors (235,289–293). Examination of these potential factors is still in the experimental stage. Likewise, the importance of changes in uterine blood flow to the conceptus in early (294) and late (170) pregnancy is presently being studied in experimental models.

From the above discussion, it can be concluded that the metabolic derangements related to hyperglycemia are a major contribution to the genesis of congenital malformations. In fact, Fuhrmann et al. (111) studied the effects of strict glucose control before conception and the incidence of neonatal complications. Of 57 infants born to 56 well-controlled mothers, only 1 was born with a fetal cardiac defect, and of 420 diabetic pregnant women (292 received treatment after 8 weeks of gestation and 128 before conception), prepregnancy glucose control resulted in a significant reduction in the rate of birth defects from 7.5% to 0.8% (111). Kitzmiller et al. (103), in a California-based study, confirmed the results of Fuhrmann et al. (111) and concluded that the prevention of marked hyperglycemia in the beginning of pregnancy by intensive management before conception reduces the frequency of major congenital anomalies among IDMs to that of the nondiabetic population. Similar findings have been reported by several other investigators (21,22,55–57,61,112,180,295,296).

These data support the concept that hyperglycemia is teratogenic. However, the actual mechanism and the target site of hyperglycemia have not been elucidated by these clinical studies. These studies point to (a) the need for detailed investigations to be performed during the critical period when malformations occur, and (b) the likelihood that the etiology and pathogenesis of malformations will be best learned from animal experimentation because of the obvious limitations for such studies being performed in humans.

EXPERIMENTAL ETIOLOGIC STUDIES

Experimental teratology dates back to the work of Hale (297) in 1933 who used dietary manipulations to induce congenital malformations. This work represents the first controlled and successful induction of congenital malformations in mammals and led to the evolution of a new field. Many investigators have used different agents and different species to induce malformations similar to those seen in humans (2,3,298).

Alloxan was the first drug used to induce diabetes in rodents. Fujimoto et al. (299) reported a high incidence of congenital anomalies and a high rate of embryo resorption in rabbits with alloxan-induced diabetes. Barashnev (300) demonstrated a time dependency in which malformations of the brain were noted only when alloxan was administered to rabbits between pregnancy days 2 and 9. The brain was reduced in weight and size, the cortex was thinner, and there was underdevelopment of the vascular network. Retarded growth of the brain capillaries was present even when the brain weight, size, and external appearance were not different from controls. He concluded that pregnancies occurring in association with a slight but persistent disturbance in carbohydrate metabolism could lead to either fetal death or fetuses with brain maldevelopment (300). This period of embryonic vulnerability was further confirmed by other investigators (58–60,168). Similar studies in rodents showed high incidences of malformations of the skeletal system, heart, and eyes as well as increased mortality of the offspring (193,301,302). Endo (195), using mice with alloxan-induced diabetes, found an increased incidence of polyploidy, aneuploidy, and chromosomal breaks in malformed offspring. They also found similar results in the blastocysts of diabetic mice (195).

The major criticism with the model of drug-induced diabetes in animals is the possibility that the embryonic malformation may be due either to the drug itself or to the drug-induced diabetic condition (303). Other investigators consider these agents, which induce diabetes, to be unlikely teratogens because of their short half-life. For example, the half-life of alloxan is about 2 to 5 minutes. Some groups have used streptozocin because it is presumed to have fewer side effects than does alloxan (65,196,231,240,303).

In one study, glucose was infused in rats to stimulate the hyperglycemic state of diabetes. However, these experiments were performed toward the latter part of pregnancy. Because the period of teratogenic vulnerability is in early pregnancy, it was not surprising that these investigators did not find an increased rate of malformations (304). However, when glucose was infused into the amniotic cavity during early gestation, malformations were observed (305). Several other hexoses have also been shown to cause malformations, although the teratogenic effects of glucose seem to be specific for the D-form. Reece et al. (229,230,255–257) have shown that the teratogenicity at increased glucose concentrations is independent of its osmolality and is related to a direct effect of the aberrant metabolic fuel. Several other investigators have supported this view (65,74,171,306–308).

Conversely, Horii et al. (309) found a significant reduction in congenital malformations and fetal mortality rate when insulin was used to treat mice with alloxan-induced diabetes. Subsequently, several investigators emphasized the importance of good metabolic control as a method of preventing embryopathy (50,58,190).

Other investigators have examined the potential teratogenic role of insulin, which remains controversial. Landauer (306) reported an increased incidence of "rumplessness," and Duraiswami (310) found a high rate of skeletal abnormalities in chickens exposed to insulin. However, they concluded that fetal maldevelopment is probably related to hyperglycemia and not to the ambient insulin concentration. Interestingly, Sadler and Horton (266) used insulin in mouse embryo culture at concentrations 500 times above a physiologic range and found no evidence of teratogenesis. It has also been shown that when rats fasted during organogenesis, fetal resorption and malformation rates increased, but this phenomenon was preventable by the supplementation of glucose and amino acids during this period (298). Therefore, the association of starvation and teratogenesis may involve deficiency of glucose or other essential substrates, or even conditions involving ketonemia. Although maternal insulin does not gain access to the fetus since it does not cross the fully developed placenta, the influence of circulating maternal insulin on the embryo and other extraembryonic membranes (e.g., through the yolk sac) during organogenesis remains unknown.

More recently, investigators have begun using spontaneously diabetic rodents in their studies of diabetic malformations. In mice, several strains are known to be spontaneously diabetic. However, they are not suitable for this type of study because they are infertile or have a high resorption rate. In 1978, Nakhooda et al. (311) first reported a spontaneously diabetic Wistar rat strain in Canada. Brownscheidle and Davis (312) and Marliss et al. (313) studied fetal malformations in the biobreeding (BB) diabetic rat and reported a 2.3% incidence of gross malformations, primarily exencephaly, anophthalmia, microphthalmia, and skeletal malformations (314). They also found that malformations occurred only when the mother was diabetic. Funaki and Mikamo (200) reported that in their colony of Chinese hamsters, the frequency of diabetes was 4.1%, and diabetes developed in 90% of the inbred generations. This group conducted an extensive, sequential study during early development from ovulation, fertilization, cleavage, and implantation to organogenesis and found no decrease in the number of ovulated eggs before implantation. However, there was a significant increase in embryonic death and gross malformations. They concluded that maternal diabetes has a deleterious effect on embryonic development during organogenesis and also causes reduced fetal growth in later developmental stages (200).

For both ethical and scientific reasons, animal experimentation is the obvious method for studying teratogenesis. However, experimentation performed under *in vivo* conditions does not permit the evaluation of separate and independent maternal influences, because several alterations in the maternal milieu act simultaneously on the conceptus. Thus, understanding the effect of independent factors is difficult. The reintroduction of the rodent conceptus culture by New (315,317–320) in 1967 revolutionized experimental teratology. This novel experimental model eliminates many complicating factors. The experimental conditions during the exposure time are precise, and absence of the maternal milieu makes the conceptus more accessible to direct observation, manipulation, and possible treatment. Currently, rat and mouse embryos can be grown in culture during the period of organogenesis with better success than other mammalian species (65,66,69,73,74,84,87,88,95,102,193,196, 228–231,240,254,259,266,303,315,316).

Deuchar (193), in one of the earliest experiments using *in vitro* culture, studied the influence of hyperglycemia on embryo development. Serum was obtained from rats made diabetic by streptozocin induction, 10-day-old embryos were cultured on watch glass covers, and no deleterious embryonic developmental effects were observed. In fact, there was "better growth" than was seen in controls (193).

Sadler (321) used whole mouse embryos at different embryonic stages of development (two to three somites and four to six somites). These embryos were cultured for 24 hours in serum obtained from rats with diabetes induced by streptozocin of differing severity. He found that embryos grown in serum from severely diabetic rats demonstrated a 60% to 90% malformation rate, whereas 28% of embryos grown in serum from moderately diabetic animals manifested malformations. Greater susceptibility toward malformations was seen in younger embryos of two to three somites (321). Several investigators studied the effect of hyperglycemia during organogenesis on rodent embryos by the addition of D-

glucose to the incubation medium and culture for 48 hours. They found the rate of malformations to be associated with increasingly elevated glucose levels in the culture medium (65–67,69,73,84,87,95,102,228–230,240).

Diverse additional factors shown to be associated with diabetic malformations have also been investigated. The suspected role of ketone bodies in diabetes-related malformations has been tested in embryo culture, where those compounds have been shown to be teratogenic (69,74,76, 77,79,80,82–84). It was also documented that synergism existed between subteratogenic levels of glucose and β-hydroxybutyrate added to the culture medium (77). Somatomedin inhibitors are found in high concentration in streptozocin-induced diabetic rats and are now being considered also as a possible teratogen (291). Sadler et al. (235), using a whole-embryo rodent culture model, were able to demonstrate that the presence of the low-molecular-weight fraction of somatomedin inhibitors was associated with an increased incidence of malformations and impaired growth.

A more recent hypothesis for the mechanism of diabetic embryopathy has been put forth by Eriksson and Borg (73,84). They have postulated that increased free oxygen radical formation is causally related to diabetes-related malformations. Support for this hypothesis comes mainly from evidence that free-oxygen-radical–scavenging enzymes are protective against glucose-induced malformations. They cultured rat embryos in media containing 10 mM of glucose to serve as controls, 50 mM of glucose (a concentration capable of producing a major malformation rate of 81%), or 50 mM glucose plus the oxygen-scavenging enzyme superoxide dismutase (SOD), catalase, or glutathione peroxidase. The addition of catalase or glutathione peroxidase to the culture media lowered malformation rates but did not return them to normal, whereas the addition of SOD returned the rate of malformations to those of the controls (73).

Using the postimplantation rat model, Eriksson and Borg (84) demonstrated the protective effect of free-oxygen-radical–scavenging enzymes in regard to malformations produced by hyperglycemia, β-hydroxybutyrate, and alpha-ketoisocaproate. The addition of SOD to the hyperglycemic medium protected against the teratogenic effects of all three agents (84). The addition of the pyruvate transport inhibitor α-cyano-4-hydroxycinnamic acid, however, provided significant protection only against the malformations induced by glucose and pyruvate, suggesting that free oxygen radicals, considered to be responsible for teratogenesis, are produced in the mitochondria because these hexoses are oxidized in the mitochondria. The authors offered the hypothesis that embryos in a diabetic milieu are exposed to too much oxidative substrate and have too little mitochondrial capacity to handle the increased load of free oxygen radicals. Furthermore, the authors proposed that increased free oxygen radical activity leads to enhanced lipid peroxidation, and this, in turn, causes an imbalance in prostaglandin synthesis. This concept provides a plausible linkage of excess production of free oxygen radicals with the myoinositol (MI)-(AA)/prostaglandin aberrant fuel phenomenon.

The notion that diabetes is associated with oxidative stress has been suggested by several authors (322–326). Increased lipid peroxidation and reactive oxygen species (ROS) generation were found in diabetic rats, measured as increased serum F2-isoprostane levels (327), and increased electron spin clearance rate (328). Both of these indicators of oxidative stress were normalized by vitamin E treatment of the diabetic rats (327,328). Cyclic voltammetric studies have indicated increased levels of lipid peroxidation in diabetic rats (329), and it has recently been demonstrated that mitochondria of vascular endothelial cells produce excess amounts of superoxide in response to hyperglycemia (330,331). Diminishing this overproduction of ROS via inhibition of electron transport, by uncoupling oxidative phosphorylation, or by addition of SOD, blocked other markers of intracellular imbalance, such as activation of protein kinase C, formation of advanced glycation end products, sorbitol accumulation, and NF-kB activation. Furthermore, embryos subjected to high glucose concentration show evidence of increased superoxide production, as measured in a Cartesian diver system (332).

In a subsequent study, an increased F2-isoprostane (8-*epi*-PGF2 alpha) concentration was found in embryonic tissue exposed to hyperglycemia *in vitro* and diabetes *in vivo* (333). This finding suggests an embryonic increase in lipid peroxidation rate that can be blocked by antioxidative treatment utilizing N-acetyl cysteine (NAC).

Adding scavenging enzymes, such as SOD, catalase, or glutathione peroxidase, to the culture medium protects rat embryos from dysmorphogenesis induced by high glucose concentrations *in vitro* (73). Teratogenic concentrations of β-hydroxybutyrate or the branched-chain amino acid analogue, alpha-ketoisocaproic acid, can be blocked by addition of SOD to the culture medium (84,102), and addition of SOD or NAC diminishes the dysmorphogenesis caused by diabetic serum (242). In a study of the early development of cranial neural crest cells, it was shown that high glucose inhibited, and NAC normalized, the migration and proliferation of these cells, and that control cells of nonneural crest origin were not affected by either treatment (334). Examination of litters of diabetic rats demonstrated lowered alpha-tocopherol (vitamin E) concentration in day-11 embryos and in the liver of day-20 fetuses (213–215).

High-amplitude mitochondrial swelling was demonstrated in embryonic neuroectoderm of embryos exposed to a diabetic environment (74), a swelling diminished by antioxidative treatment of the mother (219,220), implicating an embryonic ROS imbalance, with conceivable consequences for the rate of apoptosis in susceptible cell lineages in the embryo (335). In addition, fetuses and embryos of diabetic rodents display increased rates of DNA damage (206,207), another indication of enhanced ROS activity in the embryonic tissues.

Direct evidence of ROS excess in embryonic tissue has been difficult to demonstrate. In neuroepithelial cells, mitochondrial swelling results from exposure to a diabetic state *in vivo* or hyperglycemia *in vitro* (74,80). This high-amplitude swelling can be diminished by antioxidant supplementation (219,220). In the neuroectodermal cells, indirect evidence of superoxide production in response to hyperglycemia was found (332). This suggests that long-term exposure to high glucose creates an embryonic ROS excess either from increased ROS production (332), or from diminished antioxidant defense capacity (232,336,337). ROS excess may be relatively small, restricted to particular cell populations, and likely to vary with gestational time and nutritional status, making direct ROS determinations difficult. Nevertheless, a cyclic voltametry measurement of oxidation potential in preimplantation rodent embryos cultured in diabetic serum indicated the presence of ROS excess also at this stage (208).

In summary, despite difficulties in demonstrating ROS in embryos acutely exposed to high glucose, the combined data support the notion that the teratogenic process in the pregnancy complicated by diabetes does involve excess free radicals at a late stage, and, by blocking this excess by antioxidants the diabetes-induced dysmorphogenesis can be substantially diminished.

Abnormalities in intracellular MI and phosphoinositide metabolism have also been implicated in the pathogenesis of diabetic embryopathy. Several investigators (90,93,94, 96–101) demonstrated *in vitro* that increasing concentrations of glucose result in a parallel decrease in the MI concentration in embryos. Conversely, supplementation with MI restores the concentrations to normal values and results in a significant decrease in malformations (386,387). Furthermore, in the report of Hashimoto et al. (96), the malformation rate was reduced from 33% in the hyperglycemic medium to 6% when the *in vitro* medium was supplemented with MI. Studies by Baker et al. (90) and Hod et al. (98) noted similar results.

Khandelwal et al. (338,386,387) have performed the only *in vivo* study with MI to date. They supplemented streptozocin-induced diabetic pregnant rats with daily oral MI or AA. The rats were sacrificed on day 12, and embryos and yolk sacs were examined for evidence of malformations. They found that malformation rates were reduced from 22% to 7% with either MI or AA supplementation. Furthermore, this difference correlated with MI tissue levels in both the embryos and yolk sacs. They concluded that supplementation restores the membrane phospholipid integrity that is depleted by hyperglycemia.

A brief summary of neural tube development is presented below, as this is one of the most common forms of malformations, and serves as useful background information before a detailed discussion at the cellular level.

NORMAL DEVELOPMENT OF THE NEURAL TUBE AND YOLK SAC

During organogenesis, when organ primordia are being formed, the conceptus is most susceptible to teratogenic insults. The CNS is the first organ primordium formed and one of the most frequently affected by teratogens.

The original description of nervous system development dates back to the 19th century. However, crucial events of neurulation are still not well understood (339,340). In vertebrates, neural tube development begins by formation of a groove in the endoderm that later widens and thickens to form a neural plate. Subsequently, folding occurs toward the midline with eventual fusion or closure. Other elements forming neural tissue are neural crest cells and epidermal placodes (339). The process of neurulation involves changes in cell shape and surface molecules producing cell adhesions (341,342). There are relatively few mitotic cells in the neural plate at this stage, and proliferation is not a major factor in neurulation. Immediately after closure of the neural tube, rapid and disproportionate cell proliferation occurs, leading to the formation of the forebrain, midbrain, and hindbrain vesicles. The walls of the recently closed neural tube consist of neuroepithelial cells, which are primitive nerve cells or neuroblasts. In a transverse section of the neural tube during organogenesis, three cell layers are present: the innermost layer, close to the lumen, is the matrix or ventricular layer; next is the mantle layer; and the outermost layer is the marginal layer. Mitosis occurs in the matrix layer, with the daughter cells entering into the matrix and mantle layers. The axons of these cells grow into the marginal layer (343). The cells that make up the neuroepithelium are the epithelial, neuroglia, and nerve cells.

Throughout intrauterine life, the embryo/fetus is dependent on its extraembryonic membranes, which are derivatives of the blastocyst wall. Early studies have provided evidence that the rodent yolk sac is an important site of transport of nutrients and gases between mother and embryo during embryogenesis (344–348). Payne and Deuchar (349) examined the importance of the various yolk sac layers and demonstrated that only the visceral endodermal yolk sac layer was essential for normal growth and development. The *in vitro* culture system itself proved that an intact visceral yolk sac layer is essential for the success of the culture (315,317–320).

Reece et al. (256) proposed that before organogenesis, the newly implanted embryo receives its nutrients via a so-called histotrophic route (87,350,351) (Fig. 13-1). During organogenesis, there is a dramatic change in the route of nutrition with the establishment of the first circulation (vitelline circulation) that provides the means for a hemotrophic type of nutrition (87,256,350,351). Furthermore, in this period of development, the yolk sac provides protection, transport of nutrients, the site of origin of blood cells and vessels, germ cell primordia, and epithelia of the respiratory and digestive tracts (342,346–357). Ultrastructural studies have shown that the visceral endodermal yolk sac cells are typical absorptive epithelial cells with a brush border on the apical surface (229,356–359). These cells contain abundant rough endoplasmic reticulum indicative of active protein synthesis for export and possibly for use by the developing embryo (87,229,352,356–359). The many mitochondria present in these cells suggest that intense oxidative phosphorylation occurs, which provides a source of energy (86,228,351–353). The supranuclear region of these visceral endodermal yolk sac cells contains lysosome-like structures, coated pits, and vesicles, whereas the intranuclear region contains large stored lipid droplets (87,230,358) (Figs. 13-2 and 13-3).

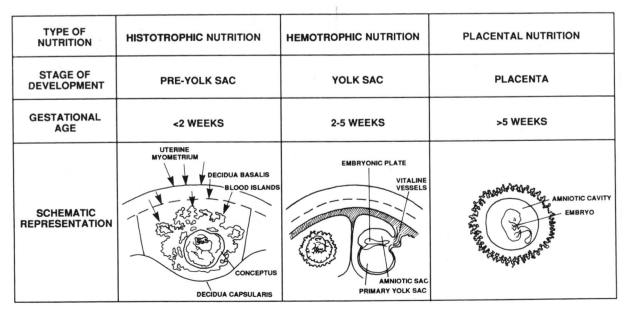

TYPE OF NUTRITION	HISTOTROPHIC NUTRITION	HEMOTROPHIC NUTRITION	PLACENTAL NUTRITION
STAGE OF DEVELOPMENT	PRE-YOLK SAC	YOLK SAC	PLACENTA
GESTATIONAL AGE	<2 WEEKS	2-5 WEEKS	>5 WEEKS
SCHEMATIC REPRESENTATION			

FIGURE 13-1. Schematic representation of the stages of yolk sac development and early developmental nutrition. (From Reece EA, Pinter E, Homko C, et al. The yolk sac theory: closing the circle on why diabetes associated malformations occur. J Soc Gynecol Invest 1994;1:3, with permission.)

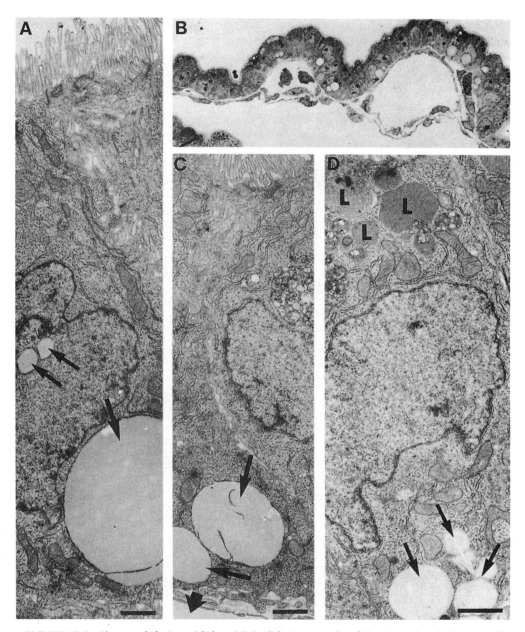

FIGURE 13-2. Electron **(A)**, **C**, and **(D)** and light **(B)** micrographs of the visceral endodermal yolk sac layer of conceptuses grown in utero (pregnancy day 12). This layer shows a wave-like surface appearance with underlying vitelline vessels and mesothelium **(B)**. The apical part of these endodermal cells contain lysosome-like structures, and the basal part contains many lipid droplets **(B)**. The visceral endodermal cells possess slender microvilli, several mitochondria, free ribosomes, a rich network of rough endoplasmic reticulum in **(A)**, **C**, **(D)** and lysosome-like structures (L). *Arrows* in **(A)**, **C**, **(D)** point out the lipid droplets in the subnuclear region and in the nucleus. The underlying capillary is shown by a *thick arrowhead* in **(C)**. The basal cell surface has many finger-like projections in **(A)** and **(C)**. Bar scale in **(A)**, **C**, and **(D)**: 1 µm. Original magnification of **(B)**: ×40. (From Pinter E, Reece EA, Leranth CZ, et al. Yolk sac failure in embryopathy due to hyperglycemia: ultrastructural analysis of yolk sac differentiation associated with embryopathy in rat conceptuses under hyperglycemic conditions. *Teratology* 1986;33:73, with permission.)

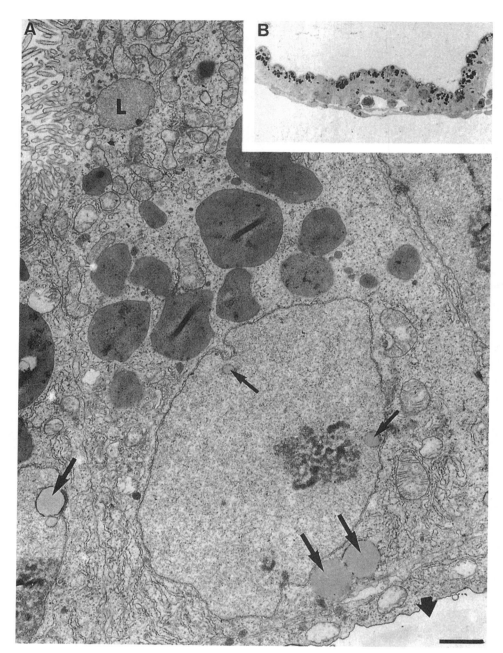

FIGURE 13-3. Electron **(A)** and light **(B)** micrographs of the visceral endodermal layer of rat yolk sac from conceptuses cultured from day 10 to 12 in male rat serum. **(B)**The visceral endodermal layer exhibits a wave-like pattern, with underlying capillaries and mesothelium. **(A)**The electron micrograph shows microvIlli and several mitochondria, rich endoplasmic reticulum, free ribosomes and many apical lysosome-like *(L)* structures with varying degrees of electron density. *Arrows* indicate that small lipid droplets at the base of the cell and in the nucleus. An *arrowhead* shows the capillary lumen **(A)**. Bar scale in **(A)**: 1 μm. Original magnification of **(B)**: ×40. (From Pinter E, Reece EA, Leranth CZ, et al. Yolk sac failure in embryopathy due to hyperglycemia: ultrastructural analysis of yolk sac differentiation associated with embryopathy in rat conceptuses under hyperglycemic conditions. *Teratology* 1986;33:73, with permission.)

The whole embryo culture system has enabled the study of neural tube and yolk sac development during a time that corresponds to postconception weeks 3 to 5 in human gestation (360). Rat embryos are explanted on pregnancy day 9.5 and cultured for 48 hours (87,254,228–230). Examination of conceptuses is performed at the end of culture. Critical events during this period include the establishment of the vitelline circulation; development of the heart, neural tube, face, optic and otic vesicles, and somites; and body rotation (361). These events are consistent, reproducible, and are similar to those observed in conceptuses grown *in vivo* (230,318,360,362,363).

The neural tube is normally closed by the end of the culture period, and normal conceptus development can be seen (Fig. 13-4 and Fig. 13-5). Light microscopic examination reveals an intact three-layered epithelium with a surrounding mesenchymal layer and ectoderm. The cells of the closed neural tube are arranged in palisades, and many of them are located at the luminal surface and show signs of mitotic activity (Fig. 13-6A). Under electron microscopy, these cells appear immature, spherical, and blast-like with scant cytoplasm, large nuclei, and few cell organelles. No cell processes are found in the neuroepithelium (Fig. 13-7).

From the supportive role of the yolk sac during organogenesis, as well as the ultrastructural features of the visceral endodermal yolk sac cells, it seems evident that the yolk sac is a crucial organ to normal embryogenesis (357,359,364). Many major events in the 4th week include formation of the CNS, primitive gut, heart, and vascular systems. A portion of the yolk sac becomes incorporated into the embryo to form the primitive gut, which contributes to the epithelial lining of the esophagus, trachea, bronchial tree, and respiratory surface of the lung. Other derivatives of the yolk sac endoderm include the epithelia of the liver, gallbladder, bile duct, pancreas, duodenum, and small and large intestine. The remaining communication is a slender vascularized stalk between the yolk sac and embryo (350,351). Hasseldahl and Larson (352,355) reported ultrastructural similarities between the liver and the yolk sac. Gitlin et al. (365–367) subsequently showed that the yolk sac in humans has a protein synthetic function before the liver assumes this role. These proteins include an α-fetoprotein, transferrin, α_1-antitrypsin, albumin, ferritin, and apolipoproteins A and B. Furthermore, the human yolk sac is a site of active and early protein production, secreting substantial amounts of apolipoproteins and a wide variety of apolipoproteins during organogenesis (368). Because the visceral endodermal yolk sac cells contain elaborate rough endoplasmic reticulum, it seems reasonable to assume that they are a major site of protein synthesis for embryonic use. Interest has been focused on the protein synthetic function

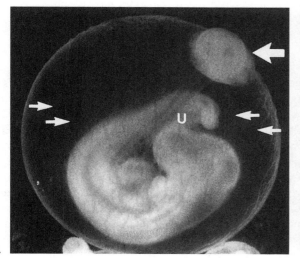
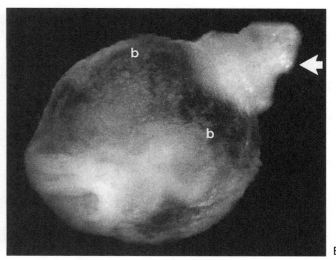

A   B

FIGURE 13-4. Whole mount photographs of conceptuses grown for 2 days in male rat serum, glucose 125 mg/dL **(A)**, or in male rat serum with D-glucose added to a final concentration of 750 mg/dL **(B)**. *Large arrow* points to the electoplacental cone. *Smaller arrows* in **(A)** point to the normal vitelline vessels that course along the fetal (inner) face of the visceral yolk sac and eventually will form the umbilical vessels *(U)*. By contrast, in **(B)**, widely dispersed, hypoplastic vitelline vessels and isolated blood islands *(B)* can be seen through the thickened opaque visceral yolk sac of the excess hyperglycemic treated conceptus. The normal embryo is seen within the visceral yolk sac of the euglycemic treated conceptus in **(A)**. The deformed embryo in the hyperglycemic treated conceptus is seen as a small dense object within the shaggy yolk sac in **(B)**. Original magnification of (A): ×160; (B), ×190. (From Pinter E, Reece EA, Leranth CZ, et al. Yolk sac failure in embryopathy due to hyperglycemia: ultrastructural analysis of yolk sac differentiation associated with embryopathy in rat conceptuses under hyperglycemic conditions. *Teratology* 1986;33:73, with permission.)

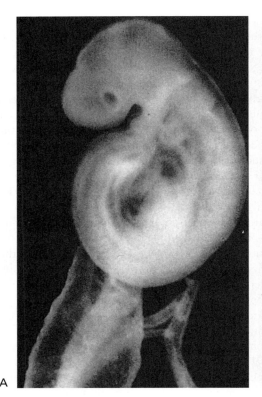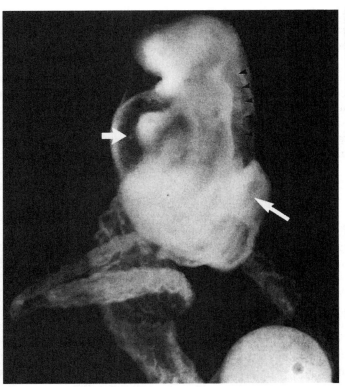

A   B

FIGURE 13-5 (A) A 12-day-old control embryo cultured in male rat serum for 2 days (days 10 to 12). Note the C-shaped form and well-developed structures. **(B)** A 12-day-old embryo cultured in hyperglycemic medium (750 µg/dL). The embryo is malformed and characterized by incomplete body rotation (*long arrow* indicating tail), heart abnormality with pericardial effusion (*broad arrow*), and widely open neural tube (*arrowheads*). The removed yolk sac is seen in **(A)** and **(B)** below the embryo. Magnification: ×200.

of the conceptus during early development (369–377). Shi et al. (368) found that the visceral endodermal yolk sac cells are the earliest intrinsic source of apolipoproteins in mouse embryos. These apolipoproteins are lipid carrier molecules and are also synthesized by the liver and the gut over the period of embryonic development. The epithelial lining of these organs is derived from the endodermal yolk sac cells. The known functions of apolipoproteins include the solubilization of lipids, the recognition and modulation of enzymes involved in lipid metabolism, and the binding of lipoproteins to their cellular receptors. Also, lipoproteins are needed to allow rapid growth of undifferentiated human teratoma cells. This fact raises the possibility that the undifferentiated, rapidly multiplying embryonic cells also have similar requirements (87,230).

ABNORMAL DEVELOPMENT OF THE NEURAL TUBE AND YOLK SAC

Studies of diabetes-related teratogenesis in the laboratories of Reece and Pinter and associates, as well as other investi-

gators, have focused on the mechanism of teratogenesis and possible target sites of action. The postimplantation whole-rat conceptus culture has been used (87,203,228–230,254, 259,315,317–320,360,378,379). Conceptuses cultured in hyperglycemic media are growth restricted and have multiple anomalies (Figs. 13-5B and 13-6B and Table 13-3). The frequency of these malformations is related to the glucose concentration (350 mg/dL, two times normal concentration = 10% to 20% malformations; 750 mg/dL, four times normal concentration = 50% malformations; 950 mg/dL, six times normal concentration = almost 100% malformations). The neural tube demonstrates failure of closure, loss of ordered cellular arrangement, and mitotic cells that are few in number and remote from the luminal surface (Fig. 13-7A). Homogeneous material is present between cells at the site of failed fusion (Fig. 13-2B). Electron microscopic examination of these areas revealed many cell processes containing mitochondria, microtubules, and lipid droplets (Figs. 13-2C and 13-5D). Morphometric analysis demonstrated that the percentage of neural tissue occupied by cell processes (neuropil) is significantly increased and that occupied by the blood vessels was significantly decreased

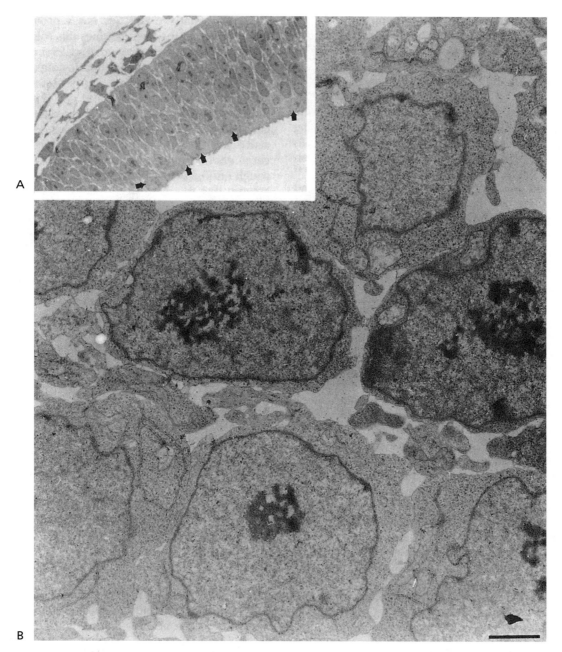

FIGURE 13-6. Light **(A)** and electron **(B)** micrographs of the neuroepithelium of a rat embryo cultured in normal male rat serum between days 10 and 12. The three layers of the neuroepithelium (ependymal, mantle, marginal) and the surrounding mesoderm can be seen. *Arrows* indicate the ependymal surface with cells tightly held together in mitosis. The mantle layer shows cells separated from each other by extracellular spaces. The electron micrograph **(B)** shows profiles with electron dense nuclei, nucleoli, and cytoplasm. The cell membranes are complex with multiple polypoid folds. Short cytoplasmic processes establish intercellular connections. Bar scale: 1 μm. Original magnification of light micrograph: ×40. (From Reece EA, Wu YK. Prevention of diabetic embryopathy in offspring of diabetic rats with use of a cocktail of deficient substrates and an antioxidant. *Am J Obstet Gynecol* 1997;176:790–797, with permission.)

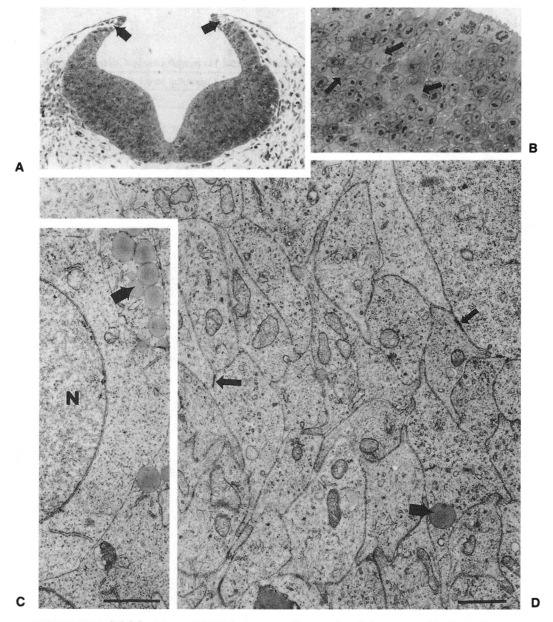

FIGURE 13-7. (A)/(B) Light and **(C)/(D)** electron micrographs of the neuroepithelium of a rat embryo cultured between days 10 and 12 in male rat serum containing added D-glucose (total concentration of 750 mg/dL). **(A)** Cross-section of an open neural tube. Note that the mesenchymal layer attaches to the neuroepithelial cell layer (*arrows*). **(B)** High-power magnification of the neuroepithelium. The neuroblasts are generally round or cuboidal and closely opposed to each other without intervening spaces. *Arrows* indicate cell-free areas containing homogeneous material. **(D)** Electron micrograph demonstrates extensive neuropil formation in the "homogeneous-like" areas indicated with *arrows* on **(B)**. These neural processes contain neurotubules and occasionally some non-membrane-bound apparent lipid droplets (*large arrow*). Between these neural processes are membrane specializations (*small arrows*). **(C)** A pair of cell bodies in detail, one of which contains a less electron-dense nucleus (N) and cytoplasm without projections, as compared with controls. Also, several lipid droplets can be observed in the cytoplasm (*large arrow*). Bar scale: 1 μm. Original magnification: **(A)**, ×10; **(B)**, ×40. (From Reece EA, Wu YK. Prevention of diabetic embryopathy in offspring of diabetic rats with use of a cocktail of deficient substrates and an antioxidant. *Am J Obstet Gynecol* 1997;176:790–797, with permission.)

TABLE 13-3. EVALUATION OF RAT CONCEPTUSES IN CONTROL AND HYPERGLYCEMIC CULTURE CONDITIONS[a]

Culture Conditions	Postincubation Conceptus Size (mm)		Embryos with Malformations
	YSD	CRL	
Group A: D-glucose = 125 mg/dl	x = 5.56	x = 5.06	None
Osmolality = 280 mOsm/kg	SD = 0.733	SD = 0.266	
Group B: D-glucose = 750 mg/dl	x = 4.51	x = 4.31	21 (50%)
Osmolality = 305 mOsm/kg	SD = 0.848	SD = 0.865	
	p < 0.001 (A vs. B)	p < 0.001 (A vs. B)	
Group C: L-glucose = 625 mg/dl	x = 5.19	x = 4.21	None
D-glucose = 125 mg/dl (total glucose = 750 mg/dl)	SD = 0.17	SD = 0.79	
Osmolality = 306 mOsm/kg	p = NS (A vs. C)	p < 0.001 (A vs. C)	

[a]Preincubation conceptus diameter about 1.00 mm, measured in the midregion between the embryonic and ectoplacental cones.
CRL, crown-rump length; YSD, yolk sac diameter.
From Witschi E. Development: prenatal vertebrae development: rat. In: Altman PL, Dittmer DS, eds. *Growth including reproduction and morphological development.* Washington, DC: Federation of American Societies for Experimental Biology, 1962:304, with permission.

(254,380) (Table 13-4) Warkany and Lemire (381) emphasized the development of abnormal vessel formation occurring as early as the 3rd week of pregnancy. The mitochondria of the neural tube in embryos from high-glucose culture media, corresponding to rat gestational age of day 11, display marked high-amplitude swelling (74). This swelling is also present to some degree in other types of embryonic cells, as well as in embryos from diabetic rats of gestational days 9 to 12, whereas it is not present in organs from day 15 fetuses of diabetic rats (74). These results highlight the embryonic mitochondria as an organelle of specific morphologic vulnerability in a diabetic environment.

The findings observed in hyperglycemic conditions are unique, because neuropil formation never occurs before complete neural tube closure. In fact, examination of normal 14-day-old embryos did not reveal the magnitude of neuropil formation that is seen in hyperglycemic conditions (254). This premature specialization that leads to loss of cellular arrangement has resulted in early divergence of neuroepithelial cell precursors. This aberration in cell development may be expected to have functional consequences because the accurate location of neurons and their processes is fundamental to the establishment of the correct patterns of neuronal connections (260,382).

In these experiments, conceptuses grown in hyperglycemic serum are not only decreased in size and malformed but have consistently poor yolk sac and embryonic vessel development (87,230,254) (Figs. 13-5B and 13-6B). The visceral endodermal yolk sac cells show the following ultrastructural alterations: the microvilli are short and broad, the mitochondria are swollen, and there is a marked decrease in rough endoplasmic reticulum. A significant reduction in the number and size of lipid droplets, with a parallel increase in the number and size of lysosome-like structures, is also present (87,230) (Fig. 13-8). These alterations are present only when the D-form of glucose is used, and are absent when L-glucose is added to the culture medium at the same concentration and osmolality (230). In the presence of hyperglycemia (always referring to D-glucose except when stated otherwise), the yolk sac endoderm demonstrates characteristic ultrastruc-

TABLE 13-4. MORPHOMETRIC ANALYSIS OF EMBRYONIC NEUROEPITHELIUM AND YOLK SAC SURFACE IN CONTROL AND EXPERIMENTAL CONDITIONS[a]

Experimental Condition	Neural Tube Surface Occupied by		Yolk Sac Surface Occupied by Blood Vessels
	Blood Vessels (%)	Neuropil (%)	
In vivo control	12.1 ± 1.8	1.5 ± 0.6	46.0 ± 5.0
In vitro control	9.7 ± 0.4	1.5 ± 0.8[b]	9.0 ± 0.9[c]
950 mg/ml D-glucose	3.1 ± 0.1[c]	13.3 ± 2.5[c]	3.9 ± 1.4[c]
950 mg/ml D-glucose + 20 µg/ml arachidonic acid	8.2 ± 0.4[b]	1.5 ± 0.4[b]	23.2 ± 8.2[b]

[a]Data are mean ± SEM from 10 semithin sections evaluated from each embryo and yolk sac.
[b]Value is significantly (p < 0.0001) different from that of experimental group, 950 mg/ml D-glucose.
[c]Value is significantly (p < 0.001) different from that of *in vitro* controls.
From Weibel RE. Stereological principles for morphometry in electron microscopic cytology. *Int Rev Cytol* 1969;26:235, with permission.

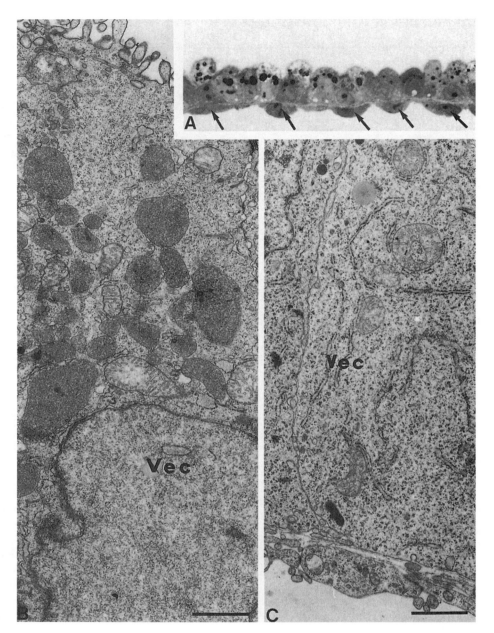

FIGURE 13-8. (A) Light and **(B)/(C)** electron micrographs of the visceral layer of rat yolk sac from an embryo cultured in male rat serum containing D-glucose (total concentration, 750 mg/dL) from day 10 to 12. The embryo had an open neural tube. **(A)** The visceral endodermal cell layer is flat, and in this area, the mesothelial cells (*arrows*) are closely opposed to the endodermal layer without capillary lumens or blood cells. Electron micrographs show the upper **(B)** and basal **(C)** part of visceral endodermal cells. These cells contain scant endoplasmic reticulum, few ribosome rosettes, and dilated mitochondria with lucent matrix. The nucleus contains less electron dense chromatin than in controls. Microvilli are short and thick. Bar scale on **(B)** and **(C)**: 1 μm. Original magnification of **(A)**: ×40. (From Pinter E, Reece EA, Leranth CZ, et al. Yolk sac failure in embryopathy due to hyperglycemia: ultrastructural analysis of yolk sac differentiation associated with embryopathy in rat conceptuses under hyperglycemic conditions. *Teratology* 1986;33:73, with permission.)

tural features of cell injury. These morphologic changes could have resulted from a variety of factors. Usually, in disease states, the cell injury is mediated via an interference in the energy supply to the cell or by damage to cell membranes (383). We found severe impairment in the development of

the yolk sac and embryonic vasculature, along with the presence of mitochondrial swelling, followed by disaggregation of polyribosomes in the rough endoplasmic reticulum, with the latest change being alterations in the lysosomes (381). All these changes were observed in the visceral endodermal yolk sac cells (87,230) (Fig. 13-8). Tentatively, the cell injury described above could occur by deprivation of appropriate oxygen supply with rapid and severe impairment in oxidative phosphorylation and a fall in adenosine triphosphate (ATP) levels with a parallel rise of inorganic phosphorus level, thus activating the glycolytic pathway and leading to the generation of lactic acid (383).

To the best of our knowledge, no information is available on alterations in protein synthetic function of the visceral yolk sac cells in hyperglycemic conditions. However, the significant

decrease in the quantity of rough endoplasmic reticulum in the yolk sac cells could reflect an alteration in protein synthesis with resultant abnormality in embryonic development.

Using scanning electron microscopy, Pinter et al. (229) also found distortion of apical microvilli (Fig. 13-9) and alterations of surface specializations of blood cells (Fig. 13-10). These findings could also reflect altered function of the cytoskeleton associated with an impairment of energy supply, changes in ion movements, and alteration in pH levels (229,384).

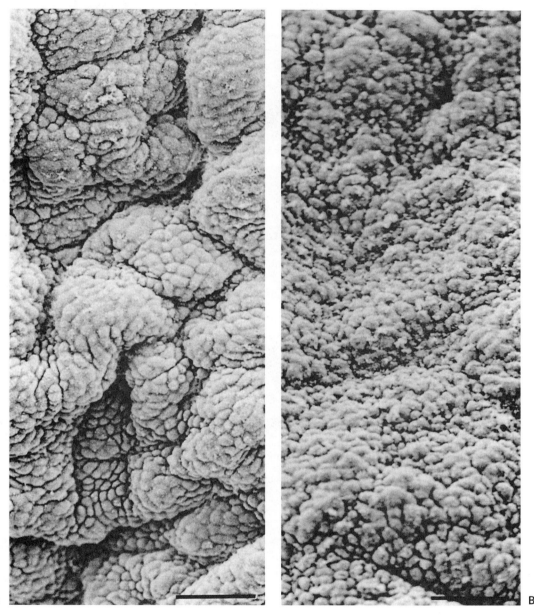

FIGURE 13-9. Scanning electron micrographs of the outer surface properties of the visceral endodermal yolk sac layer of 12-day-old conceptuses cultured in control and hyperglycemic sera. **(A)** The yolk sac of controls, with many cells forming groups sitting on underlying blood vessels and giving a wave-like appearance. **(B)** The yolk sac surface of conceptuses cultured in hypoglycemic serum (950 μg/dL). These cells have flattened surfaces, with poorly developed underlying blood vessels. Bar scale: 50 μm.

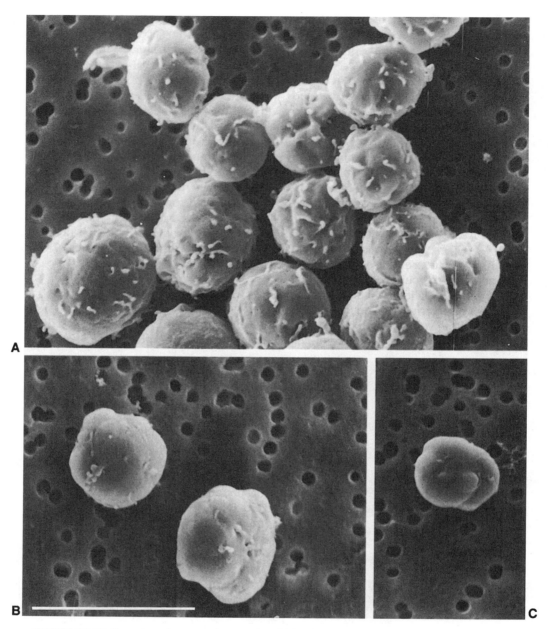

FIGURE 13-10. Scanning electron micrographs of blood cells collected from 12-day-old concep-tuses and cultured in control and hyperglycemic media. **(A)** (Controls): Many blood cells are seen characterized by enlarged surface area, crater formations, and surface infoldings or pseudopo-dia. **(B)** and **(C)** (Hyperglycemia medium): The blood cells are smooth with less prominent surface infoldings. Bar scale: 10 μm.

The above finding suggests that the yolk sac is actively involved in abnormal embryogenesis. The abnormal vascu-lature observed in hyperglycemic conditions is present dur-ing a critical phase of development when the mode of nutri-tion changes from being histotrophic to hemotropic (229,256). The alterations in vessel development may lead to poor perfusion of embryonic tissues with consequent hypoxia, acidosis, and cell injury. The abnormalities in the yolk sac tissue, which is the site of origin of epithelia of many embryonic organs, may result in developmental defects in these organs.

PREVENTION

The dysmorphogenesis found in rodent embryos exposed to high glucose concentrations *in vitro* can be diminished by addition of inositol (90,96,98), AA (86,87,228–230), or antioxidants (73,84,102,233,242) to the culture medium. In addition, the offspring of diabetic rodents show less dysmorphogenesis if the mother is supplied with inositol (99, 385,386), AA (86), or antioxidants (199,213–216,218, 387–390) during pregnancy (Fig. 13-3). Furthermore, addition of the mitochondrial pyruvate uptake inhibitor alpha-cyano-hydroxycinnamic acid to embryos cultured in high concentrations of glucose or pyruvate also diminishes dysmorphogenesis (84,102) and embryonic mitochondrial swelling (219,220). Depletion of embryonic inositol by administration of *scyllo*-inositol to the culture medium of rat embryos yields developmental damage, which can be markedly diminished by addition of inositol (101) to the medium, but not by addition of PGE_2 (419).

A culture of rat embryos with COX inhibitors, indomethacin and acetylsalicylic acid, resulted in malformations similar to those caused by high glucose culture, a maldevelopment that was blocked by supplementation of AA or PGE_2 (233). Addition of SOD or NAC diminished the COX inhibitor-induced dysmorphogenesis, analogous to the effect of the antioxidants on glucose-induced embryonic maldevelopment (233). This result, together with the finding of diminished glucose-induced embryopathy by addition of AA (86,87,228–230,233) and PGE_2 (90,233), suggest a cross-talk between teratogenic effects caused by decreased prostaglandin synthesis and ROS excess in embryos subjected to a diabetic environment, as well as between inositol and prostaglandins (90).

Supplementation of antioxidants has been shown to be beneficial for the development of embryos in a diabetes-like environment *in vivo* and *in vitro*. Dietary addition of butylated hydroxytoluene (199), vitamin E (213–216,218–220, 385,386,388,420), vitamin C (213–215), combinations of vitamins E and C (224), glutathione ester (421), and lipoic acid (389,390) diminish perturbed embryonic development *in vivo*, whereas addition of SOD (73,84,102,225), catalase (73), glutathione peroxidase (73), NAC (233,242, 333,334), and glutathione ester (232) diminish embryonic dysmorphogenesis *in vitro*.

The protection from embryonic dysmorphogenesis by these diverse agents has been amply documented. Pinter et al. (87) showed that AA supplementation to high-glucose culture medium diminished the increased malformation rate and also prevented the characteristic cytoarchitectural changes that were observed in diabetic embryopathy (Table 13-5 and Fig. 13-7). The conceptuses demonstrated normal embryonic and yolk sac vascularization and development (Fig. 13-10 and Fig. 13-11). At the cellular level, the advanced neuropil formation seen in embryos with open neural tubes (Figs. 13-7D and 13-12B) was prevented (Fig. 13-12A). The rough endoplasmic reticulum was normalized by the treatment, as were the number and size of lipid droplets and the lysosome-like structures in the endodermal yolk sac cells (54) (Fig. 13-13 and Table 13-6). Biochemical disturbances are also normalized by antiteratogenic treatment of embryos *in vitro*, using AA supplementation of high-glucose cultured embryos (228). The fatty acid content of yolk sac triglycerides was found to be similar to that of controls, and an increase in cholesterol esters in both the yolk sac and embryo was observed, with a parallel decrease in oleic acid in major lipid groups (228). The elevated oleic acid content in major lipid groups of these conceptuses indicates a relative deficiency in essential fatty acids. After 48 hours of culture, a high residual fatty acid content remained in the hyperglycemic culture medium. This fact highlights the altered absorptive functions of the yolk sac during organogenesis in the hyperglycemic conditions. In a later study, we used horseradish peroxidase as a tracer pro-

TABLE 13-5. EVALUATION OF RAT CONCEPTUSES CULTURED FROM DAYS 10 TO 12 IN CONTROL AND EXPERIMENTAL CONDITIONS[a]

Culture Conditions	After Incubation		Embryonic Malformations (%)
	Yolk Sac Diameter (mm)	Crown-Rump Length (mm)	
Group A: *In vitro* control (n = 19) (mean ± SD)	4.04 ± 0.14	3.78 ± 0.34	0
Group B: *In vitro* control + 20 μg/ml arachidonic acid (n = 18) (mean ± SD)	4.36 ± 0.42 $p < 0.003$ (A vs. B)	3.78 ± 0.40 $p < 0.004$ (A vs. B)	0
Group C: *In vitro* control + 80 μg/ml arachidonic acid (n = 6) (mean ± SD)	4.56 ± 0.3 $p < 0.001$ (A vs. C)	4.44 ± 0.38 $p < 0.001$ (A vs. C)	0
Group D: 950 mg/dl D-glucose (n = 17) (mean ± SD)	3.36 ± 0.63 $p < 0.001$ (A vs. D)	3.24 ± 0.46 $p < 0.001$ (A vs. D)	100
Group E: 950 mg/dl D-glucose + 20 μg/ml arachidonic acid (n = 20) (mean ± SD)	4.34 ± 0.57	3.78 ± 0.29	20
Group F: 950 mg/ml D-glucose + 80 μg/ml arachidonic acid (n = 16) (mean ± SD)	4.58 ± 0.12 $p < 0.001$ (D vs. F and A vs. F)	$p < 0.001$ (D vs. F and D vs. F)	0

[a]Preincubation conceptus diameter about 1.00 mm, measured in the midregion between the embryonic pole and ectoplacental cones.

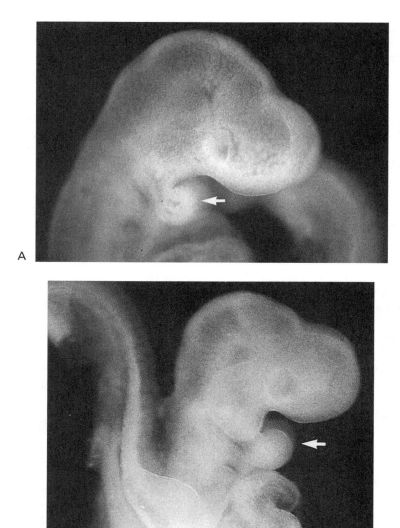

FIGURE 13-11. Magnification (×400) of head region of 12-day-old embryos cultured in control and hyperglycemic (750 µg/dL) medium. **(A)** (Control): The well-developed vascular pattern of the head, and the first branchial arch (*arrow*) of a normal embryo. **(B)** (Hyperglycemia exposed): Poorly developed vasculature of the head region in an abnormal embryo with incomplete body rotation.

tein to assess the transport function of the visceral endodermal yolk sac, cells of conceptuses cultured in both control and hyperglycemic media. We found that during hyperglycemia-induced embryopathy, there is a concomitant yolk sac failure evidenced by morphologic alterations and impaired endocytosis (255).

Diabetes mellitus is a complex metabolic disease. Disturbances in lipid metabolism are accompanied by an increase in serum lipoproteins and free fatty acids and a decrease in high-density lipoproteins (391,392). In poorly controlled diabetic individuals, high levels of serum free fatty acids are present, whereas patients with vascular complications have increased serum palmitic and oleic acids and decreased linoleic acid and AA levels (393).

Using gas-liquid chromatography, Pinter et al. (228) analyzed the fatty acid composition of the major lipid components of rat conceptuses. Analysis demonstrated an increase in triglycerides, an increased AA and oleic acid content in phospholipids and nonesterified fatty acids, and a decrease in cholesterol esters in yolk sacs exposed to hyperglycemia. Normally, the level of free AA in cytoplasm is low and is determined by the balance of hydrolysis and re-esterification of released fatty acids into other lipids (391). A high turnover of neutral lipid AA in brain has been observed, and this may be indicative of an as-yet-unexplored role of neutral lipids in AA liberation (394). These considerations suggest that dietary supplementation of linoleic acid may have a beneficial effect on the biochemi-

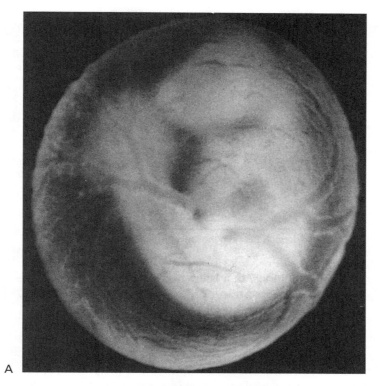

A

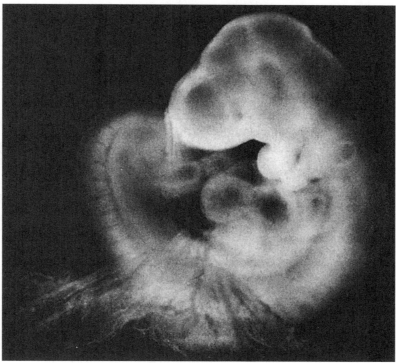

B

FIGURE 13-12. Whole mount photographs of 12-day-old conceptuses cultured for 2 days in male rat serum with added D-glucose (concentration, 950 μg/dL) and arachidonic acid (20 μg/ml). **(A)** A normal well-vascularized yolk sac. **(B)** The normal embryo after removal of the yolk sac.

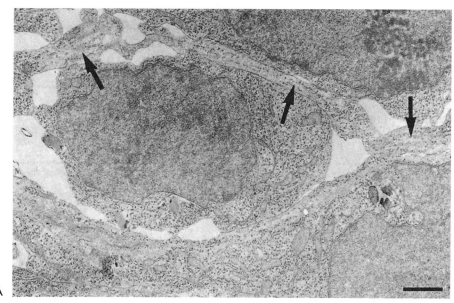

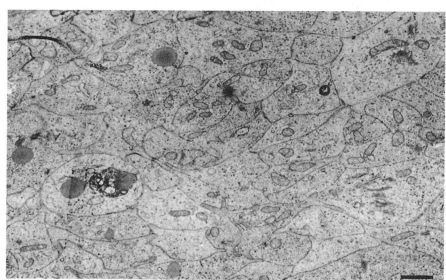

FIGURE 13-13 **(A)** The neuroepithelium dissected from the rhombencephalon area of a rat conceptus cultured from days 10 to 12 in hyperglycemic medium with added arachidonic acid (950 mg/dL of D-glucose and 20 μg/ml of arachidonic acid in male rat serum). The neuroepithelial cells show "blast-like" features: large-sized nucleus, less expanded perikaryon, few mitochondria, and free ribosome rosettes. Between the neuroepithelial cells, few cell processes (*arrows*) could be observed. **(B)** An electron micrograph taken from the rhombencephalon area of the open neural tube of a conceptus cultured from days 10 to 12 in hyperglycemic medium (950 mg/dL of D-glucose in male rat serum) without the addition of arachidonic acid. The electron micrograph demonstrates prematurely formed intercellular neuropil, a characteristic feature frequently seen in open neural tube close to the site of failed fusion. The neuropil includes interdigitating cell processes containing neurofilaments and neurotubules, some of which contain free ribosomes, mitochondria, and lipid droplets. Bar scale: 1 μm. (From Pinter E, Reece EA, Leranth CZ, et al. Yolk sac failure in embryopathy due to hyperglycemia: ultrastructural analysis of yolk sac differentiation associated with embryopathy in rat conceptuses under hyperglycemic conditions. *Teratology* 1986;33:73, with permission.)

TABLE 13-6. MORPHOMETRIC ANALYSIS OF THE VISCERAL ENDODERMAL YOLK SAC CELLS IN CONTROL AND EXPERIMENTAL CONDITIONS[a]

Experimental Conditions	Cell Volume Occupied by				
	Lysosome-like Vacuoles (%)	Rough Endoplasmic Reticulum (%)	Mitochondria (%)	Golgi Apparatus (%)	Lipid Droplets (%)
In vitro control	7.6 ± 0.5	13.1 ± 0.8	11.5 ± 0.5	1.3 ± 0.2	21.2 ± 1.9[b]
In vitro control	9.5 ± 0.4	9.2 ± 0.9	10.4 ± 0.8	1.8 ± 0.1	6.8 ± 0.6[c]
In vitro control + 20 µg/ml arachidonic acid	10.0 ± 1.2	12.9 ± 1.3	7.0 ± 0.8	2.6 ± 0.8	19.2 ± 2.0[c]
950 mg/ml D-glucose + 20 µg/ml arachidonic acid	46.2 ± 4.1[b,c]	3.4 ± 0.2[b,c]	8.2 ± 1.2	0.8 ± 0.2	1.7 ± 0.2
	8.6 ± 0.4	12.5 ± 6	10.5 ± 1.0	1.8 ± 0.1	12.2 ± 1.1[b,c]

[a]Data are mean ± SEM from 10 conceptuses in each group. All data are from 12-day-old *in vivo* and *in vitro* rat yolk sacs.
[b]Value is significantly different ($p < 0.001$) from that of *in vitro* control.
[c]Values is significantly different ($p < 0.001$) from that of the *in vivo* control.
From Weibel RE. Stereological principles for morphometry in electron microscopic cytology. *Int Rev Cytol* 1969;26:235, with permission.

cal and morphologic changes (392,393). In fact, using linoleic acid-rich diets to decrease vascular complications was reported as early as 1941 (393). These findings were confirmed in 1975 by Houtsmuller (395,396), who also demonstrated the hypoglycemic and insulin-sparing effect of this fatty acid. In a continuing *in vivo* study in our laboratory, Reece et al. (397) have fed rats safflower oil (high in linoleic acid and AA) and primrose oil (lower in linoleic acid and AA) and were able to demonstrate that both polyunsaturated fatty acids produced a lowering of the malformation rate. However, the diminution with safflower oil was significantly greater than with primrose oil (397).

Another method for prevention of anomalies was reported by Eriksson et al. (102). They used embryos from a mouse strain with increased endogenous SOD activity due to the incorporation of a transgene (hCuZnSOD) into the genome (398) and subjected these to a diabetes-like *in vitro* environment with high glucose or high β-hydroxybutyrate concentrations. It was found that transgenic embryos were more resistant to the teratogenic effects of these two compounds than the nontransgenic relatives, thus indicating that the antioxidant defense systems may play an important role in the prevention of congenital malformations. Hagay et al. (399) have subsequently confirmed this in an *in vivo* SOD transgenic diabetic mouse model, demonstrating a lower rate of malformation than in the diabetic nontransgenic animals.

In the light of the number of different therapies available *in vitro* and *in vivo* to block embryonic dysmorphogenesis, it is pertinent to ask if there exists a common pathway between the different possible teratogenic mechanisms in diabetic pregnancy. Evidently, in the hyperglycemic milieu, the intracellular levels of MI and AA decrease, and at the same time, the intracellular sorbitol concentrations increase. These processes have implications for intracellular

signaling, prostaglandin biosynthesis, and the levels of intracellular antioxidants, such as nicotinamide-adenine dinucleotide phosphate (NADPH) and (reduced) glutathione (GSH) (383,400–406). The high glucose concentration seems to induce the generation of free oxygen radicals and cause morphologic damage in the mitochondria of the embryo (74,84). The excess levels of free oxygen radicals and the decreased antioxidant defense status would allow enhanced peroxidation of embryonic lipids (407). Increased lipid peroxidation can cause a reduction in prostacyclin levels and an imbalance in prostaglandin synthesis (401), but it has also been shown that the cellular GSH content determines the rate of prostaglandin E_2 biosynthesis after oxidant stress (405). Furthermore, the hyperglycemic condition may effect DNA, either directly (206,409–412) or by changing the mode of gene expression in the embryo (413,414). It would seem that the processes are clearly interrelated and that oxidative metabolism may be of central importance. Although more work is needed to completely clarify the situation, it is of interest that antioxidant treatment has been shown to diminish the diabetes-induced complications in experimental animal models (394, 413–415).

At the present time, the mechanism of protective action of AA and MI against embryopathy is evolving. A relative AA-deficiency state seems to exist, which could adversely affect membranogenesis and membrane function (87,228). Because AA is the precursor of the prostaglandins, which are widely distributed in many cells, the protective mechanism of AA could act through this pathway (86). Arachidonate in mammalian cells is esterified to glycophospholipids and found as an essential part of membranes (366,414). Golde and Van Deenen (416) showed that AA at the second position of phosphatidylcholine should be accompanied by a saturated fatty acid, such as palmitic or stearic acid, on the first position to maintain proper membrane fluidity. This structural situation is also necessary for normal absorptive functions of the membrane for intact enzyme function (416). The cell membrane fluidity is also influenced by the intracellular concentrations of cholesterol and phospholipid, which are dependent on intracellular cholesterol esterification and influenced by *de novo* synthesis of saturated fatty acids. In the diabetic state, a decrease in desaturation of membrane lipids with consequent decrease in membrane fluidity is observed (417,418).

The available clinical and experimental data indicate that there is more than one alteration in the embryonic environment capable of inducing teratogenic development. One — perhaps the most important — alteration is the increase in glucose concentration (422), which seems to have a number of direct metabolic consequences in the embryo (423). However, there are other changes with teratogenic importance, such as increased levels of ketone bodies (424) and BCAAs (84,102), to which the mechanism of action remains to be elucidated. The study of etiologic and pathogenic factors in the genesis of congenital malformations has revealed a complex process in which the diabetic state simultaneously induces alterations in a series of teratogenically capable pathways (86,213–215,425,426). These pathways are intertwined, and several of them seem to result in an imbalance of the ROS metabolism (330,331), yielding a ROS excess in teratogenically sensitive cell populations, an imbalance ultimately causing the congenital malformations (73). This notion is important in developing therapies to counter the embryopathy. Blocking the ROS excess may be a valid way to diminish the disturbed development caused by the diabetic environment.

KEY POINTS

- Research studies indicate that congenital malformations occur in early pregnancy, are influenced by the abnormal maternal metabolic milieu, and seem to result from various combinations of factors.
- During the critical period of organogenesis, the pregnancy is hardly recognizable, making evaluation and study extremely difficult.
- The mechanism for induction of dysmorphogenesis in experimental diabetic pregnancy has been shown to include generation of free oxygen radicals and to be associated with alterations in the embryonic levels of AA, prostaglandins, and MI.
- Current investigations provide evidence that the yolk sac plays an integral role in diabetic embryopathy.
- The experimental use of several different compounds such as AA, MI, and antioxidants offer significant promise in potentially serving as a pharmacologic prophylactic against diabetic embryopathy.

REFERENCES

1. Windham GD, Edmonds LD. Current trends in the incidence of neural tube defect. *Pediatrics* 1982;70:33.
2. Kalter H, Warkany J. Congenital malformations: etiologic factors and their role in prevention. *N Engl J Med* 1983;308:424.
3. Kalter H, Warkany J. Congenital malformations. *N Engl J Med* 1983;308:491.
4. Cole SK, Smalls M. Trends in infant mortality in Scotland, 1970–1987. *J Public Health Med* 1990;12:73–80.
5. Linhart Y, Bashiri A, Maymon E, et al. Congenital anomalies are an independent risk factor for neonatal morbidity and perinatal mortality in preterm birth. *Eur J Obstet Gynecol Reprod Biol* 2000;90:43–49.
6. Mølsted-Pedersen L, Tygstrups I, et al. Congenital malformations in newborn infants of diabetic women: correlation with maternal diabetic vascular complications. *Lancet* 1964;1:1124.
7. Rusnak SL, Driscoll SG. Congenital spinal anomalies in infants of diabetic mothers. *Pediatrics* 1965;35:989.
8. Karlsson K, Kjellmer I. The outcome of diabetic pregnancies in relation to the mother's blood sugar level. *Am J Obstet Gynecol* 1972;112:213.
9. Pedersen J. *The pregnant diabetic and her newborn: problems and management*, 2nd ed. Baltimore: Williams & Wilkins, 1977.
10. Drury ML, Green AT, Stronge JM. Pregnancy complicated by clinical diabetes mellitus: a study of 600 pregnancies. *Am J Obstet Gynecol* 1977;49:519.
11. Gabbe SG. Congenital malformations in infants of diabetic mothers. *Obstet Gynecol Surv* 1977;32:125.
12. Gabbe SG, Mestman JH, Freeman RK, et al. Management and outcome of pregnancy in diabetes mellitus. Classes B to R. *Am J Obstet Gynecol* 1977;129:723.
13. Kitzmiller JL, Cloherty JP, Younger MD, et al. Diabetic pregnancy and perinatal morbidity. *Am J Obstet Gynecol* 1978;131:560.
14. Freinkel N. Metabolic implications of mild disturbances in maternal carbohydrate intolerance. *Diabetes Care* 1980;3:399.
15. Beard RW, Lowry C. Commentary: the British survey of diabetic pregnancies. *Br J Obstet Gynaecol* 1982;89:783.
16. Olofsson P, Sjöberg NO, Solum T, et al. Changing panorama of perinatal and infant mortality in diabetic pregnancy. *Acta Obstet Gynecol Scand* 1984;63:467.
17. Olofsson P, Liedholm H, Sartor G, et al. Diabetes and pregnancy: a 21–year Swedish material. *Acta Obstet Gynecol Scand* 1984;63[Suppl 122]:1.
18. Hadden DR. Diabetes in pregnancy 1985: clinical controversy. *Diabetologia* 1986;29:1.
19. Mølsted-Petersen L, Kühl C. Obstetrical management in diabetic pregnancy: the Copenhagen experience. *Diabetologia* 1986;29:13.
20. Levin ME, Rigg LA, Marshall RE. Pregnancy and diabetes. *Arch Intern Med* 1986;146:758.
21. Damm P, Mølsted-Petersen L. Significant decrease in congenital malformations in newborn infants of an selected population of diabetic women. *Am J Obstet Gynecol* 1989;161:1163.
22. Hanson U, Persson B, Thunell S. Relationship between haemoglobin A1c in early type 1 (insulin-dependent) diabetic pregnancy and the occurrence of spontaneous abortion and fetal malformation in Sweden. *Diabetologia* 1990;33:100.
23. Ramos-Arroyo MA, Rodriguez-Pinilla E, Cordero JF. Maternal diabetes: the risk for specific birth defects. *Eur J Epidemiol* 1992;8:503–508.
24. Hawthorne G, Snodgrass A, Tunbridge M. Outcome of diabetic pregnancy and glucose intolerance in pregnancy: an audit of

fetal loss in Newcastle General Hospital 1977–1990. *Diabetes Res Clin Pract* 1994;25:183–190.

25. Martinez-Frias ML. Epidemiological analysis of outcomes of pregnancy in diabetic mothers: identification of the most characteristic and most frequent congenital anomalies. *Am J Med Genet* 1994;51:108–113.
26. Pregnancy outcomes in the Diabetes Control and Complications Trial. *Am J Obstet Gynecol* 1996;174(4):1343–1353.
27. Janssen PA, Rothman I, Schwartz SM. Congenital malformations in newborns of women with established and gestational diabetes in Washington State, 1983–91. *Paediatr Perinat Epidemiol* 1996;10:52–63.
28. Kitzmiller JL, Buchanan TA, Kjos S, et al. Pre-conception care of diabetes, congenital malformations, and spontaneous abortions. *Diabetes Care* 1996;19:514–541.
29. Casson IF, Clarke CA, Howard CV, et al. Outcomes of pregnancy in insulin dependent diabetic women: results of a five year population cohort study. *BMJ* 1997;315:275–278.
30. Hawthorne G, Robson S, Ryall EA, et al. Prospective population based survey of outcome of pregnancy in diabetic women: results of the Northern Diabetic Pregnancy Audit, 1994. *BMJ* 1997;315:279–281.
31. Nielsen GL, Sorensen HT, Nielsen PH, et al. Glycosylated hemoglobin as predictor of adverse fetal outcome in type 1 diabetic pregnancies. *Acta Diabetol* 1997;34:217–222.
32. von Kries R, Kimmerle R, Schmidt JE, et al. Pregnancy outcomes in mothers with pregestational diabetes: a population-based study in North Rhine (Germany) from 1988 to 1993. *Eur J Pediatr* 1997;156:963–967.
33. Nordstrom L, Spetz E, Wallstrom K, et al. Metabolic control and pregnancy outcome among women with insulin-dependent diabetes mellitus. A twelve-year follow-up in the country of Jamtland, Sweden. *Acta Obstet Gynecol Scand* 1998;77:284–289.
34. Suhonen L, Hiilesmaa V, Teramo K. Glycaemic control during early pregnancy and fetal malformations in women with type I diabetes mellitus. *Diabetologia* 2000;43:79–82.
35. Aberg A, Westbom L, Kallen B. Congenital malformations among infants whose mothers had gestational diabetes or pre-existing diabetes. *Early Hum Dev* 2001;61:85–95.
36. Queisser-Luft A, Stolz G, Wiesel A, et al. Malformations in newborn: results based on 30,940 infants and fetuses from the Mainz congenital birth defect monitoring system (1990–1998). *Arch Gynecol Obstet* 2002;266:163–167.
37. Farrell T, Neale L, Cundy T. Congenital anomalies in the offspring of women with type 1, type 2 and gestational diabetes. *Diabet Med* 2002;19:322–326.
38. Platt KA, Owens CM. Quiz case. Congenital infantile myofibromatosis. Diaphragmatic and skeletal involvement but no visceral changes. *Eur J Radiol* 2002;43:180–182.
39. Penney GC, Mair G, Pearson DW, et al. Outcomes of pregnancies in women with type 1 diabetes in Scotland: a national population-based study. *BJOG* 2003;110:315–318.
40. Comess LJ, Bennett PH, Burch TA, et al. Congenital anomalies and diabetes in the Pima Indians of Arizona. *Diabetes* 1969;18:471.
41. Kucera J. Rate and type of congenital anomalies among offspring of diabetic women. *J Reprod Med* 1971;7:61.
42. Chung CS, Myrianthopoulos NC. Factors affecting risks of congenital malformation, II. Effect of maternal diabetes on congenital malformations. *Birth Defects* 1975;11:23.
43. Mills JL. Malformations in infants of diabetic mothers. *Teratology* 1982;25:385.
44. Simpson JL, Elias S, Martin AO, et al. Diabetes in pregnancy, Northwestern University series (1977–1981). I. *Am J Obstet Gynecol* 1983;146:263–270.

45. Ballard JL, Holroyde J, Tsang RC, et al. High malformation rates and decreased mortality in infants of diabetic mothers managed after the first trimester of pregnancy (1956–1978). *Am J Obstet Gynecol* 1984;148:1111–1118.
46. Goldman JA, Dicker D, Feldberg D, et al. Pregnancy outcome in patients with insulin-dependent diabetes mellitus with pre-conceptional diabetic control: a comparative study. *Am J Obstet Gynecol* 1986;155:293–297.
47. Miodovnik M, Mimouni F, Dignan PS, et al. Major malformations in infants of IDDM women. Vasculopathy and early first-trimester poor glycemic control. *Diabetes Care* 1988;11:713–718.
48. Becerra JE, Khoury MJ, Cordero JF, et al. Diabetes mellitus during pregnancy and the risks for specific birth defects: a population-based case-control study. *Pediatrics* 1990;85:1–9.
49. Freinkel N. Banting Lecture 1980: of pregnancy and progeny. *Diabetes* 1980;29:1023.
50. Eriksson UJ. Congenital malformations in diabetic animal models-a review. *Diabetes Res* 1984;1:57.
51. Reece EA, Homko CJ, Wu YK, et al. Metabolic fuel mixtures and diabetic embryopathy. *Clin Perinatol* 1993;20:517.
52. Baker L, Piddington R. Diabetic embryopathy: a selective review of recent trends. *J Diabetes Complications* 1993;7:204.
53. Buchanan TA, Kitzmiller JL. Metabolic interactions of diabetes and pregnancy. *Annu Rev Med* 1994;45:245.
54. Mills JL, Baker L, Goldman AS. Malformations in infants of diabetic mothers occur before the seventh gestational week: implications for treatment. *Diabetes* 1979;28:292.
55. Leslie RDG, Pyke DA, John PN, et al. Hemoglobin A1 in diabetic pregnancy. *Lancet* 1978;2:958.
56. Rosenn B, Miodovnik M, Corns CA, et al. Preconception management of insulin-dependent diabetes: improvement of pregnancy outcome. *Obstet Gynecol* 1991;77:846.
57. Miller E, Hare JW, Cloherty JP, et al. Elevated maternal hemoglobin. A1C in early pregnancy and major congenital anomalies in infants of diabetic mothers. *N Engl J Med* 1981;304:1331.
58. Baker L, Egler JM, Klein SH, et al. Meticulous control of diabetes during organogenesis prevents congenital lumbosacral defects in rats. *Diabetes* 1981;30:955.
59. Eriksson RSM, Thunberg L, Eriksson UJ. Effects of interrupted insulin treatment on fetal outcome of pregnancy diabetic rats. *Diabetes* 1989;38:764.
60. Eriksson UJ, Bone AJ, Turnbull DM, et al. Timed interruption of insulin therapy in diabetic BB/E rat pregnancy: effects on maternal metabolism and fetal outcome. *Acta Endocrinol (Copenh)* 1989;120:800.
61. Mills JL, Knopp RH, Simpson JL, et al. National Institute of Child Health and Human Development Diabetes in Early Pregnancy Study: lack of relation of increased malformation rates in infants of diabetic mothers to glycemic control during organogenesis. *N Engl J Med* 1988;318:671.
62. Buchanan TA, Denno KM, Sipos GF, et al. Diabetic teratogenesis: *in vitro* evidence for a multifactorial etiology with little contribution from glucose per se. *Diabetes* 1994;43:656.
63. Styrud J, Thunberg L, Nybacka O, et al. Correlations between maternal metabolism and deranged development in the offspring of normal and diabetic rats. *Pediatr Res* 1995;37:343.
64. Reece EA, Pinter E, Leranth CZ, et al. Ultrastructural analysis of malformations of the embryonic neural axis induced by hyperglycemic conceptus culture. *Teratology* 1985;32:363.
65. Cockroft DL, Coppola PT. Teratogenic effects of excess glucose on head-fold rat embryos in culture. *Teratology* 1977;16:141.
66. Sadler TV. Effects of maternal diabetes on early embryogenesis. II. Hyperglycemia-induced exencephaly. *Teratology* 1980;21:349.

67. Garnham EA, Beck F, Clarke CA, et al. Effects of glucose on rat embryos in culture. *Diabetologia* 1983;25:291.

68. Zusman I, Ornoy A, Yaffe P, et al. Effects of glucose and serum from streptozotocin-diabetic and non-diabetic rats on the *in vitro* development of preimplantation mouse embryos. *Isr J Med Sci* 1985;21:359.

69. Eriksson UJ. Importance of genetic predisposition and maternal environment for the occurrence of congenital malformations in offspring of diabetic rats. *Teratology* 1988;37:365.

70. Diamond MP, Harbert-Moley K, Logan J, et al. Manifestation of diabetes mellitus on mouse follicular and preembryo development: effects of hyperglycemia per se. *Metabolism* 1990;39:220.

71. Styrud J, Eriksson UJ. Effects of D-glucose and b-hydroxybutyric acid on the *in vitro* development of (pre)chondrocytes from embryos of normal and diabetic rats. *Acta Endocrinol (Copenh)* 1990;122:487.

72. de Hertogh R, Vanderheyden I, Pampfer S, et al. Stimulatory and inhibitory effects of glucose and insulin on rat blastocyst development *in vitro*. *Diabetes* 1991;40:641.

73. Eriksson UJ, Borg LAH. Protection by free oxygen radical scavenging enzymes against glucose-induced embryonic malformations *in vitro*. *Diabetologia* 1991;34:325.

74. Yang X, Borg LAH, Eriksson UJ. Altered mitochondrial morphology of rat embryos in diabetic pregnancy. *Anat Rec* 1995;241:255.

75. Bhasin S, Shambaugh GE III. Fetal fuels. V. Ketone bodies inhibit pyrimidine biosynthesis in fetal rat brain. *Am J Physiol* 1982;2431234.

76. Horton WE Jr, Sadler TW. Effects of maternal diabetes on early embryogenesis: alteration in morphogenesis produced by the ketone body. Beta-hydroxybutyrate. *Diabetes* 1983;32:610.

77. Lewis NJ, Akazawa S, Freinkel N. Teratogenesis from beta-hydroxybutyrate during organogenesis in rat embryo organ culture and enhancement by subteratogenic glucose. *Diabetes* 1983;32[Suppl I]:11A.

78. Shambaugh GE III, Angulo MC, Koehler RR. Fetal fuels. VII. Ketone bodies inhibit synthesis of purines in fetal rat brain. *Am J Physiol* 1984;247:E111.

79. Sheehan EA, Beck F, Clarke CA, et al. Effects of β-hydroxybutyrate on rat embryos grown in culture. *Experientia* 1985;41:273.

80. Horton WE, Sadler TW, Hunter ES. Effects of hyperketonemia on mouse embryonic and fetal glucose metabolism *in vitro*. *Teratology* 1985;31:227.

81. Zusman I, Yaffe P, Ornoy A. Effects of metabolic factors in the diabetic state on the *in vitro* development of preimplantation mouse embryos. *Teratology* 1987;35:77.

82. Hunter ES, Sadler IV, Wynn RE. A potential mechanism of DL-b-hydroxybutyrate-induced malformations in mouse embryos. *Am J Physiol* 1987;253172.

83. Moore DCP, Stanisstreet M, Clarke CA. Morphological and physiological effects of b-hydroxybutyrate on rat embryos grown *in vitro* at different stages. *Teratology* 1989;40:237.

84. Eriksson UJ, Borg LAH. Diabetes and embryonic malformations: role of substrate-induced free oxygen radical production for dysmorphogenesis in cultured rat embryos. *Diabetes* 1993;42:411.

85. Moley KH, Vaughn WK, Diamond MP. Manifestations of diabetes mellitus on mouse preimplantation development: effect of elevated concentration of metabolic intermediates. *Hum Reprod* 1994;9:113.

86. Goldman AS, Baker L, Piddington R, et al. Hyperglycemia-induced teratogenesis is mediated by a functional deficiency of AA. *Proc Natl Acad Sci U S A* 1985;82:8227.

87. Pinter E, Reece EA, Leranth C, et al. Arachidonic acid prevents hyperglycemia-associated yolk sac damage and embryopathy. *Am J Obstet Gynecol* 1986;155:691.

88. Engström E, Haglung A, Eriksson UJ. Effects of maternal diabetes or *in vitro* hyperglycemia on uptake of palmitic and arachidonic acid by rat embryos. *Pediatr Res* 1991;30:150.

89. Pinter E, Reece EA, Ogburn P, et al. Relative essential fatty acid deficiency in hyperglycemia-induced embryopathy. *Am J Obstet Gynecol* 1988;159:1484.

90. Baker L, Piddington R, Goldman AS, et al. Myo-inositol and prostaglandins reverse the glucose inhibition of neural tube fusion in cultured mouse embryos. *Diabetologia* 1990;33:593.

91. Goto MP, Goldman AS, Uhing MR. PGE$_2$ prevents anomalies induced by hyperglycemia or diabetic serum in mouse embryos. *Diabetes* 1992;41:1644.

92. Eriksson UJ, Naeser P, Brolin S. Increased accumulation of sorbitol in embryos of manifest diabetic rats. *Diabetes* 1986;35:1356.

93. Hod M, Star S, Passoneau J, et al. Effect of hyperglycemia on sorbital and myo-inositol content of cultured rat conceptus: failure of aldose reductase inhibitors to modify myo-inositol depletion and dysmorphogenesis. *Biochem Biophys Res Commun* 1986;140:974.

94. Sussman I, Matschinsky FM. Diabetes affects sorbitol and myo-inositol levels of neuroectodermal tissue during embryogenesis in rat. *Diabetes* 1988;37:974.

95. Eriksson UJ, Naeser P, Brolin SE. Influence of sorbitol accumulation on growth and development of embryos cultured in elevated levels of glucose and fructose. *Diabetes Res* 1989;11:27.

96. Hashimoto M, Akazawa S, Akazawa M, et al. Effects of hyperglycemia on sorbitol and myo-inositol contents of cultured embryos: treatment with aldose reductase inhibitor and myo-inositol supplementation. *Diabetologia* 1990;33:597.

97. Weigensberg MJ, Garcia-Palmer FJ, Freinkel N. Uptake of myo-inositol by early-somite rat conceptus. Transport kinetics and effects of hyperglycemia. *Diabetes* 1990;39:575.

98. Hod M, Star S, Passonneau JV, et al. Glucose-induced dysmorphogenesis in the cultured rat conceptus: prevention by supplementation with myo-inositol. *Isr J Med Sci* 1990;26:541.

99. Akashi M, Akazawa S, Akazawa M, et al. Effects of insulin and myo-inositol on embryo growth and development during early organogenesis in streptozotocin-induced diabetic rats. *Diabetes* 1991;40:1574.

100. Strieleman PJ, Connors MA, Metzger BE. Phosphoinositide metabolism in the developing conceptus. Effects of hyperglycemia and scyllo-inositol in rat embryo culture. *Diabetes* 1992;41:989.

101. Strieleman PJ, Metzger BE. Glucose and scyllo-inositol impair phosphoinositide hydrolysis in the 10.5 day cultured rat conceptus: a role in dysmorphogenesis? *Teratology* 1993;48:267.

102. Eriksson UJ, Borg LAH, Hagay Z, et al. Increased superoxide dismutase (SOD) activity in embryos of transgenic mice protects from the teratogenic effects of a diabetic environment. *Diabetes* 1993;42[Suppl 1]:85A.

103. Kitzmiller JL, Gavin LA, Gin GD, et al. Preconception care of diabetes. Glycemic control prevents congenital anomalies. *JAMA* 1991;265:731.

104. Duncan JM. On puerperal diabetes. *Trans Obstet Soc Lond* 1882;24:256.

105. Joslin EP. *Treatment of diabetes mellitus*, 3rd ed. Philadelphia: Lea & Febiger, 1923.

106. Soler NG, Walsh CH, Malins JM. Congenital malformations in infants of diabetic mothers. *Q J Med* 1976;45:303.

107. Sherman JL, Elias S, Martin AO, et al. Diabetes in pregnancy. Northwestern University series (1977–1981). I. Prospective study of anomalies in offspring of mothers with diabetes mellitus. *Am J Obstet Gynecol* 1983;146:263.

108. Miodovnik M, Mimouni F, Dignam PSJ, et al. Major malformations in infants of IDDM women. *Diabetes Care* 1988;11:713.
109. Pedersen JF, Mølsted-Petersen L, Martensen HB. Fetal growth delay and maternal hemoglobin A1C in early diabetic pregnancy. *Obstet Gynecol* 1984;64:351.
110. Rubin A, Murphy DP. Studies in human reproduction. III. The frequency of congenital malformations in the, offspring of non-diabetic individuals. *J Pediatr* 1958;53:579, 1958.
111. Fuhrmann K, Reiher H, Semmler K, et al. Prevention of congenital malformations in infants of insulin-dependent diabetic mothers. *Diabetes Care* 1983;6:219.
112. Greene MF, Hare JW, Cloherty JP, et al. First-trimester hemoglobin A1 and risk for major malformation and spontaneous abortion in diabetic pregnancy. *Teratology* 1989;39:225.
113. Tsang RC, Ballard J, Braun C. The infants of the diabetic mother: today and tomorrow. *Clin Obstet Gynecol* 1981;24:125.
114. Ballard JL, Holroyde J, Tsang RC, et al. High malformation rates and decreased mortality in infants of diabetic mothers managed after the first trimester of pregnancy (1956–1978). *Am J Obstet Gynecol* 1979;148:1111.
115. LeCorche E. Du Diabetic dans ses rapports avec la vie uterine menstruation, et al. grusesse. *Ann Gynecol* 1885;24:257.
116. White P. Pregnancy complicating diabetes. In: Joslin EP, ed. *The treatment of diabetes mellitus*, 6th ed. London: Henry Klimpton, 1937:618.
117. White P. Diabetes mellitus in pregnancy. *Clin Perinatol* 1974;1:331.
118. White P. Pregnancy and diabetes medical aspects. *Med Clin North Am* 1965;49:1015.
119. White P. Pregnancy complicating diabetes. *Am J Med* 1949;7:609.
120. Becerra JE, Khoury MJ, Cordero JF, et al. Diabetes mellitus during pregnancy and the risks for specific birth defects: a population-based case-control study. *Pediatrics* 1990;85:1.
121. Freinkel N, Metzger BE. Pregnancy as a tissue culture experience: the critical implications of maternal metabolism for fetal development. *Pregnancy metabolism, diabetes, and the fetus*. Amsterdam; New York: Excerpta Medica, 1979:109.
122. Freinkel N. Fuel-mediated teratogenesis: diabetes in pregnancy as paradigm for evaluating the developmental impact of maternal fuels. In: Serrano-Rios M, Lefebvre PJ, eds. *Diabetes 1985*. New York: Elsevier Science, 1985:563.
123. Freinkel N, Metzger BE, Phelps RL, et al. Gestational diabetes mellitus: heterogeneity of maternal age, weight, insulin secretion, HLA antigens, and islet cell antibodies and the impact of maternal metabolism on pancreatic β-cell and somatic development in the offspring. *Diabetes* 1985;34:1.
124. Adashi EY, Pinto H, Tyson JE. Impact of maternal euglycemia on fetal outcome in diabetic pregnancy. *Am J Obstet Gynecol* 1979;133:268.
125. Dignan PSJ. Teratogenic risk and counseling in diabetes. *Clin Obstet Gynecol* 1981;24:149.
126. Grix A Jr, Curry C, Hall BD. Patterns of multiple malformations in infants of diabetic mothers. *Birth Defects* 1982;18:55.
127. Neave C. Congenital malformations in offspring of diabetics. Ph.D. diss. Harvard University, 1967.
128. Naeye RL. The outcome of diabetic pregnancies: a prospective study. *Pregnancy metabolism, diabetes, and the fetus*. Amsterdam; New York: Excerpta Medica, 1979:227.
129. Reece EA, Hobbins JC. Diabetic embryopathy: pathogenesis, prenatal diagnosis and prevention. *Obstet Gynecol Surv* 1986;41:325.
130. Naftolin F, Diamond M, Pinter E, et al. A hypothesis concerning the general basis of organogenetic congenital anomalies. *Am J Obstet Gynecol* 1987;157:1.
131. Dekaban A, Magee KR. Occurrence of neurologic abnormalities in infants of diabetic mothers. *Neurology* 1958;8:193.
132. Eunpu DL, Zackai EH. Neural tube defects, diabetes, and serum alpha-fetoprotein screening. *Am J Obstet Gynecol* 1983;147:729.
133. Farquhar JW. The infant of the diabetic mother. *Postgrad Med J* 1969;45:806.
134. Milunsky A. A prenatal diagnosis of neural tube defects: the importance of serum alpha fetoprotein screening in diabetic pregnant women. *Am J Obstet Gynecol* 1982;142:1030.
135. Zacharias JF, Jenkins JH, Marion JP. The incidence of neural tube defects in the fetus and neonate of the insulin-dependent diabetic woman. *Am J Obstet Gynecol* 1984;150:797.
136. Barr M, Hanson JW, Currey K, et al. Holoprosencephaly in infants of diabetic mothers. *J Pediatr* 1983;102:565.
137. Matsunaga E, Shiota K. Holoprosencephaly in human embryos: epidemiologic studies of 150 cases. *Teratology* 1977;16:261.
138. Herre HD, Horky Z. Die Missbildungsfrequenz bei kindern diabetischer Mutter. *Zentralbl Gynakol* 1964;86:758.
139. Rowland TW, Hubbell JP, Nadas AS. Congenital heart disease in infants of diabetic mothers. *J Pediatr* 1973;83:815.
140. Khoury MJ, Becerra JE, Cordero JF, et al. Clinical-epidemiologic assessment of pattern of birth defects associated with human teratogens: application to diabetic embryopathy. *Pediatrics* 1989;84:658–665.
141. Ferencz C. On the birth prevalence of congenital heart disease. *J Am Coll Cardiol* 1990;16:1701–1702.
142. Ferencz C, Rubin JD, McCarter RJ, et al. Maternal diabetes and cardiovascular malformations: predominance of double outlet right ventricle and truncus arteriosus. *Teratology* 1990;41:319–326.
143. Albert TJ, Landon MB, Wheller JJ, et al. Prenatal detection of fetal anomalies in pregnancies complicated by insulin-dependent diabetes mellitus. *Am J Obstet Gynecol* 1996;174:1424–1428.
144. Schaefer-Graf UM, Buchanan TA, Xiang A, et al. Patterns of congenital anomalies and relationship to initial maternal fasting glucose levels in pregnancies complicated by type 2 and gestational diabetes. *Am J Obstet Gynecol* 2000;182:313–320.
145. Driscoll SG. The pathology of pregnancy complicated by diabetes mellitus. *Med Clin North Am* 1965;49:1053.
146. Crooij MG, Westhuis M, Shoemaker J, et al. Ultrasonographic measurement of the yolk sac. *Br J Obstet Gynaecol* 1983;89:931.
147. Welch JP, Aterman K. The syndrome of caudal dysplasia: a review, including etiologic considerations and evidence of heterogeneity. *Pediatr Pathol* 1984;2:313.
148. Hohl AF. Zur Pathologie des Beckens. In: *Das Schrag-ovale*. Leipzig: Wilhelm Ergleman, 1857:61.
149. His W. Die Entwicklung der ersten Nervenbahnon bei menschliche Embryo: Uebersichtliche Darstellung. *Arch Anat Physiol Anat Abt* 1887;92:368.
150. Froehlich LA, Fugikuta T. Significance of a single umbilical artery. *Am J Obstet Gynecol* 1966;4:274.
151. Churchill JA, Berendes HW, Nemore J. Neuropsychological deficits in children of diabetic mothers: a report from the collaborative study of cerebral palsy. *Am J Obstet Gynecol* 1969;105:257.
152. Bibergeil H, Gödel E, Amendt P. Diabetes and pregnancy: early and late prognosis of children of diabetic mothers. In: Camerini-Davalos RA, Cole HS, eds. *Early diabetes in early life*. New York: Academic Press, 1975:427.
153. Yssing M. Long-term prognosis of children born to mothers diabetic when pregnant. In: Comerini-Davalos RA, Cole HS, eds. *Early diabetes in early life*. New York: Academic Press, 1975:575.
154. Hayword JC, McRae KN, Dilling LA. Prognosis of infants of

diabetic mothers in relation to neonatal hypoglycemia. *Dev Med Child Neurol* 1976;18:471.

155. Stephens JA, Baker GL, Kitchell M. Outcome at ages 1, 3 and 5 years of children born to diabetic women. *Am J Obstet Gynecol* 1977;127:408.

156. Cummins M, Norrish M. Follow-up of children of diabetic mothers. *Arch Dis Child* 1980;55:259.

157. Hadden DR, Byrne E, Trotter I, et al. Physical and psychological health of children of type 1 (insulin-dependent) diabetic mothers. *Diabetologia* 1984;26:250.

158. Persson B, Gentz J. Follow-up of children of insulin-dependent and gestational diabetic mothers: neuropsychological outcome. *Acta Paediatr Scand* 1984;73:349.

159. Persson B. Longterm morbidity in infants of diabetic mothers. *Acta Endocrinol (Copenh)* 1986;277[Suppl]:156.

160. Petersen MB, Pedersen SA, Greisen G, et al. Early growth delay in diabetic pregnancy: relation to psychomotor development at age 4. *BMJ* 1988;296:598.

161. Rizzo T, Freinkel N, Metzger BE, et al. Correlations between antepartum maternal metabolism and newborn behavior. *Am J Obstet Gynecol* 1990;163:1458.

162. Silverman BL, Rizzo T, Green OC, et al. Long-term prospective evaluation of offspring of diabetic mothers. *Diabetes* 1991;40 [Suppl 2]:121.

163. Rizzo T, Metzger BE, Burns WJ, et al. Correlations between antepartum maternal metabolism and intelligence of offspring. *N Engl J Med* 1991;325:911.

164. Johansson B, Meyerson B, Eriksson UJ. Behavioral effects of an intrauterine or neonatal diabetic environment in the rat. *Biol Neonate* 1991;59:226.

165. Widness JA, Susa JB, Garcia JF. Increased erythropoiesis and elevated erythropoietin in infants of diabetic mothers and in hyperinsulinemic rhesus fetuses. *J Clin Invest* 1982;7:637.

166. Perrine SP, Greene MF, Falter DV. Delay in fetal globin switch in infants of diabetic mothers. *N Engl J Med* 1985;312:334.

167. Eriksson EJ, Dahlström E, Larsson KS, et al. Increased incidence of congenital malformations in the offspring of diabetic rats and their prevention by maternal insulin therapy. *Diabetes* 1982;31:1.

168. Eriksson UJ, Lewis NJ, Freinkel N. Growth retardation during early organogenesis in embryos of experimentally diabetic rats. *Diabetes* 1984;33:281.

169. Fulop M. Lactic acidosis in diabetic patients. *Arch Intern Med* 1976;136:137.

170. Eriksson UJ, Jansson L. Diabetes in pregnancy decreased placental blood flow and disturbed fetal developments in rats. *Pediatr Res* 1984;18:735.

171. Freinkel N, Lewis N, Akazawa S, et al. The honeybee syndrome—implications of the teratogenicity of mannose in rat embryo culture. *N Engl J Med* 1984;310:223.

172. Kennedy L, Baynes JW. Non-enzymatic glycosylation and the chronic complications of diabetes: an overview. *Diabetologia* 1984;26:93.

173. Eriksson UJ. Diabetes in pregnancy: retarded fetal growth, congenital malformations and feto-maternal concentrations of zinc, copper and managese in the rat. *J Nutr* 1984;114:477.

174. Jovanovic L, Peterson CM. Management of the pregnant, insulin-dependent diabetic woman. *Diabetes Care* 1980;3:63–68.

175. Lucas MJ, Leveno KJ, Williams ML, et al. Early pregnancy glycosylated hemoglobin, severity of diabetes, and fetal malformations. *Am J Obstet Gynecol* 1989;161:426–431.

176. Molsted-Pedersen L. Pregnancy and diabetes: a survey. *Acta Endocrinol Suppl (Copenh)* 1980;238:13–19.

177. Persson K, Ronnerstam R. Neonatal eye infections caused by

178. Reid M, Hadden D, Harley JM, et al. Fetal malformations in diabetics with high haemoglobin A1c in early pregnancy. *BMJ* 1984;289:1001.

179. Roversi GD, Canussio V, Gargiulo M, et al. The intensive care of perinatal risk in pregnant diabetics (136 cases): a new therapeutic scheme for the best control of maternal disease. *J Perinat Med* 1973;1:114–124.

180. Ylinen K, Aula P, Stenman U-H, et al. Risk of minor and major fetal malformations in diabetics with high hemoglobin Al c values in early pregnancy. *BMJ* 1984;289:345.

181. Artal R, Golde SH, Dorey F, et al. The effect of plasma glucose variability on neonatal outcome in the pregnant diabetic patient. *Am J Obstet Gynecol* 1983;147:537–541.

182. Fuhrmann K, Reiher H, Semmler K, et al. The effect of intensified conventional insulin therapy before and during pregnancy on the malformation rate in offspring of diabetic mothers. *Exp Clin Endocrinol* 1984;83:173–177.

183. Jovanovic L, Peterson CM. Optimal insulin delivery for the pregnant diabetic patient. *Diabetes Care* 1982;5[Suppl 1]:24–37.

184. Wright AD, Taylor KG, Nicholson HO, et al. Maternal blood glucose control and outcome of diabetic pregnancy. *Postgrad Med J* 1982;58:411–414.

185. Fine EL, Horal M, Chang TI, et al. Evidence that elevated glucose causes altered gene expression, apoptosis, and neural tube defects in a mouse model of diabetic pregnancy. *Diabetes* 1999;48:2454–2462.

186. Malaisse-Lagae F, Vanhoutte C, Rypens F, et al. Anomalies of fetal development in GK rats. *Acta Diabetol* 1997;34:55–60.

187. Hunter SA, Burstein SH. Receptor mediation in cannabinoid stimulated arachidonic acide mobilization and anandamide synthesis. *Life Sci* 1997;60:1563–1573.

188. Torchinsky A, Toder V, Carp H, et al. *In vivo* evidence for the existence of a threshold for hyperglycemia-induced major fetal malformations: relevance to the etiology of diabetic teratogenesis. *Early Pregnancy* 1997;3:27–33.

189. Sivan E, Lee YC, Wu YK, et al. Free radical scavenging enzymes in fetal dysmorphogenesis among offspring of diabetic rats. *Teratology* 1997;56:343–349.

190. Brownscheidle CM, Wootten V, Mathieu MH, et al. The effects of maternal diabetes on fetal maturation and neonatal health. *Metabolism* 1983;32:148.

191. Chartrel NC, Clabaut MT, Boismare FA, et al. Uteroplacental hemodynamic disturbances in establishment of fetal growth retardation in streptozocin-induced diabetic rats. *Diabetes* 1990;39:743–746.

192. Clabaut M, Stirnemann B, Bouftila B, et al. Beneficial effect induced by a beta-adrenoceptor blocker on fetal growth in streptozotocin-diabetic rats. *Biol Neonate* 1997;71:171–180.

193. Deuchar EM. Embryonic malformations in rats resulting from maternal diabetes: preliminary observations. *J Embryol Exp Morphol* 1977;41:3.

194. Diamond MP, Moley KH, Pellicer A, et al. Effects of streptozotocin- and alloxan-induced diabetes mellitus on mouse follicular and early embryo development. *J Reprod Fertil* 1989;86:1–10.

195. Endo A. Teratogenesis of diabetic mice treated with alloxan prior to conception. *Arch Environ Health* 1966;12:492.

196. Eriksson UJ, Styrud J, Eriksson RSM. Diabetes in pregnancy: genetic and temporal relationships of maldevelopment in the offspring of diabetic rats. In: Sutherland HW, Stowers JM, eds. *4th International colloquium on carbohydrate metabolism in pregnancy and the newborn.* Berlin: Springer-Verlag, 1989:51.

Chlamydia trachomatis. Scand J Infect Dis Suppl 1982;32:141–145.

197. Eriksson U, Dahlstrom E, Larsson KS, et al. Increased incidence of congenital malformations in the offspring of diabetic rats and their prevention by maternal insulin therapy. *Diabetes* 1982;31:1–6.

198. Eriksson UJ, Dahlstrom VE, Lithell HO. Diabetes in pregnancy: influence of genetic background and maternal diabetic state on the incidence of skeletal malformations in the fetal rat. *Acta Endocrinol* 1986;277:66.

199. Eriksson UJ, Siman CM. Pregnant diabetic rats fed the antioxidant butylated hydroxytoluene show decreased occurrence of malformations in offspring. *Diabetes* 1996;45:1497–502.

200. Funaki K, Mikamo K. Developmental-stage-dependent teratogenic effects of maternal spontaneous diabetes in the chinese hamster. *Diabetes* 1983;32:738.

201. Giavini E, Broccia ML, Prati M, et al. Effects of streptozotocin-induced diabetes on fetal development of the rat. *Teratology* 1986;34:81–88.

202. Giavini E, Prati M, Roversi G. Congenital malformations in offspring of diabetic rats: experimental study on the influence of the diet composition and magnesium intake. *Biol Neonate* 1990;57:207–217.

203. Buckley SK, Steele CE, New CAT. *In vitro* development of early postimplantation rate embryo. *Dev Biol* 1978;65:396.

204. Kim JN, Runge W, Wells LJ, et al. Effects of experimental diabetes on the offspring of the rat. Fetal growth birth weight gestation period and fetal mortality diabetes. *Diabetes* 1960;9:396–404.

205. Lazarow A, Kim JN, Wells LJ. Birth weight and fetal mortality in pregnant subdiabetic rats. *Diabetes* 1960;9:114–117.

206. Lee A, Plump A, DeSimone C, et al. A role for DNA mutations in diabetes-associated teratogenesis in transgenic embryos. *Diabetes* 1995;44:20.

207. Lee AT, Reis D, Eriksson UJ. Hyperglycemia-induced embryonic dysmorphogenesis correlates with genomic DNA mutation frequency *in vitro* and in vivo. *Diabetes* 1999;48:371–376.

208. Ornoy A, Kimyagarov D, Yaffee P, et al. Role of reactive oxygen species in diabetes-induced embryotoxicity: studies on pre-implantation mouse embryos cultured in serum from diabetic pregnant women. *Isr J Med Sci* 1996;32:1066–1073.

209. Pampfer S, de Hertogh R, Vanderheyden I, et al. Decreased inner cell mass proportion in blastocysts from diabetic rats. *Diabetes* 1990;39:471–476.

210. Pampfer S, Vanderheyden I, Wuu YD, et al. Possible role for TNF-alpha in early embryopathy associated with maternal diabetes in the rat. *Diabetes* 1995;44:531–536.

211. Otani H, Tanaka O, Tatewaki R, et al. Diabetic environment and genetic predisposition as causes of congenital malformations in NOD mouse embryos. *Diabetes* 1991;40:1245–1250.

212. Phelan SA, Ito M, Loeken MR. Neural tube defects in embryos of diabetic mice: role of the Pax-3 gene and apoptosis. *Diabetes* 1997;46:1189–1197.

213. Siman CM, Eriksson UJ. Vitamin C supplementation of the maternal diet reduces the rate of malformation in the offspring of diabetic rats. *Diabetologia* 1997;40:1416–1424.

214. Siman M. Congenital malformations in experimental diabetic pregnancy: aetiology and antioxidative treatment. Minireview based on a doctoral thesis. *Ups J Med Sci* 1997;102:61–98.

215. Siman CM, Eriksson UJ. Vitamin E decreases the occurrence of malformations in the offspring of diabetic rats. *Diabetes* 1997;46:1054–1061.

216. Sivan E, Reece EA, Wu YK, et al. Dietary vitamin E prophylaxis and diabetic embryopathy: morphologic and biochemical analysis. *Am J Obstet Gynecol* 1996;175:793–799.

217. Unger E, Eriksson UJ. Regionally disturbed production of cartilage proteoglycans in malformed fetuses from diabetic rats. *Diabetologia* 1992;35:517.

218. Viana M, Herrera E, Bonet B. Teratogenic effects of diabetes mellitus in the rat. Prevention by vitamin E. *Diabetologia* 1996;39:1041–1046.

219. Yang X, Borg LA, Siman CM, et al. Maternal antioxidant treatments prevent diabetes-induced alterations of mitochondrial morphology in rat embryos. *Anat Rec* 1998;251:303–315.

220. Yang X, Borg LA, Eriksson UJ. Metabolic alteration in neural tissue of rat embryos exposed to beta-hydroxybutyrate during organogenesis. *Life Sci* 1998;62:293–300.

221. Moley KH, Vaughn WK, DeCherney AH, et al. Effect of diabetes mellitus on mouse pre-implantation embryo development. *J Reprod Fertil* 1991;93:325–332.

222. de Hertogh R, Vanderheyden I, Pampfer S, et al. Maternal insulin treatment improves pre-implantation embryo development in diabetic rats. *Diabetologia* 1992;35:406–408.

223. Hunter SK, Wang Y, Rodgers VG. Bioartificial pancreas use in diabetic pregnancy. *ASAIO J* 1999;45:13–17.

224. Cederberg J, Galli J, Luthman H, et al. Increased mRNA levels of Mn-SOD and catalase in embryos of diabetic rats from a malformation-resistant strain. *Diabetes* 2000;49:101–107.

225. Eriksson UJ, Wentzel P, Minhas HS, et al. Teratogenicity of 3-deoxyglucosone and diabetic embryopathy. *Diabetes* 1998;47:1960–1966.

226. Moley KH, Chi MM, Knudson CM, et al. Hyperglycemia induces apoptosis in pre-implantation embryos through cell death effector pathways. *Nat Med* 1998;4:1421–1424.

227. Moley KH, Chi MM, Mueckler MM. Maternal hyperglycemia alters glucose transport and utilization in mouse preimplantation embryos. *Am J Physiol* 1998;275:E38–47.

228. Pinter E, Reece EA, Leranth CZ, et al. Arachidonic acid prevents hyperglycemia associated yolk sac damage and embryopathy: modifications in polyunsaturated fatty acids provide clues for pathogenesis. *Am J Obstet Gynecol* 1986;155:691.

229. Pinter E, Reece EA, Leranth CZ, et al. Surface alterations of the embryonic blood cells and the visceral endodermal yolk sac layer under hyperglycemic conditions revealed by scanning electrons microscopy. In: Proceedings of Society of Perinatal Obstetricians, 1986, p. 25 (abst).

230. Pinter E, Reece EA, Leranth CZ, et al. Yolk sac failure in embryopathy due to hyperglycemia: ultrastructural analysis of yolk sac differentiation associated with embryopathy in rat conceptuses under hyperglycemic conditions. *Teratology* 1986;33:73.

231. Sadler TV. Effects of maternal diabetes on early embryogenesis. I. The teratogenic potential of diabetic serum. *Teratology* 1980;21:339.

232. Trocino RA, Akazawa S, Ishibashi M, et al. Significance of glutathione depletion and oxidative stress in early embryogenesis in glucose-induced rat embryo culture. *Diabetes* 1995;44:992–998.

233. Wentzel P, Eriksson UJ. Antioxidants diminish developmental damage induced by high glucose and cyclooxygenase inhibitors in rat embryos *in vitro*. *Diabetes* 1998;47:677–684.

234. Ornoy A, Zusman I, Cohen AM, et al. Effects of sera from Cohen, genetically determined diabetic rats, streptozotocin diabetic rats and sucrose fed rats on *in vitro* development of early somite rat embryos. *Diabetes Res* 1986;3:43–51.

235. Sadler TW, Phillips LS, Balkan W, et al. Somatomedin inhibitors from diabetic rat serum alter growth and development of mouse embryos in culture. *Diabetes* 1986;35:861.

236. Rashbass P, Ellington SK. Development of rat embryos cultured in serum prepared from rats with streptozotocin-induced diabetes. *Teratology* 1988;37:51–61.

237. Mulder H, Fischer HR. Does thyroid function influence serum beta 2-microglobulin? *Neth J Med* 1989;34:182–188.

238. Zusman I, Yaffe P, Ornoy A. Effects of human diabetic serum

on the *in vitro* development of mouse preimplantation embryos. *Teratology* 1989;39:581–589.

239. Zusman I, Yaffe P, Raz I, et al. Effects of human diabetic serum on the *in vitro* development of early somite rat embryos. *Teratology* 1989;39:85–92.

240. Styrud J, Eriksson UJ. Development of rat embryos in culture media containing different concentrations of normal and diabetic rat serum. *Teratology* 1992;46:473.

241. Wentzel P, Eriksson UJ. Insulin treatment fails to abolish the teratogenic potential of serum from diabetic rats. *Eur J Endocrinol* 1996;134:459–466.

242. Wentzel P, Thunberg L, Eriksson UJ. Teratogenic effect of diabetic serum is prevented by supplementation of superoxide dismutase and N-acetylcysteine in rat embryo culture. *Diabetologia* 1997;40:7–14.

243. Carlsten A, Hallgren B, Jagenburg R, et al. Amino acids and free fatty acids in plasma in diabetes. II. The myocardial arteriovenous differences before and after insulin. *Acta Med Scand* 1966;179:631–639.

244. Carlsten A, Hallgren B, Jagenburg R, et al. Amino acids and free fatty acids in plasma in diabetes. I. The effect of insulin on the arterial levels. *Acta Med Scand* 1966;179:361–370.

245. Alberti KG. Letter: Intravenous insulin boluses in treatment of diabetic coma. *Lancet* 1975;2:547–548.

246. Zinman B, Stokes EF, Albisser AM, et al. The metabolic response to glycemic control by the artificial pancreas in diabetic man. *Metabolism* 1979;28:511–518.

247. Calabrese G, Bueti A, Santeusanio F, et al. Continuous subcutaneous insulin infusion treatment in insulin-dependent diabetic patients: a comparison with conventional optimized treatment in a long-term study. *Diabetes Care* 1982;5:457–465.

248. Nosadini R, Noy GA, Nattrass M, et al. The metabolic and hormonal response to acute normoglycaemia in type 1 (insulin-dependent) diabetes: studies with a glucose controlled insulin infusion system (artificial endocrine pancreas). *Diabetologia* 1982;23:220–228.

249. Capaldo B, Home PD, Massi-Benedetti M, et al. The response of blood intermediary metabolite levels to 24 hours treatment with a blood glucose-controlled insulin infusion system in type 1 diabetes. *Diabetes Res* 1984;1:187–193.

250. Beck-Nielsen H, Richelsen B, Mogensen CE, et al. Effect of insulin pump treatment for one year on renal function and retinal morphology in patients with IDDM. *Diabetes Care* 1985;8:585–589.

251. Beck-Nielsen H, Richelsen B, Schwartz Sorensen N, et al. Insulin pump treatment: effect on glucose homeostasis, metabolites, hormones, insulin antibodies and quality of life. *Diabetes Res* 1985;2:37–43.

252. Marshall MO, Heding LG, Villumsen J, et al. Development of insulin antibodies, metabolic control and B-cell function in newly diagnosed insulin dependent diabetic children treated with monocomponent human insulin or monocomponent porcine insulin. *Diabetes Res* 1988;9:169–175.

253. Goldman A, Dicker D, Feldberg D, et al. Pregnancy outcome in patients with insulin-dependent diabetes mellitus with preconceptional diabetic control: a comparative study. *Am J Obstet Gynecol* 1986;155:293.

254. Reece EA, Pinter EA, Leranth CZ, et al. Malformations of the neural tube induced by *in vitro* hyperglycemia: an ultrastructural analysis. *Teratology* 1985;32:363.

255. Reece EA, Pinter E, Leranth CZ, et al. Yolk sac failure in embryopathy due to hyperglycemia: horseradish peroxidase uptake in the assessment of yolk sac dysfunction. *Obstet Gynecol* 1989;74:755.

256. Reece EA, Pinter E, Homko C, et al. The yolk sac theory: closing the circle on why diabetes associated malformations occur. *J Soc Gynecol Invest* 1994;1:3.

257. Reece EA, Wiznitzer A, Homko CJ, et al. Synchronization of the factors critical for diabetic teratogenesis: an *in vitro* model. *Am J Obstet Gynecol* 1996;174:1284–1288.

258. Bunn HF, Haney DN, Kamin S, et al. The biosynthesis of human hemoglobin AM slow glycosylation of hemoglobin in vivo. *J Clin Invest* 1976;57:1652.

259. Sadler TV, Horton WE. Whole embryo culture. A screening technique for teratogens? *Teratogenesis Carcinog Mutagen* 1982; 2:243.

260. Reece EA, Homko CJ, Wiznitzer A. Hypoglycemia in pregnancies complicated by diabetes mellitus: maternal and fetal considerations. *Clin Obstet Gynecol* 1994;37:50.

261. Impastato DJ, Gabriel AR, Lardar EH. Electric and insulin shock therapy during pregnancy. *Dis New Syst* 1964;25:542.

262. Bergman M, Seaton TB, Auerhahn CC, et al. The incidence of gestational hypoglycemia in insulin-dependent and non-insulin-dependent diabetic women. *NY State J Med* 1986;86:174.

263. Rayburn W, Piehl E, Jacober S, et al. Severe hypoglycemia during pregnancy: its frequency and predisposing factors in diabetic women. *Int J Gynaecol Obstet* 1986;24:263.

264. Kimmerle R, Heinemann L, Delecki A, et al. Severe hypoglycemia incidence and predisposing factors in 85 pregnancies of type I diabetic women. *Diabetes Care* 1992;15:1034.

265. Ellington SKL. *In vivo* and *in vitro* studies on the effects of maternal fasting during embryonic organogenesis in the rat. *Reprod Fertil* 1980;60:383.

266. Sadler TW, Horton WE Jr. Effects of maternal diabetes on early embryogenesis: the role of insulin and insulin therapy. *Diabetes* 1983;32:1070.

267. Akazawa S, Akazawa M, Hashimoto M, et al. Effects of hypoglycemia on early embryogenesis in rat embryo organ culture. *Diabetologia* 1987;30:791.

268. Sadler TV, Hunter ES III. Hypoglycemia: how little is too much for the embryo? *Am J Obstet Gynecol* 1987;157:190.

269. Landauer W. Rumplessness of chicken embryos produced by the injection of insulin in other chemicals. *J Exp Zool* 1945;98:65.

270. Zwilling E. Association of hypoglycemia with insulin micromelia in chick embryos. *J Exp Zool* 1948;109:197.

271. Duraiswami PK. Insulin-induced skeletal abnormalities in developing chickens. *BMJ* 1950;2:384.

272. Rabinovitch AL, Gibson MA. Skeletogenesis in insulin-treated chick embryos. II. Histochemical observations, with particular reference to the tibiotarsus. *Teratology* 1972;6:51.

273. Chomette G. Entwicklungsstörungen nach Insulinschock beim trächtigen Kaninchen. *Beitr Pathol Anat* 1955;115:439.

274. Brinsmade A, Büchner F, Rübsaamen H. Missbildungen am Kaninchen embryo durch Insulininjektion beim Muttertier. *Naturwissenschaften* 1956;43:259.

275. Brinsmade AB. Entwicklungsstörungen am Kaninchen-embryo nach Glukosemangel beim trächtigen Muttertier. *Beitr Pathol Anat* 1957;117:140.

276. Smithberg M, Runner MN. Teratogenic effects of hypoglycemic treatments in inbred strains of mice. *Am J Anat* 1963;113:479.

277. Lichtenstein H, Guest GM, Warkanay J. Abnormalities in offspring of white rats given protamine zinc insulin during pregnancy. *Proc Soc Exp Biol Med* 1951;78:398.

278. Love EJ, Kinch RAH, Stevenson JAF. The effect of protamine zinc insulin on the outcome of pregnancy in the normal rat. *Diabetes* 1964;13:44.

279. Hannah RS, Moore KL. Effects of fasting and insulin on skeletal development in rats. *Teratology* 1971;4:135.

280. Buchanan TA, Schemmer JK, Freinkel N. Embryotoxic effects of brief maternal insulin-hypoglycemia during organogenesis in the rat. *J Clin Invest* 1986;78:643.

281. Ream JR Jr, Weingarten PL, Pappas AM. Evaluation of the prenatal effects of massive doses of insulin in rats. *Teratology* 1970; 3:29.

282. Steinke J, Driscoll S. The extractable insulin content of pancreas from fetuses and infants of diabetic and control mothers. *Diabetes* 1965;14:573.

283. Kathan S, Schwartz R, Adam P. Placental barrier to human insulin I125 in insulin-dependent diabetic mothers. *J Clin Endocrinol Metab* 1975;40:139.

284. Eriksson UJ, den Bieman M, Prins JB, et al. Differences in susceptibility for diabetes induced malformations in separated rat colonies of common origin. In: Proceedings of the 4th FELASA Symposium, Lyon, France, 1990:53.

285. Hurley LS, Gowan J, Swenerton H. Teratogenic effects of short-term and transitory zinc deficiency in rats. *Teratology* 1971;4: 199.

286. Eriksson UJ. Diabetes in pregnancy: retarded fetal growth, congenital malformations and feto-maternal concentrations of zinc, copper and manganese in the rat. *J Nutr* 1984;114:477.

287. Uriu-Hare JY, Stern JS, Reaven GM, et al. The effect of maternal diabetes on trace element status and fetal development in the rat. *Diabetes* 1985;34:1031.

288. Styrud J, Dahlström VE, Eriksson UJ. Induction of skeletal malformations in the offspring of rats fed a zincdeficient diet. *Upsala J Med Sci* 1986;91:29.

289. Yde H. The growth-hormone dependent sulphation factor in serum of untreated diabetics. *Lancet* 1964;2:626.

290. Winter R, Phillips LS, Klein MN, et al. Somatomedin activity and diabetic control in children with insulin dependent diabetes. *Diabetes* 1979;28:952.

291. Phillips LS, Belosky DC, Reichard LA. Nutrition and somatomedin. V. Action and measurement of somatomedin inhibitor (s) in serum from diabetic rats. *Endocrinology* 1979; 104:1513.

292. D'Ercole JA, Applewhite GT, Underwood LE. Evidence that somatomedin is synthesized by multiple tissues in the fetus. *Dev Biol* 1980;75:315.

293. Phillips LS, Bajaj VR, Fusco AC, et al. Nutrition and somatomedin. XI. Studies of somatomedin inhibitors in rats with streptozotocin-induced diabetes. *Diabetes* 1983;32:1117.

294. Wentzel P, Jansson L, Eriksson UJ. Diabetes in pregnancy: uterine blood flow and embryonic development in the rat. 2004 (*submitted for publication*).

295. Steel JM, Johnstone FD, Johnstone FD, et al. Can prepregnancy care of diabetic women reduce the risk of abnormal babies? *BMJ* 1982;185:353.

296. Elixhauser A, Weschler JM, Kitzmiller JL, et al. Cost-benefit analysis of preconception care for women with established diabetes mellitus. *Diabetes Care* 1993;16:1146.

297. Hale FL. Pigs born without eyeballs. *J Hered* 1933;24:105.

298. Kalter H, Warkany J. Experimental production of congenital malformations in mammals by metabolic procedure. *Physiol Rev* 1959;39:69.

299. Fujimoto S, Sumi T, Kwzukawa S, et al. The genesis of experimental anomalies-fetal anomalies in reference to experimental diabetes in rabbit. *J Osaka City Med Ctr* 1958;7:62.

300. Barashnev YL. Disorders of fetal brain development in maternal alloxan diabetes. *Arkh Patol* 1964;26:63.

301. Watanabe G, Ingalls TH. Congenital malformations in the offspring of alloxan-diabetic mice. *Diabetes* 1963;12:66.

302. Deuchar EM. Experimental evidence relating fetal anomalies to diabetes. In: Sutherland HW, Stowers JM, eds. *Carbohydrate metabolism in pregnancy and the newborn*. New York: Springer-Verlag, 1979:247.

303. Deuchar EM. Effects of streptozotocin on early rat embryos grown in culture. *Experientia* 1977;34:84.

304. Asplund K. Effects of intermittent glucose infusion in pregnant rats on the functional development of the foetal pancreatic B-cells. *J Endocrinol* 1973;59:287.

305. Clavert A, Wolff-Quenot MJ, Buck P. Etude de l'action embryopathigue du glucose en injection intrammniotique. *C R Soc Biol (Paris)* 1972;166:1789.

306. Landauer W. Is insulin a teratogen? *Teratology* 1972;5:129.

307. Cockroft DL, Freinkel N, Phillips LS, et al. Metabolic factors affecting organogenesis in diabetic pregnancy. *Clin Res* 1982;29: 577A(abst).

308. Buchanan TA, Freinkel N, Lewis NJ, et al. Fuel-mediated teratogenesis. Use of D-mannose to modify organogenesis in the rat embryo in vivo. *J Clin Invest* 1985;75:1927.

309. Horii K, Watanabe G, Ingalls TH. Experimental diabetes in pregnant mice: prevention of congenital malformations in offspring by insulin. *Diabetes* 1966;15:194.

310. Duraiswami P. Insulin-induced skeletal anomalies in developing chickens. *BMJ* 1950;2:384.

311. Nakhooda AF, Like AA, Chappel CI, et al. The spontaneous Wistar rat (The "BB" rat); studies prior to and during development of the overt syndrome. *Diabetologia* 1978;14:199.

312. Brownscheidle CM, Davis DL. Diabetes in pregnancy: a preliminary study of the pancreas, placenta and malformations in the BB Wistar rat. *Placenta* 1981;19[Suppl]:203.

313. Marliss EB, Nakhooda AF, Poussier P, et al. The diabetic syndrome of the "BB" Wistar rat: possible relevance to type I (insulin-dependent) diabetes in man. *Diabetologia* 1982;22: 225.

314. Scott J, Engelhard VH, Curnow RT, et al. Prevention of diabetes in BB rats. I. Evidence suggesting a requirement for mature T cells in bone marrow inoculum of neonatally injected rats. *Diabetes* 1986;35:1034.

315. New DAT. Development of explanted rat embryos in circulating medium. *J Embryol Exp Morphol* 1967;17:513.

316. Eriksson UJ, Siman CM. Pregnant diabetic rats fed the antioxidant butylated hydroxytoluene show decreased occurence of malformations in offspring. *Diabetes* 1996;45(11):1497–1502.

317. New DAT. Methods for culture of post implantation embryros of rodents. In: Daniel JC, ed. *Method in mammalian embryology*. San Francisco: Freeman, 1971:305.

318. New DAT, Coppola PT, Cockroft DL. Comparison of growth *in vitro* and *in vivo* of post-implantation rat embryos. *J Embryol Exp Morphol* 1976;36:133.

319. New DAT. Techniques for assessment of teratologic effects. *Environ Health Perspect* 1977;18:105.

320. New DAT. Whole-embryo culture and the study of mammalian embryos during organogenesis. *Biol Rev* 1978;53:81.

321. Sadler IV. Culture of early somite mouse embryos during organogenesis. *J Embryol Exp Morphol* 1979;49:17.

322. Oberley LW. Free radicals and diabetes. *Free Radic Biol Med* 1988;5:113–124.

323. Gillery P, Monboisse JC, Maquart FX, et al. Does oxygen free radical increased formation explain long term complications of diabetes mellitus? *Med Hypotheses* 1989;29:47–50.

324. Baynes JW. Role of oxidative stress in development of complications in diabetes. *Diabetes* 1991;40:405–412.

325. Schmidt AM, Weidman E, Lalla E, et al. Advanced glycation endproducts (AGEs) induce oxidant stress in the gingiva: a potential mechanism underlying accelerated periodontal disease associated with diabetes. *J Periodontal Res* 1996;31: 508–515.

326. West IC. Radicals and oxidative stress in diabetes. *Diabet Med* 2000;17:171–180.

327. Palmer AM, Thomas CR, Gopaul N, et al. Dietary antioxidant supplementation reduces lipid peroxidation but impairs vascular function in small mesenteric arteries of the streptozotocin-diabetic rat. *Diabetologia* 1998;41:148–156.

328. Sano T, Umeda F, Hashimoto T, et al. Oxidative stress measurement by *in vivo* electron spin resonance spectroscopy in rats with streptozotocin-induced diabetes. *Diabetologia* 1998;41:1355–1360.

329. Elangovan V, Shohami E, Gati I, et al. Increased hepatic lipid soluble antioxidant capacity as compared to other organs of streptozotocin-induced diabetic rats: a cyclic voltammetry study. *Free Radic Res* 2000;32:125–134.

330. Nishikawa T, Edelstein D, Brownlee M. The missing link: a single unifying mechanism for diabetic complications. *Kidney Int Suppl* 2000;77:S26–30.

331. Nishikawa T, Edelstein D, Du XL, et al. Normalizing mitochondrial superoxide production blocks three pathways of hyperglycaemic damage. *Nature* 2000;404:787–790.

332. Yang X, Borg LA, Eriksson UJ. Altered metabolism and superoxide generation in neural tissue of rat embryos exposed to high glucose. *Am J Physiol* 1997;272:E173–180.

333. Wentzel P, Welsh N, Eriksson UJ. Developmental damage, increased lipid peroxidation, diminished cyclooxygenase-2 gene expression, and lowered prostaglandin E2 levels in rat embryos exposed to a diabetic environment. *Diabetes* 1999;48:813–820.

334. Suzuki S, Ohtomo M, Satoh Y, et al. Effect of manidipine and delapril on insulin sensitivity in type 2 diabetic patients with essential hypertension. *Diabetes Res Clin Pract* 1996;33:43–51.

335. Forsberg H, Eriksson UJ, Welsh N. Apoptosis in embryos of diabetic rats. *Pharmacol Toxicol* 1998;83:104–111.

336. Menegola E, Broccia ML, Prati M, et al. Glutathione status in diabetes-induced embryopathies. *Biol Neonate* 1996;69:293–297.

337. Ishibashi M, Akazawa S, Sakamaki H, et al. Oxygen-induced embryopathy and the significance of glutathione-dependent antioxidant system in the rat embryo during early organogenesis. *Free Radic Biol Med* 1997;22:447–454.

338. Khandelwal M, Wu Y-K, Borenstein M, et al. Dietary phospholipid therapy, hyperglycemia-induced membrane changes and associated diabetic embryopathy. Paper presented at meetings of Society of Perinatal Obstetricians, January 23–28, 1995, Atlanta, GA.

339. O'Rahilly R, Gardner E. The timing and sequence of events in the development of the human nervous system, during the embryonic period proper. *Z Anat Entwick Gesch* 1971;134:1.

340. Schroeder TE. Mechanism of morphogenesis: the embryonic neural tube. *Br J Neurosci* 1971;2:183.

341. Burnside MD, Jacobson AG. Analysis of morphogenetic movements in the neuronal plate of the New Taricha torosa. *Dev Biol* 1968;18:537.

342. Edeman GM. Cell adhesion molecules. *Science* 1983;219:450.

343. Purves D, Lichtmann JW. *Principles of neural development.* Sunderland, MA: Sinauer Assoc, Inc., 1985.

344. Everett JW: Morphological and physiological studies of the placenta in the albino rat. *J Exp Zool* 1935;70:243.

345. Brunschwig AE. notes on experiments in placental permeability. *Anat Rec* 1927;34:237.

346. Leung CCK, Watabe H, Brent RL. The effect of heterologous antisera on embryonic development. *Am J Anat* 1977;148:457.

347. Freeman SJ, Beck F, Lloyd JB. The role of the visceral yolk sac in mediating protein utilization by rat embryos cultured *in vitro*. *J Embryol Exp Morphol* 1981;66:223.

348. Muglia L, Locker J. Extra pancreatic insulin gene expression in the fetal rat. *Proc Natl Acad Sci U S A* 1984;81:3635.

349. Payne GS, Deuchar EM. An *in vitro* study of function of embryonic membranes in the rat. *J Embryol Exp Morphol* 1972;27:533.

350. Moore KL. *The developing human: clinically oriented embryology.* Philadelphia: WB Saunders, 1982.

351. Sadler TW. *Langman's medical embryology*, 5th ed. Baltimore: Williams & Wilkins, 1985.

352. Hesseldahl H, Larson JF. Ultrastructure of humans yolk-sac endoderm, mesenchyme, tubules and mesothelium. *Am J Anat* 1969;126:315.

353. Hoyes AD. The human fetal yolk sac: an ultrastructural study of four specimens. *Z Zellforsch Mikrosk Anat* 1969;99: 469.

354. Moore AS, Metcalf D. Ontogeny of the hemopoietic system: yolk sac original of *in vivo* and *in vitro* colony forming cells in the developing mouse embryo. *Br J Haematol* 1970;18:279.

355. Hesseldahl H, Larson JF. Hemopoiesis and blood vessels in human yolk sac. *Acta Anat* 1971;78:274.

356. Gonzales-Cruse F. The human yolk sac and yolk sac (endodermal sinus) tremors: a review. *Prospect Pediatr Pathol* 1979;5:179.

357. Gonzales-Crussi F, Roth LM. The human yolk sac and yolk sac carcinoma. *Hum Pathol* 1976;7:675.

358. Padykula HA, Deren JJ, Wilson TH. Development of structure and function in the mammalian yolk sac. I. Developmental morphology and vitamin B12 uptake of the rat yolk sac. *Dev Biol* 1966;13:311.

359. Freeman SJ, Brent RL, Lloyd JB. The effects of teratogenic antiserum on yolk-sac function in rat embryos cultured *in vitro*. *J Embryol Exp Morphol* 1982;71:63.

360. Warner CW, Sadler IV, Shockey J, et al. A comparison of the *in vivo* and *in vitro* response of mammalian embryos to a teratogenic insult. *Toxicology* 1983;28:271.

361. Witschi E. Development: prenatal vertebrae development: rat. In: Altman PL, Dittmer DS, eds. and comps. *Growth including reproduction and morphological development.* Prepared under the auspieces of the Committee on Biological Handbooks. Washington, DC: Federation of American Societies for Experimental Biology, 1962:304.

362. Lewitt P, Rack P. Immunoperoxidase localization of glial fibrillary acidic protein in radial glial-cells and astrocytes of the developing rhesus monkey brain. *J Comp Neurol* 1980;193:815.

363. Gupta M, Gulamhusein PA, Beck F. Morphometric analysis of the visceral yolk sac endoderm in the rat *in vivo* and *in vitro*. *J Reprod Fertil* 1982;65:239.

364. Brent LR, Johnson AJ, Jensen M. The production of congenital malformations using tissue antisera. VII. Yolksac antiserum. *Teratology* 1971;4:255.

365. Gitlin D, Boseman M. Fetus-specific serum proteins in several mammals and their relation to human alpha-fetoprotein. *Biochem Physiol* 1967;32:327.

366. Gitlin D, Boseman M. Sites of serum alphafetoprotein synthesis in the human and in the rat. *J Clin Invest* 1967;46:1010.

367. Gitlin D, Perricelli A, Gitlin GM. Synthesis of alpha-fetoprotein by liver, yolk sac, and gastrointestinal tract of the human conceptus. *Cancer Res* 1972;32:979.

368. Shi W-K, Hopkin B, Thompson S, et al. Synthesis of apolipoproteins, alphafetoprotein, albumin, and transferring by the human foetal yolk sac and other foetal organs. *J Embryol Exp Morphol* 1985;85:191.

369. Dziadek M, Adamson E. Localization and synthesis of alphafetoprotein in post-implantation mouse embryos. *J Embryol Exp Morphol* 1978;43:289.

370. Adamson ED. The location and synthesis of transferrin in mouse embryos and teratocarcinoma cells. *Dev Biol* 1982;91:227.

371. Dziadek MA, Andrews GK. Tissue specificity of alpha-fetoprotein messenger RNA expression during mouse embryogenesis. *EMBO J* 1983;2:549.

372. Meehan RR, Barlow DP, Hill RE, et al. Pattern of serum protein gene expression in mouse visceral yolk sac and fetal liver. *EMBO J* 1984;3:1881.

373. Driscoll DM, Getz GS. Extrahepatic synthesis of apolipoprotein E. *J Lipid Res* 1984;25:1368.

374. Meek J, Adamson ED. Transferrin foetal and adult mouse tissues: synthesis, storage and secretion. *J Embryol Exp Morphol* 1985;86:205.

375. Lovell-Badge RH, Evans MJ, Bellairs R. Protein synthetic patterns of tissues in the early chick embryo. *J Embryol Exp Morphol* 1985;85:65.

376. Hopkins B, Sharpe CR, Baralle FE, et al. Organ distribution of apolipoprotein gene transcripts in 6–12 weeks post fertilization human embryos. *J Embryol Exp Morphol* 1986;97:177.

377. Williams CL, Priscott PK, Oliver IT, et al. Albumin and transferrin synthesis in whole rat embryo cultures. *J Embryol Exp Morphol* 1986;92:33.

378. Sanyal MK, Wiebke EA. Oxygen requirement for *in vitro* growth and differentiation of the rat conceptus during organogenesis phase of embryo development. *Biol Reprod* 1979;20:639.

379. Sanyal MK, Naftolin F. In-vitro development of the mammalian embryo. *J Exp Zool* 1986;228:235.

380. Weibel RE. Stereological principles for morphometry in electron microscopic cytology. *Int Rev Cytol* 1969;26:235.

381. Warkany J, Lemire RJ. Arteriovenous malformations of the brain: a teratologic challenge. *Teratology* 1984;29:333.

382. Lewitt P, Cooper ML, Rakic P. Coexistence of neuronal and glial precursor cells in the cerebral ventricular zone of the fetal monkey: an ultrastructural immunoperoxidase study. *J Neurosci* 1981;1:27.

383. Slauson DO, Cooper BJ. *Mechanisms of disease: a textbook of comparative general pathology.* Baltimore: Williams & Wilkins, 1982.

384. Trump BF, Berezesky IK. Cellular ion regulation and disease: a hypothesis. *Curr Top Membr Transport* 1985;25:279.

385. Reece EA, Wu YK. Prevention of diabetic embryopathy in offspring of diabetic rats with use of a cocktail of deficient substrates and an antioxidant. *Am J Obstet Gynecol* 1997;176:790–797.

386. Reece EA, Khandelwal M, Wu YK, et al. Dietary intake of myo-inositol and neural tube defects in offspring of diabetic rats. *Am J Obstet Gynecol* 1997;176:536–539.

387. Khandelwal M, Reece EA, Wu YK, et al. Dietary myo-inositol therapy in hyperglycemia-induced embryopathy. *Teratology* 1998;57:79–84.

388. Kinalski M, Sledziewski A, Telejko B, et al. Antioxidant therapy and streptozotocin-induced diabetes in pregnant rats. *Acta Diabetol* 1999;36:113–117.

389. Wiznitzer A, Furman B, Mazor M, et al. The role of prostanoids in the development of diabetic embryopathy. *Semin Reprod Endocrinol* 1999;17:175–181.

390. Wiznitzer A, Ayalon N, Hershkovitz R, et al. Lipoic acid prevention of neural tube defects in offspring of rats with streptozocin-induced diabetes. *Am J Obstet Gynecol* 1999;180:188–93.

391. Irvine RF. How is the level of free arachidonic acid controlled in mammalian cells? *Biochem J* 1982;204:3.

392. Kinsell LW, Michaels GD, Walker G, et al. Dietary linoleic acid and linoleate: effects in diabetic and non-diabetic subjects with and without vascular disease. *Diabetes* 1959;8:179.

393. Snapper I. *Chinese lessons to Western medicine.* New York: Interscience, 1941.

394. Eriksson UJ. Rat embryos exposed to a teratogenic diabetic environment *in vitro* are protected by the antioxidant N-acetylcysteine. *Eur J Endocrinol* 1994;130[Suppl 1]:20.

395. Houtsmuller AJ. Significance of linoleic acid in the metabolism and therapy of diabetes mellitus. *World Rev Nutr Diet* 1982;39:85.

396. Houtsmuller AJ. The role of fat in the treatment of diabetes mellitus. In: Vergrosen X, ed. *The role of fats in human nutrition.* London: Academic Press, 1975:231.

397. Reece EA, Wu Y-K, Wiznitzer A, et al. Dietary polyunsaturated fatty acids prevent malformations in offspring of diabetic rats. Paper presented at annual meetings of Society of Perinatal Obstetricians, San Francisco, CA, February, 8–13, 1993.

398. Epstein CJ, Avraham KB, Lovett S, et al. Transgenic mice with increased CuZn-superoxide dismutase activity: an animal model of dosage effects in Down's syndrome. *Proc Natl Acad Sci U S A* 1987;84:8044.

399. Hagay ZJ, Weiss Y, Zusman I, et al. Prevention of diabetes-associated embryopathy by overexpression of the free radical scavenger copper zinc superoxide dismutase in transgenic mouse embryos. *Am J Obstet Gynecol* 1995;173:1036–1041.

400. Lapetina EG. Regulation of arachidonic acid production: role of phospholipases C and A2. *Trends Pharmacol Sci* 1982;3:115.

401. Warso MA, Lands WEM. Lipid peroxidation in relation to prostacyclin and thromboxane physiology and pathophysiology. *Br Med Bull* 1983;39:277.

402. Wolff SP. Diabetes mellitus and free radicals. Free radicals, transition metals and oxidative stress in the aetiology of diabetes mellitus and complications. *Br Med Bull* 1993;49:642.

403. Harris C, Stark KL, Juchau MR. Glutathione status and the incidence of neural tube defects elicited by direct acting teratogens *in vitro. Teratology* 1988;37:577.

404. Harris C. Glutathione biosynthesis in the post implantation rat conceptus *in vitro. Toxicol Appl Pharmacol* 1993;120:247.

405. Kashiwagi A, Asahina T, Ikebuchi M, et al. Abnormal glutathione metabolism and increased cytotoxicity caused by H2O2 in human umbilical vein endothelial cells cultured in high glucose medium. *Diabetologia* 1994;37:264.

406. Hempel SL, Wessels DA. Prostaglandin E2 synthesis after oxidant stress is dependent on cell glutathione content. *Am J Physiol* 1994;266:C1392.

407. Simán CM, Borg LAH, Eriksson UJ. Disturbed development, low vitamin E concentration, and increased lipid peroxidation in embryos of diabetic rats. *Diabetologia* 1994;37[Suppl 1]:A171.

408. Bucala R, Model P, Cerami A. Modification of DNA by reducing sugars: a possible mechanism for nucleic acid ageing and age-related dysfunction in gene expression. *Proc Natl Acad Sci U S A* 1984;81:105.

409. Morita J, Ueda K, Nanjo S, et al. Sequence specific damage of DNA induced by reducing sugars. *Nucleic Acid Res* 1985;13:449.

410. Schreck R, Rieber P, Baeuerle PA. Reactive oxygen intermediates as apparently widely used messengers in the activation of the NF-KB transcription factor and HIV-1. *EMBO J* 1991;10:2247.

411. Cagliero E, Forsberg H, Sala R, et al. Maternal diabetes induces increased expression of extracellular matrix components in rat embryos. *Diabetes* 1993;42:975.

412. Eriksson UJ, Wentzel P, Minhas HS, et al. Teratogenicity of 3-deoxyglucosone and diabetic embryopathy. *Diabetes* 1998;47(12):1960–1966.

413. Bravenboer B, Kappelle AC, Harriers FPT, et al. Potential use of glutathione for the prevention and treatment of diabetic neuropathy in the streptozotocin-induced diabetic rat. *Diabetologia* 1992;35:813.

414. Cameron NE, Cotter MA, Archibald V, et al. Anti-oxidant and pro-oxidant effects on nerve conduction velocity, endoneurial blood flow and oxygen tension in nondiabetic and streptozotocin-diabetic rats. *Diabetologia* 1994;37:449.

415. Eriksson UJ. Antioxidants protect rat embryos from diabetes-induced dysmorphogenesis. In: International Diabetes Federation Congress Abstracts, 1994, p. 410.

416. Golde LHG, van Deenen LLH. The effect of dietary fat on the molecular species lecithin from rat liver. *Biochim Biophys Acta* 1966;125:496.

417. Zilversmit DB. A proposal linking atherogenesis to the interaction of endothelial lipoprotein lipase with triglyceride rich lipoprotein. *Circ Res* 1973;33:633.

418. Goldman AS, Goto MP. Biochemical basis of diabetic embryopathy. *Isr J Med Sci* 1991;27:469.

419. Eriksson UJ, Borg LA, Cederberg J, et al. Pathogenesis of diabetes-induced congenital malformations. *Ups J Med Sci* 2000;105:53–84.

420. Siman CM, Gittenberger-de Groot AC, Wisse B, et al. Malformations in offspring of diabetic rats: morphometric analysis of neural crest-derived organs and effects of maternal vitamin E treatment. *Teratology* 2000;61:355–367.

421. Sakamaki H, Akazawa S, Ishibashi M, et al. Significance of glutathione-dependent antioxidant system in diabetes-induced embryonic malformations. *Diabetes* 1999;48:1138–1144.

422. Cockroft DL, Coppola PT. Teratogenic effects of excess glucose on head-fold rat embryos in culture. *Teratology* 1977; 16:141–146.

423. Herrera E. Metabolic adaptations in pregnancy and their implications for the availability of substrates to the fetus. *Eur J Clin Nutr* 2000;54[Suppl 1]:S47–51.

424. Horton WE Jr, Sadler TW: Effects of maternal diabetes on early embryogenesis. Alterations in morphogenesis produced by the ketone body, B-hydroxybutyrate. *Diabetes* 1983;32:610–616.

425. Baker L, Piddington R. Diabetic embryopathy: a selective review of recent trends. *J Diabetes Complications* 1993;7: 204–212.

426. Dhanasekaran N, Wu YK, Reece EA. Signaling pathways and diabetic embryopathy. *Semin Reprod Endocrinol* 1999;17: 167–174.

PERINATAL MORTALITY AND MORBIDITY

DONALD R. COUSTAN

The pathogenesis of many of the perinatal morbidities associated with maternal diabetes, including fetal macrosomia, respiratory distress syndrome, and congenital anomalies, are presented in earlier chapters of this book. Neonatal morbidities are discussed in Chapter 33. The pathogenesis of perinatal death in pregnancies complicated by diabetes is therefore the primary concern of this chapter. In addition, suggestions are made for the prevention of both morbidity and death in these pregnancies.

PERINATAL MORTALITY

Before the discovery of insulin in 1922, those few reported pregnancies among diabetic individuals yielded a perinatal mortality rate of approximately 65% (1). However, maternal mortality rates were in the range of 30%, so fetal considerations were secondary at that time. Once insulin was available, maternal mortality rates plummeted; currently, it is reasonable to conclude that the maternal mortality risk for diabetic pregnancy is approximately equal to that of the general pregnant population plus the risk associated with having diabetes over a 9-month period. Exceptions would include those diabetic individuals with coronary artery disease (2). In addition, there have been reports of maternal mortality related to severe insulin reactions (3). Denominator figures are not available, and it cannot presently be determined whether the hypoglycemia-related death rate during pregnancy exceeds the risk to nonpregnant diabetic women.

Although maternal death rates diminished rapidly with the availability of insulin treatment for diabetes, fetal and neonatal losses were much more difficult to eliminate. Unexplained sudden fetal death was a common way for such losses to occur. In the 1930s and 1940s, approximately 20% of diabetic pregnancies ended in this manner (4–6). In the 1950s and 1960s, fetal death rates had fallen to approximately 12% (7), and by the 1970s, most centers were reporting fetal mortality rates below 3% and perinatal mortality rates below 5% (8–16). Recent case series have reported perinatal mortality rates in well-controlled type 1 diabetic pregnancies to be similar to those of the general population (17). The reasons for this decline in the perinatal mortality rate are not entirely clear. During the eight decades since the discovery of insulin, technologic advances such as blood transfusions, safer anesthesia techniques, neonatal intensive care units, fetal monitoring, amniocentesis, biochemical and biophysical antepartum testing, and ultrasonography may all have contributed to the improvement. However, an increased understanding of the effects of perturbations in maternal metabolism on the unborn fetus and techniques that allow the achievement of better metabolic control during diabetic pregnancy may have had even greater significance.

The groundbreaking publications of Harley and Montgomery (18) in 1965 and Karlsson and Kjellmer (19) in 1972 demonstrated an inverse relationship between mean maternal ambient glucose levels during the third trimester and perinatal mortality rates (Table 14-1). At the time of Karlsson and Kjellmer's publication, many centers in the United States were attempting to maintain glucose levels at around 150 mg/dL in diabetic pregnant women in the belief that maternal hypoglycemia was equally disadvantageous for the fetus as was hyperglycemia, although there was little evidence to support that view. When the pregnancies of 237 diabetic women among the 50,000 pregnancies in the Collaborative Study of Cerebral Palsy were analyzed, no effect of maternal "insulin shock" on mental or motor performance at 8 months or 4 years of age in the offspring could be demonstrated (20). Furthermore, Roversi et al. (21) maintained diabetic pregnant women at the brink of symptomatic hypoglycemia with increasing insulin doses and reported a perinatal mortality rate of 3.6%.

Jovanovic and Peterson (22) reviewed the literature in 1980, citing those studies that reported both perinatal mortality rates and mean maternal circulating glucose levels. A scatterplot of these two variables was constructed, and the line of best fit (Fig. 14-1) suggests that the optimal rate of

TABLE 14-1. PERINATAL MORTALITY RATES IN DIABETIC PREGNANCIES AS A FUNCTION OF THIRD-TRIMESTER MATERNAL INPATIENT GLUCOSE CONTROL

	Average Blood Glucose (mg/dL)		
	<100	100–150	>150
n	52	77	38
Perinatal mortality (%)	2 (3.4)[a]	12 (16)	9 (24)

[a]$p < 0.05$.
Modified from Karlsson K, Kjellmer I. The outcome of diabetic pregnancies in relation to the mother's blood sugar level. *Am J Obstet Gynecol* 1972;112:213, with permission.

perinatal survival is associated with a mean plasma glucose level of approximately 84 mg/dL. At about the same time that these data were being published and accepted, a number of centers began to explore the normal range of maternal glycemia during the third trimester (Fig. 14-2). These studies determined that normal, nondiabetic pregnant women manifest fasting plasma glucose levels averaging 74 to 88 mg/dL and postprandial values that rarely exceed 130 mg/dL at 1 hour or 120 mg/dL at 2 hours (23–25).

Although the above evidence is indirect and the appropriate randomized controlled trial of intensive metabolic management in diabetic pregnancy has not been performed to date, the weight of these data strongly suggests that maternal hyperglycemia is associated with increased perinatal mortality rates in diabetic pregnancy and that normalization of glucose levels can reduce the incidence of perinatal loss.

Because the initiation of attempts to normalize maternal glucose metabolism was coincident with the development

of methods to assess fetal condition, it is also possible that the above improvements in perinatal outcome were related to timely identification and delivery of fetuses in jeopardy, rather than to the prevention of fetal compromise. Such an explanation seems unlikely in light of the fact that the Karlsson and Kjellmer (19) series did not use antepartum fetal assessment. Furthermore, if advances in antepartum fetal monitoring (e.g., estriol measurement and nonstress and stress testing) were responsible for the noted improvements, it would be expected that approximately 10% to 20% of surviving newborns would have to be delivered expeditiously because of evidence of deteriorating fetoplacental function. In one series, in which 77% of diabetic women had mean plasma glucose levels below 120 mg/dL in the third trimester, only 2.8% of babies were delivered because of falling estriol levels or abnormal stress test results (15). In another series of 52 very tightly controlled diabetic pregnancies, none of 52 infants were delivered because of deteriorating fetal or placental function (16).

Because sudden intrauterine fetal death occurs rarely, if at all, during intensive efforts at metabolic normalization in diabetic pregnancy, this phenomenon is difficult to study. In the past, hypotheses to explain the losses included unnoticed hypoglycemia and undiagnosed ketoacidosis. However, episodes of profound maternal hypoglycemia have generally been associated with fetal survival, and it is unlikely that episodes so mild as to go unnoticed would lead to fetal death. Diabetic ketoacidosis, on the other hand, has been associated with perinatal mortality rates of 50% to 90% (26,27). It is impossible to document whether this was the mechanism for the fetal deaths reported in the past, but an alternative explanation is plausible. Myers (28) demonstrated that monkeys do not tolerate periods of hypoxia as well if they are hyperglycemic compared with euglycemic or even hypoglycemic. He found that hypoxia

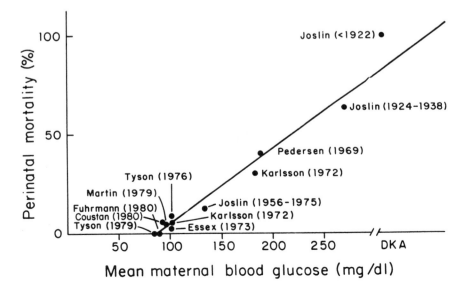

FIGURE 14-1. Perinatal mortality rate in diabetic pregnancies as a function of mean maternal blood glucose level in third trimester. (Adapted from Jovanovic L, Peterson CM. Management of the pregnant, insulin-dependent diabetic woman. *Diabetes Care* 1980;3:63, with permission.)

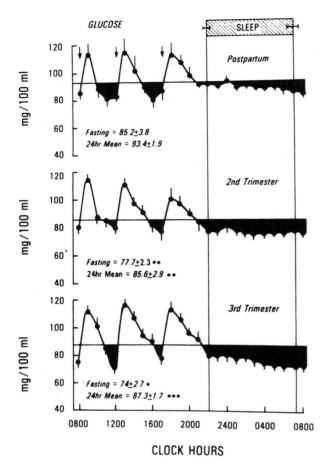

FIGURE 14-2. Diurnal glucose level excursions in six normal pregnant women during the second and third trimesters and 6 weeks postpartum. (From Cousins L, Rigg L, Hollingsworth D, et al. The 24-hour excursion and diurnal rhythm of glucose, insulin, and C-peptide in normal pregnancy. *Am J Obstet Gynecol* 1980;136:483, with permission.)

in the hyperglycemic rhesus monkey led to large accumulations of lactic acid in the central nervous system, which resulted in more severe brain damage. In studies in which sheep and rhesus monkey fetuses were made hyperinsulinemic by the direct infusion of glucose (29) or insulin (30), the high fetal insulin levels led to increased glucose and oxygen uptake across the umbilical cord, hypoxia, acidosis, and fetal death. Similarly, when large amounts of glucose were infused into normal (31–34) and diabetic (35) pregnant humans in labor, neonatal hypoxemia or acidemia (or both) occurred with increased frequency. Bradley et al. (36) obtained fetal blood by cordocentesis from diabetic pregnancies in the second and third trimesters. Although there was no difference from normal during the second trimester, the fetuses of type 1 diabetic mothers at term manifested higher lactate levels and lower pH, even before labor and delivery. Given these data, it appears likely that at least some intrauterine fetal deaths in diabetic pregnancies were caused by maternal hyper-

glycemia, which leads to fetal hyperinsulinemia and results in hypoxia and acidosis. Given lesser degrees of insult, it is possible that perinatal compromise in diabetic pregnancies may result from the same mechanism.

In summary, stillbirth occurs with increased frequency among pregnancies in diabetic mothers. There is an association between the rate of stillbirth and maternal hyperglycemia, and the incidence of this outcome has decreased steadily with improvements in diabetic control during pregnancy. The mechanism may be that of fetal hyperinsulinemia, but this has not been clearly proved. Currently, the appropriate strategy for prevention of perinatal loss is to attempt normalization of maternal glycemia, particularly during the third trimester.

PATHOPHYSIOLOGY OF PERINATAL MORBIDITY

As mentioned at the beginning of this chapter, the various types of perinatal morbidity seen in diabetic pregnancies are covered in other portions of this book. This section presents a unifying theme as to the pathophysiology of these types of morbidity, followed in the next by a plan for their prevention.

The Pedersen (37) hypothesis suggests that, in pregnant women with diabetes, maternal hyperglycemia is rapidly translated into fetal hyperglycemia. The fetal pancreas responds to this glycemic stimulus with β-cell hypertrophy and hyperplasia, and fetal hyperinsulinemia results. It is this fetal hyperinsulinemia that results in the diabetic fetopathy or perinatal morbidities seen in such pregnancies. The Pedersen hypothesis has been modified to allow for the possibility that nonglucose secretogogues for fetal pancreatic insulin may also be important (38) (Fig. 14-3).

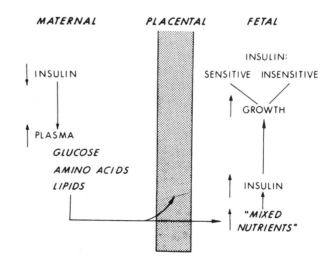

FIGURE 14-3. Genesis of fetal hyperinsulinemia according to the modified Pedersen hypothesis. (From Freinkel N. Banting lecture 1980: of pregnancy and progeny. *Diabetes* 1980;19:1023, with permission.)

As noted in Chapter 12, fetal hyperinsulinemia can induce macrosomia. Macrosomic human infants of diabetic mothers demonstrate elevated cord blood (39) and amniotic fluid (40–42) insulin levels. There is also evidence that some macrosomic infants of nondiabetic mothers may manifest high cord blood insulin levels, which suggests that the pancreas of some fetuses may be particularly responsive to seemingly normal glucose levels (43). Neonatal hypoglycemia is related to high fetal insulin levels in an obvious way. Neonatal polycythemia and hyperbilirubinemia, likewise, may be the result of fetal hyperinsulinemia, which leads to chronic hypoxia, as noted above, with a resultant increase in fetal erythropoietin (44,45). The possible influence of fetal hyperinsulinemia on respiratory distress syndrome has been thoroughly covered elsewhere. Although it has been suggested that the hydramnios seen in diabetic pregnancy is related to fetal hyperglycemia with osmotic diuresis, this has not been documented to date. The increased incidence of hypertensive disorders of pregnancy among diabetic individuals may be related to diabetic vasculopathy rather than hyperglycemia, but an increasingly likely pathophysiologic explanation is the association between insulin resistance, hyperinsulinemia, and hypertension (46–48).

STRATEGIES FOR PREVENTION

Because most complications in diabetic pregnancy are related, directly or indirectly, to maternal hyperglycemia–fetal hyperinsulinemia, it is apparent that therapeutic strategies should be directed toward normalization of maternal circulating glucose levels. As illustrated earlier, when this is done, both perinatal mortality and morbidity are reduced. They may not be reduced to levels comparable with those observed in the nondiabetic general population, suggesting that either absolute euglycemia has not been achieved or that other fetal pancreatic secretogogues must be likewise normalized. The answer to this question remains for future research to uncover.

The appropriate use of dietary prescriptions and various insulin delivery systems and schemes are discussed elsewhere in this book. A third, and extremely important, strategy toward maintenance of euglycemia is the team concept of perinatal care, beginning even prior to conception (49). It is critical that pregnant women with diabetes are cared for in centers where such patients are frequently encountered. A critical mass of personnel, programs, and facilities are necessary to offer the diabetic gravid woman the optimal chance for a good outcome. The obstetrician or internist who cares for the occasional diabetic pregnant woman simply does not have the time or the familiarity with problems specific to this group of patients to do a thorough job.

The team caring for diabetic pregnancies might consist of (a) an obstetrician who specializes in high-risk pregnancy (perinatologist) or (b) a diabetologist, internist, or obstetrician who is thoroughly familiar with modern concepts of diabetes care; (c) an ophthalmologist who is expert in detecting and treating diabetic retinopathy; (d) a nurse who devotes a significant proportion of time to patients with diabetes; (e) a dietitian; (f) a social worker; and (g) appropriate laboratory backup, including ultrasonography. A neonatologist should be part of the team, and a highly competent neonatal unit should be available in the facility where delivery is planned. In most circumstances, the major interface of the team with the patient is the diabetes nurse specialist or nurse educator, who is in frequent telephone contact with each patient, often daily, and serves as the "anchor," that is, the one who is easily available when problems arise. Consistency in obtaining the daily blood glucose results is the most important means of preventing hyperglycemia in these individuals. An immediate response to aberrations in metabolic control tends to limit these to minor problems rather than major ones, such as episodes of ketoacidosis, which may result when unacceptably high glucose values are ignored.

In some centers, the patient herself is made responsible for day-to-day adjustments in insulin dosage, with results being reported to the center at weekly or greater intervals. It has been our experience that, for many patients, this system is less than optimal. There is a tendency to assume that glucose values outside the intended range are the result of factors that are nonrecurrent and thus to put off adjustments in insulin because the glucose was high "for a reason." Although this assessment is sometimes accurate, we try to instill in our patients a sense that "fault" is not the issue and that the fetus does not "care" why its blood glucose concentration is high, only that it is elevated. Thus, having another person to report to, one who is not emotionally involved with the stresses and strains of the patient's daily life, tends to keep the patient on track toward the stated goal.

This frequent one-on-one contact (usually by telephone) has the added advantage of serving as an early warning system for complications. When the diabetic pregnant woman talks to the nurse and mentions that she has a "cold" coming on or is nauseated, the nurse takes the opportunity to review sick day management with the patient and to reinforce the need to step up surveillance of circulating glucose levels. If the patient mentions that she has, for example, "a little fluid coming out of her vagina," the nurse instructs her to come in for evaluation and not to wait for her next appointment. Thus, this contact is helpful not only for diabetic control but also for maintenance of the patient's overall obstetric state.

With the use of frequent home glucose monitoring, diet, insulin, and a team approach, it is possible to achieve euglycemia in most diabetic pregnancies and, in this way, to prevent much of the perinatal morbidity and mortality seen in former times.

KEY POINTS

■ Maternal hyperglycemia is associated with increased perinatal mortality and morbidity in diabetic pregnancies.

■ The mechanism is probably mediated by fetal hyperinsulinemia.

■ Normalization of maternal glycemia during the second half of pregnancy may reduce the incidence of perinatal loss and other adverse outcomes.

■ The diabetic team approach is the most effective way to care for diabetic pregnancies.

REFERENCES

1. Williams JW. The clinical significance of glycosuria in pregnant women. *Am J Med Sci* 1909;137:1.
2. Silfen SL, Wapner RJ, Gabbe SG. Maternal outcome in class H diabetes mellitus. *Obstet Gynecol* 1980;55:749.
3. Gabbe SG, Mestman JH, Hibbard LT. Maternal mortality in diabetes mellitus: an 18-year survey. *Obstet Gynecol* 1976;48:549.
4. Miller HC, Hurwitz D, Kuder K. Fetal and neonatal mortality in pregnancies complicated by diabetes mellitus. *JAMA* 1944;124:271.
5. White P. Pregnancy complicating diabetes. *Am J Med* 1949;7:609.
6. Hall RE, Tillman AJB. Diabetes in pregnancy. *Am J Obstet Gynecol* 1951;61:117.
7. North AF, Mazumdar S, Logrillo VM. Birth weight, gestational age, and perinatal deaths in 5,471 infants of diabetic mothers. *J Pediatr* 1977;90:444.
8. Cassar J, Gordon H, Dixon HG, et al. Simplified management of pregnancy complicated by diabetes. *Br J Obstet Gynaecol* 1978;85:585.
9. Jervell J, Moe N, Skjaerassen J, et al. Diabetes mellitus and pregnancy—management and results in Rikshospitalet, Oslo, 1970–1977. *Diabetologia* 1979;16:151.
10. Lemons JA, Vargas P, Delaney JJ. Infant of the diabetic mother: review of 225 cases. *Obstet Gynecol* 1981;57:187.
11. Soler NG, Soler SM, Matins JM. Neonatal morbidity among infants of diabetic mothers. *Diabetes Care* 1978;1:340.
12. Tevaarwerk GJM, Harding PGR, Milne KJ, et al. Pregnancy in diabetic women: outcome with a program aimed at normoglycemia before meals. *Can Med Assoc J* 1981;125:435.
13. Gabbe SG, Mestman JH, Freeman RK, et al. Management and outcome of pregnancy in diabetes mellitus, classes B to R. *Am J Obstet Gynecol* 1977;129:723.
14. Kitzmiller JL, Cloherty JP, Younger MD, et al. Diabetic pregnancy and perinatal morbidity. *Am J Obstet Gynecol* 1978;131:560.
15. Coustan DR, Berkowitz RL, Hobbins JC. Tight metabolic control of overt diabetes in pregnancy. *Am J Med* 1980;68:845.
16. Jovanovic L, Druzin M, Peterson CM. Effect of euglycemia on the outcome of pregnancy in insulin-dependent diabetic women as compared with normal control subjects. *Am J Med* 1981;71:921.
17. Wylie BR, Kong J, Kozak SE, et al. Normal perinatal mortality in type 1 diabetes mellitus in a series of 300 consecutive pregnancy outcomes. *Am J Perinatol* 2002;19:169.
18. Harley JMG, Montgomery DAD. Management of pregnancy complicated by diabetes. *BMJ* 1965;1:14.
19. Karlsson K, Kjellmer I. The outcome of diabetic pregnancies in relation to the mother's blood sugar level. *Am J Obstet Gynecol* 1972;112:213.
20. Churchill JA, Berendes HW, Nemore J. Neuropsychological deficits in children of diabetic mothers: a report from the Collaborative Study of Cerebral Palsy. *Am J Obstet Gynecol* 1969;105:257.
21. Roversi GD, Gargiulo M, Nicolini U, et al: A new approach to the treatment of diabetic pregnant women. *Am J Obstet Gynecol* 1979;135:567.
22. Jovanovic L, Peterson CM. Management of the pregnant, insulin-dependent diabetic woman. *Diabetes Care* 1980;3:63.
23. Lewis SB, Wallin JD, Kuzuya H, et al. Circadian variation of serum glucose, C-peptide imunoreactivity and free insulin in normal and insulin-treated diabetic pregnant subjects. *Diabetologia* 1976;12:343.
24. Gilmer MDG, Beard RW, Brooke F, et al. Carbohydrate metabolism in pregnancy. I. Diurnal plasma glucose profile in normal and diabetic women. *BMJ* 1975;3:399.
25. Cousins L, Rigg L, Hollingsworth D, et al. The 24-hour excursion and diurnal rhythm of glucose, insulin, and C-peptide in normal pregnancy. *Am J Obstet Gynecol* 1980;136:483.
26. Drury MI, Greene AT, Stronge JM. Pregnancy complicated by clinical diabetes mellitus: a study of 600 pregnancies. *Obstet Gynecol* 1977;49:519.
27. White P. Pregnancy and diabetes. In: Marble A, White P, Bradley R, eds. *Joslin's diabetes mellitus,* 11th ed. Philadelphia: Lea & Febiger, 1971:583.
28. Myers RE. Brain damage due to asphyxia: mechanism of causation. *J Perinat Med* 1981;9:78.
29. Phillips AF, Dubin JW, Matty PJ, et al Arterial hypoxemia and hyperinsulinemia in the chronically hyperglycemic fetal lamb. *Pediatr Res* 1982;16:653.
30. Susa JB, Gruppuso PA, Widness JA, et al. Chronic hyperinsulinemia in the fetal rhesus monkey: effects of physiologic hyperinsulinemia on fetal substrates, hormones and hepatic enzymes. *Am J Obstet Gynecol* 1984;150:415.
31. Mauad-Filho F, deMorais EN, Parente JV, et al. Effect of glucose infusion on the maternal and fetal acid-base equilibrium during labor. *J Perinat Med* 1982;10:99.
32. Kenepp NB, Shelley WC, Gabbe SG, et al. Fetal and neonatal hazards of maternal hydration with 5% dextrose before cesarean section. *Lancet* 1982;1:1150.
33. Lawrence GF, Brown VA, Parsons RJ, et al. Fetomaternal consequences of high-dose glucose infusion during labour. *Br J Obstet Gynaecol* 1982;89:27.
34. Philipson EH, Kalhan SC, Riha MM, et al. Effects of maternal glucose infusion on fetal acid-base status in human pregnancy. *Am J Obstet Gynecol* 1987;157:866.
35. Datta S, Brown WU. Acid-base status in diabetic mothers and their infants following general or spinal anesthesia for cesarean section. *Anesthesiology* 1977;47:272.
36. Bradley RJ, Brudenell JM, Nicolaides KH. Fetal acidosis and hyperlacticaemia diagnosed by cordocentesis in pregnancies complicated by maternal diabetes mellitus. *Diabetes Med* 1991;8:464.
37. Pedersen JL. *The pregnant diabetic and her newborn.* Baltimore: Williams & Wilkins, 1967.
38. Freinkel N. Banting lecture 1980: of pregnancy and progeny. *Diabetes* 1980;19:1023.
39. Weiss PAM, Hofmann H, Purstner P, et al. Fetal insulin balance: gestational diabetes and postpartal screening. *Obstet Gynecol* 1984;64:65.
40. Lin CC, River P, Mosawad AH, et al. Prenatal assessment of fetal outcome by amniotic fluid C-peptide levels in pregnant diabetic women. *Am J Obstet Gynecol* 1981;141:671.
41. Stangenberg M, Persson B, Vaclavinkova V. Amniotic fluid volumes and concentrations of C-peptide in diabetic pregnancies. *Br J Obstet Gynaecol* 1982;89:536.

42. Weiss PAM, Hofmann H, Winter R, et al. Gestational diabetes and screening during pregnancy. *Obstet Gynecol* 1984;63:776.

43. Hoegsberg B, Gruppuso PA, Coustan DR. Hyperinsulinemia in macrosomic infants of nondiabetic mothers. *Diabetes Care* 1993;16:32.

44. Widness JA, Sousa JB, Garcia JF, et al. Increased erythropoiesis and elevated erythropoietin in infants born to diabetic mothers and in hyperinsulinemic rhesus fetuses. *J Clin Invest* 1981;67:637.

45. Phillips AF, Widness JA, Garcia JF, et al. Erythropoietin elevation in the chronically hyperglycemic fetal lamb. *Proc Soc Exp Biol Med* 1982;170:42.

46. Bauman WA, Maimen M, Langer O. An association between hyperinsulinemia and hypertension during the third trimester of pregnancy. *Am J Obstet Gynecol* 1988;159:446.

47. Moller DE, Flier JS. Insulin resistance—mechanisms, syndromes and implications. *N Engl J Med* 1991;325:938.

48. Jovanovic-Peterson L, Meisel B, Bevier W. The Rubenesque pregnancy: a progression towards higher blood pressure correlates with a measure of endogenous and exogenous insulin levels. *Am J Perinatol* 1997;14:181.

49. American Diabetes Association. Position statement: Preconception care of women with diabetes. *Diabetes Care* 2003;26(suppl 1):91.

15

TESTING FOR GESTATIONAL DIABETES

MARSHALL W. CARPENTER

The association between type 2, non-insulin-dependent diabetes mellitus and a prior history of large babies, stillbirths, or neonatal deaths has been observed for several decades (1). The inference that this association is the result of subclinical maternal diabetes has been confirmed by studies that relate glucose intolerance during pregnancy and subsequent perinatal mortality or morbidity rates. The concept of gestational diabetes mellitus (GDM, pregnancy-related glucose intolerance that remits after delivery) was initially articulated in 1965 (2). Initial studies showed an association between the degree of glucose intolerance and perinatal mortality rates in selected patient series (3) and population-based studies (4,5). Subsequent observations have identified the association between the presence of GDM with fetal macrosomia (6,7); neonatal morbidities, such as hypoglycemia, polycythemia, and hyperbilirubinemia (8); and an increased risk of later maternal glucose intolerance in the nonpregnant state (9). Similarly, well-defined treatment protocols have been shown to reduce perinatal morbidity and operative delivery rates and decrease perinatal mortality rates to population norms (7,10–13), resulting in the view that GDM is a treatable disorder (14–16).

The present controversy about the utility of testing for and treating maternal glucose intolerance results from several uncertainties. First, the degree of glucose intolerance associated with fetal macrosomia is only modestly different from that of many pregnancies. Screening and diagnostic tests sufficiently sensitive to identify most pregnancies that might benefit from intervention thereby subject up to 80% of gravidas to the burden of glucose surveillance. Moreover, the diagnosis of GDM leads to increased antenatal testing and cesarean delivery rates irrespective of fetal weight, and therefore to increased maternal morbidity and health-care costs without evident benefit to the majority of women given the diagnosis. Finally, the attribution of "gestational diabetes" may affect insurability and lead to other hidden costs to the patient and society after pregnancy is concluded.

Reflective of these problems, a recent report of the U.S. Preventive Services Task Force of the Agency for Healthcare Research and Quality has reviewed the evidence that might justify screening for glucose intolerance among pregnant women (17). Its conclusion that "better quality evidence is needed to determine whether the benefits of screening for GDM outweigh the harms" has led the Task Force to recommend either no screening or "to screen only women at increased risk for GDM." The Task Force cites only "inadequate" evidence that "selective or universal screening is effective in improving important health outcomes" and that presently "reliable estimates of cost-effectiveness of screening are not possible."

This chapter discusses the development of diagnostic criteria presently used for the oral glucose tolerance test and for the intravenous glucose tolerance test (IVGTT) and screening tests, including historical factors, glycosylated hemoglobin, and other blood protein levels. Additionally, the chapter examines amniotic fluid glucose, insulin, and C-peptide, as well as postpartum evaluation of women with suspected diabetes. Finally, current medical management problems produced by selective and universal screening, and ongoing research underway to determine perinatal and obstetrical outcome-based criteria are also addressed.

REQUIREMENTS FOR DIAGNOSTIC AND SCREENING TESTS

Standards for a medical diagnostic test derive from an understanding or consensus about the natural history of the disorder to be diagnosed and the manner in which the disorder leads to morbidities of interest. Clinical and laboratory signs are used to define the disorder and form the standard against which various diagnostic tests are judged.

The studies that established the association of GDM with perinatal morbidity defined GDM based on threshold blood glucose concentrations after an oral glucose load, thereby identifying the pregnancy at risk rather than directly identifying the fetal morbidity of interest such as fetal macrosomia or metabolic compromise. In the following discussion, the glucose tolerance test (oral or intravenous) is viewed as the diagnostic test, whereas the various

TABLE 15-1. PARAMETERS OF DIAGNOSTIC TESTS

		Condition	
	Test Result	Present	Absent
Sensitivity: a ÷ (a + c)	Abnormal	a	b
Specificity: d ÷ (b + d)	Normal	c	d
Positive predictive accuracy: a ÷ (a + b)			
Negative predictive accuracy: d = (c + d)			

Note that sensitivity and specificity are independent of the prevalence of a condition [(a + c) ÷ (a + b + c + d)], whereas positive and negative predictive accuracy are a function of the condition's prevalence.

means of identifying gravid women in whom the tolerance test should be performed are viewed as screening tests.

The diagnostic (or confirmatory) test should meet several functional requirements (18). The test procedure should be clearly defined and easily performed in various clinical situations and laboratories. The interpretation of the test should be simple, even if the derivation of the limits of normality are complex and controversial (such as with the oral glucose tolerance test). The test should be evaluated for reproducibility of test function among individual subjects and among testing centers. Diagnostic (or confirmatory) tests should have a high sensitivity and specificity based on studies of subjects with known diagnoses and appropriate unaffected controls. The positive and negative predictive accuracies of the diagnostic test are evaluated by applying the test to varying populations, thereby establishing the test's clinical utility and cost (Table 15-1).

Patients may be selected for definitive testing by screening processes that may be as simple as a questionnaire or physical examination. A screening test should be well defined, easily administered, inexpensive, and reproducible. The screening test should have a high sensitivity, identifying most individuals who have the disorder, but it need not have the high specificity demanded of the diagnostic test.

ORAL GLUCOSE TOLERANCE TESTS

The oral glucose tolerance test has commonly been used in clinical investigation and practice because it models the physiologic events after a meal and is easily administered. Several earlier studies (Table 15-2) have addressed the methodologic issues of establishing norms for the oral glucose tolerance test.

Most studies lack information relating glucose tolerance test thresholds to subsequent rates of perinatal morbidity (3,5,19–22). High tolerance test criteria may define an obvious high-risk group of gravid women (5) but may not identify the larger number of pregnant women whose fetuses remain at risk from maternal glucose intolerance. Low tolerance test thresholds may inappropriately label normal-risk gravid women as having GDM. Some studies were limited by not justifying the choice of diagnostic

threshold (3,22), not defining the population tested (3,19,22), having an inadequate sample size, or choosing nonspecific outcomes such as perinatal mortality that may follow other maternal morbidities independent of GDM (3). Gillmer et al. (20) correlated the neonatal hypoglycemia rate with the total increase in blood glucose concentrations above baseline values in a 3-hour oral glucose tolerance test performed in late pregnancy, although diagnostic threshold values were not chosen. Glucose tolerance test criteria were not examined in the study.

O'Sullivan and Mahan's (23) study of the prevalence of late diabetes after gestational glucose intolerance from an unselected group of pregnancies has formed the basis for the glucose tolerance test criteria in pregnancy that are most commonly used in North America. Glucose tolerance test data from 752 subjects were used to determine statistical upper limits for normal, defined as two standard deviations (SD) above the mean for each of four glucose values in the 3-hour test. Glucose intolerance was identified when at least two test values met or exceeded these limits (Table 15-3). These parametrically derived criteria yielded the 2% prevalence of GDM sought by the investigators. O'Sullivan et al. (4) validated these criteria clinically by documenting a fourfold increased perinatal mortality rate among 187 pregnant women who were identified as having GDM in this manner and by determining a 60% prevalence of abnormal glucose tolerance 16 years later in women previously identified as having GDM (9). By this means, a criterion for glucose intolerance during pregnancy was developed that identified women at risk for poor perinatal outcome or subsequent diabetes in a small proportion of the general population of pregnant women.

In O'Sullivan's studies, whole blood was tested using the Somogyi-Nelson method for measuring reducing substances. Several later studies have attempted to transliterate his findings to present methods of glucose oxidase or hexokinase assays of plasma. Plasma glucose values have been shown to be 14% higher than those in whole blood obtained from the same samples using the same assay method (24). Amankwah et al. (25) added 13% to O'Sullivan's Somogyi-Nelson values and rounded these numbers to the nearest 5 mg/dL. The National Diabetes Data Group (NDDG) (14) reinterpreted O'Sullivan's data for glucose

TABLE 15-2. PROPOSED CRITERIA FOR ORAL GLUCOSE TOLERANCE TEST DURING PREGNANCY

Investigators[a]	Oral Glucose Load (g)	Sample Time and Glucose Values (mg/dL)							Medium	Method	Criteria for Abnormal Test
		Fasting	30 min	60 min	90 min	120 min	150 min	180 min			
Carrington et al. (3) (1957)	100					170			Whole blood	Folin-Wu	120-min value met or exceeded
O'Sullivan and Mahan (22) (1964)	100	90		165		143		127	Whole blood	Somogyi-Nelson	Two values met or exceeded
Chen et al. (18) (1972)	100	110		185		130		118	Plasma	Glucose oxidase	Three values met or exceeded
Macafee et al. (5) (1974)	50	180		180		140		180	Plasma	Glucose oxidase	120-min and any other value met or exceeded
Gillmer et al. (20) (1975)	50		+[b]	+	+	+	+	+	Plasma	Glucose oxidase	≥42 area units above baseline
Amankwah et al. (24) (1977)	100	100		180		160		140	Plasma	Glucose hexokinase	Two values met or exceeded
NDDG (14) (1979)	100	105		190		165		145	Plasma	Glucose oxidase	Two values met or exceeded
Merkatz et al. (19) (1980)	75	105		185		140		125	Plasma	Glucose oxidase	Two values met or exceeded
Mestman (21) (1980)	100	110		200		150		130	Plasma	Glucose oxidase	Two values met or exceeded
Carpenter and Coustan (28) (1982)	100	95		180		155		140	Plasma	Glucose oxidase	Two values met or exceeded

[a] Years in parentheses represent year of study publication.
[b] + = time of sampling.

TABLE 15-3. CRITERIA FOR 100-GRAM ORAL GLUCOSE TOLERANCE TEST IN PREGNANCY (MG/DL GLUCOSE)

Time	O'Sullivan and Mahan (22)[a]		1985 NDDG (14)	Carpenter and Coustan (26)	2001 ADA Criteria
	Whole Blood 100-g/3-h	Plasma 100-g/3-h	Plasma 100-g/3-h	Plasma 100-g/3-h	Plasma 75-g/2-h
Preglucose	90	105	95	95	95
1 h	165	190	180	180	180
2 h	145	165	155	155	155
3 h	125	145	140	140	—

[a]O'Sullivan and Mahan rounded chi-square + 2 SD values to nearest 5 mg/dL.

oxidase methods on plasma by increasing O'Sullivan's criteria by 15%; these criteria were reaffirmed by the American Diabetes Association (ADA) in 1985 (26).

However, neither attempt to transliterate O'Sullivan's data took into consideration the change in method in addition to the change in the medium tested. The Somogyi-Nelson method identifies other reducing substances in addition to glucose. The glucose oxidase or hexokinase methods are specific for glucose and generally result in a 5-mg/dL decrease in measured values in the range of glucose concentrations documented in these tests (27,28). A subsequently proposed criterion for the 100-g glucose tolerance test (29) reinterpreted O'Sullivan's thresholds by adjusting for both phenomena. Sacks et al. (30) performed simultaneous Somogyi-Nelson assays in whole blood and glucose oxidase assays in plasma in 994 unselected pregnant women undergoing 3-hour glucose tolerance tests, confirming that the Somogyi-Nelson assay resulted in glucose values 2% to 6% higher than the glucose oxidase assay. Patients whose glucose tolerance test results fall between the Carpenter and Coustan and NDDG criteria have the same probability of insulin treatment (26%) as those meeting the NDDG criteria (30%) (31) and the same probability of fetal macrosomia (32).

The Toronto Trihospital Gestational Diabetes Project (33) examined obstetric and perinatal outcome in 3,778 gravidas without a history of diabetes whose glucose tolerance test data were unknown to caregivers. Of these, 115 met the lower threshold Carpenter and Coustan criteria but not the NDDG criteria (borderline group) and 143 met the higher NDDG criteria. Caregivers of the former group were unaware of the patients' glucose tolerance status. Those in the latter group were identified and treated. Subjects in the borderline group delivered an infant weighing more than 4,000 g in 29% of cases, compared with 11% of treated patients and 13% of patients not meeting either set of criteria for GDM. It is reasonable to conclude, therefore, that the lower criteria for GDM continue to function well at identifying gravidas at substantial risk for fetal macrosomia, in whom intervention to achieve improved glycemic control results in normal rates of fetal macrosomia. In 2001,

the ADA adopted lower thresholds for the 3-hour/100-gram and 2-hour/75-gram oral glucose tolerance tests for GDM (Table 15-3) (34). These lower values have been reported to increase the GDM prevalence from 2.9% (35) to 5.4% (36).

In contrast to common practice in North America, much of the world uses a 75-g oral glucose tolerance test during pregnancy, according to criteria adopted by the World Health Organization (15). A multicenter study of the effect of pregnancy on the 75-g/2-hour test enlisted 1,009 mostly unselected pregnant women (37). Among subjects at more than 16 weeks' gestation, diagnostic threshold values were proposed for the fasting, 1-hour, and 2-hour values, of 126, 198, and 162 mg/dL (7, 11, and 9 mM), respectively, based on the 95th percentile for each sample. The investigators suggested that impaired glucose tolerance during pregnancy be diagnosed if the test produced an abnormal 2-hour glucose value and if either the fasting or the 1-hour limit were met. These criteria resulted in diagnosis of GDM in 10 women, and two additional diagnosed cases based on World Health Organization criteria for diabetes mellitus, for an incidence of 1.2% in a sample group with a mean maternal age of 27 years. However, the utility of these criteria for the identification of perinatal morbidity still requires examination.

In 2001 the ADA Professional Practice Committee (34) recommended that diagnostic thresholds for the 2-hour/75-gram glucose tolerance test be those of the similarly timed samples of the 3-hour/100-gram test, but without supportive clinical evidence. Weiss et al. (38) studied 30 women with a 1-hour post–75-g glucose load value of greater than 160 mg/dL and 30 women without elevated screening test glucose values. All were randomized to a 75- or 100-g repeat glucose tolerance test 3 weeks after the first test. Among those with normal first tests, the 1- and 2-hour post–glucose load glycemic level was 16 mg/dL higher at the first hour (112 vs. 128 mg/dL, p = 0.002) and 9 mg/dL higher at the second hour (104 vs. 113 mg/dL, p = 0.003), whereas the only significant difference noted among those previously identified as glucose intolerant was found at the 2-hour sample (133 vs. 149 mg/dL, p = 0.034). These data suggest that the 2001 ADA-recommended transliteration of 1- and 2-hour threshold values from the 100- to the 75-gram challenge test value (Table 15-3) may underdiagnose GDM if the 75-g stimulus is used.

HYPERGLYCEMIC GLUCOSE TOLERANCE TEST RESULTS AND PERINATAL MORBIDITY: RECENT AND ONGOING STUDIES

Questions still remain about the degree of glycemic response to an oral glucose load that has sufficient positive predictive accuracy for perinatal morbidity to justify its costs. Glucose intolerance is a continuum; even if only one value of the 3-hour glucose tolerance test is abnormal, the fetal macrosomia rate is threefold that in pregnancies with normal screening tests (39). Glycemic surveillance of such pregnancies results in a higher rate of insulin treatment, and randomized trial data demonstrate that treatment of such pregnancies reduces the macrosomia rate significantly, compared with that in nontreated controls (40). However, the correlation of glucose tolerance test results with perinatal morbidity, particularly those that have more clinical impact than the intermediate outcome of fetal macrosomia, in the context of modern obstetric practice, can only be ascertained by studying large cohorts of gravid women whose glucose tolerance is unknown to clinical care givers.

The Toronto Trihospital Gestational Diabetes Project (33) examined obstetric and perinatal outcome in 115 of 3,778 gravidas over 24 years of age without a history of diabetes whose glucose tolerance test data (meeting the 2001 but not the 1985 ADA criteria for the 3-hour/100-g oral glucose tolerance test) were unknown to caregivers. Compared with normoglycemic controls, infants weighing more than 4,000 g were delivered to 29% versus 14% of subjects (*p* <.001) and cesarean sections were performed in 30% versus 20% of subjects (*p* < 0.02). However, this 115-member cohort provided insufficient power to examine risk for birth trauma or perinatal morbidity.

A cohort study of diagnosed but unrecognized GDM (41) demonstrated a 19% (3 of 16) incidence (sixfold increase) of shoulder dystocia and a 25% (4 of 16) incidence of birth trauma (vs. 0.3%) compared with recognized, diet-treated gestational diabetic pregnancies. However, no cohorts studied in blinded fashion have been of sufficient size to allow an association of the incidence of morbid perinatal outcomes with severity of maternal glucose intolerance.

Two presently ongoing, blinded cohort studies have appropriate research design and may have sufficient power to relate maternal glucose intolerance to perinatal morbidity. The Hyperglycemia and Adverse Pregnancy Outcome study (42) is prospectively examining up to 25,000 nondiabetic gravidas in 16 centers in 11 countries, whose 75-g, 2-hour oral glucose tolerance test results are less than 105 fasting and less than 200

mg/dL at 2 hours. The study's design will identify the effect of maternal glucose intolerance on obstetric and birth outcome that is unbiased by physician response to a diagnosis of GDM based on arbitrary criteria. Primary outcomes in this study are cesarean section rate, macrosomia rate, fetal hyperinsulinemia, neonatal fatness and fat distribution, neonatal hypoglycemia, and other, less common morbidities.

The Maternal-Fetal Medicine Units Network's Mild Gestational Diabetes Study has only recently been initiated (43). This protocol will examine gravidas with midpregnancy fasting plasma glucose of less than 95 mg/dL and two of three post–100-gram oral glucose load plasma glucose concentrations meeting present ADA criteria for GDM. Its design is expected to identify possible benefit from dietary prescription and glucose surveillance compared with contemporary standard obstetric care among gravidas with mild GDM. Caregivers will be masked to subjects' glucose tolerance test data, thereby avoiding biasing physician behavior. The study's primary outcome is a composite of perinatal mortality, birth trauma, and neonatal hypoglycemia, hyperinsulinemia, and hyperbilirubinemia.

INTRAVENOUS GLUCOSE TOLERANCE TEST

The IVGTT was adapted for use in pregnancy by Silverstone et al. (44) The unit of measurement of the test, the k value, is a measure of the percentage decrease of glucose over time, according to the equation, $\log_e y = \log_e A - kt$, where y is the blood glucose concentration in milligrams per deciliter, A is the y intercept, and t is the elapsed time in minutes. The value k then becomes the index of tolerance. The disappearance curve for glucose after rapid intravenous injection is therefore a logarithmic function and can be plotted on semilogarithmic paper as a straight line. The slope, k, can be computed by dividing the difference between the natural logs of any two glucose values, A and B, by the intervening time interval in minutes multiplied by 100, according to the following equation.

$$k = \frac{\log_e A - \log_e B}{\text{time B} - \text{time A (in minutes)}} \times 100$$

The table from Posner et al. (45) provides the means of transposing the quotient of a 10-minute glucose level and a 60-minute glucose level to a k value (Table 15-4). Silverstone et al. (44,46) described mean and lower 95% confidence limit k values during the three trimesters of pregnancy, derived from a visually fitted slope based on six data points at 10-minute intervals during the 1-hour test. Subjects in these studies were known to have normal fasting blood sugar levels and be free of glycosuria. The subjects also had no family history of diabetes and no history of fetal macrosomia, liver disease, thyroid disease, cardiac disease, or hypertension. The patients were also not taking drugs that might affect their glucose tolerance. The lower limit of

TABLE 15-4. POSNER AND COLLEAGUES' INTRAVENOUS GLUCOSE TOLERANCE TEST K VALUES DERIVED FROM QUOTIENT 3

Q	k	Q	k	Q	k
1.284	0.50	1.568	0.90	1.916	1.30
1.290	0.51	1.576	0.91	1.925	1.31
1.297	0.52	1.584	0.92	1.935	1.32
1.303	0.53	1.592	0.93	1.944	1.33
1.310	0.54	1.600	0.94	1.954	1.34
1.316	0.55	1.608	0.95	1.964	1.35
1.323	0.56	1.616	0.96	1.974	1.36
1.330	0.57	1.624	0.97	1.984	1.37
1.336	0.58	1.632	0.98	1.994	1.38
1.343	0.59	1.640	0.99	2.004	1.39
1.350	0.60	1.649	1.00	2.014	1.40
1.357	0.61	1.657	1.01	2.024	1.41
1.364	0.62	1.665	1.02	2.034	1.42
1.370	0.63	1.674	1.03	2.044	1.43
1.377	0.64	1.682	1.04	2.054	1.44
1.384	0.65	1.690	1.05	2.065	1.45
1.391	0.66	1.699	1.06	2.075	1.46
1.398	0.67	1.707	1.07	2.086	1.47
1.405	0.68	1.716	1.08	2.096	1.48
1.412	0.69	1.725	1.09	2.110	1.49
1.419	0.70	1.733	1.10	2.117	1.50
1.426	0.71	1.742	1.11	2.128	1.51
1.433	0.72	1.751	1.12	2.138	1.52
1.441	0.73	1.759	1.13	2.149	1.53
1.448	0.74	1.768	1.14	2.160	1.54
1.455	0.75	1.777	1.15	2.171	1.55
1.462	0.76	1.786	1.16	2.182	1.56
1.470	0.77	1.795	1.17	2.193	1.57
1.477	0.78	1.804	1.18	2.204	1.58
1.484	0.79	1.813	1.19	2.214	1.59
1.492	0.80	1.822	1.20	2.226	1.60
1.499	0.81	1.831	1.21	2.237	1.61
1.507	0.82	1.844	1.22	2.247	1.62
1.514	0.83	1.850	1.23	2.259	1.63
1.522	0.84	1.859	1.24	2.271	1.64
1.530	0.85	1.863	1.25	2.282	1.65
1.537	0.86	1.878	1.26	2.294	1.66
1.545	0.87	1.887	1.27	2.307	1.67
1.553	0.88	1.896	1.28	2.316	1.68
1.561	0.89	1.906	1.29	2.329	1.69

Q = 10-min glucose/60-min glucose.
From Posner NA, Silverstone FA, Brewer J, et al. Simplifying the intravenous glucose tolerance test. *J Reprod Med* 1982;27:633, with permission.

normal for k in the first trimester (−2 SD) was 1.37; in the second trimester, 1.18; and in the third trimester, 1.13. Values below this level were regarded as abnormal.

O'Sullivan et al. (47) reported 232 randomly selected pregnancies tested in the third trimester and 11 weeks' postpartum with an IVGTT. They found a mean k of 2.02 in late pregnancy and 2.53 postpartum. Eleven percent of patients had third trimester values less than or equal to 1.34. Hadden et al. (48) found that 16% of selected patients had k values less than or equal to 1.40, but neither series observed an excessive perinatal morbidity or mortality rate in pregnancies with low k values.

Several studies have compared the IVGTT with an oral glucose tolerance test using varying criteria for each test in subjects with low (49) and high (46,50,51) a priori risks for GDM. These studies show a poor correlation between the two tests, although none have performed tests in a large, unselected group of pregnant women and none have related test results to perinatal morbidity.

The IVGTT offers some theoretical advantages over the oral glucose tolerance test. The k value allows easier analysis of glucose tolerance data and is, in most circumstances, independent of the method of glucose measurement. Finally, it is unaffected by variation in gastric emptying and other phenomena that may vary from patient to patient. On the other hand, the IVGTT is more expensive and is nonphysiologic in that glucose is infused in a bolus, peripherally, and is not subject to the usual influence of gastrointestinal physiology.

SCREENING TESTS

Historical and Clinical Risk Factors

Historical and clinical risk factors have been advocated as indications for oral glucose tolerance testing in pregnancy, thus functioning, as a group, as a screening test. Reproductive history (e.g., prior offspring weighing 9 pounds or more, fetal death, neonatal death, congenital anomaly, and prematurity), family history of diabetes, and clinical findings (e.g., obesity, excessive weight gain during pregnancy, glycosuria, proteinuria, and hypertension) have been advocated as factors that mandate an oral glucose tolerance test. Apart from obesity and glycosuria, O'Sullivan et al. (52) found the presence of these risk factors in 37% of an unselected indigent population. In this study, historical risk factors had a sensitivity of 0.63 in contrast to the 50-g challenge test, which had a sensitivity of 0.79 at a cutoff level of 130 mg/dL using Somogyi-Nelson methods in whole blood (~143 mg/dL by the glucose oxidase method in plasma). Others have found that historical and clinical risk factors identify only 50% of cases of GDM (53–55). Historical and clinical risk factors therefore have a high prevalence and function with a low test sensitivity, both of which are undesirable for a screening test.

The racial (genetic) background of subjects is associated with risk for GDM and, later in life, type 2 diabetes. Native Americans of the Pima (7%) and Zuni tribes (15%) have a roughly two- to fourfold prevalence compared with the 3% to 7% incidence estimated among whites in the United States. Green et al. (56) in a San Francisco cohort of 4,210 gravidas, used the 140 mg/dL threshold for the 50-g glucose screening test and the 105, 190, 165, and 145 mg/dL NDDG criteria for the 3-hour/100-g glucose tolerance test. They found a prevalence of GDM of 1.6% among non-Hispanic whites, 1.7% among blacks, 4.2% among Hispanic gravidas, 7.3% among Chinese, and 8.1% among

Pacific Islanders. Although Chinese women were older, neither maternal age nor body mass index accounted for these racial differences. In a study of 97 third trimester gravidas with elevated 50-g glucose screening test results, the relative risk for GDM was 2.3 in Asian women, compared with white women (57).

Maternal age has also been advocated as a criterion for subsequent testing. The largest study of unselected population-based screening found an incidence of GDM of 3.8% in women 30 to 34 years of age but only 0.7% in those younger than age 21 (55). In 1994, the American College of Obstetricians and Gynecologists (ACOG) advocated GDM screening by an oral glucose challenge only in women 30 years of age or older and in younger women with risk factors (58). These criteria result in a sensitivity of only 65% at a cutoff of 140 mg/dL (55) compared with an estimated screening sensitivity of 90% with universal screening during pregnancy.

The 2001 ADA Clinical Practice Recommendations (34) advocate testing for GDM as early in pregnancy "as feasible" among gravidas with "marked" obesity, prior GDM, glucosuria, or a "strong" family history of diabetes. Otherwise, this and the 2001 ACOG (59) guidelines recommend that all pregnant women should be tested at 24 to 28 weeks, except those at low probability of GDM. Those in this latter group meet all of the following criteria: age <25, "normal" weight before pregnancy, ethnicity with a "low" prevalence of GDM (other than Hispanic, Native American, Asian, Pacific Island, or African American ancestry), no known diabetes in a first-degree relative, no history of "abnormal" glucose tolerance test results, and no history of a "poor" obstetric outcome.

The direct health risks of universal pregnancy glucose tolerance screening are negligible. Consequently, the debate about universal versus selective screening for GDM is one of monetary expense. Compared with universal screening, the protocol recommended by the ADA has been estimated to miss only 3% of those with GDM, albeit reducing the number of women screened by only 10% (60). Williams et al. (35) examined a random sample of pregnant patients, finding, similarly, that selective screening only missed 4% of those with GDM. They also found that only 11% of patients met ADA criteria for low-risk status.

Poncet et al. (61) performed a cost-effectiveness analysis that compared three testing models: a 50-g glucose tolerance test applied only to "high-risk" gravidas, universal testing with a 50-g glucose tolerance test, and universal testing with a 75-g glucose tolerance test. Outcome measures included fetal macrosomia, prematurity, perinatal mortality, and maternal hypertension. They found that universal screening with the 50-g test was only 10% more expensive per "unit of additional effectiveness" than testing limited to "high-risk" gravidas. Since the relative costs of universal testing versus those of patient triage to screening are debatable, screening for GDM in all gravid women, with some sort of glucose challenge test, may be the most easily performed and reliable testing scheme.

Patients having GDM in an earlier pregnancy have a 33% to 50% risk of its recurrence in a subsequent pregnancy (62–64). Many having no documentation of glucose tolerance between pregnancies or many years since the past pregnancy may have established type 2 diabetes. An earlier diagnosis of glucose intolerance in such patients may lead to more timely intervention, reduce the risk for major fetal malformations, and allow earlier detection of fetal defects. The probability of a 1-hour, 50-g glucose test value of 140 mg/dL in a later pregnancy if a challenge test value of less than 140 mg/dL was observed in an earlier pregnancy (within 4 years) has been found to be only 1.6%, and the risk for GDM to be only 0.3% (65).

Glucose Challenge Test

Studies of the screening test criteria requiring further testing with an oral glucose tolerance test vary in patient selection, documentation of test conditions and results, and the rationale for the choice of the screening test threshold. Most describe sequential or random subject sampling, with the exception of two (19,25). Several did not provide adequate documentation of testing method (19,20,66) or did not use a uniform screening protocol (20,21,53,67). Three studies documented test parameters, so as to provide the basis for comparison with other, later studies (20,29,52).

O'Sullivan's (52) universal confirmation of the 50-g oral glucose challenge screening test and its high sensitivity for detecting GDM have led to its use as the most common screening test for GDM in North America. The test's threshold for diagnostic testing (the confirmatory 3-hour/100-g oral glucose tolerance test) has been generally advocated to be 130 to 140 mg/dL. O'Sullivan observed a 79% sensitivity at a screening threshold of approximately 143 mg/dL by present testing methods. Coustan et al. (55) tested more than 6,000 gravidas with a 50-g/1-hour oral glucose challenge test followed by 3-hour/100-g glucose tolerance testing if a threshold of 130 mg/dL was obtained by screening. They confirmed an 11% increase in test sensitivity if the threshold were lowered from 140 to 130 mg/dL. Although a high test sensitivity is desirable in a screening test, they observed that the number of women requiring a 3-hour glucose tolerance test increased by 64% if the screening test threshold was lowered from 140 to 130 mg/dL, so that 23% of screened gravidas required follow up testing. Moreover, the prevalence of GDM in the 130 to 139 mg/dL range was the same as that of the population sample tested, so no further information was imparted to caregivers of these patients by the screening test.

The post–screening test probability of gestational diabetes (positive predictive value) increases if the screening test value is more than 175 mg/dL. We have found that the positive predictive value of screening test glucose concentrations of 175 to 184 mg/dL is 50%, and that all of six subjects with screening test values greater than 184 mg/dL had confirmed gestational diabetes (29).

These data notwithstanding, additional information may be obtained by a full glucose tolerance test. If a subsequent fasting value is greater than 95 mg/dL, the diagnosis of gestational diabetes is made and no further testing is necessary. If the fasting value is sufficiently elevated, evening or nighttime insulin might be prescribed early in the course of treatment. If the fasting value is less than 95 mg/dL, the 1-hour postprandial value is sufficiently unstable to suggest that the 2- and 3-hour values may remain normal, and the patient spared the diagnosis and glucose surveillance.

Early Pregnancy Screening

The gradual impairment of insulin sensitivity during the second trimester of pregnancy results in elevated blood glucose concentrations and increased insulin/glucose ratios after meals in the normal gravid woman. Conversely, there is a decrease in fasting blood glucose in mid- to late pregnancy. These changes persist until delivery. Consequently, among asymptomatic patients without signs or history of diabetes, testing protocols suggest that screening and definitive testing for GDM be delayed until the second half of pregnancy, usually 24 to 28 weeks after the last menstrual period.

Early screening may be important in women at increased risk for glucose intolerance because of personal attributes or family history. To examine screening test function in early pregnancy, Nahum et al. (68) performed a 50-g glucose challenge test in 255 gravidas, who were not at increased risk for GDM, at 16 weeks and immediate 3-hour/100-g testing in those with values greater than 134 mg/dL. All patients not already diagnosed with GDM underwent repeat screening and diagnostic testing in the third trimester. Early testing identified 24 of 25 GDM patients. Early screening results of greater than 134 mg/dL had a positive predictive accuracy of 55% for GDM.

Glucose Polymer Challenge Tests

Glucose polymer is an inexpensive, commercially available glucose-saccharide mixture containing 3% glucose, 7% maltose, 55% maltotriose, and 85% polysaccharides. Its osmotic load is one fifth that of glucose and has been reported to be associated with less gastrointestinal symptoms. The potential improvement in patient comfort in using this preparation and its correlation with tests performed with a glucose solution have been investigated (69–72) (Table 15-5). Reece et al. (71) observed a high degree of correspondence between the two solutions used in the 1-hour challenge test (k = 0.62; *p* < 0.0001). Women expressed a preference for the Polycose drink, and had fewer gastrointestinal symptoms. A moderate level of agreement between the results of 3-hour glucose tolerance tests using the two solutions (k = 0.45; *p* < 0.001) has also been demonstrated (72). These results suggest that the glucose polymer is an effective alternative to glucose.

Testing State

Food intake prior to glucose screening tests has been shown to reduce glycemic response to the test stimulus. A 50-g oral glucose screening test was administered in the fasting state and 1 hour after a standard 600-calorie breakfast in a randomized crossover trial (73) of 46 confirmed normal subjects and 24 patients with GDM. There were no differences in test results under the two conditions among normal individuals. The test result was significantly higher among

TABLE 15-5. TESTS FOR GESTATIONAL DIABETES MELLITUS (GDM) USING GLUCOSE VERSUS POLYMER SACCHARIDE SOLUTIONS

Investigators	Methods	Results
Court et al. (49) (1984)	Single-blind trial, women at risk for GDM 50-g polymer vs. 50-g glucose tests Outcomes: symptoms, incremental area under 2-h curve	Polymer ingestion followed by fewer symptoms and associated with comparable curve area
Court et al. (50) (1985)	Open-label trial of duplicate oral tolerance tests, unselected pregnancies 100-g polymer vs. 100-g glucose Outcomes: mean plasma glucose, incremental area	Mean plasma glucose and incremental area under 2-h curve were comparable in polymer vs. glucose tests; correlation between first and second test was better using polymer solution
Reece et al. (51) (1987)	Open-label observational trial of polymer test followed by glucose test 50-g, 1-h challenge test Outcome: proprotion with abnormal tests	Polymer test abnormal in 5 of 7 glucose-abnormal tests; glucose test abnormal in 5 of 8 polymer-abnormal tests
Reece et al. (52) (1989)	Open-label observational trial of polymer test followed by glucose test 100-g, 3-h tolerance test Outcome: proprotion with abnormal tests	Polymer test abnormal in 2 of 4 glucose-abnormal tests; glucose test abnormal in 2 of 4 polymer-abnormal tests

patients with GDM if they were fasting (173.9 ± 28.8 mg/dL) than if the test followed a standard breakfast (154.8 ± 24.1 mg/dL). These findings contrast with those of Lewis et al. (74), who found that, among those with GDM, glucose levels 1 hour after a 50-g glucose ingestion were similar in the fasting state as in the 1-hour postmeal but lower in the 2-hour postmeal state. Nondiabetic subjects had higher glucose levels 1 hour after the 50-g glucose ingestion if this was performed in the fasting state. A cross-sectional study of the effect of postmeal interval on the 50-g/1-hour challenge test demonstrated an increased insulin response but no change in glycemic response when the test was performed within 3 hours of a preceding meal (75). Overall, these data suggest that, if a patient has eaten, a 130 mg/dL test threshold is appropriate to maximize test sensitivity. If it can be documented, however, that the patient is in a fasting state, then a different screening test threshold, perhaps 140 to 145 mg/dL, can yield similar test sensitivity of about 90% and potentially improve the specificity relative to the glucose tolerance test. Nevertheless, the utility of being able to perform the screening test in the context of the antepartum office visit, without regard to the timing and content of the last meal, is so great that using the test threshold of 130 mg/dL would be preferred so as to maximize test sensitivity at the cost of a slightly reduced test specificity in those patients who may be in a fasted state at the time of the screening test.

Fasting, Random, and Postmeal Glucose Studies as Screening Tests

Glucose values obtained without a glucose challenge have been investigated as screening tests. Such tests, if workable, would have the advantage of avoiding the administration of a glucose solution.

The fasting plasma glucose concentration is less likely to be elevated than postprandial values in GDM (76–78). O'Sullivan et al. (4) found that only 2% of unselected patients had fasting whole blood levels greater than or equal to 90 mg/dL. In another study of 1,697 gravid women, GDM was not identified among those having fasting plasma glucose of less than 90 mg/dL (79). However, glucose tolerance testing was performed only on women with historical risk factors and in a small sample of those without.

Stangenberg et al. (80) examined 6,969 random blood glucose levels from 1,500 pregnant women without any "signs or symptoms of diabetes." They found a mean of 83 mg/dL and a 95th percentile of 114 mg/dL. With a threshold of 116 mg/dL, 11.6% of the 1,500 subjects had an abnormal value; of those, 10 (5.8%) had an abnormal glucose tolerance test result. However, with the exception of 30 patients who had fasting glycosuria, no confirmatory testing was performed in the rest of the 1,500 patients. The overall prevalence of GDM identified in this group (0.9%)

was substantially less than that in O'Sullivan's study performed with universal confirmatory testing. This suggests that a protocol that uses random blood glucose levels may have a substantial false-negative rate.

Lind et al. (81) performed plasma glucose measurements on 2,043 patients at 28 to 32 weeks' gestation. Subjects who ate within 2 hours and those who ate more than 2 hours earlier had 99th percentile values of 109 and 100 mg/dL, respectively. In the 32 (1.4%) subjects whose levels exceeded this cutoff, 2 had unequivocal diabetes and 4 had impaired glucose tolerance, according to World Health Organization criteria (15). This low prevalence of GDM (0.26%) was partly the result of the higher glucose tolerance test criteria used in the study. That only 1.7% of the unselected screened population was actually tested with a glucose tolerance test suggests that a substantial proportion of patients with GDM in this population may have been undetected.

Coustan et al. (82) found that a standardized 600-calorie meal could be used to identify gravid women with known GDM, but only at a 1-hour postmeal glucose threshold of 100 mg/dL could a 90% test sensitivity be achieved. This threshold (mean +0.85 SD in a group of 46 nondiabetic subjects) would require confirmatory testing in more than 20% of screened subjects.

Two studies have examined candy in the form of jelly beans as a medium for glucose challenge that might be more appealing than glucose or glucose polymer solutions. The first study's (83) protocol had 157 subjects perform a usual 50-g/1-hour glucose challenge test. The same subjects ate 18 jelly beans at one sitting followed by a 1-hour plasma glucose. Testing began at 26 to 30 weeks. They then performed a 100-g/3-hour glucose tolerance test within the following 2 weeks. The reliability of the beans' weight and composition was not tested, though the investigators calculated that the chosen number provided a mixed carbohydrate load of 50 g. Thirteen (8.3%) of the subjects had gestational diabetes. Jelly beans were better tolerated than glucose solution, but neither was followed by severe symptoms. At a threshold of 140 mg/dL, the jelly bean test sensitivity was 31% compared with that of the glucose solution sensitivity of 46%.

The second study (84) used a randomized crossover design of a 50-g glucose challenge and 28 of the same brand of jelly beans (calculated to provide 50 g of "simple sugar"), each to be consumed in 10 minutes. These tests were followed by a 100-g/3-hour glucose tolerance test. Five of 136 subjects (3.7%) were diagnosed with gestational diabetes. At a threshold of 140 mg/dL, the jelly bean test sensitivity was only 20%, and that of the glucose challenge test was 60%. Only one of the five subjects with gestational diabetes had results of both tests more than 140 mg/dL. These data suggest that jelly beans provide neither a reliable nor sufficiently sensitive stimulus to identify glucose intolerance.

Glycated Blood Proteins in the Diagnosis of Gestational Diabetes

Glycated hemoglobins and other proteins have been investigated as screening tests for GDM (Table 15-6). Glycation is the slow and almost irreversible binding of glucose or a phosphorylated sugar to hemoglobin or other blood proteins. Because it is dependent on the concentration of the reactants and because the red blood cell concentration of glucose approximates that in extracellular fluid, glycated hemoglobin has been investigated as a diagnostic test for nongestationally related diabetes. Using ion exchange chromatography, nonfractionated glycohemoglobin was measured in 167 patients undergoing a glucose tolerance test and in 105 known diabetic patients (85). A significant difference in mean glycohemoglobin values could be demonstrated in the group with a normal glucose tolerance test result compared with those with an abnormal one, even if the patients appeared to maintain fasting and postprandial euglycemia apart from the tolerance test. Hall et al. (86) used affinity chromatography on fresh and postincubation aliquots of hemoglobin to measure total and stable glycohemoglobin levels on 53 patients referred for glucose testing. Those who had impaired glucose tolerance and diabetes mellitus, according to World Health Organization criteria, had significantly greater total and stable glycohemoglobin levels than those with normal glucose tolerance test results. In this small number of patients, there was no overlap in values of stable glycosylated hemoglobin when normal subjects were compared with those with impaired glucose tolerance or diabetes mellitus.

GDM, however, may not present with the same constant elevations of blood sugar levels as diabetes in nonpregnant states. Gravid women with GDM have fasting blood glucose concentrations that are low by comparison with those in nonpregnant individuals. In addition, normal nondiabetic gravid women have significantly elevated postabsorptive glucose values compared with those in the nonpregnant woman. Because of increased erythropoiesis, red blood cells are younger in pregnancy, and hemoglobin is less glycated. Finally, disturbances in glucose tolerance may have only occurred for a brief period, as a result of the hormonal milieu changing rapidly from relative insulin sensitivity to that of insulin resistance as the pregnancy progresses. For all these reasons, a measure of chronic hyperglycemia, such as glycated hemoglobin, may not be effective in distinguishing

TABLE 15-6. TESTS FOR GESTATIONAL DIABETES USING FRUCTOSAMINE OR GLYCATED HEMOGLOBIN ASSAYS VERSUS ORAL GLUCOSE CHALLENGE TESTS

Investigators	Methods	Results
Roberts et al. (74) (1983)	Observed pregnancies tested with GTT and fructosamine within 4 wk; normal fructosamine was <95th percentile for normal pregnancy; 79 gravidae tested by 100-g/3-h GTT	17 of 20 (85%) with abnormal GTT had elevated fructosamine Specificity = 95%
Roberts et al. (75) (1990)	Observed 507 unselected pregnancies tested with 28- and 36-wk 100-g GTT; fructosamine at 36 wk	Compared with 36-wk GTT, sensitivity of 28-wk GTT was 81% and for 36-wk fructosamine was 50%
Nasrat et al. (76) (1990)	Observed unselected pregnancies; tested second and third trimester with fructosamine and GTT; fructosamine abnormal at 90th percentile	Fructosamine had 50% sensitivity for abnormal GTT
Comtois et al. (77) (1989)	Compared fructosamine and fructosamine/protein; 100-g GTT in 100 pregnancies with risk for GDM	Similar fructosamine levels; fructosamine/protein elevated in only 3 of 13 women with GDM
Fadel et al. (17) (1979)	HbA_1 (microcolumn technique) in 53 normal and 22 women with GDM tested for clinical risk	$5.8 \pm 1.0\%$ vs. $7.0 \pm 1.3\%$ (ns); only 5 of 23 women with GDM had HbA_1 values ?2 SD
Shah et al. (68) (1982)	HbA_1 (ion-exchange chromatography, abnormal >8.8%); 50-g/1-h (≥140 mg/dL), 100-g GTT; 90 subjects at clinical risk	Similar HbA_1 in those with and without GDM HbA_1: sensitivity 22%, specificity 90% 50-g challenge: sensitivity 83%, specificity 56%
Anal et al. (69) (1984)	HbA_1 (ion-exchange chromatography, abnormal >7.0%); 100-g GTT (higher than ADA criteria); 82 random patients	Similar HbA_1 in those with and without GDM HbA_1: sensitivity 73%, specificity 34%
McFarland et al. (70) (1984)	HbA_1 (thiobarbituric acid technique) in 17 normal and 22 women with GDM identified by glucose screening	0.49 ± 0.07 vs. 0.54 ± 0.06 nM hydroxymethylfurfural/mg protein ($p < 0.05$); high degree of overlap between those with and without GDM
Cousins et al. (1984)	HbA_1 (fast hemoglobin test, abnormal >6.8%); 50-g/1-h (≥150 mg/dL), 100-g GTT; 806 unselected subjects	Similar HbA_1 in those with and without GDM HbA_1: sensitivity 80%, specificity 57% 50-g challenge: sensitivity about 80%, specificity 92%

ADA, American Diabetes Association; GDM, gestational diabetes mellitus; GTT, 3-hour glucose tolerance test; HbA_1, hemoglobin A_1, MAI.

normal from gestational diabetic gravid women. Hemoglobin A$_{1c}$ (HbA$_{1c}$) values in nondiabetic women have been shown to decrease during pregnancy from the first through the third trimester and then to increase postpartum (87). In another study, however, the HbA$_{1c}$ concentration was reported to be elevated in normal pregnancy (88).

Fadel et al. (89), using a microcolumn chromatographic method to identify HbA$_1$ and O'Sullivan's criteria for GDM, compared HbA$_1$ values among 23 nondiabetic nonpregnant women, 53 normal pregnant women, and 22 patients with GDM. The latter had significant elevations in HbA$_1$, although there was considerable overlap in the distribution of values among groups.

Shah et al. (90) measured HbA$_1$ using ion-exchange chromatography and applied the NDDG criteria for GDM in a group of patients with risk factors for it. Glucose tolerance tests were performed in those patients who had a 50-g oral glucose challenge test result of 140 mg/dL or more or who later presented with other clinical data suggestive of this disorder. Of the 18 patients identified with GDM, 15 had an abnormal oral challenge test result, and only 4 had an abnormal glycated hemoglobin value. This indicates a test sensitivity of 27% for glycated hemoglobin in the identification of GDM in this at-risk group. A high proportion of the elevated glycated hemoglobin values (five of nine) were found in gravid women without GDM.

Artal et al. (91) measured HbA$_1$ with ion-exchange chromatography and more restrictive criteria for an oral glucose tolerance test to define GDM in an at-risk group of gravid women. A low HbA$_{1c}$ cutoff of 7% was used as a screening test for GDM. This low HbA$_{1c}$ value gave a test sensitivity of 73% but was very nonspecific (34%). McFarland et al. (92) found no difference in glycated hemoglobin levels between 41 women with normal glucose tolerance and 12 women with GDM by the NDDG criteria.

Cousins et al. (93) performed 1-hour/50-g glucose challenge tests and assessed glycated hemoglobin levels on 806 consecutive unselected prenatal patients. This group used the NDDG criteria for GDM. The effect of the test threshold of the glucose challenge test and the HbA$_1$ test on sensitivity and specificity were compared. The investigators performed glucose tolerance testing on all subjects with a challenge test result of 150 mg/dL or more. Assuming that this scheme would identify 80% of patients with GDM, the authors calculated the specificity of the glucose challenge test to be 92% at 150 mg/dL. An HbA$_1$ threshold of 6.8 achieved a sensitivity of 80% but had a specificity of only 57% at this cutoff. If the HbA$_1$ threshold is increased (9.2%), so that a specificity of 92% is reached, the sensitivity decreases to about 36%. These data, obtained from an unselected pregnancy sample, do not support the use of glycated hemoglobin as a screening test for GDM.

It is unknown whether fractions of glycosylated hemoglobin, which have been tested in the nonpregnant population and found to be effective, would perform equally well in the identification of women with GDM. Studies in the use of the stable fraction of HbA$_{1c}$ may show this to be a more effective screening tool. Other glycosylated plasma proteins have a potential as markers for GDM. Glycosylated albumin has a shorter half-life than that of glycosylated hemoglobin and may be more effective in identifying women with an acute increase in mean daily blood glucoses. Jones et al. (94) showed a more rapid decline in glycated albumin than glycated hemoglobin among nonpregnant patients with types 1 and 2 diabetes undergoing initial insulin treatment.

Leiper et al. (95) using affinity chromatography, examined glycated albumin, glycated plasma proteins, and glycated hemoglobin in 14 insulin-dependent diabetic gravid women. A decrease of more than 50% in the former markers was noted after 4 weeks of improved metabolic control. Not until 12 weeks, however, did glycated hemoglobin levels decrease significantly.

Another marker for abnormalities of glucose hemostasis is fructosamine, an indicator of the glycation of plasma proteins. Roberts et al. (96) showed a significant difference in fructosamine levels among women with GDM versus those without GDM. Using the 95th percentile cutoff for nondiabetic gravid women, the investigators found a test sensitivity of 0.85 and specificity of 0.95 for fructosamine. However, the same investigators (97) found that, in an unspecified sample of 507 pregnant women, a 100-g glucose load at 28 weeks had a sensitivity for GDM diagnosed at 36 weeks of 81% compared with a sensitivity of 50% for fructosamine tests performed at 4-week intervals during pregnancy. Nasrat et al. (98) found no association in unselected pregnant women between fructosamine and second or third trimester fasting glucose levels or birth weight and found a fructosamine sensitivity of only 50% for GDM using the 90th percentile value. The low sensitivity of fructosamine for GDM has also been noted by other investigators (99).

AMNIOTIC FLUID STUDIES

In both normal and diabetic pregnancies, amniotic fluid glucose levels have been noted to correlate with simultaneous maternal plasma glucose concentrations and to increase acutely in response to a maternal glucose load. Insulin content or concentration in amniotic fluid is associated with increased amniotic fluid glucose and may provide a more stable marker for diabetic fetopathy. Using a solid-phase system for radioimmunologic insulin determination, Weiss et al. (100) measured total insulin concentration in amniotic fluid in 487 samples of fluid, noting a slight upward trend between 28 and 42 weeks' gestation. In a subsequent study, 75 women with a family history of diabetes underwent an oral glucose tolerance test that consisted of a glucose load of 1 g/kg and capillary blood glucose samples obtained in the fasting state and 2 hours after glucose ingestion (101). This test was performed between 20 and 28 weeks' gestation. At various times after 28 weeks, amniotic fluid total insulin concentrations were determined. Of the 25 patients with postprandial plasma glucose values in excess of 200 mg/dL, 9 showed evidence of diabetic fetopathy in the infant at birth. Another five infants with diabetic fetopathy were found among subjects with lower postprandial glucose tolerance test values. All 14 infants showing evidence of diabetic fetopathy had elevated amniotic fluid total insulin concentrations.

In addition, the proinsulin connecting peptide, C-peptide, has been measured in amniotic fluid as a marker for fetal insulin production. Assays for C-peptide offer advantages over those for insulin because C-peptide is not bound by antiinsulin antibodies, is minimally extracted by the liver, and assays are not affected by the presence of proinsulin. Amniotic fluid C-peptide concentration correlates well with standardized infant birth weight and the degree of diabetic control (102). One study found an association of total amniotic fluid content of C-peptide with the presence of neonatal morbidity but not C-peptide concentration (103).

Amniotic fluid biochemical markers for diabetic fetopathy should be distinguished from tests designed to identify gravid women with abnormal glucose tolerance. Amniotic fluid insulin sampled at 14 to 20 weeks' gestational age in women over 35 years of age has been found to be associated with both subsequent GDM and, among those with subsequently diagnosed glucose intolerance, with birth weight (104). An increase of amniotic fluid insulin concentration of one multiple of the gestational-specific median was associated with an odds ratio of 1.9 (CI 1.3–2.4, $p = 0.029$) for subsequent GDM. This weak association suggests that amniotic fluid studies would be best applied to gravidas with an already high probability of diabetic fetopathy, such as polyhydramnios, increased fetal abdominal girth, or poor maternal metabolic control.

POSTPARTUM IDENTIFICATION OF PREEXISTING GESTATIONAL DIABETES

Most women having large babies do not have glucose intolerance identifiable during the pregnancy. In circumstances in which universal screening is not performed during pregnancy, when a woman has a large offspring, postpartum testing may identify antecedent GDM. This information would allow counseling about the risk for glucose intolerance in subsequent pregnancies and later in life.

Glucose homeostasis and insulin sensitivity appear to change within the first few days after delivery. This may be due to altered diet, increased nocturnal activity, and possibly increased glucose utilization induced by lactation, as well as the abrupt decline in placental hormones. MacDon-

ald et al. (105) performed a 50-g glucose challenge in the early puerperium on 357 women who had been tested for glucose tolerance during their preceding pregnancy. They were able to document a slight decline in fasting and 2.5-hour postchallenge glucose values in the puerperium. In 12 nondiabetic women, Lind et al. (106) showed a significant decrease in fasting plasma insulin levels by the second postpartum day. They performed a glucose tolerance test in the early puerperium and again 6 weeks after delivery. Using the incremental area under the glucose tolerance curve, these investigators were able to show a continued improvement in glucose hemostasis between that noted in the early puerperium and several weeks postpartum. The probability of preceding GDM can be calculated from a 100-g/3-hour oral glucose tolerance test within 48 hours of parturition (107). In 37 subjects with GDM and 28 with screening test results of less than 130 mg/dL during pregnancy, the sum of the 1- and 2-hour incremental (the postprandial minus the fasting glucose value) glucose values at a threshold value of 110 mg/dL yielded a sensitivity of 80% and a specificity of 90% for antecedent GDM.

O'Sullivan and Mahan (23) examined the prevalence of glucose intolerance in the immediate postpartum period among women diagnosed for the first time during pregnancy as having GDM. They identified glucose intolerance by a 100-g oral glucose challenge, used the same criteria for glucose intolerance as applied during the pregnancy, and found a prevalence of 1.8%. This study is notable because these patients were sampled sequentially from a presumably normal population of indigent women. Coustan et al. (108) identified 72 gravid women with GDM using universal screening. Follow-up in these patients included a fasting and 2-hour postbreakfast test 5 weeks postpartum using fasting value of 105 mg/dL or a 2-hour postmeal value of 120 mg/dL as upper limits. Using these criteria, the investigators found an 18% prevalence of abnormal glucose tolerance among their subjects.

These data suggest delay in glucose tolerance testing of women with GDM until 5 to 6 weeks postpartum. The ADA Professional Practice Committee recommends (34) the 75-g oral glucose challenge test for diagnosis of impaired glucose tolerance in the nonpregnant state (plasma glucose values of ≥100 mg/dL and < 126 mg/dL fasting, and ≥140 mg/dL and < 200 mg/dL at 2 hours). However, the appropriate timing and utility of any glucose challenge testing for the diagnosis of preceding GDM is unknown.

C-peptide is secreted in equal molar proportions with insulin. Umbilical cord levels of C-peptide can be measured by assays that eliminate interference by transplacental passage of maternal insulin antibodies and are unaffected by fetal proinsulin. Sosenko et al. (109) measured C-peptide levels in 79 infants of diabetic mothers and 62 infants of nondiabetic mothers. They found significantly elevated cord levels in the offspring of diabetic mothers. The degree of elevation correlated well with the presence of hypoglycemia and macrosomia. The earliest assay performed was at 34 weeks.

Weiss et al. (110) measured cord blood insulin concentrations by solid-phase radioimmunoassay in 180 mature newborns to obtain a normal range of values and in 221 babies who weighed more than 4,000 g at birth. The umbilical cord insulin level in these cases correlated with increased 1- and 2-hour postprandial glucose tolerance test plasma glucose values, which suggests antecedent GDM. This suggests that either cord C-peptide or insulin levels, with appropriate documentation, may be shown to identify antecedent GDM.

GLUCOSE TOLERANCE IN TWIN PREGNANCY

The insulin resistance that characterizes the latter half of pregnancy is due in part to increased placental secretion of human chorionic somatomammotropin and to increased consumption of insulin by the placenta. A further degeneration of glucose homeostasis might thus be expected in twin pregnancy. Dwyer et al. (111) examined the function of a 100-g/3-hour glucose tolerance test in 288 patients with twins and compared the results with those of patients with singleton pregnancies at 32 to 34 weeks' gestation. Women with twin pregnancies had significantly lower fasting plasma glucose levels, but they detected no statistically significant differences in 1-, 2-, and 3-hour glucose levels after glucose ingestion. The incidence of GDM, however, was significantly higher (5.6%) than in singleton pregnancies (2.5%). Schwartz et al. (112) found a similar increased prevalence of GDM among 429 twin gestations compared with approximately 29,000 births (7.7 vs. 4.1%, $p < 0.05$) among an unselected cohort of births in a single hospital. In their cohort, fasting values among twin pregnancies were marginally lower than those among singleton pregnancies (75.2 vs. 79.7 mg/dL, $p = 0.063$).

Naidoo et al. (113) examined IVGTT results using a glucose load of 0.5 g/kg in 20 twin and 20 singleton pregnancies matched for age, parity, weight, height, and gestational age. Mean glucose disappearance rates did not differ between twin pregnancies and singleton pregnancies. Fasting insulin levels were slightly but not significantly higher in twin pregnancies than in singleton ones. However, all postinfusion insulin levels were significantly higher in twin pregnancies. These data suggest that the 50-g oral glucose challenge test may function appropriately as a screening test in women with twin pregnancies. However, because of the increased requirements for insulin secretion during a twin pregnancy, the likelihood of GDM is probably increased in pregnancies with twin fetuses.

KEY POINTS

- Although maternal glucose intolerance is associated with risks for fetal macrosomia and neonatal metabolic morbidity, the diagnosis of gestational diabetes is nonspecific and may lead to increased obstetric intervention, exposure to surgery, and problems with access to health insurance.

- Justification for screening for disease in an asymptomatic population includes low risk and high sensitivity of the test for the disease, availability of a highly specific confirmatory test, and an intervention that has improved efficacy in screened rather than symptomatic patients.

- Commonly used diagnostic criteria for the 100-g/3-hour oral glucose tolerance test identifies a 2% to 4% group that has a threefold risk for fetal macrosomia.

- Only small cohort studies have identified an association of untreated gestational diabetes and birth trauma. None have had sufficient statistical power to describe a diagnostic threshold that would identify a group of gravidas at significant risk for perinatal morbidity.

- The 50-g/1-hour oral glucose challenge test, performed without regard to meals or other dietary preparation, performs best to identify a group at significant increased risk for an abnormal 3-hour glucose tolerance test.

- Both screening and diagnostic glucose testing should be performed on equipment that provides an analytic coefficient of variation of 1% to 2% and that is tested for accuracy at regular intervals.

- Although early testing among gravidas with "marked" obesity, prior gestational diabetes, glucosuria, or a "strong" family history has been advocated, the benefits of early testing on perinatal outcome has not been determined.

REFERENCES

1. Paton DM. Pregnancy in the prediabetic patient. *Am J Obstet Gynecol* 1948;56:558.
2. Jackson WPV. Studies in prediabetes. *BMJ* 1965;2:690.
3. Carrington ER, Shuman CR, Reardon HS. Evaluation of the prediabetic state during pregnancy. *Obstet Gynecol* 1957;9:664.
4. O'Sullivan JB, Charles D, Mahan CM, et al. Gestational diabetes and perinatal mortality rate. *Am J Obstet Gynecol* 1973;116:901.
5. Macafee CAJ, Beischer NA. The relative value of the standard indications for performing a glucose tolerance test in pregnancy. *Med J Aust* 1974;1:911.
6. Dandrow RV, O'Sullivan JB. Obstetric hazards of gestational diabetes. *Am J Obstet Gynecol* 1966;96:1144.
7. Coustan DR, Imarah J. Prophylactic insulin treatment of gestational diabetes reduces the incidence of macrosomia, operative delivery, and birth trauma. *Am J Obstet Gynecol* 1984;150:836.
8. Warner RA, Cornblath M. Infants of gestational diabetic mothers. *Am J Dis Child* 1975;117:65.
9. O'Sullivan JB. Long term follow-up of gestational diabetes. In:

Camerini-Davalos RA, Cole HS, eds. *Early diabetes in early life, Third International Symposium.* San Diego: Academic, 1975.

10. Haworth JC, Dilling LAL. Effect of abnormal glucose tolerance in pregnancy on infant mortality rate and morbidity. *Am J Obstet Gynecol* 1975;122:555.

11. Gabbe SG, Mestman JH, Freeman RK, et al. Management and outcome of class A diabetes mellitus. *Am J Obstet Gynecol* 1977; 127:465.

12. O'Sullivan JB, Gellis SS, Dandrow RV, et al. The potential diabetic and her treatment in pregnancy. *Obstet Gynecol* 1966;17: 683.

13. Coustan DR, Lewis SB. Insulin therapy for gestational diabetes. *Obstet Gynecol* 1978;51:306.

14. Anonymous. National Diabetes Data Group. Classification and diagnosis of diabetes mellitus and other categories of glucose intolerance. *Diabetes* 1979;28:1039.

15. WHO Expert Committee on Diabetes Mellitus. *World Health Organization Technical Report Series 646.* Geneva: World Health Organization, 1980.

16. Frienkel N, Hadden D. Summary and recommendations of the Second International Workshop-Conference on Gestational Diabetes Mellitus. *Diabetes* 1985;34:123.

17. U.S. Preventive Services Task Force, Center for Practice and Technology Assessment, Agency for Healthcare Research and Quality. Screening for Gestational Diabetes mellitus: recommendations and rationale. *Obstet Gynecol* 2003;101:393–394.

18. Sackett DL, Haynes RB, Tugwell P. The selection of diagnostic tests. In: *Clinical epidemiology.* Boston: Little, Brown, 1985.

19. Chen W, Palav A, Tricon V. Screening for diabetes in a prenatal clinic. *Obstet Gynecol* 1972;40:567.

20. Merkatz JR, Duchon MA, Yamashita TS, et al. A pilot community based screening program for gestational diabetes. *Diabetes Care* 1980;3:453.

21. Gillmer MDG, Beard RW, Brooke FM, et al. Relation between maternal glucose tolerance and glucose metabolism in the newborn. *BMJ* 1975;3:402.

22. Mestman JH. Outcome of diabetes screening in pregnancy and perinatal morbidity in infants of mothers with mild impairment in glucose tolerance. *Diabetes Care* 1980;3:447.

23. O'Sullivan JB, Mahan CM. Criteria for the oral glucose tolerance test in pregnancy. *Diabetes* 1964;13:278.

24. Mager M, Farest G. What is "true" blood glucose? A comparison of three procedures. *Am J Clin Pathol* 1965;44:104.

25. Amankwah KS, Prentice RL, Flleury FJ. The incidence of gestational diabetes. *Obstet Gynecol* 1977;49:497.

26. Anonymous. Proceedings of the Second International Workshop-Conference on Gestational Diabetes Mellitus. *Diabetes* 1985;34:123.

27. Henry EJ. *Clinical chemistry: principles and technics,* 1st ed. New York: Hoeber Medical, 1965.

28. Niejadlik DC, Dube AH, Adamko SM. Glucose measurements and clinical correlations. *JAMA* 1973;224:1743.

29. Carpenter MW, Coustan DR. Criteria for screening tests for gestational diabetes. *Am J Obstet Gynecol* 1982;144:768.

30. Sacks DA, Abu-Fadil S, Greenspoon JS, et al. Do the current standards for glucose tolerance testing in pregnancy represent a valid conversion of O'Sullivan's original criteria? *Am J Obstet Gynecol* 1989;161:638.

31. Neiger R, Coustan DR. Are the current ACOG glucose tolerance test criteria sensitive enough? *Obstet Gynecol* 1991;78: 1117.

32. Magee MS, Walden CE, Benedette TJ, et al. Influence of diagnostic criteria on the incidence of gestational diabetes and perinatal morbidity. *JAMA* 1993;269:609.

33. Naylor CD, Sermer M, Chen E, et al. Cesarean delivery in relation to birth weight and gestational glucose intolerance: patho-

physiology or practice style? Toronto Tri-Hospital Gestational Diabetes Investigators. *JAMA* 1996;275:1165–1170.

34. Professional Practice Committee, American Diabetes Association. Clinical Practice Recommendations 2004. *Diabetes Care* 2001;2(suppl 1):S5–S10.

35. Williams CB, Yu D, Iqbal S, et al. Effect of selective screening for gestational diabetes. *Diabetes Care* 1999;22:418–421.

36. Schwartz ML, Ray WN, Lubarsky SL. The diagnosis and classification of gestational diabetes mellitus: is it time to change our tune? *Am J Obstet Gynecol* 1999;180:1560–1571.

37. Lind T, Phillips PR, for the Diabetic Study Group of the European Association for the Study of Diabetes. Influence of pregnancy on the 75-g OGTT: a prospective multicenter study. *Diabetes* 1991;40:8.

38. Weiss PAM, Haeusler M, Kainer F, et al. Toward universal criteria for gestational diabetes: relationships between seventy-five and one hundred gram glucose loads and between capillary and venous glucose concentrations. *Am J Obstet Gynecol* 1998;178: 830–835.

39. Lindsay MK, Graves W, Klein L. The relationship of one abnormal glucose tolerance test value and pregnancy complications. *Obstet Gynecol* 1989;73:103–106.

40. Langer O, Anyaegbunam A, Rustman L, et al. Management of women with one abnormal glucose tolerance test value reduces adverse outcome in pregnancy. *Am J Obstet Gynecol* 1989;161: 642.

41. Adams KM, Li H, Nelson RL, et al. Sequelae of unrecognized gestational diabetes. *Am J Obstet Gynecol* 1998;178:1321–1332.

42. HAPO Study Cooperative Research Group. The Hyperglycemia and Adverse Pregnancy Outcome (HAPO) Study. *Int J Gynaecol Obstet* 2002;78:69–77.

43. The National Institute of Child Health and Human Development Maternal-Fetal Medicine Units Network. A randomized clinical trial of treatment for mild gestational diabetes mellitus.

44. Silverstone FA, Solomons E, Rubricius J. The rapid intravenous glucose tolerance test in pregnancy. *J Clin Invest* 1961;40:2180.

45. Posner NA, Silverstone FA, Brewer J, et al. Simplifying the intravenous glucose tolerance test. *J Reprod Med* 1982;27:633.

46. Silverstone FA, Posner NA, Pomerance W, et al. Application of the intravenous and oral glucose tolerance tests in pregnancy. *Diabetes* 1971;20:476.

47. O'Sullivan JB, Snyder PJ, Sporer AC, et al. Intravenous glucose tolerance test and its modification by pregnancy. *J Clin Endocrinol Metab* 1970;31:33.

48. Hadden DR, Harley JMG, Kajtar TJ, et al. A prospective study of three tests of glucose tolerance in pregnant women selected for potential diabetes with reference to the fetal outcome. *Diabetologia* 1971;7:87.

49. Ocampo PT, Coseriu VG, Quilligan EF. Comparison of standard oral glucose tolerance test and rapid intravenous glucose tolerance test in normal pregnancy. *Obstet Gynecol* 1964;24:508.

50. Singh MM, Arshat H. Comparison of oral and intravenous glucose tolerance tests in the diagnosis of diabetes in pregnancy. *Br J Obstet Gynaecol* 1978;85:536.

51. Cooper A, Granat M, Sharf M. Glucose intolerance during pregnancy II. A comparative study of diagnostic screening methods. *Obstet Gynecol* 1979;53:495.

52. O'Sullivan JB, Mahan CM, Charles D, et al. Screening criteria for high-risk gestational diabetic patients. *Am J Obstet Gynecol* 1973;116:895.

53. Lavin JP, Barden TP, Miodovnik M. Clinical experience with a screening program for gestational diabetes. *Am J Obstet Gynecol* 1981;141:491.

54. Marquette GP, Mein VR, Niebyl JR. Efficacy of screening for gestational diabetes. *Am J Perinatol* 1985;2:7.

55. Coustan DR, Nelson C, Carpenter MW, et al. Maternal age and

screening for gestational diabetes: a population based study. *Obstet Gynecol* 1989;73:557.

56. Green, GR, Pawson IG, Schumacher LB, et al. Glucose tolerance in pregnancy: ethnic variation and influence of body habitus. *Am J Obstet Gynecol* 1990;163:86–92.

57. Gunton JE, Hitchman R, McElduff A. Effects of ethnicity on glucose tolerance, insulin resistance and beta cell function in 223 women with an abnormal glucose challenge test during pregnancy. *Aust N Z Obstet Gynaecol* 2001;41:182–186.

58. American College of Obstetricians and Gynecologists. Management of diabetes mellitus in pregnancy. American College of Obstetricians and Gynecologists Technical Bulletin No. 92. Washington, DC: American College of Obstetricians and Gynecologists, May 1986

59. American College of Obstetricians and Gynecologists Committee on Practice Bulletins. Obstetrics. American College of Obstetricians and Gynecologists Practice Bulletin: Gestational diabetes. *Obstet Gynecol* 2001;98:525–538.

60. Danilenko-Dixon DR, Van Winter JT, Nelson RL, et al. Universal versus selective gestational diabetes screening: application of the 1997 American Diabetes Association recommendations. *Am J Obstet Gynecol* 1999;181:798–802.

61. Poncet B, Touzet S, Rocher L, et al. Cost-effectiveness analysis of gestational diabetes screening in France. *Eur J Obstet Gynecol Reprod Biol* 2002;103:122–129.

62. Philipson EH, Super DM. Gestational diabetes mellitus: does it recur in subsequent pregnancy? *Am J Obstet Gynecol* 1989;160:1324–1331.

63. Gaudier FL, Hauth JC, Poist M, et al. Recurrence of gestational diabetes mellitus. *Obstet Gynecol* 1992;80:755–758.

64. Moses RG. The recurrence of rate of gestational diabetes in subsequent pregnancies. *Diabetes Care* 1996;19:1348–1350.

65. Nahum GG, Stanislaw H. Correlation between one-hour, 50-g glucose screening values in successive pregnancies. *J Reprod Med* 2002;47:564–568.

66. Lind T, McDougall AN. Antenatal screening for diabetes mellitus by random blood glucose sampling. *Br J Obstet Gynaecol* 1981;88:346.

67. Beard RW, Gillmer MDG, Oakley NW, et al. Screening for gestational diabetes. *Diabetes Care* 1980;3:468.

68. Nahum GG, Wilson SB, Stanislaw H. Early-pregnancy glucose screening for gestational diabetes mellitus. *J Reprod Med* 2002;47:656–662.

69. Court JD, Stone RP, Killip M. Comparison of glucose and glucose polymer for testing oral carbohydrate tolerance in pregnancy. *Obstet Gynecol* 1984;64:251.

70. Court JD, Mann SL, Stone PR, et al. Comparison of glucose polymer and glucose for screening and tolerance tests in pregnancy. *Obstet Gynecol* 1985;66:491.

71. Reece EA, Holford T, Tuck S, et al. Screening for gestational diabetes: one-hour carbohydrate tolerance test performed by a virtually tasteless polymer of glucose. *Am J Obstet Gynecol* 1989;156:132.

72. Reece EA, Gabrielli S, Abdalla M, et al. Diagnosis of gestational diabetes by the use of a glucose polymer. *Am J Obstet Gynecol* 1989;160:383.

73. Coustan DR, Widness JA, Carpenter MW, et al. Should the 50 gram one hour screening test for gestational diabetes be administered in the fasting or fed state? *Am J Obstet Gynecol* 1986;154:1031.

74. Lewis GF, McNally C, Blackman JD, et al. Prior feeding alters the response to the 50-g glucose challenge test in pregnancy. *Diabetes Care* 1993;16:1551.

75. Berkus MD, Stern MP, Mitchell BD, et al. Does fasting interval affect the glucose challenge test? *Am J Obstet Gynecol* 1990;163:1282.

76. Gillmer MDG, Beard RW, Brooke FM, et al. Carbohydrate metabolism in pregnancy. *BMJ* 1975;3:399.

77. Muck BR, Hommel G. Plasma insulin response following intravenous glucose in gestational diabetes. *Arch Gynakol* 1977;223:259.

78. Turner RC, Harris E, Bloom SR, et al. Relation of fasting plasma glucose concentration to plasma insulin and glucagon concentrations. *Diabetes* 1977;26:166.

79. Guttorm E. Practical screening for diabetes mellitus in pregnant women. *Acta Endocrinol (Copenh)* 1974/1975;182(suppl):11.

80. Stangenberg M, Persson B, Nordlanden E. Random capillary blood glucose and conventional selection criteria for glucose tolerance testing during pregnancy. *Diabetes Res* 1985;2:29.

81. Lind T, Anderson J. Does random blood glucose sampling outdate testing for glycosuria in the detection of diabetes during pregnancy? *BMJ* 1984;4:289.

82. Coustan DR, Carpenter MW, Widness JA, et al. The "breakfast tolerance test": screening for gestational diabetes with a standardized mixed nutrient meal. *Am J Obstet Gynecol* 1987;157:1113.

83. Boyd KL, Ross EK, Sherman SJ. Jelly beans as an alternative to a cola beverage containing fifty grams of glucose. *Am J Obstet Gynecol* 1995;173:1889–1992.

84. Lamar ME, Kuehl TJ, Cooney AT, et al. Jelly beans as an alternative to a fifty-gram glucose beverage for gestational diabetes screening. *Am J Obstet Gynecol* 1999;181:1154–1157.

85. Lev-Ran A, VanderLaan WP. Glycohemoglobins and glucose tolerance. *JAMA* 1979;241:912.

86. Hall PM, Cook JGH, Sheldon J, et al. Glycosylated hemoglobins and glycosylated plasma proteins in the diagnosis of diabetes mellitus and impaired glucose tolerance. *Diabetes Care* 1984;7:147.

87. Widness JA, Schwartz HC, Kahn CB, et al. Glycohemoglobin in diabetic pregnancy: a sequential study. *Am J Obstet Gynecol* 1979;136:1024.

88. Schwartz HC, King KC, Schwartz AL. Effects of pregnancy on hemoglobin A_{1c} in normal, gestational diabetic, and diabetic women. *Diabetes* 1976;25:1118.

89. Fadel HE, Hammond SD, Huff TA, et al. Glycosylated hemoglobins in normal pregnancy and gestational diabetes mellitus. *Obstet Gynecol* 1979;54:322.

90. Shah BD, Cohen AW, May C, et al. Comparison of glycohemoglobin determination and the one-hour oral glucose screen in the identification of gestational diabetes. *Am J Obstet Gynecol* 1982;144:774.

91. Artal R, Mosley GM, Dorey FJ. Glycohemoglobin as a screening test for gestational diabetes. *Am J Obstet Gynecol* 1984;148:412.

92. McFarland KF, Murtiashaw M, Baynes JW. Clinical value of glycosylated serum protein and glycosylated hemoglobin levels in the diagnosis of gestational diabetes mellitus. *Obstet Gynecol* 1984;64:516.

93. Cousins L, Dattel BJ, Hollingsworth DR, et al. Glycosylated hemoglobin as a screening test for carbohydrate tolerance in pregnancy. *Am J Obstet Gynecol* 1984;150:455.

94. Jones IR, Owens DR, Williams S, et al. Glycosylated serum albumin: an intermediate index of diabetic control. *Diabetes Care* 1983;6:501.

95. Leiper JM, Talwar D, Robb DA. et al. Glycosylated albumin and glycosylated proteins: rapidly changing indices of glycemia in diabetic pregnancy. *Q J Med* 1985;218:225.

96. Roberts AB, Court DJ, Henley P, et al. Fructosamine in diabetic pregnancy. *Lancet* 1983;2:998.

97. Roberts AB, Baker JR, Metcalf P, et al. Fructosamine compared with a glucose load as a screening test for gestational diabetes. *Obstet Gynecol* 1990;76:773.

98. Nasrat HA, Ajabnoor MA, Ardawi MSM. Fructosamine as a screening test for gestational diabetes mellitus: a reappraisal. *Int J Gynecol Obstet* 1990;34:27.

99. Comtois R, Desjarlais F, Nguyen M, et al. Clinical usefulness of estimation of serum fructosamine concentration as screening test for gestational diabetes. *Am J Obstet Gynecol* 1989; 160:651.

100. Weiss PAM, Lichtenegger W, Winter R, et al. Insulin levels in amniotic fluid-management of pregnancy in diabetes. *Obstet Gynecol* 1978;51:393.

101. Weiss PAM, Hofman H, Winter R, et al. Gestational diabetes and screening during pregnancy. *Obstet Gynecol* 1984; 63:776.

102. Lin CC, River P, Moawad AH, et al. Prenatal assessment of fetal outcome by amniotic fluid C-peptide levels in pregnant diabetic women. *Am J Obstet Gynecol* 1981;141:671.

103. Stangenberg M, Persson B, Vaclavinkova V. Amniotic fluid volumes and concentrations of C-peptide in diabetic pregnancies. *Br J Obstet Gynaecol* 1982;89:536.

104. Carpenter MW, Shellum C, Canick JA, et al. Amniotic fluid insulin at 14–20 weeks' gestation. *Diabetes Care* 2001;24: 1259–1263.

105. MacDonald HN, Good W, Schwarz K, et al. Serial observations of glucose tolerance in pregnancy and the early puerperium. *Br J Obstet Gynaecol* 1971;78:489.

106. Lind T, Harris VG. Changes in the oral glucose tolerance test during the puerperium. *Br J Obstet Gynaecol* 1976;83:460.

107. Carpenter MW, Coustan DR, Widness JA, et al. Postpartum testing for antecedent gestational diabetes. *Am J Obstet Gynecol* 1988;159:1128.

108. Coustan DR, Lewis SB. Insulin therapy for gestational diabetes. *Obstet Gynecol* 1978;51:306.

109. Sosenko IR, Kitzmiller JL, Loo SW, et al. The infant of the diabetic mother: correlation of increased cord C-peptide levels with macrosomia and hypoglycemia. *N Engl J Med* 1979;301:859.

110. Weiss PAM, Hofman H, Purstner P, et al. Fetal insulin balance: gestation diabetes and postpartal screening. *Obstet Gynecol* 1984;64:65.

111. Dwyer PL, Oats JN, Walstab JE, et al. Glucose tolerance in twin pregnancy. *Aust N Z J Obstet Gynaecol* 1982;22:131.

112. Schwartz DB , Daoud Y, Zazula P, et al. Gestational diabetes mellitus: metabolic and blood glucose parameters in single versus twin pregnancies. *Am J Obstet Gynecol* 1999;181:912–914.

113. Naidoo L, Jailal 1, Moodley J, et al. Intravenous glucose tolerance tests in women with twin pregnancy. *Obstet Gynecol* 1985;66:500.

MANAGEMENT OF GESTATIONAL DIABETES

DONALD R. COUSTAN

The most important step in the management of gestational diabetes mellitus (GDM) is its diagnosis. Once this has been achieved, almost every type of management protocol has been associated with a reduction in the perinatal mortality rate. This is probably a reflection of the increased maternal and fetal surveillance prompted by this diagnosis, along with general improvements in perinatal care. Currently, the perinatal mortality rate is no longer the only yardstick by which successful care is measured. The management of high-risk situations is also directed toward lowering perinatal morbidity rates. This chapter outlines a plan of management that includes the above considerations.

GOALS OF MANAGEMENT

As discussed in an earlier chapter, the perinatal mortality rate is increased in diabetic pregnancies when hyperglycemia is allowed to persist unchallenged. There is evidence that mean whole blood glucose levels above 100 mg/dL in gravidas with preexisting diabetes are associated with a significant increase in the perinatal mortality risk (1), and most centers currently strive to maintain average plasma glucose concentrations that are as near to normal as possible. We assume that the fetus whose mother experiences hyperglycemia only during pregnancy is equally sensitive to mild elevations of circulating glucose levels, as is the fetus of the long-standing diabetic woman. For this reason, to prevent perinatal loss, it is reasonable to use the same strict standards for metabolic control in the patient with GDM as in women with overt diabetes. Similarly, although perinatal deaths are reported to occur at nearly the background level in properly diagnosed and managed GDM-associated pregnancies, surveillance of the fetus for signs of compromise may be reasonable. This point remains controversial and is primarily a cost versus benefit issue.

In most large series of GDM pregnancies, even though reasonable standards for glucose control have reportedly been met, a residual increase in perinatal morbidity has remained. The morbidities reported include fetal macrosomia, operative delivery, birth trauma, and neonatal complications such as hypoglycemia, hyperbilirubinemia, plethora, and hypocalcemia. The prevention of such problems is the primary challenge remaining for those who manage pregnancies complicated by GDM.

ATTAINING THE GOALS

Dietary Therapy

The cornerstone of treatment in pregnant women with overt diabetes or GDM is diet. Specific recommendations for dietary therapy in diabetic pregnancy are given in Chapter 20 and are not repeated here. It is worthwhile, however, to reemphasize that no matter how nutritionally sound a diet prescription might be, it is useless if the patient does not follow it. Therefore, it is particularly important to be aware of cultural and individual preferences when nutritional counseling is provided.

Glucose Monitoring

Although the use of daily self-glucose monitoring has not been shown to be essential to prevent perinatal mortality in gestational diabetes, our center and most others have moved to recommending this in all but the mildest cases. More than 20% of women with GDM will manifest hyperglycemia (individual plasma glucose levels of >120 mg/dL 2 hours after a meal or >130 mg/dL 1 hour after a meal), despite the prescription of a diet appropriate for diabetic pregnancy (2–4). Presumably, these pregnancies are at increased risk for perinatal mortality, and more intensive treatment should be undertaken. The Fourth International Workshop-Conference on Gestational Diabetes Mellitus (5) reached the following conclusion: "Self-monitoring of blood glucose appears to be superior to less frequent glucose monitoring in the clinic for detection of glucose concentrations that may warrant intensification of therapy beyond standard dietary management. . . ."

Although it has been demonstrated that fasting hyperglycemia connotes a different, and more significant mechanism of disorder in maternal carbohydrate metabolism compared with isolated postprandial hyperglycemia, the fetal consequences of hyperglycemia have not been linked specifically to the time of day. Indeed, the fetus may respond with increased pancreatic insulin formation and release no matter what time hyperglycemia occurs. Freinkel (6,7) reported higher birth weights, and higher corrected birth weights, among 58 infants of GDM mothers with normal fasting plasma glucose levels than among 106 infants of normal mothers. At least four other studies of diabetic pregnancies have now demonstrated that postprandial glucose determinations are more predictive of fetal macrosomia than are fasting values (8–11). The most recent (11) was a randomized trial of preprandial versus postprandial glucose measurements among 66 individuals with gestational diabetes severe enough to warrant insulin therapy by 30 weeks' gestation. Half the subjects measured glucose fasting and prior to each meal, with the goals being values of 60 to 105 mg/dL. The other half monitored fasting and postprandially, with the goal being fasting values of 60 to 90 mg/dL and 1 hour postprandial values below 140 mg/dL. Those monitoring postprandially had a significantly greater decrease in glycohemoglobin, fewer large-for-gestational-age offspring (12% vs. 42%), fewer cesarean sections for dystocia (12% vs. 36%), and less neonatal hypoglycemia. Thus, although fasting hyperglycemia may be a relatively specific marker for general maternal hyperglycemia, it probably is not adequately sensitive, such that its absence does not preclude abnormal maternal fuel metabolism with resultant fetal hyperinsulinemia, leading to macrosomia and other morbidities. The Fourth International Workshop-Conference (5) suggested that "Postprandial glucose levels may be more closely related to fetal risks than are fasting levels. Thus, it was recommended that glucose monitoring include postprandial testing and not be confined to fasting or premeal testing."

The American Diabetes Association (12) currently recommends insulin therapy when nutritional therapy fails to maintain self-monitored glucose at the following levels:

- Fasting whole blood glucose of less than or equal to 95 mg/dL (plasma ≤105 mg/dL), or
- One-hour postprandial whole blood glucose less than or equal to 140 mg/dL (plasma ≤155 mg/dL), or
- Two-hour postprandial whole blood glucose less than or equal to 120 mg/dL (plasma ≤130 mg/dL)

When patients are performing daily self-glucose monitoring, we generally initiate insulin therapy or increase the dose if values exceed the above thresholds 20% of the time, or roughly once per day.

The use of glycosylated hemoglobin measurements as the sole means to ascertain the adequacy of diabetic control is impractical because there is a delay of up to 1 month between changes in glycemia and their reflection in glycosylated hemoglobin values. Furthermore, these measurements are not nearly sensitive enough to detect the mild degree of maternal hyperglycemia that should prompt a therapeutic response in GDM.

Oral Hypoglycemic Agents

Currently, our views of the use of oral hypoglycemic agents during pregnancy are in the process of revision (13). Sulfonylureas work by stimulating pancreatic β-cells to produce and release insulin. The first-generation sulfonylureas are known to cross the placenta and would be expected to stimulate fetal pancreatic insulin release. Because the adverse fetal consequences of maternal GDM are believed to be related to fetal hyperinsulinemia, any agent that increases fetal insulin production would be expected to worsen the outcome in such pregnancies. Using an *in vitro* isolated perfused placental cotyledon model, Elliott et al. (14) demonstrated that glyburide, one of the second-generation oral agents, crosses the human placenta minimally. Subsequently, Langer et al. (15) reported a randomized clinical trial comparing glyburide to insulin therapy in 404 GDM mothers whose hyperglycemia was deemed severe enough to require intervention prior to 33 weeks' gestation. While eight subjects assigned glyburide ultimately required insulin therapy, mean blood glucose levels were similar in the two treatment groups. Maternal outcomes (cesarean section, preeclampsia) and neonatal outcomes (macrosomia, neonatal hypoglycemia, neotatal intensive care unit admissions) were also similar in the two treatment groups. Of importance, glyburide levels were nondetectable in the cord sera of infants in the glyburide group; maternal glyburide levels were measured at delivery in 12 of the glyburide-treated mothers, and concentrations ranged from 50 to 150 ng/mL. Thus, glyburide does not appear to cross the human placenta *in vivo* to a measurable extent. Langer et al. concluded that, in the setting of gestational diabetes, glyburide and insulin are equally effective therapies. As experience with glyburide in pregnancy accumulates, its role will become better defined.

A number of other oral antidiabetic agents are currently on the market and widely used by nonpregnant individuals. Well-controlled studies with these agents are generally lacking. Metformin is widely prescribed for type 2 diabetes, as well as for clinical conditions such as polycystic ovaries and the insulin resistance syndrome. Publications of limited case series data (16,17) have claimed that metformin administered to women with polycystic ovary syndrome throughout pregnancy can reduce the likelihood of spontaneous abortion and also of gestational diabetes. Unfortunately, the outcomes in these small series were typically compared with outcomes in previous pregnancies in the same individuals, or to outcomes in groups of women with polycystic ovaries not taking metformin for unspecified reasons. It seems that metformin shows great promise in this context, but it would be advisable to await the results of randomized clinical trials before using it during pregnancy. According to the *Physicians Desk Reference* (18), there is a "partial placental barrier" to metformin. This implies that some metformin crosses the placenta. While studies in rats and rabbits did not demonstrate teratogenicity, the same was true for thalidomide. It would seem reasonable to test metformin in higher species of animals for teratogenicity. There has been one randomized trial comparing acarbose to insulin treatment of gestational diabetes, showing similar outcomes, but to date this has only appeared in abstract form (19). No data are available regarding thiazolidinedione use during pregnancy. In summary, glyburide is the only oral agent that has been evaluated and appears safe and probably effective for management of gestational diabetes.

Insulin Therapy

When permissible glucose levels have been exceeded, insulin should be instituted as outlined above. The topic of insulin therapy has been extensively covered in Chapters 3 and 19, so only those specific issues relevant to GDM are discussed here.

Pregnancy is a time of intensified central and peripheral insulin resistance. For this reason, women with GDM generally require, and tolerate, considerably higher starting doses of insulin than do nonpregnant diabetic individuals. In many centers the gravida with gestational diabetes is treated with the same insulin regimen as are those with type 1 diabetes, using frequent injections throughout the day. While such an approach is not unreasonable, we prefer to start with the simplified regimen described below, moving to more complex approaches as the need arises.

For the woman with GDM who requires insulin because of hyperglycemia despite dietary treatment, we initiate insulin therapy at a dose of 30 U per day. This is given as 20 U of NPH (neutral protamine Hagedorn) and 10 U of regular insulin, mixed in the same syringe, and injected 15 to 30 minutes before breakfast each morning. Because insulin resistance seems to reach its maximum in the third trimester, we usually start with half of the above dose if treatment is required before 28 weeks of gestation, particularly if the patient is lean. The mixture of intermediate- and short-acting insulins, given in the proportion of 2:1, is based on the pattern of insulin release in normal nondiabetic women in the third trimester of pregnancy (20) (Fig. 16-1).

If hyperglycemia persists despite the above starting dose of insulin, adjustments are made in specific components. For example, if glucose levels are high 2 hours after breakfast, the regular insulin dose is increased. If the afternoon glucose level is high, the NPH insulin dose is increased.

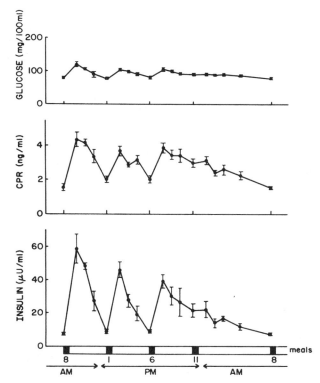

FIGURE 16-1. Serum glucose, insulin, and C-peptide (*CPR*) levels in six normal women in the third trimester of pregnancy (mean ± standard error of the mean). (From Lewis SB, Wallin JD, Kuzuya H, et al. Circadian variation of serum glucose, C-peptide immunoreactivity and free insulin in normal and insulin-treated diabetic pregnant subjects. *Diabetologia* 1976;12:343, with permission.)

Despite normal circulating glucose levels in the afternoon (when NPH insulin is at its peak of absorption), if evening or fasting glucose levels are elevated, a second insulin injection is administered just before the evening meal. Further modifications of the insulin regimen are similar to those recommended for the overt diabetic patient and are covered in Chapter 19. Symptomatic hypoglycemia is exceedingly rare, in our experience, among GDM individuals treated with this insulin regimen, unless a meal is omitted. Nevertheless, all patients are instructed in recognizing a hypoglycemic episode, in treating it, and in reporting this occurrence to us.

In recent years new insulin analogues have been introduced. Insulin lispro and insulin aspart have a more rapid absorption than does regular insulin, and are increasingly used in the management of diabetes. Although data regarding their use in pregnancy are limited, a single randomized trial compared lispro and regular insulin in 19 and 23 women with GDM, respectively (21). Patients using insulin lispro reported fewer hypoglycemic episodes, and the glucose area under the curve after a test meal was significantly lower. Importantly, when cord blood samples were analyzed, insulin lispro could not be demonstrated in the fetal circulation, suggesting that lispro insulin does not cross the placenta to a measurable extent. A single report of insulin aspart in gestational diabetes suggested a lower postbreakfast glucose area under the curve than with regular insulin; cord insulin aspart levels were not measured (22).

In the above discussion, the use of insulin was recommended when circulating glucose levels exceeded certain limits. However, current approaches to insulin therapy do not entirely eliminate such outcomes as macrosomia and neonatal hypoglycemia. Conversely, many of the patients requiring insulin treatment of gestational diabetes would probably have delivered perfectly normal babies even without insulin. Maternal glycemia is not a perfect predictor of perinatal outcome. Consequently, attempts have been made to look for better markers to identify pregnancies at greatest risk for adversity. Buchanan et al. (23) used ultrasound fetal measurements at 29 to 33 weeks' gestation in women with GDM and normal fasting glucose levels who were treated by diet alone. If the abdominal circumference exceeded the 75th percentile for gestational age, subjects were randomized to either continued diet therapy or to insulin treatment. The use of insulin was associated with a reduction in large-for-gestational age babies from 45% to 13% ($p < 0.04$), a rate similar to that which occurred when the abdominal circumference was below the 75th percentile and no insulin was given. In a subsequent randomized trial (24), the same group evaluated ultrasound abdominal circumference measurements in GDMs with fasting plasma glucose concentrations of 105 to 120 mg/dL, all of whom would ordinarily be treated with insulin. Subjects in the "standard" group were treated with insulin, whereas those in the "experimental" group received insulin only if the fetal abdominal circumference measurement was greater than or equal to the 70th percentile or if the fasting plasma glucose exceeded 120 mg/dL. Sixty-one percent of the subjects in the latter group required insulin, and circulating glucose levels were significantly lower in the former group, yet birth weights, macrosomia rates, and neonatal morbidity rates were similar in the two treatment arms. Of some concern was the finding that cesarean deliveries occurred in 33% of the experimental group, and only 15% of the standard group, a difference that was statistically significant. It is certainly plausible that different fetoplacental units may respond differently to given maternal glycemic levels, and studies such as the two cited above support evaluating the fetus as well as the mother in planning our therapy.

The benefits of any form of treatment must be weighed against the risks of that treatment. In the case of insulin for GDM, the primary risk to be considered is hypoglycemia. Symptomatic hypoglycemia in women with GDM who are treated with insulin during the third trimester is exceedingly rare unless a meal is omitted. Whether exogenous insulin contributes to other possibly adverse effects, such as are observed in patients with high circulating insulin levels due to insulin resistance syndrome, remains to be determined.

FETAL EVALUATION

Because the perinatal mortality risk of GDM has diminished markedly with more thorough screening programs and intense surveillance of glycemia, antepartum monitoring in such patients has become the subject of debate, particularly as to whether the potential benefit outweighs the cost. In 1977, Gabbe et al. (25) reported on a series of 261 women with GDM and recommended that women with uncomplicated pregnancies, GDM, and fasting euglycemia be allowed to go to 40 weeks before antepartum surveillance is instituted. Landon and Gabbe (26) reported on a second series of 97 women with GDM. Insulin was instituted if the fasting plasma glucose level exceeded 105 mg/dL on one occasion or the 2-hour postprandial plasma glucose concentration exceeded 120 mg/dL on repeated occasions; these parameters were measured weekly. Twenty-eight women (29%) required insulin. Beginning at 28 weeks' gestation, all patients recorded fetal activity daily. Antepartum surveillance with nonstress tests was begun in all patients by 40 weeks of gestation. However, those requiring insulin (29%) and those not insulin treated who had chronic hypertension (5%), pregnancy-induced hypertension (8%), or a previous stillbirth (1%) were followed with weekly nonstress tests and twice-weekly urinary estriol measurements from 34 weeks. Thus, 43% required antepartum surveillance before 40 weeks. No perinatal deaths occurred, and only six patients (6%) required intervention for suspected fetal jeopardy. These investigators recommended that antepartum fetal surveillance with nonstress tests be used before term only in insulin-requiring GDM pregnancies and in those not treated with insulin who manifest hypertension, prolonged pregnancy, and other risk factors. Another issue often debated is how often to perform antenatal fetal testing in diabetic pregnancies. In a large series (27), twice-weekly nonstress tests and amniotic fluid volume determinations were begun at 34 weeks in patients with complicated gestational diabetes, and at no later than 40 weeks in uncomplicated GDMs. There were no stillbirths within 4 days of a negative antepartum test in these 1,390 patients, but there were two stillbirths reported, at 36 and 28 weeks, respectively, in insulin-treated patients 1 week after normal tests. There was a 4.9% rate of cesarean delivery for nonreassuring fetal status.

The lack of level 1 evidence on this topic prompted the American College of Obstetricians and Gynecologists (28) to state that "There is insufficient evidence to determine the optimal antepartum testing regimen for women with relatively normal glucose levels on diet therapy and no other risk factors." In our center, we begin twice weekly nonstress tests and amniotic fluid assessments at 40 weeks' gestation when gestational diabetes is diet treated and otherwise uncomplicated. Patients whose gestational diabetes is treated with insulin or is otherwise complicated begin testing at 36 weeks or before, depending on the clinical situation.

DELIVERY

The timing and mode of delivery in diabetic pregnancies are discussed in Chapter 31. The principles enumerated for the patient with preexisting diabetes are equally applicable to those for patients with GDM. Macrosomia is every bit as much a problem here as in the offspring of "true" diabetic women.

If the gravid woman with GDM has been euglycemic and has developed no complications (such as hypertensive disorders), there is little indication for early delivery. However, if the fetus is growing rapidly near term, induction of labor may be considered before macrosomia makes vaginal delivery problematic. In a retrospective review of mostly nondiabetic mothers whose fetuses were estimated to weigh above the 90th percentile at term, Combs et al. (29) found a higher cesarean section rate with elective induction for macrosomia. Kjos et al. (30) found no difference in cesarean section rates when insulin-requiring women with GDM at 38 weeks' gestation were randomized to elective induction or expectant management.

COST-EFFECTIVENESS

Little has been written regarding the cost-effectiveness of various aspects of treatment for gestational diabetes, making it difficult to compare the relative benefit to society of investing in this type of care versus some other medical need. There has been one pilot study (31) applying cost and benefit data to the previously cited (11) randomized trial of preprandial versus postprandial glucose monitoring. The investigators demonstrated a significant improvement in the cost:benefit ratio with postprandial versus preprandial monitoring. This study also provides estimates of the costs of various approaches to management in different parts of the country, and sets a worthwhile example for future research in this area.

KEY POINTS

- The most important step in the management of GDM is the recognition of this disorder.
- All such women should be given dietary counseling.
- Women with GDM should perform fasting self-glucose monitoring and at 1 or 2 hours after each meal.
- Should hyperglycemia occur, insulin should be administered to restore glucose homeostasis and reduce perinatal risks.
- Fetal measurements may detect evolving macrosomia and help in determining the need for therapy.
- Selected oral hypoglycemic agents, such as glyburide, may have a role in the management of gestational diabetes.

- Patients with insulin-treated gestational diabetes, or with other risk factors (e.g., hypertensive disorders, poor obstetric history) should undergo fetal evaluation as if they had preexisting diabetes.

REFERENCES

1. Karlson K, Kjellmer I. The outcome of diabetic pregnancies in relation to the mother's blood sugar level. *Am J Obstet Gynecol* 1972;112:213.
2. Neiger R, Coustan DR. Are the current ACOG glucose tolerance test criteria sensitive enough? *Obstet Gynecol* 1991;78:1117.
3. Drexel H, Bichler A, Sailer S, et al. Prevention of perinatal morbidity by tight metabolic control in gestational diabetes. *Diabetes Care* 1988;11:761.
4. Goldberg JD, Franklin B, Lasser D, et al. Gestational diabetes: impact of home glucose monitoring on neonatal birth weight. *Am J Obstet Gynecol* 1986;154:546.
5. Metzger BE, Coustan DR, and the Organizing Committee. Summary and recommendations of the Fourth International Workshop-Conference on Gestational Diabetes Mellitus. *Diabetes Care* 1998;21(suppl 2):B161.
6. Freinkel N, Metzger BE. Gestational diabetes: problems in classification and implications for long-range prognosis. *Adv Exp Med Biol* 1985;189:47.
7. Freinkel N. Of pregnancy and progeny. *Diabetes* 1980;29:1023.
8. Jovanovic-Peterson L, Peterson CM, Reed GF, et al. Maternal postprandial glucose levels and infant birth weight: the Diabetes in Early Pregnancy Study. *Am J Obstet Gynecol* 1991;164:103.
9. Parfitt VJ, Clark JDA, Turner GM, et al. Maternal postprandial blood glucose levels influence infant birth weight in diabetic pregnancy. *Diabetes Res* 1992;19:133.
10. Combs CA, Gavin LA, Gunderson E, et al. Relationship of fetal macrosomia to maternal postprandial glucose control during pregnancy. *Diabetes Care* 1992;15:1251.
11. deViciana M, Major CA, Morgan MA, et al. Postprandial versus preprandial blood glucose monitoring in women with gestational diabetes requiring insulin therapy. *N Engl J Med* 1995;333:1237.
12. American Diabetes Association. Position statement on gestational diabetes mellitus. *Diabetes Care* 2003;27(suppl 1):S88.
13. Coustan DR. Oral hypoglycemic agents for the ob/gyn. *Contemp Obstet Gynecol* 2001;46:45.
14. Elliott BD, Langer O, Schenker S, et al. Insignificant transfer of glyburide occurs across the human placenta. *Am J Obstet Gynecol* 1991;165:807.
15. Langer O, Conway DL, Berkus MD, et al. A comparison of glyburide and insulin in women with gestational diabetes mellitus. *N Engl J Med* 2000;343:1134.
16. Glueck CJ, Wang P, Goldenberg N, et al. Pregnancy among women with polycystic ovary syndrome treated with metformin. *Hum Reprod* 2002;17:2858.
17. Glueck CJ, Wang P, Kobayashi S, et al. Metformin therapy throughout pregnancy reduces the development of gestational diabetes in women with polycystic ovary syndrome. *Fertil Steril* 2002;77:520.
18. *Physicians Desk Reference,* 57th ed. Montvale, NJ: Thompson PDR, 2003:1079–1085.
19. de Veciana M, Trail PA, Evans AT. A comparison of oral acarbose and insulin in women with gestational diabetes. *Obstet Gynecol* 2002;99(suppl):5.
20. Lewis SB, Wallin JD, Kuzuya H, et al. Circadian variation of

serum glucose, C-peptide immunoreactivity and free insulin in normal and insulin-treated diabetic pregnant subjects. *Diabetologia* 1976;12:343.

21. Jovanovic L, Ilic S, Pettitt D, et al. Metabolic and immunologic effects of insulin lispro in gestational diabetes. *Diabetes Care* 1999;22:1422.

22. Pettitt DJ, Ospina P, Kolaczynski JW, et al. Comparison of an insulin analog, insulin aspart, and regular human insulin with no insulin in gestational diabetes. *Diabetes Care* 2003;26:183.

23. Buchanan TA, Kjos SL, Montoro MN, et al. Use of fetal ultrasound to select metabolic therapy for pregnancies complicated by mild gestational diabetes. *Diabetes Care* 1994;17:275.

24. Kjos SL, Schaefer-Graf U, Sardesi S, et al. A randomized controlled trial using glycemic plus fetal ultrasound parameters versus glycemic parameters to determine insulin therapy in gestational diabetes with fasting hyperglycemia. *Diabetes Care* 2001; 24:1904.

25. Gabbe SG, Mestmann JH, Freeman RK, et al. Management and outcome of class A diabetes mellitus. *Am J Obstet Gynecol* 1977; 127:465.

26. Landon MB, Gabbe SG. Antepartum fetal surveillance in gestational diabetes mellitus. *Diabetes* 1985;34(suppl 2):50.

27. Kjos S, Leung A, Henry OA, et al. Antepartum surveillance in diabetic pregnancies: predictors of fetal distress in labor. *Am J Obstet Gynecol* 1995;173:1532.

28. American College of Obstetricians and Gynecologists. Gestational diabetes. *ACOG Pract Bull* 2001;30:10.

29. Combs CA, Singh NB, Khoury JC. Elective induction versus spontaneous labor after sonographic diagnosis of fetal macrosomia. *Obstet Gynecol* 1993;81:492.

30. Kjos SL, Henry OA, Montoro M, et al. Insulin-requiring diabetes in pregnancy: a randomized trial of active induction of labor and expectant management. *Am J Obstet Gynecol* 1993;169:611.

31. Kitzmiller JL, Elixhauser A, Carr S, et al. Assessment of costs and benefits of management of gestational diabetes mellitus. *Diabetes Care* 1998;21(suppl 2):B123.

17

INTERACTION BETWEEN PREGNANCY, GESTATIONAL DIABETES, AND LONG-TERM MATERNAL OUTCOME

JORGE H. MESTMAN

Over 100 years ago, Duncan (1) made three remarkable statements in the conclusions of his article on "Diabetes and Pregnancy":

1. Diabetes may come on during pregnancy.
2. Diabetes may occur only during pregnancy, absent at other times.
3. Diabetes may cease with the termination of pregnancy, recurring some time after birth.

This was the first recognition in the medical literature of what is known today as gestational diabetes and its implication, representing for a significant number of women the first manifestation of overt diabetes, mainly type 2.

Gestational diabetes mellitus (GDM), defined as carbohydrate intolerance first recognized in pregnancy, is diagnosed in 3% to 10% of pregnant women, the incidence depending on age, body weight, family history of type 2 diabetes, ethnic background, previous obstetric history, and the like. The indications for performing glucose tolerance testing (GTT) during pregnancy are based on a woman's risk factors for the potential development of GDM, risk factors similar to the ones observed in patients with the dysmetabolic syndrome or syndrome of insulin resistance (2). Indeed, the new emphasis in diagnosing GDM is not only in preventing perinatal morbidity and mortality, but also in the unique window of opportunity for the health-care professional to educate and advise the patient and her family on the different approaches to prevent or delay the onset of type 2 diabetes (3,4).

In this chapter, the following topics will be reviewed:

1. Historical evolution of the concept of gestational diabetes mellitus (GDM)
2. Prevalence of overt diabetes in women with GDM
3. Predictive factors in developing type 2 diabetes in women with GDM
4. Long-term cardiovascular complications in women with GDM

5. Relationship between GDM and insulin resistance syndrome
6. Prevention of type 2 diabetes

HISTORICAL EVOLUTION OF THE CONCEPT OF GESTATIONAL DIABETES MELLITUS

The concept that diabetes mellitus, first diagnosed during pregnancy, could represent an early manifestation of overt diabetes was entertained by early reports of increased perinatal mortality and morbidity occurring many years before the diagnosis of diabetes mellitus (5). Allen (6) in 1939 made the interesting observation of the frequent obstetric history of macrosomic infants in women diagnosed with diabetes many years after the pregnancy. Miller (7), studying autopsy material from seven infants born to mothers who did not have diabetes at the time of delivery but developed signs and symptoms of the disease months or years later, detected pathologic changes typical of those seen in infants of diabetic mothers, including hyperplasia of the islets of Langerhans, cardiomegaly, excessive extramedullary erythropoiesis, and others. The same investigator (8) compared the perinatal events in a group of mothers developing diabetes after age 40 with a nondiabetic control population. The perinatal mortality in the former was 8.3% as compared with 2.0% in the control group. In another retrospective study, Herzstein and Dolger (9) found a perinatal mortality rate of 15.4% in the 5 years preceding the diagnosis of diabetes, whereas the perinatal mortality rate was only 6% in women delivering a baby 5 to 20 years before the diagnosis of diabetes.

In 1951, Moss and Mulholland (10) performed an extensive literature review of perinatal events in women diagnosed with diabetes mellitus years after their last pregnancies; all the studies confirmed the high incidence of macrosomic infants and the high perinatal mortality years before the diagnosis of diabetes. The discrepancy among the different reports was the time elapsed between the pregnancy and the recognition of diabetes. In some series, events occurred up to 25 years before the diagnosis, while in the majority of observations it was within 5 years. Moss and Mulholland suggested "that many of these complications might have occurred in asymptomatic women with slight abnormalities in glucose intolerance." They advised a GTT for any obese women, those with a family history of diabetes, or an abnormal obstetric history or glycosuria. In view of the lack of uniformity in the diagnostic criteria for diabetes in pregnancy, they suggested "fasting blood glucose not greater than 120 mg per cc, and upper limits for 1, 2, and 3 hours of 180, 140, and 120 mg per cc, respectively."

The concern about high perinatal mortality in the prediabetic years stimulated several investigators in the field, some of whom suggested that a mild abnormality in glucose metabolism in pregnancy, not severe enough to produce symptoms, could be the cause of the high perinatal complications. This was complicated by the uncertainty in the interpretation of blood glucose during pregnancies. For example, Hoet (11) suggested maximum tolerated doses of insulin in women with an abnormal GTT in pregnancy to decrease perinatal mortality. He speculated that maternal pancreatic function also might be protected. Based on Hoet's observations, Wilkerson and Remein in Boston (12) embarked on a long-term prospective study, performing oral GTTs in a large pregnancy population. One of their aims was to study whether treatment with insulin during pregnancy in women with an abnormal GTT "would delay the onset or prevent diabetes from developing in later years in mother and child." The hypothesis of the study is shown in Table 17-1.

In 1960, Jackson (13) from South Africa suggested that a "temporary" diabetic state or significant impairment of glucose tolerance during pregnancy indicated a state of potentially permanent diabetes in the mother. He questioned whether pregnancy could be diabetogenic, based on the existing literature indicating a higher prevalence of diabetes in married than single women, in women with increased parity, and in women who have borne 10 or more children.

TABLE 17-1. EVALUATION OF THE EFFECT OF INSULIN TREATMENT ON THE OUTCOME OF PREGNANCY OF WOMEN WITH ABNORMAL CARBOHYDRATE TOLERANCE TO DETERMINE IF SUCH TREATMENT WILL:

Result in a lower rate of fetal wastage and other complications of pregnancy
Delay the onset of diabetes in pregnant women in the prediabetic stage
Decrease the chance of diabetes occurring in the live births

From Wilkerson HLC, Remein QR. Studies of abnormal carbohydrate metabolism in pregnancy. *Diabetes* 1957;6:324–326, with permission.

O'Sullivan in 1961 (14), using the same material collected by Wilkerson, published a study whose aim was "to know the frequency of asymptomatic diabetes occurring during pregnancy (gestational diabetes) and its relation to the subsequent development of diabetes." Between 1954 and 1959, 20,070 pregnant women were screened for potential diabetes. Those with positive screening including venous blood glucose of greater than 130 mg/dL 1 hour after a 50-g glucose load, a family history of diabetes, history of delivering large babies (>9 pounds), and an abnormal outcome (fetal death, neonatal death, congenital anomaly, prematurity, toxemia) in one or more pregnancies underwent a 3-hour oral GTT. The normal values using the Somogyi-Nelson technique for glucose determination were fasting 110 mg/dL, 1 hour 170 mg/dL, 2 hours 120 mg/dL, and 3 hours 110 mg/dL of venous blood. The presence of an abnormal fasting and 3-hour value or abnormal 1-, 2-, and 3-hour values were considered diagnostic of GDM. Of the initial 20,070 subjects, 8,344 women (41%) fulfilled the criteria for screening. Of these 8,344 women, 7,061 subjects followed through with a GTT, and 146 (2.06%) had an abnormal test result. O'Sullivan calculated that about 0.73% of all women registered had abnormal test results, and the corrected prevalence of GDM was 1 in 116 pregnant women (0.86%). He also performed GTTs in 378 pregnant women with negative screening, and none had a positive GTT. Therefore, the prevalence of abnormal tests in pregnancy in O'Sullivan's first publication was less than 1%.

O'Sullivan performed GTTs 6 weeks to 6 months after delivery in 126 of the 146 women with GDM. Nine had an abnormal GTT (7.1%). Extending the follow-up to 5½ years revealed that 39 (28.5%) of the 137 patients available for the study had developed diabetes. Because GDM was present in 1 of 116 pregnant women, and overt diabetes was reported in 1 of 500 or 1 of 1,000 pregnant women, O'Sullivan concluded that GDM occurred four to eight times more frequently than overt diabetes in pregnancy. He further speculated that because many patients had not been followed to this end point, the use of the life table technique could provide a statistically acceptable compensation for such losses. He then estimated the cumulative incidence of diabetes developing from GDM as 11% at 1 year, 24% at 2 years, 32% at 3 years, 42% at 4 years, and 67% at 5½ years following delivery. He concluded "that this progression dispels any doubt that the described glucose abnormality during pregnancy should be considered a variation of normal." These patients are prediabetic beyond any doubt. They are therefore suitable subjects for study of the disease while it is latent and yet easily recognizable. The far-reaching possibilities of prevention are dependent on such early recognition."

In 1964 O'Sullivan and Mahan (15) published the criteria for the diagnosis of GDM. The study was based on a group of 752 unselected women who had a 100-g oral GTT during their pregnancies. Most of the women were in the

TABLE 17-2. ORIGINAL CRITERIA FOR THE ORAL GLUCOSE TOLERANCE TEST IN PREGNANCY

Mean Blood Glucose Values of a 3 Hour Oral GTT in 752 Pregnant Women 100 g Glucose Solution Administered

	Fasting (mg/dL)	1-h (mg/dL)	2-h (mg/dL)	3-h (mg/dL)
Mean	69	103.6	91.7	79.4
Mean + 1 SD	80	134	117	103
Mean + 2 SD	90	165	143	127
Mean + 3 SD	101	196	169	151

SD, standard deviation.
From O'Sullivan JB, Mahan CM. Criteria for the oral glucose tolerance test in pregnancy. *Diabetes* 1964;13:278–285, with permission.

second and third trimesters of their gestation. They calculated the mean glucose value and 1, 2, and 3 standard deviations at fasting and at 1, 2, and 3 hours (Table 17-2). The results then were applied to a group of 1,013 women who were followed for up to 8 years after delivery. They decided to select as diagnostic of GDM the mean glucose values plus 2 SD for the following reasons: (a) "the more lenient the test (mean + 1SD) the greater will be its prevalence, with a long-term follow-up of the resulting increase in numbers posing an economic problem," and (b) "there arise the psychological ill-effects of alerting too many people in order to benefit relatively few true potential diabetics." Therefore, the criteria used for many years and still accepted in the United States and other countries as the gold standard for the diagnosis of GDM are based not on obstetric outcome, but on the development of diabetes mellitus several years after the diagnosis of GDM.

PREVALENCE OF OVERT DIABETES IN WOMEN WITH GESTATIONAL DIABETES MELLITUS

Since this first observation of overt diabetes developing years after the diagnosis of GDM, several clinical studies have confirmed the findings described above. Basic and clinical research investigations added a better understanding of the pathophysiologic basis of the relationship of GDM with the syndrome of insulin resistance.

Mestman et al. (16) followed 360 women with GDM for up to 5 years after delivery. Most women were Latino. Of 51 women with an elevated fasting glucose during pregnancy, only 4 of them reverted to a normal GTT result 6 weeks postpartum. Of 181 with an abnormal GTT result but a normal fasting glucose, 23 (12.7%) developed overt diabetes, and 59 demonstrated an abnormal GTT result with normal fasting glucose levels (32.6%).

Stowers et al. (17) followed women with GDM for up to 22 years (mean 12.9 years) with an intravenous GTT

(IVGTT). One third were treated with chlorpropamide and the others by diet alone. Thirty-five percent had an abnormal IVGTT result, and less than 7% developed overt diabetes. The use of chlorpropamide did not affect the final incidence of abnormal tests. In this study, islet cell antibodies were weakly positive in 12.5% of women, suggesting that some of them might have suffered from type 1 diabetes. Factors associated with deterioration of glucose tolerance were the patient's age at the time of pregnancy and her fasting plasma glucose [>5.8 mM (104 mg%)].

Metzger et al. (18) reported a high prevalence of abnormal GTT results within 1 year of the diagnosis of GDM. The fasting glucose value obtained in pregnancy predicted the future development of overt diabetes. Accordingly, 35% of those with a fasting glucose of less than 105 mg/dL, 43% with a fasting glucose between 106 and 129 mg/dL, and 86% with a fasting glucose of over 130 mg/dL developed overt diabetes mellitus.

Oats et al. (19) in Australia followed 485 women with the diagnosis of GDM, retesting them at intervals of from 1 to 15 years following diagnosis: 44 (9.1%) were found to have diabetes, and 82 (16.9%) had impaired glucose tolerance using the World Health Organization (WHO) criteria. Although an abnormal GTT result in the puerperium and obesity had significant association with abnormal glucose tolerance in the follow-up, the best predictive factor for the development of diabetes was the recurrence of GDM in a subsequent pregnancy.

Dornhorst et al. (20) followed 56 women with GDM of different ethnic origin for 6 to 12 years. Twenty-two developed diabetes and 14 had impaired glucose tolerance. Twenty women had a normal GTT according to the WHO criteria, but their insulin response to a glucose load was impaired. They pointed out that the high conversion to glucose intolerance or diabetes could be related to ethnicity since many of the women in their study were from the Indian subcontinent. In this regard, Motala et al. (21) from South Africa reported a progression to type 2 diabetes of 50% by 4 years after the diagnosis of GDM.

PREDICTIVE FACTORS IN THE DEVELOPMENT OF TYPE 2 DIABETES IN WOMEN WITH GESTATIONAL DIABETES MELLITUS

Not every woman diagnosed with GDM will eventually develop type 2 diabetes, although it occurs in most. The possibility of identifying those women at higher risk becomes an important public health issue, in view of recently published clinical research on the prevention of type 2 diabetes. Therefore, several investigators have studied the potential identifiable risk factors.

Kjos et al. (22) followed 671 Latino women with a history of GDM and a normal oral GTT 4 to 16 weeks postpartum. The subjects underwent at least one oral GTT within the following 7.5 years. The researchers tested 32 routine clinical parameters to discriminate between women who were at high risk and low risk for type 2 diabetes within 5 to 7 years after pregnancy. Life table analysis revealed a 47% cumulative incidence rate of type 2 diabetes 5 years after delivery. Four variables were identified as independent predictors of type 2 diabetes: (a) the area under the oral GTT curve 4 to 16 weeks postpartum; (b2) gestational age at the time of the diagnosis of GDM; (c) the area under the oral GTT glucose curve during pregnancy; and (d) the highest fasting serum glucose concentration during pregnancy. The postpartum oral GTT provided the best discrimination between high-risk and low-risk individuals [relative risk (RR) 11.5; 95% confidence interval 4.5–29.1] compared with the other three variables. In a subsequent paper by the same group (23), the investigators studied antepartum predictors of type 2 diabetes developing 11 to 26 weeks after delivery. They performed oral and intravenous GTTs and hyperinsulinemic-euglycemic clamps in 91 Latino women with GDM in the third trimester of their pregnancy. They concluded that 1-hour glucose values from the 3-hour GTT, poor pancreatic β-cell compensation for insulin resistance, and elevated endogenous glucose production during pregnancy preceded the development of type 2 diabetes in young Latino women by at least 1 to 2 years.

Peters et al. (24), in a group of Latino women with GDM, reported that an additional pregnancy increased the risk for developing type 2 diabetes. The annual incidence rate of type 2 diabetes was 30.9%, more than 2.5 times the annual incidence rate of diabetes in the cohort overall (adjusted RR 3.34). Weight gain was also independently associated with an increased risk for type 2 diabetes. The rate ratio was 1.95. The researchers concluded that repeat episodes of insulin resistance (pregnancy) might contribute to the decline in β-cell function that leads to type 2 diabetes in high-risk individuals. O'Sullivan (25) identified obesity, ethnicity, and weight gain after pregnancy as risk factors for the development of type 2 diabetes.

There is no convincing evidence that parity alone is a risk factor for the future development of type 2 diabetes (26). It is possible, as postulated by Peters et al. (24), that pregnancy has its greatest impact on the risk for type 2 diabetes in women who had already shown a propensity for glucose intolerance

Kim et al. (27) recently published a systematic review of articles between 1965 and 2001 related to GDM and the incidence of type 2 diabetes. They collected 28 studies; the cumulative incidence of diabetes ranged from 2.6 to 70% in women examined 6 weeks postpartum to 28 years postpartum. Kim et al. concluded that conversion to type 2 diabetes varied with the length of follow-up and cohort retention. Adjustment for these differences revealed a rapid increase in the cumulative incidence occurring in the first 5

years after delivery for different racial groups. They reported that the fasting glucose level during pregnancy might prove to have the greatest effect. From the review of the published articles, the investigators made several interesting observations: (a) once diagnosed with GDM, women from mixed or nonwhite cohorts seemed to progress to type 2 diabetes at similar rates; (b) the progression to type 2 diabetes increased steeply within the first 5 years after delivery and then appeared to plateau; (c) women of white ethnicity also may convert at a similar rate, but it was difficult to assess because of the relatively few studies of this population; (d) elevated fasting glucose predicted type 2 diabetes, except when more specific measures of pancreatic β-cell function were concomitantly examined; and (e) other risk factors had inconsistent or little predictive value after adjustment for other variables. According to the investigators, once women have elevated fasting glucose levels during pregnancy, their course of insulin resistance progresses at a similar rate, and that ethnicity could play an important role in determining susceptibility to initial elevation in glucose levels. They confirmed their hypothesis that much of the difference in the risk reported among studies could be explained by different lengths of follow-up, ethnic variation, and the diagnostic criteria used.

LONG-TERM CARDIOVASCULAR COMPLICATIONS IN WOMEN WITH GESTATIONAL DIABETES MELLITUS

There are few studies looking at cardiovascular complications in women with a history of GDM. In one investigation (28), 89 women with GDM were interviewed 12 to 18 years after their pregnancies: five had one abnormal value in the original GTT; 67 women were classified as class A (abnormal GTT but normal fasting glucose throughout pregnancy) and 17 had an elevated fasting glucose (class B). A total of 58 (65.2%) developed overt diabetes. The study revealed a high incidence of chronic vascular complications in the group of women who developed overt diabetes as compared with the 31 gestational diabetic women who remained euglycemic (Table 17-3). The incidence of hypertension was 44.8% versus 12.9% in the controls, 5 women had had a stroke, 4 a myocardial infarction, and 2 were on dialysis. In all of these women, the first diagnosis of diabetes was made during pregnancy, and all of them had type 2 diabetes.

O'Sullivan (29), in a preliminary analysis of the Boston Gestational Diabetes Study, showed a mortality rate that was significantly higher than that of controls up to 26 years postpartum, although he cautioned that the number of deaths was still too low to allow comfirmatory analysis. He found a higher incidence of cardiovascular risk factors among these women, including dyslipidemia and higher blood pressure than in the control group. He also reported

TABLE 17-3. INCIDENCE OF COMPLICATIONS IN WOMEN WITH GESTATIONAL DIABETES MELLITUS WHO DEVELOP OVERT DIABETES

	N	HTN	CVA	MI	Dialysis
Diabetes	58	26 (44.8)	5 (8.6)	4 (6.8)	2 (3.4)
Control	31	4 (12.9)	—	—	—

HTN, hypertension; CVA, cardiovascular accident; MI, myocardial infarction.

more electrocardiographic abnormalities in this group and three to five times more cases of myocardial infarction and angina. The final analysis of O'Sullivan 's work had not been published at the time of his death (30).

RELATIONSHIP BETWEEN GESTATIONAL DIABETES MELLITUS AND THE INSULIN RESISTANCE SYNDROME

The similarities between risk factors for the development of GDM and type 2 diabetes have been recognized in the past two decades. In addition to insulin resistance and compensatory hyperinsulinemia, abnormalities in lipid metabolism and obesity have been identified in both clinical entities. It has even been suggested that they are the same disorder (31,32).

The diagnosis of syndrome X, also known as the insulin resistance syndrome or metabolic syndrome, is based on well-defined clinical findings. It is a predictor for the development of cardiovascular complications (33) and affects 20% to 40% of the adult population depending on race and ethnicity (34). The diagnostic criteria suggested by the National Cholesterol Education Program Expert Panel (35) requires the presence of three of five of the following criteria for diagnosis: (a) blood pressure greater than or equal to 130/85 mm Hg; (b) high-density lipoprotein cholesterol (HDL) less than 40 mg/dL in men and less than 50 mg/dL in women; (c) serum triglycerides greater than 150 mg/dL; (d) abdominal obesity, defined as a waistline measuring greater than 40 inches (100 cm) in men and greater than 36 inches (92 cm) in women; and (e) fasting serum glucose greater than 110 mg/dL. Hyperinsulinemia is a constant feature. Other manifestations of metabolic syndrome are the presence of hyperuricemia, acanthosis nigricans, and polycystic ovary syndrome (PCOS). Indeed, patients with PCOS are at higher risk for developing GDM (36).

Type 2 diabetes develops in subjects with defects in insulin secretion in the presence of insulin resistance. Women with a history of GDM have been studied at different times following the index pregnancy to assess degrees of insulin action and insulin resistance in the presence of a normal GTT result (37,38). In one study (36), the researchers performed extensive investigations of carbohydrate metabolism in a group of 14 nonobese women with normal glucose tolerance and a past history of GDM. They were compared with a group of control subjects matched for both body mass index (BMI) and waist-to-hip ratio. Despite having a normal GTT result, women with a history of GDM had defects in both insulin secretion and insulin action.

The Nurse's Health Study (39), a prospective investigation initiated in 1989, followed over 100,000 female nurses for an average of 10 years. Biennial questionnaires were sent asking for lifestyle factors and health events, including pregnancies. Between 1990 and 1994, 14,613 of these nurses had at least one pregnancy, and 722 developed GDM (4.9%). Risk factors for the development of GDM were evaluated, including age, ethnicity, cigarette smoking, BMI, and weight. Predictors for the development of GDM are shown in Table 17-4. These findings are consistent with risk factors for the development of type 2 diabetes.

Bell et al. (40) compared risk factors for the development of GDM in the black population. Obese, older gravidas, as well as those with a family history of diabetes (FHD), those suffering from hypertension, and those with a family history of heart disease had a higher risk for developing GDM.

Kjos et al. (41) studied lipid metabolism in a group of Latino women with GDM followed for 36 months. At 6 to 12 weeks postpartum, serum triglycerides and HDL cholesterol were higher in those women who later developed diabetes mellitus as compared with the women who did not develop diabetes. This is consistent with findings in prediabetic patients (42).

Birth weight is inversely related to subsequent risk for type 2 diabetes (43), insulin resistance, and other features of metabolic syndrome. Both low birth weight (<2,500 g) and high birth weight are associated with the future development of type 2 diabetes as well as GDM. Birth weight has a U-shaped relationship to a woman's risk for GDM in her first pregnancy, with the highest risks associated with low and high birth weights. Odds ratios adjusted for gestational age were 2.16 for a birth weight below 2,000 g and 1.53 for a birth weight of 4,000 g or more. This study suggests that early life factors may be important in the etiology of the disorder (44).

TABLE 17-4. PREGRAVID DETERMINANTS OF GESTATIONAL DIABETES MELLITUS

Advanced maternal age
Nonwhite ethnicity
Higher body mass index
Weight gain in early adulthood
Cigarette smoking
Family history of diabetes mellitus (first-degree relative)

From Solomon CG, Willett WC, Carey VJ, et al. A prospective study of pregravid determinants of gestational diabetes mellitus. *JAMA* 1997;278:1078, with permission.

Clark et al. (45) hypothesized that GDM could manifest many of the characteristics of metabolic syndrome. They compared metabolic profiles in 52 women with GDM and 127 controls as determined by a normal 1-hour glucose screen. The group with GDM had a higher prepregnancy weight, higher prepregnancy BMI, higher C-peptide fasting and at 2 hours postprandial, higher insulin levels fasting and at 2 hours, higher fasting free fatty acid, and lower HDL cholesterol. All of the above parameters were significantly different than in control women. There were no differences in blood pressure. The investigators suggested that GDM be regarded as a component of the syndrome of insulin resistance. It provides an excellent model for the study and prevention of type 2 diabetes in a relatively young age group.

Sriharan et al. (46) measured serum sialic acid concentrations in women with a previous history of GDM and in a control group. Sialic acid, an inflammatory marker, has been shown to be a strong predictor of coronary artery disease, stroke, and cardiovascular mortality. The sialic acid concentration was associated with the 2-hour plasma glucose level after adjustment for waist-to-hip ratio and the log of serum triglycerides. The researchers speculated that their finding of a high concentration of sialic acid in women with a previous history of GDM supports the concept of GDM as part of metabolic syndrome.

The above studies strongly endorse the hypothesis that GDM has many common features with metabolic syndrome. It has important implications not only in detecting patients at risk at a younger age, but also having the potential for a preventive effect in the offspring of women with GDM. As stated by Norbert Freinkel (47) at the opening of the First International Workshop on GDM, "With GDM women, we may be able to unmask a population at greater risk for permanent diabetes under nongravid conditions and use it to evaluate the efficacy of preventive measures." This view reinforced the conclusions of O'Sullivan's paper in 1961 (14).

PREVENTION OF TYPE 2 DIABETES

Since it is known that most women with a history of GDM are at higher risk for the development of type 2 diabetes, there is a unique opportunity for the medical community to apply recent information regarding the prevention or delay in the onset of overt hyperglycemia. Several studies have shown that modifications of risk factors are effective in achieving the above goal. It has been shown that progression of IGT to type 2 diabetes occurs at a rate of 2% to 7% a year, depending on the type of population studied. It is also known that the conversion is greater in certain ethnic groups such as Latinos, Native Americans, and African Americans (48). This observation is similar to the progression of women with a history of GDM to type 2 diabetes (27).

Physical inactivity and obesity are well known risk factors for the development of type 2 diabetes. It was postulated that lifestyle modification—including losing weight, decreasing the total amount of calories consumed, increasing the amount of fiber in the diet, and increasing daily physical activity—could delay or prevent the development of type 2 diabetes in those subjects at higher risk due to obesity or family history. Indeed, two studies in the 1990s showed a significant reduction in the development of diabetes. In one group of women, it was reduced by a third through vigorous exercise independent of the family history of diabetes (49). The protective effect of regular physical activity was also shown in a prospective study of men (50). Exercise, without weight loss, increased insulin sensitivity in a recent study of sedentary middle-aged adults (51). The 6-month study consisted of walking an average of 30 minutes 3 to 7 days a week. Weight loss when sustained also has a significant benefit in reducing the conversion of IGT to diabetes mellitus (52).

In the Diabetes Prevention Program (3), 3,234 subjects over age 25 and with a BMI of 24 or higher and with a fasting serum glucose concentration of 95 to 125 mg/dL or a 2-hour value of 140 to 199 mg/dL after a 75-g glucose load were eligible for the study. They were assigned to four different groups: (a) intensive lifestyle changes under strict supervision with the aim of reducing weight by 7% with diet and 150 minutes per week of exercise; (b) treatment with metformin 850 mg twice a day and advice about meal plan and physical activity; (c) a group on troglitazone, which was discontinued because of the drug's potential for liver toxicity; and (d) a control group. The incidence of diabetes was reduced by 58% with the lifestyle intervention and by 31% with metformin as compared with placebo. These effects were similar in men and women and in all racial and ethnic groups.

In a study done in Finland (4), 552 middle-aged overweight subjects with impaired glucose tolerance were randomly assigned to either an intervention or control group. In the former, individualized counseling aimed at reducing weight and the intake of fat, increasing the intake of fiber, and increasing physical activity was provided. The cumulative incidence of diabetes after 4 years was 11% in the intervention group and 23% in the control group. During the trial, the risk for diabetes was reduced by 58% in the intervention group and was directly associated with changes in lifestyle.

The above recent studies confirm other studies that have suggested an increase in the incidence of diabetes in physically inactive individuals or those with consistent weight gain. These data should stimulate the health-care professional caring for women with a previous history of GDM to educate patients and their families on the importance of lifestyle modification to prevent or delay the onset of diabetes and reduce cardiovascular risk factors. Several studies have shown an increased incidence of obesity and abnormal glucose tolerance in the offspring of mothers with GDM, similar to the observations of children from type 2 mothers (53,54). These children may benefit from similar lifestyle modifications.

In the future, drug therapy may be used to reduce the risk for type 2 diabetes. The TRIPOD study (55) enrolled Latino women who had a previous history of GDM, but had not yet developed diabetes. The treated and placebo groups were matched for age, BMI, and parity. In the treated group, 133 women received troglitazone 400 mg a day to improve insulin sensitivity. The study was terminated after 30 months because troglitazone was found to be hepatotoxic. The incidence of overt diabetes was reduced from 12.3% in the control group to 5.4% in the treated group. The protection from diabetes persisted 8 months after the drug was stopped and was associated with preservation of pancreatic β-cell function. This beneficial effect appeared to be mediated by a reduction in the secretory demands placed on β-cells by chronic insulin resistance.

CONCLUSIONS

Type 2 diabetes mellitus has become epidemic in the past several decades owing to the advancing age of the population, a significant increased prevalence of obesity, and decreased physical activity. In the past 10 years, there has been an alarming increase, particularly in people 30 to 39 years of age (56). In addition, in adolescents, the increased diagnosis of type 2 diabetes is paralleled by the increased incidence of obesity (57). The delay in the diagnosis of type 2 diabetes is between 4 and 7 years, and at the time of diagnosis, 10% to 20% of patients have micro- and macrovascular complications (58). Diabetes mellitus is the leading cause of end-stage renal disease, blindness in the adult population, and amputation not due to trauma. Most people with type 2 diabetes also suffer from obesity, hypertension, and dyslipidemia. People with diabetes have two to five times the risk for cardiovascular disease as compared with patients without diabetes (59). Cardiovascular disease accounts for 60% of the mortality in the diabetic population. The cost of diabetes care in the United States, including its complications, is $100 billion annually. Early diagnosis and corrections of the cardiovascular risk factors have been shown to decrease micro- and cardiovascular complications (60). The American Diabetes Association has suggested metabolic targets for people with diabetes (61) (Table 17-5).

Women diagnosed with GDM are at greater risk for developing complications during gestation, affecting both mother and child. These potential complications are preventable in the majority of patients. Perinatal mortality, reported between 3% and 10% in the early literature, has been reduced to that seen in the nondiabetic population. Early diagnosis and prompt correction of maternal meta-

TABLE 17-5. SUMMARY OF RECOMMENDATIONS FOR ADULTS WITH DIABETES MELLITUS

Glycemic control	
A$_{1c}$	<7.0%[a]
Preprandial plasma glucose	90–130 mg/dL (5.0–7.2 mM)
Peak postprandial plasma glucose	<180 mg/dL (<10.0 mM)
Blood pressure	130/80 mm Hg
Lipids	
LDL	<100 mg/dL (<2.6 mM)
Triglycerides[b]	<150 mg/dL (<1.7 mM)
HDL	>40 mg/dL (1.1 M)[c]

[a]Referenced to a nondiabetic range of 4.0%–6.0% using a DCCT-based assay.
[b]Current NCEP/ATP III guidelines suggest that in patients with triglycerides ≥200 mg/dL, the non-HDL cholesterol (total cholesterol minus HDL) be used. The goal is ≤130 mg/dL.
[c]For women, it has been suggested that the HDL goal be increased by 10 mg/dL.
DCCT, Diabetes Control and Complications Trial; HDL, high-density lipoprotein; LDL, low-density lipoprotein; NCEP/ATP, National Cholesterol Education Program/adeninetriphosphate.
From the American Diabetes Association. Clinical practice recommendations 2003. *Diabetes Care* 2003;26(suppl 1):1–149, with permission.

bolic abnormalities, proper use and interpretation of tests for fetal well-being, and early care of the newborn have resulted in a dramatic improvement in maternal and fetal morbidity.

GDM is not a transient metabolic abnormality, but the first manifestation of a serious disease, type 2 diabetes. Even patients with impaired glucose intolerance are at significant risk for developing cardiovascular complications. Therefore, the physician caring for women with a previous diagnosis of GDM has the responsibility to educate patients and their families about the disease and its potential complications, and apply present medical knowledge to the evaluation, prevention, management, and treatment. Following delivery, women with previous GDM should be followed at regular intervals, having their first test for diabetes between 6 and 12 weeks postpartum. They should be encouraged to apply what they have learned during pregnancy (self-glucose monitoring, physical activity, diet principles) and to attain their ideal body weight by proper diet and exercise. Basic instruction from a nutritionist or health-care professional will allow patients to modify their meal plan to include more vegetables and fiber, and to decrease the consumption of saturated fat. Physical activity should be encouraged, with the recommendation of walking at least 45 minutes 5 to 7 days a week. Lipid determinations should be performed every 2 to 5 years and blood pressure evaluated at each medical visit. Cigarette smoking should be strongly discouraged. A family history of early cardiovascular events should be considered another important risk factor. Involvement of the community could help in achieving these important objectives.

KEY POINTS

- Prediabetes was recognized as a risk factor for neonatal morbidity and mortality in retrospective studies in the 1940s.
- O'Sullivan's early studies were aimed "to know the frequency of asymptomatic diabetes during pregnancy and its relation to the subsequent development of diabetes."
- O'Sullivan's GTT criteria were not based on perinatal events, but on the development of diabetes in women with GDM followed by an average of 8 years after delivery.
- Studies published since the 1970s have confirmed the high incidence of overt diabetes in the years following the diagnosis of GDM.
- Abnormalities in insulin secretion and sensitivity were detected in women with previous GDM, when studied postpartum, in the presence of normal glucose tolerance.
- Several researchers published clinical predictors for the development of GDM (age, BMI, ethnicity, family history of diabetes, etc.).
- Significant cardiovascular complications were reported in women in whom diabetes mellitus was diagnosed for the first time in pregnancy (GDM).
- Several characteristics of metabolic syndrome are detected at the time of the diagnosis of GDM.
- Recent publications showed that changes in lifestyle or use of insulin sensitizers drugs (metformin, thiazolidinedione) may prevent or delay the onset of overt diabetes in women with previous GDM.
- GDM is considered an early stage in the natural history of diabetes mellitus type 2. Therefore, the importance of screening programs is not only in the prevention of neonatal events, but most importantly in detecting early diabetes and preventing chronic complications.

REFERENCES

1. Duncan JM. On puerperal diabetes. *Trans Obstet Soc Lond* 1882; 24:256.
2. Reaven GM. Role of insulin resistance in human disease. *Diabetes* 1988;37:1595–1607.
3. Diabetes Prevention Program Research Group. Reduction in the incidence of type 2 diabetes with lifestyle intervention or metformin. *N Engl J Med* 2002;346:393–403.
4. Tuomilehto J, Lindstrom J, Eriksson JG, et al. Prevention of type 2 diabetes mellitus by changes in lifestyle among subjects with impaired glucose tolerance. *N Engl J Med* 2001;344:1343–1350.
5. Mestman JH. Historical notes on diabetes and pregnancy. *Endocrinologist* 2002;12:224–242.
6. Allen E. The glycosurias of pregnancy. *Am J Obstet Gynecol* 1935; 38:982–992.
7. Miller HC, Wilson HM. Macrosomia, cardiac hypertrophy, erythroblastosis and hyperplasia of the islets of Langerhans in infants born to diabetic mothers. *J Pediatr* 1943;23:251:266.
8. Miller HC. The effect of the prediabetic state on the survival of the fetus and the birth weight of the newborn infant. *N Engl J Med* 1945;233:376–378.
9. Herzstein J, Dolger H. The fetal mortality in women during the prediabetic period. *Am J Obstet Gynecol* 1946;51:420–422.
10. Moss JM, Mulholland HB. Diabetes and pregnancy with special reference ot the prediabetic state. *Ann Intern Med* 1951;34:678–691.
11. Hoet JP. Carbohydrate metabolism during pregnancy. *Diabetes* 1954;3:1–12.
12. Wilkerson HLC, Remein QR. Studies of abnormal carbohydrate metabolism in pregnancy. *Diabetes* 1957;6:324–329.
13. Jackson WPU. Diabetes, pre-diabetes, mothers and babies. *South Afr Med J* 1953;27:795–797.
14. O'Sullivan JB. Gestational diabetes: unsuspected, asymptomatic diabetes in pregnancy. *N Engl J Med* 1961;264:1082–1085.
15. O'Sullivan JB, Mahan CM. Criteria for the oral glucose tolerance test in pregnancy. *Diabetes* 1964;13:278.
16. Mestman JH, Anderson GV, Guadalupe V. Follow up study of 360 subjects with abnormal carbohydrate metabolism during pregnancy. *Obstet Gynecol* 1972;39:421.
17. Stowers JM, Sutherland HW, Kerridge DF. Long-range implications for the mother. *Diabetes* 1985;34(suppl 2):106–110.
18. Metzger BE, Bybee DE, Freinkel N, et al. Gestational diabetes mellitus. Correlation between the phenotype and genotype characteristics of the mother and abnormal glucose tolerance during the first year postpartum. *Diabetes* 1985;34(suppl 2):111–115.
19. Oats JN, Beischer NA, Grant PT. The emergence of diabetes and impaired glucose tolerance in women who had gestational diabetes. In: Weiss PAM, Coustan DR, eds. *Gestational diabetes.* New York: Springer-Verlag, 1988:199–207.
20. Dornhorst A, Bailey PC, Anyaoku V, et al. Abnormalities of glucose tolerance following gestational diabetes. *Q J Med* 1990;284:1219–1228.
21. Motala AA, Omar MAK, Gouws E. High risk of progression of NIDDM in South African Indians with impaired glucose intolerance. *Diabetes* 1993;42:556–563.
22. Kjos SL, Peters RK, Xiang AH, et al. Predicting future diabetes in Latino women with gestational diabetes. *Diabetes* 1995;44:586–591.
23. Buchanan TA, Xiang AH, Kjos SL, et al. Antepartum predictors of the development of type 2 diabetes in Latino women 11–26 months after pregnancies complicated by gestational diabetes. *Diabetes* 1999;48:2430–2436.
24. Peters RK, Kjos SL, Xiang AH, et al. Long term diabetogenic effect of single pregnancy in women with previous gestational diabetes mellitus. *Lancet* 1996;347:227–230.
25. O'Sullivan JB. Body weight and subsequent diabetes mellitus. *JAMA* 1982;248:949–952.
26. Manson JE, Rimm EB, Colditz GA, et al. Parity and incidence of non-insulin dependent diabetes mellitus. *Am J Med* 1992;93:13–18.
27. Kim C, Newton KM, Knopp RH. Gestational diabetes and the incidence of type 2 diabetes. *Diabetes Care* 2002;25:1862–1868.
28. Mestman JH. Follow up studies in women with gestational diabetes mellitus. The experience at Los Angeles County/University of Southern California Medical Center. In: Weiss PAM, Coustan DR, eds. *Gestational diabetes.* New York: Springer-Verlag, 1988:191–198.
29. O'Sullivan JB. The interaction between pregnancy, diabetes, and long-term maternal outcome. In: Reece EA, Coustan DR, eds. *Diabetes mellitus in pregnancy.* New York: Churchill Livingstone, 1995:389–397.
30. Knopp RH. John B. O'Sullivan: a pioneer in the study of gestational diabetes. *Diabetes Care* 2002;25:943–944.
31. Pendergrass M, Fazioni E, DeFronzo R. NIDDM and GDM: same disease, another name? *Diabetes Rev* 1995;3:566–583.
32. Csorba TR, Edwards AL. The genetics and pathophysiology of

type II and gestational diabetes. *Crit Rev Clin Lab Sci* 1995;32: 509–550.

33. Lakka HM, Laaksonen DE, Lakka TA, et al. The metabolic syndrome and total and cardiovascular disease mortality in middle-aged men. *JAMA* 2002;288:2709–2716.

34. Ford ES, Giles WH, Dietz WH. Prevalence of the metabolic syndrome among US adults: findings from the Third National Health and Nutrition Examination Survey. *JAMA* 2002;287: 356–359.

35. Expert Panel on Detection, Evaluation, and Treatment of High Blood Cholesterol in Adults: executive summary of the third report of the National Cholesterol Education Program (NCEP) expert panel on detection, evaluation, and treatment of high blood cholesterol in adults (Adult Treatment Panel III). *JAMA* 2001;285:2486–2497.

36. Koivunen RM, Juutinen J, Vaukhonen I, et al. Metabolic and steroidogenic alterations related to increased frequency of polycystic ovaries in women with a history of gestational diabetes. *J Clin Endocrinol Metab* 2001;86:2591–2599.

37. Ryan EA, Imes S, Liu D, et al. Defects in insulin secretion and action in women with a history of gestational diabetes. *Diabetes* 1995;44:506–512.

38. Ward WK, Johnson CLW, Beard JC, et al. Insulin resistance and impaired secretion in subjects with histories of gestational diabetes mellitus. *Diabetes* 1985;34:861–869.

39. Solomon CG, Willett WC, Carey VJ, et al. A prospective study of pregravid determinants of gestational diabetes mellitus. *JAMA* 1997;278:1078.

40. Bell DS, Barger BO, Go RC, et al. Risk factors for gestational diabetes in a black population. *Diabetes Care* 1990;13:1196–1201.

41. Kjos SL, Buchanan TA, Montoro M, et al. Serum lipids within 36 months of delivery in women with recent gestational diabetes. *Diabetes* 1991;40:142–146.

42. Haffner SM, Stern MP, Hazuda HP, et al. Cardiovascular risk factors in confirmed prediabetic individuals. Does the clock for coronary heart disease start ticking before the onset of clinical diabetes? *JAMA* 1990;263;2893–2898.

43. Phillips D. Birth weight and the future development of diabetes: a review of the evidence. *Diabetes Care* 1998;21(suppl 2): B150–B155.

44. Innes KE, Byers TE, Marshal JA, et al. Association of a woman's own birth weight with subsequent risk for gestational diabetes. *JAMA* 2002;287:2534–2541.

45. Clark CM, Qiu C, Amerman B, et al. Gestational diabetes: should it be added to the syndrome of insulin resistance? *Diabetes Care* 1997;20:867–871.

46. Sriharan M, Reichelt AJ, Opperman MLR, et al. Total sialic acid and associated elements of the metabolic syndrome in women with and without previous gestational diabetes. *Diabetes Care* 2002;25:1331–1335.

47. Freinkel N. Gestational diabetes 1979: philosophical and practical aspects of a major public health problem. *Diabetes Care* 1980; 3:399–401.

48. Edelstein SL, Knowler WC, Bain RP, et al. Predictors of progression from impaired glucose tolerance to type 2 diabetes: an analysis of six prospective studies. *Diabetes* 1997;46:701.

49. Manson JE, Rimm EB, Stampfer MJ, et al. Physical activity and incidence of non-insulin dependent diabetes mellitus in women. *Lancet* 1991;338:774–778.

50. Helmrich SP, Ragland DR, Leung RW, et al. Physical activity and reduced occurrence of non-insulin dependent diabetes mellitus. *N Engl J Med* 1991;325:147.

51. Duncan GE, Perri MG, Theriaque DW, et al. Exercise training, without weight loss, increased insulin sensitivity and postherparin plasma lipase activity in previously sedentary adults. *Diabetes Care* 2003;26:557–562.

52. Long SD, O'Brien KO, MacDonald KD Jr. Weight loss in severely obese subjects prevents the progression of impaired glucose tolerance to type II diabetes. A longitudinal interventional study. *Diabetes Care* 1994;17:372.

53. Pettitt DJ, Bennett PH, Knowler WC, et al. Gestational diabetes mellitus and impaired glucose tolerance during pregnancy: long term effects on obesity and glucose tolerance in the offspring. *Diabetes* 1985;34:119–122.

54. Pettitt DJ, Baird HR, Aleck KA, et al. Excessive obesity in offspring of Pima Indian women with diabetes during pregnancy. *N Engl J Med* 1983;308;242–245.

55. Buchanan TA, Xiang AH, Peters RK, et al. Preservation of pancreatic β-cell function and prevention of type 2 diabetes by pharmacological treatment of insulin resistance in high risk Hispanic women. *Diabetes* 2002;51;2796–2803.

56. Mokdad AH, Bowman BA, Ford ES, et al. The continuing epidemics of obesity and diabetes in the United States. *JAMA* 2001; 286;1195–1200.

57. Ludwig DS, Ebbeling CB. Type 2 diabetes mellitus in children. *JAMA* 2001;286:1427–1430.

58. Harris MI, Klein R, Welborn TA, et al. Onset of NIDDM occurs at least 4–7 years before clinical diagnosis. *Diabetes Care* 1992; 15:815–819.

59. Kannel WB, McGee DL. Diabetes and cardiovascular disease: the Framingham Study. *JAMA* 1979;241:2035–2038.

60. Gaede P, Vedel P, Larsen N, et al. Multifactorial intervention and cardiovascular disease in patients with type 2 diabetes. *N Engl J Med* 2003;348:383–393.

61. American Diabetes Association. Clinical practice recommendations 2003. *Diabetes Care* 2003;26:1–149.

18

GLUCOSE EVALUATION AND CONTROL

E. ALBERT REECE
CAROL J. HOMKO

Diabetes mellitus is a metabolic disorder that can significantly alter the environment in which the fetus develops, leading to complications such as congenital malformations, hyperinsulinism, growth aberrations, stillbirths, delayed pulmonic maturation, and even neonatal death (1).

Perinatal morbidity and mortality, however, have significantly decreased since the discovery of insulin (2–8). Before 1922, at a time when metabolic control of diabetic patients was poor, the fetal death rate was about 60% to 70%. Since the early 1970s, most centers have reported rates of 2% to 4% (6,9,10). The critical factor in this improvement has been the awareness that normalization of maternal glucose was essential to maternal and fetal health. Several studies report improved fetal outcome under a stringent program of maternal metabolic control (5,9–15). Gyves and associates (5) reported a study of 96 diabetic patients in whom the combined perinatal mortality rate was reduced from 13.5% to 4.2%. Subsequent observations by Gabbe and associates (9) lend further support to the declining trend in perinatal mortality. The major studies reveal that as the mean maternal blood glu-

cose decreases, the mortality rate also decreases. A linear regression depicting these data suggests that at a mean maternal blood glucose of 84 mg/dL, there will be no increase in infant mortality over the risk in the general population (Fig. 18-1).

Also, several investigators have reported an association between malformations and glucose control early in pregnancy while other studies have demonstrated that strict metabolic control in the periconception period can, in fact, reduce the incidence of these anomalies. Fuhrmann and colleagues (16) compared two groups of women with type 1 diabetes mellitus: 128 women who began intensive therapy before conception and 292 women in whom strict metabolic control was begun after 8 weeks' gestation. They found only one malformation (0.8%) in the group that received preconception treatment versus 22 infants (7.5%) with major congenital anomalies born to the group of late registrants. Kitzmiller and colleagues (17) reported similar results. They prospectively followed 84 women with type 1 diabetes who were recruited before conception and compared them with 110 women with type 1 diabetes who

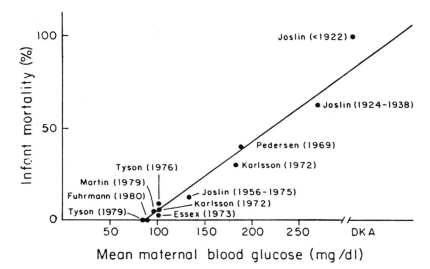

FIGURE 18-1. Mean maternal glucose control versus infant mortality rate, demonstrating that at a mean maternal blood glucose of 84 mg/dL, the risk for infant mortality is comparable with that of the general population. (From Jovanovic L, Peterson CM. Management of the pregnant, insulin-dependent diabetic woman. *Diabetes Care* 1980;3:63, with permission.)

entered care after 6 weeks' gestation. They found a significant reduction in congenital anomalies between the two groups: 1.2% in the group that achieved preconception control versus 10.9% in the group that did not. These findings have been replicated by multiple other investigators (18,19). The dominant philosophy is that preconception glycemic control can reduce the overall incidence of diabetic embryopathy, which has become the leading cause of morbidity and mortality in infants of diabetic mothers (IDMs).

Other significant advances in maternal and neonatal care, fetal surveillance, assessment of lung maturity, and the treatment of fetal and maternal complications have also contributed to improved perinatal outcomes seen in pregnancies complicated by diabetes (20). However, despite the possible roles that these advances have played in lowering perinatal mortality, the evidence provided by several controlled studies supports the current belief that good metabolic control is essential to normal fetal outcome. The aspect of diabetes care that remains debatable is what constitutes the optimal level of metabolic control in diabetic pregnancy. This subject requires the consideration of several interrelated factors, including goals for metabolic control, the definition of maternal euglycemia, and methods of glucose evaluation and control.

GOALS FOR METABOLIC CONTROL

The diabetic state during pregnancy is complicated by perturbations in the hormonal milieu that have an effect on the overall metabolism. During pregnancy, maternal glucose crosses the placenta by facilitated diffusion, whereas amino acids are actively transported. Of particular importance is the transfer to the fetus of gluconeogenic amino acids such as alanine. Maternal loss of glucose and gluconeogenic substrate to the fetus occurs simultaneously with a decrease in maternal fasting blood glucose to about 55 to 65 mg/dL, as well as a decrease in mean blood glucose to 70 to 80 mg/dL (3,21–24). However, as gestation advances, the diabetogenic effects of pregnancy are brought about by the following factors: (a) the production of increasing amounts of placental hormones that antagonize insulin action, (b) enzymes contained within the placenta itself degrading maternal insulin, and (c) enhanced production of maternal glucose in the fasted state.

Diabetogenic hormones include human placental lactogen (hPL), a polypeptide of placental origin. Circulating levels of this hormone increase progressively with increasing placental size. hPL promotes free fatty acid (FFA) production by stimulating lipolysis. FFAs, in turn, promote peripheral tissue resistance to insulin, leading to down-regulation of insulin receptors and compensatory hyperinsulinemia. In addition, insulin turnover is increased during pregnancy because of increased degradation by placental enzymes similar to liver insulinase (6,17–19).

Despite these perturbations during pregnancy, the maintenance of normal fuel metabolism remains essential to normal embryonal/fetal growth and development. Karlsson and Kjellmer (10) demonstrated the relationship between fetal outcome and glucose control, showing that the third-trimester mean maternal blood glucose was linearly correlated with the perinatal mortality rate. Mean third-trimester plasma glucose values of greater than 150 mg/dL were associated with a perinatal mortality of 23.6%, whereas mean plasma glucose concentrations between 100 and 150 mg/dL and less than 100 mg/dL were associated with rates of 15.3% and 3.8%, respectively. Similarly, a decrease in certain morbidities was also observed when the mean plasma glucose value was less than 100 mg/dL. Several other investigators have further emphasized the beneficial effects of glucose control on diabetic pregnancy outcome (5,21,25–31).

In an attempt to establish achievable glucose targets, investigators have conducted 24-hour metabolic profiles in diabetic and nondiabetic patients (16,32–34). Cousins et al. (26) conducted a longitudinal study to quantitate the progressive effects of the second and third trimesters of normal pregnancy on plasma glucose, insulin, and C-peptide. Such studies were conducted in six nonobese women with normal 3-hour glucose tolerance test results and without prenatal or postpartum complications. Hourly plasma samples were obtained throughout a 24-hour period in the second (22–26 weeks) and third (35–37 weeks) trimesters of pregnancy and again at 6 to 11 weeks after delivery. A diurnal rhythm of plasma glucose, insulin, and C-peptide was demonstrated in all study periods (Fig. 18-2). During meals, increases in plasma glucose and insulin above the 24-hour mean were small and not significantly modified by pregnancy. During the third trimester only, the peak values for both plasma glucose and insulin were significantly increased. There was also nocturnal hypoglycemia. The researchers concluded that the observation of a marked diurnal rhythm of plasma glucose and the relative nocturnal hypoglycemia in normal pregnancy provide some guidelines for the metabolic management of diabetic pregnancies.

Most recently, Parretti and colleagues (35) followed 51 ambulatory nondiabetic normal weight women without antenatal complications from 28 to 38 weeks' gestation without modifying their lifestyle or following dietary restriction. All women were taught to monitor their blood glucose before meals and 1 and 2 hours after meals. Mean blood glucose levels ranged from 74.7 ± 5.2 to 78.3 ± 5.4 mg/dL throughout the day, and postprandial levels never exceeded 105 mg/dL. These levels of glycemia were similar to the earlier studies of Cousins and others reported 20 years previously.

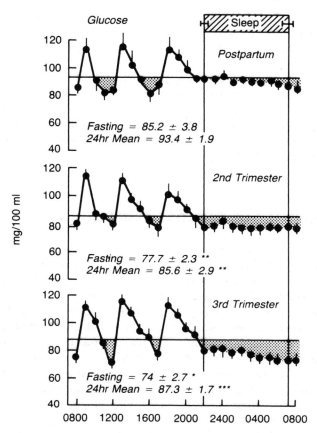

FIGURE 18-2. Excursion of plasma glucose during a 24-hour glucose profile in six normal pregnant women during the second and third trimesters of pregnancy and 6 to 11 weeks postpartum. Meals are indicated by ●. Data points reflect ± SEM. Horizontal lines represent the 24-hour mean. *$p < 0.05$; **$p < 0.01$; ***$p < 0.005$. (From Cousins L, Rigg L, Hollingsworth D, et al. The 24-hour excursion and diurnal rhythm of glucose, insulin, and C-peptide in normal pregnancy. *Am J Obstet Gynecol* 1980;136:483, with permission.)

TABLE 18-1. DIURNAL PLASMA GLUCOSE PROFILE IN NORMAL AND DIABETIC WOMEN

	Plasma Glucose (mg/dL)		
	Normal	**Chemical Diabetes**	**Insulin-Dependent Diabetes**
Mean diurnal	84	101	106
Mean daytime	88	106	117
Maximum diurnal	113	145	179
Minimum diurnal	67	76	53
Diurnal plasma glucose range	46	69	125

Modified from Gillmer MDG, Beard RW, Brooke FM, et al. Carbohydrate metabolism in pregnancy. I. Diurnal plasma glucose profile in normal and diabetic women. *BMJ* 1975;3:399, with permission.

Gillmer et al. (1,32) also studied the diurnal metabolic profile of diabetic and nondiabetic pregnant women in the third trimester of pregnancy. Patients were hospitalized during the third trimester for at least 2 weeks, and "optimal" diabetic control was achieved (Table 18-1 and Fig. 18-3). The results of their study illustrate that by using stringent metabolic control, levels of glucose control can be achieved in women with diabetes that are comparable with normal control subjects. For example, the mean daytime plasma glucose value in the diabetic subject was 117 versus 88 mg/dL in the normal group. The glycemic excursions were greater in the women with diabetes, with lower minimal plasma glucose levels at night and higher maximum plasma glucose values in the daytime (Table 18-1). From these diurnal profiles, normative data were ascertained regarding achievable glycemic control in the third trimester of pregnancy. Furthermore, these data also serve as a working definition of euglycemia in pregnancy (as described in

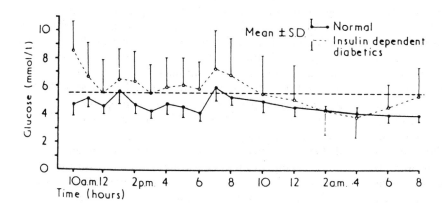

FIGURE 18-3. Diurnal glucose profiles in 13 insulin-dependent diabetic patients and 9 women with normal glucose tolerance studied between 32 and 35 weeks of pregnancy. (From Gillmer MDG, Beard RW, Brooke FM, et al. Carbohydrate metabolism in pregnancy. I. Diurnal plasma glucose profile in normal and diabetic women. *BMJ* 1975;3:399, with permission.)

Fig. 18-3), with a range from 70 to 120 mg/dL throughout the 24-hour period, with a lower level during the sleep period.

The feasibility of maintaining normal glucose profiles in women with type 1 diabetes has been studied by several investigators (11,28,36–38). Jovanovic et al. (37) reported a small series of 10 patients who were in the first trimester of their pregnancy and were maintained in tight glucose control using intensive conventional insulin therapy. These patients performed five to eight blood glucose determinations per day, and their average hemoglobin A_{1c} (HbA_{1c}) decreased from 9.4% to about 5%. The infants were described as showing no signs of macrosomia, hypoglycemia, hyperbilirubinemia, hypocalcemia, or respiratory distress. In this study, the investigators concluded that normal glycemia not only could be achieved in early pregnancy but could be maintained for prolonged periods in the outpatient setting. Normal plasma glucose levels were achieved after only 1 week of treatment. This finding greatly reduced the length of hospitalization reported in previous studies, six in which one month of strict diabetic control in a hospital was required for normalization of glucose. Kitzmiller et al. (38), using continuous subcutaneous insulin therapy, also demonstrated that good diabetic control was achievable during early pregnancy. With 24 type 1 diabetes patients, reasonable control was achieved in the fasting blood glucose (119 ± 30 mg/dL) and postprandial blood glucose (133 ± 34 mg/dL) levels. This was accompanied by an average of 2.2 ± 1.5 symptomatic hypoglycemic episodes per week. We and others have also confirmed the feasibility of stringent metabolic control throughout pregnancy and reported perinatal mortality rates of less than 5% (7,9,25,36,39,40).

The various studies discussed clearly indicate the benefit of normal glucose control throughout pregnancy, and the feasibility of tight glucose control has been demonstrated even in early pregnancy. Other questions that arise include: Does tight glucose control lead to aberrations in other metabolic fuels? Do we normalize other metabolic fuels simply by controlling glucose? Should we be measuring and controlling other metabolites as well?

Reece and associates conducted third-trimester meal studies in 22 pregnant tightly controlled diabetic women and 7 pregnant nondiabetic women to address the above questions. Determinations of FFAs, branched chain amino acid, alanine, ketones, triglycerides, cholesterol, and insulin were obtained before a standardized mixed-meal breakfast and repeated every 15 to 30 minutes for 150 minutes after the meal. Except for insulin, no significant differences between diabetic individuals and controls were observed for all metabolites assayed. This finding suggests that normalization of glucose results in normalization of other metabolic fuels. Therefore, the assessment of glucose control reflects the metabolic profile of other

insulin-sensitive fuels, which need not be measured independently. However, to achieve normalization of these metabolic fuels, increased exogenous insulin was required (41).

The results of the many aforementioned studies provide justification for stringent metabolic control during pregnancy and evidence for its feasibility. The goal of normal glycemic control throughout pregnancy has been generally adopted as part of the standard care for pregnancies complicated by diabetes.

HISTORY OF GLUCOSE EVALUATION

After the discovery and availability of insulin, it was recognized that therapy could be based on some measure of glucose levels. Repeated blood glucose measurements were feasible for hospitalized patients. However, continuous outpatient evaluation posed a problem. Urine testing for glucose was introduced, using a color change with Fehling solution (copper sulfate). This was a cumbersome process involving the boiling of urine with the solution in a test tube, as well as the use of a color change that acted as an index for the glucose content (42–44). Despite the laborious nature of this task, such a technique allowed patients an opportunity to regulate their glucose levels as outpatients. It eventually became clear that urine testing provided limited information. Although the renal threshold is lowered in pregnancy because the increase in glomerular filtration rate is not accompanied by an equivalent increase in tubular reabsorption of glucose (45), it remains considerably above the therapeutic goals established for pregnancy. In light of the above findings, improved glucose control could only be accomplished by the ascertainment of circulating blood glucose levels.

The achievement of euglycemia requires frequent daily blood glucose determinations. The introduction of portable blood glucose meters made it possible for individuals with diabetes to evaluate blood glucose with ease several times per day. The initial reports of self-monitoring of blood glucose (SMBG) appeared in early 1978 (42,44,46,47). Subsequent studies with larger numbers of subjects confirmed the initial reports that SMBG is feasible, practical, and acceptable to patients; that blood glucose determinations are sufficiently accurate for clinical use; and that glycemic control may be improved if SMBG is used as a part of a treatment program (6,22,28, 31,46–54). As a result SMBG has become the mainstay of outpatient management of pregnancies complicated by diabetes mellitus. However, certain metabolic and physiologic changes of pregnancy may interfere with the accuracy of reflectance meters. In pregnancy, glucose levels and hematocrit values are lower than in the nonpregnant state, whereas triglyceride and cholesterol levels are increased. These changes could affect meter accuracy. Harkness and colleagues (54) compared four commonly used reflectance meters against the Beckman ASTRA in 17 gravid type 1 women. All the instruments tested showed unacceptable combinations of proportional and constant bias based on laboratory standards. In a more recent study, Henry and colleagues (55) compared patient-measured glucose values on 6-second generation blood glucose meters with values obtained using a glucose analyzer. Data were collected from approximately 500 pregnant women with diabetes over a 5-year period. At the 10.5% deviation level, 34% of meter readings were out of range and 54% of these would have led to erroneous management decisions. At the 15.5% deviation level, 18% of readings were out of range, and of these, 63% would have led to erroneous treatment. The use of blood glucose meters for metabolic regulation during pregnancy should be monitored carefully for accuracy by obtaining monthly glycosylated hemoglobin levels and by periodically checking the machine against standard values. Ongoing patient education and assessment of patient technique are also crucial to maintain accuracy.

MONITORING FREQUENCY AND GLYCEMIC STANDARDS

Although it is widely accepted that the level of metabolic control achieved in the pregnancy complicated by diabetes significantly affects perinatal outcome, what constitutes optimal control is not exactly known. Landon and colleagues (56) assessed the relationship between glycemic control and perinatal outcome in 75 women with class B through D diabetes. They divided their population into two groups: women who achieved mean fasting and preprandial capillary blood glucose values of less than 110 mg/dL and those whose mean blood glucose values were greater than 110 mg/dL. They found that better blood glucose control (<110 mg/dL) significantly reduced the incidence of macrosomia, as well as several other neonatal complications. The researchers concluded that maintaining mean capillary blood glucose values of less than 110 mg/dL may reduce several major forms of morbidity in the IDM.

Langer and colleagues (57) conducted a large prospective study to determine the optimal level of glycemia for the treatment of women with gestational diabetes mellitus (GDM). Their data, collected from 246 women with GDM, demonstrated that women who achieved the lowest range of blood glucose values throughout pregnancy had a significantly lower incidence of large-for-gestational-age (LGA) and macrosomic infants. The incidence

of LGA infants increased from 9% to 24% when mean blood glucose levels exceeded 105 mg/dL. In a subsequent study (58), the same group was able to demonstrate that below a mean threshold blood glucose value of 100 mg/dL, the rates of LGA and macrosomia in GDM were comparable with those of the general population. In addition, mean blood glucose levels of less than 110 mg/dL were protective against metabolic and respiratory complications. These data would indicate that the levels of glycemia needed to reduce perinatal morbidity appear to be comparable between women with preexisting and gestational diabetes.

Combs and colleagues (59) undertook a study to determine the gestational ages at which maternal hyperglycemia is most closely related to macrosomia, as well as to determine whether fetal macrosomia is associated with elevations of fasting glucose or postprandial glucose levels, or both. The investigators examined perinatal outcomes in 111 consecutive pregnancies of women with class B through RF diabetes. Of the women in their sample, 29% delivered macrosomic infants and were compared with those without macrosomic infants. The investigators found that the incidence of macrosomia increased progressively with increasing postprandial glucose levels. Postprandial glucose levels of less than 130 mg/dL reduced the incidence of macrosomia, but levels of less than 120 mg/dL eliminated this complication. They therefore recommended a glucose level of 130 mg/dL as a reasonable target for the 1-hour postprandial glucose. These data are supported by the Diabetes in Early Pregnancy Study (60), which demonstrated that third-trimester nonfasting glucose levels are the strongest predictors of percentile birth weight in IDMs.

Furthermore, the Diabetes in Early Pregnancy Study group also found no relationship between fasting or postprandial glucose levels and macrosomia after 32 weeks' gestation. It would therefore appear that good glycemic control must be instituted by the early third trimester to prevent macrosomia. Conversely, they found that postprandial glucose values of less than 90 mg/dL were associated with increasing numbers of small-for-gestational-age (SGA) infants. Other investigators have also found a similar association between low maternal glucose levels and SGA infants in both nondiabetic women (61) and women with gestational diabetes (62).

Postprandial blood glucose levels have also been found to be a better predictor of fetal macrosomia than are fasting blood glucose levels in women with GDM. DeVeciana and co-workers (63) reported similar findings after comparing the efficacy of preprandial and postprandial glucose determinations in reducing the incidence of adverse outcomes in women with insulin-requiring gestational diabetes. Subjects were randomly assigned to have their insulin therapy adjusted according to the results of preprandial self-glucose monitoring or postprandial monitoring 1 hour after meals. Both groups demonstrated similar degrees of adherence with the monitoring protocol and had similar success in achieving the targeted glycemic control. Nevertheless, infants born to women in the preprandial monitoring group were significantly more likely to be either LGA or macrosomic than infants of mothers in the postprandial group. In addition, women in the postprandial group achieved a greater decrease in glycosylated hemoglobin values during treatment than did women in the preprandial monitoring group. The investigators concluded that adjusting insulin therapy in women with GDM according to the results of postprandial blood glucose values improves glycemic control and reduces the risk for macrosomia and other adverse outcome factors. Therefore, it is currently recommended that blood glucose measurements be performed after meals in addition to the fasting state (64).

Despite the acceptance of the importance of testing in the postprandial state, there is not consensus regarding the optimal timing of postprandial measurements (i.e., 1 vs. 2 hours).

Our group (65) has demonstrated variations in the rate of abnormal blood glucose levels comparing 1 hour to 2-hour postmeal values based on the time of day. More recently we have undertaken a prospective study to compare the rate of adverse perinatal outcomes between women with GDM monitored by 1 versus 2-hour postprandial glucose measurements (66). The preliminary results of this trial indicate that infants of women monitored by 1-hour postprandial measurements had a significantly lower incidence of macrosomia than infants of mothers monitored for 2 hours after meals.

Lastly, the optimal frequency of testing was not identified by these studies. Marked differences exist among the studies reviewed in terms of frequency of glucose monitoring ranging from four to seven times a day, up to 7 days a week. In clinical practice, the frequency of SMBG often depends on the severity of the diabetes. However, we recommend that blood glucose determinations be obtained four to eight times per day every day in patients with both preexisting and gestational diabetes. Glucose control in nonpregnant patients with diabetes has been shown to deteriorate if SMBG is reduced to less than four determinations per day (46).

METHODS OF SELF-MONITORING OF BLOOD GLUCOSE

Currently, there are multiple battery-powered portable glucose meters available for use. The meters have also been shown to have a close correlation with automated laboratory methods (67), when performed under controlled conditions. The magnitude of differences is small (±10%) when the blood glucose level is less than 300 mg/dL. Appendix Table 1 summarizes the important features of most of the glucose meters currently available. It should be noted that blood glucose meters may be calibrated to provide either whole blood or plasma readings. Whole blood–calibrated meters provide results that are approximately 10% to 12% lower than results obtained from the plasma-calibrated results.

Two types of blood glucose meters are used for self-blood glucose monitoring: reflectance meters and those that use sensor technologies. Reflectance meters use glucose oxidase–impregnated reagent strips. These strips contain a buffered mixture of glucose oxidase, peroxidase, and a chromogen system. The glucose oxidase catalyzes the oxidation of glucose to gluconic acid and hydrogen peroxide. Peroxidase then catalyzes the reaction of hydrogen peroxide with the chromogen system, producing a color that varies with the concentration of glucose originally present (40).

Sensor-type meters measure the electronic charge generated by the reaction of the glucose and the enzyme. Sensor meters are further classified based on the electrochemical principle employed: amperometry or coulomety (68). Amperometric meters use an electrochemical reaction, which in the presence of an applied potential results in electron transfer and generation of an electrical current that is proportional to the concentration of glucose. Coulometric meters use an electrochemical reaction whereby the total accumulated charge of the reaction is in proportion to the glucose concentration. With a coulometric meter, all glucose is consumed and measured (68). This newer electrochemical technology system offers two distinct advantages over conventional reflectance meters: the need for smaller blood samples and the fact that it is less effected by changes in temperature and variations in hematocrit.

Most of these second-generation glucose meters are also available with memory capacity. Studies with these meters suggest that the memory capacity improves accurate reporting and thus has an effect on the overall achievement of euglycemia. Initial work by Mazze et al. (69) reported on 19 clinic patients who used a glucometer (Ames, Elkhart, IN, U.S.A.) with a memory capacity (M-Glucometer) for 2 weeks. Approximately 26% of the logbook entries were different from capillary blood glucose results recorded by the M-Glucometer. The main source of error was omitting high glucose results and substituting lower values. In a subsequent study, patients were made aware of the memory capacity of these glucose meters, and patient performance improved significantly (70). Similar findings were reported by Langer and colleagues (71), who found that knowledge of the existence of a microchip in the reflectance meter dramatically improved patient performance and compliance in pregnant women with diabetes. It would appear that verified blood glucose determinations enhance the reliability and accuracy of self-monitored blood glucose results.

Most new meters have the capability of locally downloading the readings and graphically displaying them or sending the readings on to a health-care provider. Data management systems automatically record various aspects of diabetes control and allow the patient to store hundreds of test results and other information such as time, date, insulin type, and dose, exercise depending on the system.

All systems require a drop of blood. The patient's finger is pricked using a sharp 21- to 25-gauge lancet. A variety of lancets and lancing devices are now available. Appendix Table 2 summarizes the important features of most of the available finger-sticking devices.

An adequate drop of blood can be enhanced by placing the hand in warm water before pricking. The thumb and fourth finger have better blood supply than the remaining digits and may be preferred sites for pricking. Also, the peripheral aspects of the finger are less sensitive that the ball of the finger and may be considered preferred areas (46).

Alternate Site Testing

New glucose monitoring systems have recently been developed that allow sample extraction from sites other than the fingertip. These systems have generated a lot of interest due to the nearly painless nature of the blood acquisition. Potential sites include the forearm, upper arm, and thigh. It has been demonstrated that the glucose results from blood extracted from the arm and finger are not perfectly correlated (72). Rubbing the arm minimizes but does not totally eliminate these differences. Furthermore, changes in glucose are first observed on the finger and then the arm with a lag time of approximately 5 minutes. The greatest differences between sites have been noted when glucose levels are rapidly changing. Differences have also been noted within 2 hours after meals, an insulin dose, or exercise. On average, differences in blood glucose concentrations from the finger and arm have little influence on clinical decisions. However, at times of rapidly decreasing glucose, the difference and lag in arm readings could delay detection of hypoglycemia. Therefore, the finger tip is still recommended as the preferred site for the detection of hypoglycemia. There have been no studies specifically addressing the use of alternate site testing in pregnancy. Differences noted in the postprandial period (<2 hours) between samples obtained from the finger tip and arm raise at least a theoretical concern about use in the pregnancy complicated by diabetes.

Other Forms of Glucose Determination

Continuous Blood Glucose Monitoring

Although intermittent self-blood glucose monitoring has revolutionized diabetes self-management, it nonetheless has significant limitations and does not accurately depict the variability that may occur in blood glucose levels throughout the day. Therefore, sensors that continuously monitor glucose have long been sought as a tool to improve diabetes control. The Continuous Glucose Monitoring System (CGMS) developed by Medtronic MiniMed (Northridge, CA, U.S.A.) was the first such device to be made available for clinical use. The intended use of the CGMS is the documentation of glucose patterns and trends, rather than discrete points in time. It is a Holter-style sensor system that is designed to continuously and automatically monitor glucose values in subcutaneous tissue fluid. The monitor is connected to a tiny glucose sensor (microelectrode) that is inserted just under the skin to measure glucose. The sensor generates an electronic signal, the strength of which is proportional to the amount of glucose present in the surrounding interstitial fluid. The signal is sent to the monitor, a portable, pager-sized device that records sensor signals every 5 minutes and converts them into blood glucose readings, providing 288 readings per day for up to 3 days. The data are downloaded to a computer; software generates graphs and pie charts that present blood glucose changes. Although CGMS has proven useful for improving HbA_{1c} levels in nonpregnant persons with poorly controlled type 1 diabetes (73), a high degree of unexpected asymptomatic nighttime hypoglycemia has been reported (74,75).

Jovanovic (76) has reported on 10 women with gestational diabetes who wore the device for 72 hours. In her series, the women with GDM spent nearly 5.5 hours per day in previously unrecognized hyperglycemia. Furthermore, these elevations in blood glucose levels often occurred shortly after patients had taken blood glucose measurements that indicated glucose levels within the target range. CGMS can reveal high postprandial blood glucose levels that were previously unrecognized by intermittent self-blood glucose monitoring. As such, CGMS is a useful tool both to educate patients and improve diabetes management throughout gestation.

Glycosylated Hemoglobins

Other methods of glucose evaluation are directed toward the overall assessment of glycemic control. Some of these methods include glycosylated hemoglobin or proteins. In 1958, Allen and co-workers (77) identified three small fractions of hemoglobin A (HbA_{1a}, HbA_{1b}, HbA_{1c}) that had a faster chromatographic mobility than the remainder of the HbA. These small fractions or glycoproteins have been subsequently referred to as glycosylated hemoglobin, glycohemoglobin, or generically HbA_1. It was not until these glycohemoglobins were found to be increased in diabetic patients that their clinical usefulness was realized (78–87).

The glycosylation reaction is a slow, nonenzymatic irreversible covalent bonding of glucose to various amino acids. HbA_{1c} is the largest of these minor hemoglobins and has glucose attached to the N-terminal valine amino acid of the β chains of HbA. HbA_{1c} is structurally identical to hemoglobin A except for the presence of a glucose moiety attached to the N-terminal valine amino acid of the β chains via a Schiff base (81,88). Bunn et al. (89) showed that the Schiff base undergoes an Amadori rearrangement [i.e., a shift from an α-hydroxyaldimine (Schiff base) to a β-ketamine] to form a stable and relatively irreversible ketamine linkage. *In vivo* studies showed that glycosylation of HbA to form HbA_{1c} is a posttranslational modification of HbA_1, occurring as a slow nonenzymatic process in the circulating red blood cells (81,88). The level of glycohemoglobin represents a retrospective integration of the overall glycemic control during the 4 to 6 weeks preceding the glucose determination. This glycemic level is proportional to the time-averaged blood glucose to which the red blood cells were exposed during their lifetime (81,89–94).

The use of HbA_1 has been investigated in numerous studies. O'Shaughnessy et al. (84) measured HbA_1 in the blood of 50 normal nonpregnant women, 29 normal pregnant women, and 21 pregnant diabetic patients. In normal pregnancy, HbA_1 did not differ significantly from values in nonpregnancy or vary with the gestational age. It was also found that marked elevations in HbA_1 (elevations >10%) reliably predict poor diabetic control; that HbA_1 (90,95–97) is neither useful for fine glucose control nor useful as a screen for gestational diabetes; and that HbA_1 is not predictive of newborn birth weights. Not all studies have confirmed these results (79,84–86).

Both clinical and laboratory studies have shown a relationship between glycemic status during organogenesis, as reflected by glycohemoglobins and the incidence of birth defects (98–100). Leslie et al. (98) conducted serial studies in 25 pregnant diabetic women at 4-week intervals and at 6 weeks postpartum and found that HbA_1 decreased from the first to the third trimester, most probably as a function of glucose control. HbA_1 also increased postpartum as control was lessened. More important, however, was the observation that three of five pregnant diabetic women whose initial HbA1 was above normal gave birth to children with fatal congenital anomalies. Subsequent work by Miller et al. (99), Ylinen et al. (100), and Green et al. (101) demonstrated that HbA_1 was correlated with the malformation rate. HbA_1 therefore becomes a useful clinical tool for

grossly assessing a patient's risk for diabetes-related malformations. Most patients present to the physician in the late first or second trimester of pregnancy, beyond the time when any therapeutic intervention may be used to decrease the risk for major malformations. However, HbA_1 may be used to assess this risk as a basis for further studies, namely, α-fetoprotein or ultrasonography (or both) and as a guide for counseling.

Other investigators have examined the association among an increased prevalence of perinatal morbidity, mortality, and elevated third-trimester maternal HbA_{1c} levels. Associations among neonatal hypoglycemia, neonatal hyperbilirubinemia, neonatal hypocalcaemia, perinatal deaths, and macrosomia have all been demonstrated (102–105).

Fructosamine

Major criticisms of glycosylated hemoglobin include its long "memory," low sensitivity for mild glucose intolerance, and potential confounding factors. Therefore, several investigators have examined the use of the fructosamine assay to screen reliably for gestational diabetes and as an index of short-term control.

Fructosamine is a marker for glycosylated serum protein. This test measures the serum glycosyl protein by recognizing the Amadori rearrangement product formed by the reaction of glucose and protein molecules. The potential advantages of fructosamine include decreased day-to-day variation and apparently a shorter memory, so reequilibration to a new level requires a shorter time (106,107).

In a study by Roberts et al. (107) fructosamine was measured in 79 diabetic pregnant women and 20 women with gestational diabetes. The test detected 17 (85%) of the women with gestational diabetes and gave only 4 (5%) false-positive results. However, several other investigators have reported a lower sensitivity for the fructosamine assay in the detection of GDM.

Cefalu and colleagues (108) found no difference in baseline serum glycosylated protein levels between women with and without gestational diabetes. However, in women with pregestational diabetes followed at 2-week intervals, they found serum glycosylated protein correlated significantly with fasting blood glucose ($r = 0.81$, p 0.001) and mean outpatient blood glucose levels ($r = 0.62$; $p < 0.001$). No correlation was found between HbA_{1c} and either fasting blood glucose or mean outpatient glucose level. The researchers concluded that although the serum fructosamine is not a useful screening test for gestational diabetes, it does show potential as an objective marker of short-term glycemic control.

Parfitt and colleagues (109) also found that fructosamine predicted levels of mean blood glucose more precisely than did HbA_1 in pregnancies complicated by diabetes. However, others (110) have found serum fructosamine and HbA₁ to give comparable information regarding short-term glycemic control, whereas others have found the assay to have limited use in the management of diabetic pregnancies (111,112).

ACHIEVEMENT OF BLOOD GLUCOSE CONTROL

As stated earlier, intensive therapy regimens and the establishment of maternal euglycemia have dramatically improved fetal outcomes in pregnancies complicated by diabetes. In fact, normalization of maternal glucose control has been accepted as the main therapeutic goal of these pregnancies for several years. However, the benefits of strict metabolic control go far beyond pregnancy. Evidence from the recently completed multicenter Diabetes Control and Complications Trial suggests that tight glycemic control should be maintained for life (113).

The achievement of optimal glucose control is primarily by a combination of diet, exercise, and insulin therapy (6,22,27,37). Each mode of therapy is covered elsewhere in this text. However, a brief discussion is presented on insulin pump therapy, which is being used increasingly to simulate the pattern of normal insulin secretion.

Many series have demonstrated that continuous subcutaneous insulin infusion (CSII) can be a safe and effective means of glucose control in both pregnant and nonpregnant diabetic patients (38,114,115). A randomized clinical trial by Coustan et al. (36) was conducted among 22 type 1 diabetes patients, in which one group of 11 patients received intensive conventional therapy and the other 11 patients received CSII therapy. No significant difference between the two forms of insulin administration was observed with regard to glucose control, assessed by mean blood glucose, HbA₁, or mean amplitude of glycemic excursions, or with regard to the severity and frequency of hypoglycemia and fetal outcome. Several other investigators have reported similar findings (116,117). Most recently, Gabbe and associates (118) compared perinatal outcomes, glycemic control, and health-care costs among three groups of women: women who began insulin pump therapy during pregnancy, women treated with multiple insulin injections, and a group who were already using insulin pump therapy before pregnancy. Perinatal outcomes and health care costs were comparable among the three groups. Women who began insulin pump therapy during pregnancy did so without deterioration of glycemic control. Severe hypoglycemia was observed significantly less often in women using CSII. Furthermore, women who began pump therapy during pregnancy were very likely to continue after delivery and had significantly better postpartum glucose control than

did those women on multiple daily injections (7.2% vs. 9.1%).

The above studies should not be interpreted to suggest that CSII is without value during pregnancy. On the contrary, CSII remains a valuable means of achieving euglycemia, especially in patients with erratic eating schedules or patients who require several daily insulin injections. This study demonstrates that equivalent glucose control and fetal outcome can be achieved with either intensive conventional therapy or CSII. However, the physician will need to determine which patients will benefit from either form of therapy. In addition, a recent study demonstrated the safety and effectiveness of insulin pump therapy in women with GDM or type 2 diabetes requiring large amounts of insulin to achieve euglycemia (119).

Appendix Table 3 outlines the available insulin pumps, with descriptions of many of the features associated with each. In general, these newer generation pumps are smaller and simpler to use.

The insulin pumps discussed above are the open-loop type, in which an insulin dosage schedule is programmed into the machine to be delivered to the patient throughout the day. Obviously, a perfected closed-loop insulin pump system that is capable of detecting the blood glucose level and delivering an appropriate amount of insulin would be ideal for the treatment of diabetes. There are a few studies of closed-loop systems tested in animals and in a limited number of diabetic volunteers using a needle-type glucose sensor and a computer calculation of infusion rates of insulin or glucagon, or both (120–122). Despite encouraging preliminary work, an ideal system has not yet been achieved.

SUMMARY

The foregoing discussion has described the evolution of glucose evaluation and control as a standard form of diabetes care. Although randomized prospective studies have not proved that the reduced perinatal mortality rate was caused by the overall improvement in glycemic control, this relationship is well documented by numerous uncontrolled studies, the results are reproducible, and the concept is well accepted, precluding a randomized study in the future. With the establishment of such a premise, a variety of methods for both glucose evaluation and control have been introduced.

Recent advances with regard to glucose monitoring have been formidable. Improved techniques and further modifications of present devices, and possibly even the introduction of newer ones such as a perfected closed-loop insulin pump, will enhance current methods of glucose evaluation and control. Such improvement in devices and techniques would be expected to advance the treatment of diabetes mellitus in pregnancy closer toward levels of morbidity and mortality seen in the general population.

KEY POINTS

- Strict glycemic control in the perinconceptional period and throughout gestation can reduce the risk for congenital malformations, neonatal morbidities, and perinatal mortality.
- The goal of maintaining normal blood glucose levels throughout pregnancy is the standard of care for pregnancies complicated by diabetes.
- The achievement of euglycemia requires frequent daily self-blood glucose determinations in both the fasted and postprandial states.
- HbA$_{1c}$ and fructosamine assays are useful indicators of overall glycemic control in the diabetic pregnancy.
- Subcutaneous insulin pump therapy can be a safe and effective means of glucose control in pregnant diabetic patients.

REFERENCES

1. Gillmer MDG, Beard RW, Brooke FM, et al. Carbohydrate metabolism in pregnancy. I. Diurnal plasma glucose profile in normal and diabetic women. *BMJ* 1975;3:399.
2. Freinkel N, Dooley SL, Metzger BE. Care of the pregnant woman with insulin-dependent diabetes mellitus. *N Engl J Med* 1985;313:96.
3. Freinkel N. *Pregnancy metabolism, diabetes and the fetus.* Ciba Foundation Symposium 63 (new series). Amsterdam: Excerpta Medica, 1979:124.
4. Gabbe SG. Medical complications of pregnancy management of diabetes in pregnancy: six decades of experience. In: Pitkin RM, Zlatnik FJ, eds. *Year book of obstetrics and gynecology.* Part I: Obstetrics. Chicago: Year Book Medical, 1980:37.
5. Gyves MT, Rodman HM, Little AB, et al. A modern approach to management of pregnant diabetics: a two year analysis of perinatal outcomes. *Am J Obstet Gynecol* 1977;128:606.
6. Jovanovic L, Peterson CM. Management of the pregnant, insulin-dependent diabetic woman. *Diabetes Care* 1980;3:63.
7. Kitzmiller JL, Cloherty JP, Younger MD, et al. Diabetic pregnancy and perinatal morbidity. *Am J Obstet Gynecol* 1978;131:560.
8. Miller JM Jr, Crenshaw MC Jr, Welt SI. Hemoglobin A$_{1c}$ in normal and diabetic pregnancy. *JAMA* 1979;242:2785.
9. Gabbe SG, Mestman JH, Freeman RK, et al: Management and outcome of pregnancy in diabetes mellitus, classes B to R. *Am J Obstet Gynecol* 1977;129:723.
10. Karlsson K, Kjellmer I. The outcome of diabetic pregnancies in relation to the mother's blood sugar level. *Am J Obstet Gynecol* 1972;112:213.
11. Jovanovic L, Druzin M, Peterson CM. Effect of euglycemia on the outcome of pregnancy in insulin-dependent diabetic women as compared with normal control subjects. *Am J Med* 1981;71:921.
12. Landon MB. Diabetes mellitus and other endocrine diseases. In: Gabbe SG, Niebyl JR, Simpson JL, eds. *Obstetrics.* New York: Churchill Livingstone, 1991:1097.
13. Skyler JS, O'Sullivan MJ. Diabetes and pregnancy. In: Kohler PO, ed. *Clinical endocrinology.* New York: Wiley & Sons, 1986: 603.
14. Adashi EY, Pinto H, Tyson JE. Impact of maternal euglycemia on fetal outcome in diabetic pregnancy. *Am J Obstet Gynecol* 1979;133:268.
15. Sack RA. The large infant. *Am J Obstet Gynecol* 1969;104:195.
16. Fuhrmann K, Reiher H, Semmler K, et al. Prevention of congenital malformations in infants of insulin-dependent diabetic mothers. *Diabetes Care* 1983;6:219.
17. Kitzmiller JL, Gavin LA, Gin GD, et al. Preconception management of diabetes continued through early pregnancy prevents the excess frequency of major congenital anomalies in infants of diabetic mothers. *JAMA* 1991;265:731.
18. Goldman JA, Dicker D, Feldberg, et al. Pregnancy outcome in patients with insulin-dependent diabetes mellitus with preconceptional diabetic control: a comparative study. *Am J Obstet Gynecol* 1986;155:293.
19. Steel JM, Johnstone FD, Smith AF. Five years experience of a "prepregnancy" clinic for insulin-dependent diabetics. *BMJ* 1982;285:353.
20. Steel JM, Johnstone FD, Hepburn DA, et al. Can prepregnancy care of diabetic women reduce the risk of abnormal babies? *BMJ* 1990;301:1070.
21. Seeds AE, Knowles HC. Metabolic control of diabetic pregnancy. *Clin Obstet Gynecol* 1981;24:51.
22. Jovanovic L, Peterson CM. Optimal insulin delivery for the pregnant diabetic patient. *Diabetes Care* 1982;5:24.
23. Kitzmiller JL. The endocrine pancreas and maternal metabolism. In: Tulchinsky D, Ryan KJ, eds. *Maternal-fetal endocrinology.* Philadelphia: WB Saunders, 1980:26.
24. Knopp RH, Montes A, Childs M, et al. Metabolic adjustments in normal and diabetic pregnancy. *Clin Obstet Gynecol* 1981; 24:21.
25. Artal R, Golde SH, Dorey F, et al: The effect of plasma glucose variability on neonatal outcome in the pregnant diabetic patient. *Am J Obstet Gynecol* 1983;147:537.
26. Cousins L, Rigg L, Hollingsworth D, et al. The 24-hour excursion and diurnal rhythm of glucose, insulin, and C-peptide in normal pregnancy. *Am J Obstet Gynecol* 1980;136:483.
27. Coustan DR. Recent advances in the management of diabetic pregnant women. *Clin Perinatol* 1980;7:299.
28. Coustan DR, Berkowitz RL, Hobbins JC. Tight metabolic control of overt diabetes in pregnancy. *Am J Med* 1980;68: 845.
29. Felig P, Bergman M. Intensive ambulatory treatment of insulin-dependent diabetes. *Ann Intern Med* 1982;97:225.
30. Siperstein MD, Foster DW, Knowles HC, et al. Control of glucose and diabetic vascular disease. *N Engl J Med* 1977;296: 1060.
31. Weiss PAM, Hofmann H. Intensified conventional insulin therapy for the pregnant diabetic patient. *Obstet Gynecol* 1984; 64:629.
32. Gillmer MDG, Beard RW, Oakley NW, et al. Diurnal plasma free fatty acid profiles in normal and diabetic pregnancies. *BMJ* 1977;2:670.
33. Lewis SB, Wallin JD, Kuzuya H, et al. Circadian variation of serum glucose, C-peptide immunoreactivity and free insulin in

normal and insulin-treated diabetic pregnant subjects. *Diabetologia* 1976;12:343.

34. Rizvi J, Gillmer MDG, Oakley NW, et al. Evaluation of plasma glucose control in pregnancy complicated by chemical diabetes. *Br J Obstet Gynaecol* 1980;87:383.

35. Parretti E, Mecacci F, Psapini M, et al. Third trimester maternal glucose levels from diurnal profiles in non-diabetic pregnancies: correlation with sonographic parameters of fetal growth. *Diabetes Care* 2001;24:1319–1323.

36. Coustan DR, Reece RA, Sherwin R, et al: A randomized clinical trial of insulin pump vs. intensive conventional therapy in diabetic pregnancies. *JAMA* 1986;255:631.

37. Jovanovic L, Peterson CM, Saxena BB, et al: Feasibility of maintaining normal glucose profiles in insulin-dependent pregnant diabetic women. *Am J Med* 1980;68:105.

38. Kitzmiller JL, Younger MD, Hare JW, et al. Continuous subcutaneous insulin therapy during early pregnancy. *Obstet Gynecol* 1985;66:606.

39. Gabbe SG, Mestman JH, Freeman RK, et al. Management and outcome of class A diabetes mellitus. *Am J Obstet Gynecol* 1977;127:465.

40. Martin TR, Allen AC, Stinson D. Overt diabetes in pregnancy. *Am J Obstet Gynecol* 1979;133:275.

41. Reece EA, Coustan D, Sherwin R, et al. Does intensive glycemic control in diabetic pregnancies result in normalization of other metabolic fuels. *Am J Obstet Gynecol* 1991;165:126.

42. Sonksen PH. Home monitoring of blood glucose by diabetic patients. *Acta Endocrinol (Copenh)* 1980;94:145.

43. Sonksen PH, Judd SL, Lowy C. Home monitoring of blood glucose: method for improving diabetic control. *Lancet* 1978;1:729.

44. Sonksen PH, Judd S, Lowy C. Home monitoring of blood glucose: new approach to management of insulin-dependent diabetic patients in Great Britain. *Diabetes Care* 1980;3:100.

45. Landon MB, Gabbe SG. Glucose monitoring and insulin administration in the pregnant diabetic patient. *Clin Obstet Gynecol* 1985;28:496.

46. Skyler JS. Self-monitoring of blood glucose. *Med Clin North Am* 1982;66:1227.

47. Watford S, Gale EAM, Allison SP, et al. Self-monitoring of blood glucose. *Lancet* 1978;1:732.

48. Espersen T, Klebe JG. Self-monitoring of blood glucose in pregnant diabetics. *Acta Obstet Gynecol Scand* 1985;64:11.

49. Skyler JS, Robertson EG, Lasky IA, et al. Blood glucose control during pregnancy. *Diabetes Care* 1980;3:69.

50. Soeldner JS. Treatment of diabetes mellitus by devices. *Am J Med* 1981;70:183.

51. Peacock I, Hunter JC, Watford S, et al. Self-monitoring of blood glucose in diabetic pregnancy. *BMJ* 1979;2:1333.

52. Hanson U, Persson B, Ericksson E, et al. Self-monitoring of blood glucose by diabetic women during the third trimester of pregnancy. *Am J Obstet Gynecol* 1984;150:817.

53. Varner MW. Efficacy of home glucose monitoring in diabetic pregnancy. *Am J Med* 1983;75:592.

54. Harkness LJ, Ashwood ER, Parsons S, et al. Comparison of the accuracy of glucose reflectance meters in pregnant insulin-dependent diabetics. *Obstet Gynecol* 1991;77:181.

55. Henry MJ, Major CA, Reinsch S. Accuracy of self-monitoring of blood glucose: impact on diabetes management decisions during pregnancy. *Diabetes Educator* 2001;27:521–529.

56. Landon MB, Gabbe SG, Piana R, et al. Neonatal morbidity in pregnancy complicated by diabetes mellitus: predictive value of maternal glycemic profiles. *Am J Obstet Gynecol* 1987;156:1089.

57. Langer O, Rodriguez DA, Xenakis MJ, et al. Intensified versus conventional management of gestational diabetes. *Am J Obstet Gynecol* 1994;170:1036–1047.

58. Langer O. Is normoglycemia the correct threshold to prevent complications in the pregnant diabetic patient? *Diabetes Rev* 1996;4:2–10.

59. Combs AC, Gunderson E, Kitzmiller JL, et al. Relationship of fetal macrosomia to maternal postprandial glucose control during pregnancy. *Diabetes Care* 1992;15:1251.

60. Jovanovic-Peterson L, Peterson CM, Reed GF, et al. Maternal postprandial glucose levels and infant birth weight: the diabetes in early pregnancy study. *Am J Obstet Gynecol* 1991;164:103.

61. Abell DA. The significance of abnormal glucose tolerance (hyperglycemia and hypoglycemia) in pregnancy. *Br J Obstet Gynaecol* 1979;86:214.

62. Langer A, Levy J, Brustman L, et al. Glycemic control in gestational diabetes mellitus—how tight is tight enough: small for gestational age versus large for gestational age? *Am J Obstet Gynecol* 1989;161:646.

63. De Veciana M, Major CA, Morgan MA, et al. Postprandial versus preprandial blood glucose monitoring in women with gestational diabetes mellitus requiring insulin therapy. *N Engl J Med* 1995;333:1237–1241.

64. Metzger BE, Coustan DR. Proceedings of the Fourth Internal Workshop-Conference on Gestational Diabetes Mellitus. *Diabetes Care* 1998;21(suppl 2):B161–B168.

65. Sivan E, Weisz B, Homko CJ, et al. One or two hour postprandial glucose measurements: are they the same. *Am J Obstet Gynecol* 2001;185604–185607.

66. Weisz B, Shrim A, Homko CJ, et al. One hour versus two hour post-prandial glucose measurements in gestational diabetes—a prospective study. *Obstet Gynecol* (submitted for publication).

67. Shapiro B, Savage PJ, Lomatch D, et al. A comparison of accuracy and estimated cost of methods for home blood glucose monitoring. *Diabetes Care* 1981;4:396.

68. American Diabetes Association. Consensus statement. Self-monitoring of blood glucose. *Diabetes Care* 1996;19(suppl 1):62.

69. Mazze RS, Shamson H, Pasmantier R, et al. Reliability of blood-glucose monitoring by patients with diabetes mellitus. *Am J Med* 1984;77:211.

70. Moses RG. Assessment of reliability of patients performing SMBG with a portable reflectance meter with memory capacity (M-glucometer). *Diabetes Care* 1986;9:670.

71. Langer O, Langer N, Piper JM, et al. Cultural diversity as a factor in self-monitoring blood glucose in gestational diabetes. *J Assoc Acad Min Phys* 1995;6:73–77.

72. McGarraugh G, Price D, Schwartz S, et al. Physiologic influences on off-finger glucose testing. *Diabetes Tech Ther* 2001;3:367.

73. Bode BW, Gross TM, Thorton KR, et al. Continuous glucose monitoring used to adjust diabetes therapy improves glycosylated hemoglobin: a pilot study. *Diabetes Res Clin Pract* 1999;46:183.

74. McGowan K, Thomas W, Moran A. Spurious reporting of nocturnal hypoglycemia by CGMS in patients with tightly controlled type 1 diabetes. *Diabetes Care* 2002;25:1499.

75. Chase HP, Kim LM, Owen SL, et al. Continuous subcutaneous glucose monitoring in children with type 1 diabetes. *Pediatrics* 2001;107:222.

76. Schiaffini R, Ciampalini P, Spera S, et al. Continuous glucose monitoring in type 1 diabetic children [Abstract]. *J Pediatr Endocrinol Metab* 2001;14(suppl 3):PP51.

77. Jovanovic L. The role of continuous glucose monitoring in gestational diabetes mellitus. *Diabetes Technol Ther* 2000;2(suppl):67.

78. Allen DW, Schroder WA, Balog J. Observations on the chromatographic heterogeneity of normal adults and fetal hemoglobin: a study of the effects of crystallization and chromatography on the heterogeneity and isoleucine content. *J Am Chem Soc* 1958;80:1628.

79. Bookchin RM, Gallop PM. Structure of hemoglobin A_{1c}. Nature of the N-terminal chain blocking group. *Biochem Biophys Res Commun* 1968;32:86.

80. Ditzel J, Kjaergaard JJ. Hemoglobin A_{1c} concentrations after initial treatment for newly discovered diabetes. *BMJ* 1978;1:741.

81. Dunn PJ, Cole RA, Soeldner JS, et al. Temporal relationship of glycosylated haemoglobin concentrations to glucose control in diabetics. *Diabetologia* 1979;17:213.

82. Gabbay KH. Glycosylated hemoglobin and diabetic control. *N Engl J Med* 1976;295:443.

83. Koenig RJ, Peterson CM, Jones RL, et al. Correlation of glucose regulation and hemoglobin Al, in diabetes mellitus. *N Engl J Med* 1976;295:417.

84. Lapp CA, Huff TA, Bransome ED Jr. Detection of abnormal hemoglobin variants during glycohemoglobin analysis. *Clin Chem* 1980;26:355.

85. O'Shaughnessy R, Russ J, Zuspan FP. Glycosylated hemoglobins and diabetes mellitus in pregnancy. *Am J Obstet Gynecol* 1979;135:783.

86. Schwartz HC, King KC, Schwartz AL, et al. Effects of pregnancy on hemoglobin A_{1c} in normal, gestational diabetic and diabetic women. *Diabetes* 1976;25:1118.

87. Tahbar S. An abnormal hemoglobin in red cells of diabetics. *Clin Chim Acta* 1968;22:296.

88. Trivelli LA, Ranney HM, Lai HT. Hemoglobin components in patients with diabetes mellitus. *N Engl J Med* 1971;284:353.

89. Gabbay KH, Hasty K, Breslow JL et al. Glycosylated hemoglobins and long-term blood glucose control in diabetes mellitus. *J Clin Endocrinol Metab* 1977;44:859.

90. Bunn HF, Haney DN, Gabbay KH, et al. Further identification of the nature and linkage of the carbohydrate in hemoglobin A_{1c}. *Biochem Biophys Res Commun* 1975;67:103.

91. Bunn HF, Haney DN, Kamin S, et al. The biosynthesis of human hemoglobin A_{1c}: slow glycosylation of hemoglobin *in vivo*. *J Clin Invest* 1976;57:1652.

92. Haney DN, Bunn HF. Glycosylation of hemoglobin *in vitro*: affinity labeling of hemoglobin by glucose-6-phosphate. *Proc Natl Acad Sci U S A* 1976;73:3534.

93. Huisman RG, Dozy AM. Studies on the heterogeneity of hemoglobin. V. Binding of hemoglobin with oxidized glutathione. *J Lab Clin Med* 1962;60:302.

94. Karamanos B, Christacopoulos P, Zacharious N, et al. Rapid changes of the hemoglobin A_{1c} (HbA_{1c}) fraction following alterations of diabetic control. *Diabetologia* 1977;13:406.

95. Leslie RDG, Pyke DA, John PN, et al. How quickly can haemoglobin A_1 increase? *BMJ* 1979;2:19.

96. Gonen B, Rochman H, Rubenstein AH, et al. Haemoglobin Al: an indicator of the metabolic control of diabetic patients. *Lancet* 1977;2:734.

97. Vintzileos AM, Thompson JP. Glycohemoglobin determinations in normal pregnancy and in insulin-dependent diabetics. *Obstet Gynecol* 1980;56:435.

98. Widness JA, Schwartz HC, Thompson D, et al. Glycohemo-globin (HbA_{1c}): a predictor of birth weight in infants of diabetic mothers. *J Pediatr* 1978;92:8.

99. Leslie RDG, Pyke DA, John PN. Hemoglobin A_1 in diabetic pregnancy. *Lancet* 1978;2:958.

100. Miller E, Hare JW, Cloherty JP, et al. Elevated maternal hemoglobin A_{1c} in early pregnancy and major congenital anomalies in infants of diabetic mothers. *N Engl J Med* 1981;304:1331.

101. Ylinen K, Raivio K, Teramo K. Haemoglobin A_{1c} predicts the perinatal outcome in insulin-dependent diabetic pregnancies. *Br J Obstet Gynaecol* 1981;38:961.

102. Greene MF, Have JW, Cloherty JP, et al. First trimester hemoglobin A, and risk for major malformations and spontaneous abortion in diabetic pregnancy. *Teratology* 1989;39:225.

103. Demarini S, Mimouni F, Tsang RC, et al. Impact of metabolic control of diabetes during pregnancy on neonatal hypocalcemia: a randomized study. *Obstet Gynecol* 1994;83:918.

104. Sosenko JM, Kitzmiller JL, Fluckieger R, et al. Umbilical cord glycosylated hemoglobin in infants of diabetic mothers: relationships to neonatal hypoglycemia, macrosomia and cord serum C-peptide. *Diabetes Care* 1982;5:566.

105. Watson WJ, Herbert WN, Prior TW, et al. Glycosylated hemoglobin and fructosamine: indicators of glycemic control in pregnancies complicated by diabetes mellitus. *J Reprod Med* 1991;36:731.

106. Ylinen K, Ravio K, Teramo K. Hemoglobin A1c in diabetic pregnancies. *Br J Obstet Gynaecol* 1981;88:691.

107. Roberts AB, Court DJ, Henley P, et al. Fructosamine in diabetic pregnancy. *Lancet* 1983;2:998.

108. Baker JR, O'Connor JP, Metcalf PA, et al. The clinical utility of serum fructosamine estimation, a possible screening test for diabetes mellitus. *BMJ* 1983;287:863.

109. Cefalu WT, Prather KL, Chester DL, et al. Total serum glycosylated proteins in detection and monitoring of gestational diabetes. *Diabetes Care* 1990;13:872.

110. Parfitt NJ, Clark JD, Turner GM, et al. Use of fructosamine and glycated hemoglobin to verify self blood glucose monitoring data in diabetic pregnancy. *Diabet Med* 1993;10:162.

111. Thai AC, Lui KF, Lowes NY, et al. Serial measurements of serum fructosamine and glycosylated haemoglobin as indices of glycemic control in diabetic pregnancy. *Ann Acad Med Singapore* 1991;20:732.

112. Watson WJ, Herbert WA, Prior TV, et al. Glycosylated hemoglobin and fructosamine: indicators of glycemic control in pregnancies complicated by diabetic mellitus. *J Reprod Med* 1991;36:731.

113. Windeler J, Kobberling J. The fructosamine assay in diagnosis and control of diabetes mellitus: scientific evidence for its clinical usefulness? *J Clin Chem Clin Biochem* 1990;28:129.

114. Diabetes Control and Complications Trial Research *Group*. The effect of intensive treatment of diabetes on the development and progression of long-term, complications in insulin-dependent diabetes mellitus. *N Engl J Med* 1993;329:997.

115. Pickup JC, Keen H, Parsons JA, et al. Continuous subcutaneous insulin infusion: an approach to achieving normoglycemia. *BMJ* 1978;1:204.

116. Potter JM, Reckless JPD, Cullen DR. Subcutaneous continuous insulin infusion and control of blood glucose concentration in diabetics in third trimester of pregnancy. *BMJ* 1980;28:1099.

117. Rudolf MCJ, Coustan DR, Sherwin RS, et al. Efficacy of the insulin pump in the home treatment of pregnant diabetics. *Diabetes* 1981;30:891.

118. Gabbe SG, Holing E, Temple P, et al. Benefits, risks, costs, and patient satisfaction associated with insulin pump therapy for the

pregnancy complicated by type 1 diabetes mellitus. *Am J Obstet Gynecol* 2000;182:1283.

119. Simmons D, Thompson CF, Conroy C, et al. Use of insulin pumps in pregnancies complicated by type 2 diabetes and gestational diabetes in a multiethnic community. *Diabetes Care* 2001;24:2078.

120. Shichiri M, Kawamori R, Hakui N, et al. Closed-loop glycemic control with a wearable artificial endocrine pancreas. *Diabetes* 1984;33:1200.

121. Shichiri M, Asakawa N, Yamasaki Y, et al. Telemetry glucose monitoring device with needle-type glucose sensor: a useful tool for blood glucose monitoring in diabetic individuals. *Diabetes Care* 1986;9:298.

122. Shichiri M, Yamasaki Y, Kawamori R, et al. Wearable artificial endocrine pancreas with needle-type glucose sensor. *Lancet* 1982;2:1129.

123. American Diabetes Association. *Resource guide. Diabetes forecast.* Alexandria, VA: American Diabetes Association, 2003.

19

INSULIN TREATMENT OF THE PREGNANT PATIENT WITH DIABETES MELLITUS

MARK B. LANDON
STEVEN G. GABBE

The introduction of insulin to clinical practice in 1922 remains the most significant advancement in the treatment of pregnancy complicated by diabetes mellitus. Prior to that time, pregnancy in diabetic women was uncommon and was accompanied by high maternal and fetal mortality rates (1). Despite Priscilla White's admonition that the early use of insulin during pregnancy appeared to have its greatest impact in reducing maternal mortality and morbidity, for many years adequate techniques were not available to closely monitor blood glucose throughout gestation (2). Over the past 20 years, self-monitoring of blood glucose and intensive insulin therapy have combined to make achievement of near physiologic euglycemia a therapeutic reality for many pregnant diabetic women. The result of such efforts has been a steady decline in fetal and neonatal mortality rates; excluding major congenital malformations, the rates are now nearly equivalent to those observed in nondiabetic pregnancies (3).

Several techniques for insulin administration have been employed to achieve optimum glucose control during pregnancy (Table 19-1). The efficacy of these regimens depends on frequent glucose determinations. Self-monitoring systems provide the best means by which patients can determine their glucose control. This advancement in diabetes therapy has enabled women of reproductive age to assume a greater role in the treatment of their disease both before conception and during pregnancy. Adjustments in insulin

TABLE 19-1. TARGET GLUCOSE LEVELS DURING PREGNANCY

Time	mg/dL
Before breakfast	60–90
Before lunch, dinner, bedtime snack	60–105
After meals (2 hours)	≤120
2:00 AM to 6:00 AM	>60

dosage, diet, and exercise based on frequent monitoring of glucose levels is especially important during pregnancy when normal physiologic changes occur that can alter insulin requirements dramatically.

NORMAL INSULIN SECRETION

Insulin is required for normal carbohydrate, protein, and lipid metabolism. Individuals with type 1 diabetes mellitus do not produce sufficient quantities of this hormone and require exogenous insulin to prevent fatal ketoacidosis. In contrast, individuals with type 2 diabetes do not require exogenous insulin for survival. However, during pregnancy, many of these individuals will demonstrate marked insulin resistance, requiring supplemental insulin for adequate blood glucose control. Similarly, women with gestational diabetes mellitus may be unable to regulate glycemia with dietary manipulation alone, and may require multiple injections of insulin for this purpose.

In nondiabetic individuals, basal insulin secretion into the portal system takes place at a rate of approximately 1 unit per hour. Food intake results in a stimulated release of five to ten units of insulin from the pancreatic β-cells, such that total daily insulin secretion in a normal individual is approximately 40 units daily (4). Basal insulin secretion seems to limit hepatic glucose production in the postabsorptive state. Fasting blood glucose levels correlate well with hepatic glucose production and measures of long-term glycemic control such as glycosylated hemoglobin levels (4). Long-acting insulin preparations are prescribed to simulate basal insulin production. The endogenous insulin secretion stimulated by meals promotes disposal of ingested nutrients, primarily glucose into peripheral tissues. This phase of insulin secretion is synchronized with the rise in blood glucose in response to feeding. Once surges in postprandial glucose levels subside, there is prompt diminution in insulin secretion and a return to basal or postabsorptive levels. Premeal administration of short-acting insulin is thus physiologically important in replacement regimens designed for pregnant women with diabetes.

As with any hormone replacement, the primary goal is to achieve physiologic hormone levels at the site of hormone action. The objective of insulin replacement regimens in both the pregnant and nonpregnant states is further complicated by the need to simulate normal secretion patterns despite rapid changes in response to nutrient intake and physiologic stimuli such as exercise. Unfortunately, available insulin preparations and regimens are clearly less than physiologic. For example, the peak effects of subcutaneously administered human regular insulin are delayed until 3 to 4 hours after injection and may be present as long as 8 hours. Similarly, intermediate-acting and long-acting preparations designed to mimic basal secretion, have demonstrable peaks in their action. The administration of regular insulin by continuous subcutaneous infusion (CSII) or pump therapy has been hailed as the most suitable method to mimic normal basal insulin secretion. Yet individuals treated with this regimen, which includes both basal infusions and mealtime boluses, can demonstrate significantly elevated serum insulin levels (4).

INSULIN PREPARATIONS

Great advances have been made in the production of highly purified insulins for patient use. Today, clinicians can choose from a variety of preparations emphasizing species specificity and improved purity. Despite the production of highly purified preparations from animal sources in the form of beef or pork insulin, these types of insulin have now been largely replaced by the manufacture of human insulin by recombinant DNA technology, as well as the introduction of several genetically engineered insulin analogues. Insulin is available in short-, intermediate-, and long-acting forms that may be administered separately or mixed in the same syringe. Short-acting insulins include regular, semilente, lispro, and aspart. The intermediate-acting preparations are lente and neutral protamine Hagedorn (NPH) (Table 19-2). Insulin lispro reverses the order of amino acids proline and lysine at positions 28 and 29 in the insulin β chain to lysine and proline, whereas insulin aspart substitutes aspartic acid for proline at position 28 of the β chain. Human insulin preparations are marketed as mixtures of short- and intermediate-acting varieties in 10% steps ranging from 10%:90% to 50%:50%. Predetermined mixtures of 70% NPH and 30% regular have gained popularity, but may be of limited value in pregnancy regimens when a single component in the dosage must be changed or if intermediate-acting insulin only is to be given at bedtime. Long-acting insulin preparations include ultralente, protamine zinc, and the new analogues glargine and detemir. As with the rapid-acting genetically engineered analogues, a simple amino acid substitution produces both insulin glargine and insulin detemir. Insulin glargine substitutes glargine for asparagine at position 21 in the α chain and also adds two arginines to the carboxy-terminus of the β chain. These modifications result in insulin glargine precipitating at a neutral pH. Glargine remains soluble in formulation because it is prepared in an acidic solution. Thus, it cannot be mixed with other insulin formulations that have a neutral pH. Insulin detemir adds a fatty acid side chain to the lysine at position 29 of the β chain. The fatty acid side chain allows insulin detemir to bind to serum albumin, thus increasing its duration of action. Long-acting insulins mimic basal insulin secretion and are administered either before breakfast or dinner. Many physicians have been reluctant to use long-acting insulin during pregnancy because of its long duration of action (up to 36 hours), which, when coupled with next-day administration of mealtime short-acting insulin, might increase the risk of hypoglycemia.

Animal insulin has minor structural differences from the human hormone. Porcine insulin contains an alanine

TABLE 19-2. TYPES OF HUMAN INSULIN AND INSULIN ANALOGS

	Source	Onset (h)	Peak (h)	Duration (h)
Short acting				
Humulin R (Lilly)	Human	0.5	2–4	5–7
Velosulin-H (Novo Nordisk)	Human	0.5	1–3	8
Novolin R (Novo Nordisk)	Human	0.5	2.5–5	6–8
Lispro	Analog	0.25	0.5–1.5	6–8
Aspart	Analog	0.25	1–3	3–5
Intermediate acting				
Humulin Lente (Lilly)	Human	1–3	6–12	18–24
Humulin NPH (Lilly)	Human	1–2	6–12	18–24
Novolin L (Novo Nordisk)	Human	2.5	7–15	22
Novolin N (Novo Nordisk)	Human	1.5	4–12	24
Long acting				
Humulin Ultralente (Lilly)	Human	4–6	8–20	>36
Glargine	Analog	1.1	5	24
Determir	Analog	1–2	5	24

residue instead of threonine at the carboxy-terminus of the β chain, whereas beef insulin substitutes alanine and valine at positions 8 and 10 on the α chain (for threonine and isoleucine) (5). Thus, there is remarkable homology of sequences between human and commercially available animal insulin preparations. Because bovine insulin is less similar to human insulin than porcine, bovine insulin is more immunogenic (5). These minor differences in structure do not appear to be crucial to the binding or action of insulin. Receptor binding and cellular interactions of human insulin in fact do not differ significantly from those of beef or pork insulin (6). Amino acid substitutions, may, however, influence the tendency for dimer formation (7). Similarly, the physicochemical properties of human and animal insulins differ because of their various amino acid sequences. The addition of one extra hydroxyl group due to threonine in human insulin increases its hydrophilic and decreases its lipophilic properties compared with porcine insulin. It follows that human insulin is more soluble in aqueous solution than porcine insulin.

INSULIN PRODUCTION

The introduction of methods to mass produce human insulin has been a by-product of advances in molecular genetic technology, most importantly recombinant DNA techniques. Originally, human insulin was produced by exchanging alanine in position β30 of porcine insulin with threonine, using an enzymatic method or semisynthetic technique. Subsequently, the semisynthetic production of insulin has given way to biosynthetic production. Originally, the α and β chains were produced separately and required combination. At present, biosynthetic human proinsulin, with a three-dimensional structure identical to the natural hormone can be produced by bacterial cells. The correct three-dimensional or spherical structure is essential for receptor binding and thus biological action. The three dimensional structure of human insulin does differ slightly from porcine insulin. In practice, human proinsulin is produced and then enzymatically cleaved to insulin and C-peptide. Further purification results in biosynthetic human insulin (Fig. 19-1).

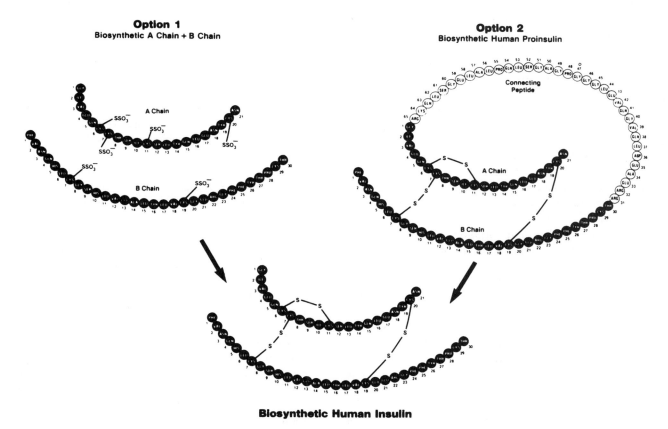

FIGURE 19-1. Two pathways for producing biosynthetic human insulin. Option 1 involves separate α- and β-chain production and subsequent combination. Option 2 involves the production of proinsulin from which C-peptide is cleaved enzymatically, resulting in insulin formation. (From Frank BH, Chance RE. Two routes for producing human insulin utilizing recombinant DNA technology. *Munch Med Wochenschr* 1982;125[Suppl 1]:S14, with permission.)

IMMUNOGENICITY OF INSULIN

The introduction of human insulin has permitted investigation of the role of antibodies to animal-derived insulin preparations in relation to pregnancy outcome. Almost all patients treated with animal-derived insulin for a period of more than 10 years will have detectable antiinsulin antibodies (5). The presence of these antibodies can significantly affect the pharmacokinetics of insulin. Normally, the plasma concentration of insulin will depend on four variables: absorption rate, endogenous insulin secretion, distribution volume, and catabolism (8). Rarely the affinity of antibodies for insulin as well as their binding capacity may be so high that little free insulin is present. In most individuals, circulating IgG antiinsulin antibodies are basically carrier proteins with varying degrees of affinity for insulin. Biologic activity is affected by this process, which results in the release of bound insulin at unpredictable times and may produce unexplained episodes of hypoglycemia. In early pregnancy, insulin antibody titers do not appear to alter insulin requirements or the ability to achieve normoglycemia (9). Mean levels of antibodies fall after a patient has been changed to a highly purified or human insulin preparation (10). The American Diabetes Association suggests that human insulin be employed for use in pregnant women and in women considering pregnancy (11). Human insulin is also recommended for the treatment of newly diagnosed diabetes or women with gestational diabetes.

While insulin antibodies do cross the placenta, they are generally cleared within the first year of life (12). There are, however, reports of persistent antibodies in the offspring of insulin-treated diabetic women (13). This raises some concern as to whether insulin antibodies might enhance the development of diabetes. There does not appear to be a correlation between cord C-peptide levels and cord insulin antibody levels, suggesting that insulin antibodies do not contribute to hyperinsulinism in the fetus. Moreover, most studies have failed to correlate fetal macrosomia or birth weight with neonatal insulin antibody levels (14). Mylvaganam's data indicate that neonatal morbidity may be increased in the offspring of mothers with higher insulin antibody titers (12). Following the observation that maternal IgG insulin antibodies can transport insulin across the placenta, Menon et al. (15) reported that type 1 diabetic women with demonstrable insulin antibodies were at increased risk for producing macrosomic infants. Unfortunately, maternal glycemic control was not analyzed in this report. Subsequently, Rosenn et al. (16) from the same institution found no difference in fetal growth characteristics in women treated with human versus animal insulin, suggesting that lower antibody production alone did not prevent fetal macrosomia.

Extremely low immunogenicity is a property of human insulin preparations and, in part, reflects the purification process. The production of semisynthetic insulin preparations has employed well-established methods used in the preparation of porcine insulin. Monocomponent porcine insulin serves as a substrate, thereby avoiding contamination with proinsulin, glucagon, pancreatic polypeptide, somatostatin, and vasoactive intestinal peptides. Recombinant DNA technology, used in the production of biosynthetic human insulin, presents a risk of contamination of the insulin product with various bacterial or yeast polypeptides. The obstacle to achieving purity has largely been overcome with intact proinsulin production in place of α- and β-chain extraction and recombination. This sophisticated purification process has resulted in human insulin preparations that are pure and free of significant contamination. Antibodies to Escherichia coli–derived peptides are thus uncommon in subjects treated with human insulin for several months (17). However, human insulin use is associated with immunogenic potential, albeit lower than that of animal-derived insulin preparations (18). IgG-insulin antibodies at very low levels can be found in approximately 50 percent of diabetic patients after exclusive treatment with biosynthetic or semisynthetic human insulin for 2 years (5). Relatively high levels of IgG insulin antibody are present in most patients who have a history of pretreatment with impure insulin preparations. Studies performed on newly diagnosed type 1 patients have surprisingly demonstrated that only two-thirds remain free of IgG insulin antibodies, whereas one-third produce low levels of antibody after treatment with semisynthetic preparations (19). A comparison between this treatment and purified porcine monocomponent insulin revealed higher antibody levels with the latter agent. A further comparison of the immunogenicity of biosynthetic insulin and purified pork insulin documented identical frequencies of antibody production in both groups during the initial 3 months; however, levels were lower in follow-up in the human insulin–treated group (20). The clinical relevance of the slightly lower immunogenic potential of human insulin compared with highly purified porcine insulin is debatable. While some have suggested that even low levels of insulin antibodies can adversely affect β-cell function, a large randomized controlled study failed to demonstrate any difference in β-cell function between human monocomponent and porcine monocomponent treated individuals (21). The mechanism by which human insulin induces antibody formation is unknown. Intravenously administered insulin is essentially nonimmunogenic. Deamidation of insulin, as well as additives, could play a role in eliciting an immune response. Transformation products such as covalently aggregated dimers, common in commercial preparations, have a slower metabolism and are highly immunogenic. Degradation products found in subcutaneous depots likely play a role as well.

As the new insulin analogues are not human insulin, the potential immunogenicity of these preparations is a concern. Interestingly, antibody response to lispro appears to be

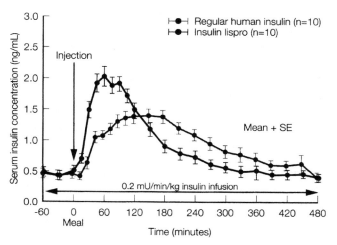

FIGURE 19-2. Comparison of serum insulin levels following infusion of insulin lispro versus human regular insulin. (From Heinemann L, Heise T, Wahl LC, et al. Prandial glycaemia after a carbohydrate rich meal in type 1 diabetic patients: using the rapid acting insulin analogue [Lys (B28), Pro (B29)] human insulin. *Diabet Med* 1996;13:625–629, with permission).

similar to regular insulin in gestational diabetic women (22). It has been postulated that the shorter action of lispro may decrease its immunogenicity. A study comparing the immunogenicity of aspart and biphasic aspart versus regular insulin also demonstrated lower levels of antibody production for these analogues (23).

The rapid-acting insulin analogues mimic physiologic insulin secretion better than rapid insulin because of their faster absorption after subcutaneous injection. Both human regular insulin and the newer analogues exist as hexamers in pharmacologic preparations. Insulin lispro and aspart disassociate into monomers at a faster rate than human regular insulin and are absorbed faster. Human regular insulin may take 80 to 120 minutes to dissociate and be absorbed, whereas the absorption for the rapid-changing analogue is approximately 40 to 50 minutes (Fig. 19-2). Insulin aspart and insulin lispro have similar pharmacokinetic profiles. Following injection, both analogues produce a sharp rise in insulin concentration and then taper off over a few hours. Insulin lispro may decline slightly faster than insulin aspart (24). In contrast with regular insulin, both analogues demonstrate a sharper peak resembling physiologic insulin secretion, whereas regular insulin has a broader peak and longer tapering time. The obvious benefit is more rapid control of postprandial excursions and avoidance of late hypoglycemia that may complicate regular insulin administration (25,26).

PHARMACOLOGIC CONSIDERATIONS

Studies investigating insulin absorption and/or insulin action are plentiful, but may be difficult to compare due to

methodologic differences, dosing variation, and the use of different sites of administration. As previously mentioned, prior use of animal insulin and subsequent antibody formation may lead to variable dissociation rates of insulin from circulating antibody complexes that can affect the bioavailability of exogenous insulin. Pharmacodynamic properties of insulin are studied by following the hypoglycemic effect of subcutaneously administered insulin over a specified time period. Because hypoglycemia may trigger a counter-regulatory response, blood glucose is best kept constant by intravenous infusion to maintain normoglycemia using euglycemic clamp techniques. Glucose requirement is thus a measure of the biological activity and potency of insulin. There is poor definition of the time-action profiles of many insulin preparations due to methodologic flaws in these studies (27). An analysis of 22 studies revealed a range of onset of action of 8 to 30 minutes for human regular insulin. Peak action varied from 45 minutes to 4 hours. Within each study, subject variation was considerable and likely reflects differences in insulin transport to target tissues (27).

Pharmacokinetic studies investigating the absorption of short-acting human versus porcine insulin have produced conflicting results with either similar absorption rates or more rapid absorption of human insulin demonstrated (28,29). Euglycemic clamp studies reveal that both insulins have similar biological activities that are dose dependent (30). The mechanism of faster absorption of human insulin in comparison to porcine regular insulin may be explained by the greater hydrophilic nature of human insulin. Alternatively, the β30 amino acid differences may effect dimer association and the tendency to dissociate.

Studies of short-acting human insulin in different concentrations report the onset of action between 15 to 30 minutes, with peak action between 150 to 180 minutes after subcutaneous injection. A slightly faster absorption was found with the U40 formulation compared with the commonly employed U100 formulation (31). Glucose infusion rates were similar with both preparations and remained greater than 50% maximal at 6 hours, indicating the longer duration of action of exogenous insulin compared to an endogenous response.

As the rapid initial delivery of insulin is vital in reducing meal-related glycemic excursions, the faster onset of action observed with the new insulin analogues lispro and aspart might be preferable to short-acting human regular insulin.

Despite apparent widespread use, little data remain on clinical experience with insulin lispro during pregnancy. In nonpregnant individuals, lispro improves metabolic control and decreases episodes of hypoglycemia. Insulin lispro is not yet approved for use in pregnancy, but it is a category B drug. While an early report raised some question regarding a possible association between insulin lispro and progression of retinopathy during pregnancy (32), recent experience suggests that this is not the case (33). There is one published report on the use of insulin aspart during pregnancy (34). Pettitt et al. (34) assessed the short-term efficacy of insulin aspart in comparison with regular human insulin in 15 women with gestational diabetes. Glycemic excursions were significantly lower with insulin aspart compared with human regular insulin. Further studies are needed to document efficacy and safety of insulin aspart, which is currently a class C drug.

Intermediate-acting human insulin preparations also show variable results when compared in pharmacologic studies with animal preparations. In an early trial, no difference in the decline of blood glucose levels could be demonstrated with human compared to animal NPH preparations (35). Subsequent observations support a more rapid onset and shorter duration of action than with corresponding animal insulins (36,37). However, disappearance rates of I125-labeled human or porcine NPH insulin do not differ significantly when administered to diabetic individuals (38). Again, differences in absorption cited above may reflect the relative hydrophilic nature of human insulin whereas other pharmacodynamic differences might be explained by interaction of the various species products with protamine.

NPH insulin appears to be absorbed at a faster rate than zinc insulin (lente insulin). A euglycemic clamp study comparing human lente and NPH demonstrated an increased metabolic effect within the first several hours following injection (39). The onset of action (half-maximal action) of four commonly prescribed human NPH preparations is within 2.5 to 3 hours with peak action at 5 to 7 hours, and duration of action (defined as >25% maximal action) between 13 and 16 hours.

More rapid absorption and shorter duration of action of intermediate-acting human insulins may have particular clinical importance in pregnant women. The administration of human NPH insulin before the evening meal might increase the likelihood of nocturnal hypoglycemia. Elevated fasting blood-glucose concentrations might also result from diminished insulin action by the following morning. Fasting glucose concentrations can be significantly lowered when the evening dose of human NPH insulin is given at bedtime instead of prior to supper (40). Human NPH insulin appears to have a distinct advantage over human lente in that it can be premixed with short-acting insulin in one syringe without a considerable change in time-action profiles. The principal effect of lente is to retard the onset of action of short-acting insulin. The delay is a result of binding of regular insulin to zinc, which results in amorphous precipitation of zinc insulin. This phenomenon does not occur with mixing of human regular and NPH insulins.

Long-acting insulin preparations have gained considerable popularity in the last several years. Ultralente human insulin has replaced bovine and porcine preparations because of a more favorable pharmacokinetic profile as well as reduced immunogenicity (41). Human zinc insulin binds water more avidly than pork insulin, which leads to better solubility of human ultralente preparations and faster absorption. The ultralente formulation with bovine insulin has a very long duration (up to 32 hours) and demonstrates no peak effect (41). In contrast, human ultralente insulin's effect peaks after 8 to 9 hours, and its duration of action is shorter than that of bovine ultralente. A study comparing time action profiles of human ultralente and human NPH revealed a peak action of 10 hours which was two-thirds that of NPH (42). Plasma insulin levels returned to baseline at 20 hours for both groups, indicating that the duration of action of human ultralente is not considerably longer than that of NPH insulin. This observation would suggest that a single daily injection of human ultralente insulin is insufficient to provide for basal need and that twice daily injections may be necessary. The high variability of insulin bioavailability of ultralente insulin preparations has resulted in limited use of these preparations during pregnancy. In most cases, we have chosen to switch women from ultra-

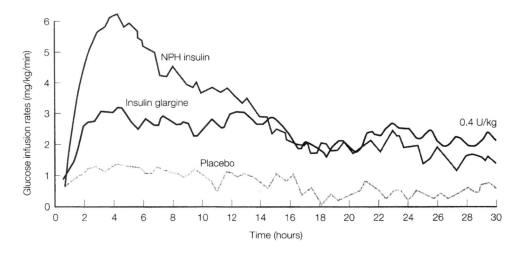

FIGURE 19-3. Pharmacokinetic comparison of insulin glargine versus NPH insulin in non-diabetic individuals utilizing glucose clamp technique. (From Linkeschova R, Heise T, Rave K, et al. Time action profile of the long-acting insulin analogue HOE 901. *Diabetes* 1999;48[Suppl 1]:A97, with permission.)

lente to NPH insulin because it has a more predictable absorption pattern and duration of action (43).

The long-acting insulin analogues glargine and detemir have been designed to more accurately mimic basal insulin secretion, yet neither has been adequately evaluated for safety or efficacy during pregnancy. Insulin glargine preparation includes the addition of zinc, which stabilizes the hexamer structure and prolongs its activity. Insulin glargine has a flat profile when compared to ultralente or NPH so that when administered with short-acting insulin, unpredictable spikes in insulin levels with resulting hypoglycemia appear to be less common (44) (Fig. 19-3). Nocturnal hypoglycemia has been reported to be reduced in type 1 diabetic pregnant women utilizing a multiple injection regimen with bedtime glargine versus NPH (45). One concern with insulin glargine is its high affinity for insulin-like growth factor (IGF) receptors (46). This interaction might potentially increase the progression of retinopathy in certain individuals. Insulin detemir may prove to be a more desirable long-acting analogue for use during pregnancy. It has a more physiologic profile than glargine and apparently less affinity for the IGF receptor when compared to regular insulin (46). In a study of nonpregnant subjects using insulin detemir, glucose excursions were lower than with NPH as were episodes of hypoglycemia (47). Clinical studies are needed to establish insulin detemir as safe for use during pregnancy.

METHODS OF INSULIN ADMINISTRATION

During pregnancy, conventional insulin therapy often needs to be abandoned in favor of intensive therapy in order to achieve the best glycemic control possible for each patient. Conventional insulin regimens have classically included one to two injections of insulin usually prior to breakfast and the evening meal, complimented by self-monitoring of blood glucose and adjustment of insulin dose according to glucose profiles. Patients are instructed on dietary composition, insulin action, recognition and treatment of hypoglycemia, adjusting insulin dosage for exercise and sick days, as well as monitoring for hyperglycemia and potential ketosis. These principles form the foundation for intensive insulin therapy in which an attempt is made to simulate physiologic insulin requirements. Insulin administration is provided for both basal needs and meals, and rapid adjustments are made in response to glucose measurements. The treatment regimen often involves three to four daily injections or the use of CSII devices. With either approach, frequent self-monitoring of blood glucose is fundamental to achieve the therapeutic objective of physiologic glucose control. Patients are instructed on an insulin dose for each meal and at bedtime if necessary. Mealtime insulin needs are determined by the composition of the meal, the premeal glucose measurement, and the level of activity

anticipated following the meal. Basal or intermediate-acting insulin requirements are determined by periodic 2 A.M. to 4 A.M. glucose measurements as well as late afternoon values that reflect morning NPH or lente action. During pregnancy, many diabetic women develop the self-management skills that are essential to an intensive insulin therapy regimen.

In patients who are not well controlled, a brief period of hospitalization is often necessary for the initiation of therapy. Individual adjustments to the regimens implemented can then be made. It is gratifying for many patients to feel that they can take charge of their own diabetic control. In our experience, patients who have previously followed a prescribed dosage regimen for years gain confidence in making adjustments in their insulin dosage after a short period of time. Patients are encouraged to contact their physician at any time if questions should arise concerning the management of their diabetes. During early pregnancy, patients are instructed to report their glucose values by telephone at least weekly.

MULTIPLE INJECTION REGIMENS

Insulin is generally administered in two to three injections. We prefer a three-injection regimen, although many patients prefer taking a combination of intermediate- and short-acting insulin before dinner and breakfast. As a general rule, the amount of intermediate-acting insulin will exceed the regular component by a two-to-one ratio. Patients usually receive two-thirds of their total dose with breakfast and the remaining third in the evening as a combined dose with dinner, or split into components with short-acting insulin at dinnertime and intermediate-acting insulin at bedtime in an effort to minimize periods of nocturnal hypoglycemia (43). These episodes frequently occur when the mother is in a relative fasting state while placental and fetal glucose consumption continue. Finally, some women may require a small dose of short-acting insulin before lunch, thus constituting a four-injection daily regimen.

Subcutaneous injection of insulin introduces numerous variables that can affect insulin absorption and in turn circulating insulin levels. Insulin absorption is clearly affected by injection site selection with absorption being diminished in the lower extremities compared with the abdominal wall. It has been demonstrated that I125-labeled rapid-acting insulin disappears 86% faster from the abdomen than from the leg (48). Thus, to maintain consistency, the type of injection site should not be changed frequently. The large abdominal surface area provides for adequate rotation while minimizing the variability associated with moving the injection from abdomen to extremity. After proper counseling, most pregnant women will accept abdominal injection. Remarkably, variation of absorption still approaches rates as high as 30% when the identical site is used and the identical dose of insulin is administered to the same individual (49).

The depth of injection and skin temperature can also affect insulin absorption. Local heat produced by exercise can accelerate absorption and consequently elevate circulating insulin levels (50). Despite efforts to achieve excellent glycemic control, variable absorption of injected insulin remains an elusive problem that can no doubt influence postprandial glucose excursions.

CONTINUOUS SUBCUTANEOUS INSULIN INFUSION

In the late 1970s, insulin delivery systems were developed that could mimic the pattern of secretion of the normal pancreas. These systems adjusted for minute-to-minute changes in blood glucose concentration. One of the first such devices, the Biostator (Miles Laboratory), is a computerized closed-loop autoanalyzer that withdraws small amounts of venous blood through a double-lumen catheter. A glucose sensor measures the glucose concentration and its rate of change over the previous 4 minutes. The amount of insulin or dextrose to be infused is determined by these data. This unit, which is the size of a microwave oven, has been used successfully for acute blood glucose regulation in small numbers of obstetric patients during the third trimester and at the time of cesarean delivery (51). Natrass et al. (52) have used a glucose-controlled insulin infusion system during labor in a small number of type 1 diabetic patients. Mean glucose concentrations ranging from 83 to 94 mg/dL were achieved without any reported complications. Such closed-loop systems remain primarily research tools because of their cost and need for an indwelling venous catheter. Additionally, their large size has prevented them from being suitable for ambulatory use. However, research continues on implantable insulin pumps with glucose monitoring, providing for an internal closed-loop system. The primary obstacle to development of such systems has been *in vivo* glucose-sensing capability. In addition, concerns regarding calibration requirements over time, occlusion of sensor tips, and selection of an optimal method for glucose measurement (glucose oxidase vs. spectroscopy) need to be addressed in future research.

While implantable open-loop insulin pumps were first employed in the early 1980s, these devices have experienced relatively little clinical use. The pumps are implanted subcutaneously, usually on the left side of the abdomen with the catheter tip being placed within the peritoneum. Clinical experience demonstrates a remarkably low incidence of electronic device failure or infection. Catheter obstruction is the most significant complication and may require a laparoscopic procedure to relieve. The major advantage of an implantable open-loop system is the precision of insulin dosage and greater initial absorption of insulin into the portal system. Currently a research tool, these devices require surgical placement and are expensive.

There has now been considerable experience with open-loop CSII during pregnancy (Table 19-3). The pump is a battery-powered unit that is usually attached to the anterior abdominal wall and may be worn during most daily activities. These systems provide continuous short-acting insulin therapy via a subcutaneous infusion. The basal infusion rate and bolus doses to cover meals are determined by frequent self-monitoring of blood glucose. A basal infusion rate is generally close to one unit per hour.

Pregnant patients will often require hospitalization before initiation of pump therapy. Women must be educated regarding the strategy of continuous infusion and have their glucose stabilized over several days. This requires that multiple blood glucose determinations be made for the prevention of periods of hyper- and hypo-glycemia. Glucose values may become normalized with minimal amplitude of daily excursions in most patients.

Episodes of severe hypoglycemia are generally reduced with pump therapy. When they occur, these events are usually secondary to errors in dose selection or failure to adhere to the required diet. The risk of nocturnal hypoglycemia, which is increased in the pregnant state, is reduced by lowering the basal rate from late evening until early morning. The basal rate can be programmed to increase in the early morning hours to counteract the "dawn phenomenon."

The mechanics of the CSII systems are relatively simple. A fine-gauge butterfly needle device is attached by connecting tubing to the pump. This cannula is reimplanted every 2 to 3 days at a different site in the anterior abdominal wall. Short-acting (regular insulin) is stored in the pump syringe. Infusion occurs at a basal rate, which can be fixed or altered for specific time of day by a computer program. For example, the basal rate can be programmed for a lower dose at

TABLE 19-3. ADVANTAGES AND DISADVANTAGES OF CONTINUOUS SUBCUTANEOUS INSULIN INFUSION IN PREGNANCY

Advantages
  Continuous basal rate delivery of insulin decreases mean
    glucose excursions
  Portable size allows for ambulatory use
  Eliminates the need for multiple daily injections
  May increase patient enthusiasm and encourage contact
    with healthcare team
Disadvantages
  Requires excellent patient compliance
  May require more intensive glucose monitoring
  Mechanical problems can produce hypo- and hyper/glycemia
  Increased potential for ketoacidosis with pump failure
  Potential infection at insertion site
  May be uncomfortable to wear in late pregnancy

night. Similarly, preprandial boluses can be delivered manually or by computer preset. Half of the total daily insulin is usually given as the basal rate and the remainder as premeal boluses infused 15 to 45 minutes before each meal. The largest bolus (30% to 35%) is administered with breakfast, followed by 25% before dinner and 15% to 20% before snacks.

Patients without any pancreatic reserve may have rapid elevations of blood glucose if there is pump failure or intercurrent infection. Since the advent of buffered insulin, insulin aggregation leading to occlusion of the silastic infusion tubing is uncommon. Initial experience with insulin pumps suggested a high risk for ketoacidosis with pump failure or intercurrent infection. Failure of the pump is associated with a steady rise in ketonemia in the nonpregnant patient. In a series of 1,880 patient-months of treatment with CSII in 101 patients, 29 episodes of ketoacidosis were encountered (53). Fifteen episodes were judged to be secondary to pump failure. Such mechanical problems, such as needle dislodgment, are less common today. However, episodes of ketoacidosis often reflect inadequate training of the patient in dealing with pump failure, such as the need for conventional insulin injection in these situations.

Increasing numbers of patients are using pumps, in large part because they provide greater flexibility in lifestyle. However, the benefits and risks associated with the use of the pump in pregnancy have not been well studied. In the largest prospective, randomized investigation, Coustan et al. (54) randomized 22 pregnant patients to intensive conventional therapy with multiple injections versus pump therapy. There were no differences between the two treatment groups with respect to outpatient mean glucose levels, glycosylated hemoglobin levels, or glycemic excursions. Gabbe et al. (55) recently reported a large retrospective cohort study of women who began pump therapy during gestation as compared to a group treated with multiple insulin injections. Patients using pumps, many with insulin lispro, had fewer hypoglycemic reactions and comparable glucose control and pregnancy outcomes. Most continued using the pump after delivery, and their control was significantly better than that of patients on multiple injections. In our practice over the last 5 years, we have begun to institute pump therapy in increasing numbers of pregnant women. We have primarily utilized insulin lispro in such cases. While studies are lacking in pregnant individuals employing CSII comparing various short-acting insulins, in nonpregnant subjects the new insulin analogues are associated with improved postprandial glycemic control (56). In one study, subjects utilizing insulin aspart had less hypoglycemia when compared to those using lispro or human regular insulin (56) (Fig. 19-4). While most pregnant women are employing lispro with pump therapy, insulin aspart is the only rapid-acting insulin analogue approved for pump use by the Food and Drug Administration.

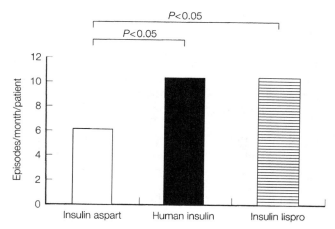

FIGURE 19-4. A comparison of the frequency of self-reported hypoglycemia in individuals utilizing continuous subcutaneous infusion therapy: insulin aspart versus human insulin and insulin lispro. (From Bode BW, Weinstein R, Bell D, et al. Comparison of insulin aspart with buffered regular insulin and insulin lispro in continuous subcutaneous insulin infusion: a randomized study in type 1 diabetes. *Diabetes Care* 2002;25:439–444, with permission.)

INSULIN REQUIREMENTS

It is well appreciated that insulin requirements rise during pregnancy largely because of the increased concentration of circulating contrainsulin hormones. Several studies have attempted to document the change in insulin dosage required to maintain tight metabolic control throughout gestation. While these reports provide insight into the characteristics of each given population, management must clearly be individualized since algorithms for insulin dosage should be based on self-reported glucose data.

Over 20 years ago, Jovanovic et al. (57) reported that constant insulin adjustment was necessary to keep up with the increasing insulin requirements of pregnancy. In a study of 40 insulin-dependent women (within 15% ideal body weight) maintained on a 30-kcal/kg diet, the total insulin dose was raised from 0.7 units/kg per day in the first trimester to 0.8 units/kg per day at week 18, 0.9 units/kg per day at week 26, and 1.0 units 1 kg per day at week 36. An increasing standard deviation was noted with advancing gestation, as the dose was more uniform at the beginning of gestation than toward the end. In this series, another 11 patients were markedly obese at the start of pregnancy; six required 1.2 units/kg per day at term; three required 2 units/kg per day at term, and two required 3 units/kg per day at term.

Langer et al. (58) have also evaluated insulin requirements in pregestational diabetic subjects. Their investigation had two unique features previously not reported: (a) patients with type 1 and type 2 diabetes were analyzed separately; and (b) all patients used a memory-based reflectance meter to ensure a means of obtaining verified self-monitored glucose values. A total of 103 patients (63 with type 1 and 40 with type 2 diabetes) were enrolled in this study. Both type 1 and type 2 patients demonstrated a triphasic insulin pattern, with type 2 diabetic women requiring significantly higher doses of insulin during each trimester (Fig. 19-5). During the first trimester no difference was found between type 1 and type 2 subjects. During the second trimester, a significant increase in insulin requirement emerged (10% for patients with type 1 diabetes compared to 33% for those with type 2 diabetes). In the third trimester, a 40% increase was found for women with type 2 diabetes. These authors speculated that increased body mass and heightened insulin resistance in type 2 patients contributed to this large adjustment in insulin requirement.

Controversy has surrounded the clinical finding of diminished or falling insulin requirements in late pregnancy. Malins (59) reported a 4.5% fetal loss rate in 67 women with no increase in insulin requirement in late pregnancy. Actual falls in insulin requirements are less common and have been associated with fetal death, if substantial. Prior to the advent of fetal monitoring, some declines in insulin requirement may have occurred because of fetal death, thus making the observation a result of the demise rather than the cause. McManus and Ryan (60) described 20 of 32 (62%) insulin-dependent women with a decline in insulin dose (12%±2%) after 36 weeks' gestation, which was associated with a longer duration of diabetes, but not with age, prepregnancy body mass index, weight gain, or maternal or fetal complications. Steel et al. (61) reported much greater decreases (over 30%) in insulin requirements,

often occurring before 36 weeks in 18 of 237 type 1 patients. In these cases, there were no abnormal fetal outcomes observed. As reported by others, Steel et al. (61) found a substantial rise in insulin dose for most type 1 pregnant women. The dose rose from a mean of 0.83±0.39 units/kg before pregnancy to a peak of 1.63±0.65 units/kg. The mean absolute increase in insulin requirement was 52 units with a greater incremental increase in the daytime insulin dose than at night. The degree of rise was significantly related to maternal weight gain between 20 to 29 weeks and initial maternal weight, and was inversely related to the duration of diabetes. Insulin dose was also unrelated to the degree of control, complications of pregnancy, White class, or perinatal outcome. This study as well as our own experience suggests that current algorithms for insulin therapy based on body weight and gestational age are inappropriate as wide variations in insulin requirements are observed in women with pregestational diabetes. An increase in insulin dosage can generally be anticipated by the second trimester, which can be related in part to weight gain and prepregnancy weight. Large falls in insulin requirements remain unexplained and may not be associated with placental failure (61). However, this unexplained phenomenon does not appear to be associated with adverse fetal outcome.

INSULIN-INDUCED HYPOGLYCEMIA

Hypoglycemia represents the limiting factor in regimens emphasizing intensive insulin therapy for patients with type 1 diabetes. Most individuals with type 1 diabetes for more than a few years have no β-cell reserve as well as deficient α-cell (glucagon) response to hypoglycemia, thus placing them at increased risk for severe hypoglycemic reactions. Women with long-standing diabetes may also demonstrate deficient epinephrine, cortisol, and growth hormone responses to insulin-induced hypoglycemia. Such individuals commonly suffer an average of one to two symptomatic episodes of hypoglycemia each week. Temporarily disabling hypoglycemia with coma or seizure occurs in as many as 25% of type 1 individuals in the course of 1 year and causes 4% of deaths due to type 1 (62). The fear of severe hypoglycemia can be psychologically disabling for some patients and frightening for healthcare providers who must guide patients seeking improved glycemic control with intensified insulin regimens.

Cryer and Gerich (62) have categorized three pathophysiologic conditions that compromise defenses against hyperinsulinemia and are associated with a high frequency of iatrogenic hypoglycemia in individuals with type 1 diabetes. These are (a) hypoglycemia unawareness — the loss of neurogenic (autonomic) warning symptoms of developing hypoglycemia; (b) defective glucose counterregulation attributable to the combined deficiencies of glucagon and

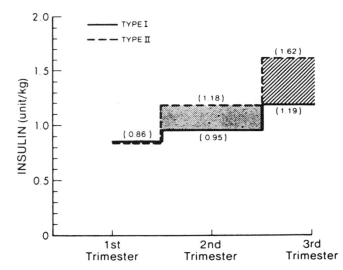

FIGURE 19-5. Triphasic pattern of insulin requirements by trimester of pregnancy for both type 1 and type 2 diabetes when corrected for weight. (From Langer O, Anyaegbunam A, Brustman L, et al. Pregestational diabetes: insulin requirements throughout pregnancy. *Am J Obstet Gynecol* 1988;159:616, with permission.)

epinephrine secretory responses to falling blood glucose concentrations; and (c) altered glycemic thresholds (lower plasma glucose concentrations required) for symptoms and activation of glucose counterregulatory systems during intensive therapy that effectively lowers overall plasma glucose concentrations. The above hypoglycemia-associated syndromes share pathophysiologic features including reduced autonomic response to hypoglycemia, yet are considered a separate entity from diabetic autonomic neuropathy.

Hypoglycemia may occur when excessive insulin is administered or not timed well in relation to meals or exercise. Less common etiologies include diminished endogenous production or reduced clearance of exogenous insulin as occurs in renal insufficiency. A review by the Diabetes Control and Complications Trial Research Group indicates that a large number of severe hypoglycemic episodes are not related to the above events (63). Thus, clinical research efforts have centered on glucose counterregulatory systems that are defective when mild or moderate hyperinsulinemia results in clinical hypoglycemia. It has also been hypothesized that recent antecedent hypoglycemia may play a role in the pathogenesis of hypoglycemia-associated autonomic insufficiency. Apparently, recent antecedent hypoglycemia results in substantially lower glucose levels required to produce both symptomatic and autonomic responses to subsequent hypoglycemia in nondiabetic individuals (64). This finding has been confirmed in patients with type 1 diabetes and thus explains how recurrent severe hypoglycemia can result in a "vicious cycle," as previous hypoglycemic episodes could reduce both hypoglycemia awareness and autonomic responses to the event (65). Avoidance of hypoglycemia in patients with type 1 diabetes who have hypoglycemia unawareness seems to ameliorate this problem, primarily by increasing β adrenegic sensitivity (66).

It has also been postulated that human insulin treatment compared with that of animal insulin may produce relative hypoglycemia unawareness. Heine et al. (67), using a hyperinsulinemic-hypoglycemic clamp technique, reported reduced autonomic symptoms and lower plasma norepinephrine levels to hypoglycemia produced by human insulin infusion compared to animal species. Other investigators have failed to confirm these results (68). One neuroglycopenic symptom, lack of concentration, may be more common during treatment with human insulin (69).

The risk of hypoglycemia during pregnancy is likely to be increased as feto-placental glucose consumption continues in the fasting state and exogenous insulin can limit other substrate availability. The effect of maternal hypoglycemia on early embryonic development has been unclear and ill defined with conflicting results reported in animal experimentation compared with human observational studies (70). Sadler and Hunter (70), using mouse embryos, demonstrated that glucose levels approximately 50% of normal were teratogenic and lower glucose concentrations

were lethal to the developing embryo. The dysmophogenic effects of hypoglycemia in rodent models may be observed with brief episodes of hypoglycemia (1 hour) during intervals coincident with the stages of neurulation. Freinkel (71) hypothesized that this period of sensitivity to hypoglycemia represented early embryonic dependence on glycolysis for metabolic energy. During late neurulation, brief periods of hypoglycemia did not produce a teratogenic effect. Freinkel (71) hypothesized that later in organogenesis, the embryo could utilize oxidative metabolism and alternative fuel sources.

Studies using a rabbit model indicate that the fetal brain is able to maintain energy metabolism during acute hypoglycemia via lactate utilization (72). There is no convincing evidence that hypoglycemia is teratogenic in human pregnancy, although caution is advised since study of subtle effects on neurobehavioral development would be difficult to execute and interpret. Of significance, however, is that both the Diabetes in Early Pregnancy Study and the California Diabetes in Pregnancy Project have failed to show an association between maternal hypoglycemic events and an increased risk for malformations in the offspring (73,74). Additionally, fetal death has not been associated with significant hypoglycemic reactions.

Our experience and that of others suggest that significant hypoglycemic episodes are more frequent during pregnancy. In a study of 35 pregnancies, significant hypoglycemia was recorded on 94 occasions (75). The risk was more pronounced during the first half of pregnancy. This observation, no doubt, stems from a combination of factors including more stringent attempts at glucose regulation following conception and increased tissue sensitivity to insulin with the attendant increase in peripheral glucose utilization. Hypoglycemia unawareness, which is associated with a reduced adrenomedullary epinephrine response to hypoglycemia, is more pronounced during gestation. Pregnant women will frequently report that hypoglycemia "sneaks up" on them faster and without warning when compared to their prepregnancy experience. Diamond et al. (76) confirmed an impaired counterregulatory hormone response to hypoglycemia in pregnant women with pregestational diabetes. Using a hypoglycemic clamp technique to lower glucose from 5.8 mM (105 mg/dL) to 2.5 mM (45 mg/dL) over 200 minutes in nine well-controlled patients, these investigators demonstrated a reduction in basal growth hormone levels and stimulated glucagon, cortisol, and epinephrine levels, when compared to nondiabetic controls. Rosenn et al. (77) have confirmed diminished counterregulatory epinephrine and growth hormone responses in clamp studies of 17 type 1 diabetic women during pregnancy. These data suggest that pregnant diabetic women do manifest a defective counterregulatory response to hypoglycemia that may be exacerbated by improved glucose control. Increasing insulin requirements and dosage may further impair this response by suppression of glucagon levels.

In contrast to the Diamond et al. (76) and Rosenn et al. (77) studies, Nisell et al. (78) reported that both hormonal and circulatory responses to acute hypoglycemia are not altered in diabetic women during pregnancy. These authors noted similar increases in epinephrine and norepinephrine as well as diminished cortisol and glucagon responses to the same degree in the group of nine diabetic women studied both during the third trimester and postpartum. Placental scintigraphy studies revealed no consistent changes in placental blood flow that was unrelated to glucose and catecholamine responses. The hormonal findings in this study might be explained in part by relatively high baseline cortisol levels during pregnancy that could prevent a further increase with hypoglycemia. However, the disparity between catecholamine responses in this study and that of Diamond et al. (76) cannot be fully explained. Nisell et al. (78) suggested that although the clamp technique allows a more precise definition of the hypoglycemic stimulus than the intravenous insulin tolerance testing used in his study, conclusions by Diamond et al. (76) could be questioned because nondiabetic control subjects were not studied during pregnancy. However, findings consistent with Diamond et al. (76) have been reported in diabetic patients under tight glycemic control.

Despite the above considerations, clinical efforts to improve glycemia during pregnancy have met with success and relatively little morbidity from insulin-induced hypoglycemia. The practitioner should carefully select those patients for whom some relaxation in glycemic control may be appropriate. With this consideration of safety in mind, patients must also be instructed to test glucose levels frequently and family members should be educated about the treatment of hypoglycemia including glucagon injections.

MANAGEMENT DURING LABOR AND DELIVERY

The goal of maintaining euglycemia during pregnancy is also important during labor and delivery. Hyperglycemia during labor significantly increases the frequency of neonatal hypoglycemia (79). Such morbidity may occur despite the presence of excellent control before the onset of labor. The intrapartum management of the diabetic patient, therefore, requires that careful attention be given to maternal glucose values, glucose infusion rate, and insulin dosage. In general, glucose determinations are made every 1 to 2 hours with a portable glucose reflectance meter at the bedside. A flow sheet to summarize these data is helpful.

Several approaches have been utilized to maintain maternal euglycemia during labor and delivery. Most investigators have employed a continuous infusion combining both insulin and glucose. Ten units of regular insulin are added to 1,000 ml of a 5% dextrose solution. An infusion rate of 100 to 125 ml/h usually results in good glucose control.

Insulin may also be infused from a syringe pump and adjusted to maintain normal glucose values. For women utilizing an insulin pump, insulin may be administered with this device. If significant hyperglycemia occurs, the pump should be discontinued and intravenous insulin administered.

Jovanovic and Peterson (80) have confirmed both the decreased need for insulin and the constant glucose requirement during the first stage of labor in a series of well-controlled patients. Using a glucose-controlled insulin infusion system, the Biostator, they demonstrated that insulin requirements fell to zero during the active first stage of labor while glucose infusion rates were maintained at 2.55 mg/kg/min to achieve blood glucose levels of 70 to 90 mg/dL. Oxytocin infusion did not appear to influence glucose control. Why insulin requirements fall during labor is poorly understood. This fall may reflect decreasing maternal levels of antiinsulin hormones produced by the placenta.

A simplified regimen has been devised by Jovanovic and Peterson (80) based on these data (Table 19-4). In well-controlled patients, the usual dose of NPH insulin is given at bedtime and the morning insulin dose is withheld. Once active labor begins or glucose levels fall below 68 mg/dL, the infusion is changed from saline to 5% dextrose and delivered at a rate of 2.5 mg/kg/min. Glucose values are recorded, and the infusion rate is adjusted accordingly. Regular insulin is administered if glucose values exceed 140 mg/dL. In general, the starting dose is 1 U/h. Insulin is often required during the second stage of labor as catecholamine levels rise.

In patients who undergo elective cesarean section, the procedure is scheduled for the early morning to simplify glucose control and maximize resources for neonatal care (Table 19-5). Patients are instructed to take their usual evening insulin dose on the day prior to delivery. The patient is given nothing by mouth, and the usual morning insulin dose is withheld. Prior to epidural anesthesia, patients should receive a "load" of a nonglucose-containing

TABLE 19-4. INSULIN MANAGEMENT DURING LABOR AND DELIVERY

Usual dose of intermediate-acting insulin is given at bedtime
Morning dose of insulin is withheld
Intravenous infusion of normal saline is begun
Once active labor begins or glucose levels fall to <70 mg/dL, the infusion is changed from saline to 5% dextrose and delivered at a rate of 2.5 mg/kg/min
Glucose levels are checked hourly using a portable reflectance meter, allowing for adjustment in the infusion rate
Regular (short-acting) insulin is administered by intravenous infusion if glucose levels are >140 mg/dL

Adapted from Jovanovic, L, Peterson CM. Insulin and glucose requirements during the first stage of labor in insulin dependent diabetic women. *Am J Med* 1983;75:607, with permission.

TABLE 19-5. INSULIN MANAGEMENT FOR ELECTIVE CESAREAN DELIVERY

Schedule for early morning to simplify glycemic control

Administer usual evening insulin dose on the day before delivery; patient ingests nothing by mouth after midnight

Usual morning insulin dose is withheld and glucose level is assessed at bedside before surgery and hourly thereafter

Dextrose is administered intravenously if glucose level is <70 mg/dL

Glycemic control is achieved and intravenous infusion of short-acting insulin

Before epidural anesthesia, patients should receive an intravenous load of a non-glucose-containing solution to reduce maternal hypotension

solution intravenously to reduce maternal hypotension. Epidural anesthesia is preferred because it enables the anesthesiologist to evaluate the mental state of the patient and detect potential hypoglycemia. After surgery, glucose levels are monitored every 2 hours and an intravenous solution of 5% dextrose is administered.

After delivery, insulin requirements are usually significantly reduced. The objective of strict control used in the antepartum period is relaxed. Patients who deliver vaginally and who are able to eat a regular diet are given one-half of their prepregnancy dose of NPH insulin on the morning of the first postpartum day. If the prepregnancy dose is unknown, we often prescribe one-third to one-half of the end of pregnancy dose. Similar reductions in insulin dosage are prescribed for women using insulin pump devices. Frequently, capillary glucose determinations help guide the insulin dosage. Sliding-scale insulin management is discouraged. Insulin should be prescribed based on careful review of previous and current glucose measurement as well as diet. If a patient has been given supplemental regular insulin in addition to the morning NPH dose, the amount of NPH insulin given on the following morning is increased by an amount equal to two-thirds of the additional regular insulin. With this method, most patients are stabilized within a few days of delivery.

Patients who undergo a cesarean delivery receive regular insulin during the first 24 to 48 hours postoperatively to maintain glucose values below 200 mg/dL. As their diet is advanced, NPH insulin is administered based on the regular insulin requirement of the preceding day. For women on pump therapy, basal insulin infusion rates are selected which represent roughly one-half of end-pregnancy doses. Similarly, boluses are reduced by a factor of one-third to one-half of end-pregnancy doses. All postpartum patients are encouraged to breast-feed. Insulin requirements may be somewhat lower in lactating women (see Chapter 32).

Most patients can be discharged from the hospital between 2 and 4 days postpartum, depending on the mode of delivery. Patients are encouraged to continue with self-monitoring techniques for glucose and to make additional adjustments in their daily insulin needs.

KEY POINTS

- Achieving optimal glucose control through utilization of insulin therapy is critical for success in the pregnancy complicated by type 1 diabetes.
- Frequent assessment of glycemic status with individual tailoring of insulin dosage is required.
- While not relaxing the objective of near physiologic control, the limitations of insulin replacement must be appreciated as well as the potential dangers of this important drug.
- The introduction of new analogues has expanded our options for treatment of insulin-dependent diabetes. These new preparations as well as awaited advancements in insulin delivery systems provide an exciting future for the care of pregnant diabetic women.

REFERENCES

1. Gabbe SG. Pregnancy in women with diabetes mellitus: the beginning. *Clin Perinatol* 1993;20:507–515.
2. White P. Diabetes in pregnancy. In: Joslin EP, ed. *The treatment of diabetes mellitus*, 4th ed. Philadelphia: Lea & Febiger, 1928.
3. Landon MB, Catalano PM, Gabbe SG. Diabetes mellitus and other endocrine diseases. In: Gabbe SG, Neibyl JR, Simpson JL, eds. *Obstetrics: normal and problem pregnancies*, 4th ed. New York: Churchill Livingston, 2002:chapter 33.
4. Galloway JA, Chance RE. Insulin agonist therapy: a challenge for the 1990s. *Clin Ther* 1990;12:460–472.
5. Schernthaner G. Immunogenecity and allergenic potential of animal and human insulins. *Diabetes Care* 1993;16:155–165.
6. Home PD, Massi-Benedetti M, Shepherd GAA, et al. A comparison of the activity and disposal of semi-synthetic human insulin and porcine insulin in normal man by the glucose clamp technique. *Diabetologia* 1982;22:41–45.
7. Gregory R, Edwards S, Yakman NA. Demonstration of insulin transformation products in insulin vials by high performance liquid chromatography. *Diabetes Care* 1991;14:42–48.
8. Binder C, Lawritzen T, Faber O, et al. Insulin pharmacokinetics. *Diabetes Care* 1984;7:188–195.
9. Jovanovic L, Mills JL, Peterson CM. Anti-insulin antibody titers do not influence control or insulin requirements in early pregnancy. *Diabetes Care* 1984;7:68–75.
10. Heding LG, Larsson Y, Luduigsson J. The immunogenicity of insulin preparation: antibody levels before and after transfer to highly purified porcine insulin. *Diabetologia* 1980;19:511–516.
11. The American Diabetes Association. Position statement: insulin administration. *Diabetes Care* 1994;16[Suppl 2]:31–34.
12. Mylvaganam R, Stowers JM, Steel JM, et al. Insulin immunogenecity in pregnancy: maternal and fetal studies. *Diabetologia* 1983;24:19–26.
13. Ziegler AG, Hillebrand B, Rabl W, et al. On the appearance of islet associated autoimmunity in offspring of diabetic mothers: a prospective study from birth. *Diabetologia* 1993;36:402–408.
14. Jovanovic L. Role of diet and insulin treatment of diabetes in pregnancy. *Clin Obstet Gynecol* 2000;43:46–55.
15. Menon RK, Cohen RM, Sperling MA, et al. Transplacental passage of insulin in pregnant women with IDDM: its role in fetal macrosomia. *N Engl J Med* 1990;323:309–315.
16. Rosenn B, Miodovnik M, Coombs CA, et al. Human versus animal insulin in the management of insulin-dependent diabetes: lack of effect on fetal growth. *Obstet Gynecol* 1991;78:590–593.

17. Baker RS, Ross JW, Schmidtke JR, et al. Preliminary studies on the immunogenecity and amount of Escherichia insulina coli polypeptides in biosynthetic human insulin produced by recombinant DNA technology. *Lancet* 1981;2(8256):1139–1142.

18. Grammer LC, Roberts M, Patterson R. IgE and IgG antibody against human (rDNA) insulin in patients with systemic insulin allergy. *J Lab Clin Med* 1985;105:108–113.

19. Schernthaner G, Borkenstein M, Fink M, et al. Immunogenicity of human insulin (Novo) or pork monocomponent insulin in HLA-DR-typed insulin dependent diabetic individuals. *Diabetes Care* 1983;6[Suppl 1]:43–48.

20. Fineberg SE, Galloway JA, Fineberg NS, et al. Immunogenicity of human insulin of recombinant DNA origin. *Diabetologia* 1983;25:465–469.

21. Marshall MO, Heding LG, Villumsen J, et al. Development of insulin antibodies, metabolic control and B-cell function in newly diagnosed insulin dependent diabetic children treated with monocomponent human insulin or monocomponent porcine insulin. *Diabetes Res* 1988;9:169–175.

22. Jovanovic L, Ilic S, Pettit DJ, et al. Metabolic and immunologic effects of insulin lispro in gestational diabetes. *Diabetes Care* 1999;22:2533–2537.

23. Lindholm A, Jensen LB, Home PD, et al. Immune responses to insulin aspart and biphasic insulin aspart in people with type 1 and type 2 diabetes. *Diabetes Care* 2002;25:876–882.

24. Hedman CA, Lindstrom T, Arnquist HJ, et al. Direct comparison of insulin lispro and aspart shows small differences in plasma insulin profiles after subcutaneous injection in type 1 diabetes. *Diabetes Care* 2001;24:1120–1121.

25. Raskin P, Guthrie RA, Leiter L, et al. Use of insulin aspart, a fast-acting insulin analog, as the mealtime insulin in the management of patients with type 1 diabetes. *Diabetes Care* 2001;23:583–588.

26. Lalli C, Ciofetta M, Del Sindeco P, et al. Long-term intensive treatment of type 1 diabetes with the rapid-acting insulin analog lispro in variable combination therapy with NPH insulin at mealtime. *Diabetes Care* 1992;22:468–477.

27. Frohnauer MK, Anderson JH. Lack of consistent definitions of the pharmacokinetics of human insulin. *Diabetes* 1991;40[Suppl 1]:460a(abst).

28. Sestoft L, Volund A, Gammeltoft S. The biological properties of human insulin. *Acta Med Scand* 1982;212:21–28.

29. Pramming S. Lauritzen T, Thorsteinsson B, et al. Absorption of soluble and isophane semi-synthetic human and porcine insulin in insulin-dependent diabetic subjects. *Acta Endocrinol* 1984;105:215–220.

30. Botterman P, Gyaram H, Wahl K, et al. Pharmacokinetics of biosynthetic human insulin and characteristics of its effect. *Diabetes Care* 1981;4:168–169.

31. Heinemann L, Chantelan EA, Starke AAR. Pharmacokinetics and pharmacodynamics of subcutaneously administered U40 and U100 formulation of regular human insulin. *Diabetic Metab* 1992;18:21–24.

32. Kitzmiller JL, Main EK, Ward B. Insulin lispro and the development of proliferative retinopathy during pregnancy. *Diabetes Care* 1999;22:873–875.

33. Buchbinder A, Miodovnik M, McElvy S. Is insulin lispro a culprit in the progression of diabetic retinopathy during pregnancy? *Am J Obstet Gynecol* 2000;182:1162–1164.

34. Pettit DJ, Kolaczynski JW, Ospina P, et al. Comparison of an insulin analog, insulin aspart and regular human insulin with no insulin in gestational diabetes mellitus. *Diabetes Care* 2003;26:183–186.

35. Galloway JA, Spradlin CT, Root MA, et al. The plasma glucose response of normal fasting subjects to neutral regular and NPH biosynthetic human and purified pork insulins. *Diabetes Care* 1981;4:183–188.

36. Owens DR, Jones IR, Birtwell AJ, et al. Study of porcine and human isophane (NPH) insulins in normal subjects. *Diabetologia* 1984;26:261–265.

37. Massi-Bendetti M, Bueti A, Mannino D, et al. Kinetics and metabolic activity of biosynthetic NPH insulin evaluated by the glucose clamp technique. *Diabetes Care* 1984;7:132–136.

38. Hilderbrandt P, Birch K, Sestoft L, et al. Dose dependent subcutaneous absorption of porcine, bovine, and human NPH insulins. *Acta Med Scand* 1984;215:69–73.

39. Francis AJ, Home PD, Hanning I, et al. Intermediate acting insulin given at bedtime: effect on blood glucose concentrations before and after breakfast. *BMJ* 1983;286:173–176.

40. Landon MB, Gabbe SG. Glucose monitoring and insulin administration in the pregnant diabetic patient. *Clin Obstet Gynecol* 1985;28:496–506.

41. Seigler DE, Olsson GM, Agramonte RF, et al. Pharmacokinetics of long acting (ultralente) insulin preparations. *Diabetes Nutr Metab* 1991;4:267–273.

42. Holman RR, Steemson J, Darling P, et al. Human ultralente insulin. *BMJ* 1984;288:665–668.

43. Fanelli CG, Pampanelli S, Porcellati F, et al. Administration of neural protamine Hagedorn insulin at bedtime versus with dinner in type 1 diabetes mellitus to avoid nocturnal hypoglycemia and improve control. A randomized, controlled trial. *Ann Intern Med* 2002;136:504–514.

44. Yki-Jarvinen H, Dresler A, Ziemen M. Less nocturnal hypoglycemia and better post-dinner glucose control with bedtime insulin glargine compared with bedtime NPH insulin during insulin combination therapy in type 2 diabetes. *Diabetes Care* 2000;23:1130–1136.

45. Devlin JT, Hothersall L, Wilkis JL. Use of insulin glargine during pregnancy in a type 1 diabetic woman. *Diabetes Care* 2002;25:1095–1096.

46. Kurtzhals P, Schaffer L, Sorensen A, et al. Correlations of receptor binding and metabolic and mitogenic potencies of insulin analogs designed for clinical use. *Diabetes* 2000;49(6):999–1005.

47. Hermansen K, Madshab S, Perrild H, et al. Comparison of the soluble basal insulin analog insulin detemir with NPH insulin: a randomized, open crossover trial in type 1 diabetic subjects on basal-bolus therapy. *Diabetes Care* 2001;24:296–301.

48. Koivisto VA, Felig P. Alterations in insulin absorption in diabetic patients. *N Engl J Med* 1989;92:59–61.

49. Galloway JA, Spradlin CT, Howey DC, et al. Intrasubject differences in pharmacokinetic and pharmacodynamic responses: the immutable problem of present-day treatment? In: Serrano-Rios M, Leferbre PJ, eds. *Diabetes 1985: proceedings of the 12th Congress of the International Diabetes Federation.* Madrid, September 1985:23–28. (Also available in International Congress Series no. 700. Amsterdam: Excerpta Medica, 1986:877–886.)

50. Zinman B, Vranic M, Albisser AM, et al. The role of insulin in the metabolic response to exercise in diabetic man. *Diabetes* 1979;28[Suppl 1]:76–81.

51. Santiago JV, Clarke WL, Arias F. Studies with a pancreatic beta cell simulator in the third trimester of pregnancies complicated by diabetes. *Am J Obstet Gynecol* 1978;132:455–460.

52. Natrass M, Alberti KGMM, Dennis KJ, et al. A glucose controlled insulin infusion system for diabetic women during labor. *BMJ* 1978;2:599–603.

53. Peden NR, Braaten JT, McKendry JBR. Diabetic ketoacidosis during long term treatment with continuous subcutaneous insulin infusion. *Diabetes Care* 1984;7:1–7.

54. Coustan DR, Reece EA, Sherwin RS, et al. A randomized clinical trial of the insulin pump vs. intensive conventional therapy in diabetic pregnancies. *JAMA* 1986;255:631–636.

55. Gabbe SG, Holing E, Temple P. Benefits, risks, costs, and patient satisfaction associated with insulin pump therapy for the preg-

nancy complicated by type 1 diabetes mellitus. *Am J Obstet Gynecol* 2000;182:1283–1285.

56. Bode BW, Weinstein R, Bell D, et al. Comparison of insulin aspart with buffered regular insulin and insulin lispro in continuous subcutaneous insulin infusion: a randomized study in type 1 diabetes. *Diabetes Care* 2002;25:439–444.

57. Jovanovic L, Druzin M, Peterson CM. Effect of euglycemia on the outcome of pregnancy in insulin-dependent diabetic women as compared with normal control subjects. *Am J Med* 1981; 7:921–927.

58. Langer O, Anyaegbunam A, Brustman L, et al. Pregestational diabetes: insulin requirements throughout pregnancy. *Am J Obstet Gynecol* 1988;159:616–621.

59. Malins J. *Clinical diabetes mellitus.* London: Eyre and Spottiswoode, 1968.

60. McManus R, Ryan EA. Insulin requirements in insulin-dependent and insulin requiring gestational diabetic women during the final month of pregnancy. *Diabetes Care* 1992;15:1323–1327.

61. Steel JM, Johnstone FD, Hume R, et al. Insulin requirements during pregnancy in women with type I diabetes. *Obstet Gynecol* 1994;83:253–258.

62. Cryer PE, Gerich JE. Hypoglycemia in insulin dependent diabetes mellitus: insulin excess and defective glucose counterregulation. In: Rifkin H, Porte D, eds. *Ellenberg and Rifkin's diabetes mellitus: theory and practice,* 4th ed. New York: Elsevier, 1990: 526–546.

63. Diabetes Control and Complications Trial Research Group. Epidemiology of severe hypoglycemia in the diabetes control and complications trial. *Am J Med* 1991;90:450–459.

64. Cryer PE. Iatrogenic hypoglycemia as a cause of hypoglycemia — associated autonomic failure in IDDM: a vicious cycle. *Diabetes* 1992;41:255–260.

65. Cryer PE. Hypoglycemia: the limiting factor in the glycemic management of type I and type II diabetes. *Diabetologia* 2002; 45:937–948.

66. Fritsche A, Stefan N, Haring H, et al. Avoidance of hypoglycemia restores hypoglycemia awareness by increasing beta-adrenergic sensitivity in type 1 diabetes. *Ann Intern Med* 2002;134:729–736.

67. Heine RJ, van der Heyden EA, van der Veen EA. Responses to human and porcine insulin in healthy subjects. *Lancet* 1989;2(8669):946–949.

68. Kern W, Lieb K, Kerner W, et al. Differential effects of human and pork insulin induced hypoglycemia on neuronal function in humans. *Diabetes* 1990;39:1091–1098.

69. Berger W, Keller U, Honegger B, et al. Warming symptoms of hypoglycemia during treatment with human and porcine insulin in diabetes mellitus. *Lancet* 1989;i;1041–1044.

70. Sadler TW, Hunter ES III. Hypoglycemia: how little is too much for the embryo? *Am J Obstet Gynecol* 1987;157:190–193.

71. Freinkel N. Diabetic embryopathy and fuel-mediated organ teratogenesis: lessons from animal models. *Horm Metab Res* 1988; 20:463–475.

72. Lapidot A, Harber S. Effect of acute insulin-induced hypoglycemia on fetal versus adult brain fuel utilization, assessed by (13)C MRS isotopomer analysis of [U-(13)C] glucose metabolites. *Dev Neurosci* 2000;22:444–455.

73. Mills JL, Knopp RH, Simpson JP, et al. Lack of relations of increased malformation rates in infants of diabetic mothers to glycemic control during organogenesis. *N Engl J Med* 1988; 318:671–676.

74. Kitzmiller JL, Gavin LA, Gin GD, et al. Preconception management of diabetes continued through early pregnancy prevents the excess frequency of major congenital anomalies in infants of diabetic mothers. *JAMA* 1991;265:731–736.

75. Kimmerle R, Heinemann L, Delecki A, et al. Severe hypoglycemia incidence and predisposing factors in 85 pregnancies of type I diabetic women. *Diabetes Care* 1992;15:1034–1037.

76. Diamond MP, Reece EA, Caprio S, et al. Impairment of counterregulatory hormone responses to hypoglycemia in pregnant women with insulin-dependent diabetes mellitus. *Am J Obstet Gynecol* 1992;166:70–77.

77. Rosenn BM, Miodovnik M, Khoury JC, et al. Counterregulatory hormonal responses to hypoglycemia during pregnancy. *Obstet Gynecol* 1996;87:568–574.

78. Nisell H, Persson B, Hanson V, et al. Hormonal, metabolic, and circulatory response to insulin-induced hypoglycemia in pregnant and nonpregnant women with insulin-dependent diabetes. *Am J Perinatol* 1994;11:231–236.

79. Taylor R, Lee C, Kyne-Grzebalski D, et al. Clinical outcomes of pregnancy in women with type 1 diabetes. *Obstet Gynecol* 2002;99:537–541.

80. Jovanovic L, Peterson CM. Insulin and glucose requirements during the first stage of labor in insulin dependent diabetic women. *Am J Med* 1983;75:607.

20

DIETARY MANAGEMENT

BARBARA LUKE

HISTORICAL PERSPECTIVE

Before the discovery of insulin by Banting and Best in 1921, the association between diabetes mellitus and pregnancy was almost nonexistent: women with diabetes had irregular ovulatory cycles and rarely conceived. Among the few who did become pregnant, the perinatal mortality rate for their infants was greater than 42% (1). Before insulin therapy, diabetic diets included regimens with as much as 85% to 90% of calories from fat, alternating with days restricted to only vegetables, fasting, or severe caloric restriction. The first physician of the preinsulin era who focused specifically on the diets of pregnant women with diabetes was Joslin (2). He recommended a low-carbohydrate and moderate fat and protein diet; fasting was advised when excessive glycosuria was present.

The use of starvation therapy during the early years of insulin availability resulted in general malnutrition, delayed puberty, anovulation, and reduced fertility in many women with diabetes (3). When insulin therapy was combined with a more liberal diet, fertility rose dramatically. The publication of exchange lists by the American Diabetes Association (ADA) in 1950 simplified the calculation and planning of diabetic diets, although the prevailing philosophy for pregnant women with diabetes limited sodium intake and restricted weight gain to 12 lb or less (4,5).

As a result of improved metabolic and dietary management of pregnant women with diabetes in recent years, perinatal mortality rates are now comparable with those of the nondiabetic general population (6), although they are still several fold higher for women with type 2 diabetes mellitus, mainly due to an excess of late fetal deaths (7). During recent years, diet therapy for diabetes has grown to include such areas as glycemic responses of various foods, soluble versus insoluble fibers, the role of monounsaturated fats, and the use of artificial sweeteners. This chapter discusses the nutritional requirements during pregnancy and the special considerations when pregnancy is complicated by diabetes.

NUTRITIONAL NEEDS DURING PREGNANCY

Metabolic Alterations of Pregnancy and Diabetes

Pregnancy itself results in alterations in metabolism, including reductions in fasting blood glucose and plasma insulin, and elevations in postprandial glucose, free fatty acids (FFAs), plasma ketones, insulin resistance, and plasma cholesterol and triglycerides. Insulin requirements during pregnancy increase two- to three-fold as a result of the rise in estrogen, progesterone, human placental lactogen, and possibly placental insulinase. Diabetes further potentiates the metabolic alterations of pregnancy. There is a relative deficiency of insulin, due to tissue resistance, decreased production, and increased degradation. Elevations in plasma glucose, FFAs, triglycerides, and branched chain amino acids result from this insulin deficiency (see Chapter 10 for more detail).

Pregestational versus Gestational Diabetes

During pregnancy, the nutritional management of pregestational and gestational diabetes differs, depending only on whether insulin is used. With insulin therapy, meal timing and the inclusion of snacks must be matched to the insulin schedule. The nutritional requirements for women with diabetes during pregnancy are the same regardless of whether they are receiving insulin therapy. Gestational diabetes mellitus is the most common metabolic disorder of pregnancy. Most women are treated with diet therapy alone, which has been shown to reduce the rate of accelerated fetal growth (8).

Recommended Dietary Allowances

In the United States, the recommended dietary allowances (RDAs) of the Food and Nutrition Board of the National

Academy of Sciences provide the foundation for dietary recommendations, including during pregnancy (9). The most current edition of the RDAs includes recommendations for 19 nutrients, as well as estimated minimum requirements (EMRs) of sodium, chloride, and potassium, and the estimated safe and adequate daily dietary intakes of biotin, pantothenic acid, copper, manganese, fluoride, chromium, and molybdenum. A summary of the 1999 dietary reference intakes for adult women before and during pregnancy is given in Table 20-1.

According to national survey data, most women of childbearing age consume diets that meet or exceed the RDAs for most nutrients (10). Nutrients most likely to be present at 80% or less of the RDA in women's diets include vitamin B6, calcium, magnesium, iron, zinc, and copper (10). Food sources rich in these nutrients (meats, poultry, fish, and dairy products) are all recommended in additional amounts during pregnancy.

The diet prescribed for pregestational or gestational diabetes has changed dramatically in recent decades and is much more like the diet of the general nondiabetic population. The challenge is to meet the nutritional requirements of pregnancy while maintaining good metabolic control of the diabetes. The current dietary prescription for patients with diabetes includes 10% to 20% of calories as protein and the remainder of calories divided between carbohydrate and fat according to the individual's glucose, lipid, and weight profile (11).

Caloric Requirement and Gestational Weight Gain

During pregnancy, energy is required for the synthesis of the fetal-placental unit and maternal tissues, resulting in a 15% to 26% increase in maternal metabolic rate (12). As recommended in the 1990 report on nutrition during pregnancy by the National Academy of Sciences (13), the caloric intake during pregnancy should be based on the pregnant woman's pregravid weight and appropriate rate of weight gain to achieve the optimal total gestational weight gain. For the normal weight woman, the caloric requirement during pregnancy is calculated as 36 kcal/kg/day (2,200 kcal/day) for the first trimester, increasing to 40 kcal/kg/day (2,500 kcal/day) during the second and third trimesters (13). Jovanovic-Peterson and Peterson (14), as well as the American Diabetes Association (11), recommend 30 kcal/kg/day for normal weight women (80% to 120% of ideal body weight), 40 kcal/kg/day for underweight women (<80% ideal body weight), and 24 kcal/kg/day for overweight women (>120% ideal body weight), based on the concept of sustaining women above the ketonuric threshold while preventing postprandial hyperglycemia. These daily caloric allowances translate into weight gains of about 25 to 35 lb, as 3.5 lb during the first trimester and about 1 lb/wk during the second and third trimesters for normal weight women; 28 to 40 lb for underweight women, as 5 lb during the first trimester and slightly more than 1 lb/wk during the second and third trimesters; and 15 to 25 lb for overweight women, as 2 lb during the first trimester and about 0.67 lb/wk during the second and third trimesters (13).

The caloric requirement and subsequent weight gain in overweight women with and without diabetes during pregnancy is controversial. Although there is concern regarding the potential adverse fetal effect of maternal ketonuria with insufficient caloric intake, studies of overweight pregnant women with diabetes have shown improved pregnancy outcomes with moderate caloric restriction (25 kcal/kg/day or 1,800 to 2,000 kcal/day) (15,16). Severe maternal ketosis, which would affect maternal acid-base balance, should be avoided because it would adversely affect both the mother and her fetus. With severe caloric restriction (<1,200 kcal/day), ketonuria may occur, and prolonged in utero exposure may be associated with neurodevelopmental problems in the offspring (17). Ketosis can be avoided by giving small, frequent meals containing slowly absorbed carbohydrates, as the attenuated insulin response induced tends to delay lipolysis and ketogenesis between meals (18). Based on their extensive research, Dornhorst and Frost (8) recom-

TABLE 20-1. SUMMARY OF DIETARY REFERENCE INTAKES FOR ADULT WOMEN, AGES 19–50 BEFORE AND DURING PREGNANCY

Nutrient	Nonpregnant	Pregnant
Protein (g/day)	50	65
Vitamin A (μg RE/day)	800	1300
Vitamin E (mg α-TE/day)	8	12
Vitamin K (μg/day)	65	65
Vitamin C (mg/day)	60	95
Iron (mg/day)	15	30
Zinc (mg)	12	15
Iodine (μg/day)	150	175
Selenium (μg/day)	55	65
Calcium (mg/day)	1000	1000
Phosphorus (mg/day)	700	700
Magnesium (mg/day)	310 (320)[a]	350 (360)
Vitamin D (μg/day)	5	5
Fluoride (mg/day)	3	3
Thiamin (mg/day)	1.1	1.4
Riboflavin (mg/day)	1.1	1.4
Niacin (mg/day)	14	18
Vitamin B-6 (mg/day)	1.3	1.9
Folate (μg/day)	400	600
Vitamin B-12 (μg/day)	2.4	2.6
Pantothenic acid (mg/day)	5	6
Biotin (μg/day)	30	30
Choline (mg/day)	425	450

[a]Values in parentheses are for ages 31–50 years, when different from recommendations for ages 19–30 years.
From National Academy of Sciences, *Dietary reference intakes.* Washington, DC: National Academy Press, 1999.

mend that women with a prepregnancy BMI above 34 (e.g., a 64″ woman with a prepregnancy weight of 200 pounds) remain weight neutral during pregnancy.

Carbohydrates

Types and Percentage of Calories

Dietary management of diabetes needs to focus on reducing postprandial hyperglycemia, thereby lessening fetal exposure. This can be achieved by either limiting carbohydrate at the expense of increasing dietary fat or by increasing the use of low glycemic index carbohydrates. The recommended carbohydrate content of the diabetic diet has risen steadily from 20% in 1921 to 55% to 60% in 1986. Higher carbohydrate recommendations have been used by various investigators, including 60%, 65%, and 85%, resulting in improved glycemic control and lowered exogenous insulin requirements (19–23). The most current ADA guidelines suggest individualization of the percentage of calories from carbohydrates (11), but levels of 40% to 50% may be more appropriate during pregnancy to maintain euglycemia (24). With the use of more low glycemic index carbohydrates, up to 60% of the total dietary energy can be given in this form without a detrimental effect on glucose tolerance (25). Low glycemic index diets are also associated with a reduction in insulin sensitivity (26). A euglycemic diet, designed to blunt postprandial hyperglycemia, has been shown to be effective. The postprandial blood glucose level is influenced by the carbohydrate content of the meal (27). In pregnancies complicated by diabetes, the postprandial blood glucose level is a major factor in the development of neonatal macrosomia (28). Women who are insulin resistant may need to reduce the carbohydrate content of their diets to 40% of calories.

Traditionally, diet therapy for diabetes has been based on the concept that there are two main classes of carbohydrates: *simple* or *refined* (glucose, sucrose, and fructose), which are rapidly absorbed and cause a relatively large rise in blood glucose, and *complex* or *starches* (such as rice, potatoes, and legumes), which are digested and absorbed more slowly and result in a smaller rise in blood glucose. Complex carbohydrates with fiber, such as whole-grain breads and cereals, brown rice, and fresh fruits and vegetables, should be substituted for simple or refined carbohydrates whenever possible. Sucrose may be used in modest amounts, depending on the degree of metabolic control. If used, it should be included in meals with other foods and preferably additional fiber.

Glycemic Index

Individuals with diabetes have traditionally been counseled to avoid simple sugars in the belief that these specific carbohydrates would result in hyperglycemia and poor meta-

bolic control of the disease. Recent studies, however, have shown that the glycemic response of a specific carbohydrate food, whether simple or complex, is influenced by three factors: (1) the amount of processing and preparation (cooked or uncooked); (2) the amount and type of dietary fiber also in the food and other foods ingested at the same meal; and (3) the nature of the carbohydrate itself, including ripeness and digestability of the starch component (29,30). For example, studies have shown that glucose, potatoes, and honey produce similar postprandial glucose responses, whereas rice, beans, and fructose yield a similar but lower glycemic response (31,32). Different glycemic responses have been observed even when a single food is prepared in different ways: whole rice results in a flatter glycemic response curve than does the ingestion of rice flour, and wheat in pasta produces a lower blood glucose than does wheat in bread (33,34). Jenkins et al. (31) suggested the use of a glycemic index to characterize foods, based on the blood glucose response to a food in comparison with the response to an equivalent amount of glucose (Table 20-2). Using this standard of evaluation, legumes, peas, and soybeans produce the lowest glycemic response, whereas potatoes and carrots elicit the highest. Also, the incorporation of simple sugars into processed foods (35) or meals (36) does not aggravate postprandial hyperglycemia. Recent studies have demonstrated a significant relationship between a diet with a high glycemic load and exacerbation of the proinflammatory process (37). To date, the glycemic index and the effect of incorporating simple sugars into the diet has been evaluated only in nonpregnant individuals with diabetes; their use in pregnancies complicated by diabetes remains to be determined.

Artificial Sweeteners

The use of sugar substitutes or artificial sweeteners is neither needed nor necessary for individuals with diabetes. They may be helpful, though, in complying with the recommendation to avoid simple sugars. Currently, four sugar substitutes or artificial sweeteners are on the market: saccharin, aspartame, acesulfame-K, and Sucralose. Saccharin, a petroleum derivative, is not metabolized by the body and is excreted unchanged by the kidneys. Stable in heat and in solution, saccharin has a relative sweetness 300 times that of sucrose. In 1977, the Food and Drug Administration (FDA) proposed a ban on saccharin because it had been shown to be a weak carcinogen in animals. Because of public opposition to the ban, Congress passed the Saccharin Study and Labeling Act, which permitted continued use of the sweetener pending further studies. Presently, the saccharin moratorium has been extended seven times. The consumption of saccharin has dropped dramatically since the introduction of aspartame in 1981. Saccharin can cross the placenta, although there is no evidence that it is harmful to the fetus.

TABLE 20-2. GLYCEMIC INDEX OF COMMON FOODS

Glycemic index ≥100%	***Glycemic index 50%–80%***
Breads, grains, and cereals	**Breads, grains, and cereals**
Bagels	Pasta
Bread stuffing	All-bran cereal
Cheerios cereal	Pumpernickel bread
Corn Chex cereal	Special K cereal
Corn flakes cereal	Sweet corn, canned
Corn chips snacks	**Fruits and vegetables**
Crispix cereal	Baked beans
French bread	Bananas
Golden Grahams cereal	Garbanzo beans
Puffed rice cereal	Grapes
Puffed wheat cereal	Kidney beans (canned)
Rice Chex cereal	Navy beans
Rice Krispies cereal	Oranges
Total cereal	Orange juice
White bread	Peas
Fruits and vegetables	Pinto beans
Baked potatoes	Popcorn
Carrots	Sweet potatoes
Instant rice	Yams
Instant potato	***Glycemic index 30%–50%***
Parsnips	**Breads, grains, and cereals**
Watermelon	Barley
Glycemic index 80%–100%	Oatmeal (slow-cooking)
Breads, grains, and cereals	Whole grain rye bread
Bran Chex cereal	**Fruits and vegetables**
Brown rice	Apples
Cream of wheat	Apple juice
Grapenuts cereal	Applesauce
Hamburger bun	Apricots (dried)
Instant mashed potatoes	Black-eyed peas
Life cereal	Chick peas
Macaroni and cheese	Grapefruit
Oat bran	Kidney beans (dried)
Rolled oats	Lentils
Rye Krisp	Lima beans
Shredded wheat	Peaches
White rice	Pears
Whole wheat bread	Tomato soup
Fruits and vegetables	**Dairy products**
Apricots	Ice cream
Mango	Milk
Papaya	Yogurt
Pineapple	***Glycemic index ≤30%***
Raisins	Cherries
	Peanuts
	Peas
	Plums
	Soybeans

Aspartame (NutraSweet) is a dipeptide of L-aspartic acid and L-phenylalanine methyl ester, which is metabolized in the intestine to aspartate, phenylalanine, and methanol. Aspartame was approved by the FDA as a tabletop sweetener and for several dry product applications in 1981 and for carbonated beverages in 1983. Aspartame is 180 to 200 times sweeter than sugar, and its use is estimated to be equal to 25% of the total sugar intake in the United States. The primary limitation of this sweetener is its susceptibility to hydrolysis and loss of sweetness at high temperatures and alkaline or neutral pH values. An encapsulated form of aspartame may soon permit the use of this sweetener in baked products, although FDA approval is still pending. The use of aspartame during pregnancy has been investigated. Aspartic acid does not readily cross the placenta, and methanol levels are only minimally elevated. Phenylalanine, the third breakdown product of aspartame, does cross the placenta, and fetal levels can be 1.3 times higher than maternal levels (38). Maternal phenylalanine levels have been found to be consistently below toxic levels, even at twice the FDA acceptable daily intake of this sweetener (38,39).

Acesulfame-K, a potassium salt of a cyclic sulfonamide, is 200 times sweeter than sugar. It is marketed under the brand names of Sunette, Sweet One, and Swiss Sweet. It has a synergistic sweetening effect with other sweeteners and an excellent shelf life and is heat stable. Like saccharin, it is not metabolized by the body and is excreted unchanged by the kidneys. In high concentrations, acesulfame-K has a bitter aftertaste. Extensive testing has not demonstrated the use of acesulfame-K to be harmful during pregnancy.

Sucralose, a nonnutritive, high-intensity sweetener made from a process that begins with sucrose, is about 600 times sweeter than sugar. It was approved in 1998 for use in baked goods, baking mixes, nonalcoholic beverages, chewing gum, and coffee and tea products, as well as many other foods. Extensive testing has shown it to be safe.

Fiber

Dietary fiber is defined as all components of food that are resistant to hydrolysis by digestion. Dietary fiber is found exclusively in plant foods, including cereal grains, legumes, and fruits and vegetables. Dietary fiber is one of two types: water soluble or water insoluble. Water-soluble fiber, such as pectins, gums, and polysaccharides, influences glucose and insulin levels by delaying the intestinal absorption of nutrients, resulting in a more gradual rise in blood glucose. Foods high in water-soluble fibers include fruits (especially citrus and apples), oats, barley, and legumes. Water-insoluble fiber, such as cellulose, lignin, and most hemicelluloses, have a greater effect on increasing gastrointestinal transit times and fecal bulk and less effect on plasma glucose and insulin levels. Foods high in water-insoluble fiber include wheat flour, cereals, and bran.

Although dietary fiber was effectively used to control hyperglycemia with the inclusion of oatmeal in the diabetic diet by von Noorden in 1903 (40), the therapeutic effects of dietary fiber on postprandial glycemic and serum insulin responses in people with diabetes were not clinically demonstrated until 1976 (41,42). Studies of nonpregnant patients with diabetes show beneficial effects of high-carbohydrate, high-fiber, low-fat diets, including decreased postprandial hyperglycemia, mean plasma glucose, glycosuria, and insulin requirement (43–46). Recent studies in pregnancy using high-carbohydrate, high-fiber diets are not in total agreement. Ney et al. (22) reported that such diets result in lower insulin requirements and better glycemic control of diabetes during pregnancy, whereas Reece et al. (47,48) did not find a significant difference between glycemic control and insulin requirements when these diets were used in pregnant patients with diabetes. Daily consumption of 20 to 35 g of dietary fiber from both soluble and insoluble fibers is recommended (11).

Protein

The recommended dietary allowance for protein is 65 g/day (9). The optimal percentage of calories from protein has not been determined, although most diets range from 12% to 20%. This allowance must provide for both the maternal physiologic adjustments and the growth and development of the fetus and placenta. The RDA for protein is generous because of uncertainties regarding the efficiency of protein storage and use during pregnancy, as well as potential adverse effects from an inadequate intake. Because most amino acids are gluconeogenic, it has traditionally been believed that high-protein diets for individuals with diabetes help stabilize glucose levels by providing a substrate for glucose production when needed. Because of the interrelationship among glucose, protein, and fatty acid metabolism, dietary protein in excess of needs will result in a compensatory increase in blood levels of glucose and fatty acids.

Fat

To achieve normoglycemia, dietary fat can be liberalized up to 40% of calories (24). High-fat diets should be avoided, as they can induce insulin resistance as well as being potentially β-cell toxic (49). Saturated fat, found mainly in animal fats, meats, hydrogenated shortenings, palm oil, coconut oil, cocoa butter, whole milk dairy products, and commercial baked goods, should be limited to one-third of fat calories or less. Monounsaturated fat, found mainly in canola oil, olive oil, and peanut oil, should account for one-third or more of calories from fat. The remaining calories from fat should come from polyunsaturated fats, as found in vegetable oils and fish oils. Supplementation with fish oil and polyunsaturated fatty acids has been shown to reduce hypertension and serum triglycerides, while also slightly increasing LDL cholesterol concentration in diabetic patients (50,51).

MEAL PLANNING APPROACHES

General Considerations

Although the nutritional needs of women with gestational diabetes and pregestational diabetes are similar, some differences do exist in approaches to meal planning. In all cases, however, food, and particularly carbohydrates, must be balanced with insulin (either exogenous or endogenous production) to achieve appropriate glycemia. Individual adjustments in meal planning according to a patient's lifestyle, exercise, cultural habits, or preferences are the cornerstone of successful nutrition counseling for diabetes.

Recommended distribution of calories among meals (Table 20-3) is similar for gestational and pregestational diabetes. However, controversy exists over the number of snacks for women with gestational diabetes (11). Some rec-

TABLE 20-3. CALORIE AND CARBOHYDRATE DISTRIBUTION TO MAINTAIN NORMOGLYCEMIA

Meal	Calories (%)
Breakfast	10–15
Snack	5–10
Lunch	20–30
Snack	5–10
Dinner	20–30
Snack	5–10

ommend three meals with only a bedtime snack for obese women with gestational diabetes (52,53). Others have advised smaller meals with appropriate between-meal snacks.

Restriction of calories at breakfast to 10% to 15% of the total is promoted by some to maintain acceptable glycemic profiles despite morning insulin resistance, particularly in gestational diabetes (11). Others (54) allow breakfast to consist of 20% to 25% of total daily calories. Avoiding fruit, fruit juices, and highly refined and processed cereals at breakfast is often necessary to maintain acceptable glycemia (11). The addition of a midmorning snack including both protein and carbohydrate is sometimes useful to prevent excessive hunger at lunch, particularly for those with a breakfast planned as 10% of total calories.

The composition of calories within a meal may also be important for maintaining postprandial glycemic control in gestational diabetes. Peterson and Jovanovic-Peterson (27) demonstrated that restricting carbohydrate content within a meal to 33%, 45%, and 40% for breakfast, lunch, and dinner, respectively, was needed to maintain glycemic control. Including sufficient carbohydrate in snacks enables total carbohydrate to reach 40% to 50% of total calories. No studies are available to address the specific types of carbohydrates or fats with regard to glycemia or pregnancy outcome. Therefore, the general guidelines for diabetes such as including high-fiber choices when possible and limiting saturated fats to 10% of calories should be followed (11).

For lean women with gestational diabetes (within 10% of ideal body weight before pregnancy), the approach is more similar to the approach for women with pregestational diabetes. Three meals and three snacks are considered optimal (ADA). Frequent meals and snacks are appropriate for both early pregnancy nausea and vomiting and third-trimester abdominal crowding, which can lead to early satiety. Snacks are used to reduce the risks of rapid decreases of blood glucose due to insulin action.

Exchange Lists

The exchange list is the most commonly used meal planning strategy (4). This approach is useful for developing consistency and promoting appropriate balance of carbohy-

drates and calories throughout the day. Meal portions, appropriate low-fat choices, and high-fiber choices are specified in the educational materials. However, some patients find that using the exchange lists for meal planning is too restrictive, particularly when eating out or on special occasions.

Carbohydrate Counting and Total Available Glucose

Other approaches such as carbohydrate counting and total available glucose (TAG) are becoming more common (55–57). These methods match insulin with the amount of carbohydrate or available glucose (58), respectively, in the diet, and are compatible with achieving the tight metabolic control desired during pregnancy. These approaches provide many patients with an increased sense of flexibility. Carbohydrate counting and TAG approaches are observed to result in fat intakes above the recommended levels (56,58). Appropriate education regarding fat with carbohydrate counting or TAG can result in appropriate nutrient intakes (56).

The choice of meal planning strategy depends on the patient's type of diabetes, educational level, lifestyle habits, motivation, and economic restraints. Many approaches are used successfully. Therefore, the important factor is application of meal planning strategies to fit an individual. Pregnant patients are often more motivated than others. Taking advantage of teachable moments is important in achieving optimal coordination of diet, insulin, and exercise regimes, and ultimately positive pregnancy and other health outcomes.

DIETARY BEHAVIOR

General Considerations

Persons with insulin-dependent diabetes mellitus often find following their diet the most difficult component of their diabetes treatment (59,60). Several specific dietary behaviors are associated with the ability to achieve lower hemoglobin A_{1c} (HbA_{1c}) levels in the Diabetes Control and Complications Trial (61). Adhering to the prescribed meal plan and making adjustments in food or insulin in response to elevated blood sugars helped to reduce HbA_{1c}. In addition, those who consistently ate their bedtime snack and followed specific guidelines to treat hypoglycemia were able to achieve slightly lower HbA_{1c} levels than those who ate extra snacks (who had higher levels of HbA_{1c}). More frequent self-monitoring of blood glucose levels is also associated with clinically and statistically better glycemic control (62).

The approaches to individualized meal planning discussed above are important to the patient's ability to adhere. In addition, all patients, but particularly patients with gestational diabetes who require insulin and women with pregestational diabetes, require continuing education to address sick day management, holidays, baby showers, and dining out. Patients using almost any meal planning strategy can be taught to adjust the insulin according to carbohydrate intake. Using these methods, blood sugar levels are maintained proactively rather than responsively, and patients can enjoy special meals while maintaining appropriate postprandial glycemia. We find that helping patients manage special occasions not only results in adequate glycemia but in a stronger patient–health care team alliance.

Treatment of Hypoglycemia

Overtreatment of hypoglycemia causes rebound hyperglycemia and may contribute to poor glycemic control. Patients who eat until they feel better have higher levels of HbA$_{1c}$ than those who eat a specific amount and then wait 15 minutes before eating more (61). Glucose tablets or gels work more quickly than milk or orange juice and result in a more similar and consistent glycemic response without rebound hyperglycemia (63). Patients should be encouraged to use glucose tablets or another specific source of 15-g carbohydrates, such as 1 cup of low-fat milk. Patients learn how much their blood sugar will rise with their specific treatment and become less likely to overtreat.

Food diaries or records periodically kept by patients are useful in identifying food choices and behaviors that affect blood glucose. Together, patients and dietitians can develop strategies to prevent hyper- and hypo-glycemia by discussing more appropriate food choices, food portions, or mealtimes. More important, patients are involved in the process of determining better ways of managing particular dietary situations. Food records draw both the dietitian's and the patient's attention to usual patterns and lifestyles and their effects on blood glucose control.

LIFESTYLE CONSIDERATIONS

Although most of our patients' lifestyles are amenable to the three-meal-and-three-snack pattern, some are not. Women who work nights and sleep until early afternoon are challenging. Careful coordination of insulin peaks and mealtimes allows patients to continue their present lifestyle while achieving acceptable glycemia. Women whose work does not allow consistent mealtimes may be adequately managed using regular insulin when meals are eaten. Women who use continuous subcutaneous insulin pumps can match their insulin to their food intake and have tremendous flexibility with mealtimes. Extensive individualization and continuing education coordinated among the dietitian, nurse, and perinatologist are the keys to successful management of patients with special lifestyle considerations.

Women may be encouraged to continue sensible exercise programs with the perinatologist's approval. The optimal time for exercise is 60 to 90 minutes after meals for both patients having either gestational or pregestational diabetes (11). Regularly scheduled exercise can be planned as part of the overall treatment and may not require alterations, but additional or occasional exercise may require additional food intake (64) (see Chapter 21).

CONCLUSION

Dietary management must be individualized. Cultural, lifestyle, economic, and educational factors influence the approach to education and composition of the diet. Resources for customizing the diabetic diet are given in Table 20-4. Methods range from emphasizing general guidelines for good nutrition (52) to structured meal planning strategies (56,58). Regardless of approach, the common goals for women with gestational and pregestational diabetes are to meet maternal and fetal nutritional needs while optimizing health and glycemia. Educating or empowering patients to manage situations can result in good glycemic control.

TABLE 20-4. DIETARY MANAGEMENT RESOURCES

Exchange lists for meal planning
Healthy food choices
Month of Meals and *Month of Meals 2*
  American Diabetes Association, Inc.
  Diabetes Information Center
  1600 Duke Street
  Alexandria, VA 22314
  800/ADA-DISC
Franz MF. *Exchanges for all occasions.* Chronimed Publishing, Minnetonka, MN: Chronimed Publishing, 1993
Total available glucose (TAG) approach
  General Clinical Research Center
  Medical University of South Carolina
  171 Ashley Avenue
  Charleston, SC 29401
Point system approach
  Diet Teach Programs, Inc.
  P.O. Box 1832
  Sun City, AZ 85372
Carbohydrate counting approach
  The complete calorie and carbohydrate counter for dining out. New York: Simon and Schuster, 1987
  Kraus B. *Calories and carbohydrates,* 10th ed. New York: New American Library, 1990
  Netzer C. *Complete book of food counts.* New York: Bantam Doubleday Dell, 1988

From Jovanovic-Peterson L. *Managing your gestational diabetes: a guide for you and your baby's good health,* Minneapolis, MN: Chronimed Publishing, 1994; American Diabetes Association. *Diabetes and pregnancy: what to expect.* Alexandria, VA: American Diabetes Association, 1995; and Milchovich SK, Dunn-Long B. *Diabetes mellitus: a practical handbook,* 6th ed. Palo Alto, CA: Bull Publishing, 1995, with permission.

KEY POINTS

- Caloric requirements during pregnancy complicated by diabetes should be based on maternal pregravid weight for height, with more calories per kilogram for underweight women and fewer calories for overweight women.

- The distribution of calories for diet therapy during pregnancy includes 10% to 20% from protein, 40% to 50% from carbohydrates (up to 60% if low glycemic carbohydrates), and the remainder in fats.

- Carbohydrates should be chosen based on their glycemic index, which reflects the relative rise in blood sugar compared an equal quantity of glucose. A diet with a high glycemic load may exacerbate the proinflammatory process.

- Artificial sweeteners may be useful in the dietary management of diabetes, but are certainly not required.

- Dietary fiber is an important component of the diet, with a recommended daily intake of 20 to 35 g.

REFERENCES

1. Williams JW. The clinical significance of glycosuria in pregnant women. *Am J Med Sci* 1909;137:1.
2. Joslin EP. *The treatment of diabetes mellitus with observations upon the disease based upon one thousand cases.* Philadelphia: Lea & Febiger, 1916.
3. Parson E, Randall LM, Wilder RM. Pregnancy and diabetes. *Med Clin North Am* 1926;10:679.
4. American Diabetes Association, American Dietetic Association. *Meal planning with exchange lists.* New York: American Diabetes Association, Inc., and American Dietetic Association, New York, 1949.
5. Ney D, Hollingsworth DR. Nutritional management of pregnancy complicated by diabetes: historical perspective. *Diabetes Care* 1981;4:647.
6. Freinkel N, Dooley SL, Metzger BE. Care of the pregnant woman with insulin-dependent diabetes mellitus. *N Engl J Med* 1985;313:96.
7. Cundy T, Gamble G, Townend K, et al. Perinatal mortality in type 2 diabetes mellitus. *Diabet Med* 2000;17:33–39.
8. Dornhorst A, Frost G. The principles of dietary management of gestational diabetes: reflection on current advice. *J Hum Nutr Diet* 2002;15:145–156.
9. National Academy of Sciences. *Dietary reference intakes.* Washington, DC: National Academy Press, 1999.
10. U.S. Department of Agriculture, Human Nutrition Information Service, Nutrition Monitoring Division. *Nationwide food consumption survey, continuing survey of food intakes by individuals.* Report no. 85-4. Hyattsville, MD: U.S. Government Printing Office, 1987.
11. American Diabetes Association. Nutrition recommendations and principles for people with diabetes mellitus. *Diabetes Care* 2000; 23:S43–S46.
12. Butte NF, Hopkinson JM, Mehta N, et al. Adjustments in energy expenditure and substrate utilization during late pregnancy and lactation. *Am J Clin Nutr* 1999;69:299–307.
13. National Academy of Sciences. Nutrition during pregnancy. Washington, D.C.: National Academy Press, 1990.
14. Jovanovic-Peterson L, Peterson CM. Dietary manipulation as a primary treatment strategy for pregnancies complicated by diabetes. *J Am Coll Nutr* 1990;9:320.
15. Algert S, Shragg P, Hollingsworth DR. Moderate caloric restriction in obese women with gestational diabetes. *Obstet Gynecol* 1985;65:487.
16. Boberg C, Gillmer MDG, Brunner EJ, et al. Obesity in pregnancy: the effect of dietary advice. *Diabetes Care* 1980;3:476.
17. Rizzo T, Metzger BE, Burns WJ. Correlations between antepartum maternal metabolism and intelligence of offspring. *N Engl J Med* 1991;325:911.
18. Wolever TMS, Bentum-Williams A, Jenkins DJ. Physiologic modulation of plasma free fatty acid concentrations by diet. *Diabetes Care* 1995;18:962–970.
19. Weinsier RL, Seeman A, Herrera G, et al. High- and low-carbohydrate diets in diabetes mellitus. *Ann Intern Med* 1974;80:332.
20. Stone DB, Connor WE. The prolonged effects of a low cholesterol, high carbohydrate diet on the serum lipids in diabetic patients. *Diabetes* 1963;12:127.
21. Brunzell JD, Lerner RL, Hazzard WR, et al. Improved glucose tolerance with high carbohydrate feeding in mild diabetes. *N Engl J Med* 1971;284:521.
22. Ney D, Hollingsworth DR, Cousins L. Decreased insulin requirement and improved control of diabetes in pregnant women given a high-carbohydrate, high-fiber, lowfat diet. *Diabetes Care* 1982;5:529.
23. Garg A, Bonanome A, Grundy SM, et al. Comparison of a high-carbohydrate diet with a high-monounsaturated-fat diet in patients with non-insulin-dependent diabetes mellitus. *N Engl J Med* 1988;319:829.
24. Jovanovic-Peterson L, Peterson CM. Dietary manipulation as a primary treatment strategy for pregnancies complicated by diabetes. *J Am Coll Nutr* 1990;9:320.
25. Fraser RB, Ford FA, Lawrence GF. Insulin sensitivity in third trimester pregnancy. A randomized study of dietary effects. *Br J Obstet Gynaecol* 1988;95:223–229.
26. Frost G, Leeds A, Trew G, Margara R, Dornhorst A. Insulin sensitivity in women at risk of coronary heart disease and the effect of a low glycemic diet. *Metabolism* 1998;47:1245–1251.
27. Peterson CM, Jovanovic-Peterson L. Percentage of carbohydrate and glycemic response to breakfast, lunch, and dinner in women with gestational diabetes. *Diabetes* 1991;40[Suppl 2]:172.
28. Jovanovic-Peterson L, Peterson CM, Reed G, et al. Maternal postprandial glucose levels predict birth weight. *Am J Obstet Gynecol* 1991;164:103.
29. Ludwig DS. The glycemic index. Physiological mechanisms relating to obesity, diabetes, and cardiovascular disease. *JAMA* 2002;287:2414–2423.
30. Foster-Powell K, Holt SHA, Brand-Miller JC. International table of glycemic index and glycemic load values: 2002. *Am J Clin Nutr* 2002;76:5–56.
31. Jenkins DJA, Wolever TMS, Taylor RH, et al. Glycemic index of foods: a physiological basis for carbohydrate exchange. *Am J Clin Nutr* 1981;34:362.
32. Crapo PA, Inset J, Sperling M, et al. Comparison of serum glucose, insulin, and glucagon responses to different types of complex carbohydrate in noninsulin-dependent diabetic patients. *Am J Clin Nutr* 1981;34:184.
33. O'Dea K, Nestel PI, Antonoff L. Physical factors influencing postprandial glucose and insulin responses to starch. *Am J Clin Nutr* 1980;33:760.
34. Jenkins DJA, Wolever TMS, Jenkins AL, et al. Glycemic response to wheat products: reduced response to pasta but no effect of fiber. *Diabetes Care* 1983;6:155.
35. Crapo PA, Scarlett JA, Kolterman OG. Comparison of the metabolic responses to fructose and sucrose sweetened foods. *Am J Clin Nutr* 1982;36:256.

36. Bantle JP, Laine DC, Castle GW, et al. Postprandial glucose and insulin responses to meals containing different carbohydrates in normal and diabetic subjects. *N Engl J Med* 1983;309:7.

37. Liu S, Manson JE, Buring JE, et al. Relation between a diet with a high glycemic load and plasma concentrations of high-sensitivity C-reactive protein in middle-aged women. *Am J Clin Nutr* 2002;75:492–498.

38. Horwitz DL, Bauer-Nehrling JK. Can aspartame meet our expectations? *J Am Diet Assoc* 1983;83:142.

39. Sturtevant FM. Use of aspartame during pregnancy. *Int J Fertil* 1985;30:85.

40. von Noorden C. Veber Hafercuren ber schwerem diabetes mellitus. *Ber Klin Wochenschr* 1903;40:817.

41. Jenkins DJA, Leeds AR, Gassull MA, et al. Unabsorbable carbohydrate and diabetes: decreased postprandial hyperglycemia. *Lancet* 1976;2:172.

42. Kiehm TG, Anderson JW, Ward K. Beneficial effects of a high carbohydrate, high fiber diet on hyperglycemic diabetic men. *Am J Clin Nutr* 1976;29:895.

43. Miranda PM, Horwitz DL. High-fiber diets in the treatment of diabetes mellitus. *Ann Intern Med* 1978;88:482.

44. Jenkins DJA, Leeds AR, Gassull MA, et al. Decrease in postprandial insulin and glucose concentrations by guar and pectin. *Ann Intern Med* 1977;86:20.

45. Anderson JW, Ward K. High-carbohydrate, high-fiber diets for insulin treated men with diabetes mellitus. *Am J Clin Nutr* 1979; 32:2312.

46. Christiansen JS, Bonnevie-Nielsen V, Svendsen PA, et al. Effect of guar gum on 24-hour insulin requirements of insulin-dependent diabetic subjects as assessed by an artificial pancreas. *Diabetes Care* 1980;3:659.

47. Reece EA, Hagay Z, Gay LJ, et al. A randomized clinical trial of a fiber-enriched diabetic diet vs the standard ADA-recommended diet in the management of diabetes mellitus in pregnancy. *J Matern-Fet Inv* 1995;5:8–12.

48. Reece EA, Hagay Z, Caseria D, et al. Do fiber-enriched diabetic diets have glucose lowering effects in pregnancy? *Am J Perinatol* 1993;10:272.

49. Boden G, Chen X. Effects of fatty acids and ketone bodies on basal insulin secretion in type 2 diabetes. *Diabetes* 1999;48: 577–583.

50. Friedberg CE, Janssen MJ, Heine RJ, et al. Fish oil and glycemic control in diabetes. A meta-analysis. *Diabetes Care* 1998;21: 494–500.

51. Yosefy C, Reuven Viskoper J, Laszt A, et al. The effect of fish oil on hypertension, plasma lipids and hemostasis in hypertensive, obese, dyslipidemic patients with and without diabetes mellitus. *Prostaglandins Leukot Essent Fatty Acids* 1999;61:83–87.

52. Abrams RS, Coustan DR. Gestational diabetes update. *Clin Diabetes* 1990;8:1.

53. Ney DM. Nutritional management of diabetes during pregnancy. *Diabetology* 1988;7:1.

54. Ney DM. Maternal nutrition and diet. In: Hollingsworth DR, ed. *Pregnancy, diabetes, and birth: a management guide*, 2nd ed. Baltimore: Williams & Wilkins, 1992.

55. Pastors JG. Alternatives to the exchanges system for teaching meal planning to persons with diabetes. *Diabetes Educ* 1992;18:57.

56. DCCT Research Group. Nutrition interventions for intensive therapy in the Diabetes Control and Complications Trial. *J Am Diet Assoc* 1993;93:768.

57. Gillespie SJ, Kulkarni KD, Daly AE. Using carbohydrate counting in diabetes clinical practice. *J Am Diet Assoc* 1998;98: 897–905.

58. Chanteleau E, Sonnenberg GE, Stanitzek-Schmidt I, et al. Diet liberalization and metabolic control in type I diabetic outpatients treated by continuous subcutaneous insulin infusion. *Diabetes Care* 1982;5:612.

59. Lockwood D, Frey ML, Gladish NA, et al. The biggest problem in diabetes. *Diabetes Educ* 1986;12:30.

60. House WC, Pendleton L, Parker L. Patients' versus physicians attribution of reasons for non-compliance with diet. *Diabetes Care* 1986;9:434.

61. Delahanty LM, Halford BN. The role of diet behaviors in achieving improved glycemic control in intensively treated patients in the Diabetes Control and Complications Trial. *Diabetes Care* 1993;16:1453.

62. Karter AJ, Ackerson LM, Darbinian JA, et al. Self-monitoring of blood glucose levels and glycemic control: the Northern California Kaiser Permanente Diabetes Registry. *Am J Med* 2001;111: 1–9.

63. Brodows RG, Williams C, Amatruda JM. Treatment of insulin reactions in diabetics. *JAMA* 1984;252:3378.

64. Pastors JG. *Nutritional care of diabetes*. San Marcos, CA: Joyce Green Pastors/Nutritional Dimension, Inc., 1992.

21

EXERCISE IN NORMAL AND DIABETIC PREGNANCIES

MARSHALL W. CARPENTER

The cardiovascular, metabolic, and endocrine responses that characterize exertion have two effects. Nutrients and oxygen are delivered to exercising muscle to sustain exertional activity, and blood flow is maintained to nonexercising tissue at sufficient levels to preserve tissue integrity and the internal environment of the exercising individual. Pregnancy also profoundly affects cardiovascular and endocrine functions. Its effects on the normal response to exercise and the effect of acute and chronic exercise on pregnancy have been examined in animal and human investigations. Diabetes mellitus alters fuel availability and, if long-standing, may compromise cardiovascular adaptation to exertion. Consequently, diabetes may affect maternal and fetal homeostasis during exercise.

Type 1 diabetes is characterized by a lack of endogenous insulin production. Consequently, the metabolic requirements of a planned exercise bout need to be anticipated by modification of exogenous insulin dose and diet before exertion. Type 1 diabetes is often complicated by deficits in counterregulatory endocrine responses and other end-organ damage, both of which may limit homeostasis during and after exercise. Type 2 diabetes mellitus is often complicated by obesity, hypertension, hyperlipidemia, and varying combinations of insulin resistance and inadequate insulin release. Cardiovascular disease may also be present as a result of these factors. Each of these characteristics may influence the risks and use of exercise in pregnancies complicated by type 2 diabetes mellitus. Gestational diabetes (GDM) is defined as glucose intolerance first identified during pregnancy (1). Consequently, individuals with GDM may manifest abnormalities in insulin release or sensitivity and varying degrees of metabolic derangement. The effect of exercise on glucose homeostasis in these patients, therefore, may vary and, in small study sample sizes, may be inconsistent. Few studies have addressed the use of exercise in maintaining maternal glycemic control during pregnancy. Regardless of the pathogenesis of maternal hyperglycemia, the goal of therapy in pregnancy complicated by diabetes remains the preservation of a normal fetal environment by maintaining "normal" metabolic control and by identifying or preventing altered perfusion of the feto-placental unit. Little is known about the effect of maternal exercise on the fetal environment. Accordingly, present recommendations regarding exercise in normal and diabetic pregnancy will likely undergo substantial modification in the future.

THE NONPREGNANT NONDIABETIC STATE

Acute Cardiovascular Effects

Exertion elicits changes in cardiorespiratory function that provide increased perfusion of, and delivery of oxygen and fuel to, exercising muscle. Oxygen uptake ($\dot{V}O_2$) is the product of oxygen delivery (expressed as cardiac output) and oxygen extraction, expressed as the arteriovenous oxygen difference ($avDO_2$). $\dot{V}O_2$ increases immediately with exertion. The rearranged Fick equation ($\dot{V}O_2$ = heart rate × stroke volume × $avDO_2$) describes the central role of these two processes in determining exercise capacity. $\dot{V}O_2$ increases to 10 to 20 times the value at rest as maximal exercise intensity is reached. Maximal $\dot{V}O_2$ ($\dot{V}O_2$ max) is reached when further increases in exercise intensity (power) elicit no further increase in whole-body $\dot{V}O_2$. At this point, further increases in exercise intensity are achieved by anaerobic glycolysis. Blood lactate levels, which begin to rise when approximately 60% $\dot{V}O_2$max is reached, rise in an accelerated fashion as $\dot{V}O_2$max is reached (Fig. 21-1). This "plateau" of $\dot{V}O_2$, defining $\dot{V}O_2$max (or maximal aerobic power), provides a benchmark against which relative intensities of physical exertion can be compared among individuals with differing aerobic capacities. For example, regardless of the level of aerobic capacity, all individuals will be found to have increasing plasma lactate at exercise intensity of greater than 60% $\dot{V}O_2$max. In most clinical circumstances, $\dot{V}O_2$max is limited by cardiac output and not by oxygen uptake by the lung.

Cardiac output increases nearly linearly with $\dot{V}O_2$ at a 6:1 ratio. Likewise, heart rate increases linearly with rising exercise intensity to two to three times resting values at $\dot{V}O_2$max. Stroke volume increases to near-peak values at

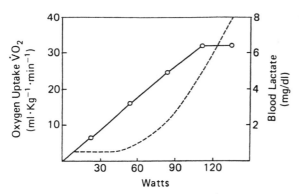

FIGURE 21-1. Characteristic oxygen uptake ($\dot{V}O_2$) and blood lactate response to incremental power output (workload). (From Carpenter MW, Sady SA. Exercise in pregnancy: effects on metabolism. In: Cowett RM, ed. *Principles of perinatal-neonatal metabolism.* New York: Springer-Verlag, 1991:237, with permission.)

approximately 40% to 50% $\dot{V}O_2$max and increases minimally at higher exercise intensities (2,3).

The proportionate distribution of cardiac output during exercise changes dramatically. This is accomplished by vasoconstriction of vascular beds not serving exercising muscle, which is associated with production of norepinephrine by the peripheral vasculature. The control of exercise-induced altered organ perfusion is not well understood. Studies of norepinephrine arteriovenous gradients across various vascular beds have suggested that, in response to exercise, norepinephrine is derived from inactive muscles, abdominal organs, fat, and myocardium, as well as exercising striated muscle, and results in vasoconstriction and reduced perfusion of nonexercising tissue (4). However, others have found that exercising muscle makes the largest absolute contribution of norepinephrine to the circulation during exertion, and have suggested that the capacity of tissues to simultaneously release and take up norepinephrine and the marked changes in relative perfusion of organs induced by exertion may invalidate earlier models based only on arteriovenous differences (5).

Reduction of flow to nonexercising tissues probably occurs within 1 to 2 minutes of the start of exertion, even at moderate intensities. Specifically, absolute (ml/min) splanchnic and renal perfusion decreases even with mild exercise and in proportion to exercise intensity. Skin perfusion is increased with moderate exercise but falls as maximal aerobic capacity is approached (6,7). The proportion of cardiac output perfusing exercising muscle at $\dot{V}O_2$max approaches 90% in trained individuals compared with much lower values in sedentary controls (8). As $\dot{V}O_2$ max is reached, avDO$_2$ increases due to increased peripheral oxygen extraction. In highly trained athletes, hemoglobin desaturation may occur at maximal exertion. Ventilation increases linearly with exertional intensity until approximately 50% $\dot{V}O_2$max, at which point the ratio of ventilation to $\dot{V}O_2$ almost doubles, going from 20 to 25 L to as much as 40 L for every 1-L increase in $\dot{V}O_2$.

Cardiovascular Effects of Chronic Exercise Training

Aerobic exercise training occurs when repeated exertion is performed "of sufficient intensity, duration and frequency to . . . improve maximal aerobic power" (8). Aerobic power is measured by observations of the body's ability to transport oxygen from the atmosphere to exercising muscle. $\dot{V}O_2$ depends on multiple cardiovascular factors, including body size, maximal heart rate (which decreases with age), stroke volume, the muscle mass used in each exercise, and the antecedent level of activity of the individual.

Cross-sectional studies of endurance athletes have commonly noted higher left ventricular end-diastolic volume without change in left ventricular wall thickness compared with sedentary controls. Longitudinal studies of sedentary subjects subjected to endurance (aerobic) training have observed only a modest 2.4% increase in end-diastolic volume (9). However, aerobic training produces an increase in $\dot{V}O_2$max up to 33% by both central and peripheral effects, depending on duration and intensity of the training program (10).

Exertional training increases aerobic capacity by modifying cardiac and peripheral vascular physiology. Cardiac changes induced by chronic exertion include increased vascularization of the myocardium, slowing of resting heart rate (secondary to increased resting stroke volume and increased resting vagal tone), and increased contribution of stroke volume to cardiac output at high exertional intensity. The peripheral effects of exercise training that result in increased aerobic capacity include increased capillary density, local avDO$_2$, and maximal blood flow rate through the trained muscle. Physiologic measurements used to identify increased aerobic power include resting pulse, stroke volume, $\dot{V}O_2$ per cardiac cycle (oxygen pulse), and observed or estimated $\dot{V}O_2$max.

Acute Endocrine Effects of Exertion

Exercise activates the sympathoadrenal system, which increases glucose production directly by stimulating glycogenolysis and gluconeogenesis. Increased glucose production is stimulated indirectly by inhibiting insulin secretion via α-adrenergic receptor stimulation and by stimulating glucagon secretion through activation of β-adrenergic receptors. Moderate exertion for 40 to 45 minutes produces a 50% fall in plasma insulin and a one-third rise in plasma glucagon while plasma glucose is rising (11). The fall in circulating insulin does not affect glucose uptake in the exercising dog. Thus, the effect of reduced insulin concentration appears to promote glucose production. Exercise can produce hypoglycemia if glucagon secretion is suppressed, but increased hepatic glucose production with exercise appears to require only basal glucagon concentrations (12).

Insulin suppression occurs with both intermittent and sustained exertion. Glucagon release is highly dependent on sustained exertion, rising 35% after 30 minutes of intense uninterrupted exertion and 300% after 81 minutes of intense uninterrupted exercise. Norepinephrine concentration rises with moderate exertional intensity, whereas epinephrine rises only with intense exertion. However, duration of exhaustive exercise does not appear to further augment the release of either hormone (13).

Acute Metabolic Effects of Exertion

The relative contribution of various fuels to sustain muscular activity is a function of prior training, nutritional status, exercise type and duration, and especially, exercise intensity. Fat is found in roughly 100-fold abundance in the body (6×10^5 kJ) compared with muscle (5×10^3 kJ) and hepatic (1.5×10^3 kJ) glycogen stores. It is oxidized preferentially at submaximal exertional intensity. This is demonstrated by changes in the respiratory exchange ratio, which is defined as the ratio of carbon dioxide production to VO_2 (CO_2/VO_2) and is an approximation, under steady-state conditions, of the ratio of carbon dioxide production to oxygen consumption in the whole animal, the respiratory quotient (RQ). As exertional intensity is increased, the respiratory exchange ratio approaches unity. Because the RQ of fat is 0.7 and that of carbohydrate is 1.0, this indicates that increased exercise intensity produces a shift from fatty acid oxidation to glycolytic oxidation. This shift appears to be a result of decreased oxygen availability, as indicated by a concomitant rise in muscle-reduced nicotinamide adenine dinucleotide (14). This is further supported by observing a rise in the respiratory exchange ratio when inspired oxygen concentration is reduced from 21% to 14% during conditions of fixed moderate exertion (15). Consequently, the duration at which near-maximal exertion can be maintained is limited by the carbohydrate stores in liver and muscle.

Net arteriovenous lactate differences in exercising muscle are noted even with mild exercise. Thus, increased plasma lactate levels noted at exercise intensity approaching maximal aerobic power indicate that muscle production of lactate exceeds lactate clearance by other muscles and liver. This may result from hormonally mediated increases in glycogenolysis and glycolysis, recruitment of fast-twitch glycolytic muscle fibers, and a redistribution of blood flow from tissues that clear lactate from circulating blood (liver) to exercising muscle. Increased lactate in tissues may suppress lipolysis, further increasing demand for carbohydrates by exercising muscle under these conditions (16). The exercise intensity at which increased lactate in plasma is measured is reproducible when measured repeatedly within individuals and is increased by endurance training.

When exercise commences, muscle adenosine triphosphate and phosphocreatine may provide enough stored energy for 6 to 8 seconds of intense muscular activity. Nonoxidative energy from glycogenolysis and glycolysis in the muscle can provide the requisite energy for 1 to 3 minutes of maximal exercise. Intense exertion, lasting more than 4 to 5 minutes, depends on blood glucose, glycerol, and free fatty acid, which diffuse from capillary to muscle mitochondria. The splanchnic production of glucose rises four-fold by 40 minutes of moderate exercise (11). Exertion lasting more than 2 hours depends on free fatty acid production. These conditions increase lipolysis and may produce a fall in blood glucose, perhaps due to exhaustion of hepatic glycogen stores.

Plasma Glucose and Glucose Uptake During and After Acute Exercise

Plasma glucose remains unchanged during brief, moderate exertion, rises 15% to 20% during intense exertion, and falls gradually during prolonged moderate work. Plasma glucose is maintained by a two- to five-fold increase in hepatic glucose production, which is increasingly derived from gluconeogenic activity as duration of exertion increases (17,18). After exhaustive exercise, glucose concentration continues to rise transiently, remaining elevated up to 30 minutes later (19).

During exercise, glucose uptake by muscle increases linearly with exercise duration and with exercise intensity, reaching 50 times resting values at maximal aerobic effort (20). This increase in muscle glucose uptake occurs even at very low insulin concentrations of 0.2 to 1.2 µU/ml, but not in the absence of circulating insulin (21).

After exertion, insulin-mediated glucose uptake is increased in exercised muscle compared with nonexercised muscle measured 4 hours after single-leg exercise in sedentary men (22). Glucose clearance is increased and postmeal glucose, insulin, and C-peptide response are reduced in patients with type 2 diabetes (23). The effect of exercise intensity may be greater than that of exercise duration on glucose tolerance following a single bout of exertion (24). Both submaximal and maximal insulin-mediated glucose uptake are increased, suggesting that both receptor (insulin sensitivity) and postreceptor (insulin responsiveness) changes occur after exertion. However, this effect cannot be demonstrated in endurance-trained athletes after a single exercise bout (25). These observations have not been confirmed in insulin-resistant women with glucose intolerance in pregnancy.

Compared to lean subjects, obese individuals demonstrate the same postexercise proportionate increase in submaximal insulin-mediated glucose uptake (about 25% over baseline values) (26). However, obese individuals demonstrate no increase in maximal insulin-mediated glucose uptake after exertion. These data suggest that some postreceptor defects in obesity may not respond to the acute effects of exertion.

Lipid Effects of Acute Exertion

Acute exertion has a variable effect on total plasma cholesterol. The most reproducible effect is at 4 to 72 hours after intense and prolonged exercise, when a lowering of cholesterol is observed. Plasma triglyceride concentration falls acutely after isolated exertion, probably due to an increase in lipoprotein lipase activity with secondary catabolism of triglycerides. This effect is marginal in individuals with low baseline plasma triglyceride levels, but may be more marked in those with hypertriglyceridemia (27).

Metabolic Effects of Exercise Training

During the 24-hour cycle of daily activity, approximately 10% of caloric consumption is used for the thermic effect of feeding, the oxidation of ingested food, and energy requirements of digestion. Physical activity can account for 15% to 30% or more of daily energy expenditure. Sixty percent to 75% of total caloric expenditure is resting metabolic rate (RMR). Consequently, changes in RMR of relatively minor proportions may have a significant effect on total caloric requirements. The acute effect of a single bout of exertion on RMR is in doubt, although very intense and prolonged exertion may be followed by a measurable increase (28). Cohort studies describe a reproducible increase in RMR in sedentary individuals subjected to training programs of weeks' duration (29,30). The reported increases of approximately 8% are much less than the 50% higher values observed in cross-sectional studies of individuals with high versus low VO_2max (31). This suggests that level of activity alone explains only a portion of the discrepancy. Genetic factors, the intensity of the exertional training, and caloric restriction, but probably not degree of obesity, influence the effect of exercise training on RMR. Nevertheless, a modest exercise-induced increase in RMR may be sufficient to improve mild glucose intolerance in gestational diabetes.

Insulin sensitivity, measured as submaximal insulin-mediated glucose uptake during a hyperinsulinemic, euglycemic clamp, returns to values found in sedentary individuals after 5 to 7 days of detraining (25,32). This is reflected in a contemporaneous fall in percentage-specific insulin binding to erythrocytes, suggesting that a reduction in insulin receptors may cause this effect. However, maximal insulin-mediated glucose uptake (insulin responsiveness) remains unchanged in the days after detraining. This suggests that an isolated exercise bout changes insulin receptor number or function but that exercise training also affects postreceptor events in muscle that are not the product of a single exercise session.

Six-week training in obese sedentary subjects, who initially demonstrated increased fasting and glucose-stimulated plasma insulin concentrations, resulted in a 26% decrease in both variables. Exercise-trained subjects also demonstrated a significant increase in total-body glucose uptake during the hyperinsulinemic, euglycemic clamp due to both increased peripheral uptake of glucose and greater suppression of hepatic glucose production (33).

Lipid Effects of Exercise Training

Chronic exertion may decrease very low-density lipoprotein triglyceride (VLDL-T) synthesis as a result of increased insulin sensitivity and a reduction in percentage of body fat. Exercise training is more effective in lowering triglyceride concentration in patients whose values are elevated before physical training. Chronic effects may result from increased skeletal muscle or adipose-tissue lipoprotein lipase activity, a reduction in hepatic triglyceride synthesis, and a reduction in adiposity.

In men, the most reproducible effect of chronic exertion on plasma cholesterol concentration is a rise in high-density lipoprotein cholesterol (HDL-C), particularly in the HDL_2 subfraction. A dose-response effect of the intensity of exertional training and increase in HDL-C has been demonstrated (34). This also correlates with exercise-related increases in insulin sensitivity and reductions in adiposity. Small decreases in low-density lipoprotein cholesterol (LDL-C) occur with moderate exercise training.

However, exercise training has demonstrated little or no effect on plasma lipids in nondiabetic sedentary women. This may be due to the lower plasma total cholesterol and LDL-C and higher HDL-C concentrations found in premenopausal, sedentary women compared with men. Women also have higher lipoprotein lipase activity than men. These sex differences may limit the observed effect of chronic exertion on lipoprotein metabolism (35,36).

Endocrine Effects of Exercise Training

The direct effect of chronic exercise on the hypothalamic-pituitary-ovarian axis and its indirect nutritional effects are beyond the scope of this chapter. Chronic exertion probably affects the acute hormonal response to individual exercise bouts. For example, the epinephrine response usually attending intense exertion may have a different effect on fuel metabolism in chronically exercised animals than in those that are sedentary. Normal rats subjected to 10 weeks of treadmill training showed a reduced glycemic response to epinephrine and diminished insulin suppression by epinephrine. Training produced no change in glucagon response to epinephrine in these rats. By contrast, training in streptozocin-induced diabetic rats produced a similar reduction in epinephrine-induced hyperglycemia but no effect on epinephrine-induced suppression of insulin release and a reduction of the two-fold increased glucagon response to epinephrine to normal (37). The changes in exercise-induced hormonal response and changes in the effects of these hormonal responses that may be caused by chronic exercise training have not been explored in pregnancy.

PREGNANT NONDIABETIC WOMEN

Cardiovascular Function at Rest

The endocrinologic and metabolic effects of pregnancy are reviewed in Chapter 10. The cardiovascular effects of pregnancy are summarized here as a necessary foundation to understanding the potential benefits and risks of acute exertion and physical training in normal and diabetic pregnancies.

Second only to the effects of acute exertion, pregnancy produces the most profound nonpathologic change in mammalian cardiovascular physiology. Cardiovascular changes have been measured as early as 6 weeks after conception in the human, when cardiac output increases by 23% and stroke volume by 20% (38–40). This may be a result of a primary reduction in peripheral vascular resistance, which has been linked to the effects of estrogen and progesterone (41). Plasma volume increases by 45% by the third trimester and red blood cell volume increases by more than 20% by mid-pregnancy (42,43), resulting in a dilutional anemia. Cardiac output increases by approximately 35% and resting $\dot{V}O_2$ increases by 13% to 30%, whereas weight increases by an average of only 13% during pregnancy. This is reflected, in part, in a decreased $avDO_2$ during pregnancy. The increase in resting $\dot{V}O_2$ during pregnancy also begins early; half of the increase observed may occur in the first trimester (44). Others have found, however, that resting $\dot{V}O_2$ increases in proportion to increased body weight; that is, $\dot{V}O_2$ per kilogram is unchanged from pregnancy to postpartum (45). End-diastolic volume and stroke volume (38,39,46) appear to increase during pregnancy. Consequently, both cardiac and hematologic changes of pregnancy may serve to increase aerobic power during pregnancy, independent of exertional training.

Acute Cardiovascular Response to Exertion

An augmentation of exercise-induced increases in $\dot{V}O_2$ has been observed inconsistently during pregnancy (46–51). Identical submaximal treadmill and cycle exercise tests performed in late pregnancy and postpartum identified a 9% increase in absolute (liters per minute) $\dot{V}O_2$ with cycle (weight-supported) exertion and a 12% higher $\dot{V}O_2$ during treadmill (weight-bearing) exertion during pregnancy compared with the exercise-produced $\dot{V}O_2$ increment measured in the postpartum state. Most (75%) of these differences were accounted for by pregnancy-related weight changes (45). The increased resting $\dot{V}O_2$ during pregnancy and the increased absolute increment in $\dot{V}O_2$ with submaximal workload means that exercise is carried out at a higher percentage of $\dot{V}O_2$max. As noted above, the identical "external" workload during pregnancy will require a higher respiratory exchange ratio (higher relative oxidation of glucose relative to fatty acids), and produce a greater sympathoadrenal response and a higher lactate plasma concentration. Also, maternal exertion during pregnancy likely augments the normal redistribution of cardiac output to exercising muscle because the exertion is taking place at a higher percentage of $\dot{V}O_2$max.

Pregnancy does not alter the 5:1 to 6:1 ratio between cardiac output and $\dot{V}O_2$ observed in the nonpregnant state (48). Pregnancy may alter the relative contribution of stroke volume and heart rate to increased cardiac output during high-intensity exertion. Increases in stroke volume may continue to contribute to increased cardiac output during incremental exertion at higher percentages of $\dot{V}O_2$max in pregnancy compared with the nonpregnant state (48). This appears to alter the predictive heart rate, the $\dot{V}O_2$ formula for $\dot{V}O_2$max during pregnancy (52). $\dot{V}O_2$max does not appear to be altered by pregnancy (52,53). However, peak age-specific pulse may be somewhat lower during pregnancy by four beats per minute.

Recovery from exertion may be impeded by pregnancy. Stroke volume falls after completion of moderate exertion to a greater degree in late pregnancy (23%) than postpartum (11%) (54). This may be due to increased venous pooling in the legs during pregnancy secondary to increased venous compliance and from partial caval obstruction from the late gravid uterus.

Acute Endocrine and Metabolic Responses to Exertion in Pregnancy

Pregnancy not only produces elevated levels of total cortisol, growth hormone, and insulin at rest, but also alters the amplitude of acute hormonal change to exertion. Norepinephrine response appears to be reduced in response to rising to a standing position during pregnancy (55), suggesting a blunted baroreceptor response. Statistically significant rises in both norepinephrine (60%) and epinephrine (47%) concentrations have been found immediately following only 15 minutes of very mild exercise (approximately twice the resting $\dot{V}O_2$) in pregnancy (56).

At greater exercise intensity and total expenditure the effect of pregnancy on hormone response is more evident. Exercise for 30 minutes at 65% of $\dot{V}O_2$max performed at 22 and 33 weeks of pregnancy and 14 weeks postpartum was performed in 12 healthy women (57). The postexertion insulin fall of approximately 30% during pregnancy was roughly twice that in the postpartum period. Glucagon rose following exercise by 33% and 10% at 22 and 33 weeks, respectively, confirming an earlier observation by Artal et al. (58) at a lower exertion intensity. Postpartum postexercise glucagon rise was again 36%. The exertional rise in total cortisol was roughly 30% during pregnancy and not significantly changed at postpartum. Growth hormone rise after exercise was markedly blunted by pregnancy. The rise with exercise at 22 and 33 weeks was 60% and 14%, respectively, compared with 286% postpartum.

Despite higher postprandial plasma glucose concentrations in pregnancy, pregnancy appears to exaggerate the fall in glucose concentrations during exertion, at least compared to postpartum observations. Thirty minutes of 65% $\dot{V}O_2$max exertion performed at 22 and 33 weeks caused a fall in glucose of 9% and 13%, respectively, but only a 1% fall in the postpartum state. Others, employing similar exercise protocols, demonstrated a 25% fall in glucose concentration to 70 mg/dL (59). Glucose values returned to pre-exertion values by 45 minutes after exertion.

Acute Effect of Maternal Exertion on Fetal Homeostasis

During brief exertion, the reduction of splanchnic perfusion is directly proportional to duration and intensity (percent $\dot{V}O_2max$) of exertion (60). In pregnant sheep, 10 minutes of exertion at 70% $\dot{V}O_2max$ reduced uterine blood flow by 8%, whereas 40 minutes of exertion at the same intensity reduced uterine blood flow by 27%. Exercise for 10 minutes at 100% $\dot{V}O_2max$ resulted in an 11% reduction in uterine blood flow. Fetal arterial oxygen tension, oxygen content, and carbon dioxide tension decreased with increasing intensity and was most marked in the 40-minute exercise protocol. Yet, under these conditions, total uterine oxygen consumption was maintained (53). A more prolonged (1 to 3 hours) treadmill exercise protocol in near-term pregnant sheep compared ewes that completed the protocol with those whose "staggering gait required assistance." There was no appreciable change in uterine blood flow in "nonexhausted" ewes. The exhausted group demonstrated a 28% decrease in uterine blood flow and a 29% reduction in fetal oxygen tension. Fetal umbilical artery oxygen content decreased 37% in this group, but this was associated with an increase in fetal oxygen extraction. Net lactate uptake by the fetus was demonstrated even in the "exhausted ewes," indicating that feto-placental oxygen uptake was still maintained even under extreme exertion intensity (61). These observed alterations in fetal environment caused by maternal exertion suggest that similar levels of maternal exertion in different environmental conditions, in other species, or in states of compromised maternal or fetal physiology may result in placental ischemia or fetal hypoxia.

Fetal bradycardia has been suspected in exercising humans even at low exertional intensity. Fetal bradycardia may be induced neurogenically by direct baroreceptor stimulation of the vagus nerve from increased fetal blood pressure or by chemoreceptor stimulation by hypoxemia and acidemia, producing increased fetal blood pressure. Fetal hypoxemia may also directly depress fetal heart rate. Consequently, because of concerns regarding the effects of human maternal exertion on fetal gas exchange, initial studies of human fetal response used clinical Doppler fetal heart rate monitors during and after maternal exertion. In these studies, fetal bradycardia was noted shortly after the initiation of even mild and moderately intense maternal exertion (62–64). These observations were probably obscured by maternal motion artifact.

Subsequent studies, using continuous two-dimensional sonographic imaging, have examined fetal heart rate response to exertion in mid-gestation and late gestation under conditions of moderate exertion and maximal voluntary effort (65,66). Incremental exertion for 18 minutes peaking at approximately 60% $\dot{V}O_2max$ in the third trimester did not produce unexplained fetal bradycardia in 85 subjects. One sustained a maternal vasovagal episode that was followed by brief fetal bradycardia (65). In contrast to findings during submaximal maternal exertion, 6- to 10-minute incremental exercise to $\dot{V}O_2max$ produced postexertional fetal bradycardia in 15 of 79 (19%) subjects immediately after cessation of peak exercise, despite continued submaximal pedaling exercise. All bradycardia episodes were abrupt in onset, variable in resolution, and unassociated with maternal blood pressure or gestational age (20 to 34 weeks). There was no protective effect of prior maternal exercise history or increased maternal aerobic capacity. All fetuses in this study demonstrated normal fetal heart rate tracings, with fetal heart rate accelerations associated with fetal movement within 30 minutes of maternal exercise cessation. Fetal bradycardia was not associated with subsequent untoward perinatal events (65). Baseline fetal heart rate appears to increase after moderate maternal exercise (67,68). Maternal exertion of at least 20 minutes duration and intensity of 50% to 60% $\dot{V}O_2max$ appears to be required to elicit this response, which appears to be more pronounced in late pregnancy. This response does not appear to be mediated by increased maternal core temperature, which was increased by only 0.3°C under the conditions of these studies.

Effects of Exercise Training

Limited information is available on the effect of chronic maternal exercise on fetal homeostasis and perinatal outcome. Most prospective studies are not randomized and are, thereby, subject to biased subject selection. Some studies used a detraining protocol rather than the training of sedentary subjects and may have introduced nutritional and body composition-related factors that could have influenced outcome. These observational cohort studies (69–75) have observed an 11% to 24% reduction in the absolute weight gain in pregnancy associated with exercise training. Most studies identified a lower birth weight among offspring of exercising subjects of 62 to 623 g. However, no studies have identified a significantly earlier gestational age at birth, or a higher incidence of prematurity among offspring of women undergoing chronic exercise training. One study showed an inverse association between exercise frequency and cesarean delivery rate (74). A nonrandomized detraining study noted a 6% cesarean rate among runners and dancers who continued to exercise compared with a rate of 30% among 44 subjects who discontinued exercise during pregnancy despite a higher birth weight in this latter group of only 407 g (67). Neither study offered information regarding the clinical decision for cesarean section.

Two randomized trials examined the association of maternal exercise with pregnancy and labor complications (69,75). No differences in gestational age, fetal growth, cesarean section rates, or fetal compromise at birth were noted. However, subject numbers of 40 and 85 in these studies were insufficient to identify many differences that may be of clinical importance.

These studies suggest that in normal human pregnancy, moderate exertion — sufficient to induce cardiovascular training effects in sedentary individuals — is not associated with evidence of acute fetal compromise. Direct measurement of fetal metabolic conditions and cardiovascular response cannot be made in human studies, however. Consequently, fetal effects of maternal exertion sufficient to influence fetal growth, body composition, or development cannot be identified with these studies. Studies of maternal exercise training and perinatal outcome have been limited by research design or small numbers of subjects. Despite these limitations, however, maternal exertion at an intensity and duration shown to produce both cardiovascular and metabolic training effects is probably unassociated with untoward fetal or maternal effects. This suggests that exercise may be investigated as a therapeutic tool in the antenatal care of women with type 2 diabetes and those with gestational diabetes. Whether the reduction in birth weight of offspring of active compared with sedentary nondiabetic athletes can be demonstrated among obese sedentary women with gestational or type 2 diabetes subjected to exercise training has not been explored. The apparent fetal safety of brief maternal exertion described in normal pregnancy has, likewise, not been examined in pregnancies complicated by long-standing diabetes.

EXERCISE IN NONPREGNANT AND PREGNANT DIABETIC PATIENTS

Exercise was reportedly prescribed as a treatment for diabetes in the first century BC by the Roman physician Celsus (76). In the modern era before insulin treatment, exercise was known to lower blood glucose and improve glucose tolerance (77,78). Although there has been a commonly held belief in the therapeutic effect of exercise in type 1 diabetes mellitus based on early observations of the augmentation of the effects of exogenous insulin by exercise (79–81), evidence to support exercise as a therapeutic tool to improve overall glycemic control in type 1 diabetes is limited (76). The powerful effects of an obligate exogenous insulin load, variable diet and absorption of food, defective counterregulation, and sympathetic neuropathy render the simple application of exertion in this disorder problematic. For example, two case series cite improved physiologic measures after an exercise training program in patients with type 1 diabetes (82,83). Exercise training, which produced improved aerobic power, resulted in normalization of

hyperglycemia and reduction of plasma ketone concentrations. Well-trained men with type 1 diabetes demonstrated normal effects of exertion on fuel metabolism. However, the behavioral demands of a consistent daily exercise program and the lack of effect of these programs beyond the duration of the research intervention have caused some authors to recommend dietary modification and careful glucose surveillance as more realistic long-term methods to effect euglycemia (84). Yet, despite the lack of data supporting its therapeutic efficacy, exercise is an important recreational feature in the lives of many diabetic patients and may sustain a sense of well-being and physical competence. Accordingly, many patients with type 1 diabetes may present the physician with the challenge of a continuing exercise training program in the context of pregnancy, with its dietary variability and the fetal imperative for near-euglycemia.

The role of exercise in the prevention and treatment of type 2 diabetes mellitus and its impact on fetal imprinting by maternal hyperglycemia (85) is much more complex. Obesity may characterize up to 90% of type 2 diabetes patients, and is more commonly that of central distribution (an increased waist/hip ratio) (86,87). Weight loss, especially when associated with diet and exercise intervention, has been associated with remission of hyperglycemia (88) and prevention of progression of impaired glucose tolerance (IGT) to type 2 diabetes (89).

Type 2 diabetes is associated with impaired hepatic sensitivity to glucose, insulin, and glucagon, with associated increased fasting hepatic glucose production and hyperglycemia (90,91). In addition, insulin-mediated peripheral disposal of glucose is reduced by as much as one-half at euglycemia, although the diabetic subject probably has normal total peripheral glucose disposal at hyperglycemic levels (92,93). Both weight loss and exercise training may modify the complex pathogenic interaction of diet, obesity, hyperlipidemia, central and peripheral insulin resistance, defective insulin release, and postreceptor cellular defects in several ways.

Scheduled exercise may reinforce behavior modification to ensure better compliance with diet and medication. Exercise training has been associated with weight reduction, an improved lipid profile, and increased aerobic power, which itself is associated with improved perfusion of chronically exercised muscle.

Nonpregnant Patients with Type 1 Diabetes Mellitus

The effect of exertion on metabolic control in type 1 diabetes is affected by the metabolic state at the initiation of exercise, the means of delivery of exogenous insulin, recent exertion, and food intake, impairment of counterregulatory hormone responses, sympathetic autonomic dysfunction, potential cardiac dysfunction, and finally, the social and psychological context in which exercise is undertaken. The metabolic response to exertion in type 1 diabetes is highly affected by metabolic state at the time of exercise. Exercise increases hyperglycemia and accelerates ketone formation when performed during marked insulin deficiency and ketosis as a result of augmented hepatic glucose production and fatty acid mobilization (94).

Moderately well-controlled and poorly controlled ketotic type 1 diabetic subjects were compared with nondiabetic controls in a 3-hour mild-intensity cycle exercise (95). Both diabetic groups demonstrated higher levels of lactate, free fatty acids, and ketones, and greater glucagon plasma concentrations than controls. Moderately well-controlled diabetic subjects experienced a fall in glucose concentration despite a rise in plasma glucagon. In ketotic, poorly controlled diabetic subjects, exercise produced a marked rise in glucose concentration and a higher level of ketone bodies and glucagon than in the moderately controlled diabetic group.

These observations suggest that exercise should be avoided under conditions of poor metabolic control, particularly in pregnancy, because the fetus may be adversely affected by maternal ketosis. Ketonemia in both nondiabetic and diabetic mothers has been associated with lower intellectual function in offspring. Maternal ketoacidosis has been associated with evidence of fetal hypoxia and an increased perinatal mortality rate (96,97). Patients who are nonketotic need not avoid exertion but should not withhold insulin before exertion.

Continuous subcutaneous insulin infusion (CSII) became popular in the 1980s. These "open-loop" systems require frequent surveillance of blood glucose and adjustment of the insulin infusion rate. Initial optimism that these devices would improve metabolic control prompted studies of the effects of this method of exogenous insulin delivery on metabolic response to exertion in diabetic patients. One study observed the expected exertion-induced fall in plasma glucose from 230 to 160 mg/dL in subjects treated with multiple subcutaneous injections of insulin (MSI) (98). Of interest, subjects treated with CSII who had preexertion glucose concentrations of 110 mg/dL, demonstrated no change in glucose concentration during or after exertion, similar to nondiabetic controls. The different responses may have been affected by preexertion euglycemia rather than the type of insulin delivery, however.

The effect of preexertional feeding was examined when euglycemic type 1 diabetic subjects with each type of insulin delivery were subjected to 45 minutes of exertion at 55% $\dot{V}O_2$max 2 hours after morning insulin and a standardized breakfast (99). In a randomized crossover design, subjects were studied at rest after their usual morning insulin dose, during exercise after their usual morning insulin dose, after the same exercise protocol after two-thirds or one-half of their usual morning insulin dose, and after no morning insulin. Figure 21-2 depicts the varying glucose and free insulin values in each protocol using subcutaneous insulin injection or CSII delivery. Both groups experienced a significant fall in plasma glucose during and after exertion with four of seven CSII subjects and three of six MSI subjects having clinical hypoglycemia. Exercise without change in pre-breakfast insulin was associated with

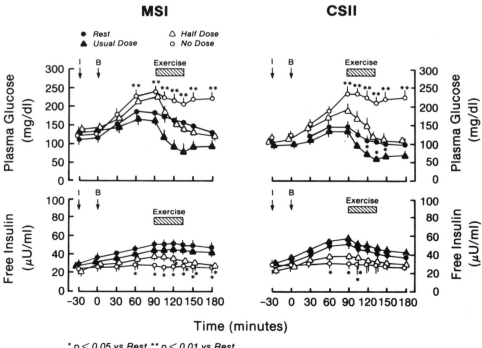

FIGURE 21-2. (Left) Plasma glucose and free insulin concentrations in patients treated with multiple subcutaneous injections of insulin (MSI) during rest and exercise studies (mean ± SEM). I, insulin administration; B, start of breakfast. **(Right)** Plasma glucose and free insulin concentration in patients treated with continuous subcutaneous infusion of insulin (CSII) during rest and exercise. (From Schiffrin A, Parikh S. Accommodating planned exercise in type I diabetic patients on intensive treatment. *Diabetes Care* 1985;8: 337, with permission.)

similar hypoglycemia in both groups, with the nadir occurring after 45 minutes (57±5 mg/dL and 65±10 mg/dL, respectively), whereas exercise after a 33% or 50% reduction in pre-breakfast insulin produced little disturbance in glucose concentrations. These studies suggest that, in euglycemic type 1 diabetic individuals, pre-meal insulin dose can be safely reduced before exertion planned 2 hours after eating. However, CSII *per se* does not appear to ensure euglycemia during and after exertion in type 1 diabetic subjects.

Pregnant Patients with Type 1 Diabetes Mellitus

Little has been published regarding exercise during pregnancy complicated by type 1 diabetes. One observational study examined two cohorts of sedentary gravidas: normal controls and subjects with type 1 diabetes assigned in a nonrandom manner to 20 minutes of "leisurely" walking three times each day or to usual activity (100). All subjects wore pedometers, and the exercisers did experience more walking. Diabetic subjects had poor metabolic control on study entry, having mean 24-hour glucose values of 174±59 and 165±55 mg/dL in exercisers and controls, respectively. Both exercising and sedentary diabetic subjects demonstrated significantly improved glycemic control at the end of the protocol (103±36 and 111±33, respectively), but prescribed walking was not associated with greater improvement. Exercise prescription did produce lower fasting cholesterol and triglyceride concentrations than in nonexercising controls.

Table 21-1 lists guidelines for exercise in women with type 1 diabetes mellitus recommended by some authors

TABLE 21-1. EXERCISE GUIDELINES FOR WOMEN WITH TYPE 1 DIABETES IN REPRODUCTIVE AGE GROUP (15/40 YEARS)

Complete history, physical examination, and screening for proliferative retinopathy, nephropathy, and cardiovascular disease

Screen for postural hypotension, tachycardia, and history of hypoglycemia without autonomic symptoms

Establish diabetic control by MSI or CSII, self-glucose monitoring, and dietary modifications

Initiate a gradual program of postprandial exercise on a regular basis in conjunction with self-glucose monitoring

Adjust preexercise insulin dose, food intake, and postexercise carbohydrate supplement

Avoid exercise during peak insulin action

Do not use exercising extremities as insulin injection sites

Alert patients to possibility of exercise-induced hypoglycemia, which may occur several hours after the completion of exercise

MSI, multiple subcutaneous injections of insulin; CSII, continuous subcutaneous insulin infusion.
From Zinman B, Vranic M. Diabetes and exercise. *Med Clin North Am* 1985;69:145, with permission.

that have applicability during pregnancy as well (94). Nondiabetic sedentary women appear to be able to initiate an exercise training program during pregnancy with the same fetal safety as active women who continue their usual exercise during pregnancy (65). Sedentary women with type 1 diabetes, however, may have undiagnosed retinopathy, nephropathy, and myocardial ischemia. We inform our patients with untreated proliferative retinopathy to delay exercise until retinal laser therapy is completed.

The effect of exercise during pregnancy on the progression of diabetic nephropathy is unknown. Although angiotensin-converting enzyme inhibitors have been shown to retard the progression of albuminuria without worsening azotemia in patients with early diabetic nephropathy, these drugs are contraindicated in pregnancy because of their association with fetal growth restriction, fetal loss, and neonatal hypotension. Consequently, pregnancy may result in increased glomerular hydraulic pressure that is untreated because of the above fetal considerations. In theory, therefore, exercise by diabetic patients with albuminuria may thereby exacerbate the progression of nephropathy. Patients with nephropathy and an interest in exercise training in pregnancy should be informed of the uncertain effects of exercise on renal function in their pregnancies.

There is no consensus regarding the appropriate method of screening for silent myocardial ischemia in gravid women with type 1 diabetes. Pregnant women with long-standing diabetes who are inclined to perform exercise training during pregnancy may be advised to undergo step or treadmill exercise testing with cardiac monitoring both during and after exertion. Especially in late pregnancy, venous return and cardiac preload may be reduced after exertion, leading to reduced stroke volume and, in the context of sympathetic neuropathy, reduced cardiac output (54). It may be useful to screen for sympathetic autonomic neuropathy. However, the effect of autonomic neuropathy on exercise safety is uncertain, particularly at modest exercise intensities.

Patients with type 1 diabetes are vulnerable to exercise-related hypoglycemia. Plasma concentrations of exogenous insulin do not fall during exertion and the usual increase in hepatic glucose production does not occur. In patients with abnormal glucagon and epinephrine counterregulatory responses, this may produce hypoglycemia. Type 1 diabetic patients who are pregnant are further prone to exercise-associated hypoglycemia for several reasons. Because of nausea or other discomforts of pregnancy, the patient's diet may be inadequate before exertion. Patients who have been successful in maintaining euglycemia during pregnancy are more vulnerable to delayed postexertional hypoglycemia, which may occur several hours after completion of exercise. Exercise training also increases insulin sensitivity in previously sedentary individuals. This may further increase the risk of unexpected hypoglycemia. Accordingly, patients should be advised to have a glucose monitor and source of glucose available to them in case of late postexertional hypoglycemia. Because of these considerations, we recommend that type 1 diabetic patients wishing to begin a new exertional program increase exercise duration and intensity gradually to allow incremental adaptations of diet and insulin dose to the exercise program.

Despite the best efforts on the part of physician and patient in avoiding hypoglycemia in pregnancy, efforts to maintain euglycemia to preserve normal embryonic and fetal development are often complicated by symptomatic neuroglycopenia, requiring support from another individual. Because hypoglycemia may occur even during exertion, we recommend that gravid women who suffer neuroglycopenia, unheralded by sympathetic symptoms, should always be accompanied by a person competent to administer subcutaneous glucagon. We recommend that all patients have available, on their person, a source of readily absorbable glucose. Some patients may prefer also to carry a reflectance meter. Some of our patients who prefer to run outdoors have a suitably equipped partner accompany them by bicycle.

Nonpregnant Patients with Type 2 Diabetes Mellitus

The therapeutic potential for exercise in type 2 diabetes mellitus is supported by both epidemiologic and experimental evidence. Chronic exercise training may be more effective in prevention of type 2 diabetes than in its treatment.

Epidemiologic studies have suggested that habitual exercise in individuals with IGT or otherwise at high risk of developing type 2 diabetes reduces the probability of developing diabetes mellitus. A 14-year cohort study demonstrated development of type 2 diabetes in 202 (3.4%) of 5,990 men (101). Risk of type 2 diabetes was reduced 6% for every 500-kcal increment in weekly energy expenditure, independent of obesity and family history of type 2 diabetes. In addition, weight gain since college and hypertension were independent risk factors for type 2 diabetes. The effect of energy expenditure was greater in those at highest risk of diabetes. Another 8-year cohort study of 87,253 female nurses aged 34 to 59 years (102) noted 1,303 new cases (1.5%) of type 2 diabetes. Among those who exercised at least weekly, the risk ratio for diabetes was 0.84 (p < 0.005) after adjusting for obesity. No dose-response relationship could be demonstrated between frequency of exercise and the development of diabetes.

Intervention trials more directly assess the effect of exercise on type 2 diabetes. The acute effect of brief exercise (four 7-minute bouts of incremental exercise) from 45 to 90 minutes after breakfast was examined in eight patients with type 2 diabetes (103). A crossover design compared a nonexertion control day with an exercise day. These patients

were treated with diet only and had fasting plasma glucose values of approximately 160 mg/dL and postprandial values of 225 mg/dL. The exercise intervention significantly reduced the area under the post-breakfast glucose curve but had no measurable effect after lunch, eaten 4 hours after breakfast. These data suggest that the effect of a single bout of exercise may not affect glucose concentrations in such patients in a clinically significant manner.

In a study of 48 men with IGT, subjects were randomized to performing twice-weekly exercise and diet modification, diet alone, or exercise alone. Weight reduction was noted among those randomized to diet alone, but improved glucose tolerance was noted only in those performing the diet/exercise protocol (88). This study suggests that an intervention combining diet and exercise is more effective in improving glycemia than weight reduction alone in those with abnormal glucose tolerance.

In a nonrandomized controlled trial of dietary and exercise intervention (89), subjects with mild type 2 diabetes and IGT who were able to complete a 5-year protocol of dietary modification and weight loss and exercise training were examined. Only those with IGT were able to maintain postprandial glycemia of less than 7 mmol/L (126 mg/dL). However, those with type 2 diabetes demonstrated a gradual rise in glycemia despite comparable reductions in postprandial hyperinsulinemia. In the IGT group, improved glucose tolerance was associated with weight reduction and increased $\dot{V}O_2$ max.

The effect of dietary modification (diet plus placebo and diet plus tolbutamide) was examined in a randomized trial of men with IGT (104). Among those completing the 10- to 12-year observation period, progression to sustained hyperglycemia (all oral glucose tolerance test values more than two standard deviations above mean values) occurred in 29% of observed controls, in 13% of those undergoing some dietary intervention without tolbutamide, and in none who continued treatment with tolbutamide. Although none of these subjects was enlisted to perform exercise, data from this and the preceding study suggest that subjects who complete protocols combining multiple interventions show improved therapeutic effect. It may be that the multiinterventional approach results in one intervention reinforcing compliance with others. Exercise may enhance dietary compliance with resulting weight loss and prevention of progressive glucose intolerance.

Studies of exercise intervention in established type 2 diabetes are less encouraging. Several investigations note an improvement in insulin sensitivity after exercise training, as demonstrated by reduced insulin and glucose concentrations after an oral glucose challenge (105), increased insulin sensitivity during a euglycemic hyperinsulinemic clamp (106), and a reduction in fasting hepatic glucose production (107,108). However, these findings are not consistently found. In particular, improvement in fasting glucose, glucose tolerance after an oral load, and glycated hemoglobin levels often cannot be demonstrated after exertional training protocols (109–111).

Pregnant Patients with Type 2 Diabetes Mellitus

Little has been published regarding exercise training in pregnant patients with type 2 diabetes. However, several conclusions may reasonably be inferred from studies of exercise intervention in nonpregnant individuals with IGT and type 2 diabetes. First, exercise appears to confer its effects only so long as training is continued, limiting effective compliance among patients who have substantial obesity or are in late pregnancy. Second, the metabolic effects of training reported among nonpregnant individuals may be less likely during gestation when the glucose intolerance of diabetes is reinforced by the metabolic effects of pregnancy. Third, effective reduction of fasting or postprandial glycemia has not been consistently demonstrated despite findings that exercise training improves several of the component metabolic defects known to contribute to type 2 diabetes. One might question whether exercise would be helpful during pregnancy, when effective prevention of macrosomia and other perinatal morbidities requires a much greater reduction of glucose (90 to 106 mg/dL) than that required in the nonpregnant patient. Consequently, exercise training in pregnancy complicated by type 2 diabetes may serve more to reinforce compliance with diet and insulin therapy than to provide a direct effect on glycemic control or fetal growth.

Pregnant Patients with Gestational Diabetes

GDM has been defined as "carbohydrate intolerance of variable severity with onset or first recognition during pregnancy" (1). The hyperglycemia that identifies GDM usually remits during the puerperium. Despite the transient and less-marked hyperglycemia noted in GDM, abnormalities of insulin secretion and action that characterize type 2 diabetes have also been identified in patients with GDM, including obesity, insulin resistance, and abnormal first-phase insulin release (112). In addition, GDM is a strong predictor for later IGT and type 2 diabetes, with the probability of subsequent development of clinical glucose intolerance within the next 2 decades in the range of 50% (113). Consequently, GDM may be considered as an early clinical manifestation of IGT and type 2 diabetes.

The therapeutic roles of exercise in this disorder are twofold. First, exercise (along with dietary and pharmacologic intervention) may be effective in preventing progressive obesity and the progression of IGT to type 2 diabetes in the same way it has been applied in other clinical trials (91). Intervention even earlier in the "natural history" of type 2 diabetes with focus on the postpartum woman may

be hypothesized to be more efficacious. More relevant to the immediate clinical circumstances of the pregnancy complicated by glucose intolerance, only limited data are available on the effect of exercise or dietary modification (or both) on maternal glucose (and other nutrient) homeostasis and on the prevention of diabetic fetopathy. The same inverse association between chronic activity level and diabetes found in nonpregnant individuals is found with respect to the incidence of GDM. An analysis of population-based birth registry data from 12,799 gravidas compared those reporting one to two exercise sessions each week with those reporting no exercise (114). The odds ratio for development of GDM in sedentary obese gravidas (body mass index >33) was 1.9 (confidence interval, 1.2–3.1) compared to those obese gravidas who reported habitual exercise. This association was not found in relatively lean gravidas.

Randomized trials of exercise training in GDM have suggested a role of maternal exercise in treatment. The first study included 41 subjects who, despite dietary therapy, had persistent fasting hyperglycemia of 105 to 140 mg/dL (115). Enrollment occurred at 28 to 33 weeks of gestational age. Patients were stratified by age and obesity before randomization. Control subjects were treated with insulin, and the exercise patients performed moderate, laboratory-observed cycle exercise three times weekly for the duration of pregnancy. Four of 21 exercise patients and 3 of 20 controls dropped out of the study and were not analyzed. Of the remainder, no differences in mean blood glucose values (94 ± 5 versus 89 ± 6 mg/dL, respectively) or birth weight ($3,369\pm534$ versus $3,482\pm502$ g, respectively) were noted.

The second randomized trial of observed exercise treatment compared 6 weeks of arm crank exercise (n = 10) to dietary therapy (n = 9) in previously untrained women with GDM, having fasting plasma glucose concentrations of 84 to 106 mg/dL (116). Exertional heart rate was kept at less than 140 beats per minute, and exercise occurred three times weekly for approximately 20 minutes. In controls, fasting plasma glucose fell during the 6-week trial from 98 ± 13 to 88 ± 6 and the 1-hour post-50-g glucose challenge value fell from 226 ± 33 to 188 ± 13 mg/dL. Greater improvement in glycemia occurred in the exercise group. Fasting plasma glucose fell during the 6-week trial from 100 ± 9 to 70 ± 7 and the 1-hour post-50-g glucose challenge value fell from 231 ± 29 to 106 ± 19 mg/dL. Because the exertional intensity and duration were relatively modest and the hand crank exertion did not require weight bearing, the protocol might have applicability even among obese, sedentary women who characteristically have GDM. Significant effects of exercise on fasting glucose concentrations were noted after only 4 weeks of exercise, suggesting that if diagnostic testing and therapeutic intervention were to be started by 24 to 28 weeks, therapeutic effects of maternal exercise on fetal macrosomia might be found.

A randomized trial of combined laboratory and home exercise versus usual activity was examined in 33 gravidas with GDM beginning at 29 and 26 weeks, respectively (117). Subjects and controls had normal preprotocol hemoglobin A1c concentrations (4.96% and 5.00%, respectively) and fasting glucose values (85 versus 84 mg/dL, respectively). The exercise protocol involved two laboratory, 30-minute, cycle ergrometry sessions at approximately 70% of VO_2max and two unsupervised sessions at similar duration and intensity each week. No differences in mean fasting glucose levels, mean 2-hour postprandial glucose values, hemoglobin A1c concentrations after 4 weeks of the protocol, incidence of insulin therapy, nor neonatal hypoglycemia could be detected. Average daily caloric intake in exercisers was significantly higher (2,301 versus 2,190 kcal, respectively at baseline). Carbohydrate intake was not reduced in exercisers during the protocol compared to controls who averaged a 15% reduction. Consequently, group differences in diet and the relatively mild character of subjects' glucose intolerance may have contributed to the lack of observed exercise training effect.

Exercise as a therapeutic intervention for fetal indications in GDM remains problematic, however. The preceding study enrolled only 19 subjects, whose motivation may have been uncharacteristic of most women with GDM. Laboratory-observed exercise is expensive and unwieldy for patients. Maintaining exercise compliance in home surroundings for sedentary, obese patients without prior exposure to exercise training for short-term protocols has not been shown to be successful in this type of patient as yet. Despite these concerns, introduction of these patients to dietary and exertional interventions during pregnancy, when health-directed motivation is high, may lay the foundation for later long-term intervention to prevent subsequent IGT or type 2 diabetes.

KEY POINTS

- Both pregnancy and exercise are associated with increased oxygen uptake, cardiac output, and cardiovascular training effects. These effects precede the development of metabolic demands of the mature conceptus.
- Pregnancy does not change the maternal cardiorespiratory nor hormonal response to exertion, except that resting oxygen uptake and cardiac output are increased in pregnancy.
- Maternal exertion for intervals of less than 30 minutes at heart rates of less than 150 beats per minute under conditions of normal hydration and cool ambient temperature has no measurable adverse effect on fetal environment or well-being. Sedentary women may safely initiate a moderate-intensity exercise training program during pregnancy.

- Maternal exercise training may improve insulin sensitivity transiently and has been shown to reduce hyperglycemia in gestational diabetic pregnancy. Chronic exercise training throughout pregnancy may reduce fetal weight and fat content among athletes.
- Exertional bouts in patients with type 1 diabetes are best preceded by a light meal and a reduction of insulin dose by 30% to 50%.
- Diabetic neuropathy, microvascular disease, and diminished counterregulatory capacity may adversely impact on maternal response to exertion. Individuals with long-standing diabetes embarking on an exercise training program should do so under close observation.

REFERENCES

1. Summary and recommendations of the Second International Workshop-Conference on Gestational Diabetes Mellitus. *Diabetes* 2985;34[Suppl 2]:123.
2. Astrand PO, Cuddy TE, Saltin B, et al. Cardiac output during submaximal and maximal work. *J Appl Physiol* 1964;19:268.
3. Karpman VL. Pumping function of the heart and blood flow in great vessels. In: *Cardiovascular system and physical exercise*. Boca Raton, FL: CRC Press, 1987:138.
4. Christensen NJ, Garbo H, Hansen JF, et al. Catecholamines and exercise. *Diabetes* 1979;28[Suppl 1]:58.
5. Peronnet F, Beliveau L, Boudreau G, et al. Regional plasma catecholamine removal and release at rest and exercise in dogs. *Am J Physiol* 1988;254:8663.
6. Horvath ES. Exercise in the treatment of NIDDM. Applications for GDM? *Diabetes* 1979;40[Suppl 1]:33.
7. Hohimer AR, Smith OA. Decreased renal blood flow in baboon during mild dynamic leg exercise. *Am J Physiol* 1979;236:1-1141.
8. Astrand PO, Rodahl K. Physical training. In: *Textbook of work physiology*, 3d ed. New York: McGraw Hill, 1986:420.
9. Peronnet F, Ferguson RI, Perrault H, et al. Echocardiography and the athlete's heart. *Physician Sports Med* 1981;9:102.
10. Saltin B, Blomqvist B, Mitchell JH, et al. Response to submaximal and maximal exercise after bed rest and training. *Circulation* 1968;38[Suppl 5]:1.
11. Felig P, Wahren J. Role of insulin and glucagon in the regulation of hepatic glucose production during exercise. *Diabetes* 1979;28[Suppl]:17.
12. Vranic M, Kawamori R. Essential roles of insulin and glucagon in regulating glucose fluxes during exercise in dogs. *Diabetes* 1978;28[Suppl 1]:45.
13. Galbo H, Holst JJ, Christensen NJ. Glucagon and plasma catecholamine responses to graded and prolonged exercise in man. *J Appl Physiol* 1975;38:70.
14. Sahlin K, Katz A, Henriksson J. Redox state and lactate accumulation in human skeletal muscle during dynamic exercise. *Biochem J* 1987;245:551.
15. Linnarsson D. Dynamics of pulmonary gas exchange and heart rate changes at start and end of exercise. *Acta Physiol Scand* 1974;415[Suppl]:24.
16. Fredholm BB. Inhibition of fatty acid release from adipose tissue by high arterial lactate concentration. *Acta Physiol Scand* 1969;330[Suppl]:77A.
17. Wahren J, Felig P, Ahlborg G, Jorfeldt L. Glucose metabolism during leg exercise in man. *J Clin Invest* 1971;50:2715.

18. Wahren J. Glucose turnover during exercise in healthy men and in patients with diabetes mellitus. Diabetes 28:82, 1979.

19. Calles J, Conningham JJ, Nelson L, et al. Glucose turnover during recovery from intensive exercise. *Diabetes* 1983;32:734.

20. Katz A, Groberg S, Sahlin K, Wahren J. Leg glucose uptake during dynamic exercise in man. *Am J Physiol* 1986;151:E65.

21. Berger M, Hagg S, Ruderman NB. Glucose metabolism in perfused skeletal muscle. Interaction of insulin and exercise on glucose uptake. *Biochem J* 1975;146:231.

22. Richter EA, Mikines KJ, Galbo H, et al. Effect of exercise in insulin action human skeletal muscle. *J Appl Physiol* 1989;66:876.

23. Larsen JJS, Dela F, Madsbad S, et al. The effect of intense exercise on postprandial glucose homeostasis in type II diabetic patients. *Diabetologia* 1999;42:1282–1292.

24. Ben-Esra, B, Jankowski C, Kendrick K, Nichols D. Effect of intensity and energy expenditure on postexercise insulin responses in women. *J Appl Physiol* 1995;79:2029–2034.

25. Mikines KJ, Sonne B, Tronier B, Galbo H. Effects of acute exercise and detraining on insulin action in trained men. *J Appl Physiol* 1989;66:704.

26. Devlin JT, Horton ES. Effects of prior high-intensity exercise on glucose metabolism in normal and insulin-resistant men. *Diabetes* 1985;34:973.

27. Oscai LB, Patterson JA, Bogard DL, et al. Normalization of serum triglycerides and lipoprotein electrophoretic patterns by exercise. *Am J Cardiol* 1981;30:775.

28. Poehlman ET. A review: exercise and its influence on resting energy metabolism in man. *Med Sci Sports Exerc* 1989;21:515.

29. Tremblay A, Fontain E, Poehlman ET, et al. The effect of exercise-training on resting metabolic rate in lean and moderately obese individuals. *Int J Obes* 1986;10:511.

30. Lennon D, Nagle F, Stratman F, et al. Diet and exercise training effects on resting metabolic rate. *Int J Obes* 1984;9:39.

31. Poehlman ET, Melby CL, Badylak SF, et al. Aerobic fitness and resting energy expenditure in young adult males. *Metabolism* 1989;38:85.

32. Burstein R, Polychronakos C, Toews CJ, et al. Acute reversal of the enhanced insulin action in trained athletes. *Diabetes* 1985;34:756.

33. DeFronzo RA, Sherwin RS, Kraemer N. Effect of physical training on insulin action in obesity. *Diabetes* 1987;36:1379.

34. Wood D, Haskell WL, Plair SN, et al. Increased exercise level and plasma lipoprotein concentrations: a one year randomized, controlled study in sedentary middle-aged men. *Metabolism* 1983;32:31.

35. Allison TH, Iammarino RM, Metz KF, et al. Failure of exercise to increase high density lipoprotein cholesterol. *J Cardiac Rehabil* 1981;1:257.

36. Wynne TP, Frey MA, Laubach LL, et al. Effect of a controlled exercise program on serum lipoprotein levels in women on oral contraceptives. *Metabolism* 1980;29:1267.

37. Nadeay A, Rousseau-Migneron S, Tancrede G, et al. Diminished glucagon response to epinephrine in physically trained diabetic rats. *Diabetes* 1985;34:1278.

38. Rubler S, Damani PM, Pinto ERL. Cardiac size and performance during pregnancy estimated with echocardiography. *Am J Cardiol* 1977;40:534.

39. Laird-Meeter K, van de Lay G, Born TH, et al. Cardiocirculatory adjustments during pregnancy: an echocardiographic study. *Clin Cardiol* 1979;2:328.

40. Capeless EL, Clapp JF. Cardiovascular change in early phase of pregnancy. *Am J Obstet Gynecol* 1989;161:1449.

41. Longo LD. Maternal blood volume and cardiac output during pregnancy: a hypothesis of endocrinologic control. *Am J Physiol* 1983;245:8720.

42. Hytten FE, Paintin DB. Increase in plasma volume during normal pregnancy. *J Obstet Gynaecol Br Cp* 1963;70:402.

43. Lund CJ, Donovan JC. Blood volume during pregnancy. *Am J Obstet Gynecol* 1967;98:393.

44. Clapp JF. Cardiac output and uterine blood flow in the pregnant ewe. *Am J Obstet Gynecol* 1978;130:419.

45. Carpenter MW, Sady SP, Sady MA, et al. Effect of maternal weight gain during pregnancy on exercise performance. *J Appl Physiol* 1990;68:1173.

46. Ueland K, Novy MJ, Peterson EN, et al. Maternal cardiovascular dynamics. *Am J Obstet Gynecol* 1969;104:856.

47. Knuttgen HG, Emerson K. Physiological response to pregnancy at rest and during exercise. *J Appl Physiol* 1974;36:549.

48. Sady SA, Carpenter MW, Thompson PD, et al. Cardiovascular response to cycle exercise during and after pregnancy. *J Appl Physiol* 1989;65:336.

49. Pernoll ML, Metcalfe J, Schlenker TT, et al. Oxygen consumption at rest and during exercise in pregnancy. *Respir Physiol* 1975;25:285.

50. Lehmann V, Regnat K. Untersuchung sur korperlighen Belastungsfahigkeit schwangeren Frauen. Der Einfluss standardisierter arbeit our Herzkreislaumsystem, Ventilation, Gasaustausch, Kohlenhydratstoffwechsel and Saure-Basenhaushalt. *Z Geburtshilfe Perinatol* 1976;180:279.

51. Blackburn MW, Calloway DH. Heart rate and energy expenditure of pregnant and lactating women. *Am J Clin Nutr* 1985;42:1161.

52. Sady SA, Carpenter MW, Sady MA, et al. Prediction of O_2max during cycle exercise in pregnant women. *J Appl Physiol* 1988;65:657.

53. Lotgering FK, Van Doorn MB, Struijk PC, et al. Exercise responses in pregnant sheep: blood gases temperatures and fetal cardiovascular system. *J Appl Physiol* 1983;55:834.

54. Morton MJ, Paul MS, Campos GR, et al. Exercise dynamics in late gestation. Effects of physical training. *Am J Obstet Gynecol* 1985;159:91.

55. Barron WM, Mujais SK, Zinaman M, et al. Plasma catecholamine responses to physiologic stimuli in normal human pregnancy. *Am J Obstet Gynecol* 1986;154:80.

56. Artal R, Platt LD, Sperling M, et al. Exercise in pregnancy. I. Maternal cardiovascular and metabolic responses in normal pregnancy. *Am J Obstet Gynecol* 1981;140:123.

57. Bessinger, RC, McMurray RG, Hackney AC. Substrate utilization and hormonal responses to moderate intensity exercise during pregnancy and after delivery. *Am J Obstet Gynecol* 1002;186:757–764.

58. Artal R, Wiswell R, Romeo Y. Hormonal responses to exercise in diabetic and nondiabetic pregnancy patients. *Diabetes* 1985;34[Suppl 2]:7880.

59. Avery MD, Walker AJ. Acute effect of exercise on blood glucose and insulin levels in women with gestational diabetes. *J Matern Fetal Med* 2001;10:52–58.

60. Rowell LB. *Human circulation: regulation during physical stress.* New York: Oxford University Press, 1986.

61. Clapp JF. Acute exercise stress in the pregnant ewe. *Am J Obstet Gynecol* 1980;136:489.

62. Artal R, Paul RH, Romeo Y, et al. Fetal bradycardia induced by maternal exercise. *Lancet* 1984;2:258.

63. Jovanovic L, Kessler A, Peterson CM. Human maternal and fetal response to graded. exercise. *J Appl Physiol* 1985;58:1719.

64. Artal R, Rutherford S, Romeo Y, et al. Fetal heart rate responses to maternal exercise. *Diabetes* 1985;34[Suppl 2]:78.

65. Carpenter MW, Sady SP, Hoegsberg B, et al. Fetal heart rate response to maternal exertion. *JAMA* 1988;259:20.

66. Lotgering FK, Van Doorn MB, Struijk PC, et al. Maximal aerobic exercise in pregnant women: heart rate, O_2 consumption, CO_2 production and ventilation. *J Appl Physiol* 1991;70:1016.

67. Carpenter MW, Sady S, Haydon B, et al. Maternal exercise duration and intensity affect fetal heart rate. Paper presented at American College of Sports Medicine annual meeting, Baltimore, 1989.

68. Collings CMS, Curet LB. Fetal heart rate response to maternal exercise. *Am J Obstet Gynecol* 1985;151:498.

69. Carr SR, Carpenter MW, Terry R, et al. Obstetrical outcome in aerobically trained women. Paper presented at Society for Perinatal Obstetricians conference, Orlando, FL, 1992.

70. Clapp JF, Dickstein S. Endurance exercise and pregnancy outcome. *Med Sci Sports Exerc* 1984;16:556.

71. Clapp JF, Capeless EL. Neonatal morphometrics after endurance exercise during pregnancy. *Am J Obstet Gynecol* 1990;163:1805.

72. Clapp JF. The course of labor after endurance exercise during pregnancy. *Am J Obstet Gynecol* 1990;163:1799.

73. Dale E, Mullinax KM, Bryan D. Exercise during pregnancy: effects on the fetus. *Can J Appl Sport Sci* 1982;7:98.

74. Hall DC, Kaufmann DA. Effects of aerobic and strength conditioning on pregnancy outcomes. *Am J Obstet Gynecol* 1987;157:1199.

75. Kulpa PJ, White BM, Visscher R. Aerobic exercise in pregnancy. *Am J Obstet Gynecol* 1987;156:1395.

76. Vranic M, Horvath S, Wahren J. Exercise and diabetes: an overview. *Diabetes* 1978;28[Suppl 1]:107.

77. Allen FM, Stillman E, Fritz R. Total dietary regulation in the treatment of diabetes. In: *Exercise monograph 11*. New York: Rockefeller Institute of Medical Research, 1919:486.

78. Hetzel KL, Long CNH. *Metabolism* of the diabetic individual during and after muscular exercise. *Proc R Soc Lond (Biol)* 1926;99:279.

79. Lawrence RD. The effects of exercise on insulin action in diabetes. *BMJ* 1926;1:648.

80. Joslin EP, Root HF, White P, et al. *The treatment of diabetes mellitus*, 5th ed. Philadelphia: Lea & Febiger, 1936.

81. Marble A, Smith RM. Exercise in diabetes mellitus. *Arch Intern Med* 1936;58:577.

82. Baevre J, Sovik O, Wisness A, et al. Metabolic responses to physical training in young insulin-dependent diabetics. *Scand J Clin Lab Invest* 1985;45:109.

83. Pruett EDR, Machlum S. Muscular exercise and metabolism in male juvenile diabetics. *Scand J Clin Lab Invest* 1973;32:139.

84. Kemmer FW, Berger M. Exercise in therapy and the life of diabetic patients. *Clin Sci* 1984;67:279.

85. Pettit DJ, Aleck KA, Baird RJ, et al. Congenital susceptibility to NIDDM. *Diabetes* 1988;37:622.

86. Kissebah AH, Vydelingum N, Murray R, et al. Relation of body fat distribution to metabolic complications of obesity. J Clin Endocrinol Metab 1983;54:254.

87. Ohlson LO, Larsson B, Svardsudd K, et al. The influence of body fat distribution on the incidence of diabetes mellitus. *Diabetes* 1985;34:1055.

88. Saltin B, Lindegrade F, Houston R, et al. Physical training and glucose tolerance in middle aged men with chemical diabetes. *Diabetes* 1979;28[Suppl 1]:30.

89. Eriksson KF, Lindgarde F. Prevention of type 2 (non-insulin-dependent) diabetes mellitus by diet and physical exercise. *Diabetologia* 1991;34:891.

90. Liljenquist JE, Mueller GL, Cherrington AD, et al. Hyperglycemia per se (insulin and glucagon withdrawn) can inhibit hepatic glucose production in man. *J Clin Endocrinol Metab* 1979;48:171.

91. Sacca L, Hendler R, Sherwin RS. Hyperglycemia inhibits glucose production in man independent of changes in glucoregulatory hormones. *J Clin Endocrinol Metab* 1978;47:1160.

92. Kolterman OG, Gray RS, Grifin J, et al. Receptor and postreceptor defects contribute to the insulin resistance in non-insulin-dependent diabetes mellitus. *J Clin Invest* 1981;68:957.

93. Revers RR, Fink R, Griffin j, et al. Influence of hyperglycemia on insulin's *in vivo* effects in type II diabetes. *J Clin Invest* 1984;73:664.

94. Zinman B, Vranic M. *Diabetes* and exercise. *Med Clin North Am* 1985;69:145.

95. Berger M, Berchtold P, Cupper JH, et al. Metabolic and hormonal effects of muscular exercise in juvenile type diabetics. *Diabetologia* 1977;13:355.

96. Lufkin G, Nelson R, Hill L, et al. An analysis of diabetic pregnancies at Mayo Clinic, 1950–79. *Diabetes Care* 1984;7:539.

97. Lobue C, Goodin RC. Treatment of fetal distress during diabetic ketoacidosis. *J Reprod Med* 1978;20:101.

98. Zinman B, Murray FT, Vranic M, et al. Glucoregulation during moderate exercise in insulin treated diabetes. *J Clin Endocrinol Metab* 1977;45:641.

99. Schiffrin A, Parikh S. Accommodating planned exercise in type I diabetic patients on intensive treatment. *Diabetes Care* 1985;8:337.

100. Hollingsworth DR, Moore TR. Postprandial walking exercise in pregnant insulin-dependent (type 1) diabetic women: reduction of plasma lipid levels but absence of a significant effect on glucemic control. *Am J Obstet Gynecol* 1987;157:1359.

101. Helmrich SP, Ragland DR, Leung RW, et al. Physical activity and reduced occurrence of non-insulin dependent diabetes mellitus. *N Engl J Med* 1991;325:147.

102. Manson JE, Rimm EB, Stampfer MJ, et al. Physical activity and incidence of non-insulin dependent diabetes mellitus in women. *Lancet* 1991;338:774.

103. Larsen JJS, Dela F, Madsbad S, et al. The effect of intense exercise on postprandial glucose homeostasis in type II diabetic patients. *Diabetologia* 1999;42:1282–1292.

104. Sartor G, Schersten B, Carlstrom S, et al. Ten year followup of subjects with impaired glucose tolerance: prevention of diabetes by tolbutamide and diet regulation. *Diabetes* 1980;29:41.

105. Holloszy JO, Schultz J, Kusnierkiewicz H, et al. Effects of exercise on glucose tolerance and insulin resistance. *Acta Med Scand* 1985;711[Suppl]:55.

106. Reitman JS, Vasquez B, Klimes I, et al. Improvement of glucose of homeostasis after exercise training in non-insulin-dependent diabetes. *Diabetes Care* 1984;7:434.

107. Jenkins AB, Furler SM, Bruce DG, et al. Regulation of hepatic glucose output during moderate exercise in non-insulin-dependent diabetes. *Metabolism* 1988;37:966.

108. Segal KR, Edano A, Albu A, et al. Effect of exercise training on insulin sensitivity and glucose metabolism in lean, obese and diabetic men. *J App Physiol* 1991;71:2402.

109. Kaplan RM, Hartwell SL, Wilson DK, et al. Effects of diet and exercise interventions on control and quality of life in non-insulin-dependent diabetes mellitus. *Gen Intern Med* 1987;2:220.

110. Ronemaa T, Mattila K, Lehtonen A, et al. A controlled randomised study on the effect of long term physical exercise on the metabolic control in type 2 diabetic patients. *Acta Med Scand* 1986;220:219.

111. Wing RR, Epstein LH, Paternostro-Bayles M, et al. Exercise in a behavioural weight control programme for obese patients with type 2 (non-insulin-dependent) diabetes. *Diabetologia* 1988;31:902.

112. Horton ES. Exercise in the treatment of NIDDM. Applications for GDM? *Diabetes* 1991;40[Suppl 2]:175.

113. O'Sullivan JB. Subsequent morbidity among gestational diabetic women. In: Sutherland HW, Stowers JM, eds. *Carbohydrate metabolism in pregnancy and the newborn*. Edinburgh: Churchill Livingstone, 1984:174.

114. Dye TD, Knox KL, Artal R, et al. Physical activity, obesity and diabetes in pregnancy. *Am J Epidemiol* 1997;146:961–965.

115. Bung P, Artal R, Khodiguian N, et al. Exercise in gestational diabetes: an optional therapeutic approach. *Diabetes* 1991;40 [Suppl 2]:182.

116. Jovanovic-Peterson L, Durak EP, Peterson CM. Randomized trial of diet versus diet plus cardiovascular conditioning on glucose levels in gestational diabetes. *Am J Obstet Gynecol* 1989; 161:415.

117. Avery MD, Leon AS, Kopher RA. Effects of a partially home-based exercise program for women with gestational diabetes. *Obstet Gynecol* 1997;89:10–15.

22

PRENATAL DIAGNOSIS AND MANAGEMENT OF CONGENITAL MALFORMATIONS IN PREGNANCIES COMPLICATED BY DIABETES

SANDRO GABRIELLI
GIANLUIGI PILU
E. ALBERT REECE

Despite the improvement in perinatal morbidity and mortality in pregnancies with well-controlled diabetes, problems related to congenital malformations persist. Most of the perinatal mortality in infants of diabetic mothers (IDMs) is now attributed to congenital anomalies, whereas most of the perinatal morbidity is related to growth aberrations.

The frequency of congenital anomalies among diabetic offspring at birth is estimated at 5% to 10%. If one assumes a 2.5% incidence of major anomalies in the overall population (1,2), this represents at least a doubling of the risk for anomalies. The pregnancies of women with gestational diabetes are not associated with an increase in anomalous offspring, whereas those of women with type 1 and type 2 diabetes are. This is not surprising, because the poorer the diabetic control during organogenesis, the greater the chance for congenital anomalies (3–6). This concept has been supported by many studies. Furthermore, there is encouraging information from several large clinical studies suggesting that strict glucose control before and immediately after conception will decrease the incidence of congenital anomalies (7).

Ultrasonography represents the most effective method to identify anomalies. It is for this reason that the sonographic assessment of fetal development is so fundamental to the management of pregnancies complicated by diabetes. Maternal diabetes is a well-recognized indication for a targeted sonographic examination of fetal anatomy at midgestation, and there is a general consensus that this examination should include a detailed survey of the fetal heart (8,9). Prenatal diagnosis by ultrasonography will have no effect on the incidence of anomalies in the offspring of women with diabetes, but it can appreciably affect how a pregnancy is managed. Women with diabetes are generally aware of their

increased likelihood to deliver anomalous infants, and a normal ultrasound examination result often allays their fears. Furthermore, the ability to perform prenatal diagnosis early in the pregnancy provides the option for early termination of pregnancy. Some fetuses with spina bifida, gastrointestinal anomalies, cardiac defects, or obstructive uropathy can benefit greatly from information provided by ultrasonography that will allow alteration in obstetric management to optimize fetal outcome.

The proportion of anomalies that will be detected by such a scan is controversial. Many studies have addressed the issue of the examination of low-risk patients with variable results. The result of targeted examinations depends largely on the criteria for selection, and the specific experience with pregnancies complicated by diabetes is limited. However, recent studies suggest that a well-performed midtrimester ultrasound examination will probably detect 70% or more of the anomalies that are identifiable at birth (10–12).

Our aim is to provide basic notions useful for the ultrasound identification of fetal anomalies, focusing on the most frequent ones. We also refer interested readers to the many detailed textbooks that have been produced on this subject (8).

CENTRAL NERVOUS SYSTEM ANOMALIES

Neural Tube Defects

These anomalies include anencephaly, spina bifida, and encephalocele. In anencephaly there is absence of the cranial vault (acrania) with secondary degeneration of the brain. Encephaloceles are cranial defects, usually occipital, with herniated fluid-filled or brain-filled cysts. In spina bifida the neural arch, usually in the lumbosacral region, is incomplete, with secondary damage to the exposed nerves. The incidence of neural tube defects (NTDs) is subject to large geographic and temporal variations; in Europe the prevalence is about 1 to 2 per 1,000 births, with a peak of 5 per 1,000 births in South Wales. Anencephaly and spina bifida, with an approximately equal prevalence, account for 95% of the cases and encephalocele for the remaining 5%.

NTDs are multifactorial disorders. Chromosomal abnormalities, single mutant genes, and maternal diabetes mellitus or ingestion of teratogens, such as antiepileptic drugs, are implicated in about 10% of the cases. Fetuses of women with diabetes have been reported to have a much higher incidence of NTDs than the general population (up to 19.5 per 1,000). Therefore, all women with diabetes should be offered a careful ultrasound examination of the fetal head and spine. Maternal serum α-fetoprotein (MSAFP) screening is also commonly recommended in the United States (13). The median MSAFP levels are lower per gestational age in women with diabetes than in the normal population, although the mechanism is still debated (13).

The sonographic diagnosis of anencephaly during the second trimester of pregnancy is based on the demonstration of absence of the cranial vault and cerebral hemispheres. The diagnosis can be made after 11 weeks, when ossification of the skull normally occurs. Ultrasonography has demonstrated that there is progression from acrania to exencephaly and finally anencephaly. In the first trimester the pathognomonic feature is acrania (Fig. 22-1), the brain being either entirely normal or at varying degrees of distortion and disruption (14).

Diagnosis of spina bifida requires the systematic examination of each neural arch from the cervical to the sacral region, both transversely and longitudinally. In the transverse scan the normal neural arch appears as a closed circle with an intact skin covering, whereas in spina bifida the arch is U shaped and there is an associated bulging meningocele (thin-walled cyst) or myelomeningocele. The extent of the defect and any associated kyphoscoliosis are best assessed in the longitudinal scan (Fig. 22-1).

The diagnosis of spina bifida has been greatly enhanced by the recognition of associated abnormalities in the skull and brain. These abnormalities include frontal bone scalloping (lemon sign) and obliteration of the cisterna magna, with either an absent cerebellum or abnormal anterior curvature of the cerebellar hemispheres (banana sign) (Fig. 22-1). These easily recognizable alterations in skull and brain morphology are often more readily attainable than detailed spinal views (15).

Encephaloceles are recognized as cranial defects with herniated fluid-filled or brain-filled cysts. They are most commonly found in an occipital location (75% of the cases) but alternative sites include the frontoethmoidal and parietal regions.

The diagnosis of an NTD, and of spina bifida in particular, is best performed by an operator who has considerable experience in this type of evaluation. Although the positive predictive accuracy of the ultrasound diagnosis of an NTD is high, the negative predictive accuracy may not be as reliable, depending on the expertise of the sonologist. Therefore, while in some centers ultrasonography is the only examination performed in patients with an elevated MSAFP, in other centers the diagnostic workup includes

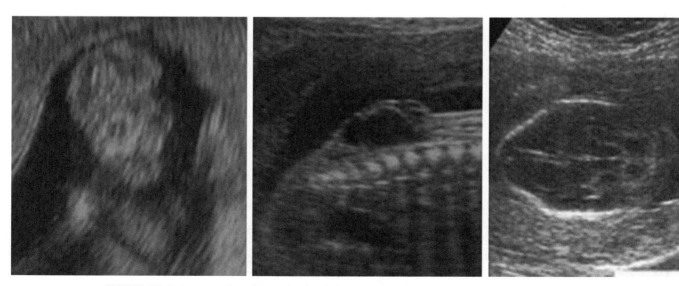

FIGURE 22-1. Sonography of neural tube defects. From left to right: typical appearance of an early stage of anencephaly (acrania) in a 12 weeks' fetus; sagittal view of myelomeningocele; and cranial signs of fetal spina bifida, frontal bossing (lemon sign), and hypoplasia of posterior fossa (banana sign).

amniocentesis for amniotic fluid α-fetoprotein and *N*-acetylcholinesterase determinations.

Anencephaly is usually fatal at or within hours of birth. In encephalocele the prognosis is inversely related to the amount of herniated cerebral tissue; overall, the neonatal mortality rate is about 40%, and more than 80% of survivors are intellectually and neurologically handicapped. In spina bifida, the surviving infants range from minimally to severely handicapped, with paralysis in the lower limbs and incontinence of bowel and bladder function; despite the associated hydrocephalus requiring surgery, intelligence may be normal.

Ventriculomegaly

The term *ventriculomegaly* is commonly used to indicate enlargement of the lateral cerebral ventricles. The incidence of this finding is unclear. Severe ventriculomegaly, or hydrocephalus, is found in less than 1 per 1,000 births. Ventriculomegaly may be the consequence of cerebral malformations, chromosomal abnormalities, or congenital infection. Genetic factors play an important role. About 25% of cases of severe ventriculomegaly occurring in males are due to X-linked transmission.

Fetal ventriculomegaly is diagnosed sonographically by the demonstration of abnormally dilated lateral cerebral ventricles. A transverse scan of the fetal head at the level of the cavum septum pellucidum will demonstrate the dilated lateral ventricles, defined by an internal diameter of the posterior horn (or atrium) of 10 mm or more. The choroid plexuses, which normally fill the lateral ventricles, are surrounded by fluid. A diameter of 10 to 15 mm indicates borderline ventriculomegaly. A diameter greater than 15 mm indicates moderate to severe ventriculomegaly (16). Certainly before 24 weeks and particularly in cases of associated spina bifida, the head circumference may be small rather than large for gestation.

Fetal or perinatal death and neurodevelopment in survivors are strongly related to the presence of other malformations and chromosomal defects. Isolated severe ventriculomegaly is associated with an increased risk of perinatal death and a 50% chance for neurologic sequelae in survivors. Although mild ventriculomegaly (atrial width of 10–15 mm) is generally associated with a good prognosis, it is also the condition with the highest incidence of chromosomal abnormalities (often trisomy 21). In addition in a few cases with apparently isolated mild ventriculomegaly, there may be an underlying cerebral maldevelopment (such as lissencephaly) or a destructive lesion (such as periventricular leukomalacia). Recent evidence suggests that in about 10% of cases there is mild to moderate neurodevelopmental delay (17).

Microcephaly

Microcephaly, a small head and brain, may result from chromosomal and genetic abnormalities, fetal hypoxia, con-

genital infection, and exposure to radiation or other teratogens, such as maternal anticoagulation with warfarin. A disproportion between the size of the skull and the face characterizes microcephaly. The brain is small, with the cerebral hemispheres affected to a greater extent than the midbrain and posterior fossa. This condition is commonly found in the presence of other brain abnormalities, such as encephalocele or holoprosencephaly. Naeye (18) has reported an increased incidence in IDMs of this relatively rare problem, which ordinarily affects only 1 in 6,200 infants.

Microcephaly should be suspected when the fetal head is more than 2 standard deviations below the mean. The diagnosis is difficult, however, for two reasons. First, there is not an absolute cut-off that distinguishes normal fetuses with constitutionally small heads from microcephalics. Second, microcephaly has a variable natural history. In many cases, the head is of normal size until late gestation and even at birth. In practice, a certain diagnosis is only possible when the head is extremely small (≤4 standard deviations below the mean) or there are associated brain abnormalities, such as holoprosencephaly. In some cases, probably a minority, the condition is rapidly recognized from midgestation (19) (Fig. 22-2). In other cases, the diagnosis is possible only in the third trimester or after birth (20). Microcephaly is an untreatable condition with a high risk for significant mental retardation. The prognosis depends largely on the underlying cause and the associated anomalies.

Holoprosencephaly

Holoprosencephaly is a spectrum of cerebral abnormalities resulting from incomplete cleavage of the forebrain. There are three types according to the degree of forebrain cleavage. The alobar type, which is the most severe, is characterized by a monoventricular cavity and fusion of the thalami. In the semilobar type, there is partial segmentation of the ventricles and cerebral hemispheres posteriorly with incomplete fusion of the thalami. In lobar holoprosencephaly, there is normal separation of the ventricles and thalami but absence of the septum pellucidum. The first two types are often accompanied by microcephaly and facial abnormalities.

Holoprosencephaly is found in about 1 per 10,000 births. Although in many cases the cause is a chromosomal abnormality (usually trisomy 13) or a genetic disorder with an autosomal-dominant or -recessive mode of transmission, the etiology is often unknown. For sporadic, nonchromosomal holoprosencephaly, the empirical recurrence risk is 6%.

In the standard transverse view of the fetal head performed for measurement of the biparietal diameter, there is a single dilated midline ventricle replacing the two lateral ventricles or partial segmentation of the ventricles. The alobar and semilobar types are often associated with facial

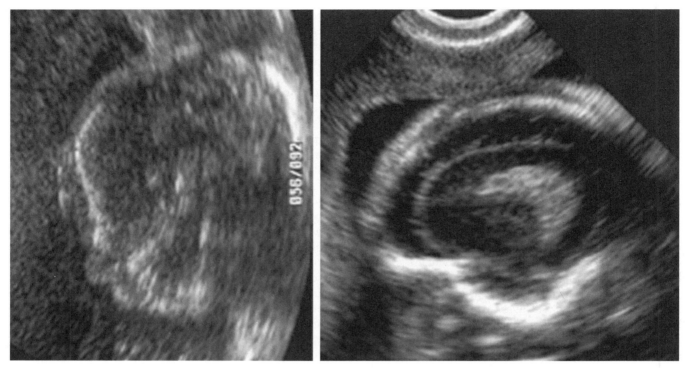

FIGURE 22-2. Sonography of severe microcephaly at 22 weeks' gestation. The head circumference was −2 standard deviations from the mean, and the definitive diagnosis was possible by noting marked flattening of the forehead (left) and increased size of the subarachnoid spaces as a consequence of cerebral hypoplasia (right).

defects, such as hypotelorism or cyclopia, a facial cleft and nasal hypoplasia or a proboscis (16). Alobar and semilobar holoprosencephaly are lethal. Lobar holoprosencephaly is associated with mental retardation.

Agenesis of the Corpus Callosum

The corpus callosum is a bundle of fibers that connects the two cerebral hemispheres. It develops at 12 to 18 weeks of gestation. Agenesis of the corpus callosum may be either complete or partial (usually affecting the posterior part). Agenesis of the corpus callosum is found in about 5 per 1,000 births. It may be due to maldevelopment or secondary to a destructive lesion. It is commonly associated with chromosomal abnormalities (usually trisomies 18, 13, and 8) and more than 100 genetic syndromes.

The corpus callosum is not visible in the standard transverse views of the brain, but agenesis of the corpus callosum may be suspected by the absence of the cavum septum pellucidum. The lateral ventricles usually are mildly enlarged and have a typical teardrop configuration. Agenesis of the corpus callosum is demonstrated in the midcoronal and midsagittal views, which may require vaginal sonography. The outcome is dependent mostly on the association with other anomalies. In about 80% of those with apparently

isolated agenesis of the corpus callosum, development is normal (21).

Dandy-Walker Complex

The Dandy-Walker complex refers to a spectrum of abnormalities of the cerebellar vermis, cystic dilation of the fourth ventricle, and enlargement of the cisterna magna. The condition is classified into (a) Dandy-Walker malformation (complete or partial agenesis of the cerebellar vermis and enlarged posterior fossa), (b) Dandy-Walker variant (partial agenesis of the cerebellar vermis without enlargement of the posterior fossa), and (c) mega–cisterna magna (normal vermis and fourth ventricle). The Dandy-Walker complex is a nonspecific end point of chromosomal abnormalities (usually trisomies 18 or 13 and triploidy), more than 50 genetic syndromes, congenital infection, or teratogens such as warfarin, but it can also be an isolated finding.

Ultrasonographically, the contents of the posterior fossa are visualized through a transverse suboccipito-bregmatic section of the fetal head. In the Dandy-Walker malformation there is cystic dilatation of the cisterna magna with partial or complete agenesis of the vermis; in more than 50% of the cases there is associated hydrocephalus and other extracranial defects. Enlarged cisterna magna is diagnosed if the vertical distance from the vermis to the inner border of the skull is more than 10 mm. Prenatal diagnosis of isolated partial agenesis of the vermis is difficult, and a false diagnosis can be made if the angle of insonation is too steep (16).

Dandy-Walker malformation is associated with a high postnatal mortality rate (~20%) and a high incidence (>50%) of impaired intellectual and neurologic development. Experience with apparently isolated partial agenesis of the vermis or enlarged cisterna magna is limited, and the prognosis for these conditions is uncertain.

CRANIOFACIAL ANOMALIES

Facial Clefts

This term refers to a wide spectrum of clefting defects (unilateral, bilateral, less commonly midline or atypical) usually involving the upper lip, the palate, or both. Cleft palate without cleft lip is a distinct disorder. Facial clefts encompass a broad spectrum of severity, ranging from minimal defects, such as a bifid uvula, linear indentation of the lip, or submucous cleft of the soft palate, to large deep defects of the facial bones and soft tissues. The typical cleft lip will appear as a linear defect extending from one side of the lip into the nostril. Cleft palate associated with cleft lip may extend through the alveolar ridge and hard palate, reaching the floor of the nasal cavity or even the floor of the orbit. Isolated cleft palate may include defects of the hard palate, the soft palate, or both. Cleft lip and palate is unilateral in about 75% of cases, and the left side is more often involved than the right side.

Facial clefting is found in about 1 per 800 births. In about 50% of cases both the lip and palate are defective, in 25% only the lip and in 25% only the palate is involved.

The face is formed by the fusion of four outgrowths of mesenchyme (frontonasal, mandibular, and paired maxillary swellings) and facial clefting is usually caused by failure of fusion of these swellings. Cleft lip with or without cleft palate is usually (>80% of cases) an isolated condition, but in 20% of cases it is associated with one of more than 100 genetic syndromes. Isolated cleft palate is a different condition and is more commonly associated with any one of more than 200 genetic syndromes. All forms of inheritance have been described, including autosomal dominant, autosomal recessive, X-linked dominant, and X-linked recessive. Associated anomalies are found in about 50% of patients with isolated cleft palate and in about 15% of those with cleft lip and palate. Chromosomal abnormalities (mainly trisomy 13 and 18) are found in 1% to 2% of cases and exposure to teratogens (such as antiepileptic drugs) in about 5% of cases. Recurrences are type specific; if the index case has cleft lip and palate there is no increased risk for isolated cleft palate, and vice versa. Median cleft lip, which accounts for about 0.5% of all cases of cleft lip, is usually associated with holoprosencephaly or the oral-facial-digital syndrome.

The sonographic diagnosis of cleft lip depends on demonstration of a groove extending from one of the nostrils to the mouth. Evaluation of the alveolar ridge helps the examining physician to determine whether the defect is limited to the lips or involves the hard palate. Both transverse and coronal planes can be used. The diagnosis of isolated cleft palate is usually impossible with antenatal ultrasonography (22).

Minimal defects, such as linear indentations of the lips or submucosal cleft of the soft palate, may not require surgical correction. Larger defects cause cosmetic, swallowing, and respiratory problems. Recent advances in surgical technique have produced good cosmetic and functional results. However, prognosis depends primarily on the presence and type of associated anomalies.

Cardiac Anomalies

Abnormalities of the heart and great arteries are among the most common congenital malformations, with an estimated incidence of 5 per 1,000 births and about 30 per 1,000 stillbirths. In general, about half are either severe or require surgery early in life and are generally referred to as major cardiac abnormalities. Defects of the cardiovascular system are among the most commonly encountered malformations in the IDM and occur much more frequently in these patients than in infants born to women with normal carbohydrate metabolism. The metabolic milieu that exists in the pregnant woman with diabetes can adversely affect normal fetal cardiac growth and development in several ways. When diabetes mellitus is present during the first trimester, there can be abnormal cardiovascular organogenesis. The congenital heart disease resulting from this metabolic abnormality appears to be related to abnormal neural crest cell migration and resulting malformations of the conotruncus. Defects such as double-outlet right ventricle (DORV) and truncus arteriosus may result (23). Because cardiac looping and septation occur between the third and sixth postconceptional weeks, maintaining strict metabolic control both before and after conception is a reasonable strategy to minimize the incidence of structural heart disease in the fetus of the woman with diabetes.

When diabetes mellitus is present in the third trimester, there is a strong association with the development of fetal hypertrophic cardiomyopathy, which may lead to left ventricular outflow tract obstruction (24–26). This hypertrophic cardiomyopathy typically resolves spontaneously within the first 6 months of postnatal life. Although debate continues, this phenomenon most likely results from fetal hyperinsulinemia in response to fetal hyperglycemia. There is reason to believe that good control of carbohydrate metabolism in the pregnant diabetic woman can decrease the likelihood of structural and functional heart disease in her offspring.

Fetal echocardiography is the primary diagnostic tool used to assess fetal cardiac structure and function. Studies from specialist centers report the diagnosis of about 80% of major defects at midgestation (9,27–29). Because abnormalities of cardiac structure and function resulting from either diabetic embryopathy or diabetic hypertrophic fetopathy can easily be demonstrated, fetal echocardiography is an important part of the prenatal evaluation of the pregnant woman with diabetes. This should be accomplished with both midtrimester scanning as well as third trimester evaluation. Earlier evaluation, at approximately 13 to 15 weeks, by either transabdominal or vaginal sonography, may be considered, because recent studies suggest that the sensitivity in the prediction of severe anomalies at this time is gestation is in the range of 50% to 70% (30). However, the examination should be corroborated by a repeat evaluation at 18 to 22 weeks of gestation.

A complete fetal echocardiographic examination should incorporate the following standard views: a demonstration of the visceral and cardiac situs, four-chamber view, ventriculoarterial connections, and the course of the great arteries. Real-time examination of cardiac structures is enhanced by the use of color Doppler. Different approaches are possible to visualize these anatomic details, and the interested reader is referred to specific works on this subject (31,32).

The echocardiographic features of the fetus with diabetic hypertrophic cardiomyopathy include restricted ventricular filling, dynamic left or right ventricular outflow tract obstruction, and global myocardial hypertrophy (25,26,33) (Fig. 22-3). Some or all of these findings may be present in any individual fetus, and to varying degrees. It is virtually unheard of to find clinically significant hypertrophic cardiomyopathy in the IDM without concomitant fetal macrosomia. The diagnosis of hypertrophic cardiomyopathy can be made using the fetal echocardiographic views mentioned above. M-mode measurements of the septal and ventricular wall may be helpful in these cases. These measurements should be taken just below the atrioventricular valves from a long-axis view of the left ventricle, taking care to orient the M-mode cursor perpendicular to the interventricular septum. Generally, the thickness of the ventricular septum should be less than 6 mm (25).

Septal Defects

Defects of the atrial and ventricular septum represent 10% to 30% of all cardiac defects, respectively. Prenatal diagnosis is challenging. Most atrial defects involve the septum secundum, which is difficult to analyze due to the physiologic presence of the foramen ovalis. Most ventricular septal defects are small and equally difficult to demonstrate antenatally (Fig. 22-4). Because they are usually associated with blood shunting across the septum, color Doppler may aid in the diagnosis, which remains difficult and is rarely made. Atrial and ventricular septal defects are not a cause of impairment of cardiac function *in utero*, because a large intracardiac right-to-left shunt is a physiologic condition in

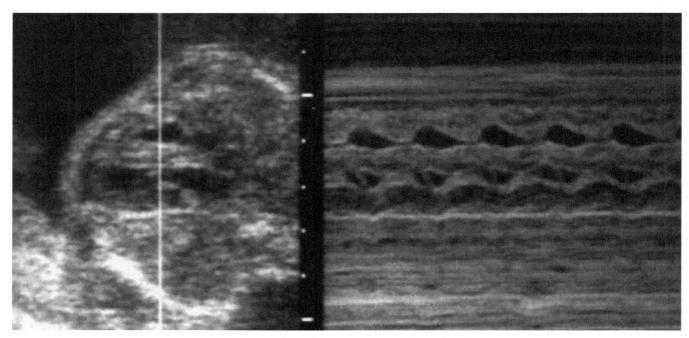

FIGURE 22-3. Sonography of fetal hypertrophic cardiomyopathy in the third trimester of pregnancy. The cardiac walls, and particularly the ventricular septum, appear thick and hypercontractile both on real-time (left) and TM-mode (right).

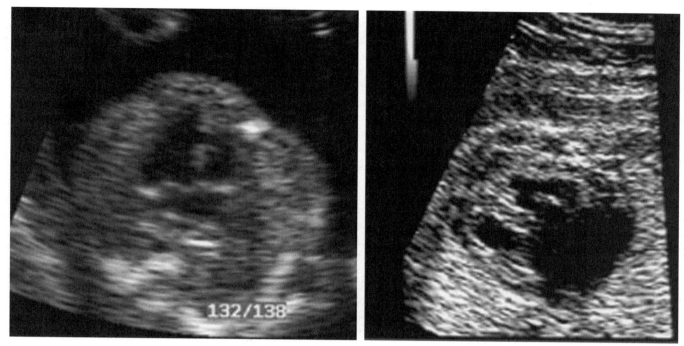

FIGURE 22-4. Sonography of fetal septal defects: muscular ventricular septal defect (left) and complete atrioventricular canal (right).

the fetus. Most affected infants are asymptomatic, even in the neonatal period. When they are not associated with other cardiac anomalies, the prognosis is excellent. Spontaneous closure is frequent. A primum atrial septal defect is the simplest form of the atrioventricular septal defects and will be considered below.

The core of the heart—that is, the apical portion of the atrial septum, the basal portion of the interventricular septum, and the medial portion of atrioventricular valves—develops from the mesenchymnal masses, or endocardial cushions. Abnormal development of these structures, commonly referred to as endocardial cushion defects, atrioventricular canal, or atrioventricular septal defects, represents about 7% of all cardiac anomalies. In the complete form, persistent common atrioventricular canal, the tricuspid and mitral valve are fused in a large single atrioventricular valve that opens above and bridges the two ventricles. In the complete form of atrioventricular canal, the common atrioventricular valve may be incompetent, and systolic blood regurgitation from the ventricles to the atria may give rise to congestive heart failure. In the partial form, there is a defect in the apical portion of the atrial septum (septum primum defect). There are two separate atrioventricular valves, but they are inserted at the same level on the ventricular septum.

Antenatal diagnosis of complete atrioventricular septal defects is usually straightforward. The four-chamber view reveals an obvious deficiency of the central core structures of the heart (Fig. 22-4). Color Doppler ultrasonography

can be useful, in that it facilitates the visualization of the central opening of the single atrioventricular valve. The atria may be dilated as a consequence of atrioventricular insufficiency. In such cases, color and pulsed Doppler ultrasonography allows identification of the regurgitant jet. The incomplete forms are more difficult to recognize. A useful hint is the demonstration that the tricuspid and mitral valves attach at the same level at the crest of the septum. The atrial septal defect is of the ostium primum type (since the septum secundum is not affected) and thus is close to the crest of the interventricular septum.

Atrioventricular septal defects do not impair the fetal circulation per se. However, the presence of atrioventricular valve insufficiency may lead to intrauterine heart failure. The prognosis of atrioventricular septal defects is poor when detected *in utero,* probably because of the high frequency of associated anomalies in antenatal series. Atrioventricular septal defects will usually be encountered either in fetuses with chromosomal aberrations (50% of cases are associated with aneuploidy, 60% being trisomy 21, 25% trisomy 18) or in fetuses with cardiosplenic syndromes. In the former cases, an atrioventricular septal defect is frequently found in association with extracardiac anomalies. In the latter cases, complex cardiac anomalies and abnormal disposition of the abdominal organs are usually found. The survival rate after surgical closure is more than 90% but in about 10% of patients a second operation for atrioventricular valve repair or replacement is necessary. Long-term prognosis is good.

Heterotaxy

In heterotaxy, also referred to as cardiosplenic syndromes, the fetus is made of either two left or two right sides. Other terms commonly used include left or right isomerism, asplenia, and polysplenia. Unpaired organs (liver, stomach, and spleen) may be absent, midline, or duplicated. Because of left atrial isomerism (and thus absence of the right atrium, which is the normal location for the pacemaker) and abnormal atrioventricular junctions, atrioventricular blocks are common. Heterotaxy represents about 2% of all congenital heart defects.

In polysplenia, the fetus has two left sides (one in normal position and the other as a mirror image); this is called left isomerism. Multiple small spleens (usually too small to be detected by antenatal ultrasonography) are found posterior to the stomach. The liver is midline and symmetric. But the stomach and aorta can be on opposite sides.

In asplenia, the fetus has two right sides (right isomerism). The liver is generally midline and the stomach right or left sided. The aorta and vena cava are on the same side (either left or right) of the spine.

Cardiac malformations are almost invariably present and are usually severe, with a tendency toward a single structure replacing normal paired structures: a single atrium, single atrioventricular valve, single ventricle, and single great vessel.

The main clue for the diagnosis of fetal heterotaxy is the demonstration of complex cardiac anomalies associated with abnormal disposition of the thoracic or abdominal organs. In polysplenia, a typical finding is interruption of the inferior vena cava with azygous continuation (there is failure to visualize the inferior vena cava, and a large venous vessel, the azygos vein, runs to the left and close to the spine and ascends into the upper thorax). Symmetry of the liver can be sonographically recognized *in utero* by the abnormal course of the portal circulation that lacks a clearly defined portal sinus bending to the right.

The heterogeneous cardiac anomalies found in association with heterotaxy are usually easily seen, but a detailed diagnosis often poses a challenge; in particular, assessment of connection between the pulmonary veins and the atrium (an element that has a major prognostic influence) can be extremely difficult. Associated anomalies include absence of the gallbladder, malrotation of the guts, duodenal atresia, and hydrops.

The outcome depends on the extent of cardiac anomalies, but tends to be poor. Atrioventricular insufficiency and severe fetal bradycardia due to atrioventricular block may lead to intrauterine heart failure.

Univentricular Heart

This term defines a group of anomalies characterized by the presence of an atrioventricular junction that is entirely connected to only one chamber in the ventricular mass. Therefore, univentricular heart includes both those cases in which two atrial chambers are connected, by either two distinct atrioventricular valves or by a common one, to a main ventricular chamber (double-inlet single ventricle) as well as those cases in which, because of the absence of one atrioventricular connection (tricuspid or mitral atresia), one of the ventricular chambers is either rudimentary or absent. Univentricular heart is rare; it represents about 1.5% of all congenital cardiac defects. Tricuspid atresia is by far the most frequent variety,

In double-outlet single ventricle, two separate atrioventricular valves are seen opening into a single ventricular cavity without evidence of the interventricular septum. In tricuspid atresia, there is only one atrioventricular valve connected to a main ventricular chamber. A small rudimentary ventricular chamber lacking an atrioventricular connection is a frequent but not constant finding.

Surgical treatment (the Fontan procedure) involves separation of the pulmonary and systemic circulations by anastomosing the superior and inferior vena cava directly to the pulmonary artery. Survivors from this procedure may develop several complications, including arrhythmias, thrombus formation, and protein-losing enteropathy. The 5-year survival rate is about 70%. The long-term outcome is uncertain.

Aortic Stenosis

Aortic stenosis represents about 3% of all cardiac defects and is commonly divided into supravalvar, valvar, and subaortic forms. The supravalvar and subaortic forms are rare and usually cannot be detected antenatally. The valvular form of aortic stenosis can be due to dysplastic, thickened aortic cusps or fusion of the commissures between the cusps. With severe valvular aortic stenosis, the left ventricle may be either hypertrophic or dilated and hypocontractile. The ascending aorta is frequently enlarged. Hyperechogenicity of the aortic valve and pulsed Doppler demonstration of increased peak velocity (usually in >1 m/s) support the diagnosis. At the color Doppler examination, high velocity and turbulence usually results in aliasing, with a mosaic of colors within the ascending aorta. Severe aortic stenosis may result in atrioventricular valve insufficiency and intrauterine heart failure. Most cases of mild to moderate aortic stenosis are probably not amenable to early prenatal diagnosis. Asymmetric septal hypertrophy and hypertrophic cardiomyopathy of fetuses of diabetic mothers resulting in subaortic stenosis occasionally have been diagnosed by demonstrating an unusual thickness of the ventricular septum.

Depending on the severity of the aortic stenosis, the association of left ventricular pressure overload and subendocardial ischemia, due to decrease in coronary perfusion, may lead to intrauterine impairment of cardiac function.

Subvalvular and subaortic forms are not generally manifested in the neonatal period. Conversely, the valvular type can be a cause of congestive heart failure in the newborn and fetus as well. Neonatal outcome depends on the severity of obstruction. If the left ventricular function is adequate, balloon valvuloplasty is performed in the neonatal period, and in about 50% of cases, surgery is necessary within the first 10 years of life because of aortic insufficiency or residual stenosis. If left ventricular function is inadequate, a Norwood-type of repair is necessary (see later section on Hypoplastic Left Heart Syndrome).

Coarctation, Tubular Hypoplasia, and Interruption of the Aortic Arch

Coarctation is a localized narrowing of the juxtaductal arch, most commonly between the left subclavian artery and the ductus. Cardiac anomalies are frequently present and include aortic stenosis and insufficiency, ventricular septal defect, atrial septal defect, transposition of the great arteries, truncus, and DORV. Noncardiac anomalies include diaphragmatic hernia, and Turner syndrome but not Noonan syndrome. Interrupted aortic arch is typically associated with a chromosome 22 microdeletion.

Coarctation or interruption of the aortic arch should be suspected when the right ventricle is enlarged (right ventricle to left ventricle ratio of more than 1.3). Narrowing of the isthmus, or the presence of a shelf, is often difficult to demonstrate because in the fetus, the aortic arch and ductal arch are close and are difficult to distinguish. In most cases, coarctation can only be suspected *in utero,* and a certain diagnosis must be delayed until after birth. The characteristic finding of an ascending aorta more vertical than usual and the impossibility to demonstrate a connection with the descending aorta suggests the diagnosis. Coarctation/interrupted aortic arch should always be considered when intracardiac lesions diverting blood flow from the left to the right heart are encountered (aortic stenosis and atresia in particular).

Critical coarctation and interruption are fatal in the neonatal period after closure of the ductus; therefore, prostaglandin therapy is necessary to maintain a patent ductus. Surgery (which involves excision of the coarcted segment and end-to-end anastomosis) is associated with a mortality rate of about 10%, and the incidence of restenosis in survivors (requiring further surgical repair) is about 15%.

For interrupted aortic arch, recent reports suggest an overall late survival rate of more than 70% after surgery.

Hypoplastic Left Heart Syndrome

Hypoplastic left heart syndrome accounts for 4% of all cardiac anomalies at birth, but it is one of the most frequent cardiac malformations diagnosed antenatally. It is a spectrum of anomalies characterized by a small left ventricle with mitral or aortic atresia or hypoplasia. Blood flow to the head and neck vessels and coronary arteries is supplied in a retrograde manner via the ductus arteriosus.

Prenatal echocardiographic diagnosis of the syndrome depends on the demonstration of a small left ventricle and ascending aorta. In most cases, the ultrasound appearance is self-explanatory, and the diagnosis an easy one. There is, however, a broad spectrum of hypoplasia of the left ventricle, and in some cases the ventricular cavity is close to normal in size. Because the four-chamber view is almost normal, these cases may be missed in most routine surveys of fetal anatomy. With closer scrutiny, however, the movement of the mitral valve will appear severely impaired to nonexistent, ventricular contractility is obviously decreased, and the ventricle often displays an internal echogenic lining that is probably due to endocardial fibroelastosis. The definitive diagnosis of the syndrome depends on the demonstration of hypoplasia of the ascending aorta and atresia of the aortic valve. Color flow mapping is an extremely useful adjunct to the real-time examination, in that it allows the demonstration of retrograde blood flow within the ascending aorta and aortic arch.

Hypoplastic left heart is well tolerated *in utero*. The patency of the ductus arteriosus allows adequate perfusion of the head and neck vessels. Intrauterine growth may be normal, and the onset of symptoms most frequently occurs after birth. The prognosis for infants with hypoplastic left heart syndrome is extremely poor, and this lesion is responsible for 25 % of cardiac deaths in the first week of life. Almost all affected infants die within 6 weeks if they are not treated. In the neonatal period, prostaglandin therapy is given to maintain ductal patency but congestive heart failure still develops within 24 hours of life. Options for surgery include cardiac transplantation in the neonatal period (with an 80% 5-year survival rate) and the three-staged Norwood repair. Stage 1 involves anastomosis of the pulmonary artery to the aortic arch for systemic outflow, placement of a systemic-to-pulmonary arterial shunt to provide pulmonary blood flow, and atrial septectomy to ensure unobstructed pulmonary venous return. Stage 2 (which is usually executed in the sixth month of life) involves anastomosis of the superior vena cava to the pulmonary arteries. Neurodevelopmental abnormalities have been reported in survivors of the Norwood operation. The survival rate of fetuses diagnosed *in utero* is in the range of 40%.

Pulmonary Stenosis and Pulmonary Atresia

Pulmonary stenosis and pulmonary atresia with intact ventricular septum (also known as hypoplastic right ventricle) represent 9% and about 2% of all cardiac anomalies, respectively.

The most common form of pulmonary stenosis is valvular, due to the fusion of the pulmonary leaflets. The hemodynamic abnormality is proportional to the degree of the stenosis. The work of the right ventricle is increased, as is its pressure, leading to hypertrophy of the ventricular walls. The same considerations formulated for the prenatal diagnosis of aortic stenosis are valid for pulmonic stenosis as well. A handful of cases recognized *in utero* have been reported in the literature thus far, mostly severe types with enlargement of the right ventricle or poststenotic enlargement or hypoplasia of the pulmonary artery.

Pulmonary atresia with intact ventricular septum in infants is usually associated with a hypoplastic right ventricle. However, cases with enlarged right ventricle and atrium have been described with unusual frequency in prenatal series. Enlargement of the ventricle and atrium is probably the consequence of tricuspid insufficiency. Prenatal diagnosis of pulmonary atresia with intact ventricular septum relies on the demonstration of a small pulmonary artery with an atretic pulmonary valve. The considerations previously formulated for the diagnosis of hypoplastic left heart syndrome apply to this condition as well.

Patients with mild stenosis are asymptomatic, and there is no need for intervention. In patients with severe stenosis, right ventricular overload may result in congestive heart failure and require balloon valvuloplasty in the neonatal period with excellent survival and normal long-term prognosis. Fetuses with pulmonary atresia and an enlarged right heart have a high degree of perinatal mortality. Infants with right ventricular hypoplasia require biventricular surgical repair, and the mortality rate is about 40%.

Conotruncal Malformations

Conotruncal malformations are a heterogeneous group of defects that involve two different segments of the heart: the conotruncus and the ventricles. Conotruncal anomalies are relatively frequent. They account for 20% to 30% of all cardiac anomalies and are the leading cause of symptomatic cyanotic heart disease in the first year of life. Prenatal diagnosis is of interest for several reasons. Given the parallel fetal circulation, conotruncal anomalies are well tolerated *in utero.* The clinical presentation occurs usually hours to days after delivery, and is often severe, representing a true emergency and leading to considerable morbidity and mortality. Yet, these malformations have a good prognosis when promptly treated, as there are two ventricles of adequate size and two great vessels, allowing biventricular surgical correction. The outcome is indeed much more favourable than with most of the other cardiac defects that are detected antenatally. Unfortunately, the recognition of these anomalies remains difficult. The four-chamber view is frequently unremarkable in these cases. A specific diagnosis requires meticulous scanning and at times may represent a challenge even for experienced sonologists.

Transposition of the great arteries (TGA) is an abnormality in which the aorta arises entirely or in large part from

the right ventricle and the pulmonary artery arises from the left ventricle. Associated cardiac lesions are present in about 50% of cases, including ventricular septal defects (which can occur anywhere in the ventricular septum), pulmonary stenosis, unbalanced ventricular size (complex transpositions), and anomalies of the mitral valve, which can be straddling or overriding.

Complete transposition is probably one of the most difficult cardiac lesions to recognize *in utero.* In most cases the four-chamber view is normal, and the cardiac cavities and the vessels have normal dimensions. A clue to the diagnosis is the demonstration that the two great vessels do not cross but arise parallel from the base of the heart (Fig. 22-5). The most useful echocardiographic view, however, is the left heart view demonstrating that the vessel connected to the left ventricle has a posterior course and bifurcates into the two pulmonary arteries. Conversely, the vessel connected to the right ventricle has a long upward course and gives rise to the brachiocephalic vessels. Corrected transposition is characterized by a double discordance, at the atrioventricular and ventriculoarterial levels. The left atrium is connected to the right ventricle, which is in turn connected to the ascending aorta. Conversely, the right atrium is connected to the left ventricle, which is in turn connected to the pulmonary artery. The derangement of the conduction tissue secondary to malalignment of the atrial and ventricular septa may result in dysrhythmias, namely complete atrioventricular block. For diagnostic purposes, the identification of the peculiar difference of ventricular morphology (moderator band, papillary muscles, insertion of the atrioventricular valves) has a prominent role. Demonstration that the pulmonary veins are connected to an atrium, which is in turn connected with a ventricle that has the moderator band at the apex, is an important clue, which is furthermore potentially identifiable even in a simple four-chamber view. Diagnosis requires meticulous scanning to carefully assess all cardiac connections, by using the same views described for the complete form. The presence of atrioventricular block increases the index of suspicion.

As anticipated from the parallel fetal circulation, complete transposition is uneventful *in utero.* After birth, survival depends on the amount and size of the mixing of the two otherwise independent circulations. Patients with transposition and an intact ventricular septum present shortly after birth with cyanosis and deteriorate rapidly. When a large ventricular septal defect is present, cyanosis can be mild. Clinical presentation may be delayed up to 2 to 4 weeks, and usually occurs with signs of congestive heart failure. When severe stenosis of the pulmonary artery is associated with a ventricular septal defect, symptoms are similar to patients with tetralogy of Fallot. The time and mode of clinical presentation with corrected transposition depend on the concomitant cardiac defects.

Surgery (which involves arterial switch to establish anatomic and physiologic correction) is usually performed

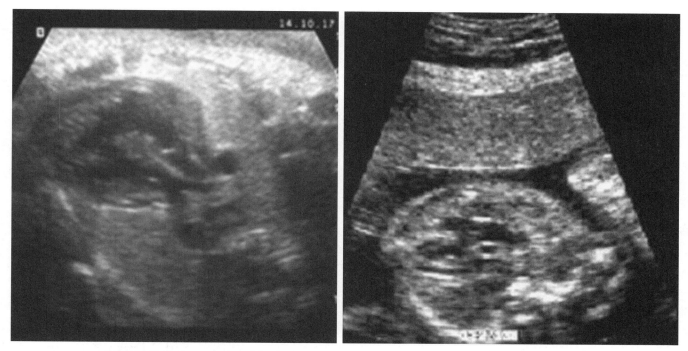

FIGURE 22-5. Sonography of fetal conotruncal anomalies. Left: the great arteries arise parallel in one fetus with complete transposition of the great arteries. Right: enlargement and overriding of the aorta on the ventricular septum suggest tetralogy of Fallot (similar findings are expected with double-outlet right ventricle).

within the first 2 weeks of life. The operative mortality rate is about 10%. Ten-year follow-up studies report normal function in the vast majority of cases. The outcome of corrected transposition depends largely on the associated cardiac defects, which are variable. Because the systemic ventricle is the right ventricle, there is a high chance for cardiac failure in adulthood.

In DORV, most of the aorta and pulmonary valve arise completely or almost completely from the right ventricle. The relationship between the two vessels may vary, ranging from a Fallot-like to a TGA-like situation (the Taussig-Bing anomaly). DORV is not a single malformation from a pathophysiologic point of view. The term refers only to the position of the great vessels that is found in association with ventricular septal defects, tetralogy of Fallot, transposition, and univentricular hearts. Pulmonary stenosis is common in all types of DORV, but left outflow obstructions, from subaortic stenosis to coarctation and interruption of the aortic arch, can also be seen.

Prenatal diagnosis of DORV can be reliably made in the fetus, but differentiation from other conotruncal anomalies can be difficult, especially with tetralogy of Fallot and TGA with ventricular septal defect. The main echocardiographic features include (a) alignment of the two vessels totally or predominantly from the right ventricle and (b) presence in most cases of bilateral coni (subaortic and subpulmonary). The hemodynamics are dependent on the anatomic type of

DORV and the associated anomalies. Because the fetal heart works as a common chamber where the blood is mixed and pumped, DORV is not associated with intrauterine heart failure. However DORV, in contrast to other conotruncal malformations, commonly occurs with extracardiac anomalies or chromosomal defects. DORV usually does not interfere with hemodynamics in fetal life. The early operative mortality rate is about 10%.

The essential features of tetralogy of Fallot are a subaortic ventricular septal defect, aorta overriding the ventricular septal defect, and infundibular stenosis of the aorta (Fig. 22-5). In about 20% of cases, there is atresia of the pulmonary valve, a condition that is commonly referred to as pulmonary atresia with ventricular septal defect. Tetralogy of Fallot can be associated with other specific cardiac malformations, including atrioventricular septal defects (found in 4% of cases) and absence of the pulmonary valve (found in <2% of cases). Hypertrophy of the right ventricle, one of the classic elements of the tetrad, is always absent in the fetus, and only develops after birth.

Echocardiographic diagnosis of tetralogy of Fallot relies on the demonstration of a ventricular septal defect in the outlet portion of the septum and an overriding aorta. Color and pulsed Doppler can be used to identify the patency of the pulmonary valve and exclude pulmonary atresia. Diagnostic problems arise at the extremes of the spectrum of tetralogy of Fallot. In cases with minor forms of right outflow obstruction and aortic overriding, differentiation from a simple ventricular septal defect can be difficult. In those cases in which the pulmonary artery is not imaged, a differential diagnosis between pulmonary atresia with ventricular septal defect and truncus arteriosus communis is similarly difficult. Abnormal enlargement of the right ventricle, main pulmonary trunk, and artery suggests absence of the pulmonary valve.

Cardiac failure is never seen in fetal life nor in the neonatal period. Even in cases of tight pulmonary stenosis or atresia, the wide ventricular septal defect provides adequate combined ventricular output, while the pulmonary vascular bed is supplied in a retrograde manner by the ductus. The only exception to this rule is found in cases with an absent pulmonary valve that may result in massive regurgitation to the right ventricle and atrium. When severe pulmonic stenosis is present, cyanosis tends to develop immediately after birth. With lesser degrees of obstruction to pulmonary blood flow, the onset of cyanosis may not appear until later in the first year of life. When there is pulmonary atresia, rapid and severe deterioration follows ductal constriction. The survival rate after complete surgical repair (which is usually performed in the third month of life) is more than 90%, and about 80% of survivors have normal exercise tolerance.

Truncus Arteriosus

A single arterial vessel that originates from the heart, overrides the ventricular septum, and supplies the systemic, pulmonary, and coronary circulations characterizes truncus arteriosus. The single arterial trunk is larger than the normal aortic root and is predominantly connected with the right ventricle in about 40% of cases, with the left ventricle in 20%, and is equally shared in 40%. The truncal valve may have one, two, or three cusps and is rarely normal. It can be stenotic or, more frequently, insufficient. A malalignment ventricular septal defect, usually wide, is an essential part of the malformation. There are three types based on the morphology of the pulmonary artery. In type 1, the pulmonary arteries arise from the truncus within a short distance from the valve, as a main pulmonary trunk, which then bifurcates. In type 2, there is no main pulmonary trunk. In type 3, only one pulmonary artery (usually the right) originates from the truncus, while a systemic collateral vessel from the descending aorta supplies the other. Similar to tetralogy of Fallot, but unlike other conotruncal malformations, in approximately 30% of cases, truncus is associated with extracardiac malformations.

Truncus arteriosus can be reliably detected with fetal echocardiography. The main diagnostic criteria are (a) a single semilunar valve overriding the ventricular septal defect and (b) direct continuity between one or two pulmonary arteries and the single arterial trunk. The semilunar valve is often thickened and moves abnormally. Doppler ultra-

sonography is of value to assess incompetence of the truncal valve. A peculiar problem found in prenatal echocardiography is demonstration of the absence of a pulmonary outflow tract and the concomitant failure to image the pulmonary arteries. In these situations a differentiation between truncus and pulmonary atresia with ventricular septal defect may be impossible.

Similar to the other conotruncal anomalies, truncus arteriosus is not associated with alteration of fetal hemodynamics. Truncus arteriosus is frequently a neonatal emergency. These patients usually have obstructed pulmonary blood flow and, with the postnatal decline in pulmonary resistance, show signs of progressive congestive heart failure. Many patients will present with cardiac failure in the first 1 or 2 weeks of life. Surgical repair (usually before the sixth month of life) involves closure of the ventricular septal defect and creation of a conduit connection between the right ventricle and the pulmonary arteries. Survival from surgery is about 90%, but the patients require repeated surgery for replacement of the conduit.

Ebstein Anomaly and Tricuspid Valve Dysplasia

An Ebstein anomaly results from faulty implantation of the tricuspid valve. The posterior and septal leaflets are elongated and tethered below their normal level of attachment on the annulus or displaced apically, away from the annulus, down to the junction between the inlet and trabecular portion of the right ventricle. The anterior leaflet is normally inserted but deformed. The resulting configuration is that of a considerably enlarged right atrium at the expense of the right ventricle. The portion of the right ventricle that is ceded to the right atrium is called the atrialized inlet of the right ventricle. It has a thin wall that may even be membranous and is commonly dilated. The tricuspid valve is usually both incompetent and stenotic. Associated anomalies include atrial septal defect, pulmonary atresia, ventricular septal defect, and supraventricular tachycardia. An Ebstein anomaly may be associated with trisomy 13 or 21, or with Turner, Cornelia de Lange, or Marfan syndrome. Maternal ingestion of lithium has also been incriminated as a causal factor.

The characteristic echocardiographic finding is that of a massively enlarged right atrium, a small right ventricle, and a small pulmonary artery. Doppler can be used to demonstrate regurgitation in the right atrium. About 25% of the cases have supraventricular tachycardia from reentrant impulse, atrial fibrillation, or atrial flutter. Differential diagnosis from pulmonary atresia with an intact ventricular septum and a regurgitant tricuspid valve or isolated tricuspid valve insufficiency is difficult and may be impossible antenatally.

Although the disease has a variable severity with some cases discovered only late in life, an Ebstein anomaly detected prenatally, when compared with cases discovered in children or adults, has a dismal prognosis, with essentially all patients dying.

THORACIC ANOMALIES

Hyperechogenic and Cystic Lungs

Fetal hyperechogenic lungs are a recently described entity. The typical finding is that of enlarged, brightly echogenic lungs displacing the mediastinum and causing an inversion of the diaphragm (34,35). Most frequently, part of one lung or one entire lung is affected, causing lateral displacement of the heart and mediastinum. Rarely, both lungs are affected, compressing the mediastinum on both sides. The pathophysiology is related to obstruction of the respiratory tree, causing accumulation of fluid and secretions in the lungs. The effects of respiratory obstruction are variable. Accumulation of fluid may lead to lung hyperplasia. Early and long-standing obstruction is probably responsible for the histologic alterations that are commonly referred to as cystic adenomatoid malformation of the lungs. The cause is variable. Obstruction may result from primary atresia, or may be the consequence of a mucus plug. A further possibility is pulmonary sequestration. In this condition, a part of the lung develops separately from the bronchi and the pulmonary circulation and is supplied through arteries that arise from the descending aorta. A differential diagnosis between these three conditions is often difficult. With lung sequestration, a specific diagnosis is possible by demonstrating with color Doppler the abnormal vessels connecting the aorta to the abnormal lung. Spontaneous regression or resolution of the increased echogenicity indicates a mucus plug as the most likely cause. When both lungs are affected, the most likely diagnosis is an obstruction of the upper airways, usually atresia of the trachea. Polyhydramnios and fetal hydrops may occur, particularly with bilateral echogenic lungs and large sequestration. Lung sequestration may also be associated with cardiac and diaphragmatic defects.

In some cases, macroscopic cysts may be associated with the increased echogenicity. Occasionally, large and multiple cysts are the dominant finding. Cystic adenomatoid malformation is usually found at birth in these cases (macrocystic variety). The pathophysiology probably overlaps echogenic lungs.

Unilateral echogenic or cystic lungs without other anomalies or hydrops have a very good outcome. The lesions usually decrease in size with gestation, and the infants are asymptomatic at birth. However, dysplastic lung tissue is usually present and must be surgically removed. Conversely, bilateral lesions or those associated with hydrops usually have a poor outcome. In these cases, drainage or shunting of the cysts may be attempted (34,35).

Pleural Effusions

Fetal pleural effusions may be an isolated finding, or they may occur in association with generalized edema and ascites. Irrespective of the underlying cause, infants affected by pleural effusions usually present in the neonatal period with severe, and often fatal, respiratory insufficiency. This is either a direct result of pulmonary compression caused by the effusions, or due to pulmonary hypoplasia secondary to chronic intrathoracic compression. The overall mortality rate of neonates with pleural effusions is 25%, with a range from 15% in infants with isolated pleural effusions to 95% in those with gross hydrops.

Isolated pleural effusions in the fetus may either resolve spontaneously or they can be treated effectively after birth. Nevertheless, in some cases severe and chronic compression of the fetal lungs can result in pulmonary hypoplasia and neonatal death. In others, mediastinal compression leads to the development of hydrops and polyhydramnios, which are associated with a high risk for premature delivery and perinatal death (36). Attempts at prenatal therapy by repeated thoracocenteses for drainage of pleural effusions have been generally unsuccessful in reversing the hydropic state, because the fluid reaccumulates within 24 to 48 hours of drainage. A better approach is chronic drainage by the insertion of thoracoamniotic shunts. This is useful both for diagnosis and treatment (37). First, the diagnosis of an underlying cardiac abnormality or other intrathoracic lesion may become apparent only after effective decompression and return of the mediastinum to its normal position. Second, it can reverse fetal hydrops, resolve polyhydramnios, and thereby reduce the risk for preterm delivery, and may prevent pulmonary hypoplasia. Third, it may be useful in the prenatal diagnosis of pulmonary hypoplasia because in such cases the lungs often fail to expand after shunting. Furthermore, it may help distinguish between hydrops due to primary accumulation of pleural effusions, with resolution of the ascites, and skin edema may resolve after shunting, and other causes of hydrops such as infection, in which drainage of the effusions does not prevent worsening of the hydrops. The survival rate after thoracoamniotic shunting is more than 90% in fetuses with isolated pleural effusions and about 50% in those with hydrops.

Diaphragmatic Hernia

Diaphragmatic hernia is found in about 1 per 4,000 births. Development of the diaphragm is usually completed by the ninth week of gestation. In the presence of a defective diaphragm, there is herniation of the abdominal viscera into the thorax at about 10 to 12 weeks, when the intestines return to the abdominal cavity. However, in some cases intrathoracic herniation of viscera may be delayed until the second or third trimesters of pregnancy. Diaphragmatic hernia is usually a sporadic abnormality. In about 50% of affected fetuses there are associated chromosomal abnormalities (mainly trisomy 18, trisomy 13, and Pallister-Killian syndrome–mosaicism for tetrasomy 12p) and other defects, mainly craniospinal defects, including spina bifida, hydrocephaly, and the otherwise rare iniencephaly, as well as cardiac abnormalities and genetic syndromes such as Fryns syndrome, de Lange syndrome, and Marfan syndrome.

Prenatally, the diaphragm is imaged by ultrasonography as an echo-free space between the thorax and abdomen. However, the integrity of the diaphragm is usually inferred from the normal disposition of the thoracic and abdominal organs. Diaphragmatic hernia can be diagnosed by the ultrasonographic demonstration of stomach, intestines (90% of the cases), or liver (50%) in the thorax and the associated mediastinal shift to the opposite side. Herniated abdominal contents, associated with a left-sided diaphragmatic hernia, are easy to demonstrate because the echo-free fluid-filled stomach and small bowel contrast dramatically with the more echogenic fetal lung. In contrast, a right-sided hernia is more difficult to identify because the echogenicity of the fetal liver is similar to that of the lung, and visualization of the gallbladder in the right side of the fetal chest may be the only way of making the diagnosis. Polyhydramnios (usually after 25 weeks) is found in about 75% of cases, and this may be the consequence of impaired fetal swallowing due to compression of the esophagus by the herniated abdominal organs. The main differential diagnosis is from echogenic/cystic lungs.

Antenatal prediction of pulmonary hypoplasia remains one of the challenges of prenatal diagnosis. This information would be vital in both counseling parents and in selecting those cases that may benefit from prenatal surgery. Poor prognostic signs are (a) increased nuchal translucency thickness at 10 to 14 weeks, (b) intrathoracic herniation of abdominal viscera before 20 weeks, and (c) severe mediastinal compression suggested by an abnormal ratio in the size of the cardiac ventricles and the development of polyhydramnios.

In the human, the bronchial tree is fully developed by the 16th week of gestation, at which time the full adult number of airways is established. In diaphragmatic hernia the reduced thoracic space available to the developing lung leads to reduction in airways, alveoli, and arteries. Thus, although isolated diaphragmatic hernia is an anatomically simple defect, which is easily correctable, the mortality rate is about 50%. The main cause of death is hypoxemia due to pulmonary hypertension resulting from the abnormal development of the pulmonary vascular bed.

In a few cases of diaphragmatic hernia, hysterotomy and fetal surgery have been performed, but this intervention has now been abandoned in favor of minimally invasive surgery. Animal studies have demonstrated that obstruction of the trachea results in expansion of the fetal lungs by retained pulmonary secretions. Endoscopic occlusion of the fetal tra-chea has also been performed in human fetuses with diaphragmatic hernia (38). A recently published prospective randomized trial did not demonstrate that *in utero* therapy was associated with better outcomes than standard care with postnatal intervention (39).

ANOMALIES OF THE ABDOMINAL WALL AND GASTROINTESTINAL TRACT

The most common gastrointestinal disorders associated with diabetes are small bowel atresia, left colon syndrome, and imperforate anus (18). Imperforate anus is thought by some to be a variation on the caudal regression theme.

Omphalocele

Omphalocele, or exomphalos, occurs in about 1 per 4,000 births, and results from failure of normal embryonic regression of the midgut from the umbilical stalk into the abdominal coeloma. The abdominal contents, including intestines and liver or spleen covered by a sac of parietal peritoneum and amnion, are herniated into the base of the umbilical cord. Less often there is an upward extension of the defect, associated with a defect in the anterior diaphragm, ectopia cordis, and embryonic fold, resulting in the pentalogy of Cantrell. In other cases, the abdominal wall defect may extend inferiorly and associate with exstrophy of the bladder or cloaca, imperforate anus, colonic atresia, and sacral vertebral defects. The Beckwith-Wiedemann syndrome (usually sporadic and occasionally familial syndrome with a birth prevalence of about 1 in 14,000) is the combination of omphalocele, macrosomia, organomegaly, macroglossia, and severe neonatal hypoglycemia. In some cases Beckwith-Wiedemann syndrome is associated with mental handicap, which is thought to be secondary to inadequately treated hypoglycemia. About 5% of affected individuals develop tumors during childhood, most commonly nephroblastoma and hepatoblastoma.

The majority of cases of omphalocele are sporadic, and the recurrence risk is usually less than 1%. However in some cases there may be an associated genetic syndrome. Chromosomal abnormalities (mainly trisomy 18 or 13) are found in about 30% of cases at midgestation and in 15% of neonates. Similarly, in Beckwith-Wiedemann syndrome, most cases are sporadic, although autosomal dominant, recessive, X-linked, and polygenic patterns of inheritance have been described.

The diagnosis of omphalocele is based on the demonstration of the midline anterior abdominal wall defect, the herniated sac with its visceral contents, and the umbilical cord insertion at the apex of the sac. The differential diagnosis includes mainly gastroschisis, in which the only herniated abdominal contents are bowel loops, not contained by an amnioperitoneal membrane.

Omphalocele is a correctable malformation in which survival depends primarily on whether or not other malformations or chromosomal defects are present. For isolated lesions, the survival rate after surgery is about 90%. The mortality rate is much higher with cephalic fold defects than with lateral and caudal defects. Whether the infants with omphalocele should be delivered by cesarean section to decrease trauma and infection to the herniated abdominal contents has been debated.

Gastroschisis

Gastroschisis is found in about 1 per 4,000 births. In gastroschisis, the primary body folds and the umbilical ring develop normally and evisceration of the intestine occurs through a small abdominal wall defect located just lateral and usually to the right of an intact umbilical cord. The loops of intestine lie uncovered in the amniotic fluid and become thickened, edematous, and matted.

Gastroschisis is a sporadic abnormality. Associated chromosomal abnormalities are rare, and although other malformations are found in 10% to 30% of the cases, these are mainly gut atresias, probably due to gut strangulation and infarction *in utero*.

Prenatal diagnosis is based on the demonstration of the normally situated umbilicus and the herniated loops of intestine, which are free floating and widely separated. About 30% of fetuses are growth restricted, but the diagnosis can be difficult because gastroschisis as such is associated with a small abdominal circumference. Postoperative survival is about 90%, and mortality is usually the consequence of short gut syndrome. Similar to omphalocele, it is debated whether these infants should be delivered by cesarean section to decrease trauma to and infection of the herniated abdominal contents.

Bladder Exstrophy and Cloacal Exstrophy

Bladder exstrophy is found in 1 per 30,000 births and cloacal exstrophy in about 1 in per 200,000 births. Bladder exstrophy is a defect of the caudal fold of the anterior abdominal wall; a small defect may cause epispadias alone while a large defect leads to exposure of the posterior bladder wall. In cloacal exstrophy, both the urinary and gastrointestinal tracts are involved. Cloacal exstrophy (also referred to as OEIS complex) is the association of an omphalocele, exstrophy of the bladder, imperforated anus, and spinal defects such as meningomyelocele. The hemibladders are on either side of the intestines.

Bladder exstrophy should be suspected when in the presence of normal amniotic fluid the fetal bladder is not visualized (the filling cycle of the bladder is normally in the range of 15 minutes); an echogenic mass is seen protruding from the lower abdominal wall, in close association with the umbilical arteries. In cloacal exstrophy, the findings are similar to bladder exstrophy (large infraumbilical defect that extends to the pelvis), but a posterior anomalous component is present. Other findings include single umbilical artery, ascites, vertebral anomalies, clubfoot, and ambiguous genitalia. In boys, the penis is divided and duplicated.

With aggressive reconstructive bladder, bowel, and genital surgery, survival is more than 80%. Bladder exstrophy is compatible with complete repair, although in some cases permanent urinary tract diversion becomes necessary. Cloacal exstrophy is a much more severe disease involving the lower abdominal tract as well and is associated with significant sequelae.

Obstruction of the Gastrointestinal Tract

Esophageal atresia is found in about 1 in 3,000 births. It is associated in about 90% of cases with tracheoesophageal fistula and results from failure of the primitive foregut to divide into the anterior trachea and posterior esophagus, events that normally occur during the fourth week of gestation.

Esophageal atresia and tracheoesophageal fistula are sporadic abnormalities. Chromosomal abnormalities (mainly trisomy 18 or 21) are found in about 20% of fetuses. Other major defects, mainly cardiac, are observed in about 50% of the cases. Tracheoesophageal fistula may be seen as part of the VATER association (vertebral and ventricular septal defects, anal atresia, tracheoesophageal fistula, renal anomalies, radial dysplasia, and single umbilical artery).

Prenatally the diagnosis of esophageal atresia is suspected when, in the presence of polyhydramnios (usually after 25 weeks), repeated ultrasonographic examinations fail to demonstrate the fetal stomach or the stomach appears permanently small (<15% of the abdominal circumference); however, gastric secretions may be sufficient to distend the stomach and make it visible. If there is an associated fistula, the stomach may also look normal. Occasionally, after 25 weeks, the dilated proximal esophageal pouch can be seen as an elongated upper mediastinal and retrocardiac anechoic structure. Usually the diagnosis is not made in the second trimester, and the condition is only suspected after 28 weeks, when polyhydramnios appears. The differential diagnosis for the combination of absent stomach and polyhydramnios includes intrathoracic compression, by conditions such as diaphragmatic hernia, and musculoskeletal anomalies causing inability of the fetus to swallow.

Survival is primarily dependent on gestation at delivery and the presence of other anomalies. Thus, for babies with an isolated tracheoesophageal fistula, born after 32 weeks, when an early diagnosis is made, avoiding reflux and aspiration pneumonitis, postoperative survival is more than 95%.

Duodenal atresia is found in about 1 per 5,000 births. It is a sporadic abnormality, although in some cases there is an autosomal-recessive pattern of inheritance. Approximately half of fetuses with duodenal atresia have associated abnormalities, including trisomy 21 in about 40% of fetuses and skeletal defects (vertebral and rib anomalies, sacral agenesis, radial abnormalities, and talipes), gastrointestinal abnormalities (esophageal atresia/tracheoesophageal fistula, intestinal malrotation, Meckel diverticulum, and anorectal atresia), as well as cardiac and renal defects.

Prenatal diagnosis is based on the demonstration of the characteristic "double bubble" appearance of the dilated stomach and proximal duodenum, commonly associated with polyhydramnios. However, obstruction due to a central web may result in only a "single bubble" representing the fluid-filled stomach. Continuity of the duodenum with the stomach should be demonstrated to differentiate a distended duodenum from other cystic masses, including choledocal or hepatic cysts. It is usually not diagnosed until after 25 weeks, suggesting that the fetus is unable to swallow sufficient volume of amniotic fluid for bowel dilatation to occur before the end of the second trimester of pregnancy. Survival after surgery in patients with isolated duodenal atresia is more than 95%.

Intestinal obstructions occur in about 1 per 2,000 births. In about half of the cases there is small bowel obstruction and in the other half anorectal atresia. Small bowel obstruction may derive from primary atresia or stenosis of the bowel, meconium ileus, and extrinsic constriction from adhesions. The most frequent site of small bowel obstruction is distal ileus, followed by proximal jejunum. In about 5% of cases, obstructions occur in multiple sites.

Although the condition is usually sporadic, in multiple intestinal atresias familial cases have been described. Associated abnormalities and chromosomal defects are rare. In contrast with anorectal atresia, associated defects such as genitourinary, vertebral, cardiovascular, and gastrointestinal anomalies are found in about 80% of cases. Meconium ileus may be associated with cystic fibrosis.

The lumen of the fetal small bowel and colon does not normally exceed 7 mm and 20 mm, respectively. Diagnosis of obstruction is usually made late in pregnancy, after 25 weeks, because dilatation of the intestinal lumen is slow and progressive. Jejunal and ileal obstructions are imaged as multiple fluid-filled loops of bowel in the abdomen (Fig. 22-6). The abdomen is usually distended, and active peristalsis may be observed. If bowel perforation occurs, transient ascites, meconium peritonitis, and meconium pseudocysts may ensue. Polyhydramnios, usually after 25 weeks, is common, especially with proximal obstructions. Similar bowel appearances and polyhydramnios may be found in fetuses with Hirschprung disease, the megacystis-microcolon-intestinal hypoperistalsis syndrome and congenital chloride diarrhea. The differential diagnosis of small bowel obstruction includes renal tract abnormalities and other intraabdominal cysts such as mesenteric, ovarian, or duplication cysts. An important clue specific for bowel obstruction is the presence of peristalsis. In anorectal atresia, prenatal diagnosis is usually difficult because the proximal bowel may not demonstrate significant dilatation and the amniotic fluid volume is usually normal; occasionally, calcified intraluminal meconium in the fetal pelvis may be seen.

The prognosis is related to the gestational age at delivery, the presence of associated abnormalities, and the site of obstruction. In those born after 32 weeks with isolated

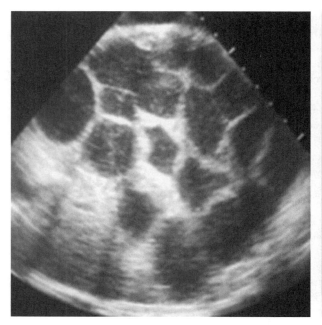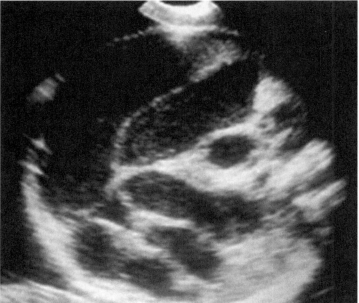

FIGURE 22-6. Sonography of small bowel obstruction in the third trimester of gestation. Multiple sonolucent areas are seen in the abdomen of these two fetuses with intestinal atresia.

obstruction requiring resection of only short segments of bowel, the survival rate is more than 95%. Loss of large segments of bowel can lead to short gut syndrome, which is a lethal condition.

ANOMALIES OF THE KIDNEYS AND URINARY TRACT

The most common renal anomalies occurring with increased frequency in diabetes are duplication of the collecting system and renal agenesis (18). Although hydronephrosis has been mentioned as being associated with diabetes, it is unclear whether this is due to a well-defined obstructive lesion.

Renal Agenesis

Bilateral renal agenesis is found in 1 per 5,000 births, while unilateral disease is found in 1 per 2,000 births.

Renal agenesis is usually an isolated sporadic abnormality, but in a few cases it may be secondary to a chromosomal abnormality or part of a genetic syndrome such as Fraser syndrome, or a developmental defect such as VACTERL association (vertebral abnormalities, anal atresia, cardiac abnormalities, tracheoesophageal fistula and/or esophageal atresia, renal agenesis and dysplasia, and limb defects). In nonsyndromic cases, the risk for recurrence is approximately 3%. However, in about 15% of cases one of the parents has unilateral renal agenesis, and in these families the risk for recurrence is increased.

Antenatally, the condition is suspected by the combination of anhydramnios and failure to visualize the fetal bladder (Fig. 22-7). Examination of the renal areas is often hampered by the oligohydramnios and the "crumpled" position adopted by these fetuses. Care should be taken to avoid mistaking perirenal fat and large fetal adrenals for the absent kidneys. The differential diagnosis includes preterm rupture of membranes, severe uteroplacental insufficiency, and obstructive uropathy or bilateral multicystic or polycystic kidneys. Vaginal sonography with a high-resolution probe is useful in these cases. Failure to visualize the renal arteries with color Doppler is another important clue to the diagnosis in difficult cases, with both bilateral and unilateral agenesis. In the absence of the kidneys, the adrenal gland appears flattened (lying down) (40) (Fig. 22-7). Prenatal diagnosis of unilateral renal agenesis is difficult because there are no major features, such as anhydramnios and empty bladder, to alert the sonographer to the fact that one of the kidneys is absent.

Bilateral renal agenesis is a lethal condition. The presence of amniotic fluid is necessary for the normal development of the lungs up to 22 to 24 weeks. Early severe oligohydramnios results typically in pulmonary hypoplasia, and infants die in the neonatal period of respiratory insufficiency. The prognosis with unilateral agenesis is normal.

Cystic Kidneys

Four main categories of cystic dysplastic kidneys are recognized. Two types can be identified with certainty via antenatal ultrasonography: multicystic kidney and cystic dys-

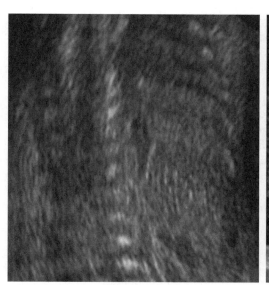 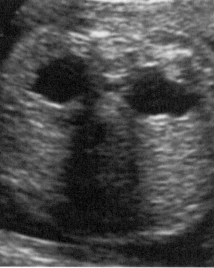 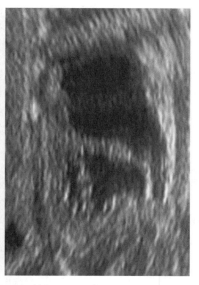

FIGURE 22-7. Sonography of renal anomalies: oligohydramnios, no demonstrable kidneys, and a flattened adrenal gland in a third-trimester fetus with renal agenesis (left); bilateral hydronephrosis (middle); and longitudinal section of one fetal kidney demonstrating two renal pelves with hydronephrosis of the upper one and suggesting ureteral duplication (right).

plasia occurring as a consequence of early and long-standing obstructive uropathy. Multicystic kidneys are usually unilateral and appear as a cluster of multiple irregular cysts of variable size with little intervening hyperechogenic stroma. In the majority of cases, this is a sporadic abnormality, but chromosomal abnormalities (mainly trisomy 18), genetic syndromes, and other defects (mainly cardiac) are present in about 50% of the cases. Isolated unilateral multicystic kidneys have a good prognosis.

Early and persistent obstruction of the lower urinary tract is associated with secondary cystic dysplasia of the kidneys that appear hyperechogenic, increased in size, and present small cysts that spread through the parenchyma. In these cases the diagnosis is made by the simultaneous demonstration of obstructive uropathy (distended bladder, convoluted ureters, pyelectasia, oligohydramnios). The prognosis is poor. Autosomal-recessive cystic kidneys (also referred to as infantile polycystic kidneys) are characterized by markedly enlarged kidneys filled with numerous cortical cysts and dilated collecting ducts. Sonographically, the kidneys are enlarged on both sides and hyperechogenic. However, these sonographic appearances may be manifest only in late gestation. Prognosis is variable. Cases appearing early in gestation are associated with oligohydramnios in the second trimester and are usually lethal due to a combination of renal failure and pulmonary hypoplasia. In other cases, the onset of the disease occurs later in gestation or after birth, and there is a variable progression toward renal failure. The infantile and juvenile types result in chronic renal failure, hepatic fibrosis, and portal hypertension; many survive into their teens and require renal transplantation.

Autosomal-dominant cystic kidneys, one of the most common genetic diseases, are usually asymptomatic until the third or fourth decade of life. Usually, sonography will not demonstrate abnormalities prior to the second or third decade. In a handful of cases, however, affected fetuses have demonstrated findings similar to the autosomal-recessive variety, enlarged and echogenic kidneys. It is clear that this disease covers a wide spectrum. The experience with prenatal diagnosis is limited. It would not seem that intrauterine presentation is necessarily associated with a poor prognosis.

Cystic kidneys are also found with many mendelian disorders, such as tuberous sclerosis, Jeune syndrome, Sturge-Weber syndrome, Zellweger syndrome, Laurence-Moon-Biedl syndrome, and Meckel-Gruber syndrome.

Hydronephrosis

Enlargement of the urinary tract usually occurs, albeit not exclusively as the consequence of obstruction. When the obstruction is complete and occurs early in fetal life, cystic renal dysplasia ensues. On the other hand, where intermittent obstruction allows for normal renal development, or when obstruction occurs in the second half of pregnancy,

hydronephrosis will result and the severity of the renal damage will depend on the degree and duration of the obstruction. Different entities with variable findings and clinical implications exist depending on the location and severity of the dilatation.

Hydronephrosis refers to dilatation of the renal pelvis (Fig. 22-7). Mild hydronephrosis, or pyelectasia, is defined by the presence of an anteroposterior diameter of the pelvis of greater than 4 mm at midgestation and greater than 7 mm in the third trimester (41). Transient hydronephrosis may be due to relaxation of smooth muscle of the urinary tract by high levels of progesterone or maternal-fetal overhydration. In the majority of cases the condition remains stable or resolves in the neonatal period. In about 20% of cases there may be an underlying pathology that requires postnatal follow-up and possible surgery. The incidence of surgery with a renal pelvis of 5 to 10 mm is in the range of 3% to 4%. Moderate hydronephrosis, characterized by an anteroposterior pelvic diameter of more than 10 mm, is almost invariably associated with calyceal dilatation, is usually progressive, and, in more than 50% of cases, requires surgery during the first 2 years of life. Sonographically, it may be difficult at times to distinguish severe hydronephrosis with significant calyceal enlargement from a multicystic kidney. A scan oriented along the coronal plane of the kidney is required to demonstrate the radial projection of the calyces around the enlarged pelvis. Sections oriented in different planes may create the false impression of multiple cysts separated by parenchymal tissue that is typical of multicystic kidney.

Hydronephrosis is usually the consequence of either ureteropelvic junction obstruction or vesicoureteric reflux. These are sporadic conditions and, although in some cases there is an anatomic cause, in most instances the underlying etiology is thought to be functional. In 80% of cases, the condition is unilateral. Rarely, associated anomalies are found, albeit a slightly increased risk of chromosomal aberrations has been suggested. Independently from the degree or progression of hydronephrosis, the prognosis is generally good. The presence of a normal amount of amniotic fluid is reassuring with regard to renal function, and no modification of standard obstetric care is required.

Hydroureteronephrosis is the combination of hydronephrosis and enlarged ureter. Of course, these findings are generally present with megacystis. However, the following discussion refers to hydroureteronephrosis with a normal bladder, which may result from either ureterovesical reflux or ureterovesical junction obstruction. Under normal conditions, the small ureter cannot be visualized with antenatal ultrasonography. The dilated ureter appears as a tortuous fluid-filled tubular structure interposed between the renal pelvis, which is variably dilated, and the bladder. Rarely, a primary megaureter will be present, with a normal renal pelvis. The outcome and management principles are similar to the ones outlined for hydronephrosis.

Ureteral duplication can be associated with hydronephrosis and megaureter. A specific diagnosis is possible when two distinct renal pelves can be seen within one kidney. Typically, there is some degree of dilatation of the upper renal pole (42,43) (Fig. 22-7).

Megacystis is defined as an abnormal enlargement of the urinary bladder, and is most frequently the consequence of urethral obstruction. Typically, it is seen in the early midtrimester and has been visualized as early as 11 weeks' gestation. The bladder is usually greatly enlarged, occupying most of the abdomen and distending it. Urethral obstruction can be caused by urethral agenesis, persistence of the cloaca, urethral stricture, or posterior urethral valves. Posterior urethral valves occur only in males and are the most common cause of bladder outlet obstruction. The condition is sporadic and is found in about 1 in 3,000 male fetuses. With posterior urethral valves, there is usually incomplete or intermittent obstruction of the urethra, resulting in an enlarged and hypertrophied bladder with varying degrees of hydroureters, hydronephrosis, a spectrum of renal hypoplasia and dysplasia, oligohydramnios, and pulmonary hypoplasia. In some cases, there is associated urinary ascites from rupture of the bladder or transudation of urine into the peritoneal cavity.

When megacystis is found in association with either a normal or increased amount of amniotic fluid, the possibility of megacystis-microcolon-intestinal hypoperistalsis syndrome should be considered. This is a sporadic abnormality characterized by a massively dilated bladder and hydronephrosis in the presence of normal or increased amniotic fluid; the fetuses are usually female. There is associated shortening and dilatation of the proximal small bowel, and microcolon with absent or ineffective peristalsis. The condition is usually lethal due to bowel and renal dysfunction.

The outcome of urethral obstruction depends on how severe and early this occurs. Complete persistent obstruction occurring in the early midtrimester (e.g., urethral atresia, early posterior urethral valves) results in massive distention of the bladder and abdominal wall (prune-belly abdomen), severe oligohydramnios, dysplastic kidneys, and pulmonary hypoplasia. Obstruction occurring in late gestation may be associated with oligohydramnios and hydronephrosis, but does not result in pulmonary hypoplasia and dysplastic kidneys. Management of early-appearing megacystis is debated. Shunting the fetal bladder is feasible, although there is not conclusive evidence that such intervention improves renal or pulmonary function beyond what can be achieved by postnatal surgery. Antenatal evaluation of renal function relies on a combination of ultrasonographic findings and analysis of fetal urine obtained by puncture of the bladder or renal pelvis. An attempt to assess the severity of renal compromise should be made before embarking on fetal therapy. Poor prognostic signs are (a) the presence of bilateral multicystic or severely hydro-

nephrotic kidneys with echogenic kidneys, suggestive of renal dysplasia; (b) anhydramnios, implying complete urethral obstruction; and (c) high urinary sodium, calcium, and β_2-microglobulin levels. In these cases, there is little chance of the infant surviving. Conversely, potential candidates for intrauterine surgery are fetuses with (a) bilateral moderately severe pelvicalyceal dilatation and normal cortical echogenicity, (b) severe megacystis and oligohydramnios, and (c) normal levels of urinary sodium, calcium, and β_2-microglobulin.

Skeletal Anomalies

Skeletal dysplasia is found in about 1 per 4,000 births; about 25% of affected fetuses are stillborn, and about 30% die in the neonatal period. Most of these anomalies are genetically determined and are not specifically associated with diabetes. Therefore, the interested reader is referred to specific texts on this subject. An exception is caudal regression or sacral agenesis syndrome, a relatively rare condition (1 in 200 to 1 in 500 pregnancies complicated by diabetes) but a rate 200 times higher than in nondiabetic pregnancies. The abnormality probably results from a defect in the midposterior axis mesoderm of the embryo occurring before the fourth week postconception. This results in the absence or hypoplasia of caudal structures. Antenatal ultrasound findings include absence of the fetal sacrum and shortening of the lower extremities. Sirenomelia (presence of only one lower extremity in association with renal agenesis) was once considered a part of the spectrum of sacral agenesis but probably is a separate entity not associated with maternal diabetes (44). Termination of pregnancy is an option that may be offered to the parents if the diagnosis is made before the period of viability; otherwise, the patient can be managed expectantly. A loss of motor function is common in infants with sacral agenesis, but sensory function is normally preserved.

CONCLUSION

Ultrasonography provides essential information about the fetus of the woman with diabetes and should be used liberally in the management of these patients. A first-trimester scan should be used to date the pregnancy and to document fetal viability; a second-trimester scan (at ~20 weeks) should allow the perinatologist to rule out most serious fetal anomalies, and a third-trimester examination will help assess fetal growth disorders. Particular attention should be directed toward ultrasound clues that might suggest fetal macrosomia or intrauterine growth restriction. In general, judicious use of ultrasonography should decrease the likelihood of surprises in a condition that is notoriously unpredictable.

KEY POINTS

- Infants of diabetic mothers have an increased likelihood of being affected by congenital anomalies. The risk is particularly high in patients with poor periconceptional metabolic control. There is a generalized increase of any type of structural anomaly, although some patterns seems to be typical of maternal diabetes.

- Apart from structural anomalies, fetal growth may be affected, particularly when the diabetes is poorly controlled in late gestation. Cardiac growth may be accelerated, leading to cardiac hypertrophy with hemodynamic alterations.

- There is a wide consensus that a targeted ultrasound examination should be performed in insulin-dependent pregnant diabetic patients. A midtrimester scan including a detailed survey of fetal anatomy and an echocardiogram are particularly recommended. Because NTDs are frequent in these pregnancies, MSAFP screening is also advised.

- The sonographic findings, prognostic figures, and management recommendations of the most frequent congenital anomalies are discussed. The exact proportion of fetal anomalies that will be revealed by a midtrimester scan is still uncertain. Probably 80% of major cardiac anomalies and most NTDs will be identified.

- Prenatal diagnosis does not prevent anomalies. However, when a severe condition is identified, pregnancy termination can be considered. Some treatable anomalies, cardiac malformations in particular, may benefit from specific perinatal treatment. Eventually, a negative scan will relieve anxiety in the parents.

REFERENCES

1. Emery AEH, Rimoin R. *Principles and practice of medical genetics.* Edinburgh: Churchill Livingstone, 1983.
2. Milunsky A. *Genetic disorders and the fetus: diagnosis, prevention, and treatment,* 3rd ed. Baltimore: Johns Hopkins University Press, 1992.
3. Becerra JE, Muin JK, Cordero JF, et al. Diabetes mellitus during pregnancy and the risks for specific birth defects: a population based case control study. *Pediatrics* 1990;85:1.
4. Fuhrmann K RH, Semmler K, et al. Prevention of congenital malformations in infants of insulin-dependent diabetic mothers. *Diabetes Care* 1983;6:219.
5. Miodovnik M, Mimouni F, St. John Dignan P, et al. Major malformations in infants of IDDM women: vasculopathy and early first-trimester poor glycemic control. *Diabetes Care* 1988;11:713–718.
6. Casson IFC, Clarke A, Howard CV, et al. Outcomes of pregnancy in insulin dependent diabetic women: results of a five year population cohort study. *BMJ* 1997;315:275–278.
7. Ray JG, O'Brien TE, Chan WS. Preconception care and the risk of congenital anomalies in the offspring of women with diabetes mellitus: a meta-analysis. *Q J Med* 2001;94(8):435–444.
8. Nyberg DA, McGahan JP, Pretorius DH, et al. *Diagnostic imaging of fetal anomalies,* 1st ed. Philadelphia: Lippincott Williams & Wilkins, 2003.
9. Allan L. Antenatal diagnosis of heart disease. *Heart* 2000;83(3):367.
10. Grandjean H, Larroque D, Levi S. Sensitivity of routine ultrasound screening of pregnancies in the Eurofetus database. The Eurofetus Team. *Ann NY Acad Sci* 1998;847:118–124.
11. Greene MF, Benacerraf BR. Prenatal diagnosis in diabetic gravidas: utility of ultrasound and maternal serum alpha-fetoprotein screening. *Obstet Gynecol* 1991;77(4):520–524.
12. Albert TJ, Landon MB, Wheller JJ, et al. Prenatal detection of fetal anomalies in pregnancies complicated by insulin-dependent diabetes mellitus. *Am J Obstet Gynecol* 1996;174(5):1424–1428.
13. Milunsky A. Prenatal diagnosis of neural tube defects. The importance of serum alpha fetoprotein screening in diabetic pregnant women. *Am J Obstet Gynecol* 1982;142:1030–1035.
14. Johnson SP, Sebire NJ, Snijders RJ, et al. Ultrasound screening for anencephaly at 10-14 weeks of gestation. *Ultrasound Obstet Gynecol* 1997;9(1):14–16.
15. Nicolaides KH, Campbell S, Gabbe SG, et al. Ultrasound screening for spina bifida: cranial and cerebellar signs. *Lancet* 1986;12(2):72–74.
16. Pilu G, Hobbins JC. Sonography of fetal cerebrospinal anomalies. *Prenat Diagn* 2002;22(4):321–330.
17. Pilu G, Falco P, Gabrielli S, et al. The clinical significance of fetal isolated cerebral borderline ventriculomegaly: report of 31 cases and review of the literature. *Ultrasound Obstet Gynecol* 1999;14(5):320–326.
18. Naeye C. Congenital malformations in offspring of diabetes [PhD Thesis]. Boston, Harvard University, 1967.
19. Pilu G, Falco P, Milano V, et al. Prenatal diagnosis of microcephaly assisted by vaginal sonography and power Doppler. *Ultrasound Obstet Gynecol* 1998;11(5):357–360.
20. Bromley B, Benacerraf BR. Difficulties in the prenatal diagnosis of microcephaly. *J Ultrasound Med* 1995;14(4):303–306.
21. Pilu G, Sandri F, Perolo A, et al. Sonography of fetal agenesis of the corpus callosum: a survey of 35 cases. *Ultrasound Obstet Gynecol* 1993;3:318–329.
22. Ghi T, Perolo A, Banzi C, et al. Two-dimensional ultrasound is accurate in the diagnosis of fetal craniofacial malformation. *Ultrasound Obstet Gynecol* 2002;19(6):543–551.
23. Ferencz C, Rubin JD, McCarter RJ, et al. Maternal diabetes and cardiovascular malformations: predominance of double outlet right ventricle and truncus arteriosus. *Teratology* 1990;41:319–323.
24. Rizzo G, Arduini D, Romanini C. Cardiac function in fetuses of type I diabetic mothers. *Am J Obstet Gynecol* 1991;164(3):837–843.
25. Rizzo G, Arduini D, Romanini C. Accelerated cardiac growth and abnormal cardiac flow in fetuses of type I diabetic mothers. *Obstet Gynecol* 1992;80(3 part 1):369–376.
26. Rizzo G, Pietropolli A, Capponi A, et al. Analysis of factors influencing ventricular filling patterns in fetuses of type I diabetic mothers. *J Perinat Med* 1994;22(2):149–157.
27. Allan L, Benacerraf B, Copel JA, et al. Isolated major congenital heart disease. *Ultrasound Obstet Gynecol* 2001;17(5):370–379.
28. Bromley B, Estroff JA, Sanders SP, et al. Fetal echocardiography: accuracy and limitations in a population at high and low risk for heart defects. *Am J Obstet Gynecol* 1992;166(5):1473–1481.
29. Achiron R, Glaser J, Gelernter I, et al. Extended fetal echocardiographic examination for detecting cardiac malformations in low risk pregnancies. *BMJ* 1992;304(6828):671–674.
30. Ghi T, Pilu G, Savelli L, et al. Sonographic diagnosis of congenital anomalies during the first trimester. *Placenta* 2003;24(suppl 2):84–87.

31. Yagel S, Cohen SM, Achiron R. Examination of the fetal heart by five short-axis views: a proposed screening method for comprehensive cardiac evaluation. *Ultrasound Obstet Gynecol* 2001; 17(5):367–369.

32. Chaoui R, McEwing R. Three cross-sectional planes for fetal color Doppler echocardiography. *Ultrasound Obstet Gynecol* 2003;21(1):81–93.

33. Rizzo G, Pietropolli A, Capponi A, et al. Echocardiographic studies of the fetal heart. *J Perinat Med* 1994;22(suppl 1):46–50.

34. Cacciari A, Ceccarelli PL, Pilu GL, et al. A series of 17 cases of congenital cystic adenomatoid malformation of the lung: management and outcome. *Eur J Pediatr Surg* 1997;7(2):84–89.

35. Adzick NS, Harrison MR, Crombleholme TM, et al. Fetal lung lesions: management and outcome. *Am J Obstet Gynecol* 1998; 179(4):884–889.

36. Estroff JA, Parad RB, Frigoletto FDJ, et al. The natural history of isolated fetal hydrothorax. *Ultrasound Obstet Gynecol* 1992;2(3): 162–165.

37. Becker R, Arabin B, Novak A, et al. Successful treatment of primary fetal hydrothorax by long-time drainage from week 23. Case report and review of the literature. *Fetal Diagn Ther* 1993;8(5):331–337.

38. Sydorak RM, Harrison MR. Congenital diaphragmatic hernia: advances in prenatal therapy. *World J Surg* 2003;27(1):68–76.

39. Harrison MR, Keller RL, Hawgood SB, et al. A randomized trial of fetal endoscopic tracheal occlusion for severe fetal congenital diaphragmatic hernia. *N Engl J Med* 2003;349(20): 1916–1924.

40. Hoffman CK, Filly RA, Callen PW. The "lying down" adrenal sign: a sonographic indicator of renal agenesis or ectopia in fetuses and neonates. *J Ultrasound Med* 1992;11(10): 533–536.

41. Sairam S, Al-Habib A, Sasson S, et al. Natural history of fetal hydronephrosis diagnosed on mid-trimester ultrasound. *Ultrasound Obstet Gynecol* 2001;17(3):191–196.

42. Whitten SM, McHoney M, Wilcox DT, et al. Accuracy of antenatal fetal ultrasound in the diagnosis of duplex kidneys. *Ultrasound Obstet Gynecol* 2003;21(4):342–346.

43. Abuhamad AZ, Horton CEJ, Horton SH, et al. Renal duplication anomalies in the fetus: clues for prenatal diagnosis. *Ultrasound Obstet Gynecol* 1996;7(3):174–177.

44. Twickler D, Budorick N, Pretorius D, et al. Caudal regression versus sirenomelia: sonographic clues. *J Ultrasound Med* 1993; 12(6):323–330.

23

DIAGNOSIS AND MANAGEMENT OF ABNORMAL FETAL GROWTH

ODED LANGER

INTRODUCTION

The growth potential of the developing fetus under normal conditions is determined by several components, including genetic, environmental, nutritional, and endocrinologic factors, as well as the proper functioning of the placental supply line (1). Any conditions that interfere with this growth potential, most significantly diabetes in pregnancy and diseases associated with vasculopathy, may cause abnormal growth of the fetus. When physiologic levels of maternal glucose were not achieved in diabetic patients, excessive fetal growth resulted in a 25% to 42% macrosomia rate (2). Moreover, distinct levels of glycemic control are associated with small-for-gestational age (SGA) (<10th percentile) and large-for-gestational age (LGA) (>90th percentile) infants in gestational diabetes (GDM). When normoglycemia was achieved, the incidence of LGA ranged from 1.4 to 9%.

In general, in growth-restricted and macrosomic fetuses, morbidity and mortality rates are increased. The macrosomic infant is also predisposed to shoulder dystocia and traumatic birth injury (3). For these reasons, the identification and timely delivery of abnormally grown fetuses (LGA/SGA) and an understanding of their relationship to glycemic control could provide the foundation for optimal management. Despite extensive ultrasonographic knowledge regarding measurement of macrosomic and growth-restricted fetuses (4–7), a paucity of information exists regarding the types and the timing of onset of accelerated/restricted fetal growth in the pregnant diabetic patient (8–10).

The need for early gestational dating in pregnancies complicated by diabetes is obvious because alterations in fetal growth are related to fetal age, and women with advanced diabetes are rarely permitted to go post term. Clinical decisions on lung maturity testing, elective delivery, and methods of delivery are all based on gestational age and weight of the fetus. Biometric methodology attempts to insert precision into the process of adequately identifying the affected infant. However, these measurements are not sufficiently rigorous and can, therefore, provide both false positive and false negative results during routine clinical use. These sonographic measures attempt to identify an abnormal outcome rather than to antenatally detect the compromised infant. Until such time that a marker exists that clearly defines the infant compromised by abnormal growth, the process will remain unsatisfactory.

FIRST TRIMESTER BIOMETRY

It is in the second half of pregnancy that the fetus of a diabetic patient can be differentiated from that of a normal woman. The only exception to this rule occurs for SGA in the first trimester. Traditionally, measurements of the crown-rump length (CRL) have been considered the most accurate method of gestational age estimation. As a single measurement, the CRL is one of the most precise dating methods (±4 to 7 days) until the 12th week of gestation, after which the measurement becomes less accurate because of variable degrees of fetal flexion. The CRL is obtained by measuring the long axis of the embryo.

Pedersen and Molsted-Pederson (11) reported evidence that challenges the accuracy of CRL in dating diabetic pregnancies. Of 99 women with diabetes, 38 had embryos whose CRLs at 7 to 14 weeks were more than 6 days below the mean for gestation. Seven of these fetuses (27%) with "early growth restriction" were later diagnosed as being anomalous. Although this observation is of significant interest in the understanding and, perhaps, identification of diabetes-related anomalies, it casts doubt on the accuracy of CRL in diabetic patients because almost one in three nonanomalous embryos of women with diabetes had early growth restriction. The patients in the Pedersen and Molsted-Pederson (11) studies had 28- to 30-day cycles before becoming pregnant; nevertheless, this did not preclude them from ovulating late in the conception cycle.

A subsequent study was reported by Keys et al. (12) in patients whose date of conception was established either by basal body temperature chart or ovulation induction drugs. These authors found no evidence of growth restriction.

Cousins et al. (13) also performed longitudinal CRL measurements in 20 control pregnancies and 20 pregnancies complicated by diabetes. Like Keys et al. (12), they found no differences between the two groups, including the growth of the two anomalous fetuses in the study. The Diabetes in Early Pregnancy Study (14) also did *not* find statistically significant differences between fetuses with malformations compared with those without malformations. Therefore, although a fetus growing in an abnormal metabolic milieu may be at increased risk for growth restriction as well as malformation, there is no reproducible evidence indicating that an early growth delay is associated with malformed infants.

SECOND TRIMESTER BIOMETRY

Biparietal Diameter

When ultrasound was first used in obstetrics, one of the early fetal parameters that could be consistently measured was the biparietal diameter (BPD). In fact, even after static B-mode images became possible to interpret, many authors thought that the BPD was the gold standard for gestational age estimation and should be measured from an A-mode image. Therefore, many nomograms of the BPD appeared in the literature. They are all reasonably accurate (±7 to 10 days) through the 26th week of gestation. With the improvements of ultrasound imaging, many other measurements of fetal dimensions have been conducted, and nomograms of other fetal biometric parameters have been introduced (15).

Biparietal diameter measurements correlate poorly with the development of SGA and LGA. Sensitivity rates range between 50% and 60%. Head circumference measurements may be preferable to BPD measurements because the latter are influenced by the fetal lie and position as well as the normal variations that occur in fetal head shape during pregnancy (15).

Abdominal Circumference

Diabetes seems to preferentially affect the abdominal circumference (AC) more than the BPD or long bone length. Thus, this measurement is particularly useful in identifying either macrosomic or growth-restricted fetuses. The fetal liver is the organ most affected by variations in fetal nutrition and should therefore be chosen as the place for AC measurement. However, errors in sonographic measurements, especially AC, have a large inter- and intra-observer variability.

AC measurements less than the 25th percentile have a sensitivity of 83% to 86% and a specificity of 79% to 80% in the detection of SGA. Other predictors of low birth weight include the ponderal index or morphometric ratios, although these are less sensitive in detecting symmetrical SGA. The choice of percentile used to define abnormal AC measurements influences the predictive value of the test. Decreasing the percentile value to the tenth percentile decreases the sensitivity of the test, but improves the specificity (15).

Occipitofrontal Diameter

The occipitofrontal diameter (OFD) should be obtained in the same plane used for the BPD. An axial plane of the head is obtained at 15 to 20 degrees from the horizontal plane. The thalami, septum cavum pellucidum, and the third ventricle are identifiable at that level. The distance from the mid-echogenic plane of the occipital bone to the mid-echogenic plane of the frontal bone is then measured. Although most ultrasound units have similar axial resolutions, they may vary in their lateral resolutions. The antero-posterior (axial) resolution is less than 2 mm in most ultrasound machines, whereas the degree of lateral resolution is generally greater and ranges from 3 to 5 mm. The head circumference measurement can be calculated using both the short diameter (BPD) and the long diameter (OFD): (BPD + OFD)/2 × 3.14. It can also be measured by tracing the sonographic image directly on the screen (15).

Transverse Cerebellar Diameter

Transverse cerebellar diameter (TCD) has become a standard measurement for evaluating the fetal head and somatic growth. The cerebellum is an intracranial structure located in the posterior fossa of the fetal head. Morphologically, it has a butterfly-like shape and is easy to identify sonographically.

Measurements of the TCD are independent of the fetal head and thus remain an accurate method of estimating gestational age. Because the posterior fossa is not affected by external pressure, measurements of the TCD should provide more precise information about fetal growth than other measurements of the bony fetal head. Furthermore, Reece et al. (16) have reported that the TCD is not significantly affected by growth restriction, Hill et al. (17) found that the TCD remained relatively unchanged in macrosomic fetuses, and thus is a useful marker for determination of gestational age in pregnancies complicated by diabetes and aberrant growth.

Long Bones

Gestational age can also be estimated from measurements of the fetal long bones such as femur, humerus, tibia, and ulna. Length of the femur and other long bones show a correlation with gestational age, approximately that obtained from the BPD. Hadlock et al. (18) have shown that combining biometric data results in a more accurate prediction of gestational age than using one measurement alone, provided outliers are excluded from this average. When dating pregnancies, one must be aware of an occasional familial tendency toward large heads or short limbs that may alter the mean biometric estimate of gestational age. For example, if the BPD or femur length is not consistent with every other variable, it would be better to delete this outlier and average the clustered biometric data than to include all measurements in an overall estimation of gestational age.

DEVIANT FETAL GROWTH

Large and small fetuses are in most cases (70%) constitutional and influenced by genetic factors. The Gaussian distribution of fetal weight, even in the nondiabetic population, will result in 10% being LGA (above the 90th percentile) and 10% SGA (below the 10th percentile). In the pregnant diabetic woman, the "toxic effects" of glucose on fetal development will cause accelerated growth (hyperglycemia) or fetal growth restriction (tight glycemic control and/or the presence of vasculopathy). These rates increase two- to four-fold for each growth deviance.

The etiology of macrosomia is thought to be secondary to fetal hyperinsulinemia resulting from maternal hyperglycemia. The fetal pancreas is stimulated by elevated blood glucose to increase production of insulin. Pedersen et al. (19) proposed that the concomitant presence of excessive substrate and insulin enhance fetal glycogen synthesis, lipogenesis, and protein synthesis. There are experimental data supporting insulin as the primary growth hormone (1).

The macrosomic infant is at greater risk for several perinatal complications. Macrosomia is generally defined as a birth weight in excess of 4,000 g and an LGA weight above the 90th percentile for gestational age. Infants weighing more than 4,000 g account for 8% to 10% of all deliveries, whereas birth weight in excess of 4,500 g occurs in approximately 1% of pregnancies (20). Fetuses of women with diabetes are at high risk of birth trauma not only because of their tendency toward macrosomia but also because of their disproportionately greater growth of the body compared with the head. In fact, increased weight of insulin-sensitive tissues, including liver, pancreas, heart, lungs, and adrenals has been demonstrated in the infant of the diabetic mother.

Conversely, it has also been demonstrated that women with diabetes are at increased risk of delivering a small-for-gestational-age infant. This form of deviant fetal growth has also been related to disturbances in maternal fuel metabolism. The risk of growth restriction increases with the severity of the mother's diabetic vascular state, and an association has been demonstrated between growth restriction and poor maternal renal function and hypertension.

The growth of the fetal head and femur follows a pattern similar to that of "normal" fetuses. It is after week 26 to 28 of gestation that the abnormal growth patterns become evi-

dent and are mostly confined to the AC. Ogata et al. (9) studied 23 women with diabetes in pregnancy and showed ultrasonographically that accelerated abdominal growth can be detected at 28 to 32 weeks' gestation and that it diverges from the predicted curve at this stage. Landon et al. (10) studied 31 women with type 1 diabetes mellitus using serial ultrasound examinations in the third trimester, and demonstrated a divergent growth pattern (acceleration of AC growth) at week 32 in fetuses destined to be LGA at birth. In a large research sample (21), we identified two distinct abnormal fetal growth patterns in the infants of pregnant diabetic mothers by estimated fetal weight and AC growth velocity throughout the third trimester. The reliability of fetal weight estimation was reflected in the overall error of less than 10%. The results of our study support the existence of both early and late accelerated growth patterns in the fetuses of gestational and pregestational diabetic women. These patterns are inherently different from the growth patterns exhibited by macrosomic fetuses of nondiabetic postdate patients. Furthermore, our study described the presence of varied types of delayed growth patterns discernible by sonographic measurements among type 1 DM, GDM, and control subjects.

The existence of two distinct excessive growth patterns in the LGA infants was revealed by assessment with serial ultrasonography. At 30 weeks' gestation, an early accelerated growth pattern was detected in 23% of the LGA infants. In 77% of LGA fetuses, the late accelerated growth pattern was observed. Growth escalation began at 33 weeks' gestation and reached the 90th percentile at 36 weeks' gestation. Head circumference (HC), femur length (FL), and corresponding daily growth rates were comparable for LGA and appropriate for gestational age (AGA) infants of diabetic mothers. The distinctive factors for identification of the macrosomic infant *in utero* are an enlarged AC and its corresponding daily growth rate. Other organs affected by the diabetic fetopathy leading to restricted or accelerated growth may be used as potential markers for these deviant growth patterns. These may include subcutaneous fat in the cheek, skin fold thickness, and liver size.

LGA infants of diabetic mothers exhibited a significantly greater daily growth rate in AC than did the AGA infants. Within the early accelerated growth pattern, the growth rate for AC remained constant throughout the third trimester. At 30 weeks' gestation, the AC of these fetuses was already above the 95th percentile. In infants manifesting the late accelerated growth pattern, acceleration of growth in AC occurred later in the third trimester and reached the 95th percentile at 35 weeks' gestation. In this growth pattern, the daily growth rate in AC was significantly greater during the second half of the third trimester (weeks 36 to 40) than during the first half. Mean blood glucose in the two growth patterns were comparable: in the early pattern 107±16 mg/dL, and in the late pattern 116±18 mg/dL. Thus, differences in glycemic profile cannot be attributed to either early or late onset of accelerated growth (21) (Table 23-1).

Fetal growth is multifactorial. However, in the diabetic pregnancy, fetal growth complications are considered to be the result of hyperglycemia, one of the foundations of diabetic fetopathy. Insulin is the foremost regulatory hormone for fetal growth. Although present at 8 to 10 weeks' gestation, fetal insulin remains relatively inactive until week 20 of gestation (22). Furthermore, in the human fetal liver, insulin receptors are maximized between 19 and 25 weeks' gestation. In addition, there is an increased affinity for insulin in late gestation (23). The growth rate of the fetus up to 25 to 27 weeks' gestation is independent of circulating insulin levels. It is late in gestation that the major effects of insulin on delayed and accelerated fetal growth and fat deposition occur (1).

This physiologic process is consistent with findings of distinct time-related abnormal growth patterns (LGA fetuses) (21). In addition, our results corroborated prior research that abdominal measurements are the most reliable indicator for the detection of macrosomia *in utero* (5,24). In macrosomic infants of nondiabetic mothers, constitutional (symmetric) macrosomia is the common finding that reflects genetic effects on growth. These fetuses were at the 75th percentile throughout the third trimester, with HC, FL, and FL/AC ratio approximating the 90th percentile for a given gestational age. This finding confirms those of Hadlock et al. (4), who described larger morphometric measurements for LGA infants of normal mothers than in LGA infants of diabetic mothers.

Shoulder dystocia is a critical obstetric complication, with potential long-term consequences for both mother and infant and often medical/legal repercussions for the obstetrician and/or perinatologist. Fetal macrosomia remains a strong risk factor for shoulder dystocia (25–29),

and it has been demonstrated that macrosomic infants of diabetic mothers are at even higher risk for shoulder dystocia than those of nondiabetic mothers (26,29).

Several studies have demonstrated that adiposity is higher in infants of diabetic mothers (30–32). Modanlou et al. (33) described larger shoulder circumference in macrosomic infants of diabetic mothers in comparison to nondiabetic control subjects. It may well be that extra fat is concentrated in the upper body of these infants and this weight disproportion may increase their risk of shoulder dystocia.

Macrosomic infants of diabetic mothers may have different anthropometric and body composition characteristics than those of nondiabetic patients. Osler (30) described higher body fat percentile in 12 infants of diabetic mothers, but did not indicate whether they were macrosomic infants. Modanlou et al. (33) showed that the mean weight of macrosomic infants of diabetic mothers was higher than that of control infants and that shoulder circumference was significantly larger. In a study by Ballard et al. (34), infants of diabetic mothers displayed "disproportional macrosomia" defined by increased ponderal index more often than infants of nondiabetic mothers.

Brans et al. (32) described thicker skin folds in macrosomic infants of type 1 diabetic mothers in comparison to infants of nondiabetic and type 2 diabetic mothers. Vohr and McGarvey (31) found that LGA infants of diabetic mothers had significantly thicker skin folds than LGA control infants. Although these studies addressed adiposity, they did not describe anthropometric and body composition characteristics in the same macrosomic infants of diabetic mothers. In our study (35), we described the characteristics that can potentially contribute to shoulder dystocia in macrosomic infants of diabetic mothers: body composition and anthropometric characteristics on the same macrosomic infants (Table 23-2).

TABLE 23-1. COMPARISON OF GROWTH RATES IN LGA AND AGA FETUSES

	LGA		AGA
	Early	Late	
Mean blood glucose (mg/dL)			
27–35.9 wk	107.8 ± 19.00	116.0 ± 18.00	99.9 ± 15.00
36–42 wk	106.5 ± 17.00	114.5 ± 18.00	98.9 ± 14.00
Daily weight gain (g)[a]			
27–35.9 wk	45.2 ± 13.00	39.6 ± 17.00	29.3 ± 19.00
36–42 wk[b]	49.6 ± 14.00	44.6 ± 15.00	31.1 ± 23.00
Abdominal circumference (mm)[c]			
27–35.9 wk	1.81 ± 0.68	1.28 ± 0.42	1.13 ± 0.26
36–42 wk[d]	2.09 ± 0.22	1.67 ± 0.51	1.02 ± 0.17

[a]$p < 0.0003$ SGA vs. AGA vs. LGA.
[b]$p < 0.003$ within SGA period 1 vs. period 2.
[c]$p < 0.001$ SGA vs. AGA vs. LGA; $p < 0.0008$ early LGA vs. late SGA for periods 1 and 2.
[d]$p < 0.0003$ within LGA late period 1 vs. period 2.
AGA, appropriate for gestational age; LGA, large for gestational; SGA, small for gestational age.
Adapted from Langer O, Kozlowski S, Brustman L. Abnormal growth patterns in diabetes in pregnancy: a longitudinal study. *Isr J Med Sci* 1991;27:516–523, with permission.

TABLE 23-2. NEONATAL CHARACTERISTICS

	Diabetic Patients (n = 16)	Controls (n = 58)	p
Gestational age at delivery (wk)	39.4 ± 1.5	40.6 ± 1.3	0.001
Birth weight (g)	4294 ± 270	4290 ± 228	NS
Ponderal index	2.9 ± 0.3	2.9 ± 0.4	NS
Length (cm)	53.1 ± 2.3	53.3 ± 2.1	53.1 ± 2.3
Circumference (cm)			
Shoulder	42.2 ± 1.8	41.1 ± 1.8	0.04
Chest	36.8 ± 1.1	36.9 ± 2.0	NS
Abdomen	36.3 ± 1.4	35.7 ± 1.4	NS
Head circumference/shoulder circumference	0.85 ± 0.04	0.88 ± 0.04	0.02
Head circumference/abdominal circumference	0.97 + 0.03	0.98 + 0.04	NS
Extremity circumference (cm)			
Upper	13.5 ± 1.1	12.9 ± 0.9	0.04
Lower	17.9 ± 1.0	17.0 ± 1.2	0.008
Skinfolds (mm)			
Triceps	7.5 ± 1.5	5.4 ± 1.2	<0.0001
Subscapular	6.8 ± 2.0	5.4 ± 1.3	0.002
Flank	6.5 ± 1.5	5.6 ± 1.2	0.01
Fat mass (g)	1012 ± 292	762 ± 243	0.0009
Fat-free mass (g)	3282 ± 267	3519 ± 236	0.001
Percent body fat	23.5	17.7	0.0004

[a]Calculated using Dauncey method.
NS, not significant.
Adapted from MacFarland MB, Trylovich CG, Langer O. Anthropometric differences in macrosomic infants of diabetic and nondiabetic mothers. *J Matern Fetal Med* 1998;7:292–295, with permission.

ESTIMATED FETAL WEIGHT

Shoulder dystocia, brachial plexus injury, and clavicular fracture are complications associated with macrosomia and increase in frequency with increasing birth weight. The frequency of these complications in infants of diabetic mothers is two- to three-fold higher at any given birth weight than among deliveries of infants of nondiabetic mothers (36–38). Moreover, not only are infants of diabetic mothers at significantly increased risk for shoulder dystocia (29), but in one study, 80% of shoulder dystocia in diabetic pregnancies occurred at birth weights of 4,000 g or more.

Fetal weight between 4,250 to 4,500 g poses a sufficiently high risk of severe fetal compromise that it may justify delivery by cesarean section in the diabetic mother even if it involves maternal morbidity and additional medical expense. For these reasons, greater efforts need to be directed toward the identification of fetal growth abnormalities in fetuses of diabetic mothers.

The management plan for the route of delivery should be based on an estimated fetal weight (EFW). To obtain an EFW by sonography, several standard measurements of the fetus are made and these are entered into a formula that attempts to relate fetal size to weight. The EFW is used to diagnose SGA; it is more accurate than AC, BPD, HC, FL/AC ratio, amniotic fluid index, and Doppler velocimetry in predicting low birth weight (39,40). EFW measurements have sensitivities for diagnosing SGA that range from 87% to 90% with specificities of 80% to 87% (39,41) (Table 23-3). Estimated fetal weight separates LGA and SGA infants from the majority of normally grown babies; it does not differentiate the constitutionally small or large babies from the functionally impaired fetus. An option to identify the growth-impaired fetus is a calculation of ponderal index and Doppler velocimetry studies. An LGA fetus by weight estimation but with a normal ponderal index is most likely a constitutional LGA fetus. An SGA fetus with normal Doppler velocity studies is most likely a constitutional SGA fetus.

The practitioner's intention in obtaining an EFW is usually to employ fetal weight cutoffs for selecting cases that can be delivered vaginally with a low risk of birth trauma versus cases in whom the risk of trauma is high enough to warrant delivery by cesarean section. To date, there are numerous logarithmic formulas for estimating fetal weight, but a lack of uniformity and inaccuracy in measurement. A recent study of 31 formulas (42) for EFW had comparably poor accuracy for the prediction of macrosomia. Sonographic EFW has a relatively poor positive predictive value (i.e., 64%) (43), and virtually all EFW formulas systematically overestimate birth weight. The imprecision of the formulas to account for fat deposits in fetuses and difficulties in measuring AC of diabetic mothers may explain the inaccuracies in EFW (Table 23-4).

TABLE 23-3. IDENTIFICATION OF SMALL- AND APPROPRIATE-FOR GESTATIONAL AGE FETUSES (N = 292) WITH ULTRASOUND WITHIN 10 DAYS OF DELIVERY[a]

Statistics	Parameter (%)					
	BPD	AC	FL	FL/AC	PI	EFW
Sensitivity	73	97	45	55	53	66
Specificity	70	60	98	74	70	94
Predictive value of						
Positive results[b]	51	51	89	48	44	88
	(21)	(21)	(64)	(20)	(18)	(65)
Negative results[b]	86	97	81	79	78	87
	(96)	(99)	(94)	(94)	(92)	(96)
Prevalence	43	43	43	43	43	43

AC, abdominal circumference; BPD, biparietal diameter; EFW, estimated fetal weight; FL, femur length; PI, ponderal index.
[a]Prenatal intrauterine growth retardation: BPD, AC, FL, and EFW <10th percentile.
[b]Values in parentheses assume a prevalence of 10%.
From Hadlock FP, Harrist RB, Carpenter RJ. Sonographic estimation of fetal weight. The value of femur length in addition to head and abdomen measurements. *Radiology* 1984;150:535–540, with permission.

Despite a lack of compelling evidence evaluating the efficacy of ultrasound to determine fetal weight and select a route of delivery based on the results, sonographic estimation of fetal size at term is often used in the management of diabetic pregnancies. All of the above 31 formulas are better at predicting macrosomia than predictions based on gestational age alone. Despite its limitations, sonographic EFW may play a significant role in clinical decision making for determining optimal time and route of delivery. In a survey to evaluate the use of estimated fetal weight prior to delivery in diabetic women, it was found that 75% of perinatologists and 66% of general obstetricians used this technology for their clinical decision making (44).

The Shephard formula (45) (BPD + AC) and the Hadlock formula (46) (AC + FL) are the most commonly used equations for measuring EFW. However, it should be noted that the infant of the diabetic mother has a body morphometry significantly different from that of the general fetal population. Tamura et al. (47) found that estimates of fetal weight at term in type 1 diabetic women could be in error by as much as 900 g when comparing actual to estimated fetal weight. Therefore, a fetus weighing 4,000 g at birth could have had an estimated weight of as little as 3,100 g or as much as 4,900 g. Benson et al. (48) tried to devise customized formulas to estimate fetal weight. In practical terms, if estimated fetal weight is

TABLE 23-4. DIAGNOSIS OF MACROSOMIA BY ULTRASOUND

Investigations	No. of Patients	Parameters Measured	Criteria	Sensitivity (%)	Specificity (%)	PV + (%)	PV − (%)
Wladimiroff, 1978	30	BPD Fetal chart area	>90 percentile BW	47	95		
Elliot, 1982	23	Chest diameter-BPD	>4,000 g	87		61	
Bracero, 1985	50	BPD, AD, FL	>90 percentile BW				
		AD/FL		79	80	83	76
		AD/BPD		83	60	71	75
Tamura, 1986	67	AC, EFW	>90 percentile BW	71	71	88	89
Rosavik, 1986	21	Multiple	>90 percentile BW	81	85		
Benson, 1987	20	BPD, FL, AD, AC	>4,000 g	77	84		
Bochner, 1987	41	AC (30–33 wk)	>90th percentile BW	88	83	56	96
Miller, 1988	58	BPD, FL, AC, EFW	≥4,000 g	24–53	94–98	52–71	88–92
Benacerraf, 1988	324	BPD, OFD, AD, EFW	≥4,000 g	65	90		
Landon, 1989	32	BPD, HC, AC, FL, EFW	≥90th percentile	58–84	75–85	68–79	75–89
Chervenak, 1989	81	BPD, FL, AC, EFW	>4,000 g	61	91	70	87

PV +, predictive value, positive; PV −, predictive value, negative; BPD, biparietal diameter; AD, abdominal diameter; FL, femur length; AC, abdominal circumference; EFW, estimated fetal weight; OFD, occipitofrontal diameter; BW, birthweight.
From Tamura RK, Sabbagha RE, Dooley SL, et al. Real time ultrasound estimation of weight in fetuses of diabetic gravid women. *Am J Obstet Gynecol* 1985;153:57–60, with permission.

greater than 4,000 g, then only 77% of newborns, using an equation based on femur and abdominal circumference, would actually weigh more than 4,000g. In 1995, McLaren et al. (49), studying patients with type 1 diabetes, confirmed that estimation of weight utilizing AC and FL was as accurate as more complex formulas, although only 65% were correctly estimated within 10% of actual birth weight. An estimated fetal weight of 4,700 g was required for the obstetrician to be 90% sure that the actual fetal weight would be above approximately 4,000 gm. The inherent inaccuracies of ultrasonography alone to determine EFW limit the precision and the strict clinical utility of these measurements.

The use of EFW with the inclusion of morphometry may enhance the detection of macrosomia in the fetus of a diabetic mother. In 1987, Tamura et al. (6) found that when AC + EFW were greater than the 90th percentile, macrosomia was present in approximately 88% of neonates. Landon et al. (50) further expanded the inclusion of morphometry by studying enlarged asymmetric fetuses' subcutaneous fat thickness surrounding the trunk and upper extremities during the third trimester. In one study, humeral soft tissue measurements greater than 13 mm at term were significantly more predictive of LGA infants when compared with customary EFW formulas or body proportionality indices such as FL/AC. Sood et al. (51) confirmed greater humeral soft tissue thickness and found that they were more sensitive than EFW in predicting macrosomia in infants with a large ponderal index, and also in predicting shoulder dystocia.

In another study by Landon et al. (10), serial ultrasound examinations during the third trimester measured growth for HC and AC + FL. AC growth was clearly accelerated from 32 weeks in fetuses destined to be LGA, while no statistical difference was found between LGA and AGA fetuses in HC + FL growth. They calculated that AC growth of more than 1.2 cm/wk was the optimal cutoff point for detecting LGA fetuses. At this threshold, there was a sensitivity of 83.3% and a specificity of 85.4%. Abramowicz et al. (52), again directing attention to evaluation of soft tissue thickness, measured cheek-to-cheek diameter in abnormal fetal growth. They found greater sensitivity than EFW in predicting macrosomia (88% vs. 71%) but less specificity (75% vs. 91%). It has been suggested that the disproportion between the head size and the extended shoulder diameter, including subcutaneous tissue, can be the explanation for the higher rate of shoulder dystocia in infants of diabetic mothers. Elliot et al. (53) proposed a macrosomia index calculated by subtracting the BPD from the chest diameter, while Cohen et al. (54) suggested measuring the difference between abdominal diameter and BPD. Both indices have not been extensively used because of wide variations in measurement, failure to add to the accuracy of previously proposed methods, and no independent validation.

INTRAUTERINE GROWTH RESTRICTION

Intrinsic fetal abnormalities or substrate deprivation due to advanced maternal vascular disease may be the causes of growth restriction in infants of diabetic mothers. These infants display loss of adipose tissue, oligohydramnios, utero-placental insufficiency, fetal distress, and intrauterine death. Infants of mothers with advanced vascular disease and hypertension exhibit extrinsic growth failure especially of abdominal girth.

Small-for-gestational-age infants are not a homogeneous population. The symmetrical (reduction of size in all organs) and asymmetrical (long, wasted body with relatively normal head growth) groups have been described (7). Fetal growth restriction has been reported in human and animal studies in relation to low levels of glycemia and possible reduction of nutrient availability to the fetus in the pregnant diabetic woman (55). We reported that morphometric growth parameters were comparable in SGA fetuses of both type 1 diabetic women (mean blood glucose 120±18 mg/dL) and hypertensive nondiabetic subjects, resulting in asymmetric growth delay. The etiology of growth restriction in these groups may be the result of vasculopathy as shown by estimated fetal growth weight patterns and AC growth (21) (Table 23-5).

There is a direct association between neonatal size and levels of glycemic control, suggesting a metabolic etiology for growth restriction. A 20% rate of intrauterine growth restriction was observed in subjects with GDM and a mean blood glucose of 81±6 mg/dL (2). In another study, a previously undisclosed growth restricted pattern was noted in GDMs. These infants were small in all morphometric parameters when compared to type 1 diabetic patients and control groups. However, the AC was larger in SGA infants of women with GDM (41st percentile) and diminished in type 1 diabetic patients and hypertensive nondiabetic SGA (6th percentile) infants. This finding of relatively normal AC may be the result of the effect of insulin on the fetal liver. In contrast, in type 1 diabetic women, the combined effect of vasculopathy and glucose toxicity results in a long, wasted fetal body. Therefore, AC as an indicator of growth restriction should be used with caution in GDM subjects (21).

Doppler Fetal Surveillance

Pulsed Doppler has been investigated as a means to assess blood flow in the uterine artery and in various parts of the fetal circulatory system. Early results have strongly supported the potential of this method to identify the small-for-date fetus that is hypoxic or nutritionally deprived (56). The pathophysiologic rationale for using Doppler velocimetry in fetal growth restriction is based on the fetal hemodynamic response to chronic nutritional and cardiovascular stress. This response includes redistribution of flow favoring the

TABLE 23-5. COMPARISON OF GROWTH RATES IN SGA AND AGA FETUSES

	SGA		
	GDM	Type 1 Diabetes	AGA
Mean blood glucose (mg/dL)			
27–35.9 wk	91.0 ± 14.00	115.3 ± 21.00	99.9 ± 15.00
36–42 wk	92.0 ± 16.00	105.8 ± 18.00	98.9 ± 14.00
Daily weight gain (g)[a]			
27–35.9 wk	14.9 ± 12.50	15.1 ± 13.00	29.3 ± 19.00
36–42 wk[b]	7.4 ± 14.20	4.6 ± 14.00	31.1 ± 23.00
Abdominal circumference (mm)[c]			
27–35.9 wk	0.96 ± 0.32	0.89 ± 0.46	1.13 ± 0.26
36–42 wk[d]	0.91 ± 0.35	0.79 ± 0.14	1.02 ± 0.17

[a]$p < 0.0003$ SGA vs. AGA vs. LGA.
[b]$p < 0.003$ within SGA period 1 vs. period 2.
[c]$p < 0.001$ SGA vs. AGA vs. LGA; $p < 0.0008$ early LGA vs. late SGA for periods 1 and 2.
[d]$p < 0.0003$ within LGA late period 1 vs. period 2.
AGA, appropriate for gestational age; LGA, large for gestational age; SMA, small for gestational age.
Adapted from Langer O, Kozlowski S, Brustman L. Abnormal growth patterns in diabetes in pregnancy: a longitudinal study. *Isr J Med Sci* 1991;27:516–523, with permission.

brain, heart, and adrenals rather than the muscles, viscera, skin, and other less critical tissues and organs (57). It remains controversial whether diagnostic efficacy of Doppler sonography encompasses pregnancies with diabetes. Doppler studies attempting to identify fetuses affected by SGA have not been shown to significantly improve the positive and negative predictive values obtained by standard biometric parameters (58) (Table 23-6).

In SGA fetuses, there is a decrease in resistance in the cerebral vessels, resulting in an increase in the diastolic component of the middle cerebral artery waveform. This causes a decrease in the pulsatility index (PI), systolic/diastolic (S/D) ratio, and resistance index (RI). The umbilical artery that indirectly reflects the status of the placental circulation will initially display an increased PI, S/D ratio, and RI in the face of fetal compromise followed by an absent or reversed end-diastolic flow. It appears that in the sequence of progressive hypoxia in growth-restricted fetuses, the umbilical artery waveform indices rise to greater than the 95th confidence levels before fetal heart rate monitoring, fetal movement, and breathing are affected. Usually by the time there is absent diastolic flow, other clinical parameters become abnormal. While Bracero et al. (59) noted a significant positive correlation between umbilical arterial S/D and mean serum glucose values ($r = 0.52$, $p < 0.001$) in a mixed population of GDM and type 1 diabetic mothers, this finding was refuted by Landon et al. (60). In a study of 35 insulin-dependent women, Landon et al. (60) found no significant correlation between mean third-trimester umbilical arterial S/D, glycosylated hemoglobin ($r = 0.25$) or mean blood glucose levels ($r = 0.15$). Diabetic pregnancies compromised by vasculopathy and hypertensive complications may benefit from the use of Doppler velocimetry of the umbilical artery to evaluate the growth-restricted fetus. However, it is as yet inconclusive if such surveillance is efficacious in the fetus at risk in the absence of such complications. To date, Doppler ultrasound is useful as a means of corroborating other diagnostic tests but does not appear superior to current biometric parameters in predicting or detecting growth restriction.

TABLE 23-6. COMPARISON OF STANDARD DIAGNOSTIC TESTS IN PREDICTION OF SMALL-FOR-GESTATIONAL/AGE NEONATES (PREVALENCE 50.0%)

	MCA (%)	UA (%)	Cerebral/Umbilical Ratio (%)
Sensitivity	11.1	40.0	40.0
Specificity	97.7	91.1	100.0
Positive predictive value	83.3	81.8	100.0
Negative predictive value	52.3	60.2	62.5
Accuracy	54.4	65.5	70.0

MCA, middle cerebral artery; UA, umbilical artery.
From Ardvini D, Rizzo G, Romaini C, et al. Fetal blood flow velocity waveforms as predictors of growth retardation. *Obstet Gynecol* 1987;70:7, with permission.

MANAGEMENT AND OUTCOME

The purpose of the treatment of any medical condition in pregnancy is to decrease the maternal and fetal morbidity and mortality attributed to the disease. Diabetes in pregnancy is a disorder associated with abnormal glucose metabolism represented by elevated blood glucose. GDM represents the milder form of glucose abnormality on the diabetes continuum extending in severity to type 2 and type 1 diabetes. Moreover, maternal hyperglycemia, regardless of its source or level of severity, poses a threat to the well-being of the unborn fetus. The association between maternal hyperglycemia and adverse pregnancy outcome has been well documented in the literature (61–64). Therefore, the foundation of management of diabetes in pregnancy is to decrease the glucose level to near-normoglycemic values, because the majority of fetal complications are the result of the diabetic fetopathy represented by fetal hyperinsulinemia.

Various methods have been proposed to evaluate the level of glycemia in pregnancy, including mean blood glucose, and preprandial and postprandial blood glucose with determinations at diverse testing times (1 hour, 1.5 hours, and 2 hours after meals). Furthermore, various criteria are used to initiate glyburide or insulin therapy when diet therapy fails in GDM. Some investigators have suggested a threshold of fasting plasma glucose at different levels (90, 95, 105mg/dL, etc.), while others have recommended that an amniotic fluid insulin level or fetal anthropometric measurements, specifically AC, be used.

Buchanan et al. (65) used ultrasound measurements of the fetal AC to identify infants at high risk for macrosomia. They demonstrated that maternal insulin therapy reduced excessive fetal growth and adiposity. Our group in several studies characterized the relationship between LGA infants and glycemic control. In one study, we showed that among women with GDM, those who achieved blood glucose levels of less than 87mg/dL had a lower incidence of macrosomic infants. An average blood glucose of 87 to 105 mg/dL doubled the incidence for the development of large infants. When the glucose threshold was higher than 105mg/dL, the incidence of large infants quadrupled in comparison to the group with a mean glucose of less than 87mg/dL (66). In another study, we found that the incidence of LGA was reduced to a range of 1.4% to 9% when normoglycemia was achieved. Additionally, we demonstrated that when maternal level of glycemic control is below 87mg/dL, 23% of the infants were growth restricted. These data suggest that in non-vascular-compromised diabetic mothers, "overtreatment" can result in a metabolic form of SGA. Thus, the physician needs to be aware of the consequences of over- and under-treatment of the pregnant diabetic patient (2,55).

In a large-scale study, we evaluated the effect of intensified insulin therapy compared to the conventional approach. We found similar pregnancy outcome to nondiabetic control individuals for the intensified treated group (blood glucose) and a two- to five-fold increase in adverse outcomes for the conventional group (67). These data support the hypothesis that pharmacologically treatable factors controlling maternal glycemia are important determinants of the risk of aberrant growth in pregnancies complicated by diabetes. It should be noted that although different criteria exist for starting pharmacological treatment, both fetal and maternal metabolic characteristics controlling glucose will be the determining factors for achieving the desired outcome of pregnancy. Various glucose thresholds have been identified for different neonatal and maternal complications for both gestational and pregestational diabetes. These thresholds should be considered in the management plan of the diabetic patient (68,69).

As mentioned above, macrosomia, with its related complications and especially shoulder dystocia during delivery, are of primary concern in the management of the diabetic patient during labor. Shoulder dystocia rates in infants of diabetic women are as high as 10% overall and as high as 25% to 50% in macrosomic infants in contrast to rates of 0.5% to 1% in nondiabetic patients (26). When actual birth weight is 4,000 g or more, the risk for shoulder dystocia is increased 3.6-fold in infants of diabetic women. Anthropometric differences between macrosomic and non-macrosomic infants can be used to explain the varied shoulder dystocia rates (33,35).

Elective cesarean delivery has been proposed by several investigators in order to avoid shoulder dystocia and its accompanying trauma (26,29,33,53,70). However, diabetic women are infrequently analyzed as a separate group regardless of their propensity for this complication. We compared (29) diabetic women with nondiabetic women for risk of shoulder dystocia and found that the rate of shoulder dystocia was significantly different when stratified by birth weight between the groups. Overall, when the birth weight was 4,000 g or higher, 84% versus 60% of shoulder dystocia was accounted for in the diabetic and nondiabetic groups, respectively. Therefore, avoiding vaginal delivery of macrosomic infants of diabetic mothers would significantly decrease the rate of shoulder dystocia. What still remains, however, is the question of what will be the effect of the cesarean section rate utilizing this type of protocol since the prediction of macrosomia by ultrasonography remains imperfect (5,48,53,71,72).

We attempted to provide reasonable answers for the above question for choosing the method and timing of delivery in diabetic mothers (73). In a prospective study of 2,604 diabetic women, those with an ultrasonographic fetal weight estimated to be more than 4,250 g underwent elective cesarean delivery, while women with LGA and fetal weight less than 4,250 g underwent induction of labor. The rate of shoulder dystocia was significantly lower after instituting this protocol (2.4% vs. 1.1%; odds ratio, 2.2). The cesarean section rate increased significantly (21.7% vs. 25.1%) between the pre-protocol and protocol period. Correct identification for the presence of macrosomia was made in 87% of the cases. The rate of shoulder dystocia was 7.4% in macrosomic infants not identified by ultrasound examination and delivered vaginally. During the 3-year period of the study, only 57 patients underwent unnecessary cesarean section, which contributed 0.5% to the overall cesarean section rate in our institution. Therefore, an estimated weight threshold of 4,250 g as an indication for elective delivery for diabetic women reduces the rate of shoulder dystocia by at least 50% without a clinically meaningful increase in the cesarean section rate.

Using receiver-operating characteristic curves of sonographic EFW for prediction of macrosomia, it was shown that at the inflexion-point cutoff level of 3,711 g, sensitivity, specificity, and positive and negative predictive values of EFW for birth weight of <4,000 g, were 85%, 72%, 49%, and 94%, respectively. At the inflexion point cutoff level of 4,192 g for birth weight of <4500 g, these values were 83%, 92%, 30%, and 99%, respectively. The relative risk for birth weight of <4,000 g was 7.99, and for birth weight of <4,500 g, 39.50, both significant (74).

Kjos et al. (75) evaluated expectant management of GDMs and type 2 diabetic patients. They concluded that expectant management after the 38th week of gestation did not reduce the incidence of cesarean delivery. Moreover, there was an increased rate of LGA (23% vs. 10%) and a higher but not significant increase in shoulder dystocia (3% vs. 0.0%) in the expectant group. These two studies support

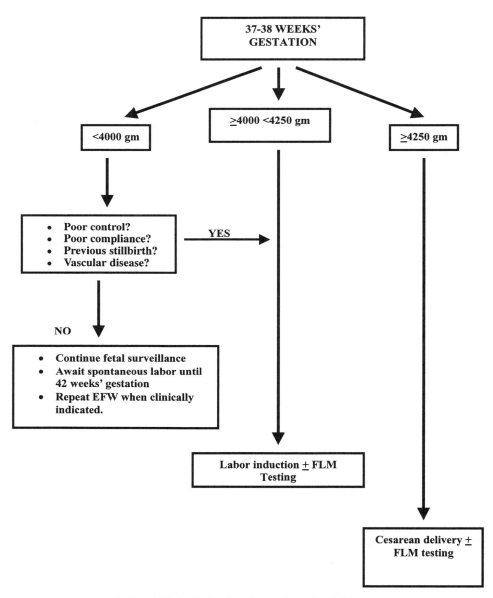

FIGURE 23-1. Optimal timing and mode of delivery.

the concept that ultrasound weight estimation and elective delivery may be beneficial in selecting the time and mode of delivery in the diabetic patient.

Since it is difficult to predict shoulder dystocia with an acceptable degree of accuracy, the goal of the obstetrician should be its prevention (25,26,76). We may improve prevention by adhering to a strategy that incorporates the following: (a) improvement of glycemic control to reduce the macrosomia rate (67); (b) induction of labor when a LGA fetus is suspected (77); and (c) elective cesarean delivery of macrosomic fetuses to avoid the trauma of shoulder dystocia during vaginal delivery (26,29,33,53,70). However, even with the most appropriate protocol, the physician needs to recognize the patient's distinctiveness since the decision regarding delivery mode is based on the size of the woman's pelvis, the progress of labor, and the woman's obstetric history.

Just as macrosomia represents one end of the abnormal growth spectrum, fetal growth restriction represents the opposite end. Elective delivery of a premature, growth-restricted fetus may not improve the neonate's condition. In these cases, rest, reduction of maternal risk factors (e.g., hypertension, smoking cessation), nutritional supplementation, and reevaluation of the stringency of glycemic control will benefit the fetus. Elective delivery should be considered only in the presence of lung maturity testing or evidence of specific abnormal fetal surveillance testing.

The prognosis for future growth and development for any neonate whose birth weight is less than the tenth percentile for gestational age depends on the physiologic significance of the associated cause. Infants who are SGA on a constitutional basis enjoy a good prognosis, although there appears to be an increase in perinatal mortality, even in this group. The long-term outcome is most significantly influenced by the etiologic basis for growth restriction. An infant whose birth weight is less than the tenth percentile for gestational age on a deprivational basis should also enjoy a good prognosis if delivery occurs without perinatal compromise. In general, symmetric SGA is likely to be followed by slow growth after birth, whereas infants with asymmetric SGA are more likely to achieve normal growth patterns after birth. However, if the length of the fetus is also affected, the infant is likely to remain small (78). In summary, abnormal fetal biometry alone should not be considered a reason for intervention. Noninvasive fetal function tests such as Doppler studies can assist us in detection of the compromised growth-restricted fetus requiring intervention. However, conservative management of the mature growth-restricted fetus is not warranted in the pregnant diabetic patient (Fig. 23-1).

CONCLUSION

Fetal growth in the pregnant diabetic woman can be considered the result of an interaction between the genetic

drive to grow and constraints provided by the limitation of substrate availability. Varied abnormal growth configurations exist in relation to type of diabetic disease and level of glycemic control. Macrosomia is a result of excess substrate availability, and growth restriction occurs as the appropriate adaptation to limited substrate availability or the presence of vasculopathy. Therefore, serial sonographic measurements need to be performed throughout pregnancy. In the first trimester, CRL measurements are performed for dating and to document fetal viability; in the middle of the second trimester (at approximately 20 weeks) AC and fetal weight estimation will enhance identification of the constitutionally large or small infant and should allow the perinatologist to rule out most serious fetal anomalies. During the third trimester, sonographic measurements at 28 to 30 weeks, 34 to 36 weeks, and 38 to 39 weeks' gestation will assist in the selection of the treatment modality, such as insulin or glyburide, and the detection of the abnormal growth pattern of the over- or under-sized fetus.

KEY POINTS

- Fetal growth in the pregnant diabetic woman is the result of an interaction between the genetic drive to grow and constraints provided by the limitation of substrate availability.
- Fetal growth during the first and second semesters accounts for about 20% of fetal weight with the majority occurring in the third semester influenced mainly by environmental and nutritional factors.
- Large and small fetuses are in most cases (70%) constitutional and influenced by genetic factors.
- The CRL is obtained by measuring the long axis of the embryo and may be associated with future restricted fetal growth and congenital anomalies.
- Diabetes seems to preferentially affect the AC more than the BPD or long bone length; therefore, AC is particularly useful in identifying either macrosomic or growth-restricted fetuses.
- The choice of percentile used to define abnormal AC measurements influences the predictive value of the test.
- An abnormal growth pattern after 26 to 28 weeks' gestation becomes evident and is mostly confined to abdominal circumference (AC).
- There are two distinct excessive growth patterns in the LGA infants — early accelerated growth at 30 weeks' gestation (23% LGA) and late accelerated growth after 33 to 36 weeks' gestation (77% LGA).
- Serial ultrasound measurements need to be performed during pregnancy to identify the growth-deviant fetus.
- Estimated fetal weight separates LGA and SGA infants from the majority of normally grown babies; it does not differentiate the constitutionally small or large babies from the functionally impaired fetus.

- Level of glycemic control that should be targeted to maximize perinatal outcome is mean blood glucose between 87 to 105 mg/dL; deviation from this range will result in either growth-restricted or macrosomic fetuses.

REFERENCES

1. Gluckman PD. The role of pituitary hormones, growth factors and insulin in the regulation of fetal growth. In: Clarke JR, ed. *Oxford reviews of reproductive biology.* Oxford: Oxford University Press, 1986:8.
2. Langer O, Levy J, Brustman L, et al. Glycemic control in gestational diabetes mellitus — how tight is tight enough: small for gestational age versus large for gestational age? *Am J Obstet Gynecol* 1989;161:646–653.
3. Modanlou HD, Dorchester WI, Thorosian A. Macrosomia-maternal fetal and neonatal implications. *Obstet Gynecol* 1980; 55:420.
4. Hadlock FP, Harrist RB, Feameyhough TC, et al. Use of femur length/abdominal circumference ratio in detecting the macrosomic fetus. *Radiology* 1985;154:503.
5. Deter RL, Hadlock FP. Use of ultrasound in the detection of macrosomia: a review. *J Clin Ultrasound* 1985;13:519–524.
6. Tamura RK, Sabbagha RE, Depp R, et al. Diabetic macrosomia: accuracy of third trimester ultrasound. *Obstet Gynecol* 1987;67: 828.
7. Campbell S, Thoms A. Ultrasound measurement of the fetal head to abdomen circumference ratio in the assessment of growth retardation. *Br J Obstet Gynaecol* 1977;84:165–174.
8. Basel D, Lederer R, Diamant YZ. Longitudinal ultrasonic biometry of various parameters in fetuses with abnormal growth rate. *Acta Obstet Gynecol Scand* 1987;66:143–149.
9. Ogata ES, Sabbagha R, Metzger BE, et al. Serial ultrasonography to assess evolving fetal macrosomia. *JAMA* 1980;243: 2405–2408.
10. Landon MB, Mintz MC, Gabbe SG. Sonographic evaluation of fetal abdominal growth: predictor of the large-for-gestational age in pregnancies complicated by diabetes mellitus. *Am J Obstet Gynecol* 1989;160:115–121.
11. Pedersen JF, Molsted-Pederson L. Early growth retardation in diabetic pregnancy. *BMJ* 1979;1:18.
12. Keys TC, Cousins L, Moore TR. Early fetal growth in insulin dependent diabetics. Proceedings of the 32nd Annual Meeting of the Society for Gynecological Investigation, Phoenix, AZ, March 1985.
13. Cousins LC, Keys TC, Schorzman L, et al. Ultrasonographic assessment of early fetal growth in insulin-treated diabetic pregnancies. *Am J Obstet Gynecol* 1988;159:1186.
14. Brown ZA, Mills JL, Metzger BE. Early sonographic evaluation for fetal growth delay and congenital malformations in pregnancies complicated by insulin-requiring diabetes. *Diabetes Care* 1992;15:613.
15. Tamura RK. Diabetes mellitus and accelerated fetal growth. In: Sabbagha RE, ed. *Diagnostic ultrasound applied to obstetrics and gynecology.* Philadelphia: JB Lippincott, 1994:165.
16. Reece EA, Goldstein I, Pilu G. Fetal cerebellar growth unaffected by intrauterine growth retardation: a new parameter for prenatal diagnosis. *Am J Obstet Gynecol* 1987;157:632.
17. Hill LM, Guzick D, Fries J. The transverse cerebellar diameter in estimating gestational age in the large-for-gestational-age fetus. *Obstet Gynecol* 1990;75:981.
18. Hadlock FP, Harrist RB, Shah YP. Estimating fetal age using

19. Pedersen IM, Tystrup I, Pedersen J. Congenital malformations in newborn infants of diabetic women. Correlation with maternal diabetic vascular complications. *Lancet* 1964;1:1124.
20. Houchang D, Modanlou HD, Dorchester WI. Macrosomia — maternal, fetal and neonatal implications. *Obstet Gynecol* 1980; 55:420.
21. Langer O, Kozlowski S, Brustman L. Abnormal growth patterns in diabetes in pregnancy: a longitudinal study. *Isr J Med Sci* 1991;27:516–523.
22. Adam PAJ, Teramo K, Raiha N, et al. Human fetal insulin metabolism early in gestation: responses to acute elevation of the fetal glucose concentration and placental transfer of human insulin I-131. *Diabetes* 1969;18:409–416.
23. Neufeld ND, Scott M, Kaplan SA. Ontogeny of the mammalian receptor. *Dev Biol* 1980;78:151–160.
24. Benson CB, Doubilet PM, Saltzman DH, et al. Femur length/abdominal circumference ratio: poor predictor of macrosomic fetuses in diabetic mothers. *J Ultrasound Med* 1986;5: 141–144.
25. McFarland MB, Hod M, Piper JM, et al. Are labor abnormalities more common in shoulder dystocia? *Am J Obstet Gynecol* 1995; 173:1211–1214.
26. Acker BD, Sachs BP, Friedman EA. Risk factors for shoulder dystocia. *Obstet Gynecol* 1985;66:762–768.
27. Benedetti TJ, Gabbe SG. Shoulder dystocia: a complication of fetal macrosomia and prolonged second stage of labor with mid-pelvic delivery. *Obstet Gynecol* 1978;53:526–529.
28. Sandmire HF, O'Halloin TJ. Shoulder dystocia: It incidence and associated risk factors. *Int J Gynaecol Obstet* 1988;26:65–73.
29. Langer O, Berkus MD, Huff RW, et al. Shoulder dystocia: should the fetus weighing ≥ 4000 grams be delivered by cesarean section? *Am J Obstet Gynecol* 1991;165:831–837.
30. Osler M. Body fat of newborn infants of diabetic mothers. *Acta Endocrinologica* 1960;34:277–286.
31. Vohr BR, McGarvey ST. Growth patterns of large-for-gestational-age and appropriate-for-gestational-age infants of gestational diabetic mothers and control mothers at age 1 year. *Diabetes Care* 1997;20:1066–1072.
32. Brans YW, Shannon DL, Hunter MA. Maternal diabetes and neonatal macrosomia: neonatal anthropometric measurements. *Early Hum Dev* 1983;8:297–305.
33. Modanlou HD, Komatsu G, Dorchester W, et al. Large-for-gestational-age neonates: anthropometric reasons for shoulder dystocia. *Obstetric Gynecol* 1982;60:417–423.
34. Ballard JL, Rosenn B, Khoury JC, Miodovnik M. Diabetic fetal macrosomia: significance of disproportionate growth. *J Pediatr* 1993;122:155–159.
35. McFarland MB, Trylovich CG, Langer O. Anthropometric differences in macrosomic infants of diabetic and nondiabetic mothers. *J Matern Fetal Med* 1998;7:292–295.
36. Nesbitt TS, Gilbert WM, Herrchen B. Shoulder dystocia and associated risk factors with macrosomic born in California. *Am J Obstet Gynecol* 1998;179:476–480.
37. Gilbert WM, Nesbitt TS, Danielsen B. Associated factors in 1611 cases of branchial plexus injury. *Obstet Gynecol* 1999;93: 536–540.
38. Roberts SW, Hernandez C, Maberry MC, et al. Obstetric clavicular fracture: the enigma of normal birth. *Obstet Gynecol* 1995;86:978–981.
39. Dudley NJ, Lamb MP, Hatfield JA. Estimated fetal weight in the detection of the small-for-gestational age fetus. *J Clin Ultrasound* 1990;18:387–393.
40. Laurin J, Persson PH. Ultrasound screening for detection of

multiple parameters: a prospective evaluation in a racially mixed population. *Am J Obstet Gynecol* 1987;156:955.

intra-uterine growth retardation. *Acta Obstet Gynecol Scand* 1987;66:493–500.

41. Divon MY, Guidetti DA, Braverman JJ. Intrauterine growth retardation — A prospective study of the diagnostic value of real-time sonography combined with umbilical artery flow velocimetry. *Obstet Gynecol* 1988;72:611–614.

42. Combs CA, Rosenn B, Miodovnik M, et al. Sonographic EFW and macrosomia: is there an optimum formula to predict diabetic fetal macrosomia? *J Matern Fetal Med* 2000;9:55–61.

43. Mohadevan N, Pearace M, Steer P. The proper measure of intrauterine growth retardation is function not size. *Br J Obstet Gynaecol* 1994;101: 1032–1035.

44. Landon MB, Gabbe SG, Sachs L. Management of diabetes mellitus and pregnancy: a survey of obstetricians and maternal-fetal specialists. *Obstet Gynecol* 1990;75:635–640.

45. Shepherd MJ. An evaluation of two equations for predicting fetal weight by ultrasound. *Am J Obstet Gynecol* 1982;142:47–52.

46. Hadlock FP, Harrist RB, Carpenter RJ. Sonographic estimation of fetal weight. The value of femur length in addition to head and abdomen measurements. *Radiology* 1984;150:535–540.

47. Tamura RK, Sabbagha RE, Dooley SL, et al. Real time ultrasound estimation of weight in fetuses of diabetic gravid women. *Am J Obstet Gynecol* 1985;153:57–60.

48. Benson CB, Doubilet OM, Saltzman DM. Sonographic determination of fetal weight in diabetic pregnancies. *Am J Obstet Gynecol* 1987;156:441–444.

49. McLaren RA, Puckett JL, Chauhan SP. Estimators of birth weight in pregnant women requiring insulin: a comparison of seven sonographic models. *Obstet Gynecol* 1995;85:565–569.

50. Landon MB, Sonek J, Foy P. Sonographic measurement of fetal humeral soft tissue thickness in pregnancy complicated by GDM. *Diabetes* 1991;40[Suppl 2]:66–70.

51. Sood AK, Yancey M, Richards D. Prediction of fetal macrosomia using humeral soft tissue thickness. *Obstet Gynecol* 1995;85: 937–940.

52. Abramowicz JS, Sherer DM, Woods JR. Ultrasonographic measurement of cheek-to-cheek diameter in fetal growth disturbances. *Am J Obstet Gynecol* 1993;169:405–408.

53. Elliot JP, Garite TJ, Freeman RK. Ultrasonic prediction of fetal macrosomia in diabetic patients. *Obstet Gynecol* 1982;60:159–162.

54. Cohen B, Penning S, Major C, et al. Sonographic prediction of shoulder dystocia in infants of diabetic mothers. *Obstet Gynecol* 1996;88:10–13.

55. Langer O, Damus K, Maiman M, et al. A link between relative hypoglycemia-hypoinsulinemia during oral glucose tolerance tests and intrauterine growth retardation. *Am J Obstet Gynecol* 1986;155:711–716.

56. Laurin J, Marsal K, Persson PH. Ultrasound measurement of fetal blood flow in predicting fetal outcome. *Br J Obstet Gynecol* 1987;94:90.

57. Peeters LLH, Sheldon RE, Jones MD. Blood flow to fetal organ as a function of arterial oxygen content. *Am J Obstet Gynecol* 1979;135:637.

58. Arduini D, Rizzo G, Romaini C, et al. Fetal blood flow velocity waveforms as predictors of growth retardation. *Obstet Gynecol* 1987;70:7.

59. Bracero L, Schulman H, Fleischer A, et al. Umbilical artery velocimetry in diabetes and pregnancy. *Obstet Gynecol* 1986;68: 654–658.

60. Landon MB, Gabbe SG, Bruner JP, et al. Doppler umbilical artery velocimetry in pregnancy complicated by insulin-dependent diabetes mellitus. *Obstet Gynecol* 1989;73:961–985.

61. Combs CA, Gavin LA, Dunderson E. Relationship of fetal macrosomia to maternal postprandial glucose control during pregnancy. *Obstet Gynecol* 1966;27:683–689.

62. Jovanovic-Peterson L, Peterson CM, Reed GF. Maternal postprandial glucose levels and infant birth weight: the Diabetes in Early Pregnancy Study. *Am J Obstet Gynecol* 1991;164:103–111.

63. Langer O. Prevention of macrosomia. *Bailliere's Clin Gynecol* 1991;5:333–347.

64. Langer O. Management of gestational diabetes. *Clin Perinatol* 1993;20:603–617.

65. Buchanan TA, Kjos SL, Montoro MN. Prophylactic insulin in gestational diabetes. *Obstet Gynecol* 1987;70:587.

66. Langer O, Mazze RS. The relationship between large-for-gestational age infants and glycemic control in women with gestational diabetes. *Am J Obstet Gynecol* 1988;59:1478–1483.

67. Langer O, Rodriguez DA, Xenakis EMJ, et al. Intensified versus conventional management of gestational diabetes. *Am J Obstet Gynecol* 1994;170:1036–1047.

68. Langer O. Is normoglycemia the correct threshold to prevent complications in the pregnant diabetic patient? *Diabetes Rev* 1996;4:2–10.

69. Langer O, Conway DL. Level of glycemia and perinatal outcome in pregestational diabetes. *J Matern Fetal Med* 2000;9:35–41.

70. Parks DG, Ziel HK. Macrosomia:a proposed indication for primary cesarean section. *Obstet Gynecol* 1978;52:407–409.

71. Delpapa EH, Meuller-Heubach F. Pregnancy outcome following ultrasound of diagnosis of macrosomia. *Obstet Gynecol* 1991;78:340–343.

72. Levine A, Lockwood CJ, Brown B, et al. Sonographic diagnosis of the large-for-gestational age fetus at term: Does it make a difference? *Obstet Gynecol* 1992;79:55–58.

73. Conway DL, Langer O. Elective delivery of infants with macrosomia in diabetic women: reduced shoulder dystocia versus increased cesarean deliveries. *Am J Obstet Gynecol* 1998;178; 922–925.

74. O'Reilly-Green CP, Divon MY. Receiver operating characteristic curves of sonographic estimated fetal weight for prediction of macrosomia in prolonged pregnancies. *Ultrasound Obstet Gynecol* 1997;9:403–408.

75. Kjos SL, Henry OA, Montoro M, et al. Insulin-requiring diabetes in pregnancy: a randomized trial of active induction of labor and expectant management. *Am J Obstet Gynecol* 1993;168: 611–615.

76. Gross TL, Sokol RJ, Williams T, et al. Shoulder dystocia: a fetal-physician risk. *Am J Obstet Gynecol* 1987;156:1408–1418.

77. Boyd ME, Usher RH, McLean FH. Fetal macrosomia: prediction, risks, proposed management. *Obstet Gynecol* 1983;61: 715–722.

78. Brook CGD. Consequences of intrauterine growth retardation. *BMJ* 1983;286:164.

24

FETAL BIOPHYSICAL AND BIOCHEMICAL TESTING

BARAK M. ROSENN
MENACHEM MIODOVNIK

The purpose of antenatal fetal evaluation is to detect changes in fetal biophysical parameters that are associated with fetal compromise and may warrant intervention. Antenatal fetal testing has been justified in maternal and fetal clinical conditions that are associated with an increased risk of fetal compromise, such as maternal hypertensive disorders or fetal growth restriction. Because diabetes mellitus has long been known to increase the risk of fetal demise, antenatal testing has become a commonly practiced modality of surveillance in these pregnancies during the third trimester. It is noteworthy, however, that there are no data from prospective randomized trials to indicate that a policy of antenatal fetal biophysical testing in these pregnancies improves perinatal outcome. In fact, there are only four randomized trials of antenatal fetal testing in high-risk pregnancies. Only one of these included pregnancies complicated by diabetes, and none showed any benefit in terms of perinatal outcome (1). Furthermore, there is no consensus regarding the optimal method or regimen of antenatal testing in pregnancies complicated by diabetes and a broad range of management schemes have been suggested.

IS MATERNAL DIABETES ASSOCIATED WITH FETAL HYPOXIA?

When pregnancy is associated with factors predisposing to fetal hypoxia, it is reasonable to try to obtain early evidence of fetal compromise through antenatal biophysical testing. Diabetes is associated with several pathologic changes that may result in fetal hypoxia. In women with type 1 diabetes, thickening of the basement membrane in the chorionic villi may impede transplacental diffusion of oxygen to the fetus (2). Uterine blood flow to the placenta may also be decreased, particularly in pregnancies complicated by diabetic vasculopathy (3). But it appears that the most important risk factors for fetal hypoxia in diabetes are hyperglycemia and hyperinsulinemia. In animal models, fetal hyperglycemia is associated with a 30% increase in oxygen consumption (4), lactic acidosis, and fetal death (5). Even in the absence of hyperglycemia, fetal hyperinsulinemia *per se* is associated with a significant increase in glucose oxidation and oxygen consumption (6). Indeed, studies in human pregnancies complicated by diabetes have demonstrated a significant association between fetal cord blood insulin levels and acidemia (7), and significant fetal acidemia even in the absence of hypoxemia (8). Moreover, blood levels of erythropoietin are increased in macrosomic infants of mothers with diabetes, suggesting chronic intrauterine hypoxia (9). Histologic studies of placentas from diabetic pregnancies have led to similar conclusions. In a study of term deliveries in 132 women with gestational diabetes mellitus (GDM) and 159 uncomplicated pregnancies, Salafia and Silberman (10) found that umbilical vasculitis, suggestive of tissue hypoxia, was highly correlated with abnormal fetal heart rate (FHR) patterns in the pregnancies complicated by diabetes. Thus, there is ample evidence to suggest that maternal diabetes, resulting in fetal hyperglycemia and hyperinsulinemia, increases the risks of fetal hypoxia and academia.

IS MATERNAL DIABETES ASSOCIATED WITH AN INCREASED RISK OF PERINATAL MORTALITY?

In the past, prior to the widespread institution of perinatal programs for the diagnosis and management of diabetes during pregnancy, stillbirth and perinatal mortality were common complications in these pregnancies. Advances in understanding the importance of maternal glycemic control and improved care of both the mother and the neonate seem to have led to significant improvements in the outcomes of these pregnancies. In 1989, the St. Vincent declaration, published by the World Health Organization and the International Diabetes Federation, included as a 5-year goal, "the outcome of diabetic pregnancy should approximate that of the nondiabetic pregnancy" (11). Despite the aforementioned improvements in perinatal outcome in diabetic pregnancies, it is doubtful whether this goal has been achieved.

Table 24-1 summarizes data from several recent studies involving women with pregestational diabetes (both type 1 and type 2) from various parts of the world. Most of these studies demonstrate a higher rate of perinatal mortality compared to controls, with only one notable exception (18). Only a few provide details on the percentage of losses attributed to congenital malformations, but in most cases it is apparent that the majority of losses are not related to malformations. Thus, it appears that despite widespread efforts in controlling diabetes and providing the best prenatal care, the goals of the St. Vincent declaration have not yet been achieved.

There is some debate whether GDM increases the risk of perinatal mortality. One might assume that poorly controlled GDM would be associated with a higher risk of perinatal mortality and that strict glycemic control would decrease that risk, but there are very few data to support this premise. A recent study from Australia (20) provides indirect evidence on the matter. In a large retrospective analysis of 116,303 pregnancies from 1971 through 1994, outcome of pregnancy was correlated with the results of a standard 2-hour 50-g glucose tolerance test (GTT) administered during the third trimester. From 1971 through 1980, the cutoff values for the definition of GDM were a 1-hour value >10mmol/L (180 mg/dL), and a 2-hour value >7.8mmol/L (140 mg/dL). Women with mild degrees of hyperglycemia on the GTT, which at the time did not meet criteria for the diagnosis of GDM, received routine prenatal care and had a perinatal mortality rate of 26 per 1,000. However, from 1981 onward, the cutoff values for diagnosis of GDM were lowered to a 1-hour value >9mmol/L (162 mg/dL) and a 2-hour value >7mmol/L (126 mg/dL). Among the women with mild hyperglycemia that met the new criteria for GDM, but that would not have met the old criteria, the perinatal mortality rate decreased from 26 per 1,000 to 7 per 1,000. As expected, this change in diagnostic criteria did not affect the perinatal mortality rate among women who had more severe degrees of hyperglycemia on the GTT:

18 per 1,000 in the earlier period, and 20 per 1,000 during the later period. Interestingly, the institution of more intensive management of GDM in 1991 lowered the perinatal mortality rate even further in both groups, to 5 per 1,000 and 4 per 1,000 in the severely hyperglycemic and mildly hyperglycemic groups, respectively. The cause of the improved perinatal outcome cannot be directly determined; it may be due to improved glycemic control, closer patient surveillance, antenatal fetal testing, or a combination of all of the above. This study demonstrates that undiagnosed (and therefore untreated) GDM, even of a mild degree, is associated with increased perinatal mortality, and that stricter control of GDM is associated with a lower perinatal mortality rate.

Further indirect evidence that untreated GDM may be associated with an increased rate of perinatal mortality comes from a recent study (21). The investigators identified a group of 3,958 women with GDM and a control group matched by year of delivery, maternal age, and parity. There was no significant difference in the stillbirth rate between these two groups. However, review of the previous pregnancies in these women revealed a stillbirth rate that was 56% higher among the group of women who were subsequently diagnosed with GDM in their next pregnancies. The authors concluded that this significantly poorer outcome may have been due to the presence of undiagnosed and, therefore, untreated GDM.

These two large studies provide an idea of the benefit to be gained by defining a group of women at increased risk for perinatal loss and managing them accordingly. It does, however, demonstrate that the overall risk of perinatal mortality in GDM is small, and that any study attempting to prove or disprove the effect of a specific strategy on modifying this risk would require a very large number of subjects. For example, if the perinatal mortality rate among a risk group is 10 per 1,000, an intervention demonstrating a 50% reduction in that risk to 5 per 1,000 would require randomization of 10,400 subjects (5,200 in each arm) providing 80% power to detect a significant difference at an alpha error level of 0.05. It is, therefore, not surprising that there are no published prospective randomized studies

TABLE 24-1. PERINATAL MORTALITY IN PREGNANCIES COMPLICATED BY PREGESTATIONAL DIABETES

Author	Country	Study Period	N	PNM Diabetes	PNM Controls	% Attributed to CM
Hanson 1993 (12)	Sweden	1982–1985	491	31.0	7.0	—
Cnattingius 1994 (13)	Sweden	1983–1986	914	22.0	9.0	—
Hawthorne 1997 (14)	England	1994	111	48.0	8.9	—
Casson 1997 (15)	England	1990–1994	462	36.1	8.3	—
Cundy 2000 (type 1) (16)	New Zealand	1985–1997	160	12.5	12.5	0%
Cundy 2000 (type 2) (16)	New Zealand	1985–1997	434	46.1	12.5	14.3%
Platt 2002 (17)	England	1995–1999	547	43.0	8.4	35%
Wylie 2002 (18)	Canada	1989–1999	300	6.6	31.0	—
Penney 2003 (19)	Scotland	1998–1999	273	27.8	7.6	—

CM, congenital malformations; PNM, perinatal mortality per 1,000 live births.

examining strategies for antenatal fetal surveillance in GDM pregnancies. Nonetheless, women nowadays expect perfect outcomes of their pregnancies. For the woman with GDM who experiences a stillbirth, any strategy that might have prevented this mishap would have been worthwhile, however marginal its effect might be on the overall rate of perinatal mortality. The actual benefit to be derived from such strategies, and their overall cost-benefit ratio, are issues that remain to be studied.

HOW DOES MATERNAL DIABETES AFFECT FETAL BIOPHYSICAL CHARACTERISTICS?

Most studies suggest that several aspects of fetal behavioral patterns in diabetic pregnancies are different compared to the behavior of fetuses in nondiabetic pregnancies, reflecting a delayed maturation of the central nervous system. In a study of 20 women with type 1 diabetes, Mulder and Visser (22) found a 1- to 2-week delay in the emergence of all of the normal fetal movement patterns, particularly in the women who had poor glycemic control in early pregnancy. In contrast, fetal breathing movements were observed at an earlier age than in nondiabetic controls. During the third trimester, fetuses of mothers with diabetes have fewer fetal movements and FHR accelerations but more breathing movements compared to controls (23–25). The normal cyclic fetal motility observed during the third trimester is also disrupted in diabetic pregnancies, and this seems to be related to fluctuations in maternal glucose levels (26). Doherty and Hepper (27) studied habituation patterns in fetuses of mothers with diabetes by performing repetitive vibro-acoustic stimulation. They found that these fetuses took longer to habituate compared to controls, once again reflecting delayed maturation of the central nervous system.

It is not entirely clear whether these altered patterns of fetal activity are solely the result of altered fetal development in the face of maternal diabetes, or whether they are affected by acute perturbations of maternal (and therefore fetal) glucose levels. Some studies suggest that fetal behavior is unaffected by acute changes in maternal glucose levels (28–30), while others report increased (31–33) or decreased (34,35) fetal activity in the presence of maternal hyperglycemia.

Several studies have examined the effect of maternal diabetes on the FHR pattern. Tincello et al. (36) studied computerized fetal heart rate recordings in 26 women with type 1 diabetes throughout the third trimester. They found that these tracings demonstrated delay in fetal maturation compared to uncomplicated pregnancies, reflected in a greater incidence of absent high variability, as well as differences in short-term variability, basal heart rate, accelerations, and frequency of fetal movements. Similar findings were reported by Allen and Kisilevsky (34). Weiner et al. (37) compared FHR patterns in women with well-controlled GDM or pregestational diabetes and nondiabetic controls. They found that FHR variability and frequency of accelerations were significantly reduced in the diabetic pregnancies and increased at a lower rate during the third trimester compared to controls.

Many clinicians believe that maternal oral intake may improve the appearance of a nonreactive nonstress test. In fact, there is conflicting evidence regarding this matter. Zimmer et al. (38) found that ingestion of 50 g oral glucose in 27 healthy pregnant women at 37 to 40 weeks' gestation was followed by a decrease in FHR indices of variation. Similarly, Holden et al. (39) found that maternal hyperglycemia did not stimulate FHR accelerations. Other authors found increased reactivity (40,41), increased mean FHR (42), or no difference (43) after ingestion of glucose.

Hypoglycemia in pregnant women with diabetes does not appear to have adverse effects on fetal biophysical measures. Reece et al. (44) performed insulin-induced hypoglycemic clamp studies in pregnant women with type 1 diabetes, lowering the blood glucose concentration to 45 mg/dL. During hypoglycemia, there was a nonsignificant increase in fetal limb and body movements, and no changes in fetal breathing movements or FHR. Other authors reported that insulin-induced maternal hypoglycemia was associated with increased frequency and amplitude of FHR accelerations (45) and fetal activity (39).

In summary, there are conflicting data on the effects of diabetes on fetal biophysical characteristics, making it difficult to determine the significance of abnormal biophysical parameters at various gestational ages. Overall, it appears that maternal diabetes and hyperglycemia may be associated with maturational delay of fetal behavioral patterns concomitant with increased breathing activity. However, it is unclear how these changes should affect the interpretation of biophysical testing of fetal well-being.

DOPPLER FLOW VELOCIMETRY STUDIES IN PREGNANCIES COMPLICATED BY DIABETES

In obstetrics, the Doppler principle is used to determine the volume and velocity of blood flow through fetal and maternal blood vessels. Various indices of flow have been developed, including the systolic/diastolic (S/D) ratio, pulsatility index (PI), and resistance index (RI), all based on the relationship between the systolic and diastolic flow through a given blood vessel and providing information on downstream resistance. In high-risk pregnancies, such as those complicated by fetal growth restriction or preeclampsia, changes in placental vasculature impedance and redistribution of blood flow in the fetus may be associated with changes in Doppler velocity waveforms. Additionally, maternal vascular pathology may be associated with abnormal waveforms in the maternal uterine arteries and may provide information on the risk of developing preeclampsia.

Indeed, several studies have demonstrated that Doppler waveform analysis is a useful diagnostic tool in high-risk pregnancies. Whether it provides any clinically useful information in pregnancies complicated by diabetes is a matter of controversy.

Studies in pregnant ewes demonstrate that chronic fetal hyperglycemia is associated with a 30% increase in fetal oxygen consumption (4), and acute maternal hypoglycemia produces redistribution of fetal blood flow to vital organs (46). Moreover, in pregnant ewes rendered diabetic by streptozocin, fetal brain and renal perfusion increase significantly without any change in umbilical-placental blood flow (47). These observations suggest that in the presence of maternal diabetes, placental perfusion does not change to meet the increased oxygen demands of the fetus, and Doppler waveforms of the umbilical arteries remain unchanged in the face of fetal hypoxia. Salvesen et al. (48) have confirmed these findings in human pregnancies complicated by diabetes. They found that in 65 pregnant women with diabetes, Doppler studies of umbilical and fetal vessels were essentially normal except in the few cases complicated by preeclampsia or fetal growth restriction, while umbilical venous pH values were significantly lower than normal.

The association of abnormal Doppler indices with vasculopathy, hypertension, and fetal growth restriction in diabetic pregnancies has been demonstrated by several investigators. Landon et al. (49) studied 35 pregnant women with type 1 diabetes and found abnormal umbilical artery waveforms in 50% of women with vascular disease compared to 12% of women without hypertension or nephropathy. In the group with vasculopathy, four of the five fetuses were growth restricted. Similarly, Dicker et al. (50) examined 108 women with type 1 diabetes, and found normal umbilical artery Doppler indices except in women with vasculopathy and in those who developed preeclampsia or fetal growth restriction. Reece et al. (51) evaluated 56 pregnant women with diabetes, 14 of whom had varying degrees of vasculopathy. In the group with vasculopathy, umbilical artery S/D ratios, PI, and RI were significantly higher than in women without vasculopathy and in nondiabetic controls. In a large series of 128 women with diabetes, Johnstone et al. (52) found nine women with abnormal umbilical artery waveforms, six of whom had either vasculopathy or preeclampsia.

In contrast to these studies, Fadda et al. (53) observed that among 67 normotensive pregnant women with insulin-dependent diabetes, 34% had abnormal Doppler indices of the umbilical artery and these were associated with increased risk of perinatal complications. These authors also studied 89 pregnancies complicated by GDM and found that 13% had abnormal Doppler indices without fetal growth restriction or preeclampsia. These pregnancies were also associated with a higher incidence of perinatal complications (54). Olofsson et al. (55) found a higher umbilical artery resistance index in a study of 40 women with diabetes compared to controls. In a study of 207 pregnancies with diabetes, Bracero et al. (56) noted that abnormal Doppler studies obtained within 1 week of delivery are better predictors of adverse outcome compared to the nonstress test (NST) or biophysical profile (BPP). Thus, there is lack of agreement on whether abnormal indices of Doppler flow velocimetry are associated with diabetes, per se, or only with diabetes complicated by vascular disease. Most authors, however, agree that the sensitivity of Doppler studies in determining fetal compromise in pregnancies complicated by diabetes is rather low, ranging from 32% to 61% (52,53,56).

Whether the quality of glycemic control affects Doppler flow indices and perinatal outcome is also a matter of controversy. Although Bracero et al. (57) first reported a significant correlation between umbilical artery S/D ratios and mean maternal blood glucose concentrations, other investigators have not found evidence of such a correlation (49–52,58). Also, in hypoglycemic clamp studies, where maternal blood glucose concentrations of pregnant women with type 1 diabetes were lowered to 40 to 45 mg/dL, very slight or inconsistent changes in umbilical artery Doppler indices were observed (44,45). Thus, most of the published data suggests no correlation between maternal glycemic control and changes in Doppler indices, in accordance with data from animal studies.

In summary, it appears that Doppler studies of the fetoplacental vasculature have limited clinical value in the antenatal surveillance of pregnancies complicated by diabetes. As in nondiabetic pregnancies, these studies are primarily useful in cases of fetal growth restriction, maternal vascular disease, and preeclampsia. It is also clear that in many cases, adverse perinatal outcome occurs following documentation of normal Doppler studies, reflecting the dissociation between fetal hypoxia and feto-placental blood flow in these pregnancies.

ANTENATAL FETAL TESTING IN PREGNANCIES COMPLICATED BY DIABETES

From the data presented in the previous paragraphs, it should be clear that there are no randomized clinical trials to prove the necessity or the efficacy of any scheme of antenatal testing to improve perinatal outcome in pregnancies complicated by diabetes. However, there are several published studies describing the outcome of pregnancy following specific protocols of antenatal testing.

Fuentes and Chez (59) reviewed the literature on antenatal fetal surveillance in pregnancies complicated by insulin-requiring diabetes, including patients with preexisting diabetes as well as patients with insulin-treated GDM. In the analysis, the authors included only pregnancies with well-controlled, uncomplicated diabetes, without evidence of microvascular disease, hypertension, or clinical fetopathy. The seven studies surveyed included a total of 491 patients who were subjected to various methods of antenatal testing, including NST, contraction stress test (CST), BPP, either alone or in combination, and performed either weekly or twice a week. In 17 women (3.5%), abnormal testing resulted in induction of labor or delivery by cesarean section, and stillbirth occurred in an additional seven pregnancies (1.4%), two of which were associated with congenital malformations incompatible with life. Three stillbirths occurred in patients with type 1 diabetes within 1 week of reassuring testing. These data demonstrate that in uncomplicated diabetes, the incidence of abnormal fetal testing is low, but stillbirth may occur even following reassuring fetal testing.

Kjos et al. (60) examined the predictive value of antepartum fetal surveillance for fetal distress in labor in pregnancies complicated by diabetes. In this study, a nonreactive NST was followed by a BPP, and 13% of the 1,501 women studied were admitted for delivery due to nonreassuring testing. The factors most predictive of cesarean delivery for fetal distress were presence of decelerations, nonreactivity during the NST, and increasing severity of diabetic classification. There were no stillbirths within 4 days of reassuring testing, but there were two cases of intrauterine fetal demise at 36 and 38 weeks, 1 week after reassuring testing, in women who had missed their preceding interval testing session. Not surprisingly, this study does not allow us to deduce whether antenatal testing had an impact on pregnancy outcome, because it is impossible to determine what the outcome would have been without intervention in the patients that were delivered due to nonreassuring testing.

Johnson et al. (61) reported their experience using biophysical scoring as the primary mode of antenatal testing; they had no stillbirths among 188 pregnancies complicated by GDM, and a 2.7% rate of required delivery for nonreassuring testing. Girz et al. (62) reported their experience with 389 women with GDM undergoing antenatal testing weekly from 28 to 34 weeks, and then twice a week until delivery. In this study, 7% of women were delivered due to nonreassuring testing. There were three stillbirths within 72 hours of reassuring testing, demonstrating that antenatal testing is not necessarily a guarantee for good outcome.

Several studies have demonstrated that when diabetes is complicated by microvascular or macrovascular disease, there is a much higher risk of abnormal fetal testing requiring intervention. Landon et al. (63) found that intervention was prompted by abnormal fetal testing in 40% of women with nephropathy or hypertension, but only in 2% of women without these risk factors. Using the CST as the primary mode of antenatal testing in women with diabetes, Lagrew et al. (64) found that intervention was necessary in 11% of women without microvascular disease, compared to 19% of those with retinopathy or nephropathy. In the lat-

ter group, 50% of the patients requiring intervention due to nonreassuring testing were delivered prior to 34 weeks' gestation.

SHOULD WOMEN WITH UNCOMPLICATED DIABETES UNDERGO ANTENATAL TESTING?

A major problem in determining the value of fetal testing in women with diabetes is that much of the published literature on antenatal fetal surveillance relates to women with pregestational, insulin-requiring diabetes. In these pregnancies, it has been demonstrated that maternal vascular disease, hypertension, and poor glycemic control are associated with an increased risk of poor perinatal outcome, facts that might justify the institution of antenatal fetal testing. It is unclear whether these data can be extrapolated to include women with uncomplicated, well-controlled diabetes or well-controlled GDM. If the risk of poor perinatal outcome is not increased in these pregnancies, then the benefit of antenatal testing may be questionable. On the other hand, glycemic control may not be the only determining factor related to fetal compromise. As mentioned previously, fetal biophysical parameters are altered in pregnancies complicated by diabetes, and these changes do not necessarily correlate with short- or long-term maternal glycemic control (23). Even though there are currently no solid data with which to resolve these issues, some authors have argued that women with uncomplicated GDM who are controlled on diet alone are at very low risk for adverse fetal outcome, and therefore do not require antenatal testing prior to 40 weeks' gestation, while those who are not well controlled or who are treated with insulin incur a greater risk and warrant antenatal testing starting at some point in the third trimester (65). The rationale underlying this approach is that GDM that is severe enough to require insulin therapy in order to achieve good glycemic control is, presumably, associated with a higher risk of fetal compromise, but GDM controlled well on diet alone is not. There are limited published data to support this premise (66).

Beyond the question of perinatal risk in women whose diabetes is well controlled, a fundamental question would be how to define well-controlled diabetes. This is an issue that often generates debate, even among specialists in maternal-fetal medicine. A pregnant woman might be considered in good control by one clinician, but not by another. The clinician's decision to initiate or withhold insulin therapy in GDM does not necessarily reflect the true severity of the disease. Rather, it depends on many subjective variables on which there is still much debate and disagreement, such as when and how often capillary glucose values should be obtained, what levels of pre- and postprandial glucose should be achieved, and at what glucose concentrations should insulin therapy be initiated. Some clinicians even believe that sonographic parameters, and not glucose levels, might be better indicators of fetal pathology (67,68).

WHAT IS THE BEST SCHEME OF ANTENATAL TESTING IN PREGNANCIES COMPLICATED BY DIABETES?

None of the three common modalities of antenatal testing (NST, CST, and BPP) appears to have any clear-cut advantage over the others in pregnancies complicated by diabetes. Olofsson et al. (69) found an incidence of 3.7% pathologic NSTs among 2,672 tests performed. They determined that a normal NST predicted a reassuring (>7) 5-minute Apgar score in 99% of cases, and a reassuring intrapartum FHR tracing in approximately 80% of cases. They also found that the CST had no distinct advantage over the NST except for fewer false positive or abnormal test results. These authors also concluded that, in general, the specificity of the NST is good (i.e., most healthy fetuses have reassuring tracings) but that the sensitivity (i.e., percentage of compromised fetuses with an abnormal NST) and the positive predictive value of an abnormal test are poor. Dicker et al. (70) reached very similar conclusions with respect to the BPP. In their series, an abnormal BPP score (<8) was obtained in 2.9% of the tests, and a normal BPP predicted a 5-minute Apgar score of >7 in 99% of cases. They also found that the specificity of the BPP is generally good, but that the sensitivity and positive predictive value of abnormal tests results are poor.

Bracero et al. (56) compared the performance of the NST to that of the BPP and Doppler velocimetry in predicting adverse pregnancy outcome in pregnancies complicated by diabetes. Using a very broad definition of the term, 36.2% of pregnancies resulted in an adverse outcome. The relative risk (RR) of adverse outcome was very similar in women with a BPP of <6 (RR = 1.7) and in those with a nonreassuring NST (RR = 1.6). Interestingly, an umbilical artery S/D ratio of >3.0 was the best predictor of adverse outcome, with an RR of 2.6.

The paucity of data on the value of antenatal fetal testing in pregnancies complicated by diabetes has led to adoption of various management schemes by clinicians that range from no testing until 40 weeks for women with diet-controlled GDM to twice-a-week fetal testing from 28 weeks onward for women with complicated diabetes. Many variations exist, including once-a-week testing, incorporating the BPP into the management scheme, alternating between the BPP and the NST, and so forth. The Fourth International Workshop on GDM, convened in 1997, offered the following suggestions (71):

> Decisions regarding the commencement and frequency of fetal surveillance should be influenced by the severity of maternal hyperglycemia and the presence of other adverse clinical factors. Non stress testing should be considered from 32 weeks for insulin-treated GDM and near term for GDM managed with diet alone. Mothers with GDM should be taught to monitor fetal movements during the last 8–10 weeks of pregnancy.

Given these general recommendations, it is not surprising that the regimens for antenatal fetal surveillance, as they appear in the literature, differ greatly among authors. It is clear that no one strategy has been universally adopted; the timing, frequency, and the method of fetal testing all seem to depend on the choice of the practitioner. Our own approach is summarized in Table 24-2. Although these recommendations have not stemmed from prospective randomized studies, it is highly unlikely that any such data will be generated in the future. Even though antenatal testing cannot guarantee the favorable outcome of a pregnancy, it seems prudent to employ the limited techniques available at this time to provide a degree of reassurance for the patient and her provider and to allow the diabetic pregnancy to continue, safely allowing further fetal maturation.

TABLE 24-2. SUGGESTED PROTOCOL FOR ANTENATAL FETAL TESTING IN PREGNANCIES COMPLICATED BY DIABETES

1. All women with diabetes are instructed to monitor fetal movements daily in the third trimester.
2. Women with uncomplicated preexisting diabetes or GDM who achieve good glycemic control on diet, insulin, or oral hypoglycemic therapy undergo fetal testing twice a week from 34 weeks onward.
3. Women with preexisting diabetes or GDM who fail to achieve good glycemic control on diet, insulin, or oral hypoglycemic therapy undergo fetal testing twice a week from 30 to 31 weeks onward.
4. Women with complicated diabetes (microvascular or macrovascular disease, hypertension, or fetal growth restriction) undergo fetal testing twice a week from 28 to 29 weeks onward.
5. It appears that the NST or BPP are equally acceptable as modalities of antenatal fetal testing. Umbilical artery Doppler studies may also be used in cases of complicated diabetes with evidence of fetal growth restriction.

BPP, biophysical profile; GDM, gestational diabetes mellitus; NST, nonstress test.

TESTING FOR FETAL LUNG MATURITY IN PREGNANCIES COMPLICATED BY DIABETES

Maternal diabetes has long been considered a predisposing factor for respiratory distress syndrome (RDS) in the neonate. In the past, many pregnant women with diabetes were delivered prior to term (at 35 to 36 weeks' gestation) in order to avoid the risk of term stillbirth, increasing the incidence of iatrogenic RDS. In 1976, Robert et al. (72) demonstrated that the overall risk of RDS in infants of mothers with diabetes was 23.4%, more than 20 times higher than in nondiabetic controls. Even after controlling for risk factors such as gestational age and route of delivery, the relative risk of RDS in infants of mothers with diabetes remained high at 5.6.

The alleged high incidence of RDS in infants of mothers with diabetes may be due to a direct effect of maternal diabetes on fetal lung development, but the precise mechanism involved in delayed lung maturation remains to be elucidated. Animal studies addressing this issue have been conducted in monkeys (73), rats (74), rabbits (75), and sheep (76), and all have confirmed that fetal lung maturation is delayed in the presence of maternal diabetes. *In vitro* studies have shown that insulin inhibits the accumulation of surfactant protein A and B messenger RNA in human fetal lung tissue (77,78), thereby inhibiting production of surfactant by type 2 cells in the fetal lung. Indeed, the levels of surfactant protein A in the amniotic fluid of pregnancies complicated by diabetes are significantly lower than in nondiabetic control subjects (79). It has been shown, however, that the selective inhibition of surfactant-associated protein 35 (SAP-35) can be overcome by good control of diabetes (80).

Clinical studies suggest that the increased incidence of RDS in infants of mothers with diabetes is associated with poor glycemic control. Landon et al. (81) studied 43 women with pregestational diabetes who maintained good glycemic control during pregnancy (mean capillary blood glucose <110 mg/dL) and 32 women who maintained poor glycemic control (>110 mg/dL). Only one of the six infants in the good control group who delivered at 35 to 36 weeks' gestation developed RDS compared to four of the seven infants in the poor control group. Langer et al. (82) found that intensified treatment of pregnant women with GDM (mean glucose 98±16 mg/dL), when compared to conventional treatment (mean glucose 123±17 mg/dL), is associated with a decreased risk of RDS that is similar to the risk in a nondiabetic population: 2.3% versus 6.2%. Similarly, in a large group of 621 women with diabetes, Piper et al. (83) found that all cases of RDS beyond 32 weeks' gestation occurred in women with poor glycemic control (mean glucose >105 mg/dL) and that no cases of RDS occurred beyond 37 weeks' gestation.

These observations suggest that pregnant women with diabetes who maintain good glycemic control throughout pregnancy may deliver at 38 to 39 weeks' gestation without

an increased risk of neonatal RDS. If the woman has a compromised fetus, it would make sense to incur the risk of RDS rather than the risk of a term stillbirth. If an elective delivery is planned prior to 39 weeks' gestation, it is appropriate to obtain laboratory documentation of fetal lung maturity (FLM), raising the following questions:

1. Does diabetes affect the results of FLM tests?
2. Does glycemic control affect the results of FLM tests?
3. Do immature FLM tests predict RDS in diabetic pregnancies?

There is considerable controversy on whether diabetes and glycemic control affect results of FLM tests. While several authors found that diabetes is associated with delayed maturity of FLM tests (84–89), others have not found any difference between pregnancies complicated by diabetes and controls (90–96). Berkowitz et al. (94) compared FLM results in 501 women with GDM and 561 nondiabetic controls. They found no differences between the two groups with respect to the lecithin/sphyngomyelin (L/S) ratio or the mean percent PG at any gestational age. Similarly, Fadel et al. (93) found no differences in FLM indices between women with or without diabetes. Piazze et al. (91) studied a group of 45 women with diabetes and found no differences between women with well-controlled diabetes and controls in any of the following FLM tests: shake test, lamellar body count, L/S ratio, and presence of phosphatidylglycerol (PG).

In contrast, Moore (86) studied 295 women with diabetes and 590 matched controls and found that in women with GDM, the onset of PG production is delayed from 35.9±1.1 weeks to 37.3±1.0 weeks. In women with overt diabetes, the delay was even longer, to 38.7±0.9 weeks. This delay was not associated with the level of glycemic control or fetal macrosomia.

Piper and Langer (87) also found that FLM is delayed in women with diabetes, but noted an association with glycemic control: women with poorly controlled diabetes had delayed FLM test results at every gestational age compared to nondiabetic controls. In women with well-controlled diabetes, there were no statistically significant differences compared to controls at each stratum of gestational age, but overall, they too were more likely, as a group, to have immature FLM results (odds ratio, 2.11; confidence interval, 1.3–3.4).

Even though the likelihood of immature FLM tests may be higher in women with diabetes, the ability of an immature test to predict neonatal lung disease is poor. In a study of 526 women with diabetes, Kjos et al. (97) found that the positive predictive value of an immature L/S test was 15%, and that of an immature PG test was only 9% for RDS. Only five infants had surfactant-deficient RDS, and all five were delivered before 34 weeks' gestation.

In summary, it appears that positive FLM test results may be delayed in pregnancies complicated by diabetes, particularly in the presence of poor glycemic control. However, the majority of infants delivered after 34 weeks' gestation will not have RDS even in the presence of an immature FLM test.

KEY POINTS

- Fetal hyperglycemia and hyperinsulinemia are associated with fetal hypoxia and acidosis.
- Maternal diabetes is associated with an increased risk of perinatal mortality.
- Untreated or poorly controlled diabetes carries the highest risk of perinatal mortality.
- Diabetes is associated with a maturational delay of fetal neurobehavioral patterns and biophysical indices.
- Acute hypoglycemia does not affect fetal biophysical patterns.
- It is unclear how acute hyperglycemia affects fetal biophysical patterns.
- Doppler velocimetry studies are not useful for assessing fetal well-being in most pregnancies complicated by diabetes. Doppler velocimetry studies may be helpful in the presence of maternal vasculopathy and/or intrauterine growth restriction.
- There are few prospective randomized trials demonstrating that antenatal fetal testing improves perinatal outcome in diabetic pregnancies.
- Most clinicians institute some form of antenatal testing in pregnancies complicated by diabetes based on the severity of diabetes and the quality of glycemic control.
- The appearance of biochemical markers of fetal lung maturity may be delayed in the fetus whose mother has diabetes.
- The vast majority of fetuses born after 34 weeks' gestation do not have RDS if the mother has well-controlled diabetes.

REFERENCES

1. Pattison N, McCowan L. Cardiotocography for antepartum fetal assessment. Cochrane Review. The Cochrane Library, Issue 2. Chichester, UK: John Wiley and Sons, 2002.
2. Bjork O, Persson B. Villous structure in different parts of the cotyledon in placentas of insulin dependent diabetic women. *Acta Obstet Gynecol Scand* 1984;63:37–43.
3. Nylund L, Lunell NO, Lewande R, et al. Utero placental blood flow in diabetic pregnancies. *Am J Obstet Gynecol* 1982;144: 298–302.
4. Philipps AF, Porte PJ, Stabinsky S, et al. Effects of chronic fetal hyperglycemia upon oxygen consumption in the ovine uterus and conceptus. *J Clin Invest* 1984;74:279–286.
5. Shelly JH, Bassett JM, Milner RD. Control of carbohydrate metabolism in the fetus and newborn. *Br Med Bull* 1975;31:37.
6. Hay WW, DiGiacomo JE, Meznarich HK, et al. Effect of glucose and insulin on fetal glucose oxidation and oxygen consumption. *Am J Physiol* 1989;256:E704–E713.
7. Salvesen DR, Brudenell JM, Proudler A, et al. Fetal pancreatic

8. beta-cell function in pregnancies complicated by maternal diabetes mellitus: relationship to fetal acidemia and macrosomia. *Am J Obstet Gynecol* 1993;168:1363–1369.
8. Bradley RJ, Brudenell JM, Nicolaides KH. Fetal acidosis and hyperlactinemia diagnosed by cordocentesis in pregnancies complicated by maternal diabetes mellitus. *Diabet Med* 1991;8: 464–468.
9. Jazayeri A, O'Brien WF, Tsibris JC, et al. Are maternal diabetes and pre-eclampsia independent stimulators of erythropoeitin production? *Am J Perinatol* 1998;15:577–580.
10. Salafia CM, Silberman L. Placental pathology and abnormal fetal heart rate patterns in gestational diabetes. *Pediatr Pathol* 1989;9: 513–520.
11. World Health Organisation, International Diabetes Federation. Diabetes care and research in Europe: the St Vincent Declaration. *Diabet Med* 1990;34:655–661.
12. Hanson U, Persson B. Outcome of pregnancies complicated by type 1 insulin-dependent diabetes in Sweden: acute pregnancy complications, neonatal mortality and morbidity. *Am J Perinatol* 1993;10:330–334.
13. Cnattingius S, Berne C, Nordstrom ML. Pregnancy outcome and infant mortality in diabetic patients in Sweden. *Diabet Med* 1994;11:696–700.
14. Hawthorne G, Robson S, Ryall EA, et al. Prospective population based survey of outcome of pregnancy in diabetic women: results of the Northern Diabetic Pregnancy Audit, 1994. *BMJ* 1997; 315:279–281.
15. Casson IF, Clarke CA, Howard CV, et al. Outcomes of pregnancy in insulin dependent diabetic women: results of a five-year population cohort study. *BMJ* 1997;315;275–278.
16. Cundy T, Gamble G, Townend K, et al. Perinatal mortality in Type 2 diabetes mellitus. *Diabet Med* 2000;17:33–39.
17. Platt MJ, Stanisstreet M, Casson IF, et al. St Vincent's Declaration 10 years on: outcomes of diabetic pregnancies. *Diabet Med* 2002;19:216–220.
18. Wylie BR, Kong J, Kozak SE, et al. Normal perinatal mortality in type 1 diabetes mellitus in a series of 300 consecutive pregnancy outcomes. *Am J Perinatol* 2002;19:169–176.
19. Penney GC, Mair G, Pearson DWM. Outcomes of pregnancies in women with type 1 diabetes in Scotland: a national population-based study. *BJOG* 2003;110:315–318.
20. Beischer NA, Wein P, Sheedy MT, et al. Identification and treatment of women with hyperglycaemia diagnosed during pregnancy can significantly reduce perinatal mortality rates. *Aust N Z J Obstet Gynaecol* 1996;36:239–247.
21. Moses RG. The recurrence rate of gestational diabetes in subsequent pregnancies. *Diabetes Care* 1996;19:1348–1350.
22. Mulder EJ, Visser GH. Growth and motor development in fetuses of women with type-1 diabetes. II. Emergence of specific movement patterns. *Early Hum Dev* 1991;25:107–115.
23. Devoe LD, Youssef AA, Castillo RA, et al. Fetal biophysical activities in third trimester pregnancies complicated by diabetes mellitus. *Am J Obstet Gynecol* 1994;171:298–303.
24. Mulder EJ, Leiblum DM, Visser GH. Fetal breathing movements in late diabetic pregnancy: Relationship to fetal heart rate patterns and Braxton-Hicks contractions. *Early Hum Dev* 1995; 43:225–232.
25. Mulder EJ, O'Brien MJ, Lems YL, et al. Body and breathing movements in near-term fetuses and newborn infants of type I diabetic women. *Early Hum Dev* 1990;24:131–132.
26. Robertson SS, Dierker LJ. Fetal cyclic motor activity in diabetic pregnancies: sensitivity to maternal blood glucose. *Dev Psychobiol* 2003;42:9–16.
27. Doherty NN, Hepper PG. Habituation in fetuses of diabetic mothers. *Early Hum Dev* 2000;59:85–93.

28. Bocking AD. Observations of biophysical activities in the normal fetus. *Clin Perinatol* 1989;16:583–594.

29. Lewis PJ, Trudinger BJ, Mangez J. Effect of maternal glucose ingestion on fetal breathing and body movements in late pregnancy. *Br J Obstet Gynaecol* 1978;85:86–89.

30. Natale R, Richardson B, Patrick J. The effect of maternal hyperglycemia on gross body movements in human fetuses at 32 to 34 weeks' gestation. *Early Hum Dev* 1983;8:13–20.

31. Aladjem S, Feria A, Rest J, et al. Effect of maternal glucose load on fetal activity. *Am J Obstet Gynecol* 1979;134:276–280.

32. Eller DP, Stramm SL, Newman RB, et al. The effect of maternal intravenous glucose administration on fetal activity. *Am J Obstet Gynecol* 1992;167:1071–1074.

33. Miller FC, Skiba H, Klapholz H. The effect of maternal blood sugar levels on fetal activity. *Obstet Gynecol* 1978;52:662–665.

34. Allen CL, Kisilevsky BS. Fetal behavior in diabetic and nondiabetic pregnant women: an exploratory study. *Dev Psychobiol* 1999;35:69–80.

35. Edelberg SC, Dierker L, Kalhan S, et al. Decreased fetal movements with sustained maternal hyperglycemia using the glucose clamp technique. *Am J Obstet Gynecol* 1987;156:1101–1105.

36. Tincello D, White S, Walkinshaw S. Computerised analysis of fetal heart rate recordings in maternal type I diabetes mellitus. *BJOG* 2001;108:853–857.

37. Weiner Z, Thaler I, Farmakides G, et al. Fetal heart rate patterns in pregnancies complicated by maternal diabetes. *Eur J Obstet Gynecol Reprod Biol* 1996;70:111–115.

38. Zimmer EZ, Paz Y, Goldstick O, et al. Computerized analysis of fetal heart rate after maternal glucose ingestion in normal pregnancy. *Eur J Obstet Gynecol Reprod Biol* 2000;93:57–60.

39. Holden KP, Jovanovic L, Druzin ML, et al. Increased fetal activity with low maternal blood glucose levels in pregnancies complicated by diabetes. *Am J Perinatol* 1984;1:161–164.

40. Graca LM, Meirinho M, Sanches JF, et al. Modification of fetal reactivity for an intravenous glucose load to the mothers. *J Perinat Med* 1981;9:286–292.

41. Gillis S, Connors G, Potts P, et al. The effect of glucose on Doppler flow velocity waveforms and heart rate pattern in the human fetus. *Early Hum Dev* 1992;30:1–10.

42. Bocking A, Adamson L, Carmichael L, et al. Effect of intravenous glucose injection on human maternal and fetal heart rate at term. *Am J Obstet Gynecol* 1984;148:414–420.

43. Druzin ML, Foodim J. Effect of maternal glucose ingestion compared with maternal water ingestion on the nonstress test. *Obstet Gynecol* 1986;67:425–426.

44. Reece EA, Hagay Z, Roberts AB, et al. Fetal Doppler and behavioral responses during hypoglycemia induced with the insulin clamp technique in pregnant diabetic women. *Am J Obstet Gynecol* 1995;172:151–155.

45. Björklund AO, Adamson UKC, Almström, NHH, et al. Effects of hypoglycaemia on fetal heart activity and umbilical artery Doppler velocity waveforms in pregnant women with insulin-dependent diabetes mellitus. *Br J Obstet Gynaecol* 1996;103:413–420.

46. Crandell SS, Fisher DJ, Morriss FH Jr. Effects of ovine maternal hyperglycemia on fetal regional blood flows and metabolism. *Am J Physiol* 1985;249:E454–E460.

47. Dickinson JE, Meyer BA, Palmer SM. Fetal vascular responses to maternal glucose administration in streptozocin-induced ovine diabetes mellitus. *J Obstet Gynaecol Res* 1998;24:325–333.

48. Salvesen DR, Freeman J, Brudenell JM, et al. Prediction of fetal acidaemia in pregnancies complicated by maternal diabetes mellitus by biophysical profile scoring and fetal heart rate monitoring. *BJOG* 1993;100:227–233.

49. Landon MB, Gabbe SG, Bruner JP, et al. Doppler umbilical

50. Dicker D, Goldman JA, Yeshaya A, et al. Umbilical artery velocimetry in insulin dependent diabetes mellitus (IDDM) pregnancies. *J Perinat Med* 1990;18:391–395.

51. Reece EA, Hagay Z, Assimakopoulos E, et al. Diabetes mellitus in pregnancy and the assessment of umbilical artery waveforms using pulsed Doppler ultrasonography. *J Ultrasound Med* 1994;12:73–80.

52. Johnstone FD, Steel JM, Haddad NG, et al. Doppler umbilical artery flow velocity waveforms in diabetic pregnancy. *Br J Obstet Gynaecol* 1992;99:135–140.

53. Fadda GM, Cherchi PL, D'Antona D, et al. Umbilical artery pulsatility index in pregnancies complicated by insulin-dependent diabetes mellitus without hypertension. *Gynecol Obstet Invest* 2001;51:173–177.

54. Fadda GM, D'Antona D, Ambrosini G, et al. Placental and fetal pulsatility indices in gestational diabetes mellitus. *J Reprod Med* 2001;46:365–370.

55. Olofsson P, Lingman G, Marshal K, et al. Fetal blood flow in diabetic pregnancy. *J Perinat Med* 1987;15:545–553.

56. Bracero LA, Figueroa R, Byrne DW, et al. Comparison of umbilical Doppler velocimetry, nonstress testing, and biophysical profile in pregnancies complicated by diabetes. *J Ultrasound Med* 1996;15:301–308.

57. Bracero L, Schulman H, Fleischer A, et al. Umbilical artery velocimetry in diabetes and pregnancy. *Obstet Gynecol* 1986;68:654–658.

58. Grunewald C, Divon M, Lunell NO. Doppler velocimetry in last trimester pregnancy complicated by insulin-dependent diabetes mellitus. *Acta Obstet Gynecol Scand* 1996;75:804–808.

59. Fuentes A, Chez RA. Role of fetal surveillance in diabetic pregnancies. *J Matern Fetal Med* 1996;5:85–88.

60. Kjos SL, Leung A, Henry OA, et al. Antepartum surveillance in diabetic pregnancies: predictors of fetal distress in labor. *Am J Obstet Gynecol* 1995;173:1532–1539.

61. Johnson JM, Lange IR, Harman CR, et al. Biophysical profile scoring in the management of the diabetic pregnancy. *Obstet Gynecol* 1988;72:841–846.

62. Girz BA, Divon MY, Merkatz IR. Sudden fetal death in women with well-controlled, intensively monitored gestational diabetes. *J Perinatol* 1992;12:229–233.

63. Landon MB, Langer O, Gabbe SG, et al. Fetal surveillance in pregnancies complicated by insulin-dependent diabetes mellitus. *Am J Obstet Gynecol* 1992;167:617–621.

64. Lagrew DC, Pircon RA, Towers CV, et al. Antepartum fetal surveillance in patients with diabetes: when to start? *Am J Obstet Gynecol* 1993;168:1820–1826.

65. Landon MB, Gabbe SG. Fetal surveillance and timing of delivery in pregnancy complicated by diabetes mellitus. *Obstet Gynecol Clin North Am* 1996;23:109–123.

66. Landon MB, Gabbe SG. Antepartum fetal surveillance in gestational diabetes mellitus. *Diabetes* 1985;34[Suppl 2]:50–54.

67. Buchanan TA, Kjos SL, Montoro MN, et al. Use of fetal ultrasound to select metabolic therapy for pregnancies complicated by mild gestational diabetes. *Diabetes Care* 1994;17:275–283.

68. Kjos SL, Schaefer-Graf U, Sardesi S, et al. A randomized controlled trial using glycemic plus fetal ultrasound parameters versus glycemic parameters to determine insulin therapy in gestational diabetes with fasting hyperglycemia. *Diabetes Care* 2001;24:1904–1910.

69. Olofsson P, Sjoberg NO, Solum T. Fetal surveillance in diabetic pregnancy. I. Predictive value of the nonstress test. *Acta Obstet Gynecol Scand* 1986;65:241–246.

70. Dicker D, Feldberg D, Yeshaya A, et al. Fetal surveillance in

insulin-dependent diabetic pregnancy: predictive value of the biophysical profile. *Am J Obstet Gynecol* 1988;159:800–804.

71. Aerts L, Dornhorst A, Haffner S, et al. Long-range implications and management after pregnancy. Proceedings of the Fourth International Workshop-Conference on Gestational Diabetes mellitus. *Diabetes Care* 1998;21:B166–B167.

72. Robert MF, Neff RK, Hubbell JP, et al. Association between maternal diabetes and the respiratory distress syndrome in the newborn. *N Engl J Med* 1976;294:357–360.

73. Susa JB, McCormick KL, Widness JA, et al. Chronic hyperinsulinemia in the fetal rhesus monkey: effects of fetal growth and composition. *Diabetes* 1979;28:1058–1063.

74. Rhoades RA, Filler DA, Vannata B. Influence of maternal diabetes on lipid metabolism in neonatal rat lung. *Biochem Biophys Acta* 1979;572:132–138.

75. Sosenko IR, Lawson EE, Demottay V, et al. Functional delay in lung maturation in fetuses of diabetic rabbits. *J Appl Physiol* 1980;48:643–647.

76. Warburton D. Chronic hyperglycemia reduces surface active material flux in tracheal fluid of fetal lambs. *J Clin Invest* 1983;71:550–555.

77. Synder JM, Mendelson CR. Insulin inhibits the accumulation of the major lung surfactant apoprotein in human fetal lung explants maintained in vitro. *Endocrinology* 1987;120:1250–1257.

78. Dekowski SA, Snyder JM. Insulin regulation of messenger ribonucleic acid for the surfactant-associated proteins in human fetal lung in vitro. *Endocrinology* 1992;131:669–676.

79. Synder JM, Kwun JE, O'Brien JA, et al. The concentration of the 35kDa surfactant apoprotein in amniotic fluid from normal and diabetic pregnancies. *Pediatr Res* 1988;24:728–734.

80. McMahan MJ, Mimouni F, Miodovnik M, et al. Surfactant associated protein (SAP-35) in amniotic fluid from diabetic and non-diabetic pregnancies. *Obstet Gynecol* 1987;70:94–98.

81. Landon MB, Gabbe SG, Piana R, et al. Neonatal morbidity in pregnancy complicated by diabetes mellitus: predictive value of maternal glycemic profiles. *Am J Obstet Gynecol* 1987;156:1089–1095.

82. Langer O, Rodriguez DA, Xenakis EMJ, et al. Intensified vs. conventional management of gestational diabetes. *Am J Obstet Gynecol* 1994;170:1036–1047.

83. Piper JM, Xenakis EM, Langer O. Delayed appearance of pulmonary maturation markers is associated with poor glucose control in diabetic pregnancies. *J Matern Fetal Med* 1998;7:148–153.

84. Ojomo EO, Coustan DR. Absence of evidence of pulmonary maturity at amniocentesis in term infants of diabetic mothers. *Am J Obstet Gynecol* 1990;163:954–957.

85. Gluck L, Kulovich MV. Lecithin/sphingomyelin ratios in amniotic fluid in normal and abnormal pregnancy. *Am J Obstet Gynecol* 1973;115:539–546.

86. Moore TR. A comparison of amniotic fluid fetal pulmonary phospholipids in normal and diabetic pregnancy. *Am J Obstet Gynecol* 2002;186:641–650.

87. Piper JM, Langer O. Does maternal diabetes delay fetal pulmonary maturity? *Am J Obstet Gynecol* 1993;168:783–786.

88. Piper JM, Samueloff A, Langer O. Outcome of amniotic fluid analysis and neonatal respiratory status in diabetic and non-diabetic pregnancies. *J Reprod Med* 1995;40:780–784.

89. Hallman M, Teramo K. Amniotic fluid phospholipids profile as a predictor of fetal maturity in diabetic pregnancies. *Obstet Gynecol* 1979;54:703–707.

90. Ferroni KM, Gross TL, Sokol RJ, et al. What affects fetal pulmonary maturation during diabetic pregnancy? *Am J Obstet Gynecol* 1984;150:270–274.

91. Piazze JJ, Anceschi MM, Maranghi L, et al. Fetal lung maturity in pregnancies complicated by insulin-dependent and gestational diabetes: a matched cohort study. *Eur J Obstet Gynecol Reprod Biol* 1999;83:145–150.

92. Bent AE, Gray JH, Luther ER, et al. Assessment of fetal lung maturity: relationship of gestational age and pregnancy complications to phosphatidylglycerol levels. *Am J Obstet Gynecol* 1982;142:664–669.

93. Fadel HE, Saad SA, Nelson GH, et al. Effect of maternal-fetal disorders on lung maturation. *M J Obstet Gynecol* 1986;155:544–553.

94. Berkowitz K, Reyes C, Saadat P, et al. Fetal lung maturation: comparison of biochemical indices in gestational diabetic and nondiabetic pregnancies. *J Reprod Med* 1997;42:793–800.

95. Amon E, Lipshitz J, Sibai BM, et al. Quantitative analysis of amniotic fluid phospholipids in diabetic pregnant women. *Obstet Gynecol* 1986;68:373–378.

96. Tabsh KM, Brinkman CR, Bashore RA. Lecithin;sphingomyelin ratio in pregnancies complicated by insulin-dependent diabetes mellitus. *Obstet Gynecol* 1982;59:353–358.

97. Kjos SL, Walther FJ, Montoro M, et al. Prevalence and etiology of respiratory distress in infants of diabetic mothers: predictive value of fetal lung maturation tests. *Am J Obstet Gynecol* 1990;163:898–903.

25

DIABETIC KETOACIDOSIS IN PREGNANCY

MARTIN N. MONTORO

Diabetic ketoacidosis (DKA) is an acute, life-threatening, medical emergency. Fortunately, the mortality from DKA in the general population has steadily decreased over the years to less than 2%, although it remains higher in those younger than 5 or older than 50 years (1,2). In pregnancy, a maternal mortality rate of 4% to 15% has been reported, also higher than in the general population (3). Fortunately, no maternal deaths have been reported in the most recent publications (4–8). The frequency of DKA during pregnancy has been reported to be 1.7% to 3% (4–8). While DKA has historically been considered to be a complication of type 1 diabetes, it has been increasingly reported in individuals who appear to have type 2 diabetes (9). Rare cases of DKA in gestational diabetes have been reported as well (10,11). In addition, DKA during pregnancy may lead to fetal death. Indeed, the perinatal mortality until 10 to 15 years ago was reported to be as high as 90%. More recent fetal mortality rates have varied from 10% to 35%, still significantly elevated (4–8).

This chapter will review the consequences of ketosis with and without acidosis and DKA during pregnancy. The review includes the pathophysiology, clinical signs and symptoms, precipitating factors, diagnosis, prevention, and treatment of this potentially catastrophic complication of diabetes.

KETOSIS WITHOUT OVERT ACIDOSIS

There is no information about the long-term consequences of maternal DKA in fetuses surviving this acute diabetic complication. However, several studies have reported lower IQ in infants of mothers who had ketonuria during pregnancy (12–14). In a more recent study, ketonuria alone did not seem to correlate with subsequent intellectual development unless there was a concomitant elevation of plasma concentrations of beta-hydroxybutyrate or free fatty acids. The offspring of mothers with higher levels of those two fuels during the third trimester had lower scores of behav-

ioral and intellectual development at 2 and 5 years of age (15). Therefore, since even mild abnormalities of maternal glucose metabolism may adversely affect intellectual development, optimal control of diabetes should be achieved throughout gestation.

PATHOPHYSIOLOGY

DKA is characterized by an absolute or relative deficiency of insulin combined with excessive amounts of counterregulatory hormones such as glucagon, catecholamines, cortisol, and growth hormone. In the absence of insulin, there is a dramatic elevation of glucagon, which in turn antagonizes insulin action particularly in adipose tissue and the liver. This combination of factors causes insulin-sensitive tissues (e.g., adipose tissue, liver, skeletal muscle) to increase lipolysis. The increased levels of counterregulatory hormones stimulate gluconeogenesis and ketone formation, which precipitate DKA. DKA itself is the cause of added severe stress and perpetuates the cycle. An additional effect of insulin deficiency is the release of massive amounts of free fatty acids (FFA). In the liver, FFA undergo beta-oxidation leading to unrestrained ketoacid (beta-hydroxybutarate and acetoacetate) production, as well as gluconeogenesis, which further contributes to hyperglycemia. There is increased proteolysis as well causing higher plasma levels of amino acids, which also serve as precursors for gluconeogenesis and additional glucose production. Glucose transporters (GLUT) may also have a supporting role in the development of hyperglycemia. GLUT 2 transports glucose in and out of liver cells, and GLUT 4 is responsible for glucose uptake by muscle and fat cells. Both are reduced by lack of insulin (16).

Excessive amounts of ketones lead to acidosis, and hyperglycemia causes osmotic diuresis with loss of electrolytes, volume depletion, and dehydration. Decreased cardiac output, hypotension, and even shock may ensue. Without adequate tissue perfusion, lactic acid may accumulate and will further contribute to the acidosis. In an effort to compensate for the falling pH, there is a shift of hydrogen ions into the cells, causing the exit of intracellular potassium into the extracellular space. Under these conditions the measured levels of serum potassium, which may be normal or even high at presentation, are not an accurate reflection of the intracellular depletion of potassium, which can be severe.

It is generally acknowledged that diabetic pregnant women may develop DKA faster than when not pregnant. Pregnancy is characterized by "accelerated starvation." Fat breakdown and ketosis as well as protein catabolism occur much faster than outside of pregnancy (Chapter 10). Pregnant women also have a decreased buffering capacity due to increased alveolar minute ventilation, resulting in a compensatory increase in renal excretion of bicarbonate. Whether the increased levels of several diabetogenic hormones (e.g., human placental lactogen, free cortisol, prolactin, progesterone) might also play a role remains to be seen. Persistent nausea and vomiting in early pregnancy have been suggested as a contributing factor as well (7). However, nausea and vomiting are also a common complication of the DKA itself.

PRECIPITATING FACTORS

Precipitating factors include infections, omission of insulin during an acute illness, insulin pump failure, noncompliance, failure to recognize new onset of diabetes, drug and alcohol use, and medications such as steroids and adrenergic agonists. In our own series, almost a third of the cases had unrecognized new onset diabetes. Their illness went undetected for 1 to 3 weeks until they were severely ill, and their symptoms were attributed to influenza or a viral syndrome (6). This group accounted for 57% of the fetal deaths. Others have also reported new onset of diabetes presenting as DKA during pregnancy (17).

CLINICAL PRESENTATION

DKA usually develops progressively over a period of 3 to 7 days. Alcohol ingestion may precipitate a much more rapid onset, sometimes even overnight. Common symptoms include polyuria, polydipsia, blurred vision, anorexia, nausea, vomiting, weight loss, abdominal pain, changes in mental status ranging from drowsiness to coma, Kussmaul's respirations (rapid, deep, sighing), ketotic (fruity) odor, signs of volume depletion (dry mucous membranes, poor skin turgor), tachycardia, and orthostatic hypotension. However, the skin is generally warm. The temperature is usually normal or below normal. While infection should be suspected if fever is present, a normal temperature does not exclude infection. The nausea, vomiting, and

abdominal pain are due to ketone bodies. Hypokalemia may cause (or worsen if already present) gastroparesis and even ileus. Hyperventilation, an effort to compensate for metabolic acidosis, is more marked when the pH is less than 7.2. In severe cases, symptoms and signs of shock may be present.

LABORATORY DIAGNOSIS

The laboratory diagnosis is based on the same criteria as outside of pregnancy except that even profound DKA may be present despite normal or only mildly elevated serum glucose levels. It is important not to dismiss the diagnosis of DKA in a pregnant woman simply because her serum glucose is not significantly elevated. This relative euglycemia may lead to misdiagnosis and inappropriate therapy (4). Other diagnostic criteria are the same as for nonpregnant women, and include an arterial pH of less than 7.3, serum bicarbonate of less than 15 mEq/L, an elevated anion gap, and positive serum ketones. Leukocytosis is common and does not necessarily indicate infection. A left shift in the differential is more suggestive of infection.

The anion gap is usually 15 or higher in DKA and can be calculated by this formula: $Na - (Cl + HCO_3) = 8$ to 12. However, it may also be elevated in other conditions such as lactic acidosis, chronic renal failure, rhabdomyolysis, and acid ingestion (salicylate overdose, ethylene glycol, methanol, formaldehyde, sulfur, toluene, and paraldehyde). Mental status correlates better with the serum osmolality than with other metabolic derangements. An osmolality of 320 mOsm/L or higher is clinically significant. Coma may occur at 340 mOsm/L or higher. The serum osmolality can be calculated by the formula: $2(Na + K) + (glucose/18)$. Another calculation, helpful in estimating water deficits, is the corrected serum Na level. Hyperglycemia usually dilutes plasma Na by 1.6 mEq/L for every 100-mg/dL increase in glucose (18). An initial level of serum Na that is normal or elevated indicates massive water loss. The formula to calculate the corrected sodium level follows: measured $[Na + 1.6 \times$ plasma glucose (mg/dL) $- 100]/100$. In pure metabolic acidosis the PCO_2 level given in the arterial blood gas (ABG) report should be equal to the last two numbers of the arterial pH. A lower-than-predicted PCO_2 indicates respiratory alkalosis and may be a clue to sepsis. If the PCO_2 is higher than predicted, suspect respiratory acidosis. If hypoxemia is also present, suspect pneumonia or adult respiratory distress syndrome.

DIFFERENTIAL DIAGNOSIS

The differential diagnosis of coma in a pregnant diabetic woman is no different from that outside of pregnancy. It includes drug or alcohol overdose, encephalopathy, hyperosmolar syndrome, hypoglycemia, uremic coma, trauma, infection, psychosis, syncope, and seizures.

PREVENTION

DKA indicates a breakdown of medical management. Prevention is of the utmost importance and patient education, particularly about sick-day management, and cannot be emphasized enough. Frequent blood glucose measurements aimed at maintaining adequate hydration and insulin dosages could prevent most cases of DKA. All published reports include a large number of patients who lost their appetite and stopped injecting insulin. Patients tend to skip their insulin dose if they are not going to eat a full meal. Patients may fail to appreciate the significance of vomiting and dehydration. In this setting, being able to test for urine ketones is highly advisable. Ideally, all patients should be able to contact a healthcare provider early in the course of their disease. Alertness to the symptoms of diabetes may help to promptly identify patients with new onset diabetes. Otherwise, their symptoms may go unrecognized until they are severely ill and at higher risk for fetal death (6,17).

TREATMENT

Patients in DKA should be in an intensive or special care unit, and the fetus continuously monitored as well. A careful flow sheet to guide management is indispensable. It should indicate dates, times, serial levels of glucose, electrolytes, ABG, anion gap, insulin given, fluid intake, and urine output.

Fluid and electrolyte losses should be replaced first to restore extracellular volume. Once fluid replacement is initiated, insulin is given, usually intravenously. At high levels of glucose (>250 mg/dL) non-glucose-containing fluid is satisfactory. On the other hand, as glucose falls below 250 mg/dL, a combination of insulin and glucose-containing fluids will be necessary. Insulin will start the reversal of the abnormal metabolism in the adipose tissue and the liver toward normal. It will also restore glucose transporters and inhibit counterregulatory hormones. If identified, precipitating factors, particularly infections, should be managed promptly. The importance of frequent testing and readjustment of therapy as necessary cannot be overemphasized.

FLUIDS AND ELECTROLYTES

One common error made in the treatment of DKA is the failure to administer adequate fluids. With sufficient fluid replacement, there is more rapid improvement, and fewer electrolyte and acid-base disturbances. The total fluid deficit usually averages 5 to 6 L (6,16), and should be replaced quickly during the first few hours of treatment. Replacement should take into account not only the amounts infused but also urine produced and insensible losses. In general, the first 1 to 3 liters are given as 0.9% normal saline (NS) except when the initial Na is normal or high, in which case 1/2 NS should be given from the outset. The rate for the first 4 hours should be 500 to 1,000 ml/hr and 250 to 500 ml/hr for the next 4 hours. A dextrose solution should be started when the blood glucose is 250 mg/dL or lower. In pregnant women in DKA with relatively low serum glucose levels, dextrose solutions should be given from the outset. In most cases, the actual deficit is of free water, which is better replaced by hypotonic saline or dextrose in water. The latter may be given after the extracellular volume has been repleted and hyperglycemia has been brought under control. In the past, the rapid administration of fluids, especially hypotonic fluids, was thought to increase the risk of cerebral edema. This is not evident in more recent reports (19,20). Cerebral edema seems to be the result of reduced blood volume and arterial carbon dioxide leading to cerebral vasoconstriction, ischemia, and hypoxia, and is probably related to the duration and severity of the DKA (20). Because hyperchloremia almost always develops in the course of the treatment of DKA, some authors prefer lactated Ringer's instead of saline solutions. However, there is no evidence that hyperchloremia is detrimental. In fact, poorly controlled diabetic patients may not respond well to lactate infusions.

INSULIN

Insulin therapy should be initiated promptly after fluid replacement has begun. Fluids alone will not reverse DKA. Only regular insulin should be used, administered by continuous, low-dose intravenous infusion. If the insulin infusion can be prepared in a timely manner, there is no need for an insulin bolus. However, if any delay is expected, a bolus (usually 10 units) is recommended. High doses of insulin have been associated with a greater likelihood for hypoglycemia and hypokalemia later in the course of treatment.

The general insulin requirements are 0.1 units per kilogram of body weight per hour. The infusion must be adjusted as often as necessary in response to not only the serum glucose levels measured every 1 to 2 hours initially, but also to the anion gap, arterial pH, and other biochemical parameters. The recommended rate of glucose fall should be more than 10% per 1 to 2 hours, usually 60 mg/dL per hour. There is no advantage to rapidly lowering the serum glucose level, but if the therapeutic goals are not met, the insulin infusion rate should be increased as needed to achieve a gradual glucose reduction.

POTASSIUM

Usual potassium deficits are 3 to 5 mmol/kg or higher. Potassium will shift back into the cells rapidly, as soon as proper therapy is underway. These changes should be anticipated and the therapy readjusted as needed in order to maintain normal levels throughout. Potassium is not generally given until treatment has been ongoing for 2 to 4 hours, except if the initial level is already low. Most patients require 20 to 40 mEq/hour. A general guide is to give 40 mEq/hr if the serum potassium is less than 3 mEq/L, 30 mEq/hr if less than 4 mEq/L, and 20 mEq/hr if less than 5 mEq/L. The rate of administration will need to be readjusted according to serum potassium levels and urinary output as well as renal and cardiac function. Extreme caution should be exercised in patients with oliguria or anuria.

BICARBONATE

Bicarbonate administration is generally considered unnecessary if pH is higher than 7.1. Some authors do not recommend it unless the pH is less than 7.0. Clearer indications are the concomitant presence of lactic acidosis or life-threatening hyperkalemia reflected by changes in the electrocardiogram. Concerns associated with liberal use of bicarbonate include paradoxical lowering of intracellular pH by CO_2 diffusion, impaired oxygenation due to a shift in the oxygen dissociation curve, hypertonicity, sodium overload, additional risk of hypokalemia, cerebral dysfunction (19), and late alkalemia. However, if hypotension is also present, some authors recommend bicarbonate administration to all patients with a pH of 7.2 or more. Under these circumstances, the increased responsiveness of the left ventricle and the vascular system would outweigh any possible deleterious effect of alkalinization.

PHOSPHATES

Routine replacement is not universally recommended. Those in favor of replacement claim that phosphate administration prevents or minimizes muscular weakness, rhabdomyolysis, hemolytic anemia, and respiratory depression, and improves oxygen delivery to the tissues by the action of 2,3 diphosphoglycerate, which helps to shift the oxygen dissociation curve to the left. The recommended replacement is 2.5 mg of elemental phosphorus per kilogram of actual weight over a period of 6 hours. There are 90 milligrams (3 mmol) of elemental phosphorus in each milliliter of potassium phosphate (KPO_4) as well as 4 mEq of potassium. Most protocols recommend alternating potassium chloride with potassium phosphate during the course of the treatment.

COMPLICATIONS OF DKA

Maternal death from diabetic ketoacidosis is rare at present, given proper treatment. It is reported at between 0% to 10% with better outcomes in more recent reports. Mortality can result from DKA itself, a complication of the treatment, or another disease process, usually the precipitating factor. If hypotension and/or shock are present, the reason could be volume depletion and acidosis. If after adequate fluid replacement hypotension persists, sepsis or a myocardial infarction should be suspected. A silent myocardial infarction would be unusual in women of childbearing age except in those with preexisting vascular disease (e.g., longstanding diabetes, hypertension, nephropathy). Other potential complications include pulmonary edema, particularly in pregnant women receiving large quantities of fluids, adrenergic agonists for premature labor, and steroids in an effort to accelerate lung maturation. Steroids under these conditions could be very dangerous because they could markedly worsen the diabetes and even induce ketoacidosis (21,22).

Other complications include hyperlipidemia, pancreatitis, hypokalemia, hypoglycemia, hyperchloremia, hypocalcemia, renal failure, and vascular thrombosis. Cerebral edema (19,20) is a feared complication more commonly reported in children and young adults but may occur at any age. It should be suspected in patients who develop neurologic deficits or worsening of coma after an initial improvement, or if there is failure to recover neurologically despite a good biochemical response.

One of the crucial moments in the treatment of DKA occurs when the patient is ready to resume oral intake and is converted to subcutaneous insulin. If not done properly, worsening or even recurrence of the DKA may occur. Intravenous insulin disappears from the plasma quickly. Therefore, subcutaneous insulin must be injected long enough before stopping the insulin drip to ensure that there will be adequate insulin levels to prevent a setback in treatment. Before resuming oral intake, the gastrointestinal tract must have recovered. Most patients do well once the plasma CO_2 is 20 mEq/L or more, provided there are no other complicating factors (e.g., gastric dilatation or erosive gastritis).

DKA AND PREGNANCY OUTCOME

No maternal deaths have been reported in the most recent publications. While fetal deaths have also declined, fetal mortality is still significantly elevated (4–6). Reports of fetal autopsies have not shown a discernible cause of death, which suggests a metabolic derangement as the most likely cause. Several potential causes include: (a) maternal hypovolemia and catecholamine excess causing decreased uterine blood flow; (b) hyperglycemia decreases myocardial contractility in experimental animals; and (c) the maternal acidosis and electrolyte disturbances will also be directly reflected in the fetus since ketoacids cross the placenta freely. A nonreassuring fetal heart rate demonstrating late decelerations will usually resolve as maternal condition improves. Several papers have reported examples of fetal distress that subsided after successful treatment of the maternal DKA (6,23). Transient, abnormal fetal blood flow has been detected by Doppler ultrasonography (24).

We attempted to determine the differences between women who had a fetal demise and those who were successfully treated and went on to deliver a live fetus (6). In our series, 65% delivered a live fetus and 35% had a fetal demise. Those with a fetal demise had more advanced gestational age (24 vs. 31 weeks); higher glucose levels (374 vs. 830 mg/dL); higher BUN (14 vs. 23 mg/dL); and higher osmolality (295 vs. 311 mmol/kg). They also required more insulin (127 vs. 202 units) and their DKA took longer to resolve (28 vs. 38 hours). Even the values that did not reach significance tended to be worse in patients with a fetal demise, suggesting that it is more likely to occur in cases with more severe acidosis and in whom the treatment is delayed for whatever reason. If the fetus is still alive on admission, every effort should be made to start treatment promptly, since, as noted above, fetal distress may subside if the mother is properly treated. We observed no fetal losses once therapy was initiated, and there were no maternal deaths.

Despite the severity of DKA, a high index of suspicion will lead to a rapid diagnosis and timely treatment, thus ensuring the best possible outcome for both mother and fetus. Adequate preventive measures as outlined or, if necessary, prompt therapy in the early stages of the disease will further improve the outcome.

KEY POINTS

- DKA during pregnancy carries a higher mortality risk (4% to 15%) than outside of pregnancy (<2%).
- Fetal mortality remains high (10% to 35%) and there is little information about possible long-term sequelae in survivors of an acute episode except that their intellectual and behavioral development may be impaired.
- DKA is usually seen in type 1 diabetes, but it is increasingly recognized that there are some individuals who appear to have type 2 diabetes who may develop DKA in a manner similar to those with type 1 diabetes. A few cases of DKA in women with gestational diabetes have been reported as well.
- During pregnancy, DKA develops much faster than outside of pregnancy and, in addition, it may occur with only slight elevations, and even with normal levels, of serum glucose. These peculiarities may lead to misdiagnosis and to delayed or inappropriate treatment. Fetal mortality is higher in those with more severe acidosis and delays in treatment.

- Precipitating factors, clinical presentation, and laboratory and differential diagnoses are similar to DKA outside of pregnancy. Several cases of new-onset type 1 diabetes during pregnancy have been reported when the symptoms went unrecognized until the women were severely ill; those women experienced a high rate of fetal death. Awareness of the symptoms of uncontrolled diabetes may help in recognizing patients with new-onset of diabetes at a much earlier stage of their disease when treatment is more likely to be successful.
- Pregnant women with DKA should be treated early and aggressively in an intensive care unit and the fetus closely monitored as well. The therapy should be readjusted as frequently as indicated by clinical and frequent laboratory parameters. Treatment of precipitating factors, particularly infections, should be done promptly as well.
- In general, the occurrence of DKA is a sign of a breakdown of medical management. Diabetes education, including sick-day management, and easy access to a healthcare provider are extremely important. In most instances, DKA could be prevented or, if not, treated in the very early stages when the danger for mother and fetus is much lower.

REFERENCES

1. Connell FA, Louden JM. Diabetes mortality in persons under 45 years of age. *Am J Public Health* 1983;73:1174–1177.
2. Wetterhal SF, Olson DR, De Stafano F, et al. Trends in diabetes and diabetic complications. *Diabetes Care* 1992;15:960–967.
3. Gabbe SG, Mestman JH, Hibbard LT. Maternal mortality in diabetes mellitus: an 18–year survey. *Obstet Gynecol* 1976;48:549–551.
4. Cullen MT, Reece EA, Homko CJ, et al. The changing presentations of diabetic ketoacidosis during pregnancy. *Am J Perinatol* 1996;13:449–451.
5. Chauhan SP, Perry KG Jr, McLaughlin BN, et al. Diabetic ketoacidosis complicating pregnancy. *J Perinatol* 1996;16:173–175.
6. Montoro MN, Myers VP, Mestman JH, et al. Outcome of pregnancy in diabetic ketoacidosis. *Am J Perinatol* 1993;10:17–20.
7. Rodgers BD, Rodgers DE. Clinical variables associated with diabetic ketoacidosis during pregnancy. *J Reprod Med* 1991;36:797–800.
8. Kilvert JA, Nicholson HO, Wright AD. Ketoacidosis in diabetic pregnancy. *Diabet Med* 1993;10:278–281.
9. Umpierrez GE, Kelley JP, Navarrete JE, et al. Hyperglycemic crisis in urban blacks. *Arch Intern Med* 1997;157:669–675.
10. Maislos M, Harman-Bohem I, Weitzman S. Diabetic ketoacidosis: a rare complication of gestational diabetes. *Diabetes Care* 1992;15:968–970.
11. Clark JDA, Mc Connell A, Hartog M. Normoglycemic ketoacidosis in a woman with gestational diabetes. *Diabet Med* 1991;8:388–389.
12. Churchill JA, Berendes HW, Nemore J. Neuropsychological deficits in children of diabetic mothers: a report from the Collaborative Study of Cerebral Palsy. *Am J Obstet Gynecol* 1969;105:257–268.
13. Stehbens JA, Baker GL, Kitchell M. Outcome of ages 1, 3, and

5 years of children born to diabetic women. *Am J Obstet Gynecol* 1977;127:408–413.

14. Rudolf M, et al. Maternal ketosis and its effects on the fetus. *Clin Endocrinol Metab* 1983;12:413–428.

15. Rizzo T, Metzger BE, Burns WJ, et al. Correlations between antepartum maternal metabolism and intelligence of the offspring. *N Eng J Med* 1991;325:911–916.

16. Fleckman AM. Diabetic ketoacidosis. *Endocrinol Metab Clin North Am* 1993;22:181–207.

17. Sills IN, Rapaport R. New onset IDDM presenting with diabetic ketoacidosis in a pregnant adolescent. *Diabetes Care* 1994;17:904–905.

18. Katz MA. Hyperglycemia-induced hyponatremia — calculation of expected serum sodium depression. *N Engl J Med* 1973;289:843–844.

19. Glaser N, Barnett P, McCaslin I, et al. Risks factors for cerebral edema in children with diabetic ketoacidosis. *New Engl J Med* 2001;344:264–269.

20. Dunger DB, Edge JA. Predicting cerebral edema during diabetic ketoacidosis. *N Engl J Med* 2001;344:302–303.

21. Phuapradit W, Saropala N, Roungsipragarn R. Diabetic ketoacidosis in pregnancy. *J Med Assoc Thai* 1993;76:288–291.

22. Bedalov A, Balasubramanyam A. Glucocorticoid-induced ketoacidosis in gestational diabetes: Sequela of the acute treatment of preterm labor. *Diabetes Care* 1997;20:922–924.

23. O'Shaughnessy MJ, Beingesser KR, Khieu WU. Diabetic ketoacidosis in pregnancy with a recent normal screening test. *West J Med* 1999;170:115–118.

24. Takahashi Y, Kawabata I, Shinohara A, et al. Transient fetal blood flow redistribution induced by maternal ketoacidosis diagnosed by Doppler ultrasonography. *Prenat Diagn* 2000;20:524–525.

26

OBSTETRIC COMPLICATIONS IN DIABETIC PREGNANCIES

LARRY COUSINS

Pregnancy complicated by any class of diabetes is known to be associated with an increased incidence of various obstetric complications. This chapter will summarize the published experience from a recent review (1994–2003) regarding obstetric complications among diabetic pregnant women and compare them with earlier reviews from 1965 to 1985 (1) and 1986 to 1993 (2). To identify the most recent published experience with maternal morbidity among diabetic pregnancies, a PubMed computerized literature search of the English-language literature from 1994 to the present was performed. The PubMed searches were constructed similarly to those from the earlier periods. Specifically, the English-language literature was searched for *diabetes mellitus, pregnancy and maternal obstetrical complications, maternal morbidity, individual pregnancy complications* [i.e., *pregnancy-induced hypertension* (PIH), *preeclampsia, chronic hypertension, diabetic ketoacidosis, hydramnios-polyhydramnios, preterm delivery, cesarean section,* etc.], and *maternal mortality.* The bibliography of individual references found in the computerized search were reviewed for possible inclusion. Selected references from the bibliographies were also reviewed to identify articles that may not have come up in the computerized search. To be considered for inclusion in the compiled data, it was necessary for a report to meet the following criteria:

1. The article was published in English between 1994 and 2003.
2. The diabetic patients were identified according to White's classification or the National Diabetes Data Group (NDDG) classification, or were categorized as having gestational diabetes mellitus (GDM) or pregestational diabetes.
3. The reports cited a specific rate for one or more of the maternal complications of interest.

The intent of both the previous and the current literature reviews was to determine or define:

1. The incidence of the specific maternal complications.
2. Whether in the report nondiabetic comparative data (control) were provided.

3. Was there a difference in the incidence of complications either between diabetic and nondiabetic groups or between various diabetic classes?
4. If there was an increased incidence of a particular complication among diabetic patients, determine whether the published literature explained the mechanism for the increased rate of complications.
5. Whether there has been a change in the incidence of individual complications over time, that is, from the earliest to the middle to the latest review.

Differences in emphasis were noted between the reports from the more recent period and the earlier intervals. More recently, some reports now use exclusively the NDDG classification system for type 1 and type 2 diabetes rather than the White classification. There appears to be more clear-cut categorization in the latest period of hypertensive complications among diabetic pregnant women. In the current review, more specific definitions for pregnancy-induced hypertension and preeclampsia were more frequent than in the earlier reviews. In the most recent review there were many references dealing with the issues of the relationship of glycemic control to preterm delivery and to hypertensive complications. Preterm labor was not included in the current review because of the lack of usable data, as well as the recognized ambiguity of that clinical entity. In the more recent publications, investigators appear to be more attentive to differentiating between total and spontaneous preterm delivery rates. Other complications not addressed in the current review are spontaneous abortion (no or minimal data), chronic hypertension with superimposed preeclampsia (no or minimal data), and the medical complications (retinopathy, nephropathy, and neuropathy). As in the prior reviews, the published literature between 1994 and 2003 included many articles with unusable data for a variety of reasons, for example, incomplete definition of their diabetic or control cases and nonclassification of overt diabetics into the White or NDDG classes.

Chi-square analysis of the compiled data was used to test the hypothesis that the presence of an individual complication and the subject categories are independent. If $p < 0.05$,

TABLE 26-1. COMPARISONS FOR 1965–1985, 1986–1993, AND 1994–2003[a] REVIEWS OF OBSTETRIC COMPLICATIONS AMONG PREGNANCIES IN WOMEN WITH DIABETES MELLITUS

Years Searched	1965–1985	1986–1993	1994–2003
No. of "relevant" references	52	56	65
No. of references with usable data[b]	24	25	32
No. of reports with nondiabetic comparison data	8	13	18
No. of complications with diabetic and nondiabetic comparison rates	6	14	10
No. of diabetic-nondiabetic comparisons of individual complications	16	33	44
Total diabetic pregnancies	5,288	6,070	12,360
Cases of GDM/overt diabetes	1,781/3,375	2,401/3,677	6,700/4,688
Cases of White class B, C	2,126	1,055	983
Cases of White class D, F, R	960	711	1,657
Cases of White class B–R	N/A	N/A	848
Cases of NDDG type 2	N/A	N/A	545
Cases of NDDG type 1	N/A	N/A	1,627

[a]Data from current review.
[b]See text for specific computer search instructions and inclusion criteria.
N/A, not applicable.

the hypothesis that the subject categories and the complication are independent was rejected. The subject categories were gestational, White classes B and C combined, White classes D, F, and R combined, NDDG type 1 and type 2 diabetes mellitus, and nondiabetic controls. Table 26-1 summarizes the reviewed data from the current and previous series (1,2). The number of cases for the various categories of overt diabetes noted for the 1994 to 2003 reviews are mutually exclusive of each other. The noteworthy differences indicated in Table 26-1 between the earlier reviews (1,2) and the current review from 1994 to 2003 include the marked increase in the total number of diabetic pregnancies reported and the inclusion of data for NDDG type 2 and type 1 patients.

Table 26-2 summarizes the reviewed data from the earlier (1,2) and the most recent series. The diabetic categories were gestational, White classes B and C combined, and classes D, F, and R combined. The table provides the compiled number of cases and incidence rates for specific complications in the various diabetic categories.

Tables 26-3 and 26-4 summarize the studies that report specific complications among various White and NDDG classes and nondiabetic control subjects. The chi-square analysis of diabetic versus control comparison in an individual report is indicated. Where reported, the odds ratios, relative risks, and 95% confidence intervals are noted.

PREECLAMPSIA AND PREGNANCY-INDUCED HYPERTENSION

The incidence of preeclampsia and PIH among the patients categorized as having GDM or White class B-R ranged from 8.8% among the patients with GDM to 41% among those with class D or greater (Table 26-2). The pattern seen in the earlier series with the highest incidence of preeclampsia/PIH occurring in the higher White class patients was repeated in the current series. The statistical analysis of the presence of preeclampsia and PIH and diabetic categories is highly significant (Table 26-2), indicating that these hypertensive complications and the diabetic categories are not independent. In the most recent series, investigators have more consistently differentiated between preeclampsia (PIH with proteinuria) and PIH (i.e., without proteinuria) than was done in the earlier series. Attention to this detail and larger series have emphasized the relationship between an increasing incidence of preeclampsia and White diabetic class D and higher. Sibai et al. (18) observed a stepwise increase in the incidence of preeclampsia from class B (10.8%), to C (22.0%), to D (21.4%), to F-R (36.2%) ($p < 0.0001$). Overall, there was no change from GDM to class B-C. White class is not the only variable influencing the incidence of preeclampsia. Other factors that have been associated with increased incidence of preeclampsia include nulliparity, increased urinary albumin excretion, and increased hemoglobin A_{1c} (HbA_{1c}) levels (23). In the current series, five reports compared White class B and C patients to White class D-R subjects from the same institution (2,6,8,13,18). Without exception, the incidence of preeclampsia/PIH was significantly greater in White class D-R.

Preeclampsia/PIH contributes to the increased rate of preterm delivery in pregnancies complicated by diabetes. It was noted in the 1986 to 1993 (2) review that hypertensive complications were the second most common cause for nonspontaneous, medically indicated preterm delivery.

TABLE 26-2. NUMBER OF PREGNANCIES COMPLICATED BY DIABETES MELLITUS REPORTED AND INCIDENCE OF SPECIFIC COMPLICATIONS ACCORDING TO YEARS OF REVIEW AND DIABETIC CATEGORIES

Outcome	GDM		Class B and C		Class ≥ D		p^a
	No.	%	No.	%	No.	%	
PE/PIH (3–24)[b]							
1965–1985	791	10.0	729	8.0	350	15.7	<0.005
1986–1993	1,530	13.7	488	14.1	304	27.0	<0.005
1994–2003[c]	4,378	8.8	668	21.3	575	41.0	<0.005
CHT (3,4,25,26)							
1965–1985	142	9.9	411	8.0	118	16.9	<0.02
1986–1993	81	2.5	—	—	—	—	—
1994–2003	3,076	6.1	—	—	—	—	—
DKA							
1965–1985	169	0	400	8.3	282	7.1	<0.005
1986–1993	277	0.7	—	—	—	—	—
1994–2003	—	—	—	—	—	—	—
Hydramnios (13,16,27)							
1965–1985	133	5.3	199	17.6	167	18.6	<0.005
1986–1993	656	2.0	—	—	—	—	—
1994–2003	1,223	6.7	185	6.5	103	8.7	NSD
Pyelonephritis (13,22)							
1965–1985	124	4.0	356	2.2	264	4.9	NSD
1986–1993	247	1.2	—	—	—	—	—
1994–2003	149	1.3	185	2.7	103	5.2	NSD
PTD: spontaneous (13,28–30)							
1965–1985	—	—	—	—	—	—	—
1986–1996	166	14.6	118	28.0	113	24.0	<0.025
1994–2003	705	6.2	338	17.2	241	19.9	<0.001
PTD: total (6,12,14,20,26,27,31,32)							
1965–1985	—	—	—	—	—	—	—
1986–1993	717	7.3	224	19.0	205	37.6	<0.001
1994–2003	678	8.0	124	34.7	339	46.0	<0.001
C/S: primary (3,9,13,22)							
1965–1985	532	12.4	359	44.0	97	56.7	<0.005
1986–1993	255	15.1	—	—	—	—	—
1994–2003	3,484	15.4	185	26.3	103	37.8	<0.001
C/S: total (5,9,14,16,20,21,26,31,33,34)							
1965–1985	800	20.4	554	41.9	175	58.3	<0.005
1986–1993	1,155	23.4	—	—	—	—	—
1994–2003	1,481	31.1	—	—	109	76.1	<0.001
Maternal mortality (MM) ratio (pregnancy-related mortalities/100,000 live births)							
1965–1985	All diabetic women (3/2,614)		MM ratio = 115		—		—
1986–1993	All diabetic women (9/6,070)		MM ratio = 148		—		—
1994–2003	All diabetic women (5/12,360)		MM ratio = 40		—		—

[a]Chi-square analysis for independence of complication and diabetic category.
[b]References for 1994–2003 review.
[c]Current review.
—, no data; C/S, cesarean section; DKA, diabetic ketoacidosis; GDM, gestational diabetes mellitus; NSD, no significant difference; PE/PIH, preeclampsia/pregnancy-induced hypertension; PTD, preterm delivery.

Cundy and associates' (26) report supports this finding. The incidence of preterm delivery among their subjects without hypertension was 3.5%, whereas pregnancies complicated by chronic hypertension had a 10.6% preterm delivery rate and in those patients with preeclampsia without chronic hypertension, the incidence of preterm delivery was 23.1% ($p < 0.001$).

Table 26-3 lists reports with comparative rates of preeclampsia and PIH in diabetic and nondiabetic women. In the current series there were 10 studies with GDM and control data. Five of the ten studies (9,11,19,20,22) concluded that the incidence of preeclampsia/PIH was significantly greater in patients with GDM than in the control group. However the other five studies failed to find a statistically

TABLE 26-3. WITHIN-STUDY COMPARISONS OF SPECIFIC COMPLICATIONS RATES IN DIABETIC PREGNANCIES COMPLICATED BY DIABETES MELLITUS AND CONTROL PREGNANCIES

Outcome	Class	Diabetes Mellitus No.	%	Control No.	%	OR or RR 95% CI	p[a]	Investigators
PE/PIH	GDM	141/2,461	5.8	374/4,922	7.6	—	NSD	Langer et al., 1994 (3)
	GDM	10/197	5	12/197	6.2	—	NSD	Schaffir et al., 1995 (4)
	GDM	12/143	8.4	144/2,940	4.9	—	0.1	Naylor et al., 1996 (5)
	GDM	146/874	17	7,532/6,209	12	—	<0.001	Casey et al., 1997 (9)
	GDM	7/65	10.8	2/153	1.3	—	<0.01	Jang et al., 1997 (11)
	GDM	10/81	12.4	260/3,381	7.7	—	0.09	Joffe et al., 1998 (15)
	GDM	28/143	19.6	15/143	10.5	—	<0.05	Jensen et al., 2000 (20)
	GDM	16/57	21.9	1,632/21,377	7.1	—	<0.05	Roach et al., 2000 (19)
	GDM	8/149	5.3	18/298	6	—	NSD	Rizk et al., 2001 (22)
	GDM	6/218	2.8	0/108	0	—	<0.01	Vambergue et al., 2002 (24)
PE/PIH	Type 2	63/244	25.8	—	7.8	—	—	Zhu et al., 1997 (12)
		38/164	23.2	1,632/21,377	7.1	—	<0.05	Roach et al., 2000 (19)
	Type 1	52/178	29.2	—	7.8	—	—	Zhu et al., 1997 (12)
		101/491	20.6	—	5.0	—	<0.05	Hanson and Persson, 1998 (17)
		117/683	17.1	23/854	2.7	—	<0.0001	Hiilesmaa et al., 2000 (21)
	B–F, R	114/288	39.6	4/150	2.7	—	<0.003	Reece et al., 1998 (13)
		79/616	12.8	23/854	2.7	—	<0.0001	Hiilesmaa et al., 2000 (21)
	F, FR	38/67	57	23/854	2.7	—	<0.0001	Hiilesmaa et al., 2000 (21)
CHT	GDM	11/197	5.6	7/197	3.6		NSD	Schaffir et al., 1995 (4)
	GDM	146/2,461	5.9	305/4,922	6.2		NSD	Langer et al., 1994 (3)
Hydramnios	GDM	39/824	4.8	>120,000	0.7	7.23 (5.0–10.5)	<0.001	McMahon et al., 1998 (16)
	B–F, R	21/288	7.3	1/150	0.7	—	<0.05	Reece et al., 1998 (13)
Pyelonephritis	GDM	2/149	1.3	3/298	1.0	—	NSD	Rizk et al., 2001 (22)
	B–F, R	10/288	3.5	0/150	0	—	<0.05	Reece et al., 1998 (13)

[a]Chi-square analysis for independence of complication and diabetic category.
—, no data; CHT, chronic hypertension; CI, confidence interval; GDM, gestational diabetes mellitus; NSD, no significant difference; OR, odds risks; PE/PIH, preeclampsia/pregnancy-induced hypertension; RR, relative risks.

TABLE 26-4. WITHIN-STUDY COMPARISONS OF PRETERM DELIVERY AND CESAREAN DELIVERY COMPLICATION RATES IN PREGNANCIES COMPLICATED BY DIABETES MELLITUS AND CONTROL PREGNANCIES

Outcome	Class	Diabetes Mellitus No.	%	Control No.	%	OR or RR 95% CI	p[a]	Investigators
PTD: spontaneous (<37 wk)	GDM	34/555	6.2	946/14,552	6.5	—	NSD	Bar-Hava et al., 1997 (28)
	B–F, R	43/288	14.9	10/150	6.7	—	<0.05	Reece et al., 1998 (13)
	B–F, R	74/461	16.1	288/2,738	10.5	1.6 (1.2–2.2)	<0.05	Sibai et al., 2000 (29)
<35 wk	B–F, R	41/461	8.9	122/2,738	4.5	2.1 (1.4–3.0)	<0.05	Sibai et al., 2000 (29)
PTD: indicated (<35 wk)	B–F, R	101/461	21.9	92/2,738	3.4	8.1 (6–11)	<0.05	Sibai et al., 2000 (29)
	B–F, R	34/461	7.4	45/2,738	1.6	4.8 (3.0–7.5)	<0.05	Sibai et al., 2000 (29)
PTD: total	GDM	15/143	10.5	7/143	4.9	—	NSD	Jensen et al., 2000 (20)
	B–F, R	175/461	38	380/2,738	13.9	2.7 (2.3–3.2)	<0.05	Sibai et al., 2000 (29)
<35 wk	B–F, R	75/461	16.3	167/2,738	6.1	2.7 (2.1–3.4)	—	Sibai et al., 2000 (29)
C/S: primary	GDM	399/2,461	16.2	541/4,922	11	—	<0.01	Langer et al., 1994 (3)
	GDM (Multiple)	12/52	23	71/1,142	6.2	—	<0.001	Naylor et al., 1996 (5)
	GDM	117/874	13.4	4,917/61,209	8	—	<0.001	Casey et al., 1997 (9)
	GDM	22/149	14.7	21/298	7	—	<0.01	Rizk et al., 2001 (22)
	B–F, R	88/288	30.6	19/150	12.5	—	<0.05	Reece et al., 1998 (13)
C/S: repeat	GDM	18/127	14.2	183/3,123	5.9	—	<0.002	Naylor et al., 1996 (5)
	GDM	143/874	16	5,306/61,209	9	—	<0.001	Casey et al., 1997 (9)
C/S: total	GDM	48/143	33.6	585/2,940	20.2	—	<0.001	Naylor et al., 1996 (5)
	GDM	260/874	30	10,223/61,209	17	—	<0.001	Casey et al., 1997 (9)
	GDM	21/116	18.1	357/4,526	7.9	—	<0.05	Aberg et al., 2001 (34)
	GDM	47/143	32.9	30/143	21.0	—	<0.05	Jensen et al., 2000 (20)
	B–F	524/683	76.7	161/854	18.8	—	<0.0001	Hiilesmaa et al., 2000 (21)

—, no data; CHT, chronic hypertension; CI, confidence interval; C/S, cesarean section; GDM, gestational diabetes mellitus; NSD, no significant difference; OR, odds risks; PE/PIH, preeclampsia/pregnancy-induced hypertension; PTD, preterm delivery; RR, relative risks.

significantly difference in the preeclampsia/PIH rates. Closer attention to the selection of control subjects and whether the control subjects were matched to the patients with GDM for factors believed to predispose to preeclampsia/PIH (e.g., race, age, prepregnancy body mass index or weight, and parity) does not resolve the question. Schaffir (4) used controls and patients with GDM matched for race, age, parity, and prepregnancy weight and reported no significant difference between GDM and control groups. Rizk (22) matched controls and patients with GDM for age and parity, and Joffe (1998) made adjustments for race and body mass index in analyzing their results. Neither of these investigators found rate differences between groups. Langer et al. (3) did not match controls and patients with GDM, but noted that controls were younger and less obese than the patients with GDM, and therefore their pregnancies would be less likely to be complicated by preeclampsia or PIH. However, Jang (11) matched controls to patients with GDM for age and prepregnancy body mass index and found a significant difference between groups. Roach (19) performed a log regression for maternal age, parity, and body mass index and noted a significant difference between groups as well. Jensen matched controls to patients with GDM for age, parity, and prepregnancy body mass index and reported statistically significant differences between groups. Based on the available information, it appears that the question whether GDM increases the risk for preeclampsia/PIH remains to be definitively answered.

By contrast, among pregestational diabetic patients, all studies that included data from nondiabetic subjects found significantly higher rates of preeclampsia and PIH among the pregestational diabetic women, whether classified by the White system or that of the NDDG classification schema (Table 26-3). The differences between diabetic women and control subjects were remarkable, with crude calculations of relative risks among diabetic women ranging from 3 to 20.

There is increasing information linking suboptimal glycemic control in pregnancy to the development of increased blood pressure. Combs et al. (35) reported that among pregestational diabetic patients whose 12- to 16-week glycosylated hemoglobin value was greater than 9%, the adjusted odds ratio for the later development of preeclampsia was 1.4 compared with those diabetic patients with a level of 9% or less ($p < 0.05$). In the current review, a number of other reports supported the earlier findings of Combs et al. Hsu (8) followed serial glycosylated hemoglobin levels in 123 type 1 diabetic patients and found that high hemoglobin A_{1c} levels at any time in pregnancy were associated with an increased incidence of preeclampsia. They suggested that the best strategy to reduce the frequency of preeclampsia in type 1 diabetic pregnancies is improving glycemic control before gestation. In a population-based study of 491 type 1 diabetic subjects, Hanson et al. (17) reported that high hemoglobin A_{1c} in early pregnancy (median 9 weeks) was independently (of nephropa-

thy and retinopathy) and significantly ($p < 0.01$) associated with preeclampsia/PIH. They concluded that the poor glycemic control in early pregnancy was associated with an increased risk for preeclampsia in nonproteinuric type 1 diabetic pregnancies. Hiilesmaa (21) followed 683 consecutive type 1 diabetic patients. Using multiple logistic regression analysis, glycemic control (as reflected by hemoglobin A_{1c}), nulliparity, retinopathy, and duration of diabetes were statistically significant, independent predictors of preeclampsia. The adjusted odds ratios for preeclampsia were 1.6 [95% confidence interval (CI) 1.3–2.0] for each 1% increment in HbA$_{1c}$ in early gestation (median 7 weeks) and 0.6 (95% CI 0.5–0.8) for each 1% decrement achieved during the first half of pregnancy. Changes in glucose control in the second half of pregnancy did not significantly alter the risk for preeclampsia. Risk for PIH, in contrast to preeclampsia, was not associated with glycemic control. Lauszus (23) studied type 1 diabetic subjects with 24-hour ambulatory blood pressure monitoring as well as urinary albumin excretion, hemoglobin HbA$_{1c}$, and various demographic end points. Ambulatory blood pressure was significantly related to HbA$_{1c}$ levels throughout pregnancy. The investigators concluded that poor glycemic control was associated with preeclampsia. Cundy et al. (26) studied both type 1 and type 2 diabetic subjects and found that poor glucose control at presentation was a risk factor for hypertension in both groups. HbA$_{1c}$ levels of greater than 9.0% (compared with <7.0%) at presentation had a relative risk for hypertension in pregnancy of 1.92 (95% CI 1.12–3.27). Joffe (15) found that the glucose level 1 hour after a 50-g oral glucose challenge was positively correlated with the likelihood of preeclampsia in nondiabetic women ($p < 0.0001$). In conclusion, it seems clear that suboptimal glucose control during pregnancy predisposes to the new onset of hypertension in pregnancy. These more recent reports support the suggestion that improved glucose control preconceptionally may reduce the risk for hypertension developing in pregnancy.

CHRONIC HYPERTENSION

Between 1994 and 2003, three studies reported the incidence of chronic hypertension among GDM pregnancies. Rates ranged from 5.6% (4) to 7.2% (25). The largest study by Langer and associates (3) found an incidence of 5.9% for chronic hypertension among patients with GDM. Among the over 3,000 patients with GDM in the current review, the cumulative incidence of chronic hypertension was 6.1% (Table 26-2). There were no reports of the incidence of chronic hypertension among pregestational diabetics and White classes. Among 100 consecutive, singleton type 2 diabetic patients, Cundy (26) found a 15% incidence of chronic hypertension compared with a 6% incidence among 100 consecutive, singleton type 1 diabetic patients.

Langer et al. (3) noted no difference in the incidence of chronic hypertension between conventionally managed versus intensively managed patients with GDM. Likewise, they found no difference between GDM patients and controls in the incidence of chronic hypertension (Table 26-3). Of note in this study, the controls were younger and less obese than the patients with GDM. Schaffir (4) matched 197 controls for age, race, parity, and prepregnancy weight to 197 GDM subjects and reported no statistically significant difference in the incidence of chronic hypertension. Anyaegbunam (25) reported that chronic hypertensive patients with GDM were significantly older or heavier and more often underwent induction than nonhypertensive patients with GDM. In summary, it appears that there is no difference in the incidence of chronic hypertension between patients with GDM and controls if appropriate matching for age, weight, and other variables occurs.

DIABETIC KETOACIDOSIS

Historically, diabetic ketoacidosis has been one of the most significant complications in pregnancy. When it occurs, it represents not only a significant risk for morbidity and mortality for the mother, but also for the fetus. The morbidity due to ketoacidosis may have lessened during the interval of the current review as compared with earlier studies. Chauhan (36) reported on the experience at the University of Mississippi; first before and then after initiation of an aggressive management protocol among diabetic gravidas. In the preintervention period (1976–1981), 227 type 1 diabetic women manifested 51 episodes of diabetic ketoacidosis (DKA) (22%). Eighteen fetal deaths occurred (35%). In the interval following initiation of the aggressive management protocol (1986–1991), 301 type 1 diabetic patients had nine episodes of DKA (3%). One of the nine DKA episodes resulted in death of the fetus (11%). Interestingly, despite the reduction in the incidence of DKA and fetal death, the mean serum glucose and pH at presentation did not differ between the two intervals. The findings of Chauhan et al. (36) were consistent with those of Cullen (37), who reported an incidence of DKA of 2% among 520 diabetic pregnancies treated between 1985 and 1995. In the reported experience of Cullen et al. (37), 4 of the 11 patients with ketoacidosis had glucose levels of less than 200 mg/dL at presentation.

Despite the reduction in the incidence of DKA episodes among overt diabetic patients, episodes of DKA still occur that should be preventable. Precipitating causes for DKA remain infections (urinary, viral), noncompliance with recommended insulin management protocols (especially with nonadherence to recommendations during "sick days"), dietary indiscretion, β agonist and glucocorticoid use, and unsatisfactory clinical management (38). In a known pregnancy with a compliant patient receiving care, DKA is usu-

ally preventable. In most instances, prevention can be accomplished without hospitalization. Prevention of DKA among diabetic gravid women requires optimal glycemic control in the well subject, patient compliance with medical recommendations, increased attention to self blood glucose monitoring, insulin dosage adjustments when illness occurs, and early and increased frequency of communication between caregiver and patient during times of illness. If despite these steps, glycemic control significantly deteriorates, prompt hospitalization and aggressive inpatient management are indicated.

HYDRAMNIOS

Hydramnios occurs more frequently among pregnancies complicated by diabetes than among controls (Table 26-3). It appears that in the current review, the incidence of hydramnios complicating overt diabetic pregnancies decreased compared with earlier reports (1) (Table 26-2). In the recent review, two articles presented usable data. McMahon (16) reported a population-based, longitudinal study of 824 women diagnosed with GDM in Nova Scotia, Canada, between 1980 and 1993. The 4.8% incidence of hydramnios was seven times greater than that of the nondiabetic population. Reece et al. (13) described 288 pregestational diabetic pregnancies. The 7.3% incidence of hydramnios among overt diabetic patients was 10-fold higher than the incidence in the nondiabetic control group. Reece et al. (13) found no difference in the incidence of hydramnios between diabetic groups with and without microvascular disease (8.7% and 6.5%, respectively).

Hypothetical mechanisms to explain the increased incidence of hydramnios among diabetic pregnancies include (a) maternal hyperglycemia-induced fetal hyperglycemia resulting in osmotic diuresis by the fetus; (b) glucose transfer across the placenta between a hyperglycemic maternal compartment and the fetal compartment, which would then drive fluid toward the fetal compartment; (c) volume expansion and an increase in glomerular filtration leading to increased fetal urine production; and (d) an imbalance between fetal swallowing and urination. Rosenn et al. (39) found the presence of hydramnios to be significantly associated with elevated maternal glucose levels. Gycosylated hemoglobin levels were significantly higher in all trimesters among subjects with hydramnios as compared to the group without hydramnios. Bar-Hava (27) examined the association between amniotic fluid volume and recent glucose status in GDM. The investigators performed serial amniotic fluid index (AFI) measurements along with capillary blood glucose determinations in 399 patients with GDM. Patients served as their own control, and glucose assessments preceding normal and elevated AFI values were compared. They found that pregnancies with AFI-documented hydramnios (>20 cm) had significantly higher mean glucose values 1 day before (114.7 mg/dL vs. 102.8 mg/dL, p < 0.01) and 1 week before (111.0 mg/dL vs. 102.0 mg/dL, p < 0.05). In conclusion, the incidence of hydramnios is more common among diabetes-complicated pregnancies than controls, and the increase is related to maternal hyperglycemia, by mechanisms yet to be fully defined.

PYELONEPHRITIS

Despite the concern that diabetic patients have higher rates of infectious complications than nondiabetic patients, the published reports regarding pyelonephritis have been mixed (Table 26-3). Rizk (22) compared the incidence of urinary tract infections between 149 patients with GDM and 298 controls. In this comprehensive study of urinary tract infections, they found no difference between patients with GDM and controls in recurrent bacteriuria or acute cystitis. *Escherichia coli* was the most common organism producing urinary tract infections, accounting for 71% of all infections. Reece et al. (13) found a difference in the incidence of pyelonephritis between 288 pregestational diabetics and 150 controls. In contrast to earlier reports, this article reported a 3.5% rate of pyelonephritis among the diabetic women but none among the control subjects (p < 0.05). The diabetic subjects in the report of Reece et al. were categorized into those with and without microvascular disease. They found no difference in the incidence of pyelonephritis between these two diabetes subgroups. Categorizing diabetic patients into those who achieved satisfactory glucose control and unsatisfactory control, there was no difference in the incidence in pyelonephritis in these subgroups, 3.4% and 3.8%, respectively.

SPONTANEOUS PRETERM DELIVERY

The overall clinical significance of preterm delivery may be greater among diabetic patients than controls because of other associated problems, for example, hyperglycemia-induced fetal distress, delayed organ system function, risk for neonatal hypoglycemia, and hyperbilirubinemia, among others. Indicated preterm delivery is that required by the obstetric circumstances, such as severe preeclampsia or ominous fetal biophysical assessment. An increased awareness of the significance of spontaneous preterm delivery is suggested by the increased reporting of such cases in the current review (Table 26-2). The compiled data both in this review as well as in the earlier review (2) indicate that the incidence of spontaneous preterm delivery is influenced by diabetic class and is significantly more common in pregnancies complicated by pregestational diabetes than GDM. The limited information available regarding GDM suggests that the incidence of spontaneous preterm delivery is not different from that in controls. Bar-Hava (28) studied 555

intensively treated patients with GDM. The objective was to correlate glycemic control in GDM with spontaneous preterm delivery as compared with the outcomes in 14,552 control subjects. These investigators found no difference in the incidence of spontaneous preterm delivery between the total group of patients with GDM and controls (Table 26-4). They also looked at the glycemic profiles of the 34 patients with GDM who had spontaneous preterm deliveries and compared those to 68 patients with GDM delivered at term. The glycemic profiles were not significantly different between groups. Reece and associates (13) described 288 class B-R diabetic patients and compared their outcomes to 150 nondiabetic controls. They also compared the spontaneous preterm delivery rate among the diabetic patients with and without microvascular disease. The incidence of spontaneous preterm delivery in those without microvascular disease was 13.0% as compared to 18.4% in those with microvascular disease. Regarding the issue of the relationship of glycemic control to spontaneous preterm delivery rates, the data reported by Reece et al. (13) are instructive. In the pregestational diabetic group with satisfactory glucose control, the incidence of spontaneous preterm delivery was 11.4% as compared with 30.8% in those who did not achieve satisfactory glucose control (p < 0.05). Kovilam (30) examined the role of glycemic control in spontaneous preterm delivery in type 1 diabetic patients. Using logistic regression analysis, they examined the association between hemoglobin A_1 in 53 women with spontaneous preterm delivery and 200 women who delivered at term. Hemoglobin A_1 levels were higher in the spontaneous preterm group than the term group throughout pregnancy. The differences reached statistical significance in the first trimester. Their data indicated that each 1% increase in glycohemoglobin A_1 increased spontaneous preterm delivery by 37%.

The mechanism explaining an increased risk for spontaneous preterm delivery among pregestational diabetes remains to be defined. Studies relating the increased risk for spontaneous preterm delivery with increasing glycohemoglobin levels on glucose profiles must be considered. It appears that hyperglycemia from the second trimester onward may lead to activation of key steps in the initiation of parturition resulting in preterm delivery. Suboptimal glucose control or other factors among pregestational diabetic women that predispose to infection is another possible mechanism. Investigators have reported increased prostaglandin E–like material from the platelets of diabetic patients (40). Increased prostaglandin secretion resulting from poor glycemic control may increase spontaneous preterm delivery rates. If hyperglycemia enhanced susceptibility loci in the genes governing preterm delivery, this could conceivably increase a woman's risk for spontaneous preterm delivery (41). Many questions remain regarding the association of glycemic control and spontaneous preterm delivery.

PRETERM DELIVERY

Indicated

Indicated preterm delivery or delivery for maternal or fetal reasons other than spontaneous preterm labor or ruptured membranes has only recently received attention in the literature. Sibai and associates (29) reported that 21.9% of White class B-R patients delivered preterm because of maternal-fetal indications. This figure compares with a 3.4% rate among 2,738 control subjects. The odds ratio of 8.1 with a 95% confidence interval of 6 to 11 is noteworthy (Table 26-4). These results relate to preterm delivery defined as delivery at less than 37 weeks' gestation. If the criterion of delivery at less than 35 weeks was used, patients with pregestational diabetes still had a significantly greater likelihood of having an indicated preterm delivery with an odds ratio of 4.8 (Table 26-4). The most common reason for an indicated preterm delivery was preeclampsia in this group of pregestational diabetic patients.

Total

Total preterm delivery rates are significantly increased in pregestational diabetic and GDM groups (Table 26-2), as compared with control subjects (Table 26-4). This pattern is similar to the pattern seen in earlier reviews (2). Eight articles provided useful data for the current review (6,12,14,20,26,29,31,32). Of these reports, all but Jensen's (20) dealt with pregestational diabetic women. Among the articles focusing on the experience of patients with pregestational diabetes, several provided special emphasis on diabetic nephropathy (White class F). In Kimmerle's (31) report, among 150 pregestational diabetic pregnancies, there were 37 class F patients. The total preterm delivery rate (<34 weeks) among the class F group was 31%, significantly greater (*p* < 0.05) than that observed in patients without nephropathy. They noted that among the White class F patients, four deaths occurred in 4 to 10 years following their study. They did not report whether the deaths happened during or after pregnancy, nor whether they were pregnancy related. Miodovnik (6) described 182 insulin-dependent diabetic patients who delivered between 1978 and 1991, including 46 with class F diabetes. Using less than 37 weeks as the criterion for preterm delivery, the preterm delivery rate approached 57% among the class F group as compared with 25% for class B-R (*p* < 0.01). Revising the definition of preterm to less than 34 weeks, the incidence was still significantly greater among the class F patients (22%) than the class B-R patients (10%, *p* < 0.03). Furthermore, among the class F subjects, end-stage renal disease was reached in a median of 6 years following pregnancy. There were five deaths among this patient group in the follow-up period. The investigators did not define the time period during which the mortalities occurred. Zhu (12) described 482 pregestational diabetic pregnancies

(type 1, 203; type 2, 279; class B-D, 406; class R, 66; class F, 10). The total preterm delivery rate in the class RF group was 69.5%, significantly greater than the rate seen in classes B through D (30.5%, *p* < 0.0001). The investigators pointed out that in patients with nephropathy, severe preeclampsia was the primary factor contributing to adverse perinatal outcomes.

Of the reports providing total preterm delivery rates among pregestational diabetic women, only Sibai (29) reported control data. The total preterm delivery rates (<37 weeks) for their 461 class B-F diabetic patients was 38%, significantly greater than the rate of 13.9% among controls (Table 26-4). Revising the criteria for preterm delivery to less than 35 weeks, the incidence among the diabetic group was 16.3% and for controls again significantly lower at 6.1%. Ekbom (32) described 240 women with pregestational diabetes, including 11 class F patients with a 91% incidence of total preterm delivery, significantly greater than the rates in class B and C (35%) and D and R (42%) patients. This important article examined the relationship of urinary albumin excretion to maternal and perinatal outcomes. The investigators noted that urinary albumin excretion and increased HbA$_{1c}$ were independent predictors of preterm delivery. Lastly, Cundy (26) studied 100 consecutive type 2 and 100 consecutive type 1 diabetic gravidas. The preterm delivery rates (≤35 weeks) were 12% among the type 1 and 6% among the type 2 groups. The adverse effect of hypertension was emphasized. Among the type 1 patients, 10 of the 45 with hypertension delivered prematurely (22.2%), significantly greater than the preterm delivery rate (3.6%, *p* < 0.02) among the 55 type 1 patients without hypertension. The overall preterm delivery rate among the type 1 diabetic patients was significantly greater than that among type 2 subjects (*p* < 0.005).

CESAREAN DELIVERY

Primary

The likelihood of primary cesarean delivery progressively increases from GDM patients to those with pregestational diabetes. Similarly, the rate of primary cesarean delivery among pregestational diabetes patients with vascular disease is greater than that among those without vasculopathy (Table 26-2). A similar pattern was seen in an earlier review (1). Among reports with control data, in all diabetic categories studied, the incidence of primary cesarean delivery is significantly greater than that of controls (Table 26-4). Among patients with GDM, the relative risk for primary cesarean delivery compared with controls is approximately 1.5 to 3.5 (Table 26-4). Langer et al. (3), in addition to reporting a statistically significant difference between the total group of GDM and control subjects (*p* < 0.01), also found a significantly higher rate of primary cesarean delivery (19%) among conventionally treated GDM patients compared with the rate seen in intensively treated GDM patients (13%) ($p < 0.01$). Reece (13) reported a 2.5-fold higher incidence of primary cesarean delivery among a group of 288 women with pregestational diabetes (Table 26-4). When the diabetic subjects were classified into those without or with microvascular disease, the incidence of primary cesarean section was 26.3% and 37.8%, respectively.

Repeat

In the current review, two articles provided sufficient information from which to calculate repeat cesarean delivery rates (5,9). In the prospective study of Naylor et al. (5), 18 of 127 GDM patients (by NDDG criteria) were delivered by repeat cesarean delivery (14.2%). Among the patients with a negative 1-hour glucose screen and those with a positive 1-hour glucose screen but a negative glucose tolerance test result, 5.9% had a repeat cesarean delivery. Casey et al. (9) compared the incidence of repeat cesarean delivery in 874 patients with GDM to a large control group. The incidence of repeat cesarean delivery among patients with GDM was 13.4% as compared with the control rate of 9% ($p < 0.001$).

Total

Total cesarean delivery rates were dramatically higher in the compiled data among patients within White classes D, F, and R than among patients with GDM (Table 26-2). No studies defined pregestational diabetes sufficiently to have a rate for White classes B and C. Of the articles that compared diabetic groups to nondiabetic controls (5,9,20,21, 34), all but Hiilesmaa (21) dealt with GDM subjects. Hiilesmaa (21) reported a total cesarean delivery rate of 76.7% among White classes B through F. In part, Hiilesmaa's extraordinarily high total cesarean delivery rate is explained by the investigators' practice of "always doing elective cesarean sections in White's class D and higher." Among the GDM groups, the total cesarean delivery rates ranged from 18.1% (34) to 33.6% (5). Crude estimates of relative risks of total cesarean delivery in the patients with GDM ranged from 1.5 to 2.3.

The analysis by Naylor et al. (5) of cesarean delivery rates and the factors influencing those rates is informative. These investigators performed a prospective cohort study in which all subjects had a 1-hour glucose screening test as well as a 3-hour 100-g oral glucose tolerance test at 28 weeks' gestation. Of the 3,778 patients tested, 143 met NDDG criteria for GDM. These women received the usual care for GDM (diet, monitoring, etc.). Physicians were blinded to glucose test results for all others, including 115 untreated women with "borderline" GDM by the Carpenter and Coustan criteria. These investigators found no difference in the indications for cesarean delivery across the four glucose tolerance categories (negative 1-hour glucose screen; positive 1-hour glucose screen/negative glucose tolerance test result; positive glucose tolerance test result by Carpenter and Coustan criteria; positive glucose tolerance test result by NDDG criteria). There were no differences across the glucose tolerance categories and the proportions of women with breech presentation, dystocia, or fetal distress. However, significantly more women with GDM had undergone a previous cesarean delivery (8.4%, 8.7%, 14.0%, and 17.3%, respectively; $p = 0.002$). The subjects with recognized GDM had a lower rate of vaginal births after a prior cesarean delivery (18%) compared to the women with normal oral glucose tolerance ($p > 0.2$). Among multiparous women with GDM, the primary cesarean delivery rate was 23% compared to 6.2% for women with normal oral glucose tolerance test results ($p < 0.001$) (Table 26-4). Interestingly, Naylor et al. (5) found that among patients with GDM receiving usual care, there is a marked reduction in macrosomia compared with untreated subjects with borderline GDM. Women known to have GDM had persistently high cesarean delivery rates regardless of whether normal fetal weight was achieved. Among patients with borderline GDM, the cesarean delivery rate was high in the presence of macrosomia (45.5%) but was similar to that of the control subjects (23.5%) when the infant weighed 4,000 g or less. Multivariate modeling including maternal age, race, parity, body mass index, history of preeclampsia, current preeclampsia, gestational age, and previous cesarean delivery did not eliminate the increased cesarean delivery rate seen in GDM (by NDDG criteria). In summary, this sophisticated analysis is consistent with the hypothesis that recognition of the diagnosis of GDM influences clinical practice toward cesarean delivery. These findings are consistent with the suggestions of Goldman et al. (42) and Suhonen and Teramo (43), investigators who earlier reported that cesarean delivery rates among patients with GDM are higher than among controls despite the absence of differences between the groups in macrosomia rates, the incidence of large-for-gestational-age infants, or labor abnormalities.

It is suggested that in the absence of other complications (Table 26-5), pregnancies complicated by GDM should be

TABLE 26-5. FACTORS INFLUENCING THE TIMING OF DELIVERY OF PREGNANCIES COMPLICATED BY DIABETES MELLITUS

Suboptimal glycemic control
Maternal hypertension
Macrosomia
Decreased fetal activity
Suspicious fetal biophysical test
Poor maternal compliance
Maternal vascular disease
Hydramnios
Poor obstetric history
Prior intrauterine demise

followed expectantly. The elements of a coordinated management plan should include (a) meticulous glucose control (mean fasting capillary or blood glucose level of ≤95 mg/dL and mean 1-hour postprandial capillary glucose level of ≤130 mg/dL; (b) daily fetal movement counts from 28 weeks' gestation; (c) late pregnancy (38 weeks) ultrasonography for estimated fetal weight, amniotic fluid index; and (d) anthropometric assessment and antenatal testing if the patient is undelivered at 40 weeks' gestation (44).

In the absence of superimposed complications (Table 26-5), this expectant management approach is also advocated for patients with pregestational diabetes as well. Routine preterm delivery is not appropriate. The avoidance of early delivery, coupled with meticulous attention to maternal and fetal status, is safe and allows the fetus and labor mechanism to mature and the inducibility of the cervix to improve. The presence of one or more of the risk factors listed in Table 26-5 may require preterm delivery. However, in the absence of such risk factors, the major concerns regarding the management approach outlined above include concern about fetal demise and macrosomia with increased risk for shoulder dystocia. The former is minimized by establishment of euglycemia, monitoring the pregnancy for maternal and fetal complications, and antenatal assessment. Risk for shoulder dystocia may be minimized by careful evaluation of mother and fetus. Late pregnancy ultrasonography at 38 weeks allows for an estimate of fetal weight and assessment of head/body proportions. This ultrasound information, maternal physical examination, maternal past obstetric history, and then judicious intrapartum management will prevent the vast majority of intrapartum complications. A suspicion of macrosomia (based on fundal height measurement, Leopold's assessment, or late pregnancy ultrasonography) or fetal head/trunk disproportion, especially when coupled with any dysfunctional labor pattern, warns the obstetrician against injudicious use of forceps or vacuum extraction.

PREDELIVERY HOSPITALIZATION DAYS

Outpatient evaluation and management of pregnancies complicated by diabetes is currently the standard (44). In most instances, hospitalization is unnecessary as long as the patient is involved in a comprehensive patient evaluation care program, and is motivated, compliant, and does not develop superimposed maternal or fetal complications (Table 26-5). In the current review, no reports were found with the data reporting predelivery hospitalization days. In the review covering 1986 to 1993, Gregory (45) and Nagy (46) reported a reduction in predelivery hospitalization days for subjects with pregestational diabetes and GDM. Gregory (45) explained the reduction by an increased experience in outpatient management by the diabetes team and the introduction of outpatient fetal biophysical assessment.

Anecdotally, I would point out that, should there be reduced availability of a perinatal team experienced in outpatient care, a general reduction in the resources available to medically disadvantaged patients, and consequently more frequent semiemergent or emergent diabetic patient referrals, an increase in hospitalization for patient education, evaluation, and care will be inevitable.

MATERNAL MORTALITY

In the current review, there was a single report with information on maternal mortality. Leinonen et al. (47) reported on five pregnancy-related deaths among 972 women with type 1 diabetes (1975–1997) in Finland. Three of the five had no vascular complications other than retinal microaneurysms. Two of the five had diabetic nephropathy. Deaths were attributed to a high spinal anesthesia (one case), brainstem infarction after a cesarean delivery (one case), hypoglycemia (two cases), and ketoacidosis and intoxication (one case). All the deaths occurred during or within 42 days of pregnancy. The two hypoglycemia-precipitated deaths occurred in early pregnancy (14 weeks 5 days and 10 weeks 1 day), prompting the investigators to emphasize the importance of focusing on hypoglycemia during early pregnancy.

Kimmerle (31) and Miodovnik (6) commented on four and five deaths, respectively, among their pregestational diabetic subjects. In neither report was the time of the death defined nor did they indicate whether the death was pregnancy related. It is unclear whether these deaths would qualify as maternal deaths, defined as death resulting from obstetric complications in pregnancy, labor, or the puerperium, and from interventions, omissions, incorrect treatment, or a chain of events resulting from any of these factors (48).

The maternal mortality ratio (i.e., the number of maternal deaths that result from the reproductive process per 100,000 live births) was 8.5 in the United States in 1994 (48).

As shown in Table 26-2, the calculated maternal mortality ratio in the current review was less than in the earlier review but still dramatically higher than in the general population (2).

KEY POINTS

- Hypertensive complications (preeclampsia, PIH, chronic hypertension) are more common in pregestational diabetic patients than nondiabetic women.
- There is increasing information linking elevated glucose levels to the development of hypertensive complications.
- The incidence of episodes of diabetic ketoacidosis and the perinatal morbidity/mortality risks per episode may be decreased with aggressive medical management.

- Hydramnios remains significantly more common among all classes of diabetic patients than control subjects. The mechanism explaining this increased incidence of hydramnios among diabetic patients is related to maternal hyperglycemia, although the details of that mechanism remain to be defined.

- Spontaneous preterm delivery, to be differentiated from indicated preterm delivery, is more common in pregestational diabetic patients than among GDM and nondiabetic women. A mechanism explaining the increased risk for spontaneous preterm delivery in these patients remains to be defined.

- Indicated preterm delivery, frequently due to preeclampsia, is significantly more common in women with pregestational diabetes.

- Rates for primary cesarean delivery are not independent of diabetic class.

- The risk for maternal mortality in pregnancies complicated by diabetes is many times that of the general obstetric population.

ACKNOWLEDGMENT

I gratefully acknowledge the assistance of Barbara Blackman in the preparation of the manuscript.

References

1. Cousins LM. Pregnancy complications among diabetic women: review 1965–1985. *Obstet Gynecol Surv* 1987;42:140–147.
2. Cousins LM. In: Reece EA, Coustan DR, eds. *Obstetric complications in diabetes mellitus in pregnancy.* New York: Churchill Livingstone, 1995.
3. Langer O, Rodriguez DA, Xenakis EMJ, et al. Intensified versus conventional management of gestational diabetes. *Am J Obstet Gynecol* 1994;170;1036–1047.
4. Schaffir JA, Lockwood CJ, Lapinski R, et al. Incidence of pregnancy-induced hypertension among gestational diabetics. *Am J Perinatol* 1995;12:252–254.
5. Naylor CB, Sermer M, Chen E, et al. For the Toronto Tri-Hospital Gestational Diabetes Investigators. Cesarean delivery in relation to birth weight in gestational glucose intolerance. Pathophysiology or practice style? *JAMA* 1996;275:1165–1170.
6. Miodovnik M, Rosenn BM, Khoury JC, et al. Does pregnancy increase the risk of poor development and progression of diabetic nephropathy? *Am J Obstet Gynecol* 1996;174:1180–1191.
7. Gordon M, Landon MV, Samuels P, et al. Perinatal outcome in long-term follow-up associated with modern management of diabetic nephropathy. *Obstet Gynecol* 1996;87:401–409.
8. Hsu CD, Tan HY, Hong SF, et al. Strategies for reducing the frequency of preeclampsia in pregnancies with insulin-dependent diabetes mellitus. *Am J Perinatol* 1996;13:265–268.
9. Casey BM, Lucas MJ, McIntire DD, et al. Pregnancy outcomes in women with gestational diabetes compared with the general obstetric population. *Obstet Gynecol* 1997;90:869–873.
10. Ekbom P. Copenhagen Pre-eclampsia in Diabetic Pregnancy Study Group. Pre-pregnancy microalbuminuria predicts pre-eclampsia in insulin-dependent diabetes mellitus. *Lancet* 1999; 353:377.
11. Jang HC, Cho NH, Min YK, et al. Increased macrosomia and perinatal morbidity independent of obesity in advanced age in Korean women with GDM. *Diabetes Care* 1997;20:1582–1588.
12. Zhu L, Nakadayashi M, Takeda Y. Statistical analysis of perinatal outcomes in pregnancy complicated by diabetes mellitus. *J Obstet Gynecol Res* 1997;23:555–563.
13. Reece EA, Sivan E, Francis G, et al. Pregnancy outcomes among women with and without microvascular disease (White's classes B to FR) versus non-diabetic controls. *Am J Perinatol* 1998;15: 549–555.
14. Reece EA, Leguizamon G, Homko C. Stringent controls in diabetic nephropathy associated with optimization of pregnancy outcomes. *J Matern Fetal Med* 1998;7:213–216.
15. Joffe GM, Esterlitz JR, Levine RJ, et al. The relationship between abnormal glucose tolerance and hypertensive disorders of pregnancy in healthy nulliparous women. *Am J Obstet Gynecol* 1998; 179:1032–1037.
16. McMahon MG, Ananth CV, Liston RM. Gestational diabetes mellitus. Risk factors, obstetrical complications and infant outcomes. *J Reprod Med* 1998;43:372–378.
17. Hanson U, Persson B. Epidemiology of pregnancy-induced hypertension in preeclampsia in type 1 (insulin-dependent). *Acta Obstet Gynecol Scand* 1998;77:620–624.
18. Sibai BM, Caritis S, Hauth J, et al. Risks of preeclampsia and adverse neonatal outcomes among women with pre-gestational diabetes mellitus. *Am J Obstet Gynecol* 2000;182:364–369.
19. Roach BJ, Hin LY, Tam WH, et al. The incidence of pregnancy-induced hypertension among patients with carbohydrate intolerance. *Hypertens Pregnancy* 2000;19:183–189.
20. Jensen DM, Sorensen B, Feilberg-Jorgensen N, et al. Maternal and perinatal outcomes in 143 Danish women with gestational diabetes and 143 controlled with a similar risk profile. *Diabet Med* 2000;17:281–286.
21. Hiilesmaa V, Suhonen L, Teramo K. Glycemic control is associated with preeclampsia but not with pregnancy-induced hypertension in women with type 1 diabetes mellitus. *Diabetologia* 2000;43:1534–1539.
22. Rizk DE, Mustafa N, Thomas L. The prevalence of urinary tract infections in patients with gestational diabetes mellitus. *Int Urogynecol J Pelvic Floor Dysfunc* 2001;12:317–321.
23. Lauszus FF, Rasmussen OW, Lousen T, et al. Ambulatory blood pressures predictor of preeclampsia in diabetic pregnancies with respect to urinary albumin excretion rate and glycemic regulation. *Acta Obstet Gynecol Scand* 2001;80:1096–1103.
24. Vambergue A, Nuttens C, Goeusse P, et al. Pregnancy induced hypertension in women with gestational carbohydrate intolerance: the Diagest Study. *Eur J Obstet Gynecol Reprod Biol* 2002;102:31–35.
25. Anyaegbunam AM, Scarpelli S, Mikhail MS. Chronic hypertension in gestational diabetes: influence on pregnancy outcome. *Gynecol Obstet Invest* 1995;39:167–170.
26. Cundy T, Slee F, Gamble G, et al. Hypertensive disorders in pregnancy in women with type 1 and type 2 diabetes. *Diabet Med* 2002;19:482–489.
27. Bar-Hava I, Scarpelli SA, Barnhard Y, et al. Amniotic food volume reflects recent glycemic status in gestational diabetes mellitus. *Am J Obstet Gynecol* 1994;171:952–955.
28. Bar-Hava I, Barnhard Y, Scarpelli SA, et al. Gestational diabetes in pre-term labor: is glycemic control a contributing factor? *Eur J Obstet Gynecol Reprod Biol* 1997;73:111–114.
29. Sibai BM, Caritis FM, Hauth JC, et al. Preterm delivery in women with pre-gestational diabetes mellitus or chronic hypertension relative to women with uncomplicated pregnancies. The National Institute of Child Health & Human Development, Maternal-Fetal Medical Units Networks. *Am J Obstet Gynecol* 2000;183:1520–1524.

30. Kovilam O, Khoury J, Miodovnik M, et al. Spontaneous preterm delivery in type 1 diabetic pregnancy: the role of glycemic control. *J Matern Fetal Med* 2002;11:245–248.

31. Kimmerle R, Zass RP, Cupisti S, et al. Pregnancies in women with diabetic nephropathy: long-term outcome for mother and child. *Diabetologia* 1995;38:227–235.

32. Ekbom P, Damm P, Feldt-Rasmussen B, et al. Pregnancy outcome in type 1 diabetic women with microalbuminuria. *Diabetes Care* 2001;24:1739–1744.

33. Dunne FP, Brydon PA, Proffitt M, et al. Fetal and maternal outcomes in Indo-Asian compared to Caucasian women with diabetes in pregnancy. *Q J Med* 2002;93:813–818.

34. Aberg A, Rydhstroem H, Frid A. Impaired glucose tolerance associated with adverse pregnancy outcome: a population-based study in southern Sweden. *Am J Obstet Gynecol* 2001;184:77–83.

35. Combs CA, Rosenn B, Kitzmiller JL, et al. Early pregnancy proteinuria in diabetes related to pre-eclampsia. *Obstet Gynecol* 1993;82:802–807.

36. Chauhan SP, Perry KG, McLaughlin BN, et al. Diabetic ketoacidosis complicating pregnancy. *J Perinatol* 1996;16:173–175.

37. Cullen MT, Reece EA, Homko CJ, et al. The changing presentations of diabetic ketoacidosis during pregnancy. *Am J Perinatol* 1996;13:449–451.

38. Rodgers BD, Rodgers DE. Clinical variables associated with diabetic ketoacidosis during pregnancy. *J Reprod Med* 1991;36:797–800.

39. Rosenn B, Miodovnik M, Combs CA, et al. Poor glycemic control and antepartum obstetric complications in women with insulin-dependent diabetes. *Int J Gynecol Obstet* 1993;43:21–28.

40. Halushka PV, Lurie D, Colwell JA. Increased synthesis of prostaglandin E like material by platelets from patients with diabetes mellitus. *N Engl J Med* 1977;297:1306–1310.

41. Hoffman JD, Ward K. Genetic factors in preterm delivery. *Obstet Gynecol Surv* 1999;54:203–210.

42. Goldman M, Kitzmiller JL, Abrams B, et al. Obstetrics complications with GDM. Effects of maternal weight. *Diabetes* 1991;40(suppl 2):79–82.

43. Suhonen L, Teramo K. Hypertension in preeclampsia in women with gestational glucose intolerance. *Acta Obstet Gynecol Scand* 1993;72:269–272.

44. Guidelines for Care. Sweet Success, California Diabetes and Pregnancy Program. Department of Health Services, Maternal and Child Health Branch. State of California, 1998.

45. Gregory R, Scott AR, Mohajer M, et al. Diabetic pregnancy 1977–1990: have we reached a plateau? *J Coll Physicians Lond* 1992;26:162–166.

46. Nagy G. Management of gestational diabetes. *Zentralbl Gynakol* 1993;115:147–153.

47. Leinonen PJ, Hiilesmaa VK, Kaaja RJ, et al. Maternal mortality in type 1 diabetes. *Diabetes Care* 2001;24:1501–1502.

48. Cunningham FG, MacDonald PC, Grant NF, et al., eds. *Williams obstetrics,* 20th ed. Stamford, CT: Appleton & Lange, 1997.

27

HYPERTENSIVE DISORDERS IN PREGNANCY

ANDREA C. HINTON
BAHA M. SIBAI

DEFINITIONS AND DIAGNOSIS OF HYPERTENSIVE DISORDERS IN PREGNANCY

Hypertensive disorders are the most common medical complication in pregnancy. Hypertension affects 5% to 10% of all pregnancies (1,2). Hypertensive disorders in pregnancy include chronic hypertension, gestational hypertension, and preeclampsia. Review of the literature reveals that 70% of hypertensive disorders in pregnancy are due to gestational hypertension, whereas the other 30% are due to chronic hypertension (1). Hypertensive complications in pregnancy can range from mild elevations of blood pressure to severe hypertension with multiorgan failure. Hypertension is defined as a systolic blood pressure of at least 140 mm Hg, or a diastolic blood pressure of at least 90 mm Hg. These values must be present on two separate occasions approximately 6 hours apart. Both chronic hypertension and gestational hypertension can be diagnosed using these criteria. In women with chronic hypertension, the blood pressure elevations should occur prior to pregnancy or before 20 weeks' gestation. Women with chronic hypertension are more likely to develop superimposed preeclampsia during their antepartum course.

Superimposed preeclampsia is defined as an exacerbation of hypertension with the new development of proteinuria. Gestational hypertension, on the other hand, is the elevation of blood pressure during the second half of pregnancy, or in the first 24 hours postpartum (2). This can occur without proteinuria and without symptoms. Generally, normalization of blood pressure will occur during the postpartum period, usually within 10 days. Treatment is not warranted in most cases, although 40% of women with preterm gestational hypertension can progress to preeclampsia. In addition, women with gestational hypertension are at increased risk to develop elevated blood pressures in subsequent pregnancies. These women are also at increased risk for developing essential hypertension later in life.

Preeclampsia is a systemic disease that can manifest in multiple organ systems. The classic triad of hypertension, proteinuria, and symptoms defines it. These symptoms include headaches, visual disturbances, epigastric pain or right upper quadrant pain, and shortness of breath or tightness behind the sternum. In some women, it might be associated with organ dysfunction (3). Multiple risk factors have been identified in the development of preeclampsia. These include nulliparity, thrombophilia, and obesity, a prior pregnancy complicated by preeclampsia, and pregestational diabetes (3–5) (Table 27-1). Gestational hypertension and preeclampsia can be further subdivided into mild and severe. The distinction between mild and severe is based on the degree of hypertension, the severity of proteinuria, and the involvement of other organ systems. The onset of persistent symptoms such as headache, visual changes, right upper quadrant pain, abdominal pain, nausea or vomiting, and shortness of breath will make the diagnosis severe irrespective of other findings. The criteria for mild and severe hypertension and preeclampsia are presented in Table 27-2.

HYPERTENSION AND DIABETES MELLITUS

The prevalence of hypertension in the diabetic population is approximately 1.5 to 3 times higher than that in the general population (4). Hypertension complicates the management of a diabetic patient in 20% to 60% of cases. In fact, cardio-

TABLE 27-1. RISK FACTORS FOR PREECLAMPSIA

Nulliparity
Pregestational Diabetes
Thrombophilia
Molar pregnancy
Fetal hydrops
Multifetal gestation
Chronic hypertension/renal disease
Obesity
Prior preeclampsia
Family history of preeclampsia

TABLE 27-2. CLASSIFICATION OF HYPERTENSIVE DISORDERS IN PREGNANCY

Diagnosis	Systolic BP (mm Hg)	Diastolic BP (mm Hg)	Symptoms	Laboratory Findings
Mild gestational hypertension	140–159	90–109	No	Normal
Severe gestational hypertension	≥160	≥110	±	Normal or abnormal
Mild preeclampsia	140–159	90–109	±	Proteinuria ≥300 mg/24 h
Severe preeclampsia	≥160	≥110	Yes	Proteinuria ≥5 g/24 h
				Thrombocytopenia
				Oliguria
				Pulmonary edema

BP, blood pressure.

vascular disease is the leading cause of mortality in diabetes, responsible for approximately 86% of all deaths (6). The development of hypertension differs between type 1 and type 2 diabetes. In type 1 diabetes, hypertension may be noted several years after the initial diagnosis of diabetes. The onset of hypertension in this group may signal the onset of diabetic nephropathy, ultimately affecting 30% of this population (6). In type 2 diabetes, the patients tend to be older and more obese, with hypertension often present at the time of diagnosis (7). In some cases of type 2 diabetes, the presence of nephropathy may be the first sign of hypertension (6).

Women with diabetes and hypertension have a greatly increased risk for cardiovascular events, renal insufficiency, and diabetic retinopathy. Most studies in the literature assess complications from hypertension and diabetes separately, looking at only a subset of patients that have both disease processes. In general, it is well known that there is an increased risk for cardiovascular disease with chronic hypertension. It has also been noted that, if the systolic or diastolic blood pressure increases approximately 5 mm Hg above the normal range, the resulting increase in cardiovascular disease is about 20% to 30% (8). In the diabetic population, diabetic retinopathy is noted to progress more rapidly with a diastolic blood pressure greater than 70 mm Hg (9).

In 2003, the Joint National Committee on Prevention, Detection, Evaluation, and Treatment of High Blood Pressure revised recommendations concerning the management of hypertension in the general population. The committee also recommended a target blood pressure in diabetic patients of less than 130 mm Hg systolic and less than 80 mm Hg diastolic (10). Although the standard definition of hypertension is 140/90 mm Hg, it is apparent from the multiple studies including diabetic patients that this cut-off value is too high.

HYPERTENSION IN THE DIABETIC PREGNANT WOMAN

Preeclampsia is a complication that can be seen in approximately 10% to 20% of diabetic pregnancies (11–13). This is of concern due to the increased perinatal mortality and morbidity associated with the onset of preeclampsia in such women. The risk factors for preeclampsia in women with diabetes include duration of pregestational diabetes, concurrent chronic hypertension, poor glycemic control prior to 20 weeks' gestation, nulliparity, the presence of microalbuminuria, and the presence of nephropathy (3,14) (Table 27-3).

DIAGNOSIS OF PREECLAMPSIA IN WOMEN WITH PREGESTATIONAL DIABETES

The diagnosis of preeclampsia can be difficult to make in the diabetic patient due to preexisting hypertension and proteinuria. Preeclampsia in the pregestational diabetic who is normotensive and nonproteinuric can be diagnosed by the onset of blood pressure elevations greater than 140/90 mm Hg associated with proteinuria of at least 300 mg per 24 hours or thrombocytopenia (platelet count <100,000). In diabetic women with hypertension but without baseline proteinuria, preeclampsia is diagnosed when there is new onset of proteinuria (>300 mg/24 hours). If the patient has no hypertension, but proteinuria early in pregnancy, preeclampsia is evidenced by the onset of hypertension or thrombocytopenia. In those diabetic patients with both proteinuria and hypertension prior to pregnancy or at less than 20 weeks' gestation, the presence of preeclampsia can be determined by new onset of thrombocytopenia, a severe exacerbation of hypertension with exacerbation of proteinuria, or symptoms (15) (Table 27-4).

TABLE 27-3. RISK FACTORS FOR PREECLAMPSIA IN WOMEN WITH TYPE 1 DIABETES

Duration of diabetes
Chronic hypertension
Microalbuminuria prior to pregnancy
Glycemic control prior to pregnancy
Nulliparity
Minimal proteinuria (190–499 mg/day) before 20 wk
Nephropathy

TABLE 27-4. RATE OF PREECLAMPSIA IN WOMEN WITH TYPE 1 DIABETES (EXCLUDING NEPHROPATHY)

Investigators	Number of Women	White's Classification	Number with Preeclampsia	Percent with Preeclampsia
Garner et al. (9)	107	B, C	13	12.2
Greene et al. (11)	361	B-R	86	23.8[a]
Hanson and Persson (21)	463	B-R	53	11.5
Miodovnik et al. (25)	136	B-R	12	9.0
Kovilam et al. (26)	238	B-D	36	15
Sibai et al. (12)	404	B-D	71	17.3
Total	**1,709**		**271**	**15.9**

[a]Includes women with pregnancy-induced hypertension.

ROLE OF INSULIN RESISTANCE AND HYPERTENSIVE DISORDERS OF PREGNANCY

Insulin resistance is a normal physiologic change in pregnancy. This phenomenon is not well understood, but is noted to increase significantly in the third trimester. It has been suggested that both gestational hypertension and pre-eclampsia are associated with a greater degree of insulin resistance (16,17). Insulin resistance may affect blood pressure through sympathetic nervous system activation, sodium retention, or endothelial dysfunction. Increased insulin resistance is noted in the third trimester, a time when gestational hypertension and preeclampsia are noted to occur (16,17). Several studies have shown that the rate of gestational hypertension and preeclampsia are increased in women with gestational diabetes; however, this remains controversial since it has not been observed in all studies (18).

Joffe et al. (19) analyzed the relationship of hyperinsulinemia and hypertensive disorders in pregnancy in 3,689 women. In this population, women with abnormal glucose tolerance were found to have increased rates of both gestational hypertension and preeclampsia. From these results, it appears that insulin resistance may play a role in the patho-

physiology of hypertensive disorders in pregnancy. These findings were confirmed by Vambergue et al. (20), who analyzed data from 218 women with gestational diabetes, 130 with glucose intolerance/one abnormal value on the 3-hour glucose challenge, and 108 controls. The women with gestational diabetes were noted to have an increased rate of gestational hypertension. Among women with gestational diabetes, 14.2% developed gestational hypertension and 2.8% developed preeclampsia. On the other hand, in women with glucose intolerance, 10.8% had gestational hypertension, but no cases of preeclampsia were noted. These data suggest that gestational diabetes is an independent risk factor for gestational hypertension and preeclampsia.

Women with pregestational diabetes are also at increased risk for developing hypertensive disorders during their pregnancy. The reported rate of hypertensive disorders in diabetic women ranges from 9% to 66% (3) in the literature. In general, the incidence of preeclampsia is noted to be associated with diabetes severity (Table 27-5). Several different types of hypertension have been noted to occur more frequently in diabetic pregnancies. Cundy et al. (7) found an increased incidence of all hypertensive disorders of pregnancy in both type 1 and type 2 diabetes. The incidence of hypertensive disorders was similar between type 1 and type

TABLE 27-5. RATE OF PREECLAMPSIA IN WOMEN WITH DIABETIC NEPHROPATHY

Investigators	No. of Women	No. with Preeclampsia	% with Preeclampsia
Hanson and Persson (21)	31	18	58
Greene et al. (11)	59	39	66
Reece et al. (27)	31	11	35
Gordon et al. (28)	45	24	53
Miodovnik et al. (25)	46	30	65
Kovilam et al. (26)	73[a]	32	44
Sibai et al. (12)	48	17	36
Total	333	171	51

[a]Includes women with class R/F diabetes.

2 diabetes, but they differed in terms of the type of hypertension that developed. Women with type 1 diabetes were noted to develop preeclampsia more frequently than those with type 2 diabetes, whereas women with type 2 diabetes had a higher rate of chronic hypertension.

Siddiqi et al. (12) evaluated the rate of gestational hypertension and preeclampsia in 175 women with insulin-dependent diabetes: 88 patients were class B or C, and 87 patients were classes D through RF. These women were followed from approximately 9 weeks' gestation until delivery. The overall rate of gestational hypertension was 15.4%. In patients with class B or C diabetes, the rate of gestational hypertension was 9%, whereas in classes D through RT the rate was 22%. Women who developed gestational hypertension were noted to have higher serum creatinine levels and higher urinary protein excretion than those women who did not develop gestational hypertension. Interestingly, the creatinine clearance did not differ significantly between these two groups. The investigators also noted that patients who developed gestational hypertension had significantly higher preprandial blood glucose levels in the first trimester than the group without gestational hypertension. The glycohemoglobin levels were also noted to be significantly elevated between 14 and 20 weeks' gestation in the group with gestational hypertension as compared to those without gestational hypertension. The investigators concluded that poor glycemic control and advanced diabetic classification are both independent risk factors for the development of gestational hypertension and preeclampsia.

Rudge et al. (21) evaluated the frequency and the type of hypertensive disorders in 168 pregnant women with diabetes: 54% of the cases were complicated by chronic hypertension, 30% developed gestational hypertension, and 8% developed preeclampsia.

The type of hypertensive disorder was associated with the White classification. Women with gestational diabetes were more likely to have chronic hypertension, whereas those with classes B and C diabetes were more likely to develop gestational hypertension. Preeclampsia was more likely to develop in those with vascular abnormalities (classes D through RT). Table 27-5 summarizes the rate of preeclampsia in women with type 1 diabetes without nephropathy (3).

PREECLAMPSIA IN WOMEN WITH INCIPIENT NEPHROPATHY

The diagnosis of preeclampsia can be difficult to make in women with diabetes and preexisting proteinuria. Microalbuminuria is defined as urinary albumin excretion of 30 to 300 mg/day. The presence of microalbuminuria, an early sign of diabetic vascular disease, places the patient at risk for progression to overt diabetic nephropathy (22). Microalbuminuria is associated with elevations in blood pressure due to ongoing vascular disease. It has been shown that women with

microalbuminuria are at an increased risk for developing preeclampsia. Ekbom and associates (23) studied 203 women with pregestational diabetes: 85% had normal urinary albumin excretion, 11% had microalbuminuria, and 5% had diabetic nephropathy. The rate of preeclampsia was significantly increased in those with microalbuminuria and in those with diabetic nephropathy. Microalbuminuria was noted to increase to the nephrotic range in many of these women.

Multiple studies have demonstrated that diabetic nephropathy is a major risk factor for preeclampsia. Nephropathy is defined as either persistent dipstick-positive proteinuria, urinary albumin excretion greater than 300 mg/day, or total urinary protein excretion of more than 500 mg/day. Combs et al. (22) evaluated the rate of preeclampsia in women with pregestational diabetes. Women with early pregnancy proteinuria of 190 to 499 mg/day were found to have an increased rate of preeclampsia when compared to women with less than 190 mg of protein per day. The rate of superimposed preeclampsia was not found to be significantly different when comparing those women with existing proteinuria of less than 500 mg/day and those with overt nephropathy of greater than 500 mg of protein per day. The incidence of gestational hypertension was also noted to increase dramatically in the group with 190 to 499 mg of protein per day. Using multivariate analysis, the investigators found that nulliparity, proteinuria greater than 190 mg/day, and an elevated glycohemoglobin level increased the risk for developing preeclampsia. The investigators also suggested that women with baseline proteinuria of 190 mg/day may have incipient diabetic nephropathy. The rate of preeclampsia in women with diabetic nephropathy varies from 35% to 66% (3) (Table 27-4). The differences in rates reflect the difficulty in making a diagnosis of preeclampsia in such women.

Glycemic control also plays a role in the development of preeclampsia. It is hypothesized that poor glycemic control leads to a restriction of the proliferation of cytotrophoblasts during the first trimester and to the decreased conversion of maternal spiral arteries to large sinusoidal vessels. When this occurs, there is insufficient uteroplacental circulation. Hanson and Persson (24) evaluated 491 diabetic pregnancies to determine the relationship between glycemic control and hypertensive disorders. They found that poor glycemic control in early pregnancy correlated with an increased rate of subsequent preeclampsia. The preeclamptic group (n = 53) had significantly higher glycohemoglobin values early in pregnancy. A glycohemoglobin level 8 standard deviations above the mean value was associated with a higher rate of preeclampsia.

MANAGEMENT OF HYPERTENSION IN DIABETIC WOMEN

In women with diabetes who are not pregnant, behavioral management may be attempted initially if the blood pressure is less than 140/90 mm Hg, including sodium restriction, weight reduction, and physical activity. Although weight reduction can be an effective measure in the initial therapy of mild to moderate hypertension in women without diabetes, there has not been a randomized control trial that has addressed this issue in diabetes. Even so, the results from weight reduction studies in the general population can be extrapolated to the diabetic population. Weight loss and dietary restriction of sodium have been shown to be effective in significantly lowering blood pressure. Results from controlled trials concerning essential hypertension and moderate sodium restriction show that there is a 5 mm Hg systolic decrease and a 2 to 3 mm Hg diastolic decrease in mean blood pressure with a moderate sodium restriction of 2,300 mg of sodium per day. Sodium restriction also seems to potentiate the action of pharmacologic agents, resulting in a better response to the pharmacologic agent when used concomitantly (6).

DRUG THERAPY OF HYPERTENSION IN DIABETIC WOMEN

The goal of antihypertensive therapy in nonpregnant patients is to reduce the morbidity and mortality that is associated with uncontrolled hypertension. Control of blood pressure will result in significant reduction of cardiovascular complications such as congestive heart failure, coronary artery disease, and stroke, as well as microvascular complications such as nephropathy and retinopathy.

Nephropathy is a real concern in diabetic patients with hypertension. Approximately 20% of diabetic patients will develop end-stage renal disease with time. African Americans are five times more likely to develop renal disease than their white counterparts, and Asians have increased rates of end-stage renal disease (6). When comparing normotensive diabetic patients and hypertensive diabetic patients, it has been shown that those who are normotensive have slower progression to nephropathy (6).

The Hypertension Optimal Treatment study addressed antihypertensive therapy in patients with diabetes (25). In this large-scale trial, 18,790 patients were evaluated, 1,501 with diabetes. The patients were assigned to one of three groups: diastolic blood pressure of less than 90, less than 85, or less than 80 mm Hg. A calcium channel blocker was used as the initial treatment. The group with diastolic blood pressure of less than 80 mm Hg had the lowest rate of complications and a significant reduction in cardiovascular events. The vast majority of patients were treated with at least two antihypertensives. From this trial, it is apparent that hypertension in diabetic patients must be aggressively controlled if we are to decrease morbidity and mortality from microvascular and cardiovascular disease (25).

Antihypertensive agents exert their activity through one of the following mechanisms: decreased cardiac output, decreased peripheral vascular resistance, centrally decreased

TABLE 27-6. USE OF ANTIHYPERTENSIVES IN PREGNANCY

Medication	Dose	Maximum Dose
Methyldopa	250–500 mg p.o. every 6–12 h	4 g/24 h
Labetalol	100 mg p.o. b.i.d.	2,400 mg/24 h
Thiazide	12.5 mg p.o. b.i.d.	50 mg/24 h
Nifedipine	10–20 mg p.o. every 4–6 h	240 mg/24 h

blood pressure, diuresis, and inhibition of angiotensin production. Drugs commonly used in pregnancy are listed in Table 27-6.

CENTRALLY ACTING DRUGS

Methyldopa is the most commonly used antihypertensive in pregnancy. It acts by inhibiting the sympathetic drive. The safety of methyldopa is well documented. No congenital malformations are associated with its use. Maternal side effects include drowsiness, somnolence, and dry mouth. However, this drug is generally not effective in women with diabetes and hypertension, so more potent agents are usually necessary.

β-BLOCKERS

β-blockers work primarily by reducing cardiac output through β-adrenergic blockade. The drugs in this group are a heterogeneous mixture that exert their effects depending on receptor selectivity, lipid solubility, and sympathomimetic action. Labetalol is a nonselective β-blocker and a postsynaptic $α_1$-blocker. It has less of a β-blocking effect and therefore does not reduce cardiac output. Maternal side effects include tremors, headache, and scalp tingling.

CALCIUM CHANNEL BLOCKERS

Calcium channel blockers act by inhibiting extracellular calcium influx into cells through slow calcium channels, resulting in decreased peripheral vascular resistance. Calcium channel blockers are not known to be teratogenic. Adverse maternal and fetal outcomes are associated with sublingual use of nifedipine: maternal myocardial infarction, and profound hypotension. Maternal side effects include headache, palpitations, and flushing.

VASODILATORS

Vasodilators act by direct vasodilatation. Hydralazine is a potent vasodilator. It can be used orally as well as intravenously to manage a hypertensive crisis. No congenital effects are associated with hydralazine. Maternal side effects include headache, palpitations, tachycardia, a lupuslike syndrome, and fluid retention. It can cause neonatal thrombocytopenia.

DIURETICS

Diuretics act by reducing total body sodium and have a vasodilatory effect. Although diuretics are not absolutely contraindicated in pregnancy, their potential effects on decreasing intravascular volume and possibly causing uteroplacental perfusion must be taken into consideration. No congenital defects have been associated with the use of diuretics.

Thiazide diuretics only minimally lower blood pressure. Maternal side effects include hyponatremia, acute pancreatitis, and an elevation in blood uric acid levels. Fetal thrombocytopenia is also associated with the use of thiazide diuretics.

Furosemide may be used in combination with other antihypertensive agents, but is rarely used as the sole agent. Furosemide should be limited to the management of pulmonary edema in the preeclamptic patient and fluid overload in the postpartum patient.

ANGIOTENSIN-CONVERTING ENZYME INHIBITORS

Angiotensin-converting enzyme (ACE) inhibitors act by competitively inhibiting the conversion of angiotensin I to angiotensin II, reducing the production of angiotensin II and aldosterone, with a resultant decrease in peripheral vascular resistance (26). In addition, ACE inhibitors reduce intraglomerular hypertension and decrease oxidative stress (26). ACE inhibitors also decrease hyperfiltration and albuminuria. Unfortunately, a high degree of morbidity and mortality in fetuses and newborns has been documented in

TABLE 27-7. FETAL AND NEONATAL COMPLICATIONS WITH USE OF ANGIOTENSIN-CONVERTING ENZYME INHIBITORS

Fetal
  Skull hypoplasia
  Limb contractures
  Oligohydramnios
  Intrauterine growth restriction
  Renal failure
  Lung hypoplasia
Neonatal
  Patent ductus arteriosus
  Renal failure
  Respiratory distress syndrome due to lung hypoplasia
  Prolonged hypotension
  Neonatal death

Adapted from How HY, Sibai BM. Use of angiotensin-converting enzyme inhibitors in patients with diabetic nephropathy. *J Matern Fetal Med* 2002;12:402–407, with permission.

women who have been treated with ACE inhibitors (Table 27-7). In the fetus, the use of ACE inhibitors is associated with an increased risk for intrauterine demise, renal dysgenesis, oligohydramnios, pulmonary hypoplasia, and fetal growth restriction (26). These effects are not believed to be due to a teratogenic effect. The use of ACE inhibitors in pregnancy may be warranted in certain high-risk groups as a last resort, but complete safety in the first trimester cannot be assured. However, low-dose and short-acting ACE inhibitors are recommended. ACE inhibitors are associated with maternal hypotension, hyperkalemia, glycosuria, proteinuria, and renal failure. Their use can also be associated with neutropenia and liver damage (26).

PREVENTION OF PREECLAMPSIA

Interventions that could prevent preeclampsia would directly impact maternal and perinatal mortality and morbidity. Many studies have investigated methods to prevent preeclampsia. Consideration has been given to low-salt diets, diuretics, bed rest, and control of maternal weight gain. Unfortunately, none of these interventions have proven to be beneficial. Several studies evaluated the use of low-dose aspirin and calcium supplementation for the prevention of preeclampsia (27). The National Institute of Child Health and Human Development Network of Maternal-Fetal Medicine Units (27) evaluated the use of low-dose aspirin in women at high risk for preeclampsia: 462 women with pregestational diabetes were assigned to either the low-dose aspirin or placebo groups. The results for all women at high risk showed no differences in the rate of preeclampsia between the aspirin and placebo groups. The National Institute of Child Health and Human Development Network of Maternal-Fetal Medicine Units also evaluated women who were nulliparas, with chronic hypertension, and with diabetes (28). Study patients were randomized at 13 to 32 weeks' gestation. However, the results were reported for all women at high risk, including those with diabetes, and no separate analysis was performed for the women with diabetes. In this study, low-dose aspirin did not reduce the rate of preeclampsia.

Currently, it appears that aggressive treatment of maternal blood pressure prior to pregnancy and during gestation along with intensive control of maternal blood glucose to achieve euglycemia before 20 weeks' gestation and the prevention of microalbuminuria may be most effective in preventing gestational hypertension and preeclampsia in type 1 and type 2 diabetes.

KEY POINTS

- Hypertensive disorders affect 5% to 10% of all pregnancies. These include chronic hypertension, gestational hypertension, and preeclampsia/eclampsia.

- Hypertension complicates diabetic management in 20% to 60% of cases in the general population.
- Preeclampsia develops in 10% to 20% of diabetic pregnancies.
- Risk factors for preeclampsia in women with diabetes include duration of pregestational diabetes, concurrent chronic hypertension, poor glycemic control prior to 20 weeks' gestation, and the presence of microalbuminuria or nephropathy.
- Based on the current literature, gestational diabetes can be considered an independent risk factor for the development of gestational hypertension and preeclampsia.
- The incidence of preeclampsia increases as the severity of pregestational diabetes increases.
- The presence of microalbuminuria, urinary albumin excretion of 30 to 300 mg/day, prior to pregnancy increases the risk for developing preeclampsia.
- Nephropathy, urinary protein excretion of more than 300 mg/day, is a major risk factor for preeclampsia.
- Poor glycemic control may cause a restriction of the proliferation of cytotrophoblasts in the first trimester and a decreased conversion of maternal spiral arteries to large sinusoidal vessels, leading to insufficiency in the uteroplacental circulation.
- Pharmocologic agents that may be used in pregnancy to control blood pressure include methyldopa, β-blockers, calcium channel blockers, and vasodilators.
- Low-dose and short-acting ACE inhibitors may be used as a last resort in pregnancy to control hypertension. Women treated with ACE inhibitors must be followed closely for the development of hypotension, hyperkalemia, and oligohydramnios.
- Fetal complications that may occur with the use of ACE inhibitors include skull hypoplasia, limb contractures, intrauterine growth restriction, renal failure, and lung hypoplasia.
- Neonatal complications that may occur with the use of ACE inhibitors include renal failure, respiratory distress, prolonged hypotension, patent ductus arteriosus, and neonatal death.
- Aggressive control of maternal blood pressure prior and during gestation along with intensive control of maternal blood sugars to achieve euglycemia before 20 weeks' gestation are the most effective strategies to decrease hypertensive disorders in diabetic women.

REFERENCES

1. Report of the National High Blood Pressure Education Program. Working group report on high blood pressure in pregnancy. *Am J Obstet Gynecol* 2000;183(suppl):1–22.
2. American College of Obstetricians and Gynecologists Committee on Practice Bulletins-Obstetrics. Diagnosis and management of preeclampsia and eclampsia. *Obstet Gynecol* 2001;98:159–167.
3. Sibai BM. Risk factors, pregnancy complications, and prevention of hypertensive disorders in women with pregravid diabetes mellitus. *J Matern Fetal Med* 2000;9:62–65.
4. Caritis SN, Sibai BM, Hauth J, et al. Predictors of pre-eclampsia in women at high risk. National Institute of Child Health and Human Development Network of Maternal-Fetal Medicine Units. *Am J Obstet Gynecol* 1998;179:946–951.
5. Sibai BM, Ewell M, Levine RJ, et al. Risk factors associated with preeclampsia in healthy nulliparous women. National Institute for Child Health and Human Development Network of Maternal-Fetal Medicine Units Calcium for Preeclampsia Prevention Study Group. *Am J Obstet Gynecol* 1997;177(5):1003–1010.
6. Arauz-Pacheco C, Parrott MA, Raskin P. The treatment of hypertension in adult patients with diabetes. *Diabetes Care* 2002;25(1):134–147.
7. Cundy T, Slee F, Gamble G, et al. Hypertensive disorders of pregnancy in women with type I and type II diabetes. *Diabet Med* 2002;19:482–489.
8. MacMahon S, Peto R, Cutler J, et al. Blood pressure, stroke, and coronary heart disease. Part 1. Prolonged differences in blood pressure: prospective observational studies corrected for regression dilution bias. *Lancet* 1990;335:765–774.
9. Janka HU, Warram JH, Rand LI, et al. Risk factors for progression of background retinopathy in long-standing IDDM. *Diabetes* 1989;38:460–464.
10. Chobanian AV, Bakris GL, Black HR, et al. The Seventh Report of the Joint National Committee on Prevention, Detection, Evaluation, and Treatment of High Blood Pressure. JAMA 2003;289(19):2560–2571.
11. Garner PR, D'Alton ME, Dudley DK, et al. Preeclampsia in diabetic pregnancies. *Am J Obstet Gynecol* 1990;163:505–508.
12. Siddiqi T, Rosenn B, Mimouni F, et al. Hypertension during pregnancy in insulin dependent diabetic women. *Obstet Gynecol* 1991;77:514–519.
13. Greene MF, Hare JW, Krache M, et al. Prematurity among insulin-requiring diabetic gravid women. *Am J Obstet Gynecol* 1989;161:106–111.
14. Gordon M, Landon MB, Samuels P, et al. Perinatal outcome and long-term follow-up associated with modern management of diabetic nephropathy. *Obstet Gynecol* 1996;87:401–409.
15. Sibai BM, Caritis S, Hauth J, et al. Risks of preeclampsia and adverse neonatal outcomes among women with pregestational diabetes mellitus. National Institute of Child Health and Human Development Network of Maternal–Fetal Medicine Units. *Am J Obstet Gynecol* 2000;182:364–369.
16. Kuhl C. Insulin secretion and insulin resistance in pregnancy and GDM: implications for diagnosis and management. *Diabetes* 1991;40:18–24.
17. Solomon CG, Seely EW. Hypertension in pregnancy, a manifestation of the insulin resistance syndrome? *Hypertension* 2001;37:232–239.
18. Schaffir JA, Lockwood CJ, Lapinski R, et al. Incidence of pregnancy-induced hypertension among gestational diabetics. *Am J Perinatol* 1995;12(4):252–256.
19. Joffe GM, Esterlitz JR, Levine RJ, et al. The relationship between abnormal glucose tolerance and hypertensive disorders of pregnancy in healthy nulliparous women. The Calcium for Prevention of Preeclampsia Study Group. *Am J Obstet Gynecol* 1998;179:1032–1037.
20. Vambergue A, Nuttens MC, Goeusse P, et al. Pregnancy induced hypertension in women with gestational carbohydrate intolerance: the Diagest study. *Eur J Obstet Gynecol Reprod Biol* 2002;102:31–35.
21. Rudge M, Calderon I, Ramos M, et al. Hypertensive disorders in pregnant women with diabetes mellitus. *Gynecol Obstet Invest* 1997;44:11–15.
22. Combs CA, Rosenn B, Kitzmiller JL, et al. Early pregnancy pro-

teinuria in diabetes related to preeclampsia. *Obstet Gynecol* 1993;82:802–807.

23. Ekbom P, Damm P, Feldt-Rasmussen B, et al. Pregnancy outcome in type I diabetic women with microalbuminuria. *Diabetes Care* 2001;14:1739–1744.

24. Hanson U, Persson B. Epidemiology of pregnancy induced hypertension and preeclampsia in type I (insulin-dependent) diabetic pregnancies in Sweden. *Acta Obstet Gynecol Scand* 1998;77:620–624.

25. Hansson L, Zanchetti A, Carruthers SG, et al. Effects of intensive blood-pressure lowering and low-dose aspirin on patients with hypertension: principal results of the Hypertension Optimal Treatment randomized trial. *Lancet* 1998;351:1755–1762.

26. How HY, Sibai BM. Use of angiotensin-converting enzyme inhibitors in patients with diabetic nephropathy. *J Matern Fetal Med* 2002;12:402–407.

27. Caritis S, Sibai BM, Hauth J, et al. Lose-dose aspirin to prevent preeclampsia in women at high risk. National Institute of Child Health and Human Development Network of Maternal-Fetal Medicine Units. *N Engl J Med* 1998;338:701–705.

28. CLASP Collaborative Group. A randomized trial of low-dose aspirin for the prevention and treatment of pre-eclampsia among 9368 pregnant women. *Lancet* 1994;343:619–629.

28

DIABETIC RETINOPATHY

LOIS JOVANOVIC

Before 1922, few infants of diabetic mothers survived (1). With the advent of insulin, the infant survival rate improved, but it was not until the 1980s that the mortality rate decreased to a rate near that of the general population (2). Although infant survival seems to be directly related to the degree of maternal glucose control (3,4), there is still controversy regarding the impact of pregnancy per se on the maternal health status (5–9). This chapter specifically covers the literature on pregnancies complicated by diabetic retinopathy and attempts to tease out the variables that influence the natural history of retinopathy during pregnancy.

NATURAL HISTORY OF DIABETIC RETINOPATHY IN NONPREGNANT INDIVIDUALS

Diabetic retinopathy is the result of retinal arteriolar and capillary endothelial cell injury, basement membrane thick-ening, and pericyte damage (10). Diabetic retinopathy is a progressive disorder and is generally divided into three stages: normal, nonproliferative, and proliferative (11). For research purposes, these stages are subdivided into several grades based on a specific set of defined criteria and objective findings (12), as summarized in Table 28-1.

The nonproliferative type is also known as background retinopathy (Fig. 28-1). An intermediate category, known as preproliferative retinopathy, is used, as are more subtle gradings of the severity of the changes in retinopathy (Fig. 28-2). Proliferative retinopathy requires the growth of new capillaries on the retina (Fig. 28-3). These may extend into the vitreous and rupture, causing vitreous hemorrhage, which is usually only a minor visual threat. The hemorrhage appears as a sudden unilateral clouding or loss of vision. It typically resolves over a period of several weeks. If the blood in the vitreous organizes and does not clear, vision may be impaired. It is for this reason that the surgical procedure of vitrectomy was developed. The real threat to vision is that, subsequent to the hemorrhage, there will be scarring and

TABLE 28-1. GRADING SYSTEM FOR DIABETIC RETINOPATHY: MODIFIED AIRLIE HOUSE DIABETIC RETINOPATHY CLASSIFICATION BASED ON THE SEVEN STANDARD FUNDUS PHOTOGRAPHS

Clinical Grouping	Description of Retina
Normal	No retinopathy
Minimal background	Microaneurysms or blot hemorrhages only
Mild background	Hemorrhages easily visible with an ophthalmoscope and questionable presence of hard exudates, soft exudates, and intraretinal microvascular abnormalities, and/or venous beading
Moderate background	Numerous hemorrhages and definite presence of both hard and soft exudates with obvious intraretinal microvascular abnormalities and venous beading; lesions localized to less than two fields of the seven standard fields of the fundus photographs
Severe background	Same lesions as moderate, but presence of these lesions in greater than or equal to two fields of the fundus photographs
Proliferative retinopathy	Presence of neovascularization

From the Early Treatment Diabetic Retinopathy Study Research Group. Grading diabetic retinopathy from stereoscopic color fundus photographs: an extension of the modified Airlie House classification. ETDRS report number 10. *Ophthalmology* 1991;98:786, with permission.

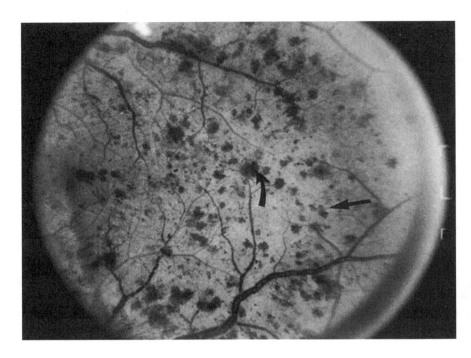

FIGURE 28-1. Microaneurysms and dot and blot hemorrhages in the retina. Hemorrhages are large and have irregular margins. Smaller hemorrhages cannot be distinguished from microaneurysms.

traction detachment of the retina, resulting in permanent visual loss.

By and large, background retinopathy does not threaten vision. It is characterized by the appearance of venous dilatation, hard exudates, retinal edema, microaneurysms, and small red dot hemorrhages in the retina. Unless these occur in the perimacular area, visual symptoms do not occur. Background retinopathy is extremely common in diabetes and is practically universal if carefully sought after the patient has had the disease for 20 years. Background retinopathy is usually not clinically apparent in casual examinations with the ophthalmoscope in patients who have had diabetes for less than 10 years.

Preproliferative retinopathy is a transitional stage toward proliferative retinopathy. Fortunately, not all background retinopathy progresses to proliferative retinopathy. When

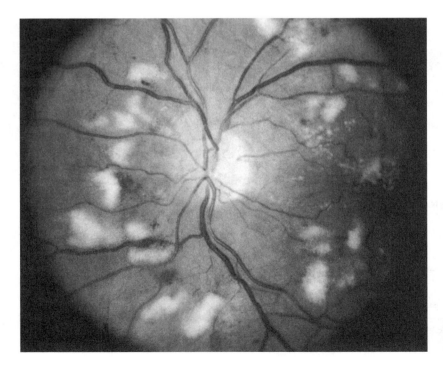

FIGURE 28-2. Multiple cotton-wool spots surround the optic disc in a pregnant diabetic woman.

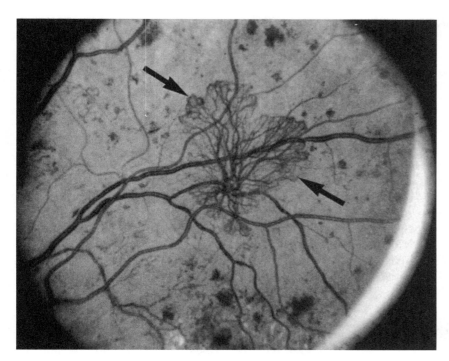

FIGURE 28-3. A neovascular frond (*arrows*) of proliferative diabetic retinopathy that is made up of irregular, small vessels.

this transitional stage occurs, there is increasing evidence that early and vigorous photocoagulation may prevent subsequent proliferation and visual loss. The characteristic lesions in preproliferative retinopathy are intraretinal microvascular abnormalities and soft, or cotton-wool, exudates.

A subgroup of patients with preproliferative diabetic retinopathy may develop vision loss from complications involving the macula. Diabetic macular edema is a frequent complication of severe proliferative diabetic retinopathy (13) and is recognized as the leading cause of legal blindness in patients with type 2 diabetes mellitus. In the early stages of diabetic macular edema, a breakdown of the inner blood-retinal barrier occurs, resulting in the characteristic accumulation of extracellular fluid in the macula (14). Abnormal vessel permeability results in leakage of water, blood cells, proteins, and lipoproteins into the surrounding retinal tissue. It has been estimated that over a 10-year period, clinically significant diabetic macular edema will develop in 10% of patients with diabetes (15).

The mechanisms that cause retinal damage appear similar to the more general effect of diabetes on the systemic microvascular system. Putative mechanisms include circulatory damage and ischemia, endothelial deposits, platelet plugs, cholesterol plaques, myofibril hypertrophy, and hyperglycemia-induced hypercoagulation (16). The evidence that retinopathy is a consequence of excessive elevation of blood glucose levels and the sequelae of these elevations is consistent with a demonstrated inhibition of retinopathy by strict glycemic control in diabetic dogs (17). Unfortunately, retinopathy in humans is not as easily stud-

ied. It is clear that the duration of diabetes is a strong risk factor for diabetic retinopathy. The Wisconsin Epidemiologic Study of Diabetic Retinopathy (WESDOR) found that the prevalence of retinopathy in patients with an onset of diabetes before age 30 was 17% after 5 years and up to 97.5% at greater than 15 years' duration (18,19). The severity of retinopathy was related to the duration of diabetes, level of glycosylated hemoglobin, age at examination, presence of proteinuria, and higher diastolic blood pressure. Similar prevalence data have been reported in several other studies (20–24). Although WESDOR researchers did not address pregnancy per se, they did find that the number of previous pregnancies did not affect prevalence rates of retinopathy.

ROLE OF HYPERGLYCEMIA AS A CAUSE OF DIABETIC RETINOPATHY

Evidence directly indicating the importance of metabolic control has become available as a result of prospective studies of diabetes in human subjects. Two randomized, prospective trials have been performed. The first was a study from Sweden in which 102 patients with insulin-dependent diabetes mellitus (type 1 diabetes mellitus), nonproliferative retinopathy, normal serum creatinine concentrations, and unsatisfactory blood glucose control were randomly assigned to intensified insulin treatment or standard insulin treatment (25). They were then evaluated at 1.5, 3, 5, and 7.5 years. The two groups maintained a separation in their glycosylated hemoglobin levels of 1.4%

(p = 0.001). Over the study period, the two groups had a significant difference in the prevalence of proliferative retinopathy requiring photocoagulation (27% vs. 52%, p = 0.01). The second study confirmed the first study but had a sample size 10 times larger. The latter study, the Diabetes Control and Complications Trial, was a multicenter investigation funded by the National Institutes of Health that finally provided the definitive answer as to the relationship of retinopathy and glucose levels in nonpregnant subjects (26). This trial recruited 1,441 type 1 diabetic patients and randomized them into two groups of glycemic control. Those patients in the standard care group maintained a mean glycosylated hemoglobin of 9.0%, and those patients in the intensive care group a mean glycosylated hemoglobin of 7.2%. The intensive care group had a 50% lower prevalence rate of new-onset retinopathy or progression of retinopathy compared with that in the standard case group.

RAPID NORMALIZATION OF GLUCOSE

Several studies have also shown dramatic reversal of diabetic retinopathy after only 2 to 3 months of insulin infusion pump therapy (27–30). Although these studies are promising, other reports have implicated rapid normalization of blood glucose level as a causal factor in accelerating diabetic retinopathy (26,31). This progression of retinopathy has been characterized mainly by the appearance of nerve fiber layer infarctions and intraretinal vascular lesions, which appear to be secondary to decreased blood flow.

The effects of normalization of blood glucose levels on various stages of preexisting diabetic retinopathy are unknown. The risk for returning an abnormal retinal circulation that has adapted to an elevated blood glucose level to an environment of normal blood glucose level is undetermined. The current methods of achieving tight control of glucose levels also result in episodes of hypoglycemia, whose effects on preexisting diabetic retinopathy are unknown. Hypoglycemia has been implicated as a causative factor in the development of vitreous hemorrhage in proliferative diabetic retinopathy (32,33), but these cases are anecdotal.

Preliminary reports and our own experience suggest that retinopathy may continue to progress after the achievement of tight control of glucose levels. These reports are unable to determine whether the natural progression of the disease was unaffected or normalization of blood glucose levels actually adversely affected diabetic retinopathy. In our cases (presented later), the onset of visual symptoms appeared to be related to the achievement of good control of blood glucose levels.

Drash et al. (34) reported on four children with Mauriac syndrome (marked hyperglycemia and growth retardation) who initially presented with minimal diabetic retinopathy. When the diabetes was controlled, the degree of retinopa-

thy progressed rapidly in all four, with the development of microaneurysms, hemorrhages, exudates, and macular edema. The three older children went on to develop proliferative retinopathy, and one patient became blind in one eye. These findings, although distressing, may be related to the association of the appearance of diabetic complications with the onset of puberty. All these patients were prepubertal when first seen and progressed through puberty during the period of diabetic control.

Tamborlane et al. (35) reported equally disturbing vitreous hemorrhages in 2 of 10 patients, 1 within 3 months after the start of tight control of glucose levels. The ages of these 2 patients were not stated, and both started with proliferative retinopathy. Nevertheless, these two case studies have led at least one advocate of tight control of glucose levels to recommend that such control not be attempted in patients with a history of underinsulinization and severe retinopathy (36).

In our own experience, two patients with well-documented control of blood glucose levels reported changes in vision shortly after the normalization of these levels (37). However, our third patient with background retinopathy had macular edema that developed 2 weeks after acute normalization of her twice-normal glucose levels and resolved completely after 9 months of maintenance of normoglycemia with an insulin infusion pump.

These observations suggest that, as a prevention measure against retinopathy, normoglycemia may be the treatment goal for diabetic nonpregnant patients. In patients with predisposed retinae, acute normalization of blood glucose levels should be avoided. Instead, the process should proceed with caution. Once normoglycemia is achieved, however, its maintenance may be accompanied by improvement in the diseased retina.

The lessons to be learned from the studies of nonpregnant diabetic patients are as follows:

1. The duration of diabetes is closely associated with the presence of retinopathy (38).
2. Hyperglycemia, as documented by an elevated hemoglobin A_{1c} level, is associated with an increased risk for retinopathy (25,26).
3. The severity of retinopathy at the beginning of an observation period is thought to be significant in predicting subsequent changes in retinopathy (39).
4. Current age or age at the time of the examination has been found to be related to the severity of retinopathy (38).
5. Hormonal influences may potentiate retinopathy (40).
6. Hypertension potentiates retinopathy (41).
7. Rapid normalization of blood glucose may accelerate retinopathy (34,35).
8. Smoking accelerates retinopathy.

We now turn to the diabetic pregnant woman and look for evidence of a "pregnancy risk factor" for diabetic retinopathy over and above those observations in nonpregnant populations.

DOES PREGNANCY CHANGE THE NATURAL HISTORY OF DIABETIC RETINOPATHY

Peptide and steroid hormones have been implicated as playing an etiologic role in diabetic retinopathy for decades (40,42). Regression of proliferative retinopathy in patients with pituitary infarctions has been reported (41,42). This observation resulted in the use of hypophysectomy as a treatment for patients with proliferative retinopathy. Although the retinopathy did regress, the life span of these patients was shortened, perhaps secondary to the steroid doses needed to sustain viability. The hypothesis that growth hormone might be the primary villain was strengthened when Merimee et al. (43) observed that ateliotic dwarfs, who are totally deficient in growth hormone, do not develop retinopathy, even with more than 15 years of documented hyperglycemia.

Pregnancy is associated with a marked elevation in human placental lactogen, which has many growth hormone–like effects (44). Because of this and elevations in other hormones that cause vascular changes, such as estrogen, progesterone, and cortisol, pregnancy may in fact accelerate retinopathy.

Hypertension has also been linked to the severity of retinopathy (18,19,45–48). Studies in which antihypertensive agents have been used to slow the progression of diabetic nephropathy have also suggested that such therapy might retard the progression of retinopathy (48,49). In our own study, in which we used a nonmydriatic camera to screen for diabetic retinopathy in the diabetic population in Santa Barbara County, we noted that those patients with evidence of retinopathy had significantly higher blood pressure than did those patients who had no evidence of retinopathy (50). The relationship of hypertension to retinopathy may be particularly important during pregnancy because, in up to 20% of type 1 diabetic women, pregnancy-induced hypertension develops (51). Rosenn et al. (52) reported progression of retinopathy in 51 of 154 pregnancies among type 1 diabetic women. They found that hypertension, be it pregnancy-induced or preexisting chronic hypertension, was the most important risk factor associated with progression of retinopathy in pregnancy. Using logistic regression analysis, these investigators showed that the association of hypertension with the progression of retinopathy persisted after controlling for the effects of poor glycemic control and of rapid changes in glycemic control.

Investigators have reported differing findings regarding the effects of pregnancy per se on diabetic retinopathy. Many reports show that, for women with minimal or no retinopathy at the onset of pregnancy, although there may be minor progression, vision-threatening retinopathy generally does not occur. Of 234 pregnancies followed at the Rikshospitalet in Oslo, Norway, from 1970 to 1977, new incidence or progression of retinopathy during pregnancy was reported in 68 pregnancies (53). Rodman et al. (54) reported that 85% of patients with background retinopathy experienced progression during pregnancy. Soubrane et al. (55) followed the course of diabetic retinopathy by repeated fluorescein angiography during pregnancy in 22 diabetic women. The mean number of microaneurysms increased consistently throughout pregnancy and decreased after pregnancy, but not to the number encountered before pregnancy. Other observers have also reported that progression seemed to be accelerated during pregnancy (56,57). By contrast, Stephens et al. (58) found that, of 114 pregnancies in 78 diabetic women, retinopathy developed during only 2 pregnancies.

When a woman starts her pregnancy with more severe retinopathy, the likelihood that retinopathy will progress increases. Thus, the duration of diabetes is an independent risk factor for the progression of retinopathy in pregnancy. Dibble et al. (21) reported that, in 3 of 19 patients with only background retinopathy, proliferative changes developed during pregnancy. Horvat et al. (59) conducted a 12-year prospective study during which they surveyed 107 women with latent diabetes and 160 with clinical diabetes. In the latter group, background retinopathy was present or occurred during gestation in 40 women. Vision remained stable in all except 4 patients (10%), who progressed to proliferative retinopathy. Only 1 woman had new vessels develop in one eye during pregnancy, whereas the other 3 had proliferative changes noted after completing their pregnancies. Eleven women had proliferative retinopathy, with one case appearing *de novo* during pregnancy. These individuals had an average duration of diabetes of 21 years in contrast to 13.5 years for women with background retinopathy. In this study, retinopathy was noted to fluctuate during the index and subsequent pregnancies. Not infrequently, changes occurred in both directions at one time, with one part of the eye getting better while another part worsened. The investigators concluded that pregnancy was not associated with an increased risk to the mother of retinal changes and visual loss.

Moloney and Drury (56) followed 53 pregnant patients with type 1 diabetes by retinal photography every 6 weeks and for 6 months postpartum. Thirty-three (62%) had retinopathy at first examination, and in eight others (15%) it developed as pregnancy advanced. They reported progressive changes as gestation progressed with a moderate increase in microaneurysms, hemorrhages in 30 (56.6%), and soft exudates in 15 (28.3%). Four women had neovascularization for the first time with further deterioration with advancing pregnancy. By 6 months after delivery, background changes had regressed to control levels, and neovascularization showed some regression. Again, development and progression of retinopathy were related to the

TABLE 28-2. PROGRESSION OF DIABETIC RETINOPATHY IN PREGNANCY STRATIFIED BY INITIAL RETINAL FINDINGS

Investigators	No. of Pregnancies	No. (%) with Progression Given the Initial Findings		
		None	Background	Proliferative
Horvat et al. (59), 1980	160	13/118 (11)	11/35 (31)	1/7 (14)
Moloney and Drury (56), 1982	53	8/20 (40)	15/30 (50)	1/3 (33)
Dibble et al. (21), 1982	55	0/23 (0)	3/19 (16)	7/13 (54)
Ohms (60), 1984	100	4/50 (8)	15/48 (31)	1/2 (50)
Rosenn et al. (52), 1992	154	18/78 (23)	28/68 (41)	5/8 (63)

duration of diabetes, and every pregnant patient who had diabetes for 10 years or longer had retinopathy. Increased doses of insulin and polyhydramnios were risk factors for retinal hemorrhage. Of interest, low fasting blood glucose levels (better control) late in pregnancy were associated significantly with soft exudates. Pregnancy had no visible effect in the retinae of patients who had diabetes for less than 2 years, but thereafter, it did accelerate the development of retinopathy. Also in conjunction with a strict metabolic control management protocol during pregnancy, the course of retinopathy changed with an increase in hemorrhages and soft exudates. These changes were of short duration and usually resolved within 6 weeks (54).

Table 28-2 summarizes the above reports in which diabetic retinopathy was assessed before and after pregnancy and presents findings of progression based on the initial examination (21,52,56,59,60). These studies clearly show that the severity of retinopathy at the onset of pregnancy is an independent risk factor for progression. When a woman had no retinopathy early in pregnancy, the risk for progression varied from 0% to 40%. When a woman had background retinopathy at the start of her pregnancy, her risk for progression increased from 16% to 50%; however, when a woman had proliferative retinopathy at the start of her pregnancy, her risk was as high as 63%.

PROSPECTIVE TRIALS IN PREGNANCY

Differences in the conclusions reported from some of these studies may have resulted from lack of objective recording and assessment of the retinal lesions and inappropriate comparison groups or none at all. Klein et al. (61) conducted a prospective study to determine the effect of pregnancy on diabetic retinopathy. The control group for the type 1 diabetic pregnant women was composed of nonpregnant type 1 diabetic women. After adjusting for glycosylated hemoglobin, current pregnancy was significantly associated with progression ($p < 0.005$). Diastolic blood pressure had a lesser effect on the probability of progression. This group also reported that, when the duration of diabetes is controlled for in the analysis, parity is not a risk factor for retinopathy.

Price et al. (62) found that the course of pregnancy is closely related to the severity of the eye disease at the start of the pregnancy. Those patients without retinopathy do not develop significant retinopathy and have relatively uncomplicated pregnancies. Those patients with retinopathy tended also to have progressive eye disease and obstetric complications. Of note, the infant outcome was satisfactory despite the high-risk pregnancies.

Larinkari et al. (42) followed 40 consecutive pregnant women with type 1 diabetes randomized at the end of the first trimester to receive conventional insulin treatment or constant subcutaneous insulin infusion (CSII). Nine women randomized to CSII declined the treatment. Two of 18 women who were receiving conventional treatment had some deterioration of retinopathy, compared with 5 of 13 in the CSII group and 3 of 9 who declined pump treatment. In most women, retinal deterioration was mild, but two patients who received CSII developed acute ischemic retinopathy, which progressed to a proliferative stage despite laser treatment. The decrease in hemoglobin A_{1c} level in these two patients was among the greatest and fastest in the study. These findings are analogous to those mentioned earlier in this chapter in poorly controlled nonpregnant patients after the institution of tight glucose control.

Serup (64) described the influence of pregnancy on diabetic retinopathy in a prospective study in Copenhagen initiated in 1979. In this protocol, three ophthalmologic examinations were performed during pregnancy and three in the year after delivery. Of the 145 women enrolled in the study, about half of the patients with retinopathy had deterioration during pregnancy. All improved to some extent after delivery. In a few women with background retinopathy at the onset of pregnancy, proliferative retinopathy developed, which commonly disappeared during the early postpartum period. No severe changes with respect to vitreous hemorrhages or severe proliferative changes occurred. In only one case was postpartum photocoagulation necessary to arrest retinal proliferative changes at the optic disc. Thus, Serup (64) agreed with Moloney and Drury (56) that pregnancy may interfere with the spontaneous course of diabetic retinopathy, resulting in a deterioration during pregnancy followed by some regression after delivery. Complete remission was noted in women who did not have retinopathy at conception but in whom it developed during gestation. These findings led to the conclusion that treatment with photocoagulation during pregnancy and in the 8 to 12 months after delivery should be restricted. This is in contrast to the approach of others who advise treatment before, during, and after pregnancy for proliferative retinopathy (64).

Phelps et al. (66) noted that, in pregnancies managed by intensive therapy to normalize the blood glucose level, 55% of retinal abnormalities worsened. Deterioration of background retinopathy correlated significantly with the levels of plasma glucose at entry and with the improvement in glycemia achieved. They concluded that the abrupt institution of improved diabetic control during pregnancy might be one factor in the deterioration of background retinopathy of pregnancy.

In a preliminary report of the Diabetes in Early Pregnancy Study Group, the eyes of 18 pregnant type 1 diabetic women were photographed in the first and third trimesters of pregnancy to evaluate the effect of normoglycemia on retinopathy (66). The mean duration of diabetes was 18 years. All women achieved normoglycemia within 1 month of conception and maintained normoglycemia to term. Retinopathy was photographically documented monthly with seven standard stereoscopic fields. In 21 of 36 eyes (58.3%), the level of retinopathy increased. Of 12 patients who had hemoglobin A_{1c} levels lower than 7.0% (normal <7.0%), 8 increased at least one level in one or both eyes (66.7%). Renal disease (50% depression of the creatinine clearance rate and proteinuria greater than 150 mg/24 h) appeared to be associated with progression to more severe levels of retinopathy. Eight of nine patients who had cystoid macular edema had proteinuria greater than 1.0 g per 24 hours. Photocoagulation therapy prevented loss of ambulatory vision. A report of the entire study population of diabetic women in the Diabetes in Early Pregnancy Study Group (68) showed that patients with mild or more severe retinopathy at conception were at high risk for progression of retinopathy during pregnancy. The rates of progression from nonproliferative retinopathy to proliferative retinopathy were nearly 7% and 30% in patients whose baseline retinopathy levels were mild and moderate, respectively. Elevated glycosylated hemoglobin levels at entry more than six standard deviations above the mean of a normal pregnant population were associated with a statistically significant increased risk for progression. Among women with the highest initial glycosylated hemoglobin concentrations, those who improved the most in metabolic control during early pregnancy were the most likely to progress ($p = 0.03$) (67). In the Diabetes in Early Pregnancy study, as in the study by Phelps et al. (66), rapid normalization of blood glucose may have been a major independent variable in the progression of retinopathy.

Although gestational diabetic women do not have a risk for diabetic retinopathy during pregnancy because of the recent onset of their hyperglycemia, 50% of these women have marked tortuosity of their retinal vessels (69) (Fig. 28-4). This tortuosity is probably not a result of the pregnancy

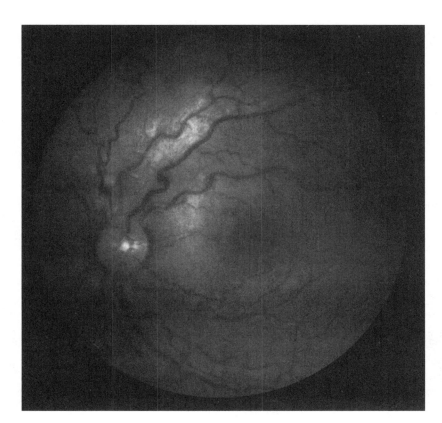

FIGURE 28-4. Retina of a 35-year-old woman with the diagnosis of gestational diabetes mellitus. Note the corkscrew development of the smaller retinal vessels. Tortuosity of the retinal vessels does not necessarily infer any form of retinopathy. It may actually be a genetic marker for glucose intolerance in some persons.

because it did not regress up to 1 year postpartum. It is hypothesized that retinal vessel tortuosity may be a marker for those women in whom type 2 diabetes will develop because 50% of women with gestational diabetes do go on to have frank diabetes as they age (69). Further reports are necessary to confirm this hypothesis. In contrast to the increased risk for progression of retinopathy in long-standing type 1 and type 2 diabetic women who become pregnant and who have their blood glucose levels normalized quickly, gestational diabetic women were previously thought to not have a problem with diabetic retinopathy. However, Kitzmiller et al. (70) recently suggested that when the blood glucose level is normalized quickly using insulin lispro, even diabetic women with no retinopathy may have progression of pathology. He hypothesized that because pregnancy is associated with an increased serum concentration of growth-promoting factors when the blood glucose level is rapidly decreased, there is increased retinal extravasation of serum proteins.

NEW INSULIN ANALOGUES

The new insulin analogues (71) are reported to be safe for use in pregnancy. They do have insulin-like growth factor-1 (IGF-1) activity. Hill et al. (75) found that a potent mitogen and angiogenic factor normally absent from the adult circulation became detectable by 14 weeks' gestation and was highest at 22 to 32 weeks' gestational age. A placental growth hormone variant has been observed to increase throughout pregnancy, along with human somatomammotropin, or prolactin (73). Maternal IGF-1 production has also been shown to increase significantly above nonpregnant levels (74). It is well known that diabetes mellitus is associated with perturbations of growth hormone IGF-1 in cases of poor metabolic control (75).

Human insulin binds to the IGF-1 receptor with an affinity of 0.1% to 0.2% that of IGF-1. A comparison of lispro and human insulin was made to determine the relative IGF-1 receptor binding affinity in human placental membranes, skeletal muscle, smooth muscle cells, and mammary epithelial cells. Lispro had slightly higher affinity for the human placental membranes when compared with human insulin (1.3 times greater than human insulin). No other differences were observed in any other cell lines. Despite the suggested increased affinity, it should be noted that the absolute affinity for the IGF-1 receptor is extremely low for both lispro and human insulin. Concentrations more than 1,000 times above normal physiologic range are needed to reach 50% receptor binding. IGF-1 is a much larger protein chain than insulin, and there is a 49% homology between human insulin and IGF-1. The reversal of the B28 and B29 amino acids in lispro increases this homology to 51%, because of the analogous position in the IGF molecule. As noted above, insulin lispro has nearly the same affinity for the IGF-1 receptor as does human insulin, and the dissociation kinetics of insulin lispro on the insulin receptor are identical to those of insulin, indicating that insulin lispro should have no excess mitogenic effect via either the IGF-1 or insulin receptor (70,76). Patients in the report by Kitzmiller et al. (70) all had elevated levels of IGF-1 due to poor control of their diabetes and to pregnancy, independent of the possible IGF-1 activity of lispro. Furthermore, anecdotal cases cannot be used to infer a cause-effect relationship (77). In controlled clinical trials of over 2,000 patients with lispro insulin, no significant differences in retinopathy were observed. However, there were no pregnant women in these trials (77–80).

In a busy clinic, the ability to completely examine the retinae is compromised. Mild background retinopathy may be missed, even in the best of settings. Any retinopathy increases the risk for progression, especially if the blood glucose level is elevated. Rather than recommending angiography to all women before each pregnancy is planned, in the absence of retinopathy on retinal examination, it is prudent to improve the glucose control slowly. Preconceptional care programs allow the slow normalization of blood glucose. Pregnancy is planned only after the blood glucose levels have been stabilized in the normal range for at least 6 months (79–81). If a patient presents pregnant, with high glycosylated hemoglobin levels, regardless of the retinal status, as suggested by these cases, then a retinal specialist needs to be on the team, be vigilant, and treat any developing angiopathy while the blood glucose is normalized.

If we did have an insulin analogue that was not immunogenic, had the rapid action of lispro, and had less IGF-1 activity than human insulin, such an insulin would become the treatment of choice. Insulin aspart, an insulin analogue that has been shown to produce a peak blood level at 40 minutes and lowers postprandial glucose levels significantly better than human insulin, has only 69% the IGF-1 activity of human insulin. However, use of insulin aspart in pregnancy must await the results of ongoing clinical trials to prove that it does not cause an immunoglobulin G (IgG) response and does not cross the placenta. A report on a small series of gestational diabetic women treated with insulin aspart has been published (80), and it appears to be safe and efficacious.

Long-acting insulin analogues have only recently been used in clinical practice. The first clinically available long-acting insulin analogue is insulin glargine. Insulin glargine has a glycine substitution in the α chain at the 21 position and two glargines attached to the β-chain terminal at position 30. It has been shown to provide peakless, sustained, predictable 24-hour action. There are no clinical trials using insulin glargine in pregnancy. Of note, insulin glargine has a sixfold increase in IGF-1 activity as compared with human insulin. Another insulin analogue that is currently in clinical trials is insulin detemir. Here again there are no trials using this insulin in pregnancy, but the studies show that detemir has the same IGF-1 activity as human insulin.

The clinician has to keep in mind that the most important concern is normalization of maternal blood glucose levels. Before 1985, we used impure, animal insulin with a result that the IgG antibody levels rose the longer the women were treated. Purified human insulin has now been available for over 15 years. We have a new generation of type 1 diabetic women who have never been treated with animal insulins and thus have negligible antibodies. Before we begin to give these women insulin analogues we must prove that they (a) do not cause an immunologic response, (b) do not cross the placenta, (c) do not increase the risk for congenital anomalies or spontaneous abortions, and (d) do not significantly increase the serum IGF-1 levels or accelerate diabetic retinopathy.

WHEN TO TREAT PREGNANT DIABETIC WOMEN WITH LASER THERAPY

A retina that has been treated with photocoagulation therapy for proliferative diabetic retinopathy is shown in Fig. 28-5. There are no randomized trials of pregnant women with retinopathy in which photocoagulation therapy has been the study variable. We can only learn from the trials reported in nonpregnant patients (79). The Diabetic Retinopathy Study recommended photocoagulation ther-

apy for significant neovascularization of the optic nerve head and in those patients with any neovascularization in the presence of vitreous hemorrhage. The controversy about photocoagulation therapy during pregnancy concerns the known observations that retinopathy regresses postpartum and thus photocoagulation therapy may not be necessary (61). Most centers treat significant neovascularization rather than risk a retinal hemorrhage. The definitive study remains to be presented.

KEY POINTS

- Pregnancy per se is an independent risk factor that accelerates retinopathy.
- Hypertension potentiates this acceleration.
- Hyperglycemia at the start of pregnancy also potentiates this acceleration.
- Rapid normalization of blood glucose markedly accelerates the progression of retinopathy.
- The duration of diabetes and state of the retina at the beginning of the pregnancy influence the rate of acceleration.
- Increased growth-promoting factors of pregnancy increase the risk for retinopathy.
- If an insulin analogue has increased growth-promoting factor characteristics, the use during pregnancy may be reconsidered.

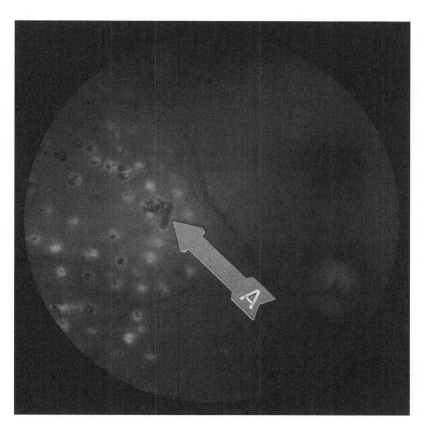

FIGURE 28-5. This woman received photocoagulation or laser therapy for neovascularization of her retinal vessels. Laser treatment appears on the photograph as dark and light spots (*arrow A* on the retina).

- A retinal specialist with expertise in retinopathy during pregnancy should be on the team to care for a type 1 or type 2 diabetic pregnant women, especially if she begins the pregnancy with any level of retinopathy.
- Prudent therapy suggests that treatment in pregnancy should be planned to allow normalization of blood glucose slowly, bringing the glycosylated hemoglobin to less than 6 standard deviations above the mean of a normal population over a period of at least 6 to 9 months before conception. In addition, while awaiting clinical trials, photocoagulation treatment for proliferative retinopathy that presents during pregnancy would appear prudent, despite the possibility that retinopathy may regress spontaneously postpartum.
- Postpartum, diabetic retinopathy usually regresses, but closely monitoring the retinal status is merited if the woman desires to breast-feed, for elevated prolactin levels are also associated with an increased risk for retinopathy progression.

REFERENCES

1. Jovanovic L, Peterson CM. Optimal insulin delivery for the pregnant diabetic patient. *Diabetes Care* 1982;5(suppl 1):24.
2. Coustan DR. Management of the pregnant diabetic. In: Olefsky JM, Sherwin RS, eds. *Diabetes mellitus: management and complications.* New York: Churchill Livingstone, 1985:311.
3. Karlsson K, Kjellmer I. The outcome of diabetic pregnancies in relation to the mother's blood sugar level. *Am J Obstet Gynecol* 1972;112:213.
4. Jovanovic L, Druzin M, Peterson CM. Effect of euglycemia on the outcome of pregnancy in insulin-dependent diabetic women as compared with normal control subjects. *Am J Med* 1981;71:921.
5. White P. Pregnancy and diabetes, medical aspects. *Med Clin North Am* 1965;49:1015.
6. Cassar J, Kohner EM, Hamilton AM, et al. Diabetic retinopathy and pregnancy. *Diabetologia* 1978;15:105.
7. Hare JW, White P. Pregnancy in diabetes complicated by vascular disease. *Diabetes* 1977;26:953.
8. Sharma WK, Archer DB, Hadden DR, et al. Morbidity and mortality in patients with diabetic retinopathy. *Trans Ophthalmol Soc UK* 1980;100:83.
9. Carstensen LL, Frost-Larsen K, Fuglebjerg S, et al. Does pregnancy influence the prognosis of uncomplicated insulin-dependent juvenile-onset diabetes mellitus? *Diabetes Care* 1982;5:1.
10. Palmberg P, Smith M, Waltman S, et al. The natural history of retinopathy in insulin-dependent juvenile-onset diabetes. *Ophthalmology* 1981;88:613.
11. Early Treatment Diabetic Retinopathy Study Research Group. *Manual of Operations, Early Treatment Diabetic Retinopathy Study, 5-1-5-10.* Baltimore: Maryland Medical Research Institute, 1985.
12. Early Treatment Diabetic Retinopathy Study Research Group. Grading diabetic retinopathy from stereoscopic color fundus photographs: an extension of the modified Airlie House classification. ETDRS report number 10. *Ophthalmology* 1991;98:786.
13. Riiordan-Eva, Vaughan DG. Eye. In: Tierney LM, McPhee SJ, Papadakis MA, eds. *Current medical diagnosis and treatment,* 34th ed. Norwalk, CT: Appleton & Lange, 1995:144–168.
14. Antcliff RJ, Marshall J. The pathogenesis of edema in diabetic maculopathy. *Semin Ophthalmol* 1999;14:223–232.
15. Klein R, Klein BEK, Moss SE, et al. The Wisconsin epidemiological study of diabetic retinopathy. XVII: The 14-year incidence and progression of diabetic retinopathy and associated risk factors in type 1 diabetes. *Ophthalmology* 1998;105:1801–1815.
16. Bresnick GH, Davis MD, Myers FL, et al. Clinicopathologic correlations in diabetic retinopathy. II. Clinical and histologic appearance of retinal capillary microaneurysms. *Arch Ophthalmol* 1977;95:1215.
17. Engerman RL. Animal models of diabetic retinopathy. *Trans Am Acad Ophthalmol Otolaryngol* 1976;81:710.
18. Klein R, Klein BEK, Moss S, et al. The Wisconsin Epidemiologic Study of Diabetic Retinopathy. III. Prevalence and risk of diabetic retinopathy when the age at diagnosis is less than thirty years. *Arch Ophthalmol* 1984;102:520.
19. Klein R, Klein BEK, Moss S, et al. The Wisconsin Epidemiologic Study of Diabetic Retinopathy. III. Prevalence and risk of diabetic retinopathy when the age at diagnosis is greater than thirty years. *Arch Ophthalmol* 1984;102:527.
20. Job D, Eschwege E, Guyot-Argenton C, et al. Effect of multiple daily insulin injections on the course of diabetic retinopathy. *Diabetes* 1976;25:463.
21. Dibble CM, Kochenour NK, Worley RJ, et al. Effect of pregnancy on diabetic retinopathy. *Obstet Gynecol* 1982;59:699.
22. Pirart J. Diabète et complications dégénératives. Présentation d'une étude prospective portant sur 4400 cas observés entre 1947 et 1973. *Diabetes Metab* 1977;3:97.
23. Cunha-Vaz JG, Fonseca JR, Faria De Abreu JR, et al. Detection of early retinal changes in diabetes by vitreous fluorophotometry. *Diabetes* 1979;28:16.
24. Waltman SR, Oestrick C, Krupin T, et al. Quantitative vitreous fluorophotometry: a sensitive technique for measuring early breakdown of the blood retinal barrier in young diabetic patients. *Diabetes* 1978;27:85.
25. Reichard P, Nilsson B-Y, Rosenqvist U. The effect of long-term intensified treatment on the development of microvascular complications of diabetes mellitus. *N Engl J Med* 1993;329:304.
26. The Diabetes Control and Complications Trial Research Group (DCCT). The effect of intensive treatment of diabetes on the development and progression of long-term complications in insulin-dependent diabetes mellitus. *N Engl J Med* 1993;29:977.
27. Lawson PM, Champion MC, Canny C, et al. Continuous subcutaneous insulin infusion (CSII) does not prevent progression of proliferative and preproliferative retinopathy. *Br J Ophthalmol* 1982;66:762.
28. Irsigler K, Kritz H, Najemnik C. Reversal of florid diabetic retinopathy. *Lancet* 1979;2:1068.
29. Kohner EM. The effect of diabetes on retino-vascular function. *Acta Diabetol* 1971;8(suppl 1):135.
30. Van Ballegooie E, Hooymans JMM, Timmerman Z, et al. Rapid deterioration of diabetic retinopathy during treatments with continuous subcutaneous insulin infusion. *Diabetes Care* 1984;7:236.
31. Brinchmann-Hansen O, Dahl-Jorgensen K, Hanssen KF, et al. Effects of intensified insulin treatment on various lesions of diabetic retinopathy. *Am J Ophthalmol* 1985;100:644.
32. Murata M, Yoshimoto H. Morphological study of the pathogenesis of retinal cottonwool spot. *Jpn J Ophthalmol* 1983;27:362.
33. Tasman W. Diabetic vitreous hemorrhage and its relationship to hypoglycemia. *Mod Probl Ophthalmol* 1979;20:413.
34. Drash AL, Daneman D, Travis L. Progressive retinopathy with improved metabolic control in diabetic dwarfism (Mauriac's syndrome). *Diabetes* 1980;29(suppl 2):1A.

35. Tamborlane WV, Puklin JE, Bergman M, et al. Long-term improvement of metabolic control with the insulin pump does not reverse diabetic microangiopathy. *Diabetes Care* 1982; 5(suppl 1):58.

36. Engerman RL. Perspectives in diabetes: pathogenesis of diabetic retinopathy. *Diabetes* 1989;38:1203.

37. Jovanovic-Peterson L, Peterson CM. Diabetic retinopathy. *Clin Obstet Gynecol* 1991;34:516.

38. Klein R, Klein BEK, Moss SE, et al. Retinopathy in young-onset diabetic patients. *Diabetes Care* 1985;8:311.

39. Groop LC, Teir S, Koskimies PH, et al. Risk factors and markers associated with proliferative retinopathy in patients with insulin-dependent diabetes. *Diabetes* 1986;35:1397.

40. Barnes AJ, Kohner EM, Johnston DG, et al. Severe retinopathy and mild carbohydrate intolerance: possible role of insulin deficiency and elevated circulating growth hormone. *Lancet* 1985;1: 1465.

41. Rand LI, Krolewski AS, Aiello LM, et al. Multiple factors in the prediction of risk of diabetic retinopathy. *N Engl J Med* 1985; 313:1433.

42. Larinkari J, Laatikainen L, Ranta T. Metabolic control and serum hormone levels in relationship to retinopathy in diabetic pregnancy. *Diabetologia* 1982;22:327.

43. Merimee TJ, Zapf J, Froesch ER. Insulin-like growth factors: studies in diabetics with and without retinopathy. *N Engl J Med* 1983;309:527.

44. Peterson LP, Kundu N. Endocrine assessment of high-risk pregnancies. *Obstet Gynecol Ann* 1980;9:169.

45. Kostraba JN, Klein R, Dorman JS, et al. The epidemiology of Diabetes Complications Study IV. Correlates of diabetic background and proliferative retinopathy. *Am J Epidemiol* 1991;133: 381.

46. Janka HU, Warram JH, Rand LJ, et al. Risk factors for progression of background retinopathy in longstanding IDDM. *Diabetes* 1989;38:460.

47. Chase HP, Garg SK, Jackson WE, et al. Blood pressure and retinopathy in type I diabetes. *Ophthalmology* 1990;97:155.

48. Norgaard K, Feldt-Rasmussen B, Deckert T. Is hypertension a major independent risk factor for retinopathy in type I diabetes? *Diabet Med* 1991;8:334.

49. Jackson WE, Holmes DL, Garg SK, et al. Angiotensin-converting enzyme inhibitor therapy and diabetic retinopathy. *Ann Ophthalmol* 1992;24:99.

50. Lewis JM, Jovanovic-Peterson L, Ahmadizadeh I, et al. The Santa Barbara County Diabetic Screening Feasibility Study: significance of diabetes duration and systolic blood pressure. *J Diabet Complications* 1994;8:51.

51. Cousins L. Pregnancy complications among diabetic women: review 1965–1985. *Obstet Gynecol Surv* 1987;42:140.

52. Rosenn B, Miodovnik M, Kranias G, et al. Progression of diabetic retinopathy in pregnancy: association with hypertension in pregnancy. *Am J Obstet Gynecol* 1992;166:1214.

53. Jervell J, Moe N, Skjaeraasen J, et al. Diabetes mellitus and pregnancy: management and results at Rikshospitalet, Oslo, 1970–1977. *Diabetologia* 1979;16:151.

54. Rodman HM, Singerman LJ, Aiello LM. Diabetic retinopathy: effects of pregnancy and laser therapy, abstracted. *Diabetes* 1980; 29:1A.

55. Soubrane G, Canivet J, Coscas G. Influence of pregnancy on the evolution of background retinopathy. *Int Ophthalmol Clin* 1985; 8:249.

56. Moloney JBM, Drury IM. The effect of pregnancy on the natural course of diabetic retinopathy. *Am J Ophthalmol* 1982;93: 745.

57. Rodman HM, Singerman LJ, Aiello LM, et al. Diabetic retinopathy and its relationship to pregnancy. In: Merkatz ER, Adams PAJ, eds. *The diabetic pregnancy: a perinatal perspective.* Orlando, FL: Grune & Stratton, 1979:321.

58. Stephens JW, Page OC, Hare RL. Diabetes and pregnancy: a report of experiences in 119 pregnancies over a period of ten years. *Diabetes* 1963;12:213.

59. Horvat M, Maclean H, Goldberg L, et al. Diabetic retinopathy in pregnancy: a 12-year prospective survey. *Br J Ophthalmol* 1980;64:398.

60. Ohrt V. The influence of pregnancy on diabetic retinopathy. *Acta Endocrinol (Copenh)* 1986;112(suppl 277):122.

61. Mein BEK, Moss SE, Klein R. Effect of pregnancy on progression of diabetic retinopathy. *Diabetes Care* 1990;13:34.

62. Price JH, Hadden DR, Archer DB, et al. Diabetic retinopathy in pregnancy. *Br J Obstet Gynaecol* 1984;91:11.

63. Larinkari J, Laatikainen L, Ranta T, et al. Metabolic control and serum hormone levels in relationship to retinopathy in diabetic pregnancy. *Diabetologia* 1982;22:327.

64. Serup L. Influence of pregnancy on diabetic retinopathy. *Acta Endocrinol (Copenh)* 1986;112(suppl 277):122.

65. Klein BEK. Diabetic retinopathy during pregnancy. In: Jovanovic L, ed. *Controversies in the field of pregnancy and diabetes.* New York: Springer-Verlag, 1988:77.

66. Phelps RL, Sakol P, Metzger BE, et al. Changes in diabetic retinopathy during pregnancy: correlations with regulation of hyperglycemia. *Arch Ophthalmol* 1986;104:1806.

67. Chang S, Fuhrmann M, Jovanovic L. The Diabetes in Early Pregnancy Study Group (DIEP): pregnancy, retinopathy, normoglycemia: a preliminary analysis. *Diabetes* 1985;(suppl):353A.

68. The Diabetes in Early Pregnancy Study Group. Metabolic control and progression of retinopathy, abstracted. Presented at the National American Diabetes Association Meeting, New Orleans, LA, June 11, 1994.

69. Boone MI, Farber ME, Jovanovic-Peterson L, et al. Increased retinal vascular tortuosity in gestational diabetes mellitus. *Ophthalmology* 1989;96:251.

70. Kitzmiller J, Main E, Ward B, et al. Insulin lispro and the development of proliferative diabetic retinopathy during pregnancy. *Diabetes Care* 1999;22:874.

71. DiMarchi RD, Chance RE, Long HB, et al. Preparation of an insulin with improved pharmacokinetics relative to human insulin through consideration of structural homology with insulin-like growth factor-1. *Horm Res* 1994;41(suppl 2): 93–96.

72. Merimee TJ, Zapf J, Froesch ER. Insulin-like growth factors: studies in diabetics with and without retinopathy. *N Engl J Med* 1983;309:527–531.

73. Larinkari J, Laatikainen L, Ranta T. Metabolic control and serum hormone levels in relationship to retinopathy in diabetic pregnancy. *Diabetologia* 1982;22:327–331.

74. Jovanovic L, Ilic S, Pettitt DJ, Hugo K, et al. The metabolic and immunologic effects of insulin lispro in gestational diabetes. *Diabetes* 1998;47(suppl 1):190.

75. Hill DJ, Clemmons DR, Riley SC, et al. Immunohistochemical localization of insulin like growth factors and IGF binding proteins-1,-2, and -3 in human placenta and fetal membranes. *Placenta* 1993;14:1–12.

76. MacLeod JN, Worsley I, Ray Y, et al. Human growth hormone variant is a biologically active somatogen and lactogen. *Endocrinology* 1991;128:1298–1302.

77. Gluckman PD. The endocrine regulation of fetal growth in late gestation: the role of insulin-like growth factors. *J Clin Endocrinol Metab* 1995;80:1047–1050.

78. Holly JMP, Amiel SA, Sandhu RR, et al. The role of growth hormone in diabetes mellitus. *J Endocrinol* 1988;118:353–364.

79. Llewelyn J, Slieker LJ, Zimmermann JL. Pre-clinical studies on insulin lispro. *Drugs Today* 1998;34(suppl C):11–21.

80. Anderson JH, Brunelle RL, Koivisto VA. Reduction of postprandial hyperglycemia and frequency of hypoglycemia in IDDM patients on insulin-analog treatment. *Diabetes* 1997;46: 265–270.

81. Laatikainen L, Teramo K, Hieta-Heikurainen H, et al. A controlled study of the influence of continuous subcutaneous insulin infusion treatment on diabetic retinopathy during pregnancy. *Acta Med Scand* 1987;221:367–376.

82. Pettitt DJ, Ospina P, Kolaczynski JW, et al. Comparison of an insulin analog, insulin aspart, and regular human insulin with no insulin in gestational diabetes mellitus. *Diabetes Care* 2003;26: 183–186.

29

CLINICAL DIABETIC NEPHROPATHY BEFORE AND DURING PREGNANCY*

JOHN L. KITZMILLER

Diabetic nephropathy (DN), with its link to cardiovascular disease (CVD), is a major factor in deaths related to diabetes mellitus and the leading cause of very costly end-stage renal disease (ESRD) (1,2). Intensified control of blood glucose (BG) and blood pressure (BP) can prevent or delay the onset of nephropathy in women with type 1 or type 2 diabetes (3–5). New information about the pathogenesis of the early stages of DN has led to renoprotective therapies that block or retard progression of the disease and reduce cardiovascular morbidity and mortality (6,7). Thus, it is essential for women at risk for DN to receive optimal global care (behavioral, nutritional, pharmacologic) at all stages of their lives, and especially in preparation for pregnancy.

DN is the most important complication of diabetes that affects the outcome of pregnancy. Associated perinatal problems include congenital malformations, fetal growth retardation, stillbirth, and preterm delivery with associated neonatal disorders. Maternal hazards consist of possible renal failure during or after pregnancy, superimposed preeclampsia, the frequent association of nephropathy with proliferative retinopathy and macular edema, and the risk for eventual morbidity or death from macrovascular disease. Despite the possible complications, such women and their mates frequently desire to have a child. Optimal outcomes for mothers and babies are produced when a multidisciplinary approach is used at a perinatal center with perinatologists, nephrologists, diabetologists, and neonatologists interacting effectively. Patient care must be supported by diabetes educators, dietitians, medical social workers, and obstetric nurses who specialize in high-risk pregnancy. With such an approach, perinatal outcome has improved dramatically for women with DN, but concerns persist about preservation of maternal health.

Thus, there are many challenges regarding DN and pregnancy. To consider them, we must understand the natural history and pathogenesis of this disorder. There has been a continuing acceleration of information and hypotheses about DN. There are new data on genetic susceptibility to DN (8,9); on structure-function relationships in the kidneys in the progressing stages of DN (10–12); on the possible damaging role of hyperfiltration, increased glomerular pressure, and vasoactive substances early in the course of diabetes (13–17); on the identification of incipient nephropathy as microalbuminuria at a stage when preventive care is possible (18,19); and on interacting biochemical pathways that link hyperglycemia and associated pathogenic factors to changes in the kidneys and vasculature (20–23) and influence treatment (24,25). An expanded review of current literature on these topics is available in the online version of the text.

Obstetricians who care for women with DN often view the pregnancy as such an important time that the perspective of the natural or remedied course of DN is lost. Optimal long-term maternal and child health occurs when health-care providers consider the full continuum of the stages of living with diabetes proceeding through the childbearing years. The effectiveness of medical therapy in the years before pregnancy strongly influences the degree of complications noted during gestation. In addition, the rationale and goals of treatment during pregnancy must include effects on long-term maternal health as well as short-term perinatal outcome.

DEFINITION AND EPIDEMIOLOGY

Overt clinical DN is diagnosed in women with either type 1 or type 2 diabetes mellitus on the basis of persistent proteinuria [>0.5 g/24 h total urinary protein excretion (TPE) or >200 µg/min or >300 mg/24 h urinary albumin excretion (UAE)] in the absence of infection or evidence of other renal or urinary tract disorders (1,2,26). Because women

---

*Due to space limitations, this is an annotated version of this chapter. The complete text, including expanded sections on epidemiology and genetics, basic renal structure and function, pathologic structure/function studies, pathogenesis, and therapeutic interventions is updated quarterly and is available online at JKITZ.net.

with type 2 diabetes and proteinuria may have nondiabetic renal pathology (27,28), the coexistence of diabetic retinopathy has been used in the absence of renal biopsies to presume the diagnosis of DN, although the majority of proteinuric type 2 diabetic women without retinopathy have diabetic glomerular-tubulointerstitial changes (29,30). Progression of DN is characterized by hypertension, declining glomerular filtration rate (GFR) by 4 to 12 mL/min per yr, and eventual ESRD with uremia (1,2,26).

Renal failure is a major cause of death for diabetic adults of all ages (31,32), but albuminuria also predicts increased mortality from myocardial infarction and congestive heart failure, especially in women, with both types of diabetes (33–35). Because of the high morbidity and mortality rates, research has focused on early changes in renal function and structure that could predict advanced DN and identify subjects for treatment to prevent DN and associated CVD (6,7,19,36).

The concept of incipient DN is defined by repetitive subclinical increases in UAE known as microalbuminuria, although some patients show early abnormalities in renal function and structure without significant increases in UAE (37,38). The diagnosis of microalbuminuria is best made using a timed daytime or 24-hour urine collection without strenuous exercise (two of three samples with UAE 20–199 mg/min or 30–299 mg/24 h) (39,40). Simpler screening tests for microalbuminuria in spot urine samples have been proposed, to be measured in first morning urine samples due to the diurnal variation in UAE. Spot urine albumin concentration is less reliable than the urine albumin/creatinine ratio (UACR) (>3.5 mg/mM or >30 mg/g, for females), but variability in UACR can be substantial due to differences in creatinine excretion related to muscle mass, gender, age, and lack of standardization of creatinine assays (41,42). Spot UACR is a sensitive screening test but a poor predictor of quantitative UAE (43).

The prevalence of microalbuminuria in type 1 diabetes varies from 6% to 52% (41,44–48), depending on postpubertal duration of diabetes (45,49), baseline UAE greater than 10 μg/min, greater than 10 mg/d (41,46–49), level of glycemic control marked by even modestly elevated glycohemoglobin (41,47–52), elevated BP in some studies (46, 53,54), elevated fasting triglyceride (TG) and low-density lipoprotein (LDL) cholesterol (41,54,55), and current smoking (48,52,56,57). Viberti provided a good assessment of the use of risk markers versus risk determinants in early DN (58). Low birth weight has been inadequately studied as a risk factor for increased prevalence of microalbuminuria in type 1 diabetes (57,59,60), but maternal smoking during pregnancy and parental hypertension were independent predictors of microalbuminuria in a nested case control study, especially in the setting of current poor glycemic control (57). Hyperglycemia is seen as a necessary but not completely sufficient cause of the renal changes leading to microalbuminuria.

In follow-up of cases of microalbuminuria, 10% to 56% will regress to normal UAE, perhaps as a result of improved glycemic control and other renoprotective therapies (47,48,61,62), although these patients may progress back to persistent microalbuminuria (63). Prospective studies conducted before widespread use of glycemic monitoring indicated that most type 1 diabetic women with microalbuminuria eventually progressed to macroalbuminuria or proteinuria (DN) (18,19,64,65). Since then, prospective studies in settings of improved metabolic control have shown that 14% to 25% of type 1 diabetic adults with baseline microalbuminuria progress over 4 to 10 years to clinical DN, compared to 0% to 6% of patients with normal albuminuria at baseline (48,61,62,66–68). Progression is independently associated with baseline UAE in the upper normal range and slightly elevated baseline and prevailing hemoglobin A$_{1c}$ (HbA$_{1c}$) levels (61,66–68), and with elevated BP in some but not all studies (67,68). It has been debated whether modest hypertension precedes or accompanies the progression of microalbuminuria.

In prospective longitudinal studies of diabetic children and adolescents, the cumulative incidence of persistent microalbuminuria is 10% to 20% (69–72). These studies provide insight into the determinants of microalbuminuria in the early years of type 1 diabetes. Hyperglycemia is a predictor for its development and progression (70–74), and other risk factors include female gender, early puberty, elevated systolic BP (69–75), plus increased kidney volume (75) and glomerular hyperfiltration (76,77). The reasons for the increase in albuminuria associated with early puberty (72,78, 79) are unclear—discussion focuses on worsening glycemic control, sex steroids, growth hormone, and insulin-like growth factor-1. Young diabetic females should be screened for microalbuminuria annually by age 12.

For women with type 2 diabetes, microalbuminuria is found in sequential urine samples in 6% to 26% of newly diagnosed patients in cross-sectional studies (80–82), although the actual duration of diabetes is uncertain. In the UK Prospective Diabetes Study (UKPDS) of 585 newly diagnosed patients with type 2 diabetes, 17% had microalbuminuria, 3.8% macroalbuminuria, and 37% were hypertensive (83). Independent correlates of UAE included systolic BP and fasting plasma glucose and TG, although only 10% of the variance in UAE was explained (83). Microalbuminuria may subsequently regress to normal levels with improved glycemic control in type 2 patients. The prevalence of persistent microalbuminuria in patients with established and treated type 2 diabetes in various parts of the world was 17% to 33% in the 1980s and 1990s (80,81, 84–92), but the clinical characteristics of the microalbuminuric subjects may vary by ethnic group (87,89–93). Diabetic retinopathy is identified in the majority of these patients. In prospective longitudinal studies of type 2 subjects with baseline normal UAE, persistent microalbuminuria develops in 16% to 35% over 6 to 20 years (81,

84–86,91,92). Predictors of the development of microalbuminuria in type 2 diabetes include baseline UAE in the upper normal range (84,91,92), chronic hyperglycemia (82,84,85,92), slight elevations in BP in some studies (81,85,87,91,92) and hyperlipidemia in others (84,85,88), and markers of inflammation (93–96) including highly sensitive complement-reactive protein (97,98). Progression to overt DN occurs in 9% to 45% of women with type 2 diabetes and microalbuminuria (incipient DN) over 2 to 20 years of follow-up, compared with 0.8% to 4.1% in patients normoalbuminuric at baseline, and progression in type 2 diabetes is associated with poor glycemic control, increasing BP, increased body mass index (BMI), and hyperlipidemias (91,84–86,91,92).

Microalbuminuria in type 2 diabetes is more predictive of CVD and related mortality than of ESRD (99–104), except in East Asia, where the rate of coronary artery disease is relatively low (89,93,103). The link between increased UAE and risk for CVD is not fully understood, and may represent common susceptibility to hyperglycemic effects on endothelium, blood vessels, and glomerular-tubular structures. For many investigators, the data suggest that microalbuminuria is a sign of widespread vascular injury or inflammation in patients with both types of diabetes (94,95,105,106) as well as in nondiabetic patients with essential hypertension (107,108). Due to the strong association between microalbuminuria and CVD in type 2 diabetes, Stehouwer and others propose that microalbuminuria is a marker of a pathophysiologic process induced by hyperglycemia that causes both renal albumin loss and atherothrombosis (95).

Ongoing changes in diabetes management may be yielding a declining prevalence of DN in type 1 diabetes in some regions (1,3,6). Until the 1980s, macroalbuminuria developed gradually over 20 to 30 years in 30% to 50% of type 1 diabetic women, and at least 50% of cases progressed to ESRD by 10 years of proteinuria (44,109,110). More recent data from Scandinavia (111–113) and the United States (45,110,114) show cumulative incidences of DN after 10 to 24 years of type 1 diabetes to be 11% to 34%, with a slower increase after 20 to 24 years. The incidence peaks at 12 to 17 years of type 1 diabetes, and is highest in women diagnosed in their youth who develop microalbuminuria early in the course of diabetes, or in the age interval of 25 to 35 years (45,109–111,113,115), demonstrating the relevance to childbearing. As with microalbuminuria, modifiable risk factors associated with DN in type 1 diabetes include hyperglycemia, current smoking, and baseline elevated BP (110,112,114,116). Low birth weight may also be a risk factor for development of DN (117). In one area of Sweden with near normal glycohemoglobin values in most type 1 patients with diabetes onset before age 15, the cumulative incidence of DN after 20 years of diabetes decreased from 28% in those with diabetes onset during 1961to 1965 to 5.8% in those with diabetes onset during

1971 to 1975 (118). This is similar to prevalences of DN of 3.7% to 6.5% after 15 years of type 1 diabetes in recent nationwide multicenter studies in Italy (119), Denmark (120), and Spain (121). These surveys provide hope that current strategies of renoprotection (1,3,6) may prevent the development of DN and its costly complications.

In cross-sectional studies of type 2 diabetes, the prevalence of DN (macroalbuminuria or proteinuria) has a wide range of 3% to 37%, depending on earlier decade of diagnosis and longer duration of diabetes (122–125), level of hyperglycemia (114,116,122,126,127), hypertension (114, 116,122,127,128), smoking (116,125), and ethnic or national background (90,116,124,125,128–130). High prevalence rates are found in patients of Native American (116,131), Mexican (129), and African origin (90,124, 128), and in India (91), Hong Kong (116), and Japan (125). These risk factors hold for women with type 2 diabetes as well as men (84,90,116,122). Follow-up studies of type 2 patients with no proteinuria at baseline for 10 years showed that 12% to 30% developed DN in the 1980s (114,123). The modifiable risk factors of level of glycohemoglobin and BP, smoking, and hyperlipidemias were independently related to the development of DN (84,114,123, 125). In a selected group of Danish type 2 patients with normoalbuminuria at baseline, 3% developed DN over 6 years (84). Several studies showed that the risk for developing DN is greatest in those patients diagnosed with type 2 diabetes at a younger age, even when controlling for duration of known glycemic exposure (90,122,125). Thus, all type 2 patients of any age should be screened regularly for albuminuria.

Progression to ESRD occurred in 2% to 5% of type 1 diabetic patients followed for a median of 8 to 25 years in population-based studies, similar to 1% to 5% in type 2 diabetic patients (114,132,133). The higher yield came from the World Health Organization multinational study of vascular disease in diabetes, which included patients from populations with a high prevalence of diabetes, hypertension, and renal disease (133). All the studies agreed that the risk factors for renal failure include duration of diabetes, glycemic control, elevated BP, smoking, hyperlipidemia, and the comorbidities of diabetic retinopathy and CVD (114,132,133). Although the risk for renal failure may be somewhat greater in patients with type 1 than type 2 diabetes (114,134), the majority of patients with diabetic ESRD entering treatment have type 2 diabetes, due to the much greater prevalence of type 2 diabetes in all populations (134–137). In Western countries with multiracial populations there is an excess risk for diabetic ESRD in minority groups (134–139). Whether this is due to genetic or social differences such as access to care (136) or response to antihypertensive treatment (139) is unclear, but the clinical importance is that programs attempting to reduce the huge costs of ESRD must target minority groups.

As predicted by the link between microalbuminuria and CVD, clinical DN is also associated with CVD (coronary artery disease, heart failure, and stroke) (34,109,123,126, 127), and as noted, the leading cause of mortality has become CVD rather than uremia in patients with DN, except in Japan (104,112,140–142). Assessment of CVD risk in diabetes "must include 'diabetes-related' variables such as glycemic control, proteinuria, and retinopathy, as well as the classic risk factors, blood pressure, smoking and dyslipidemia" (142), and treatment plans should target all of these factors.

Familial Relationships and Genetic Predispositions to Diabetic Nephropathy

Because approximately 50% of patients with type 1 diabetes may never develop DN despite decades of hyperglycemia, research focuses on factors that influence the susceptibility to nephropathy. An early study found that 24 of 29 diabetic siblings of probands with DN had albuminuria compared with only 2 of 12 diabetic siblings of probands free of DN (143). Other diabetic sibling studies confirmed the familial clustering of DN, suggesting a major gene effect (144,145). In the Diabetes Control and Complications Trial (DCCT), there was an increased risk for albuminuria in first-degree relatives of albuminuric versus nonalbuminuric type 1 subjects in the secondary intervention cohort (146). Familial clustering of nephropathy is also described in type 2 diabetes in various populations in Europe (147,148), Japan (149), and the Americas (150–155).

Approaches to identification of genes involved in the development, progression, or protection from nephropathy in type 1 and type 2 diabetes have been reviewed (156–159). Krowlewski proposed that genetic susceptibility must result from DNA sequence differences called polymorphisms/mutations, or disease alleles in (or linked to) regulatory or structural parts of one or more genes. He described possible models of gene effects interacting with poor glycemic control: (a) a major gene effect due to polymorphisms in one gene; (b) moderate gene effects due to mutations in any one of several genes with similar additive effects, with the most frequent disease allele having a more major role (perhaps one predisposing to onset of DN and others to progression or response to treatment); and (c) polygenic effects in which poor glycemic control interacts with DNA sequence differences in many loci, each contributing minor effects to the overall susceptibility to DN. The manifestation of a particular susceptibility genotype can vary in different populations and depend on the intensity or the cumulative exposure to hyperglycemia (157). Continuing searches of DNA sequence variants in the human genome, linked to specific phenotypic analysis in large prospective studies, will probably define multifactorial contributions of these and other candidate genes to the micro- and macrovascular disease associated with DN.

PATHOLOGIC RENAL STRUCTURE AND FUNCTION IN DIABETES

Consideration of the pathologic findings in the kidney in diabetes is based on recent advances in understanding renal structure and function. The glomerular capillary tuft is made up of three cell types: fenestrated endothelium, visceral epithelium (the octopus-shaped podocytes), and mesangium. The glomerular capillaries derive from a richly innervated afferent arteriole, which divides into branches: each branch forms a lobular network of anastomosing capillaries, with each lobule supported by mesangium. The capillaries then merge to form the efferent arteriole, which again divides to form a second capillary network surrounding the tubules. Glomerular capillary pressure (P_{gc}) is affected by afferent and efferent arteriolar pressure and flow (160), and counterforces generated by the envelope of the glomerular basement membrane (GBM), contractile mesangial processes, and the podocyte foot processes (FPs) maintain glomerular stability (161). There is little turnover of glomerular cells in the healthy adult kidney. Various protein effectors and bioactive receptors are demonstrated in the endothelial and mesangial cells and the podocytes. Podocytes are specialized for protein secretion, play a key role in the biogenesis of GBM, and can reabsorb some of the filtered protein. Podocyte failure with effacement of the FPs (162) "decisively accounts for the initiation of progressive renal diseases, as well as for the maintenance of the progression to end-stage renal failure" (163). Very thin slit diaphragms between the foot processes (Fig. 29-1) provide cell-cell contact between the podocytes and are dynamic sites of glomerular permselectivity, probably via rectangular pores (4×14 nm) about the size of albumin (164). Nephrin and podocin are recently discovered proteins that are major components of the slit diaphragm complex (165). Interference with proteins of the slit diaphragms cause effacement of the FPs and proteinuria (164,165).

A complex network of two types of extracellular matrix (ECM; GBM and mesangial matrix) supports the glomerular cells. The GBM is an amorphous scaffold made up mostly of a compact meshwork of type IV collagen, glycoproteins, and stabilizing proteoglycans (166). Proteoglycans consist of protein cores with attached long carbohydrate side chains like heparan sulfate; the side chains impart a negative charge (167). The concept that anionic sites in the internal and external layers of the GBM provide a barrier to negatively charged proteins has become controversial (168). The sulfate radicals hold water in between the polysaccharide chains of the proteoglycans and maintain the GBM as a hydrated gel matrix, which contributes to a constant solute flow across the gel membrane.

Proximal convoluted tubule epithelial cells (PTEC) have an internal apical microvillous brush border that greatly increases the luminal surface and a prominent intracellular digestive tract (endocytosis and lysosomes) for limited reab-

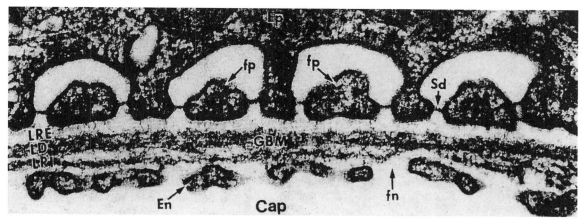

FIGURE 29-1. Electron micrograph of the ultrafiltration unit. Note foot processes (*fp*) of epithelial cell (*Ep*) with intervening slit diaphragms (*Sd*), glomerular basement membrane (*GBM*), and fenestrated (*fn*) endothelium (*En*). The GBM consists of lamina densa (*LD*) and lamina rarae interna (*LRI*) and externa (*LRE*). (Original magnification × 50,000.) (From Kanwar YS. *Semin Nephrol* 1991;11:390, with permission.)

sorption of filtered protein (169). Insulin is digested both by the peritubular and microvillous sides of the cells, but albumin is rapidly taken up by shared tubular brush border receptors for albumin and LDL called megalin and cubulin (170,171). Albumin is broken down in the lysosomes, and degradation products are released into the peritubular side.

Despite research into the structural determinants of glomerular permeability to macromolecules, uncertainty remains about permselectivity in the normal human kidney and the multiple causes of proteinuria in disease (168,169, 172). Selectivity implies filtration of molecules smaller than albumin and retention of others based on size, charge, and shape, and does not account for tubular reabsorption. Deen et al. (172) and Tryggvason and Wartiovaara (165) described the basic structural unit for filtrate flow as the endothelial fenestrae (50–100 nm) covered by negatively charged glycocalyx, the GBM meshwork gel, and the filtration slit diaphragm made up of nephrin bridging (~43 nm wide) the podocyte FPs. Formerly the GBM was considered the primary size and charge-selective sieve of the glomerulus based on irregular "pores" among the polymer meshwork and the negative repelling charge of the gycosaminoglycans (165) but there is controversy regarding the charge selectivity of the GBM or the glomerular unit (163,168,172). Current models of human permselectivity indicate that the major site of size selectivity is the slit diaphragm with pores measuring 4 × 14 nm (165,172). The best-fit model for glomerular sieving is heteroporous membranes perforated by a lower size distribution of restrictive pores (mean radius 4.4 nm) and a parallel upper distribution of larger shuntlike pores (172). It was concluded that "the selectivity of proteinuria is a complex function of both filtration properties of the glomerular barrier and of tubular reabsorptive capacity, and the contribution of each of these variables cannot be determined" (173).

The renal interstitium comprises the extravascular intertubular spaces of the renal parenchyma, containing cells and extracellular substances that modulate almost all exchange among the tubular and vascular elements of the kidney, influence glomerular filtration through effects on tubuloglomerular feedback, affect growth and differentiation of parenchymal cells, and determine the compliance of the peritubular vasculature. Alterations in the interstitium are key to progression of chronic renal disease (174). The interstitial cells include fibroblast-like cells often adjacent to macrophages, lipid-laden cells with receptors for angiotensin II and bradykinin, dendritic cells from the bone marrow that present antigens to T lymphocytes, and perivascular cells (pericytes). The extracellular components comprise a matrix of a hydrated gel of various glycosaminoglycans and glycoproteins (fibronectin, laminin) within reticular fibers of collagens, the aqueous pathway for water and solute exchange (174).

Renal biopsy studies of young patients early in the course of diabetes reveal enlargement of the glomerulus by hypertrophy shortly after diagnosis of diabetes (175,176) and increased thickness of the GBM by 2 years of disease, compared with nondiabetic controls, in advance of detectable hypertension, albuminuria, or reduced filtration (177,178). Enlargement of the glomerular capillary wall area (the filtration surface of the peripheral GBM) seems to be the initial morphologic correlate of elevated GFR and filtration fraction (FF) found over the first decade of type 1 diabetes (12,176,179). Mesangial expansion (of matrix more than cells) (180) can be measured after a few more years, and is related to thickening of GBM (12,181,182) (Fig. 29-2), nocturnal mean arterial pressure (183), and increasing UAE (177,181,184), and to eventual reduction of filtration surface (Fig. 29-3) and decline in GFR (Fig.

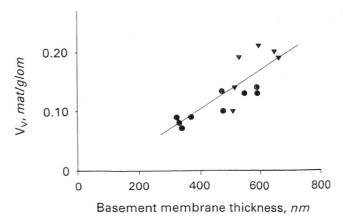

FIGURE 29-2. Relationship between peripheral basement membrane thickness and mesangial matrix as a fraction of glomerulus in type 1 diabetes; $r = 0.82$, $p = 0.0001$. Symbols: ●, normoalbuminuria; ▼, microalbuminuria. [From Walker JD, Close CF, Jones SL, et al. Glomerular structure in type-1 (insulin-dependent) diabetic patients with normo- and microalbuminuria. *Kidney Int* 1992;41:741, with permission.]

29-4) (177,185,186). Interstitial fractional volume is reduced early in diabetes, probably due to tubular enlargement without concomitant interstitial expansion, which occurs later (12,187,188). Osterby and colleagues observed a marked increase in interstitial volume as a diffuse fibrosis with mostly extracellular material, after 7 to 18 years of type 1 diabetes at the stage of early albuminuria (189). All of these changes seem specific for diabetes, because nondiabetic identical twins of diabetic subjects have normal glomerular and tubular morphology (190). Kidneys from nondiabetic donors transplanted into normotensive diabetic patients develop the same lesions (without morphologic evidence of transplant rejection), but this does not occur in nondiabetic transplant recipients (191,192).

ECM components accumulate in the expanding mesangial matrix and GBM of diabetic patients, perhaps at the expense of decreased heparan sulfate-proteoglycan (HSPG) measured in the internal and external lamina of GBM in type 1 patients with clinical proteinuria (193–195). The number of podocytes is reduced as DN progresses (196) and the podocyte FPs widen and then efface (197) as a correlate of increasing albuminuria. As disease advances, podocytes may be lost and measured in the urine (198). As noted by Mauer, arteriolar hyalinosis may progress to "exudative" fibrinoid or hyaline lesions. "Capillary loops can sometimes develop microaneurysms, which appear to be the forerunners of K-W nodules" (182). As DN progresses, similar to other chronic renal diseases, tubulointerstitial injury is seen to include tubular atrophy, interstitial fibrosis with increased cellularity due to infiltration of lymphocytes/macrophages, and transition of PTEC to myofibroblasts, plus arterioscle-

rosis (187,199–204). Percentage glomeruli occluded, tubular atrophy, and degree of mesangial and interstitial fibrosis all correlate with further decline in GFR (182,184,205, 206).

The Pima Indians of Arizona offer a unique population for study of glomerular structure since they develop type 2 diabetes at an early age with its onset diagnosed prospectively, and they "are not afflicted by equally early development of hypertension, atherosclerosis, or nondiabetic renal disease" (207). Renal biopsies in patients with a range of albuminuria from normal to high revealed doubled glomerular volume and high GFR in early diabetes (compared with non-Pima controls) and significant increases in GBM thickness and fractional volumes of mesangium and interstitium (207). The patients with clinical proteinuria had a marked increase in global sclerosis, with reduced number and density of podocytes of larger cell volume and widened FP. Thus, the endothelial and mesangial cells can

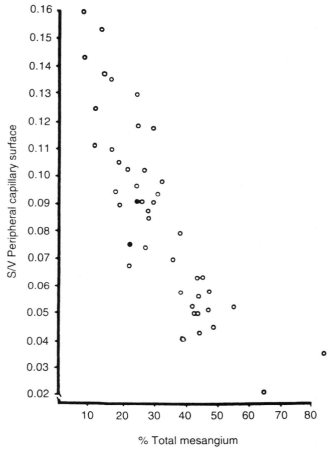

FIGURE 29-3. Relationship between the total percentage mesangium and the surface density (*S/V*) of the peripheral capillary filtration surface. (Modified from Mauer SM. Structural-functional correlations of diabetic nephropathy [Review]. *Kidney Int* 1994;45:612, with permission.)

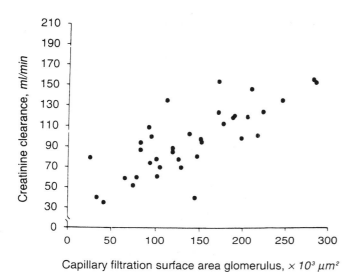

FIGURE 29-4. Direct correlation between capillary filtration surface area per glomerulus and glomerular filtration rate estimated by creatinine clearance. (Modified from Mauer SM. Structural-functional correlations of diabetic nephropathy [Review]. *Kidney Int* 1994;45:612, with permission.)

proliferate as part of glomerular hypertrophy, but podocytes cannot as they "stretch" to cover more surface area (like neurons). In a later study of a subset with microalbuminuria, reduced podocyte number on the baseline biopsy was the strongest predictor of progression of albuminuria because mesangial volume fraction had a modest effect (208). Australian type 2 diabetic patients with proteinuria showed reduced expression of the podocyte-specific protein nephrin in renal biopsies compared with nondiabetic controls, and the nephrin messenger RNA expression was inversely related to degree of proteinuria (209). This finding is consistent with the proposed role of nephrin in maintaining pore structure in the slit diaphragms (165,210).

CLINICAL COURSE OF DIABETIC NEPHROPATHY

The follow-up studies of renal function and structure carried out in subjects with diabetes of short to longer duration now allow us to differentiate early and advanced stages of the development of DN in susceptible patients. Five stages of DN have been described by Mogensen for type 1 diabetes: (a) early hypertrophy-hyperfunction; (b) early glomerular lesions without albuminuria; (c) incipient nephropathy characterized by microalbuminuria; (d) overt clinical nephropathy characterized by macroproteinuria, declining glomerular filtration, and worsening hypertension; and (e) end-stage diabetic renal disease with uremia (Table 29-1). (44,211). The format of the table may suggest that patients regularly progress from one stage to the next, but that is no longer true given intensified glycemic control and pharmacologic treatment. For this reason some of the older studies provide the clearest picture of the natural history of DN. There is overlap of some of the clinicopatho-

logic features from one stage to the next, so we must not think of the stages as hard and fast categories. Mogensen's diagram of the probable progression of changes in renal function in type 1 diabetes is reproduced in Fig. 29-5.

Mogensen's 1983 classification (44,211) is compared in Table 29-1 with the stages of chronic kidney disease (CKD) promulgated by the National Kidney Foundation (NKF) in 2002 (212) and adopted by the American Heart Association (AHA) (213). Mogensen's classification emphasizes the early development of DN, and the NKF's is based on impaired GFR. In the NKF/AHA documents, CKD is defined as either (a) kidney damage for more than 3 months, as confirmed by kidney biopsy or markers of kidney damage such as proteinuria, abnormal urinary sediment, or abnormalities on imaging studies; or (b) GFR less than 60 mL/min/1.73 m² for more than 3 months, with or without signs of kidney damage. This GFR was selected as the cut-off value for definition of CKD because it represents a reduction by more than half of the normal value of approximately 125 mL/min/1.73 m² in young men and women. Kidney failure was defined as GFR less than 15 mL/min/1.73 m² or treatment by dialysis. This definition is not synonymous with ESRD, which is an administrative term in the United States signifying eligibility for coverage by Medicare for payment for dialysis and transplantation (213).

Renal Hypertrophy and Glomerular Hyperfiltration

At the time of diagnosis of type 1 diabetes in adults and young patients, there is usually increased kidney size (75, 214,215), glomerular volume (175,176) and renal plasma flow (RPF), with hyperfiltration marked by GFR greater than 125 to 150 mL/min/1.73 m² (means +2 SDs for non-

TABLE 29-1. CLASSIFICATION OF THE CLINICAL STAGES OF DIABETIC NEPHROPATHY

Mogensen 1983 Stages	Clinical-Pathologic Findings	NKF/AHA 2002/2003 CKD Stages by GFR
I	Renal hypertrophy; glomerular hyperfiltration GFR >130 mL/min/m²	Kidney damage plus GFR
II	Normal UAE; increased GBM thickness and mesangial expansion; increased GFR persists if insufficient glycemic control	
III (incipient DN)	Microalbuminuria 30–299 mg/24 h (GFR declines if progression)	
IV (overt DN)	Macroalbuminuria >300 mg/24 h	1. GFR ≥90 mL/min/m²
Early	Clinical proteinuria 2+ or >500 mg/24 h Mesangial and interstitial expansion	2. GFR 60–89 mL/min/m²
Intermediate	GFR 30–70 mL/min/m²; hypertension Podocyte loss; glomerulosclerosis, increasing rate of glomerular closure; interstitial fibrosis, tubular atrophy	3. Moderate, GFR 30–59 mL/min/m²
Advanced	Nephrotic syndrome; GFR 10–30 mL/min/m² Hypertrophy of remaining glomeruli	4. Severe, GFR 15–29 mL/min/m²
V (ESRD)	Uremia; GFR 0–10 mL/min/m² Generalized glomerular closure Dialysis	5. Kidney failure, <15 mL/min/m² or dialysis

AHA, American Heart Association; CKD, chronic kidney disease, DN, diabetic nephropathy, ESRD, end-stage renal disease; GFR, glomerular filtration rate, NKF, National Kidney Foundation; UAE, urinary albumin excretion.
Data from references 44 and 211–213.

Diabetic nephropathy
Intervention in microalbuminuria

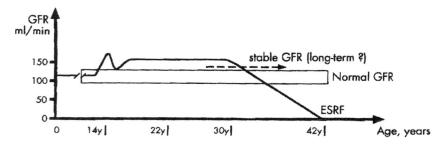

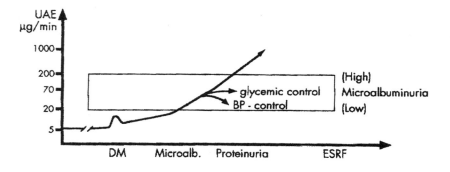

FIGURE 29-5. Urinary albumin excretion rate (*UAE*) and glomerular filtration rate (*GFR*) in the course of diabetes. Usually, daytime blood pressure (*BP*) starts to increase in type 1 diabetes mellitus after an increase in UAE, indicating incipient diabetic nephropathy (microalbuminuria). When UAE reaches 70 μg/min (101 mg/24 h), GFR starts to decline. Overt diabetic nephropathy is characterized by proteinuria and often by large increases in BP and further linear decline in GFR. The figure also shows that microalbuminuria and GFR can be stabilized by antihypertensive treatment (*AHT*) and excellent glycemic control. *ESRF,* end-stage renal failure. (Modified from Mogensen CE. *Diabetes Metab* 1989;15:343, with permission.)

diabetic controls in individual laboratories) (216,217). This is accompanied by glomerular hypertrophy with an enlarged capillary surface area (176,179), and presumed increased intraglomerular pressure, based on elevated FF (Δ GFR > Δ RPF) (218) and glomerular micropuncture studies in experimental diabetes (219). At this early stage, there is no abnormal proteinuria in the resting state, but exercise produces a fivefold increase in the rate of urinary excretion of albumin (220). Although an acute increase in plasma glucose in nondiabetic subjects causes a transient increase in GFR and RPF (221), hyperfiltration in diabetic patients is more related to chronic hyperglycemia (222). Indeed, improved glycemic control with insulin treatment reverses the elevations in GFR and exercise-induced albuminuria (218,223,224). The increased size of kidney, glomeruli, and tubules may persist despite reduction of GFR with intensified glycemic control (225), and factors other than glomerular hypertrophy must be responsible for hyperfiltration, which is also documented early in the course of type 2 diabetes (226). The large number of investigations of the mechanisms of hyperfiltration related to hyperglycemia and tubular reabsorption, vasoactive and growth factors, pressure and shear stress, and cytokines have been reviewed by several investigators (16,17,227–231).

Progression of Glomerulopathy with Normal Albuminuria

Over the first 3 to 9 years of diabetes, at least in patients with imperfect control of hyperglycemia, a proportion of type 1 patients maintain a persistent hyperfiltration with GFR greater than RPF (15,77,179,232,233). In these early years of diabetes, there is a gradual increase in the thickness of the GBM, often followed by mesangial expansion (175, 186,234). Long-term hyperfiltration without simultaneous hyperfusion (increased FF) predicted GBM thickness and mesangial matrix expansion on subsequent renal biopsies of adolescent type 1 patients (179,235). In a 17- to 27-year follow-up study of 29 adult type 1 diabetic patients, 4 of 6 developing DN had initial elevated GFR or FF (236). Glomerular hyperfiltration seems to best predict DN in young type 1 patients (77,179). In the largest follow-up study of 64 adolescents, the PPV of initial GFR of greater than 125 mL/min/1.73 m^2 for combined incipient and overt DN was 53%, and the negative predictive value of less than 125 mL/min/m^2 was 95% (76).

In these studies HbA$_{1c}$ levels predicted progression, but clinic BP did not. Ambulatory monitoring of young type 1 patients with hyperfiltration showed that nocturnal BP levels above the 90th centile of controls predicted glomerulopathy changes and persistent microalbuminuria (183); the latter confirmed findings in adults with type 1 diabetes (237,238). At this stage of diabetes there is progression in exercise-induced proteinuria with increased albumin excretion related to increases in systolic BP (211,239) and

increased plasma prorenin of uncertain origin as a precursor to albuminuria (240). Despite the glomerular hyperfiltration and increased GBM thickness in most inadequately controlled diabetic persons after 5 years of disease, clinical nephropathy develops in 20% to 40% of subjects, but not in the others.

There is a subset of mostly female patients with longstanding type 1 diabetes and moderately decreased creatinine clearance (CrCl) without albuminuria (37,241) who have more advanced diabetic glomerular lesions than normoalbuminuric women with normal GFR (242). Their lesions consist of increased GBM width and volume of mesangial cells and matrix. It is not clear if these patients had hyperfiltration earlier in the course of diabetes, but in the largest study the group had increased prevalence of hypertension and diabetic retinopathy (242). The reason for the female preponderance in this subset of patients is also unclear. Endogenous CrCl was used to estimate GFR in these studies, which if carefully performed correlate reasonably well with reference methods (243–246). Use of serum cystatin-C as an indicator of GFR is under increasing study and may replace calculations based on Cr as an estimate of CrCl (247–249).

Incipient Nephropathy Characterized by Microalbuminuria

At this stage in type 1 diabetic patients, GFR is well preserved and may remain above normal, with increased capillary surface area seen in structural studies (211). In the absence of intensified treatment, the degree of microalbuminuria increases over several years with an annual increase in UAE of approximately 50% at the Steno Diabetes Center in Denmark and in Australia in the 1980s (39%–46% progressing to DN) (37,250). The annual increase in UAE has declined to 8% per year since then (25% developing macroalbuminuria) (48), and most recently the 20-year cumulative incidence of microalbuminuria was 14.1% and 10.2% for macroalbuminuria in 244 type 1 patients with onset of diabetes during 1979 to 1984 (251). GFR remains stable in normotensive patients with nonprogressive or disappearing microalbuminuria (66), but declines slowly (2.2 mL/min/yr) in those gradually developing DN over 5 to 10 years (37,252). In some adolescent patients with previous hyperfiltration, a steeper annual decline of 11 mL/min/yr was observed (253). Basal UAE of 45 to 100 mg/day predicts a high rate of DN without special intervention (66). Microalbuminuric type 1 patients usually demonstrate subclinical elevations in 24-hour systolic BP, nighttime heart rate and systolic and diastolic pressures, and left ventricular hypertrophy (LVH) compared with normoalbuminuric subjects (254–258). The annual change in UAE correlated significantly with the annual increase in 24-hour systolic BP in microalbuminuric type 2 diabetic patients (259). The prevalence of hypertension in 1988 in Denmark in female

TABLE 29-2. PREVALENCE OF STAGE 2 HYPERTENSION STRATIFIED BY AGE IN FEMALE CONTROLS AND TYPE 1 DIABETIC PATIENTS WITH DIFFERENT LEVELS OF URINARY ALBUMIN EXCRETION (DENMARK IN 1988)

| Group | N | % Blood Pressure >160/95 mm Hg or Treatment | | | |
		Age 20–29 yr	30–39 yr	40–49 yr	50–59 yr
Controls	5,525	1.4	1.7	7.6	13.1
Type 1 diabetes					
Normoalbuminuria (<30 mg/24 h)	579	0.7	2.2	8.6	14.1
Microalbuminuria (30–299 mg/24 h)	95	7.4	26.7	33.3	33.3
Macroalbuminuria (>299 mg/24 h)	90	78.3	86.5	100	80.0

Modified from Norgaard K, Feldt-Rasmussen, Borch-Johnson K, et al. Prevalence of hypertension in type 1 (insulin-dependent) diabetes mellitus. *Diabetologia* 1990;33:407, with permission.

microalbuminuric type 1 diabetic patients grouped by age is given in Table 29-2.

Progressing microalbuminuria is associated with glomerular structural changes (260–264), as noted in the section on pathological structure/function studies. The mechanisms of albuminuria in type 1 and type 2 diabetes are not completely understood, and it is probable that no single factor is responsible. Human studies have focused on the contribution of glomerular hemodynamics (265,266), on the nature of the glomerular "barrier" to permeability (267,268), on failure of reabsorption of albumin at the proximal tubule (269–271), and on the influence of glycation or lipid binding on filtration of albumin (272). The recent finding of smaller podocyte filtration slits (197) with less nephrin expression (209,210) may be revealing.

Overt Clinical Nephropathy Characterized by Macroalbuminuria (UAE >300 mg/24 h) or Proteinuria (TPE >500 mg/24 h), declining GFR by 1.0 to 12 mL/min/yr, and Worsening Hypertension

Studies of glomerular permeability in diabetic patients with macroalbuminuria show an increased large shunt defect (>50 nm) (268,273,274,275), and the nonselective proteinuria (276,277) overwhelms the tubular reabsorptive capacity and reaches nephrotic levels of more than 3 g/24 h. The heavy proteinuria may represent the dysfunction of the slit diaphragms between the podocyte FPs (278). There is evidence that the overflow albuminuria has toxic effects on the tubules and is associated with interstitial fibrosis (279–281), which is the final common pathway for all progressive glomerular disorders. The glomerular structural correlates (279,282) of the functional changes of overt clinical DN are described in the section on Pathologic Renal Structure and Function.

Progression of overt nephropathy in type 1 DN is a multifactorial process, now influenced by available strategies of intervention. Hypertension is common in these patients (Table 29-2). Genetic susceptibility to progression of DN and response to treatment is discussed above. The rate of decline in GFR (1–12 mL/min/yr) is related to glycohemo-

globin and BP levels (283–286) and serum cholesterol (287). Impaired autoregulation of GFR in DN means that "failure of the afferent arteriole to constrict in the setting of elevated BP can lead to enhanced transmission of the systemic pressure into the glomerular capillary network, and glomerular hypertension" (288). On the other hand, Mauer stated that systemic hypertension is not necessary for the emergence of the advanced lesions of DN, and that "the nephropathic lesions of diabetes are not, alone, a sufficient cause of the hypertension" in patients with GFR greater than 40 mL/min (283). Independent risk factors predicting progression of nephropathy after adjustment for treatment group included baseline proteinuria of greater than 3 g/day, serum Cr greater than 130 μM (1.2 mg/dL), elevated serum glucose, peripheral edema, age at onset of DM >16 years, and parental history of diabetes in an analysis of 409 patients enrolled in a trial of an angiotensin-converting enzyme (ACE) inhibitor (289). Female patients did not have a slower rate of decline in renal function as they do in other renal diseases, so diabetes seems to remove any gender protection against nephropathy as well as CVD (290–292). In type 1 patients with nonnephrotic macroalbuminuria, there are diurnal variations in GFR, albuminuria, and BP, with lowest values during sleep at night (293). Type 1 patients with GFR less than 60 mL/min and expanded extracellular volume lacked a nocturnal decline in arterial pressure, probably related to latent fluid retention (294). Anemia is much more common in DN patients with serum Cr less than 180 μM (1.7 mg/dL) than in similar patients with glomerulonephritis, and it is associated with increased proteinuria and lack of erythropoietin response (295).

Progression of clinical DN in type 2 diabetes is influenced by the usual greater age and BMI of patients (296) and the more heterogeneous nephropathology (297,298). The UKPDS investigators described the development and progression of nephropathy over 10 years (median) in 5,097 type 2 patients (299). Progression from micro- to macroalbuminuria occurred at 2.8% per year, and from macroalbuminuria to elevated serum Cr of greater than 175 μM (1.6 mg/dL) or renal replacement therapy at 2.3% per year, which was less than the annual rate to death from any cause of 4.6%. The annual probability of remaining in the stage of macroalbuminuria was 93.1%, and a model-derived estimate of the time spent in that stage was 9.7 years (300). In other recent European studies of type 2 DN (mean age 52–58 years) in treatment, the annual loss of glomerular function (ΔGFR 5–6 mL/min/yr) correlated with postprandial BG, systolic BP, TG level (296,297,300), and more with baseline GBM width and mesangial volume than with baseline UAE, Cr, or mean arterial pressure (MAP) (262). In contrast, in the more homogeneous and younger Pima Indians, GFR declined by 35% over 4 years (Δ 11.2 mL/min/yr) despite treatment, and renal insufficiency developed in 30% (Cr >177 μM, >2.0 mg/dL) (301,302).

End-Stage Renal Disease with Uremia

End-stage renal failure is characterized by generalized glomerular and tubular closure and interstitial fibrosis, along with marked decreases of GFR (CrCl <15 mL/min/ 1.73 m^2) and increasing plasma Cr and blood urea nitrogen (302). Albumin excretion may decrease as a result of nephron closure (211). The degree of azotemia is related to the percentage of sclerotic glomeruli that are occluded; it is also possible to observe capillary closure within nonsclerotic glomeruli (10,303,304). Worsening hypertension accompanies and contributes to the renal failure. Comparisons of the course to ESRD in type 1 and type 2 patients suggest that the clinical progression of DN is similar for both types after development of proteinuria, although hypertension and CVD are more common with type 2 (305–307). Type 1 and type 2 patients start dialysis at similar times in the course of DN, with 71% to 75% starting due to fluid overload and symptoms of uremia (306). ESRD is overrepresented in African-American (305) and Asian diabetic populations (308). The burden of type 2 diabetic renal disease is illustrated by the UKPDS, in which 14 of 37 patients with baseline macroproteinuria progressed to ESRD in the median follow-up of 10 years, and only 24 of 37 were still alive (299). The median survival of 3.0 years for 51 patients on renal replacement therapy in this study is similar to an observed value of 2.7 years among diabetic dialysis patients in France (309). Continuing hyperglycemia is deleterious during the course of ESRD (310).

THERAPEUTIC INTERVENTIONS TO PREVENT DIABETIC NEPHROPATHY AND DELAY OR HALT ITS PROGRESSION

Multiple strategies for renoprotection in chronic, otherwise progressive renal diseases including DN are evolving through observational analysis of the risk factors for development and progression, experimental testing of hypotheses, rigorous therapeutic trials, and applications in the clinical setting (6,311–314). Acknowledging that effective

treatments of renal disease may decrease proteinuria or slow the decline in GFR, Brenner reserves the term *renoprotection* to mean a reduction in ESRD, up to now an elusive goal (315). It is widely held that whatever the origin of most renal injuries, the final common pathways of progressive glomerulosclerosis and tubulointerstitial fibrosis are similar and must be blocked or reversed to prevent ESRD. Nevertheless, the metabolic derangements of imperfectly treated diabetes have specific effects on the development and progression of DN. Taking into account the stages of DN, Parving (6) and Viberti (316) categorize treatment strategies as (a) primary prevention modalities applied to any normoalbuminuric diabetic patient at risk, including the reversal of glomerular hyperfiltration, (b) secondary prevention modalities applied to diabetic patients with a high risk (e.g. microalbuminuria) of the development of DN, and (c) tertiary preventive treatment of overt DN to prevent or delay the development of ESRD. Those treatment strategies involve control of BG, BP, and protein and salt intake, as well as specific pharmacologic interventions based on the emerging understanding of the many renopathogenic pathways in diabetes. Brenner, Parving, Remuzzi, and others concluded that comprehensive, mutifactorial approaches to treatment will be required to prevent ESRD as well as the major killer, CVD (6,312,316–322), "employing multiple therapies directed at different aspects of the pathogenesis of progressive renal injury" (315).

There is a huge, rapidly evolving literature on experimental and human studies of the pathogenesis of early and advanced DN, and only a few key references and reviews can be cited here. Knowledge of this work is important to understand the rationale of the many therapeutic interventions being evaluated for renoprotection in diabetes. A review of the bulk of the experimental studies is available in the complete online text.

Glycemic Control

Glucose Uptake of Glomerular Cells

An increased rate of renal intracellular glucose metabolism promotes the pathologic changes of DN (323). Of the large gene family of tissue-specific facilitative, rate-limiting glucose transporters, glucose transporter 1 (GLUT-1) is constitutively expressed in both the glomerular and tubular compartments, and it is the major transporter permissive factor for mesangial injury caused by hyperglycemia (324). Mesangial cells obtained from diabetic patients exhibit increased GLUT-1 levels (325). GLUT-4 is also expressed in cultured mesangial cells and podocytes but is lost with repeated cell transfer (326), and the sodium-glucose cotransporter SGLT-1 is expressed in mesangial and PTEC (327). High glucose exposure induces GLUT-1 expression and activity in mesangial as opposed to systemic endothelial cells, facilitating increased glucose uptake and glycolysis, and apparently no responsive decrease in GLUT-4 transporters will diminish the glucose uptake as in skeletal muscle (328). Glomerular hypertension or mechanical stretching of human mesangial cells also induces overexpression of GLUT-1 and increased basal glucose uptake (329). High glucose flux through facilitative glucose transporters on endothelial and mesangial cells overwhelms the mitochondrial electron transport system, with biochemical changes as detailed by Brownlee and others (20–23,330,331).

Five main molecular mechanisms have been implicated in glucose-mediated vascular and renal damage (Fig. 29-6): increased polyol pathway flux (332), increased flux through the hexosamine pathway (333–335), activation of protein kinase C isoforms via *de novo* synthesis of the lipid second messenger diacylglycerol (336,337), activation of the proinflammatory transcription factor nuclear factor κB (338), and increased intracellular formation of advanced glycation end products and activation of their receptor (RAGE) (339–341). Brownlee and colleagues have shown that these mechanisms reflect the hyperglycemia-induced overproduction of superoxide by the mitochondrial transport chain (Fig. 29-7) via its indirect inhibition of the multifunctional enzyme GADPH (330,342–344). Excess superoxide produces DNA strand breaks that activate poly(ADP-ribose)

polymerase (PARP), which then inhibits GADPH activity. Inhibition of PARP blocked hyperglycemia-induced activation of multiple pathways of vascular damage (345). The interactions of these pathways in renal cells are being explored to explain glomerular and tubulointerstitial pathology. There are several recent reviews of the roles of oxidant and carbonyl stress in DN (346–349), and Himmelfarb has emphasized oxidant stress as a unifying concept of CVD in uremia (22).

Effects of High Ambient Glucose on Renal Cells in Culture and In Vivo

The damaging effects of the glucose-induced biochemical pathways are mediated by a large number of growth and vasoactive factors, cytokines, kinases, and transcription factors (20–23,350,351a), which produce the pathologic features of hypertrophy, ECM accumulation, podocyte loss, inflammation and cellular transformation, glomerulosclerosis, and interstitial fibrosis. The major players are listed in Table 29-3 and key supporting references are given. The diagram by Ritz (319) illustrates some of these mechanisms of endothelial and renal cell damage in hyperglycemia (Fig.

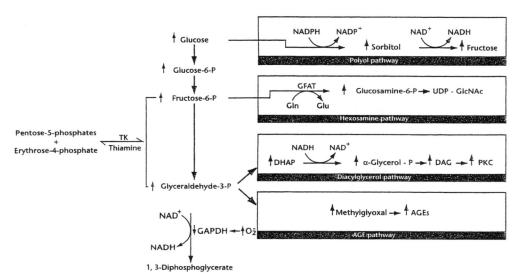

FIGURE 29-6. Mechanisms by which hyperglycemia-induced mitochondrial superoxide production accentuates four pathways of hyperglycemic damage. Excess superoxide partially inhibits the glycolytic enzyme GAPDH, thereby diverting upstream metabolites from glycolysis into pathways of glucose overutilization. This results in increased flux of DHAP to diacylglycerol (*DAG*), an activator of protein kinase C, and of triose phosphates to methylglyoxal, the main intracellular advanced glycation end product precursor. Increased flux of fructose-6-phosphate to UDP-*N*-acetylglucosamine increases modification of transcription proteins by O-linked *N*-acetylglucosamine (*GlcNAc*) with increased production of cytokines such as plasminogen activator inhibitor-1 and transforming growth factor-β. Increased glucose flux through the polyol pathway consumes NADPH and depletes the antioxidant glutathione. Thiamine or benfotiamine can block the four pathways of hyperglycemic damage by activation of the thiamine-dependent pentose phosphate pathway enzyme, transketolase (*TK*). *P,* phosphate; *GFAT,* glutamine-fructose-6-P-amidotransferase; *DHAP,* dihydroxyacetone phosphate. (Modified from Brownlee M. Biochemistry and molecular cell biology of diabetic complications. *Nature* 2001;414:813, and Hammes H-P, Du X, Edelstein D, et al. Benfotiamine blocks three major pathways of hyperglycemic damage and prevents experimental diabetic retinopathy. *Nature Med* 2003;9:294, with permission.)

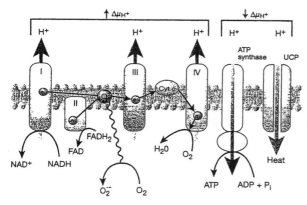

FIGURE 29-7. Production of superoxide by the mitochondrial electron-transport chain. Increased hyperglycemia-derived electron donors from the trichloroacetic acid cycle (NADH and FADH) generate a high mitochondrial membrane potential (DmH⁺) by pumping protons across the mitochondrial inner membrane. This inhibits electron transport at complex III, increasing the half-life of free radical intermediates of coenzyme Q (ubiquinone), which reduce O_2 to superoxide. (Modified from Brownlee M. Biochemistry and molecular cell biology of diabetic complications. *Nature* 2001;414:813, with permission.)

29-8). Current investigations focus on development of specific inhibitors of these biochemical and cytokine pathways that could be used safely in human studies.

Clinical Trials of Intensified Glycemic Control

Because epidemiologic studies link nephropathy to duration of poor glycemic control in both types of diabetes, the hypothesis that strict glycemic control would prevent the development of DN or slow the progression of renal dysfunction has been tested several times. A metaanalysis of seven randomized studies comparing the effect of intensive versus conventional BG control showed the increase in UAE in normoalbuminuric type 1 diabetic patients to be significantly reduced (odds ratio 0.34) with intensive treatment (373). In the DCCT, the development of microalbuminuria was reduced by 34% with intensive glycemic control over 6.5

years (374), and the benefit was consistent in subgroups defined by age, duration of diabetes, baseline HbA$_{1c}$, retinopathy level, and CrCl of ±130 mL/min/1.73 m² (3). Development of microalbuminuria continued to be reduced in patients in the original intensive therapy group 4 to 6 years after close-out of the DCCT (375,376). At evaluation of 1,349 participants 7 to 8 years after close-out, the previous intensive treatment group had significantly less albuminuria, azotemia (Cr >1.9 mg/dL), and hypertension than the previous conventional treatment group (377) (Table 29-4).

A randomized 6-year study of intensive insulin treatment of type 2 diabetic patients in Japan, similar in design to the DCCT, also showed beneficial reduction in the development of microalbuminuria (378). In the UKPDS (4) of a large number of subjects with type 2 diabetes, intensive BG control with sulfonylureas or insulin significantly reduced the progression of microalbuminuria after 9 to 12 years (34% progressed in conventional treatment, 23% progressed in intensive treatment, $p < 0.001$; mean HbA$_{1c}$ 8.4 at 10 years with conventional treatment, 7.8 with intensive treatment) (4). There has been controversy about whether there is a glycemic threshold below which renal complications will not occur, but investigators now agree we should target BG levels as close to normal as possible without incapacitating hypoglycemia.

Antihypertensive Treatment

Blood pressure in adults 18 years or older is now classified as normal (systolic <120 and diastolic <80 mm Hg), prehypertension (systolic 120–139 or diastolic 80–89 mm Hg), stage 1 hypertension (systolic 140–159 or diastolic 90–99 mm Hg), and stage 2 hypertension (systolic >160 or diastolic >100 mm Hg) (379). Ambulatory monitoring provides BP information during daily activities and sleep that correlates better than office measurements with target organ injury. Ambulatory BP values obtained by automatic devices or patient self-measurement are often lower than office measurements (380), and mean values by continuous

TABLE 29-3. MEDIATORS THOUGHT TO BE INVOLVED IN THE PATHOGENESIS OF DIABETIC NEPHROPATHY

Mediators	Key Supporting References
Insulin-like growth factor-1 (IGF-1)	351
Transforming growth factor-β (TGF-β) and matrix metalloproteinases (MMP-2 and -3)	352–356
Platelet-derived growth factor (PDGF)	357,358
Connective tissue growth factor (CTGF)	359,360
Vascular endothelial growth factor (VEGF)	361–363a
Plasminogen activator inhibitor-1 (PAI-1)	364
Monocyte chemoattractant proteins (MAP,MCP)	365,366
Angiotensin-2 (AngII)	367–370
Nitric oxide (NO)	371,372

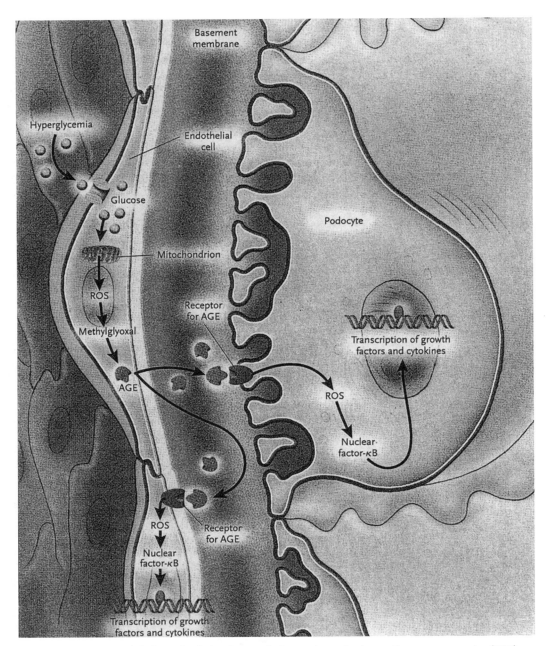

FIGURE 29-8. Model of renal cellular damage in hyperglycemia via reactive oxygen species (*ROS*) and advanced glycation end products (*AGE*). Hyperglycemia drives more glucose into endothelial cells, causing excessive generation of ROS in mitochondria; these in turn favor the generation of methylglyoxal and AGE. These end products are bound by specific receptors, causing a burst of further ROS and activation of the transcription factor κB and, ultimately, transcription of injurious growth factors and cytokines on endothelial cells as well as neighboring cells, such as those within the kidney, mesangial cells, podocytes, and proximal tubular cells. (Modified from Ritz E. Albuminuria and vascular damage—the vicious twins [Essay]. *N Engl J Med* 2003;348:2349, with permission.)

TABLE 29-4. SUSTAINED EFFECT OF PREVIOUS INTENSIFIED GLYCEMIC CONTROL OF TYPE 1 DIABETES ON KIDNEY OUTCOMES 7 TO 8 YEARS AFTER CLOSE-OUT OF THE DCCT

Outcome	Original DCCT Treatment Group, No. (%)		
	Conventional (n = 673)	Intensive (n = 676)	p
Developed new microalbuminuria[a]	87/550 (15.8%)	39/572 (6.8%)	<0.001
Developed new macroalbuminuria[a]	59/630 (9.4%)	9/632 (1.4%)	<0.001
CrCl <70 mL/min/1.73 m^2	(4%)	(<1%)	<0.001
Serum creatinine >2 mg/dL	19 (2.8%)	5 (0.7%)	0.004
Prevalence of hypertension[b]	(40.3%)	(29.9%)	<0.001
Using ACE inhibitors	(29.0%)	(21.6%)	

[a]Denominator is number in each treatment group without microalbuminuria (<40 mg/24 h) or macroalbuminuria (<300 mg/24 h) at the end of the DCCT.
[b]Prevalence of hypertension (>140/90 mm Hg) 11% in both groups at the end of the DCCT.
ACE, angiotensin converting enzyme; CrCl, creatinine clearance; DCCT, Diabetes Control and Complications Trial.
Modified from the Writing Team for the Diabetes Control and Complications Trial/Epidemiology of Diabetes Interventions and Complications Research Group. Sustained effect of intensive treatment of type 1 diabetes mellitus on development and progression of diabetic nephropathy. The Epidemiology of Diabetes Interventions and Complications Study. JAMA 2003;290:2159, with permission.

monitoring of greater than 135/85 mm Hg in awake individuals and greater than 120/75 mm Hg during sleep qualify as hypertension. These guidelines are abstracted from the recent Seventh Report of the Joint National Committee on Prevention, Evaluation, and Treatment of High Blood Pressure (379).

Hypertension frequently accompanies chronic renal insufficiency of any cause, including DN. Several longitudinal studies of type 1 diabetic patients show that stage 1 hypertension usually appears when there is already evidence of incipient DN (microalbuminuria), suggesting that hypertension is a consequence of the renal disease rather than the cause of it (60,77,254, 257–259). Nevertheless, subtle changes in diurnal or systolic BP can be a factor in (381,382) or accompany (383) the development of diabetic microalbuminuria, and an increase in BP with an increase in UAE may represent concomitant manifestations of common processes responsible for the development of nephropathy and CVD in diabetic patients (316,319,384). Ambulatory 24-hour BP (385) and nocturnal systolic BP (256) correlate with LVH in diabetic patients with microalbuminuria. There is widespread agreement that uncontrolled hypertension accelerates the progression from incipient to overt nephropathy and on to ESRD. Even modest BP elevations to greater than 120/80 are shown to cause worsening of DN and CVD (6,386,387). The hypothesis that strict control of arterial pressure might slow the progression of nephropathy has been extensively investigated.

Using multiple linear regression analysis of 100 controlled and uncontrolled studies up to 1993, Kasiske et al. assessed the relative effect of different antihypertensive agents on proteinuria and renal function in patients with diabetes. Regardless of the agent used, the analysis indicated that reduction of MAP resulted in both a decrease in urinary protein excretion and a sparing of GFR (+3.7 mL/min for each reduction of 10

mm Hg in MAP) (388). An updated metaanalysis came to similar conclusions (389). Since then the UK Prospective Type 2 Diabetes Study found that the subjects randomized to tight control of BP (mean over 9 years 142/82 mm Hg) with one to five agents, compared with less tight control (9-year mean 154/87 mm Hg), had a lower frequency of microalbuminuria (20.3% vs. 28.5%; p < 0.01), as well as less retinopathy and stroke (5,390). Control of systolic BP provided the major beneficial effect in this landmark study, including significant reduction in myocardial infarction (391). Double-blind randomized studies in hypertensive, normoalbuminuric type 2 patients comparing the effect of ACE inhibitors versus a long-acting dihydropyridine calcium channel blocker (CCB) (392,393) or β-adrenergic blockade (5,394) demonstrated a similar beneficial renoprotective effect of BP reduction with and without ACE inhibition (6,395). Double-blind randomized placebo-controlled trials of ACE inhibitors in normotensive, normoalbuminuric type 1 and type 2 patients reduced the development of microalbuminuria (396–398). ACE inhibitors also produced long-term benefit in reducing microalbuminuria in "normotensive" type 2 diabetic subjects (399–401).

ACE inhibition ameliorates glomerular hyperfiltration in experimental and clinical models and reduces intraglomerular pressure by preferential dilation of the efferent arteriole (402–404). A favorable local effect of ACE inhibitors on intrarenal hemodynamics and UAE is seen when diabetic subjects have been hyperglycemic with an enhanced renin-angiotensin-aldosterone system (405,406). Nonhemodynamic renal effects of ACE inhibitors in models of diabetes include preservation of glomerular barrier function and HSPG content (407,408), reduction of transforming growth factor-β (TGF-β) and TGF-β receptor levels (409,410), and attenuation of AGE production (411). Whether ACE inhibitors retard progression of DN to a greater degree than we could expect with control of systemic BP remains controversial, since most clinical trials used standardized office BP but did not account for ambulatory/diurnal BP (6,412). The effect of ACE inhibitors in type 1 diabetes on preventing progression to macroalbuminuria and maintaining stable GFR lasted more than 8 years in a continuing study in Copenhagen (413,414).

Use of ACE inhibitors is considered essential in patients with DN (415–417), but side effects such as cough and possible hyperkalemia limit the use of ACE inhibitors in some diabetic patients. Enzymes other than ACE, such as chymase (370,418), can produce angiotensin II, suggesting that ACE inhibitor treatment may have an incomplete antagonistic effect on the intrarenal renin-angiotensin system (ACE inhibitor escape) (419). These problems may be obviated by treating with angiotensin II type 1 receptor blockers. Several studies demonstrated that angiotensin II receptor-1 blockade (ARB) reduced UAE in both hypertensive and normotensive type 2 diabetic patients with micro- and macroalbuminuria (420,421), probably independently of lowering office BP (422–424). In clinical DN in type 1 diabetes, losartan treatment was similar to ACE inhibitors in lowering BP and proteinuria and slowing the decline in GFR (425). In large randomized trials in type 2 diabetic patients with microalbuminuria or DN, ARB was effective in reducing albuminuria and risk for azotemia (422,426,427). ARB may have intrinsic renoprotective actions in addition to its antihypertensive effects (428). After withdrawal of long-term ARB, persistent reduction of microalbuminuria suggested that reversal of renal structural or biochemical abnormalities might be responsible, because ARB-induced hemodynamic changes did not continue (429). The combination of ARB with ACE inhibitors might produce more complete antagonism of tissue angiotensin effects (430), and preliminary studies of combined therapy showed improved renal effects compared to monotherapy (428,431,432). Long-term studies on large numbers of diabetic patients are needed to determine benefit of combined treatment on reducing ESRD and CVD.

The role of CCBs in providing renal and cardiovascular protection to diabetic subjects has also been widely studied (433), and different types of CCBs have varying effects on albumin excretion (434,435) and renal hemodynamics (436,437). Because reduction of proteinuria contributes to renoprotection in the treatment of chronic renal disease (6, 322,438), nondihydropyridine CCBs are preferred in diabetes because they may reduce albuminuria more effectively (434,435,437).

Role of Low-Protein Diet, Lipid-Lowering Agents, and Peroxisome Proliferator–Activated Receptor Ligands (Thiazolidinediones, Glitazones) in Diabetic Nephropathy

In experimental and clinical models of diabetes, high protein intake was associated with increased P_{gc}, GFR, and protein-

uria (439–444). Three randomized trials found that a low-protein diet (0.6–0.8 g/kg body weight) maintained over 0.5 to 3 years resulted in decreased proteinuria and a slowing of the decrease of GFR in patients with DN (445–447), and improved glomerular permeability and hemodynamics in diabetic subjects at risk for DN (448). However, systemic BP counteracts the benefit of low protein even in the absence of hypertension, and about half of subjects show low compliance with the low-protein diet (448). A metaanalysis of 13 randomized controlled trials including 1,919 patients with diabetic and nondiabetic renal disease concluded that there was a relatively weak magnitude effect of dietary protein restriction on slowing the rate of renal function decline, although the effect might be greatest in the diabetic patients (449). A secondary analysis of the relationship between achieved protein intake and the progression of advanced renal disease (GFR 13–24 mL/min/1.73 m^2) in the Modification of Diet in Renal Disease randomized study demonstrated a slower decline in GFR and longer time to renal failure in the groups with intake below 0.75 gm/kg/day (450).

Lipid-Lowering Agents: "Pleiotropic" Effects of Statins

In type 1 diabetes, only minor compositional changes in the classic cholesterol lipoproteins are associated with albuminuria, but elevated UAE is associated with increased concentrations of total TGs, the highly atherogenic intermediate-density lipoprotein (IDL) and small dense LDL particles, with no differences in gender (451). Type 2 diabetic patients with persisting microalbuminuria exhibit elevated TG to high-density lipoprotein (HDL) ratios and increased small, dense LDL particles, independent of confounding factors (452–455). Mesangial cells have receptors for apo- and lipoproteins (456), and LDL can stimulate mesangial proliferation (457), fibronectin and superoxide production (458), and chemoattractant expression and monocyte adhesion (459,460). Statins are competitive inhibitors of 3-hydroxy-3-methylglutaryl coenzyme A (HMG-CoA) reductase (461,462), resulting in decreased cholesterol biosynthesis, and in type 2 diabetes they reduce the oxidative modification of plasma IDL and LDL fractions and have other pleiotropic effects (463–465). Experimental studies suggest a benefit of statins on diabetic renal pathology, but no large trial of the effect of lipid reduction on the progression of renal disease has been performed. Thirteen prospective controlled trials with small numbers of patients have been subjected to metaanalysis to determine the effects of antilipemic agents on GFR and albuminuria (466). Subjects in seven of the studies had type 2 diabetes, treated with fibrates to lower TGs versus placebo in two and statins versus placebo in five. Combined results of all the studies using a random effects model showed a significant slowing of decline in GFR with reduction of plama lipids and lipoproteins over the duration of the studies, but inconsistent effects on albuminuria.

Agents Binding to Peroxisome Proliferator–Activated Receptor Nuclear Receptors: Glitazones

Thiazolidinediones, insulin-sensitizing agents also known as TZDs or glitazones, are high-affinity synthetic ligands for peroxisome proliferator–activated receptor-γ (PPAR-γ) (467,468), which is expressed in renal cells (469). Experimental studies suggest that glitazones might ameliorate diabetic glomerulopathy, albuminuria, and mesangial hypertrophy and ECM production, independent of insulin-sensitizing effects (470–472). In preliminary studies, treatment of microalbuminuric type 2 diabetic patients also reduced albuminuria (473,474), as well as decreased urinary podocyte excretion, suggesting protection against podocyte injury in early-stage DN (475). Further clinical trials are needed to define the role of glitazones in the prevention and management of DN, probably in concert with antihypertensive agents and statins.

Clinical Guidelines for Management of Diabetic Patients with Hypertension or Albuminuria

Antihypertensive Treatment

Based on the randomized controlled trials and metaanalyses cited above and elsewhere, recent health organization guidelines published in North America are concordant in urging a treatment goal BP of less than 130/80 mm Hg for hypertensive patients with diabetes, or CKD defined as albuminuria greater than 300 mg/day, for the purpose of reducing renal insufficiency and CVD (379,476–478). Lifestyle modifications to manage hypertension include weight reduction to a BMI of 18.5 to 24.9; diet rich in fruits, vegetables, and low-fat dairy products with a reduced content of saturated and total fat; reduction of dietary sodium intake to no more than 100 mEq/L (2.4 g Na or 6 g NaCl); regular aerobic physical activity such as brisk walking at least 30 min/day, most days of the week; cessation of smoking; and limiting consumption of alcohol to no more than one drink per day for women.

Most diabetic patients with hypertension or renal disease require two or more antihypertensive medications to achieve the treatment goal BP, added or changed in stepwise fashion, with the fewest side effects possible (6,319,379, 476). Lists of single and combination antihypertensive drugs and trade names available in the United States in 2003 and their dosages are provided in the Joint National Committee (JNC) 7 report (379). Initial therapy with ACE inhibitors and/or ARB plus a thiazide diuretic is suggested, with substitution of a loop diuretic if serum Cr is greater than 1.8 mg/dL (476). Long-acting nondihydropyridine CCBs are suggested as next-line agents. Beta-adrenergic blockers are useful if the baseline pulse exceeds 83 and are preferred if the patient has angina, heart failure, or arrhythmia (476). If BP is still not at goal, an amlodipine-like CCB or a long-acting α-blocker may be added at night (476). Clinical caveats include avoiding the combination of β-blocker with a nondihydropyridine CCB in the elderly or those with conduction abnormalities, and not to use clonidine with β-blockers for numerous reasons, including the risk for severe bradycardia (476). Once doses are titrated, use of fixed combination medications are useful to reduce pill counts and pharmacy copayments (476). Low-dose aspirin use (75 mg/day, enteric coated) is indicated in diabetic patients with CVD risk factors, including hypertension, dyslipidemia, and micro- or macroalbuminuria (479), but it should be witheld until BP is controlled, due to the danger of hemorrhagic stroke (379).

As stated in JNC 7, "the most effective therapy prescribed by the most careful clinician will control hypertension only if patients are motivated. Motivation improves when patients have positive experiences with and trust in the clinician. Empathy builds trust and is a potent motivator"(379). A patient-centered strategy to achieve the mutually agreed BP goal "and an estimation of the time needed to reach the goal are important . . . all members of the health care team must work together to influence and reinforce instructions to improve patients' lifestyles and BP control" (379). As reported in detail by the National Kidney Foundation Working Group, the patient's willingness to comply with any given treatment regimen is based on her beliefs regarding the disease, the practitioner, the type of treatment, and numerous cultural and familial factors, of which the health-care professionals must become aware (476). The same management principles are essential in achieving effective BG control. Clinicians must believe and act as if there is no excuse for inadequate control of BP and BG (both hypo- and hyper-) if costly morbidity is to be avoided and premature mortality prevented.

Protein Intake and Lipid-Lowering Therapy

Current guidelines conclude that the recommended daily allowance limit for total protein intake of 0.8 g/kg/day should be followed in diabetic patients at risk for DN, and that once the GFR begins to decline in DN, restriction of total protein intake to 0.6 g/kg/day "may prove useful in slowing the decline of GFR in selected patients" (478). It is controversial whether nutritional deficiency and muscle weakness will occur in many individuals so treated (480, 481).

In the absence of satisfactory trials, current guidelines suggest that patients with DN be treated similarly to other diabetic patients for CVD risk reduction and using therapeutic lifestyle changes for LDL greater than 100 mg/dL (2.59 mM). Pharmacologic treatment for an LDL greater than 130 mg/dL (3.37 mM) should be started and a target LDL of less than 100 mg/dL (2.59 mM) established (482–484). In individuals with elevated serum TG greater than 200 mg/dL, the most recent Adult Treatment Panel III report of the National Cholesterol Education Program identified non-HDL cholesterol less than 130 mg/dL (LDL + IDL + very-low-density lipoprotein cholesterol) or its surrogate total apolipoprotein B less than 90 mg/dL as secondary targets of therapy (482,483). Non-HDL cholesterol provides the cholesterol content of LDL + TG-rich lipoproteins, and total apolipoprotein B is a measure of total particle number in these lipoproteins. If TG is less than 200 mg/dL, LDL cholesterol "contains the bulk of `atherogenic cholesterol' and thus is a sufficient target alone" (485).

EVALUATION OF PATIENTS WITH DIABETIC NEPHROPATHY BEFORE CONCEPTION

The potential problems of DN and pregnancy require the application of preconception care. Clinicians caring for diabetic women need to recognize that they may become pregnant, and that poor control of hyperglycemia and hypertension determines many of the risks to mother and offspring, which can be reduced through intensified multifactorial interventions before conception and throughout pregnancy. In the preconception management of women with established diabetes, evaluation for microvascular disease and hypertension is critical. If overt DN is diagnosed, the patient should be thoroughly counseled regarding measures used to improve outcomes of pregnancy and the pos-

sible vascular complications and life expectancy, so that there can be an informed decision on whether to attempt pregnancy. The previous widespread practice of advising women with DN not to attempt pregnancy due to a low probability of a healthy infant and the likelihood that nephropathy will worsen is not supported by modern data. Management of women with DN prior to and during pregnancy is outlined in Table 29-5.

Renoprotective or antihypertensive therapy is indicated for patients with microalbuminuria or overt nephropathy (6), and agents used should be effective and safe in early pregnancy (486–489). Although probably not teratogenic (490,491), ACE inhibitors or angiotensin II receptor blockers are contraindicated during pregnancy because they are associated with proximal tubular dysgenesis and neonatal renal failure (492–494). The hypothesis that use of ACE inhibitors in the preconception period will also decrease complications during pregnancy (495,496) should be tested in controlled trials in women with excellent glycemic control. In a study of eight women with presumed DN, Jovanovic found that normoglycemia achieved by early pregnancy also resulted in stable renal function and low complication rates (497). Diltiazem and other calcium entry blockers are possibly best avoided during the first trimester because some data indicate an association with fetal limb defects [possibly related to reduced uteroplacen-

---

TABLE 29-5. MANAGEMENT OF DIABETIC NEPHROPATHY BEFORE AND DURING PREGNANCY

At all times
   Prevent hyperglycemia without untoward hypoglycemia
   Control hypertension <130/80 mm Hg; angiotensin inhibition or receptor blocker plus
      long-acting non-dhp CCB or β-blocker as needed prior to pregnancy; delete ACE inhibitors
      and ARB during pregnancy
   Controlled carbohydrate, fat, and protein diet
   Target LDL <100 mg/dL; delete statins, fibrates, and glitazones in pregnancy
   Adequate rest
Prior to pregnancy
   Measure renal function; ophthalmologic examination
   Cardiovascular evaluation (history, examination, EKG, echocardiogram as needed)
   Thyroid evaluation; hepatitis B surface antigen
   Counseling and education
First trimester
   Measure renal function; ophthalmologic examination
   Sonogram for dating
Second trimester
   Measure renal function (12, 24 wk)
   Maternal expanded serum α-fetoprotein (15–18 wk)
   Detailed sonogram with fetal echocardiogram (20–22 wk)
Third trimester
   Monthly sonogram for fetal growth and AFI
   Weekly nonstress test (26 wk)
   Ophthalmologic examination
   Measure renal function (36 wk); consider labs for PET
   Delivery planning

ACE inhibitor, angiotensin converting enzyme inhibitor; AFI, amniotic fluid index; ARB, antiotensin receptor blocker; EKG, electrocardiogram; LDL, low-density lipoprotein; non-dhp CCB, nondihydropyridine calcium channel blocker; PET, preeclamptic toxemia.

tal blood flow (498)], but not confirmed as teratogenic in a larger survey (499). Diltiazem may have benefits for glomerular function not possessed by dihydropyridine CCBs (436,437,500,501). Agents believed to be relatively safe for early pregnancy include α-methyldopa, clonidine, and β-adrenergic antagonists with low lipid solubility (486–489).

Ophthalmologic examination is especially important for women with nephropathy because most also have diabetic retinopathy. Hyperglycemia induces retinal ischemia, and relatively rapid insulinization and normalization of BG may elevate growth factor levels (e.g., insulin-like growth factor-1, vascular endothelial growth factor, fibroblast growth factor) associated with worsening of retinopathy (502–508). In the presence of background or proliferative retinopathy, normalization of BG may take a few months in the preconception period. Proliferative retinopathy should be in remission or laser treated before pregnancy is attempted. In women with background retinopathy at the beginning of pregnancy, the risk for development of neovascularization during gestation is 7% to 10% in hyperglycemic (509–511) or hypertensive women (512).

COURSE OF NEPHROPATHY DURING PREGNANCY

GFR increases by 40% to 80% in normal and uncomplicated diabetic pregnancy, as reflected by increasing CrCl and decreasing serum Cr (513,514). The increase in GFR occurs in the first weeks of pregnancy (515) in advance of the expansion of plasma volume (516), and reaches an increment of 40% to 50% by the end of the first trimester (513). The glomerular hyperfiltration and increase in renal plasma flow (RPF) is maximal at 26 to 30 weeks' gestation (517), then RPF declines significantly by term pregnancy (but not to control levels) in subjects lying on their sides, while GFR by inulin clearance does not (514,518). Therefore, FF must increase in late normal pregnancy as osmotic pressure declines (513). Because there is a slight decline in endogenous CrCl from 29 to 37 weeks (from 141 to 126

mL/min), it is possible there is reduced tubular secretion of Cr in late pregnancy, at the same time there is enhanced net tubular reabsorption of uric acid and a slight decrease in uric acid clearance (518–520). Extensive studies in various pregnant models of experimental nephropathy never showed increased P_{gc} secondary to pregnancy (516), which is reassuring because hyperfiltration and hypertension in the glomerulus is considered a prerequisite for human DN.

With DN in pregnancy, the expected increase in CrCl is seen in only about one third of patients, as summarized in Table 29-6 (497,521,522). The decrease in CrCl in another third of DN patients probably reflects the underlying natural progression of nephropathy, or accelerating hypertension. Initial serum Cr of 1.0 to 1.5 mg/dL (109–163 μM) was associated with a decline in CrCl during pregnancy in 12 women with DN, whereas in 9 patients with initial serum Cr greater than 1.5 mg/dL (163 μM), CrCl remained stably low at 41 to 65 mL/min (523). About one third of DN patients show an increase in serum Cr by the third trimester, when inverse serum levels are used as an indicator of GFR, related to reduced renal function at baseline or superimposed preeclampsia (524–528). An increase in serum Cr during pregnancy in a large number of women with DN was associated with "crossover" from a hyperdynamic cardiac output to a vasoconstricted state in a preliminary report (529). Jovanovic found that prevention of hyperglycemia and hypertension allowed a normal increase in CrCl during pregnancy in eight diabetic women with subnormal values prior to conception (497), but Biesenbach et al. observed that mean CrCl declined by 16% during the first two trimesters in seven proteinuric diabetic women with subnormal CrCl prior to pregnancy (37–73 mL/min/1.73 m²), despite intensified glycemic control and antihypertensive therapy during pregnancy (530). Preliminary data on use of serum cystatin C as an alternate indicator of GFR during pregnancy are inconsistent (531–534), and data are unavailable for pregnant women with DN.

The excretion of albumin (UAE) increases only slightly in normal pregnancy (514,535–539), whereas TPE increases by 40% to 200%, albeit to less than 300 mg/24 h (540–542) (Table 29-7). Albumin represents a small fraction of TPE.

TABLE 29-6. CHANGES IN CREATININE CLEARANCE (CRCL) IN 44 WOMEN WITH DIABETIC NEPHROPATHY WITH MEASUREMENTS IN BOTH FIRST AND THIRD TRIMESTER OF PREGNANCY

First Trimester		Third Trimester		
CrCl	n (%)	Increased >25%	Stable	Decreased >15%
>90 mL/min	14 (32%)	3 (21%)	5 (36%)	6 (43%)
60–89 mL/min	20 (45.5%)	9 (45%)	6 (30%)	5 (25%)
<60 mL/min	10 (22.5%)	2 (20%)	6 (60%)	2 (20%)
Total	44 (100%)	14 (32%)	17 (39%)	13 (29%)

Data stratified by CrCl in first trimester.
Data from references 497, 521, and 522.

TABLE 29-7. AVERAGE LEVELS OF ALBUMINURIA AND PROTEINURIA BEFORE, DURING, AND AFTER NORMAL AND TYPE 1 DIABETIC PREGNANCIES WITHOUT CLINICAL NEPHROPATHY

	Nonpregnant	Third Trimester	4[a]–6[b] mo Postpartum
11 normal controls[a]			
UAE (mg/24 hr)	9	12	13
TPE (mg/24 hr)	117	262	174
7 patients with normoalbuminuria type 1[b]			
UAE	12	71	13
TPE	73	417	96
7 patients with microalbuminuria type 1[b]			
UAE	80	478	114
TPE	233	2350	239

[a]Roberts et al., 1996 (542).
[b]Biesenbach and Zasgornik, 1989 (549).
TPE, total protein excretion; UAE, urinary albumin excretion.

The increase in TPE is presumably due to increased GFR and limited tubular reabsorption.

In diabetic women without microalbuminuria in early pregnancy (<30 mg/24 h), UAE increases slightly in the second trimester and sometimes greatly in the third trimester, whereas urinary TPE may increase to greater than 300 mg/24 h (543–545). Of course, some cases of proteinuria may be explained by mild preeclampsia, which clouds the interpretation of changes in renal function in pregnant diabetic women. In the setting of the DCCT, only 10 of 180 type 1 diabetic women in either treatment group developed microalbuminuria (>40 mg/24 h) during pregnancy (507). With microalbuminuria before pregnancy in diabetic women, the increase in albumin and total protein excretion during gestation is even greater (546–548) (Table 29-7). Most investigators have observed that microalbuminuria in early pregnancy predicts a risk for superimposed preeclampsia of 35% to 60% compared with 6% to 14% in diabetic women without microalbuminuria (546,549–552).

With clinical DN (macroalbuminuria or proteinuria) diagnosed prior to pregnancy, albuminuria and total proteinuria often increase dramatically during gestation, even without associated hypertension, frequently exceeding 10 g/24 h in the third trimester. Although some of this increase may reflect the underlying progression of nephropathy, protein excretion usually subsides after delivery, but not necessarily to preconception levels (521,525,530,553). It is unknown if temporary heavy overload proteinuria in diabetic pregnancy contributes to later tubulointerstitial fibrosis via upregulation of vasoactive and inflammatory genes, as it does in other clinical and experimental models (322,438). Follow-up studies of women with DN are discussed in the last section of this chapter.

During pregnancy, ambulatory BP monitoring of nondiabetic women has been used to predict hypertensive complications in the third trimester with fairly low sensitivity and specificity (554,555). In type 1 diabetic pregnant women, midpregnancy cutoffs of greater than 105 mm Hg nighttime systolic (556) or greater than 122 mm Hg daytime systolic (551) provided the best sensitivity/specificity for third trimester hypertension. However, a careful study in Denmark showed that UAE of 30 to 299 mg/24 h was a better predictor of preeclamptic toxemia (PET; new hypertension and proteinuria) in type 1 diabetes than diurnal BP (patients with treated hypertension were excluded) (549). In a study of early pregnancy TPE in American diabetic women (mixed type 1 and type 2), 27% of 45 women with microproteinuria (190–499 mg/24 h) were treated for chronic hypertension compared with 39% in 62 patients with 500 mg/24 h and only 6% in 204 women with TPE of less than 190 mg/24 h (547). In this study patients with both early pregnancy microproteinuria and chronic hypertension had the highest frequency (~50%) of superimposed PET.

Significant factors predicting the development of hypertension in pregnancy in a New Zealand study of pooled groups of 100 each of type 1 and 2 diabetes included nulliparity [relative risk (RR) 1.5], smoking (RR 0.39), duration diabetes greater than10 years (RR 1.87), earliest HbA$_{1c}$ greater than 9.0 (RR 1.9), retinopathy (RR 1.8), earliest UAE 30 to 300 mg/24 h (RR 1.8), earliest systolic BP 116 to 129 mm Hg or higher (RR 2.1), and earliest diastolic BP greater than 80 mm Hg (RR 2.5) (557). Many of these parameters are probably interrelated. Primary PET was more common in type 1 (19%) than in type 2 (7%) diabetes, whereas the latter cases had more chronic hypertension and micro- and macroalbuminuria. Similar predictors of hypertensive disorders in pregnant women with type 1 diabetes were identified in large Swedish and North American multicenter studies (558–560).

Maternal characteristics identified in early pregnancy in 225 cases of clinical DN reported during 1981 through 1996 include approximately 50% frequencies of proliferative retinopathy, anemia, and hypertension. Reduced CrCl

TABLE 29-8. FREQUENCY OF RENAL PARAMETERS DURING AND AFTER PREGNANCY IN WOMEN WITH DIABETIC NEPHROPATHY

	Hypertension	Urinary Protein Excretion >5 g/day	Decreased CrCl or Increased Cr[a]	Renal Failure	Death
Early preg	42%	9%	34%	0	0
Late preg	71%	26%	26%	0	0
Follow-up	60%	17%	43%	23%[b]	5.6%

[a]Creatinine clearance (CrCl) <80 mL/min, Cr >1.2 mg/dL (106 μ*M*).
[b]Of 195 women followed 1–10 years, median 2.6 years.
Data from references 497,521–523,526,527,553,561–564.

(<80 mL/min) was recorded in 45% of cases, and 15% of the total had serum Cr greater than 1.2 mg/dL (>106 μ*M*) (497,521–523,526,527,553,561–564) (Table 29-8). Low-level proteinuria (<1 g total protein/24 h before 20 weeks' gestation) was detected in many of the women, which may dilute the cases of "true" DN; therefore, the frequencies of anemia, hypertension, proliferative diabetic retinopathy, and impaired glomerular filtration probably should be higher. Of 146 diabetic women with greater than 1 g total protein/24 h in early pregnancy, 57 (39%) had impaired renal function at that stage of gestation [serum Cr >1.2 mg/dL (106 μ*M*) or CrCl <80 mL/min], and 37% of the total group showed a further decline of more than 15% during later pregnancy (Table 29-9). Three subsequent series reported since 1996 show similar proportions of these maternal complications (528,544,565). Pregnancy is probably contraindicated in women with DN if serum Cr is above 2.0 mg/dL (177 μ*M*) or CrCl is below 50 mL/min before or in early pregnancy, because of the high rate of maternal and fetal complications, unless renal transplantation can be performed prior to pregnancy.

Maternal anemia results from both decreased erythropoietin production by damaged glomeruli and the physiologic hemodilution of pregnancy. The degree of anemia is related to the severity of nephropathy as reflected in lower CrCl and is not usually associated with abnormal iron studies (521). Exogenous erythropoietin can be used to treat anemia unresponsive to iron and folate replacement (566–569). Asymptomatic bacteriuria is more common in diabetic than nondiabetic women, leading to a greater risk for urinary tract infection (570–573), but there is controversy over screening and treatment outside of pregnancy (574,575). During pregnancy, screening and preventive treatment of women with hypertension or DN is justified due to the deleterious effects of pyelonephritis (521). Although paradoxically PET in the third trimester may be less common in nondiabetic women who smoke cigarettes (559,576), smoking should be strongly discouraged in diabetic women due to impaired fetal oxygenation in mid-pregnancy and hazardous effects on progression of DN (577–579).

DN can progress to ESRD during pregnancy, although this is unusual. Of 195 women followed after pregnancy and summarized in Table 29-8, none progressed to end-stage disease during pregnancy. There is experience with both hemodialysis and continuous ambulatory peritoneal dialysis in pregnancy, but analyzed cases include few diabetic women (580–587). In about one fourth of reported cases of dialysis in pregnancy, the patients conceived prior to starting dialysis. They either were close to needing dialy-

TABLE 29-9. COURSE OF DIABETIC NEPHROPATHY DURING AND AFTER PREGNANCY COMPARING PATIENTS WITH PRESERVED VERSUS IMPAIRED RENAL FUNCTION IN EARLY PREGNANCY

	Initial Renal Function		
	Preserved	Impaired[a]	Cr >2.0 mg/dL (>177 μ*M*)
Number	70	57	(6)
Decline during pregnancy	12 (17%)	21 (37%)	(1)
Renal failure after pregnancy[b]	4/57 (7%)	27/55 (49%)	(3)
Died	2 (3.5%)	5 (9.1%)	(0)

N less than in Table 29-8 due to lack of renal function data in first trimester. Note the limited number of cases with severe azotemia in early pregnancy.
[a]Cr >1.2 mg/dL (>106 μ*M*), CrCl <80 mL/min.
[b]Denominator is number evaluated 1–10 years after pregnancy.
Data from references 497,521,522,524,527,553, and 561–564.

sis prior to the unplanned gestation or had a rapid decline in renal function during pregnancy (581). In this group termination of pregnancy rarely rescues the kidneys (588), and "unless transplant is a certainty, the pregnancy may be the woman's last chance to have a child" (581). In women using dialysis prior to conception, treatment of anemia with erythropoietin or blood transfusion is usually required (589). In a U.S. national registry survey of pregnancy in dialysis patients with ESRD of various causes (36.6% primary glomerular diseases, 26.3% lupus or other vasculitis, 7.4% diabetes, 6.6% interstitial diseases, 14.2% other), BP was normal in only 21%, and severe hypertension (BP >170/110 mm Hg) was noted at some time during pregnancy or postpartum in 48% (581). There were five episodes of peritonitis in 59 pregnancies in women treated with peritoneal dialysis; there were 245 pregnancies in women using hemodialysis, and two maternal deaths in the entire group, which is "lower than the average for dialysis patients of child-bearing age as a whole" (581). Therefore, the risk for death in a dialysis patient who becomes pregnant is not increased by the pregnancy, but "the severity of the illness in the women with hypertensive crisis is evidence that pregnancy is a dangerous undertaking for a pregnant patient" (581).

DIABETIC NEPHROPATHY AND PERINATAL OUTCOME

Despite the dramatic improvements in perinatal outcome in pregnancies of diabetic women (590), complications remain more frequent when DN is present. Examining the pooled results of 13 clinical series published during 1981 through 1996 (495,497,521,522,524,526,527,553,561, 562–564,591), of 265 infants born to women with DN, nearly two thirds were preterm deliveries prior to 37 weeks' gestation, 72.5% were delivered by cesarean section, and respiratory distress syndrome was diagnosed in 24.5% of liveborn infants. Fetal growth restriction was noted in 14.3%, and the major correlates of small size for dates were the degree of maternal hypertension and impaired renal function (521,522,563). Major congenital malformations were diagnosed in 7.6% of the 265 infants. The frequencies of these perinatal complication were similar in 90 pregnancies reported in 1981 through 1988 compared with 175 reported in 1992 through 1996 (Table 29-10), and in the subsequent reports of Reece et al. (565) and Biesenbach and colleagues (592). Perinatal mortality rates were 55.5 per 1,000 and 34.3 per 1,000 in the earlier and later groups, respectively. Overall, 95.8% of infants survived to leave the neonatal intensive care unit.

These clinical results would probably be somewhat worse in women with "true" clinical DN diagnosed prior to pregnancy. At least 16% of the pooled cases probably had only microalbuminuria preconception, because they were

TABLE 29-10. DIABETIC NEPHROPATHY AND PERINATAL OUTCOME IN TWO ERAS IN WHICH PERINATAL TECHNOLOGY WAS USED

Year of Report	1981–1988	1992–1996
Infants	90	175
Perinatal survival	94.4%	96.6%
Fetal growth restriction	13.3%	14.9%
Preterm delivery	57.8%	64.6%
Cesarean delivery	68.9%	74.3%
Respiratory distress syndrome	25.6%	24.2%
Major congenital malformations	7.8%	7.7%

Data from references 495,497,521,522,524,526,527,553,561–564, and 591.

included in the DN reports based on less than 1 g/day total protein excretion in the first trimester. Limiting the analysis of perinatal mortality to 223 cases with greater than 1 g/day total urinary protein excretion in the first trimester, perinatal mortality rates were 54.8 per 1,000 in 1982 through 1988 compared with 71.4 per 1,000 in 1992 through 1996. Major congenital malformations and severe fetal growth restriction were responsible for most of the perinatal deaths.

Perinatal morbidity is related to the severity of DN as illustrated in Table 29-11. Selecting out cases from the pooled series with sufficient detail for analysis (521,522, 562,563), 19 women had greater than 1 g/day total urinary protein with preserved renal function in early pregnancy, compared with 41 proteinuric diabetic women with CrCl less than 80 mL/min or serum Cr greater than 1.2 mg/dL (>106 μM). The latter group had much higher rates of fetal growth restriction, PET, fetal distress causing delivery, and serious prematurity. Analyzing initial serum Cr in 60 pregnancies with DN, Khoury et al. confirmed high rates of fetal growth restriction, preterm birth at less than 32 weeks' gestation, and attendant neonatal complications in 9 women with levels above 1.5 mg/dL (133 μM), even though superimposed PET (44.4%) was no higher than in 39 women with serum Cr less than 1.0 mg/dL (<88.4 μM) (523). The data are useful for counseling women with DN prior to pregnancy. Similar results and clinical relationships are reported for pregnancies in women with other chronic glomerular or tubulointerstitial diseases (585,593–597). It is controversial whether fetal outcome is determined by type of glomerulopathy (e.g., focal and segmental glomerulosclerosis being worse) (598) or primarily by risk factors associated with nephropathy, such as degree of hypertension or level of renal impairment (594,596).

Perinatal outcome in women with ESRD on dialysis is poor, with few pregnancies reaching term or normal birth weight; published series include patients with all forms of renal failure, including diabetes (581–583,585,587,599). In the largest national registry series, only 42% of 320 pregnancies resulted in surviving infants, but survival was better

TABLE 29-11. PERINATAL OUTCOME RELATED TO RENAL STATUS IN EARLY PREGNANCY IN WOMEN WITH DIABETIC NEPHROPATHY

	Protein Excretion 0.3–0.9 g/24 h	Initial Renal Function with TPE >1 g/24 h	
		Preserved	Impaired[a]
Number	18	19	41
Fetal growth restriction	1 (6%)	1 (5%)	11 (27%)
PET	2 (11%)	4 (21%)	15 (37%)
Fetal distress	1 (6%)	4 (21%)	12 (29%)
Fetal death	1	1	1
Delivery at 24–33 wk	4 (22%)	5 (26%)	18 (38%)
Uncomplicated	10 (56%)	6 (32%)	9 (24%)

[a]Cr >1.2 mg/dL (>106 μM) or creatinine clearance <80 mL/min.
PET, preeclamptic toxemia; TPE, total protein excretion.
Data combined from cases reported in references 521,522,562, and 563.

at 73.6% in women who conceived before starting dialysis (581). The same differential perinatal survival was seen in a survey in Belgium (583). In women becoming pregnant already on dialysis, there is a continuum of midtrimester fetal loss (21%), often with severe growth restriction, or preterm delivery before 28 weeks' gestation in 18% (581, 582). Obstetric complications include polyhydramnios and placental abruption (582,583,587,589). Pregnancy outcome does not seem to differ between women using hemodialysis versus continuous ambulatory peritoneal dialysis, but is worse with severe hypertension in either group (581,587). The high rate of congenital malformations of 14.7% reported in the U.S. registry (581) was not observed in three smaller contemporary reports (none in 49 pregnancies) (582,583,587). Hou has published useful guidelines for the management of dialysis and pregnancy (600).

Superimposed PET is a leading cause of prematurity in pregnant women with diabetes (558,560,601,602) and DN (521,522,562,563). With preexisting DN, it may not be possible to clinically distinguish "true" PET from a simple worsening of hypertension and proteinuria. Edema and hyperuricemia are not helpful in the differential diagnosis because they are common in patients with renal disease or PET. Hypoalbuminemia commonly results from excessive proteinuria in PET and leads to generalized edema. If thrombocytopenia or elevated transaminases are found, these laboratory values support a diagnosis of superimposed PET in women with DN. As a practical matter, it is generally necessary to observe the patient at hospital bed rest, with or without antihypertensive therapy. We lack controlled studies of the timing of delivery in women with DN with or without PET. The decision to deliver the infant must balance the gestational age, the severity of the maternal condition, and indicators of fetal well-being.

Unfortunately no controlled trials of treatment of hypertensive pregnant women with DN have been reported. The Canadian Hypertension Society Consensus Conference recommended a threshold of 140/90 mm Hg to start antihypertensive treatment during pregnancy (603). An Australasian consensus group recommended maintaining BP between 110 and 140 mm Hg systolic and 80 and 90 mm Hg diastolic for pregnant women with chronic or gestational hypertension (604). A U.S. National Heart, Lung, and Blood Institute consensus group recommended that antihypertensive treatment be used during pregnancy only for BP levels greater than 150 to 160 mm Hg systolic and/or greater than 100-110 mm Hg diastolic, in order to prevent maternal vascular accidents during pregnancy, since treatment effects on perinatal outcome at lower levels of BP were inconclusive in controlled trials in nondiabetic hypertensive women (605). The group reasoned that untreated nondiabetic women would be at low risk for cardiovascular complications within the short time frame of pregnancy. On the other hand, there is increasing focus on the potential implications of hypertension in pregnancy on long-term cardiovascular and renal risk in women (530,606–608). Many investigators follow evidence-based guidelines recommending treatment for nonpregnant diabetic women with hypertension or micro/macroalbuminuria (319,379,476,609) and continue during pregnancy with agents that are safe for the fetus (610,611). Such agents include methyldopa, β-adrenergic blockers other than atenolol, nondihydropyridine CCBs, clonidine, and perhaps prazocin (612). There is concern about impaired fetal growth with atenolol (487,613,614), even though one controlled trial demonstrated less superimposed preeclampsia using atenolol in hypertensive women with elevated cardiac output (615). Suggested BP targets to guide therapy outside of pregnancy are less than 140/90 mm Hg for nondiabetic patients and less than 130/80 mm Hg for diabetic subjects (319,379,476,609). Some believe the use of the latter target during nondiabetic pregnancy may contribute to fetal growth restriction (611).

As noted, fetal growth delay is related to placental pathology, maternal hypertension, or its treatment. Serial sonography is indicated to evaluate fetal growth. In addition, fetal heart rate monitoring or biophysical assessment should be used because growth restriction or fetal hyperglycemia-hypoxia-acidosis (616) is frequently associated with evidence of fetal distress. For women with clinical DN, weekly nonstress testing should begin at 26 weeks' gestation and move to twice-weekly testing at 34 weeks, but earlier if there is growth delay. Vaginal delivery is preferred if there is no evidence of fetal distress and no obstetric contraindication.

PREGNANCY AFTER RENAL TRANSPLANTATION

Ogburn et al. compiled the experience of nine diabetic women from several centers who became pregnant after renal transplantation for DN (617). All were treated with prednisone and azathioprine, and no transplant rejections occurred during pregnancy. Complications were frequent, including PET in six, fetal distress in six, and preterm delivery in all of the women. Armenti and the U.S. National Transplant Pregnancy Registry (NTPR) reported 28 pregnancies in diabetic renal transplant recipients after cyclosporine (CsA) was added to the immunosuppression regimen to decrease acute rejection (618). Rejection was observed in 4% and graft dysfunction in 11%. Preeclampsia was diagnosed in 17%, although 59% had hypertension; 47% of the infants had neonatal complications.

Most studies of pregnancy after renal transplantation included limited numbers of diabetic women among patients with other renal diseases (619,620). GFR increases by approximately 30% during pregnancy in women with renal allografts, but not to the extent of normal controls, and the gradual decline in CrCl the last 6 weeks of gestation is similar to controls (619,621). The extent of increase in CrCl is dependent on preconception levels (621). Early reports of fetal growth delay with CsA (622,623) were not confirmed in other small studies (624,625) and are difficult to compare with results in larger surveys. These report a prevalence of low birth weight of 23% to 63% and delivery at less than 37 weeks in 38% to 75%, but most do not provide data on size for dates, so the contribution from prematurity to low birth weight is unclear (585,619,620,626, 627). Perinatal mortality ranged from 30 to 270 per 1,000 in pregnancies after renal allografts across several decades, but the high figures were in early pregnancies without recent improvements in perinatal management and antihypertensive-immunosuppressive therapy (619,620,626,628). Many of the perinatal losses were in poorly controlled diabetic women. Prevention of infection is especially important in these immunosuppressed diabetic patients, and monthly urine cultures are recommended (585).

Predictors of increased risk for premature delivery include increased creatinine level, hypertension before 28 weeks' gestation (619,620,626), and graft dysfunction in the peripartum period (629). Azathioprine is not associated with excess congenital malformations (585), and the prevalence rate with CsA was 4.1%, but the odds ratio of 3.83 compared with other agents was not significant due to small numbers (627). The NTPR also found no excess fetal malformations in 154 pregnancies (630). Concern for toxic effects of maternal CsA treatment on fetal-placental function was not borne out in a study of nitric oxide synthase, endothelin-1, and tissue factor in human placentas (631).

There is limited information on perinatal effects of the newer immunosuppressant tacrolimus (632), the potentially reprotoxic mycophenolate mofetil (633), and the immunoglobulin G muromonab-CD3 (OKT3) (634). A preliminary registry study of pregnancy outcomes with the newer immunosuppressive agents neoral and tacrolimus showed rates of hypertension, PET, and prematurity similar to those in previous studies (635). In a survey of 175 children exposed to CsA *in utero* and followed to preschool and early school age, 16% were noted to have delays or need educational support (636). This may not be significantly greater than for premature infants in the general population. Continuous fetal exposure to CsA seemingly impairs development or maturation of lymphocytes, with effects still apparent at 1 year of age, but none of six infants had clinical evidence of an immunodeficient state (637). There is also concern about possible remote effects of maternal immunosuppression causing autoimmune or reproductive disorders in daughters of treated mothers (638,639), but long-term follow-up studies are incomplete. Also under investigation is the impact and potential mechanisms for effects of female gender on many aspects of renal transplantation (640,641).

Combined kidney-pancreas transplantation prior to pregnancy has been reported several times (642–645), and the NTPR also reported 23 pregnancies after combined transplantation (646). In this group 25% had PET while 91% were hypertensive; 70% of deliveries were premature. Two thirds of these gravidas were treated for some type of infections. Barrou et al. reviewed 19 cases of pregnancy after simultaneous pancreas-kidney transplantation reported to the International Pancreas Transplant Registry in the CsA era (647). There were 19 live births with average birth weight 2,150 ± 680 g and two major congenital malformations. Only one pancreas graft and one kidney graft were lost after pregnancy in two different recipients.

Beyond these studies, there has been hypothetical concern that pregnancy may adversely affect renal graft survival (621,624). The NTPR reported an 11% frequency of rejection episodes during pregnancy or within 3 months postpartum in 197 CsA-treated pregnancies (620). CsA blood levels declined during pregnancy in groups with and without rejection. In a series of 29 women in southern Spain, renal function remained stable during pregnancy in 72%, postpartum renal allograft deterioration was detected in 8 patients (28%), and 5 required reinitiation of dialysis at 4 months to 5 years after pregnancy (625). Studies with long-term follow-up found no difference in graft survival or function between women who became pregnant and matched controls who did not (629,648,649). Pancreas-kidney graft loss over two years postpartum occurred in 6 of 37 diabetic women, and loss was not related to maternal or neonatal variables (650). On the other hand, renal graft failure seems to be greater after 2 or more pregnancies (651), an effect possibly related to pregnancy-induced anti-HLA immunization detected only by flow cytometric evaluation (652).

Lindheimer and Katz (653) and Hou (585) provide guidelines on preconception counseling of women with renal transplants. Women should wait 2 years posttransplantation with immunosuppression at maintenance levels (prednisone <15 mg/day, azathioprine <2 mg/kg/day, CsA <5 mg/kg/day) and no evidence of active graft rejection. This requires effective contraception. Renal function should show serum Cr less than 1.5 mg/dL (133 μM) (653) or less than 2.0 mg/dL (177 μM) (585) with 24-hour urine TPE less than 500 mg. BP and BG levels should be well controlled with medication.

EFFECT OF PREGNANCY ON THE SUBSEQUENT PROGRESSION OF DIABETIC NEPHROPATHY

Characteristics of DN in pregnancy such as hyperfiltration, hypertension, or heavy proteinuria might damage glomeruli, tubules, and interstitium and accelerate the postpartum progression of DN to ESRD. In a pooled series of 195 women experiencing pregnancies with DN and having renal function assessed 1 to 10 years afterward, 23% were in renal failure and 5.6% had died (Table 29-8). The frequency of progression to renal failure after pregnancy was 49% in the group of women with impaired renal function in early pregnancy, compared with 7% if serum Cr was less than 1.2 mg/dL (<106 μM) or CrCl exceeded 80 mL/min in early gestation (497,521,522,524–527,553,561–564) (Table 29-9). A similar risk for postpregnancy decline of renal function based on pre- or early pregnancy CrCl was also reported by Biesenbach, and he speculated that inadequate antihypertensive therapy may have contributed to the decline in renal function (530).

Three early studies assessed the decline in CrCl after pregnancy in women with nephropathy (521,525,564). All three found that CrCl declined an average of about 10 mL/min/yr, similar to the average rate in men and women with DN at that time (654–656). More recently, the annual decline in GFR in DN has improved to 2 to 5 mL/min/yr due to advances in renoprotection (6). Rossing and col-

leagues at the Steno Diabetes Center in Denmark conducted an observational study of female patients who developed DN during 1984 to 1989 and were followed until death or the year 2000 (657). The decline in CrCl over a median of 10 years postpartum was 3.2 ± 3.4 mL/min/yr in 17 parous patients versus 3.2 ± 5.1 mL/min/yr in 42 women never pregnant. Miodovnik observed that increasing parity did not exacerbate the risk for renal failure after pregnancy (564), and the EURODIAB Type 1 Complications Survey (658) and the Pittsburgh Epidemiology of Diabetes Complications case control study (659) found that parity was not related to the incidence of micro- or macroalbuminuria. In the DCCT, pregnancy had no effect on the end-of-study prevalence of albuminuria (507). Purdy et al. thought that 5 of 11 women with DN and moderate renal insufficiency had an accelerated rate of decline in renal function during pregnancy, but in follow-up for a mean of 2 years postpartum the group of 11 had slightly less decline in inverse Cr than 11 similar patients without pregnancy (527). Mackie and colleagues (526) and Kaaja et al. (660) also found no evidence for accelerated decline of renal function after pregnancy in diabetic women compared with nonpregnant patients. Based on these admittedly limited data sets, physicians can counsel diabetic women with mild-to-moderate impairment of renal function about their long-term prognosis after pregnancy. It is hoped that intensified multifactorial therapeutic interventions aimed at renoprotection early in the course of nephropathy, before, during, and after pregnancy will continue to improve this outlook.

ACKNOWLEDGMENT

I am grateful for the excellent library services of Janet Bruman at the Natividad Medical Center in Salinas and Judy Gehman at the San Jose Medical Center, California.

REFERENCES

1. Rossing P. Promotion, prediction, and prevention of progression of nephropathy in type 1 diabetes mellitus [Review]. *Diabet Med* 1998;15:900.
2. Ritz E, Orth SR. Nephropathy in patients with type 2 diabetes mellitus [Review]. *N Engl J Med* 1999;341:1127.
3. Diabetes Control and Complications Trial Research Group. Effect of intensive therapy on the development and progression of diabetic nephropathy in the Diabetes Control and Complications Trial. *Kidney Int* 1995;47:1703.
4. UK Prospective Diabetes Study Group. Intensive blood glucose control with sulphonylureas or insulin compared with conventional treatment and risk of complications in patients with type 2 diabetes. *Lancet* 1998;352:837.
5. UK Prospective Diabetes Study Group. Tight blood pressure control and risk of macrovascular and microvascular complications in type 2 diabetes. *BMJ* 1998;317:703.
6. Parving H-H, Hovind P, Rossing K, et al. Evolving strategies for

renoprotection: diabetic nephropathy [Review]. *Curr Opin Nephrol Hypertens* 2001;10:515.

7. Grundy SM, Howard B, Smith S, et al. AHA Prevention Conference VI: Diabetes and cardiovascular disease. Executive summary. *Circulation* 2002;105:2231.

8. Trevisan R, Viberti G. Genetic factors in the development of diabetic nephropathy [Review]. *J Lab Clin Med* 1995;126:342.

9. Krowlewski AS, Fogarty DG, Warram JH. Hypertension and nephropathy in diabetes mellitus: what is inherited and what is acquired? [Review]. *Diabetes Res Clin Pract* 1998;39(suppl):1.

10. Osterby R, Gall M-A, Schmitz A, et al. Glomerular structure and function in proteinuric type 2 (non-insulin-dependent) diabetic patients. *Diabetologia* 1993;36:1064.

11. Fioretto P, Steffes MW, Sutherland DER, et al. Sequential renal biopsies in insulin-dependent diabetic patients: structural factors associated with clinical progression. *Kidney Int* 1995;48:1929.

12. Drummond K, Mauer M, for the International Diabetic Nephropathy Study Group. The early natural history of nephropathy in type 1 diabetes. II. Early renal structural changes in type 1 diabetes. *Diabetes* 2002;51:1580.

13. Mogensen CE. Early glomerular hyperfiltration in insulin-dependent diabetes and late nephropathy. *Scand J Clin Lab Invest* 1986;46:201.

14. Nowack R, Raum E, Blum W, et al. Renal hemodynamics in recent onset type 2 diabetes. *Am J Kidney Dis* 1992;20:342.

15. Yip JW, Jones SL, Wiseman MJ, et al. Glomerular hyperfiltration in the prediction of nephropathy in IDDM. A 10-year follow-up study. *Diabetes* 1996;45:1729.

16. O'Bryan GT, Hostetter TH. The renal hemodynamic basis for diabetic nephropathy [Review]. *Semin Nephrol* 1997;17:93.

17. Hostetter TH. Hypertrophy and hyperfunction of the diabetic kidney [Essay]. *J Clin Invest* 2001;107:161.

18. Viberti G, Jarrett R, Mahmud U, et al. Microalbuminuria as a predictor of clinical nephropathy in insulin-dependent diabetes mellitus. *Lancet* 1982;1:1430.

19. Mogensen CE. Microalbuminuria predicts clinical proteinuria and early mortality in maturity-onset diabetes. *N Engl J Med* 1984;310:356.

20. Cooper ME. Interaction of metabolic and hemodynamic factors in mediating experimental diabetic nephropathy [Review]. *Diabetologia* 2001;44:1957.

21. Scheetz MJ, King GL. Molecular understanding of hyperglycemia's effects for diabetes complications [Review]. *JAMA* 2002;288:2579.

22. Himmelfarb J, Stenvinkel P, Ikizler TA, et al. The elephant in uremia: oxidant stress as a unifying concept of cardiovascular disease in uremia. *Kidney Int* 2002;62:1524.

23. Haneda M, Koya D, Isono M, et al. Overview of glucose signaling in mesangial cells in diabetic nephropathy [Review]. *J Am Soc Nephrol* 2003;14:1374.

24. Ziyadeh FN, Sharma K. Combating diabetic nephropathy [Essay]. *J Am Soc Nephrol* 2003;14:1355.

25. Wolf G, Ritz E. Diabetic nephropathy in type 2 diabetes. Prevention and patient management [Review]. *J Am Soc Nephrol* 2003;14:1396.

26. Parving H-H. Iniation and progression of diabetic nephropathy. *N Engl J Med* 1996;335:1682.

27. Olsen S, Mogensen CE. How often is NIDDM complicated with non-diabetic renal disease? An analysis of renal biopsies and the literature. *Diabetologia* 1996;39:1638.

28. Mazzucco G, Bertani T, Fortunato M, et al. Different patterns of renal damage in type 2 diabetes mellitus: a multicentric study on 393 biopsies. *Am J Kidney Dis* 2002;39:713.

29. Schwartz MM, Lewis EJ, Leonard-Martin T, et al. Renal pathology patterns in type II diabetes mellitus: relationship with retinopathy. *Nephrol Dial Transplant* 1998;13:2547.

30. Christensen PK, Larsen S, Horn T, et al. Causes of albuminuria in patients with type 2 diabetes without diabetic retinopathy. *Kidney Int* 2000;58:1719.

31. Rossing P, Hougaard P, Borch-Johnsen K, et al. Predictors of mortality in insulin-dependent diabetes: 10 year observational followup study. *BMJ* 1996;313:779.

32. Ritz E, Rychlik I, Locatelli F, et al. End-stage renal failure in type 2 diabetes: a medical catastrophe of worldwide dimensions. *Am J Kidney Dis* 1999;34:795.

33. Stephenson JM, Kenny S, Stevens LK, et al. Proteinuria and mortality in diabetes: the WHO multinational study of vascular disease in diabetes. *Diabet Med* 1995;12:149.

34. Wang S-L, Head J, Stephens L, et al. Excess mortality and its relation to hypertension and proteinuria in diabetic patients: the WHO Multinational study of Vascular Disease in Diabetes. *Diabetes Care* 1996;19:305.

35. Weia U, Turner B, Gibney J, et al. Long-term predictors of coronary artery disease and mortality in type 1 diabetes. *Q J Med* 2001;94:623.

36. Messent JWC, Elliott TG, Hill RD, et al. Prognostic significance of microalbuminuria in insulin-dependent diabetes mellitus: a twenty-three year follow-up study. *Kidney Int* 1992;41:836.

37. Tsalamandris C, Allen TJ, Gilbert RE, et al. Progressive decline in renal function in diabetic patients with and without albuminuria. *Diabetes* 1994;43:649.

38. Caramori ML, Fioretto P, Mauer M. The need for early predictors of diabetic nephropathy risk. Is albumin excretion rate sufficient? *Diabetes* 2000;49:1399.

39. Wiegmann TB, Chonko AM, Barnard MJ, et al. Comparison of albumin excretion rate obtained with different times of collection. *Diabetes Care* 1990;13:864.

40. Mogensen CE, Vestbo E, Poulsen PL, et al. Microalbuminuria and potential confounders. A review and some observations on variability of urinary albumin excretion. *Diabetes Care* 1995;18:572.

41. Chaturvedi N, Bandinelli S, Mangili R, et al. Microalbuminuria in type 1 diabetes: rates, risk factors and glycemic threshold. *Kidney Int* 2001;60:219.

42. Bakker AJ. Detection of microalbuminuria. Receiver operating characteristic curve analysis favors albumin-to-creatinine ratio over albumin concentration. *Diabetes Care* 1999;22:307.

43. Houlihan CA, Tsalamandris C, Akdeniz A, et al. Albumin to creatinine ratio: a screening test with limitations. *Am J Kidney Dis* 2002;39:1183.

44. Mogensen CE, Schmitz O. The diabetic kidney: from hyperfiltration and microalbuminuria to endstage renal failure. *Med Clin North Am* 1988;72:1465.

45. Warram JH, Gearin G, Laffel, et al. Effect of duration of type 1 diabetes on the prevalence of stages of diabetic nephropathy defined by urinary albumin/creatinine ratio. *J Am Soc Nephrol* 1996;7:930.

46. The Microalbuminuria Collaborative Study Group. Predictors of the development of microalbuminuria in patients with type 1 diabetes mellitus: a seven-year prospective study. *Diabet Med* 1999;16:918.

47. Tabei BP, Al-Kassab AS, Ilag LL, et al. Does microalbuminuria predict diabetic nephropathy? *Diabetes Care* 2001;24:1560.

48. Rossing P. Risk factors for development of incipient and overt diabetic nephropathy in type 1 diabetic patients. *Diabetes Care* 2002;25:859.

49. Powrie JK, Watts GF, Ingham JN, et al. Role of glycemic control in the development of microalbuminuria in patients with insulin-dependent diabetes. *BMJ* 1994;309:1608.

50. Diabetes Control and Complications Trial Research Group. The absence of a glycemic threshold for the development of

long-term complications: the perspective of the Diabetes Control and Complications Trial. *Diabetes* 1996;45:1289.

51. Orchard TJ, Forrest KY, Ellis D, et al. Cumulative glycemic exposure and microvascular complications in insulin-dependent diabetes mellitus: the glycemic threshold revisited. *Arch Intern Med* 1997;157:1851.

52. Scott LJ, Warram JH, Hanna LS, et al. A nonlinear effect of hyperglycemia and current cigarette smoking are major determinants of the onset of microalbuminuria in type 1 diabetes. *Diabetes* 2001;50:2842.

53. Poulsen PL, Hansen KW, Mogensen CE. Ambulatory blood pressure in the transition from normo- to microalbuminuria. A longitudinal study in IDDM patients. *Diabetes* 1994;43:1248.

54. Coonrod BA, Ellis D, Becker DJ, et al. Predictors of micro-albuminuria in individuals with IDDM: Pittsburgh Epidemiology of Diabetes Complications study. *Diabetes Care* 1993;16:1376.

55. Sibley SD, Hokanson JE, Steffes MW, et al. Increased small dense LDL and intermediate-density lipoprotein with albuminuria in type 1 diabetes. *Diabetes Care* 1999;22:1165–1170.

56. Chaturvedi N, Stephensen JM, Fuller JH: The relationship between smoking and microvascular complications in the EURODIAB IDDM Complications Study. *Diabetes Care* 1995;18:785.

57. Rudberg S, Stattin E-L, Dahlquist G. Familial and perinatal risk factors for micro- and macroalbuminuria in young IDDM patients. *Diabetes* 1998;47:1121.

58. Viberti G. Outcome variables in the assessment of progression of diabetic kidney disease. *Kidney Int* 1994;45(suppl 45):121.

59. Vestbo E, Damsgaard EM, Froland A, et al. Birth weight and cardiovascular risk factors in an epidemiological study. Diabetologia 1996;39:1598.

60. Mogensen CE. Microalbuminuria, blood pressure and diabetic renal disease: origin and development of ideas. *Diabetologia* 1999;42:263.

61. Almdal T, Norgaard K, Feldt-Rasmussen B, et al. The predictive value of microalbuminuria in IDDM. A five-year followup study. *Diabetes Care* 1994;17:120.

62. Bojestig M, Arnquist HJ, Karlberg BE, et al. Glycemic control and prognosis in type 1 diabetic patients with microalbuminuria. *Diabetes Care* 1996;19:313.

63. Bach LA, Gilbert, Cooper ME, et al. Prediction of persistent microalbuminuria in patients with diabetes mellitus. *J Diabet Complications* 1993;7:67.

64. Mogensen CE, Christensen CK. Predicting diabetic nephropathy in insulin-dependent patients [Essay]. *N Engl J Med* 1984;311:89.

65. Mathiesen ER, Oxenboll B, Johansen K, et al. Incipient nephropathy in type 1 (insulin-dependent) diabetes. *Diabetologia* 1984;26:406.

66. Mathiesen ER, Feldt-Rasmussen B, Hommel E, et al. Stable glomerular filtration rate in normotensive IDDM patients with stable microalbuminuria. A 5-year prospective study. *Diabetes Care* 1997;20:286.

67. Warram JH, Scott LJ, Hanna LS, et al. Progression of microalbuminuria to proteinuria in type 1 diabetes. Nonlinear relationship with hyperglycemia. *Diabetes* 2000;49:94.

68. Royal College of Physicians of Edinburgh Diabetes Register Group. Near-normal urinary albumin concentrations predict progression to diabetic nephropathy in type 1 diabetes mellitus. Diabetic Med 2000;17:782.

69. Janner M, Eberhard Knill SE, Diem P, et al. Persistent microalbuminuria in adolescents with type 1 (insulin-dependent) diabetes mellitus is associated to early rather than late puberty. Results of a prospective longitudinal study. *Eur J Pediatr* 1994;153:403.

70. Rudberg S, Dahlquist G. Determinants of progression of microalbuminuria in adolescents with IDDM. *Diabetes Care* 1996;19:369.

71. Jones CA, Leese GP, Kerr S, et al. Development and progression of microalbuminuria in a clinic sample of patients with insulin dependent diabetes mellitus. *Arch Dis Child* 1998;78:518.

72. Schultz CJ, Konopelska-Bahu T, Dalton RN, et al. Microalbuminuria prevalence varies with age, sex, and puberty in children with type 1 diabetes followed from diagnosis in a longitudinal study. *Diabetes Care* 1999;22:495.

73. Holl RW, Grabert M, Thon A, et al. Urinary excretion of albumin in adolescents with type 1 diabetes. Persistent versus intermittent microalbuminuria and relationship to duration of diabetes, sex, and metabolic control. *Diabetes Care* 1999;22:1555.

74. Levy-Marchal C, Shaler C, Cahane M, et al. Risk factors of microalbuminuria in children and adolescents with type 1 diabetes. GECER Study Group. *J Pediatr Endocrinol Metab* 2000;13:613.

75. Lawson ML, Sochett EB, Chait PG, et al. Effect of puberty on markers of glomerular hypertrophy and hypertension in IDDM. *Diabetes* 1996;45:51.

76. Rudberg S, Persson B, Dahlquist G. Increased glomerular filtration rate as a predictor of diabetic nephropathy—an 8-year prospective study. *Kidney Int* 1992;41:822.

77. Chiarelli F, Verrotti A, Morgese G. Glomerular hyperfiltration increases the risk of developing microalbuminuria in diabetic children. *Pediatr Nephrol* 1995;9:154.

78. Barkai L, Vamosi I, Lukacs K. Enhanced progression of urinary albumin excretion during puberty. *Diabetes Care* 1998;21:1019.

79. Schultz CJ, Neil HAW, Dalton RN, et al., on behalf of the Oxford Regional Prospective Study Group. Risk of nephropathy can be detected before the onset of microalbuminuria during the early years after the diagnosis of type 1 diabetes. *Diabetes Care* 2000;23:1811.

80. Patrick AW, Leslie PJ, Clarke BF, et al. The natural history and associations of microalbuminuria in type 2 diabetes during the first year after diagnosis. *Diabet Med* 1990;7:902.

81. Niskanen LK, Penttila I, Parviainen M, et al. Evolution, risk factors, and prognostic implications of albuminuria in NIDDM. *Diabetes Care* 1996;19:486.

82. Sosenko JM, Hu D, Welty T, et al. Albuminuria in recent-onset type 2 diabetes. The Strong Heart Study. *Diabetes Care* 2002;51:1078.

83. UK Prospective Diabetes Study Group. UK Prospective Diabetes Study (UKPDS). X. Urinary albumin excretion over 3 years in diet-treated type 2 (non-insulin-dependent) patients, and association with hypertension, hyperglycemia and hypertriglyceridemia. *Diabetologia* 1993;36:1021.

84. Gall M-A, Hougaard P, Borch-Johnson K, et al. Risk factors for development of incipient and overt diabetic nephropathy in patients with non-insulin dependent diabetes mellitus: prospective, observational study. *BMJ* 1997;314:783.

85. Ravid M, Brosh D, Ravid-Safran, et al. Main risk factors for nephropathy in type 2 diabetes mellitus are plasma cholesterol levels, mean blood pressure, and hyperglycemia. *Arch Intern Med* 1998;158:998.

86. de Grauw WJC, van de Lisdonk EH, van Gerwen WHEM, et al. Microalbuminuria in patients with type 2 diabetes mellitus from general practice: course and predictive value. *Diabet Med* 2001;18:139.

87. Nelson RG, Pettitt DJ, Baird HR, et al. Pre-diabetic blood pressure predicts urinary albumin excretion after the onset of type 2 (non-insulin-dependent) diabetes mellitus in Pima Indians. *Diabetologia* 1993;36:998.

88. Gerstein HC, Mann JFE, Pogue J, et al. Prevalence and determinants of microalbuminuria in high-risk diabetic and non-dia-

betic patients in the Heart Outcomes Prevention Evaluation Study. *Diabetes Care* 2000;23(suppl 2):B35.

89. Lee K-U, Park JY, Kim SW, et al. Prevalence and associated features of albuminuria in Koreans with NIDDM. *Diabetes Care* 1995;18:793.

90. Dasmahapatra A, Bale A, Raghuwanshi MP, et al. Incipient and overt diabetic nephropathy in African Americans with NIDDM. *Diabetes Care* 1994;17:297.

91. John L, Sunder Rao PSS, Kanagasabapathy AS. Rate of progression of albuminuria in type II diabetes. Five-year prospective study from South India. *Diabetes Care* 1994;17:888.

92. Park J-Y, Kim H-K, Chung YE, et al. Incidence and determinants of microalbuminuria in Koreans with type 2 diabetes. *Diabetes Care* 1998;21:530.

93. Islam N, Kazmi F, Chusney GD, et al. Ethnic differences in correlates of micro-albuminuria in NIDDM. The role of the acute-phase response. *Diabetes Care* 1998;21:385.

94. Festa A, D'Agostino R, Howard G, et al. Inflammation and microalbuminuria in nondiabetic and type 2 diabetic subjects: the Insulin Resistance Atherosclerosis Study. *Kidney Int* 2000; 58:1703.

95. Stehouwer CDA, Gall M-A, Twisk JWR, et al. Increased urinary albumin excretion, endothelial dysfunction, and chronic low-grade inflammation in type 2 diabetes. Progressive, interrelated, and independently associated with risk of death. *Diabetes* 2002;51:1157.

96. Pearson TA, Mensah GA, Alexander RW, et al. Markers of inflammation and cardiovascular disease. Application to clinical and public health practice. A statement for health care professionals from the Centers for Disease Control and Prevention and the American Heart Association. *Circulation* 2003;107: 499.

97. Colhoun HM, Schalkwijk C, Rubens MB, et al. C-reactive protein in type 1 diabetes and its relationship to coronary artery calcification. *Diabetes Care* 2002;25:1813.

98. Ridker PM. Clinical application of C-reactive protein for cardiovascular disease detection and prevention [Review]. *Circulation* 2003;107:363.

99. Mattock MB, Barnes DJ, Viberti GC, et al. Microalbuminuria and coronary heart disease in NIDDM. An incidence study. *Diabetes* 1998;47:1786.

100. Marso SP, Ellis SG, Tuzcu M, et al. The importance of proteinuria as a determinant of mortality following percutaneous coronary revascularization in diabetics. *J Am Coll Cardiol* 1999;33: 1269.

101. Gerstein HC, Mann JFE, Yi Q, et al. Albuminuria and risk of cardiovascular events, death, and heart failure in diabetic and nondiabetic individuals. *JAMA* 2001;286:421.

102. Spoelstra-de Man AME, Brouwer CB, Stehouwer CDA, et al. Rapid progression of albumin excretion is an independent predictor of cardiovascular mortality in patients with type 2 diabetes and microalbuminuria. *Diabetes Care* 2001;24:2097.

103. Sasaki A, Horiuchi N, Hasagawa K, et al. Persistent albuminuria as an index of diabetic nephropathy in type 2 diabetic patients in Osaka, Japan: incidence, risk factors, prognosis and causes of death. *Diabetes Res Clin Pract* 1989;7:299.

104. Vaur L, Gueret P, Lievre M, et al. Development of congestive heart failure in type 2 diabetic patients with microalbuminuria or proteinuria. Observations from the DIABHYCAR (type 2 DIABetes, Hypertension, CArdiovascular Events and Ramipril) study. *Diabetes Care* 2003;26:855.

105. Deckert T, FeldtRasmussen B, BorchJohnsen K, et al. Albuminuria reflects widespread vascular damage: the Steno hypothesis. *Diabetologia* 1989;32:219.

106. Beckman JA, Creager MA, Libby P. Diabetes and atherosclero-

sis. Epidemiology, pathophysiology, and management [Review]. *JAMA* 2002;287:2570.

107. Clausen P, Feldt-Rasmussen B, Jensen G, et al. Endothelial haemostatic factors are associated with progression of urinary albumin excretion in clinically healthy subjects: a 4-year prospective study. *Clin Sci* 1999;97:37.

108. Jager A, van Hinsburgh VWM, Kostense PJ, et al. von Willenbrand factor, C-reactive protein and 5-year mortality in diabetic and non-diabetic subjects: the Hoorn Study. *Arterioscler Thromb Vasc Biol* 1999;19:3071.

109. Andersen AR, Christiansen JS, Andersen JK, et al. Diabetic nephropathy in type 1(insulin-dependent) diabetes mellitus: an epidemiological study. *Diabetologia* 1983;25:496.

110. Krolewski AS, Warram JH, Christlieb AR, et al. The changing natural history of nephropathy in type I diabetes. *Am J Med* 1985;78:785.

111. Kofoed-Enevoldsen A, Borch-Johnsen K, Kreiner S, et al. Declining incidence of persistent proteinuria in type I (insulin-dependent) diabetic patients in Denmark. *Diabetes* 1987;36: 205.

112. Rossing P, Rossing K, Jacobsen P, et al. Unchanged incidence of diabetic nephropathy in IDDM patients. *Diabetes* 1995;44: 739.

113. Tuomilehto J, Borch-Johnsen K, Molarius A, et al. The unchanging incidence of hospitalization for diabetic nephropathy in a population-based cohort of IDDM patients in Finland. *Diabetes Care* 1997;20:1081.

114. Klein R, Klein BEK, Moss SE, Cruickshanks KJ. Ten-year incidence of gross proteinuria in people with diabetes. *Diabetes* 1995;44:916.

115. Forsblom CM, Groop PH, Ekstrand A, et al. Predictive value of microalbuminuria in patients with insulin-dependent diabetes of long duration. *BMJ* 1992;305:1051.

116. Bennett PH, Lee ET, Lu M, et al. Increased albumin excretion and its associations in the WHO Multinational Study of Vascular Disease in Diabetes. *Diabetologia* 2001;44(suppl 2):37.

117. Rossing P, Tarnow L, Nielsen SF, et al. Low birth weight: a risk factor for development of diabetic nephropathy? *Diabetes* 1995;44:1405.

118. Bojestig M, Arnqvist HJ, Hermansson G, et al. Declining incidence of nephropathy in insulin-dependent diabetes mellitus. *N Engl J Med* 1994;330:15.

119. Mangili R, Deferrari G, DiMario U, et al. Arterial hypertension and microalbuminuria in IDDM: the Italian Microalbuminuria Study. *Diabetologia* 1994;37:1015.

120. Olsen BS, Johannesen J, Sjolie AK, et al. Metabolic control and prevalence of microvascular complications in young Danish patients with type 1 diabetes mellitus. *Diabet Med* 1999;16:79.

121. Esmatjes E, DeAlvaro F, for the Estudio Diamante investigators. Incidence of diabetic nephropathy in type 1 diabetic patients in Spain: "Estudio Diamante." *Diabetes Res Clin Pract* 2002;57:35.

122. Bruno G, Cavallo-Perin P, Bargero G, et al. Prevalence and risk factors for microalbuminuria and macroalbuminuria in an Italian population-based cohort of NIDDM subjects. *Diabetes Care* 1996;19:43.

123. Larson TS, Santanello N, Shahinfar S, et al. Trends in persistent proteinuria in adult-onset diabetes. A population-based study. *Diabetes Care* 2000;23:51.

124. Gitter J, Langefeld CD, Rich SS, et al. Prevalence of nephropathy in black patients with type 2 diabetes mellitus. *Am J Nephrol* 2002;22:35.

125. Yokoyama H, Okudaira M, Otani T, et al. High incidence of diabetic nephropathy in early-onset Japanese NIDDM patients. Risk analysis. *Diabetes Care* 1998;21:1080.

126. Ballard DJ, Humphrey LL, Melton LJ, et al. Epidemiology of

persistent proteinuria in type 2 diabetes mellitus. Population-based study in Rochester, Minnesota. *Diabetes* 1988;37:405.

127. Gall M-A, Rossing P, Skott P, et al. Prevalence of micro- and macro- albuminuria, arterial hypertension, retinopathy and large vessel disease in European type 2 (non-insulin-dependent) diabetic patients. *Diabetologia* 1991;34:655.

128. Goldschmid MG, Domin WS, Ziemer DC, et al. Diabetes in urban African-Americans. II. High prevalence of microalbuminuria and nephropathy in African-Americans with diabetes. *Diabetes Care* 1995;18:955.

129. Haffner SM, Mitchell BD, Pugh JA, et al. Proteinuria in Mexican-Americans and non-hispanic whites with NIDDM. *Diabetes Care* 1989;12:530.

130. Samanta A, Burden AC, Feehally J, et al. Diabetic renal disease: differences between Asian and white patients. *BMJ* 1986;293:366.

131. Nelson RG, Knowler WC, Pettitt DJ, et al. Incidence and determinants of elevated urinary albumin excretion in Pima Indians with NIDDM. *Diabetes Care* 1995;18:182.

132. Humphrey LL, Ballard DJ, Frohnert PP, et al. Chronic renal failure in non-insulin-dependent diabetes mellitus. *Ann Intern Med* 1989;111:788.

133. Colhoun HM, Lee ET, Bennett PH, et al. Risk factors for renal failure: the WHO multinational study of vascular disease in diabetes. *Diabetologia* 2001;44(suppl 2):46.

134. Cowie CC, Port FK, Wolfe RA, et al. Disparities in incidence of diabetic end-stage renal disease according to race and type of diabetes. *N Engl J Med* 1989;321:1074.

135. Stephens GW, Gillespey JA, Clyne D, et al. Racial differences in the incidence of end-stage renal disease in types I and II diabetes mellitus. *Am J Kidney Dis* 1990;15:562.

136. Pugh JA, Medina RA, Cornell JC, et al. NIDDM is the major cause of diabetic end-stage renal disease. More evidence from a tri-ethnic community. *Diabetes* 1995;44:1375.

137. Burden A, McNally P, Feehally J, et al. Increased incidence of end-stage renal failure secondary to diabetes mellitus in Asian ethnic groups in the United Kingdom. *Diabet Med* 1992;9:641.

138. Chandie Shaw PK, Vandenbroucke JP, Tjandra YI, et al. Increased end-stage diabetic nephropathy in Indo-Asian immigrants living in the Netherlands. *Diabetologia* 2002;45:337.

139. Earle KA, Porter K, Olsberg J, et al. Variation in the progression of diabetic nephropathy according to racial origin. *Nephrol Dial Transplant* 2001;16:286.

140. Tuomilehto J, Borch-Johnsen K, Molarius A, et al. Incidence of cardiovascular disease in type 1 (insulin-dependent) diabetic subjects with and without diabetic nephropathy in Finland. *Diabetologia* 1998;41:784.

141. Morrish NJ, Wang S-L, Stevens LK, et al. Mortality and causes of death in the WHO multinational study of vascular disease in diabetes. *Diabetologia* 2001;44(suppl 2):14.

142. Fuller JH, Stevens LK, Wang S-L, and the WHO Multinational Study Group. Risk factors for cardiovascular mortality and morbidity: the WHO multinational study of vascular disease in diabetes. *Diabetologia* 2001;44(suppl 2):54.

143. Seaquist ER, Goetz FC, Rich S, et al. Familial clustering of diabetic kidney disease. Evidence for genetic susceptibility to diabetic nephropathy. *N Engl J Med* 1989;320:1161.

144. Borch-Johnsen K, Norgaard K, Hommel E, et al. Is diabetic nephropathy an inherited complication? *Kidney Int* 1992;41:719.

145. Quinn M, Angelico MC, Warram JH, et al. Familial factors determine the development of diabetic nephropathy in patients with IDDM. *Diabetologia* 1996;39:940.

146. Diabetes Control and Complications Trial Research Group. Clustering of long-term complications in families with diabetes

in the Diabetes Control and Complications Trial. *Diabetes* 1997;46:1829.

147. Faronato PP, Maoili M, Tonolo G, et al. Clustering of albumin excretion rate abnormalities in Caucasian patients with NIDDM. *Diabetologia* 1997;40:816.

148. Forsblom CM, Heritability of albumin excretion rate in families of patients with type II diabetes. *Diabetologia* 1999;42:1359.

149. Takeda H, Ohita K, Hagiwara M, et al. Genetic predisposition factors in non-insulin dependent diabetes with persistent albuminuria. *Tokai J Exp Clin Med* 1990;17:99.

150. Pettitt DJ, Saad MF, Bennett PH, et al. Familial predisposition to renal disease in two generations of Pima Indians with type 2 (non-insulin-dependent) diabetes mellitus. *Diabetologia* 1990;33:438.

151. Freedman BI, Tuttle AB, Spray BJ. Familial predisposition to nephropathy in African-Americans with non-insulin-dependent diabetes. *Am J Kidney Dis* 1995;25:710.

152. Canani LH, Gerchman F, Gross JL. Familial clustering of diabetic nephropathy in Brazilian type 2 diabetic patients. *Diabetes* 1999;48:909.

153. Fogarty DG, Rich SS, Hanna L, et al. Urinary albumin excretion in families with type 2 diabetes is heritable and genetically correlated to blood pressure. *Kidney Int* 2000;57:250.

154. Imperatore G, Knowler WC, Pettitt DJ, et al. Segregation analysis of diabetic nephropathy in Pima Indians. *Diabetes* 2000;49:1049.

155. Fogarty DG, Hanna LS, Wantman M, et al. Segregation analysis of urinary albumin excretion in families with type 2 diabetes. *Diabetes* 2000;49:1057.

156. Fujisawa T, Ikegami H, Kawaguchi Y, et al. Meta-analysis of association of insertion/deletion polymorphism of angiotensin 1–converting enzyme gene with diabetic nephropathy and retinopathy. *Diabetologia* 1998;41:47.

157. Krowlewski AS. Genetics of diabetic nephropathy: evidence for major and minor gene effects. *Kidney Int* 1999;55:1582.

158. Rogus JJ, Warram JH, Krowlewski AS. Genetic studies of late diabetic complications. The overlooked importance of diabetes duration before complication onset. *Diabetes* 2002;51:1655.

159. Iyengar SK, Fox KA, Schachere M, et al. Linkage analysis of candidate loci for end-stage renal disease due to diabetic nephropathy. *J Am Soc Nephrol* 2003;14(suppl):195.

160. Navar LG, Nishiyama A. Intrarenal formation of angiotensin II [Review]. *Contrib Nephrol* 2001;135:1.

161. Kriz W, Elger M, Mundel P, et al. Structure-stabilizing forces in the glomerular tuft. *J Am Soc Nephrol* 1995;5:1731.

162. Mundel P, Shankland SJ. Podocyte biology and response to injury [Review]. *J Am Soc Nephrol* 2002;13:3005.

163. Pavenstadt H, Kriz W, Kretzler M. Cell biology of the glomerular podocyte [Review]. *Physiol Rev* 2003;83:253.

164. Reiser J, von Gersdorff, Simons M, et al. Novel concepts in understanding and management of glomerular proteinuria [Review]. *Nephrol Dial Transplant* 2002;17:951.

165. Tryggvason K, Wartiovaara J. Molecular basis of glomerular permselectivity. *Curr Opin Nephrol Hypertens* 2001;10:543.

166. Miner JH. Renal basement membrane components [Review]. *Kidney Int* 1999;56:2016.

167. Raats CJI, van den Born J, Berden JHM. Glomerular heparan sulfate alterations: mechanisms and relevance for proteinuria [Review]. *Kidney Int* 2000;57:385.

168. Russo LM, Bakris GL, Comper WD. Renal handling of albumin: a critical review of basic concepts and perspective [Review]. *Am J Kidney Dis* 2002;39:899.

169. D'Amico G, Bazzi C. Pathophysiology of proteinuria [Review]. *Kidney Int* 2003;63:809.

170. Birn H, Fyfe JC, Jacobsen C, et al. Cubulin is an albumin binding protein important for renal tubular albumin reabsorption. *J Clin Invest* 2000;105:13353.

171. Verroust PJ, Birn H, Nielsen R, et al. The tandem endocytic receptors megalin and cubulin are important proteins in renal pathology. *Kidney Int* 2002;62:745.

172. Deen WM, Lazzara MJ, Myers BD. Structural determinants of glomerular permeability. *Am J Physiol* 2001;281:F579.

173. Blouch K, Deen WM, Fauvel J-P, et al. Molecular configuration and glomerular size selectivity in healthy and nephritic humans. *Am J Physiol* 1997;273:F430.

174. Lemley KV, Kriz W. Anatomy of the renal interstitium [Review]. *Kidney Int* 1991;39:370.

175. Osterby R. Early phases in the development of diabetic nephropathy. A quantitative electron microscopic study. *Acta Med Scand Suppl* 1975;574:1–80.

176. Kroustrup JP, Gunderson HJG, Osterby R. Glomerular size and structure in diabetes mellitus. III. Early enlargement of the capillary surface. *Diabetologia* 1977;13:207.

177. Ellis EN, Warady BA, Wood EG, et al. Renal structural-functional relationships in early diabetes mellitus. *Pediatr Nephrol* 1997;11:584.

178. Rudberg S, Osterby R. Diabetic glomerulopathy in young IDDM patients [Review]. *Horm Res* 1998;50(suppl 1):17.

179. Berg UB, Torbjornsdotter TB, Jaremko G, et al. Kidney morphological changes in relation to long-term renal function and metabolic control in adolescents with IDDM. *Diabetologia* 1998;41:1047.

180. Steffes MW, Bilous RW, Sutherland DER, et al. Cell and matrix components of the glomerular mesangium in type I diabetes. *Diabetes* 1992;41:679.

181. Walker JD, Close CF, Jones SL, et al. Glomerular structure in type-1 (insulin-dependent) diabetic patients with normo- and microalbuminuria. *Kidney Int* 1992;41:741.

182. Mauer SM. Structural-functional correlations of diabetic nephropathy [Review]. *Kidney Int* 1994;45:612.

183. Torbjornsdotter TB, Jaremko GA, Berg UB. Ambulatory blood pressure and heart rate in relation to kidney structure and metabolic control in adolescents with type I diabetes. *Diabetologia* 2001;44:865.

184. Bangstad H-J, Osterby R, Hartmann A, et al. Severity of glomerulopathy predicts long-term urinary albumin excretion rate in patients with type 1 diabetes and microalbuminuria. *Diabetes Care* 1999;22:314.

185. Osterby R, Parving H-H, Nyberg G, et al. A strong positive correlation between glomerular filtration rate and filtration surface in diabetic nephropathy. *Diabetologia* 1988;31:265.

186. Steffes MW, Osterby R, Chavers B, et al. Mesangial expansion as a central mechanism for loss of kidney function in diabetic patients [Review]. *Diabetes* 1989;38:1077.

187. Katz A, Caramori MLA, Sisson-Ross S, et al. An increase in the cell component of the cortical interstitium antedates interstitial fibrosis in type 1 diabetic patients. *Kidney Int* 2002;61:2058.

188. Lane PH, Steffes MW, Fioretto P, et al. Renal interstitial expansion in insulin-dependent diabetes mellitus. *Kidney Int* 1993;43:661.

189. Osterby R, Hartmann A, Nyengaard JR, et al. Development of renal structural lesions in type-1 diabetic patients with microalbuminuria. Observations by light microscopy in 8-year follow-up biopsies. *Virchows Arch* 2002;440:94.

190. Steffes MW, Sutherland DER, Goetz FC, et al. Studies of kidney and muscle biopsy specimens from identical twins discordant for type I diabetes mellitus. *N Engl J Med* 1985;312:1282.

191. Mauer SM, Goetz FC, McHugh LE, et al. Long-term study of normal kidneys transplanted into patients with type I diabetes. *Diabetes* 1989;38:516.

192. Osterby R, Nyberg G, Hedman L, et al. Kidney transplantation in type 1 (insulin-dependent) diabetic patients. Early glomerulopathy. *Diabetologia* 1991;34:668.

193. Makino H, Shikata K, Hironaka K, et al. Ultrastructure of nonenzymatically glycated mesangial matrix in diabetic nephropathy. *Kidney Int* 1995;48:517.

194. Tamsma JT, Van Den Born J, Bruijn JA, et al. Expression of glomerular extracellular matrix components in human diabetic nephropathy: decrease of heparan sulfate in the glomerular basement membrane. *Diabetologia* 1994;37:313.

195. Edge ASB, Spiro RG. A specific structural alteration in the heparan sulphate of human glomerular basement membrane in diabetes. *Diabetologia* 2000;43:1056.

196. White KE, Bilous RW, Marshall SM, et al. Podocyte number in normotensive type 1 diabetic patients with albuminuria. *Diabetes* 2002;51:3083.

197. Bjorn SF, Bangstad H-J, Hanssen KF, et al. Glomerular epithelial foot processes and filtration slits in IDDM patients. *Diabetologia* 1995;38:1197.

198. Nakamura T, Ushiyama C, Suzuki S, et al. Urinary excretion of podocytes in patients with diabetic nephropathy. *Nephrol Dial Transplant* 2000;15:1379.

199. Ueno M, Kawashima S, Nishi S, et al. Tubulointerstitial lesions in non-insulin dependent diabetes mellitus. *Kidney Int* 1997;52 (suppl 63):191.

200. Gilbert RE, Cooper M. The tubulointerstitium in progressive diabetic kidney disease: more than an aftermath of glomerular injury? [Review]. *Kidney Int* 1999;56:1627.

201. Essawy M, Soylemezoglu O, Muchaneta-Kubara EC, et al. Myofibroblasts and the progression of diabetic nephropathy. *Nephrol Dial Transplant* 1997;12:43.

202. Yang J, Liu Y. Dissection of key events in tubular epithelial to myofibroblast transition and its implications in renal interstitial fibrosis. *Am J Pathol* 2001;159:1465.

203. Zeisberg M, Maeshima Y, Mosterman B, et al. Renal fibrosis: extracellular matrix microenvironment regulates migratory behavior of activated tubular epithelial cells. *Am J Pathol* 2002; 160:2001.

204. Rastaldi MP, Ferrario F, Giardino L, et al. Epithelial-mesenchymal transition of tubular epithelial cells in human renal biopsies. *Kidney Int* 2002;62:137.

205. Osterby R. Glomerular structural changes in type 1 (insulin-dependent) diabetes mellitus: causes, consequences, and prevention [Review]. *Diabetologia* 1992;35:803.

206. Gunderson HJG, Osterby R. Glomerular size and structure in diabetes mellitus. II. Late abnormalities. *Diabetologia* 1977;13: 43.

207. Pagtalunan ME, Miller PL, Jumping-Eagle S, et al. Podocyte loss and progressive glomerular injury in type II diabetes. *J Clin Invest* 1997;99:342.

208. Meyer TW, Bennett PH, Nelson RG. Podocyte number predicts long-term urinary albumin excretion in Pima Indians with type II diabetes and microalbuminuria. *Diabetologia* 1999;42: 1341.

209. Langham RG, Kelly DJ, Cox AJ, et al. Proteinuria and the expression of the podocyte slit diaphragm protein, nephrin, in diabetic nephropathy: effects of angiotensin converting enzyme inhibition. *Diabetologia* 2002;45:1572.

210. Doublier S, Salvidio G, Lupia E, et al. Nephrin expression is reduced in human diabetic nephropathy. Evidence for a distinct role for glycated albumin and angiotensin II. *Diabetes* 2003;52: 1023.

211. Mogensen CE, Christensen CK, Vittinghus E. The stages in diabetic renal disease, with emphasis on the stage of incipient diabetic nephropathy. *Diabetes* 1983;32(suppl 2):64.

212. National Kidney Foundation. K/DOQI clinical practice guide-

lines for chronic kidney disease: evaluation, classification, and stratification. *Am J Kidney Dis* 2002;39(suppl 1):1.

213. Sarnak MJ, Levey AS, Schoolwerth AC, et al. Kidney disease as a risk factor for development of cardiovascular disease. A statement from the American Heart Association Councils on Kidney in Cardiovascular Disease, High Blood Pressure Research, Clinical Cardiology, and Epidemiology and Prevention. *Hypertension* 2003;42:1050.

214. Mogensen CE, Anderson MJF. Increased kidney size and glomerular filtration rate in early juvenile diabetes. *Diabetes* 1973;22:706.

215. O'Hayon BE, Cummings EA, Daneman D, et al. Does dietary protein intake correlate with markers suggestive of early diabetic nephropathy in children and adolescents with type 1 diabetes mellitus? *Diabet Med* 2000;17:708.

216. Christiansen JS, Gammelgaard J, Tronier B. Kidney function and size in diabetics before and during initial insulin treatment. *Kidney Int* 1982;21:683.

217. Mauer M, Drummond K, for the International Diabetic Nephropathy Study Group. The early natural history of nephropathy in type 1 diabetes. I. Study design and baseline characteristics of the study participants. *Diabetes* 2002;51:1572.

218. Mogensen CE. Glomerular filtration rate and renal plasma flow in short-term juvenile diabetes mellitus. *Scand J Clin Lab Invest* 1971;28:91.

219. Hostetter TH, Rennke HG, Brenner BM. The case for intrarenal hypertension in the initiation and progression of diabetic and other glomerulopathies. *Am J Med* 1982;72:375.

220. Viberti GC, Bilous RW, Mackintosh D, et al. Monitoring glomerular function in diabetic nephropathy: a prospective study. *Am J Med* 1983;74:256.

221. Claris-Appiani A, Assael BM, Tirelli AS, et al. Sodium excretion and hyperfiltration during glucose infusion in man. *Am J Nephrol* 1990;10:103.

222. Mogensen CE. Glomerular filtration rate and renal plasma flow in normal and diabetic man during elevation of blood sugar levels. *Scand J Clin Lab Invest* 1971;28:177.

223. Wiseman MJ, Saunders AJ, Keen H, et al. Effect of blood glucose control on increased glomerular filtration rate and kidney size in insulin-dependent diabetes. *N Engl J Med* 1985;312:617.

224. Tuttle KR, Bruton JL, Perusek MC, et al. Effect of strict glycemic control on renal hemodynamic response to amino acids and renal enlargement in insulin-dependent diabetes mellitus. *N Engl J Med* 1991;324:1626.

225. Hannedouche TP, Delgado AG, Gnionsahe DA, et al. Renal hemodynamics and segmental tubular sodium reabsorption in early type 1 diabetes. *Kidney Int* 1990;37:1126.

226. Lemley KV, Abdullah I, Myers BD, et al. Evolution of incipient nephropathy in type 2 diabetes mellitus. *Kidney Int* 2000;58:1228.

227. Brenner BM, Lawler EV, Mackenzie HS. The hyperfiltration theory: a paradigm shift in nephrology [Review]. *Kidney Int* 1996;49:1774.

228. Wolf G, Ziyadeh FN. Molecular mechanisms of diabetic renal hypertrophy [Review]. *Kidney Int* 1999;56:393.

229. Lansang MC, Hollenberg NK. Renal perfusion and the renal hemodynamic response to blocking the renin system in diabetes. Are the forces leading to vasodilation and vasoconstriction linked? *Diabetes* 2002;51:2025.

230. Fioretto P, Sambataro M, Cipollina MR, et al. Atrial natriuretic peptide in the pathogenesis of sodium retention in IDDM with and without glomerular hyperfiltration. *Diabetes* 1992;41:936.

231. Vallon V, Blantz RC, Thomson S. Glomerular hyperfiltration and the salt paradox in early type 1 diabetes mellitus: a tubulocentric view [Review]. *J Am Soc Nephrol* 2003;14:530.

232. Brochner-Mortensen J, Ditzel J. Glomerular filtration rate and

extracellular fluid volume in insulin-dependent patients with diabetes mellitus. *Kidney Int* 1982;21:696.

233. Caramori MLA, Gross JL, Pecis M, et al. Glomerular filtration rate, urinary albumin excretion rate, and blood pressure changes in normoalbuminuric normotensive type 1 diabetic patients. *Diabetes Care* 1999;22:1512.

234. Chavers BM, Bilous FW, Ellis EN, et al. Glomerular lesions and urinary albumin excretion in type 1 diabetes without overt proteinuria. *N Engl J Med* 1989;320:966.

235. Rudberg S, Osterby R, Dahlquist G, et al. Predictors of renal morphological changes in the early stage of microalbuminuria in adolescents with IDDM. *Diabetes Care* 1997;20:265.

236. Lervang H-H, Jensen S, Brochner-Mortensen J, et al. Early glomerular hyperfiltration and the development of late nephropathy in type 1 (insulin-dependent) diabetes mellitus. *Diabetologia* 1988;31:723.

237. Pecis M, Azevedo MJ, Gross JL. Glomerular hyperfiltration is associated with blood pressure abnormalities in normotensive normoalbuminuric IDDM patients. *Diabetes Care* 1997;20:1329.

238. Lurbe E, Redon J, Kesani A, et al. Increase in nocturnal blood pressure and progression to microalbuminuria in type 1 diabetes. *N Engl J Med* 2002;347:797.

239. Viberti GC, Bilous RW, Mackintosh D, et al. Monitoring glomerular function in diabetic nephropathy: a prospective study. *Am J Med* 1983;74:256.

240. Deinum J, Ronn B, Mathiesen E, et al. Increase in serum prorenin precedes onset of microalbuminuria in patients with insulin-dependent diabetes mellitus. *Diabetologia* 1999;42:1006.

241. Lane PH, Steffes MW, Mauer SM. Glomerular structure in IDDM women with low glomerular filtration rate and normal urinary albumin excretion. *Diabetes* 1992;41:581.

242. Caramori ML, Fioretto P, Mauer M. Low glomerular filtration rate in normoalbuminuric type 1 diabetic patients. An indicator of more advanced glomerular lesions. *Diabetes* 2003;52:1036.

243. Ellis EN, Steffes MW, Goetz F, et al. Glomerular filtration surface in type I diabetes mellitus. *Kidney Int* 1986;29:889.

244. Caramori ML, Kim Y, Huang C, et al. Cellular basis of diabetic nephropathy. 1. Study design and renal structural-functional relationships in patients with long-standing type 1 diabetes. *Diabetes* 2002;51:506.

245. Lemann L Jr, Bidani AK, Bain RP, et al. Use of the serum creatinine to estimate glomerular filtration rate in health and early diabetic nephropathy. *Am J Kidney Dis* 1990;16:236.

246. Giovannetti S, Barsotti G. In defense of creatinine clearance. *Nephron* 1991;59:11.

247. Dharnidharka VR, Kwon C, Stevens G. Serum cystatin C is superior to serum creatinine as a marker of kidney function: a meta-analysis. *Am J Kidney Dis* 2002;40:221.

248. Tan GD, Lewis AV, James TJ, et al. Clinical usefulness of cystatin C for the estimation of glomerular filtration rate in type 1 diabetes: reproducibility and accuracy compared with standard measures and iohexol clearance. *Diabetes Care* 2002;25:2004.

249. Buysschaert M, Joudi I, Wallemacq P, et al. Performance of serum cystatin-C versus serum creatinine in subjects with type 1 diabetes. *Diabetes Care* 2003;26:1320.

250. Mathiesen ER, Ronn B, Storm B, et al. The natural course of microalbuminuria in insulin-dependent diabetes: a 10-year prospective study. *Diabet Med* 1995;12:482.

251. Hovind P, Tarnow L, Rossing K, et al. Decreasing incidence of severe diabetic microangiopathy in type 1 diabetes. *Diabetes Care* 2003;26:1258.

252. Bangstad H-J, Osterby R, Rudberg S, et al. Kidney function and glomerulopathy over 8 years in young patients with type 1 (insulin-dependent) diabetes mellitus and microalbuminuria. *Diabetologia* 2002;45:253.

253. Rudberg S, Osterby R. Decreasing glomerular filtration rate—

an indicator of more advanced diabetic glomerulopathy in the early course of microalbuminuria in IDDM adolescents? *Nephrol Dial Transplant* 1997;12:1149.

254. Moore WV, Donaldson DL, Chonko AM, et al. Ambulatory blood pressure in type 1 diabetes mellitus. Comparison to presence of incipient nephropathy in adolescents and young adults. *Diabetes* 1992;41:1035.

255. Watschinger B, Brunner C, Wagner A, et al. Left ventricular diastolic impairment in type 1 diabetic patients with microalbuminuria. *Nephron* 1993;63:145.

256. Rutter MK, McComb JM, Forster J, et al. Increased left ventricular mass index and nocturnal systolic blood pressure in patients with type 2 diabetes mellitus and microalbuminuria. *Diabet Med* 2000;17:321.

257. Lafferty AR, Werther GA, Clarke CF. Ambulatory blood pressure, microalbuminuria, and autonomic neuropathy in adolescents with type 1 diabetes. *Diabetes Care* 2000;23:533.

258. Cohen CN, Albanesi FM, Goncalves MF, et al. Microalbuminuria, high blood pressure burden, and the nondipper phenomenon. An interaction in normotensive type 1 diabetic patients. *Diabetes Care* 2001;24:790.

259. Nielsen S, Schmitz A, Poulsen PL, et al. Albuminuria and 24-h ambulatory blood pressure in normoalbuminuric and microalbuminuric NIDDM patients. A longitudinal study. *Diabetes Care* 1995;18:1434.

260. Walker JD, Close CF, Jones S, et al. Glomerular structure in type-1 (insulin-dependent) diabetic patients with normo- and microalbuminuria. *Kidney Int* 1992;41:741.

261. Fioretto P, Steffes MW, Mauer M. Glomerular structure in nonproteinuric IDDM patients with various levels of albuminuria. *Diabetes* 1994;43:1358.

262. Nosadini R, Velussi M, Brocco E, et al. Course of renal function in type 2 diabetic patients with abnormalities of albumin excretion rate. *Diabetes* 2000;49:476.

263. Adler SG, Kang S-W, Feld S, et al. Glomerular mRNAs in human type 1 diabetes: biochemical evidence for microalbuminuria as a manifestation of diabetic nephropathy. *Kidney Int* 2001;60:2330.

264. Osterby R, Hartmann A, Nyengaard JR, et al. Development of renal structural lesions in type-1 diabetic patients with microalbuminuria. Observations by light microscopy in 8-year follow-up biopsies. *Virchows Arch* 2002;440:94.

265. Anderson S, Vora JP. Current concepts of renal hemodynamics in diabetes. *J Diabet Complications* 1995;9:314.

266. Imanishi M, Yoshioka K, Konishi Y, et al. Glomerular hypertension as one cause of albuminuria in type II diabetic patients. *Diabetologia* 1999;42:999.

267. Scandling JD, Myers BD. Glomerular size-selectivity and microalbuminuria in early diabetic glomerular disease. *Kidney Int* 1992;41:840.

268. Oberbauer R, Nenov V, Weidekamm C, et al. Reduction in mean glomerular pore size coincides with the development of large shunt pores in patients with diabetic nephropathy. *Exp Nephrol* 2001;9:49.

269. Holm J, Hemmingsen L, Nielsen NV. Low-molecular-mass proteinuria as a marker of proximal renal tubular dysfunction in normo- and microalbuminuric non-insulin-dependent diabetic subjects. *Clin Chem* 1993;39:517.

270. Schultz CJ, Dalton RN, Neil HAW, et al. Markers of renal tubular dysfunction measured annually do not predict risk of microalbuminuria in the first few years after diagnosis of type 1 diabetes. *Diabetologia* 2001;44:224.

271. Osicka TM, Houlihan CA, Chan JG, et al. Albuminuria in patients with type 1 diabetes is directly linked to changes in the lysosome-mediated degradation of albumin during renal passage. *Diabetes* 2000;49:1579.

272. Kowluru A, Kowluru R, Bitensky MW, et al. Suggested mechanism for the selective excretion of glucosylated albumin: the effects of diabetes mellitus and aging on this process and the origins of diabetic microproteinuria. *J Exp Med* 1987;166:1259.

273. Gall M-A, Rossing P, Kofoed-Enevoldsen A, et al. Glomerular size- and charge selectivity in type 2 (non-insulin-dependent) diabetic patients with diabetic nephropathy. *Diabetologia* 1994; 37:195.

274. Anderson S, Blouch K, Bialek J, et al. Glomerular permselectivity in early stages of overt diabetic nephropathy. *Kidney Int* 2000;58:2129.

275. Bakoush O, Tencer J, Tapia J, et al. Higher urinary IgM excretion in type 2 diabetic nephropathy compared to type 1 diabetic nephropathy. *Kidney Int* 2002;61:203.

276. Jerums G, Allen TJ, Cooper ME. Triphasic changes in selectivity with increasing proteinuria in type 1 and type 2 diabetes. *Diabet Med* 1989;6:772.

277. Yoshioka K, Imanishi M, Konishi Y, et al. Glomerular charge and size selectivity assessed by changes in salt intake in type 2 diabetic patients. *Diabetes Care* 1998;21:482.

278. Shirata I, Hishiki T, Tomino Y. Podocyte loss and progression of diabetic nephropathy [Review]. *Contrib Nephrol* 2001;134:69.

279. Taft JL, Nolan CJ, Yeung SP, et al. Clinical and histological correlations of decline in renal function in diabetic patients with proteinuria. *Diabetes* 1994;43:1046.

280. Remuzzi G. Nephropathic nature of proteinuria [Review]. *Curr Opin Nephrol Hypertens* 1999;8:655.

281. Walls J. Relationship between proteinuria and progressive renal disease [Review]. *Am J Kidney Dis* 2001;37(suppl 2):13.

282. Osterby R, Gunderson HJG, Nyberg G, et al. Advanced diabetic glomerulopathy: quantitative structural characterization of nonoccluded glomeruli. *Diabetes* 1987;36:612.

283. Mauer SM, Sutherland DER, Steffes MW. Relationship of systemic blood pressure to nephropathology in insulin-dependent diabetes. *Kidney Int* 1992;41:736.

284. Jerums G, Allen TJ, Tsalamandris C, et al. Relationship of progressively increasing albuminuria to apoprotein(a) and blood pressure in type 1 (insulin-dependent) diabetic patients. *Diabetologia* 1993;36:1037.

285. Rossing P, Hommel E, Smidt UM, et al. Impact of arterial blood pressure and albuminuria on the progression of diabetic nephropathy in IDDM patients. *Diabetes* 1993;42:715.

286. Alaveras AEG, Thomas SM, Sagriotis A, et al. Promoters of progression of diabetic nephropathy: the relative roles of blood glucose and blood pressure control. *Nephrol Dial Transplant* 1997; 12(suppl 2):71.

287. Hovind P, Rossing P, Tarnow L, et al. Progression of diabetic nephropathy. *Kidney Int* 2001;59:702.

288. Christensen PK, Hansen HP, Parving H-H. Impaired autoregulation of GFR in hypertensive non-insulin dependent diabetic patients. *Kidney Int* 1997;52:1369.

289. Breyer JA, Bain RP, Evans JK, et al. Predictors of the progression of renal insufficiency in patients with insulin-dependent diabetes and overt diabetic nephropathy. *Kidney Int* 1996;50: 1651.

290. Orchard TJ, Dorman JS, Maser RE, et al. Prevalence of complications in IDDM by sex and duration. Pittsburgh Epidemiology of Diabetes Complications Study II. *Diabetes* 1990;39: 1116.

291. Neugarten J, Acharya A, Silbiger SR. Effect of gender on the progression of nondiabetic renal disease: a meta-analysis. *J Am Soc Nephrol* 2000;11:319.

292. Stenvinkel R, Wanner C, Metzger T, et al. Inflammation and outcome in end-stage renal failure: does female gender constitute a survival advantage? *Kidney Int* 2002;62:1791.

293. Hansen HP, Hovind P, Jensen BR, et al. Diurnal variations of

glomerular filtration rate and albuminuria in diabetic nephropathy. *Kidney Int* 2002;61:163.

294. Mulec H, Blohme G, Kullenberg K, et al. Latent overhydration and nocturnal hypertension in diabetic nephropathy. *Diabetologia* 1995;38:216.

295. Bosman DR, Winkler AS, Marsden JT, et al. Anemia with erythropoietin deficiency occurs early in diabetic nephropathy. *Diabetes Care* 2001;24:495.

296. Hasslacher C, Bostedt-Kiesel A, Kempe HP, et al. Effect of metabolic factors and blood pressure on kidney function in proteinuric type 2 (non-insulin-dependent) diabetic patients. *Diabetologia* 1993;36:1051.

297. Christensen PK, Gall M-A, Parving H-H. Course of glomerular filtration rate in albuminuric type 2 diabetic patients with or without diabetic glomerulopathy. *Diabetes Care* 2000;23(suppl 2):B14.

298. Wong TYH, Choi PCL, Szeto CC, et al. Renal outcome in type 2 diabetic patients with or without coexisting nondiabetic nephropathies. *Diabetes Care* 2002;25:900.

299. Adler AI, Stevens RJ, Manley SE, et al. Development and progression of nephropathy in type 2 diabetes: the United Kingdom Prospective Diabetes Study (UKPDS 64). *Kidney Int* 2003;63:225.

300. Gall M-A, Nielsen FS, Smidt UM, et al. The course of kidney function in Type 2 (non-insulin-dependent) diabetic patients with diabetic nephropathy. *Diabetologia* 1993;36:1071.

301. Myers BD, Nelson RG, Tan M, et al. Progression of overt nephropathy in non-insulin-dependent diabetes. *Kidney Int* 1995;47:1781.

302. Nelson RG, Bennett PH, Beck GJ, et al. Development and progression of renal disease in Pima Indians with non-insulin-dependent diabetes mellitus. *N Engl J Med* 1996;335:1636.

303. Osterby R, Gunderson HJG, Horlyck A, et al. Diabetic glomerulopathy. structural characteristics of the early and advanced stages. *Diabetes* 1983;32(suppl 2):79.

304. Osterby R, Gunderson HJG, Nyberg G, et al. Advanced diabetic glomerulopathy. Quantitative structural characterization of non-occluded glomeruli. *Diabetes* 1987;36:612.

305. Ordonez JD, Hiatt RA. Comparison of type II and type I diabetics treated for end-stage renal disease in a large prepaid health plan population. *Nephron* 1989;51:524.

306. Pugh JA, Medina R, Ramirez R. Comparison of the course to endstage renal disease of type 1 (insulin-dependent) and type 2 (non-insulin-dependent) diabetic nephropathy. *Diabetologia* 1993; 36:1094.

307. Muhlhauser I, Overmann H, Bender R, et al. Predictors of mortality and end-stage diabetic complications in patients with type 1 diabetes mellitus on intensified therapy. *Diabet Med* 2000; 17:727.

308. Burden AC, McNally PG, Feehally J, et al. Increased incidence of end-stage renal failure secondary to diabetes mellitus in Asian ethnic groups in the United Kingdom. *Diabet Med* 1992;9:641–645.

309. Charra B, VoVan C, Marcelli D, et al: Diabetes mellitus in Tassin, France: remarkable transformation in incidence and outcome of ESRD in diabetes. *Adv Renal Replace Ther* 2001;8:42.

310. Melin J, Hellberg O, Fellstrom B. Hyperglycemia and renal ischemia-reperfusion injury. *Nephrol Dial Transplant* 2003;18:460.

311. DeJong PE, Navis G, de Zeeuw D. Renoprotective therapy: titration against urinary protein excretion [Commentary]. *Lancet* 1999;354:352.

312. Ruggenenti P, Schieppati A, Remuzzi G. Progression, remission, regression of chronic renal diseases [Review]. *Lancet* 2001;357:1601.

313. Weir MR. Progressive renal and cardiovascular disease: optimal treatment strategies [Review]. *Kidney Int* 2002;62:1482.

314. Noronha IL, Fujihara CK, Zatz R. The inflammatory component in progressive renal disease—are interventions possible? [Review]. *Nephrol Dial Transplant* 2002;17:363.

315. Brenner BM. Retarding the progression of renal disease [Review]. *Kidney Int* 2003;64:370.

316. Viberti G, Chaturvedi N. Angiotensin converting enzyme inhibitors in diabetic patients with microalbuminuria or normoalbuminuria. *Kidney Int* 1997;52(suppl 63):32.

317. Gaede P, Vedel P, Parving H-H, et al. Intensified multifactorial intervention in patients with type 2 diabetes mellitus and microalbuminuria: the Steno type 2 randomized study. *Lancet* 1999;353:617.

318. Gaede P, Vedel P, Larsen N, et al. Multifactorial intervention and cardiovascular disease in patients with type 2 diabetes. *N Engl J Med* 2003;348:383.

319. Ritz E. Albuminuria and vascular damage—the vicious twins [Essay]. *N Engl J Med* 2003;348:2349.

320. Wald NJ, Law MR. A strategy to reduce cardiovascular disease by more than 80%. *BMJ* 2003;326:1419.

321. Law MR, Wald NJ, Morris JK, et al. Value of low dose combination treatment with blood pressure lowering drugs: analysis of 354 randomized trials. *BMJ* 2003;326:1427.

322. Schieppati A, Remuzzi G. The future of renoprotection: frustration and promises. *Kidney Int* 2003;64:1947.

323. Mogyorosi A, Ziyadeh FN. GLUT1 and TGF-β: the link between hyperglycemia and diabetic nephropathy. *Nephrol Dial Transplant* 1999;14:2827.

324. Heilig C, Zaloga C, Lee M, et al. Immunogold localization of high affinity glucose transporter isoforms in normal rat kidney. *Lab Invest* 1995;73:674.

325. Liu ZH, Chen ZH, Li Y-J, et al. Phenotypic alterations of live mesangial cells in patients with diabetic nephropathy obtained from renal biopsy specimen. *J Am Soc Nephrol* 1999;10:A0669.

326. Heilig CW, Brosius FC, Henry DN. Glucose transporters of the glomerulus and the implications for diabetic nephropathy [Review]. *Kidney Int* 1997;51(suppl 60):91.

327. Wakisaka M, He Q, Spiro MJ, et al. Glucose entry into rat mesangial cells is mediated by both Na$^+$-coupled and facilitative transporters. *Diabetologia* 1995;38:291.

328. Heilig C, Liu Y, England R, et al. D-glucose stimulates mesangial cell GLUT1 expression, basal, and IGF1-sensitive glucose uptake in rat mesangial cells: implications for diabetic nephropathy. *Diabetes* 1997;46:1030.

329. Gnudi L, Viberti GC, Raij L, et al. Link between hemodynamic and metabolic factors in glomerular injury? *Hypertension* 2003;42:19.

330. Brownlee M. Biochemistry and molecular cell biology of diabetic complications. *Nature* 2001;414:813.

331. Reusch JEB. Diabetes, microvascular complications, and cardiovascular complications: what is it about glucose? *J Clin Invest* 2003;112:986.

332. Derylo B, Babazono T, Glogowski E, et al. High glucose-induced mesangial cell altered contractility: role of the polyol pathway. *Diabetologia* 1998;41:507.

333. Schleicher ED, Weigert C. Role of hexosamine biosynthetic pathway in diabetic nephropathy. *Kidney Int* 2000;58(suppl):13.

334. Goldberg HJ, Whiteside CI, Fantus IG. The hexosamine pathway regulates the plasminogen activator inhibitor-1 gene promoter and Sp1 transcriptional activation through protein kinase C β and δ. *J Biol Chem* 2002;277:33833.

335. Babaei-Jadidi R, Karachalias N, Ahmed N, et al. Prevention of incipient diabetic nephropathy by high-dose thiamine and benfotiamine. *Diabetes* 2003;52:2110.

336. Way KJ, Katai N, King GL. Protein kinase C and the development of diabetic vascular complications [Review]. *Diabet Med* 2001;18:945.

337. Whiteside CI, Dlugosz JA. Mesangial cell protein kinase C isozyme activation in the diabetic milieu [Review]. *Am J Physiol* 2002;282:F975.

338. Yerneni KK, Bai W, Khan B, et al. Hyperglycemia-induced activation of nuclear transcription factor kappaB in vascular smooth muscle cells. *Diabetes* 1999;48:855.

339. Singh R, Barden A, Mori T, et al. Advanced glycation end-products: a review. *Diabetologia* 2001;44:129.

340. Wendt T, Tanji N, Guo J, et al. Glucose, glycation, and RAGE: implications for amplification of cellular dysfunction in diabetic nephropathy. *J Am Soc Nephrol* 2003;14:1383.

341. Wendt TM, Tanji N, Guo J, et al. RAGE drives the development of glomerulosclerosis and implicates podocyte activation in the pathogenesis of diabetic nephropathy. *Am J Pathol* 2003; 162:1123.

342. Du, XL, Edelstein D, Rosetti L, et al. Hyperglycemia-induced mitochondrial superoxide overproduction activates the hexosamine pathway and induces plasminogen activator inhibitor-1 expression by increasing Sp1 glycolysylation. *Proc Natl Acad Sci U S A* 2000;97:12222.

343. Nishikawa T, Edelstein D, Du XL, et al. Normalizing mitochondrial superoxide production blocks three pathways of hyperglycemic damage. *Nature* 2000;404:787.

344. Hammes H-P, Du X, Edelstein D, et al. Benfotiamine blocks three major pathways of hyperglycemic damage and prevents experimental diabetic retinopathy. *Nature Med* 2003;9:294.

345. Du X, Matsumura T, Edelstein D, et al. Inhibition of GADPH activity by poly(ADP-ribose) polymerase activates three major pathways of hyperglycemic damage in endothelial cells. *J Clin Invest* 2003;112:1049.

346. Lyons TJ, Jenkins AJ. Glycation, oxidation, and lipoxidation in the development of the complications of diabetes: a carbonyl stress hypothesis. *Diabetes Rev* 1997;5:365.

347. Baynes JW, Thorpe SR. Role of oxidative stress in diabetic complications. A new perspective on an old paradigm. *Diabetes* 1999;48:1.

348. Ceriello A, Morocutti A, Mercuri F, et al. Defective intracellular antioxidant enzyme production in type 1 diabetic patients with nephropathy. *Diabetes* 2000;49:2170.

349. Hodgkinson AD, Bartlett T, Oates PJ, et al. The response of antioxidant genes to hyperglycemia is abnormal in patients with type 1 diabetes and diabetic nephropathy. *Diabetes* 2003;52:846.

350. Flyvberg A. Putative pathophysiological role of growth factors and cytokines in experimental diabetic kidney disease. *Diabetologia* 2000;43:1205.

351a. Wolf G: Molecular mechanisms of diabetic mesangial cell hypertrophy: a proliferation of novel factors [Reviews]. *J Am Soc Nephrol* 2002;13:2611.

351. Berfield AK, Andress DL, Abrass CK. IGF-1-induced lipid accumulation impairs mesangial cell migration and contractile function. *Kidney Int* 2002;62:1229.

352. Sakharova OV, Taal MW, Brenner BM. Pathogenesis of diabetic nephropathy: focus on transforming growth factor-β and connective tissue growth factor [Review]. *Curr Opin Nephrol Hypertens* 2001;10:727.

353. Schnaper HW, Hayashida T, Poncelet A-C. It's a SMAD world: regulation of TGF-β signaling in the kidney [review]. *J Am Soc Nephrol* 2002;13:1126.

354. Huang C, Kim Y, Caramori MLA, et al. Cellular basis of diabetic nephropathy II. The transforming growth factor-β system and diabetic nephropathy lesions in type 1 diabetes. *Diabetes* 2002;51:3577.

355. Li JH, Huang XR, Zhu H-J, et al. Role of TGF-β signaling in extracellular matrix production under high glucose conditions. *Kidney Int* 2003;63:2010.

356. Sharpe CC, Hendry BM. Signaling: focus on Rho in renal disease [review]. *J Am Soc Nephrol* 2003;14:261.

357. Ghosh SS, Gehr TWB, Ghosh S, et al. PPARγ ligand attenuates PDGF-induced mesangial cell proliferation: role of MAP kinase. *Kidney Int* 2003;64:52.

358. Langham RG, Kelly DJ, Maguire J, et al. Over-expression of platelet-derived growth factor in human diabetic nephropathy. *Nephrol Dial Transplant* 2003;18:1392.

359. Gupta S, Clarkson MR, Duggan J, et al. Connective tissue growth factor: potential role in glomerulosclerosis and tubulointerstitial fibrosis. *Kidney Int* 2000;58:1389.

360. Finckenberg P, Inkinen K, Ahonen J, et al. Angiotensin II induces connective tissue growth factor gene expression via calcineurin-dependent pathways. *Am J Pathol* 2003;163:355.

361. Eremina V, Sood M, Haigh J, et al. Glomerular-specific alterations of VEGF-A expression lead to distinct congenital and acquired renal diseases. *J Clin Invest* 2003;111:707.

362. Kang D-H, Johnson RJ. Vascular endothelial growth factor: a new player in the pathogenesis of renal fibrosis [Review]. *Curr Opin Nephrol Hypertens* 2003;12:43.

363. Ziyadeh FN, Wolf G. Why should an angiogenic factor modulate tubular structure in diabetic nephropathy? Some answers, more questions [Essay]. *Kidney Int* 2003;64:758.

363a. Ferrara N, Gerber H-P, LeCouter J. The biology of VEGF and its receptors [Review]. *Nature Med* 2003;9:669.

364. Eddy AA. Plasminogen activator inhibitor-1 and the kidney [Review]. *Am J Physiol* 2002;283:F209.

365. Rovin BH, Phan LT. Chemotactic factors and renal inflammation. *Am J Kidney Dis* 1998;31;1065.

366. Wada T, Furuichi K, Sakai N, et al. Up-regulation of monocyte chemoattractant protein-1 in tubulointerstitial lesions of human diabetic nephropathy. *Kidney Int* 2000;58:1492.

367. Wolf G, Ziyadeh FN. The role of angiotensin II in diabetic nephropathy: emphasis on nonhemodynamic mechanisms. *Am J Kidney Dis* 1997;29:153.

368. Chen S, Wolf G, Ziyadeh FN. The renin-angiotensin system in diabetic nephropathy [Review]. *Contrib Nephrol* 2001;135:212.

369. Tikellis C, Johnston CI, Forbes JM, et al. Characterization of renal angiotensin-converting enzyme 2 in diabetic nephropathy. *Hypertension* 2003;41:392.

370. Huang XR, Cgen WY, Truong LD, et al. Chymase is upregulated in diabetic nephropathy: implications for an alternative pathway of angiotensin-mediated diabetic renal and vascular disease. *J Am Soc Nephrol* 2003;14:1738.

371. Trachtman H, Futterweit S, Pine E, et al. Chronic diabetic nephropathy: role of inducible nitric oxide synthase. *Pediatr Nephrol* 2002;17:20.

372. Komers R, Anderson S. Paradoxes of nitric oxide in the diabetic kidney. *Am J Physiol* 2003;284:F1121.

373. Wang PH, Lau J, Chalmers TC. Meta-analysis of effects of intensive blood-glucose control on late complications of type 1 diabetes. *Lancet* 1993;341:1306.

374. Diabetes Control and Complications Trial Research Group. The effect of intensive treatment of diabetes on the development and progression of long-term complications in insulin-dependent diabetes mellitus. *N Engl J Med* 1993;329:977.

375. Diabetes Control and Complications Trial/Epidemiology of Diabetes Interventions and Complications Research Group. Retinopathy and nephropathy in patients with type 1 diabetes four years after a trial of intensive therapy. *N Engl J Med* 2000; 342:381.

376. Writing Team for the Diabetes Control and Complications Trial/Epidemiology of Diabetes Interventions and Complica-

tions Research Group. Effect of intensive therapy on the microvascular complications of type 1 diabetes mellitus. *JAMA* 2002;287:2563.

377. Writing Team for the Diabetes Control and Complications Trial/Epidemiology of Diabetes Interventions and Complications Research Group. Sustained effect of intensive treatment of type 1 diabetes mellitus on development and progression of diabetic nephropathy. The Epidemiology of Diabetes Interventions and Complications Study. *JAMA* 2003;290:2159.

378. Ohkubo Y, Kishikawa H, Araki E, et al. Intensive insulin therapy prevents the progression of diabetic microvascular complications in Japanese patients with non-insulin-dependent diabetes mellitus: a randomized prospective 6-year study. *Diabetes Res Clin Pract* 1995;28:103.

379. Chobanian AV, Bakris GL, Black HR, et al. The Seventh Report of the Joint National Committee on Prevention, Detection, Evaluation, and Treatment of High Blood Pressure. The JNC 7 Report [Review]. *JAMA* 2003;289:2560.

380. Masding MG, Jones JR, Bartley E, et al. Assessment of blood pressure in patients with type 2 diabetes: comparison between home blood pressure monitoring, clinic blood pressure measurement and 24-h ambulatory blood pressure monitoring. *Diabet Med* 2001;18:431.

381. Berrut G, Hallab M, Bouhanick B, et al. Value of ambulatory blood pressure monitoring in type I (insulin-dependent) diabetic patients with incipient diabetic nephropathy. *Am J Hypertens* 1994;7:222.

382. Knudsen ST, Poulsen PL, Hansen KW, et al. Pulse pressure and diurnal blood pressure variation: association with micro- and macrovascular complications in type 2 diabetes. *Am J Hypertens* 2002;15:244.

383. Microalbuminuria Collaborative Study group, UK. Intensive therapy and progression to clinical albuminuria in patients with insulin dependent diabetes mellitus and microalbuminuria. *BMJ* 1995;311:973.

384. Ritz E. Cardiovascular risk factors and urinary albumin: vive la petite difference [Essay]. *J Am Soc Nephrol* 2003;14:1415.

385. Page SR, Manning G, Ingle AR, et al. Raised ambulatory blood pressure in type 1 diabetes with incipient microalbuminuria. *Diabet Med* 1994;11:877.

386. Chase HP, Garg SK, Harris A, et al. High-normal blood pressure and early diabetic nephropathy. *Arch Intern Med* 1990;150:639.

387. Orchard TJ, Forrest KY-Z, Kuller LH, et al. Lipid and blood pressure treatment goals for type 1 diabetes. 10-year incidence data from the Pittsburgh Epidemiology of Diabetes Complications Study. *Diabetes Care* 2001;24:1053.

388. Kasiske BL, Kalil RSN, Ma JZ, et al. Effect of antihypertensive therapy on the kidney in patients with diabetes: a meta-regression analysis. *Ann Intern Med* 1993;118:129.

389. Weidmann P, Schneider M, Bohlen L. Therapeutic efficacy of different antihypertensive drugs in human diabetic nephropathy: an updated meta-analysis. *Nephrol Dial Transplant* 1995;10 (suppl 9):39.

390. UK Prospective Diabetes Study Group. Efficacy of atenolol and captopril in reducing risk of macrovascular and microvascular complications in type 2 diabetes:UKPDS 39. *BMJ* 1998;317:713.

391. Adler AI, Stratton IM, Neil HA, et al. Association of systolic blood pressure with macrovascular and microvascular complications of type 2 diabetes (UKPDS 36): prospective observational study. *BMJ* 2000;321:412.

392. Tatti P, Pahor M, Byington RP, et al. Outcome results of the Fosinopril versus Amlodipine Cardiovascular Events randomized Trial (FACET) in patients with hypertension and NIDDM. *Diabetes Care* 1998;21:597.

393. Estacio RO, Jeffers BW, Gifford N, et al. Effect of blood pressure control on diabetic microvascular complications in patients with hypertension and type 2 diabetes. *Diabetes Care* 2000;23 (suppl 2):B54.

394. Gray A, Clarke P, Raikou M, et al. An economic evaluation of atenolol vs. captopril in patients with type 2 diabetes (UKPDS 54). *Diabet Med* 2001;18:438.

395. Parving H-H, Jacobsen P, Rossing K, et al. Benefits of long-term antihypertensive treatment on prognosis in diabetic nephropathy. *Kidney Int* 1996;49:1778.

396. Euclid Study Group. Randomized placebo-controlled trial of lisinopril in normotensive patients with insulin-dependent diabetes and normoalbuminuria or microalbuminuria. *Lancet* 1997;349:1787.

397. Ravid M, Brosh D, Levi Z, et al. Use of enalapril to attenuate decline in renal function in normotensive, normoalbuminuric patients with type 2 diabetes mellitus. *Ann Intern Med* 1998;128:982.

398. Heart Outcomes Prevention Evaluation (HOPE) Study Investigators. Effects of ramipril on cardiovascular and microvascular outcomes in people with diabetes mellitus: results of the HOPE study and MICROHOPE substudy. *Lancet* 2000;355:253.

399. Sano T, Kawamura T, Matsumae H, et al. Effects of long-term enalapril treatment on persistent microalbuminuria in well-controlled hypertensive and normotensive NIDDM patients. *Diabetes Care* 1994;7:420.

400. Ravid M, Lang R, Rachmani R, et al. Long-term renoprotective effect of angiotensin-converting enzyme inhibition in non-insulin-dependent diabetes mellitus. A 7-year follow-up study. *Arch Intern Med* 1996;156:286.

401. Ahmad J, Siddiqui MA, Ahmad H. Effective postponement of diabetic nephropathy with enalapril on normotensive type 2 diabetic patients with microalbuminuria. *Diabetes Care* 1997;20:1576.

402. Komers R, Cooper ME. Acute renal hemodynamic effects of ACE inhibition in diabetic hyperfiltration: role of kinins. *Am J Physiol* 1995;268:F588.

403. Kimura G, Brenner BM. Indirect assessment of glomerular capillary pressure from pressure-natriuresis relationship: comparison with direct measurements reported in rats. *Hypertens Res* 1997;20:143.

404. Imanishi M, Yoshioka K, Okumura M, et al. Mechanism of decreased albuminuria caused by angiotensin converting enzyme inhibitor in early diabetic nephropathy. *Kidney Int* 1997;52(suppl 63):198.

405. Jenkins DAS, Cowan P, Collier A, et al. Blood glucose control determines the renal hemodynamic response to angiotensin converting enzyme inhibition in type 1 diabetes. *Diabet Med* 1990;7:252.

406. McKenna K, Smith D, Barrett P, et al. Angiotensin-converting enzyme inhibition by quinapril blocks the albuminuric effect of atrial natriuretic peptide in type 1 diabetes and microalbuminuria. *Diabet Med* 2000;17:219.

407. Morelli E, Loon N, Meyer T, et al. Effects of converting-enzyme inhibition on barrier function in diabetic glomerulopathy. *Diabetes* 1990;39:76.

408. Reddi AS, Ramamurthi R, Miller M, et al. Enalapril improves albuminuria by preventing glomerular loss of heparan sulfate in diabetic rats. *Biochem Med Metab Biol* 1991;45:119.

409. Sharma K, Eltayeb BO, McGowan TA, et al. Captopril-induced reduction of serum levels of transforming growth factor-β1 correlates with long-term renoprotection in insulin-dependent diabetic patients. *Am J Kidney Dis* 1999;34:818.

410. Hill C, Logan A, Smith C, et al. Angiotensin converting enzyme inhibitor suppresses glomerular transforming growth factor β receptor expression in experimental diabetes in rats. *Diabetologia* 2001;44:495.

411. Miyata Y, van Ypersele de Strihou C, Ueda Y, et al. Angiotensin II receptor antagonists and angiotensin-converting enzyme inhibitors lower *in vitro* the formation of advanced glycation end products: biochemical mechanisms. *J Am Soc Nephrol* 2002; 13:2478.

412. Kurtz TW. False claims of blood pressure-independent protection by blockade of the renin angiotensin aldosterone system? *Hypertension* 2003;41:193.

413. Mathiesen ER, Hommel E, Hansen HP, et al. Randomized controlled trial of long term efficacy of captopril on preservation of kidney function in normotensive patients with insulin dependent diabetes and microalbuminuria. *BMJ* 1999;319:24.

414. Tarnow L, Rossing P, Jensen C, et al. Long-term renoprotective effect of nisoldipine and lisinopril in type 1 diabetic patients with diabetic nephropathy. *Diabetes Care* 2000;23:1725.

415. ACE Inhibitors in Diabetic Nephropathy Trialist Group. Should all patients with type 1 diabetes mellitus and microalbuminuria receive angiotensin-converting enzyme inhibitors? A meta-analysis of individual patient data. *Ann Intern Med* 2001; 134:370.

416. Wilner WA, Hebert LA, Lewis EJ, et al. Remission of nephrotic syndrome in type 2 diabetes: long-term follow-up of patients in the captopril study. *Am J Kidney Dis* 1999;34:308.

417. Hovind P, Rossing P, Tarnow L, et al. Remission of nephrotic-range albuminuria in type 1 diabetic patients. *Diabetes Care* 2001;24:1972.

418. Huang XR, Chen WY, Truong LD, et al. Chymase is upregulated in diabetic nephropathy: implications for an alternative pathway of angiotensin-mediated diabetic renal and vascular disease. *J Am Soc Nephrol* 2003;14:1738.

419. Hollenberg NK, Fisher NDL, Price DA. Pathways for angiotensin II generation in intact human tissue: evidence from comparative pharmacological interruption of the renin system. *Hypertension* 1998;32:387.

420. Lacourciere Y, Belanger A, Godin C, et al. Long-term comparison of losartan and enalapril on kidney function in hypertensive type 2 diabetics with early nephropathy. *Kidney Int* 2000;58:762.

421. Andersen S, Tarnow L, Cambien F, et al. Long-term renoprotective effects of losartan in diabetic nephropathy: interaction with ACE insertion/deletion genotype? *Diabetes Care* 2003;26: 1501.

422. Parving HH, Lehnert H, Brochner-Mortensen J, et al. The effect of irbesartan on the development of diabetic nephropathy in patients with type 2 diabetes. *N Engl J Med* 2001;345:870.

423. Viberti G, Wheeldon NM, for the Microalbuminuria Reduction with Valsartan (MARVAL) Study Investigators. Microalbuminuria reduction with valsartan in patients with type 2 diabetes mellitus. A blood-pressure-independent effect. *Circulation* 2002;106:672.

424. Suzuki K, Souda S, Ikarishi T, et al. Renoprotective effects of low-dose valsartan in type 2 diabetic patients with diabetic nephropathy. *Diabetes Res Clin Pract* 2002;57:179.

425. Andersen S, Tarnow L, Rossing P, et al. Renoprotective effects of angiotensin II blockade in type 1 diabetic patients with diabetic nephropathy. *Kidney Int* 2000;57:601.

426. Brenner BM, Cooper ME, De Zeeuw D, et al. Effects of losartan on renal and cardiovascular outcomes in patients with type 2 diabetes and nephropathy. *N Engl J Med* 2001;345:861.

427. Lewis EJ, Hunsicker LG, Clarke WR, et al. Renoprotective effect of the angiotensin-receptor antagonist irbesartan in patients with nephropathy due to type 2 diabetes. *N Engl J Med* 2001;345:851.

428. Rossing K, Jacobsen P, Pietraszek L, et al. Renoprotective effects of adding angiotensin II receptor blocker to maximal recommended doses of ACE inhibitor in diabetic nephropathy. A

429. randomized double-blind crossover trial. *Diabetes Care* 2003; 26:2268.

429. Andersen S, Brochner-Mortensen JB, Parving H-H, for the Irbesartan in Patients with Type 2 Diabetes and Microalbuminuria Study Group. Kidney function during and after withdrawal of long-term irbesartan treatment in patients with type 2 diabetes and microalbuminuria. *Diabetes Care* 2003;26:3296.

430. Komine N, Khang S, Wead LM, et al. Effect of combining an ACE inhibitor and an angiotensin II receptor blocker on plasma and kidney tissue angiotensin II levels. *Am J Kidney Dis* 2002; 39:159.

431. Mogensen CE, Neldam S, Tikkanen I, et al. Randomized controlled trial of dual blockade of renin-angiotensin system in patients with hypertension, microalbuminuria, and non-insulin-dependent diabetes: the candesartan and lisinopril microalbuminuria (CALM) study. *BMJ* 2000;321:1440.

432. Jacobsen P, Andersen S, Jensen BR, et al. Additive effect of ACE inhibition and angiotensin II receptor blockade in type I diabetic patients with diabetic nephropathy. *J Am Soc Nephrol* 2003;14:992.

433. Nosadini R, Tonolo G. Cardiovascular and renal protection in type 2 diabetes mellitus: the role of calcium channel blockers [Review]. *J Am Soc Nephrol* 2002;13(suppl):216.

434. Bakris GL, Smith A. Effects of sodium intake on albumin excretion in patients with diabetic nephropathy treated with long-acting calcium antagonists. *Ann Intern Med* 1996;125:201.

435. Smith AC, Toto R, Bakris GL. Differential effects of calcium channel blockers on size selectivity of proteinuria in diabetic glomerulopathy. *Kidney Int* 1998;54:889.

436. Griffin KA, Picken M, Bakris GL, et al. Comparative effects of selective T- and L-type calcium channel blockers in the remnant kidney model. *Hypertension* 2001;37:1268.

437. Hayashi K, Ozawa Y, Fujiwara K, et al. Role of actions of calcium antagonists on efferent arterioles—with special references to glomerular hypertension [review]. *Am J Nephrol* 2003;23:229.

438. Rossing P, Hommel E, Smidt UM, et al. Reduction in albuminuria predicts diminished progression in diabetic nephropathy. *Kidney Int* 1994;45(suppl 45):145.

439. Zatz R, Meyer TW, Rennke HG, et al. Predominance of hemodynamic rather than metabolic factors in the pathogenesis of diabetic glomerulopathy. *Proc Natl Acad Sci U S A* 1985;82: 5963.

440. Fioretto P, Trevisan R, Giorato C, et al. Type 1 insulin-dependent diabetic patients show an impaired renal hemodynamic response to protein intake. *J Diabet Complications* 1988;2:27.

441. Jones SL, Kontessis P, Wiseman M, et al. Protein intake and blood glucose as modulators of GFR in hyperfiltering diabetic patients. *Kidney Int* 1992;41:1620.

442. Jameel N, Pugh JA, Mitchell BD, et al. Dietary protein intake is not correlated with clinical proteinuria in NIDDM. *Diabetes Care* 1992;15:178.

443. Toeller M, Buyken A, Heitkamp G, et al. Protein intake and urinary albumin excretion rates in the EURODIAB IDDM Complications Study. *Diabetologia* 1997;40:1219.

444. Knight EL, Stampfer MJ, Hankinson SE, et al. The impact of protein intake on renal function decline in women with normal renal function or mild renal insufficiency. *Ann Intern Med* 2003;138:460.

445. Brouhard BH, LaGrone L. Effect of dietary protein restriction on functional renal reserve in diabetic nephropathy. *Am J Med* 1990;89:427.

446. Zeller K, Whittaker E, Sullivan L, et al. Effect of restricting dietary protein on the progression of renal failure in patients with insulin-dependent diabetes. *N Engl J Med* 1991;324:78.

447. Raal FJ, Kalk WJ, Lawson M, et al. Effect of moderate dietary protein restriction on the progression of overt diabetic

nephropathy: a six-month prospective study. *Am J Clin Nutr* 1994;60:579.

448. Dullaart RPF, Beusekamp BJ, Meijer S, et al. Long-term effects of protein-restricted diet on albuminuria and renal function in IDDM patients without clinical nephropathy and hypertension. *Diabetes Care* 1993;16:483.

449. Kasiske BL, Lakatua JDA, Ma JZ, et al. A meta-analysis of the effects of dietary protein restriction on the rate of decline in renal function. *Am J Kidney Dis* 1998;31:954.

450. Levey AS, Adler S, Caggiula AW, et al. Effects of dietary protein restriction on the progression of advanced renal disease in the Modification of Diet in Renal Disease Study. *Am J Kidney Dis* 1996;27:652.

451. Groop P-H, Elliott T, Ekstrand A, et al. Multiple lipoprotein abnormalities in type 1 diabetic patients with renal disease. *Diabetes* 1996;45:974.

452. Niskanen L, Uusitupa M, Sarlund H, et al. Microalbuminuria predicts the development of serum lipoprotein abnormalities favoring atherogenesis in newly diagnosed type 2 (non-insulin-dependent) diabetic patients. *Diabetologia* 1990;33:237.

453. UK Prospective Diabetes Study Group. Urinary albumin excretion over 3 years in diet-treated type II (non-insulin-dependent) diabetic patients, and association with hypertension, hyperglycemia and hypertriglyceridemia. *Diabetologia* 1993;33:237.

454. Reverter JL, Senti M, Rubies-Prat J, et al. Relationship between lipoprotein profile and urinary albumin excretion in type II diabetic patients with stable metabolic control. *Diabetes Care* 1994;17:189.

455. Hirano T, Naito H, Kurokawa M, et al. High prevalence of small LDL particles in non-insulin-dependent diabetic patients with nephropathy. *Atherosclerosis* 1996;123:57.

456. Takemura T, Yoshioka K, Aya N, et al. Apolipoproteins and lipoprotein receptors in glomeruli in human kidney diseases. *Kidney Int* 1993;43:918.

457. Nishida Y, Oda H, Yorioka N. Effect of lipoprotein on mesangial cell proliferation. *Kidney Int Suppl* 1999;56:51.

458. Chen H-C, Guh J-Y, Shin S-J, et al. Effects of pravastatin on superoxide and fibronectin production of mesangial cells induced by low-density lipoprotein. *Kidney BP Res* 2002;25:2.

459. Rovin BH, Tan LC. LDL stimulates mesangial fibronectin production and chemoattractant expression. *Kidney Int* 1993;43: 218.

460. Chana RS, Wheeler DC. Fibronectin augments monocyte adhesion to low-density-lipoprotein-stimulated mesangial cells. *Kidney Int* 1999;55:179.

461. Istvan ES, Diesenhofer J. Structural mechanism for statin inhibition of HMG-CoA reductase. *Science* 2001;292:1160.

462. Liao JK. Isoprenoids as mediators of the biological effect of statins. *J Clin Invest* 2002;110:285.

463. Harada N, Kashiwaga A, Nishio Y, et al. Effects of cholesterol-lowering treatments on oxidative modification of plasma intermediate density lipoprotein plus low density lipoprotein fraction in type 2 diabetic patients. *Diabetes Res Clin Pract* 1999;43:111.

464. McFarlane SI, Muniyappa R, Francisco R, et al. Pleiotropic effects of statins: lipid reduction and beyond [Review]. *J Clin Endocrinol Metab* 2002;87:1451.

465. Shishehbor MH, Brennan M-L, Aviles RJ, et al. Statins promote potent systemic antioxidant effects through specific inflammatory pathways. *Circulation* 2003;108:426.

466. Fried LF, Orchard TJ, Kasiske BL, for the Lipids and Renal Disease Progression Study Group. Effect of lipid reduction on the progression of renal disease: a meta-analysis. *Kidney Int* 2001; 59:260.

467. Plutsky J. PPARs as therapeutic targets: reverse cardiology? *Science* 2003;302:406.

468. Lee C-H, Chawla A, Urbiztondo N, et al. Transcriptional repression of atherogenic inflammation: modulation by PPARδ. *Science* 2003;302:453.

469. Nicholas SB, Kawano Y, Wakino S, et al. Expression and function of peroxisome proliferator-activated receptor-γ in mesangial cells. *Hypertension* 2001;37(part 2):722.

470. Isshiki K, Haneda M, Koya D, et al. Thiazolidinedione compounds ameliorate glomerular dysfunction independent of their insulin-sensitizing action in diabetic rats. *Diabetes* 2000;49: 1022.

471. McCarthy KJ, Routh RE, Shaw W, et al. Troglitazone halts diabetic glomerulosclerosis by blockade of mesangial expansion. *Kidney Int* 2000;58:2341.

472. Arima S, Kohagura K, Takeuchi K, et al. Biphasic vasodilator action of troglitazone on the renal microcirculation. *J Am Soc Nephrol* 2002;13:342.

473. Imano E, Kanda T, nakatani Y, et al. Effect of troglitazone on microalbuminuria in patients with incipient diabetic nephropathy. *Diabetes Care* 1998;21:2135.

474. Nakamura T, Ushiyama C, Shimada N, et al. Comparative effects of pioglitazone, glibenclamide, and voglibose on urinary endothelin-1 and/or urinary albumin excretion in diabetes patients. *J Diabet Complications* 2000;14:250.

475. Nakamura T, Ushiyama C, Osada S, et al. Pioglitazone reduces urinary podocyte excretion in type 2 diabetes patients with microalbuminuria. *Metabolism* 2001;50:1193.

476. Bakris GL, Williams M, Dworkin L, et al. for the National Kidney Foundation Hypertension and Diabetes Executive Committees Working Group. Preserving renal function in adults with hypertension and diabetes: a consensus approach. *Am J Kidney Dis* 2000;36:646.

477. American Diabetes Association. Treatment of hypertension in adults with diabetes [Position statement]. *Diabetes Care* 2003; 26(suppl 1):80.

478. American Diabetes Association. Diabetic nephropathy [Position statement]. *Diabetes Care* 2003;26(suppl 1):94.

479. American Diabetes Association. Aspirin therapy in diabetes [Position statement]. *Diabetes Care* 2003;26(suppl 1):87.

480. Schichiri M, Hishio Y, Ogura M, et al. Effect of low-protein, very-low-phosphorus diet on diabetic renal insufficiency with proteinuria. *Am J Kidney Dis* 1991;18:26.

481. Brodsky IG, Robbins DC, Hiser E, et al. Effects of low-protein diets on protein metabolism in insulin-dependent diabetes mellitus patients with early nephropathy. *J Clin Endocrinol Metab* 1992;75:351.

482. Expert Panel on Detection, Evaluation, and Treatment of High Blood Cholesterol in Adults. Executive Summary of the Third Report of the National Cholesterol Education Program (NCEP) Expert Panel on Detection, Evaluation, and Treatment of High Blood Cholesterol in Adults (Adult Treatment Panel III). *JAMA* 2001;285:2486.

483. Grundy S, for the NCEP Expert Panel. Detection, evaluation, and treatment of high blood cholesterol in adults (Adult Treatment Panel III). Final report. *Circulation* 2002;25:3143.

484. American Diabetes Association. Management of dyslipidemia in adults with diabetes [Position statement]. *Diabetes Care* 2003;26(suppl 1):83.

485. Grundy SM. Low-density lipoprotein, non-high-density lipoprotein, and apolipoprotein B as targets of lipid-lowering therapy [essay]. *Circulation* 2002;106:2526.

486. Conway DL, Langer O. Selecting antihypertensive therapy in the pregnant woman with diabetes mellitus. *J Matern Fetal Med* 2000;9:66.

487. Magee LA. Treating hypertension in women of child-bearing age and during pregnancy. *Drug Safety* 2001;24:457.

488. Rosenthal T, Oparil S. The effect of antihypertensive drugs on the fetus. *J Hum Hypertens* 2002;16:293.

489. Sibai BM. Diagnosis and management of gestational hypertension and preeclampsia. *Obstet Gynecol* 2003;102:181.

490. Lip GYH, Churchill D, Beevers M, et al. Angiotensin-converting enzyme inhibitors in early pregnancy. *Lancet* 1997;350: 1446.

491. Burrows RF, Burrows EA. Assessing the teratogenic potential of angiotensin-converting enzyme inhibitors in pregnancy. *Aust NZ J Obstet Gynaecol* 1998;38,306.

492. Magee LA, Ornstein MP, Von Dadelszen P. Management of hypertension in pregnancy. *BMJ* 1999;318:1322.

493. Saji H, Yamanaka M, Hagiwara A, et al. Losartan and fetal toxic effects. *Lancet* 2001;357:36319.

494. Cox RM, Anderson JM, Cox P. Defective embryogenesis with angiotensin II receptor antagonists in pregnancy. *Br J Obstet Gynaecol* 2003;110:1038.

495. Hod M, van Dijk DJ, Karp M, et al. Diabetic nephropathy and pregnancy: the effect of ACE inhibitors prior to pregnancy on maternal outcome. *Nephrol Dial Transplant* 1995;10:2328.

496. Bar JB, Schoenfeld A, Orvieto R, et al. Pregnancy outcome in patients with insulin dependent diabetes mellitus and diabetic nephropathy treated with ACE inhibitors before pregnancy. *J Pediatr Endocrinol Metab* 1999;12:659.

497. Jovanovic R, Jovanovic L. Obstetric management when normoglycemia is maintained in diabetic pregnant women with vascular compromise. *Am J Obstet Gynecol* 1984;149:617.

498. Danielsson BR, Reiland S, Rundqvist E, et al. Digital defects induced by vasodilating agents: relationship to reduction in uteroplacental blood flow. *Teratology* 1989;40:351.

499. Magee LA, Conover B, Schick B, et al. Exposure to calcium channel blockers in human pregnancy: a prospective, controlled, multicentre cohort study. *Teratology* 1994;49:372.

500. Demarie BK, Bakris GL. Effects of different classes of calcium antagonists on proteinuria in diabetic subjects. *Ann Intern Med* 1990;113:987.

501. Slataper R, Vicknair N, Sadler R, et al. Comparative effects of different antihypertensive treatments on the progression of diabetic renal disease. *Arch Intern Med* 1993;153:973.

502. Brinchmann-Hansen O, Dahl-Jörgensen K, Hanssen KF, et al. Effects of intensified insulin treatment on various lesions of diabetic retinopathy. *Am J Ophthalmol* 1985;100:644.

503. Bereket A, Lang CH, Blethen SL, et al. Effect of insulin on the insulin-like growth factor system in children with new-onset insulin-dependent diabetes mellitus. *J Clin Endocrinol Metab* 1995;80:1312.

504. Attia N, Caprio S, Jones TW. Changes in free insulin-like growth factor-1 and leptin concentrations during acute metabolic decompensation in insulin withdrawn patients with type 1 diabetes. *J Clin Endocrinol Metab* 1999;84:2324.

505. Pfeiffer A, Spranger J, Meyer-Schwickerath R, et al. Growth factor alterations in advanced diabetic retinopathy: a possible role of blood retina breakdown. *Diabetes* 1997;46(suppl 2):26.

506. Hill DJ, Flyvberg A, Arany E, et al. Increased serum levels of serum fibroblast growth factor-2 in diabetic pregnant women with retinopathy. *J Clin Endocrinol Metab* 1997;82:1452.

507. Diabetes Control and Complications Trial Research Group. Effect of pregnancy on microvascular complications in the Diabetes Control and Complications Trial. *Diabetes Care* 2000;23: 1084.

508. Lauszus FF, Klebe JG, Bek T, et al. Increased serum IGF-I during pregnancy is associated with progression of diabetic retinopathy. *Diabetes* 2003;52:852.

509. Klein BEK, Moss SE, Klein R. Effect of pregnancy on progression of diabetic retinopathy. *Diabetes Care* 1990;13:34.

510. Chew EY, Mills JL, Metzger BE, et al. The diabetes and early pregnancy study. Metabolic control and progression of retinopathy. *Diabetes Care* 1995;18:631.

511. Axer-Siegel R, Hod M, Fink-Cohen S, et al. Diabetic retinopathy during pregnancy. *Ophthalmology* 1996;103:1815.

512. Rosenn B, Miodovnik M, Kranias G, et al. Progression of diabetic retinopathy in pregnancy: association with hypertension in pregnancy. *Am J Obstet Gynecol* 1992;166:1214.

513. Krutzen E, Olofsson P, Back SE, et al. Glomerular filtration rate in pregnancy: a study in normal subjects and in patients with hypertension, preeclampsia and diabetes. *Scand J Clin Lab Invest* 1992;52:387.

514. Moran P, Baylis PH, Lindheimer MD, et al. Glomerular ultrafiltration in normal and preeclamptic pregnancies. *J Am Soc Nephrol* 2003;14:648.

515. Davison JM, Noble MCB. Serial changes in 24-hour creatinine clearance during normal menstrual cycles and the first trimester of pregnancy. *Br J Obstet Gynaecol* 1981;88:10.

516. Baylis C. Glomerular filtration rate in normal and abnormal pregnancies. *Semin Nephrol* 1999;19:133.

517. Davison JM, Dunlop W. Renal hemodynamics and tubular function in normal human pregnancy. *Kidney Int* 1980;18:152.

518. Ezimokhai M, Davison JM, Philips PR, et al. Non-postural serial changes in renal function during the third trimester of normal human pregnancy. *Br J Obstet Gynaecol* 1981;88:465.

519. Dunlop W, Davison JM. The effect of normal pregnancy upon the renal handling of uric acid. *Br J Obstet Gynaecol* 1977;84: 13.

520. Olofsson P, Krutzen E, Nilsson-Ehle P. Iohexol clearance for assessment of glomerular filtration rate in diabetic pregnancy. *Eur J Obstet Gynecol Reprod Med* 1996;64:63.

521. Kitzmiller JL, Brown ER, Phillippe M, et al. Diabetic nephropathy and perinatal outcome. *Am J Obstet Gynecol* 1981; 141:741.

522. Reece EA, Coustan DR, Hayslett JP, et al. Diabetic nephropathy: pregnancy performance and fetomaternal outcome. *Am J Obstet Gynecol* 1988;159:56.

523. Khoury JC, Miodovnik M, LeMasters G, et al. Pregnancy outcome and progression of diabetic nephropathy. What's next? *J Matern Fetal Neonat Med* 2002;11:238.

524. Grenfell A, Brudenell JM, Doddridge MC, et al. Pregnancy in diabetic women who have proteinuria. *Q J Med* 1986;59:379.

525. Reece EA, Winn HN, Hayslett JP, et al. Does pregnancy alter the rate of progression of diabetic nephropathy? *Am J Perinatol* 1990;7:193.

526. Mackie ADR, Doddridge MC, Gamsu HR, et al. Outcome of pregnancy in patients with insulin-dependent diabetes mellitus and nephropathy with moderate renal impairment. *Diabet Med* 1996;13:90.

527. Purdy LP, Hantsch CE, Molitsch ME, et al. Effect of pregnancy on renal function in patients with moderate-to-severe diabetic renal insufficiency. *Diabetes Care* 1996;19:1067.

528. Dunne FP, Chowdhury TA, Hartland A, et al. Pregnancy outcome in women with insulin-dependent diabetes mellitus complicated by nephropathy. *Q J Med* 1999;92:451.

529. Carr D, Binney G, Brown Z, et al. Relationship between hemodynamics, renal function, and pregnancy outcome in class F diabetes. *Am J Obstet Gynecol* 2002;187(suppl):152.

530. Biesenbach G, Grafinger P, Stoger H, et al. How pregnancy influences renal function in nephropathic type 1 diabetic women depends on their pre-conception creatinine clearance. *J Nephrol* 1999;12:41.

531. Dworkin LD. Serum cystatin C as a marker of glomerular filtration rate. *Curr Opin Nephrol Hypertens* 2001;10:551.

532. Cataldi L, Mussap M, Bertelli L, et al. Cystatin C in healthy women at term pregnancy and in their infant newborns: relationship between maternal and neonatal serum levels and reference values. *Am J Perinatol* 1999;16:287.

533. Strevens H, Wide-Swensson D, Grubb A. Serum cystatin C is a

better marker for preeclampsia than serum creatinine or serum urate. *Scand J Clin Lab Invest* 2001;61:575.

534. Strevens H, Wide-Swensson D, Torffvit O, et al. Serum cystatin C for assessment of glomerular filtration rate in pregnant and non-pregnant women. Indications of altered filtration process in pregnancy. *Scand J Clin Lab Invest* 2002;62:141–148.

535. Pedersen EB, Rasmussen AB, Johannsen P, et al. Urinary excretion of albumin, beta-2-microglobulin and light chains in pre-eclampsia, essential hypertension in pregnancy, and normotensive pregnant and non-pregnant control subjects. *Scand J Clin Lab Invest* 1981;41:777.

536. Lopez-Espinoza I, Humphreys S, Redman CWG. Urinary albumin excretion in pregnancy. *Br J Obstet Gynecol* 1986;93:176.

537. Wright A, Steele P, Bennett JR, et al. The urinary excretion of albumin in normal pregnancy. *Br J Obstet Gynaecol* 1987;94:408.

538. Misiani R, Marchesi D, Tiraboschi G, et al. Urinary albumin excretion in normal pregnancy and pregnancy-induced hypertension. *Nephron* 1991;59:416.

539. Bernard A, Thielemans N, Lauwerys R, et al. Selective increase in the urinary excretion of protein 1 (Clara cell protein) and other low molecular weight proteins during normal pregnancy. *Scand J Clin Lab Invest* 1992;52:871.

540. Cheung CK, Lao T, Swaminathan R. Urinary excretion of some proteins and enzymes during normal pregnancy. *Clin Chem* 1989;35:1978.

541. Higby K, Suiter CR, Phelps JY, et al. Normal values of urinary albumin and total protein excretion during pregnancy. *Am J Obstet Gynecol* 1994;171:984.

542. Roberts M, Lindheimer MD, Davison JM. Altered glomerular permselectivity to neutral dextrans and heteroporous membrane modeling in human pregnancy. *Am J Physiol* 1996;270:F338.

543. McCance DR, Traub AI, Harley JMG, et al. Urinary albumin excretion in diabetic pregnancy. *Diabetologia* 1989;32:236.

544. Biesenbach G, Zasgornik J. Incidence of transient nephrotic syndrome during pregnancy in diabetic women with and without pre-existing microalbuminuria. *BMJ* 1989;299:366.

545. MacRury SM, Pinion S, Quin JD, et al. Blood rheology and albumin excretion in diabetic pregnancy. *Diabet Med* 1995;12:51.

546. Winocour PH, Taylor RJ. Early alterations of renal function in insulin-dependent diabetic pregnancies and their importance in predicting preeclamptic toxaemia. *Diabetes Res* 1989;10:159.

547. Combs CA, Rosenn B, Kitzmiller JL, et al. Early-pregnancy proteinuria in diabetes related to preeclampsia. *Obstet Gynecol* 1993;82:802.

548. Biesenbach G, Zasgornik J, Stoger H, et al. Abnormal increases in urinary albumin excretion during pregnancy in IDDM women with preexisting albuminuria. *Diabetologia* 1994;37:905.

549. Ekbom P, Damm P, Norgaard K, et al. Urinary albumin excretion and 24-hour blood pressure as predictors of pre-eclampsia in type I diabetes. *Diabetologia* 2000;43:927.

550. Schroder W, Heyl W, Hill-Grasshof B, et al. Clinical value of detecting microalbuminuria as a risk factor for pregnancy-induced hypertension in insulin-treated diabetic pregnancies. *Eur J Obstet Gynecol Reprod Biol* 2000;94:155.

551. Lauszus FF, Rasmussen OW, Lousen T, et al. Ambulatory blood pressure as predictor of preeclampsia in diabetic pregnancies with respect to urinary albumin excretion rate and glycemic regulation. *Acta Obstet Gynecol Scand* 2001;80:1096.

552. Ekbom P, Damm P, Feldt-Rasmussen, et al. Pregnancy outcome in type 1 diabetic women with microalbuminuria. *Diabetes Care* 2001;24:1739.

553. Gordon M, Landon MB, Samuels P, et al. Perinatal outcome and long-term follow-up associated with modern management of diabetic nephropathy. *Obstet Gynecol* 1996;87:401.

554. Walker SP, Higgins JR, Brennecke SP. Ambulatory blood pressure monitoring in pregnancy. *Obstet Gynecol Surv* 1998;53:636.

555. Higgins JR, de Swiet M. Blood-pressure measurement and classification in pregnancy. *Lancet* 2001;357:131.

556. Flores L, Levy I, Aguilera E, et al. Usefulness of ambulatory blood pressure monitoring in pregnant women with type 1 diabetes. *Diabetes Care* 1999;22:1507.

557. Cundy T, Slee F, Gamble G, et al. Hypertensive disorders of pregnancy in women with type 1 and type 2 diabetes. *Diabet Med* 2002;19:482.

558. Hanson U, Persson B. Epidemiology of pregnancy-induced hypertension and preeclampsia in type 1 (insulin-dependent) diabetic pregnancies in Sweden. *Acta Obstet Gynecol Scand* 1998;77:620.

559. Caritis S, Sibai B, Hauth J, et al. Predictors of preeclampsia in women at high risk. National Institute of Child Health and Human Development Network of Maternal-Fetal Medicine Units. *Am J Obstet Gynecol* 1998;179:946.

560. Sibai BM, Caritis S, Hauth J, et al. Risks of preeclampsia and adverse neonatal outcomes among women with pregestational diabetes mellitus. *Am J Obstet Gynecol* 2000;182:364.

561. Dicker D, Feldberg, Peleg D, et al. Pregnancy complicated by diabetic nephropathy. *J Perinat Med* 1986;14:299.

562. Biesenbach G, Stoger H, Zasgornik J. Influence of pregnancy on progression of diabetic nephropathy and subsequent requirement of renal replacement therapy in female type I diabetic patients with impaired renal function. *Nephrol Dial Transplant* 1992;7:105.

563. Kimmerle R, Zass R-P, Cupisti S, et al. Pregnancies in women with diabetic nephropathy: long-term outcome for mother and child. *Diabetologia* 1995;38:227.

564. Miodovnik M, Rosenn BM, Khoury JC, et al. Does pregnancy increase the risk for development and progression of diabetic nephropathy? *Am J Obstet Gynecol* 1996;174:1180.

565. Reece EA, Leguizamon G, Homko C. Stringent controls in diabetic nephropathy associated with optimization of pregnancy outcomes. *J Matern Fetal Med* 565;7:213.

566. McGregor E, Stewart G, Junor BJ, et al. Successful use of recombinant human erythropoietin in pregnancy. *Nephrol Dial Transplant* 1991;6:292.

567. Yankowitz J, Piraino B, Laifer A, et al. Use of erythropoietin in pregnancies complicated by severe anemia of renal failure. *Obstet Gynecol* 1992;80:485.

568. Braga J, Marques R, Branco A, et al. Maternal and perinatal implications of the use of human recombinant erythropoietin. *Acta Obstet Gynecol Scand* 1996;75:449.

569. Muruyama H, Shimada H, Obayashi H, et al. Requiring higher doses of erythropoietin suggests pregnancy in hemodialysis patients. *Nephron* 1998;79:413.

570. Balasoiu D, van Kessel KC, van Kats-Renaud HJ, et al. Granulocyte function in women with diabetes and asymptomatic bacteriuria. *Diabetes Care* 1997;20:392.

571. Geerlings SE, Stolk RP, Camps MJL, et al. Risk factors for symptomatic urinary tract infection in women with diabetes. *Diabetes Care* 2000;23:1737.

572. Geerlings SE, Stolk RP, Camps MJL, et al. Consequences of asymptomatic bacteriuria in women with diabetes mellitus. *Arch Intern Med* 2001;161:1421.

573. Geerlings SE, Meiland R, van Lith EC, et al. Adherence of type 1-fimbriated *Escherichia coli* to uroepithelial cells. More in diabetic women than in control subjects. *Diabetes Care* 2002;25:1405.

574. Davison JM, Sprott MS, Selkon JB. The effect of covert bacteriuria in schoolgirls on renal function at 18 years and during pregnancy. *Lancet* 1984;2:651.

575. Harding GKM, Zhanel GG, Nicolle LE, et al. Antimicrobial treatment in diabetic women with asymptomatic bacteriuria. *N Engl J Med* 2002;347:1576.

576. Eskenazi B, Fenster L, Sidney S. A multivariate analysis of risk factors for preeclampsia. *JAMA* 1991;266:237.

577. Muhlhauser I, Bender R, Bott U, et al. Cigarette smoking and progression of retinopathy and nephropathy in type 1 diabetes. *Diabet Med* 1996;13:536.

578. Baggio B, Budakovic A, Dalla Vestra M, et al. Effects of cigarette smoking on glomerular structure and function in type 2 diabetic patients. *J Am Soc Nephrol* 2002;13:2730.

579. Chuahiran T, Wesson DE. Cigarette smoking predicts faster progression of type 2 established diabetic nephropathy despite ACE inhibition. *Am J Kidney Dis* 2002;39:376.

580. Hou S. Frequency and outcome of pregnancy in women on dialysis. *Am J Kidney Dis* 1994;23:60.

581. Okundaye I, Abrinko P, Hou S. Registry of pregnancy in dialysis patients. *Am J Kidney Dis* 1998;31:766.

582. Romao JE, Luders C, Kahhale S, et al. Pregnancy in women on chronic dialysis. A single-center experience with 17 cases. *Nephron* 1998;78:416.

583. Bagon JA, Vernaeve H, De Muylder X, et al. Pregnancy and dialysis. *Am J Kidney Dis* 1998;31:756.

584. Chan WS, Okun N, Kjellstrand CM. Pregnancy in chronic dialysis: a review and analysis of the literature. *Int J Artif Organs* 1998;21:259.

585. Hou S. Pregnancy in chronic renal insufficiency and end-stage renal disease. *Am J Kidney Dis* 1999;33:235.

586. Toma H, Tanabe K, Tokumoto T, et al. Pregnancy in women receiving renal dialysis or transplantation in Japan: a nationwide survey. *Nephrol Dial Transplant* 1999;14:1511.

587. Chao A-S, Huang J-Y, Lien R, et al. Pregnancy in women who undergo long-term hemodialysis. *Am J Obstet Gynecol* 2002;187:152.

588. Jones DC, Hayslett JP. Outcome of pregnancy in women with moderate or severe renal insufficiency. *N Engl J Med* 1996;335:226.

589. Hou SH, Orlowski J, Pahl M, et al. Pregnancy in women with end stage renal disease: treatment of anemia and preterm labor. *Am J Kidney Dis* 1993;21:16.

590. Kitzmiller JL. Sweet success with diabetes. The development of insulin therapy and glycemic control for pregnancy [Review]. *Diabetes Care* 1993;16(suppl 3):107.

591. Holley JL, Bernardini J, Quadri KHM, et al. Pregnancy outcomes in a prospective matched control study of pregnancy and renal disease. *Clin Nephrol* 1996;45:77.

592. Biesenbach G, Grafinger P, Zasgornik J, et al. Perinatal complications and three-year followup of infants of diabetic mothers with diabetic nephropathy stage IV. *Renal Failure* 2000;22:573.

593. Cunningham FG, Cox SM, Harstad TW, et al. Chronic renal disease and pregnancy outcome. *Am J Obstet Gynecol* 1990;163:453.

594. Lindheimer MD, Katz AI. Pregnancy in the renal transplant patient. *Am J Kidney Dis* 1992;19:173.

595. Abe S, Amagasaki Y, Kaniski K, et al. The influence of antecedent renal disease on pregnancy. *Am J Obstet Gynecol* 1985;153:508.

596. Jungers P, Houillier P, Chauveau D, et al. Pregnancy in women with reflux nephropathy. *Kidney Int* 1996;50:593.

597. Jungers P, Chauveau D, Choukroun G, et al. Pregnancy in women with impaired renal function. *Clin Nephrol* 1997;47:281.

598. Packham DK. Aspects of renal disease and pregnancy. *Kidney Int* 1992;44(suppl 42):64.

599. Rizzoni G, Ehrich JH, Broyer M, et al. Successful pregnancies in women on renal replacement therapy: report from the EDTA Registry. *Nephrol Dial Transplant* 1992;7:279.

600. Hou S. Pregnancy in women on dialysis. In: Nissenson AR, Fine RN, eds. *Dialysis therapy*, 3rd ed. Philadelphia: Hanley & Belfus, 2002:519–522.

601. Greene MF, Hare JW, Krache M, et al. Prematurity among insulin-requiring diabetic gravid women. *Am J Obstet Gynecol* 1989;161:106.

602. Garner PR, D'Alton ME, Dudley DK, et al. Preeclampsia in diabetic pregnancies. *Am J Obstet Gynecol* 1990;163:505.

603. Rey E, LeLorier J, Burgess E, et al. Report of the Canadian Hypertension Society Conference. 3. Pharmacologic treatment of hypertensive disorders in pregnancy. *Can Med Assoc J* 1997;157:1245.

604. Brown MA, Hague WM, Higgins J, et al. The detection, investigation and management of hypertension in pregnancy: full consensus statement. *Aust N Z J Obstet Gynaecol* 2000;40:139.

605. National High Blood Pressure Education Program Working Group on High Blood Pressure in Pregnancy. Report of the National High Blood Pressure Education Program Working Group on High Blood Pressure in Pregnancy. *Am J Obstet Gynecol* 2000;183:1.

606. Seely EW. Hypertension in pregnancy: a potential window into long-term cardiovascular risk in women. *J Clin Endocrinol Metab* 1999;84:1858–1861.

607. Irgens HU, Reisaeter L, Irgens LM, et al. Long term mortality of mothers and fathers after preeclampsia: population based cohort study. *BMJ* 2001;323:1213.

608. Kestenbaum B, Seliger SL, Easterling TR, et al. Cardiovascular and thrombolic events following hypertensive pregnancy. *Am J Kidney Dis* 2003;42:982.

609. Mosca L, Grundy SM, Judelson D, et al. Guide to preventive cardiology for women. AHA/ACC Scientific Statement: Consensus Panel Statement. *Circulation* 1999;99:2480.

610. American Diabetes Association. Position statement: standards of medical care for patients with diabetes mellitus. *Diabetes Care* 2004;28(suppl 1):39.

611. Von Dadelszen P, Ornstein MP, Bull SB, et al. Fall in mean arterial pressure and fetal growth restriction in pregnancy hypertension: a meta-analysis. *Lancet* 2000;355:87.

612. Sibai BM. Chronic hypertension in pregnancy. *Obstet Gynecol* 2002;100:369.

613. Lydakis C, Lip GYH, Beevers M, et al. Atenolol and fetal growth in pregnancies complicated by hypertension. *Am J Hypertens* 1999;12:541–547.

614. Easterling TR, Carr DB, Brateng D, et al. Treatment of hypertension in pregnancy: effect of atenolol on maternal disease, preterm delivery, and fetal growth. *Obstet Gynecol* 2001;98:427.

615. Easterling TR, Brateng D, Schmucker B, et al. Prevention of preeclampsia: a randomized trial of atenolol in hyperdynamic patients before onset of hypertension. *Obstet Gynecol* 1999;93:725.

616. Salvesen DR, Higueras MT, Brudenell M, et al. Doppler velocimetry and fetal heart studies in nephropathic diabetics. *Am J Obstet Gynecol* 1992;167:1297.

617. Ogburn PL Jr, Kitzmiller JL, Hare JW, et al. Pregnancy following renal transplantation in class T diabetes mellitus. *JAMA* 1986;225:911.

618. Armenti VT, McGrory CH, Cater J, et al. The national transplantation registry: comparison between pregnancy outcomes in diabetic cyclosporine-treated female kidney recipients and CyA-treated female pancreas-kidney recipients. *Transplant Proc* 1997;29:669.

619. Sturgiss SN, Davison JM. Perinatal outcome in renal allograft recipients: prognostic significance of hypertension and renal function before and during pregnancy. *Obstet Gynecol* 1991;78:573.

620. Armenti VT, Ahlswede KM, Ahlswede BA, et al. Variables

affecting birthweight and graft survival in 197 pregnancies in cyclosporine-treated female kidney transplant recipients. *Transplantation* 1995;59:476.

621. Davison JM. The effect of pregnancy on kidney function in renal allograft recipients. *Kidney Int* 1985;27:74.

622. Pirson Y, Van Lierde M, Ghysen J, et al. Retardation of fetal growth in patients receiving immunosuppressive therapy. *N Engl J Med* 1985;313:328.

623. Pickrell MD, Sawers R, Michael J. Pregnancy after renal transplantation: severe intrauterine growth retardation during treatment with cyclosporine A. *BMJ* 1988;296:825.

624. Salmela KT, Kyllonen LEJ, Holmberg C, et al. Impaired renal function after pregnancy in renal transplant recipients. *Transplantation* 1993;56:1372.

625. Queipo-Zaragoza JA, Vera-Donoso CD, Soldevila A, et al. Impact of pregnancy on kidney transplant. *Transplant Proc* 2003;35:866.

626. Cararach V, Carmona F, Monleon FJ, et al. Pregnancy after renal transplantation: 25 years experience in Spain. *Br J Obstet Gynecol* 1993;100:122.

627. Oz B, Hackman R, Einarson T, et al. Pregnancy outcome after cyclosporine therapy during pregnancy: a meta-analysis. *Transplantation* 2001;71:1051.

628. Ahlswede KM, Armenti VT, Moritz MJ, et al. Premature births in female transplant recipients: degree and effect of immunosuppressive regimen. *Surg Forum* 1992;43:524.

629. Sturgiss SN, Davison JM. Effect of pregnancy on long-term function of renal allografts. *Am J Kidney Dis* 1992;19:167.

630. Armenti VT, Ahlswede KM, Ahlswede BA, et al. National Transplantation Pregnancy Registry—outcomes of 154 pregnancies in cyclosporine-treated female kidney transplant recipients. *Transplantation* 1994;57:502.

631. Di Paolo S, Monno R, Stallone G, et al. Placental imbalance of vasoactive factors does not affect pregnancy outcome in patients treated with cyclosporine A after transplantation. *Am J Kidney Dis* 2002;39:776.

632. Kainz A, Harabacz I, Cowlrick IS, et al. Review of the course and outcome of 100 pregnancies in 84 women treated with tacrolimus. *Transplantation* 2000;70:1718.

633. Pergola PE, Kancharia A, Riley DJ. Kidney transplantation during the first trimester of pregnancy: immunosuppression with mycophenolate mofetil, tacrolimus, and prednisone. *Transplantation* 2001;71:994.

634. Eisenberg JA, Armenti VT, McGrory CH, et al. National Transplantation Pregnancy Registry (NTPR): use of muromonab-CD3 (OKT3) during pregnancy in female transplant recipients. *Am Soc Transplant Phys* 1997;20:108.

635. Armenti VT, Coscia LA, Dunn SR, et al. National Transplantation Pregnancy Registry: pregnancy outcomes in female kidney recipients treated with Neoral vs. Tacrolimus based regimens. *Transplantation* 2000;69(suppl):322.

636. Stanley CW, Gottlieb R, Zager R, et al. Developmental well-being in offspring of women receiving cyclosporine post-renal transplant. *Transplant Proc* 1999;31:241.

637. Di Paolo S, Schena A, Morrone LF, et al. Immunologic evaluation of infants from cyclosporine treated kidney transplanted mothers during the first year of life. Analysis of lymphocyte subpopulations and immunoglobulin serum levels. *Transplantation* 2000;69:2049.

638. Scott JR, Branch DW, Holman J. Autoimmune and pregnancy complications in the daughter of a kidney transplant patient. *Transplantation* 2002;73:815.

639. Armenti VT, Moritz MJ, Coscia LA, et al. Parenthood after transplantation: what are the risks? [Essay]. *Transplantation* 2002;73:677.

640. Neugarten J, Silbiger SR. The impact of gender on renal transplantation. *Transplantation* 1994;58:1145.

641. Meier-Kriesche H-U, Ojo AO, Leavey SF, et al. Differences in etiology for graft loss in female renal transplant recipients. *Transplant Proc* 2001;33:1288.

642. Tyden G, Bratterstrom C, Bjorkman U, et al. Pregnancy after combined pancreas-kidney transplantation. *Diabetes* 1989;39 (suppl 1):43.

643. Skannal DG, Miodovnik M, Dungy-Poythress LJ, et al. Successful pregnancy after combined renal-pancreas transplantation: a case report and literature review. *Am J Perinatol* 1996;13:383.

644. Van Winter JT, Ogburn PL Jr, Ramin KD, et al. Pregnancy after pancreatic-renal transplantation because of diabetes. *Mayo Clinic Proc* 1997;72:1044.

645. Karaitis LK, Nankivell BJ, Lawrence S, et al. Successful obstetric outcome after simultaneous pancreas and kidney transplantation. *Med J Aust* 1999;170:368.

646. McGrory CH, Groshek MA, Sollinger HW, et al. Pregnancy outcomes in female pancreas-kidney transplants. *Transplant Proc* 1999;31:652.

647. Barrou BM, Gruessner AC, Sutherland DE, et al. Pregnancy after pancreas transplantation in the cyclosporine era: report from the International Pancreas Transplant Registry. *Transplantation* 1998;65:524.

648. First MR, Combs CA, Weiskittel P, et al. Lack of effect of pregnancy on renal allograft survival or function. *Transplantation* 1995;59:472.

649. Tanabe K, Kobayashi C, Takahashi K, et al. Long-term renal function after pregnancy in renal transplant recipients. *Transplant Proc* 1997;29:1567.

650. Wilson GA, Coscia LA, McGrory CH, et al. National Transplantation Pregnancy Registry: postpregnancy graft loss among female pancreas-kidney transplants. *Transplant Proc* 2001;33:1667.

651. Mahanty HD, Cherikh WS, Chang GJ, et al. Influence of pretransplant pregnancy on survival of renal allografts from living donors. *Transplantation* 2001;72:228.

652. Rebibou J-M, Chabod J, Alcalay D, et al. Flow cytometric evaluation of pregnancy-induced anti-HLA immunization and blood transfusion-induced reactivation. *Transplantation* 2002;74:537.

653. Lindheimer MD, Katz AI. Pregnancy in the renal transplant patient [Review]. *Am J Kidney Dis* 1992;19:173.

654. Mogensen CE. Progression of nephropathy in long-term diabetics with proteinuria and effect of initial antihypertensive treatment. *Scand J Clin Lab Invest* 1976;36:383.

655. Parving H-H, Smidt UM, Friisberg B, et al. A prospective study of glomerular filtration rate and arterial blood pressure in insulin-dependent diabetics with diabetic nephropathy. *Diabetologia* 1981;20:457.

656. Austin SM, Lieberman JS, Newton LD, et al. Slope of serial glomerular filtration rate and the progression of diabetic renal disease. *J Am Soc Nephrol* 1993;3:1358.

657. Rossing K, Jacobsen P, Hommel E, et al. Pregnancy and progression of diabetic nephropathy. *Diabetologia* 2002;45:36.

658. Chaturvedi N, Stephenson JM, Fuller JH, et al. The relationship between pregnancy and long-term maternal complications in the EURODIAB IDDM complications study. *Diabet Med* 1995;12:494.

659. Hemachandra A, Ellis D, Lloyd CE, et al. The influence of pregnancy on IDDM complications. *Diabetes Care* 1995;18:950.

660. Kaaja R, Sjoberg L, Hellstedt T, et al. Long-term effects of pregnancy on diabetic complications. *Diabet Med* 1996;13:165.

30

DIABETIC NEUROPATHY AND CORONARY HEART DISEASE

GUSTAVO F. LEGUIZAMÓN
E. ALBERT REECE

Diabetic neuropathy is a heterogeneous group of abnormalities involving both the autonomic and peripheral nervous systems. It can occur in patients with type 1 and type 2 diabetes with a significant impact on quality of life and life expectancy. This entity has long been underestimated especially among pregnant women and as a consequence there is a paucity of data regarding its occurrence during pregnancy. The purpose of this chapter is to review the clinical features and principles of management of diabetic neuropathy, so that the reader will become familiar with and be able to recognize this common diabetic complication. Its occurrence during pregnancy is reviewed and general counseling and management guidelines are addressed. Finally, the association of coronary artery disease (CAD) and pregnancy with class H diabetes is reviewed as well.

Knowledge of the pathophysiology of neuropathy is still evolving, but its occurrence and progression seem to be a multifactorial process. Several hypotheses are currently under investigation, such as metabolic insult, autoimmune process, and vascular insufficiency, as well as neurohormonal deficiencies (1,2). The importance of hyperglycemia, however, was recently highlighted by Perkins et al. (3) who demonstrated that the severity of neuropathy is correlated with the degree of glycemic control. A hyperglycemic state could provoke sorbitol accumulation through the activation of the polyol pathway, leading to direct neuronal damage or decreased blood flow (4).

Several authors have described different classifications for diabetic neuropathy. As our understanding of the different syndromes included under the term diabetic neuropathy evolved, new classification schemes were suggested. In 1958, Sullivan (5) identified two different entities based on their etiologies: a more frequent, diffuse, symmetrical form and a less common focal asymmetrical pattern (5). In 1988, the San Antonio consensus conference was held to standardize the nomenclature and assessment of diabetic neuropathy. It was recommended that at a minimum, a sign, a symptom, and an abnormal finding on the electrodiagnostic tests must be present to make the diagnosis of neuropathy. Furthermore, the consensus supported that at least one parameter of the following areas must be tested to classify diabetic neuropathy: use of standardized scales of clinical measures, quantitative sensory testing (QST), autonomic nervous system testing, and nerve conduction studies. Correctly, the classification and staging system depicted in Table 30-1 is most widely accepted (6).

CLINICAL MANIFESTATIONS OF DIABETIC NEUROPATHY

The clinical presentation of diabetic neuropathy is often difficult to classify, and significant overlap is frequently found among the various syndromes. However, it is reasonable to assess the symptoms and signs according to whether they correspond to the somatic or autonomic nervous system.

Somatic Neuropathies
Symmetrical Distal Polyneuropathy

This form is the most common of the diabetic neuropathies. Its onset is usually gradual, and it affects predominately sensory or sensorimotor fibers. Its pathologic hallmark is progressive nerve fiber loss as well as microangiopathy in the vasa nervosum (7). It mainly affects lower extremities with predilection for the distal sensorimotor fibers in a glove or stocking distribution. Frequently, patients describe symptoms as numbness in the feet relieved by walking or massage; it can also be referred to as a sensation of walking on air or pillows. The signs observed on examination are loss of vibratory as well as light touch and pinprick sensation, occasionally followed by weakness. Approximately 10% of these patients suffer the syndrome of painful peripheral neuropathy, which consists of pain of variable severity in their feet or legs. It can also be mild and

TABLE 30-1. CLASSIFICATION AND STAGING OF DIABETIC NEUROPATHY

Subclinical Neuropathy
Abnormal electrodiagnostic tests
   Decrease nerve conduction velocity
   Decrease amplitude of evoked muscle or nerve action potential
Abnormal quantitative sensory testing
   Vibrator tactile
   Thermal warming/cooling
   Other
Abnormal autonomic function tests
   Abnormal cardiovascular reflexes
   Altered cardiovascular reflexes
   Abnormal biochemical responses to hypoglycemia
Clinical Neuropathy
Diffuse somatic neuropathy
   Distal symmetric sensorimotor polyneuropathy
      Primarily small-fiber neuropathy
      Primarily large-fiber neuropathy
      Mixed
   Autonomic neuropathy
      Cardiovascular autonomic neuropathy
      Abnormal pupillary function
      Gastrointestinal autonomic neuropathy
         Gastroparesis
         Constipation
         Diabetic diarrhea
         Anorectal incontinence
      Genitourinary autonomic neuropathy
         Bladder dysfunction
         Sexual dysfunction
      Hypoglycemia unawareness/unresponsiveness
      Sudomotor dysfunction
Focal neuropathy
   Mononeuropathy
   Mononeuropathy multiplex
   Amyotrophy

Note: Based on the San Antonio convention for neuropathy. To be diagnosed, patients must have a minimum of a sign or a symptom, and an abnormal electrodiagnostic test.
From Vinik AI, Holland MI, Le Beau JM, et al. Diabetic neuropathies. *Diabetes Care* 1992;15:1926–1975, with permission.

TABLE 30-2. TORONTO CLINICAL SCORING SYSTEM

Symptom Score	Reflex Scores	Sensory Test Scores
Foot	Knee reflexes	Pinprick
Pain	Ankle reflexes	Temperature
Numbness		Light touch
Tingling		Vibration
Weakness		Position
Ataxia		
Upper limb symptoms		

Symptoms scores: present = 1; absent = 0. Reflex scores: absent = 2; reduced = 1, normal = 0. Sensory score: abnormal = 1; normal = 0.

referred to as burning or aching, or severe and disabling characterized as stabbing or an electric shock-like sensation.

This condition should be evaluated with a complete neurologic examination in combination with electrodiagnostic testing and standardized clinical scoring systems. Recently, to provide a simple and objective measure of the presence and severity of diabetic peripheral neuropathy, the Toronto Clinical Scoring System was developed and validated. One of the advantages of this system is that it is not time consuming and can be performed in the office as a screening tool by the clinician. The results range from a minimum of 0 (absence of neuropathy) to a maximum of 19. As depicted in Table 30-2, six points correspond to symptoms, eight to lower limb reflexes, and five to sensory tests (8).

Electrodiagnostic testing further describes this entity and provides sensitive and specific, as well as reproducible measures of the presence and severity of neuropathy (9). The tests most widely used are nerve conduction studies (NCS), although electromyography is also an alternative. Both motor and sensory NCS in upper and lower limbs are recommended, including evaluation of motor function of the medial, ulnar, peroneal, and tibial nerves, as well as sensory function of the medial, ulnar, and sural nerves.

QST is a noninvasive procedure that can add a quantitative rather than a qualitative measure of sensation. It is usually designed to assess perception of vibration and thermal and light touch. The main drawback of QST is its reliance on the patient's subjective interpretation (10). Furthermore, lack of standardization and low specificity make this method less accurate than NCS studies (11).

The most effective treatment and prevention of symmetrical distal polyneuropathy rely on tight glycemic control. In 1993, the results of the Diabetes Control and Complications Trial (DCCT) (12) demonstrated that patients with type 1 diabetes benefit from glucose control irrespective of the presence or absence of neuropathy. Among patients without evidence of neuropathy at baseline, intensive therapy reduced the appearance of neuropathy at 5 years by 69% (to 3%, versus 10% in the conventional-therapy group; $p = 0.006$), and for those with established disease by 57% (to 7%, vs. 16%). Studies on subjects with type 2 diabetes support similar benefits (13,14). Other nonspecific measures, such as use of analgesics or antidepressants, are also frequently employed. Avoidance of chronic potent analgesics, like opiates, is important since addiction or significant side effects could cause more harm than benefit. During pregnancy, to minimize fetal risks, acetaminophen is preferred. Finally, local treatment modalities such as cold soaks, especially during the evening, as well as massages, can improve symptoms and are unlikely to cause side effects (7).

Cranial Neuropathy

This clinical presentation is restricted to a single nerve. It usually occurs among older women with long-standing disease, and presents with an acute onset, most commonly affecting the oculomotor nerve (III) with the following symptoms: pain around the eye and ipsilateral headache, diplopia and external eye divergence, ophthalmoplegia, and ptosis. Finally, the pupil is not dilated, which is key in differentiating this diagnosis from a complicated aneurysm or tumor. Therefore, in the absence of other neurologic findings, diagnosis can be made without the utilization of radiologic procedures allowing avoidance of unnecessary fetal exposure during pregnancy. Treatment is conservative, consisting of covering the affected eye and administrating analgesics. Nonsteroidal antiinflammatory drugs (NSAIDs) are best avoided in the pregnant patient (15). Complete recovery is expected in 6 to 8 weeks.

Radiculopathy or Truncal Mononeuropathy

This presentation may compromise single or multiple nerves. For the clinician involved in the care of diabetic women, it is important to become familiar with the clinical presentation to avoid unnecessary diagnostic and therapeutic procedures. The patient usually complains of unilateral deep aching pain in a radicular distribution, frequently mimicking an acute abdominal or thoracic process. In pregnant patients, the presentation may be confused with labor or renal urolithiasis and, in the older patient, this condition may be mistaken for angina or the initial symptoms of herpes zoster. Treatment is based on supportive measures, especially in the young pregnant patient. Topical lidocaine patches, amitryptiline, and gabapentin have been used in nonpregnant women (7). Spontaneous resolution is expected within 3 months.

Neuropathic Fractures

Patients with diabetes may have difficulty with spontaneous and often painless fractures of the bones in the foot (Charcot fractures); peripheral neuropathy is almost always clinically evident in these patients. Because the fractures are usually painless, they go unnoticed initially allowing further damage to occur. Altered neural function and input to the bone is involved in the pathogenesis. The foot may be red and swollen, suggesting the presence of infection, which can be virtually excluded by the absence of ulceration of the skin. This point is particularly important because the radiographic appearance suggests osteomyelitis. Since the treatment of refractory osteomyelitis is often amputation, it is obviously critical not to make this diagnosis erroneously. The treatment for a Charcot foot is primarily elevation of the foot without weight bearing to allow healing of the fractures. Casting may be required. Healing is often slow and may take several months. Assiduous avoidance of weight bearing is important to prevent compounding the damage and increasing the degree of deformity. Unfortunately, such patients often do have a residual deformity of the foot.

Because they have a neuropathic foot, they are also prone to neuropathic ulceration and additional fractures. The most common deformity, a rocker bottom foot, results from fractures of the metatarsal bones and distortion of the arch.

This complication may occur in young women and therefore, it may be seen in pregnancy. A report of nine women who became pregnant after prior renal transplantation included two with neuropathic fractures of the foot (16). In this special situation, the use of corticosteroid therapy along with the alterations in vitamin D and calcium metabolism associated with renal failure may have contributed to dissolution of bone.

Autonomic Neuropathies

The autonomic nervous system can also be compromised by diabetes, leading to severe morbidity and mortality. In fact, among diabetic subjects with cardiovascular autonomic neuropathy, the 5-year mortality rate is increased by five-fold when compared with diabetic individuals without this complication (17). Significant variability is observed in the prevalence of diabetic neuropathy across different studies. For instance, cardiovascular autonomic neuropathy (CAN) has been reported to occur from a rather low prevalence of 7.7% among well-controlled patients with recently diagnosed type 1 diabetes (18), to as high as 50% to 90% among those with more advanced disease (19,20). These inconsistencies can be explained by the heterogenicity of the cohorts, and diagnostic modalities used as well as criteria utilized to diagnose diabetic neuropathy (1).

Autonomic neuropathy can have a wide range of clinical manifestations. The systems most commonly involved with their associated symptoms are summarized below:

Cardiovascular: resting tachycardia, exercise intolerance, and orthostatic hypotension.
Gastrointestinal: abnormal esophageal motility, gastroparesis, diarrhea, and constipation.
Genitourinary: neurogenic bladder, sexual dysfunction (defective lubrication).

Furthermore, hypoglycemia unawareness and pupillomotor deficits can be present.

As in the evaluation of somatic neuropathy, the American Diabetes Association (ADA) encourages using noninvasive, quantitative, and standardized measurement techniques. The recommended tests for the evaluation of autonomic neuropathy focus on the different systems affected by diabetes.

CAN may be evaluated by the determination of the *beat-to-beat heart rate variation* also known as R-R variation. This parameter is measured with the patient resting and breathing at a rate of six times per minute while the difference between maximum and minimum heart rate is recorded. A decrease in R-R variation with deep breathing is a sign of sympathetic neuropathy (9).

Another method to detect CAN is the *Valsalva maneuver*. The patient is asked to blow against a 40-mm Hg resistance for 15 seconds and an EKG is performed before, during, and after this procedure. The Valsalva ratio represents the longest R-R interval to the shortest R-R interval. Since the physiologic response of increased heart rate during strain and increased blood pressure with reflex bradycardia on release is altered in the presence of diabetic neuropathy, a Valsalva ratio of 1:10 or less is frequently observed.

Finally, *postural blood pressure testing* consists of determining the blood pressure while the patient is resting in a supine position and again after 1 and 5 minutes of standing. The presence of symptoms together with a decrease of at least 20 mm Hg of the systolic blood pressure is considered a positive test (9).

Gastroparesis consists of an abnormal motility pattern of the stomach secondary to autonomic neuropathy. This condition interferes with food absorption and is therefore associated with difficulties in blood glucose control. On occasion, overt symptoms like nausea and vomiting are present. Although its diagnosis is not well standardized, the finding of food in the stomach after 8 to 12 hours of fasting is sufficient for the diagnosis. Endoscopy serves to rule out other causes of vomiting, and a detailed history regarding a pharmacologic etiology is essential. Finally, isotope scintigraphy to measure solid-phase gastric emptying may be indicated. Since this condition deserves special consideration during pregnancy, this topic will be reviewed in the next section. In nonpregnant women, management of gastropathy could be based on changes in the feeding pattern including six meals a day, avoiding ingestion of large amounts of food at a single meal, and also avoiding a diet with a high-fat content. The use of metoclopramide to control vomiting can also be considered. When gastropathy occurs during pregnancy, nausea and vomiting may be severe, and parenteral nutrition may be necessary.

PREGNANCY AND DIABETIC NEUROPATHY

Because many women are delaying pregnancy, clinicians are now caring for patients suffering from diabetes of long duration. When these women present for preconceptional care, the issues of whether pregnancy accelerates the progression or induces the occurrence of diabetic neuropathy is of utmost importance. The paucity of data available in the literature highlights that this issue may have been underestimated.

During an uncomplicated pregnancy, the physiologic adaptation of the cardiovascular system is complex and requires adequate adjustments of the autonomic nervous system. Overall, there is an increase in heart rate, and cardiac output is enhanced by 40%. Because of the mechanical compression exerted by the uterus on the inferior vein cava, significant adjustment is needed to avoid frequent hypotension. For instance, in the supine position, cardiac output is 30% less than in the lateral recumbent position. Nevertheless, the potential collateral effects are blunted by a rise in the systemic vascular resistance (21). The physiologic adaptation to pregnancy could be hampered in patients suffering from diabetic neuropathy. Airaksinen and Salmela (22) evaluated pregnant women with type 1 diabetes to determine whether their diabetic condition was associated with impaired cardiac adjustment to the demands of pregnancy. The authors found a markedly smaller increase in the heart rate, stroke volume, and consequently in the cardiac output (1.3 L/min vs. 3.4 L/min, p < 0.01) than among nondiabetic controls. Another significant issue regards the accuracy of diagnostic tests to detect autonomic neuropathy during pregnancy. The heart rate change with breathing performed under standardized conditions is considered one of the most accurate tests to diagnose CAN in nonpregnant women. However, during pregnancy this response is blunted (23), thus making the diagnosis of autonomic diabetic neuropathy for the first time during pregnancy a challenge.

Few authors have evaluated the impact of pregnancy on diabetic neuropathy. Early investigations suggested that pregnancy could enhance the progression of neuropathy (24). However, in 1995 the EURODIAB type 1 complications study (25) compared the impact of parity among 1,358 nonpregnant women with type 1 diabetes. The authors concluded that parity does not influence the long-term prevalence or severity of diabetic autonomic neuropathy. Hemachandra el al. (26) conducted two nested, pair-matched case control studies based on the Epidemiology of Diabetes Complication study population: patients in this cohort were examined at baseline and at 2 and 4 years after inclusion for the presence of distal sensory-motor neuropathy. In the first study, the prevalence of neuropathy in 80 diabetic women who achieved pregnancy was compared with the control subjects corresponding to women who remained nulligravid at the 4-year follow-up. The authors concluded that the long-term prevalence of distal symmetric polyneuropathy was not increased by parity. In the second study, the short-term effect (<2 years) was evaluated. Interestingly, the incidence of neuropathy was ten times higher for parous women than for the nulliparous controls (41.7% vs. 4.8%; odds ratio, 10.00; confidence interval, 1.10–100). Therefore, this study indicates that although pregnancy may accelerate the development of neuropathy in the short term, there is no evidence of poorer prognosis in the long run (26).

Finally, Lapolla et al. (27) also addressed the issue of the potential influence of pregnancy on diabetic neuropathy. In their study, controls consisted of one group of matched nonpregnant diabetic women and another of matched nondiabetic pregnant women. This design avoids the potential confusion of the normal blunted autonomic response reported in uncomplicated pregnancies (23). The patients

TABLE 30-3. PREGNANCIES COMPLICATED BY DIABETIC GASTROPATHY

Reference	Age (Years)	Years Since Diabetes Diagnosis	Comorbidities	Outcome
Hare and White (30)	34	13	Severe vomiting Malnutrition Pulmonary edema Bacteremia	Chorioamnionitis Stillbirth
Macleod et al. (24)	30	15	Severe vomiting Malnutrition Cardiac arrest Aspiration	Intrauterine growth restriction Stillbirth
Macleod et al. (24)	25	12	Severe vomiting Parenteral nutrition	None
Steel (31)	25	14	Severe vomiting Intravenous replacement	None
Steel (31)	32	19	Vomiting Hypertension Diarrhea	Prematurity
Guy et al. (32)	27	11	Severe vomiting	Pregnancy termination

were evaluated for somatic and autonomic neuropathy three times during pregnancy and at 6 months follow-up. The authors concluded that women with mild or no evidence of neuropathy are not adversely affected by pregnancy. Another interesting finding was the improvement in conduction velocities observed in pregnant diabetic women towards the third trimester. Since the DCCT trial demonstrated that tight glucose control significantly decreases disease progression (12), a possible explanation for this unexpected finding is the improved glycemic control achieved during pregnancy (27).

We may therefore conclude, based on the available literature, that pregnancy is not a risk factor for the development or progression of either autonomic or somatic diabetic neuropathy.

Whether diabetic autonomic neuropathy affects pregnancy outcome has not been well studied. Three aspects of autonomic neuropathy can theoretically affect pregnancy outcome: (a) inability of the cardiovascular system to adjust to the hemodynamic demands of pregnancy; (b) interference with safe achievement of tight glucose control secondary to hypoglycemia unawareness; and (c) gastric dismotility and its implication on glucose absorption. Airaksinen et al. (28) conducted a prospective study in women with type 1 diabetes comparing outcomes in 23 pregnancies with autonomic dysfunction and 77 pregnancies without such complications. The authors reported that even after achieving similar glycemic control by the third trimester, no difference in the rates of hypoglycemic episodes between the two groups was observed. Furthermore, no statistically significant increase in any particular complication was observed in the study groups. This finding, however, must be interpreted with caution since it could be the result of the small sample studied. A thorough

analysis of maternal and fetal outcomes reveals that perinatal mortality, congenital malformations, polyhydramnios, preterm delivery, preeclampsia, hypoglycemic episodes, and ketoacidosis occurred at least twice as frequently in patients with diabetic neuropathy compared with control subjects. Not surprisingly, when the authors assessed complications as a single outcome variable, they observed a significant increase among pregnant diabetic women with neuropathy. Furthermore, this association was independent of metabolic control, duration of disease, and the presence of nephropathy (28).

Perhaps the most worrisome aspect of diabetic autonomic neuropathy during pregnancy is the occurrence of gastroparesis diabeticorum. Severe gastroparesis may result in significant maternal and fetal morbidity. Gastroparesis symptoms can be enhanced in early pregnancy by hyperemesis or morning sickness and in the third trimester by the mechanical stress induced by the enlarged uterus, causing severe nausea and vomiting. This condition, when severe, has been associated with significant maternal complications such as pulmonary edema or aspiration, the need for parenteral nutrition, and poor glucose control. Furthermore, significant fetal complications have been recognized: intrauterine growth restriction, preterm labor, and fetal loss (29). Severe gastroparesis complicating pregnancy is unusual, and only a few cases have been published in the world's literature (24,30–32) (Table 30-3).

Based on these serious complications, Macleod et al. (24) suggested that pregnancy should be considered a relative contraindication in patients with severe diabetic gastroparesis. Furthermore, the fact that autonomic function tests could be altered during pregnancy highlights the importance of preconception screening for gastroparesis in women of reproductive age. This will allow identification of more severe cases and proper counseling regarding potential maternal and perinatal morbidity and mortality.

CORONARY ARTERY DISEASE

Although CAD is uncommon among women in their reproductive years, diabetes mellitus carries an increased risk for this population. In fact, the estimated incidence of myocardial infarction during the childbearing age for the general population is approximately 1 in 10,000 pregnancies, while 1 in 350 women with type 1 diabetes develop CAD (33,34). Several mechanisms have been proposed for the early development of CAD among diabetics: (a) carbohydrate-induced elevation of very low-density lipoprotein; (b) hyperinsulinemia-induced stimulation of smooth muscle cell proliferation; (c) sorbitol-induced cellular damage; and (d) diabetes-induced abnormalities in cells, platelets, or lipoproteins metabolism (35).

Hare and White (30) first defined class H diabetes as diabetes complicating pregnancy of any duration or age of onset that is accompanied by CAD. From 1953 to date, 24 cases of class H diabetes have been reported in the literature (30,36–49) (Table 30-4). Eleven myocardial infarctions (46%) occurred before pregnancy, and 11 (46%) during

pregnancy. Finally, two (8%) occurred during the puerperium. Only three cases had a coronary artery bypass graft (CABG) before pregnancy. The analysis of these data is limited for several reasons, most importantly, because the number of patients is small and the available information on residual cardiac function is incomplete. With these limitations in mind, three general observations can be made. First, there were no maternal deaths among patients who had a CABG before pregnancy versus 38% in those who did not receive such preconception care. Similar differences are observed for fetal mortality. Second, maternal mortality was extremely high (73%) among patients reported before 1980, with a dramatic improvement thereafter (no maternal deaths). Third, the timing of the occurrence of the infarction appears to be important, since there were no maternal deaths associated with preconception events, but a mortality rate of 62% when it occurred during pregnancy or the puerperium (Table 30-5). The benefit of a CABG performed before pregnancy in properly selected women seems to be supported, and is possibly related to the increased survival observed. However, this cannot be evaluated thoroughly. While patients who underwent surgery before conception had a survival rate of 100%, these cases were reported *after* 1980 when the overall survival rate for patients with and without bypass surgery was zero.

TABLE 30-4. PUBLISHED CASES ON CLASS H DIABETES

Author	Age	Type of CAD	Time of Occurrence (Trimester)	Mode of Delivery	Maternal Outcome	Fetal Outcome
Brock (1953)	34	MI	First	Vaginal	Survived	Survived
Siegler (1956)	38	MI	First	Vaginal	Survived	Survived
Delaney (1970)	32	MI	Third	—	Died	—
White (1972)	35	MI	First	—	Died	Aborted
	35	MI	First	—	Died	Aborted
	35	MI	First	—	Died	Aborted
Hibbard (1975)	36	MI	First	—	Died	Aborted
Hare (1977)	—	MI	Before pregnancy	—	Survived	Survived
	—	MI	Third	—	Died	Survived
	—	MI	Puerperium	—	Died	Survived
	—	MI	Puerperium	—	Died	Died
Silfen (1980)	23	MI	Before pregnancy	Cesarean section	Survived	Survived
Gast (1985)	28	MI	Before pregnancy	Vaginal	Survived	Survived
	23	MI	Before pregnancy	Cesarean section	Survived	Survived
	36	MI	Before pregnancy	Vaginal	Survived	Died
Reece (1986)	32	Angina Occlusion LAD	Before pregnancy	Cesarean section	Survived	Survived
Sheikh (1993)	32	MI	Second	Vaginal	Survived	Survived
Spencer (1994)	38	MI	Second	Cesarean section	Survived	Survived
Wilson (1994)	30	MI	Before pregnancy	Cesarean section	Survived	Survived
	31	MI	Before pregnancy	Cesarean section	Survived	Survived
Pombar (1995)	29	MI	Before pregnancy	Cesarean section	Survived	Survived
Gordon (1996)	28	MI	Second	Cesarean section	Survived	Survived
Bagg (1999)	37	MI	Before pregnancy	Cesarean section	Survived	Survived
	36	MI	Before pregnancy	Vaginal	Survived	Survived

CAD, coronary artery disease; LAD, left anterior descending; MI, myocardial infarction.

TABLE 30-5. DEPICTS MATERNAL AND FETAL SURVIVAL ACCORDING TO PERIOD OF TREATMENT AND PRESENCE OF CABG AND TIMING OF EVENT

	1980 (Overall)		CABG		Time of AMI Relative to Pregnancy	
	Before	After	(−)	(+)	Before	During and After
Maternal mortality	73% (8/11)	0% (0/12)	38% (8/21)	0% (0/3)	0% (0/11)	62% (8/13)
Fetal loss	50% (5/10)	0% (0/12)	30% (6/20)	0% (0/3)	9% (1/11)	42% (5/12)

AMI, acute myocardial infarction; CABG, coronary artery bypass graft.

Improved understanding of the cardiovascular physiology of the pregnant woman as well as advances in management of these high-risk patients and their neonates may have played a role in the improvement of maternal and fetal survival. Furthermore, it appears that preconception correction of CAD may help to improve cardiac tolerance to the pregnant state with a subsequent prolongation of pregnancy and diminished morbidity from prematurity.

Management of class H diabetic pregnancies should include careful glycemic regulation to avoid hypoglycemia and therefore catecholamine release and tachycardia with subsequent increased myocardial demands (50). Gast and Riggs (42) recommended fasting blood glucose values of 70 mg/dL and 2-hour postprandial below 120 mg/dL. The mode of delivery should be individualized, since in reviewing the literature, there are no data supporting any particular route. In fact, among the published reports, 40% of patients were delivered vaginally and 60% by cesarean section. Some investigators have suggested the use of vacuum or forceps extraction to shorten the duration of the second stage of labor and to decrease the Valsalva maneuver (44). Continuous cardiac monitoring should be performed during labor (42). Swan-Ganz catheter placement to improve hemodynamic monitoring has been recommended (44); however, success has been achieved without its utilization. If the patient is allowed to go into labor, continuous epidural anesthesia should be used to avoid pain-related stress.

KEY POINTS

■ Adequate management of pregnancies complicated by class H diabetes requires a multidisciplinary approach.

■ Preconceptional evaluation and possibly treatment of patients with CAD with a bypass graft may improve maternal and perinatal outcomes.

■ Review of the recent literature on class H diabetes reveals that pregnancy does not appear to have as ominous a prognosis as was once reported.

■ Given the relatively high maternal mortality rate, pregnancy should still be considered relatively contraindicated until further information confirms a more favorable trend.

REFERENCES

1. Vinik AI, Maser E, Mitchell BD. Diabetic autonomic neuropathy. *Diabetes Care* 2003;26:1553–1579.
2. Vinik AI. Diagnosis and management of diabetic neuropathy. *Clin Geriatr Med* 1999;15:293–320.
3. Perkins BA, Greene DA, Bril V. Glycemic control is related to the morphological severity of diabetic sensorimotor polyneuropathy. *Diabetes Care* 2001;24:748–752.
4. Greene DA, Lattimer SA, Sima AA. Are disturbances of sorbitol, phosphoinositide, and Na+ K+ATPase regulation involved in pathogenesis of diabetic neuropathy? *Diabetes* 1988;37:688–693.
5. Sullivan JF. The neuropathies of diabetes. *Neurology* 1958;8:243–249.
6. Vinik AI, Holland MT, LeBeau JM, et al. Diabetic neuropathies. *Diabetes Care* 1992;15:1926–1975.
7. Bloomgarden ZT. Neuropathy, womens' health, and socioeconomic aspects of diabetes. *Diabetes Care* 2002;25:1085–1094.
8. Bril V, Perkins BA. Validation of the Toronto Clinical Scoring System for diabetic polyneuropathy. *Diabetes Care* 2002;25:2048–2052.
9. Kahn R. Proceedings of a consensus development conference on standardized measures in diabetic neuropathy. Clinical measures. *Diabetes Care* 1992;15:1081–1083.
10. Gelber DA, Pfeifer MA, Broadstone VL, et al. Components of variance of vibratory and thermal threshold testing in normal and diabetic subjects. *J Diabetes Complications* 1995;9:170–176.
11. Perkins BA, Bril V. Diabetic neuropathy: a review emphasizing diagnostic methods. *Clin Neurophysiol* 2003;114 (7):1161–1175.
12. The Diabetes Control and Complications Trial Research Group. The effect of intensive treatment of diabetes on the development and progression of long-term complications in insulin-dependent diabetes mellitus. *N Engl J Med* 1993;329:977–986.
13. Klein R, Klein BEK, Moss SE. Relation of glycemic control to diabetic microvascular complications in diabetes mellitus. *Ann Intern Med* 1996;124:90–96.
14. Ohkubo Y, Kishikawa H, Araki E, et al. Intensive insulin therapy prevents the progression of diabetic microvascular complications in Japanese patients with non-insulin-dependent diabetes mellitus: a randomized prospective 6-year study. *Diabetes Res Clin Pract* 2995;28:103–117.
15. Stika CS, Gross GA, Leguizamón G. A prospective randomized safety trial of celecoxib for treatment of preterm labor. *Am J Obstet Gynecol* 2002;187:653–660.
16. Ogburn PL, Kitzmiller JL, Hare JW et al. Pregnancy following renal transplantation in class T diabetes mellitus. *JAMA* 1986;255:911.
17. Ziegler D. Cardiovascular autonomic neuropathy: clinical manifestations and measurement. *Diabetes Rev* 1999;7:300–315.
18. Ziegler D, Gries FA, Spuler M, et al. The epidemiology of diabetic neuropathy. *J Diabetes Complications* 1992;6:49–57.

19. Ewing DJ, Campbell IW, Clark BF. Assessment of cardiovascular effects in diabetic autonomic neuropathy and prognostic implications. *Ann Intern Med* 1980;92:308–311.

20. Kennedy WR, Navarro X, Sutherland DER. Neuropathy profile of diabetic patients in a pancreas transplantation program. *Neurology* 1995;45:773–780.

21. Van Oppen A, Stigter R, Bruinse H. Cardiac output in normal pregnancy: a critical review. *Obstet Gynecol* 1996;87:310.

22. Airaksinen KEJ, Salmela PI. Pregnancy is not a risk factor for a deterioration of autonomic nervous function in diabetic women. *Diabet Med* 1993;10:540.

23. Airaksinen KEJ, Salmela PI, Markku J, et al. Effect of pregnancy on autonomic nervous function and heart rate in diabetic and nondiabetic women. *Diabetes Care* 1987;10:748–751.

24. Macleod AF, Smith SA, Sonksen PH, et al. The problem of autonomic neuropathy in diabetic pregnancy. *Diabet Med* 1990;7:80.

25. Chaturvedi N, Stephenson JM, Fuller JH, et al. The relationship between pregnancy and long term maternal complications in the EURODIAB IDDM complications study. *Diabet Med* 1995;12:494–499.

26. Hemachandra A, Ellis D, Lloyd K, et al. The influence of pregnancy on IDDM complications. *Diabetes Care* 1995;18:950–954.

27. Lapolla A, Cardone C, Negrin P, et al. Pregnancy does not induce or worsen retinal and peripheral nerve dysfunction in insulin-dependent diabetic women. *J Diabetes Complications* 1998;12:74–80.

28. Airaksinen KEJ, Anttila LM, Linnaluoto MK, et al. Autonomic influence on pregnancy outcome in IDDM. *Diabetes Care* 1990;13:756.

29. Hagay Z, Weissman A. Management of diabetic pregnancy complicated by coronary artery disease and neuropathy. *Obstet Gynecol Clin North Am* 1996;23:205–220.

30. Hare JW, White P. Pregnancy in diabetes complicated by vascular disease. *Diabetes* 1977;26:953.

31. Steel JM. Autonomic neuropathy in pregnancy [Letter]. *Diabetes Care* 1989;12:170–171.

32. Guy RJC, Dawson JL, Garrett JT, et al. Diabetic gastroparesis from autonomic neuropathy: surgical considerations and changes in vagus nerve morphology. *J Neurol Neurosurg Psychiatry* 1984;47:686–691.

33. Fletcher E, Knox EW, Morton P. Acute myocardial infarction in pregnancy. *BMJ* 1967;3:586.

34. Sullivan JM, Ramanathan KB. Management of medical problems in pregnancy—severe cardiac disease. *N Engl J Med* 1985;313:304.

35. Stout RW. Insulin and atheroma—an update. *Lancet* 1987;1(8541):1077.

36. Brock HJ, Russel NG, Randall CL. Myocardial infarction in pregnancy: report of a case with normal spontaneous vaginal delivery seven months later. *JAMA* 1953;152:1030.

37. Siegler AM, Hoffman J, Bloom O. Myocardial infarction complicating pregnancy. *Obstet Gynecol* 1956;7:306.

38. Delaney JJ, Ptacek J. Three decades of experience with diabetic pregnancies. *Am J Obstet Gynecol* 1970;106:550.

39. White P. Life cycle of diabetes in youth. *J Am Med Women Assoc* 1972;27:293.

40. Hibbard LT. Maternal mortality due to cardiac disease. *Clin Obstet Gynecol* 1975;18:27.

41. Silfen SL, Wapner RJ, Gabbe SG. Maternal outcome in class H diabetes mellitus. *Obstet Gynecol* 1980;55:749.

42. Gast MJ, Riggs LA. Class H diabetes and pregnancy. *Obstet Gynecol* 1985;66:5–7.

43. Reece EA, Egan JFX, Coustan DR, et al. Coronary artery disease in diabetic pregnancies. *Am J Obstet Gynecol* 1986;154:150–151.

44. Sheikh AU, Harper MA. Myocardial infarction during pregnancy: management and outcome of two pregnancies. *Am J Obstet Gynecol* 1993;169:279–284.

45. Spencer J, Gadalla F, Wagner W, et al. Cesarean section in a diabetic patient with a recent myocardial infarction. *Can J Anaesth* 1994;41:516–618.

46. Wilson JD, Moore G, Chipps D. Successful pregnancy in patients with diabetes following myocardial infarction. *Aust N Z J Obstet Gynaecol* 1994;34:604–606.

47. Pombar X, Strassner HT, Fenner PC. Pregnancy in a women with Class H diabetes and previous coronary artery bypass graft. Part 2. A case report and review of the literature. *Obstet Gynecol* 1995;85:825–829.

48. Gordon MC, Landon MB, Boyle J. Coronary artery disease in insulin dependent diabetes mellitus of pregnancy (Class H): A review of the literature. *Obstet Gynecol Surv* 1996;51:437–444.

49. Bagg W, Henley PG, Macpherson P, et al. Pregnancy in women with diabetes and ischaemic heart disease. *Aust NZ J Obstet Gynecol* 1999;39:99–102.

50. Hankins GD, Wendel GD, Leveno KJ, et al. Myocardial infarction during pregnancy: a review. *Obstet Gynecol* 1985;65:139–146.

31

DELIVERY: TIMING, MODE, AND MANAGEMENT

DONALD R. COUSTAN

One of the most critical and controversial aspects of perinatal medicine is the precise timing of the delivery. Furthermore, once a decision has been made to accomplish delivery, the clinician must decide between abdominal and vaginal routes. In the woman with diabetes mellitus, the management of glucose metabolism during cesarean section or labor appears to be an important determinant of at least some types of neonatal morbidity. In 1966, *Williams Obstetrics* (1) contained the following statement:

> Because of the increase in fetal death as term approaches there is widespread belief that pregnancy should be terminated either by the induction of labor or by cesarean section about three weeks prior to term. The choice between cesarean section and induction of labor depends upon the level of the presenting part and the condition of the cervix.

As to the management of diabetes during labor, the above textbook recommends that "it is well to give the equivalent of 10 g of glucose approximately every hour" (1).

A great many changes have occurred in the approach to these issues during the past 40 years, and this chapter outlines current recommendations.

TIMING

With the improvements in management of the pregnancy complicated by diabetes discussed in earlier chapters, the necessity for early intervention to deliver such pregnancies has diminished remarkably. In the past, the high intrauterine fetal death rate after 36 to 37 weeks of gestation more than outweighed the risks of respiratory distress syndrome (RDS) occurring in infants of diabetic mothers (IDMs) delivered after this gestational age. However, the convergence of both advancing perinatal technology and improved understanding of the relationship between meticulous maternal diabetic control and the prevention of perinatal death, has enabled the clinician to individualize decision making, allowing most diabetic women to proceed to term or near term before planned delivery.

The development of neonatal intensive care units has improved the survival chances for infants born prematurely, particularly those who have RDS. Furthermore, the development and utilization of tests of fetoplacental function, which include antepartum fetal monitoring, such as the nonstress test, contraction stress test, biophysical profile, and fetal movement counting, have allowed the evolution of a strategy to identify those diabetic pregnancies at lowest risk of fetal deterioration, thereby avoiding the neonatal and maternal risks of untimely intervention. Conversely, these tests allow appropriate intervention in those pregnancies with evidence of fetal risk.

In addition to identification of those pregnancies in which the fetus is compromised, it has also become possible to measure the likelihood of a particular fetus to develop RDS if delivered at a given point in time. The measurement of surfactant components in amniotic fluid has become a standard method of assessing fetal pulmonic maturity, critical for timing the elective delivery of a patient with diabetes. This technology allows the avoidance of iatrogenic RDS when delivery can be safely postponed. It is particularly helpful when antepartum biophysical assessment of fetal well-being is equivocal or when other indications for delivery are present but not absolute.

In parallel with the abovementioned advances in fetal assessment has come the elucidation of the relationship between the achievement of maternal euglycemia and a marked reduction in perinatal mortality rates. It is thus clear that the approach to timing delivery can be two-pronged: (a) we can prevent the necessity for intentional early delivery in most cases by strict metabolic control of maternal diabetes; and (b) we can identify those few fetuses still at high risk of perinatal death with antepartum testing. What remains is the vast majority of pregnancies complicated by diabetes in which there is no specific indication for delivery at a given time. The principle that should guide our determination of the optimal date for intervention in these individuals is one that is familiar to every doctor and medical student: *primum non nocere*—first, do no harm. As discussed later in this chapter, vaginal delivery is preferable to cesarean section if all other factors are equal. Therefore, a management scheme that will optimize the chances for a normal vaginal delivery without increasing perinatal mortality and morbidity is desirable. On the other hand, perinatal risk increases when pregnancies, in general, go much beyond term, and most clinicians are reluctant to allow women with diabetes to continue pregnancies beyond the estimated date of confinement. Although in the well-controlled and otherwise uncomplicated case this position may be emotional rather than data based, it is unlikely to change in the near future, particularly with medicolegal concerns lurking in the conscious or subconscious of every practicing obstetrician. Therefore, the following approach has evolved in our diabetes center.

1. Delivery is accomplished even without documented lung maturity if maternal or fetal compromise places the life of either mother or fetus at significant risk, such as proven severe fetal compromise at a time when fetal survival after delivery is considered possible, currently around 24 weeks at our center. A typical situation would be one in which maternal eclampsia or severe preeclampsia is present, maternal well-being is compromised by continuing the pregnancy, and little improvement in fetal outcome is anticipated because the fetus is growth restricted and a nonreassuring tracing is documented. In such situations, the likelihood of extrauterine survival must be weighed against the severity of fetal or maternal compromise.

2. Delivery is recommended as soon as lung maturity can be documented when there is a significant maternal or fetal problem, but neither poses an immediate risk, such as when there is poor or undocumented maternal metabolic control, a maternal hypertensive disorder of pregnancy or worsening preexisting hypertension, intrauterine growth restriction, previous classical cesarean section, or equivocal antepartum assessment of fetal condition.

3. In patients who do not fulfill any of the above criteria, elective delivery (whether by induction of labor or repeat cesarean section) is *considered* at 39 weeks' gestation to decrease the expense and anxiety associated with continuing the pregnancy, if the cervix is clinically "ripe" and gestational age is well established (American College of Obstetricians and Gynecologists, Educational Bulletin #230). If earlier elective delivery is planned, as in uncomplicated pregnancies, fetal lung maturity should be documented by studies of amniotic fluid. If the cervix is unfavorable, amniocentesis is not attempted because fetal pulmonic maturity would not lead to elective induction of labor under these circumstances.

A number of studies have suggested that RDS is no more common in IDMs whose glucose metabolism has been well controlled during pregnancy than among normal controls (3,4), and that false-positive test results at term are no more likely in IDMs than in normal pregnancies. These data would suggest that if fetal hyperinsulinemia can be avoided by meticulous control of maternal blood glucose levels, RDS in near term IDMs is not likely. The study by Piper and Langer (5), showing a greater prevalence of immature lung profiles in poorly controlled than in well-controlled diabetic pregnancies, would tend to confirm this. It is almost certainly true that in pregnancies complicated by diabetes, as in other pregnancies, the single most important determinant of pulmonic maturity is gestational age.

It should be apparent that, in this scheme, the White class of maternal diabetes does not enter into clinical decision making as to timing of delivery. Although it is undoubtedly true that women with vascular disease are more likely to have adverse outcomes such as perinatal death, this increased risk is most likely associated with problems such as hypertension and intrauterine growth restriction, which would themselves prompt early delivery. Conversely, if a particular woman whose diabetes has been in excellent metabolic control, has normal blood pressure, and has an appropriately growing fetus with normal antenatal monitoring parameters, it would be unreasonable to induce labor, possibly increasing the likelihood of a cesarean section, at a predetermined number of weeks before term merely because she has had diabetes for 20 years rather than 19 years.

In a patient with diabetes, the otherwise uncomplicated pregnancy that reaches 40 weeks' gestation with a cervix unfavorable for induction can present a dilemma. The options include continuing the pregnancy while awaiting cervical change; using methods such as prostaglandin, Foley catheter, or laminaria to effect cervical ripening; or proceeding with a primary cesarean section. Except in the presence of macrosomia (discussed later in this chapter), we almost never choose the last of the options. In the absence of significant macrosomia, the performance of a cesarean section without labor seems extreme. Although the efficacy of cervical ripening among diabetic pregnancies at 40 weeks or more has not been unequivocally demonstrated, this option is often chosen to alleviate the anxiety of both patient and obstetrician after 40 weeks. The above approach to the timing of delivery should allow most patients to deliver at or beyond the 38 weeks generally accepted as "term."

MODE

There has been considerable controversy concerning the appropriate mode of delivery for pregnancies complicated by diabetes over the years. During the first 70 years of the last century, many experts advocated almost routine cesarean section for such pregnancies and reported cesarean section rates of 65% or more (6–9) at a time when overall cesarean section rates in most hospitals were below 5%.

Other experts disagreed and reported cesarean section rates of approximately 16% (7,10–12).

During the 1970s, overall cesarean section rates in the United States increased for many reasons outside the scope of this chapter. At the same time, the advances in management discussed earlier enabled clinicians to feel more and more comfortable in allowing pregnancies to proceed closer to term in women with diabetes. These two trends would be expected to have opposing effects on cesarean section rates for pregnancies complicated by diabetes. In a selective review of 17 series of overt diabetic pregnancies published between 1975 and 1985, cesarean section rates varied between 19% and 83% (13–29). When all results were combined, 995 of 2,138 (47%) deliveries were performed by cesarean section. It was not possible to distinguish the characteristics of diabetes management that predisposed to higher or lower cesarean rates. The cesarean section rate for diabetic pregnancy at the National Maternity Hospital in Ireland increased from 19% in 1983 (29) to 28% in 1992 (30). A 1993 prospective nationwide study in Sweden found the overall cesarean section rate for pregnancies complicated by diabetes to be 45% versus 12% for control pregnancies (31), and a 1991 multicenter prospective survey in France reported a 60% cesarean section rate for women with preexisting diabetes (32). In a 1990 survey of 273 American subspecialists in maternal-fetal medicine, only 31% reported cesarean rates for insulin-dependent diabetic women to be 25% or less; 58% estimated that their rates were between 26% and 50%; and 10% reported rates above 50% (33). Over the past 10 years, cesarean section rates in the North American general population have risen markedly. Approximately one-fourth of American women are now delivered abdominally. A recent publication from Vancouver reported a cesarean section rate of 47% among 300 women with type 1 diabetes (34).

Cesarean section may be considered as an adverse outcome for the mother, given the greater incidence of infectious morbidity among women with diabetes compared with that in the general population (35,36), and the increased maternal mortality rates ascribed to cesarean section. In addition, the total cost of cesarean section exceeds that of vaginal delivery, and maternal discomfort is arguably greater. From the fetal-neonatal point of view, there is a clear increase in the incidence of RDS when delivery is by cesarean (37,38). Thus, all other things being equal, vaginal delivery is preferable to cesarean section.

Certain complications that are more likely to occur in the pregnancy complicated by diabetes may necessitate cesarean delivery, making the higher than usual cesarean section rates likely to continue. Among these are the association of hypertensive disorders of pregnancy with maternal diabetes that may make early intervention necessary at a time when cervical ripening has not occurred and the uterus is not as likely to respond to oxytocin stimulation. Likewise, the greater likelihood of fetal compromise in the diabetic woman whose glucose metabolism is suboptimally controlled may necessitate early intervention and cesarean section.

The increased incidence of fetal macrosomia, with the accompanying risk of shoulder dystocia, prompts many clinicians to opt for cesarean section when the estimated fetal weight exceeds certain limits. This is understandable, particularly in view of the fact that the macrosomic IDM is likely to have a body that is disproportionately large in relation to its head size, thus predisposing to shoulder dystocia at any given birth weight (39,40). Shoulder dystocia has been reported to occur in 3% (41) to 12% (42) of deliveries that result in neonates weighing 4,000 g or more, and in 8.4% (42) to 14.6% (43) of those weighing more than 4,500 g. In one study, 31% of diabetic women who had babies weighing 4,000 g or more experienced shoulder dystocia (42). In another study, 21% of infants weighing more than 4,000 g and undergoing midpelvic vaginal delivery after a prolonged second stage had shoulder dystocia (41). Thus, diabetes, macrosomia, midpelvic delivery, and a prolonged second stage all appear to be risk factors for shoulder dystocia. Shoulder dystocia is of greatest concern because of the possibility that Erb's palsy may result. Erb's palsy was found in the offspring of 10 in 1,000 diabetic pregnancies compared with 0.6 in 1,000 normal controls (44). This has prompted many obstetricians to resort to elective cesarean section when IDMs are estimated to weigh 4,000 g or more or 4,500 g or more.

Problems associated with this type of plan include the poor predictive value of clinical estimates of fetal weight when macrosomia is present (45,46), and the lack of agreement as to the accuracy of ultrasound measurements for such predictions. In babies who weigh 4,000 to 4,500 g, the usually acceptable 10% error in ultrasound fetal weight estimation may lead to under- or over-estimation by 400 to 450 g. This problem has prompted a number of proposals for predicting shoulder dystocia, including ultrasonic measurement of anthropometric data (39), such as abdominal circumference (47), the difference between chest diameter and biparietal diameter (48), the rate of abdominal growth (49), magnetic resonance imaging of fetal fat (50), and ultrasound imaging (51) or computed tomographic scanning (52) of shoulder soft tissue width. No such system has been tested thoroughly enough in a prospective manner at this time to allow evaluation of its function as a screening test for shoulder dystocia. Therefore, ultrasound estimation of fetal weight is currently the most accurate method available and continues to be relied on for clinical decision making. It should be noted that the use of a relatively inaccurate method to diagnose macrosomia has drawbacks as well as benefits and that overdiagnosis may increase morbidity by prompting unnecessary interventions (53). Conway and Langer (54) reported a case series of 2,604 women with gestational and preexisting diabetes managed before and after the institution of a policy requiring elective cesarean section when estimated fetal weight exceeded 4,250 grams. The rate of shoulder dystocia was reduced from 2.4% to 1.1%, while the cesarean section rate increased from 22% to 25%. The authors subsequently pointed out that their experience suggested that one would have to perform four additional cesarean sections to prevent one shoulder dystocia (55). Rouse et al. (56) carried out a decision analysis in order to determine the potential costs and effectiveness of performing cesarean section without labor when estimated fetal weight exceeded various thresholds in diabetic and nondiabetic pregnancies. They attempted to take into account all important factors including the inaccuracy of ultrasound, the likelihood of permanent Erb's palsy when shoulder dystocia occurs, and the costs associated with cesarean section and vaginal delivery. For mothers with diabetes, if a policy of cesarean section for estimated fetal weight of 4,000 grams or more were instituted, it would require 489 cesarean sections at a cost of $880,000 to prevent one permanent Erb's palsy. A policy of elective cesarean section at an estimated fetal weight of 4,500 grams would require 443 cesarean sections at a cost of $930,000 to prevent one permanent Erb's palsy. In nondiabetic populations, the costs would be many times greater, with 3,695 cesarean sections at a cost of $8.7 million to prevent one permanent Erb's palsy at an estimated fetal weight exceeding 4,500 grams. The authors consider the merits of such an approach in pregnancies complicated by diabetes to be "debatable."

Given the risks of macrosomia, a reasonable option might be to induce labor before the appearance of fetal overgrowth in the hope of preventing morbidity. A retrospective study found that elective induction of labor in fetuses estimated to be above the 90th percentile for weight increased the cesarean section rate without preventing shoulder dystocia (57). However, a randomized prospective clinical trial of induction when diabetic pregnancies reached 38 weeks demonstrated a reduction in macrosomia and shoulder dystocia without an increase in cesarean sections (58). In a report of a case series before and after the institution of a protocol for inducing labor at 38 to 39 weeks in insulin-treated diabetic women (59), the incidence of shoulder dystocia fell from 5% (7 of 133 deliveries) prior to the protocol to 1% (1 of 74 deliveries) after institution of the protocol. This difference was not statistically significant. However, the authors also found that five of the seven shoulder dystocias encountered prior to the protocol occurred in patients delivering beyond 40 weeks gestation, supporting the value of induction in preventing shoulder dystocia.

Decision making as to the mode of delivery in a pregnancy complicated by overt diabetes is guided by the following principles:

1. Diabetes is not an *a priori* indication for cesarean section, although its complications may necessitate this route of delivery.

2. In general, the closer to term a pregnancy is allowed to continue, the greater is the likelihood of a vaginal delivery.

3. The decision for cesarean section is made on obstetric indications.

4. To minimize the risk of shoulder dystocia, the fetal weight should be estimated with as much accuracy as possible before a decision is made as to the mode of delivery. We consider the following to be indications for cesarean section without a trial of labor: Estimated fetal weight more than 4,500 g in most instances or estimated fetal weight of 4,000 to 4,500 g, depending on history, clinical assessment of the pelvis, and progress of labor. Midforceps or midcavity vacuum deliveries in such patients should be avoided, if possible, particularly after a long second stage. A history of shoulder dystocia, unless the estimated fetal weight is significantly lower than the birth weight of the previous baby, would also indicate cesarean delivery.

The relationship between cesarean section rates and diabetic status may be confounded considerably by physician preconceptions regarding risk. A prospective cohort study by the Toronto Tri-Hospital Group (60) compared 143 treated gravidas with known gestational diabetes (GDM) with 115 untreated gravidas whose glucose tolerance test abnormality met less stringent criteria for GDM, and whose caregivers were blinded to the results. A normal control group of 2,940 subjects with normal diabetes screening tests was also included. Neonatal macrosomia (birth weight >4 kg) was present in 10% of the treated GDM pregnancies (similar to the 14% rate in normal controls), and 29% of the untreated GDMs (p < 0.001), suggesting that whatever treatment was offered to the GDMs was effective in preventing fetal overgrowth. However, the cesarean section rate in treated GDMs was 34%, similar to that in the untreated GDMs (30%) and almost 50% higher than in normal controls (p < 0.001). Of interest, cesarean section in the untreated blinded GDMs was directly related to macrosomia, whereas it was unrelated to macrosomia in the treated GDMs. These findings suggest that caregivers' perception of the risk of GDM, probably shoulder dystocia, influenced them to perform cesarean sections at a higher rate despite the successful prevention of excess macrosomia. On the other hand, a case series from Australia (61) revealed similar cesarean section rates for GDM and normal control women when adjusted for age and parity.

MANAGEMENT OF DIABETES DURING LABOR AND DELIVERY

The principle guiding the management of maternal diabetes during labor and delivery is the maintenance of maternal euglycemia. Animal studies have demonstrated that maternal-fetal hyperglycemia may be associated with increasing fetal lactate levels and oxygen consumption, with subsequent acidosis and occasional fetal death (62,63). It has also been suggested that the combination of hyperglycemia and hypoxia in primates may predispose to brain damage (64). In human studies, the infusion of large amounts of glucose into normal (65,66) and diabetic (67) women about to undergo cesarean section has been associated with fetal and neonatal acidemia.

One of the more common neonatal morbidities in IDMs is neonatal hypoglycemia resulting from fetal and neonatal hyperinsulinemia. Although the pancreas of the fetus of the diabetic mother may be more responsive to hyperglycemia, even the normal fetus responds to maternal hyperglycemia with an outpouring of insulin (68). The administration of intravenous glucose solutions during labor, leading to maternal hyperglycemia, has been associated with neonatal hypoglycemia in both diabetic (69–71) and normal (72) pregnancies. Thus, the continued meticulous control of maternal glycemia during labor is necessary to avoid neonatal hypoglycemia.

In the past, it was customary to administer subcutaneous short-acting insulin to diabetic women in labor, using a lower dose than the daily pregnancy amount. Given that even short-acting insulin does not reach a peak of absorption for a few hours, it is not surprising that euglycemia was difficult to maintain during labor. In 1977, West and Lowy (73) described the use of a continuous intravenous infusion of glucose and low-dose (1 to 2 units/h) insulin as a means to control glycemia during labor. Soon thereafter, numerous centers reported satisfactory results with this system, although neonatal hypoglycemia was not entirely eliminated (74–76). In the first study, glucose was infused at a rate of 8.3 g/h, and all 15 patients required at least 1.4 units/h of insulin throughout the labor (73). In the later studies, lower rates of glucose infusion were used (5 to 6 g/h), and lower infusion rates of insulin were necessary. In fact, some patients required no insulin.

In 1978, Nattrass et al. (77) reported the use of an artificial pancreas during labor in three laboring insulin-dependent diabetic women. The average infusion rates to maintain normoglycemia were 0.7 to 6.7 units/h of insulin and 3.0 to 6.4 g/h of glucose. By contrast, Jovanovic and Peterson (78) reported that 12 pregnant women with insulin-dependent diabetes managed with an artificial pancreas required no insulin during active first-stage labor despite glucose infusion rates of approximately 10 g/h. Golde et al. (79) used glucose infusion rates of 6 g/h in 33 women with insulin-dependent diabetes during oxytocin induction of labor. One-half of the patients required no insulin to maintain euglycemia; the other half required insulin infusions of 0.6 to 1.2 units/h or more. It is thus apparent that at least some women with diabetes require no insulin during active labor; others may need more intensive treatment. It is most important to monitor maternal glucose levels hourly during this dynamic period of labor and to be prepared to add insulin if hyperglycemia occurs.

Our current approach to the metabolic management of diabetes during labor is based on the goal of maternal euglycemia at delivery and acknowledges the caloric requirements attributable to the work of labor and that laboring women should not be allowed to ingest food because of the potential hazard of aspiration if anesthesia is required. Although the rapid infusion of large volumes of glucose-containing solutions has been demonstrated to give rise to fetal lactic acidosis as noted above, more recent studies of normal laboring gravidas have demonstrated no decrease in cord pH levels with the infusion of 5% glucose solutions at rates of 125 to 200 ml/h (80,81). Furthermore, a greater likelihood of the development of ketonemia during labor has been demonstrated in women with gestational diabetes than in normal controls, supporting the need for caloric support (82).

1. On the day before induction of labor when the patient has been in satisfactory metabolic control, the existing insulin and meal regimen is followed to ensure that euglycemia will be present on the morning of induction.
2. On the morning of induction, withhold insulin and breakfast.
3. Start an intravenous infusion of 5% dextrose in half-normal saline, at a rate of 125 ml/h, using an infusion pump.
4. Measure the glucose level at the bedside every 1 to 2 hours, maintaining a glucose concentration between 70 and 120 mg/dL.
5. If the glucose level exceeds 120 mg/dL, add 10 U of regular insulin to 1,000 ml of dextrose 5% in half-normal saline and continue the infusion rate of 125 ml/h. This yields an insulin dose of approximately 1.25 units/h.
6. Further adjustments in insulin dosage are made by doubling or halving the insulin concentration but keeping the infusion rate constant.
7. Another option is to use a separate infusion line for insulin in a nonglucose-containing solution, and to piggyback this into the glucose infusion. Such an approach requires three infusion pumps: one for glucose, one for insulin, and a third for oxytocin.
8. If spontaneous labor occurs, the procedure is the same. However, the patient may be less likely to require insulin, since she may have taken some intermediate-acting insulin before the onset of labor.

When elective cesarean section is planned, the procedure is simpler. The patient is instructed to follow her usual meal and insulin regimen on the day and evening before surgery. If it is assumed that the patient has been in good metabolic control, she should awaken on the morning of cesarean section with a normal blood glucose level. An intravenous line is inserted, and normal saline without glucose is infused. The diabetic patient's cesarean section should be the first one on the morning schedule, commencing at an early hour so that no perturbations in glucose metabolism have yet occurred. Once the baby has been delivered, glucose with or without insulin can be infused as needed.

With the approach outlined above, it is possible to maintain normal or near-normal glucose levels in most laboring diabetic women and prevent the sudden surge of fetal insulin release at the time of delivery that might increase the risk of neonatal hypoglycemia. Occasionally, this meticulous control of circulating glucose levels during labor can be abruptly negated by the infusion of a large quantity of glucose-containing solution just before the initiation of conduction anesthesia to prevent maternal hypotension. It is thus important that the entire healthcare team, including nurses and anesthesiologists, be aware of the importance of maintaining maternal euglycemia. Because it is usually necessary to expand the mother's intravascular volume before an epidural or spinal anesthetic is administered, nonglucose-containing solutions should be used.

KEY POINTS

- Lung maturity need not be documented when maternal or fetal compromise places the life of either at significant risk.

- Deliver as soon as fetal lung maturity can be documented when there is a significant maternal or fetal problem, but no immediate risk to the life of either.

- If elective delivery earlier than 39 weeks' gestation is planned in an otherwise uncomplicated diabetic pregnancy, fetal lung maturity should be documented.

- Diabetes is not an indication for cesarean delivery, but its complications may be.

- The decision for cesarean section is made on obstetric indications.

- Estimated fetal weight of >4,500 grams may be considered an indication for cesarean section without a trial of labor in a diabetic gravida; when estimated fetal weight is between 4,000 and 4,500 grams, the decision may be individualized.

- The goal of diabetes management in labor is the attainment of euglycemia in the mother, to prevent hypoglycemia in the neonate.

REFERENCES

1. Eastman NJ, Hellman LM. *Williams obstetrics*, 13th ed. New York: Appleton & Lange, 1966.
2. Ojomo EO, Coustan DR. Absence of evidence of pulmonary maturity at amniocentesis in term infants of diabetic mothers. *Am J Obstet Gynecol* 1990;163:954.
3. Mimouni F, Miodovnik M, Whitsett JA, et al. Respiratory distress syndrome in infants of diabetic mothers in the 1980s: no direct adverse effect of maternal diabetes with modern management. *Obstet Gynecol* 1987;69:191.
4. Kjos SL, Walther FJ, Montoro M, et al. Prevalence and etiology of respiratory distress in infants of diabetic mothers: predictive value of fetal lung maturation tests. *Am J Obstet Gynecol* 1990; 163:898.
5. Piper JM, Langer O. Does maternal diabetes delay fetal pulmonary maturity? *Am J Obstet Gynecol* 1993;168:783.
6. White P. Pregnancy complicating diabetes. *Am J Med* 1949;6: 609.
7. Pedowitz P, Shlevin EL. Review of management of pregnancy complicated by diabetes and altered carbohydrate metabolism. *Obstet Gynecol* 1964;23:716.
8. Harley JMG, Montgomery DAD. Management of pregnancy complicated by diabetes. *BMJ* 1965;1:14.
9. Schwartz RH, Kyle GC. Timing of delivery in the pregnant diabetic patient. *Obstet Gynecol* 1969;34:787.
10. Jones WS. Diabetes in pregnancy. *Am J Obstet Gynecol* 1953;66: 322.
11. Hall RE, Tillman AJB. Diabetes in pregnancy. *Am J Obstet Gynecol* 1951;61:1107.
12. Delaney JJ, Ptacek J. Three decades of experience with diabetic pregnancies. *Am J Obstet Gynecol* 1970;106:550.
13. Brearley BF. The management of pregnancy in diabetes mellitus. *Practitioner* 1975;215:644.
14. Ayromlooi J, Mann LI, Weiss RR, et al. Modern management of the diabetic pregnancy. *Obstet Gynecol* 1977;49:137.
15. Boehm FH, Graber AL, Hicks MML. Coordinated metabolic and obstetric management of diabetic pregnancy. *South Med J* 1978;71:37.
16. Cassar J, Gordon H, Dixon HG, et al. Simplified management of pregnancy complicated by diabetes. *Br J Gynaecol* 1978;85: 585.
17. Gabbe SG, Lowensohn RI, Wu PYK, et al. Current patterns of neonatal morbidity and mortality in infants of diabetic mothers. *Diabetes Care* 1978;1:335.
18. Goldstein AI, Cronk DA, Garite T, Amlie RN. Perinatal outcome in the diabetic pregnancy: a retrospective analysis. *J Reprod Med* 20:61, 1978.
19. Kitzmiller JL, Cloherty JP, Younger MD, et al. Diabetic pregnancy and perinatal morbidity. *Am J Obstet Gynecol* 1978; 131:560.
20. Jervell J, Moe N, Skjaeraasen J, et al. Diabetes mellitus and pregnancy—management and results at Rikshospitalet, Oslo, 1970–1977. *Diabetologia* 1979;16:151.
21. Martin TR, Allen AC, Stinson D. Overt diabetes in pregnancy. *Am J Obstet Gynecol* 1979;133:275.
22. Roversi GD, Gargiulo M, Nicolini U, et al. A new approach to the treatment of diabetic pregnant women: report of 479 cases seen from 1963 to 1975. *Am J Obstet Gynecol* 1979;135:567.
23. Coustan DR, Berkowitz RL, Hobbins JC. Tight metabolic control of overt diabetes in pregnancy. *Am J Med* 1980;68:845.
24. Haukkamaa M, Nilsson CG, Luukkainen T. Screening, management, and outcome of pregnancy in diabetic mothers. *Obstet Gynecol* 1980;55:596.
25. Tevaarwerk GJM, Harding PGR, Milne KJ, et al. Pregnancy in diabetic women: outcome with a program aimed at normoglycemia before meals. *CMAJ* 1981;125:435.
26. Fadel HE, Hammond SD. Diabetes mellitus in pregnancy: management and results. *J Reprod Med* 1982;27:56.
27. Traub AI, Harley JMG, Montgomery DAD, et al. Pregnancy and diabetes—the improving prognosis. *Ulster Med J* 1983;52:118.
28. Piras G, Cherchi PL, Delfino F, et al. Diabetes in pregnancy. an epidemiologic study by Department of Obstetrics and Gynecology of Sassari University from 1974 to 1983. *Clin Exp Obstet Gynecol* 1985;12:26.
29. Drury MI, Stronge JM, Foley ME, et al. Pregnancy in the diabetic patient: timing and mode of delivery. *Obstet Gynecol* 1983;62:279.

30. Rasmussen MJ, Firth R, Foley M, et al. The timing of delivery in diabetic pregnancy: a 10-year review. *Aust N Z J Obstet Gynaecol* 1992;32:313.

31. Hanson U, Persson B. Outcome of pregnancies complicated by type 1 insulin-dependent diabetes in Sweden: acute pregnancy complications, neonatal mortality and morbidity. *Am J Perinatol* 1993;10:330.

32. Gestation and Diabetes in France Study Group. Multicenter survey of diabetic pregnancy in France. *Diabetes Care* 1991;14:994.

33. Landon MB, Gabbe SG, Sachs L. Management of diabetes mellitus and pregnancy: a survey of obstetricians and maternal-fetal specialists. *Obstet Gynecol* 1990;75:635.

34. Wylie BR, Kong J, Kozak SE, et al. Normal perinatal mortality in type 1 diabetes mellitus in a series of 300 consecutive pregnancy outcomes. *Am J Perinatol* 2002;19:169–176.

35. Diamond MP, Entman SS, Salyer SI, et al. Increased risk of endometritis and wound infection after cesarean section in insulin-dependent women. *Am J Obstet Gynecol* 1986;155:297.

36. Stamler EF, Cruz ML, Mimouni F, et al. High infectious morbidity in pregnant women with insulin-dependent diabetes: an understated complication. *Am J Obstet Gynecol* 1990;163:1217.

37. Usher RH, Allen AC, McLean FH. Risk of respiratory distress syndrome related to gestational age, route of delivery, and maternal diabetes. *Am J Obstet Gynecol* 1971;111:826.

38. Robert MF, Neff RK, Hubbell JP, et al. Association between maternal diabetes and the respiratory distress syndrome in the newborn. *N Engl J Med* 1976;294:357.

39. Modanlou HD, Komatsu G, Dorchester W, et al. Large-for-gestational-age neonates: anthropometric reasons for shoulder dystocia. *Obstet Gynecol* 1982;60:417.

40. Langer O, Berkus M, Huff RW, et al. Shoulder dystocia: should the fetus weighing ≥4000 grams be delivered by cesarean section? *Am J Obstet Gynecol* 1991;165:831.

41. Benedetti TJ, Gabbe SG. Shoulder dystocia: a complication of fetal macrosomia and prolonged second stage of labor with mid-pelvic delivery. *Obstet Gynecol* 1978;52:526.

42. Acker DB, Sachs BP, Friedman EA. Risk factors for shoulder dystocia. *Obstet Gynecol* 1982;60:417.

43. Spellacy WN, Miller S, Winegar A, et al. Macrosomia: maternal characteristics and infant complications. *Obstet Gynecol* 1985;66:762.

44. Acker DB, Gregory KD, Sachs BP, et al. Risk factors for Erb-Duchenne palsy. *Obstet Gynecol* 1988;71:389.

45. Benson CB, Doubilet PM, Saltzman DH. Sonographic determination of fetal weights in diabetic pregnancies. *Am J Obstet Gynecol* 1987;156:441.

46. Miller JM, Brown HL, Khawli OF, et al. Fetal weight estimates in diabetic gravid women. *J Clin Ultrasound* 1988;16:569.

47. Ogata ES, Sabbagha RE, Metzger BE, et al. Serial ultrasonography to assess evolving fetal macrosomia: studies in 23 pregnant diabetic women. *JAMA* 1980;243:2405.

48. Elliott JP, Garite TJ, Freeman RK, et al. Ultrasonic prediction of fetal macrosomia in diabetic patients. *Obstet Gynecol* 1982;60:159.

49. Landon MB, Mintz MC, Gabbe SG. Sonographic evaluation of fetal abdominal growth: predictor of the large-for-gestational-age infant in pregnancies complicated by diabetes mellitus. *Am J Obstet Gynecol* 1989;160:115.

50. Jovanovic-Peterson L, Crues J, Durak E, et al. Magnetic resonance imaging in pregnancies complicated by gestational diabetes predicts infant birth weight ratio and neonatal morbidity. *Am J Perinatol* 1993;10:432.

51. Mintz MC, Landon MB, Gabbe SG, et al. Shoulder soft tissue width as a predictor of macrosomia in diabetic pregnancies. *Am J Perinatol* 1989;6:240.

52. Kitzmiller JL, Mall JC, Gin GD, et al. Measurement of fetal shoulder width with computed tomography in diabetic women. *Obstet Gynecol* 1987;70:941.

53. Levine AB, Lockwood CJ, Brown B, et al. Sonographic diagnosis of the large for gestational age fetus at term: does it make a difference? *Obstet Gynecol* 1992;79:55.

54. Conway DL, Langer O. Elective delivery of infants with macrosomia in diabetic women: reduced shoulder dystocia versus increased cesarean deliveries. *Am J Obstet Gynecol* 1998;178:922–925.

55. Conway DL, Langer O. Letter to the editor reply. *Am J Obstet Gynecol* 1998;179:837.

56. Rouse DJ, Owen J, Goldenberg RL, et al. The effectiveness and costs of elective cesarean delivery for fetal macrosomia diagnosed by ultrasound. *JAMA* 1996;276:1480–1486.

57. Combs CA, Singh NB, Khoury JC. Elective induction versus spontaneous labor after sonographic diagnosis of fetal macrosomia. *Obstet Gynecol* 1993;81:492.

58. Kjos SL, Henry OA, Montoro M, et al. Insulin-requiring diabetes in pregnancy: a randomized trial of active induction of labor and expectant management. *Am J Obstet Gynecol* 1993;169:611.

59. Lurie S, Insler V, Hagay ZJ. Induction of labor at 38 to 39 weeks of gestation reduces the incidence of shoulder dystocia in gestational diabetic patients Class A2. *Am J Perinatol* 1996;13:293–296.

60. Naylor CD, Sermer M, Chen E, et al. Cesarean delivery in relation to birth weight and gestational glucose intolerance: pathophysiology or practice style? *JAMA* 1996;275:1165–1170.

61. Moses RG, Russell KG, Knights SJ, et al. Gestational diabetes: is a higher cesarean section rate inevitable? *Diabetes Care* 2000;23:15–17.

62. Robillard JE, Sessions C, Kennedy RI, et al. Metabolic effects of constant hypertonic glucose infusion in well-oxygenated fetuses. *Am J Obstet Gynecol* 1978;130:199.

63. Phillips AF, Rosenkrantz TS, Raye J. Consequences of perturbations of fetal fuels in ovine pregnancy. *Diabetes* 1985;34[Suppl 2]:32.

64. Myers RE. Brain damage due to asphyxia: mechanism of causation. *J Perinat Med* 1981;9:78.

65. Kenepp NB, Kumar S, Shelley WC, et al. Fetal and neonatal hazards of maternal hydration with 5% dextrose before cesarean section. *Lancet* 1982;1(8282):1150.

66. Philipson EH, Kalhan SC, Riha MM, et al. Effects of maternal glucose infusion on fetal acid-base status in human pregnancy. *Am J Obstet Gynecol* 1987;157:866.

67. Datta S, Kitzmiller JL, Naulty JS, et al. Acid-base status in diabetic mothers and their infants following spinal anesthesia for cesarean section. *Anesth Analg* 1982;61:662.

68. Cordero L Jr, Grunt JA, Anderson GG. Hypertonic glucose infusion in labor. *Am J Obstet Gynecol* 1970;107:560.

69. Light IJ, Keenan WJ, Sutherland JM. Maternal intravenous glucose administration as a cause of hypoglycemia in the infant of the diabetic mother. *Am J Obstet Gynecol* 1972;113:345.

70. Anderson O, Hertel J, Schmolker L, et al. Influence of the maternal plasma glucose concentration at delivery on the risk of hypoglycaemia in infants of insulin-dependent diabetic mothers. *Acta Paediatr Scand* 1985;74:268.

71. Soler NG, Soler SM, Matins JM. Neonatal morbidity among infants of diabetic mothers. *Diabetes Care* 1978;1:340.

72. Grylack LJ, Chu SS, Scanlon JW. Use of intravenous fluids before cesarean section: effects of perinatal glucose, insulin, and sodium homeostasis. *Obstet Gynecol* 1985;63:654.

73. West TET, Lowy C. Control of blood glucose during labour in diabetic women with combined glucose and low-dose insulin infusion. *BMJ* 1977;1:1252.

74. Yeast JD, Porreco RP, Ginsberg HN. The use of continuous insulin infusion for the peripartum management of pregnant diabetic women. *Am J Obstet Gynecol* 1978;131:861.

75. Caplan RH, Pagliara AS, Beguin EA, et al. Constant intravenous

insulin infusion during labor and delivery in diabetes mellitus. *Diabetes Care* 1982;5:6.

76. Bowen DJ, Daykin AP, Nacekievill ML, et al. Insulin dependent diabetic patients during surgery and labour: use of continuous intravenous insulin-glucose-potassium infusions. *Anaesthesia* 1984;39:407.

77. Nattrass M, Alberti KGMM, Dennis KJ, et al. A glucose-controlled insulin infusion system for diabetic women during labour. *BMJ* 1978;2:599.

78. Jovanovic JL, Peterson CM. Insulin and glucose requirements during the first stage of labor in insulin-dependent diabetic women. *Am J Med* 1983;75:607.

79. Golde SH, Good-Anderson B, Montoro M, et al. Insulin requirements during labor: a reappraisal. *Am J Obstet Gynecol* 1982;144:556.

80. Fisher AJ, Huddleston JF. Intrapartum maternal glucose infusion reduces umbilical cord academia. *Am J Obstet Gynecol* 1997;177:765–769.

81. Cerri V, Tarantini M, Schena V, et al. Intravenous glucose infusion in labor does not affect maternal and fetal acid-base balance. *J Matern Fetal Med* 2000;9:204–208.

82. Sameshima H, Kamitomo M, Kajiya S, et al. Ketonemic tendency in gestational diabetic pregnancy in labor. *J Matern Fetal Invest* 1996;6:87–90.

32

POSTPARTUM MANAGEMENT, LACTATION, AND CONTRACEPTION

SIRI L. KJOS
THOMAS A. BUCHANAN

During pregnancy, women with diabetes receive intensive and frequent medical care to closely monitor their glycemic control and fetal well-being. In contrast, during the periods after and in between pregnancies, reproductive health issues are relatively ignored as both physicians and the new mother relax their vigilance. While the new mother focuses her attention on her newborn, the responsibility for her care often shifts from specialists back to generalists. There are also few well-recognized care guidelines and evidence-based studies dealing with postpartum care, lactation, and contraception in diabetic women. However, after delivery, the healthcare team has a unique window of opportunity to educate and encourage the diabetic woman to extend her successfully applied skills and habits from pregnancy for maintaining euglycemia and to work together to develop a reproductive health plan. For women with preexisting diabetes, the primary goal should be continued euglycemia to prevent diabetic sequelae. For women with gestational diabetes, the objectives include the prevention of diabetes by implementing lifestyle changes and outlining a plan of periodic testing for diabetes. Equally vital is education regarding reproductive health and planning or preventing subsequent pregnancies by using effective contraception. The goal of this chapter is to discuss these topics to enable the practitioner to develop an individualized care plan.

THE PUERPERIUM

Glycemic Control

Immediately following delivery there is a loss of placental hormones, creating a temporary window of improved insulin sensitivity. During the first few days after delivery, women with type 1 diabetes generally require little insulin. Glycemic control is often best achieved by utilizing a variable dosing scale based on premeal glucose levels and anticipated carbohydrate intake. Recovery after cesarean delivery, rapid weight loss and establishment of lactation all contribute to glycemic instability. Relaxing glycemic targets (>120–150 mg/dL) helps avoid hypoglycemic episodes. When resuming daily insulin, the initial total dose generally can be calculated at 0.5 to 0.6 U/kg daily. In women using continuous insulin infusion or pump therapy, it is safer to start at half the nonpregnant basal rate and slowly adjust the dosing pattern as a new equilibrium becomes established. Breast-feeding requires >500 additional Kcal/day and can abruptly lower maternal glucose levels. Frequent glycemic assessment will be needed to monitor the changing metabolic status.

Similarly, women with type 2 diabetes will often have adequate glycemic control immediately postpartum without medical therapy. Resuming oral antidiabetic medication may not immediately be necessary. A schedule for monitoring glucose levels at home during the puerperium should be established. Generally, monitoring fasting glucose levels is sufficient. Medical therapy should be initiated when diet and exercise therapy does not lower fasting glucose levels (<130 mg/dL). Oral antidiabetic medications are contraindicated in breast-feeding mothers and insulin therapy should be prescribed when overt fasting hyperglycemia is present, starting at >0.6 U/kg based on postpartum weight.

Working together, the patient's obstetrician or perinatologist and medical physician should establish a care plan for glycemic monitoring, exercise, medical therapy, and follow-up. If a diabetic woman was not regularly receiving diabetic care prior to pregnancy, a referral for continued medical care is necessary.

The majority of women with gestational diabetes will have normal glucose levels immediately postpartum and monitoring with a fasting serum glucose level is sufficient. By definition, gestational diabetes includes women with mild glucose intolerance as well as those with probable asymptomatic diabetes unrecognized prior to pregnancy. Those at highest risk include women with an initial fasting glucose level greater than 126 mg/dL, and those diagnosed during the first trimester, with a history of prior gestational diabetes or impaired glucose tolerance (1). Postpartum diabetes should be excluded prior to hospital discharge with a fasting glucose level of less than 126 mg/dL. Rarely is insulin or antidiabetic medication indicated until an adequate trial of diet, exercise, and weight reduction has been implemented.

BREAST-FEEDING

After delivery all women with type 1, type 2, or gestational diabetes should be reevaluated to assess their caloric intake to achieve or maintain ideal body weight and to meet any additional caloric demands of breast-feeding. Breast-feeding should be encouraged in women with preexisting and gestational diabetes, realizing that breast-feeding may be hampered by postoperative recovery and initial separation of the mother from her newborn (2). Milk volume and biochemical markers for lactation—that is, lactose, citrate, sodium, and total protein—appear to be delayed approximately 24 hours in type 1 diabetic women (3). Breast-feeding within the first 12 hours has been shown to stimulate the onset of lactogenesis in type 1 diabetic women (2). Furthermore, women can be reassured that the quality of breast milk does not appear to be adversely affected in diabetic women who are in good metabolic control and good health (4,5). Successful and continued breast-feeding beyond 6 weeks as well as lower fasting glucose levels have been demonstrated when appropriate caloric intake (30–32 Kcal/kg) is maintained (6). Lower maternal glucose levels and lower diabetes rates during the postpartum period have also been found in breast-feeding women with prior gestational diabetes (7).

POSTPARTUM COUNSELING

Prior to discharge from the hospital, when the concepts and habits to maintain good glucose control are fresh, counseling to encourage continued diabetic care and good health habits should be done. Large controlled clinical trials in both type 1 and type 2 diabetic patients have demonstrated that strict glycemic control significantly reduces the risk of developing or the progression of microvascular complications (8,9). In type 1 patients, strict control achieved by multiple injections or pump therapy nearly as stringent as strategies recommended during pregnancy prevented or reduced the development or progression of retinopathy by 76% and 54%, respectively; prevented or reduced the development of microalbuminuria and albuminuria by 39% and 54%, respectively; and prevented clinical neuropathy by 60% (8). There was no glycemic threshold for an increased risk of complications; rather the risk was a continuum with increasing glucose levels. In type 2 patients treated intensively with mono- or multi-drug therapy

including insulin, sulfonylurea compounds, or metformin, the risk of developing microvascular complications decreased by 25% (9). Again the relationship to glycemia was continuous. With each percentage point reduction in glycosylated hemoglobin, the rate of microvascular complications decreased by 35%, myocardial infarction by 18%, and diabetes-related death by 25% (10–12). A further twofold reduction in cardiovascular risk and microvascular complications was achieved by adequate blood pressure control with either angiotensin-converting enzyme inhibitors or β-blocker therapy (13). Clearly, women with either type 1 or type 2 diabetes should be strongly encouraged to maintain near-normal glucose levels and to schedule frequent and regular visits with their medical provider.

Equally important is counseling women with prior gestational diabetes regarding their greater than 50% risk for developing diabetes within the next 2 decades. Rates vary, generally paralleling the background rate of type 2 diabetes in various ethnic groups, with high-risk groups such as Latina women who have 5-year diabetes rates of 60% (14). After delivery at the 4- to 8-week postpartum visit, all women should undergo testing for diabetes (Table 32-1) by either a fasting plasma glucose level or 2-hour oral glucose tolerance test. The presence of postpartum impaired glucose tolerance (2-hour glucose 140–199 mg/dL) identifies women at greatest risk of developing diabetes (e.g., 16% annual risk in Latina women) (14). While glucose tolerance testing provides greater sensitivity in early detection of diabetes prior to the development of fasting hyperglycemia, it is unclear whether early treatment will improve long-term outcome. The frequency at which diabetes testing should be performed has not clearly been established, and caregivers should consider the presence of other risk factors such as obesity, ethnicity, early gestational age at diagnosis, and fasting hyperglycemia during pregnancy. According to the American Diabetes Association, prior gestational diabetes merits early testing below the screening age of 45 and testing more frequent than every 3 years (1). A fasting plasma glucose level performed in conjunction with an annual physical would satisfy these guidelines. Importantly, women with prior gestational diabetes should be screened

TABLE 32-1. DIAGNOSIS OF DIABETES MELLITUS IN NONPREGNANT ADULTS

Classification	Normal (mg/dL)	Impaired (Prediabetes) (mg/dL)	Diabetes (mg/dL)
Fasting plasma glucose[a]	<110	110–125	≥126
2-hour glucose (OGTT)[b]	<140	141–199	≥200

[a]Measured on plasma in a certified clinical laboratory.
[b]75-g oral glucose tolerance test.
From Report of the Expert Committee on the Diagnosis and Classification of Diabetes Mellitus. *Diabetes Care* 2004;27[Suppl 1]: IS5–S10.

before planning a subsequent pregnancy. Asymptomatic fasting hyperglycemia as low as 120 mg/dL has been associated with a twofold increase in the risk of major malformations in infants (15). Lastly, women should be encouraged to adopt lifestyle changes that decrease insulin resistance. Increased physical activity and weight reduction have been shown to reduce the risk of diabetes by 40% to 60% in adults with impaired glucose tolerance (16,17). Although similar randomized trials have not yet been conducted in women with prior gestational diabetes, they should be encouraged to walk or engage in moderate exercise for 30 minutes a day and achieve ideal body weight. Recently, insulin-sensitizing drug therapy in high-risk women with prior gestational diabetes has been shown to delay or prevent the development of diabetes by a reduction in insulin resistance (18).

CONTRACEPTION

Plans for a future pregnancy and contraceptive counseling should be reviewed at every medical visit during the reproductive life of a woman with diabetes. Today, women have a wide variety of safer, more effective options for controlling fertility. Although more prospective contraceptive studies in diabetic women need to be done, the practitioner can be reassured based on existing studies in diabetic women and extrapolation from several large prospective studies in healthy women. The contraception prescription in women with current diabetes mellitus, type 1 or type 2, or in prediabetic women with previous gestational diabetes mellitus must take into account the metabolic effects and lifestyle demands unique to each woman.

HORMONAL CONTRACEPTION

Hormonal contraceptives can be divided into those that contain only a progestin or those that contain both a progestin and an estrogen. They can further be classified by the route of delivery: orally as a progestin-only or combination oral contraceptive, transdermally as a combination patch or vaginal ring, intramuscularly as a progestin-only or combination formula, and subcutaneously as a progestin-only implant or inside the uterine cavity via a progestin-containing intrauterine device. The metabolic impact is not only influenced by the delivery route but also by the dosage and potency of the various hormonal formulations. Understanding these metabolic effects allows the proper selection to meet not only the demands of diabetes but also the patient's lifestyle. Several methods have recently become available and thus data regarding their effect on carbohydrate metabolism and diabetes are still lacking. Tables 32-2 to 32-4 provide a summary of clinical guidelines for contraceptive prescription in diabetic women.

Oral Contraceptives

Low-Dose Combination Oral Contraceptives

Estrogen doses should be minimized to decrease the risk of thromboembolic complications (19,20) and hypertension (21), both of which are mediated through a dose-dependent increase in clotting factors and angiotensinogen. Current estrogen-containing preparations (≤35 µg) have not been associated with an increased risk of myocardial infarction, pulmonary embolism, or cerebral vascular accidents in healthy women (22,23). However, in hypertensive women, there is an excess risk of myocardial infarction with combination oral contraceptive use (24). Combination preparations should not be prescribed in hypertensive women. In women with pregestational diabetes or previous gestational diabetes, blood pressure should be monitored regularly.

The progestin component of combination oral contraceptives varies widely in its dosage and potency. Levonorgestrel and its "third-generation" derivatives—norgestimate, desogestrel, and gestodene—are approximately 10-fold more potent than norethindrone, and thus are marketed in a lower dose. The progestin component is responsible for the adverse effect on glucose tolerance and increased insulin resistance (25,26). In healthy women, preparations containing either the "third-generation" progestins (27,28), or lower doses of the older progestins—norethindrone (<0.50 mg) and levonorgestrel (triphasic)—have also decreased the androgenic side effects on both carbohydrate and lipid metabolism (29,30). These preparations, except for the triphasic levonorgestrel, actually have beneficial effects on lipid metabolism, reducing LDL cholesterol by 10% to 12% and increasing HDL cholesterol by 5% to 16% (29,31–33).

The net effect of combination oral contraceptives on carbohydrate and lipid metabolism appears to depend on the molar concentration ratio of estrogen to progestin (34). Today's low-dose combination preparations, whether containing the newer progestins or lower doses of the old progestins, tend to have an estrogen-dominant metabolic effect. They have been shown to have minimal effect on glucose tolerance, serum insulin, or glucagon levels in healthy women (27,35–38). The lowest potency/dosage of both estrogen and progestin should always be selected.

Progestin-Only Oral Contraceptive

Commonly referred to as the "mini-pill," the progestin-only oral contraceptive is available in two preparations, norethindrone (0.35 mg) or levonorgestrel (0.075 mg), and both have lower progestin doses than the combination oral contraceptives. These preparations have minimal effect on carbohydrate and lipid metabolism (29). In women who have contraindications to estrogen (e.g., a history of hypertension or thrombosis), progestin-only oral methods may be prescribed.

TABLE 32-2. GUIDELINES FOR ORAL CONTRACEPTIVE USE IN WOMEN WITH PRIOR GESTATIONAL DIABETES AND OVERT DIABETES

	Prior History of Gestational Diabetes Mellitus	Diabetes Mellitus (Type 1 or Type 2)
Oral contraceptives *Combination OC* first choice	Lowest progestin dose/potency and low estrogen dose (20–35 mcg ethynil estradiol)	Lowest progestin dose/potency and low estrogen dose (20–35 mcg ethynil estradiol)
Progestin-only OC	Do not use progestin-only OC while breastfeeding	Acceptable
Care guidelines		
OC refill schedule	4 cycles, 9 cycles, then annual refill (13 cycles)	4 cycles, 5 cycles, 4 cycles …
Clinic Visits	3 months, 9 months then annually	3 months, then every 4 months
Diabetes testing and glucose monitoring	Postpartum fasting plasma glucose or 75 g OGTT; then annual fasting plasma glucose If develop diabetes, initiate diabetes therapy and follow diabetes OC guidelines If develop impaired fasting or glucose tolerance, intensify lifestyle changes	If not self-monitoring glucose: fasting and HbA$_{1c}$ at baseline, then every 4 months If self-monitoring glucose, review glycemic control, HbA$_{1c}$ at baseline, then every 4 months If glycemic control worsens, evaluate compliance with diabetic therapy. Stress importance of contraception while in poor glycemic control.
Cardiovascular screen (fasting lipid profile)	Routine screening every 5 years (wait at least 3 months postpartum)	Annually (wait at least 3 months postpartum)
Monitor	Weight, blood pressure every visit	Weight, blood pressure every visit
Patient education	Continue ADA diet with caloric adjustment to achieve ideal body weight Daily exercise Refer to nutritionist if gain >5 lb/yr	ontinue ADA diet with caloric adjustment to achieve ideal body weight Reinforce importance of planned pregnancy when in health and glycemia is optimized
Desires pregnancy	Test for diabetes: If no diabetes, provide routine preconception counseling If diabetes, initiate preconception care to achieve euglycemia and target weight goals	Preconception care to achieve euglycemia Medical evaluation for pregnancy Discontinue contraception after medical evaluation and HbA$_{1c}$ <7.0%
Complications or change in status	*Test for diabetes* *Diet counseling to achieve ideal body weight, daily cardiovascular exercise*	*Improve glycemic control* *Diet counseling to achieve ideal body weight, daily cardiovascular exercise*
Develop hypertension >130/85 mmHg on 2 occasions	Add low-salt diet Switch to progestin-only OCs or nonhormonal method Assess cardiovascular risk factors: test for diabetes, hyperlipidemia Reassess for medical therapy after lifestyle changes instituted (1–3 months)	Add low-salt diet Switch to progestin-only OCs or nonhormonal method Assess cardiovascular risk factors: test for diabetes, hyperlipidemia Reassess for medical therapy after lifestyle changes instituted (1–3 months)
Develop elevated serum triglycerides ≥500 mg/dL	Add lipid-lowering diet Switch to progestin-only OCs or nonhormonal method or switch to lowest estrogen dose OC (20 mcg ethinyl estradiol) Assess cardiovascular risk factors for medical therapy Evaluate for hypothyroidism	Add lipid-lowering diet Switch to progestin-only OCs or nonhormonal method or switch to lowest estrogen dose OC (20 mcg ethinyl estradiol) Assess cardiovascular risk factors for medical therapy Evaluate for hypothyroidism
Hypercholesteremia	Lipid-lowering diet Switch to lowest dose/potency progestin containing OC (3rd generation progestins) or nonhormonal method Assess cardiovascular risk factors: Reassess for medical therapy based on risk factors and after lifestyle changes	Lipid-lowering diet Switch to lowest dose/potency progestin containing OC (3rd generation progestins) or nonhormonal method Assess cardiovascular risk factors Reassess for medical therapy based on risk factors and after lifestyle changes
Preexisting hypertension	Estrogen-containing methods contraindicated Progestin-only OC or nonhormonal method	Estrogen-containing methods contraindicated Progestin-only OC or nonhormonal method
Multiple risk factors	Recommend nonhormonal contraception	Recommend nonhormonal contraception

ADA, American Diabetes Association; OC, oral contraceptive; OGTT, oral glucose tolerance test.

TABLE 32-3. GUIDELINES FOR NONORALLY ADMINISTERED HORMONAL CONTRACEPTIVE USE IN WOMEN WITH PRIOR GESTATIONAL AND OVERT DIABETES

Methods	Special Notes
Injectables	
Progestin only: Depo-medroxyprogesterone acetate	Injection every 3 months. Associated with increased weight gain, elevated fasting glucose and insulin levels in healthy women
Estradiol cypionate/medroxyprogesterone (Lunelle®)	Monthly injections
Progestin implants	
Etonogestrel	Up to 3 years
(Norplant®)[2]	Up to 5 years, off market in United States
Transdermal combination	
Transdermal patch (OrthoEvra®)	Change patch weekly for 3 weeks, 1 week free
Vaginal ring (NuvaRing®)	3 weeks use, 1 week free

Care Guidelines	Prior History of Gestational Diabetes Mellitus	Diabetes Mellitus (Type 1 or Type 2)
All second-line methods secondary to lack of studies	DMPA: Advisable to avoid progestin-only methods while breastfeeding	
Diabetes testing	Follow same guidelines as for oral contraceptives 3 months, 9 months, then annually	Follow same guidelines as for oral contraceptives every 3–4 months
Clinic visits	Follow same guidelines as for oral contraceptives	Follow same guidelines as for oral contraceptives
Cardiovascular screen	Follow same guidelines as for oral contraceptives	Follow same guidelines as for oral contraceptives
Patient education	Follow same guidelines as for oral contraceptives	Follow same guidelines as for oral contraceptives
Desires pregnancy	Follow same guidelines as for oral contraceptives	Follow same guidelines as for oral contraceptives
Complications or change in status	*Test for diabetes*	Improve glycemic control
	Diet counseling to achieve ideal body weight, daily cardiovascular exercise	Diet counseling to achieve ideal body weight, daily cardiovascular exercise
Develop hypertension, >130/85 mmHg on 2 occasions	Progestin-only methods have not been found to affect blood pressure; increased weight gain may be a cofactor	Progestin-only methods have not been found to affect blood pressure; increased weight gain may be a cofactor
Develop elevated serum triglycerides ≥500 mg/dL	Lipid-lowering diet	Lipid-lowering diet
	Progestin-only methods have minimal effect on triglycerides or lipids in healthy women	Progestin-only methods have minimal effect on triglycerides or lipids in healthy women
Hypercholesteremia	Recommend nonhormonal contraception as first choice	Recommend nonhormonal contraception as first choice
Preexisting hypertension or multiple risk factors	Follow same guidelines as for oral contraceptives	Follow same guidelines as for oral contraceptives

Oral Contraceptive Use and Preexisting Diabetes Mellitus

Several prospective short-term studies in women with type 1 diabetes have found that both low-dose combination (39,40) and progestin-only oral contraceptives (41) have a minimal effect on glycemic control, lipid metabolism, and cardiovascular risk factors (42,43).

Currently there are no long-term prospective studies evaluating the effect of oral contraceptive use on diabetic sequelae associated with type 1 diabetes. Cross-sectional (44) and case control (45) studies have not found any increased risk of or progression of retinopathy, renal disease, or hypertension with past or current use of oral contraceptives after controlling for known risk factors.

To date no studies have examined oral contraceptive use in women with type 2 diabetes. Generally, older and obese women with type 2 diabetes exhibit varying degrees of diminished pancreatic β-cell response to glucose in addition to impaired peripheral insulin action. Glycemic control may be achieved by diet therapy and weight loss alone, or it may require the addition of oral antihyperglycemic medication and/or additional insulin.

In women with type 1 or type 2 diabetes, formulations with the lowest-dose estrogen plus the lowest dose/potency progestin or progestin-only oral contraceptive should be prescribed. Women with type 1 or type 2 diabetes using hormonal contraceptives should be monitored more frequently for changes in weight, blood pressure, and glycemic control (Table 32-2). A shared monitoring schedule to coincide with her routine diabetic monitoring should be established between the patient's gynecologist and internist.

Oral Contraceptive Use in Women with Previous Gestational Diabetes Mellitus

The lowest dose/potency of progestins and estrogens should be prescribed to minimize adverse effects on glucose toler-

TABLE 32-4. GUIDELINES FOR INTRAUTERINE DEVICE USE IN WOMEN WITH PRIOR GESTATIONAL AND OVERT DIABETES

Type	Special Notes
Copper medicated (Cu380T)	Up to 10 years of continuous use
	Safety and low risk of pelvic inflammatory disease supported in large randomized; controlled trials
	Studies support use in type 1 and type 2 diabetic women
	Associated with increased menses
	Metabolically neutral
Progestin medicated (Levonorgestrel IUS)	Up to 5 years or continuous use
	Decreased menstrual flow
	Minimal systemic hormonal effect
	Both devices are excellent for multiparous women at low risk for sexually transmitted disease

Care Guidelines	Prior History of Gestational Diabetes Mellitus	Diabetes Mellitus (Type 1 or Type 2)
Diabetes testing	Follow same guidelines as for oral contraceptives	Annual HbA$_{1c}$ and evaluation of glycemia
Clinic visit	6-week pelvic exam after insertion, annual	6-week pelvic exam after insertion, annual
	Follow same guidelines as for oral contraceptives	Follow same guidelines as for oral contraceptives
Monitoring	Test for sexually transmitted diseases prior to insertion, then annually	Test for sexually transmitted diseases prior to insertion, then annually
	Aggressively treat vaginal infections	Aggressively treat vaginal infections
Cardiovascular screen	Follow same guidelines as for oral contraceptives	Follow same guidelines as for oral contraceptives
Patient education	Teach early signs of symptoms of pelvic inflammatory disease and sexually transmitted diseases	Teach early signs of symptoms of pelvic inflammatory disease and sexually transmitted diseases
Desires pregnancy	Follow same guidelines as for oral contraceptives	Follow same guidelines as for oral contraceptives
Complications or change in status	*Test for diabetes*	*Improve glycemic control*
	Diet counseling to achieve ideal body weight, daily cardiovascular exercise	*Diet counseling to achieve ideal body weight, daily cardiovascular exercise*
Develop hypertension, hypercholesteremia or hypertriglyceridemia	First-choice method because of lack of metabolic effects; no contraindications to continued usage	First-choice method because of lack of metabolic effects; no contraindications to continued usage
Preexisting hypertension or multiple risk factors	First-choice method because of lack of metabolic effects; no contraindications to continued usage	First-choice method because of lack of metabolic effects; no contraindications to continued usage

ance and serum lipids. Short-term prospective studies have not demonstrated any adverse effect of low dose/potency combination oral contraceptives on glucose or lipid metabolism (46–48). A long-term controlled study found that continued use of two combination oral contraceptives, one with monophasic norethindrone (40 μg) and the other with triphasic levonorgestrel (50–125 μg), did not influence the development of diabetes, with virtually identical 3-year cumulative incidence rates for those using oral contraceptives (25.4%) compared to nonhormonal methods (26.5%) (49). However, breast-feeding women using progestin-only oral contraceptives had a threefold increased risk to develop diabetes. Thus, women with prior gestational diabetes may not be ideal candidates for progestin-only oral contraceptives while breast-feeding, but rather should use a nonhormonal method or wait 6 to 8 weeks after the establishment of lactation to begin a low-dose combination method. The use of progestin-only oral contraception in nonlactating women with prior gestational diabetes has not been examined. Regardless of method, all women with prior gestational diabetes should be tested for diabetes every 1 to 3 years (1) (Table 32-2).

Nonorally Administered Hormonal Contraception

The advantage of the nonorally administered hormonal methods is their longer action and thereby improved efficacy, as they do not require daily administration. Recently, several new long-acting hormonal contraceptives have become available, including a monthly combination injection (Lunelle™, estradiol cypionate 5 mg/medroxyprogesterone 25 mg); a weekly transdermal combination patch (OrthoEvra®, norelgestromin 6 mg/ethinyl estradiol 0.75 mg); and a 3-week intravaginal combination ring (NuvaRing®, etonogestrel 125 μg/ethinyl estradiol 15 μg). Currently no studies have addressed their effect on carbohydrate and lipid metabolism. These methods would be expected to have similar profiles to low-dose oral contraceptives. The two long-acting progestins for which data are available for healthy women are intramuscular medroxyprogesterone (DMPA) (Depo-provera®, 150 mg every 3 months) and the subcutaneous levonorgestrel implant (Norplant®). The sustained release of progestin inhibits ovulation, as do oral contraceptives. Similar to the progestin-only oral contraceptives, both do not increase liver globulins, that is, clotting factors or angiotensinogen and have not been associated with increased thromboembolic risk or blood pressure (28,50,51). The effect of these agents on carbohydrate tolerance in prediabetic or diabetic women is not clear. Healthy women using depo-medroxyprogesterone have been found to have a statistically but not clinically significant deterioration in glucose tolerance (50–52), and lower serum triglyceride and HDL cholesterol levels (53,54). As prescribed for contraception, depo-medroxyprogesterone is a relatively high-dose progestin and has been associated with significant annual weight gain. No metabolic studies have been reported in prediabetic or diabetic women. Norplant®, no longer marketed in the United States, has been associated with a statistically but not clinically significant increase in glucose and insulin levels during glucose tolerance testing in healthy users (55). Again, no studies have examined its action in diabetic women.

In the absence of data, none of the long-acting, nonorally administered hormonal methods can be recommended as first-line methods in women with diabetes or prior gestational diabetes. When contraindications to estrogen are present, the progestin-only oral contraceptive in non-breast-feeding women would be preferable. However, in select patients where daily compliance is problematic, such as a sexually active teenager with type 1 diabetes, a highly efficacious long-acting method may be preferable. When prescribing these methods in either diabetic or prediabetic women, periodic glucose and lipid monitoring similar to those recommended for oral contraceptives are recommended (Table 32-3).

INTRAUTERINE DEVICES

Two types of medicated IUDs are currently available (Table 32–4), the copper-medicated IUD (CuT380A), effective for up to 10 years, and the levonorgestrel system (Mirena®), effective for up to 5 years. The copper-medicated IUDs have not been associated with an increased risk of pelvic inflammatory disease after the first 20 days postinsertion. A meta-analysis of 13 randomized clinical trials in over 23,000 users found an overall incidence of 1.6 cases per 1,000 women (56). Pelvic inflammatory disease and tubal infertility have been associated with a risk of exposure to sexually transmitted disease (e.g., multiple sexual partners, history of pelvic inflammatory disease, or nulliparous women below the age of 25) (57–59). Accordingly, the use of IUDs should be restricted to women at low risk of exposure to sexually transmitted disease, such as monogamous, parous women without a history of recent sexually transmitted disease.

No prospective studies examining copper-medicated intrauterine IUDs in diabetic women—either type 1

(60,61) or type 2 (62)—or nonmedicated devices (63–65) have found any evidence for an increased rate of pelvic infection or decreased efficacy with IUD use. However, caution must be exercised. Because the risk of pelvic inflammatory disease is extremely low in the general population, it is highly unlikely that large enough studies in diabetic women can ever be conducted to demonstrate the absence of an increased risk of pelvic infection (62). General gynecological principles should be adhered to for proper patient selection, insertion, and monitoring in diabetic women (Table 32-4). None of the studies involving diabetic women used prophylactic antibiotics with insertion or removal, and it seems unlikely that prophylaxis would add any benefit.

Because the IUDs have little or no systemic effects and are metabolically neutral, they offer an ideal method for diabetic women with vascular disease such as hypertension, retinopathy, or hyperlipidemia.

CONCLUSION

After delivery, a physician has a unique opportunity to extend the intensive patient relationship from pregnancy into a long-term relationship during the patient's remaining reproductive years. Patient education, counseling, and care are key to either preventing unwanted pregnancies or planning future pregnancies in optimal maternal health and glycemic control. Effective contraceptive options are key to achieving both of these goals.

KEY POINTS

- Contraception and pregnancy planning should be reviewed at every medical visit during the reproductive years.
- During the early postpartum period, insulin needs and glucose levels decrease.
- Breast-feeding should be encouraged in women with diabetes and prior gestational diabetes.
- The lowest dose and potency of progestin should be selected to minimize adverse effects on carbohydrate and lipid metabolism.
- Low-dose combination oral contraceptives and progestin-only oral contraceptives can be prescribed for diabetic women with close monitoring.
- Low-dose combination oral contraceptives do not increase the risk of developing diabetes in women with prior gestational diabetes.
- Progestin-only oral contraceptives may not be appropriate in breast-feeding women with prior gestational diabetes.
- The intrauterine device is an excellent contraceptive method for properly selected diabetic women at low risk for sexually transmitted diseases.

■ Nonorally administered hormonal contraceptive methods are second-line contraceptive choices due to the absence of data and experience.

REFERENCES

1. Report of the Expert Committee on the Diagnosis and Classification of Diabetes Mellitus. *Diabetes Care* 2002;25[Suppl 1]: S5–S20.
2. Ferris AM, Neubauer SH, Bendel RB, et al. Perinatal lactation protocol and outcome in mothers with and without insulin-dependent diabetes mellitus. *Am J Clin Nutr* 1993;58:43–48.
3. Hartmann P, Cregan M. Lactogenesis and the effects of insulin-dependent diabetes mellitus and prematurity. *J Nutr* 2001;131: 3016S–3020S.
4. Lammi-Keefe CJ, Jonas CR, Ferris AM, et al. Vitamin E in plasma and milk of lactating women with insulin dependent diabetes mellitus. *J Pediatr Gastroenterol Nutr* 1995;20: 305–309.
5. Neubauer SH, Ferris AM, Chanse CG, et al. Delayed lactogenesis in women with insulin-dependent diabetes mellitus. *Am J Clin Nutr* 1993;58:54–60.
6. Ferris AM, Dalidowitz CK, Ingardia DM, et al. Lactation outcome in insulin-dependent diabetic women. *J Am Diet Assoc* 1988;88:317–322.
7. Kjos SL, Henry O, Lee RM, et al. The effect of lactation on glucose and lipid metabolism in women with recent gestational diabetes. *Obstet Gynecol* 1993;82:451–455.
8. The Diabetes Control and Complications Trial Research Group. The effect of intensive therapy of diabetes on the development of long-term complications in insulin-dependent diabetes mellitus. N Engl J Med 1993;329:977–986.
9. United Kingdom Prospective Diabetes Study 24: a 6-year randomized controlled tial comparing sulfonylurea, insulin and metfromin therapy in patients with newly diagnosed type 2 diabetes that could not be controlled with diet. *Ann Intern Med* 1998;128:165–175.
10. American Diabetes Association. Implications of the United Kingdom Prospective Diabetes Study: reviews/commentaries/ position statement: position statement. *Diabetes Care* 1998; 21:2180–2184.
11. UK Prospective Diabetes Study Group. Intensive blood-glucose control with sulphonylureas or insulin compared to conventional treatment and risk of complications in patients with type 2 diabetes (UKPDS 33). *Lancet* 1998;353:837–853.
12. UK Prospective Diabetes Study Group. Intensive blood-glucose control with metformin of risk of complications in overweight patients with type 2 diabetes (UKPDS 34) *Lancet* 1998;352: 854–865.
13. UK Prospective Diabetes Study Group. Tight blood pressure control and risk of macrovascular and microvascular complications in type 2 diabetes (UKPDS 38). *BMJ* 1998;317:703–713.
14. Kjos SL, Peters RK, Xiang A, et al. Predicting future diabetes in Latino women with gestational diabetes. Utility of early postpartum glucose tolerance testing. *Diabetes* 1995;44:586–591.
15. Schaefer UM, Songster G, Xiang A, et al. Congenital malformations in offspring of women with hyperglycemia first detected during pregnancy. *Am J Obstet Gynecol* 1997:177: 1165–1171.
16. Tuomilehto J, Lindstrom J, Eriksson JG, et al. Prevention of type 2 diabetes mellitus by changes in lifestyle among subjects with impaired glucose tolerance. *N Engl J Med* 2001;344: 1343–1350.
17. Pan XR, Li GW, Hu YH, et al. Effects of diet and exercise in preventing NIDDM in people with impaired glucose tolerance. The Da Qing IGT and Diabetes Study. *Diabetes Care* 1997; 20:537–544.
18. Buchanan TA, Xiang AH, Peters RK, et al. Preservation of pancreatic beta-cell function and prevention of type 2 diabetes by pharmacological treatment of insulin resistance in high-risk Hispanic women. *Diabetes* 2002;51:2796–2803.
19. Further analysis of mortality in oral contraceptive users: Royal Colleage of General Practitioners' oral contraception study. *Lancet* 1981:541–546.
20. Stampfer MJ, Willet WC, Colditz GA, et al. A prospective study of past use of oral contraceptives agents and risk of cardiovascular diseases. *N Engl J Med* 1988;319:1313–1317.
21. Wilson ES, Cruickshank J, McMaster M, et al. A prospective controlled study of the effect on blood pressure of contraceptive preparations containing different types of dosages and progestogen. *Br J Obstet Gynaecol* 1984;91:1254–1260.
22. Porter JB, Hunter JR, Jick H, et al. Oral contraceptives and nonfatal vascular disease. *Obstet Gynecol* 1985;66:1–4.
23. Porter JB, Jick H, Walker AM. Mortality among oral contraceptive users. *Obstet Gynecol* 70:1987,70:29–32.
24. Rosenberg L, Palmer JR, Lesko SM, et al. Oral contraceptive use and the risk of myocardial infarction. *Am J Epidemiol* 1990; 131:1009–1016.
25. Perlman JA, Russell-Briefel R, Ezzati T, et al. Oral glucose tolerance and the potency of contraceptive progestins. *J Chronic Dis* 1985;338:857–864.
26. Spellacy W. Carbohydrate metabolism during treatment with estrogen, progestogen and low-dose oral contraceptive preparations on carbohydrate metabolism. *Am J Obstet Gynecol* 1982; 142:732–734.
27. Bringer J. Norgestimate: a clinical overview of a new progestin. *Am J Obstet Gynecol* 1992;166:1969–1977.
28. Kjaer K, Lebech A-M, Borggaard B, et al. Lipid metabolism and coagulation of two contraceptives: correlation to serum concentrations of levonorgestrel and gestodene. *Contraception* 1989; 40:665–673.
29. Gosland IF, Crook D, Simpson R, et al. The effects of different formulations of oral contraceptive agents on lipid and carbohydrate metabolism. *N Engl J Med* 1990;323:1375–1381.
30. Wahl P, Walden C, Knopp R, et al. Effect of estrogen/progestin potency on lipid/lipoprotein cholesterol. *N Engl J Med* 1981; 308:862.
31. Kjaer K, Lebech A-M, Borggaard B, et al. Lipid metabolism and coagulation of two contraceptives: correlation to serum concentrations of levonorgestrel and gestodene. *Contraception* 1989; 40:665–673.
32. Kloosterboer HJ, van Wayjen RG, van del Ende A. Comparative effects of monophasic desogestrel plus ethinyl estradiol and triphasic levonorgestrel plus ethinylestradiol on lipid metabolism. *Contraception* 1986;34:125.
33. Percival-Smith RK, Morrison BJ, Sizto R, et al. The effect of triphasic and biphasic oral contraceptive preparations on HDL-cholesterol and LDL-cholesterol in young women. *Contraception* 1987;35:179.
34. Kalkhoff RK. Metabolic effects of progesterone. *Am J Obstet Gynecol* 1982;142:735.
35. Loke DFM, Ng CSA, Samsioe G, et al. A comparative study of the effects of a monophasic and a triphasic oral contraceptive containing ethinyl estradiol and levonorgestrel on lipid and lipoprotein metabolism. *Contraception* 1990;42:535–554.
36. Petersen KR, SKouby SO, Pederson RG. Desogestrel and gestodene in oral contraceptives: 12 months' assessment of carbohydrate and lipoprotein metabolism. *Obstet Gynecol* 1991;78: 666–672.

37. Spellacy WN, Buhi WC, Birk SA. Carbohydrate metabolism prospectively studied in women using a low estrogen oral contraceptive for six months. *Contraception* 1979;20:137–148.

38. van der Vange N, Kloosterboer HJ, Haspels AA. Effect of seven low-dose combined oral contraceptive preparations on carbohydrate metabolism. *Am J Obstet Gynecol* 1987;156(4):918–922.

39. Skouby SO, Molsted-Pedersen, Kuhl C, et al. Oral contraceptives in diabetic women: metabolic effects of four compounds with different estrogen/progestogen profiles. *Fertil Steril* 1986; 46:858–64.

40. Skouby SO, Jensen BM, Kuhl C, et. al. Hormonal contraception in diabetic women: acceptability and influence on diabetes control and ovarian function of a nonalkylated estrogen/progestogen compound. *Contraception* 1985;32:23–31.

41. Radberg T, Gustafson A, Skryten A, et al. Oral contraception in diabetic women. Diabetes control, serum and high density lipoprotein lipids during low-dose progestogen, combined oestrogen/progestogen and non-hormonal contraception. *Acta Endocrinol* 1981;98:246–251.

42. Peterson KR, Skouby SO, Sidelmann J, et al. Effects of contraceptive steroids on cardeovascular risk factors in women with insulin-dependent diabetes mellitus. *Am J Obstet Gynecol* 1994; 171:400–405.

43. Petersen KR, Skouby SO, Sidelmann J, et al. Assessment of endotherlial function during oral contraception in women with insulin-dependent diabetes mellitus. *Metabol Clin Exp* 1994;43: 1379–1383.

44. Klein BEK, Moss SE, Klein R. Oral contraceptives in women with diabetes;*Diabetes Care* 1990;13:895–898.

45. Garg SK, Chase HP, Marshal G, et al. Oral contraceptives and renal and retinal complications in young women with insulin-dependent diabetes mellitus. *JAMA* 1994;271:1099–1102.

46. Skouby SO, Anderson O, Saurbrey N, et al. Oral contraception and insulin sensitivity: in vivo assessment in normal women and women with previous gestational diabetes. *J Clin Endocrinol Metab* 1987;64:519–523.

47. Skouby SO, Kuhl C, Molsted-Pedersen, et al. Triphasic oral contraception: Metabolic effects in normal women and those with previous gestational diabetes. *Am J Obstet Gynecol* 1985, 153:495–500.

48. Kjos SL, Shoupe D, Douyan S, et al. Effect of low-dose oral contraceptives on carbohydrate and lipid metabolism in women with recent gestational diabetes: results of a controlled, randomized, prospective study. *Am J Obstet Gynecol* 1990;163:1822–1827.

49. Kjos SL, Peters RK, Xiang A, et al. Contraception and the risk of type 2 diabetes mellitus in Latina women with prior gestational diabetes mellitus. *JAMA* 1998;280:533–538.

50. Toppozada HK, Koetswang S, Aimakhu VE, et al. World Health Organization Expanded Programme of Research, Development and Research Training in Human Reproduction Task Force on Long-Acting Systemic Agents for the Regulation of Fertility. Multinational comparative clinical evaluation of two long-acting injectable contraceptive steroids: northisterone enanthate and medroxyprogesterone acetate. Final report. *Contraception* 1983;28:1–20.

51. World Health Organization Expanded Programme of Research, Development and Research Training in Human Reproduction Task Force on Long-Acting Systemic Agents for the Regulation of Fertility. Multinational comparative clinical evaluation of two long-acting injectable contraceptive steroids: norethisterone enanthate and medroxyprogesterone acetate. Final report. *Contraception* 1983;28:1–20.

52. Liew DFM, Ng CSA, Yong YM, et al. Long-term effects of depo-provera on carbohydrate and lipid metabolism. *Contraception* 1985;31:51–59.

53. Deslypere JP, Thiery N, Vermeulen A. Effect of long-term hormonal contraception in plasma lipids. *Contraception* 1985;31: 633.

54. Fahmy K, Khairy M, Allam G, et al. Effect of depo-medorxyprogesterone acetate on coagulation factors and serum lipids in Egyptian women. *Contraception* 1991;44:431–434.

55. Konje JC, Otolorin EO, Ladipo AO. The effect of continuous subdermal levonorgestrel (Norplant) on carbohydrate metabolism. *Am J Obstet Gynecol* 1992;166:15–19.

56. Farley TMM, Rosenberg MJ, Rowe PJ, et al. Intrauterine devices and pelvic inflammatory disease: an international perspective. *Lancet* 1992;339:785–788.

57. Lee NC, Rubin GL, Ory HW, et al. Type of intrauterine device and the risk of pelvic inflammatory disease. *Obstet Gynecol* 1983;62:1–6.

58. Lee NC, Rubin GL. The intrauterine device and pelvic inflammatory disease revisited: New results form the Women's Health Study. *Obstet Gynecol* 1988;72:1–6.

59. Cramer DW, Schiff I, Schoenbaum SC, et al. Tubal infertility and the intrauterine device. *N Engl J Med* 1985;312:941–947.

60. Skouby SO, Molsted-Pedersen L, Kosonen A. Consequences of intrauterine contraception in diabetic women. *Fertil Steril* 1984;42:568–572.

61. Kimmerle R, Weiss R, Berger M, et al. Effectiveness, safety and acceptablilty of a copper intrauterine device (CU Safe 300) in type I diabetic women. *Diabetes Care* 1993;16:1227–1230.

62. Kjos SL, Ballagh SA, La Cour M, et al. The copper T380A intrauterine device in women with type II diabetes mellitus. *Obstet Gynecol* 1994;84:1006–1009.

63. Gosen C, Steel J, Ross A, et al. Intrauterine contraception in diabetic women. *Lancet* 1982;1:530–535.

64. Lawless M, Vessey MP. Intrauterine device use by diabetic women. *Br J Fam Plann* 1982;7:110–111.

65. Wiese J. Intrauterine contraception in diabetic women. *Fertil Steril* 1977;28:422–425.

33

NEONATAL OUTCOME AND CARE

WILLIAM OH

Basic research and clinical investigations have generated new information during the past 3 to 4 decades that enhanced our understanding of morbidities encountered in infants of diabetic mothers (IDMs). Although optimal medical and obstetric management can reduce the incidence and severity of the perinatal complications in the newborn (1), such an ideal situation is difficult to achieve because of many factors, including lack of patient compliance. Therefore, it is important that clinicians who provide care to these infants understand the pathophysiology, diagnosis, and management of the various neonatal complications.

Figure 33-1 shows our current understanding of the pathophysiology of the various neonatal complications. When maternal diabetes goes undetected or if good control of diabetes is not achieved, maternal episodic hyperglycemia leads to fetal episodic hyperglycemia, possible enhanced placental transfer of amino acids, and increased availability of fatty acids to the fetus. The episodic fetal hyperglycemia is due to the direct relationship between the maternal and fetal blood glucose concentrations (2). In mammalian species, the fetus derives most of its caloric and metabolic needs from glucose, transported from the mother across the placenta by facilitated diffusion (3–5). It is also known that the endocrine system in the fetus is autonomous so that fetal hyperglycemia is associated with fetal hyperinsulinism and with hypertrophy and hyperplasia of the β-cells of the fetal pancreas. There is strong evidence suggesting that insulin serves as the primary growth factor for the fetus (6,7). Therefore, in the presence of an abundant supply of substrate, the hyperinsulinemic state accelerates fetal growth, leading to macrosomia. The presence of fetal macrosomia, in turn, sets the stage for shoulder dystocia and an increased risk for birth injury and asphyxia during delivery. It has been shown that, in the nonhuman primate, chronic fetal hyperinsulinemia is associated with fetal macrosomia and selective organomegaly (8). In spite of increasing understanding of the pathophysiology and the management of diabetes during pregnancy, the incidence of macrosomia in IDMs appears to be unchanged (9). Cardiomyopathy has been observed, and

the morphologic cardiac abnormality has been correlated with functional changes. Using the echocardiographic technique, Walther et al. (10) demonstrated an inverse correlation between the thickness of the atrioventricular septum and cardiac output in IDMs. The functional aberration is transient and is usually resolved at the end of the first week of life. However, in some cases, the condition may be severe causing compromise in cardiac function and serious consequences (11). Another important clinical aspect of fetal macrosomia in IDMs is its relationship to obesity in later childhood. Vohr et al. (12) demonstrated a direct correlation between neonatal macrosomia and obesity during the adolescent period. This report was based on a group of infants born during the 1960s with a relatively small sample size. However, more recently, Vohr et al. (13) prospectively tracked a cohort of children born to mothers with gestational diabetes through 4 to 7 years of age. They found that those who were macrosomic infants born to mothers with gestational diabetes have a significantly higher height, weight, and body mass index when compared with appropriately matched controls. A similar relationship has been shown in an animal model in which neonatal macrosomia, a result of mild maternal hyperglycemia, was associated with obesity in young adult rats (14–16). Furthermore, the obesity was also associated with glucose intolerance (17,18), which raised the potential association between maternal diabetes, fetal macrosomia, later childhood obesity, and the development of glucose intolerance (type 2 diabetes) in young obese adult subjects.

Fetal hyperinsulinemia appears to be an important factor in the pathogenesis of the respiratory distress syndrome (RDS), which occurs more frequently in IDMs than it does in the offspring of nondiabetic mothers at similar gestational ages (19). Several studies have shown the inhibitory effect of insulin on surfactant production, which provides an experimental rationale for the increased risk of RDS (20–23). Furthermore, fetal hyperinsulinemia is also the mechanism involved in the increased risk of neonatal hypoglycemia in these infants (24).

The mechanism for the increased risks of polycythemia and hyperviscosity in IDMs is less well defined. It has been

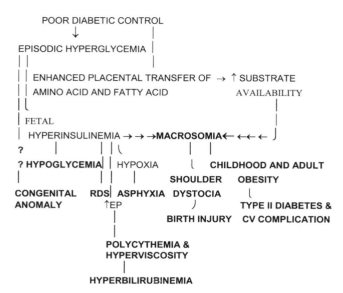

POOR DIABETIC CONTROL

EPISODIC HYPERGLYCEMIA

ENHANCED PLACENTAL TRANSFER OF → ↑ SUBSTRATE
AMINO ACID AND FATTY ACID   AVAILABILITY

FETAL
HYPERINSULINEMIA → → →MACROSOMIA← ←← ←

? HYPOGLYCEMIA   HYPOXIA   CHILDHOOD AND ADULT
                        SHOULDER   OBESITY

CONGENITAL   RDS ASPHYXIA DYSTOCIA
ANOMALY   ↑EP   TYPE II DIABETES &
                   BIRTH INJURY   CV COMPLICATION

POLYCYTHEMIA &
HYPERVISCOSITY

HYPERBILIRUBINEMIA

FIGURE 33-1. Proposed pathogenesis of neonatal complications in infants of diabetic mothers. Ep, erythropoietin; RDS, respiratory distress syndrome.

shown that fetal hypoxia stimulates fetal erythropoietin production (25), resulting in an increase in erythropoiesis. Such an association has been documented in infants of diabetic mothers as shown by higher cord serum erythropoietin levels among IDMs when compared with control subjects (Fig. 33-2), although the precise relationship to

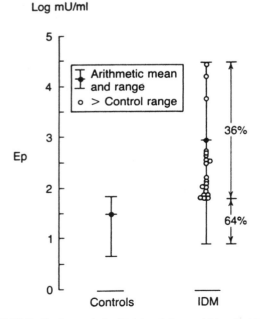

Log mU/ml

FIGURE 33-2. Erythropoietin (Ep) levels in cord blood of infants of diabetic mothers (IDM). (From Widness JA, Susa JB, Garcia JF, et al. Increased erythropoiesis and elevated erythropoietin in infants born to diabetic mothers and in hyperinsulinemic rhesus fetuses. *J Clin Invest* 1981;67:637. With permission.)

polycythemia and hyperviscosity was not shown in this report. Using the chronic sheep preparation as an animal model, Stonestreet et al. (26) showed that fetal hypersulinemia is associated with increased fetal blood volume. Furthermore, the increased blood volume may also be explained on the basis of acute fetal distress and asphyxia. It has been shown previously that in the presence of an intact umbilical circulation, fetal distress or birth asphyxia is associated with "intrauterine placental transfusion," that is, with an increase in fetal blood volume derived from the placenta (27–29). After the acute expansion of blood volume at birth, a process of adjustment between circulating blood volume and circulatory capacity occurs that results in hemoconcentration. Under these circumstances, some infants may have polycythemia and hyperviscosity on the basis of high hematocrit and blood viscosity (30).

The precise mechanism for the increased incidence of neonatal hypocalcemia in IDMs is unknown but presumed to be related to some degree of hypoparathyroid state (31). There are other complicating factors such as prematurity, birth asphyxia, and respiratory distress with acidosis that may adversely influence calcium and phosphate homeostasis during the first few days of life leading to hypocalcemia.

The higher incidence of hyperbilirubinemia in the offspring of diabetic mothers probably stems from the higher red blood cell volumes and an increased amount of "physiologic hemolysis" during the first days of life. There is currently no other mechanism that accounts for the higher incidence of hyperbilirubinemia in IDMs except for an interesting observation that, in breast-fed IDMs, there is an increased level of β-glucuronidase in the mother's serum and breast milk (32). This raised the possibility of a greater degree of enterohepatic shunt leading to higher serum bilirubin levels in the infants.

Other neonatal conditions for which the pathogenesis remains to be elucidated in the offspring of diabetic women include the increased incidence of congenital malformations. However, it has been suggested that hyperglycemia may contribute to an imbalance in fetal milieu during embryogenesis (33), and that good control of diabetes during preconception and first trimester of pregnancy significantly reduces the incidence of congenital anomalies in infants (34). Other studies have not confirmed this association (35).

It is clear from this overview of the pathogenesis of perinatal morbidity that if obstetric and medical management of diabetes is optimal during pregnancy and if the maternal blood glucose level is controlled throughout the period of gestation, the opportunity exists to reduce the perinatal morbidity and mortality in IDMs. The decreased perinatal mortality rate that has been achieved in association with careful maternal metabolic control is clear evidence that maternal management and diabetic status play an important role in the neonatal outcome (36–39).

Clinical abnormalities seen in IDMs usually occur in a predictable temporal sequence. There is a usual age of onset

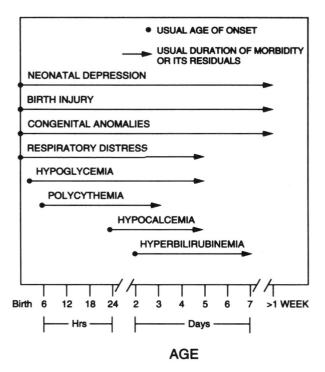

FIGURE 33-3. Usual age of onset and duration of neonatal complications in infants of diabetic mothers.

and duration for each of the common complications. As shown in Figure 33-3, neonatal depression, birth injury, and most congenital malformations are readily detectable at the time of birth by a careful assessment and physical examination of the infant in the delivery room. Respiratory distress, irrespective of cause, usually occurs soon after birth and characteristically persists for 3 to 5 days unless complications such as pneumothorax or pneumonitis prolong its course. Hypoglycemia usually develops during the first 3 hours of life, with a peak incidence at 1.5 hours after birth. In most instances, the hypoglycemia is transient in nature, and the blood glucose concentration returns to normal by 3 to 5 days of age. Because hemoconcentration occurs maximally at 3 to 6 hours of life, polycythemia and hyperviscosity usually present at this age. Therefore, a capillary hematocrit should be performed at that time as a screen of these complications. With treatment (by partial exchange transfusion), polycythemia and hyperviscosity generally occur around 24 hours and resolve at 3 to 5 days of age. Hyperbilirubinemia generally occurs around the second or third day and lasts through the first week of life.

NEONATAL MACROSOMIA

Neonatal macrosomia or large for gestational age is a situation in which the birth weight exceeds the 90th percentile of the mean at a certain gestational age. Lindsay et al. (40)

recently studied the secular changes (4 decades since 1965) in the incidence of macrosomia in indigenous infants of gestational diabetic mothers. They found that the incidence is higher prior to 1965 but it has not changed very much since then despite improvement in the management of diabetes. This observation suggests that clinicians should continue to have a high awareness and surveillance of this morbidity in caring for IDMs. The condition can be identified at birth and, with the aid of fetal ultrasonography, is often identified before birth (41). The recognition of fetal macrosomia is important because it is often associated with a number of perinatal morbidities, including birth injury (often related to shoulder dystocia), cardiomyopathy, neonatal depression, respiratory distress, hypoglycemia, and hyperbilirubinemia. In regard to birth injury, a recent study showed that mode of delivery (vaginal or cesarean delivery) does not affect the incidence of birth injury in macrosomic infant (42,43). Thus, in evaluating infants at birth, signs of birth injury should be considered irrespective of mode of delivery.

The relationship between neonatal macrosomia and obesity in later childhood has been discussed previously. In a recent study involving relatively small sample size, Plagemann et al. (44) showed that breast-feeding IDM led to a higher body weight and impaired glucose tolerance at age 2 years (44). This observation requires further confirmation. It is clear that there is inadequate evidence to allow for more definitive anticipatory guidance in regard to the role of the dietary and nutritional management of the infants to prevent the development of childhood obesity and glucose intolerance.

NEONATAL DEPRESSION

Depression at birth is a common problem in IDMs if the control of diabetes during pregnancy is not optimal. As indicated in the previous discussion, fetal hyperinsulinemia is associated with fetal hypoxemia, probably on the basis of increased fetal metabolic demand that is not adequately compensated by increased placental oxygen transfer. Fetal status should be monitored, and if fetal distress or nonreassuring biophysical profile is present, appropriate timing of delivery is essential to avoid fetal demise or significant fetal distress that eventually may lead to neonatal depression. If fetal macrosomia is present, there is an increased likelihood that dystocia and difficulty during delivery may contribute to the occurrence of neonatal depression. Thus, with a history of poor control of the diabetic condition, evidence of compromise in fetal status and fetal macrosomia, the possibility of neonatal depression should be strongly suspected and anticipated. Facilities, equipment, and personnel for neonatal resuscitation should be available during delivery of this infant for the prompt management of neonatal depression. Management consists of maneuvers to prevent cold injury, maintain airway, and establish cardiopulmonary function. After vaginal delivery, the umbilical cord is best clamped at 15 to 30 seconds after the delivery of the fetal body to avoid excessive placental transfusion.

SHOULDER DYSTOCIA AND BIRTH INJURY

The presence of fetal macrosomia in a mother with a small- to normal-sized pelvis may result in prolonged labor, shoulder dystocia, and birth injury. In a population-based study, it was shown that shoulder dystocia is associated with increased risk of birth injury, neonatal depression, and length of hospital stay (45). Some of the more common birth injuries in the macrosomic IDMs include Erb's palsy, fractured clavicle, facial paralysis, phrenic nerve injury, and intracranial hemorrhage in the form of intracerebral bleeding or subdural hematomas.

The symptoms and signs of these various types of birth injury are well known to most clinicians. An awareness of such potential complications makes them readily identifiable soon after birth. For instance, facial palsies and Erb's paralysis can be detected by physical examination; phrenic nerve injuries are recognizable by the presence of respiratory distress together with asymmetric excursions of the hemidiaphragms during respiration. A fractured clavicle can be suspected by a lack of movement in the upper extremity on the side of injury and confirmed by radiologic examination. The diagnosis of intracranial hemorrhage is sometimes more difficult to make. A history of a difficult delivery in a macrosomic infant with birth depression in whom marked hypo- or hyper-tonia later develops associated with seizures should alert the clinician to the potential for intracranial pathologic conditions, including intracranial hemorrhage. When intracranial hemorrhage is suspected, cranial ultrasonography may be useful in arriving at this diagnosis. Computed tomographic scan can also identify other forms of intracranial hemorrhage. The medical management of these birth injuries is largely supportive because many of the injuries resolve over time. However, it should be pointed out that bleeding disorders in the intracranial areas might have longer-lasting effects and sequelae.

CONGENITAL MALFORMATIONS

The incidence of congenital malformations in infants of diabetic mothers is significantly higher than in the normal newborn population. The precise reason for this increased risk of congenital anomalies is unknown, but it has been theorized that a "disturbed homeostatic state" during embryonic development resulting from poor maternal metabolic control, may serve as a contributing factor (33,46). The two most common groups of malformations encountered are those that involve the cardiovascular and skeletal systems, especially of the neural axis. Among the cardiovascular anomalies, transposition of the great vessels, atrial and ventricular septal defects, endocardial cushion defects, and coarctation of the aorta are most common. Caudal regression syndrome (caudal dysplasia, sacral agenesis), although rare, is commonly associated with IDMs (47). Clinicians attending the IDM immediately after birth should be alert to these possibilities, and careful physical examination is essential for prompt detection. In cases in which strong possibilities for congenital malformations are present, diagnostic studies, including chest radiography, ultrasonography with echocardiography, and electrocardiography, should be done in cases where cardiac anomalies are suspected.

Another condition recently shown to be associated with IDM is DiGeorge anomaly (48,49). The presence of a cardiac anomaly such as coarctation of the aorta should prompt a diagnostic study for this condition.

RESPIRATORY DISTRESS

Respiratory distress is also a common neonatal morbidity in the IDM. Causes of respiratory distress are not limited to RDS or hyaline membrane disease. "Retained lung fluid" secondary to cesarean birth (50), transient tachypnea of the newborn (51), hypoglycemia, and polycythemia and hyperviscosity (52) are some of the other known etiologic factors for respiratory difficulties in the newborn period. However, these metabolic and transitional causes of respiratory distress are usually benign and transient in nature and most often resolve by the second or third day of life. RDS, on the other hand, can be more severe, particularly for those infants who are born prematurely. In the prenatal assessment of fetal lung maturity in the diabetic pregnancy, the conventional value of a mature amniotic fluid lecithin/sphingomyelin (L/S) ratio of 2:1 may often be misleading. In IDMs, an amniotic fluid L/S ratio of 2.0 may not necessarily indicate lung maturity because many of these fetuses lack phosphatidyl glycerol (PG), one of the phospholipids in the lung that serves an important role in maintaining alveolar stability (53). In normal pregnancy, fetal lung maturation is associated with a parallel increase in the various specific phospholipids (e.g., lecithin, PG, phosphatidylinositol, and phosphatidylserine). In IDMs, for yet unknown reasons, there is delay in maturation of the PG synthesis system so that one may have a relatively normal L/S ratio with lack of PG, which leads to the development of RDS. Some investigators recommend using a L/S ratio of greater than 3.0 as an indicator of lung maturity for the IDM (54). The most direct method to assess the level of lung maturity is to analyze both L/S ratio and PG. In many perinatal centers, the latter is routinely done in the clinical laboratory.

The management of IDMs with respiratory distress is supportive and is similar to the management of an infant with respiratory difficulty who is not an IDM. The use of surfactant replacement therapy has been shown to be effective in the treatment of infants with RDS (55). However, its efficacy has not been shown specifically in IDMs. Nevertheless, because the pathophysiology of RDS is similar in IDMs and non-IDMs, there is no reason to suspect that surfactant replacement therapy will not be equally effective in the treatment of RIDS in IDMs. Thus, in the presence of prematurity, evidence of fetal lung immaturity, and classic clinical signs of RDS (tachypnea, chest retraction, and typical radiologic findings of homogeneous granular infiltrate and air bronchogram), the use of surfactant therapy in IDMs is appropriate.

NEONATAL HYPOGLYCEMIA

This is the most common and well-defined metabolic complication in IDMs. The major contributing factor to the hypoglycemia is hyperinsulinemia. The hyperinsulinemia leads to suppressed endogenous glucose production (56) by decreased gluconeogenesis and glycogenolysis that occurs despite an abundance of glycogen stores in the liver and myocardium (57). Hyperinsulinemia also leads to increased peripheral glucose utilization.

The peak age of onset for hypoglycemia is at 1 to 1.5 hours of life. The frequency of this complication is greater in infants born to insulin-dependent mothers (58), in infants whose mother's diabetic status is poor during pregnancy, and in those whose mothers receive large doses of intravenous glucose during labor or at the time of delivery (59). Many IDMs with hypoglycemia may be asymptomatic particularly in the first few hours of life because of availability of alternative substrates for cerebral metabolism. In those who are symptomatic, the manifestations may be nonspecific in nature. These manifestations include jitteriness, twitching of the extremities, apnea, tachypnea, and in extreme cases, seizures. The condition is confirmed by a determination of the plasma glucose level, and hypoglycemia is diagnosed when the plasma glucose concentration is less than 35 mg/dL in a term infant or less than 25 mg/dL in a preterm infant. All IDMs should have semiquantitative assessment of blood for glucose level at hourly intervals during the first 3 hours of life. If the screening results show a blood glucose level below 40 mg/dL, a plasma sample for glucose determination by the clinical laboratory should be obtained. The infant may be given an intravenous glucose infusion at a dose of 5 to 6 mg/kg/min, preferably through a peripheral vein. If the plasma glucose concentration confirms the diagnosis of hypoglycemia, the glucose infusion can be continued. If the plasma glucose value is normal and a repeat determination at 6 to 12 hours of age reveals normal results, the intravenous glucose can be discontinued if the infant's condition is stable and oral feeding is feasible. Otherwise, the intravenous glucose infusion can be continued and gradually tapered as the infant's ability to feed orally increases.

Early initiation of oral feeding (4 to 6 hours of age) is useful for earlier establishment of glucose and calcium homeostasis. However, it should not be done if the infant's cardiopulmonary status is unstable. The risk of aspiration is real and should be avoided.

The use of bolus hypertonic glucose infusion should be avoided because the hyperinsulinemia induced by a rise in plasma glucose level may lead to rebound hypoglycemia (59). In infants with symptomatic hypoglycemia, a bolus dose of 200 mg/kg of 10% glucose may be given intravenously over a 5- to 10-minute period followed by continuous infusion with a dose that is indicated above. It has been shown that this method of glucose therapy provides a prompt increase in serum glucose concentration with no risk of a rebound hypoglycemia (60). The use of glucagon during the first 6 hours of life has been proposed at a dosage of 300 μg per kilogram of body weight (61); however, there appears to be no real advantage to glucagon infusion. Glucagon administration may produce a brisk rise in blood glucose concentration so that the risk of rebound hypoglycemia is present and may constitute a potential disadvantage for this therapeutic regimen. Epinephrine has also been used in the treatment of neonatal hypoglycemia on the basis of its glycogenolytic property; however, it has the disadvantages of producing untoward cardiovascular side effects and lactic acidosis in an infant who may already have cardiopulmonary difficulties.

In most instances, neonatal hypoglycemia in the IDM is a transient condition; however, occasionally, the hypoglycemia may persist beyond the second or third day of life and may require the use of additional therapeutic agents, such as glucocorticoids. If hypoglycemia still persists despite adequate therapy, other underlying causes, such as β-cell hyperplasia (nesidioblastosis) or islet cell tumor, should be entertained. The prognosis for IDMs with hypoglycemia is usually favorable, and when the problem is treated promptly, neurologic sequelae are minimal.

POLYCYTHEMIA AND HYPERVISCOSITY

The precise incidence of polycythemia complicating the newborn period in IDMs has not been well documented. However, it is accepted by most clinicians that this morbidity is fairly common. The mechanism is based on a hypoxia-induced increase in erythropoietin and subsequent enhanced erythropoiesis. If fetal hypoxia occurs during labor, there is an increased possibility of placental transfusion and hypervolemia. In the presence of hypervolemia and subsequent hemoconcentration, a rise in hematocrit ensues. Those infants with a venous hematocrit value that exceeds two standard deviations (65%) are considered to be polycythemic.

Clinically, infants with polycythemia appear plethoric; the condition is often initially suspected on the basis of the newborn's appearance, and is confirmed by hematocrit determination. In this respect, it is important to consider the site of blood sampling because it is well known that capillary blood generally yields higher hemoglobin and hematocrit values than venous blood (62,63). Figure 33-4 shows the correlation between capillary and venous hematocrits in term newborn infants during the first 24 hours of life. It may be used as a guide for estimating the venous hematocrit when a capillary blood measurement is used for screening purposes. It should be emphasized, however, that to establish the diagnosis of polycythemia definitively, a venous blood hematocrit is required.

It has been shown that the venous blood hematocrit and blood viscosity are directly related (64). When the hematocrit value exceeds 65%, the viscosity of the blood exceeds two standard deviations above the normal range, hence constituting a state of hyperviscosity (64). Although it is ideal to diagnose hyperviscosity by actual measurement of blood viscosity (65), many clinical laboratories may not have this service available. Thus, it is often assumed that an infant who evidences polycythemia also has hyperviscosity. It

should be emphasized that this is not an entirely valid assumption.

The clinical manifestations of polycythemia are nonspecific in nature, mainly because the symptom complex may be attributed to one or more of the following factors:

Effects of perinatal asphyxia. Because perinatal asphyxia is often the primary event that leads to polycythemia and hyperviscosity, many polycythemic infants may have signs and symptoms relating to perinatal asphyxia

Effects of transudation of fluid from intravascular into extravascular (interstitial) space of various organs. The clearest evidence for this is the association of less efficient respiratory functions in infants with large placental transfusions. In the presence of acute expansion of blood volume, the newborn compensates by hemoconcentration, resulting in transvascular movement of fluid into interstitial tissue, including that of the lung (66). The latter gives rise to low lung compliance and tachypnea.

Effect of hyperviscosity itself. This in turn may impede the velocity of blood flow in various microcirculatory beds.

The treatment of polycythemia or hyperviscosity consists of a partial exchange transfusion during which blood is

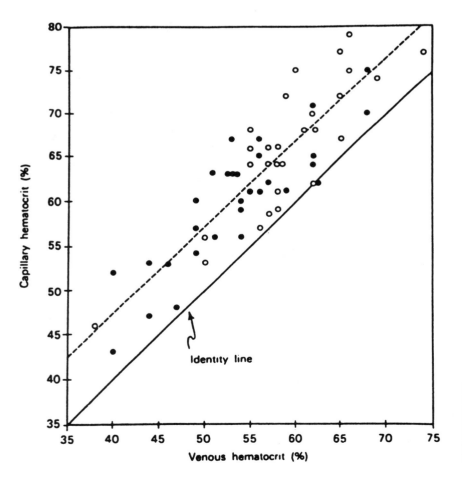

FIGURE 33-4. Correlation between capillary and venous hematocrit in normal newborn infants during first 6 hours of life. (Adapted from Oh W, Lind J. Venous and capillary hematocrit in newborn infants and placental transfusion. *Acta Paediatr Scand* 1966;56:197. With permission.)

removed and replaced by an equal quantity of a volume expander such as plasma, plasmanate, or salt-poor albumin. The formula used is as follows:

Blood volume to be exchanged = Observed hematocrit − Desired hematocrit × Blood volume (90 ml) × Body weight (kg) / Observed hematocrit

Three to 4 hours after the procedure is done, it is prudent to reexamine the neonate's venous blood hematocrit and viscosity. If both parameters are still abnormally high, a repeat partial exchange transfusion may be indicated.

NEONATAL HYPOCALCEMIA

Neonatal hypocalcemia is the other common metabolic problem encountered in IDMs. The mechanism of hypocalcemia in this group of infants remains unclear. It has been suggested that a state of relative maternal hyperparathyroidism plays a role (67). Although it has been shown that an elevated immunoreactive parathyrin level exists in normal pregnant women (68), the precise parathyroid status in the diabetic mother has not been well defined. Another predisposing factor that could contribute to the increased incidence of hypocalcemia in IDMs is the greater frequency of respiratory distress with acidosis. It has been shown that during a state of acidosis, calcium ions may diffuse from the intracellular into the extracellular fluid, including the intravascular compartment, hence producing an apparently normal serum calcium level. When acidosis is corrected either by treatment or through spontaneous recovery from the respiratory difficulties, the calcium ion reequilibrates into the intracellular fluid compartment, resulting in an abrupt fall in the serum calcium concentration. This may account for the fact that the peak age of onset of hypocalcemia is in the second or third day of life, coinciding with the usual recovery phase from respiratory distress (69). Hypoglucagonemia has also been implicated as another possible contributing factor to the hypocalcemia in IDMs (70). However, this hypothesis has yet to be confirmed. An association between hypomagnesemia and hypocalcemia has been proposed. However, magnesium administration to prevent hypocalcemia was shown to be ineffective in a randomized trial (71). Although IDMs with hypocalcemia may be asymptomatic, their hypocalcemia is usually treated with calcium supplementation administered either intravenously or orally. There are no follow-up data established in regard to the potential harmful or innocuous nature of asymptomatic hypocalcemia during the neonatal period.

HYPERBILIRUBINEMIA

It is well established that hyperbilirubinemia is a common problem in IDMs. It was previously believed that this was due mainly to prematurity because, in the past, most IDMs were delivered before term. It has been shown, however, that even when matched for gestational age, the IDM has a higher risk of hyperbilirubinemia than does the normal infant (72). The reason for this increased risk of jaundice is not known, but polycythemia with an associated increase in the breakdown of red blood cells is considered to be a contributing factor. In spite of this higher incidence of jaundice, the risk of kernicterus in IDMs does not appear to be unusually high. One hypothesis invoked to explain this observation in IDMs makes use of their suppressed lipolytic response to adrenergic-provoking stimuli such as hypothermia, hypoglycemia, stress, and so forth. It has been speculated that the increased risk of kernicterus in infants with hyperbilirubinemia under situations of stress results from a reduction of bilirubin-binding capacity secondary to epinephrine-induced elevations in free fatty acids (73,74). Therefore, reducing the lipolytic response to stress in IDMs may provide a degree of protection from kernicterus because the bilirubin-binding capacity will not be altered even in the presence of stress. More recently, there is increasing evidence that the risk of kernicterus in full-term infants with nonhemolytic jaundice is extremely low (75). This observation is probably applicable to IDMs because most of these infants are full term and the hyperbilirubinemia is due to causes other than hemolysis. It should be pointed out that with early hospital discharge of term and near-term newborns and less concern among clinicians about the possibility of bilirubin encephalopathy in nonhemolytic jaundice, there is a surge in the incidence of bilirubin encephalopathy in this group of infants (76). There is a need of heighten vigilance in this regard to prevent the occurrence of bilirubin encephalopath in term or nearterm infants with nonhemolytic jaundice.

The management of hyperbilirubinemia in IDMs is similar to that in other infants. The main goal is to prevent kernicterus by keeping the serum bilirubin levels within the range of safety by phototherapy and, if needed, by exchange transfusion.

LONG-TERM NEURODEVELOPMENTAL OUTCOME

There is a paucity of data regarding long-term neurodevelopmental outcomes of IDMs. A study by Hadden et al. (77) showed no difference in mental, emotional, and academic performance of a group of children born to mothers with type 1 diabetes when compared with a well-matched group of children born to nondiabetic mothers (77). Similar results were found by Persson and Gentz (78) who followed a group of children born to diabetic mothers at 5 years of age. Another study (79) evaluating a group of children born to mothers with diabetic nephropathy showed a significantly high incidence of neonatal morbidities and psychomotor retardation (7 of 35 children followed at 5 years of age). Using event-related potential, Nelson et al. (80) demonstrated a deficit in recognition memory in a group of IDM at 6 months of age. It is likely that the long-term neurodevelopmental outcome of IDMs will depend on a variety of factors such as types of diabetes, incidence and severity of perinatal complications, socio economic status etc. Future studies are clearly needed to address this important issue.

REFERENCES

1. Brecher A, Tharakan TM, Williams AA, et al. Perinatal mortality in diabetic patients undergoing antepartum fetal evaluation: a case control study. *Matern Fetal Neonatal Med* 2002;122: 423–427.
2. Spellacy WN, Goetz FC, Greenberg BZ, et al. The human placental gradient for plasma insulin and blood glucose. *Am J Obstet Gynecol* 1964;90:753.
3. Widdas WF. Transport mechanisms in the foetus. *Br Med Bull* 1961;17:107.
4. Karvonen MJ, Raiha N. Permeability of placenta of the guinea pig to glucose and fructose. *Acta Physiol Scand* 1954;31:194.
5. Battaglia FC, Hellegers AE, Heiler CG, et al. Glucose concentration gradients across the maternal surface, the placenta, and the amnion of the rhesus monkey (*Macaca mulatta*). *Am J Obstet Gynecol* 1964;88:22.
6. Hill DE. Effect of insulin on fetal growth. *Semin Perinatol* 1978;2:319.
7. Picon L. Effect of insulin on growth and biochemical composition of the rat fetus. *Endocrinology* 1967;81:1419.
8. Susa JB, Schwartz R. Effects of hyperinsulinemia in the primate fetus. *Diabetes* 1985;34:36.
9. Hod M, Merlob P, Friedman S, et al. Gestational diabetes mellitus. A survey of perinatal complications in the 1980s. *Diabetes* 1991;40[Suppl 2]:74.
10. Walther FJ, Siassi B, King J, et al. Cardiac output in infants to insulin-dependent diabetic mothers. *J Pediatr* 1985;107:109.
11. Sardesai MG, Gray AA, Mcgrath MM, et al. Fatal hypertrophic cardiomyopathy in the fetus of a woman with diabetes. *Obstet Gynecol* 2001;98:925–927.
12. Vohr BR, Lipsitt LP, Oh W. Somatic growth of children of diabetic mothers with reference to birth size. *J Pediatr* 1980;97: 196.
13. Vohr BR, McGarvey ST, Tucker R. Effects of maternal gestational diabetes on offspring adiposity at 4–7 years of age. *Diabetes Care* 1999;22:1284–1291.
14. Gelardi NL, Cha CJ, Oh W. Evaluation of insulin sensitivity in obese offspring of diabetic rats by hyperinsulinemic-euglycemic clamp. *Pediatr Res* 1991;30:40.
15. Cha C-JM, Gelardi NL, Oh W. Accelerated growth and abnormal glucose tolerance in young female rats exposed to fetal hyperinsulinemia. *Pediatr Res* 1987;21:83.
16. Gelardi NL, Cha C-JM, Oh W. Glucose metabolism in adipocytes of obese offsprings of mild hyperglycemic rats. *Pediatr Res* 1990;28:641.
17. Oh W, Cha C-JM, Gelardi NL. The cross generation effect of neonatal macrosomia in rat pups of streptozotocin induced diabetes. *Pediatr Res* 1991;29:606.
18. Vileisis RA, Oh W. Enhanced fatty acid synthesis in hyperinsulinemic rat fetuses. *J Nutr* 1983;113:246.
19. Robert MF, Neff RK, Hubbel JP, et al. Association between diabetes and the respiratory distress syndrome in the newborn. *N Engl J Med* 1976;294:357.
20. Smith BT, Giroud LJP, Robert MF, et al. Insulin antagonism of cortisol action on lecithin synthesis by cultured fetal lung cells. *J Pediatr* 1975;87:953.
21. Neufeld ND, Servanian A, Barrett CT, et al. Inhibition of surfactant production by insulin in fetal rabbit lung slices. *Pediatr Res* 1979;13:752.
22. Epstein MF, Farrell PM, Chez RA. Fetal lung lecithin metabolism in the glucose-intolerant rhesus monkey pregnancy. *Pediatrics* 1976;57:722.
23. Morishige WK, Uetake CA, Greenwood FC, et al. Pulmonary insulin responsivity: in vivo effects of insulin binding to lung receptors in normal rats. *Endocrinology* 1977;100:1710.
24. Cornblath M, Schwartz R. *Disorders of carbohydrate metabolism in infancy*, 2nd ed. Philadelphia: WB Saunders, 1976.
25. Widness JA, Susa JB, Garcia JF, et al. Increased erythropoiesis and elevated erythropoietin in infants born to diabetic mothers and in hyperinsulinemic rhesus fetuses. *J Clin Invest* 1981;67: 637.
26. Stonestreet BS, Goldstein M, Oh W, et al. Effects of prolonged hyperinsulinemia on erythropoiesis in fetal sheep. *Am J Physiol* 1989;257:81199.
27. Oh W, Omori K, Emmanouilides GC, et al. Placenta to lamb fetus transfusion in utero during acute hypoxia. *Am J Obstet Gynecol* 1975;122:316.
28. Flod NE, Ackerman BD. Perinatal asphyxia and residual placental blood volume. *Acta Paediatr Scand* 1971;60:433.
29. Yao AC, Wist A, Lind J. The blood volume of the newborn infant delivered by caesarean section. *Acta Paediatr Scand* 1967; 56:585.
30. Oh W. Neonatal polycythemia and hyperviscosity. *Pediatr Clin North Am* 1986;33:523.
31. Cruikshank DP, Pitkin RM, Verner MW, et al. Calcium metabolism in diabetic mother, fetus and newborn. *Am J Obstet Gynecol* 1983;145:1010–1016.
32. Sirota L, Ferrera M, Lerer N, et al. Beta glucuronidase and hyperbilirubinemia in breast fed infants of diabetic mothers. *Arch Dis Child* 1992;67:760.
33. Kappy MS, Clarke DW, Boyd FT Jr, et al. Insulin is a growth promoter of the developing brain: possible implications for the infant of diabetic mother. *Compr Ther* 1986;12:57–61.
34. Jovanovic L, Druzin M, Peterson CM. Effects of euglycemia on the outcome of pregnancy in insulin-dependent diabetic women as compared with normal control subjects. *Am J Med* 1980;68:105.
35. Gabbe SG, Mestman JH, Freeman RK, et al. Management and outcome of pregnancy in diabetes mellitus, classes B to R. *Am J Obstet Gynecol* 1977;129:723.
36. Karlsson K, Kjellmer I. The outcome of diabetic pregnancies in relation to the mother's blood sugar level. *Am J Obstet Gynecol* 1972;112:213.
37. Coustan DR, Berkowitz RI, Hobbins JC. Tight metabolic control of overt diabetes in pregnancy. *Am J Med* 1980;68:845.
38. Cousins L. Congenital anomalies among infants of diabetic mothers. *Am J Obstet Gynecol* 1983;147:333.
39. Fuhrmann K, Reiher H, Semmler K, et al. The effect of intensified conventional insulin therapy before and during pregnancy on the malformation rate in offspring of diabetic mothers. *Exp Clin Endocrinol* 1984;83:173.
40. Lindsay RS, Hanson RL, Bennett PH, et al. Secular trends in birth weight, BMI, and diabetes in the offspring of diabetic mothers. *Diabetes Care* 2000;23:1249–1254.
41. Miller JM, Brown HL, Khawli OF, et al. Fetal weight estimates in diabetic gravid women. *J Clin Ultrasound* 1988;16:569–572.

42. Kolderup LB, Laros RB, Musci TJ. Incidence of persistent birth injury in macrosomic infants: association with mode of delivery. *Am J Obstet Gynecol* 1998;178:195.

43. Conway DL. Delivery of the macrosomic infant: cesarean section versus vaginal delivery. *Semin Perinatol* 2002;26:225–231.

44. Plagemann A, Harder T, Franke K, et al. Long-term impact of neonatal breast-feeding on body weight and glucose tolerance in children of diabetic mothers. *Diabetes Care* 2002;25:16–22.

45. Nesbitt TS, Gilbert WM, Herrchen. Shoulder dystocia and associated risk factors with macrosomic infants born in California. *Am J Obstet Gynecol* 1999;179:476–480.

46. Kylinen P, Stenman U-H, Kesaniemi-Kuokkanen T, et al. Risk of minor and major fetal malformations in diabetics with high haemoglobin A$_{1c}$ values in early pregnancy. *BMJ* 1984;289:345.

47. Welch JP, Aterman K. The syndrome of caudal dysplasia: a review, including etiologic considerations and evidence of heterogeneity. *Pediatr Pathol* 1984;2:313–327.

48. Novak RW, Robinson HB. Coincident DiGeorge anomaly and renal agenesis and its relation to maternal diabetes *Am J Med Genet* 1995;55:513–514.

49. Wilson TA, Blethen SL, Vallone A, et al. DiGeorge anomaly with renal agenesis in infants of mothers with diabetes *Am J Med Genet* 1993;47:1078–1082.

50. Milner AD, Saunders RA, Hopkin IE. Effects of delivery by caesarean section on lung mechanics and lung volume in the human neonate. *Arch Dis Child* 1978;53:545.

51. Avery ME, Gatewood OB, Brumley G. Transient tachypnea of the newborn: possible delayed resorption of fluid at birth. *Am J Dis Child* 1966;1111:380.

52. Richardson DW. Transient tachypnea of the newborn associated with hypervolemia. *CAMJ* 1970;103:70.

53. Meuller-Beubach E, Caritis SN, Edelstone DI, et al. Lecithin/sphingomyelin ratio in amniotic fluid and its value for the prediction of neonatal respiratory distress syndrome in pregnant diabetic women. *Am J Obstet Gynecol* 1978;130:28.

54. Cunningham MD, Desai NS, Thompson SA, et al. Amniotic fluid phosphatidylglycerol in diabetic pregnancies. *Am J Obstet Gynecol* 1978;131:719.

55. Mercier CE, Soil RF. Clinical trials of natural surfactant extract in respiratory distress syndrome. *Clin Perinatol* 1993;20:711.

56. Kalhan SC, Savin SM, Adam PAJ. Attenuated glucose production rate in newborn infants of insulin dependent diabetic mothers. *N Engl J Med* 1977;296:375.

57. Cardell BS. The infants of diabetic mothers. A morphological study. *Br J Obstet Gynaecol* 1953;60:834.

58. Chen CH, Adam PAJ, Laskowski DE, et al. The plasma free fatty acid composition and blood glucose of normal and diabetic pregnant women and of their newborns. *Pediatrics* 1965;36:843.

59. Haworth JC, Dilling LA, Vidyasagar D. Hypoglycemia in infants of diabetic mothers. Effect of epinephrine therapy. *J Pediatr* 1973;82:94.

60. Lilien LD, Pildes RS, Sainivasan G, et al. Treatment of neonatal hypoglycemia with minibolus and intravenous glucose infusion. *J Pediatr* 1980;97:295.

61. Wu PYK, Modanlou H, Karelitz M. Effect of glucagon on blood glucose homeostasis in infants of diabetic mothers. *Acta Paediatr Scand* 1975;64:441.

62. Oettinger L Jr, Mills WB. Simultaneous capillary and venous hemoglobin determinations in the newborn infant. *J Pediatr* 1949;35:362.

63. Oh W, Lind J. Venous and capillary hematocrit in newborn infants and placental transfusion. *Acta Paediatr Scand* 1966;56:197.

64. Gross GP, Hathaway EW, Boyle E. Hyperviscosity in the neonate. *J Pediatr* 1973;82:2004.

65. Wells RE, Denton R, Merrill EW. Measurement of viscosity of biologic fluids by cone-plate viscometer. *J Lab Clin Med* 1961;57:646.

66. Oh W, Wallgren G, Hanson JS, et al. The effects of placental transfusion on respiratory mechanics of normal term newborn infants. *Pediatrics* 1967;40:6.

67. Tsang RC, Kleinman LL, Sutherland JM, et al. Hypocalcemia in infants of diabetic mothers. *J Pediatr* 1972;80:384.

68. Cushard WG Jr, Creditor MA, Canterbury JM, et al. Physiologic hyperparathyroidism in pregnancy. *J Clin Endocrinol Metab* 1972;34:767.

69. Tsang RC, Oh W. Neonatal hypocalcemia in low birth weights infants. *Pediatrics* 1970;45:773.

70. Bergman L. Studies on early neonatal hypocalcemia. *Acta Pediatr Scand* 1974;[Suppl 248]:5.

71. Mehta KC, Kalkwarf HO, Mimouni F, et al. Randomized trial of magnesium administered to prevent hypocalcemia in infants of diabetic mothers. *J Perinatol* 1998;18:352.

72. Taylor PM, Wofson JH, Bright NH, et al. Hyperbilirubinemia in infants of diabetic mothers. *Biol Neonate* 1963;5:289.

73. Schiff D, Aranda JV, Chan G, et al. Metabolic effects of exchange transfusions. I. Effect of citrated and heparinized blood on glucose, nonesterified fatty acids, 2-(4-hyporoxy-benzeneazo)benzoic acid binding, and insulin. *J Pediatr* 1971;78:603.

74. Brown AK. Variations in the management of neonatal hyperbilirubinemia. Impact of our understanding of fetal and neonatal physiology. *Birth Defects* 1970;6:22.

75. Newman TB, Maisels MJ. Evaluation and treatment of jaundice in the term newborn: a kinder, gentler approach. *Pediatrics* 1992;89:809.

76. Brown AK, Johnson KL. Loss of concern about jaundice and the reemergence of kernicterus in full term infants in the era of managed care. In: Fanaroff A, Klaus M, eds. *Yearbook of neonatal perinatal medicine.* St. Louis, MO: 1996:xvii–xxviii.

77. Hadden DR, Byrne E, Trotter I, et al. Physical and psychological health of children of type I (insulin dependent) diabetic mothers. *Diabetologia* 1984;26:250–254.

78. Persson B, Gentz J. Follow up of children of insulin-dependent and gestational diabetic mothers. Neuropsychological outcome *Acta Paediatr Scand* 1984;73:349–358.

79. Kimmerle R, Zass RP, Cupisti S, et al. Pregnancies in women with diabetic nephropathy. Long-term outcome for mother and child. *Diabetologia* 1995;38:227–235.

80. Nelson CA, Wewerka S, Thomas KM, et al. Neurocognitive sequelae of infants of diabetic mothers. *Behav Neurosci* 2000;114:950–956.

LONG-TERM OUTCOME OF INFANTS OF DIABETIC MOTHERS

DANA DABELEA
PETER H. BENNETT
DAVID J. PETTITT

The infant of the diabetic mother eventually becomes the child, the adolescent, and the adult offspring of the diabetic mother. The legacy of the diabetic intrauterine environment, acquired during gestation, cannot be ignored. It is widely recognized now that the effects of the diabetic intrauterine environment extend beyond those apparent at birth (1,2).

Long-term changes that may result from development in a diabetic intrauterine environment can be grouped into three categories:

Anthropometric. Growth rates are excessive during the latter stages of gestation and also during childhood and early adulthood, resulting in development of *macrosomia*, *overweight*, and *obesity*.

Metabolic. Glucose homeostasis is deregulated and glucose tolerance is more likely to be abnormal than that observed in offspring of nondiabetic women, resulting in development of *impaired glucose tolerance* and *diabetes mellitus*.

Neurologic and psychological. Offspring of such pregnancies often have neurologic deficits, which are usually relatively minor, but which may be significant; psychological and intellectual development may also be affected (3).

ANTHROPOMETRIC CONSEQUENCES

As is evident from standardized growth curves, there is great variation in height and weight among growing children, even within a family. For a given height, the heaviest "normal" individuals may weigh almost twice as much as the lightest. Consequently, factors that affect growth may need to exert a very large effect to cause an otherwise average child to meet some arbitrary definition for obesity, and a child genetically destined to be near the low end of the scale may end up well above the mean without appearing abnormal. Thus, individual children within the normal range for

height and weight may be very different from what they would have been without an antecedent insult. Nevertheless, the offspring born after the onset of diabetes in their mothers are, on average, heavier for their height than the offspring of nondiabetic women.

In 1953, White et al. (4) at the Joslin Clinic reported "superiority of growth in stature and weight" in the offspring of women with diabetes. Subsequently, reports from many parts of the world confirmed and documented excessive growth in the offspring of diabetic women after the first few years of life. In 1959, Hagbard et al. (5) reported the stature of 239 children with an average age of 5 years who were born after the onset of their mothers' diabetes and 68 with an average age of 16 years who were born before the onset of the diabetes. Since the two groups of children were of quite different ages, each was compared with age-appropriate normal data. Those born after the mothers developed diabetes were significantly shorter and significantly heavier than normal for their age, while those born before showed no deviation from normal. Cummins and Norrish (6) reported the heights and weights for 50 offspring of diabetic women aged 4 to 13 years. The children tended to be tall and heavy, with 68% being above the 50th percentile for height and 70% being above the 50th percentile for weight. In addition, there was an excess of children with excessive weight for height—32 percent were above the 90th percentile for weight while only 20% were over the 90th percentile for height. Vohr et al. (7) examined 7-year-old offspring of diabetic and control women and found that the offspring of diabetic women were significantly more likely to have a weight for height index above 1.2. Most of these heavy children had been large for gestational age at birth, probably indicating poor diabetes control during pregnancy. Gerline et al. (8) examined heights and weights of infants of diabetic mothers at birth, during the first year of life and annually up to age 4 years. They found that by age 4 years, the children of mothers with poor metabolic control during pregnancy were significantly heavier and had a significantly higher weight for height ratio than the off-spring of women who had been well controlled. The difference was smallest at 6 months and increased progressively during the 4 years of observation. Interestingly, the differences were larger in the female offspring.

Many of these studies, however, have not specified the type of diabetes present in the mothers, have used mixed samples, or had limited the data to offspring of women with either gestational or type 2 diabetes. Recently, Weiss et al. (9) studied the offspring of women with type 1 diabetes and reported that they have a significantly higher body mass index and symmetry index than the offspring of control women. These measures of obesity were significantly correlated with fasting and post-load blood glucose.

THE PIMA INDIAN STUDY

Some of the most informative data come from the longitudinal follow-up study of offspring of diabetic Pima Indian women (10–15). Data from Pima Indians who were examined at birth and then followed repeatedly during childhood (10) reveal that the offspring of diabetic women are larger for gestational age at birth (Fig. 34-1). They are heavier for height at every age before age 20 years than are the offspring of prediabetic women (i.e., women who developed diabetes only after the child was born) or of nondiabetic women (i.e., women who never developed diabetes). Relative weight in these latter two groups is similar. Up to 20 years of age, offspring of diabetic mothers had a much higher prevalence of severe obesity, defined as ≥140% of the standard weight for height, than those of prediabetic and nondiabetic mothers (16) (Fig. 34-2). Afterward, the differences between the offspring of diabetic women and the other two groups are much less, reflecting the high rates of obesity that are present in this population regardless of the intrauterine environment (17). However, at older ages, the obese offspring of the diabetic women are likely to have been obese much longer than the obese offspring of the

nondiabetic and prediabetic women. As duration of obesity is a risk factor for diabetes in this population (18), this will inevitably increase the risk for developing diabetes in the offspring of diabetic women.

From the data presented in Fig. 34-1, it is not clear whether the diabetic intrauterine environment leads to childhood obesity directly or simply results in a large birth weight that in turn leads to the childhood obesity. However, from Fig. 34-3 it can be seen that even the normal birth-weight offspring of the diabetic women were heavier by age 5 to 9, 10 to 14, and 15 to 19 years than the offspring of nondiabetic and prediabetic women (12).

Evidence that excess growth experienced by offspring of diabetic mothers is not due to genetic factors alone comes from several reports. First, obesity is no more common in the offspring of women in whom diabetes developed after delivery than in those of nondiabetic women (10,19). Second, obesity in the offspring of diabetic women cannot be accounted for by maternal obesity (10,12). Third, the excessive growth seen in the offspring of diabetic mothers is not found in offspring of diabetic fathers in either the Joslin Clinic or the Pima Indians series (2). The comparison between offspring of diabetic and prediabetic women is an attempt to control for any potential confounding effect of a genetic predisposition to obesity and diabetes and the relationship between exposure to the maternal diabetic environment and obesity and diabetes in the offspring. However, the ideal way to approach this question is to examine sibling pairs in which one sibling is born before and one is born after the onset of their mother's diabetes (20) (Fig. 34-4). The mean body mass index in the 62 Pima Indian non-diabetic siblings born after the onset of the mother's diabetes (i.e., offspring of diabetic women) was significantly higher than among the 121 nondiabetic siblings who were not exposed to diabetes *in utero* (i.e., born before the onset of the mother's diabetes).

There is some suggestion that relative hyperinsulinemia may be a precursor to childhood obesity. At age 5 to 9 years, Pima offspring of women with diabetes or impaired glucose

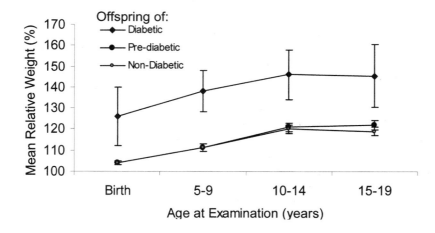

FIGURE 34-1. Mean relative weight in offspring by age and timing of mother's diabetes. (From Pettitt DJ, Knowler WC, Bennett PH, et al. Obesity in offspring of diabetic Pima Indian women despite normal birthweight. *Diabetes Care* 1987;10:76–80, with permission from the American Diabetes Association.)

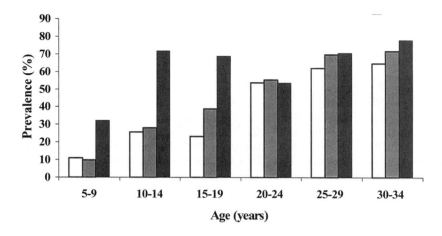

FIGURE 34-2. Prevalence of severe obesity (weight ≥140% of standard weight for height) in offspring by age and timing of mother's diabetes. *Open bars*, offspring of nondiabetic mothers; *hatched bars*, offspring of prediabetic mothers; *solid bars*, offspring of diabetic mothers. (From Dabelea, D, Knowler WC, et al. Effect of diabetes in pregnancy on offspring: follow-up research in the Pima Indians. *J Matern Fetal Med* 2000;9:83–88, with permission.)

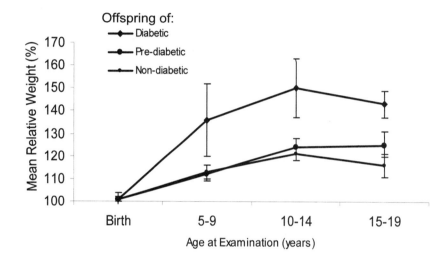

FIGURE 34-3. Mean relative weight in offspring by age and timing of mother's diabetes in normal birth-weight offspring (birth weight = 90% to 109% of the median weight for gestational age). (From Pettitt DJ, Baird HR, Aleck KA, et al. Excessive obesity in offspring of Pima Indian women with diabetes during pregnancy. *N Engl J Med* 1983;308:242–245, with permission.)

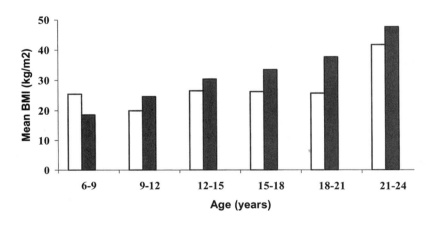

FIGURE 34-4. Mean BMI by age in siblings exposed (*solid bars*) and not exposed (*open bars*) to diabetic intrauterine environment. (From Dabelea D, Hanson RL, Lindsay RS, et al. Intrauterine exposure to diabetes conveys risks for type 2 diabetes and obesity: a study of discordant sibships. *Diabetes* 2000;49: 2208–2211, with permission from the American Diabetes Association.)

tolerance during pregnancy have higher fasting insulin concentrations than the offspring of women with better glucose tolerance during pregnancy (14). Although this difference is not apparent at older ages, a follow-up of children and adolescents found that the fasting insulin concentration at ages 5 to 9 years was significantly correlated with the rate of weight gain during follow-up (21).

DIABETES IN PREGNANCY CENTER AT NORTHWESTERN UNIVERSITY IN CHICAGO

The Diabetes in Pregnancy Center has conducted the other longitudinal study reporting excessive growth in the offspring of women with diabetes during pregnancy (22,23). In this study, amniotic fluid insulin was collected at 32 to 38 weeks of gestation. At the age of 6 years there was a significant association between the amniotic fluid insulin and childhood obesity, as estimated by the symmetry index. The insulin concentrations in 6-year-old children who had a symmetry index of less than 1.0 (86.1 pmol/l) or between 1.0 and 1.2 (69.9 pmol/l) were half the level measured in the more obese children who had a symmetry index greater than 1.2 (140.5 pmol/l; $p < 0.05$ for each comparison). Children who were born during this study were examined at birth, at age 6 months, and annually to age 8 years (23). The symmetry index, which was normal at 1 year of age, deviated increasingly from the norm during follow-up so that by age 8 the mean symmetry index was almost 1.3, that is, the children were on average 30% heavier than expected for their height.

This study has added unique insight into the cause of excessive growth and provided confirming evidence that the diabetic intrauterine environment plays an important role. Amniotic fluid insulin is of fetal origin and is directly correlated with the amount of fetal insulin produced. Fetal insulin, in turn, is correlated with the amount of circulating glucose, which is of maternal origin and is directly correlated with mother's diabetes control. Thus, this study demonstrates a direct correlation between an objective measure of the diabetic intrauterine environment and the degree of obesity in children and adolescents (24).

Although the two studies detailed above are of very different design and the patient populations are quite different, the effect on the offspring is similar. The age-specific symmetry index in offspring from both studies (14,23) is presented in Fig. 34-5 (25). From birth to age 8 years, the offspring of diabetic women from the Diabetes in Pregnancy Center in Chicago, while less obese than the Pima offspring of diabetic women, have a steady increase in their mean symmetry index that parallels that seen in the Pimas. After age 5 years, the symmetry index in the Chicago group exceeds that in the Pima children whose mothers did not have diabetes during pregnancy.

METABOLIC CONSEQUENCES

Standard methods for the diagnosis of diabetes and impaired glucose tolerance require the ingestion of a specific carbohydrate load in asymptomatic individuals (26). Such tests have seldom been performed in clinical practice in children, even for those whose parents have diabetes. Surveys of populations and selected groups, however, have allowed an evaluation of glucose tolerance in children in relation to their mothers' glucose tolerance or diabetes status at the time of pregnancy.

Reports from several countries document high rates of diabetes in the offspring of diabetic parents. Many studies of the familial occurrence of diabetes, however, have not distinguished between parental diabetes that developed before and after the pregnancy. Consequently, children who are the products of metabolically normal pregnancies but whose mothers eventually developed diabetes are often included along with those whose mothers had diabetes during pregnancy. Nevertheless, studies that look at the offspring of women with diabetes generally find higher rates of diabetes than in those of nondiabetic women (27–32).

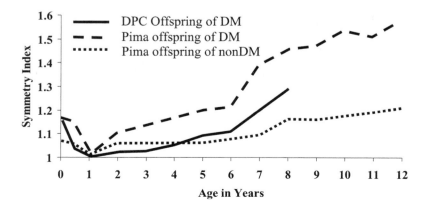

FIGURE 34-5. Symmetry index by age in offspring of diabetic mothers from the Diabetes in Pregnancy Center (*Silverman ODM*), offspring of diabetic Pima Indians (*Pima ODM*), and offspring of nondiabetic Pima Indians (*Pima ONDM*). (Pettitt DJ. Summary and comment on: Silverman BL, Rizzo T, Green OC, et al. Long-term prospective evaluation of offspring of diabetic mothers. *Diabetes* 1991;40[Suppl 2]:121–25. *Diabetes Spectrum* 1992;5:39–40, with permission from the American Diabetes Association.

The rates of diabetes in the offspring of diabetic women range from 5 to 225 times the rates in the general population. Although it is generally accepted that diabetes is familial, transmission does not follow simple Mendelian patterns and appears to be influenced by both the environment and the genetic background (33–35). How much of the excess diabetes in the offspring of diabetic mothers can be attributed to heredity and how much can be attributed to the environment is not clear, but there is evidence that the intrauterine environment plays an important role. Inheritance of a "diabetes gene" or genes may be necessary in order for the environment to have an effect.

Only in longitudinal studies that follow women who have normal glucose tolerance during pregnancy but who subsequently develop diabetes, can women be identified in retrospect as prediabetic. The term "prediabetes" as used here includes women with normal glucose tolerance who subsequently develop diabetes. It is not to be confused with the more recently popularized use of "prediabetes" to describe individuals with impaired fasting glucose and/or impaired glucose tolerance. Comparison of the offspring of prediabetic pregnancies with those of diabetic pregnancies identifies differences that are likely to be the effect of the diabetic intrauterine environment. High rates of diabetes have generally been found in the offspring of diabetic fathers, but it has been recognized for some time, as stated by White (19) in 1960, that the "maternal environment, prenatal, natal and post natal, had a greater influence upon the second generation than did the diabetic paternal environment." The maternal environment has also been shown to have a much greater effect on the occurrence of diabetes in Pima Indians (32), as described below.

The Pima Indians of Arizona have the highest reported prevalence and incidence of type 2 diabetes compared to any other group in the world. Individuals at particular risk include those whose parents developed diabetes at an early age (36) and those whose mothers had diabetes during pregnancy (32). For more than 30 years, Pima Indian women have had oral glucose tolerance tests during pregnancy as well as on a routine basis approximately every 2 years. Consequently, extensive maternal diabetes information based on glucose data rather than on assessment of family history of diabetes is available for offspring of women who had diabetes before or during pregnancy (diabetic mothers), as well as of those who developed diabetes only after pregnancy (prediabetic mothers) or who remained nondiabetic.

The prevalence of type 2 diabetes by age group in offspring of diabetic, prediabetic, and nondiabetic mothers (16) is presented in Fig. 34-6. By age 5 to 9 and 10 to 14 years, diabetes was present almost exclusively among the offspring of diabetic women. In all age groups, there was significantly more diabetes in the offspring of diabetic women than in those of prediabetic and nondiabetic women, and there were much smaller differences in diabetes prevalence between offspring of prediabetic and nondiabetic women. The small differences may be due to differences in the genes inherited from the mothers, while the large difference in prevalence between the offspring of diabetic and prediabetic mothers, which have presumably inherited the same genes from their mothers, is the consequence of exposure to the diabetic intrauterine environment (37). These differences persisted after adjusting for presence of diabetes in the father, age at onset of diabetes in either parent, and obesity in the offspring. A significant correlation between the 2-hour post-load plasma glucose in 15- to 24-year-old Pima women and their mother's 2-hour glucose during pregnancy has also been described (14), suggesting that the diabetic intrauterine environment has effects on the offspring's plasma glucose above and beyond genetic or other familial effects.

The congenital effects acquired during development *in utero* may be confounded by genetic factors. Women who develop diabetes at an early age might carry more susceptibility genes than those who develop the disease later in life and, therefore, they might transmit greater genetic suscep-

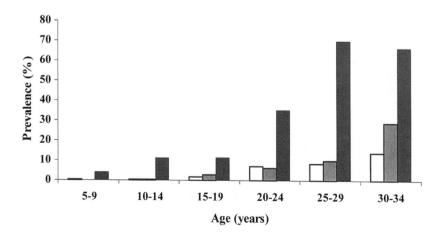

FIGURE 34-6. Prevalence of type 2 diabetes, by mother's diabetes during and following pregnancy in Pima Indians aged 5 to 34 years. *Open bars,* offspring of nondiabetic mothers; *hatched bars,* offspring of pre-diabetic mothers; *solid bars,* offspring of diabetic mothers. (From Dabelea D, Knowler WC, Pettitt DJ. Effect of diabetes in pregnancy on offspring: follow-up research in the Pima Indians. *J Matern Fetal Med* 2000;9:83–88, with permission.)

tibility to their offspring. Thus, the greater frequency of diabetes in the offspring of diabetic pregnancies might be due to greater genetic susceptibility in such offspring. To determine the role of exposure to the diabetic intrauterine environment that is in addition to genetic transmission of susceptibility, the prevalence of type 2 diabetes was compared in Pima Indian siblings born before and after their mother developed diabetes (20). Families were selected that had at least one sibling born before and at least one after the mother was diagnosed with type 2 diabetes. Nineteen families with 58 siblings and 28 sibling pairs discordant both for diabetes and diabetes exposure *in utero* were informative for the analysis. In 21 of the 28 sibling pairs, the diabetic sibling was born after the mother's diagnosis of diabetes and in only 7 of the 28 pairs was the diabetic sibling born before (odds ratio, 3.0; p < 0.01) (Fig. 34-7). In contrast, among 84 siblings and 39 sibling pairs from 24 families of diabetic fathers, the risk for type 2 diabetes was similar in the sibling pairs born before and after father's diagnosis of diabetes (Fig. 34-7). Thus, within the same family, siblings born after the mother's diagnosis of diabetes have a much greater risk of developing diabetes at an early age than siblings born before the diagnosis of diabetes in the mother. Since siblings born before and after carry a similar risk of inheriting the same susceptibility genes, the different risk reflects the effect of intrauterine exposure associated with or directly due to hyperglycemia. Since these differences were not seen in the families of diabetic fathers, it is unlikely that these findings are due to cohort or birth order effects.

In Pima Indian children aged 5 to 19 years, the prevalence of type 2 diabetes has increased two- to three-fold over the last 30 years (38). The percent of children who have been exposed to diabetes *in utero* has also increased significantly over the same time period and this was associated with a doubling of the prevalence of diabetes in children that may be attributed to this exposure (from 18.1% in 1967–1976 to 35.4% in 1987–1996). The "epidemic" of type 2 diabetes in Pima Indian children was almost entirely accounted for, statistically, by the increasing exposure to diabetes during pregnancy and the increase in obesity. Exposure to intrauterine maternal hyperglycemia was the strongest single risk factor for type 2 diabetes in Pima Indian youth (odds ratio, 10.4; p < 0.0001).

Recently, Stride et al. (39) have shown that in MODY 3 associated with mutations in the HNF-1α gene, the age of diabetes diagnosis in the offspring is lower when the mother was diagnosed before pregnancy compared to when the mother was diagnosed after pregnancy (15 vs. 27 years). This suggests that nongenetic effects are important determinants of the age of diagnosis, even in single gene disorders such as HNF-1α MODY 3. Thus, exposure to the diabetic intrauterine environment, with alterations of fetal fuels, predisposes the child to the development of diabetes later in life, an effect that is in addition to that of any inherited susceptibility genes.

The Diabetes in Pregnancy Study at Northwestern University in Chicago enrolled offspring of women with pregestational diabetes (both insulin dependent and non-insulin dependent) and gestational diabetes from 1977 to 1983. Plasma glucose and insulin were measured both fasting and after a glucose load yearly from age 1.5 years in offspring of diabetic mothers and one time at ages 10 to 16 years in control subjects (40). On their most recent evaluation (age 12.3 years), offspring of diabetic mothers had a significantly higher prevalence of impaired glucose tolerance (IGT) than the age- and sex-matched control group (19.3% vs. 2.5%) (Fig. 34-8), and two female offspring had developed type 2 diabetes at ages 7 and 11 years. Interestingly, in this cohort, the predisposition to IGT was associated with maternal hyperglycemia, regardless of whether it was caused by gestational diabetes or preexisting insulin-dependent or non-insulin-dependent diabetes. Moreover, excessive insulin secretion *in utero*, assessed

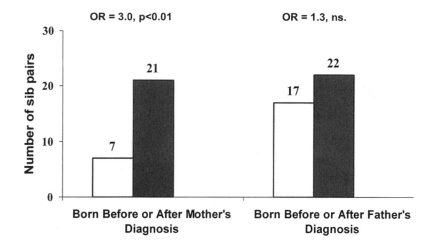

FIGURE 34-7. Pima Indian sibling pairs discordant for diabetes and exposure to diabetes *in utero*. (From Dabelea D, Pettitt DJ. Intrauterine diabetic environment confers risks for type 2 diabetes mellitus and obesity in the offspring, in addition to genetic susceptibility. *J Pediatr Endocrinol Metab* 2001;14:1085–1091, with permission.)

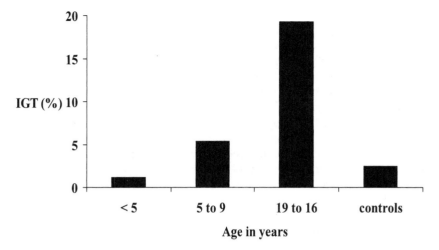

FIGURE 34-8. Prevalence of impaired glucose tolerance in offspring of diabetic mothers in three age groups and in control subjects aged 10 to 16 years. (From Silverman BL, Metzger BE, Cho NH, et al. Impaired glucose tolerance in adolescent offspring of diabetic mothers. *Diabetes Care* 1995;18:611–617, with permission from the American Diabetes Association.

by the amniotic fluid concentration measured at 32 to 38 weeks' gestation was a strong predictor of IGT in childhood.

A greater influence of the maternal environment is not always apparent. Warram et al. (31) reported higher rates of type 1 diabetes among the offspring of diabetic fathers than of diabetic mothers with type 1 diabetes. They speculated that women with diabetes may experience selective intrauterine loss of fetuses that inherit the susceptibility. This would not occur if the parent with diabetes were the father and would lead to the survival of a larger percentage of infants in whom diabetes eventually develops in offspring of diabetic fathers than of diabetic mothers. The hypothesis is that the fetus who inherits the susceptibility to type 1 diabetes is less likely to survive the pregnancy if the mother also has this susceptibility. Other studies of the familial occurrence of type 1 diabetes in children have also found that a greater proportion had diabetic fathers than diabetic mothers (41,42). There are other possible explanations for this finding (37): genetic transmission with differential susceptibility (imprinting) depending on which parent supplies the predisposing genes, or true maternal protection against type 1 diabetes in the offspring.

A role for genetic imprinting in the pathogenesis of diabetes has been suggested by recent studies. Using family-based association methods in parent-offspring trios with type 2 diabetes, Huxtable et al. (43) reported a relationship between the insulin gene and type 2 diabetes that was mediated exclusively through paternally transmitted, class III, variable number, tandem repeat (VNTR) alleles. An association among paternal, but not maternal, type 2 diabetes, low birth weight, and type 2 diabetes was reported in Pima Indian offspring (44). In this population, allelic variation of the insulin gene (class III *INS* VNTR) was associated with lower birth weight and with increased prevalence of type 2 diabetes (45). Moreover, significant linkage disequilibrium was found between the *23 Hph1* T allele of the INS gene

and birth weight, and the effects of paternally transmitted T alleles were greater than those of maternally transmitted alleles (45).

A report from the Framingham Offspring Study (46) showed that paternal and maternal type 2 diabetes conferred equivalent risks for offspring type 2 diabetes. Offspring of diabetic mothers with an age of onset less than 50 years, however, had a much higher risk for both type 2 diabetes and IGT compared with offspring of diabetic fathers. Based on comparable effect sizes among maternal and paternal type 2 diabetes, the authors concluded that fathers may transmit unique genetic factors of similar strength to maternal environmental effects.

In the cohort of adolescent offspring of diabetic mothers followed by Silverman et al. (40), the predisposition to IGT was associated with maternal hyperglycemia, and not with the type of diabetes in the mother. In a study in Germany, the prevalence of IGT was similarly increased in infants (ages 1 to 4 years) and children (ages 5 to 9 years) of mothers with pregestational type 1 diabetes and in those of mothers with gestational diabetes (47). These data support the hypothesis that the effects of maternally transmitted diabetes genes are modified by congenital influences, regardless of the type of diabetes present in the mother, as suggested by the results of the MODY 3 study (39). The metabolic effects of the diabetic intrauterine environment on the fetus might, therefore, be similar regardless of whether the mother has type 1 or type 2 diabetes.

The mechanisms by which exposure to diabetes *in utero* increases the risk of IGT and type 2 diabetes are still uncertain. A higher frequency of maternal than of paternal transmission of diabetes has been demonstrated in GK rats (48). In these rats the diabetic syndrome is produced by strepotozotocin injection or glucose infusion. They do not have any genetic predisposition for diabetes, nor can their diabetes be classified as type 1 or 2. These studies have demonstrated that hyperglycemia in the mother during pregnancy leads to impairment of glucose tolerance and decreased insulin action and secretion in adult offspring (49–54).

Several studies performed in newborns of diabetic mothers have shown an enhanced insulin secretion to a glycemic stimulus in these neonates (55,56) and, consistent with these findings, Van Assche and Gepts (57) and Heding et al. (58) described hyperplasia of the beta cells in newborns of diabetic mothers. Whether this is a transient phenomenon, as suggested by Isles et al. (59), or leads to IGT later in life when insulin resistance becomes important, is still uncertain. Impaired insulin secretion (60,61) has also been proposed as a possible mechanism. Among 104 normal glucose tolerant Pima Indian adults, insulin secretion rates were lower in individuals whose mothers had developed diabetes before the age of 35 years compared with those whose parents remained nondiabetic until the age of 49 years. The acute insulin response was approximately 40% lower in individuals whose mothers had diabetes during pregnancy than in those whose mothers developed diabetes at an early age but after the birth of the subject (62). These results suggest that exposure to the diabetic intrauterine environment is associated with impaired insulin secretion. Based on the observation made in rats and supported by the Pima Indian findings, it may be hypothesized that exposure to hyperglycemia during critical periods of fetal development "programs" the developing pancreas in a way that leads to a subsequent impairment in insulin secretion.

NEUROLOGIC AND PSYCHOLOGICAL CONSEQUENCES

Reports of neurologic problems of the children of diabetic women have included impaired visual motor function, low intelligence, Erb's palsy, seizure disorder, cerebral palsy, mental retardation, speech disturbances, reading difficulties, behavior disturbance, psychosis, and deafness (6, 63–75). Mechanisms potentially involved in the occurrence of such problems include birth trauma, especially trauma to the head and neck because of large infant size and shoulder dystocia (75); prolonged, severe neonatal hypoglycemia, which may damage the central nervous system with potentially permanent deficits (65,76); neonatal hyperbilirubinemia, which leads to kernicterus (67); and abnormal fuel metabolism during gestation, which may cause long-term aberrations in neurologic and psychological development. In addition, even though infants of diabetic women exhibit generalized macrosomia, the brain is underweight for gestational age (68,77).

Major cerebral dysfunction has been related to more severe diabetes in pregnancy (29). In the newborn offspring of women with well-controlled diabetes, Rizzo et al. (73)

found a significant inverse correlation between maternal glycemia during pregnancy and newborn behavior. A correlation between acetonuria during pregnancy and diminished intelligence quotients (IQ) in the offspring of diabetic mothers has been reported in at least two studies (69,70). In one of them, birth weight was also predictive of IQ, with smaller infants at birth having lower IQ scores at age 5 years (69). Rizzo et al. (74) found no correlation between maternal acetonuria and the child's IQ, but reported an inverse correlation between maternal second trimester β-hydroxybutyrate concentrations and the offspring's mental development index scores at age 2 years. The mothers of these children had well-controlled diabetes during pregnancy and only infrequent acetonuria. Although hypoglycemia may result in potentially permanent damage to the central nervous system, no relationship was found between neonatal hypoglycemia in the offspring of diabetic women and low IQ (71). The offspring of diabetic women fared better on follow-up than did hypoglycemic infants whose mothers did not have diabetes (65). It appears either that the underlying cause of the hypoglycemia in these infants was different, or that early recognition and treatment of the infant of the diabetic mother was responsible for the difference (i.e., it may not be the hypoglycemia *per se* that causes the problem in most cases).

The offspring born to women enrolled between 1977 and 1983 in the Northwestern University Diabetes in Pregnancy Center follow-up study (24) were followed longitudinally to evaluate the behavioral and intellectual influences of intrauterine exposure to diabetes. Direct correlations between mild maternal ketonemia in the second and third trimester and poorer performances on Mental Development Index of the Bayley Scales of Infant Development at age 2, on the Stanford-Binet Intelligence Scales at ages 3 to 5 years (74), and on the Bruininks-Oseretsky Test of Motor Proficiency at 6 to 9 years (78) were found. The associations between exposure to maternal diabetes *in utero* and psychomotor and cognitive functions in childhood were independent of socioeconomic status and ethnicity, and were similar regardless of gestational or pregestational maternal diabetes status. Moreover, they were not explained by perinatal morbidities occurring more frequently in newborns born to mothers with diabetes.

Delivery of very large infants by cesarean section and control of blood glucose concentrations throughout gestation may prevent neurologic problems in the offspring of diabetic women (67,76). Sells et al. (79) compared neurodevelopment through 36 months of age in offspring of women with type 1 diabetes and control infants. Infants of mothers with tight glycemic control during pregnancy had similar neurologic test results to the control infants, while offspring of mothers with poorer glycemic control during pregnancy scored less well on tests of language development.

PROJECTIONS FOR THE FUTURE

The effects of maternal diabetes on the child may be viewed as a vicious cycle (80,81). Children whose mothers had type 2 diabetes during pregnancy are at increased risk of becoming obese and developing diabetes at young ages. Many of these female offspring already have diabetes or abnormal glucose tolerance by the time they reach their childbearing years, thereby perpetuating the cycle. Although rigorous control of diabetes during pregnancy has been shown to decrease infant mortality, reduce the prevalence of macrosomia, and normalize the delivery and postpartum course for the mother (82–85), there is little evidence that this leads to long-term benefits for the offspring. Indeed, even levels of abnormal glucose tolerance that are not diagnostic of diabetes in the nonpregnant state are associated with slightly higher glucose concentrations and more obesity in the offspring (11,14). However, Dorner et al. (86) speculated that treatment of diabetes and IGT in pregnant women, along with the prevention of overnutrition in the newborn, by preventing hyperinsulinism in the fetus and newborn during differentiation and maturation of the neuroendocrine system, may be responsible for the decrease in the prevalence of childhood diabetes seen in Berlin. Enzi et al. (87) provided evidence that the excess obesity seen in the offspring of women with diabetes during the pregnancy may not be inevitable. They followed infants whose diabetic mothers had been receiving strict low-calorie diets during pregnancy. Those with normal birth weight who had been receiving carefully controlled diets to age 1 year were not obese by that time. They concluded that overnutrition *in utero*, such as occurs with maternal diabetes, does not have long-lasting effects on adiposity if the birth weight is normal and infant overfeeding is prevented. A recent longitudinal study in the Pima Indians attempted to longitudinally observe the impact of improved diabetes care during pregnancy—based on the historical improvements in the management of diabetes—on the risk of adult obesity and type 2 diabetes (88). The authors concluded that the increased risk for obesity and type 2 diabetes associated with the diabetic pregnancy does not seem to diminish with time, in spite of presumed improvements in management of diabetic pregnancy.

In the past, high perinatal mortality claimed many offspring of diabetic women, especially in pregnancies with the greatest perinatal difficulties and poorly controlled diabetes. Long-term follow-up, therefore, was limited to the survivors who may not have been as severely affected as those who died *in utero* or in infancy. Today, infant survival is the norm, even for infants of women with severe diabetes that is difficult to control. The long-term effects in the offspring of diabetic women who are being born today, therefore, may differ from those reported previously. However, the long-term outcome in the future may be no better than in the past because children, who in former times would have died *in utero*, now survive. It is also likely that offspring of diabetic mothers will be affected at early ages with excess complications, given their increased risk of diabetes and their earlier age at onset.

Long-term studies of diabetic pregnancy outcomes based on glucose control data are needed (89) to evaluate whether intensive glucose control during pregnancy can break this vicious cycle. The challenge for the future is to determine whether a degree of diabetic control can be achieved throughout pregnancy that would prevent the developing fetus from recognizing that its mother has diabetes. If this is achievable, it will in turn probably reduce the prevalence of diabetes in the next generation of pregnancies and, therefore, be beneficial for future generations as well as the immediate offspring.

KEY POINTS

- Exposure to the diabetic intrauterine environment predisposes the offspring to overweight and obesity, IGT, and diabetes mellitus, and can affect psychological and intellectual development.
- These effects seem to occur regardless of the type of mother's diabetes during pregnancy (gestational or pre-existing type 1 or type 2 diabetes).
- These consequences are in addition to any genetic susceptibility that is inherited, although the mechanisms by which exposure to diabetes *in utero* increases the risk of IGT and type 2 diabetes are still uncertain.
- It is not known whether there are ethnic-specific responses to such exposure.
- The effects of maternal diabetes on the child may be viewed as a vicious cycle, and may partly explain the epidemic of obesity and type 2 diabetes in children.
- The challenge for the future is to see whether a degree of diabetic control can be achieved throughout pregnancy that would break the vicious cycle, therefore reducing the prevalence of diabetes in the next generation.

REFERENCES

1. Freinkel N. Banting lecture 1980: of pregnancy and progeny. *Diabetes* 1980;29:1023–1026.
2. Pettitt DJ, Bennett PH. Long-term outcome of infants of diabetic mothers. In: Reece EA, Coustan D, eds. *Diabetes mellitus in pregnancy: principles and practice.* New York: Churchill Livingstone, 1988:559–575.
3. Dabelea D, Pettitt DJ. Long-term implications: child and adult. In: Hod M, Jovanovic L, Di Renzo GC, et al., eds. *Textbook of diabetes and pregnancy.* Martin Dunitz, 2003:305–317.
4. White P, Koshy P, Duckers J. The management of pregnancy complicating diabetes and of children of diabetic mothers. *Med Clin North Am* 1953;39:1481–1484.

5. Hagbard L, Olow I, Reinand T. A follow-up study of 514 children of diabetic mothers. *Acta Paediatrica* 1959;48:184–197.

6. Cummins M, Norrish M. Follow-up of children of diabetic mothers. *Arch Dis Child* 1980;55:259–264.

7. Vohr BR, Lipsitt LP, Oh W. Somatic growth of children of diabetic mothers with reference to birth size. *J Pediatr* 1980;97:196–199.

8. Gerline G, Arachi S, Gori MG, et al. Developmental aspects of the offspring of diabetic mothers. *Acta Endocrinologica* 1986;[Suppl 277]:150–155.

9. Weiss PAM, Scholz HS, Haas J, et al. Long-term follow-up of infants of mothers with type 1 diabetes. *Diabetes Care* 2000;23:905–911.

10. Pettitt DJ, Baird HR, Aleck KA, et al. Excessive obesity in offspring of Pima Indian women with diabetes during pregnancy. *N Engl J Med* 1983;308:242–245.

11. Pettitt DJ, Bennett PH, Knowler WC, et al. Gestational diabetes mellitus and impaired glucose tolerance during pregnancy: Long-term effects on obesity and glucose tolerance in the offspring. *Diabetes* 1985;34[Suppl 2]:119–122.

12. Pettitt DJ, Knowler WC, Bennett PH, et al. Obesity in offspring of diabetic Pima Indian women despite normal birthweight. *Diabetes Care* 1987;10:76–80.

13. Pettitt DJ, Knowler WC. Diabetes and obesity in the Pima Indians: a cross-generational vicious cycle. *J Obesity Weight Regulation* 1988;7:61–75.

14. Pettitt DJ, Bennett PH, Saad MF, et al. Abnormal glucose tolerance during pregnancy in Pima Indian women: long-term effects on the offspring. *Diabetes* 1991;40[Suppl 2]:126–130.

15. Dabelea D, Pettitt DJ. Intrauterine diabetic environment confers risks for type 2 diabetes mellitus and obesity in the offspring, in addition to genetic susceptibility. *J Pediatr Endocrinol Metab* 2001;14:1085–1091.

16. Dabelea D, Knowler WC, Pettitt DJ. Effect of diabetes in pregnancy on offspring: follow-up research in the Pima Indians. *J Matern Fetal Med* 2000;9:83–88.

17. Price RA, Charles MA, Pettitt DJ, et al. Obesity in Pima Indians: large increases among post-world war II birth cohorts. *Am J Physical Anthropol* 1993;92:473–479.

18. Everhart JE, Pettitt DJ, Bennett PH, et al. Duration of obesity increases the incidence of NIDDM. *Diabetes* 1992;41:235–240.

19. White P. Childhood diabetes: its course, and influence on the second and third generations. *Diabetes* 1960;9:345–348.

20. Dabelea D, Hanson RL, Lindsay RS, et al. Intrauterine exposure to diabetes conveys risks for type 2 diabetes and obesity: a study of discordant sibships. *Diabetes* 2000;49:2208–2211.

21. Odeleye OE, de Courten M, Pettitt DJ, et al. Fasting hyperinsulinemia is a predictor of increased body weight gain and obesity in Pima Indian children. *Diabetes* 1997;46:1341–1345.

22. Metzger BE, Silverman BL, Freinkel N, et al. Amniotic fluid insulin concentration as a predictor of obesity. *Arch Dis Child* 1990;65:1050–1052.

23. Silverman BL, Rizzo T, Green OC, et al. Long-term prospective evaluation of offspring of diabetic mothers. *Diabetes* 1991;40[Suppl 2]:121–125.

24. Silverman BL, Rizzo TA, Cho NH, et al. Long-term effects of the intrauterine environment: the Northwestern University Diabetes in Pregnancy Center. *Diabetes Care* 1998;21[Suppl 2]:B142–149.

25. Pettitt DJ. Summary and comment on: Silverman BL, Rizzo T, Green OC, et al. Long-term prospective evaluation of offspring of diabetic mothers. *Diabetes* 1991;40[Suppl 2]:121–25. *Diabetes Spectrum* 1992;5:39–40.

26. World Health Organization. Definition, diagnosis and classification of diabetes mellitus and its complications. Part 1. Report of a WHO consultation: diagnosis and classification of diabetes mellitus. Geneva: World Health Organization, 1999.

27. Simpson NE. Diabetes in the families of diabetics. *CAMJ* 1968;98:427–429.

28. Simpson NE. Heritabilities of liability to diabetes when sex and age at onset are considered. *Ann Hum Genet* 1969;32:283–286.

29. Yssing M. Long-term prognosis of children born to mothers diabetic when pregnant. In: Camerini-Davalos RA, Cole HS, eds. *Early diabetes in early life*. San Diego, CA: Academic Press, 1975:575–590.

30. Bibergeil H, Godel E, Amendt P. Diabetes and pregnancy: early and late prognosis of children of diabetic mothers. In: Camerini-Davalos RA, Cole HS, eds. *Early diabetes in early life*. San Diego, CA: Academic Press, 1975:427–441.

31. Warram JH, Krolewski AS, Gottlieb MS, et al. Differences in risk of insulin-dependent diabetes in offspring of diabetic mothers and diabetic fathers. *N Engl J Med* 1984;311:149–152.

32. Pettitt DJ, Aleck KA, Baird HR, et al. Congenital susceptibility to NIDDM: role of intrauterine environment. *Diabetes* 1988;37:622–625.

33. Neel JV. Diabetes mellitus—a geneticist's nightmare. In: Creutzfeldt W, Köbberling J, Neel JV, eds. *The genetics of diabetes mellitus*. New York: Springer-Verlag, 1976:1–14.

34. Friedman JM, Fialkow PJ. The genetics of diabetes mellitus. In: Steinberg AG, Bearn AG, Motulsky AG, et al., eds. *Progress in medical genetics*, vol. 4. Philadelphia: WB Saunders, 1980:199–215.

35. Rotter JI, Rimoin DL. The genetics of the glucose intolerance disorders. *Am J Med* 1981;70:116–119.

36. Hanson RL, Elston RC, Pettitt DJ, et al. Segregation analysis on non-insulin-dependent diabetes mellitus in Pima Indians: evidence for a major gene effect. *Am J Hum Genet* 1995;57:160–170.

37. Pettitt DJ. Diabetes in subsequent generations. In: Dornhorst A, Hadden DR, eds. *Diabetes and pregnancy: an international approach to diagnosis and management*. Chichester: John Wiley & Sons, 1996:367–376.

38. Dabelea D, Hanson RL, Bennett PH, et al. Increasing prevalence of type 2 diabetes in American-Indian children. *Diabetologia* 1998;41:904–910.

39. Stride A, Shepherd M, Frayling TM, et al. Intra-uterine hyperglycaemia is associated with an earlier diagnosis of diabetes in hepatocyte nuclear factor-1 alpha gene mutation carriers. *Diabetes Care* 2002;25:2287–2291.

40. Silverman BL, Metzger BE, Cho NH, et al. Impaired glucose tolerance in adolescent offspring of diabetic mothers. *Diabetes Care* 1995;18:611–617.

41. Wagener DK, Sacks JM, LaPoret RE, et al. The Pittsburgh study of insulin-dependent diabetes mellitus. *Diabetes* 1982;31:136–139.

42. Lee ET, Anderson PS Jr, Bryan J, et al. Diabetes, parental diabetes and obesity in Oklahoma Indians. *Diabetes Care* 1985;8:107–112.

43. Huxtable SJ, Saker PJ, Haddad L, et al. Analysis of parent-offspring trios provides evidence for linkage and association between the insulin gene and type 2 diabetes mediated exclusively through paternally transmitted class III variable number tandem repeat alleles. *Diabetes* 2000;49:126–130.

44. Lindsay RS, Dabelea D, Roumain J, et al. Type 2 diabetes and low birth weight: the role of paternal inheritance in the association of low birth weight and diabetes. *Diabetes* 2000;49:445–449.

45. Lindsay RS, Hanson RL, Weidrich C, et al. The insulin gene variable number tandem repeats class I/III polymorphism is in linkage disequilibrium with birth weight but not type 2 diabetes in the Pima population. *Diabetes* 2003;52:187–193.

46. Meigs JB, Cupples AL, Wilson PWF. Parental transmission of type 2 diabetes. The Framingham Offspring Study. *Diabetes* 2000;49:2201–2207.

47. Plagemann A, Harder T, Kohlhoff R, et al. Glucose tolerance and insulin secretion in children of mothers with pregestational IDDM or gestational diabetes. *Diabetologia* 1997;40:1094–1100.

48. Gauguier D, Nelson I, Bernard C, et al. Higher maternal than paternal inheritance of diabetes in GK rats. *Diabetes* 1994;43:220–224.

49. Bihoreau MT, Ktorza A, Kinebanyan MF, et al. Impaired glucose homeostasis in adult rats following intrauterine exposure to mild hyperglycemia during late gestation. *Diabetes* 1986;35:979–984.

50. Gauguier D, Bihoreau MT, Ktorza A, et al. Inheritance of diabetes mellitus as consequence of gestational hyperglycemia in rats. *Diabetes* 1990;39:734–739.

51. Aerts L, Van Assche FA. Is gestational diabetes an acquired condition? *J Dev Physiol* 1979;1:219–225.

52. Aerts L, Van Assche FA. Endocrine pancreas in the offspring of rats with experimentally induced diabetes. *J Endocrinol* 1981;88:81–88.

53. Aerts L, Sodoyez-Goffaux F, Sodoyez JC, et al. The diabetic intrauterine milieu has a long-lasting effect on insulin secretion by B cells and on insulin uptake by target tissues. *Am J Obstet Gynecol* 1988;259:1287–1292.

54. Grill V, Johansson B, Jalkanen P, et al. Influence of severe diabetes mellitus early in pregnancy in the rat: effects on insulin sensitivity and insulin secretion in the offspring. *Diabetologia* 1991;34:373–378.

55. Gentz J, Lunell NO, Olin P, et al. Glucose tolerance in overweight babies and infants of diabetic mothers [Letter]. *Acta Paediatr Scand* 1967;56:228–229.

56. Pildes PS, Hart RJ, Warrner R, et al. Plasma insulin response during oral glucose tolerance tests in newborns of normal and gestational diabetic mothers. *Pediatrics* 1969;44:76–83.

57. Van Assche FA, Gepts W. The cytological composition of the foetal endocrine pancreas in normal and pathological conditions. *Diabetologia* 1971;7:434–444.

58. Heding LG, Perrson B, Strangenberg M. β-cell function in newborn infants of diabetic mothers. *Diabetologia* 1980;19:427–430.

59. Isles TE, Dickson M, Farquhar JW. Glucose tolerance and plasma insulin in newborn infants of normal and diabetic mothers. *Acta Paediatr Scand* 1968;57:460–461.

60. Hultquist GT, Olding LB. Pancreatic-islet fibrosis in young infants of diabetic mothers. *Lancet* 1975;2:1015–1018.

61. Wilson CA, Weyer C, Knowler WC, et al. Acute insulin secretion is impaired in adult offspring of diabetic pregnancies. *Diabetes* 1999;48[Suppl 1]:A300.

62. Gautier JF, Wilson C, Weyer C, et al. Low acute insulin secretory responses in adult offspring of people with early onset type 2 diabetes. *Diabetes* 2001;50:1828–1833.

63. Pedersen J. Future years of surviving babies. In: Pedersen J, ed. *The pregnant diabetic and her newborn*, 2nd ed. Copenhagen: Munksgaard, 1977:223–241.

64. Sack RA. The large infant. *Am J Obstet Gynecol* 1969;104:195–206.

65. Knobloch H, Sotos JF, Sherard ES Jr et al. Prognostic and etiologic factors in hypoglycemia. *Pediatrics* 1967;70:876–881.

66. Peevy KJ, Landaw SA, Gross SJ. Hyperbilirubinemia in infants of diabetic mothers. *Pediatrics* 1980;66:417–222.

67. Cowett RM, Schwartz R. The infant of the diabetic mother. *Pediatr Clin North Am* 1982;29:1213–1218.

68. Driscoll SG, Benirschke K, Curtis GW. Neonatal deaths among infants of diabetic mothers. *Am J Dis Child* 1960;100:818–822.

69. Stehbens JA, Baker GL, Kitchel M. Outcome at ages 1, 3, and 5 years of children born to diabetic women. *Am J Obstet Gynecol* 1977;127:408–413.

70. Churchill JA, Berendes HW, Newmore J. Neuropsychological deficits in children of diabetic mothers. *Am J Obstet Gynecol* 1969;105:257–263.

71. Persson B, Gentz J. Follow-up of children of insulin-dependent and gestational diabetic mothers. *Acta Paediatr Scand* 1984;73:349–353.

72. Naeye RL, Chez RA. Effects of maternal acetonuria and low pregnancy weight gain on children's psychomotor development. *Am J Obstet Gynecol* 1981;139:189–193.

73. Rizzo T, Freinkel N, Metzger BE, et al. Correlations between antepartum maternal metabolism and newborn behavior. *Am J Obstet Gynecol* 1990;163:1458–1462.

74. Rizzo T, Metzger BE, Burns WJ, et al. Correlations between antepartum maternal metabolism and intelligence of offspring. *N Engl J Med* 1991;325:911–918.

75. Dor N, Mosberg H, Stern W, et al. Complications in fetal macrosomia. *N Y State J Med* 1984;84:302–304.

76. Pildes RS. Infants of diabetic mothers. *N Engl J Med* 1973;289:902–905.

77. Hill DE. Effect of insulin on fetal growth. *Semin Perinatol* 1978;2:319–322.

78. Rizzo TA, Dooley SL, Metzger BE, et al. Prenatal and perinatal influences on long-term psychomotor development in offspring of diabetic mothers. *Am J Obstet Gynecol.* 1995;173:1753–1758.

79. Sells CJ, Robinson NM, Brown Z, et al. Long-term developmental follow-up of infants of diabetic mothers. *J Pediatr* 1994;125:S9–S17.

80. Pettit DJ, Knowler WC. Diabetes and obesity in the Pima Indians: a cross-generational vicious cycle. *J Obesity Weight Regul* 1988;7:61–65.

81. Knowler WC, Pettit DJ, Saad MF, et al. Diabetes mellitus in the Pima Indians: incidence, risk factors and pathogenesis. *Diabetes Metab Rev* 1990;6:1–13.

82. Karlsson K, Kjellmer I. The outcome of diabetic pregnancies in relation to the mother's blood sugar level. *Am J Obstet Gynecol* 1972;112:213–217.

83. Gyves MT, Rodman HM, Little AB, et al. A modern approach to management of pregnant diabetics: a two-year analysis of perinatal outcomes. *Am J Obstet Gynecol* 1977;128:606–611.

84. Coustan DR, Berkowtiz RL, Hobbins JC. Tight metabolic control of overt diabetes in pregnancy. *Am J Med* 1980;68:845–849.

85. Jovanovic L, Druzin M, Peterson CM. Effect of euglycemia on the outcome of pregnancy in insulin-dependent diabetic women as compared with normal control subjects. *Am J Med* 1981;71:921–927.

86. Dorner G, Steindel E, Thoelke H, et al. Evidence for decreasing prevalence of diabetes mellitus in childhood apparently produced by prevention of hyperinsulinism in the foetus and newborn. *Exp Clin Endocrinol* 1984;84:134–139.

87. Enzi G, Inelmen EM, Rubaltelli FF, et al. Postnatal development of adipose tissue in normal children on strictly controlled calorie intake. *Metabolism* 1982;31:1029–1034.

88. Lindsay RS, Hanson RL, Bennett PH, et al. Secular trends in birth weight, BMI, and diabetes in the offspring of diabetic mothers. *Diabetes Care* 2000;23:1249–1254.

89. Jovanovic L. A tincture of time does not turn the tide. *Diabetes Care* 2000;23:1219–1220.

APPENDIX

APPENDIX TABLE 1. SUMMARY OF IMPORTANT FEATURES OF MOST OF THE AVAILABLE GLUCOSE METERS

Name and Manufacturer	Test Strip Used	Range (mg/dL)	Test Time (Seconds)	Warranty	Features
Accu-Chek Active (Roche Diagnostics)	Accu-Chek Active	10–600	5	3 years	Uses small sample size. Simple, 2-step procedure. Meter turns on automatically when strip inserted. Results downloadable.
Accu-Chek Advantage (Roche Diagnostics)	Accu-Chek Advantage or Accu-Chek Comfort Curve	10–600	26	3 years	Uses Comfort Curve test strips with small sample size, capillary action, & large target area. 100-value memory with time & date has download capability.
Accu-Chek Compact (Roche Diagnostics)	Accu-Chek Compact	10–600	15	3 years	Storage of drum inside monitor; underdosed strip detection; minimum sample size of 3.5 uL (microliters); 100-value memory with time, date, & 7-day averaging. Downloadable.
Accu-Chek Complete (Roche Diagnostics)	Accu-Chek Advantage or Accu-Chek Comfort Curve	10–600	26	3 years	2-step test procedure. Collects, stores, & analyzes up to 1,000 values. "ATM-like" push-button selection. Software is available to upload test results.
Accu-Check Voicemate (Roche Diagnostics)	Accu-Chek Comfort Curve	10–600	20	3 years	For the blind & visually impaired. Clear, step-by-step voice guide. Touchable strips. No cleaning required. Lilly brand insulin identification.
Ascensia DEX 2 Diabetes Care System (Bayer Corporation, Diagnostics Division)	Ascensia Autodisc; 10 test strips in one disc	20–600	30	5 years	Disc-based monitor; Performs 10 tests without reloading. Disc automatically calibrates monitor for 10 tests. Sensor actively draws just the amount of blood it needs. Advanced data management.
Ascensia Elite Diabetes Care System (Bayer Corporation, Diagnostics Division)	Ascensia Elite	20–600	30	5 years	No buttons; turns on when test strip is inserted. Blood touched to the tip of test strip is automatically drawn into the test chamber. 20-test memory & 3-minute automatic shutoff.
Ascenia Elite XL Diabetes Care System (Bayer Corporation, Diagnostics Division)	Ascensia Elite	20–600	30	5 years	No operating buttons; turns on when test strip is inserted. 120-test memory with date, time, & 14-day average. 3-minute automatic shutoff.
Assure (Hypoguard)	Assure	30–550	35	3 years	Data-management system; biosensor technology; 180-test memory; large touch-screen display.
Assure II (Hypoguard)	Assure II	30–550	30	3 years	Large display, 2-step test, automatic on/off, large test strip, capillary action.

APPENDIX TABLE 1 *(continued)*

Name and Manufacturer	Test Strip Used	Range (mg/dL)	Test Time (Seconds)	Warranty	Features
ExacTech (Abbott Laboratories, MediSense Products)	ExacTech	40–450	30	4 years	Credit card size & shape; simple 3-step testing procedure; biosensor technology; no cleaning, wiping, or timing; last reading recall & calibration code.
ExacTech RSG (Abbott Laboratories, MediSense Products)	ExacTech RSG	40–450	30	4 years	Requires no calibration or coding; simple 3-step testing procedure; biosensor technology; no cleaning or maintenance required.
Focus Blood Glucose Monitoring System (QuestStar Medical, Inc.)	Focus	25–500	15–35	Lifetime	Hands-off automatic calibration. Display provides word prompts for guidance. Automatic hematocrit & temperature corrections for assured accuracy. Stores up to 225 results with time, date, insulin type, & dosage. Average glucose reading. Clock. Data port allows down-loading to PC. Prompts in 10 languages.
FreeStyle (TheraSense)	FreeStyle	20–500	15	5 years	Virtually painless testing using small blood sample (1/3 uL). Offers various testing sites, including forearm, upper arm, thigh, calf, hand, & finger. Unaffected by oxygen, common interfering substances & by hematocrit from 0% to 60%. Strip inserting automatically turns meter on. Samples pulled into strip by capillary action. Sample can be retaken, using same sampling area for up to 60 seconds. Confirmation beeps let you know the strip is full. 250-test memory, date & time, and 14-day average. Data downloadable.
FreeStyle Tracker (TheraSense)	FreeStyle	20–500	15	5 years	FreeStyle meter integrated into a personal digital assistant (PDA) providing automatic storage of up to 2,500 glucose results into an electronic logbook along with user-entered insulin, carbohydrate, exercise, & medication info. Offers many testing sites, including forearm, upper arm, thigh, calf, hand, & finger, Small blood sample (1/3 uL). Various reporting methods for comprehensive trend analysis. 2,500-item food list with carb values per serving size, insulin tables, prescribed regimen table, & reminder alarms for checking glucose or keeping appointments. Data uploadable.

APPENDIX TABLE 1 *(continued)*

Name and Manufacturer	Test Strip Used	Range (mg/dL)	Test Time (Seconds)	Warranty	Features
Hypoguard Advance (Hypoguard)	Hypoguard Advance	20–600	15	3 years	Large display, 2-step test, automatic on/off, 100-test emory, compact meter, and special carrying case.
MediSense 2 Card (Abbott Laboratories)	MediSense 2 or Precision Q.I.D.	20–600	20	4 years	Provides same features as MediSense 2 Pen Sensor. Credit card size, extra large display window. Uses same sensor test strips.
MediSense 2 Pen Sensor (Abbott Laboratories)	MediSense 2 or Precision Q.I.D.	20–600	20	4 years	Biosensor technology; automatic start with "hands-off" testing; no cleaning, no wiping, no blotting, no timing; pen-size; extended memory; individually wrapped test strips.
One Touch Basic (LifeScan)	One Touch	0–600	45	3 years	75-test memory with optional display of date & time; simple, 3-step test procedure; large, easy-to-handle test strips; single-button coding.
One Touch InDuo (LifeScan)	One Touch Ultra	20–600	5	3 years	Combined blood glucose meter & insulin dosing system. Less painful alternate site testing (arm), tiny blood sample, 150-test memory with date & time. 14- & 30-day test averaging. No cleaning. Insulin doser uses 3 ml PenFill insulin cartridges and NovoFine max 8 mm length needles. Doses in 1- to 70-unit increments. Remembers last dose and elapsed time.
One Touch Profile (LifeScan)	One Touch	0–600	45	5 years	3-step testing with no timing, wiping, or blotting; large display in English, Spanish, or 17 other languages; stores last 250 results with date & time; 14- & 30-day test average; insulin programming; event labeling.
One Touch SureStep (LifeScan)	SureStep	0–500	15–30	3 years	Single-button testing; blue dot confirms sample before test; touchable test strip; off-meter dosing; large display with universal symbols, 150-test memory with date & time; 14- & 30-day test averaging; data downloadable.
One Touch Ultra (LifeScan)	One Touch Ultra	20–600	5	3 years	Alternate site testing; fast test time; tiny blood sample; easy blood application with FastDraw Design test strip, including confirmation window small meter size; 150-test memory with date & time; 14- & 30-day test averaging; no cleaning necessary; data downloadable.

(continued)

APPENDIX TABLE 1 *(continued)*

Name and Manufacturer	Test Strip Used	Range (mg/dL)	Test Time (Seconds)	Warranty	Features
Prestige IQ (Home Diagnostics, Inc.)	Prestige Smart System	25–600	10–50	5 years	Fast, accurate results, data management including date, time, and 14- & 30-day averaging; easy-to-read, large digital display; Internet uploading capabilities allow patients to track, graph, record, & share test results.
Supreme II (Hypoguard)	Supreme	30–600	50	3 years	Large display, universal symbols, . true off-meter dosing (blood can also be applied while strip is inside the meter), absorbent test strip, color chart comparison, 100-test memory
Prestige LX (Home Diagnostics)	Prestige Smart System	25–600	10–50	5 years	Easy to use. 3 simple steps; one coding button. Large, easy-to-read display. 365-test memory.
Precision Xtra (Abbott Laboratories, MediSense Products)	Precision Xtra	20–500	20 sec glucose 30 sec ketones	4 years	Also measures ketone levels. Requires small drop of blood. Patented fill-trigger virtually eliminates risk of short sampling. Not affected by common medications. Has lighting features that make testing easier in low-light situations; 450-result memory with time & date and 1-, 2-, & 4-week averaging.
QuickTek (Hypoguard)	QuickTek	20–600	10–30	3 years	Large display, compact meter, 250-test memory with time & date, large test strip for easy handling, small sample size 3.5 uL, 2-step testing.
ReliOn (Wal-Mart Pharmacies)	ReliOn	20–600	20	4,000 tests	No wiping, blotting, timing, or cleaning. Requires only a 4-uL blood sample size.
Sof-Tact Diabetes Management System (Abbott Laboratories, MediSense Products)	Sof-Tact	30–450	20	2 years	Integrated alternate site meter. Test on forearm & upper arm. 450-result memory with date & time; 1-, 2-, & 4-week averaging. Compatible with Precision Link 2.3 and higher. Preload feature allows patients to load meter with test strip and lancet up to 8 hours in advance of testing.

APPENDIX TABLE 2. SUMMARY OF IMPORTANT FEATURES OF THE AVAILABLE LANCING DEVICES

Name (Manufacturer/Distributor)	Features
Accu-Chek Softclix Lancet Device (Roche Diagnostics)	Features 11 depth settings providing precise control of penetration depth while maximizing comfort.
Accu-Chek Soft Touch Lancet Device (Roche Diagnostics)	Five depth selections with an adjustable dial.
Ascensia Microlet Adjustable Lancing Device (Bayer Corporation, Diagnostics Division)	Ergonomic design has easy cocking mechanism and 5 adjustable settings to control depth of puncture.
Ascensia Microlet Vaculance Lancing Device (Bayer Corporation, Diagnostics Division)	Vacuum action draws blood to skin surface, allowing patient to perform alternate site testing.
Auto-Lancet (Palco Labs)	Finger-lancing device with adjustable tip that adjusts to match different skin type.
Auto-Lancet Mini (Palco Labs)	Compact mini design. Adjustable tip allows five depth levels.
Autolet Mini (Owen Mumford)	Two devices in one package; two depth platforms offer choice of blood flow, contour grips assist handling.
Autolet Lite (Owen Mumford)	Finger lancet device with three platform depths: 1.8 mm, 2.4 mm, 3.0 mm, self-arming; lancet ejection.
Autolet Clinisafe (Owen Mumford)	Finger lancet device with 20 platforms (10 each of different depths), 10 Unilet lancets, and vinyl wallet.
BD Lancet Device (BD)	Compatible with most lancets; comes with three BD Ultra-Fine lancets.
E–Z Lets II (Palco Labs)	Sterile, single-use, disposable device; automatically retracts.
Gentle-Lance Lancet Device (Futura Medical Corporation)	Pen-style device with five adjustable settings for maximum comfort.
Glucolet Automatic Lancing Device (Bayer Corporation, Diagnostics Division)	Multilingual instruction insert.
Haemolance Plus (Hypoguard)	Single-use disposable lancet. After use, the needle automatically retracts.
Haemolance (Hypoguard)	Single-use disposable lancet with built-in needle protection system; needle retracts automatically.
Lasette Plus Assisted Blood Sampling Device (Cell Robotics, Inc.)	Needleless capillary blood sampling system based on laser technology. Appropriate for individuals who fear frequent needle use.
Lite Touch Lancing Device (Medicore)	Stainless steel for durability. Adjustable; uses most lancets.
MPD Pro Lancet (Medical Plastic Devices)	Self-contained safety lancet rendered inoperative after one use; automatically retracts to prevent needlestick accidents.
Penlet II Automatic Blood Sampling Device (LifeScan)	Pen-shaped; hands-off lancet removal system to minimize possibility of sticks.
Prestige Lite Touch Lancing Device (Home Diagnostics)	Highly portable; lightweight. Five depth settings for optimal skin penetration.
QuickLance (Hypoguard, Inc.)	All-in-one lancing system; does not require a separate lancing device or lancet; test anywhere discreetly.
Safe-T-Lance Plus (Futura Medical)	Single-use lancet with retractable needle.
Select Lite Lancing Device (Hypoguard)	Pen-shaped device is compatible with most lancets; adjustable tip; five settings.
Tenderlett (ITC)	Surgical blade produces shallow 1.75-mm incision; permanently retracting steel blade.
Tenderlett Jr. (ITC)	Same features and action as the Tenderlett, but produces a shallower 1.25-mm incision for use with children.
Tenderlett Toddler (ITC)	Same features and action as the Tenderlett, but produces a shallower 0.85-mm incision.
UltraTLC Adjustable Lancing Device (Abbott Laboratories)	Adjustable tip provides five penetration depth settings; pen-shaped.
Unistik 1 (Owen Mumford)	Single-use device; lancet automatically retracts for safety.
Unistik 2 (Owen Mumford)	Single-use for safety and disposability; punctures and retracts automatically.

APPENDIX TABLE 3. FEATURES OF INSULIN PUMPS

Pump Name	Pump Model (Manufacturer)	Weight (oz)	Battery Type/ Life	Basal #	Basal Range (U/hr)	Smallest Bolus	Occlusion Alarm	Over-Delivery Alarm	Near-Empty Alarm	Features
Animas IR 1000	Animas	3.5	Four 1.5-volt silver oxide batteries, type 257 or equivalent, 6–8 week life	Up to 12 basal rates in four personalized programs plus a temporary basal rate	0.05–9.9	0.1 units	Yes	Yes	Yes	User-friendly menu-driven programming; basal delivery every 3 mins; precise basal rate adjustment in 0.05 units/hr to ensure precision delivery; audio bolus button, user-defined safety limit; pump memory includes last 255 boluses; alarms & daily totals; waterproof; backlight for easy viewing; multiple languages; enclosed lead screw; interchangeable fashion covers in various colors; pump clip; insurance assistance; 24-hr, toll-free customer service staffed by medical professionals; customized education programs; PC download via IR port
D-TRON	Disetronic Medical Systems	4.2 (including battery)	3-volt lithium battery (2-month life)	24 basal rates plus temporary basal rate increases	0.0–25	0.1 units	Yes	Yes	n/a	PC download (IR port, bi-direction communication between pump and PC); free computer-based training CD; 5-bolus alternatives; audible bolus delivery; adjustable volume; whisper-quiet stepper motor; flexible "automatic" off; large backlit display; continuous safety checks; vibrating standard bolus confirmation; 24-hr, toll-free telephone support; insurance assistance, guaranteed pump replacement by next business day

	Manufacturer	Weight (oz)	Battery	Basal rate profiles	Basal rate range	Increment				Comments
H-TRONplus	Disetronic Medical Systems	3.5 (including battery)	Two 3-volt silver oxide batteries (1-month life)	24 profiles	0.0–99.0	0.1 units	Yes	Yes	n/a	Patient receives two pumps; 3-minute insulin delivery system; audible bolus delivery; glass and plastic cartridges available; free training video; 24-hour, toll-free telephone support; insurance assistance; color choice, durable clip case, and other accessories available
MiniMed 508	MiniMed Technologies, Inc.	3.5	Three 1.5-volt silver oxide batteries. Four- to 6-week life.	48 profiles plus temporary basal rate	0.1–35.0	0.1 units	Yes	Runaway	Yes	Multiple bolus options include: normal for immediate delivery; square wave, Bio-Pulse delivery; controlled 0.1-unit insulin pulses clinically equivalent to 3-minute basal delivery. Remote control. MiniGlo backlight, choice of alarms; child block (makes unintended programming impossible) and self-test features. Downloadable memory includes approximately 90 days delivery history. Water-resistant. Toll-free help line. Free videos, educational material, and insurance assistance.
MiniMed Paradigm	MiniMed Technologies, Inc.	3.4	1 standard AAA battery; 4-week life (depending on usage)	3 patterns with up to 48 profiles and temporary basal rate	0.1–35.0	0.1 units	Yes	Yes	Runaway	E-Z path programming. Watertight to 8 feet for 24 hours. Easy to fill and load reservoirs. Bio-Pulse delivery; controlled 0.1-unit insulin pulses, clinically equivalent to 3-minute basal delivery. Slow bolus (1.5 unit/minute maximum). Multiple bolus options include: normal for immediate delivery; square wave bolus for delivery over an extended period of time; dual wave. Remote control. MiniGlo backlight, safety block, and self-test features. Downloadable memory includes approximately 90 days delivery history. Toll-free help line. Free videos, educational material, and insurance assistance.

SUBJECT INDEX

Page numbers in *italics* denote figures; those followed by "t" denote tables